CAMERA

Following A Simple Concept

MASTERS

Producing An Extraordinary Result

ORDER FORM

Prices are for current editions only.
Call 1-800-FILMBKS or 213/471-8066 for more information.

YES! PLEASE SEND THE FOLLOWING BOOKS:

QTY.	ANNUAL DIRECTORIES	PRICE	CA. TAX	TOTAL
_____	FILM DIRECTORS—8th Ed.	$59.95	$4.95	$_____
_____	PRODS/STUDIOS/ AGENTS & CASTING DIRECTORS—3rd Ed.	49.95	4.12	$_____
_____	CINEMATOGRAPHERS PRODUCTION DESIGNERS COSTUME DESIGNERS & FILM EDITORS—3rd Ed.	49.95	4.12	$_____
_____	FILM WRITERS—3rd Ed.	49.95	4.12	$_____
_____	FILM COMPOSERS—1st Ed.	29.95	2.47	$_____
_____	TV WRITERS—2nd Ed.	49.95	4.12	$_____
_____	TV DIRECTORS - 1st Ed.	29.95	2.47	$_____
_____	FILM ACTORS GUIDE—1st Ed.	49.95	4.12	$_____
_____	SPECIAL EFFECTS & STUNTS—2nd Ed.	39.95	3.30	$_____

SUBTOTAL $_____
ADD IN SHIPPING $_____
TOTAL ORDER $_____

UPS SHIPPING CHARGES
CONT. USA/CANADA
First Directory $6.00 $10.00
Add'l. Directory $2.50 $ 5.00

SHIPPING CHARGES (Overseas)	AIRMAIL	SURFACE
Film Directors	$45.00	$12.50
Other Directories	$35.00	$12.50

For Faster Service
Call 213/471-8066 (CA) or
1/800-FILMBKS

FAX ORDERS ACCEPTED: 213/471-4969

PAYMENT IS BY:
Check _____ Money Order_____ Visa_____ MC ____ AMEX_____
Card No._____Exp. Date_____
Signature_____
(exactly as it appears on your card)

SHIP BOOKS TO:
NAME_____
COMPANY _____ PHONE (very imp't.!)_____
ADDRESS _____
CITY/STATE/ZIP_____

ORDER FORM

Prices are for current editions only.
Call 1-800-FILMBKS or 213/471-8066 for more information.

YES! PLEASE SEND THE FOLLOWING BOOKS:

QTY.	ANNUAL DIRECTORIES	PRICE	CA. TAX	TOTAL
_____	FILM DIRECTORS—8th Ed.	$59.95	$4.95	$_____
_____	PRODS/STUDIOS/ AGENTS & CASTING DIRECTORS—3rd Ed.	49.95	4.12	$_____
_____	CINEMATOGRAPHERS PRODUCTION DESIGNERS COSTUME DESIGNERS & FILM EDITORS—3rd Ed.	49.95	4.12	$_____
_____	FILM WRITERS—3rd Ed.	49.95	4.12	$_____
_____	FILM COMPOSERS—1st Ed.	29.95	2.47	$_____
_____	TV WRITERS—2nd Ed.	49.95	4.12	$_____
_____	TV DIRECTORS - 1st Ed.	29.95	2.47	$_____
_____	FILM ACTORS GUIDE—1st Ed.	49.95	4.12	$_____
_____	SPECIAL EFFECTS & STUNTS—2nd Ed.	39.95	3.30	$_____

SUBTOTAL $_____
ADD IN SHIPPING $_____
TOTAL ORDER $_____

UPS SHIPPING CHARGES
CONT. USA/CANADA
First Directory $6.00 $10.00
Add'l. Directory $2.50 $ 5.00

SHIPPING CHARGES (Overseas)	AIRMAIL	SURFACE
Film Directors	$45.00	$12.50
Other Directories	$35.00	$12.50

For Faster Service
Call 213/471-8066 (CA) or
1/800-FILMBKS

FAX ORDERS ACCEPTED: 213/471-4969

PAYMENT IS BY:
Check _____ Money Order_____ Visa_____ MC ____ AMEX_____
Card No._____Exp. Date_____
Signature_____
(exactly as it appears on your card)

SHIP BOOKS TO:
NAME_____
COMPANY _____ PHONE (very imp't.!)_____
ADDRESS _____
CITY/STATE/ZIP_____

ORDER FORM

Prices are for current editions only.
Call 1-800-FILMBKS or 213/471-8066 for more information.

YES! PLEASE SEND THE FOLLOWING BOOKS:

QTY.	ANNUAL DIRECTORIES	PRICE	CA. TAX	TOTAL
_____	FILM DIRECTORS—8th Ed.	$59.95	$4.95	$_____
_____	PRODS/STUDIOS/ AGENTS & CASTING DIRECTORS—3rd Ed.	49.95	4.12	$_____
_____	CINEMATOGRAPHERS PRODUCTION DESIGNERS COSTUME DESIGNERS & FILM EDITORS—3rd Ed.	49.95	4.12	$_____
_____	FILM WRITERS—3rd Ed.	49.95	4.12	$_____
_____	FILM COMPOSERS—1st Ed.	29.95	2.47	$_____
_____	TV WRITERS—2nd Ed.	49.95	4.12	$_____
_____	TV DIRECTORS - 1st Ed.	29.95	2.47	$_____
_____	FILM ACTORS GUIDE—1st Ed.	49.95	4.12	$_____
_____	SPECIAL EFFECTS & STUNTS—2nd Ed.	39.95	3.30	$_____

SUBTOTAL $_____
ADD IN SHIPPING $_____
TOTAL ORDER $_____

UPS SHIPPING CHARGES
CONT. USA/CANADA
First Directory $6.00 $10.00
Add'l. Directory $2.50 $ 5.00

SHIPPING CHARGES (Overseas)	AIRMAIL	SURFACE
Film Directors	$45.00	$12.50
Other Directories	$35.00	$12.50

For Faster Service
Call 213/471-8066 (CA) or
1/800-FILMBKS

FAX ORDERS ACCEPTED: 213/471-4969

PAYMENT IS BY:
Check _____ Money Order_____ Visa_____ MC ____ AMEX_____
Card No._____Exp. Date_____
Signature_____
(exactly as it appears on your card)

SHIP BOOKS TO:
NAME_____
COMPANY _____ PHONE (very imp't.!)_____
ADDRESS _____
CITY/STATE/ZIP_____

ORDER FORM

Prices are for current editions only.
Call 1-800-FILMBKS or 213/471-8066 for more information.

YES! PLEASE SEND THE FOLLOWING BOOKS:

QTY.	ANNUAL DIRECTORIES	PRICE	CA. TAX	TOTAL
_____	FILM DIRECTORS—8th Ed.	$59.95	$4.95	$_____
_____	PRODS/STUDIOS/ AGENTS & CASTING DIRECTORS—3rd Ed.	49.95	4.12	$_____
_____	CINEMATOGRAPHERS PRODUCTION DESIGNERS COSTUME DESIGNERS & FILM EDITORS—3rd Ed.	49.95	4.12	$_____
_____	FILM WRITERS—3rd Ed.	49.95	4.12	$_____
_____	FILM COMPOSERS—1st Ed.	29.95	2.47	$_____
_____	TV WRITERS—2nd Ed.	49.95	4.12	$_____
_____	TV DIRECTORS - 1st Ed.	29.95	2.47	$_____
_____	FILM ACTORS GUIDE—1st Ed.	49.95	4.12	$_____
_____	SPECIAL EFFECTS & STUNTS—2nd Ed.	39.95	3.30	$_____

SUBTOTAL $_____
ADD IN SHIPPING $_____
TOTAL ORDER $_____

UPS SHIPPING CHARGES
CONT. USA/CANADA
First Directory $6.00 $10.00
Add'l. Directory $2.50 $ 5.00

SHIPPING CHARGES (Overseas)	AIRMAIL	SURFACE
Film Directors	$45.00	$12.50
Other Directories	$35.00	$12.50

For Faster Service
Call 213/471-8066 (CA) or
1/800-FILMBKS

FAX ORDERS ACCEPTED: 213/471-4969

PAYMENT IS BY:
Check _____ Money Order_____ Visa_____ MC ____ AMEX_____
Card No._____Exp. Date_____
Signature_____
(exactly as it appears on your card)

SHIP BOOKS TO:
NAME_____
COMPANY _____ PHONE (very imp't.!)_____
ADDRESS _____
CITY/STATE/ZIP_____

NO POSTAGE
NECESSARY IF
MAILED IN THE
UNITED STATES

BUSINESS REPLY CARD
FIRST CLASS PERMIT NO. 4842, BEVERLY HILLS, CA.

POSTAGE WILL BE PAID BY:

LONE EAGLE PUBLISHING CO.
9903 Santa Monica Blvd. #204
Beverly Hills, CA 90212-9942

NO POSTAGE
NECESSARY IF
MAILED IN THE
UNITED STATES

BUSINESS REPLY CARD
FIRST CLASS PERMIT NO. 4842, BEVERLY HILLS, CA.

POSTAGE WILL BE PAID BY:

LONE EAGLE PUBLISHING CO.
9903 Santa Monica Blvd. #204
Beverly Hills, CA 90212-9942

NO POSTAGE
NECESSARY IF
MAILED IN THE
UNITED STATES

BUSINESS REPLY CARD
FIRST CLASS PERMIT NO. 4842, BEVERLY HILLS, CA.

POSTAGE WILL BE PAID BY:

LONE EAGLE PUBLISHING CO.
9903 Santa Monica Blvd. #204
Beverly Hills, CA 90212-9942

CINEMATOGRAPHERS, PRODUCTION DESIGNERS, COSTUME DESIGNERS AND FILM EDITORS

GUIDE

Third Edition

CINEMATOGRAPHERS, PRODUCTION DESIGNERS, COSTUME DESIGNERS
AND
FILM EDITORS

GUIDE

Third Edition

Compiled and Edited by David Pecchia

LONE EAGLE

**CINEMATOGRAPHERS, PRODUCTION DESIGNERS,
COSTUME DESIGNERS AND FILM EDITORS GUIDE
THIRD EDITION**

LONE EAGLE PUBLISHING CO.
2337 Roscomare Road, Suite Nine
Los Angeles, CA 90077-1815
213/471-8066

Printed in the United States of America

Book designed by Liz Ridenour

This book was entirely typeset using an Apple Macintosh SE, Apple Macintosh II, LaserwriterPlus, Microsoft Word, Microsoft Excel, and Aldus Pagemaker.

Printed by McNaughton & Gunn, Saline, Michigan 48176

ISBN: 0-943728-43-6

NOTE: We have made every reasonable effort to ensure that the information contained herein is as accurate as possible. However, errors and omissions are sure to occur and are unintentional. We would appreciate your notifying us of any which you may find.

* Lone Eagle Publishing is a division of Lone Eagle Productions, Inc.

LONE EAGLE PUBLISHING STAFF
Publishers ....Joan V. Singleton
                              Ralph Singleton
Editorial Director ....Bethann Wetzel
Advertising Director ....Lori Copeland
Customer Service ....Steven Keyes
Editorial Assistant ....Steve LuKanic
Art Director ....Heidi Frieder
Computer Consultant ....Glenn Osako

LETTER FROM THE PUBLISHERS

When Susan Avallone decided to concentrate her efforts on the very time-consuming job of editing our FILM WRITERS GUIDE, we were fortunate enough to have David Pecchia step into her job as editor of this tome. His years of experience writing about the film industry for the entertainment-industry section of the Los Angeles *Times* (*The Calendar*), among other publications, proved that David had the interest. Ah, but did he have the talent and the ability to root out all the information needed to complete a volume such as this?

You be the judge. This Third Edition of CINEMATOGRAPHERS, PRODUCTION DESIGNERS, COSTUME DESIGNERS and FILM EDITORS GUIDE is over 450 pages long. There is even more of what you have asked us for in the past: listings, credits, contacts. The index has been combined into one extremely useful section—almost 200 pages long! In a flash, you can tell who's who in each of the four categories for thousands of movies.

The one area in which we will continue to ask—no, *beg*—for your help is with contacts. Only you can tell us how someone looking to hire you can reach you, and reach you fast. Often in this industry, if a first choice isn't easily reachable, they'll choose the next person on their list. If your name is one of those without any contact information next to it, do yourselves (and us) a favor and let us know so we can update it for the next edition as well as give it out to those who call our office looking for your credits.

A computerized version of our directories is in the development stage. We'd love to hear from you as to what you would like included. As always, though, we appreciate your comments and suggestions.

Joan V. Singleton and Ralph S. Singleton
Publishers

DATTNER

& ASSOCIATES

A talent agency representing cinematographers

12210 NEBRASKA AVE., SUITE 45 LOS ANGELES, CA 90025
Contact:Fay Dattner Phone 213- 447-5986

TABLE OF CONTENTS

INTRODUCTION

In a conventional situation, this would be the portion of the book where those who assisted the author are properly thanked. In many cases, these very people receiving thanks also earned wages for their efforts on behalf of the author, but tradition dictates that they grab some ink, just the same.

This book is quite different, however. I, David Pecchia, will hereby take *all* the credit for the **Third Edition of CINEMATOGRAPHERS, PRODUCTION DE-SIGNERS, COSTUME DESIGNERS AND FILM EDITORS GUIDE** you now hold in your anxious little hands.

First off, I hired myself, then devised the concept. I then scoured the trades, made the required phone calls, and proceeded to initiate the interviews. Following this, I carefully edited down the myriad words until they were publication-worthy. Finally, after a recuperative weekend in Palm Springs, I got down to the business of chopping down the necessary number of trees to facilitate the mass production of this work.

Ok, ok...I have embellished a wee bit.

Indeed there are people to be thanked and I'd be thrilled to death if you read the forthcoming accolades slowly and carefully.

Beth Wetzel was my main conduit (and favorite Scrabble opponent) over at the friendly offices of Lone Eagle Publishing. Every time I called in to flake on a deadline, lovely Beth would assure me my work was worth waiting for. Whoops, there I go again.

Joan Singleton and hubby, Ralph, need to be especially praised. After all, they believed everything I told them at the initial interview and hired me anyway. Susan Avallone, who edited and slaved over the Second Edition of the CPCE was particularly generous with her time when I took this project on. So I hope these kind words will suffice in lieu of a royalty percentage.

My four interview subjects are in my heart with Steve LuKanic who painstakingly transcribed the whole mess.

There then. Now you've got the *real* story.

What I've obtained from this endeavor is a better sense as to the big picture associated with a motion picture. To be sure, Vittorio Storaro and Gordon Willis and Vilmos Zsigmond command your attention by what they've accomplished with a few lights and some Panavision equipment. But now I know how incredibly much talent a Jordan Cronenweth (*BLADE RUNNER*) or an Owen Roizman (*THE FRENCH CON-NECTION*) possesses. This is equally true across all CPCE categories.

This book continues to provide an easy, practical and comprehensive reference to cinematographers, production designers, costume designers, film editors and their work. The **CINEMATOGRAPHERS, PRODUCTION DESIGNERS, COSTUME DE-SIGNERS and FILM EDITORS GUIDE** emphasizes professionals who are currently active in the industry and their feature film credits over the past ten years. We do include credits for selected deceased persons in the main listing section, as well as in the index. Their credits are noted with a "†" by the person's name.

This edition includes many more contacts as well as a designation for guild and/or union members. Although we have worked extremely diligently to uncover as many contacts as we can, it is an impossibility to find contacts for all. For those looking to get in touch with someone in this directory, we suggest calling the appropriate guild and/or union to locate the person if no contact information is provided, or has changed since publication. We also encourage those with incomplete listings, and their agents, to provide us with up-dated information for future editions.

Although the main focus of this directory is the feature film world, there is a sampling of television credits. The rule of thumb has been to include television credits for those who work in features, but not for those whose credits are solely in television. This book does not include credits for music videos, commercials, industrials or stage productions; we do, however, include credits for a few noteworthy short films (e.g., *Tummy Trouble*).

A FEW WORDS OF CLARIFICATION

CINEMATOGRAPHERS:

The credits listed here are only for Directors of Photography, not for other types of photography (Additional, Second Unit, Aerial, etc.) The only other credit included is "Visual Consultant"—a rare designation for a special contribution.

PRODUCTION DESIGNERS:

The focus of this section is on those professionals with credits as Production Designer. However, since the title, "Production Designer" is an honorary one granted to a film's Art Director by the film's producer, and many features do not have a Production Designer, we have also included Art Director credits. The notation, "AD" follows the credit. In many instances where there was more than one Art Director, the "Supervising Art Director" credit is also noted, as well as Art Director for a specific location, e.g., *Art Director—Japan*.

COSTUME DESIGNERS:

Where there is not a Costume Designer for a feature, we have listed the Wardrobe Supervisor or Men's Costumer and Women's Costumer. Many times a designer is hired to do the wardrobe for one particular star. We have included those credits, also. We only include Assistant Costumer credits when the person has additional credits as a Costumer.

FILM EDITORS:

This section lists Film Editors only and not the many other types of Editors that work on a film (Sound, ADR, Music, Special Effects, etc.). Supervising Editor (SE) and Co-Editor (CE) are included and noted, although Assistant and Associate Editors are not.

In order for the **CINEMATOGRAPHERS, PRODUCTION DESIGNERS, COSTUME DESIGNERS and FILM EDITORS GUIDE** to continue growing and improving with each edition, we need your comments and criticism—pro and con. Please continue to send us your feedback so we can keep making the guide a better reference tool.

It pleased me to know, as I plowed through the mountains of hard copy, both faxed and published. that this guide is not solely read for hiring purposes. Any film buff, in any town at any age strolling through any walk of life can leaf through this coffee table enhancer and derive enjoyment.

My fun was bolstered, too, by the fact that film reviewers and copy editors alike and publications across the nation keep these Lone Eagle must-haves close to their work stations. In my many years with the Los Angeles <u>Times</u>, I've certainly had occasion to consult **MICHAEL SINGER'S FILM DIRECTORS: A COMPLETE GUIDE** as an invaluable aid toward my film writing assignments.

So enjoy this guide as often as you can, and start saving your pennies for the Fourth Edition.

Thank you,

David Pecchia

KEY TO ABBREVIATIONS

(TF) = TELEFEATURE
Motion pictures made for television with an on-air running time of 1-1/2 hours to 4-1/2 hours on commercial television; or 1 hour to 4 hours on non-commercial television.

(CTF) = CABLE TELEFEATURE
Motion pictures made for cable television with an on-air running time of 1 hour to 4 hours.

(MS) = MINI-SERIES
Motion pictures made for television with an on-air running time of 4-1/2 hours and more on commercial television; or 4 hours or more on non-commercial television.

(CMS) = CABLE MINI-SERIES
Motion pictures made for cable television with an on-air running time of 4 hours or more.

(TVS) = TELEVISION SERIES
Episodic television on commercial television.

(PILOT) = PILOT
Motion picture made for television specifically as an introduction to a potential series.

(TV) = TELEVISION
A general category for television specials, variety shows, etc., that do not fall under the other television categories.

(CTV) = CABLE TELEVISION
A general category for cable television specials, variety shows, etc., that do not fall under the other cable television categories.

ACTT = Association of Cinematographs, Television & Allied Technicians.
ASC = American Society of Cinematographers
BSC = British Society of Cinematographers
CSC = Candian Society of Cinematographers
ACS = Australian Society of Cinematographers
AIC = Association of Italian Cinematographers
ACE = Association of Cinema Editors
IATSE = International Alliance of Theatrical & Stage Employees
NABET = National Association of Broadcast Employees & Technicians

KEY TO SYMBOLS

★ = after a film title denotes an Academy Award nomination
★★ = after a film titles denotes an Academy Award win.
☆ = after a film title denotes an Emmy Award nomination.
☆☆ = after afilm titles denotes an Emmy Award win.
† = denotes deceased person
* = denotes *known* Union or Guild Affiliation. (Absence of an asterisk should not be interpreted automatically to mean the person is not a member of a Union or Guild.)

C L O S E - U P

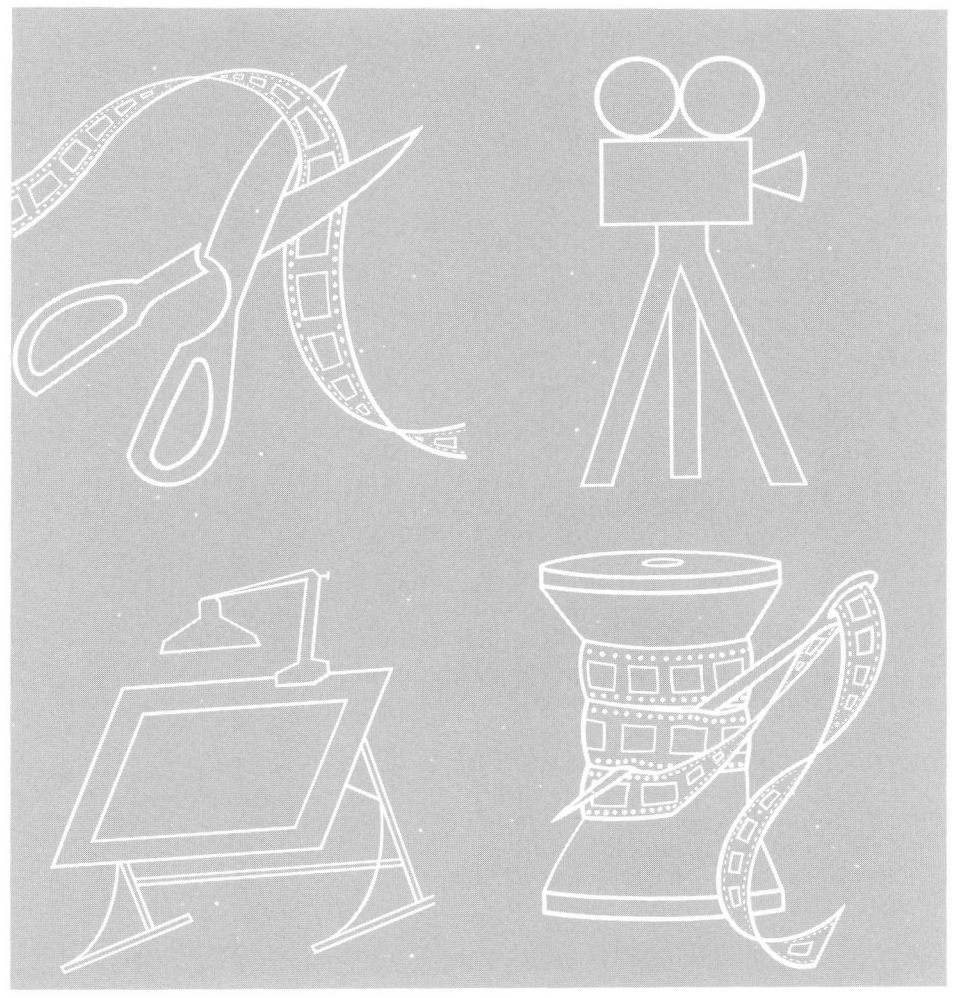

I N T E R V I E W S

OWEN ROIZMAN

O WEN ROIZMAN IS YET ANOTHER NEW YORKER WHO has wound up in Los Angeles. He and his wife have one child, a son of 22. Among Owen's acclaimed credits: *THE FRENCH CONNECTION, THE EXORCIST, NETWORK, ABSENCE OF MALICE, TOOTSIE* and the upcoming *GRAND CANYON.*

David Pecchia: Let's open up with *GRAND CANYON*. You're not doing travelogues now, are you?

Owen Roizman: No (*laughs.*) It's a story written by Lawrence Kasdan (*THE BIG CHILL, THE ACCIDENTAL TOURIST.*) It's about people. Life. Existence in Los Angeles. It has nothing to do with the Grand Canyon except as metaphor.

Sort of Steve Martin's *L.A. STORY* turned on its head, is what I've heard.

Yeah, it's like the more dramatic side of *L.A. STORY.* Larry calls it a "dramatic comedy." It's about people, and how they affect one another. A very touching, moving story. It's smooth reading. And when you finish reading it you're left with a lot of thoughts. Great characters: blacks, whites, you know...the horrors of L.A. and the wonders of it. It's just a nice little story. I don't know how well it'll do commercially, but I know it's a picture that critics will like because I think it's very well written.

Any special look you're trying to give this project?

No. Larry said we should go places we haven't been before, which is really hard to do. I'm kind of keeping it natural and simple. We're not fussing with it. If the light changes or something, we're not worrying about it. It's not a big budget film and we're trying to get it done on time so we're letting a lot of things go and just not worrying so much whether things go together perfectly or not. We're going through it and shooting a lot of long lenses. Even interiors. Larry really likes the feeling of long lenses so we're not sitting back and looking at sets and backgrounds and things like that. We're just using them as the background for people.

Long lens shots also save time, do they not?

Sometimes and sometimes not because you really have to deal with a lot of focus things, interesting compositions and things like that. We're trying to move the camera a lot, even with the long lenses. I'm shooting some scenes where we're just dollying all over the place with the long lenses during some sequences. So that takes time to carefully lay out. So I don't really think it's a time saver but it's interesting. It's fun. It's free. I think it's got a real free look to it.

Certain directors of photography keep the camera in constant motion. What's Owen Roizman's guide to camera movement?

A lot of that's dictated by the scene. I think that anybody who moves the camera all over the place, all the time, is really just taking a technical approach to it. Every scene requires a different approach. If the scene will work better by moving the camera a lot, getting across the point of the scene, then it's better to be stylish. And if it's better just to sit back with a wide lens, not move it and be absolutely static, then that works, too. I don't think you should just move the camera for the sake of it. It should be approached by how the staging is done, the actor's intention...the pace of it. The camera just has to capture all that stuff. So I don't believe in following any formulas.

You're not one to show off?

I never like to do that.

You and Larry met for the first time on *I LOVE YOU TO DEATH*. Obviously you two saw eye to eye.

His feeling, as he's conveyed to me, is he doesn't want to work with anybody else, and, frankly, that's the way I feel right now. I'd be happy if I only worked with him. I think he's great.

Well, there's no reason Larry can't keep the two of you busy into the next millennium. He's quite a director.

He's a wonderful director and a great human being. He's a great writer and he's terrific to be around. And, he's a lot of fun. I really look forward to going to work every day and very rarely have I had that feeling in all my years in the business.

What *did* get you into this crazy business?

Actually, I grew up in the business in a way because my father was a cinematographer. But I had no idea at all that that's what I wanted to do and I had no particular interest in it. I wanted to play baseball. That's all I ever wanted to do, and all I ever thought about.

Ever get close to the big leagues?

Yeah, I got close but when I hurt my arm that was the end of my career. I was a pitcher and till that day I was doing well. Made all-scholastic in high school. Went on to play college ball but that was after my arm had been shot. So I really didn't do much after high school.

Still throw the ball around a little?

No, no. I play golf. Also played tennis for a long time. I'm an athlete, but no more baseball.

What events led up to your hitching up with William Friedkin?

I started in the commercial business and did them for about ten years. I was an assistant, an operator, and then I did a very low budget film called *STOP* that a friend of mine produced but was never released. He gave me the opportunity to do it. It was that picture that got me *THE FRENCH CONNECTION*. Somebody recommended me to Friedkin when he found out Billy was looking for a cinematographer for *FRENCH CONNECTION*. Friedkin had seen my commercial reel, and loved it, and said, "But can he do a feature?" So I screened *STOP* for him and he loved what I did with it. So he offered me *THE FRENCH CONNECTION*.

Why don't you, for undoubtedly the millionth time, tell us all about the chase sequence.

When we first got together at the beginning of the picture, Phil D'Antoni, who produced the film, and had also produced *BULLITT*, got us all in a room. He said, "Look, I want this chase sequence to be the best ever done." It was all planned up front to be a big chase. Then he said, "I want it to be better than the one in *BULLITT*, which until then was probably the best one. So we very carefully laid it out with the stunt coordinator, Friedkin, myself and whoever else was involved. We shot, usually using five cameras at a time, for about five weeks to get the chase. That's including the exteriors, and the stuff on the subway train, and all the second unit work that went into it. There were five major stunts that we did. The rest of it was just the icing on the cake. The running, the shots of the faces and the excitement of the whole thing basically was five major stunts. Each of the shots involved five cameras; three of them usually mounted on the car for each pass and then five outside the car for other takes.

Did you operate at all or were you basically just orchestrating the mayhem?

I sometimes operated, but mostly just orchestrated it. Once in a while I'd be on the main camera, but in general on the film, a lot of time I operated the second camera when we used two cameras. We did have a main operator and I had two first assistants the whole picture, besides the second assistant, so that whenever we put up the second camera I had a good first assistant with me. We did probably 70% of the picture hand-held.

This being your first legitimate feature, did you have any sort of clue as to the enduring impact the film would make?

Well, I'll tell you a great story relating to that. When I read the script, I thought it was an absolutely fantastic script. It was a knockout script and I was really excited about it. Until then, I didn't realize that you get to read so many bad scripts because this was one of the first scripts I'd been handed and read. And I loved it. Anyway, we finished the picture and they were editing. They edited it out here in California while I was still living in New York. So I called up Friedkin one day, when he was in the editing room with Phil. Billy picked up the extension so I was talking with the two of them at once and I said, "So, what's going on? How's the picture?" And Friedkin says "Well, you know it's just about finished and we're going to start testing it out a bit and see what we've got." So I said "Well, you know, give me a feeling for it. What do you think? Is it good? Is it a piece of garbage?...What?" I had no idea. And they said "No way is it a piece of garbage. I mean, we don't know how good it is. We can't tell at this point." So, I mean, obviously it wasn't a piece of garbage. It was pretty astounding. But we really had no idea at the time it was going to come out and be that monumental. I felt we were making a pretty good picture. We were excited about the dailies, the acting and the whole ambience and feel to it. But you just don't know till it's out there.

So Owen Roizman's career began to move along faster than Popeye Doyle's Chevy did under that overpass.

I was already on to my next picture. I had been offered a show before THE FRENCH CONNECTION was finished based on word of mouth...and the dailies. Some directors had looked at the dailies. I remember one day the production man-

---

"I've done multiple pictures with several directors and the second time's always easier. It's a very close collaboration, and I don't think that a great looking film can be produced if he's impervious to suggestion. You have to agree on things. If you don't agree, you shouldn't be working together."—Owen Roizman

---

ager came by and mentioned something like, "You'll be going up for the envelope on this one," and I was thinking, how can he say something like that? How can he tell anything? I didn't have any idea it would get nominated. I was just doing what I did and trying to capture the mood of it. And it just worked.

Tell us a bit about the director/cinematographer collaboration.

It's a very close relationship. At least it should be. I mean, it doesn't always work that way. It depends on the director. But the way I like to do it, and the only directors I've ever enjoyed working with are the ones with whom I could collaborate. You start right from the very beginning. If you've never worked with the guy before it's just discussions up front about his philosophies on filmmaking and your philosophies on filmmaking. How you want that picture to come across. What the look should be. The feeling and mood. What's acceptable. What's not acceptable. What can you reach for, what can't you reach for, etc. And once you've worked with him, at least the second time, anyway, usually by then you know each other pretty well. I've done multiple pictures with several directors and the second time's always easier. It's a very close collaboration, and I don't think that a great looking film can be produced if he's impervious to suggestion. You have to agree on things. If you don't agree, you shouldn't be work-

ing together. Naturally, there are going to be disagreements during the course of it, but if it's a good collaboration, they're friendly disagreements, and they're creative disagreements. But not personality disagreements.

Do you generally get along with your directors?

I had some disagreements with Billy Friedkin while we were doing the THE EXORCIST about certain things. But even there, not a lot. I usually have the attitude that the director's the boss and it's his film and if he says he wants something a certain way, then I usually do it. I'll usually let him know if I don't agree, but I'll still do it his way. I think he has the right to have it his way. I very rarely disagree with directors.

So Friedkin called you back for THE EXORCIST. Did the pressures and tumult surrounding that shoot make THE FRENCH CONNECTION seem like a walk in the park?

THE EXORCIST was probably the most strenuous shoot I've been on. It was a very difficult film to do. The nature of the material was difficult. We were way over budget, and there was a lot of pressure from the studio. Billy wouldn't settle for anything less than perfect. So he put a lot of pressure on everybody to do their best work so there was a lot of tension. It was just hard, real hard, and I was very happy to see it end.

Did you think audiences would line up to see Linda Blair have trouble holding down her pea soup?

Again, it was just a fantastic book and a great, great script. And I usually go on the theory, and, so far I think I've been right, that if it reads well it's going to play well. If it doesn't read well, it usually doesn't work. Some have but not really, not down to the core. And so with THE EXORCIST, we knew it was good material and it was just a matter of whether it was all believable. Or not. And at that time we had no idea. It was kind of like telling a joke if you know the punchline. You hear the joke over and over again, and after a while you stop laughing. With this, we knew what was going to happen, so the tension wasn't there for us while we were doing it. We had no idea how the audience was going to accept it. But, boy, did they ever!

This time out, Friedkin had you lighting sets in sub-zero temperatures during the exorcism segment. How does that affect an F-stop?

Well, we really approached it as if we were shooting outside in sub-zero freezing temperatures. The only difference was that when we arrived in the morning, they had the set cooled down to about 20 degrees below zero, and we found out that because of the lack of humidity, we couldn't photograph an actor's breath. I mean, it could be 30 degrees above outside and you'll see breath because of the humidity but on a stage like that, where the air conditioning is doing the cooling, there's no humidity. I don't know if we even tried to put humidity in the room or not, but a person's breath wouldn't show if it wasn't way below zero. So we'd get in there at 20 below and line up the shots and start lighting it, but with the air conditioners going you couldn't hear anything, so we had to shut them down to do the lighting. We'd then light for whatever time it took and tried to use as small lights as possible as to not get too much heat going on the set. That was before they had cool lights. We'd finish lighting and then everybody would empty out and they'd turn the air conditioners back on and freeze it up again. Sometimes we'd have to wait a couple hours before getting a take.

Ordeal. With a capital "O."

Yes, it was, so it was very time consuming and the exorcism alone took a couple of months to shoot. It was just a tedious, one shot at a time kind of deal. So that's how we approached it. And we had to winterize the cameras and do everything that we would do as if we were shooting outside. That includes dressing the same.

Parkas, wool socks and all?

You got it.

Another director with whom you've worked repeatedly is Sydney Pollack. Tell us how that collaboration originated.

I guess he had seen stuff of mine, or somebody had recommended me to him. Maybe a combination of the two. He asked me to do *THREE DAYS OF THE CONDOR*. I did it, naturally, and we got along, made a good film, and that was it. After that, he just wanted me to shoot with him, so the only two pictures that I haven't done of his since I met him was *BOBBY DEERFIELD*, which he did in Europe and he used a European cameraman. Then there was *OUT OF AFRICA*, which he

asked me to do but I couldn't. I had just opened my own commercial production company had other people involved so I really couldn't shut down to go do *OUT OF AFRICA*.

It would seem that Friedkin and Pollack work under a separate directing dynamic.

Like night and day. Totally different. A lot of it is in personality, too, in the way they shoot things. Sydney's a great actor's director. Also, he knows technically what he wants. He's very good technically. He knows editing very well. He understands lenses, camera movement and what all that stuff will do and how he wants it to work for him. Sydney has a great understanding of it all. Billy has a good sense of filmmaking and shoots a little more from the hip even though he's well prepared. He has a shot list made up and things like that, but he's a little more spontaneous, I think, than Sydney who's a little more calculated and more reserved.

What happened to *HAVANA*?

The script (*Roizman slowly forms a laugh.*) That's what it came down to. After Sydney sent it to me to read I called him up and said, "I have problems with the script." We had a big falling out for a while there. Then we had a long talk about it because I basically was hesitant to do it because of the problems I had with the script. He was a little pissed at me that I would even question the script considering our relationship. Maybe he's right, maybe not, but I was going to be giving up a lot of my life for that project so I put faith in him that he would make it work. And that's it, in a nutshell. The acting was good, sets were good and I think it looked good. All the other elements worked, except the story.

Any desires to work with a director you may respect but haven't had a chance to meet?

At this stage in my career, there are a couple people I'm comfortable with. I'd just as soon enjoy my work and know that I'm going to enjoy it and I don't feel like necessarily taking a chance with new people. Because, even though they may be great filmmakers, I don't know if I'd like being around them, and at this point it's just as important for me to be around people I like. To enjoy my work. Enjoy myself...my life. Earlier in my career it would have been different, but right now, I prefer working with people I know.

And with your track record, you do

have that luxury.

Yeah. I have a few people that call me back, and it's nice. It's very nice.

You've been nominated for an Academy Award a number of times, Owen. Does it matter if you eventually win one?

Well, the first time, when I was doing *THE FRENCH CONNECTION* and somebody said, "You're gonna be getting a nomination for this," I said "Aww, that's fine. I'm not interested in that stuff." But I didn't realize how much I was going to enjoy being nominated (*laughs*). Sure, I'd love to win one. Everybody wants to be recognized. Why not? I don't think that I'm going to approach every film with the idea that maybe this is the one. I just think those things happen when you hook up with a good film, good people, good acting. You might just be lucky enough to with an Oscar for it.

Of which of your peers are you a fan?

Oh, [Vittorio] Storaro, of course. Besides being a good friend I think he's just a genius. I think Gordie Willis and his contribution with the style of the *GODFATHER* movies is just monumental. He's a tremendous cinematographer. And I love Caleb Deschanel's work...*THE NATURAL, BEING THERE*. It's a shame he's given it up for directing because he's a great cinematographer. Jordan Cronenweth... I'm a great fan of Jordie's. He's probably one of the most underrated cinematographers in the business. People don't realize how good he is, but he's brilliant.

You mentioned Deschanel's move on to directing. Is this adjustment in your game plan at all?

I really don't want to direct films. I've directed TV commercials for, God, thirty years almost, and had my own production company directing and shooting filmed commercials. And I get great satisfaction from directing them, but as far as directing a film, I don't really have the desire to do it. I don't know, sometimes I think I'd be a good director, but I don't really have the patience right now to spend that big a chunk of my life involved in a picture. I'd rather shoot it, take off for a while. Shoot another one, take off for a while. I like my free time.

Ron Phillips

LAWRENCE G. PAULL

ARRY PAULL ORIGINALLY ASPIRED TO BE A NEW YORK CITY architect but somehow ended up designing movie sets. Another, no lesser, task of Paull's is making a movie location look like it's not a movie location. Larry lives in Los Angeles with his publicist wife, Marcie Bolotin, and has provided the look to such films as: *THE NAKED APE; BLADE RUNNER,* for which he was nominated for the prestigious Academy Award and won the British Academy Award; *BACK TO THE FUTURE;* as well as this summer's hit starring Billy Crystal— *CITY SLICKERS* He is currently working on *MEMOIRS OF AN INVISIBLE MAN* starring Chevy Chase and Darryl Hannah, directed by John Carpenter.

David Pecchia: Let's start with *BLADE RUNNER.* How did Ridley Scott come to know of you?

Lawrence G. Paull: My background had been, on the last several films, a small amount of special effects work. By the time *BLADE RUNNER* came up, I had finished working with Douglas Trumbull—the special effects/visual effects coordinator on a film that never got made called *PYRAMID* over at MGM. Douglas had finished *BRAINSTORM* with David Snyder [Paull's co-production designer on *BLADE RUNNER.*] Ridley did not know anybody in the United States and was looking for a very young, talented, aggressive designer who would work for peanuts, okay? (*We both laugh.*) My name came up because I had worked for the associate producer before. I had seen *ALIEN* just a month or two before and was excited and enthused. Basically, it was a series of right connections and I felt Ridley liked my background. The script was really right up my alley. I happened to be an architect as well as a city planner, and I had a lot of opinions on what was going to happen to the city...you know, the deterioration, the massive flux of minorities into the inner city, which is nothing new. It was just presented in a much more dynamic way. And a much more visual way. I mean, I can take you downtown any Friday or Saturday night over on Broadway and it looks like parts of *BLADE RUNNER,* except the signs are in Spanish, not in Chinese and Japanese.

So your background in architecture pretty much helped you...

Well, I don't know. After the meeting, I then met with Ridley's associate who, on the side, said, "I want you to know, it's going to be a terribly tough show. It's gonna kill you because Ridley's background is design." Well, Ridley had a lot of strong opinions...and so did I. And there were times during the show when he and I clashed.

Over a particular look?

Various things. Some sets, some details...just various different items, but I think it was a very good collaboration.

Sometimes friction can generate good stuff.

Well, I mean, there was a certain amount of friction because it was a very expensive movie—more than anybody anticipated. With a man like Ridley you pull out all the stops because you know you're going to have a director back you up every inch of the way, as opposed to other, many different kinds of directors. Some directors look at the style of the film as very, very important. Others, it's sort of "whatever you want to do is fine."

Now how did you and David divvy up the duties. Obviously a few matte paintings were required?

There were a lot of matte paintings, and a lot of miniatures. And this was one of the areas where I let David interface for me in dealing with the "miniature wranglers." As David had worked with Doug Trumbull before...as I said, he was on *BRAINSTORM*...it made sense for him to do all the interfacing. I brought all the miniature makers, including their key man, Mark Stetson, down to the back lot, and walked them through it. We gave them drawings of all the exterior sets, so they got the feeling of the architectural quality that we were after—this retro-fitted style that was very indicative of the breakdown of the mechanical aspects of the buildings.

David had been my assistant on two earlier shows—at Universal—and he was part of my design team at that time. David handled what we did down at the Bradbury Building, such as the Ennis-Brown house, as well as the room that had all the eyes and the chambers. But that was built on location in a meat locker. A freezer. A big open freezer.

On location in L.A.?

On location in L.A. We found an available meat storage locker that was available for rent. We built the set at the studio, prefabbed it, took it to the meat locker, set it up, put all the walls together, and brought the effects guys in and proceeded to hose the set down with Hudson spray guns with water over a period of five days—until the whole set was like dripping icicles. And also, while we did that, we gradually turned the temperature down to five degrees above zero. It was a very complicated process. Nothing on this film was simple, that goes without saying. Every element of the design was worked out, from streetlights to newspapers to vending machines to telephones to every aspect of the design. You know, I'm the first one to say I didn't do everything. You couldn't. Either that or you'd be dead at the end of the movie or part way through. But you do get involved in everything you can and all the important things, and you learn to delegate a lot of things to people that you have confidence in who are in tune with what you're doing.

But, at all times, David had instructions as to what should be accomplished at his end?

Absolutely. Also, we still had a drafting room to run, too. We had two illustrators and four or five set designers. So, it was a real busy show, to say the least.

But it came out looking brilliant. I mean, it's just a wonderful thing to look at.

Thank you.

Okay, so let's move on. Futuristic settings.

Well, first of all, I don't consider *BLADE RUNNER* a futuristic film, okay? Every time a press person would talk to me abouth the film, I would say, "No, it's not a film set in the future. We're doing a period piece. It just happens to be forty years from now as opposed to forty years ago." Conceptually, the film is set forty years from now and has buildings of that time, which is 2019, still has buildings of 1980 or '81, and it still had buildings of 1930 and 1935. So, there was this variety of design and architecture that existed in the environment, and it was my job as a designer to make sure that the audience was aware of that type of thing—that it wasn't just how you think of futuristic projects, that everything is slick and modern and new. It wasn't meant to be that way. So, no, and by the way, no, it's not. *BLADE RUNNER* was a very challenging project just because of the scope and the scale and the thought process that went into it. I've had other shows that were just as difficult for different reasons, such as *BACK TO THE FUTURE* and *ROMANCING THE STONE*. They were difficult, because here we're in Mexico for five months, and it's raining like hell, and part of the mountain slides down on the shooting company, and everybody waves their hands, "I'm alright!" Or, you try and communicate to your carpenters, and even though I speak Spanish, obviously, it's my error of communication because they didn't get what I was talking about, and even though I have an English and Spanish-speaking art director with me, it was just tough. And *BACK TO THE FUTURE* was tough, because we built everything and did all these things and all these sets from 1955, and I'm getting ready to go into the 1984 or '85 sequence, and I get a phone call that says, "Stop!" But I didn't know that they were re-casting the movie. So, whatever you built, you have to re-build. So there are different films that are tough in different ways. *BLADE RUNNER* was the toughest because it was the most design-provoking. I'd never had a director who was that "into it." I'd never taken on a project that big before.

Okay, so *GANDHI* wins the production design Oscar and *BLADE RUNNER* doesn't. Tell me your thoughts on that.

Well, *GANDHI* won because the

Academy saw it and voted for it, you see. The Academy didn't see *BLADE RUNNER*. *BLADE RUNNER* was not successful at the box office. It was a downer.

Didn't it do like $40 million or so?

No, it did $28 million. At least initially. It was disappointing. And to say the least, I now was told by people who were in the know that, Larry, you're not gonna win.

"I don't consider BLADE RUNNER a futuristic film, okay? It's not a film set in the future. We're doing a period piece. It just happens to be forty years from now as opposed to forty years ago."

—*Larry Paull*

It's that simple. Plus, it wasn't the Academy's kind of movie. The Academy, by and large, likes these kinds of epic-type movies. I find it fascinating that I managed to win the British Academy Award, and Stuart [Craig] didn't. But then he won the American Academy Award. I just find it all fascinating.

When you were very young, what were your thoughts about the Academy Award thing? Let's talk about your youth.

Well, I was a movie nut. I used to go to the movies every weekend and see all the westerns and the serials and all the Buck Rogers stuff. And on Friday nights, when I was a teenager, I used to go to a theatre in Chicago on the north side where we all hung out. From the time I was about 16, I had fantasies of becoming a film designer, an art director. And when I was bumbling about through college, on and off studying architecture, and not happy with myself or with what I was doing, I interviewed with a commercial house in Chicago. They offered me a job. I was all excited. At the age of 20, I was going to become a set designer. Then they called up and said—at

that time they still had the draft—"Has Larry finished his military obligation?" My mother answered the phone and she said, "Military? Oh, no, he's not been in the army." So they hired the other person. So, I went back to college after I got out of the service and got my degree, and then I started my Master's Degree in city planning and ran out of money and out of scholarships. Then I came to California to be an architect...basically, to do my hallowed work routine. And within a year I found out that didn't work. At least it didn't work for me. And, within about a year and a half, I had met a couple of people at Columbia.

So you were destined to become a filmmaker. At least a set maker.

I always wanted to be in the film business, always as a designer. I see a lot of people in this business in various areas whose interest, whose desire, whose fantasy is always to do something other than they do. A lot of people want to direct. I've never had that desire. I really get off on what I do, and back around 15 or 18 years ago, I was offered a job as an associate producer with a rather well-established production company here. Not a studio, but an independent production company. I passed, because the area I wanted to be in is where I'm at.

How'd you land your first feature?

My [now ex-]wife, Karen, worked for Bob Evans at Paramount. Al Ruddy had a producing deal at Paramount before his next picture, *LITTLE FAUSS AND BIG HALSY*. He got to know Karen... he wanted to stay on her good side so he'd have access to Evans, and this is sort of how you can do it, through an executive's assistant. Anyway, he promised me the show in front of Bob Evans, without consulting the director, Sidney Furie, who was not too happy about the choice. There was no money to do anything. Whatever I wanted to do, I literally did it myself. Be it age-down signs, buildings, whatever. I had to do it. Two of the characters who played Michael J. Pollard's parents had this lunch wagon—a "roach coach," you see. One day, the transportation guy says, "Larry, where do you want this?" And I said, "What's that?" "Oh, this is the 'roach coach.'" "But guys, there're no counters in it, there's no door opening cut." "But Larry, I just bought it for $3,000, do what you want with it." "Ungh?" And all of a sudden I'm sitting there with no painter, no construction people, no nothing. Except I had one thing; the brains that God gave me. And I went through the Yellow Pages, and all of a sudden I found a body shop that would cut what I wanted done. I found a sheet metal shop to build all the counters and the little grill and all that. I found sign writers. It took two weeks, but lo and behold, there was a roach coach. It was done by the sweat of my brow, and for peanuts. That was sort of my first show.

Which begs another question. Now they're spending, $40 and $50 million on shows. *LITTLE FAUSS AND BIG HALSY* cost what, about $2 million?

Two and a half.

Is it easier for you, the production designer, to have that much money? Kind of the "blank check syndrome?"

No matter what you have, it's not a blank check. No matter what you have, there's always a budget, and there's always X amount for this set and X amount for that set. The bottom line may be bigger, but there is a big difference between shooting on location and shooting on stage. There's just no two ways about it. When you're shooting on stage, what you have is the advantage of controlling everything you do, and designing the sets for the action. When you go on location, you not only compromise your art, as the designer—because you can only do X amount with various locations—you also compromise what the director can do with that location. So what happens is, a lot of times when you shoot sequences on locations, the action gets modified to fit the location. As opposed to when you're on the back lot or on stage, you design settings to fulfill the needs of the script. The point is, we cannot talk about the cost of a production. You weigh that, and then you take out what is called a bulk line, which are producers, the directors, the writers, the stars, and the supporting players. All of a sudden, on a lot of films, that above-the-line is equal to and a lot of times more than the cost to make the movie. So, it may seem like I may be working on a big, big film, but in fact, I'm not. I mean, the money is going into areas that the studio or whoever's financing the film deem necessary, be it to get this actor or that director or this producer or that writer or whatever. And that package is costing X amount of money.

Films are very top-heavy these days.

Yeah, they're very, very top-heavy. And the more top-heavy they get with certain actors who want to be protected from the public, so to speak, or who do not want to have a lot of exposure to the public, the more you find them on sound stages, because the actor—the star—feels more comfortable in a controlled environment. He doesn't have to worry about someone saying, "Oh, can I have your autograph?" Or this guy saying, "Hey, I hear you're not really as tough as you are in the movies, are ya? Well, let's duke it out here in the alley!" And I've seen that happen! It's very interesting. And also, as a designer, it's a lot more fun to design sets. There's no two ways about it, it's a lot more fun. I mean, location scouting is not at the top of my list on what I want to do four or five days a week.

Were you at all tentative on your first shows?

Oh, yeah, absolutely. I was scared to death!

When did that start to let up?

Well, on the first show I was really paranoid. On my second show, *THE HIRED HAND*, I was chosen by both the producer and the director, so I had a much freer hand to design. Also, I felt more a part of that whole film unit kind of collaboration. And it was a very interesting experience because Vilmos Zsigmond turned out to be the cameraman, it was Peter Fonda's directorial debut, and that was with his company right after EASY RIDER, so we had a lot of fun. We really all had a lot of fun, because everybody was able to do their thing, so to speak, and most people thought we just found everything in New Mexico. Because it was a Peter Fonda film, they thought, "Oh, you just go out and find the stuff, it's just there." And it's not.

I guess the easier time people thought you had on a film, the better job you've done.

Yes. For the most part, that is true. Sometimes, it's not true, because for the real high-profile design films, you have to do "look-at-me" in books. You have to, and I'm not saying it always works, but let's just say, most recently, with *DICK TRACY*. The look, the style of the sets were the co-star of the movie, there's no two ways about it. The co-star of *BLADE*

RUNNER was the look and the style of the film, there's no two ways about that either.

But people expect that. It's like, they're plunking down their seven bucks, or whatever.

Except most films don't call for that type of thing. This film [*THE MEMOIRS OF AN INVISIBLE MAN* starring Chevy Chase and Darryl Hannah as directed by John Carpenter.] has some of that. That building over there [points to drawing on wall] is a six-story highrise building, and we're gonna make it look like a partially invisible six-story building. So, that's the challenge here. We're building partially invisible sets, and I've never done partially invisible sets. We'll have walls that are gone, and walls hanging in mid-air.

That's what makes your job fun. With each particular film, you can express a particular look.

Yes, exactly. This is the other reason I left architecture. In architecture, you can be on a project for two years and see it finished. In film, the average film is anywhere from six to ten months for me, from pre-production through production. Some films last over a year, a year and a quarter sometimes, but most times not. You know, you're in and you're out. Twelve, thirteen weeks of pre-production, twelve weeks of shooting, hello, goodbye, see you on the next film, maybe. You're out of there. Another advantage of working in film is that you are able to mimic, you're able to set standards, and you reach a very large audience of people. And that's what's really fun. Six or seven months, and then you move on. You find a whole new group of people, and you start basically all over again on a totally different kind of project. And that's what's great about it.

When you hear that a Vilmos Zsigmond's going to be lighting your sets, is that pleasing to know?

Oh, yes. Or who I have right now is Bill Fraker. I'm absolutely enthralled to be able to collaborate with Bill Fraker, you know, because I know what I'm doing is going to be shot and lit properly, in the manner and feeling to which it was designed. And I know it sounds a little pompous, but it's real, real true. I've had experiences where I've designed shows, and I've thought, "I've done a wonderful job," and you go to dailies, and I want to go stick my head in a bucket of shit. I mean, it's

9

poorly lit, they use Musco lights when they shouldn't use Musco lights. Or, instead of seeing the whole set, you just see close-ups, and you wanna die! So a lot has to do with who you collaborate with, and a lot of times, the person who's putting that collaborative group together is the director, so you can only hope and pray that he puts the right people together.

CITY SLICKERS. Tell us a little bit about that.

Well, *CITY SLICKERS* is a modern-day western, and it's initially set in New York, and there are these three buddies who go on Walter Mitty-type vacations once a year. The film opens up at the running of the bulls in Pamplona. When I read that, I thought, "Oh, my God, where are we going to do this?" Anyway, the three guys come back to New York and decide the next year they'll go out west on a vacation where they'll be part of a cattle drive going from New Mexico to Colorado. And I was the envy of just about every production designer in this town, because no one does westerns anymore, and I love westerns. I did one years ago, and I worked on another one as an assistant, and it was a lot of fun. I'd gone to New Mexico before on a show, and I'd also gone down there riding. So it's a modern-day western set in the the Old West. So, I designed a ranch— there are two ranches in the show...both were built. The first one is in Abique, New Mexico, which is right where Georgia O'Keeffe lived for many, many years. Again, the director's first response when he got there was, "My God, Larry, it's big!" And I said, "Yeah, it's big." And "The West" *is* big. I wanted the ranch, the barn, the scale of the house to be big, you know, and these guys were like...I think I made the producer wince when I said one of my favorite westerns was "Giant," which was another modern-day western. But a lot of *CITY SLICKERS* takes place on this cattle drive, the bulk of which was done in Colorado. But the show was very, very busy design-wise, because Billy [Crystal]'s apartment was on stage, the studio, the ranches were set pieces. An interior bunkhouse was built, an interior chuckhouse was built, the inside of the barn. It was a good sized film. We had five nights at this place called Diablo Canyon, which is an outdoor canyon. And the director asked me, "Can't you do this on stage, Larry?" So, I designed a little cave set that turned out to fill up an entire stage. It was huge. Besides doing the five nights worth of work there, then I started revamping it into other caves, other rock sets, because we had all these campsites throughout the film. They never wanted to leave the stage again. Ever.

What are your favorite Larry Paull-designed movies?

One of my earlier favorites was a film called *THE BINGO LONG TRAVELLING ALL-STARS AND MOTOR KINGS.* That was a lot of fun. It was a real creative time. Obviously, one of my other favorites, design-wise, is *BLADE RUNNER.*

You seem very content.

I'm still of the opinion that, where else but in the movie business can you have so much fun, be very well paid, and just really enjoy what you are doing. I understand I'm naive in certain ways, but I do understand that I am sort of unique in as much that I enjoy what I do, because most people don't. I sort of feel lucky. With it comes a lot of aggravation, but I think aggravation comes with anything that one does, and you just sort of have to move by it. I'd be very, very unhappy if I was not doing what I am doing.

W℞C WARNER RESEARCH COLLECTION

Research

for motion pictures, television, advertising
and other creative mediums

...Story ideas...hard-to-find books... architecture...fashion...
...furnishings... ...history...license plates... technical manuals...
...and more

By appointment
(818) 953-9743
FAX (818) 953-8639

Burbank Public Library
110 N. Glenoaks Blvd. at Olive Avenue
Burbank, CA 91502-1203

Separate entrance at rear

Christine Loss

GLORIA GRESHAM

LORIA GRESHAM WAS RAISED IN INDIANAPOLIS, INDIANA, but soon found herself battling the masses in New York City. Gloria's presently married to a film producer and they call both New York and Los Angeles home. Though this costume designer spends a bit more time in Los Angeles, she stresses that she tends to miss New York while in California. Gloria was responsible for the threads in *AUTHOR, AUTHOR; THE NATURAL; FLETCH; MIDNIGHT RUN; WHEN HARRY MET SALLY...* and *THE WAR OF THE ROSES,* to mention but a sampling.

David Pecchia: How did you come to do *BEETHOVEN*?

Gloria Gresham: Well, Ivan Reitman is producing, so that's really how I came to it...that is through Ivan, Joe Medjuck and Michael Gross, who are the producers. I was doing another film, a big period film actually, and that fell out. When that happened, they were doing a couple of things...they're very generous and gracious to me, and they said, "Come, do either one or both of them. Whatever you want to do."

You had done *TWINS* and *GHOSTBUSTERS* with these guys.

And *KINDERGARTEN COP.* And I also had done *MIDNIGHT RUN* with Chuck [Grodin], so it just felt good and I said, "Sure, I'll come and do this." They're nice people.

Who's directing this?

Steve Rash [*Editor's note: Brian Levant took over directing chores when Rash departed due to "creative differences."*]

Alright. Let's delve back into your youth here. At a young age, were you interested in movies? Did you want to make them?

No, I started in the theatre. I still have my apartment in New York on 57th Street, and, no, when I was in high school and in college, I was in the theatre department. I always thought I would go to New York...which I did, and all the formative years were in New York. I spent the first ten years working on Broadway and off-Broadway, and then sort of gravitated toward filmmaking and assisted on a number of pictures as a design assistant, and then eventually came out here. And here I am.

Any desire to go back to the Broadway stage?

Yes, a little bit. Just recently, though, I've felt it. Kathleen Turner did *Cat on a Hot Tin Roof* last year, and we were talking about different things, and I said, "I would love to come back and do a play." So, you know, it might happen. Next year, maybe.

But in the theatre, once the play starts its run, your services become obsolete, right?

That's right. And that's one of the things that made me gravitate toward film more and more. I worked on a lot of Broadway shows that opened on Tuesday and closed on Thursday, you know, and even if a film is not well-received, or, at the moment people don't like it, it's always there to look at later and to review. It's not lost, it's not gone forever, which is the way it is with a theatrical production. But I still like sitting in a dark theatre at dress rehearsal.

What brought you into the feature area of filmmaking?

I always worked in features, even when I was assisting in New York.

Films made for tv?

No. Once I assisted designer Ruth Morley, who passed away recently, on a little television movie.. Then I assisted on a couple of feature films, one more television thing, a few more features, and then that sort of led me to some more assisting with Tony Walton. Then I got *URBAN COWBOY,* mainly because of Ali MacGraw, and that was the beginning. I mean, it's not as if it was all real easy, or as if I've been made Chairman of the Board of some big company, because tomorrow

is like anything. It's like actors or directors or anybody working in this unpredictable business..

You're suddenly and repeatedly out of work, right?

Absolutely. They don't know your name.

***URBAN COWBOY* was a big project. How did it come about?**

I was doing a movie with Ali called, *JUST TELL ME WHAT YOU WANT,* directed by Sidney Lumet, and I was working with Tony [Walton.] I was the co-costume designer on it, and Ali was the star. Bob Evans, who is her ex-husband and the father of her only child—they're really good friends— was producing, so Ali said to him, "You have to know her, you have to meet her, and she's terrific, she has to do this!" So I flew out here and had an interview with Jim Bridges and met the producers, and, you know, it just happened. It was great.

And was *ZORRO, THE GAY BLADE* soon after that? That would be a likely dream endeavor of your profession.

No. I had a little down time after *URBAN COWBOY.* In fact, I went back to New York and thought, "Oh, this is great, I'm off to a wonderful beginning here," and then nothing happened for months and months.

That's...pretty frightening.

It was. It was, really.

But the film did pretty well, didn't it?

But the film wasn't released yet. When you finish, there's a big lapse of time between the time you finish shooting and the time the film comes out.

But I think people in the industry know the buzz, the early word on films. Dailies are seen and talked about quite a few months before the finished product hits the theaters.

I went back to New York. I didn't come here, and I think that made a difference, too. In retrospect, I think if I had been out here it might have helped. But I was a New Yorker. I came out from New York to do it, I went back to New York and then eventually...for a long time, I was bicoastal. For about five years. Now I basically am here and go back to New York just from time to time. But I did *THE ESCAPE ARTIST* for Zoetrope, Francis Coppola's company, and then I did *ZORRO, THE GAY BLADE,* which was a big period film.

How did that one go? You were still a little green, right?

It was fun. I like George Hamilton very much, and he's very entertaining. The thing about George is he knows clothes, and he knows what looks good on him so he had ideas about things. And it was good. I enjoyed it.

So he would suggest things, and if something didn't look right on him, he would let you know?

Yes, he would, and always with a sense of humor. And then, also, he's very bright. I think he's very creative.

Let's talk about Barry Levinson You did *DINER* and then...

TIN MEN and *THE NATURAL* and *AVALON.*

Kind of a ten year collaboration, off and on.

We got out of sync this year, though.

Oh, really...for *BUGSY*?

Well, what happened...by the time they called...it would have been excellent. I'll tell you what I said. I said "You should have called a week sooner!" By the time they called, I was already committed to *FULLY LOADED* [now known as *V. I. WARSHAWSKI,* starring Kathleen Turner] and it was impossible to get out of it.

How did you meet up with Barry? Did he hear about you through your other shows?

No, through Mark Johnson, who has produced every film that Barry's done. Mark and I went back to these early days when I was assisting other designers, and Mark was a second assistant director. I was a design assistant, so we were both assistant types.

Running around a lot, right?

Yeah, and I didn't even quite realize at the time what a fan Mark was of my work and how I worked and everything, but he was, and he introduced me to Barry, and of course, it was the first film Barry directed. It was the first film Mark produced, and so

I think Mark wanted somebody that he really felt he could trust, and so that's how I came into the picture. Basically, I didn't even interview with Barry. Mark just said, "I think...."

Well, it worked out fine.

Yes, it did.

Now, let's talk about the collaboration between director and costumer. You read the script, obviously, and then

> *"...the more pictures that are made and the more good pictures, profitable pictures that are made, the better it is for all of us. Everybody. Because indirectly, even if you're not involved in a big hit, it helps the industry. It helps the town, so you just want everything to do well."—Gloria Gresham*

you confer with the director. How do you work out the look of the actors?

Every project is different, obviously. A period project is approached slightly differently than a modern film, but first you start with the script. That's the most important thing. And then the next step is to have a meeting with your director, and some directors have more ideas about the clothes than others. Some are more willing to leave it to you, others want to be really involved and come to fittings. I think it's better, quite frankly, when there's more collaboration, because then you don't have surprises when you get on the set, like, "Oh, you've ruined my movie, what else do you have?" You know, that kind of thing. But, certainly, the actor has to bring something to it, because you can sit around and speculate all you want about how a character should look, or what you think of this and that, and then the actor or the actress can come in with their perspective, because after all, they are the ones who speak the words, and they are the ones who wear the clothes. So eventually that does come into the equation, too. And once again, it's different; some actors just stand back and say, "Do it" and others have very opinionated ideas.

And again, I think that works well for you, because you don't want those

surprises.

No, I don't. And actually, I like the whole...it is a creative process. And it's always a work in progress, and that's the reason if somebody has an idea up until the eleventh hour, and it's a good idea, I will try to accommodate it—within the parameters of what we can do and what we can't.

What if you just hate the idea? Does that happen? I mean, when you think something is not working?

Oh, a lot of times. A few times, I lied. There are times when I think it's not right. I find, in the early stages, one way to squelch it: If I am really right, then they'll see it when I show them what they want. Sometimes they want something which I don't think is right. But we go and get it, or we get a picture of it, or we get a sketch of it, or we do whatever, and then I show it to them, and they go, "Oh, you're right." So it saves a lot of arguments. Instead of me saying, "I don't think so," I do my best to get it, whatever it is, because—and sometimes I'm wrong, you know—it looks great, whatever it is. But if I really feel secure in the fact that this is a mistake, I'll plunge ahead and show them. That's my main way of getting through—to go ahead and do it and then let the cards fall where they may.

Now, on *THE NATURAL* you worked with Bernie Pollack, right? Sidney's brother?

Yes.

Okay. How did you two merge your style?

Well, Redford wanted Bernie and Barry wanted me, and it was a big enough picture, and the casting was so light, especially for the female leads, Glenn [Close] and Kim Basinger. I mean, Kim was cast literally three, four days before she worked in period costumes. I wasn't in New York...I was someplace visiting my husband over the weekend. They called and they said she's working on Tuesday, and I said, "You're kidding!" So it was the same thing with all of us. But it worked out just fine that Bernie was really really busy with the men and the baseball uniforms and all of that. So actually, in a really unusual situation, because it's not common to have two costume designers on the same film...I thought it worked out just fine.

And did you speak with Mr. Redford about what he was wearing and what the attire contrast with the female leads would be? Or what he would like it to be?

No. First of all, I wouldn't speak to the actor about it, I would speak to Bernie about it. I would speak to the designer about it. That would not be correct decorum, first of all, to speak to the actor. No, I spoke to Bernie about things. But actually, in that kind of picture, quite frankly, the women set the tone anyway because the men's wardrobe is for the most part pretty muted, you know. In a period picture it seems really dark. The fabrics are much heavier. Even in summertime they're darker, like wool fabrics, that's what people wore then. So, most of the color came from, I think, a lot of the style...

The frills and the brightness and so forth?

Well, I don't know if it was bright, but I think in some ways you get a better sense of period. You know, it was such a strong male picture.

Now, when your agent or manager tells you about a project that he or she wants you to do, what are the first questions that you ask? Are you interested in who's directing?

That's practically the first question. Well, the first question is, "Is it modern or is it period?" That's the first question. And most of the time, they turn out to be modern. Especially after *AVALON*, I really wanted to do another period picture. And I will soon, but...not this week. And then you want to know who's directing it. And then you also want to know if there's some casting that they have in mind, and you can read it with that person in mind. I remember when I read *RAIN MAN* which eventually I didn't do. Barry directed it, but I was working on it when Marty Brest was directing it, and by the time Barry got it, once again, I was on another project so I couldn't come do it. But I remember reading it knowing that it was Dustin and Tom and I couldn't put it down. I thought Dustin was born to do this. And so, it does add a dimension if you can also know that when you're reading it. But otherwise, then you make your own idea.

Does it bother you at all, does it hurt or disappoint you when a film you've

worked on doesn't do well at the box office?

Well, yes, because, I mean, no matter what it is, you've worked hard, so you want people to see it. And sometimes, you know as you're doing it, though, that it's not going to work out as well as other films. I've been very fortunate. I think one of the reasons is that I have worked with good directors, i.e., Rob Reiner, Barry Levinson, Ivan Reitman. And I've done a number of pictures, so that helps. I think the main thing is the director. Somebody asked me recently what other directors would I like to work with, and I thought for a minute and I couldn't think of anybody! It was horrible! Now I can, but...

Scorsese...?

Exactly. It was like, I thought that's a very, very good question, and why can't you answer that, Gloria. But, does it hurt me? It hurts me, it hurts the industry because the more pictures that are made and the more good pictures, profitable pictures that are made, the better it is for all of us. Everybody, because indirectly, even if you're not involved in a big hit, it helps the industry. It helps the town, so you just want everything to do well.

Mr. Schwarzenegger and Mr. DeVito wore some terrific outfits in *TWINS*. I thought those matching suits added a bit of spark to the characters.

We had to key that all to Danny, because Arnold can wear just about anything, and Danny, obviously, because he's not as tall and doesn't...I mean everybody knows that it's no secret that shorter people have to be more careful about how they dress themselves. Basically, the thing was whatever looked good on Danny than Arnold had to wear it. Well, you can't—you shouldn't—put Danny DeVito in anything except something that has really clean, simple lines, so that's what we did. Then Arnold had to wear it.

He had no problems with that?

No, because he's fabulous. First of all, as I said, he looks good in everything, and he's such a gentleman and so professional. I can't say enough for him. But in that particular instance, it was really Ivan who was the guiding light. But they both just sat back, even though they're pretty opinionated in their lives, and they trusted Ivan.

Any films in recent memory that you would have killed to work on? Anything

that you've seen in the past five or ten years that you really thought was really grand and thought, "Why wasn't I on that show?"

Oh, you see that all the time, I guess. I mean, I would have loved to have done *CHARIOTS OF FIRE* or the first *GODFATHER*. That kind of thing. And even now, not being able to do *BUGSY* with Barry was a real heartbreak, you know. But there wasn't anything I could do about it. And you do another picture.

Is it easier to work with a director you know?

Yes, definitely. Definitely. Because you always have to go through that period, and also with actors, too, you have to go through that period of learning to trust one another. But even at that, every time you do a project, you still have to prove yourself...again. Because the requirements are different and they still have pressures, and nobody is going to let you do something that's a mistake. I found even though I'd done three other pictures with Barry, I was still nervous about doing the right thing for *AVALON* and being sure that he was happy. And so, I don't think you ever get over that.

Okay, finally, what are your favorite three Gloria Gresham costumed films? Blow your horn a bit here, if you will.

You know, obviously *AVALON* and *DINER*. Definitely *DINER* was a real turning point for me. It was a film where I felt I made a large contribution, and we had a very small budget, and even now I look at it and I think, "Wow!" And I like the film so much, and I like the soundtrack from it so much. So, I can only give you two, because the third, well, in a way, it might have been *URBAN COWBOY* only because it was so much fun to do, and also it marked such a beginning for me.

GEORGE   BOWERS

GEORGE BOWERS HAILS FROM THE BRONX SECTION OF New York City, having been born there in 1944. George and his wife, Eileen, who also works in the editing field, now reside in Los Angeles with their two daughters. Mr. Bowers directed *MY TUTOR* and handled editing chores on such films as: *THE ADVENTURES OF BUCKAROO BANZAI: ACROSS THE EIGHTH DIMENSION; THE STEPFATHER; SHOOT TO KILL; HARLEM NIGHTS*; and this year's hit, *SLEEPING WITH THE ENEMY*.

David Pecchia: So what did George Bowers want to be when he grew up?

George Bowers: Film editing was definitely the first choice and I guess it happened when I was about fourteen, fifteen years old. There was a family friend who lived in my neighborhood, a guy by the name of Hugh Robertson, who was a black man and was nominated for an Academy Award for editing *MIDNIGHT COWBOY* years ago. He was my first influence in the business. At the time of growing up I was in the Bronx and Hugh was a guy who used to drive a great Pontiac convertible—black, with red interior. Hugh dressed well and he worked downtown making films. That was the magic of it all. He did all this working downtown and not taking numbers. Like, where I grew up, anybody who drove big cars and Cadillacs and stuff and wore fancy clothes was definitely taking numbers or doing something else. So this was a good influence on me in terms of someone who did something legitimate and did well by it. He was a family friend and I kind of knew, because at about fifteen he took me down to the cutting rooms and I started seeing it. I kind of knew then he was going to get me into the business. So that was that deal.

Did you suffer the usual editorial path? That is, internship, apprenticeship, assistantship, etc?

I'd say yes, in terms of apprenticing, definitely. I started off first sitting down for a week learning how to splice. People would give me some film to practice with, using the splicer and stuff like that. Moved on to being an assistant. I kind of made a jump from assistant to editing very quickly, so I think I spent probably only about a year being an assistant. I never

really assisted on a feature. We were doing lots of documentaries, lots of trailers, featurettes and commercials and sound effects, too, and somehow I just got thrown by being in a small editorial company where we had two editors. As third in command, I got thrown in the back cutting trailers early on so I did a big jump from assisting into editing. It was more or less being thrown into the hot seat, making mistakes and having people show you and correct you. To just do it.

Sounds like someone "up there" likes you. It's easier to win the lottery than to get in the Editor's Guild.

It's real hard, especially out here. I guess the way the system goes, people get to be an apprentice and then they get to be an assistant for years and years and years before they get a jump. Somehow, in New York, there's an urgency. It's also like that out here, but it's like your father's in editing so you get a job or you get into it because your family's in it so you know that's the way you're going. In New York you got to go out of your way to find film editing, you know what I mean? There're multitudes of things to do, and how the hell can you find editing in there? You really have to go out of your way to find editing, and then jump fast. It's real hard to find someone back east who stays in the system too long. Everybody's climbing that ladder, trying to cut, stuff like that. So I kind of got a fast jump into editing.

Is trailer cutting a good training ground?

Cutting trailers gave me a good sense of taste, because it has to be interesting—dialogue and drama. When you do features, sometimes it's the dialogue that takes the pace, how it's going, the sense of

the dialogue. In trailers and stuff like that you are creating everything.

What are some of the qualities one must possess to be a good editor?

This is kind of a hard question. To be a good editor is sort of like what i have learned in the last twenty five, thirty years doing it, you know what I mean? Strong sense of story, what's important in the story and what isn't. After a while, a sense of timing, dramatics, choosing the right performance, when to cut, good sense of organization, planning and working well with other people, getting people to work for you. To do things for you in a nice way.

Is there a managerial aspect to it in terms of delegating jobs in your job? You need things done and you have to get them done without being a jerk?

Absolutely. And being a little bit of a diplomat. When someone else is a jerk you have to cover for them. Or the sense, the urgency of the film is so crazy you've got to overwork people. Whatever. There is a hell of a lot to do in planning, you know, and knowing when things have to be done and sort of getting them done correctly.

I've been told you directed some blaxploitation films early in your career. Why couldn't you continue directing?

To start off with, I've directed four motion pictures of which only one was black. So I never really started out with the intention of directing black films only. It was with the intention of directing films period. I guess I could have continued directing films but I realized that when I started off doing a lot of low budget films and directing films in twenty days, feature length motion pictures, you kind of realize its not really a lot of time. You're not going to be discovered for fancy footwork. You're not laying out interesting dolly moves and crane shots. There are no cranes, and you find yourself standing up on high places and stuff like that. Chairs or whatever. You've got to improvise a lot. There's not a hell of a lot you are going to do in twenty days that really is going to knock somebody on their ass to say what a great job you've done. Then it's a matter of the little companies and how much they can push it, you know? I think a film also needs publicity. If you can't sell a film there is almost no use making it in today's market. People have to know about it. A small company can't buy TV ads so no one's going to see it. So making low budget films, again that's the reason they call them low budget. And non union. You don't make any money. It's hard enough to jump into bigger films let alone being a black director, you know? It makes it much more difficult. I directed a couple of *Dukes of Hazzard.* But when my agent would get calls, he would get calls saying, "George, they need a black director." It's like they have a quota to fill or the show is on its last lap and some of the more successful TV directors know the show's not going to go or do any more re-runs, so to make that quota look better let's put in a minority. It's not like they need a *good* director, they need a *black* director. You get a little tired of it. Since editing was my first love and the first thing I did well, I went back to that and started making a good living. It's easier at the moment—and at times its easier to get employed—in editing than it was getting a directing gig because of some of the other things involved, which I guess we should go into. I wouldn't direct just to direct because I've already done it. If someone offers me a script tomorrow it's got to be the script. It's got to be the money involved. It's got to be the company. It doesn't make any difference to direct the same things that I have directed—that doesn't grab me. It's got to be the real possibility of doing something significant or else it's not worth it. I'd rather edit.

Tell us how directing helped your editing?

I don't think directing helped my editing eye. I think editing helped directing, because you kind of know what you need in the end, what you need to have in order to put this thing together.

What directing did do for me, though, was to gave me great appreciation of the process.I think I was much more understanding when I would have a scene. In other words, I knew more of what the director went through to get that scene and I just understood the process better. Sometimes as an editor, one sits down and bitches about why he or she didn't get that angle or why he or she didn't get that extra

shot. Now you kind of understand, and if you know you are working with a good director, if you got it that's great and if you didn't get it then that's about it. If you really need it you can ask him to go back, and if you know you are never going back to location that's the end of it and you try to make the scene work without it.

Do you secretly harbor a desire to direct that great script?

I hope so. Directing takes a lot out of

> *When you're editing, if you don't know what you're doing it's going to be pretty damn obvious real quick. You can't fake that stuff, you know what I mean? If you're sitting down in front of the Kem and you're putting some sloppy stuff together, any fool can see you don't know what the hell you are doing.—George Bowers*

you, it's a lot of planning. It's much, much harder than editing. It's hours, hours, decisions, questions every minute. It takes a lot to put it together. A lot of technical knowledge, and, unless the film has a chance of really going somewhere, I don't think it's worth it. I've done those films, I've made those films. And it hurts when you carry the ball, and then someone else can't carry the ball. Or when someone can't see what you did with twenty days and half a million dollars.The film makes a profit or whatever and they say, well it didn't really look that great. Well the "noble" films, you know, take 55 days to shoot. So it's a hard game. I'd love to do something but it is just getting very commercial. You can make the film for low money but it costs so much to do the publicity and prints. It's so much now, its a matter of whose going to trust you to invest that $25 million. I started out doing films for a half a million dollars. Publicity, prints and advertisements were probably under two million dollars. You can't do that stuff anymore. Prints and advertising...it has to be $10 million dollars to launch in movie theaters. And I think the choices of directors is a lot fewer now. There're just fewer films being made for that kind of money going out.

There are precious few blacks working in above-the-line capacities in this

business. **What is your theory?**

A friend of mine I once directed said to me, "You know, George, not one of my films has made a dime and they keep giving me more money. They keep offering me more salary and they keep giving me bigger budget films." Okay. So the answer really is it's a white boys club, you know what I mean? It's real hard for blacks to get into directing. Let me back this up. It's too much money involved and I don't think the people want to share that. I don't think those in power want to share that. No, it's too much money, it's too much power. You can look around and say there are lots of black brain surgeons, why can't there be some executives? I've run into a few executives that I didn't think could be brain surgeons. Too much money, too much power. They don't want to give it up. It's America.It's better, but it's still America. It's getting a little better.

Is it better for blacks in the editing field?

No. Is it easier? Is it a little easier for blacks in the editing field? No, it's not better for blacks in any field. It's not easier because editing to me is harder than directing. Editing is harder than directing in a real sense and I know that contradicts what I said before. When you're editing if you don't know what you're doing it's going to be pretty damn obvious real quick. You can't fake that stuff, you know what I mean? If you're sitting down in front of the Kem and you're putting some sloppy stuff together, any fool can see you don't know what the hell you are doing. A lot of people can direct, be it somebody's assistant, a relative, a son, a wife, husband. You can be a singer, a movie star and get to direct. And you get a lot of talented people to support you all the way down the line. Good a.d.'s, cameramen, good editors, you know? They make you look good. Editing is more of a skill, a craft, that you have to learn. It takes much longer. Directing is something to hold you up in certain instances. Even though I still agree that the process of directing, if you're a real director is much harder, you really have to work hard at it. But you can walk through the directing without any technical training. There's no school to go to to become a director. Look at TV. A lot of TV actors. A lot of TV shows begin with 22 episodes. After a while there are only eight shots left for DGA members because every actor want to get two shots. They want to write one and they want to direct two. The production manager wants to direct one because he wants to get some residuals, the medical benefits and so on down the line. And, actually, when an actor is directing, somehow the show gets going while they're off changing clothes. And adding makeup. Sometimes it's the crew and the cameramen who end up shooting the show.

How did the wacky *THE ADVENTURES OF BUCKAROO BANZAI: ACROSS THE EIGHTH DIMENSION* come into your life?

An old friend of mine, Richard Marks, was first contacted by [director] Rick Richter to clean up, doctor or fix *BUCKAROO BANZAI* because it had been edited by someone else and it didn't work out. It wasn't happening. So Richie was in a time crunch. We had to do it in a short amount of time. Richie, being from New York, had seen my work. It was the first time we worked together but I guess he respected my work, and we sort of co-edited. So that is how that happened. When you doctor a film, when you fix up a film, generally— unless the other person is a total idiot—an attempt has been made to put the film in some kind of structure. You look at it. You can always tell what's wrong with it, in terms of editing. At least the structure is there then you can go back in and look at what hasn't been used and find out why those choices were made. Or find other choices. That's generally what we do. Then we go back in and we can find other ways of doing it by seeing the things we thought would be better. And you can change pace and change scenes entirely. But I wouldn't say throw out totally what was done—you know, re-tool it. You never go back to dailies right from the beginning. To do dailies is to back and look at it all again from the top. You go into the things and look at what was left at the end and you can tell, generally if you have a good film. If the right choices have been made or, if not. It was a fun film to work on. It was kooky. It was crazy, and that's what was interesting about it. It was a cartoon. It was almost like you couldn't do wrong because it was supposed to be crazy so it worked out that way. It was all fun, it was

all in jest. The characters were bigger than life, they were real cartoons. John Lithgow was great. He had a great character so it was real good . It was real interesting working with him. And Richter was very, very interesting and nice to work with. Very nice man. A very smart guy.

***THE STEPFATHER* was a disturbing little thriller that certainly didn't disturb its investors. Do you feel partly responsible for its success?**

The film's success? Of course I helped it. Joe Ruben [*THE STEPFATHER's* director] is a very old friend. I edited his first film in New York, the first film he ever did...a thing called *THE SISTER IN LAW*. And,*THE POM-POM GIRL was* his second film out here in California. The way we work is very simple; he shoots and I put it together. He looks at what I do, and then together we make it better. Be it his eye or my eye, whatever, we just try to tighten up the pace, change shots, and it usually works out well that way. The first cut is usually longer— two and a half hours— and then you cut it down to under two hours. It's always a little fat. There're always a few scenes that are never going to stay in the movie, especially if the script is fat and they hadn't edited it before it was shot. Or they just don't work out. The scenes don't advance the story. No one wants to get tired sitting there. There is only so much time in a movie before you get tired of looking at it

So you two just get together and come up with the best film it can be.

Again, Joe works very closely with me after I cut the film. He gets in there very, very closely and we just keep making it better, by going over it over and over.

Do you ever show a rough cut of the film to someone who might not be so close to it? For objectivity's sake?

No. No. I know what's going to work. I don't think you get feedback that way, by showing it to your friends, asking your friends what they think. Your friends will probably lie to you anyway. I think at this stage we know, and if we don't know we ought to get out of the business. If he's shot it, he has done as good as he can do, and together I do the best I can do along with him. Hopefully, we can do good work together. So, we wouldn't run it by anyone else; we would look at it ourselves. And, I think, just reworking, looking for new

things, not being afraid to try a different angle is a process to editing, the way to do it. But I must say that right now it's getting easier to really be able to choose the right performances. To know exactly what you are going for. There are sometimes when you are working with Joe, in dailies and in shooting, he can't really tell me what he wants and what takes to use unless it's something very obvious or something he loves. Generally, he doesn't say much at all. A lot of that is he wants to see what I am going to do with it. He has an idea but I may give him something better than he has in mind and, then, after seeing that, that may spark something else off with him or maybe that wasn't so great, so let's go back to something he had in mind. But I guess you go on in years, and I am never that far off. It's never that bad. When we showed Joe the first rough cut of the last film we did, *SLEEPING WITH THE ENEMY*, we were both very happy. It looked great to us and we really couldn't come up with any great ways of changing it. We looked at it, and he was disturbed because it kind of looked too good for him and we tried to go back into it. It took us a while. We couldn't come up with any great changes. It really took about three weeks before we could get back into the film and find ways of making it better. This was a great rough cut but he felt and, rightly so, that we definitely could make it better.

On *HARLEM NIGHTS*, you certainly had your Moviola full, what with not one, but three comedy legends. Did Eddie Murphy, Richard Pryor and Redd Foxx improv you to death?

Well, to be quite truthful, for Eddie Murphy it's quite different. Eddie is an extremely good actor, so he doesn't improv when he's acting. Whatever bit of hilarious stuff that he does he's probably going to do the same way, exactly, the next time. He's a very good actor in that way? If you do eight takes you are not going to get eight different things. His timing is very good. Wherever he laughs or cracks or whatever he does or whatever movements that he does, he doesn't have to repeat every time.

It wasn't really just people, characters one-upping each another. Things like that happen with lesser-trained actors. In the film, we would try things like that, but these guys are professionals and what they did, they did consistently throughout the film. It was pretty good.

In other cases—like I'll just venture off to say in shooting a TV show—things like that have happened. The Sheriff and the Mayor on *Dukes of Hazzard.* Now these guys improvised, you know what I mean? You didn't know what they were going to say. And sometimes they were very good and it was very funny and sometimes it wasn't so funny; but they wouldn't do the same thing twice. But that's just an example, when improv doesn't help you. It makes it difficult in terms of editing, whereas in *HARLEM NIGHTS* the guys wouldn't wander off too far.

Will you consult your director as to which takes work better for you?

Yes. Then again sometimes its pretty obvious. You really get into a rhythm. You can just really see it. It stands out. I can see what it is. I pick it up. Now, maybe later on in the course of editing, ignored takes may be reconsidered. Again, working with Joe Ruben, I did five films with him, and we'd go through the process. I know what he likes and what he doesn't like. And he trusts me. I can put it together and then we can see what he does or doesn't like. For example, when we did *TRUE BELIEVER,* Jimmy [Woods] was a very intense actor. Sometimes we had to pull back a little from the performance because he was so intense. In terms of choosing the dailies, I would have three or four takes of real intense and then maybe we would give them a couple of takes of a little easier. The director is there for a reason, and those who don't act like that get a reputation and then they don't look like good people to work with.

Is a flexible director a good director?

Most directors are open to suggestions, no question about it. Why would they hire you if they weren't? I haven't really run into too many people that were not open to suggestions. At this point in my life I wouldn't work for them. Life's too short.

When I was younge, I wouldn't say that. But now I say, " Screw it. Life is too short to get jerked around."

Do you notice editing and pace when you're just out for an evening at the movies?

When you are out at a movie, I just sit back and enjoy it. I can tell when it is bad. I can tell when the editing is bad because the timing is off. Look at MTV. It will drive you crazy. Just when you are about to see something that you want to look at it's gone. The good looking girl on the left—just when you are about to see her again...she's gone. You say, "Holy shit!" So sometimes they ruin a beautiful shot. I would say let it go a little bit more. But generally I just go to look at the movie. In general, I want to see things and I am there to take it all in. I want to know if it's good camera work. I want to know if the acting is good, if the director is doing a good job, stuff like that. But that's just part of a good movie. That's the whole process.

Have any films you've seen just jumped out at you in terms of beautiful editing?

Well, *LAWRENCE OF ARABIA* is the only film that the last time I went to see it, I went to see it again.

How did Eddie Murphy come up with you for his directing bow, *HARLEM NIGHTS*?

I think the people working around Eddie, when he was directing that film, knew he wanted a black editor. And at that time there were a lot of people at Paramount who knew me. Head of editorial had done a couple of films there and Ralph Singleton, one of the producers of the film, knew me from many years ago, on the second film I ever touched back in New York. So it was the first time we had worked together in years, but he remembered me and I got a call. People called me.

Did Eddie freely solicit your views on this, his very first directing show?

Eddie didn't talk a lot. I think he did have a vision of what he wanted, so he didn't ask a lot of questions or give a lot of suggestions. He did a pretty good job and, again, we certainly had some people on the set to help him. I think he trusted me a lot. Quite a few people help put the film together. He was very cooperative in that. I mean, Eddie didn't come to the mix a lot. He did trust. There was much he didn't know about filmmaking, but I think he did trust people to do that job and he certainly trusted me. He would allow me to mix the film and show it to him and then at the end suggest if the music was too loud here or if he had to go back and think it out. He didn't get involved in the day to day hands on all the way. He would have suggestions for things and sometimes I would try them. Sometimes they worked, sometimes they didn't. He was very accessible. He would suggest something, I might disagree with it, but I would do it anyway and then show it to him. Then I let him see what his vision of it was, and I would suggest that we do something else. He was very approachable to work with in that way.

CINEMATOGRAPHERS

LISTINGS

CINEMATOGRAPHERS
PRODUCTION
DESIGNERS,
COSTUME
DESIGNERS AND
FILM EDITORS
GUIDE

C
I
N
E
M
A
T
O
G
R
A
P
H
E
R
S

CINEMATOGRAPHERS
ACADEMY AWARDS & NOMINATIONS
1977-1990

★★ = denotes winner in the category

1977
CLOSE ENCOUNTERS OF THE
   THIRD KIND .... Vilmos Zsigmond ★★
ISLANDS IN THE STREAM ..... Fred J. Koenekamp
JULIA .... Douglas Slocombe
LOOKING FOR
   MR. GOODBAR .... William A. Fraker
THE TURNING POINT .... Robert Surtees

1978
DAYS OF HEAVEN .... Nestor Almendros ★★
HEAVEN CAN WAIT .... William A. Fraker
SAME TIME, NEXT YEAR .... Robert Surtees
THE DEER HUNTER .... Vilmos Zsigmond
THE WIZ .... Oswald Morris

1979
1941 .... William A. Fraker
ALL THAT JAZZ .... Giuseppe Rotunno
APOCALYPSE NOW .... Vittorio Storaro ★★
KRAMER VS. KRAMER .... Nestor Almendros
THE BLACK HOLE .... Frank Phillips

1980
COAL MINER'S DAUGHTER .... Ralf D. Bode
RAGING BULL .... Michael Chapman
TESS .... Geoffrey Unsworth and
                         Ghislain Cloquet ★★
THE BLUE LAGOON .... Nestor Almendros
THE FORMULA .... James Crabe

1981
EXCALIBUR .... Alex Thomson
ON GOLDEN POND .... Billy Williams
RAGTIME .... Miroslav Ondricek
RAIDERS OF THE
   LOST ARK .... Douglas Slocombe
REDS .... Vittorio Storaro ★★

1982
DAS BOOT .... Jost Vacano
E.T. THE EXTRA-TERRESTRIAL ...... Allen Daviau
GANDHI .... Billy Williams and Ronnie Taylor ★★
SOPHIE'S CHOICE .... Nestor Almendros
TOOTSIE .... Owen Roizman

1983
FANNY AND ALEXANDER .... Sven Nykvist ★★
FLASHDANCE .... Don Peterman
THE RIGHT STUFF .... Caleb Deschanel
WARGAMES .... William A. Fraker
ZELIG .... Gordon Willis

1984
A PASSAGE TO INDIA .... Ernest Day
AMADEUS .... Miroslav Ondricek
THE KILLING FIELDS .... Chris Menges ★★
THE NATURAL .... Caleb Deschanel
THE RIVER .... Vilmos Zsigmond

1985
MURPHY'S ROMANCE .... William A. Fraker
OUT OF AFRICA .... David Watkin ★★
RAN .... Takao Saito, Masaharu Ueda
                      and Asakazu Nakai
THE COLOR PURPLE .... Allen Daviau
WITNESS .... John Seale

1986
A ROOM WITH A VIEW .... Tony Pierce-Roberts
PEGGY SUE GOT
   MARRIED .... Jordan Cronenweth
PLATOON .... Robert Richardson
STAR TREK IV: THE VOYAGE
   HOME .... Don Peterman
THE MISSION .... Chris Menges ★★

1987
BROADCAST NEWS .... Michael Ballhaus
EMPIRE OF THE SUN .... Allen Daviau
HOPE AND GLORY .... Philippe Rousselot
MATEWAN .... Haskell Wexler
THE LAST EMPEROR .... Vittorio Storaro ★★

1988
MISSISSIPPI BURNING .... Peter Biziou ★★
RAIN MAN .... John Seale
TEQUILA SUNRISE .... Conrad L. Hall
THE UNBEARABLE LIGHTNESS
   OF BEING .... Sven Nykvist
WHO FRAMED ROGER
   RABBIT? .... Dean Cundey

1989
THE ABYSS .... Mikael Salomon
BLAZE .... Haskell Wexler
BORN ON THE FOURTH
   OF JULY .... Robert Richardson
THE FABULOUS
   BAKER BOYS .... Michael Ballhaus
GLORY .... Freddie Francis ★★

1990
AVALON .... Allen Daviau
DANCES WITH WOLVES .... Dean Semler ★★
DICK TRACY .... Vittorio Storaro
THE GODFATHER PART III .... Gordon Willis
HENRY AND JUNE .... Philippe Rousselot

★★★★

A

HISHAM ABED
THE NATURAL HISTORY OF PARKING LOTS   Little
   Deer Productions, 1989

BARRY ABRAMS
HOLLYWOOD ON TRIAL (FD)   Lumiere, 1976
HERE COME THE TIGERS   American International,
   1978
FRIDAY THE 13TH   Paramount, 1980
A STRANGER IS WATCHING   MGM/UA, 1982

THOMAS (TOM) ACKERMAN
Agent: The Gersh Agency, Inc., Beverly Hills -
   213/274-6611, New York - 212/997-1818

ROADHOUSE 66   Atlantic Releasing Corporation, 1984
FOXFIRE LIGHT   Ramblin International, 1981
NEW YEAR'S EVIL   Cannon, 1981
GIRLS JUST WANT TO HAVE FUN   New World, 1985
BACK TO SCHOOL   Orion, 1986
BEETLEJUICE   Warner Bros., 1988
NATIONAL LAMPOON'S CHRISTMAS VACATION
   Warner Bros., 1989

MARSHALL ADAMS
DEADLY DANCER   Action International Pictures/AIP
   Home Video, 1990 w/Voya Mikulic

CLAUDE AGOSTINI
SUNDAY LOVERS   MGM/United Artists, 1981
QUEST FOR FIRE   20th Century Fox, 1982
TOO SHY TO TRY   Quartet, 1983
LES COMPERES   European International, 1984
THE BAY BOY   Orion, 1985
SWORD OF GIDEON (CTF)   Alliance Entertainment/
   Les Films Ariane/HBO Premiere Films/CTV/Telefilm
   Canada/Rogers Cablesystems/Radio-Canada, 1986
THE ARROGANT   Cannon, 1989

LLOYD AHERN II
DANIELLE STEEL'S 'FINE THINGS' (TF)   NBC
   Productions/The Cramer Company, 1990
DAUGHTER OF THE STREETS (TF)   20th Century
   Fox Film Corporation/Adam Productions, 1990

MAC AHLBERG
NOCTURNA   Compass International, 1979
HELL NIGHT   Aquarius, 1981
PARASITE   Embassy, 1982
THE SEDUCTION   Avco Embassy, 1982
MY TUTOR   Crown International, 1983
CHAINED HEAT   Jensen Farley Pictures, 1983
METALSTORM: THE DESTRUCTION OF JARED-SYN
   Universal, 1983
YOUNG WARRIORS   Cannon, 1983
GHOULIES   Empire Pictues, 1985
RE-ANIMATOR   Empire Pictures, 1985
THE DUNGEONMASTER   Empire Pictures, 1985
PRIME RISK   Almi Pictures, 1985
FUTURE COP   *TRANCERS*   Empire Pictures, 1985

ELIMINATORS   Empire Pictues, 1986
FROM BEYOND   Empire Pictures, 1986
GHOST WARRIOR   *SWORDKILL*   Empire Pictures,1986
HOUSE   New World, 1986
ZONE TROOPERS   Empire Pictures, 1986
DOLLS   Empire Pictures, 1987
HOUSE II: THE SECOND STORY   New World, 1987
PULSE POUNDERS   Empire Pictures, 1988
PRISON   Empire Pictures, 1988
GHOST TOWN   Trans World Entertainment, 1988
DEEPSTAR SIX   Tri-Star, 1989
THE HORROR SHOW   MGM/UA, 1989
ROBOT JOX   Empire/Triumph Releasing, 1990
OSCAR   Buena Vista, 1991

ROBERT ALAZRAKI
LOVE SONGS   Spectrafilm, 1986
FAMILY BUSINESS   European Classics, 1987
MY FATHER'S GLORY   Gaumont, 1991

ROMANO ALBANI
INFERNO   20th Century Fox, 1980
TERRORVISION   Empire Pictures, 1986
TROLL   Mariam Films, 1986
BLOOD LINK   Zadar Films, 1986
THE SLEAZY UNCLE   Ellepi Films, 1989
OBSESSION: A TASTE FOR FEAR   Titanus Produzione/
   Reteitalia, 1989

ARTHUR ALBERT
Phone: 212/691-5907

THE NIGHT OF THE COMET   Atlantic Releasing
   Corporation, 1984
THE BOYS NEXT DOOR   New World, 1985
ODD JOBS   Tri-Star, 1986, w/Peter Lyons Collister
STREETS OF GOLD   20th Century Fox, 1986
THE SQUEEZE   Tri-Star, 1987
THE PRINCIPAL   Tri-Star, 1987
MISS FIRECRACKER   Corsair Pictures, 1989
HEART CONDITION   New Line Cinema, 1990

MARYSE ALBERTI
POISON   Zeitgeist Films, 1991

JOSE LUIS ALCAINE
Agent: Smith Gosnell Nicholson & Associates -
   Pacific Palisades, 213/459-0307

DEMONS IN THE GARDEN   Spectrafilm, 1984
RUSTLER'S RHAPSODY   Paramount, 1985
WOMEN ON THE VERGE OF A NERVOUS
   BREAKDOWN   Orion Classics, 1988
ATAME   *TIE ME UP! TIE ME DOWN!*   Miramax, 1990
TWISTED OBSESSION   IVE, 1990

NESTOR ALMENDROS, ASC *
East Coast Card
Agent: Smith Gosnell Nicholson & Associates -
   Pacific Palisades, 213/459-0307

LA COLLECTIONNEUSE   Pathe Contemporary, 1967
THE WILD CHILD   United Artists, 1970
MY NIGHT AT MAUD'S   Pathe Contemporary, 1970
CLAIRE'S KNEE   Columbia, 1971
TWO ENGLISH GIRLS   Janus, 1972
CHLOE IN THE AFTERNOON   Columbia, 1972
IDI AMIN DADA (FD)   Tinc, 1974
COCKFIGHTER   *BORN TO KILL*   New World, 1974

AI

CINEMATOGRAPHERS
PRODUCTION
DESIGNERS,
COSTUME
DESIGNERS AND
FILM EDITORS
GUIDE

C
I
N
E
M
A
T
O
G
R
A
P
H
E
R
S

AI
**CINEMATOGRAPHERS
PRODUCTION
DESIGNERS,
COSTUME
DESIGNERS AND
FILM EDITORS
GUIDE**

C
I
N
E
M
A
T
O
G
R
A
P
H
E
R
S

THE STORY OF ADELE H.   New World, 1975
THE MARQUIS OF O....   New Line, 1976
THE MAN WHO LOVED WOMEN   Cinema 5, 1977
MISTRESS   Gaumont, 1978
MADAME ROSA   Atlantic Releasing Corporation,1978
DAYS OF HEAVEN ★★   Paramount, 1978
GOIN' SOUTH   Paramount, 1978
PERCEVAL   New Yorker, 1978
THE GREEN ROOM   United Artists, 1978
LOVE ON THE RUN   New World, 1979
KRAMER VS. KRAMER ★   Columbia, 1979
BLUE LAGOON ★   Columbia, 1980
THE LAST METRO   United Artists Classics, 1980
THE VALLEY OBSCURED BY CLOUDS   Michael
   Kaplan/Circle Associates, 1981
STILL OF THE NIGHT   MGM/UA, 1982
SOPHIE'S CHOICE ★   Universal/AFD,1982
VIVEMENT DIMANCHE   Spectrafilm, 1983
PAULINE AT THE BEACH   Orion, 1983
CONFIDENTIALLY YOURS   Spectrafilm, 1984
PLACES IN THE HEART   Tri-Star, 1984
HEARTBURN   Paramount, 1986
NADINE   Tri-Star, 1987
MES PETITES AMOUREUSES   New Yorker, 1987
NEW YORK STORIES ("Life Lessons")   Buena
   Vista,1989

JOHN A. ALONZO, ASC*
BLOODY MAMA   American International, 1970
VANISHING POINT   20th Century Fox, 1971
HAROLD AND MAUDE   Paramount, 1971
SOUNDER   20th Century Fox, 1972
LADY SINGS THE BLUES   Paramount, 1972
PETE 'N' TILLIE   Universal, 1972
GET TO KNOW YOUR RABBIT   Warner Bros., 1972
CHINATOWN ★   Paramount, 1974
THE FORTUNE   Columbia, 1975
ONCE IS NOT ENOUGH   Paramount, 1975
FAREWELL, MY LOVELY   Avco Embassy, 1975
I WILL, I WILL ... FOR NOW   20th Century Fox, 1976
THE BAD NEWS BEARS   Paramount, 1976
BLACK SUNDAY   Paramount, 1976
WHICH WAY IS UP?   Universal, 1977
BEYOND REASON   Allwyn Pictures/Arthur M.
   Sarkissian, 1977
CASEY'S SHADOW   Columbia, 1978
THE CHEAP DETECTIVE   Columbia, 1978
NORMA RAE   20th Century Fox, 1979
TOM HORN   Warner Bros., 1980
BACK ROADS   Warner Bros., 1981
ZORRO, THE GAY BLADE   20th Century Fox, 1981
BLUE THUNDER   Columbia, 1983
CROSS CREEK   Universal/AFD, 1983
SCARFACE   Universal, 1983
THE HIT   Island Alive, 1984, British
TERROR IN THE AISLES (FD)   Universal, 1984
RUNAWAY   Tri-Star, 1984
OUT OF CONTROL   New World, 1985
JO JO DANCER, YOUR LIFE IS CALLING
   Columbia,1986
50 YEARS OF ACTION! (FD)   DMS Productions
   Services, 1986, w/Caleb Deschanel &
   Chuck Clifton
NOTHING IN COMMON   Tri-Star, 1986
OVERBOARD   MGM/UA, 1987
REAL MEN   MGM/UA, 1987
ROOTS: THE GIFT (TF)   David L. Wolper Productions/
   Warner Bros. TV, 1988
PHYSICAL EVIDENCE   Columbia, 1989

STEEL MAGNOLIAS   Tri-Star, 1989
INTERNAL AFFAIRS   Paramount, 1990
THE GUARDIAN   Universal, 1990
NAVY SEALS   Orion, 1990

JAMIE ANDERSON
HOLLYWOOD BOULEVARD   New World, 1976
MALIBU BEACH   Crown International, 1978
PIRANHA   New World, 1978

THEIRRY ARBOGAST
NIKITA   Gaumont, 1990

FERNANDO ARGUE
9 1/2 NINJAS   Republic Pictures Home Video, 1991

ARLEDGE ARMENAKI
BLACKOUT   Ambient Light Entertainment/Overseas
   Film Group, 1989
CRACK HOUSE   Silverman Entertainment/
   Cannon, 1989

CHUCK ARNOLD
BLIND FAITH-PARTS I & II (TF)   NBC
   Productions, 1990
WEB OF DECEIT (CTF)   Wilshire Court Productions/
   Sankan Productions, 1990
THE CHASE (TF)   Steve White Productions, 1991

RICARDO ARONOVICH
Agent: Smith Gosnell Nicholson & Associates -
   Pacific Palisades, 213/459-0307

PROVIDENCE   Cinema 5, 1977
THE OUTSIDER   Paramount, 1979
CLAIR DE FEMME   Gaumont, 1979
YOU BETTER WATCH OUT   Edward R. Pressman
   Productions, 1980
CHANEL SOLITAIRE   United Film Distribution, 1981
MISSING   Universal, 1982
HANNA K.   Universal, 1983
LE BAL   Almi Classics, 1984
THE MAN INSIDE   New Line Cinema, 1990

HOWARD ATHERTON
FATAL ATTRACTION   Paramount, 1987
THE BOOST   Hemdale, 1988
MERMAIDS   Orion, 1990

BERNARD AUROUX
FALSE IDENTITY (TF)   LBS/RKO Pictures, 1990

B

HANANIA BAER

Agent: Smith Gosnell Nicholson & Associates -
PacificPalisades, 213/459-0307

A KILLER IN THE FAMILY (TF)   Stan Margulies
Productions/Sunn Classic Pictures, 1983
ECHOES   Continental, 1983
BREAKIN'   MGM/UA/Cannon, 1984
NINJA III: THE DOMINATION,   Cannon 1984
BREAKIN' 2 ELECTRIC BOOGALOO   Tri-Star, 1984
NIGHT PATROL   New World, 1984, w/Jurg Walthers
THE CARTIER AFFAIR (TF)   Hill-Mandelker
Productions, 1984
OBSESSED WITH A MARRIED WOMAN (TF)
Sidaris-Camhe Productions/The Feldman-
Meeker Co., 1985
ALWAYS   Samuel Goldwyn Company, 1985
AMERICAN NINJA   Cannon, 1985
BAD GUYS   Interpictures, 1986
PRINCE OF BEL AIR (TF)   Leonard Hill Films, 1986
SAMARITAN (TF)   Levine-Robins Productions/Fries
Entertainment, 1986
BROTHERHOOD OF JUSTICE (TF)   Guber-Peters
Productions/Phoenix Entertainment Group, 1986
ASSASSINATION   Cannon, 1987
MASTERS OF THE UNIVERSE   Cannon, 1987
SOMEONE TO LOVE   International Rainbow
Pictures/Castle Hill Productions, 1987
POKER ALICE (TF)   New World TV, 1987
AN ENEMY AMONG US (TF)   Helios
Productions, 1987
STRANGE VOICES (TF)   Forrest Hills Productions/
Dacks-Geller Productions/TLC, 1987
THE KING OF LOVE (TF)   Sarabande Productions/
MGM-UA TV, 1987
A FRIENDSHIP IN VIENNA (CTF)   Finnegan-Pinchuk
Productions,, 1988
ELVIRA: MISTRESS OF THE DARK   New
World, 1988
SEVEN HOURS TO JUDGMENT   Trans World
Entertainment, 1988
THE KID WHO LOVED CHRISTMAS (CTF)
Paramount TV/Eddie Murphy TV Enterprises, 1990
LEONA HELMSLEY: THE QUEEN OF MEAN (TF)
DIVING IN   Skouras, 1990
MURDER IN PARADISE (TF)   Columbia Pictures
TV/Bill McCutchen Productions, 1990
EATING   International Rainbow Pictures, 1990
DIVING IN   Skouras Pictures, 1991

KING BAGGOT

CHEECH & CHONG'S NEXT MOVIE   Universal, 1979
THE HAND   Orion/Warner Bros., 1981
BEATLEMANIA   American Cinema, 1981
SOME KIND OF HERO   Paramount, 1982
FAST-WALKING   Pickman Films, 1982
SECOND THOUGHTS   Universal, 1983
DOCTOR DETROIT   Universal, 1983
THE LAST STARFIGHTER   Universal, 1984
REVENGE OF THE NERDS   20th Century Fox, 1984

OH, GOD! YOU DEVIL   Warner Bros., 1984
GOTCHA!   Universal, 1985
TOUGH GUYS   Buena Vista, 1986
VICE VERSA   Columbia, 1988
DREAM A LITTLE DREAM   Vestron, 1989
LITTLE VEGAS   I.R.S., 1990
SHE SAID NO (TF)   Spectacor Films/Steve White
Productions, 1990
A MOTHER'S COURAGE: THE MARY THOMAS
STORY (TF)   Walt Disney TV/Chet Walker
Enterprises/Interscope, 1990

JOHN BAILEY, ASC*

Agent: Bauer Benedek Agency - Los Angeles ,
213/275-2421

THE MAFU CAGE   Clouds Productions, 1979
BOULEVARD NIGHTS   Warner Bros., 1979
AMERICAN GIGOLO   Paramount, 1980
ORDINARY PEOPLE   Paramount, 1980
HONKY TONK FREEWAY   Universal/AFD, 1981
CONTINENTAL DIVIDE   Universal, 1981
CAT PEOPLE   Universal, 1982
THAT CHAMPIONSHIP SEASON   Cannon, 1982
WITHOUT A TRACE   20th Century Fox, 1983
THE BIG CHILL   Columbia, 1983
RACING WITH THE MOON   Paramount, 1984
THE POPE OF GREENWICH VILLAGE
MGM/UA, 1984
MISHIMA: A LIFE IN FOUR CHAPTERS   Warner
Bros., 1985
SILVERADO   Columbia, 1985
CROSSROADS   Columbia, 1986
BRIGHTON BEACH MEMOIRS   Universal, 1986
SWIMMING TO CAMBODIA   Cinecom, 1987
TOUGH GUYS DON'T DANCE   Cannon, 1987
(Visual Consultant)
LIGHT OF DAY   Tri-Star, 1987
VIBES   Columbia, 1988
THE ACCIDENTAL TOURIST   Warner Bros., 1988
TIME FLIES WHEN YOU'RE ALIVE (CTF)   HBO
Showcase/Kings Road Entertainment, 1989
MY BLUE HEAVEN   Hawn-Sylbert/Warner
Bros., 1990

IAN BAKER

Agent: Paul Gerard Agency - Newport Beach,
714/644-7950

LIBIDO   Producers & Directors Guild of Australia, 1973
THE DEVIL'S PLAYGROUND   Entertainment
Marketing, 1976
THE CHANT OF JIMMIE BLACKSMITH   New
Yorker, 1980
BARBAROSA   Universal/AFD, 1982
ICEMAN   Universal, 1984
THE CLINIC   Satori, 1985
PLENTY   20th Century Fox, 1985
ROXANNE   Columbia, 1987
A CRY IN THE DARK   Warner Bros., 1988
THE PUNISHER   New World, 1989
EVERYBODY WINS   Orion, 1990
THE RUSSIA HOUSE   Pathe Entertainment/
MGM/UA, 1990

JOHN BAKER

CHAMPION-SWEET DANGER (TF)   Consolidated
Productions/BBC TV, 1990

Ba

CINEMATOGRAPHERS
PRODUCTION
DESIGNERS,
COSTUME
DESIGNERS AND
FILM EDITORS
GUIDE

C
I
N
E
M
A
T
O
G
R
A
P
H
E
R
S

Ba

CINEMATOGRAPHERS
PRODUCTION
DESIGNERS,
COSTUME
DESIGNERS and
FILM EDITORS
GUIDE

C
I
N
E
M
A
T
O
G
R
A
P
H
E
R
S

26

ROBERT M. BALDWIN
Agent: Tobias-Skouras & Associates, Inc. -
    Los Angeles, 213/277-6211
Phone: 516/331-8962

THE WEREWOLF OF WASHINGTON   Diplomat, 1973
THE EXTERMINATOR   Avco Embassy, 1980
THE SOLDIER   Embassy, 1982
EXTERMINATOR 2   Cannon, 1984,
    w/Joseph Mangine
ZOMBIE ISLAND MASSACRE   Troma, 1985
BASKET CASE 2   Shapiro Glickenhaus
    Entertainment, 1990
FRANKENHOOKER   Shapiro Glickenhaus
    Entertainment, 1990

MICHAEL BALLHAUS, ASC
Agent: Lawrence A. Mirisch, Triad Artists, Inc. -
    Los Angeles, 213/556-2727

SATAN'S BREW   New Yorker, 1976
SUMMER GUESTS   Constantin, 1976
MOTHER KUSTERS GOES TO HEAVEN
    New Yorker, 1977
DESPAIR   New Line Cinema, 1978
KALEIDOSKOP: VALESKA GERT (FD)   1979
THE MARRIAGE OF MARIA BRAUN
    New Yorker, 1979
DEAR MR. WONDERFUL   Joachim con Vietinghoff
    Produktion/Westdeutscher Rundfunk/Sender
    Freis Berlin, 1982
THE STATIONMASTER'S WIFE   Teleculture, 1983
MALOU   Quartet, 1983
SHEER MADNESS   R5/S8, 1983
BABY, IT'S YOU   Paramount, 1983
RECKLESS   MGM/UA, 1984
THE AUTOGRAPH   Cine-International, 1984
OLD ENOUGH   Orion Classics, 1984
HEARTBREAKERS   Orion, 1984
AFTER HOURS   The Geffen Co./Warner Bros., 1985
DEATH OF A SALESMAN (TF)   Roxbury and Punch
    Productions, 1985
THE COLOR OF MONEY   Buena Vista, 1986
UNDER THE CHERRY MOON   Warner Bros., 1986
THE GLASS MENAGERIE   Cineplex Odeon, 1987
BROADCAST NEWS H   20th Century Fox, 1987
THE HOUSE ON CARROLL STREET   Orion, 1988
BAJA OKLAHOMA (CTF)   HBO Pictures, 1988
THE LAST TEMPTATION OF CHRIST
    Universal, 1988
DIRTY ROTTEN SCOUNDRELS   Orion, 1988
WORKING GIRL   20th Century Fox, 1988
THE FABULOUS BAKER BOYS ★   20th Century
    Fox, 1989
POSTCARDS FROM THE EDGE   Columbia, 1990
GOODFELLAS   Warner Bros., 1990
GUILTY BY SUSPICION   Warner Bros., 1991
WHAT ABOUT BOB?   Buena Vista, 1991

MICHAEL BARNARD
THE INVISIBLE KID   Taurus Entertainment, 1988

CUSI BARRIO
HOUR OF THE ASSASSIN   Concorde, 1987
CRIME ZONE   Concorde, 1989
HEROES STAND ALONE   Concorde, 1989

GEORGE BARTELS
AMERICAN NINJA 3: BLOOD HUNT   Cannon, 1989

ANDRZEJ BARTKOWIAK
DEADLY HERO   Avco Embassy, 1976
PRINCE OF THE CITY   Orion/Warner Bros., 1981
DEATHTRAP   Warner Bros., 1982
THE VERDICT   20th Century Fox, 1982
DANIEL   Paramount, 1983
TERMS OF ENDEARMENT   Paramount, 1983
GARBO TALKS   MGM/UA, 1984
PRIZZI'S HONOR   20th Century Fox, 1985
POWER   20th Century Fox, 1986
THE MORNING AFTER   20th Century Fox, 1986
NUTS   Warner Bros., 1987
TWINS   Universal, 1988
FAMILY BUSINESS   Tri-Star, 1989
Q & A   Tri-Star, 1990

JAMES BARTLE
HEART OF THE STAG   New World, 1984
THE QUIET EARTH   Skouras Pictures, 1985
THE GOOD WIFE   Atlantic Releasing Corporation, 1987
MY BEST FRIEND IS A VAMPIRE   Kings Road, 1988
A DANGEROUS LIFE (CMS)   McElroy & McElroy
    Prods./Film Accord, 1988
BROTHERHOOD OF THE ROSE (TF)   NBC
    Productions, 1989

PAUL BARTON
POSITIVE I.D.   Universal, 1987

CRAIG BASSUK
DEATHROW GAMESHOW   Crown International, 1987

JOHN BATEMAN
CHALLENGE THE WIND   Vidmark/Sell
    Entertainment, 1990

FRED BATKA
LITTLE DARLINGS   Paramount, 1980
THE NIGHT THE LIGHTS WENT OUT IN GEORGIA
    Avco Embassy, 1981, w/Bill Butler

LORENZO BATTAGLIA
THE BARBARIANS   Cannon, 1987
WITCHERY   Filmirage, 1989

MARIO BATTISTONI
THE ICICLE THIEF   Aries Releasing, 1990

BOJAN BAZELLI
Agent: The Gersh Agency, Inc., Beverly Hills -
    213/274-6611, New York - 212/997-1818

CHINA GIRL   Vestron, 1987
PATTY HEARST   Atlantic Releasing Corporation,1988
PUMPKINHEAD   MGM/United Artists, 1988
TAPEHEADS   Avenue Pictures, 1988
THE COMEBACK (TF)   CBS Entertainment, 1989
THE HAUNTING OF SARAH HARDY (TF)   1989
BIG MAN ON CAMPUS   Vestron, 1989
SOMEBODY HAS TO SHOOT THE PICTURE (CTF)
    Scholastic Productions/MCA TV/Frank Pierson Films/
    Alan Barnette Productions, 1990
KING OF NEW YORK   New Line Cinema, 1990
CURIOSITY KILLS (CTF)   MCA TV Entertainment/
    Dutch, 1990

FRANK BEASCOECHEA, ASC *
West Coast Card
Agent: Smith Gosnell Nicholson & Associates - PacificPalisades, 213/459-0307

BUCK ROGERS   Universal, 1979
ISABEL'S CHOICE (TF)   Stuart Miller-Pantheon TV, 1981
NADIA (TF)   Dave Bell Productions/Tribune Entertainment Company/Jadran Film, 1984
STARK (TF)   CBS Entertainment, 1985
CHASE (TF)   CBS Entertainment, 1985
A FATHER'S HOMECOMING (TF)   NBC Productions, 1988
NO HOLDS BARRED   New Line Cinema, 1989
NICK KNIGHT (pilot)   1989
IN THE LINE OF DUTY: A COP FOR THE KILLING (TF)   WIN/Brittcadia Productions/Patchett Kaufman Entertainment, 1990
SNOW KILL (CTF)   Wilshire Court Productions, 1990
MIRACLE LANDING (TF)   CBS Entertainment Productions, 1990

AFFONSO BEATO
Agent: Lawrence A. Mirisch, Triad Artists, Inc. - Los Angeles, 213/556-2727

THE BOSS'S SON   Circle Associates, 1978
CIRCLE OF POWER *MYSTIQUE*   Televicine, 1983
THE TWO WORLDS OF ANGELITA   First Run Features, 1983
HAPPILY EVER AFTER   European Classics, 1986
THE BIG EASY   Columbia, 1987
GREAT BALLS OF FIRE!   Orion, 1989
ENID IS SLEEPING   Vestron, 1991

ETIENNE BECKER
ONE DEADLY SUMMER   Universal Classics, 1984

TERRY BEDFORD
JABBERWOCKY   Cinema 5, 1977

PAUL BEESON
STARCRASH   New World, 1979
THE UNIDENTIFIED FLYING ODDBALL   Buena Vista, 1979
HAWK THE SLAYER   ITC, 1980
SILVER DREAM RACER   American Cinema 5, 1980
JANE AND THE LOST CITY   New World, 1987

PETER BENISON, CSC
Agent: Gerald K. Smith - Los Angeles, 213/849-5388
Address: 2297 Oxford Ave., Montreal, Quebec, Canada H4A 2X7, 514/484-0714

UPS AND DOWNS   JAD International, 1983
MEATBALLS III   TMS Pictures, 1986
MAKE MINE CHARTREUSE (TF)   1986
BALLERINA & THE BLUES (TF)   1986
WHISPERS   ITC Entertainment Group/Live Home Video, 1990

GIANFRANCO BERGAMINI
COUNTERFEIT COMMANDOS   Aquarius, 1981
RAGE   Gel International, 1986

GABRIEL BERISTAIN
Agent: Sandra Marsh Management - Sherman Oaks, 818/905-6961

CARAVAGGIO   Cinevista, 1986
ARIA (Bill Bryden & Ken Russell segments)   Miramax, 1987
THE COURIER   Vestron, 1988
TROUBLES   Little Bird Productions/London Weekend TV, 1988
KILLING DAD   Scottish Television Enterprises, 1989
WAITING FOR THE LIGHT   Epic Productions/Triumph, 1990

JOHN BERRIE
HOW TO MAKE LOVE TO A NEGRO WITHOUT GETTING TIRED   Angelika Films, 1990

GRAHAM BERRY
POWAQQATSI   Cannon, 1988, w/Leonidas Zourdoumis

RENATO BERTA
FULL MOON IN PARIS   Orion Classics, 1984
L'HOMME BLESSE   Promovision International, 1985
RENDEZ-VOUS   Spectrafilm, 1987
L'ANNEE DES MEDUSES   European Classics, 1987
AU REVOIR, LES ENFANTS   Orion Classics, 1988
TWISTER   Vestron, 1989

JOHN BEYMER
MURDER IN BLACK AND WHITE (TF)   Titus Productions, 1990
SHATTERED DREAMS (TF)   Carolco TV/Roger Gimbel Productions, 1990

ADRIAN BIDDLE
ALIENS   20th Century Fox, 1986
THE PRINCESS BRIDE   20th Century Fox, 1987
WILLOW   MGM/UA, 1988
THE TALL GUY   Miramax, 1990
THELMA & LOUISE   Pathe/MGM, 1991

DONALD BIRNKRANT, ASC
TANK   Universal, 1984
BROTHERS-IN-LAW (TF)   1985

JOSEPH BIROC, ASC *
IT'S A WONDERFUL LIFE   Liberty Films, 1946
HUSH, HUSH SWEET CHARLOTTE ★   20th Century Fox, 1964
WHATEVER HAPPENED TO AUNT ALICE?   Cinerama Releasing Corporation, 1969
TOO LATE THE HERO   Cinerama Releasing Corporation, 1970
BRIAN'S SONG (TF) ★★   Screen Gems/Columbia TV, 1971
THE TOWERING INFERNO ★★   20th Century Fox, 1974, w/Fred Koenekamp
HUSTLE   Paramount, 1975
THE DUCHESS & THE DIRTWATER FOX   20th Century Fox, 1976
THE CHOIRBOYS   Universal, 1977
BEYOND THE POSEIDON ADVENTURE   Warner Bros., 1979
AIRPLANE!   Paramount, 1980
...ALL THE MARBLES   MGM/United Artists, 1981
HAMMETT   Orion/Warner Bros., 1982, w/Philip Lathrop
AIRPLANE II: THE SEQUEL   Paramount, 1982
FATHER OF HELL TOWN (TF)   1985
A DEATH IN CALIFORNIA (TF)   Mace Neufeld Productions/Lorimar Productions, 1985

Bi

CINEMATOGRAPHERS
PRODUCTION
DESIGNERS,
COSTUME
DESIGNERS and
FILM EDITORS
GUIDE

C
I
N
E
M
A
T
O
G
R
A
P
H
E
R
S

PETER BIZIOU, BSC *
BUGSY MALONE   Paramount, 1976,
    w/Michael Seresin
MONTY PYTHON'S LIFE OF BRIAN   Orion/Warner
    Bros., 1979
TIME BANDITS   Avco Embassy, 1981
PINK FLOYD - THE WALL   MGM/UA, 1982
ANOTHER COUNTRY   Orion Classics, 1984
9 1/2 WEEKS   MGM/UA, 1986
A WORLD APART   Atlantic Releasing
    Corporation, 1988
MISSISSIPPI BURNING ★★   Orion, 1988
ROSENCRANTZ & GUILDENSTERN ARE DEAD
    Cinecom, 1991

CHISTIAN BLACKWOOD
THELONIUS MONK: STRAIGHT, NO CHASER
    Warner Bros., 1990

BENJAMIN BLAKE
COLD FEET   Cinecom, 1984

STEPHEN ASHLEY BLAKE, SOC
Phone: 818/780-0962, 212/465-3381

DEADLY PREY   A.I.P., 1986
NIGHT WARS   A.I.P., 1987
VICE ACADEMY   Trans World Entertainment, 1988
ORDER OF THE EAGLE   Eagle Productions, 1988
BATTLE GROUND   A.I.P., 1989
TERMINAL FORCE   Austin Entertainment, 1989
BEVERLY HILLS VAMP   Austin Entertainment, 1990
DREAMERS   Midsummer Productions, 1991

CYRUS BLOCK
BROKEN BADGES (TF)   Stephen J. Cannell
    Productions, 1990

PATRICK BLOSSIER
VAGABOND   International Film Exchange, 1986
BETRAYED   MGM/UA, 1988
MUSIC BOX   Carolco Pictures/Tri-Star, 1989
DOCTEUR PETIOT   DR. PETIOT   Canal Plus/M.S.
    Productions-Sara Films-Cine 5/AAA, 1990

RALF D. BODE, ASC *
West & East Coast Cards
Agent: Smith Gosnell Nicholson & Associates -
    Pacific Palisades, 213/459-0307

THERE IS NO THIRTEEN   Film Ventures
    International, 1977
SATURDAY NIGHT FEVER   Paramount, 1977
SLOW DANCING IN THE BIG CITY   United
    Artists, 1978
JUST OUT OF REACH   1979
RICH KIDS   United Artists, 1979
COAL MINER'S DAUGHTER ★   Universal, 1980
DRESSED TO KILL   Filmways, 1980
RAGGEDY MAN   Universal, 1981
THE PRESIDENT'S WOMEN   Krona, 1981
A LITTLE SEX   Universal, 1982
GORKY PARK   Orion, 1983
FIRSTBORN   Paramount, 1984
BRING ON THE NIGHT (FD)   Samuel Goldwyn
    Company, 1985
THE WHOOPEE BOYS   Paramount, 1986

VIOLETS ARE BLUE   Columbia, 1986
CRITICAL CONDITION   Paramount, 1987
THE BIG TOWN   Columbia, 1987
DISTANT THUNDER   Paramount, 1988
THE ACCUSED   Paramount, 1988
COUSINS   Paramount, 1989
UNCLE BUCK   Universal, 1989
ONE GOOD COP   Buena Vista, 1991

JEAN BOFFETY
QUINTET   20th Century Fox, 1979
BOLERO   Double 13/Sharp Features, 1982
EDITH AND MARCEL   Miramax, 1984

HASKELL B. BOGGS
WHERE PIGEONS GO TO DIE (TF)   World International
    Network/Michael Landon Productions, 1990

LUDEK BOGNER
BUSTED UP   Shapiro Entertainment, 1987
MURDER ONE   Miramax, 1988
AGE-OLD FRIENDS (CTF)   HBO/Granger
    Productions, 1990

WILLY BOGNER
FIRE AND ICE   Concorde, 1987

ALAN BOLLINGER
BEYOND REASONABLE DOUBT   Satori, 1983
CAME A HOT FRIDAY   Orion Classics, 1985

PHILIP BONHAM-CARTER
SHE'S BEEN AWAY   BBC Films, 1989

JEAN-JACQUES BOUHON
3 MEN AND A CRADLE   Samuel Goldwyn
    Company, 1986

RICHARD BOWEN
Agent: Tobias-Skouras & Associates, Inc. - Los Angeles,
    213/277-6211

STREET MUSIC   Specialty, 1982
BELIZAIRE THE CAJUN   Skouras Pictures, 1986
STACKING   Spectrafilm, 1987, w/Paul Elliott
THE WIZARD OF LONELINESS   Skouras Pictures, 1988
ANIMAL BEHAVIOR   Millimeter Films, 1989
WHEELS OF TERROR (CTF)   Wilshire Court
    Productions/Once Upon A Time Productions, 1990

ED BOWES
BORN IN FLAMES   First Run Features, 1983,
    w/Al Santana

RUSSELL BOYD, ACS
Agent: Smith Gosnell Nicholson & Associates -
    PacificPalisades, 213/459-0307

THE MAN FROM HONG KONG   The Movie Company/
    Golden Harvest, 1975
PICNIC AT HANGING ROCK   Atlantic Releasing
    Corporation, 1975
SUMMER OF SECRETS   Greater Union Film
    Distributors, 1976
THE SINGER AND THE DANCER   Columbia, 1977
BREAK OF DAY   Greater Union Film Distributors, 1977
THE LAST WAVE   World Northal, 1978
DAWN   Hoyts, 1979

CHAIN REACTION   Hoyts, 1980
GALLIPOLI   Paramount, 1981
STARSTRUCK   Cinecom, 1982
THE YEAR OF LIVING DANGEROUSLY
   MGM/UA, 1983
TENDER MERCIES   Universal/AFD, 1983
PHAR LAP   20th Century Fox, 1984
A SOLDIER'S STORY   Columbia, 1984
MRS. SOFFEL   MGM/UA, 1984
BETWEEN WARS   Satori, 1985
BURKE AND WILLS   Hemdale 1985
"CROCODILE" DUNDEE   Paramount, 1986
HIGH TIDE   Tri-Star, 1987
THE RESCUE   Buena Vista, 1988
"CROCODILE" DUNDEE II   Paramount, 1988
IN COUNTRY   Warner Bros., 1989
ALMOST AN ANGEL   Ironbark Films/Paramount, 1990

JULIO BRAGADO
RAGE OF HONOR   Trans World Entertainment, 1987

MICHEL BRAULT
THRESHOLD   20th Century Fox International
   Classics, 1983
LOUISIANA (CTF)   ICC/Antenne-2/Superchannel/
   CTV/Societe de Development de L'Industrie
   Cinematographique Canadienne, 1983
NO MERCY   Tri-Star, 1987
DEAD MEN OUT (CTF)   Citadel Entertainment, 1989

JONATHAN BRAUN
ONE MORE CHANCE   Cannon, 1983

DOMINIQUE BRENGUIER
MR. FROST   SVS/AAA-Hugo/Triumph
   Releasing, 1990

JULES BRENNER
OUTLAW BLUES   Warner Bros., 1977
WHEN YOU COMIN' BACK RED RYDER?
   Columbia, 1979
THE LAST WORD   Samuel Goldwyn
   Company, 1979
THE RETURN OF THE LIVING DEAD   Orion, 1985
TEEN WOLF TOO   Atlantic Releasing
   Corporation, 1987
1969   Atlantic Releasing Corporation, 1988
SINS OF THE MOTHER (TF)   Corapeake
   Productions, 1991

DAVID BRIDGES
PRIVATE INVESTIGATIONS   MGM/UA, 1987,
   w/Bryan Duggan
WALKER   Universal, 1987
LIP SERVICE (CTF)   Cinehaus, 1988
THE FULFILLMENT OF MARY GRAY (TF)   Mary
   Gray Inc./Lee Caplin Prods., 1989
LOVE HURTS   Vestron, 1989

ROBERT BRINKMANN
Agent: The Gersh Agency, Inc., Beverly Hills -
   213/274-6611, New York - 212/997-1818

KANDYLAND   New World, 1987
U2: RATTLE AND HUM (b&w)   Paramount, 1988

KEN BRINSLEY
BEJEWELLED (CTF)   TVS Productions, 1991

RICHARD E. BROOKS
NATURAL ENEMIES   Cinema 5, 1979
NIGHTMARE AT SHADOW WOODS   Film Concept
   Group, 1987
MORGAN STEWART'S COMING HOME   New Century/
   Vista, 1987

RONALD W. BROWNE
Agent: The Gersh Agency, Inc. - Beverly Hills,
   213/274-6611

THREE AMIGOS   Orion, 1986
ANYTHING BUT LOVE (Pilot)   1989
COACH (Pilot)   1989
THE MARSHALL CHRONICLES (Pilot)   Viacom
   Television/Sweetum Productions, 1989
WORKING GIRL (Pilot)   20th Century Fox TV/Patchett
   Kaufman Entertainment, 1990

BOBBY BUKOWSKI
Agent: The Doug Apatow Agency, 10559 Blythe Ave. -
   Los Angeles, CA 90064

THE WAY IT IS   Spring Films, 1986
ANNA   Vestron, 1987
KISS DADDY GOOD NIGHT   Beast of Eden, 1987
LOLA LA LOCA   1988
LIFE UNDER WATER (TF)   American Playhouse, 1989
THOUSAND PIECES OF GOLD   American Playhouse/
   Maverick Films/Kelly/Yamamoto/Film Four
   International, 1990
MEN OF RESPECT   Columbia, 1991
DANGEROUS OBSESSION   Panorama
   Entertainment, 1991

DON BURGESS
Agent: The Gersh Agency, Inc., Beverly Hills -
   213/274-6611, New York - 212/997-1818

RUCKUS   1982
THE NIGHT STALKER   Almi Pictures, 1987
DEATH BEFORE DISHONOR   New World, 1987
SUMMER CAMP NIGHTMARE   Concorde, 1987
WORLD GONE WILD   Lorimar, 1988
TOO YOUNG THE HERO (TF)   Pierre Cossette
   Productions/The Lansburg Company, 1988
UNDER THE BOARDWALK   New World, 1989
BLIND FURY   Tri-Star, 1990
BREAKING POINT (CTF)   Avnet-Kerner
   Company, 1990
THE COURT-MARTIAL OF JACKIE ROBINSON (CTF)
   Turner Network Television/von Zerneck Sertner
   Films, 1990

HANS BURMANN
SANDINO   TVE-Umanzor-Beta Films-Reteitalia-Granada
   TV/RTVE-Miguel Littin Productions, 1990

KEN BURNS
THE CIVIL WAR I-IX   WETA-Washington, D.C./Florentine
   Films, 1990, w/Allen Moore and Buddy Squires

DAN BURSTALL
SQUIZZY TAYLOR   Satori, 1984
KANGAROO   Cineplex Odeon, 1987
WEEKEND WITH KATE   Phillip Emanuel
   Productions, 1990

CINEMATOGRAPHERS
PRODUCTION
DESIGNERS,
COSTUME
DESIGNERS and
FILM EDITORS
GUIDE

C
I
N
E
M
A
T
O
G
R
A
P
H
E
R
S

CINEMATOGRAPHERS
PRODUCTION
DESIGNERS,
COSTUME
DESIGNERS and
FILM EDITORS
GUIDE

THOMAS BURSTYN, CSC

Agent: Suzanne Depoe, Creative Technique,
   416/466-4173
Address: 768 Quest Rue, St. Paul, Montreal,
   Quebec H3C 1M4, 514/878-3606

THE LOST TRIBE   Meridian Films/Film
   InvestmentCorporation of New Zealand/New
   Zealand FilmCommission, 1983
HEAVENLY BODIES   MGM/UA, 1985
DARK OF THE NIGHT   Castle Hill Productions, 1986
NATIVE SON   Cinecom, 1986
BROKEN VOWS (TF)   Brademan-Self Productions/
   Robert Halmi Inc., 1987
FORD: THE MAN AND THE MACHINE (MS)
   Lantana Productions/Filmline International
   Productions/Robert Halmi, Inc., 1987
FOXFIRE (TF)   Marian Rees Associates, 1987
TADPOLE AND THE WHALE   New World Mutual, 1988
PROMISED A MIRACLE (TF)   Dick Clark Productions/
   Republic Pictures/Roni Weisberg Productions, 1988
THE CHEETAH   Buena Vista, 1989
LEAP OF FAITH (TF)   Hart, Thomas & Berlin
   Productions, 1988
THE COLD FRONT   Cold Front Productions, 1989
NIGHT WALK (TF)   Galatea Productions/CBS
   Entertainment Productions, 1990
THE DREAMER OF OZ   Bedrock Production/Adam
   Productions/Spelling Entertainment, 1990
TOY SOLDIERS   Tri-Star Pictures, 1991

GEOFF BURTON

THE FOURTH WISH   South Australian Film
   Corporation, 1975
STORM BOY   South Australian Film Corporation, 1976
BORN TO RUN   Buena Vista, 1976
THE PICTURE SHOW MAN   Roadshow
   Distributors, 1977
BLUE FIN   Roadshow Distributors, 1978
STIR   Hoyts, 1980
MIDNITE SPARES   Filmco Australia, 1983
THE YEAR MY VOICE BROKE   Avenue Pictures, 1987
THE TIME GUARDIAN   Hemdale, 1987
ROMERO   Four Seasons Entertainment, 1989
BANGKOK HILTON (CTF)   Kennedy-Miller, 1990

STEPHEN H. BURUM, ASC*

West Coast Card
Agent: Smith Gosnell Nicholson & Associates -
   Pacific Palisades, 213/459-0307

DEATH VALLEY   Universal, 1982
THE ESCAPE ARTIST   Orion/Warner Bros., 1982
THE ENTITY   20th Century Fox, 1983
THE OUTSIDERS   Warner Bros., 1983
SOMETHING WICKED THIS WAY COMES   Buena
   Vista , 1983
RUMBLE FISH   Universal, 1983
UNCOMMON VALOR   Paramount, 1983, w/Ric Waite
BODY DOUBLE   Columbia, 1984
ST. ELMO'S FIRE   Columbia, 1985
THE BRIDE   Columbia, 1985
8 MILLION WAYS TO DIE   Tri-Star, 1986
NUTCRACKER: THE MOTION PICTURE   Atlantic
   Releasing Corporation, 1986
THE UNTOUCHABLES   Paramount, 1987
ARTHUR 2 ON THE ROCKS   Warner Bros., 1988
CASUALTIES OF WAR   Columbia, 1989
THE WAR OF THE ROSES   20th Century Fox, 1989
HE SAID, SHE SAID   Paramount, 1991

DICK BUSH

Agent: Sandra Marsh Management - Sherman Oaks,
   818/905-6961

CULLODEN (TF)   BBC, 1964
SONG OF SUMMER (TF)   BBC, 1969
ISADORA   Universal, 1969
LAUGHTER IN THE DARK   Lopert, 1969
WHEN DINOSAURS RULED THE EARTH   Warner
   Bros., 1969
TOOMORROW   FRD, 1970
THE BLOOD ON SATAN'S CLAW   Cannon, 1971
TWINS OF EVIL   Universal, 1972
SAVAGE MESSIAH   MGM, 1972
PHASE IV   Paramount, 1974
MAHLER   Mayfair, 1974
IN CELEBRATION   American Film Theatre, 1975
CLOUDS OF GLORY: WILLIAM AND DOROTHY (TF)
   Granada TV, 1978
TOMMY   Columbia, 1975
SORCERER   Universal/Paramount, 1977,
   w/John M. Stephens
THE HOUND OF THE BASKERVILLES   Atlantic
   Releasing Corporation, 1979
YANKS   Universal, 1979
THE LEGACY   Universal, 1979, w/Alan Hume
ONE TRICK PONY   Warner Bros., 1980
FALLING IN LOVE AGAIN   Inernational Picture Show
   Company, 1980, w/Michael Mileham
THE FAN   Parmaount, 1981
VICTOR/VICTORIA   MGM/United Artists, 1982
TRAIL OF THE PINK PANTHER   MGM/United
   Artists, 1982
CURSE OF THE PINK PANTHER   MGM/United
   Artists, 1983
THE PHILADELPHIA EXPERIMENT   New World, 1984
CRIMES OF PASSION   New World, 1984
THE JOURNEY OF NATTY GANN   Buena Vista, 1985
NAZI HUNTER: THE BEATE KLARSFELD STORY (TF)
   William Kayden Productions/Orion TV/Silver Chalice/
   Revcom/George Walker TV/TF1/SFP, 1986
THE QUICK AND THE DEAD (CTF)   HBO Pictures/
   Joseph Cates Company, 1987
DESPERADO (TF)   Walter Mirisch Productions/Charles
   E. Sellier Productions/Universal TV, 1987
ASSAULT AND MATRIMONY (TF)   Michael Filerman
   Productions/NBC Productions, 1987
THE LAIR OF THE WHITE WORM   Vestron, 1988
LITTLE MONSTERS   MGM/UA, 1989
STAYING TOGETHER   Hemdale, 1989
SWITCH   Warner Bros., 1991

BILL BUTLER, ASC*

(Wilmer C. Butler)
West Coast & Midwest Cards
Agent: Smith Gosnell Nicholson & Associates -
   Pacific Palisades, 213/459-0307

THE RAIN PEOPLE   Warner Bros., 1969
DRIVE, HE SAID   Columbia, 1971
HICKEY AND BOGGS   United Artists, 1972
THE CONVERSATION   Paramount, 1974
THE EXECUTION OF PRIVATE SLOVIK (TF)
   Universal TV, 1974
ONE FLEW OVER THE CUCKOO'S NEST ★
   United Artists, 1975, w/Haskell Wexler
JAWS   Universal, 1975
LIPSTICK   Paramount, 1976, w/William A. Fraker
THE BINGO LONG TRAVELING ALL-STARS & MOTOR
   KINGS   Universal, 1976

ALEX & THE GYPSY   20th Century Fox, 1976
RAID ON ENTEBBE (TF) ☆☆   Edgar J. Scherick
    Associates/20th Century Fox TV, 1977
MARY WHITE (TF)   Radnitz/Mattel Productions, 1977
THE DEMON SEED   MGM/UA, 1977
CAPRICORN ONE   Warner Bros., 1978
DAMIEN - OMEN II   20th Century Fox, 1978
GREASE   Paramount, 1978
UNCLE JOE SHANNON   United Artists, 1978
ICE CASTLES   Columbia, 1979
ROCKY II   United Artists, 1979
CAN'T STOP THE MUSIC   AFD, 1980
IT'S MY TURN   Columbia, 1980
THE NIGHT THE LIGHTS WENT OUT IN GEORGIA
    Avco Embassy, 1981, w/Fred Batka
STRIPES   Columbia, 1981
ROCKY III   MGM/UA, 1982
THE STING II   Universal, 1983
THE THORN BIRDS (MS) ☆   David L. Wolper-Stan
    Margulies Productions/Edward Lewis Productions/
    Warner Bros. TV, 1983
A STREETCAR NAMED DESIRE (TF)   Keith Barish
    Productions, 1984
BEER   Orion, 1985
ROCKY IV   MGM/UA, 1985
BIG TROUBLE   Columbia, 1986
WILDFIRE   Zupnick Enterprises/Jody Ann
    Productions, 1987
BILOXI BLUES   Universal, 1988
CHILD'S PLAY   MGM/UA, 1988
WHEN WE WERE YOUNG (Pilot)   1989
GRAFFITI BRIDGE   Paisley Park/Warner Bros., 1990

MICHAEL C. BUTLER

CHARLEY VARRICK   Universal, 1973
HARRY AND TONTO   20th Century Fox, 1974
RANCHO DeLUXE   United Artists, 1975
92 IN THE SHADE   United Artists, 1975
THE MISSOURI BREAKS   United Artists, 1976
TELEFON   MGM/United Artists, 1977
JAWS II   Universal, 1978
WANDA NEVADA   United Artists, 1979
A SMALL CIRCLE OF FRIENDS   United Artists, 1980
SMOKEY AND THE BANDIT, PART II   Universal, 1980
THE CANNONBALL RUN   20th Century Fox, 1981
MEGAFORCE   20th Century Fox, 1982
DANCE OF THE DWARFS   Dove, Inc., 1983

FRANK BYERS

FLOWERS IN THE ATTIC   New World, 1987, w/Gil
    Hubbs
THE WRONG GUYS   New World, 1988
FREEWAY   New World, 1988
TWIN PEAKS (TF)   Spelling Entertainment/
    Propaganda Films, 1990
ARCHIE: TO RIVERDALE AND BACK AGAIN (TF)
    DIC Enterprises/Patchett Kaufman Entertainment
    Productions, 1990

BOBBY BYRNE

Agent: The Gersh Agency, Inc. - Beverly Hills,
    213/274-6611

FIRST LOVE   Paramount, 1977
SMOKEY AND THE BANDIT   Universal, 1977
HOOPER   Warner Bros., 1978
THE END   United Artists, 1978
THE LAST WALTZ   United Artists, 1978,
    (Additional DP w/Laszlo Kovacs, David Myers,
    Hiro Narita, Michael Watkins & Vilmos Zsigmond)

BLUE COLLAR   Universal, 1978
THE VILLAIN   Columbia, 1979
HEAD OVER HEELS   *CHILLY SCENES OF WINTER*
    United Artists, 1979
CALIFORNIA DREAMING   American International, 1979
WALK PROUD   Universal, 1979
THOSE LIPS, THOSE EYES   United Artists, 1980
PATERNITY   Paramount, 1981
THINGS ARE TOUGH ALL OVER   Columbia, 1982
GOING BESERK   Univesal, 1983
SIXTEEN CANDLES   Universal, 1984
BULL DURHAM   Orion, 1988
STEALING HOME   Warner Bros., 1988
THE LEMON SISTERS   Miramax, 1990

C

JOHN CABRERA

PAPER TIGER   Joseph E. Levine Presents, 1976
WIDOW'S NEST   Navarro Productions, 1977
JAGUAR LIVES!   American International, 1979
CONAN THE BARBARIAN   Universal, 1982,
    w/Duke Callaghan
NIGHT OF THE ZOMBIES   MPM, 1984
TRIUMPHS OF A MAN CALLED HORSE   Jensen Farley
    Pictures, 1984, w/John Alcott
HUNDRA   Film Ventures International, 1984
YELLOW HAIR AND THE FORTRESS OF GOLD
    Crown International, 1984
BLACK ARROW (CTF)   Harry Alan Towers Productions/
    Pan-Atlantic Pictures Productions, 1985
HONEYMOON ACADEMY   Trans World Entertainment/
    Triumph, 1990

DUKE CALLAGHAN

Agent: Sanford-Skouras & Gross - Los Angeles,
    213/208-2100

THE SCALPHUNTERS   United Artists, 1968
JEREMIAH JOHNSON   Warner Bros., 1972
THE YAKUZA   Warner Bros., 1975
THE LAST HARD MEN   20th Century Fox, 1976
CONAN THE BARBARIAN   Universal, 1982,
    w/John Cabrera
LOVELINES   Tri-Star, 1984

JERRY G. CALLAWAY

GUNSMOKE: THE LAST APACHE (TF)   Galatea
    Productions/CBS Entertainment Productions, 1990

THOMAS L. CALLAWAY

SLAVE GIRLS FROM BEYOND INFINITY   Urban
    Classics, 1987, w/Ken Wiatrak
SLUMBER PARTY MASSACRE II   Concorde, 1987
ASSAULT OF THE KILLER BIMBOS   Empire
    Pictures, 1988
ACTION U.S.A.   Stewart & Berger Inc., 1989
LADY AVENGER   Marco Colombo, 1989
STEEL & LACE   Cinema Home Video/Paragon Arts/
    Fries, 1990
CARTEL   Promark/Cobra Entertainment/Shapiro
    Glickenhaus, 1990

Ca

CINEMATOGRAPHERS
PRODUCTION
DESIGNERS,
COSTUME
DESIGNERS AND
FILM EDITORS
GUIDE

C
I
N
E
M
A
T
O
G
R
A
P
H
E
R
S

Ca

CINEMATOGRAPHERS
PRODUCTION
DESIGNERS,
COSTUME
DESIGNERS AND
FILM EDITORS
GUIDE

C
I
N
E
M
A
T
O
G
R
A
P
H
E
R
S

JOHN CAMPBELL
MALA NOCHE   Frameline, 1987

BRIAN CAPENER
WORKING TRASH   Westgate Productions/Aurora
    Development Fund/FNM Company, 1990

ROBERT CARAMICO, ASC
Agent: The Miller Agency - Burbank, 818/843-1511

THE DOBERMAN GANG   Dimension, 1973
THE DARING DOBERMANS   Dimension, 1973
NO WAY BACK   Atlas, 1976
JOSHUA   Lone Star, 1976
SLUMBER PARTY '57   Cannon, 1977
THE HAPPY HOOKER GOES TO WASHINGTON
    Cannon, 1977

JACK CARDIFF, BSC
Agent: Grace Lyons Management - Los Angeles,
    213/655-5100

A MATTER OF LIFE AND DEATH   Universal, 1946
BLACK NARCISSUS   Universal, 1947
THE RED SHOES   Eagle-Lion, 1948
UNDER CAPRICORN   Warner Bros., 1949
THE BLACK ROSE   20th Century Fox, 1950
PANDORA AND THE FLYING DUTCHMAN
    MGM, 1951
THE AFRICAN QUEEN   United Artists, 1952
THE VIKINGS   United Artists, 1958
FANNY ★   Warner Bros., 1961
WAR AND PEACE   Continental, 1968
THE LAST DAYS OF POMPEII   RKO Radio, 1935
RIDE A WILD PONY   1975
CROSSED SWORDS   THE PRINCE AND THE
    PAUPER   20th Century Fox, 1977
DEATH ON THE NILE   Paramount, 1978
THE 5TH MUSKETEER   Columbia, 1979
AVALANCHE EXPRESS   20th Century Fox, 1979
A MAN, A WOMAN AND A BANK   Avco
    Embassy, 1979
THE AWAKENING   Orion/Warner Bros., 1980
THE DOGS OF WAR   United Artists, 1981
GHOST STORY   Universal, 1981
THE WICKED LADY   MGM/UA, 1983
SCANDALOUS   Orion, 1984
THE FAR PAVILIONS (CMS)   Geoff Reeve &
    Associates/Goldcrest, 1984
CONAN THE DESTROYER   Universal, 1984
STEPHEN KING'S CAT'S EYE   MGM/UA, 1985
RAMBO: FIRST BLOOD PART II   Tri-Star, 1985
TAI-PAN   DEG, 1986
MILLION DOLLAR MYSTERY   DEG, 1987

RUSSELL CARPENTER
Agent: Grace Lyons Management - Los Angeles,
    213/655-5100

SOLE SURVIVOR   International Film Marketing, 1984
THE WIZARD OF SPEED AND TIME   Shapiro
    Glickenhaus Entertainment, 1988
CRITTERS 2: THE MAIN COURSE   New Line
    Cinema, 1988
LADY IN WHITE   New Century/Vista, 1988
CAMERON'S CLOSET   SVS Films, 1989
DEATH WARRANT   MGM/UA, 1990
SOLAR CRISIS   Gakken Publishing-NHK Enterprises/
    Shochiku-Fuji, 1990
THE PERFECT WEAPON   Paramount, 1991

STEPHEN CARPENTER
PRANKS   New Image, 1982
THE POWER   Film Ventures International, 1984
THE DORM THAT DRIPPED BLOOD   New Image, 1984
TORMENT   New World, 1986
THE KINDRED   FM Entertainment, 1987

JAMES L. CARTER
Phone: 818/780-9272

HOME MOVIES   United Artists Classics, 1980
SWEET SIXTEEN   CIF, 1983
PARADISE MOTEL   Saturn International, 1985
DARK EYES   Island Pictures, 1987, Italian-French
TERMINAL ENTRY   United Film Distribution, 1987
IN DANGEROUS COMPANY   Manson
    International, 1988
DEADLY WEAPON   Empire Pictures, 1989
LEATHERFACE: THE TEXAS CHAINSAW MASSACRE III
    New Line Cinema, 1989
BACK TO BACK   Concorde, 1990
PLAYROOM   Smart Egg, 1990
SPACED INVADERS   MARTIANS!!!   Smart Egg/Silver
    Screen Partners IV/Touchstone/Buena Vista, 1990
HURRICANE   I.R.S. Media, 1991

CHRISTOPHER CHALLIS, BSC
MR. QUILP   Avco Embassy, 1975
THE INCREDIBLE SARAH   Avco Embassy, 1976
THE DEEP   Columbia, 1977
FORCE 10 FROM NAVARONE   American
    International, 1978
THE RIDDLE OF THE SANDS   Satori, 1979
THE MIRROR CRACK'D   AFD, 1980
EVIL UNDER THE SUN   Universal/AFD, 1982
TOP SECRET!   Paramount, 1984
SECRETS   Samuel Goldwyn Company, 1984
STEAMING   New World, 1984

MARC CHAMPION
OUT OF THE BLUE   Discovery, 1982
ANGELA   Embassy, 1984

MICHAEL CHAPMAN*
THE LAST DETAIL   Columbia, 1973
THE WHITE DAWN   Paramount, 1974
TAXI DRIVER   Columbia, 1976
THE FRONT   Columbia, 1976
THE NEXT MAN   Allied Artists, 1976
FINGERS   Brut Productions, 1978
THE LAST WALTZ   United Artists, 1978
INVASION OF THE BODY SNATCHERS   Untied
    Artists, 1978
HARDCORE   Columbia, 1979
THE WANDERERS   Orion/Warner Bros., 1979
RAGING BULL ★   United Artists, 1980
PERSONAL BEST   Warner Bros., 1982
DEAD MEN DON'T WEAR PLAID   Universal, 1982
THE MAN WITH TWO BRAINS   Warner Bros., 1983
THE LOST BOYS   Warner Bros., 1987
SHOOT TO KILL   Buena Vista, 1988
GOTHAM (CTF)   Showtime/Phoenix Entertainment
    Group/Keith Addis & Associates, 1988
SCROOGED   Paramount, 1988
GHOSTBUSTERS II   Columbia, 1989
QUICK CHANGE   Devoted/Warner Bros., 1990
KINDERGARTEN COP   Universal, 1990

RON CHAPMAN
SHOCK 'EM DEAD   Academy Entertainment, 1991

ROBERT CHAPPELL
THE THIN BLUE LINE   Miramax, 1988,
   w/Stefan Czapsky

DOMINIQUE CHAPUIS
SUGAR CANE ALLEY   Orion Classics, 1984
SHOAH (FD)   New Yorker, 1985, w/Jimmy
   Glasberg & William Lubchansky
TEA IN THE HAREM   Cinecom, 1986
A KILLING AFFAIR   Hemdale, 1988
THE LITTLE THIEF   Miramax, 1989

RODNEY CHARTERS
PSYCHO IV: THE BEGINNING (CTF)   Smart Money
   Productions, 1990

CLAUDIO CHEA
CROSSOVER DREAMS   Miramax, 1985

MICHAEL CHIN
CHAN IS MISSING   New Yorker, 1982
DIM SUM: A LITTLE BIT OF HEART   Orion
   Classics, 1985
FORBIDDEN CITY, USA   1989

STEVE CHIVERS
HARDWARE   Millimeter Films, 1990

DANA CHRISTIAANSEN
SECOND SIGHT   Warner Bros., 1989

JOAN CHURCHILL
COMIC BOOK CONFIDENTIAL   Cinecom, 1989,
   w/Robert Fresco

RICHARD CIUPKA, CSC
Address: 71 Cornwall St., Town of Mount Royal,
   Montreal, Quebec H3P 1M6, 514/738-9996

ATLANTIC CITY   Paramount, 1980
YESTERDAY   Cinepix, 1980
DIRTY TRICKS   Avco Embassy, 1981
MELANIE   Jensen Farley Pictures, 1983
THE TERRY FOX STORY   20th Century Fox, 1983
THE BLOOD OF OTHERS (CMS)   HBO Premiere
   Films/ICC/Filmax Productions, 1984
HEARTSOUNDS (TF)   Embassy TV, 1984
SECRET WEAPONS (TF)   Goodman-Rosen
   Productions/ITC Productions, 1985

JOSEP M. CIVIT
SILENT NIGHT, DEADLY NIGHT III: BETTER
   WATCH OUT!   Quiet Films, 1989

DAVID CLAESSEN
THE TELEPHONE   New World, 1988

CURTIS CLARK
West Coast card, Local 659
Agent: The Doug Apatow Agency, 10559 Blythe Ave. -
   Los Angeles, CA 90064, 213/202-6888

THE DRAUGHTSMAN'S CONTRACT   United Artists
   Classics, 1983

AND NOTHING BUT THE TRUTH   Castle Hill
   Productions, 1984
ALAMO BAY   Tri-Star, 1985
SESAME STREET PRESENTS FOLLOW THAT BIRD
   Warner Bros., 1985
13 AT DINNER (TF)   1985
MADE IN THE U.S.A.   DEG, 1986
EXTREMITIES   Atlantic Releasing Corporation, 1987
THY KINGDOM COME...THY WILL BE DONE (FD)
   Roxie Films, 1988
DOMINICK AND EUGENE   Orion, 1988
TRIUMPH OF THE SPIRIT   Nova International
   Films, 1989
TALENT FOR THE GAME   Paramount, 1991

EARL CLARK
THE YOUNG RIDERS (TF)   MGM-UA TV/Ogiens-Kane
   Company/Pendragon Entertainment, 1990

TERRY COLE
THREE KINDS OF HEAT   Cannon, 1987
A GHOST IN MONTE CARLO (CTF)   Gainsborough
   Pictures/The Grade Company, 1990

PETER LYONS COLLISTER
Agent: The Gersh Agency, Inc. - Beverly Hills,
   213/274-6611; New York, 212/997-1818

THE SUPERNATURALS   Republic Entertainment/
   Sandya Howard Productions, 1985
AVENGING ANGEL   New World, 1985
EYE OF THE TIGER   Scotti Bros., 1986
KBG: THE SECRET WAR   *LETHAL*   Cinema
   Group, 1986
GETTING EVEN   American Distribution Group, 1986
ODD JOBS   Tri-Star, 1986, w/Arthur Albert
HE'S MY GIRL   Scotti Bros., 1987
CAN'T BUY ME LOVE   Buena Vista, 1987
YOU CAN'T HURRY LOVE   MCEG, 1988,
   w/John Schwartzman
HALLOWEEN 4: THE RETURN OF MICHAEL MYERS
   Galaxy International, 1988
PULSE   Columbia, 1988
ALL'S FAIR   MovieStore Entertainment, 1989
LIMIT UP   MCEG, 1990
JURY DUTY: THE COMEDY (TF)   Spectacor Films/
   Steve White Productions, 1990
PROBLEM CHILD   Imagine Entertainment/
   Universal, 1990

CHUCK COLWELL
THRASHIN'   Fries Entertainment, 1986
THE TRIAL OF THE INCREDIBLE HULK (TF)   1989
THE DEATH OF THE INCREDIBLE HULK (TF)   New
   World TV/Bixby-Brandon Productions, 1990

DAVID CONNELL
ALL THE RIVERS RUN (CMS)   Crawford Productions/
   Nine Network, 1984, Australian
THE AVIATOR   MGM/UA, 1985
SLATE, WYN & ME   Hemdale, 1987
LES PATTERSON SAVES THE WORLD   Hoyts
   Distribution, 1987
HEAVEN TONIGHT   Boulevard Films, 1990
THE NEVERENDING STORY II: THE NEXT CHAPTER
   Time-Warner/Warner Bros., 1990

DOUG CONNELL
DEF-CON 4   New World, 1985, w/Les Krizan

Co

CINEMATOGRAPHERS
PRODUCTION
DESIGNERS,
COSTUME
DESIGNERS AND
FILM EDITORS
GUIDE

C
I
N
E
M
A
T
O
G
R
A
P
H
E
R
S

Co

CINEMATOGRAPHERS
PRODUCTION
DESIGNERS,
COSTUME
DESIGNERS and
FILM EDITORS
GUIDE

C I N E M A T O G R A P H E R S

JOHN CONNERS *
West Coast & Midwest Cards
Agent: The Gersh Agency, Inc. - Beverly Hills,
213/274-6611; New York, 212/997-1818

A NIGHT IN THE LIFE OF JIMMY REARDON   20th
Century Fox, 1988
SHADOWS IN THE STORM   Vidmark
Entertainment, 1989
SHORT TIME   Gladden/20th Century Fox, 1990

JACK CONROY
MY LEFT FOOT   Miramax Films, 1989
THE FIELD   Granada Film/Avenue Pictures, 1990
THE LOVE SHE SOUGHT (TF)   Arnold
Productions, 1990

JAMES A. CONTNER
CRUISING   United Artists, 1980
GILDA LIVE (FD)   Warner Bros., 1980 w/Ted Churchill,
Alan Metzger & Peter Norman
TIMES SQUARE   AFD, 1980
NIGHTHAWKS   Universal, 1981
SO FINE   Warner Bros., 1981
EDDIE MACON'S RUN   Universal, 1983
TOUGH ENOUGH   20th Century Fox, 1983
JAWS 3-D   Universal, 1983
WHERE THE BOYS ARE   Tri-Star, 1984
THE FLAMINGO KID   20th Century Fox, 1984
BERRY GORDY'S THE LAST DRAGON   Tri-Star, 1985
LET'S GET HARRY   Tri-Star, 1986
HEAT   New Century/Vista, 1987
MONKEY SHINES   Orion, 1988

BROWN COOPER
ICE HOUSE   Upfront Films, 1989

ROBIN COPPING
THE PIRATE MOVIE   20th Century Fox, 1982

JOHN COQUILLON
INSIDE OUT   Warner Bros., 1976
ECHOES OF A SUMMER   Cine Artists, 1976
THE 39 STEPS   International Picture Show
Company, 1978
MR. PATMAN   Film Consortium, 1980
THE CHANGELING   AFD, 1980
FINAL ASSIGNMENT   Almi Cinema 5, 1980
THE AMATEUR   20th Century Fox, 1982
THE OSTERMAN WEEKEND   20th Century Fox, 1983
THE LAST PLACE ON EARTH (TF)   1985
LACE 2 (MS)   Lorimar Productions, 1985
GOING UNDERCOVER   Miramax, 1985
CLOCKWISE   Universal, 1986
ABSOLUTION   Trans World Entertainment, 1988

PIO CORRADI
CANDY MOUNTAIN   International Film
Exchange, 1987
ALPINE FIRE   Vestron, 1987

CHARLES CORRELL, ASC*
MOVING VIOLATIONS   20th Century Fox, 1976
NATIONAL LAMPOON'S ANIMAL HOUSE
Universal, 1978
FAST BREAK   Columbia, 1979
IN GOD WE TRUST   Universal, 1980
DIE LAUGHING   Orion/Warner Bros., 1980
NATIONAL LAMPOON GOES TO THE MOVIES   1981
CHEECH & CHONG'S NICE DREAMS   Columbia, 1981
THE WINDS OF WAR (MS) ☆☆   Paramount TV/Dan
Curtis Productions, 1983
STAR TREK III: THE SEARCH FOR SPOCK
Paramount, 1984
THE JESSE OWENS STORY (TF)   Harve Bennett
Productions/Paramount TV, 1984
JOY OF SEX   Paramount, 1984
WALLENBERG: A HERO'S STORY (TF)   Dick Berg-
Stonehenge Productions/Paramount TV, 1985
REVENGE OF THE NERDS II   20th Century Fox, 1987
FACE TO FACE (TF)   Robert Halmi Productions, 1990

JOHN A. CORSO
NY Local 644
Business: Champoux-Corso, Inc., 501 E. 87th St., #5-B,
New York, NY 10128, 212/472-0309
Representative: Louis D'Agostino - New Yrok,
212/244-2121

SHADOWLAND   Tak, 1986
SENIOR WEEK   Vestron, 1988
METAMORPHOSIS   InterContinental Releasing, 1990

MICHAEL COULTER
THAT SINKING FEELING   Samuel Goldwyn
Company, 1979
GREGORY'S GIRL   Samuel Goldwyn Company, 1982
NO SURRENDER   Circle Releasing Corporation, 1986
GOSPEL ACCORDING TO VIC   Skouras Pictures, 1987
THE GOOD FATHER   Skouras Pictures, 1987
HOUSEKEEPING   Columbia, 1987
THE DRESSMAKER   Shedlo/Freeway, 1988
BREAKING IN   Samuel Goldwyn Company, 1989
DIAMOND SKULLS   Film Four, 1989
BEARSKIN: AN URBAN FAIRYTALE   Film Four
International, 1989

RAOUL COUTARD
PASSION   United Artists Classics, 1983
DANGEROUS MOVES   Arthur Cohn Productions, 1984
FIRST NAME: CARMEN   Spectrafilm, 1984
LA CRABE TAMBOUR   Interama, 1984
BETHUNE: THE MAKING OF A HERO   Parmentier-
Belstar/Filmline International-August 1st Film Studio,
1990, w/Mike Molloy

GRAEME COWLEY
SMASH PALACE   Atlantic Releasing Corporation, 1982

VINCENT G. COX
ACT OF PIRACY   Major Arts/Marton Holding, 1990
ANY MAN'S DEATH   INI Entertainment, 1990

TODD CROCKETT
ALLIGATOR EYES   Castle Hill, 1990

JORDAN CRONENWETH, ASC*
West Coast Card
Agent: Smith Gosnell Nicholson & Associates -
Pacific Palisades, 213/459-0307

BREWSTER McCLOUD   MGM, 1970
PLAY IT AS IT LAYS   Universal, 1972
COUNT YOUR BULLETS   Brut Productions, 1972
BIRDS OF PREY (TF)   Tomorrow Entertainment, 1973
THE FRONT PAGE   Universal, 1974

ZANDY'S BRIDE   Warner Bros., 1974
THE NICKEL RIDE   20th Century Fox, 1975
GABLE AND LOMBARD   Universal, 1976
ROLLING THUNDER   American International, 1977
CITIZEN'S BAND   *HANDLE WITH CARE*
   Paramount, 1977
ONE IN A MILLION: THE RON LeFLORE STORY (TF)
   Roger Gimbel Productions/EMI TV, 1978
AND I ALONE SURVIVED (TF)   Jerry Leider-OJL
   Prods., 1978
TRANSPLANT (TF)   Time-Life Producitons, 1979
ALTERED STATES   Warner Bros., 1980
CUTTER'S WAY   United Artists Classics, 1981
BEST FRIENDS   Warner Bros., 1982
BLADE RUNNER   The Ladd Company/Warner
   Bros., 1982
STOP MAKING SENSE (FD)   Cinecom International/
   Island Alive, 1984
JUST BETWEEN FRIENDS   Orion, 1986
PEGGY SUE GOT MARRIED ★   Tri-Star, 1986
GARDENS OF STONE   Tri-Star, 1987
U2: RATTLE AND HUM (color)   Paramount, 1988
STATE OF GRACE   Cinehaus/Orion, 1990

WILLIAM CRONJAGER
Agent: The Miller Agency - Santa Clarita,
   818/843-7335

VIGILANTE FORCE   United Artists, 1976
THE RETURN OF FRANK CANNON (TF)   QM
   Productions, 1980
BORN TO BE SOLD (TF)   Ron Samuels, 1981

NAT CROSBY
MADAME SOUSATZKA   Universal, 1988
A PRIVATE LIFE   BBC/Totem, 1989
PAPER MASK   Film Four International, 1991

GREGORY M. CUMMINS
PATTI ROCKS   FilmDallas, 1988
HOMETOWN BOY MAKES GOOD (CTF)
   HBO, 1990

DEAN CUNDEY, ASC *
West Coast Card
Agent: The Gersh Agency, Inc., Beverly Hills -
   213/274-6611, New York - 212/997-1818

BARE KNUCKLES   Intercontinental, 1978
HALLOWEEN   Compass International, 1978
ROLLER BOOGIE   United Artists, 1979
ROCK 'N' ROLL HIGH SCHOOL   New World, 1979
THE FOG   Avco Embassy, 1980
GALAXINA   Crown International, 1980
WITHOUT WARNING   Filmways, 1980
HALLOWEEN II   Universal, 1981
ESCAPE FROM NEW YORK   Avco Embassy, 1981
ANGELS BRIGADE   Arista, 1981
THE THING   Universal, 1982
HALLOWEEN III: SEASON OF THE WITCH
   Universal, 1982
SEPARATE WAYS   Crown International, 1983
PSYCHO II   Universal, 1983
D.C. CAB   Universal, 1983
M.A.D.D.: MOTHERS AGAINST DRUNK
   DRIVING (TF)   Universal TV, 1983
ROMANCING THE STONE   20th Century Fox, 1984
INVITATION TO HELL (TF)   Moonlight
   Productions II, 1984

IT CAME UPON THE MIDNIGHT CLEAR (TF)
   Schenck-Cardea Productions/Columbia TV/LBS
   Communications, 1984
JAWS OF SATAN   United Artists, 1984
BACK TO THE FUTURE   Universal, 1985
WARNING SIGN   20th Century Fox, 1985
BIG TROUBLE IN LITTLE CHINA   20th Century
   Fox, 1986
PROJECT X   20th Century Fox, 1987
BIG BUSINESS   Buena Vista, 1988
WHO FRAMED ROGER RABBIT ★   Buena Vista, 1988
ROAD HOUSE   MGM/UA, 1989
BACK TO THE FUTURE II   Universal, 1989
BACK TO THE FUTURE III   Universal, 1990
NOTHING BUT TROUBLE   Warner Bros., 1991

ALEC CURTIS
NOT A PENNY MORE, NOT A PENNY LESS-
   PARTS 1 & 2 (CTF)   Paramount-Revcom/BBC, 1990

STEFAN CZAPSKY
ON THE EDGE   Skouras Pictures, 1986
THE THIN BLUE LINE   Miramax, 1988,
   w/Robert Chappell
VAMPIRE'S KISS   Hemdale, 1989
FLASHBACK   Paramount, 1990
SONS   Pacific Pictures, 1990
CHILD'S PLAY 2   Universal, 1990
EDWARD SCISSORHANDS   20th Century Fox, 1990

D

JOHN DALEY
CLOSE RELATIONS (CTF)   Lionheart
   Television, 1990

DOMINIQUE DALMASSO
GOING PLACES   Interama, 1974

DENNIS DALZELL
Agent: Grace Lyons Management - Los Angeles,
   213/655-5100
Phone: 818/842-3204

SIDEWINDER 1   Avco Embassy, 1977
HARD COUNTRY   Associate Film Distribution, 1981
BUSTIN' LOOSE   Universal, 1981
JIMMY THE KID   New World, 1983
THE OUTLAWS (TF)   Limekin and Templar Productions/
   Universal TV, 1984
FALSE WITNESS (TF)   New World TV/Valente-Kritzer-
   EPI Productions, 1990

LEE DANIEL
NEVER LEAVE CANADA   South of Canada, 1989

MARK DANIELS
PRIVILEGE   Zeitgeist Films, 1991

Da

CINEMATOGRAPHERS
PRODUCTION
DESIGNERS,
COSTUME
DESIGNERS AND
FILM EDITORS
GUIDE

C
I
N
E
M
A
T
O
G
R
A
P
H
E
R
S

Da

CINEMATOGRAPHERS
PRODUCTION
DESIGNERS,
COSTUME
DESIGNERS AND
FILM EDITORS
GUIDE

C
I
N
E
M
A
T
O
G
R
A
P
H
E
R
S

JEFF DARLING
Agent: Jill Nicholas, Top Technicians, P.O. Box 1035,
    DEE WHY N.S.W., 2099 Australia, 612/981-1622;
    fax - 612/971-2880

A PLACE AT THE COAST Daedalus Films, 1986
PRINCESS KATE (TF) Unthank Films, 1987
THE CROSSING Beyond International, 1989
YOUNG EINSTEIN Warner Bros., 1989

ALLEN DAVIAU, ASC*
STREETS OF L.A. (TF) George Englund
    Productions, 1979
THE BOY WHO DRANK TOO MUCH (TF) MTM
    Enterprises, 1980
RAGE (TF) Diane Silver Productions/Charles Fries
    Productions, 1980
E.T.: THE EXTRATERRESTRIAL ★ Universal, 1982
TWILIGHT ZONE - THE MOVIE (Segments 2 & 4)
    Warner Bros., 1983
HARRY TRACY Quartet Films Inc., 1983
LEGS (TF) The Catalina Production Group/Radio City
    Music Hall Productions/Comworld Productions, 1983
THE FALCON AND THE SNOWMAN Orion, 1985
THE COLOR PURPLE ★ Warner Bros., 1986
HARRY AND THE HENDERSONS Universal, 1987
EMPIRE OF THE SUN ★ Warner Bros., 1987
AVALON ★ Baltimore Pictures/Tri-Star, 1990
DEFENDING YOUR LIFE Warner Bros., 1991

ZOLTAN DAVID
CALL ME Vestron, 1988
DEADLY OBSESSION Distant Horizon, 1989

ANDREW DAVIS
OVER THE EDGE Orion/Warner Bros., 1979

BENJAMIN DAVIS
SLEEPAWAY CAMP United Film Distribution, 1983
SUDDEN DEATH Marvin Films, 1985

ELLIOT DAVIS
Agent: Tobias-Skouras & Associates - Los Angeles,
    213/277-6211

INDEPENDENCE DAY Unifilm, 1977
BROKEN ENGLISH Lorimar, 1981
VAMP New World, 1986
SUMMER HEAT Atlantic Releasing Corporation, 1987
MILES FROM HOME Cinecom, 1988
SIGNS OF LIFE Avenue Pictures, 1989
BLOODHOUNDS OF BROADWAY Columbia, 1989
LOVE AT LARGE Orion, 1990
MORTAL THOUGHTS Columbia Pictures, 1991

ERNEST DAY, BSC
Agent: Tobias-Skouras & Associates - Los Angeles,
    213/277-6211

RUNNING SCARED Paramount, 1972
VISIT TO A CHIEF'S SON United Artists, 1974
GHOST IN A NOONDAY SUN Columbia, 1974
MADE International Co-productions, 1975
THE SONG REMAINS THE SAME (FD) Warner
    Bros., 1976
REVENGE OF THE PINK PANTHER United
    Artists, 1979
SPHINX Orion/Warner Bros., 1981
A PASSAGE TO INDIA ★ Columbia, 1984

DECEPTIONS (TF) Louis Randolph Productions/
    Consolidated Productions/Columbia TV, 1985
AS SUMMERS DIE (CTF) HBO Premiere Films/
    Chris-Rose Productions/Baldwin/Aldrich Productions/
    Lorimar-Telepictures Productions, 1986
SUPERMAN IV: THE QUEST FOR PEACE Warner
    Bros., 1987
BURNING SECRET Vestron, 1988
PARENTS Vestron, 1989, w/Robin Vidgeon
YOUNG CATHERINE-PARTS I & II (CMS) Consolidated
    Entertainment, 1991
FIRE! TRAPPED ON THE 37TH FLOOR (TF) Papazian/
    Hirsch Productions, 1991

ROGER DEAKINS, BSC
Agent: Sandra Marsh Management - Sherman Oaks,
    818/905-6961

BLUE SUEDE SHOES Kendon Films, 1980
ANOTHER TIME, ANOTHER PLACE Samuel Goldwyn
    Company, 1983
1984 Atlantic Releasing Corporation, 1984
RETURN TO WATERLOO New Line Cinema, 1985
THE INNOCENT TVS Ltd./Tempest Films, 1985
SID & NANCY Samuel Goldwyn Company, 1986
SHADEY Skouras Pictures, 1986
DEFENSE OF THE REALM Hemdale, 1987
PERSONAL SERVICES Vestron, 1987
WHITE MISCHIEF Columbia, 1987
STORMY MONDAY Atlantic Releasing
    Corporation, 1988
THE KITCHEN TOTO Cannon, 1988
PASCALI'S ISLAND Avenue Pictures, 1988
MOUNTAINS OF THE MOON Tri-Star, 1990
THE LONG WALK HOME New Visions Pictures/
    Miramax Films, 1990
AIR AMERICA Indie Prod/Carolco/Tri-Star, 1990
BARTON FINK 20th Century Fox, 1991
HOMICIDE Triumph, 1991

RICARDO DE ANGELIS
MAN FACING SOUTHEAST FilmDallas, 1987

AUSTIN DE BESCHE
RETURN OF THE SECAUCUS SEVEN Libra/Specialty
    Films, 1980
LIANNA United Artists Classics, 1983

JAN DE BONT
Agent: The Gersh Agency, Inc., Beverly Hills -
    213/274-6611, New York - 212/997-1818

TURKISH DELIGHT Cinemation, 1973
KEETJE TIPPEL Cinema National, 1975
MAX HAVELAAR 1976
PRIVATE LESSONS Jensen Farley Pictures, 1981
ROAR 1981
I'M DANCING AS FAST AS I CAN Paramount, 1982
CUJO Warner Bros., 1983
ALL THE RIGHT MOVES 20th Century Fox, 1983
BAD MANNERS GROWING PAINS New World, 1984
THE FOURTH MAN Spectrafillm, 1984
THE RAY MANCINI STORY (TF) 1985
FLESH + BLOOD Orion, 1985
THE CLAN OF THE CAVE BEAR Warner Bros., 1986
THE JEWEL OF THE NILE 20th Century Fox, 1985
RUTHLESS PEOPLE Buena Vista, 1986
WHO'S THAT GIRL? Warner Bros., 1987
LEONARD PART 6 Columbia, 1987
DIE HARD 20th Century Fox, 1988
BERT RIBGY, YOU'RE A FOOL Warner Bros., 1989

BLACK RAIN   Paramount, 1989
THE HUNT FOR RED OCTOBER   Paramount, 1990
FLATLINERS   Stonebridge Entertainment/
   Columbia, 1990

DE BORMAN
MURDER ON LINE ONE   Silent Fiction Film
   Productions/Independant Feature Films Ltd./
   Academy Entertainment, 1990

ANDREW DE GROOT
DOGS IN SPACE   Skouras Pictures, 1987

BRUNO DE KEYZER
Agent: Smith Gosnell Nicholson & Associates -
   Pacific Palisades, 213/459-0307

A SUNDAY IN THE COUNTRY   MGM/UA
   Classics, 1984
SINCERELY CHARLOTTE   New Line Cinema, 1986
THE MURDERS IN THE RUE MORGUE (TF)
   RobertHalmi, Inc./International Film
   Productions, 1986
'ROUND MIDNIGHT   Warner Bros., 1986
LITTLE DORRIT   Cannon, 1988
BEATRICE   Samuel Goldwyn Company, 1987
REUNION   Ariane Films/Burning Secret
   Productions, 1989
LA VIE ET RIEN D'AUTRE   *LIFE AND NOTHING BUT*
   Hachette Premiere/AB Films/A2, 1989
DECEMBER BRIDE   Film Four International, 1991
IMPROMPTU   Hemdale Films, 1991

ANGHEL DECCA
Agent: Dattner & Associates - Los Angeles,
   213/447-5986

THE RETURN OF SUPERFLY   Crash Pictures/Triton
   Pictures, 1990
HANGIN' WITH THE HOMEBOYS   New Line
   Cinema, 1991

MICHAEL DELAHOUSSAYE
Address: 1836 Grace Ave., Los Angeles, CA 90028,
   213/466-4740

THEY STILL CALL ME BRUCE   Shapiro
   Entertainment, 1987
ACROSS THE TRACKS   Rosenbloom
   Entertainment, 1990

TOM DELILLO
END OF THE NIGHT   In Absentia, 1990

TONINO DELLI COLLI, AIC
SEVEN BEAUTIES   Cinema 5, 1976
THE PURPLE TAXI   Parafrance, 1977
TILL MARRIAGE DO US PART   Franklin Media, 1977
VIVA ITALIA   Cinema 5, 1978
CARO PAPA   Dean Film/AMLF/Prospect Film, 1979
TRAVELS WITH ANITA   *LOVERS AND LIARS*
   United Artists, 1979
SUNDAY LOVERS   MGM/United Artists, 1980
TRENCHCOAT   Buena Vista, 1983
TALES OF ORDINARY MADNESS   Fred Baker
   Films, 1983
ONCE UPON A TIME IN AMERICA   The Ladd Co./
   Warner Bros., 1984

THE NAME OF THE ROSE   20th Century Fox, 1986
GINGER & FRED   MGM/UA, 1986, w/Ennio Guarnieri
THE VOICE OF THE MOON   Penta Distribuzione, 1989

THOMAS DEL RUTH, ASC *
Agent: The Gersh Agency, Inc., Beverly Hills -
   213/274-6611, New York - 212/997-1818

SHE'S DRESSED TO KILL (TF)   Grant-Case-McGrath
   Enterprises/Barry Weitz Films, 1979
THE LAST CONVERTIBLE (MS)   Roy Huggins
   Productions/Universal TV, 1979
MARK, I LOVE YOU (TF)   The Aubrey Company, 1980
MOTEL HELL   United Artists, 1980
UNDERGRAD ACES   Filmways, 1981
DEATH WISH II   Filmways, 1982, w/Richard Kline
GET CRAZY   Embassy, 1983
WHO WILL LOVE MY CHILDREN? (TF)   ABC Circle
   Films, 1983
SOMETHING ABOUT AMELIA (TF)   Leonard Goldberg
   Productions, 1984
PAPER DOLLS (TF)   Mandy Productions/
   MGM-UA TV, 1984
IMPULSE   20th Century Fox, 1984
FANDANGO   Warner Bros., 1985
THE BREAKFAST CLUB   Universal, 1985
STAND BY ME   Columbia, 1986
QUICKSILVER   Columbia, 1986
THE RUNNING MAN   Tri-Star, 1987
CROSS MY HEART   Universal, 1987
SATISFACTION   20th Century Fox, 1988
DREAM BREAKERS (TF)   CBS Entertainment
   Prods., 1989
LOOK WHO'S TALKING   Tri-Star, 1989
LOOK WHO'S TALKING TOO   Tri-Star, 1990

PETER DEMING
Agent: Sandra Marsh Management, 14930 Ventura Blvd.,
   #200 - Sherman Oaks, 818/905-6961
Home: 2243 Cheremoya Ave., Los Angeles

EVIL DEAD 2   Rosebud Releasing Corporation, 1987
HOLLYWOOD SHUFFLE   Samuel Goldwyn
   Company, 1987
IT TAKES TWO   MGM/UA, 1988
PURPLE PEOPLE EATERS   Concorde, 1988
FROM HOLLYWOOD TO DEADWOOD   Island
   Pictures, 1989
WHY ME?   Epic Pictures/Triumph, 1990
MARTIANS GO HOME   Taurus Entertainment, 1990
HOUSE PARTY   New Line Cinema, 1990
BOOK OF LOVE   New Line Cinema, 1991
DROP DEAD FRED   New Line Cinema, 1991
SCORCHERS   Miramax, 1991
MY COUSIN VINNY   20th Century Fox, 1991
DROP DEAD FRED   New Line Cinema, 1991

THOMAS S. DeNOVE
THE LAST HORROR FILM   Twin Continental, 1982
HUNTER'S BLOOD   Concorde, 1987
COLD STEEL   CineTel, 1987
KIDNAPPED   Virgin Vision, 1987
LIBERTY & BASH   Chippewa/Chariot 7 Productions/Fries
   Home Video, 1990
SATAN'S PRINCESS   Paramount Home Video, 1991

ALEX DE ROCHE
THE NASTY GIRL   Miramax Films, 1990

De

CINEMATOGRAPHERS
PRODUCTION
DESIGNERS,
COSTUME
DESIGNERS AND
FILM EDITORS
GUIDE

C
I
N
E
M
A
T
O
G
R
A
P
H
E
R
S

CINEMATOGRAPHERS
PRODUCTION
DESIGNERS,
COSTUME
DESIGNERS and
FILM EDITORS
GUIDE

**C
I
N
E
M
A
T
O
G
R
A
P
H
E
R
S**

PASQUALINO DE SANTIS
ROMEO AND JULIET ★★ Paramount, 1968
MIDNIGHT PLEASURES 1975
L'INNOCENTE Rizzoli, 1976
THE IMMORTAL BACHELOR 1978
ILLUSTRIOUS CORPSES 1981
THREE BROTHERS New World, 1982
L'ARGENT Cinecom, 1984
MISUNDERSTOOD MGM/UA, 1984
CARMEN Triumph, 1984
SHEENA Columbia, 1984

CALEB DESCHANEL, ASC*
MORE AMERICAN GRAFFITI Universal, 1979
THE BLACK STALLION United Artists, 1979
BEING THERE United Artists, 1979
LET'S SPEND THE NIGHT TOGETHER (FD)
    Embassy, 1982, w/Gerald Feil
THE RIGHT STUFF H The Ladd Company/Warner
    Bros., 1983
THE NATURAL ★ Tri-Star, 1984
THE SLUGGER'S WIFE Columbia, 1985
50 YEARS OF ACTION! (FD) DMS Production
    Services, 1986, w/John Alonzo & Chuck Clifton

JAMES DEVIS
THERE GOES THE BRIDE Vanguard, 1980
DEATH HUNT 20th Century Fox, 1981
TAKE THIS JOB AND SHOVE IT Avco Embassy, 1981

TOM DICILLO
Agent: The Gersh Agency, Inc., Beverly Hills -
    213/274-6611, New York - 212/997-1818

PERMANENT VACATION Cinethesia, 1981
STRANGER THAN PARADISE Samuel Goldwyn
    Company, 1984
BURROUGHS (FD) Citifilmworks, 1984, w/others
VARIETY Horizon Films, 1985
THE BEAT Vestron, 1987
END OF THE NIGHT In Absentia Productions, 1990

ERNEST DICKERSON, ASC
Agent: The Gersh Agency, Inc., Beverly Hills -
    213/274-6611, New York - 212/997-1818

BROTHER FROM ANOTHER PLANET
    Cinecom, 1984
KRUSH GROOVE Warner Bros., 1985
SHE'S GOTTA HAVE IT Island Pictures, 1986
ENEMY TERRITORY Empire Pictures, 1987
EDDIE MURPHY RAW Paramount, 1987
SCHOOL DAZE Columbia, 1988
DO THE RIGHT THING Universal, 1989
DEF BY TEMPTATION Bonded Filmworks
    Productions/Troma, 1990
MO' BETTER BLUES 40 Acres and a Mule
    Filmworks/Universal, 1990
JUNGLE FEVER 40 Acres and a Mule Filmworks/
    Universal, 1991

BILLY DICKSON
VESTIGE OF HONOR (TF) Spanish Trails
    Productions/Envoy Productions/Dan Wigutow
    Productions/Desperado Pictures, 1990
TAGGET (CTF) Mirisch Films, 1991

FRANCO DI GIACOMO
LIBERA AMORE MIO Roberto Loyolo Cinematografica,
    1973
LA STANZA DEL VESCOVO *BISHOP'S BEDROOM*
    Merope Film/Carlton Film Export/Societe Nouvelle
    Prodis, 1977
FIGHTING BACK Paramount, 1982
AMITYVILLE II: THE POSSESSION Orion, 1982
THE MEADOW New Yorker, 1982
THE NIGHT OF THE SHOOTING STARS United Artists
    Classics, 1982
VICTORY MARCH Summit, 1983
A BOY FROM CALABRIA International Film
    Exchange, 1987
DARK EYES Island Pictures, 1987

MARIO DI LEO
THE EVIL New World, 1978
BREAKER! BREAKER! American International, 1978
NIGHTMARES Universal, 1983, w/Gerald Perry
    Finnerman
SUDIE AND SIMPSON (CTF) Hearst Entertainment
    Productions/Donald March Productions/Freed-Laufer
    Productions, 1990

BILL DILL
Agent: The Doug Apatow Agency, 10559 Blythe Ave. -
    Los Angeles, LA 90064, 213/202-6888

SIDEWALK STORIES Island Pictures, 1989
THE FIVE HEARTBEATS 20th Century Fox, 1991

ANDREW DINTENFASS
Agent: The Gersh Agency, Inc., Beverly Hills -
    213/274-6611, New York - 212/997-1818

ABOUT LAST NIGHT... Tri-Star, 1986
MEMORIES OF ME MGM/UA, 1988
SHANNON'S DEAL (TF) Stan Rogow Productions/NBC
    Productions, 1989

CARLO DI PALMA
TOGETHER Quartet, 1981
THE TRAGEDY OF A RIDICULOUS MAN Warner
    Bros., 1982
THE BLACK STALLION RETURNS MGM/UA, 1983
GABRIELA MGM/UA Classics, 1984
OFF BEAT Buena Vista, 1986
HANNAH AND HER SISTERS Orion, 1986
THE SECRET OF MY SUCCESS Universal, 1987
RADIO DAYS Orion, 1987
SEPTEMBER Orion, 1987
ALICE Rollins-Joffe/Orion, 1990

ROXANNE DI SANTO
CRIMINAL ACT *TUNNELS* Film Ventures, 1989

ALAN DOBERMAN
VOICE OF THE HEART (CTF) Portman
    Productions, 1990

STEPHEN DOBSON, ACS
Agent: Smith Gosnell Nicholson & Associates -
    Pacific Palisades, 213/459-0307

HEARTBREAK HOTEL Buena Vista, 1988
GROUND ZERO Avenue Pictures, 1988

E

CINEMATOGRAPHERS
PRODUCTION
DESIGNERS,
COSTUME
DESIGNERS AND
FILM EDITORS
GUIDE

C
I
N
E
M
A
T
O
G
R
A
P
H
E
R
S

ALAIN DOSTIE
IRON EAGLE II   Tri-Star, 1988
THE GUNRUNNER   New World, 1989

ROBERT DRAPER
TALES FROM THE DARKSIDE: THE MOVIE
    Paramount, 1990
IN BROAD DAYLIGHT (TF)   Force Ten
    Productions, 1991

STUART DRYBURGH
AN ANGEL AT MY TABLE   Circle Releasing, 1990

MITCHELL DUBIN
MEET THE APPLEGATES   Triton Pictures, 1991

STEVEN DUBIN
COP   Atlantic Releasing Corporation, 1988
THE WICKEDEST WITCH (TF)   Boo You
    Productions, 1990

GUY DUFAUX
THE DELINE OF THE AMERICAN EMPIRE
    Cineplex Odeon, 1986
BLIND TRUST   Cinema Group, 1987
NIGHT ZOO   FilmDallas, 1987
MILK AND HONEY (TF)   ABC Distribution
    Company, 1989
PIN   New World, 1989
JESUS OF MONTREAL   Max Films/UGC, 1989

BRIAN DUGGAN
COLD FEET   Avenue Pictures, 1989

BERT DUNK*
East Coast Card & West Coast Restricted Card
Agent: Smith Gosnell Nicholson & Associates -
    Pacific Palisades, 213/459-0307

CAGNEY & LACEY (TF)   Mace Neufeld Productions/
    Filmways, 1981
KLONDIKE FEVER   1982
HANK WILLIAMS: THE SHOW HE NEVER GAVE
    Simcom/Film Consortium of Canada, 1982
THE INCUBUS   Film Ventures International, 1982
CLASS OF 1984   United Film Distribution, 1982
ILLUSIONS (TF)   CBS Entertainment, 1983
HIGHPOINT   New World, 1984
MURDER TIMES SEVEN (TF)   Pendick/Titus
    Productions, 1990
RICH MEN, SINGLE WOMEN (TF)   Aaron Spelling
    Productions, 1990

ANDREW DUNN
Agent: Sandra Marsh Management - Sherman Oaks,
    818/905-7434

CHATAHOOCHIE   Hemdale, 1989
STRAPLESS   Miramax, 1990
BLACKEYES   BBC, 1990
L.A. STORY   Tri-Star, 1991

ROBERT EBINGER
STUDENT BODIES   Paramount, 1981
LIES   International Film Marketing, 1983
SCHOOL SPIRIT   Concorde, 1985

RICHARD J. EDESA
LINE OF FIRE: THE MORRIS DEES STORY (TF)
    Bo James Entertainment, 1991

DAVID EGGBY, ACS
Agent: Smith Gosnell Nicholson & Associates -
    Pacific Palisades, 213/459-0307

MAD MAX   American International, 1979
THE NAKED COUNTRY   Naked Country
    Productions, 1984
BULLAMAKANKA   Bullmakanka Productions, 1984
A THOUSAND SKIES (MS)   Dimssey Ginn Ltd., 1985
DREAM WEST (MS)   Sunn Classic Pictures, 1986
KANSAS   Trans World Entertainment, 1988
THE BLOOD OF HEROES   *THE SALUTE OF THE
    JUGGER*   Kings Road, 1990
QUIGLEY DOWN UNDER   Pathe-MGM/UA, 1990
WARLOCK   Trimark, 1991

JACOB ELESARI
PENNY ANTE   Andrew Solt Productions, 1990

CHUY ELIZONDO
STOLEN: ONE HUSBAND (TF)   King Phoenix
    Entertainment, 1990
DARK SHADOWS PARTS I-II (Pilot)   Dan Curtis
    Television Productions, 1991, (Part two only)

IAN ELKIN
THE LAST WINTER   Rode Pictures, 1989
THE OUTSIDE CHANCE OF MAXIMILIAN GLICK
    South Gate Entertainment, 1989

PAUL ELLIOTT
Agent: Sandra Marsh Management - Sherman Oaks,
    818/905-6961

THE TOMB   Trans World Entertainment, 1986
ARMED RESPONSE   CineTel, 1986
STACKING   Spectrafilm, 1987, w/Richard Bowen
CYCLONE   CineTel, 1987
RACHEL RIVER   Taurus Entertainment, 1989
976-EVIL   New Line Cinema, 1989
FAR FROM HOME   Vestron, 1989
EQUAL JUSTICE (PILOT)   Orion TV Entertainment/
    Thomas Carter Company, 1989
WELCOME HOME, ROXY CARMICHAEL
    ITC/Paramount, 1990
THE LOST CAPONE (CTF)   Patchett Kaufman
    Entertainment, 1990
DADDY'S DYIN'...WHO'S GOT THE WILL?   Propaganda
    Films/MGM/UA, 1990
MY GIRL   Columbia, 1991
THE FINAL VERDICT (CTF)   TNT, 1991

EI

CINEMATOGRAPHERS
PRODUCTION
DESIGNERS,
COSTUME
DESIGNERS and
FILM EDITORS
GUIDE

C
I
N
E
M
A
T
O
G
R
A
P
H
E
R
S

FREDERICK ELMES*
West Coast Card
Agent: Smith Gosnell Nicholson & Associates -
   Pacific Palisades, 213/459-0307

THE KILLING OF A CHINESE BOOKIE   Faces
   International, 1976
ERASERHEAD   Libra, 1978
OPENING NIGHT   Faces International, 1979
VALLEY GIRL   Atlantic Releasing Corporation, 1983
BLUE VELVET   DEG, 1986
ALLAN QUATERMAIN AND THE LOST CITY OF GOLD
   Cannon, 1987, w/Alex Phillips
RIVER'S EDGE   Island Pictures, 1987
HEAVEN (FD)   Island Pictures, 1987
PERMANENT RECORD   Paramount, 1988
MOONWALKER   Warner Bros., 1989, w/John Hora
WILD AT HEART   Samuel Goldwyn Company, 1990

ROBERT ELSWIT
Agent: Tobias-Skouras & Associates - Los Angeles,
213/277-6211

WALTZ ACROSS TEXAS   Atlantic Releasing
   Corporation, 1982
THE END OF AUGUST   Quartet, 1982
SUMMERSPELL   Summerspell Productions, 1983
TIGER TOWN   Buena Vista, 1984
THE SURE THING   Embassy, 1985
MOVING VIOLATIONS   20th Century Fox, 1985
DESERT HEARTS   Samuel Goldwyn Company, 1985
TRICK OR TREAT   DEG, 1986
AMAZING GRACE AND CHUCK   Tri-Star, 1987
RETURN OF THE LIVING DEAD PART II
   Lorimar, 1988
MARGARET BOURKE-WHITE (TF)   Turner Network
   Television, 1989
DREAMSTREET (Pilot)   1989, w/Thomas Olgeirson
HOW I GOT INTO COLLEGE   20th Century Fox, 1989
HEART OF DIXIE   Orion, 1989
BAD INFLUENCE   Epic Productions/Triumph, 1990
OPPOSITES ATTRACT (TF)   von Serneck-Sertner
   Films/Rastar Productions/Bar-Gene
   Productions, 1990
KILLING IN A SMALL TOWN (TF)   Hearst
   Entertainment Productions/The IndieProd
   Company, 1990
PARIS TROUT   Viacom Pictures, 1991

BRYAN ENGLAND
WEEKEND PASS   Crown International, 1984
THE PARTY ANIMAL   International Film
   Marketing, 1985
PRIVATE PROPERTY   Park Lane Productions,
   1985, w/Bob Brownell
HUNK   Crown International, 1987
FRIDAY THE 13TH PART VIII - JASON TAKES
   MANHATTAN   Paramount, 1989
WICKED STEPMOTHER   MGM/UA, 1989
I, MADMAN   Trans World Entertainment, 1989

ROBERT ENNIS
HOME IS WHERE THE HART IS   Atlantic Releasing
   Corporation, 1987

TEO ESCAMILLA
BLOOD WEDDING   Libra, 1981
THE NEST   Quartet, 1982
THE UNKNOWN GOD   1982

SWEET HOURS   New Yorker, 1982
CARMEN   Orion Classics, 1983
IT'S NEVER TOO LATE   Films Inc., 1984
EL AMOR BRUJO   Orion Classics, 1986
ON THE LINE   Miramax, 1987
BERLINE BLUES   Cannon, 1989

LAURO ESCOREL
Agent: Lawrence A. Mirisch, Triad Artists, Inc. -
   Los Angeles, 213/556-2727

LUCIO FLAVIO   Unifilm/Embrafilme, 1978
AMADA AMANTE   1979
BYE BYE BRAZIL   Carnaval/Unifilm, 1980
THEY DON'T WEAR BLACK TIE   New Yorker, 1983
QUILOMBO   New Yorker, 1986
IRONWEED   Tri-Star, 1987
BETTER DAYS AHEAD   1990

DENIS EVSTIGNEEV
TAXI BLUES   Lenfilm Leningrad, 1991

MIKE FASH
Agent: The Gersh Agency, Inc., Beverly Hills -
   213/274-6611, New York - 212/997-1818

BRITANNIA HOSPITAL   United Artists Classics, 1982
BETRAYAL   20th Century Fox International
   Classics, 1983
RED MONARCH   Enigma Films/Goldcrest Films &
   Television Ltd., 1983
SUCCESS IS THE BEST REVENGE   Triumph/
   Columbia, 1984
PRIVATE SESSIONS (TF)   The Belle Company/
   Seltzer-Gimbel Productions/Raven's Claw Productions/
   Comworld Productions, 1985
THE WHALES OF AUGUST   Alive Films, 1987
IN THE LINE OF DUTY: THE FBI MURDERS (TF)
   Telecom Entertainment, 1988
GLORY! GLORY! (CMS)   Atlantis Films Ltd./
   Orion TV, 1989
ORPHEUS DESCENDING (CTF)   Nederlander TV AND
   Film Productions, 1990
SARAH, PLAIN AND TALL (TF)   Self Help
   Productions, 1991

GERALD FEIL
HE KNOWS YOU'RE ALONE   MGM/United Artists, 1980
FRIDAY THE 13TH - PART 3   Paramount, 1982
LET'S SPEND THE NIGHT TOGETHER (FD)   Embassy,
   1982, w/Caleb Deschanel
SILENT MADNESS   Almi Pictures, 1984
SAVAGE DAWN   MAG Enterprises/Gregory Earls
   Productions, 1985

JOHN FENNER
TEENAGE MUTANT NINJA TURTLES   Limelight/Golden
   Harvest/New Line Cinema, 1990

JOAO FERNANDES
THE NESTING   Feature Films, 1981
THE KIRLIAN WITNESS   Sarno, 1981
THE LAND OF NO RETURN   International Picture
    Show, 1981
THE BIG SCORE   Almi Pictures, 1983
FRIDAY THE 13TH - THE FINAL CHAPTER
    Paramount, 1984
THE ROSEBUD BEACH HOTEL   Almi Pictures, 1984
MISSING IN ACTION   Cannon, 1984
INVASION U.S.A.   Cannon, 1985
PRETTYKILL   Spectrafilm, 1987
BRADDOCK: MISSING IN ACTION III   Cannon, 1988
RED SCORPION   Shapiro Glickenhaus, 1989
MOTHER, MOTHER   1989
DELTA FORCE 2   Cannon Films, 1990

ANGEL LUIS FERNANDEZ
WHAT HAVE I DONE TO DESERVE THIS?
    Cinevista, 1985
LAW OF DESIRE   Cinevista, 1987

GIANCARLO FERRANDO
(John McFerrand)
THE THIEF   1981
THE SWORD OF THE BARBARIANS   Cannon, 1983
AFTER THE FALL OF NEW YORK   Almi
    Pictures, 1985
WARRIOR OF THE LOST WORLD   Vista
    International, 1985
DETECTIVE SCHOOL DROPOUTS   Cannon, 1986
MONSTER SHARK   Cinema Shares, 1986
HANDS OF STEEL   Almi Pictures, 1986
THE MESSENGER   Snizzlefritz Distribution, 1987,
    w/Craig Greene

RICK FICHTER
BRIDE OF RE-ANIMATOR   Wildstreet Pictures/
    50th St. Films, 1991

A. JAFA FIELDER
DAUGHTERS OF THE DUST   American
    Playhouse, 1991

STEVEN FIERBERG
Agent: The Gersh Agency, Inc., Beverly Hills -
    213/274-6611, New York - 212/997-1818

VORTEX   B Movies, 1982
FORTY-DEUCE   Island Alive, 1982
THE FIRST TIME   New Line Cinema, 1983
STREETWALKIN'   Concorde, 1985
SEVEN MINUTES IN HEAVEN   Warner Bros., 1986
TALES FROM THE DARKSIDE (Pilot)   1987
TONIGHT'S THE NIGHT (TF)   IndieProd Productions/
    Phoenix Entertainment Group, 1987
A NIGHTMARE ON ELM STREET 4   New Line
    Cinema, 1988
SPIKE OF BENSONHURST   FilmDallas, 1988
SHARING RICHARD (TF)   Houston Motion
    Picture Entertainment/CBS Entertainment, 1988
HELL HIGH   MGM Enterprises, 1989
SCENES FROM THE CLASS STRUGGLE IN BEVERLY
    HILLS   Cinecom, 1989
ORIGINAL SIN (TF)   Larry Thompson Organization/
    New World TV, 1989
CRIMINAL JUSTICE (CTF)   Elysian Films/HBO
    Showcase, 1990

GABRIEL FIGUEROA
THE NIGHT OF THE IGUANA ★   MGM, 1964
THE CHILDREN OF SANCHEZ   Lone-Star, 1978
UNDER THE VOLCANO   Universal, 1984

HECTOR FIGUEROA*
Agent: The Miller Agency - Santa Clarita, 818/843-7335

SCARED STRAIGHT - ANOTHER STORY (TF)   Golden
    West TV, 1980
THE MANIONS OF AMERICA (MS)   Roger Gimbel
    Productions/EMI TV/Argonaut Films Ltd., 1981
TOMORROW'S CHILD (TF)   20th Century Fox TV, 1982
MEMORIAL DAY (TF)   Charles Fries Productions, 1983
SPACE - PARTS 1 - 5 (MS)   Stonehenge Productions/
    Paramount TV, 1985
CHALLENGE OF A LIFETIME (TF)   1985
STITCHES   International Film Marketing, 1985
THE RETURN OF MICKEY SPILLANE'S MIKE
    HAMMER (TF)   Jay Bernstein Productions/
    Columbia TV, 1986
THE OUTSIDERS (Pilot)   Papazian-Hirsch Entertainment/
    Zoetrope Studios, 1989

VILKO FILAC
Agent: The Gersh Agency, Inc., Beverly Hills -
    213/274-6611, New York - 212/997-1818

WORKERS LIFE   Forum Film, 1986
THE TIME OF THE GYPSY   *GYPSY CARAVAN*
    Forum Film, 1989
THE FORGOTTEN (TF)   Wilshire Court
    Prodcutions, 1991

BRUCE L. FINN
KILL CRAZY   Media Home Entertainment, 1991

GERALD PERRY
FINNERMAN, ASC
NIGHTMARES   Universal, 1983, w/Marco Di Leo
SMORGASBORD   Warner Bros., 1985

ROBERT FIORE
PUMPING IRON (FD)   Cinema 5, 1977
CAN SHE BAKE A CHERRY PIE?   Castle Hill
    Productions/Quartet Films, 1983

GERRY FISHER, BSC *
East Coast Card
Agent: Smith Gosnell Nicholson & Associates - Pacific
    Palisades, 213/459-0307

SECRET CEREMONY   Universal, 1968
THE GO-BETWEEN   Columbia, 1971
A DOLL'S HOUSE   Tomorrow Entertainment, 1973
THE OFFENCE   United Artists, 1973
JUGGERNAUT   United Artists, 1974
BUTLEY   American Film Theatre, 1974
THE ROMANTIC ENGLISH WOMAN   New World, 1975
BRANNIGAN   United Artists, 1975
THE ADVENTURE OF SHERLOCK HOLMES'
    SMARTER BROTHER   20th Century Fox, 1975
ACES HIGH   Cinema Shares International, 1976
MR. KLEIN   20th Century Fox/Lira, 1976
THE ISLAND OF DR. MOREAU   American
    International, 1977
THE LAST REMAKE OF BEAU GESTE   Universal, 1977

CINEMATOGRAPHERS
PRODUCTION
DESIGNERS,
COSTUME
DESIGNERS AND
FILM EDITORS
GUIDE

C
I
N
E
M
A
T
O
G
R
A
P
H
E
R
S

FI

CINEMATOGRAPHERS
PRODUCTION
DESIGNERS,
COSTUME
DESIGNERS and
FILM EDITORS
GUIDE

C
I
N
E
M
A
T
O
G
R
A
P
H
E
R
S

THE ROADS OF THE SOUTH   Parafrance, 1978
FEDORA   United Artists, 1979
WISE BLOOD   New Line Cinema, 1979
THE NINTH CONFIGURATION   Warner Bros., 1980
DON GIOVANNI   Gaumont/New Yorker, 1980
WOLFEN   Orion/Warner Bros., 1981
VICTORY   Lorimar/Paramount, 1981
LOVESICK   Warner Bros., 1983
YELLOWBEARD   Orion, 1983
SAMSON AND DELILAH (TF)   Catalina Production
    Group/Comworld Productions, 1984
THE HOLCROFT COVENANT   Universal, 1985
HIGHLANDER   20th Century Fox, 1986
MAN ON FIRE   Tri-Star, 1987
RUNNING ON EMPTY   Warner Bros., 1988
DEAD BANG   Warner Bros., 1989
BLACK RAINBOW   Goldcrest, 1989
THE FOURTH WAR   Kodiak Films/New Age
    Releasing, 1990
THE EXORCIST III   Morgan Creek/20th
    Century Fox, 1990

JOHN FLECKENSTEIN
THE MEN'S CLUB   Atlantic Releasing
    Corporation, 1986

JOHN C. FLINN III
THE OPERATION (TF)   Viacom/Moress-Nanas-Golden
    Entertainment, 1990

FRANK FLYNN
HOT RESORT   Cannon, 1985
MASTER BLASTER   Artist Entertainment Group, 1987

ROBERT D. FORGES
THE CURSE   Trans World Entertainment, 1987

JOEY FORSYTE
ALEXA   Platinum Pictures, 1989
NEW YEAR'S DAY   International Rainbow
    Pictures, 1989

RON FORTUNATO
HOWARD BEACH: MAKING THE CASE FOR
    MURDER (TF)   Patchett-Kaufman Entertainment
    Productions, 1990

WILLIAM A. FRAKER, ASC*
Agent: The Gersh Agency, Inc., Beverly Hills -
    213/274-6611, New York - 212/997-1818

ROSEMARY'S BABY   Paramount, 1968
PAINT YOUR WAGON   Paramount, 1969
THE DAY OF THE DOLPHIN   Avco Embassy, 1973
COONSKIN (AF)   Bryanston, 1974
RANCHO DeLUXE   United Artists, 1975
ALOHA, BOBBY AND ROSE   Columbia, 1975
LIPSTICK   Paramount, 1976, w/Bill Butler
GATOR   United Artists, 1976
THE KILLER INSIDE ME   Warner Bros., 1976
EXORCIST II: THE HERETIC   Warner Bros., 1977
LOOKING FOR MR. GOODBAR ★   Paramount, 1977
AMERICAN HOT WAX   Paramount, 1978
HEAVEN CAN WAIT ★   Paramount, 1978
OLD BOYFRIENDS   Avco Embassy, 1979
1941 ★   Universal, 1979
THE HOLLYWOOD KNIGHTS   Columbia, 1980

DIVINE MADNESS (FD)   The Ladd Company/Warner
    Bros., 1980
SHARKEY'S MACHINE   Orion/Warner Bros., 1981
THE BEST LITTLE WHOREHOUSE IN TEXAS
    Universal, 1982
WARGAMES ★   MGM/UA, 1983
IRRECONCILABLE DIFFERENCES   Warner Bros., 1984
PROTOCOL   Warner Bros., 1984
MURPHY'S ROMANCE ★   Columbia, 1985
FEVER PITCH   MGM/UA, 1985
SPACECAMP   20th Century Fox, 1986
BURGLAR   Warner Bros., 1987
BABY BOOM   MGM/UA, 1987
CHANCES ARE   Tri-Star, 1989
AN INNOCENT MAN   Buena Vista, 1989
THE FRESHMAN   Tri-Star, 1990

FREDDIE FRANCIS
Home: 12 Ashley Drive, Jersey Road, Osterley,
    Middlesex 7W7 5QA, England
Agent: CCA Personal Management Ltd., 4 Court Lodge,
    48 Sloane Square, London SW1W 8AT, England,
    01/730-8857

SONS AND LOVERS ★★   20th Century Fox, 1960
THE ELEPHANT MAN   Paramount, 1980
THE FRENCH LIEUTENANT'S WOMAN   United
    Artists, 1981
THE JIGSAW MAN   United Film Distribution, 1984
MEMED, MY HAWK   Filmworld Distribution, 1984
DUNE   Universal, 1984
CODE NAME: EMERALD   MGM/UA, 1985
DARK TOWER   Spectrafilm, 1987
CLARA'S HEART   Warner Bros., 1988
HER ALIBI   Warner Bros., 1989
BRENDA STARR   New World, 1989, w/Peter Stein
GLORY ★★   Tri-Star, 1989
THE PLOT TO KILL HITLER (TF)   David L. Wolper
    Productions, 1990

TOM FRASER
Phone: 213/395-1795
Contact: The Irv Schechter Company - Beverly Hills,
    213/278-8070

WIRED TO KILL   American Distribution Group, 1986
HOLLYWOOD ZAP   Troma, 1986
THE UNNAMEABLE   Vidmark Entertainment, 1987
ALIEN FROM L.A.   Cannon, 1988
JOURNEY TO THE CENTER OF THE EARTH   Cannon,
    1989, w/David Watkin
DEAD MEN DON'T DIE   Waymar Productions/Trans
    Atlantic Pictures, 1990
CHOPPER CHICKS IN ZOMBIE TOWN   Troma, 1991

ROBERT FRESCO
COMIC BOOK CONFIDENTIAL   Cinecom, 1989,
    w/Joan Churchill
LAST TRAIN HOME (CTF)   Great North Productions/
    Atlantis Films, 1990

RON FRICKE
KOYAANISQATSI   New Cinema, 1983

JOSEPH FRIEDMAN
ANGELO MY LOVE   Cinecom, 1983

MARTIN FUHRER
Agent: Smith Gosnell Nicholson & Associates - Pacific Palisades, 213/459-0307

NANOU   Umbrella-Caulfield Films Ltd./National Film Finance Corporation/Curzon Film Distribution Ltd./ French Ministry of Culture, 1986
LORD OF THE FLIES   Castle Rock/Columbia, 1990

TAK FUJIMOTO
Agent: Tobias-Skouras & Associates - Los Angeles, 213/277-6211

BADLANDS   Warner Bros., 1974
BOOTLEGGERS   Howco International, 1974
CAGED HEAT   New World, 1974
DEATH RACE 2000   New World, 1975
CANNONBALL   New World, 1976
DR. BLACK, MR. HYDE   Dimension, 1976
BAD GEORGIA ROAD   Dimension, 1976
CHATTER-BOX   American International, 1977
REMEMBER MY NAME   Columbia, 1978
LAST EMBRACE   United Artists, 1979
STONY ISLAND   World Northal, 1980
WHERE THE BUFFALO ROAM   Universal, 1980
BORDERLINE   AFD, 1980
MELVIN AND HOWARD   Universal, 1980
NATIONAL LAMPOON GOES TO THE MOVIES   1981
HEART LIKE A WHEEL   20th Century Fox, 1983
SWING SHIFT   Warner Bros., 1984
SEDUCED (TF)   Catalina Production Group/ Comworld Productions, 1985
PRETTY IN PINK   Paramount, 1986
FERRIS BUELLER'S DAY OFF   Orion, 1986
BACKFIRE   New Century/Vista, 1987
SOMETHING WILD   Orion, 1987
SWEET HEARTS DANCE   Tri-Star, 1988
MARRIED TO THE MOB   Orion, 1988
COCOON: THE RETURN   20th Century Fox, 1988
CAST THE FIRST STONE (TF)   Columbia Pictures TV/ Mench Productions, 1990
MIAMI BLUES   Orion, 1990
THE SILENCE OF THE LAMBS   Orion, 1991

G

RICARDO JACQUES GALE
BLOODFIST   Concorde, 1989
CORPORATE AFFAIRS   Concorde-New Horizons, 1990

TIMOTHY GALFAS
Agent: Scott Harris, Harris & Goldberg - Los Angeles, 213/553-5200

BOGARD   L-T Films, 1975
THE LORD OF THE RINGS (AF)   United Artists, 1978
SUMMER LOVERS   Filmways, 1982
RHINESTONE   20th Century Fox, 1984
DEFENSE PLAY   Kodiak Films, 1986
COLLISION COURSE   DEG, 1988

RONALD VICTOR GARCIA
Contact: 213/459-3547

HOT POTATO   Warner Bros., 1976
ONE FROM THE HEART   Columbia, 1982
RAINY DAY FRIENDS   Signature Productions, 1986
DOIN' TIME   Warner Bros., 1986
THE NIGHT BEFORE   Kings Road Productions, 1987
NIGHTBREAKER (TF)   Symphony Pictures, 1989
NAKED LIE (TF)   Shadowplay Films/Phoenix Entertainment, 1989
DISORGANIZED CRIME   Buena Vista, 1989
TWIN PEAKS (Pilot)   Worldwide Enterprises/Propaganda Films/Lynch-Frost Productions, 1989
SIDE OUT   Tri-Star, 1990
MATTERS OF THE HEART (CTF)   MCA TV Entertainment/Tahse-Bergman Productions, 1990
THE BRIDE IN BLACK (TF)   New World TV/Barry Weitz Films, 1990
DARK AVENGER (TF)   A/L Productions/Columbia Pictures Television, 1990
EL DIABLO (CTF)   Wizan/Black Films Productions, 1990

GREG GARDINER
FAR OUT MAN   New Line Cinema, 1990, w/Eric Woster

MIKE GARFATH
LAMB   Film Forum, 1986
CAR TROUBLE   CineTel Films, 1986
A PRAYER FOR THE DYING   Samuel Goldwyn Company, 1987
SOURSWEET   Skouras Pictures, 1988
WE THINK THE WORLD OF YOU   Cinecom, 1989
NUNS ON THE RUN   HandMade/20th Century Fox, 1990

JOAN GELPI
COUNTERFORCE (TF)   Golden Sun/ESME, 1991

HARVEY GENKINS
FIVE DAYS FROM HOME   Universal, 1978
H.O.T.S.   Derio Productions, 1979
THUNDER RUN   Cannon, 1986
OMEGA SYNDROME   New World, 1987
SILENT NIGHT, DEADLY NIGHT - PART II   Ascot Entertainment Group, 1987
THE GARBAGE PAIL KIDS MOVIE   Atlantic Releasing Corporation, 1987
THE GUMSHOE KID   Argus Entertainment/ Skouras, 1990

LASZLO GEORGE, CSC
Address: 8616 East Worthington Dr., San Gabriel, CA 91755, 213/271-1686 or Toronto 416/651-5357

RUNNING   Universal, 1979
NOTHING PERSONAL   American International, 1980
CIRCLE OF TWO   World Northal, 1981
PAROLE (TF)   RSO Films, 1982
MAZES AND MONSTERS (TF)   1982
DRAW! (CTF)   HBO, 1984
THE BEAR   Embassy, 1984
THE UNDERGRADS (CTF)   Sharmhill Productions/The Disney Channel, 1985
THE PARK IS MINE (CTF)   HBO Premiere Films/Astral Film Productions/ICC, 1985
A LETTER TO THREE WIVES (TF)   20th Century Fox TV, 1985
MURDER IN SPACE (CTF)   Robert Cooper Productions/ Zenith Productions/CTV Network, 1985

Gi

CINEMATOGRAPHERS
PRODUCTION
DESIGNERS,
COSTUME
DESIGNERS and
FILM EDITORS
GUIDE

C
I
N
E
M
A
T
O
G
R
A
P
H
E
R
S

VANISHING ACT (TF)   Robert Cooper
    Productions, 1986
YOUNG AGAIN (TF)   Sharmhill Productions/Walt
    Disney Productions, 1986
A MASTERPIECE OF MURDER (TF)   20th Century
    Fox TV, 1986
MANY HAPPY RETURNS (TF)   Alan M. Levin & Steven
    H. Stern Films, 1986
STRANGER IN MY BED (TF)   Taft Entertainment TV/
    Edgar J. Scherick Productions, 1986
HANDS OF A STRANGER (TF)   Taft Entertainment
    TV, 1987
ROLLING VENGEANCE   Apollo Pictures, 1987
A STONING IN FULLHAM COUNTY (TF)   The
    Landsburg Co., 1988
SWIM SUIT (TF)   Musifilm Productions, 1989
TARZAN IN MANHATTAN (TF)   1989
ALWAYS REMEMBER I LOVE YOU (TF)
    Stephen J. Cannell Productions/Gross-Weston
    Productions, 1990
STORM AND SORROW (CTF)   Hearst Entertainment
    Productions/Accent Entertainment, 1990,
    w/Ivan Mark
LAST FLIGHT OUT (TF)   NBC Productions/Co-Star
    Entertainment/The Mannheim Company, 1990
ROXANNE: THE PRIZE PULITZER (TF)   Qintex
    Entertainment, 1990
THE KENNEDYS OF MASSACHUSETTS (TF)
    Orion TV/Edgar J. Scherick Associates
    Productions, 1990
DANIELLE STEEL'S 'KALEIDOSCOPE' (TF)   NBC
    Productions/The Cramer Company, 1990

RODNEY GIBBONS
MY BLOODY VALENTINE   Paramount, 1981
THE AMITYVILLE CURSE   Allegro Films, 1990

PAUL GIBSON
THE GAME   Curtis Films/Visual Perspectives, 1989

STAN GILBERT
WITHOUT HER CONSENT (TF)   Carla Singer
    Productions/Half Pint Productions/Raymond Katz
    Enterprises, 1990

BLASCO GIURATO
CINEMA PARADISO   Miramax, 1989
TUTTI STANNO BENE   EVERYBODY'S FINE
    Miramax, 1990

PIERRE-WILLIAM GLENN
SMALL CHANGE   New World, 1976
THE JUDGE AND THE ASSASSIN   Libra, 1976
THE THREAT   Parafrance, 1977
AVALANCHE   New World, 1978
A LITTLE ROMANCE   Orion/Warner Bros., 1979
SERIE NOIRE   THRILLER STORY   Gaumont, 1979
LOULOU   Gaumont, 1980
L'ENTOURLOUPE   THE SWINDLE   CCFC, 1980
UNE SEMAINE DE VACANCES   A WEEK'S VACATION
    Paramount, 1980
CLEAN SLATE   COUP DE TORCHON   Biograph/
    Quartet/Frank Moreno, 1981
DEATH WATCH   Quartet, 1982
A WEEK'S VACATION   Biograph International, 1982
L'ETOILE DU NORD   United Artists Classics, 1983
CHOICE OF ARMS   Summit, 1983
DEATHWATCH   Quartet, 1984
MISSISSIPPI BLUES (FD)   Film Forum, 1985

CHILDREN OF CHAOS   1989
A DRY WHITE SEASON   MGM/UA, 1989, w/Kevin Pike

JAMES M. GLENNON
Agent: The Gersh Agency, Inc., Beverly Hills -
    213/274-6611, New York - 212/997-1818

PRISONERS   20th Century Fox, 1984
THE WILD LIFE   Universal, 1984
EL NORTE   Cinecom/Island Alive, 1984
UP THE CREEK   Orion, 1984
SECOND SIGHT - A LOVE STORY (TF)   Entheos
    Unlimited Productions/T.T.C. Productions, 1984
MY WICKED, WICKED WAYS (TF)   1985
SMOOTH TALK   Spectrafilm, 1985
FLIGHT OF THE NAVIGATOR   Buena Vista, 1986
ONE MORE SATURDAY NIGHT   Columbia, 1986
A TIME OF DESTINY   Columbia, 1988
LEMON SKY (TF)   American Playhouse, 1988
FLYING BLIND (TF)   NBC Productions, 1990
A SHOW OF FORCE   Golden Harvest/Paramount, 1990

PAUL GLICKMAN
TRACKS   Castle Hill Productions, 1976
THE PRIVATE FILES OF J. EDGAR HOOVER   American
    International, 1978
PERFECT STRANGERS   BLIND ALLEY   New Line
    Cinema, 1984
THE STUFF   New World, 1985

RICHARD C. GLOUNER, ASC
Phone: 818/894-2028

GRIFFIN AND PHOENIX (TF)   ABC Circle Films, 1976
THE GUMBALL RALLY   Warner Bros., 1976
THE GONG SHOW MOVIE   Universal, 1980
THE MAN WITH BOGART'S FACE   20th Century
    Fox, 1980
SUMMER (Pilot)   1984
HOT CHILD IN THE CITY   Mediacom Filmworks, 1987
ANOTHER CHANCE   W.A. Productions, 1987
MIRACLE AT BEEKMAN'S PLACE (TF)   EM/BE Inc.
    Productions, 1988
CHAMELEONS (TF)   Glen Larson Productions/NBC
    Productions, 1990

GODFREY A. GODAR
THE BOYS IN COMPANY C   Columbia, 1978
GAME OF DEATH   Columbia, 1979
GYMKATA   MGM/UA, 1985
HOWLING IV...THE ORIGINAL NIGHTMARE   Allied
    Entertainment, 1988

KEITH GODDARD
TWENTY-ONE   Anglo International Films, 1991

STEPHEN GOLDBLATT, ASC *
West & East Coast Cards
Agent: Smith Gosnell Nicholson & Associates - Pacific
    Palisades, 213/459-0307

BREAKING GLASS   Paramount, 1980
OUTLAND   The Ladd Company/Warner Bros., 1981
THE HUNGER   MGM/UA, 1983
THE COTTON CLUB   Orion, 1984
YOUNG SHERLOCK HOLMES   Paramount, 1985
THE RETURN OF THE SOLDIER   European
    Classics, 1985

LETHAL WEAPON   Warner Bros., 1987
EVERYBODY'S ALL-AMERICAN   Warner Bros., 1988
LETHAL WEAPON 2   Warner Bros., 1989
JOE VERSUS THE VOLCANO   Amblin Entertainment/
    Warner Bros., 1990

PAUL H. GOLDSMITH
Agent: Dattner & Associates - Los Angeles,
    213/447-5986

HOMEWORK   Jensen Farley Pictures, 1982
WAVELENGTH   New World, 1983
THE KILLING TIME   New World, 1987
BIG TIME   The American Playhouse, 1988
WINNIE (TF)   All Girl Productions/NBC Prods., 1988
WHAT'S ALAN WATCHING? (Pilot)   1989
A SHOCK TO THE SYSTEM   Corsair Pictures, 1990
AGAINST THE LAW (TF)   MGM-UA TV/Sarabande
    Productions, 1990

DAVID GOLIA
HADLEY'S REBELLION   American Film
    Distributors, 1984
KAMIKAZE HEARTS   Legler/Bashore, 1986
NO RETREAT, NO SURRENDER   Cannon, 1986,
    w/John Huneck
THE ROSARY MURDERS   New Line Cinema, 1987
MIDNIGHT   SVS Films, 1989
BAD JIM   21st Century, 1990

IRV GOODNOFF
DADDY'S DEADLY DARLING   Aquarius, 1984
THE IRON TRIANGLE   Scotti Bros., 1989

ROBIN GOODWIN
SWAMP THING   Embassy, 1982

MICHAEL GORNICK
MARTIN   Libra Films, 1978
DAWN OF THE DEAD   United Film Distribution, 1979
KNIGHTRIDERS   United Film Distribuiton, 1981
CREEPSHOW   Warner Bros., 1982
DAY OF THE DEAD   United Film Distribution, 1985

RICCARDO GRASSETTI
ONLY ONE SURVIVED (TF)   RAI TV/CBS
    Entertainment, 1990

GARY GRAVER
GRAND THEFT AUTO   New World, 1977
MOONSHINE COUNTY EXPRESS   New World, 1977
DEATHSPORT   New World, 1978
SUNNYSIDE   American International, 1979
SMOKEY BITES THE DUST   New World, 1981
THE GLOVE   PN International, 1981
HOLLYWOOD HIGH PART II   Lone Star, 1981
MORTUARY   Film Ventures, 1983
THEY'RE PLAYING WITH FIRE   New World, 1984
PARTY CAMP   Lightning Pictures, 1987
COMMANDO SQUAD   Trans World
    Entertainment, 1987
PHANTOM EMPIRE   American Independent, 1987
DEEP SPACE   Trans World, 1987
MOB BOSS   American Independent/Vidmark, 1990
SPIRITS   Cinema Group, 1990

STEPHEN W. GRAY
SAVANNAH SMILES   Embassy, 1982
BASIC TRAINING   MovieStore, 1985

RICHARD GREATREX
KNIGHTS AND EMERALDS   Warner Bros., 1986
WAR REQUIEM   Movie Visions, 1989
FOR QUEEN AND COUNTRY   Atlantic Releasing
    Corporation, 1989

JACK N. GREEN
Agent: The Gersh Agency, Inc., Beverly Hills - 213/274-
    6611, New York - 212/997-1818

HEARTBREAK RIDGE   Warner Bros., 1986
LIKE FATHER, LIKE SON   Tri-Star, 1987
THE DEAD POOL   Warner Bros., 1988
BIRD   Warner Bros., 1988
PINK CADILLAC   Warner Bros., 1989
RACE FOR GLORY   New Century/Vista, 1989
WHITE HUNTER, BLACK HEART   Warner Bros., 1990
THE ROOKIE   Malpaso/Warner Bros., 1990

ADAM GREENBERG
Agent: The Gersh Agency, Inc., Beverly Hills -
    213/274-6611, New York - 212/997-1818

DIAMONDS   Avco Embassy, 1975
THE PASSOVER PLOT   Atlas, 1977
OPERATION THUNDERBOLT   1977
IT'S A FUNNY, FUNNY WORLD   Noah Films, 1978
THE URANIUM CONSPIRACY   Noah Films, 1978
GOING STEADY   Noah Films, 1979
THE BIG RED ONE   United Artists, 1980
LEMON POPSICLE   Noah Films, 1981
SAFARI 3000   MGM/UA, 1982
PARADISE   Embassy, 1982
THE LAST AMERICAN VIRGIN   Cannon, 1982
10 TO MIDNIGHT   Cannon, 1983
OVER THE BROOKLYN BRIDGE   MGM/UA/
    Cannon, 1984
THE AMBASSADOR   MGM/UA/Cannon, 1984
THE TERMINATOR   Orion, 1984
ONCE BITTEN   Samuel Goldwyn Company, 1985
WAR AND LOVE   Cannon, 1985
IRON EAGLE   Tri-Star, 1986
WISDOM   20th Century Fox, 1986
THE LADIES CLUB   New Line Cinema, 1986
JOCKS   Crown International, 1987
A WALK ON THE MOON   Benenson/Midwest Film
    Productions, 1987
LA BAMBA   Columbia, 1987
THREE MEN AND A BABY   Buena Vista, 1987
NEAR DARK   DEG, 1987
ALIEN NATION   20th Century Fox, 1988
SPELLBINDER   MGM/UA, 1988
TURNER AND HOOCH   Buena Vista, 1989
WORTH WINNING   20th Century Fox, 1989
LOVE HURTS   Vestron, 1990
GHOST   Paramount, 1990
THREE MEN AND A LITTLE LADY   Interscope/Jean
    Francois LePetit/Touchstone/Buena Vista, 1990

ROBBIE GREENBERG, ASC
Agent: Bauer Benedek Agency - Los Angeles,
    213/275-2421

YOUNGBLOOD   American International, 1978
THE LATHE OF HEAVEN (TF)   WNET-13 Television
    Laboratory/Taurus Film, 1980
BUTCHER, BAKER, NIGHTMARE MAKER   *NIGHT
    WARNING*   Comworld, 1981
TIME WALKER   New World, 1982

Gr

CINEMATOGRAPHERS
PRODUCTION
DESIGNERS,
COSTUME
DESIGNERS AND
FILM EDITORS
GUIDE

C
I
N
E
M
A
T
O
G
R
A
P
H
E
R
S

Gr

CINEMATOGRAPHERS
PRODUCTION
DESIGNERS,
COSTUME
DESIGNERS and
FILM EDITORS
GUIDE

C
I
N
E
M
A
T
O
G
R
A
P
H
E
R
S

THE WINTER OF OUR DISCONTENT (TF)   Lorimar
    Productions, 1983
THIS GIRL FOR HIRE (TF)   Barney Rosenzweig
    Productions/Orion TV, 1983
MY MOTHER'S SECRET LIFE (TF)
    Furia-Oringer Productions/ABC Circle Films, 1984
SWEET DREAMS   Tri-Star, 1985
MOVERS AND SHAKERS   MGM/UA, 1985
CREATOR   Universal, 1985
SECOND SERVE (TF)   Linda Yellen Productions/
    Lorimar Telepictures, 1986
THE MILAGRO BEANFIELD WAR   Universal, 1988
FAR NORTH   Alive Films, 1988

CRAIG GREENE

THE OFFSPRING   TMC Pictures, 1987
THE MESSENGER   Snizzlefritz Distribution, 1987,
    w/Giancarlo Ferrando

KENNETH C. GREGG

THE MAGIC SEASON OF ROBERTSON DAVIES
    Canadian Broadcasting Corporation, 1990

DAVID GRIBBLE

Agent: Smith Gosnell Nicholson & Associates -
    Pacific Palisades, 213/459-0307

MONKEY GRIP   Cinecom, 1982
LOVE IS NEVER SILENT (TF)   Marian Rees
    Associates, 1985
FAST TALKING   Cinecom 1985
ADAM: HIS SONG CONTINUES (TF)   Alan Landsburg
    Productions, 1986
AMERICAN HARVEST (TF)   Ruth-Stratton
    Productions/The Finnegan Company, 1987
OFF LIMITS   20th Century Fox, 1988
TAP   Tri-Star, 1989
CADILLAC MAN   Orion, 1990

KAREN GROSSMAN

Agent: Lawrence A. Mirisch, Triad Artists, Inc. -
    Los Angeles, 213/556-2727

THE SLAYER   21st Century, 1982
THUNDER ALLEY   Cannon, 1985
HAMBURGER...THE MOTION PICTURE   FM
    Entertainment, 1986
MODERN GIRLS   Atlantic Releasing Corporation, 1986
TRADING HEARTS   Cineworld Enterprises, 1988
RETURN TO GREEN ACRES (TF)   Orion TV/Jaygee
    Productions, 1990
SHADOWZONE   Full Moon/JGM Enterprises, 1990

FRANCIS GRUMMAN

BULLETPROOF   CineTel Films, 1987
MURDER BY NUMBERS   Burnhill, 1990
GOIN' TO CHICAGO   Poor Robert Productions, 1990

ALEXANDER GRUSZYNSKI

Agent: Tobias-Skouras & Associates - Los Angeles,
    213/277-6211

A SAVAGE HUNGER THE OASIS   Shapiro
    Entertainment, 1984
ALMOST YOU   TLC Films/20th Century Fox, 1984
THE LAST INNOCENT MAN (CTF)   HBO Pictures/
    Maurice Singer Productions, 1987
UNDER COVER   Cannon, 1987

PROMISED LAND   Vestron, 1988, w/Ueli Steiger
BAD DREAMS   20th Century Fox, 1988
THE WOMEN OF BREWSTER PLACE (TF)   Harpo
    Productions/Phoenix Entertainment, 1989
TREMORS   Universal, 1990
BY DAWN'S EARLY LIGHT (CTF)   Paravision
    International/HBO, 1990
STONE COLD   Columbia Pictures, 1991

ENNIO GUARNIERI

THE CASSANDRA CROSSING   Avco Embassy, 1977
LA TRAVIATA   Universal Classics, 1983
GINGER & FRED   MGM/UA, 1986, w/Tonino Delli Colli
OTELLO   Cannon, 1986
DANCERS   Cannon, 1987

OLIVIER GUENEAU

SWEET REVENGE (CTF)   Chrysalide Film/Canal Plus/
    The Movie Group, 1990

PILI FLORES GUERRA

FULL FATHOM FIVE   Concorde, 1990

MARK GUNNING

KOREA: THE UNKNOWN WAR (TF)   WGBH-TV, Boston/
    Thames Television, 1990, w/Frank Haysom

DAVID GURFINKEL

THE FOX IN THE CHICKEN COOP   Hashu'alim
    Ltd., 1978
THE MAGICIAN OF LUBLIN   Cannon, 1979
ENTER THE NINJA   Cannon, 1981
REVENGE OF THE NINJA   MGM/UA/Cannon, 1983
SAHARA   MGM/UA, 1984
THE NAKED FACE   MGM/UA, 1984
RAPPIN'   Cannon, 1985
MATA HARI   Cannon, 1985
AMERICA 3000   Cannon, 1985
THE DELTA FORCE   Cannon, 1986
OVER THE TOP   Cannon, 1987
RUMPELSTILTSKIN   Cannon, 1987
APPOINTMENT WITH DEATH   Cannon, 1988
SALSA   Cannon, 1988
A MAN CALLED SARGE   Cannon Pictures, 1990
HELD HOSTAGE: THE SIS AND JERRY LEVIN
    STORY (TF)   Paragon Entertainment, 1991

MANFRED GUTHE

Agent: Smith Gosnell Nicholson & Associates -
    Pacific Palisades, 213/459-0307

CURTAINS   Jensen Farley Pictures, 1983,
    w/Robert Paynter
DEADLINE   New Image, 1984
TOO OUTRAGEOUS!   Spectrafilm, 1987
AMERIKA (MS)   ABC Circle Films, 1987

H

RON HAGEN
Agent: Smith Gosnell Nicholson & Associates - Pacific
    Palisades, 213/459-0307

A PLACE TO CALL HOME (TF)   Big Deal Productions/
    Crawford Productions/Embassy TV, 1987
THE ROOM UPSTAIRS (TF)   Marian Rees Associates/
    The Alexander Group, 1987
AARON'S WAY: THE HARVEST (TF)   Blinn-
    Thorpe Productions/Lorimar Telepictures, 1988
THE FAR COUNTRY (MS)   Crawford
    Productions, 1987

DANIEL HAINEY
AMERICAN NIGHTMARE   Mano, 1984
PLAIN CLOTHES   Paramount, 1988
BIG TIME   Alive Films, 1988

JACQUES HAITKIN
HOT TOMORROWS   American Film Institute, 1978
THEY WENT THAT-A-WAY & THAT-A-WAY
    International Picture Show, 1978
THE PRIZE FIGHTER   New World, 1979
THE PRIVATE EYES   New World, 1980
ST. HELENS   New World, 1981
GALAXY OF TERROR   New World, 1981
ANGEL OF H.E.A.T.   Summa Vista, 1982
THE HOUSE WHERE EVIL DWELLS   MGM/UA, 1982
LAST PLANE OUT   New World, 1983
MAKING THE GRADE   MGM/UA/Cannon, 1984
A NIGHTMARE ON ELM STREET   New Line
    Cinema, 1984
THE LOST EMPIRE   JGM Enterprises, 1985
THE IMAGEMAKER   Castle Hill Productions, 1985
A NIGHTMARE ON ELM STREET PART 2: FREDDY'S
    REVENGE   New Line Cinema, 1985
QUIET COOL   New Line Cinema, 1986
MY DEMON LOVER   New Line Cinema, 1987
THE HIDDEN   New Line Cinema, 1987
CHERRY 2000   Orion, 1988
LUCKY STIFF   New Line Cinema, 1989
CAGE   New Century/Vista, 1989
SHOCKER   Universal, 1989
BURIED ALIVE (CTF)   MCA Entertainment, 1990

CONRAD L. HALL, ASC *
INCUBUS   1961
WILD SEED   Universal, 1965
MORITURI ★   20th Century Fox, 1965
HARPER   Warner Bros., 1966
THE PROFESSIONALS ★   Columbia, 1966
DIVORCE AMERICAN STYLE   Columbia, 1967
IN COLD BLOOD ★   Columbia 1967
COOL HAND LUKE   Warner Bros., 1967
THE HAPPY ENDING   United Artists, 1969
HELL IN THE PACIFIC   Cinerama Releasing
    Corporation, 1968
TELL THEM WILLIE BOY IS HERE   Universal, 1969
BUTCH CASSIDY AND THE SUNDANCE KID ★★
    20th Century Fox, 1969

ELECTRA GLIDE IN BLUE   United Artists, 1973
THE DAY OF THE LOCUST ★   Paramount, 1975
SMILE   United Artists, 1975
MARATHON MAN   Paramount, 1976
BLACK WIDOW   20th Century Fox, 1987
TEQUILA SUNRISE ★   Warner Bros., 1988
CLASS ACTION   20th Century Fox, 1991

VICTOR HAMMER
Agent: The Gersh Agency, Inc., Beverly Hills -
    213/274-6611, New York - 212/997-1818

DIVE   Warner Bros., 1990
LEAN ON ME   Warner Bros., 1989
SOUVENIRS   Columbia, 1991

WONG WING HANG
THE KILLER   Circle Releasing, 1991, w/Peter Pao

RICHARD HANNAH
THE STAR CHAMBER   20th Century Fox, 1983

PETER HANNAN, ASC, BSC
FLAME   Goodtime Enterprises, 1975
THE HAUNTING OF JULIA   Discovery Films, 1977
THE STUD   Trans-American, 1978
MOON OVER THE ALLEY   British Film Institute, 1980
THE MISSIONARY   Columbia, 1982
BRIMSTONE AND TREACLE   United Artists
    Classics, 1982
MONTY PYTHON'S THE MEANING OF LIFE
    Universal, 1983
THE RAZOR'S EDGE   Columbia, 1984
DANCE WITH A STRANGER   Samuel Goldwyn
    Company, 1985
INSIGNIFICANCE   Island Alive 1985
TURTLE DIARY   Samuel Goldwyn Company, 1985
CLUB PARADISE   Warner Bros., 1986
HALF MOON STREET   20th Century Fox, 1986
WITHNAIL AND I   Cineplex Odeon, 1987
THE LONELY PASSION OF JUDITH HEARNE   Island
    Films, 1987
A HANDFUL OF DUST   New Line Cinema, 1988
HOW TO GET AHEAD IN ADVERTISING   Warner
    Bros., 1989
NOT WITHOUT MY DAUGHTER   Pathe Entertainment/
    MGM/UA, 1991

GARY HANSEN
WE OF THE NEVER NEVER   Triumph, 1983

FRANK HARRIS
THE PATRIOT   Crown International, 1986
LOW BLOW   Crown International, 1986
CATCH THE HEAT   Trans World Entertainment, 1987,
    w/Nicho Nissim

MARK HARRIS
MINISTRY OF VENGEANCE   Concorde, 1989

STUART HARRIS
WETHERBY   MGM/UA Classics, 1985

GEOFF HARRISON
CHANDLER (TF)   R.M. Associates, 1991

Ha

CINEMATOGRAPHERS
PRODUCTION
DESIGNERS,
COSTUME
DESIGNERS AND
FILM EDITORS
GUIDE

C
I
N
E
M
A
T
O
G
R
A
P
H
E
R
S

Ha

CINEMATOGRAPHERS
PRODUCTION
DESIGNERS,
COSTUME
DESIGNERS AND
FILM EDITORS
GUIDE

C
I
N
E
M
A
T
O
G
R
A
P
H
E
R
S

HARVEY HARRISON, BSC
Agent: Sandra Marsh Management - Sherman Oaks,
818/905-6961

TODAY MEXICO - TOMORROW THE WORLD
Shillingford & Company/Rank, 1970
WHITE ROCK (FD)   EMI, 1977
THE BURNING   Filmways, 1982
AMIN: THE RISE AND FALL   Twin Continental, 1983
G'OLE! (FD)   Warner Bros., 1983
CHEECH & CHONG: STILL SMOKIN'
Paramount, 1983
CHEECH & CHONG'S THE CORSICAN BROTHERS
Orion, 1984
AMERICAN GOTHIC   Vidmark, 1987
CASTAWAY   Cannon, 1987
SALOME'S LAST DANCE   Vestron, 1988
ARIA (Nicolas Roeg Segment)   RCA VP/Virgin
Vision, 1987
A CONNECTICUT YANKEE IN KING ARTHUR'S
COURT (TF)   Consolidated Entertainment/
Schaefer-Karpf Productions, 1990
THE WITCHES   Warner Bros., 1990

ROBERT B. HAUSER, ASC
Agent: The Miller Agency - Santa Clarita,
818/843-7335

THE ODD COUPLE   Paramount, 1968
A MAN CALLED HORSE   National General, 1970
LE MANS   National General, 1970
WILLARD   Cinerama Releasing Corporation, 1971
FINAL CHAPTER - WALKING TALL   American
International, 1977
TWILIGHT'S LAST GLEAMING   Allied Artists, 1977
MEAN DOG BLUES   American International, 1978
THE FRISCO KID   Warner Bros., 1979
WHEN HELL WAS IN SESSION (TF)   Aubrey-
Hamner Productions, 1979
CHRISTMAS LILIES OF THE FIELD (TF)
Rainbow Productions/Osmond Productions, 1979
FUGITIVE FAMILY (TF)   Aubrey-Hamner
Productions, 1980
ALCATRAZ: THE WHOLE SHOCKING STORY (TF)
Pierre Cossette Productions, 1980
TERROR AMONG US (TF)   David Gerber
Company, 1981
THE DAY THE LOVING STOPPED (TF)   Monash-
Zeitman Productions, 1981
NO PLACE TO HIDE (TF)   Metromedia
Producers Corporation, 1981
KILLJOY (TF)   Lorimar Productions, 1981
SEVEN BRIDES FOR SEVEN BROTHERS (TF)   David
Gerber Company/MGM-UA TV, 1982
AIRWOLF (TF)   Belisarius Productions/
Universal TV, 1984
JESSIE (TF)   Lindsay Wagner Productions/
MGM-UA TV, 1984

GORDON HAYMAN
DARK TOWER   Spectrafilm, 1989

JAMES HAYMAN
TOKYO POP   Spectrafilm, 1988
THE STRANGER WITHIN (TF)   Goodman-Rosen
Productions/New World Television, 1990
IRON AND SILK   Sun Productions, 1990

FRANK HAYSOM
KOREA: THE UNKNOWN WAR (TF)   WGBH-TV,
Boston/Thames Television, 1990, w/Mark Gunning

KEVIN HAYWARD
TEARAWAY   Spectrafilm, 1987

JACK HAZAN
RUDE BOY   Atlantic Releasing Corporation, 1980
A BIGGER SPLASH   Buzzy Enterprises, 1984
SOPHISTICATED LADY   Davids Film Company
Production, 1989

BRIAN HEBB
HUMONGOUS   Embassy, 1982
COWBOYS DON'T CRY   Cineplex Odeon, 1989
ON THIN ICE: THE TAI BABILONIA STORY (TF)
Spectacor Films/Janet Faust Krusi Films/Bernard
Rothman Productions, 1990
RUNNING AGAINST TIME (CTF)   MCA TV
Entertainment/Finnegan-Pinchuk Productions, 1990

BRIAN HEFFRON
THE IMPORTED BRIDEGROOM   Lara Classics, 1990

BERND HEINL
BAGDAD CAFE   Island Pictures, 1988
FROM THE DEAD OF NIGHT (TF)   Shadowplay Films/
Phoenix Entertainment, 1989
ROSALIE GOES SHOPPING   Futura Film Verlag/
Pelemele Film, 1989
DISTURBED   Live Entertainment/Odyssey
Distribution, 1990
MURDER C.O.D. (TF)   The Kushner-Locke Company/
Perry Lafferty Productions, 1990
MY HEROES HAVE ALWAYS BEEN COWBOYS
Samuel Goldwyn Company, 1991

JOHN HENDRICKS
HOLLYWOOD VICE SQUAD   Cinema Group, 1986

DAVID HERRINGTON
Address: 54 Baltray Crescent, Don Mills, Ontario
M3A 2H4, 416/447-9820

THE HOUSEKEEPER   Castle Hill Productions, 1987
LOVE & MURDER   Norstar Entertainment, 1989
A QUIET LITTLE NEIGHBORHOOD, A PERFECT LITTLE
MURDER (TF)   Saban International/Neal and Gary
Productions, 1990
PRIMO BABY   Victory Film, 1990
COMMON GOUND-PARTS I & II (TF)   Lorimar
Telepictures/Daniel H. Blatt Productions, 1990

JOHN HERZOG
HELLO MARY LOU: PROM NIGHT II   Samuel Goldwyn
Company, 1987

GREGG HESCHONG
A CRY IN THE WILD   Concorde-New Horizons, 1990

JACK HILDYARD
MOHAMMED, MESSENGER OF GOD   Tarik, 1977
THE WILD GEESE   Rank, 1978
LION OF THE DESERT   United Film Distribution, 1981
THE ZANY ADVENTURES OF ROBIN HOOD (TF)
Bobka Productions/Charles Fries Entertainment, 1984

ELLIS ISLAND (MS)   Pantheon Pictures/Telepictures
    Productions, 1984
FLORENCE NIGHTINGALE (TF)   Cypress Point
    Productions, 1985

PAUL HIPP
IN SEARCH OF HISTORIC JESUS   Sunn
    Classic, 1979
HANGAR 18   Sunn Classic, 1980
THE PRESIDENT MUST DIE   Jensen Farley
    Pictures, 1981
PSYCHO FROM TEXAS   New American, 1982

ALEC HIRSCHFELD
SPACE RAIDERS   New World, 1983
LOVE LETTERS   New World, 1984

GERALD HIRSCHFELD, ASC
Agent: The Gersh Agency, Inc., Beverly Hills -
    213/274-6611, New York - 212/997-1818

FAIL-SAFE   Columbia, 1967
GOODBYE, COLUMBUS   Paramount, 1969
DIARY OF A MAD HOUSEWIFE   Universal, 1970
T.R. BASKIN   Paramount, 1971
ONE SUMMER LOVE   American International, 1976
TWO-MINUTE WARNING   Universal, 1976
THE CAR   Universal, 1977
THE WORLD'S GREATEST LOVER   20th Century
    Fox, 1977
COMA   MGM/United Artists, 1978, w/Victor Kemper
THE BELL JAR   Avco Embassy, 1979
AMERICATHON   United Artists, 1979
WHY WOULD I LIE?   MGM/United Artists, 1980
NEIGHBORS   Columbia, 1981
MY FAVORITE YEAR   MGM/UA, 1982
TO BE OR NOT TO BE   20th Century Fox, 1983
THE HOUSE OF GOD   United Artists, 1984
HEAD OFFICE   Tri-Star, 1985
LOVE LIVES ON (TF)   Script-Song Productions/
    ABC Circle Films, 1985
MALONE   Orion, 1987
THE NEON EMPIRE   Fries Entertainment, 1987
CHILD IN THE NIGHT (TF)   Jayhawk, 1990

ZORAN HOCHSTATTER
THE HAUNTING OF MORELLA   Concorde, 1990
DECEPTIONS   Republic Pictures, 1990
TRANSYLVANIA TWIST   Concorde, 1990

ADAM HOLENDER, ASC*
West & East Coast Cards
Agent: Smith Gosnell Nicholson & Associates -
    Pacific Palisades, 213/459-0307

MIDNIGHT COWBOY   Universal, 1969
PUZZLE OF A DOWNFALL CHILD   Universal, 1970
PANIC IN NEEDLE PARK   20th Century Fox, 1971
THE EFFECT OF GAMMA RAYS ON MAN-IN-
    THE-MOON MARIGOLDS   20th Century Fox, 1973
MAN ON A SWING   Paramount, 1974
IF EVER I SEE YOU AGAIN   Columbia, 1978
THE SEDUCTION OF JOE TYNAN   Universal, 1979
PROMISES IN THE DARK   Orion/Warner Bros., 1979
SIMON   Orion/Warner Bros., 1980
THE IDOLMAKER   United Artists, 1980
THE SHADOW BOX (TF)   The Shadow Box Co., 1980
THE BOY WHO COULD FLY   20th Century Fox, 1986,
    w/Steven Poster

THREESOME (TF)   CBS Entertainment, 1984
STREET SMART   Cannon, 1987
TO KILL A PRIEST   Columbia, 1988
THE DREAM TEAM   Universal, 1989
SEA OF LOVE   Universal, 1989

JOHN HORA, ASC*
West Coast Card
Agent: Smith Gosnell Nicholson & Associates - Pacific
    Palisades, 213/459-0307

FURTHER ADVENTURES OF THE WILDERNESS
    FAMILY - PART II   Pacific International, 1978
THE HOWLING   Avco Embassy, 1981
LIAR'S MOON   Crown International, 1982
TWILIGHT ZONE - THE MOVIE (Segment 3)   Warner
    Bros., 1983
GREMLINS   Warner Bros., 1984
EXPLORERS   Paramount, 1985
MOONWALKER   Warner Bros., 1989,
    w/Frederick Elmes
LOVERBOY   Tri-Star, 1989
GREMLINS 2: THE NEW BATCH   Amblin/
    Warner Bros., 1990

LOUIS HORVATH
STRANGE BEHAVIOR   World Northal, 1981
STRANGE INVADERS   Orion, 1983

GIL HUBBS
Agent: Smith Gosnell Nicholson & Associations -
    Pacific Palisades, 213/459-0307

ENTER THE DRAGON   Warner Bros., 1973
GOLDEN NEEDLES   American International, 1974
BOBBIE JO AND THE OUTLAW   American
    International, 1976
GUYANA TRAGEDY: THE STORY OF JIM JONES (TF)
    The Konigsberg Company, 1980
FORCE: FIVE   American Cinema, 1981
THIS IS ELVIS (FD)   Warner Bros., 1981
TWIRL (TF)   Charles Fries Productions, 1981
THE LAST NINJA (TF)   Paramount TV, 1983
JEALOUSY (TF)   Charles Fries Productions/Alan Sacks
    Productions, 1983
SCORNED AND SWINDLED (TF)   Cypress
    Point Productions, 1984
THE SKY'S THE LIMIT (TF)   Palance-Levy
    Productions, 1984
CHILDREN OF THE NIGHT (TF)   Robert Guenette
    Productions, 1985
STARCROSSED (TF)   Fries Entertainment, 1985
TERROR AT LONDON BRIDGE (TF)
CALIFORNIA GIRLS (TF)   ABC Circle Films, 1985
NORTH BEACH & RAWHIDE (TF)   CBS
    Entertainment, 1985
THE RIGHT OF THE PEOPLE (TF)   Big Name Films/
    Fries Entertainment, 1986
SWORD OF HEAVEN   Trans World Entertainment, 1985
16 DAYS OF GLORY (FD)   Paramount, 1986, w/others
FLOWERS IN THE ATTIC   New World, 1987,
    w/Frank Byers
GODDESS OF LOVE (TF)   Phil Margo Enterprises/New
    World TV/Phoenix Entertainment Group, 1988

DAVID HUE
TWISTED JUSTICE   Seymour Borde & Associates, 1990

Hu

CINEMATOGRAPHERS
PRODUCTION
DESIGNERS,
COSTUME
DESIGNERS AND
FILM EDITORS
GUIDE

C
I
N
E
M
A
T
O
G
R
A
P
H
E
R
S

Hu

CINEMATOGRAPHERS
PRODUCTION
DESIGNERS,
COSTUME
DESIGNERS and
FILM EDITORS
GUIDE

C
I
N
E
M
A
T
O
G
R
A
P
H
E
R
S

MICHEL HUGO, ASC
Agent: Tobias-Skouras & Associates - Los Angeles,
    213/277-6211

THE APRIL FOOLS   National General, 1969
NUMBER ONE   United Artists, 1969
THE PHYNX   Warner Bros., 1970
FOOLS   Cinerama Releasing Corporation, 1970
ONE IS A LONELY NUMBER   MGM, 1972
R.P.M.   Columbia, 1970
BLESS THE BEASTS AND CHILDREN   Columbia, 1971
TROUBLE MAN   20th Century Fox, 1972
MURPH THE SURF   American International, 1975
BUG   Paramount, 1975
ODE TO BILLY JOE   Warner Bros., 1976
THE MANITOU   Avco Embassy, 1978
GORP   American International, 1980
THE MOUNTAIN MEN   Columbia, 1980
THE OCTAGON   American Cinema, 1980
PANDEMONIUM   MGM/UA, 1982

ALAN HUME
THE LAND THAT TIME FORGOT   American
    International, 1975
CLEOPATRA JONES AND THE CASINO OF GOLD
    Warner Bros., 1975
AT THE EARTH'S CORE   American International, 1976
THE PEOPLE THAT TIME FORGOT   American
    International, 1977
GULLIVER'S TRAVELS   EMI, 1977
THE AMSTERDAM KILL   Columbia, 1978
WARLORDS OF ATLANTIS   Columbia, 1978
CARRY ON EMMANUELLE   Hemdale, 1978
ARABIAN ADVENTURE   AFD, 1979
THE LEGACY   Universal, 1979, w/Dick Bush
BEAR ISLAND   Taft International, 1980
WATCHER IN THE WOODS   Buena Vista, 1980
CAVEMAN   United Artists, 1981
FOR YOUR EYES ONLY   United Artists, 1981
EYE OF THE NEEDLE   United Artists, 1981
RETURN OF THE JEDI   20th Century Fox, 1983
OCTOPUSSY   MGM/UA, 1983
SUPERGIRL   Tri-Star, 1984
A VIEW TO A KILL   MGM/UA, 1985
LIFEFORCE   Tri-Star, 1985
RUNAWAY TRAIN   Cannon, 1985
THE SECOND VICTORY   Filmworld Distributors, 1987
HEARTS OF FIRE   Lorimar, 1987
A FISH CALLED WANDA   MGM/United Artists, 1988
JACK THE RIPPER (MS)   Euston Films, 1988
WITHOUT A CLUE   Orion, 1988
THE TENTH MAN (TF)   William Self Productions/
    Rosemont Productions, 1988
SHIRLEY VALENTINE   Paramount, 1989
JUDITH KRANTZ'S TILL WE MEET AGAIN-
    PARTS I & II (MS)   Yorkshire TV/Steve
    Krantz Productions, 1990
SECRET WEAPON (CTF)   TVS/ABC Australia/
    Griffin-Elysian Films Production, 1990
EVE OF DESTRUCTION   Orion, 1991

TOM D. HURWITZ
WASN'T THAT A TIME!   United Artists Classics, 1982,
    w/Jim Brown & Daniel Ducovny
WHITE ELEPHANT   1985
DOWN AND OUT IN AMERICA (FD)   Joseph
    Feury Productions, 1986
HARD CHOICES   Lorimar, 1986
CREEPSHOW 2   New World, 1987, w/Dick Hart

PETER HYAMS
Agent: Creative Artists Agency - Beverly Hills,
    213/288-4545

2010   MGM/UA, 1984 (also directed)
RUNNING SCARED   MGM/UA, 1986 (also directed)
THE PRESIDIO   Paramount, 1988 (also directed)
NARROW MARGIN   Carolco/Tri-Star, 1990 (also
    directed)

ARTHUR IBBETSON
Agent: London Management - London, England,
    011/441/493-1610

THE HORSE'S MOUTH   United Artists, 1959, British
THE CHALK GARDEN   Universal, 1964, British
PRETTY POLLY   Universal, 1968, British
INSPECTOR CLOUSEAU   United Artists, 1968, British
WHERE EAGLES DARE   MGM, 1969, British
ANNE OF THE THOUSAND DAYS ★   Universal, 1969
WILLY WONKA AND THE CHOCOLATE FACTORY
    Paramount, 1971, British
MISTRESS PAMELA   Fanfare, 1974, British
BRIEF ENCOUNTER (TF)   Carlo Ponti Productions/Cecil
    Clarke Productions, 1974, British
OUT OF SEASON   Athenaeum, 1975, British
THE SELL OUT   Hemdale, 1976
SPECTRE (TF)   20th Century Fox TV, 1977
ALL THINGS BRIGHT AND BEAUTIFUL   IT SHOULDN'T
    HAPPEN TO A VET   World Northal, 1978
A LITTLE NIGHT MUSIC   New World, 1978
THE MEDUSA TOUCH   Warner Bros., 1978
THE PRISONER OF ZENDA   Universal, 1979
HOPSCOTCH   Avco Embassy, 1980
NOTHING PERSONAL   American International, 1980
LITTLE LORD FAUNTLEROY (TF)   Norman Rosemont
    Productions, 1980
WITNESS FOR THE PROSECUTION (TF)   1982
THE BOUNTY   Orion, 1984
SANTA CLAUS: THE MOVIE   Tri-Star, 1985

TONY IMI, BSC
Agent: Stella Richards, 01/736-7786

IT'S NOT THE SIZE THAT COUNTS   Joseph Brenner
    Associates, 1974
THE SLIPPER AND THE ROSE: THE STORY OF
    CINDERELLA   Universal, 1976
INTERNATIONAL VELVET   MGM/United Artists, 1978
BRASS TARGET   MGM/United Artists, 1978
THE SEA WOLVES   Paramount, 1980
ffolkes   Universal, 1980
BREAKTHROUGH   Maverick Pictures International, 1981
NIGHT CROSSING   Buena Vista, 1982
NATE AND HAYES   Paramount, 1983
ENEMY MINE   20th Century Fox, 1985
NOT QUITE PARADISE   New World, 1985
EMPIRE STATE   Virgin/Miracle, 1987
BUSTER   Hemdale, 1988
BABYCAKES (TF)   Konigsberg/Sanitsky Co., 1989

WIRED   Taurus Entertainment, 1989
OPTIONS   Vestron, 1989, w/James Robb
COINS IN THE FOUNTAIN (TF)   The Konigsberg-
   Sanitsky Company/JE Entertainment-RTL
   Productions/Michael Filerman Productions, 1990
FIRE BIRDS   Nova International Films/Touchstone/
   Buena Vista, 1990
THE OLD MAN AND THE SEA (TF)   Rorkshire TV/
   Green Pond Productions/Storke Enterprises, 1990
THE LAST TO GO (TF)   Freyda Rothstein Productions/
   Interscope, 1991
FOURTH STORY (CTF)   Viacom Pictures, 1991

PETER INDERGAND
FACE OF THE ENEMY   Tri-Culture Pictures, 1990

DAVID INSLEY
POLYESTER   New Line Cinema, 1981
TWO FOR THE MONEY   Bonner Films, 1985
ADVENTURE OF THE ACTION HUNTERS
   Troma, 1987
HAIRSPRAY   New Line Cinema, 1988
CRY BABY   Imagine Entertainment/Universal, 1990

JUDY IROLA
NORTHERN LIGHTS   CineManifest/New Front
   Films, 1978
WORKING GIRLS   Miramax, 1986
DEAD END KIDS   Film Forum, 1986

LOUIS IRVING
DEATH OF A SOLDIER   Scotti Bros., 1986
HOWLING III   Square Pictures, 1987
COMMUNION   MCEG, 1989

MARK IRWIN, CSC
Phone: 213/849-5388

STARSHIP INVASIONS   Warner Bros., 1977
BLOOD AND GUTS   Ambassador, 1978
THE BROOD   New World, 1979
FAST COMPANY   Topar, 1979
SCANNERS   Avco Embassy, 1981
NIGHT SCHOOL   Paramount, 1981
FUNERAL HOME   MPM, 1982
VIDEODROME   Universal, 1983
THE DEAD ZONE   Paramount, 1983
SPASMS   Producers Distribution Company, 1983
SPECIAL PEOPLE: BASED ON A TRUE STORY (TF)
   Joe Cates Productions/CTV Broadcasting
   Corporation, 1984
THE PROTECTOR   Warner Bros., 1985
THE FLY   20th Century Fox, 1986
YOUNGBLOOD   MGM/UA, 1986
ARTIE SHAW: TIME IS ALL YOU'VE GOT (FD)
   Bridge Films, 1986, w/Jim Aquila
THE HANOI HILTON   Cannon, 1987
PASS THE AMMO   New Century/Vista, 1988
THE BLOB   Tri-Star, 1988
BAT 21   Tri-Star, 1988
LOVE AT STAKE   BURNIN' LOVE   Tri-Star, 1988
FRIGHT NIGHT PART 2   New Century/Vista, 1989
CALL ME ANNA (TF)   Mianna Pearce/
   Finnegan-Pinchuk Productions, 1990
I COME IN PEACE   Vision pdg/Triumph, 1990
HEAT WAVE (CTF)   Propaganda Films/
   Avnet-Kerner Company, 1990
CLASS OF 1999   Original Pictures/Lightning
   Pictures/Taurus Entertainment, 1990

PAINT IT BLACK   Vestron, 1990
SO PROUDLY WE HAIL (TF)   CBS Entertainment
   Productions/Lionel Chetwynd Productions, 1990
ROBOCOP 2   Orion, 1990
NOT OF THIS WORLD (TF)   Barry & Enright
   Productions, 1991

LEVIE ISAACS
SUNDOWN: THE VAMPIRE IN RETREAT
   Vestron, 1989
I'M DANGEROUS TONIGHT (CTF)   BBK
   Productions, 1990
SPONTANEOUS COMBUSTION   Taurus
   Entertainment, 1990

MARK IVAN
DAUGHTER OF DARKNESS (TF)   King Phoenix
   Entertainment, 1990

J

PETER JAMES, ACS, CSC
Agent: Smith Gosnell Nicholson & Associates -
   Pacific Palisades, 213/459-0307
Address: 112 Sparkall Ave., Toronto, Ontario M4K 1G8,
   416/966-3500

CADDIE   Atlantic Releasing Corporation, 1976
THE IRISHMAN   Forest Home Films, 1978
THE KILLING OF ANGEL STREET   Satori, 1983
THE WILD DUCK   Orion, 1983
REBEL   Vestron, 1986
ECHOES OF PARADISE   SHADOWS OF THE PEACOCK
   Castle Hill Productions/Quartet Films, 1987
THE RIGHT HAND MAN   FilmDallas, 1987
DRIVING MISS DAISY   Warner Bros., 1989
MR. JOHNSON   Avenue Pictures, 1990

TONY JANNELLI
LONGTIME COMPANION   American Playhouse/Samuel
   Goldwyn Company, 1990

JOHNNY E. JENSEN
WHEN YOU REMEMBER ME (TF)   Warner Bros.
   Television/David L. Wolper Productions, 1990
BARE ESSENTIALS (TF)   Republic Pictures TV, 1991

PETER JESSOP
JEEVES AND WOOSTER PARTS I-IV (TF)   Granada/
   Picture Partnership, 1990
MURDER BY THE BOOK (CTF)   Benbow Evans
   Productions/TVS International, 1990

ROBERT C. JESSUP, ASC
Agent: The Miller Agency - Santa Clarita, 818/843-7335

RACE WITH THE DEVIL   20th Century Fox, 1975
DRIVE-IN   Columbia, 1976
A SMALL TOWN IN TEXAS   American
   International, 1976
THE WHITE LIONS (TF)   Alan Landsburg
   Productions, 1979

Je

CINEMATOGRAPHERS
PRODUCTION
DESIGNERS,
COSTUME
DESIGNERS AND
FILM EDITORS
GUIDE

CINEMATOGRAPHERS

CINEMATOGRAPHERS
PRODUCTION
DESIGNERS,
COSTUME
DESIGNERS AND
FILM EDITORS
GUIDE

THE BIG BRAWL   Warner Bros., 1980
DEADLY BLESSING   United Artists/Polygram, 1981
SILENT RAGE   Columbia, 1982, w/Neil Roach
SPLIT IMAGE   Orion, 1982
COWBOY (TF)   Bercovici-St. Johns Productions/
   MGM TV, 1983
LICENSE TO KILL (TF)   Marian Rees Associates/D.
   Petrie Productions, 1984
HE'S NOT YOUR SON (TF)   CBS Entertainment, 1984
TARGET   Warner Bros., 1985
THE BILL JOHNSON STORY (TF)   1985
POISON IVY (TF)   NBC Productions, 1985
PORKY'S REVENGE   20th Century Fox, 1985
STORMIN' HOME (TF)   CBS Entertainment, 1985
SINS OF INNOCENCE (TF)   1986
GUILTY OF INNOCENCE: THE LENELL GETER
   STORY (TF)   Embassy TV, 1986
CATCH THE HEAT   *FEEL THE HEAT*   Trans World
   Entertainment, 1987
DESPERADO (TF)   Walter Mirisch Productions/Charles
   E. Sellier Productions/Universal TV, 1987
LONGARM (TF)   Universal TV, 1988

THOMAS JEWELL
PEACEMAKER   Fries Entertainment, 1990

THOMAS JEWETT
Agent: Bruce E. Fritzberg, The Production Agency,
   8489 W. 3rd St. - Los Angeles, 213/651-1858

HOLD BACK THE DARKNESS   Act of Faith
   Productions, 1978
ONE LAST CHANCE   Cannon Films, 1978
THE SECRET SELF   Astrial Productions, 1982
THE CENSUSTAKER   Argentum Productions, 1985
HOME REMEDY   Xero Productions, 1986
THE DEADLY INTRUDER   Intruder Productions, 1986
THE CELLAR   Indian Neck Productions, 1987
WITCHTRAP   Mentone Pictures, 1987
TRUST ME   Cinecom Pictures, 1989
PEACEMAKER   Fries Entertainment, 1989
INSTANT KARMA   Desert Wind Films/Rosenbloom
   Entertainment/MGM, 1990
MIKY   Tapestry Films, 1990

SHELLY JOHNSON
MAID TO ORDER   New Century/Vista, 1987
NIGHTFLYERS   New Century/Vista, 1987
JACK'S BACK   Cinema Group, 1988
EVERYBODY'S BABY: THE RESCUE OF JESSICA
   McCLURE (TF)   Interscope Productions/The
   Campbell Soup Company, 1989
ANGEL OF DEATH (TF)   Once Upon A Time
   Films, 1990
JOSHUA'S HEART (TF)   Spectacor, 1990
THE GIRL WHO CAME BETWEEN THEM (TF)
   Saban-Scherick, 1990

DENNIS E. JONES
PACIFIC HEIGHTS   Morgan Creek/20th Century
   Fox, 1990

MARIO GARCIA JOYA
RIO NEGRO   Flach Film/Yavita Film, 1990

JON JOST
ALL THE VERMEERS IN NEW YORK   American
   Playhouse Theatrical Films,
   1990 (also directed/edited)

JEFF JUR
THE ROOMMATE   Rubicon Film Productions, 1985
STATIC   Sandstar Releasing Co., 1985
SCREEN TEST   CineTel Films, 1986
SOUL MAN   New World, 1986
DIRTY DANCING   Vestron, 1987
STRANDED   New Line Cinema, 1987
THE BIG PICTURE   Columbia, 1989
REVEALING EVIDENCE (TF)   Universal/T.W.S.
   Productions, 1990
HIDER IN THE HOUSE   Vestron, 1990

JURGEN JURGES
EFFI BRIEST   New Yorker, 1974
JOHN GLUECKSTADT   1975
FEAR OF FEAR   1976
CHRISTIANE F.   1981
A WOMAN IN FLAMES   Almi Pictures, 1984
GERMANY PALE MOTHER   New Yorker, 1984
MAN UNDER SUSPICION   Spectrafilm, 1985,
   w/Renato Fortunato
50/50   New Line Cinema, 1986

SAVAS KALOGERAS
CRAZY MOON   Miramax, 1987
FALLING OVER BACKWARDS   Ranfilm Productions/
   Astral Films, 1990

JANUSZ KAMINSKI
THE RAIN KILLER   Califilm/Concorde, 1990
THE TERROR WITHIN II   Concorde, 1991

MICHAEL KARP
BLOOD SALVAGE   High Five Productions/
   Paragon Arts, 1990

AVRAHAM KARPICK
SURVIVAL GAME   Trans World Entertainment, 1987
BEAUTY AND THE BEAST   Cannon, 1987
THE FURTHER ADVENTURES OF TENNESSEE BUCK
   Trans World Entertainment, 1988
RIVER OF DEATH   Cannon, 1989
PUSS IN BOOTS   Cannon, 1989
ODD BALL HALL   Ravenhill, 1989
DELTA FORCE   Global, 1990
WORLDS APART   Orbit International, 1990
S.E.A.L.S.   21st Century, 1991

KARL KASES
MINDWALK   Mindwalk Productions/Atlas Company, 1990

STEPHEN M. KATZ
Agent: Harris & Goldberg Talent Agency - Los Angeles,
   213/553-5200

ANGELS HARD AS THEY COME   1971
THE PEACE KILLERS   1971
THE STUDENT TEACHERS   New World, 1973
YOUR THREE MINUTES ARE UP   1973

PRISONERS   1973
BEST FRIENDS   Crown International, 1973
THE FOUR DEUCES   Avco Embassy, 1974
MESSIAH OF EVIL   International Cinefilm, 1975
SWITCHBLADE SISTERS   Centaur, 1975
LAS VEGAS LADY   Crown International, 1976
THE POM-POM GIRLS   Crown International, 1976
BITTERSWEET LOVE   Avco Embassy, 1976
JOYRIDE   American International, 1977
THE KENTUCKY FRIED MOVIE   United Film
    Distribution, 1977
OUR WINNING SEASON   American
    International, 1978
THE BLUES BROTHERS   Universal, 1980
THE LITTLE DRAGONS   Aurora, 1980
COMING SOON (CTD)   Universal Pay TV, 1983
'NIGHT, MOTHER   Universal, 1986
LAST RESORT   Concorde/Cinema Group, 1986,
    w/Alex Nepomaniaschy
NICE GIRLS DON'T EXPLODE   New World, 1987
SISTER, SISTER   New World, 1988
18 AGAIN   New World, 1988
AND GOD CREATED WOMAN   Vestron, 1988
WHO'S HARRY CRUMB?   Tri-Star, 1989
BACKSTREET DREAMS   O'Malley Film/Vidmark, 1990

LLOYD   KAUFMAN

WAITRESS   *SOUP TO NUTS*   Troma, 1982
STUCK ON YOU   Troma, 1983
THE FIRST TURN-ON!   Troma, 1983
THE TOXIC AVENGER   Troma, 1985,
    w/James London

STEPHEN   KAZMIERSKI

LISTEN UP   Warner Bros., 1990

JAMES   B.   KELLEY

OUTRAGEOUS!   Cinema 5, 1977
HAPPY BIRTHDAY GEMINI   United Artists, 1980

VICTOR   J.   KEMPER, ASC *

West Coast Card
Agent: The Gersh Agency, Inc., Beverly Hills -
    213/274-6611, New York - 212/997-1818

THE HOSPITAL   United Artists, 1971
WHO IS HARRY KELLERMAN AND WHY IS HE
    SAYING ALL THOSE THINGS ABOUT ME?
    National General, 1971
THE CANDIDATE   Warner Bros., 1972
LAST OF THE RED HOT LOVERS   Paramount, 1972
THE REINCARNATION OF PETER PROUD
    American International, 1975
DOG DAY AFTERNOON   Warner Bros., 1975
STAY HUNGRY   United Artists, 1976
THE LAST TYCOON   Paramount, 1976
MIKEY AND NICKY   Paramount, 1976, w/Lucien
    Ballard, Jack Cooperman & Jerry File
SLAP SHOT   Universal, 1977
AUDREY ROSE   United Artists, 1977
OH, GOD!   Warner Bros., 1977
THE ONE AND ONLY   Paramount, 1978
COMA   MGM/United Artists, 1978,
    w/Gerald Hirschfeld
EYES OF LAURA MARS   Columbia, 1978
MAGIC   20th Century Fox, 1978
...AND JUSTICE FOR ALL   Columbia, 1979
THE JERK   Universal, 1979
NIGHT OF THE JUGGLER   Columbia, 1980
THE FINAL COUNTDOWN   United Artists, 1980

XANADU   Universal, 1980
THE FOUR SEASONS   Universal, 1981
CHU CHU AND THE PHILLY FLASH   20th Century
    Fox, 1981
PARTNERS   Paramount, 1982
AUTHOR! AUTHOR!   20th Century Fox, 1982
MR. MOM   20th Century Fox, 1983
NATIONAL LAMPOON'S VACATION   Warner Bros.,1983
THE LONELY GUY   Universal, 1984
CLOAK AND DAGGER   Universal, 1984
THE ATLANTA CHILD MURDERS (TF)   Mann-Rafshoon
    Productions/Finnegan Associates, 1985
SECRET ADMIRER   Orion, 1985
CLUE   Paramount, 1985
PEE-WEE'S BIG ADVENTURE   Warner Bros., 1985
WALK LIKE A MAN   MGM/UA, 1987
HOT TO TROT   Warner Bros., 1988
COHEN AND TATE   Nelson Entertainment, 1989
SEE NO EVIL, HEAR NO EVIL   Tri-Star, 1989
CRAZY PEOPLE   Paramount, 1990
THE HARD WAY   Universal, 1991
FX 2: THE DEADLY ART OF ILLUSION   Orion, 1991

FRANCIS   KENNY

Agent: The Gersh Agency, Inc., Beverly Hills -
    213/274-6611, New York - 212/997-1818

SALVATION!   Circle Releasing Corporation, 1987
CAMPUS MAN   Paramount, 1987
HEATHERS   New World, 1989
UNSUB (Pilot)   1989
TENNESSEE WILLIAMS' SWEET BIRD OF YOUTH (TF)
    Atlantic/Kushner-Locke Productions, 1990
NEW JACK CITY   Warner Bros., 1991

JOHN   KENWAY

FELLOW TRAVELLER (CTF)   British Film Institute/BBC
    Television/HBO Showcase, 1990

GLEN   KERSHAW

FATAL SKIES   AIP Home Video, 1990

ROLF   KESTERMANN

KNIGHTS OF THE CITY   New World, 1986
SURF NAZIS MUST DIE   Troma, 1987
DISORDERLIES   Warner Bros., 1987
CASUAL SEX?   Universal, 1988

CHIRINE   EL   KHADEM

SMITHEREENS   New Line Cinema, 1982

GARY   B.   KIBBE *

West Coast Card
Agent: The Gersh Agency, Inc., Beverly Hills -
    213/274-6611, New York - 212/997-1818

PRINCE OF DARKNESS   Universal, 1987
THEY LIVE   Universal, 1988

JAN   KIESSER *

West Coast Card
Agent: Smith Gosnell Nicholson & Associates -
    Pacific Palisades, 213/459-0307

RETURN ENGAGEMENT   Island Alive, 1983
PURPLE HEARTS   The Ladd Co./Warner Bros., 1984
CHOOSE ME   Island Alive, 1984
THE RIVER RAT   Paramount, 1984

Ki

CINEMATOGRAPHERS
PRODUCTION
DESIGNERS,
COSTUME
DESIGNERS AND
FILM EDITORS
GUIDE

C
I
N
E
M
A
T
O
G
R
A
P
H
E
R
S

Ki

CINEMATOGRAPHERS
PRODUCTION
DESIGNERS,
COSTUME
DESIGNERS and
FILM EDITORS
GUIDE

C
I
N
E
M
A
T
O
G
R
A
P
H
E
R
S

VICTIMS FOR VICTIMS (TF)   Daniel L. Paulson-Loehr
    Spivey Productions/Orion TV, 1984
FRIGHT NIGHT   Columbia, 1985
THE CHECK IS IN THE MAIL   Ascot
    Entertainment, 1986
SOME KIND OF WONDERFUL   Paramount, 1987
MADE IN HEAVEN   Lorimar, 1987
CLEAN AND SOBER   Warner Bros., 1988
DAD   Universal, 1989

JEFFREY L. KIMBALL*
West Coast Card
Agent: Smith Gosnell Nicholson & Associates -
    Pacific Palisades, 213/459-0307

THE LEGEND OF BILLIE JEAN   Tri-Star, 1985
TOP GUN   Paramount, 1986
BEVERLY HILLS COP II   Paramount, 1987
REVENGE   Columbia, 1990
JACOB'S LADDER   Carolco/Tri-Star, 1990

ALAR KIVILO, CSC
Address: 126 Shuter St., Suite 1, Toronto, Ontario M5A
    1V8, 416/360-1106

DA   FilmDallas, 1988

RICHARD H. KLINE, ASC
Agent: The Gersh Agency, Inc., Beverly Hills -
    213/274-6611, New York - 212/997-1818

HANG 'EM HIGH   United Artists, 1968
CAMELOT ★   Warner Bros., 1967
THE BOSTON STRANGLER   20th Century Fox, 1968
GAILY, GAILY   United Artists, 1969
THE MOONSHINE WAR   MGM, 1970
THE ANDROMEDA STRAIN   Universal, 1971
KOTCH   Cinerama Releasing Corporation, 1971
HAMMERSMITH IS OUT   Cinerama Releasing
    Corporation, 1972
THE MECHANIC   United Artists, 1972
SOYLENT GREEN   MGM, 1972
THE TALL BLONDE MAN WITH ONE BLACK SHOE
    Cinema 5, 1972
THE HARRAD EXPERIMENT   Cinerama Releasing
    Corporation, 1973
THE TERMINAL MAN   Warner Bros., 1974
MANDINGO   Paramount, 1975
WON TON TON, THE DOG WHO SAVED HOLLYWOOD
    Paramount, 1976
KING KONG ★   Paramount, 1976
THE FURY   20th Century Fox, 1978
WHO'LL STOP THE RAIN   United Artists, 1978
TILT   Warner Bros., 1979
STAR TREK - THE MOTION PICTURE
    Paramount, 1979
TOUCHED BY LOVE   Columbia, 1980
THE COMPETITION   Columbia, 1980
TRISTAN AND ISOLT   Clar Productions, 1981
BODY HEAT   The Ladd Co./Warner Bros., 1981
DEATH WISH II   Filmways, 1982, w/Thomas Del Ruth
MAN, WOMAN AND CHILD   Paramount, 1983
BREATHLESS   Orion, 1983
DEAL OF THE CENTURY   Warner Bros., 1983
ALL OF ME   Universal, 1984
HARD TO HOLD   Universal, 1984
THE MAN WITH ONE RED SHOE   20th Century
    Fox, 1985
HOWARD THE DUCK   Universal, 1986
TOUCH AND GO   Tri-Star, 1987

MY STEPMOTHER IS AN ALIEN   WEG, 1988
DOWNTOWN   20th Century Fox, 1990

NICK KNOWLAND
PING PONG   Samuel Goldwyn Company, 1987
SEPARATE BUT EQUAL (TF)   1991

GEORGE KOBLASA
CLASS CRUISE (TF)   Portoangelo Productions, 1990
COLUMBO GOES TO COLLEGE (TF)
    Universal TV, 1990
COLUMBO: MURDER CAN BE HAZARDOUS TO YOUR
    HEALTH (TF)   Universal City Studios, 1991

DOUGLAS KOCH
I'VE HEARD THE MERMAIDS SINGING   Miramax, 1987
NIGHT FRIEND   Cineplex Odeon, 1988
FRIENDS, LOVERS & LUNATICS   Fries
    Entertainment, 1989

FRED J. KOENEKAMP, ASC*
West Coast Card
Agent: Smith Gosnell Nicholson & Associates -
    Pacific Palisades, 213/459-0307

PATTON ★   20th Century Fox, 1970
FOREIGN EXCHANGE (TF)   Halsan Productions, 1970
BILLY JACK   Warner Bros., 1971, w/John Stephens
PAPILLON   Allied Artists, 1973
THE TOWERING INFERNO ★★   20th Century Fox,
    1974, w/Joseph Biroc
DOC SAVAGE, THE MAN OF BRONZE   Warner
    Bros., 1975
POSSE   Paramount, 1975
THE WILD McCULLOCHS   American International, 1975
WHITE LINE FEVER   Columbia, 1975
SECOND CHANCE   United Artists Classics, 1976
EMBRYO   Cine Artists, 1976
FUN WITH DICK AND JANE   Columbia, 1977
THE DOMINO PRINCIPLE   Avco Embassy, 1977,
    w/Ernest Laszlo
ISLANDS IN THE STREAM ★   Paramount, 1977
THE OTHER SIDE OF MIDNIGHT   20th Century
    Fox, 1977
THE BAD NEWS BEARS IN BREAKING TRAINING
    Paramount, 1977
THE SWARM   Warner Bros., 1978
THE CHAMP   MGM/United Artists, 1979
THE AMITYVILLE HORROR   American
    International, 1979
LOVE AND BULLETS   AFD, 1979,
    w/Anthony B. Richmond
WHEN TIME RAN OUT   Warner Bros., 1980
THE HUNTER   Paramount, 1980
FIRST FAMILY   Warner Bros., 1980
FIRST MONDAY IN OCTOBER   Paramount, 1981
CARBON COPY   Avco Embassy, 1981
WRONG IS RIGHT   Columbia, 1982
YES, GIORGIO   MGM/UA, 1982
IT CAME FROM HOLLYWOOD (FD)   Paramount, 1982
TWO OF A KIND   20th Century Fox, 1983
THE ADVENTURES OF BUCKAROO BANZAI: ACROSS
    THE 8TH DIMENSION   20th Century Fox, 1984
OBSESSIVE LOVE (TF)   Onza Inc./Moonlight
    Productions, 1984
CITY KILLER (TF)   Stan Shpetner Productions, 1984
A TOUCH OF SCANDAL (TF)   Doris M. Keating
    Productions/Columbia TV, 1984
AMOS (TF)   The Byrna Company/Vincent Pictures, 1985

NOT MY KID (TF)   Beth Polson Productions/Finnegan
    Associates, 1985
FAST FORWARD (TF)   Columbia, 1985
PLEASURES (TF)   Catalina Production Group/
    Columbia TV, 1986
NEWS AT ELEVEN (TF)   Turman-Foster Productions/
    Finnegan Associates, 1986
STEWARDESS SCHOOL   Columbia, 1987
HARD TIME ON PLANET EARTH (Pilot)   1989
LISTEN TO ME   WEG, 1989
WELCOME HOME   Columbia, 1989
FLIGHT OF THE INTRUDER   Paramount, 1991

PHILIP KOLAHAN
INITIATION: SILENT NIGHT, DEADLY NIGHT 4
    Silent Films/Live Home Video, 1990

LAJOS KOLTAI
Agent: Smith Gosnell Nicholson & Associates -
    Pacific Palisades, 213/459-0307

RIDDANCE   Studio Hunnia, 1973
ADOPTION   Studio Hunnia, 1975
JUST LIKE AT HOME   Studio Hummia, 1978
A PRICELESS DAY   Budapest Studio, 1979
MEPHISTO   Analysis, 1980
CONFIDENCE   New Yorker, 1981
TIME STANDS STILL   Libra, 1982
THE STUD FARM   New Yorker, 1982
COLONEL REDL   Orion Classics, 1985
GABY - A TRUE STORY   Tri-Star, 1987
HANUSSEN   Hungarofilms, 1988
HOMER AND EDDIE   Kings Road, 1989
DESCENDING ANGEL (CTF)   Freyda Rothstein
    Productions, 1990
PERFECT WITNESS (CTF)   Granger Productions/
    HBO Pictures, 1990
WHITE PALACE   Mirage-Double Play/Universal, 1990

EDMOND L. KOONS
Agent: Grace Lyons Management - Los Angeles,
    213/655-5100

A PERFECT COUPLE   20th Century Fox, 1979
HEALTH   20th Century Fox, 1980
SKAG (TF)   NBC, 1980
THE JAYNE MANSFIELD STORY (TF)   Alan Landsburg
    Productions, 1980
MODERN PROBLEMS   20th Century Fox, 1981
A WHALE FOR THE KILLING (TF)   Play Productions/
    Beowulf Productions, 1987
P.K. AND THE KID   Castle Hill Productions, 1987
THE LONG JOURNEY HOME (TF)   Andrea
    Baynes Productions/Grail Productions/Lorimar-
    Telepictures, 1987

LASZLO KOVACS, ASC *
West Coast Card
Agent: Smith Gosnell Nicholson & Associates -
    Pacific Palisades, 213/459-0307

HELL'S ANGELS ON WHEELS   American
    International, 1967
PSYCH-OUT   American International, 1968
THE SAVAGE SEVEN   American International, 1968
TARGETS   Paramount, 1968
A MAN CALLED DAGGER   MGM, 1968
SINGLE ROOM FURNISHED   Crown
    International, 1968

EASY RIDER   Columbia, 1969
THAT COLD DAY IN THE PARK   Commonwealth
    United, 1969
FIVE EASY PIECES   Columbia, 1970
GETTING STRAIGHT   Columbia, 1970
ALEX IN WONDERLAND   MGM, 1970
THE LAST MOVIE   Universal, 1971
THE MARRIAGE OF A YOUNG STOCKBROKER
    20th Century Fox, 1971
WHAT'S UP, DOC?   Paramount, 1972
POCKET MONEY   National General, 1972
THE KING OF MARVIN GARDENS   Columbia, 1972
SLITHER   MGM, 1972
STEELYARD BLUES   1972
A REFLECTION OF FEAR   Columbia, 1973
PAPER MOON   Paramount, 1973
FOR PETE'S SAKE   Columbia, 1974
HUCKLEBERRY FINN   United Artists, 1974
FREEBIE AND THE BEAN   Warner Bros., 1974
SHAMPOO   Columbia, 1975
AT LONG LAST LOVE   20th Century Fox, 1975
BABY BLUE MARINE   Columbia, 1976
HARRY & WALTER GO TO NEW YORK
    Columbia, 1976
NICKELODEON   Columbia, 1976
NEW YORK, NEW YORK   United Artists, 1977
THE LAST WALTZ   United Artists, 1978, Additional DP
    w/Bobby Byrne, David Myers, Hiro Narita, Michael
    Watkins & Vilmos Zsigmond
F.I.S.T.   United Artists, 1978
PARADISE ALLEY   Universal, 1978
THE RUNNER STUMBLES   20th Century Fox, 1979
BUTCH AND SUNDANCE: THE EARLY DAYS   20th
    Century Fox, 1979
HEART BEAT   Orion/Warner Bros., 1979
INSIDE MOVES   AFD, 1980
THE LEGEND OF THE LONE RANGER
    Universal/AFD, 1981
THE TOY   Columbia, 1982
FRANCES   Universal/AFD, 1982
CRACKERS   Universal, 1984
GHOSTBUSTERS   Columbia, 1984
MASK   Universal, 1985
LEGAL EAGLES   Universal, 1986
LITTLE NIKITA   Columbia, 1988
SAY ANYTHING   20th Century Fox, 1989

JON KRANHOUSE
BRAINWAVES   MPM, 1983, w/Uli Lommel
FRIDAY THE 13TH PART VI: JASON LIVES
    Paramount, 1986
KICKBOXER   Pathe Entertainment, 1989

RICHARD KRATINA
MONEY, POWER, MURDER (TF)   CBS Entertainment/
    Skids Productions, 1990

HENNING KRISTIANSEN
BABETTE'S FEAST   Orion Classics, 1987

WILLY KURANT*
West & East Coast Cards
Agent: Smith Gosnell Nicholson & Associates -
    Pacific Palisades, 213/459-0307

MASCULINE FEMININE   Royal Films International, 1966
LE DEPART   Pathe Contemporary, 1967
THE IMMORTAL STORY   Fleetwood Films, 1968
THE DEEP   1969, unfinished

CINEMATOGRAPHERS
PRODUCTION
DESIGNERS,
COSTUME
DESIGNERS AND
FILM EDITORS
GUIDE

C
I
N
E
M
A
T
O
G
R
A
P
H
E
R
S

Ku

CINEMATOGRAPHERS
PRODUCTION
DESIGNERS,
COSTUME
DESIGNERS and
FILM EDITORS
GUIDE

C
I
N
E
M
A
T
O
G
R
A
P
H
E
R
S

THE NIGHT OF THE FOLLOWING DAY
    Universal, 1969
MICHAEL KOLHAS   Columbia, 1969
OUTSIDE CHANCE (TF)   NW Productions/
    Miller-Begun Productions, 1978
HARPER VALLEY P.T.A.   April Fools, 1978
TAG   New World, 1982
TUFF TURF   New World, 1985
A STATE OF EMERGENCY   Esstar Productions, 1986
FLAGRANT DESIRE   Hemdale, 1986
UNDER SATAN'S SON   Alive Films, 1987
STORMY SUMMER   Slay Productions/Films A2 SGGC
    AFE, 1990

TOYOMICHI KURITA

TROUBLE IN MIND   Alive Films, 1986
THE MODERNS   Alive Films, 1988
POWWOW HIGHWAY   HandMade Films, 1988
A RAGE IN HARLEM   Miramax, 1991

L

DANIEL LACAMBRE

BATTLE BEYOND THE STARS   New World, 1979
THE LADY IN RED   New World, 1979
HUMANOIDS FROM THE DEEP   New World, 1980
SATURDAY THE 14TH   New World, 1981
THE DIRT BIKE KID   Concorde, 1985

EDWARD LACHMAN

Agent: The Gersh Agency, Inc. - Beverly Hills,
    213/274-6611

LIGHTNING OVER WATER   Pari Films, 1980
UNION CITY   Kinesis Ltd., 1980
SAY AMEN, SOMEBODY   United Artists Classics,
    1983, w/Don Lenzer
THE LITTLE SISTER   American Playhouse, 1985
TOKYO-GA   Gray City, 1985
DESPERATELY SEEKING SUSAN   Orion, 1985
ORNETTE: MADE IN AMERICA (FD) 1985,
    w/Arthur J. Ornitz
STRIPPER (FD)   20th Century Fox, 1986
MOTHER TERESA (FD)   Toho International, 1986,
    w/Sandi Sissel
TRUE STORIES   Warner Bros., 1986
MAKING MR. RIGHT   Orion, 1987
LESS THAN ZERO   20th Century Fox, 1987

JOHN LAMBERT

ETERNITY   Paul Entertainment, 1990

GIUSEPPE LANCI

NOSTALGHIA   Grange Communications, 1984
HENRY IV   Orion Classics, 1985
CAMORRA   Cannon, 1985
EVERY TIME WE SAY GOODBYE   Tri-Star, 1986
GOOD MORNING, BABYLON   Vestron, 1987
DEVIL IN THE FLESH   Orion Classics, 1987
FRANCESCO   Karol Film/RAI/Royal Film, 1989

NORMAN LANGLEY

HOUSE OF THE LONG SHADOWS   Cannon, 1984
FOREVER YOUNG   Cinecom, 1986
WILT   LWT/Talkback, 1989
JEKYLL & HYDE (TF)   King Phoenix Entertainment/
    London Weekend TV/David Wickes TV, 1990

STEVAN LARNER, ASC*

West Coast Card
Agent: Smith Gosnell Nicholson & Associates -
    Pacific Palisades, 213/459-0307

PIPE DREAMS   Avco Embassy, 1976
ROOTS (MS) ☆   Wolper Productions, 1977
GRAY LADY DOWN   Universal, 1978
ALMOST SUMMER   Universal, 1978
THE BUDDY HOLLY STORY   Columbia, 1978
GOLDENGIRL   Avco Embassy, 1979
CADDYSHACK   Orion/Warner Bros., 1980
TWILIGHT ZONE - THE MOVIE (Prologue & Segment 1)
    Warner Bros., 1983
THE WINDS OF WAR (MS) ☆☆   Paramount TV/Dan
    Curtis Productions, 1983
HAPPY ENDINGS (TF)   Motown Productions, 1983
V: THE FINAL BATTLE (TF)   Blatt-Singer Productions/
    Warner Bros. TV, 1984
THE MYSTIC WARRIOR (MS)   David L. Wolper-Stan
    Margulies Productions/Warner Bros. TV, 1984
ANATOMY OF AN ILLNESS (TF)   Hamner Productions/
    CBS Entertainment, 1984
FATAL VISION (TF)   NBC Productions, 1984
NORTH AND SOUTH (MS) ☆   Wolper Productions/
    Warner Bros. TV, 1985
CONVICTED: A MOTHER'S STORY (TF)   NBC
    Productions, 1987
INHERIT THE WIND (TF) ☆   Vincent Pictures
    Productions/David Greene-Robert Papazian
    Productions, 1988
STUDIO 5B (Pilot)   1989
WHAT EVER HAPPENED TO BABY JANE? (TF)   Steve
    White Productions, 1991

DALE LARSON

SEXBOMB   Phillips & Mora Entertainment, 1989

JACEK LASKUS

Agent: Camera Masters - Venice, 213/306-0810

FAR FROM POLAND (FD)   Film Forum, 1984
PARTING GLANCES   Cinecom, 1986
SQUARE DANCE   Island Pictures, 1986
HEART   New World, 1987, w/Derek Wolski
THE CAINE MUTINY COURT MARTIAL (TF)   CBS
    Entertainment, 1988
DIRTY DANCING (Pilot)   1988
STEPFATHER II   ITC Entertainment/Millimeter
    Films, 1989

WALTER LASSALLY

THE WILD PARTY   American International, 1975
AUTOBIOGRAPHY OF A PRINCESS (TF)   Merchant
    Ivory Productions, 1975
THE CLOWN   Constantin, 1976
THE GREAT BANK HOAX *SHENANIGANS*   Warner
    Bros., 1977
HULLABALOO OVER GEORGIE AND BONNIE'S
    PICTURES   Corinth, 1979
SOMETHING SHORT OF PARADISE   American
    International, 1979

THE PILOT   Summit, 1981
TOO FAR TO GO   Zoetrope, 1982
PRIVATE SCHOOL   Universal, 1983
HEAT AND DUST   Universal Classics, 1983
THE BOSTONIANS   Almi Pictures, 1984
THE PERFECT MURDER   Merchant Ivory
    Productions, 1988
THE DECEIVERS   Cinecom, 1988
THE BALLAD OF THE SAD CAFE   Angelika
    Films, 1991

ANDREW LASZLO, ASC*
West & East Coast Cards
Agent: Smith Gosnell Nicholson & Associates -
    Pacific Palisades, 213/459-0307
Phone: 516/671-7910

ONE POTATO, TWO POTATO   Cinema 5, 1964
YOU'RE A BIG BOY NOW   7 Arts, 1966
THE NIGHT THEY RAIDED MINSKY'S   United
    Artists, 1968
POPI   United Artists, 1969
LOVERS AND OTHER STRANGERS
    Cinerama Releasing Corporation, 1970
THE OWL AND THE PUSSYCAT   Columbia, 1970
THE OUT-OF-TOWNERS   Paramount, 1970
TO FIND A MAN   Columbia, 1972
CLASS OF '44   Warner Bros., 1973
COUNTDOWN AT KUSINI   Columbia, 1976
THIEVES   Paramount, 1977, w/Arthur Ornitz
SOMEBODY KILLED HER HUSBAND   Columbia,
    1978, shared credit
THE WARRIORS   Paramount, 1979
THE FUNHOUSE   Universal, 1981
SOUTHERN COMFORT   20th Century Fox, 1981
FIRST BLOOD   Orion, 1982
I, THE JURY   20th Century Fox, 1982
STREETS OF FIRE   Universal, 1984
THIEF OF HEARTS   Paramount, 1984
THAT'S DANCING! (FD)   MGM/UA, 1985,
    w/Paul Lohmann
REMO WILLIAMS: THE ADVENTURE BEGINS
    Orion, 1985
POLTERGEIST II: THE OTHER SIDE
    MGM/UA, 1986
INNERSPACE   Warner Bros., 1987
STAR TREK V: THE FINAL FRONTIER
    Paramount, 1989
GHOST DAD   Universal, 1990

PHILIP LATHROP, ASC*
West Coast Card
Agent: Smith Gosnell Nicholson & Associates -
    Pacific Palisades, 213/459-0307

LONELY ARE THE BRAVE   Universal, 1982
EXPERIMENT IN TERROR   Warner Bros., 1962
THE PINK PANTHER   United Artists, 1964
THE AMERICANIZATION OF EMILY ★   MGM, 1964
THE CINCINNATI KID   MGM, 1965
POINT BLANK   MGM, 1967
FINIAN'S RAINBOW   Warner Bros., 1968
THEY SHOOT HORSES, DON'T THEY?   Cinerama
    Releasing Corporation, 1969
EARTHQUAKE ★   Universal, 1974
MAME   Warner Bros., 1974
THE PRISONER OF SECOND AVENUE   Warner
    Bros., 1975
HARD TIMES   Columbia, 1975
THE KILLER ELITE   United Artists, 1975

THE BLACK BIRD   Columbia, 1975
SWASHBUCKLER   Universal, 1976
AIRPORT '77   Universal, 1977
A DIFFERENT STORY   Avco Embassy, 1978
THE DRIVER   20th Century Fox, 1978
MOMENT BY MOMENT   Universal, 1978
THE CONCORDE - AIRPORT '79   Universal, 1979
FOOLIN' AROUND   Columbia, 1980
LITTLE MISS MARKER   Universal, 1980
LOVING COUPLES   20th Century Fox, 1980
A CHANGE OF SEASONS   20th Century Fox, 1980
ALL NIGHT LONG   Universal, 1981
HAMMETT   Orion/Warner Bros., 1982, w/Joseph Biroc
JEKYLL AND HYDE...TOGETHER AGAIN
    Paramount, 1982
NATIONAL LAMPOON'S CLASS REUNION   20th
    Century Fox, 1982
CELEBRITY (MS) ☆   NBC Productions, 1984
PICKING UP THE PIECES (TF) ☆   CBS
    Entertainment, 1985
MALICE IN WONDERLAND (TF) ☆☆   ITC
    Productions, 1985
LOVE ON THE RUN (TF)   NBC Productions, 1985
THE LIBERATORS (TF)   Kenneth Johnson Productions/
    Brian Grazer Productions/Warner Bros. TV, 1985
DEADLY FRIEND   Warner Bros., 1986
SIX AGAINST THE ROCK (TF)   Schaefer-Karpf-Epstein
    Productions/Gaylord Production Co., 1987
LITTLE GIRL LOST (TF) ☆   Marian Rees
    Associates, 1988

BART LAU
IT HAD TO BE YOU   Limelite Studios, 1989

RONALD M. LAUTORE
GOOD COPS, BAD COPS (TF)   Commonwealth Films/
    Kushner-Locke Company, 1990
CHILDREN OF THE BRIDE (TF)   Leonard Hill
    Films, 1990

VERNON LAYTON
McVICAR   Crown International, 1982

JOHN LEBLANC
ANGEL TOWN   Imperial Entertainment/Taurus
    Entertainment, 1990

CLAUDE LECOMTE
SUNDAY LOVERS   United Artists, 1981
VOYAGE EN DOUCE   *SENTIMENTAL JOURNEY*
    New Yorker, 1981
BETTER LATE THAN NEVER   Warner Bros., 1983
JUST THE WAY YOU ARE   MGM/UA, 1984
LA PETITE BANDE   Triumph, 1984
THE DIARY OF A MADMAN   Lydie Media, 1987

RICK LEE
A TIME TO REMEMBER   Tra-Zan Group/
    Filmworld, 1990

JASON LEHEL
TANK MALLING   Pointlane Films Production, 1989

A. NORMAN LEIGH
THE BRINK'S JOB   Universal, 1978
SCHIZOID   Cannon, 1980
DEADLY FORCE   Embassy, 1983, w/David Myers

Le

CINEMATOGRAPHERS
PRODUCTION
DESIGNERS,
COSTUME
DESIGNERS AND
FILM EDITORS
GUIDE

C
I
N
E
M
A
T
O
G
R
A
P
H
E
R
S

Le

CINEMATOGRAPHERS
PRODUCTION
DESIGNERS,
COSTUME
DESIGNERS and
FILM EDITORS
GUIDE

C
I
N
E
M
A
T
O
G
R
A
P
H
E
R
S

RICHARD LEITERMAN, CSC
Address: Windforce Productions Ltd., 14 Birch Ave.,
Toronto, Ontario M4V 1C9, 416/928-9029

THE FAR SHORE   1976
WHO HAS SEEN THE WIND   Astral Bellevue, 1977
TICKET TO HEAVEN   United Artists Classics, 1981
SILENCE OF THE NORTH   Universal, 1982
MOTHER LODE   Agmemnon Films, 1982
UTILITIES   New World, 1983
HE'S FIRED, SHE'S HIRED (TF)   CBS, 1984
MY AMERICAN COUSIN   Spectrafilm, 1985
RAD   Tri-Star, 1986
WATCHERS   Universal, 1988
THE SQUAMISH FIVE   CBC Film, 1989
STEPHEN KING'S "IT" (TF)   Lorimar TV/Green-Epstein
    Productions/Konigsberg-Sanitsky Productions, 1990
DEAD RECKONING (CTF)   MCA Entertainment/
    Houston Lady Production Company, 1990
CADENCE   Northern Lights Entertainment/
    International Movie Group/Republic Pictures/
    New Line Cinema, 1991
AND THE SEA WILL TELL (TF)   Columbia Pictures
    Television, 1991

JEAN-YVES LEMENER
A MAN AND A WOMAN: 20 YEARS LATER   Warner
    Bros., 1986
THE FATAL IMAGE (TF)   Hearst Entertainment
    Productions/Ellipse Programme, 1990

JAMES LEMMO
ONE DOWN TWO TO GO   Almi Pictures, 1982
THE LAST FIGHT   Best Film & Video, 1983
FEAR CITY   Chevy Chase Distribution, 1985
RELENTLESS   New Line Cinema, 1989
MANIAC COP 2   Movie House Sales Co./Fadd
    Enterprises, 1990
THE FATAL IMAGE (TF)   Hearst Entertainment
    Productions/Ellipse Programme, 1990

DENIS LENOIR
Agent: The Gersh Agency, Inc., Beverly Hills -
    213/274-6611, New York - 212/997-1818

DADDY NOSTALGIE   *DADDY NOSTALGIA*   Clea
    Productions/Little Bear/Solyfic Company, 1990

DEAN LENT
BORDER RADIO   Coyote Films, 1987
THE HORSEPLAYER   Relentless Entertainment, 1989
GENUINE RISK   I.R.S., 1990

MIKLOS LENTE, CSC
Address: 1589 The Queensway, Unit 14, Toronto, Ontario
    M82 5W9, 416/521-2211

IN PRAISE OF OLDER WOMEN   Avco Embassy, 1978
HAPPY BIRTHDAY TO ME   Columbia, 1981
AGENCY   Jensen Farley Pictures, 1981
SCREWBALLS   New World, 1983
COUNTDOWN TO LOOKING GLASS (CTF)   L & B
    Productions/Primedia Productions, 1984
BEDROOM EYES   Aquarius Releasing, 1984
THE LITTLE KIDNAPPERS (CTF)   Canadian Broadcast-
    ing Corporation/Disney Channel/Jones 21st Century
    Entertainment/Resnick Margellos Productions, 1990

JOHN R. LEONETTI
Agent: The Gersh Agency, Inc., Beverly Hills -
    213/274-6611, New York - 212/997-1818

THE BROTHERHOOD   Trans World Entertainment, 1990
THE COOPERSMITH (TF)   Universal TV, 1990

MATTHEW F. LEONETTI, ASC
Agent: The Gersh Agency, Inc., Beverly Hills - 213/274-
    6611, New York - 212/997-1818

MR. BILLION   20th Century Fox, 1977
THE CHICKEN CHRONICLES   Avco Embassy, 1977
BREAKING AWAY   20th Century Fox, 1979
RAISE THE TITANIC   AFD, 1980
EYEWITNESS   20th Century Fox, 1981
POLTERGEIST   MGM/UA, 1982
FAST TIMES AT RIDGEMONT HIGH   Universal, 1982
THE BUDDY SYSTEM   20th Century Fox, 1984
THE ICE PIRATES   MGM/UA, 1984
JESSIE (Pilot)   1984
SONGWRITER   Tri-Star, 1984
FAST FORWARD   Columbia, 1985
WEIRD SCIENCE   Universal, 1985
JAGGED EDGE   Columbia, 1985
COMMANDO   20th Century Fox, 1985
JUMPIN' JACK FLASH   20th Century Fox, 1986
DRAGNET   Universal, 1987
EXTREME PREJUDICE   Tri-Star, 1987
RED HEAT   Tri-Star, 1988
ACTION JACKSON   Lorimar, 1988
JOHNNY HANDSOME   Tri-Star, 1989
HARD TO KILL   Warner Bros., 1990
ANOTHER 48 HRS.   Eddie Murphy Productions/
    Paramount, 1990

JEAN LEPINE
VINCENT & THEO   Hemdale, 1990

ANDREW LESNIE
THE DELINQUENTS   Warner Bros., 1990

PETER LEVY, ASC
Agent: Lloyd H. Segan, Irvin Arthur Associates -
    Los Angeles, 213/276-7493

DANGEROUS GAME   Hemdale, 1989
A NIGHTMARE ON ELM STREET, PART 5 - THE
    DREAM CHILD   New Line Cinema, 1989
PREDATOR 2   Gordon-Silver-Davis/20th
    Century Fox, 1990

DAVID LEWIS
Agent: Dattner & Associates - Los Angeles,
    213/447-5986

THE NIGHT HAVE EYES PART II   Peter Locke, 1984
UHF   Orion, 1989
THE SLEEPING CAR   Triax/Vidmark, 1990
NIGHT ANGEL   Paragon Arts International/Fries
    Entertainment, 1990

DENIS LEWISTON
THE SQUEEZE   Warner Bros., 1977
NIGHT GAMES   Avco Embassy, 1980
BLUEBERRY HILL   MGM, 1988
NIGHT OF THE DEMONS   Paragon, 1988
DANGEROUS CURVES   Vestron, 1989
THE SEX TAPES (TF)   von Zerneck/Sertner Films, 1989

GORE VIDAL'S BILLY THE KID (TF)   Turner Network
    Television, 1989
MADHOUSE   Orion, 1990
THE BIG ONE: THE GREAT LOS ANGELES
    EARTHQUAKES-PARTS I & II (TF)
    von Zerneck-Sertner Films, 1990
MONTANA (CTF)   Roger Gimbel Productions/Zoetrope
    Studios/HBO Productions, 1990
PEOPLE LIKE US-PARTS 1 & 2 (TF)   ITC Productions/
    CM Two Productions, 1990

PIERRE L'HOMME
QUARTET   New World, 1981
MY LITTLE GIRL   Hemdale, 1987
MAURICE   Cinecom, 1987
CYRANO DE BERGERAC   Orion Classics, 1990

STEPHEN LIGHTHILL
West Coast card, Local 659
Agent: The Doug Apatow Agency, 10559 Blythe Ave. -
    Los Angeles, CA 90064, 213/202-6888

THE SPIRIT OF '76   Commercial Pictures/Black
    Diamond/Columbia, 1990
BERKELEY IN THE SIXTIES   P.O.V. Theatrical
    Films, 1990

JOHN LINDLEY
Agent: The Gersh Agency, Inc. - Beverly Hills,
    213/274-6611

GIRLS OF THE WHITE ORCHID (TF)   Hill-Mandelker
    Films, 1983
THE DEMON MURDER CASE (TF)   Dick
    Clark Productions/Len Steckler Productions, 1983
THE GOODBYE PEOPLE   Embassy, 1983
LILY IN LOVE   New Line Cinema, 1985
KILLER PARTY   MGM/UA, 1986
HOME OF THE BRAVE   Cinecom, 1986
IN THE MOOD   Lorimar, 1987
THE SERPENT & THE RAINBOW   Universal, 1987
THE STEPFATHER   New Century/Vista, 1987
SHAKEDOWN   Universal, 1988
TRUE BELIEVER   Columbia, 1989
FIELD OF DREAMS   Universal, 1989
IMMEDIATE FAMILY   Columbia, 1989
VITAL SIGNS   20th Century Fox, 1990
SLEEPING WITH THE ENEMY   20th Century
    Fox, 1991

GERRY LIVELY
GIRLFRIEND FROM HELL   Queens Cross
    Productions/IVE (Live Entertainment), 1990

WALT LLOYD
DANGEROUSLY CLOSE   Cannon, 1986
DOWN TWISTED   Cannon, 1987
THE WASH   Skouras Pictures, 1988
SEX, LIES, AND VIDEOTAPE   Miramax, 1989
OUT ON THE EDGE (TF)   1989
TO SLEEP WITH ANGER   SVS, 1990
EXTREME CLOSE-UP (TF)   Robert Greenwald
    Productions/Bedford Falls Productions, 1990
PUMP UP THE VOLUME   SC Entertainment/New
    Line Cinema, 1990

BRYAN LOFTUS
Agent: Sandra Marsh Management - Sherman Oaks,
    818/905-6961

THE COMPANY OF WOLVES   Cannon, 1985
THE ASSAM GARDEN   Film Forum, 1986
ZINA   Film Forum, 1986
JAKE SPEED   New World, 1986
SIESTA   Lorimar, 1987

BRUCE LOGAN
IDAHO TRANSFER   Cinemation 1975
CRAZY MAMA   New World, 1975
JACKSON COUNTY JAIL   New World, 1976
I NEVER PROMISED YOU A ROSE GARDEN
    New World, 1977
STUNTS   New Line Cinema, 1977
DRACULA'S DOG   Crown International, 1978
THE INCREDIBLE SHRINKING WOMAN
    Universal, 1981
TRON   Buena Vista, 1982

DIETRICH LOHMANN
Agent: The Gersh Agency, Inc., Beverly Hills -
    213/274-6611, New York - 212/997-1818

SILHOUETTE (CTF)   Dutch Productions/MCA Television
    Entertainment, 1990
THE ROSE AND THE JACKAL (CTF)   PWD Productions/
    Spectacor Films/Steve White Productions, 1990
DARK SHADOWS PARTS I-II (Pilot)   Dan Curtis
    Television Productions, 1991 (Part one only)

PAUL LOHMANN
Agent: Grace Lyons Management - Los Angeles,
    213/655-5100

CATCH A PEBBLE   World Wide, 1971
EXTREME CLOSE-UP   National General, 1973
LET THE GOOD TIMES ROLL (FD)   Columbia, 1973
COFFY   American International, 1973
CALIFORNIA SPLIT   Columbia, 1974
NASHVILLE   Paramount, 1976
SILENT MOVIE   20th Century Fox, 1976
BUFFALO BILL AND THE INDIANS or SITTING BULL'S
    HISTORY LESSON   United Artists, 1976
THE WHITE BUFFALO   United Artists, 1977
HIGH ANXIETY   20th Century Fox, 1977
AN ENEMY OF THE PEOPLE   Warner Bros., 1978
STRAIGHT TIME   Warner Bros., 1978
NORTH DALLAS FORTY   Paramount, 1979
TIME AFTER TIME   Orion/Warner Bros., 1979
METEOR   American International, 1979
HIDE IN PLAIN SIGHT   MGM/United Artists, 1980
CHARLIE CHAN & THE CURSE OF THE DRAGON
    QUEEN   American Cinema, 1981
MOMMIE DEAREST   Paramount, 1981
LOOKER   The Ladd Company/Warner Bros., 1981
ENDANGERED SPECIES   MGM/UA, 1982
KIDCO   20th Century Fox, 1983
THE DOLLMAKER (TF)   Finnegan Associates/IPCFilms
    Inc./Dollmaker Productions, 1984
LUST IN THE DUST   New World, 1984
DELTA PI *MUGSY'S GIRLS*   Pegasus, 1985
THAT'S DANCING! (FD)   MGM/UA, 1985,
    w/Andrew Laszlo
FREE RIDE   Galaxy, 1985
I'LL BE HOME FOR CHRISTMAS (TF)   NBC
    Productions, 1988

Lo

CINEMATOGRAPHERS
PRODUCTION
DESIGNERS,
COSTUME
DESIGNERS AND
FILM EDITORS
GUIDE

CINEMATOGRAPHERS

Lo

CINEMATOGRAPHERS
PRODUCTION
DESIGNERS,
COSTUME
DESIGNERS and
FILM EDITORS
GUIDE

C
I
N
E
M
A
T
O
G
R
A
P
H
E
R
S

THE OUTSIDE WOMAN (TF)   Green-Epstein
    Productions, 1989
A FAMILY FOR JOE (Pilot)   NBC Productions/
    Grosso-Jacobson Productions, 1990
JOHNNY RYAN (TF)   NBC Productions/MGM/UA/Dan
    Curtis TV Productions, 1990
THE MYSTERY OF FLIGHT 1501 (TF)   Consolidated/
    Citadel/Schaefer-Karpf Productions, 1990

RAOUL LOMAS
STACY'S KNIGHTS   Crown International, 1983
CHILDREN OF THE CORN   New World, 1984

ULLI LOMMEL
A TASTE OF SIN   Ambassador, 1983
BRAINWAVES   MGM/UA, 1983, w/Jon Kranhouse
THE DEMONSVILLE TERROR   MPM, 1983

JAMES LONDON
THE TOXIC AVENGER   Troma, 1985,
    w/Lloyd Kaufman
THE TOXIC AVENGER PART II   Troma, 1989
THE TOXIC AVENGER PART III: THE LAST
    TEMPTATION OF TOXIE   Troma, 1990

MICHAEL LONZO
THE WILD PONY (TF)   Sullivan Films, Inc., 1982
HEARTBREAKER   Monorex, 1983

GORDON LONSDALE
A GIRL OF THE LIMBERLOST (TF)   Sascha
    Schneider Productions, 1990

CLAUS LOOF
NOBODY'S PERFECT   Panorama Film International/
    Steve Ader Productions/Moviestore, 1990

GERARD LOUBEAU
BURIED ALIVE   Breton Film Productions/21st Century
    Films/RCA Columbia Pictures Home Video, 1990
MASTER OF DRAGONARD HILL   Cannon, 1990

WILLIAM LUBTCHANSKY
LOVE ON THE GROUND   Spectrafilm, 1986
NEXT SUMMER   European Classics, 1986
CLASS RELATIONS   New Yorker Films, 1987
THE MAHABHARATA   Les Productions du Zeme
    Etage, 1989

IGOR LUTHER
THE HANDMAID'S TALE   Warner Bros., 1990
DEATH OF A SCHOOLBOY   Neue Studio Film
    GMBH, 1991

BERNARD LUTIC
THE AVIATOR'S WIFE   New Yorker, 1981,
    w/Roman Windig
THE WELL-MADE MARRIAGE   United Artists
    Classics, 1982
ENTRE NOUS   United Artists Classics, 1983
HEAT OF DESIRE   Triumph, 1984
REVOLUTION   Warner Bros., 1985
THE RETURN OF THE MUSKETEERS
    Universal, 1990

JULIO MACAT
HOME ALONE   John Hughes/20th Century Fox, 1990
ONLY THE LONELY   20th Century Fox, 1991

PETER MACDONALD
SECRET PLACES   TLC Films/20th Century Fox, 1984
SOLARBABIES   MGM/UA, 1986
HAMBURGER HILL   Paramount, 1987
SHAG: THE MOVIE   Hemdale, 1989

PETER MACKAY
THE FACE OF FEAR (TF)   Warner Bros./Lee Rich
    Productions/Papazian-Hirsch Productions, 1990

KENNETH MACMILLAN
Agent: Sandra Marsh Management - Sherman Oaks,
    818/905-6961

SMILEY'S PEOPLE (MS)   BBC/Paramount TV, 1982
THE AERODROME (TF)   BBC, 1983
THE GHOST WRITER (TF)   WGBH-Boston/Malone-Gill
    Productions/BBC, 1984
BLEAK HOUSE (MS)   BBC, 1985
PAST CARING (TF)   BBC, 1985
HOTEL DU LAC (TF)   Channel Four, 1986
DAY AFTER THE FAIR (TF)   BBC/Bill Kenright Films Ltd./
    Arts & Entertainment Network, 1987
THE LITTLE MATCH GIRL (TF)   NBC Productions,1987
PACK OF LIES (TF)   Robert Halmi, Inc., 1987
A MONTH IN THE COUNTRY   Orion Classics, 1987
A SUMMER STORY   Atlantic Releasing
    Corporation/ITC, 1988
HENRY V   Renaissance Films, 1989
THE TREE OF HANDS   Greenpoint/Granada/British
    Screen, 1989
KING RALPH   Mirage/Universal, 1991

GLEN MACPHERSON
CLARENCE (CTF)   Television New Zealand/The Family
    Channel (Canada)/Family Channel/North Star
    Entertainment/South Pacific Pictures/Atlantis
    Films, 1990

SIMON MAGGS
MOTHER LOVE-PARTS I-III (MS)   WGBH Boston/BBC
    TV, 1990, w/Nigel Walters

TOMASZ MAGIERSKI
BAIL JUMPER   Angelika Films, 1990

SOPHIE MAINTIGNEUX
SUMMER   Orion Classics, 1986
KING LEAR   Cannon, 1987

HARRY MAKIN, CSC
Address: 368A King St. East, Toronto, Ontario M5A 1K9,
    416/366-8843

HARD FEELINGS   Astral Bellevue, 1981

IF YOU COULD SEE WHAT I HEAR   Jensen Farley
    Pictures 1982
HANG TOUGH   Astral Bellevue Pathe/Moviestore
    Entertainment, 1990

FIROUZ MALEKZADER
THE RUNNER   International Home Cinema, 1990

JOSEPH MANGINE
SQUIRM   American International, 1976
VAN NUYS BLVD.   Crown International, 1979
LOVE IN A TAXI 1980
MOTHER'S DAY   United Film Distributors, 1980
ALLIGATOR   Group 1, 1980
THE SWORD AND THE SORCERER   Group 1, 1982
ALONE IN THE DARK   New Line Cinema, 1982
DREAMLAND   First-Run Features, 1983
EXTERMINATOR 2   Cannon, 1984, w/Robert Baldwin
NEON MANIACS   Bedford Entertainment, 1986,
    w/Oliver Wood

ISIDORE MANKOFSKY, ASC*
Agent: Grace Lyons Management - Los Angeles,
    213/655-5100

TRICK BABY   Universal, 1973
HOMEBODIES   Avco Embassy, 1974
THE ULTIMATE THRILL   General Cinema, 1974
THE MUPPET MOVIE   AFD, 1979
GOLDIE AND THE BOXER (TF)   Orenthal
    Productions/Columbia TV, 1979
THE JAZZ SINGER   AFD, 1980
SOMEWHERE IN TIME   Universal, 1980
JACQUELINE BOUVIER KENNEDY (TF)   ABC
    Circle Films, 1981
IN THE CUSTODY OF STRANGERS (TF)
    Moonlight Productions/Filmways, 1982
SUZANNE   20th Century Fox, 1982, Canadian
QUARTERBACK PRINCESS (TF)   CBS
    Entertainment, 1983
SILENCE OF THE HEART (TF)   David A. Simons
    Productions/Tisch-Avnet Productions, 1984
THE BURNING BED (TF)   Tisch-Avnet
    Productions, 1984
MISFITS OF SCIENCE (TF)   James D. Parriott
    Productions/Universal TV, 1985
EWOKS: THE BATTLE FOR ENDOR (TF)
    Lucasfilm Ltd., 1985
BETTER OFF DEAD   Warner Bros., 1985
ONE CRAZY SUMMER   Warner Bros., 1986
"SAY YES"   Cinetel, 1986
LITTLE SPIES (TF)   Walt Disney TV, 1986
NUTCRACKER: MONEY, MADNESS AND
    MURDER (MS)   Green Arrow Productions/
    Warner Bros. TV, 1987
BILLIONAIRE BOYS CLUB (TF)   Donald March/
    Gross-Weston Productions/ITC Productions, 1987
DAVY CROCKETT: RAINBOW IN THE THUNDER (TF)
    Echo Cove Productions/Walt Disney TV, 1988
CLINTON AND NADINE   HBO Pictures/ITC, 1988
FATAL JUDGMENT (TF)   Jack Farren Prod./
    Group W Prods., 1988
A VERY BRADY CHRISTMAS (TF)   Sherwood
    Schwartz Co., 1988
SKIN DEEP   20th Century Fox, 1989
PARENT TRAP III (TF)   Walt Disney TV, 1989
LITTLE WHITE LIES (TF)   New World TV/The
    Larry A. Thompson Organization, 1990
POLLY-COMIN' HOME (TF)   Echo Cove/Disney, 1990

APPEARANCES (TF)   Touchstone TV/Echo Cove
    Productions, 1990
LOVES, LIES AND MURDER-PARTS I & II (TF)   Republic
    Pictures, 1991

MICHAEL D. MARGULIES, ASC
Agent: Tobias-Skouras & Associates - Los Angeles,
    213/277-6211

MINNIE AND MOSKOWITZ   Universal, 1971, w/Alric
    Edens & Arthur J. Ornitz
BRUTE COPS   General Films, 1971
THE BABY   Scotia International, 1973, British
DIRTY MARY, CRAZY LARRY   20th Century Fox, 1974
THE RIVER NIGER   Cine Artists, 1976
THE MAGIC OF LASSIE   International Picture
    Show, 1978
MY BODYGUARD   20th Century Fox, 1980
SIX WEEKS   Universal, 1982
POLICE ACADEMY   The Ladd Company/Warner
    Bros., 1984
16 DAYS OF GLORY (FD)   Paramount, 1986, w/others
STUCK WITH EACH OTHER (TF)   Nexus
    Productions, 1990
REPOSSESSED   New Line Cinema/Seven Arts, 1990

IVAN MARK
STORM AND SORROW (CTF)   Hearst Entertainment
    Productions/Accent Entertainment, 1990,
    w/Laszlo George

PETER MARKLE
THE PERSONALS   New World, 1982

BARRY MARKOWITZ
THE BIG BANG   Kanter-Toback, 1989
TORN APART   City Lights/Castle Hill, 1990

ARTHUR D. MARKS
BAD GIRLS DORMITORY   Films Around the World, 1986
BREEDERS   Empire Pictures, 1986
NECROPOLIS   Empire Pictures, 1987
SHE'S BACK   Vestron, 1989
THE OCCULTIST   Empire, 1989

JACQUES MARQUETTE, ASC
Agent: The Miller Agency - Santa Clarita, 818/843-7335

THREE IN THE ATTIC   American International, 1968
THE TROUBLE WITH GIRLS   MGM, 1969
FUZZ   United Artists, 1972
RETURN TO MACON COUNTY   American
    International, 1975
BURNT OFFERINGS   United Artists, 1976

JEFF MART
RUSH WEEK   RCA/Columbia Pictures Home
    Video, 1991

JACK A. MARTA
DUEL   Universal, 1983

F. SMITH MARTIN
AMERICAN BORN   PM Home Video, 1990

Ma

CINEMATOGRAPHERS
PRODUCTION
DESIGNERS,
COSTUME
DESIGNERS AND
FILM EDITORS
GUIDE

C
I
N
E
M
A
T
O
G
R
A
P
H
E
R
S

Ma

CINEMATOGRAPHERS
PRODUCTION
DESIGNERS,
COSTUME
DESIGNERS AND
FILM EDITORS
GUIDE

C
I
N
E
M
A
T
O
G
R
A
P
H
E
R
S

NINO G. MARTINETTI
GOLDEN BRAID   1990

MARCELLO MASCIOCCHI
YOR, THE HUNTER FROM THE FUTURE
    Columbia, 1983
TREASURE OF THE FOUR CROWNS   Cannon,
    1983, w/Giuseppe Ruzzolini

STEVE MASON
LUIGI'S LADIES   TraLaLa Films, 1989

JAMES MATHERS
Agent: Gerald K. Smith & Associates - Burbank,
    213/849-5388
Address: P.O. Box 1973, Studio City, CA 91604,
    818/762-2214

OUTLAW FORCE   Trans World Entertainment, 1987
TAKE TWO   TBJ Films, 1987
THE GAME   TBJ Films, 1989
MEMORIAL DAY   Concorde Releasing/Warner
    Home Video, 1989
ZADAR, COW FROM HELL!   Stone Peach
    Productions, 1989
LAST CALL   Amritraj Entertainment/Prism
    Entertainment/Paramount Home Video, 1990
SYNGENOR   Syngenor/American Cinema Marketing
    Group/South Gate Entertainment, 1990
HIDDEN VIEW (TF)   LBS, 1990
NIGHT EYES   Amritraj-Baldwin, 1990

HARRY MATHIAS*
West Coast Card
Agent: Smith Gosnell Nicholson & Associates -
    Pacific Palisades, 213/459-0307

PRAY TV   *K-GOD*   Filmways, 1980
CREATURE   Cardinal Releasing, 1985
MY CHAUFFEUR   Crown International, 1986
TIMESTALKERS (TF)   Fries Entertainment/
    Newland-Raynor Productions, 1987
ERNEST GOES TO CAMP   Buena Vista, 1987,
    w/Jim May
PHANTOM OF THE MALL   Fries Distribution, 1989
BEVERLY HILLS BRATS   Taurus Entertainment, 1989
DREAM DATE (TF)   Frederic Golchan/Robert Kosberg
    Productions, 1990

THOMAS MAUCH
STROSZEK   New Yorker, 1977
SIGNS OF LIFE   New Yorker, 1981
FITZCARRALDO   New World, 1982
WAR AND PEACE   TeleCulture, 1983, shared credit
THE BLIND DIRECTOR   Spectrafilm, 1986
DEADLINE   Skouras Pictures, 1987,
    w/Amnon Salomon

BRADFORD MAY*
West Coast Card
Agent: Triad Artists, Inc. - Los Angeles, 213/556-2727

WHO GETS THE FRIENDS (TF)   CBS
    Entertainment, 1988
DOWNPAYMENT ON MURDER (TF)   Adam
    Productions/20th Century Fox TV, 1987
DO YOU REMEMBER LOVE? (TF)   Dave Bell
    Productions, 1985

PRIVATE EYE (Pilot)   1987
OUT ON A LIMB (MS)   Stan Margulies Company/ABC
    Circle Films, 1987
BROTHERLY LOVE (TF)   CBS Entertainment, 1985
THE MONSTER SQUAD   Tri-Star, 1987
FAVORITE SON (MS) II   NBC Productions, 1988
APT PUPIL   New Century/Vista, 1990

DONALD McALPINE, ASC
Agent: The Gersh Agency, Inc., Beverly Hills -
    213/274-6611, New York - 212/997-1818

BARRY McKENZIE HOLDS HIS OWN   Satori, 1975
THE GETTING OF WISDOM   Atlantic Releasing
    Corporation, 1977
THE ODD ANGRY SHOT   Roadshow Distributors, 1979
PATRICK   Cinema Shares International, 1979
MY BRILLIANT CAREER   Analysis, 1980
THE CLUB   Roadshow, 1980
BREAKER MORANT   New World/Quartet, 1980
THE EARTHLING   Filmways, 1981
MONEY MOVERS   South Australian Film
    Corporation, 1981
DON'T CRY, IT'S ONLY THUNDER   Sanrio, 1982
TEMPEST   Columbia, 1982
PUBERTY BLUES   United Artists Classics, 1983
BLUE SKIES AGAIN   Warner Bros., 1983
NOW AND FOREVER   Inter Planetary, 1983
HARRY & SON   Orion, 1984
MOSCOW ON THE HUDSON   Columbia, 1984
KING DAVID   Paramount, 1985
DOWN AND OUT IN BEVERLY HILLS   Buena
    Vista, 1986
PREDATOR   20th Century Fox, 1987
THE FRINGE DWELLERS   Atlantic Releasing
    Corporation, 1987
ORPHANS   Lorimar, 1987
MOVING   Warner Bros., 1988
MOON OVER PARADOR   Universal, 1988
SEE YOU IN THE MORNING   Warner Bros., 1989
PARENTHOOD   Universal, 1989
STANLEY & IRIS   MGM/UA, 1990
CAREER OPPORTUNITIES   Universal Pictures, 1991
THE HARD WAY   Universal, 1991

JAMED McCALMONT
VOODOO DAWN   Academy Entertainment, 1990

LARRY McCONKEY
COOL RUNNINGS: THE REGGAE MOVIE   R5/S8, 1986
WHITE OF THE EYE   Palisades Entertainment, 1988

TOM McDONOUGH
ENORMOUS CHANGES AT THE LAST MINUTE   TLC
    Fllms International, 1985

BRUCE McGOWAN
LETTERS TO BREZHNEV   Cirlce Releasing
    Corporation, 1985

MICHAEL McGOWAN
TOO LATE THE HERO (TF)   Viacom Enterprises/
    Premiere Limited Productions, 1990

MARTIN McGRATH
E.A.R.T.H. FORCE (TF)   Paramount Network TV, 1990

DANIEL McKINNY

PERRY MASON: THE CASE OF THE DESPERATE DECEPTION (TF)   Viacom/Dean Hargrove Productions/Fred Silverman Productions, 1990
PERRY MASON: THE CASE OF THE POISONED PEN (TF)   Viacom/Dean Hargrove Productions/Fred Silverman Productions, 1990
PERRY MASON: THE CASE OF THE DEFIANT DAUGHTER (TF)   Viacom/Dean Hargrove Productions/Fred Silverman Productions, 1990

AUSTIN McKINNEY

GETTING IT ON!   Comworld, 1983
LORDS OF THE DEEP   Concorde, 1989
AFTER SCHOOL   Moviestore Entertainment, 1989

JOHN McLEAN

TOUCH AND GO   Greater Union Film Distributors, 1980
ESCAPE 2000   New World, 1983

NICK McLEAN

Agent: The Gersh Agency, Inc., Beverly Hills - 213/274-6611, New York - 212/997-1818

STAYING ALIVE   Paramount, 1983
STROKER ACE   Universal, 1983
CITY HEAT   Warner Bros., 1984
CANNONBALL RUN II   Warner Bros., 1984
STICK   Universal, 1984
THE GOONIES   Warner Bros., 1985
TWICE IN A LIFETIME   The Yorkin Company, 1985
SHORT CIRCUIT   Tri-Star, 1986
SPACEBALLS   20th Century Fox, 1987
MAC AND ME   Orion, 1988
B-MEN (TF)   D.W.T. Productions/Lorimar-Telepictures, 1989

IAN McMILLAN

GIVE MY REGARDS TO BROAD STREET   20th Century Fox, 1984

JOHN McPHERSON, ASC *

West Coast Card
Agent: Smith Gosnell Nicholson & Associates - Pacific Palisades, 213/459-0307

JUST ONE OF THE GUYS   Columbia, 1985
ELEANOR ROOSEVELT: FIRST LADY OF THE WORLD (TF)   Murbill Productions/Embassy TV, 1986
JAWS - THE REVENGE   Universal, 1987
BATTERIES NOT INCLUDED   Universal, 1987
SHORT CIRCUIT 2   Tri-Star, 1988
FLETCH LIVES   Universal, 1989

STEVE McWILLIAMS

DAN TURNER, HOLLYWOOD DETECTIVE (TF)   LBS/Fries Entertainment, 1990

PHIL MEHEUX

BLACK JOY   Hemdale, 1977
THE MUSIC MACHINE   Norfolk International Pictures/Target International Pictures, 1979
SCUM   Berwick Street Films, 1979
THOSE GLORY, GLORY DAYS   Cinecom, 1980
THE FINAL CONFLICT   20th Century Fox, 1981, w/Robert Paynter
THE LONG GOOD FRIDAY   Embassy, 1982
THE FINAL OPTION   MGM/UA, 1983
BEYOND THE LIMIT   *THE HONORARY CONSUL*   Paramount, 1983
EXPERIENCE PREFERRED BUT NOT ESSENTIAL   Samuel Goldwyn Company, 1983
MORONS FROM OUTER SPACE   Universal, 1985
THE FOURTH PROTOCOL   Lorimar, 1987
CRIMINAL LAW   Tri-Star, 1989
RENEGADES   Universal, 1989

CHRIS MENGES

Agent: Leading Artists, Inc. - Beverly Hills, 213/858-1999
Address: 7 Wesleyan Place, London NW5, England, 01/267-6875

BLACK JACK   Boyd's Company, 1979
THE GAMEKEEPER   ATV, 1980, w/Charles Stewart
WARLORDS OF THE 21ST CENTURY   *BATTLETRUCK*   New World, 1982
DANNY BOY   *ANGEL*   Triumph/Columbia, 1983
LOCAL HERO   Warner Bros., 1983
COMFORT AND JOY   Universal, 1984
THE KILLING FIELDS ★★   Warner Bros., 1984
WINTER FLIGHT   Cinecom, 1984
A SENSE OF FREEDOM   Island Pictures, 1985
MARIE   MGM/UA, 1985
THE MISSION ★★   Warner Bros., 1986
WALTER AND JUNE   *LOVING WALTER*   Film Forum, 1986
SHY PEOPLE   Cannon, 1987
HIGH SEASON   Hemdale, 1988
SINGING THE BLUES IN RED   Angelika Films, 1988

JOHN METCALFE

SPACED OUT   Miramax, 1981, w/Peter Sinclair
HORROR PLANET   *INSEMINOID*   Almi Pictures, 1982
JAMES JOYCE'S WOMEN   Universal, 1985
THE AMERICAN WAY   Miramax, 1987
RAWHEAD REX   Empire Pictures, 1987

REXFORD METZ, ASC *

West Coast Card
Agent: Smith Gosnell Nicholson & Associates - Pacific Palisades, 213/459-0307

JIM, THE WORLD'S GREATEST   Universal, 1976, shared credit
THE GAUNTLET   Warner Bros., 1977
EVERY WHICH WAY BUT LOOSE   Warner Bros., 1978
THE SKY TRAP (TF)   Walt Disney Productions, 1979
SERIAL   Paramount, 1980
FORCED VENGEANCE   MGM/United Artists, 1982
THE BABYSITTER (TF)   Moonlight Productions/Filmways, 1980
ERNIE KOVACS: BETWEEN THE LAUGHTER (TF)   ABC Circle Films, 1984
DEADLY MESSAGES (TF)   Columbia TV, 1985
THIS WIFE FOR HIRE (TF)   The Belle Company/Guillaume-Margo Productions/Comworld Productions, 1985
LETTING GO (TF)   Adam Productions/ITC Productions, 1985
SILENT WITNESS (TF)   Robert Greenwald Productions, 1985
THE MIDNIGHT HOUR (TF)   ABC Circle Films, 1985
THE DEFIANT ONES (TF)   MGM-UA TV, 1986
NECESSITY (TF)   Barry-Enright Productions/Alexander Productions, 1988

Me

CINEMATOGRAPHERS
PRODUCTION
DESIGNERS,
COSTUME
DESIGNERS AND
FILM EDITORS
GUIDE

C
I
N
E
M
A
T
O
G
R
A
P
H
E
R
S

Me

CINEMATOGRAPHERS
PRODUCTION
DESIGNERS,
COSTUME
DESIGNERS AND
FILM EDITORS
GUIDE

C
I
N
E
M
A
T
O
G
R
A
P
H
E
R
S

ALAN METZGER

THAT'S THE WAY OF THE WORLD *SHINING STAR*
  United Artists, 1975
ANDY WARHOL'S BAD New World, 1977
VOICES MGM/United Artists, 1979
GILDA LIVE Warner Bros., 1980, w/Ted Churchill,
  James Contner & Peter Norman
BELOW THE BELT Atlantic Releasing
  Corporation, 1980
KOJAK: THE BELARUS FILE (TF)
  Universal TV, 1985

PETER MIDDLETON

THE TEMPEST World Northal, 1980

PIERRE MIGNOT

COME BACK TO THE 5 & DIME JIMMY DEAN,
  JIMMY DEAN Cinecom, 1982
STREAMERS United Artists Classics, 1983
SECRET HONOR Cinecom, 1985
THE LAUNDROMAT (CTF) Byck-Lancaster
  Productions/Sandcastle 5 Productions, 1985
FOOL FOR LOVE Cannon, 1985
THE BOY IN BLUE 20th Century Fox, 1986
MARIA CHAPDELAINE The Movie Store, 1986
BEYOND THERAPY New World, 1987
O.C. AND STIGGS MGM/UA, 1987

VOYA MIKULIC

DEADLY DANCER Action International Pictures/AIP
  Home Video, 1990, w/Marshall Adams

ALEC MILLS, BSC

Agent: Grace Lyons Management - Los Angeles,
  213/655-5100

BIDDY Sands Films Ltd., 1983, British
SHAKAZULU (MS) Harmony Gold/
  Tele-Munchen, 1985
HOT TARGET Crown International, 1985
KING KONG LIVES DEG, 1986
THE LIVING DAYLIGHTS MGM/UA, 1987
LIONHEART Orion, 1987
LICENCE TO KILL MGM/UA, 1989

CHARLES MILLS

BOYZ N THE HOOD Columbia, 1991

DOUGLAS MILSOME, BSC

Agent: Grace Lyons Management - Los Angeles,
  213/655-5100

WILD HORSES Satori, 1984
FULL METAL JACKET Warner Bros., 1987
THE BEAST Columbia, 1988
LONESOME DOVE (MS) ☆ Motown Prods./Quintex
  Entertainment, 1989
HAWKS Skouras Pictures, 1989
GREAT EXPECTATIONS (TF) The Disney Channel/
  Harlech TV/Primetime TV, 1989
MILY OF SPIES-PARTS I & II (TF) King Phoenix
  Entertainment, 1990
DESPERATE HOURS Dino De Laurentiis
  Communications/MGM/UA, 1990
IF LOOKS COULD KILL Warner Bros., 1991

CHARLES D. (CHUCK) MINSKY*

West Coast Card
Agent: Smith Gosnell Nicholson & Associates -
  Pacific Palisades, 213/459-0307

RADIOACTIVE DREAMS DEG, 1986
APRIL FOOL'S DAY Paramount, 1986
WEEKEND WARRIORS The Movie Store, 1986
CHINA BEACH (Pilot) 1988
SILENCE AT BETHANY Keener Productions/American
  Playhouse Theatrical Films, 1988
CAPITAL NEWS (Pilot) 1990
PRETTY WOMAN *3000* Buena Vista, 1990

JANUSZ MINSKI

GRIM PRAIRIE TALES East-West Film Partners
  Productions, 1990

AMIR MOKRI

Agent: Smith Gosnell Nicholson & Associates -
  Pacific Palisades, 213/459-0307

HOUSE OF THE RISING SUN Platinum Pictures, 1985
SLAM DANCE Island Pictures, 1987
EAT A BOWL OF TEA Columbia, 1989
BLUE STEEL MGM/UA, 1990
LIFE IS CHEAP...BUT TOILET PAPER IS EXPENSIVE
  Silverlight Entertainment, 1990
WHORE Trimark Pictures, 1991
QUEENS LOGIC New Visions, 1991

MIKE MOLLOY

Agent: Jill Nicholas, Top Technicians Pty. Ltd.,
  P. O. Box 1035, DEE WHY N.S.W., 2099 Australia,
  612/981-1622 or fax - 612/971-2880

MAD DOG Cinema Shares International, 1976
SUMMERFIELD Greater Union Film Distributors, 1977
THE SHOUT Films Inc., 1979
THE HUMAN FACTOR United Artists, 1979
THE KIDNAPPING OF THE PRESIDENT Crown
  International, 1980
SHOCK TREATMENT 20th Century Fox, 1981
THE RETURN OF CAPTAIN INVINCIBLE
  New World, 1983
THE HIT Island Alive, 1985
LINK Thorn EMI/Cannon, 1986
SCANDAL Miramax, 1989
BETHUNE: THE MAKING OF A HERO Parmentier-
  Belstar/Filmline International-August 1st Film Studio,
  1990, w/Raoul Coutard

JAMES MOMEL

MS. 45 Navaron, 1981
MADMAN Jensen Farley Pictures, 1982

FELIX MONTI

Agent: Sandra Marsh Management - Sherman Oaks,
  818/905-6961

THE OFFICIAL STORY Historias
  Cinematograficas, 1985
TANGOS: THE EXILE OF GARDEL New Yorker, 1986
SUR Pacific Productions/Cinesur/Instituto de
  Cinematografica, 1987
OLD GRINGO Columbia, 1989

VINCENT MONTON, ACS

Agent: Jill Nicholas, Top Technicians Pty. Ltd.,
  P. O. Box 1035, DEE WHY N.S.W., 2099 Australia,
  612/981-1622 or fax - 612/971-2880

THE TRUE STORY OF ESKIMO NELL *DICK DOWN
  UNDER* Quest Films/Filmways Australasian
  Distributors, 1975, Australian
FANTASM Filmways Australasian, 1977, Australian
THE TRESPASSERS Filmways, 1976
RAW DEAL Greater Union Film Distributors, 1977
THE DAY AFTER HALLOWEEN *SNAP-SHOT*
  Group 1, 1979
NEWSFRONT New Yorker, 1979
THIRST Greater Union Film Distributors, 1979
NORMAN LOVES ROSE Atlantic Releasing
  Corporation, 1981
ROAD GAMES Avco Embassy, 1981
HEATWAVE New Line Cinema, 1983
TREASURE OF THE YANKEE ZEPHYR Film Ventures
  International/Artists Releasing Corporation, 1984
MOVING OUT Satori, 1985
THE HIJACKING OF THE ACHILLE LAURO (TF)
  Tamara Asseyev Prods./Spectacor Films/New World
  Television, 1989

ALLEN MOORE

THE CIVIL WAR I-IX WETA-Washington, D.C./
  Florentine Films, 1990, w/Ken Burns and
  Buddy Squires

FREDERICK MOORE*

West Coast Card
Agent: Smith Gosnell Nicholson & Associates -
  Pacific Palisades, 213/459-0307

THE MAN WHO WASN'T THERE Paramount, 1983
BEVERLY HILLS BUNTZ (Pilot) 1987
NIGHTINGALES (Pilot) 1988
FIRE AND RAIN (CTF) Wilshire Court
  Productions, 1989
THANKSGIVING DAY (TF) Zacharias-Buhai
  Productions/NBC Productions, 1990

RICHARD MOORE, ASC

THE WILD ANGELS American International, 1966
WILD IN THE STREETS American International, 1968
THE SCALPHUNTERS United Artists, 1968
THE REIVERS National General, 1969
WINNING Universal, 1969
MYRA BRECKINRIDGE 20th Century Fox, 1970
WUSA Paramount, 1970
SOMETIMES A GREAT NOTION *NEVER GIVE
  AN INCH* Universal, 1971
THE STONEKILLER Columbia, 1973
THE LIFE AND TIMES OF JUDGE ROY BEAN National
  General, 1973
ANNIE Columbia, 1982

TED MOORE

DR. NO United Artists, 1962
FROM RUSSIA WITH LOVE United Artists, 1963
GOLDFINGER United Artists, 1964
THUNDERBALL United Artists, 1965
A MAN FOR ALL SEASONS ★★ Columbia, 1966
DIAMONDS ARE FOREVER United Artists, 1973
LIVE AND LET DIE United Artists, 1973
THE MAN WITH THE GOLDEN GUN United
  Artists, 1974

SINBAD AND THE EYE OF THE TIGER Columbia, 1977
ORCA Paramount, 1977
DOMINIQUE Sword and Sorvery Productions, 1979
CLASH OF THE TITANS United Artists, 1981
PRIEST OF LOVE Filmways, 1981

DONALD M. MORGAN, ASC*

West Coast Card
Agent: Smith Gosnell Nicholson & Associates -
  Pacific Palisades, 213/459-0307

SHEILA LEVINE IS DEAD AND LIVING IN NEW YORK
  Paramount, 1975
LET'S DO IT AGAIN Warner Bros., 1975
ONE ON ONE Warner Bros., 1977
A PIECE OF THE ACTION Warner Bros., 1977
I WANNA HOLD YOUR HAND Universal, 1978
SKATETOWN, U.S.A. Columbia, 1979
ELVIS (TF) ☆ Dick Clark Productions, 1979
USED CARS Columbia, 1980
AMBER WAVES (TF) Time-Life Productions, 1980
OFF THE MINNESOTA STRIP (TF) Cherokee
  Productions/Universal TV, 1980
FREEDOM (TF) Hill-Mandelker Films, 1981
MURDER IN TEXAS (TF) Dick Clark Productions/Billy
  Hale Films, 1981
CRISIS AT CENTRAL HIGH (TF) Time-Life
  Productions, 1981
OFF THE WALL Jensen Farley Pictures, 1983
CHRISTINE Columbia, 1983
HYSTERICAL Embassy, 1983
MEATBALLS PART II Tri-Star, 1984
STARMAN Columbia, 1984
LOVE AND LIES (TF) ITC Entertainment/Fredya
  Rothstein Productions, 1990
MURDER IN MISSISSIPPI (TF) David L. Wolper
  Productions, 1990

KEN MORGAN

THE INVESTIGATION: INSIDE A TERRORIST
  BOMBING (CTF) Granada Television, 1990
CROSSING TO FREEDOM (TF) Granada TV/
  Stan Margulies Productions/Procter & Gamble
  Productions, 1990

RHETT MORITA

Agent: The Gersh Agency, Inc., Beverly Hills -
  213/274-6611, New York - 212/997-1818

INTO THE FIRE S.C. Entertainment, 1987
BLOOD RELATIONS S.C. Entertainment, 1988
PROM NIGHT III: THE LAST KISS Norstar, 1990
JOHNNY SUEDE Vega/Sundance Institute, 1991

JOHN A. MORRILL

BROTHERS Warner Bros., 1977
THE DARK Film Ventures International, 1977
KINGDOM OF THE SPIDERS Dimension, 1977
THE DAY TIME ENDED Compass International, 1979

MARK MORRIS

THINK BIG Concorde, 1990

OSWALD MORRIS, BSC

OLIVER! ★ Columbia, 1968
FIDDLER ON THE ROOF ★★ United Artists, 1971
THE MACKINTOSH MAN Warner Bros., 1973
THE MAN WHO WOULD BE KING Allied Artists, 1975

Mo

CINEMATOGRAPHERS
PRODUCTION
DESIGNERS,
COSTUME
DESIGNERS AND
FILM EDITORS
GUIDE

C
I
N
E
M
A
T
O
G
R
A
P
H
E
R
S

Mo

CINEMATOGRAPHERS
PRODUCTION
DESIGNERS,
COSTUME
DESIGNERS and
FILM EDITORS
GUIDE

C
I
N
E
M
A
T
O
G
R
A
P
H
E
R
S

SEVEN PER-CENT SOLUTION   Universal, 1976
EQUUS   United Artists, 1977
THE WIZ ★   Universal, 1978
JUST TELL ME WHAT YOU WANT   Warner
   Bros., 1980
THE GREAT MUPPET CAPER   Universal/AFD, 1981
THE DARK CRYSTAL   Universal/AFD, 1982

REGINALD H. MORRIS, CSC
Address: 255 Bamburgh Circle, #308, Scarborough,
   Ontario M1W 3T6, 416/497-9266 or 213/849-2363

BLACK CHRISTMAS   Warner Bros., 1975
THE FOOD OF THE GODS   American
   International, 1976
SHADOW OF THE HAWK   Columbia, 1976,
   w/John Holbrook
SECOND WIND   Health And Entertainment Corp. of
   America, 1976
EMPIRE OF THE ANTS   American International, 1977
WELCOME TO BLOOD CITY   EMI, 1977
MARIE-ANNE   1978
MURDER BY DECREE   Avco Embassy, 1979
THE SHAPE OF THINGS TO COME   Film
   Ventures International, 1979
MIDDLE AGE CRAZY   20th Century Fox, 1980
TRIBUTE   20th Century Fox, 1980
PHOBIA   Paramount, 1981
PORKY'S   20th Century Fox, 1982
MURDER BY PHONE   New World, 1982
LOVE   Velvet Films, 1982, shared credit
PORKY'S II: THE NEXT DAY   20th Century Fox, 1983
A CHRISTMAS STORY   MGM/UA, 1983
TURK 182   20th Century Fox, 1985
LOOSE CANNONS   Tri-Star, 1990
LADY IN A CORNER (TF)   1990

PETER MOSS*
West Coast Card
Agent: Smith Gosnell Nicholson & Associates -
   Pacific Palisades, 213/459-0307

FLASHPOINT   Tri-Star, 1984
STRANDED (TF)   Tim Flack Productions/
   Columbia TV, 1986

ROBBY MULLER
Agent: Smith Gosnell Nicholson & Associates -
   Pacific Palisades, 213/459-0307

SUMMER IN THE CITY (DEDICATED TO
   THE KINKS)   1970
THE GOALIE'S ANXIETY AT THE PENALTY KICK
   Bauer International, 1972
THE SCARLET LETTER   Bauer International, 1973
ALICE IN THE CITIES   New Yorker, 1974
THE WRONG MOVE   New Yorker, 1975
KINGS OF THE ROAD   Bauer International, 1976
THE AMERICAN FRIEND   New Yorker, 1977
MYSTERIES   Cine Vog, 1979
SAINT JACK   New World, 1979
HONEYSUCKLE ROSE   Warner Bros., 1980
THEY ALL LAUGHED   20th Century Fox, 1981
THE GLASS CELL   Roxy/Solaris, 1981
LES TRICHEURS   Films du Galatee, 1983
REPO MAN   Universal, 1984
PARIS, TEXAS   20th Century Fox, 1984
BODY ROCK   New World, 1984
CLASS ENEMY   Teleculture, 1984

FINNEGAN BEGIN AGAIN (CTF)   HBO Premiere
   Films/Zenith Productions/Jennie & Co. Film
   Productions, 1985
TO LIVE AND DIE IN L.A.   MGM/UA, 1985
LONGSHOT   Orion, 1986
DOWN BY LAW   Island Pictures, 1986
THE BELIEVERS   Orion, 1987
BARFLY   Cannon, 1987
THE LITTLE DEVIL   Columbia, 1988
MYSTERY TRAIN   Orion, 1989

BRIANNE MURPHY, ASC
FATSO   20th Century Fox, 1980
HIGHWAY TO HEAVEN (TVS) ☆   1984
MY DAD CAN'T BE CRAZY...CAN HE? (TF)   Rosebud
   Productions, 1989
IN THE BEST INTERESTS OF THE CHILD (TF)
   Papazian-Hirsch Entertainment, 1990

FRED MURPHY
Agent: The Gersh Agency, Inc., Beverly Hills -
   213/274-6611, New York - 212/997-1818

NOT A PRETTY PICTURE   Films Inc., 1976
THE GARDNER'S SON (TF)   RIP/Filmhaus, 1977
GIRLFRIENDS   Warner Bros., 1978
LOCAL COLOR   1978
HEARTLAND   Levitt-Pickman, 1979
TELL ME A RIDDLE   Filmways, 1980
IMPOSTERS   First Run Features, 1981
Q   United Film Distribution, 1982
THE STATE OF THINGS   Gracy City, 1983,
   w/Henri Alekan
TOUCHED   Lorimar Productions/Wildwood
   Partners, 1983
EDDIE AND THE CRUISERS   Embassy, 1983
KEY EXCHANGE   20th Century Fox, 1985
THE TRIP TO BOUNTIFUL   Island Pictures/Film
   Dallas, 1985
DEATH OF AN ANGEL   20th Century Fox, 1985
HOOSIERS   Orion, 1986
THE DEAD   Vestron, 1987
BEST SELLER   Orion, 1987
FIVE CORNERS   Cineplex Odeon, 1987
FRESH HORSES   WEG, 1988
FULL MOON IN BLUE WATER   Trans World
   Entertainment, 1988
NIGHT GAME   Trans World Entertainment, 1989
ENEMIES, A LOVE STORY   20th Century Fox, 1989
THE FINAL DAYS (TF)   The Samuels Film
   Company, 1990
FUNNY ABOUT LOVE   Paramount, 1990
SCENES FROM A MALL   Buena Vista, 1991

MICHAEL D. MURPHY
COACH   Crown International, 1978
SILENT SCREAM   American Cinema, 1980,
   w/David Shore
BEACH GIRLS   Crown International, 1982
MIRRORS   First American, 1984

PAUL MURPHY, ACS
Agent: Smith Gosnell Nicholson & Associates -
   Pacific Palisades, 213/459-0307

DEAD END DRIVE-IN   New World, 1986
BLISS   New World, 1986
EMERALD CITY   Limelight Productions, 1989
I'LL TAKE ROMANCE (TF)   New World Television, 1990
BLUE DESERT   Neo Films, 1991

DAVID MYERS
THE MYSTERIOUS MONSTERS   Schick Sunn
    Classics, 1976
WELCOME TO L.A.   United Artists/Lions Gate, 1977
RENALDO & CLARA   Circuit Films, 1978
FM   Universal, 1978
THE LAST WALTZ   United Artists, 1978
    (Additional DP w/Bobby Byrne, Laszlo Kovacs,
    Hiro Narita, Michael Watkins & Vilmos Zsigmond)
THE SECRET LIFE OF PLANTS   Paramount, 1978,
    w/Ghislain Cloquet & Peter Smokler
SAMMY STOPS THE WORLD (FD)   Elkins, 1979
DIE LAUGHING   Orion/Warner Bros., 1980
ROADIE   United Artists, 1980
ZOOT SUIT   Universal, 1982
HUMAN HIGHWAY   1982
DEADLY FORCE   Embassy, 1983, w/Norman Leigh
GOSPEL (FD)   20th Century Fox, 1984
UFORIA   Universal, 1985
HARD TRAVELING   New World, 1986

ASAKAZU NAKAI
RAN ★   1985, w/Takao Saito & Masaharu Ueda

ARMANDO NANNUZZI
LA CAGE AUX FOLLES II   United Artists, 1981
LA NUIT DE VARENNES   Triumph, 1983
NANA   Cannon, 1983
BEYOND GOOD AND EVIL   Films Inc., 1984
STEPHEN KING'S SILVER BULLET   Paramount, 1985
MAXIMUM OVERDRIVE   DEG, 1986
THE CALLER   Empire Pictures, 1987
FRANKENSTEIN UNBOUND   Mount Company/
    20th Century-Fox, 1990, w/Michael Scott

DANIELE NANNUZZI
YOUNG TOSCANINI   Carthago Films/Canal Plus/
    FR3/La Sept/Italian International Pics/RAI, 1988
BUY AND CELL   Empire Pictures, 1988

HIRO NARITA
Agent: The Gersh Agency, Inc. - Beverly Hills,
    213/274-6611

FAREWELL TO MANZANAR (TF)   Korty Films/
    Universal TV, 1976
THE LAST WALTZ   United Artists, 1978
    (Additional DP w/Bobby Byrne, Laszlo Kovacs,
    David Myers, Michael Watkins & Vilmos Zsigmond)
NEVER CRY WOLF   Buena Vista, 1983
PRINCE JACK   Castle Hill Productions, 1984
GO TELL IT ON THE MOUNTAIN (TF)   Learning in
    Focus, 1984
SOLOMON NORTHRUP'S ODYSSEY (TF)   Past
    America Inc., 1985
SYLVESTER   Columbia, 1985
FIRE WITH FIRE   Paramount, 1986
NO MAN'S LAND   Orion, 1987
HONEY, I SHRUNK THE KIDS   Buena Vista, 1989
MOTHERS, DAUGHTERS AND LOVERS (TF)   Katz-
    Huyck-Films Productions/NBC Productions, 1989

ANDRE NEAU
THE RETURN OF MARTIN GUERRE   European
    International, 1983
WAITING FOR THE MOON   Skouras Pictures, 1987

MICHAEL NEGRIN
TOUCH OF A STRANGER   Raven-Star Pictures, 1990
DICE RULES   Seven Arts, 1991

SOL NEGRIN, ASC
East & West Coast cards
Agent: Bob Shapiro, 213/859-8877
Address: 873 Custer St., Valley Stream, NY 11580,
    516/825-2406

AMAZING GRACE   UA, 1974
A QUESTION OF ANSWERS (TF) ☆   Universal Pictures
    Television, 1975
THE LAST TENANT (TF)   Titus Productions, 1978
MORE THAN FRIENDS (TF)   Reiner-Mishkin
    Productions/Columbia TV, 1978
...AND YOUR NAME IS JONAH (TF)   Charles Fries
    Productions, 1979
WOMEN AT WEST POINT (TF)   Green-Epstein
    Productions/Alan Sacks Productions, 1979
NERO WOLF (Pilot)   1980
O'MALLEY (Pilot)   1981
REPEAT PREFORMANCE (TF)   NBC Productions,
    1989 (New York segments)
BLOODRUSH   *PRESENCE OF EVIL*   Brisun
    Entertainment, 1990

ALEX NEPOMNIASCHY
Agent: Grace Lyons Management - Los Angeles,
    213/655-5100

WANTED DEAD OR ALIVE   New World, 1986
LAST RESORT   Concorde, 1986, w/Stephen Katz
POLTERGEIST III   MGM/UA, 1988
LISA   MGM/UA, 1990
ONE POINT OF VIEW   O.P.V. Productions, 1990
AFTER THE SHOCK (CTF)   Wilshire Court
    Productions, 1990
MURDEROUS VISION (CTF)   Wilshire Court
    Productions, 1991

TOM NEUWIRTH
LADY BEWARE   Scotti Bros., 1987
BRIDGE TO SILENCE (TF)   Fries Entertainment, 1989
A KILLER AMONG US (TF)   Dave Bell Associates Inc.
    Productions, 1990
FALL FROM GRACE (TF)   NBC Productions, 1990
THIS GUN FOR HIRE (CTF)   BBK Productions, 1991

ROBERT C. NEW
Agent: Camera Masters - Venice, 213/306-0810

PROM NIGHT   Avco Embassy, 1980
SPRING FEVER   Comworld, 1983,
    w/Christopher Bonniere & Paul Mitchrick
THE ZOO GANG   New World, 1985
VENDETTA   Concorde, 1986
NIGHT OF THE CREEPS   Tri-Star, 1986

JOHN C. NEWBY
DEAD WOMEN IN LINGERIE   Seagate Films/Monarch
    Home Video, 1990

Ne

CINEMATOGRAPHERS
PRODUCTION
DESIGNERS,
COSTUME
DESIGNERS AND
FILM EDITORS
GUIDE

CINEMATOGRAPHERS

Ne

CINEMATOGRAPHERS
PRODUCTION
DESIGNERS,
COSTUME
DESIGNERS and
FILM EDITORS
GUIDE

C
I
N
E
M
A
T
O
G
R
A
P
H
E
R
S

ANTHONY NEWTON
RUSSIAN TERMINATOR   Areno Home Video, 1991

YURI NEYMAN
Agent: Dattner & Associates - Beverly Hills,
    213/653-4188

LIQUID SKY   Cinevista, 1983
D.O.A.   Buena Vista, 1988
GINGER ALE AFTERNOON   Skouras Pictures, 1989
FRAMED (CTF)   HBO Pictures, 1990
BACK IN THE USSR   Largo Entertainment, 1991

MARK NORRIS
HANGFIRE   Motion Picture Corporation of
    America, 1991

DANNY NOWAK
Home: 103-857 Beatty St., Vancouver, B.C., V6B2M6,
    604/669-3456

EMPIRE OF THE ASH III   North American
    Pictures, 1988
FLESH GORDON MEETS THE COSMIC
    CHEERLEADERS   Maurice Smith
    Productions, 1990
SILHOUETTE   North American Pictures, 1990

BRUNO NUYTTEN
THE BRONTE SISTERS   Gaumont, 1979
FRENCH POSTCARDS   Paramount, 1979
BRUBAKER   20th Century Fox, 1980
LIKE A TURTLE ON ITS BACK   New Line
    Cinema, 1981
UNDER SUSPICION   *GARDE A VUE*
    Fred Baker, 1982
POSSESSION   Limelight International, 1983
LIFE IS A BED OF ROSES   Spectrafilm, 1984
DETECTIVE   Spectrafilm, 1985
JEAN DE FLORETTE   Orion Classics, 1987
MANON OF THE SPRING   Orion Classics, 1987

SVEN NYKVIST, ASC
CRIES AND WHISPERS ★★   New World, 1973
THE TERRORISTS *RANSOM*   20th Century
    Fox, 1975
BLACK MOON   20th Century Fox 1975
THE MAGIC FLUTE   Surrogate, 1975
FACE TO FACE   Paramount, 1976
THE TENANT   Paramount, 1976
THE SERPENT'S EGG   United Artists, 1977
AUTUMN SONATA   New World, 1978
KING OF THE GYPSIES   Paramount, 1978
HURRICANE   Paramount, 1979
STARTING OVER   Paramount, 1979
FROM THE LIFE OF THE MARIONETTES
    Universal/AFD, 1980
WILLIE AND PHIL   20th Century Fox, 1980
THE POSTMAN ALWAYS RINGS TWICE
    Paramount, 1981
CANNERY ROW   MGM/United Artists, 1982
FANNY & ALEXANDER ★   Embassy, 1983
STAR 80   The Ladd Company/Warner Bros., 1983
SWANN IN LOVE   Orion Classics, 1984
AFTER THE REHEARSAL   Triumph, 1984
AGNES OF GOD   Columbia, 1985
THE UNBEARABLE LIGHTNESS OF BEING ★
    Orion, 1988

ANOTHER WOMAN   Orion, 1988
NEW YORK STORIES ("Oedipus Wrecks")   Buena
Vista, 1989
CRIMES AND MISDEMEANORS   Orion, 1989

RENE OHASHI, CSC
Address: 564 Palmerston Ave., Toronto, Ontario
    M6G 2P7, 416/536-4680

SWEET LORRAINE   Angelika Films, 1987
SHADOW DANCING   Shapiro Glickenhaus, 1988
MILLENNIUM   20th Century Fox, 1989

DARYN OKADA
Agent: Grace Lyons Management - Los Angeles,
    213/655-5100

WITNESS TO A KILLING   Taprobane Pictures, 1987
PHANTASM II   Universal, 1988
SURVIVAL QUEST   Starway International/
    MGM/UA, 1989
BLIND VENGEANCE (CTF)   MCA TV Entertainment/
    Spanish Trail, 1990
BORIS & NATASHA   MCEG, 1990

THOMAS OLGEIRSON
UNDER COVER (TF)   Sacret/Paint Rock
    Productions, 1991

MARTY OLLSTEIN
PENITENTIARY   Jerry Gross Organization, 1980
PENITENTIARY III   Cannon, 1987

WOODY OMENS, ASC
Agent: Valentine, 818/982-8289
Address: 6647 Morella Ave., North Hollywood, CA
    91606, 213/876-4040

ISHI, THE LAST OF HIS TRIBE (TF)   Edward & Mildred
    Lewis Productions, 1978
STONE (TF)   Stephen J. Cannell Productions, 1979
THE MAN IN THE SANTA CLAUS SUIT (TF)   Dick Clark
    Productions, 1979
MADAME X (TF)   Levenback-Riche Productions/
    Universal TV, 1981
HISTORY OF THE WORLD, PART 1   20th
    Century Fox, 1981
FIRE ON THE MOUNTAIN (TF)   Bonnard
    Productions, 1982
MAGNUM, P.I. (TF) ☆   1981
FACTS OF LIFE GOES TO PARIS (TF)
    Embassy TV, 1982
GRACE KELLY (TF)   The Kota Company/
    Embassy TV, 1983
POLICEWOMAN CENTERFOLD (TF)   Moonlight
    Productions, 1983
WHY ME? (TF)   Lorimar Productions, 1984
THE RED LIGHT STING (TF)   1984
LIME STREET (Pilot)   1985

EVERGREEN (MS) ☆ Edgar J. Scherick Associates/
    Metromedia Producers Corporation, 1985
BLADE IN HONG KONG (TF) Terry Becker
    Productions, 1985
AN EARLY FROST (TF) ☆☆ NBC Productions, 1985
HEART OF THE CITY (Pilot) ☆☆ 1986
I SAW WHAT YOU DID (TF) ☆☆ Universal, 1988
COMING TO AMERICA Paramount, 1988
HARLEM NIGHTS Paramount, 1989

MIROSLAV ONDRICEK

Agent: The Gersh Agency, Inc., Beverly Hills -
    213/274-6611, New York - 212/997-1818

IF... Paramount, 1969
TAKING OFF Universal, 1971
SLAUGHTERHOUSE-FIVE Universal, 1971
O LUCKY MAN! Warner Bros., 1973
HAIR United Artists, 1979
RAGTIME ★ Paramount, 1981
THE WORLD ACCORDING TO GARP Warner
    Bros., 1982
THE DIVINE EMMA United Artists Classics, 1983
SILKWOOD 20th Century Fox, 1983
AMADEUS ★ Orion, 1984
HEAVEN HELP US Tri-Star, 1985
F/X Orion, 1986
BIG SHOTS 20th Century Fox, 1987
FUNNY FARM Warner Bros., 1988
VALMONT Orion, 1989
AWAKENINGS Columbia, 1990

PAUL ONORATO*

NABET - Australia
Agent: Smith Gosnell Nicholson & Associates -
    Pacific Palisades, 213/459-0307

SIDECAR RACERS Universal, 1975
ABBA - THE MOVIE Warner Bros., 1977
ALL AT SEA (TF) 1977
TIM Satori, 1979
IN SELF DEFENSE (TF) Leonard Hill Films, 1987
TRICKS OF THE TRADE (TF) Leonard Hill
    Films, 1988
THE STORY OF THE BEACH BOYS: SUMMER
    DREAMS (TF) Leonard Hill Films, 1990
TAKEN AWAY (TF) Hart, Thomas & Berlin
    Productions, 1990
DEADLY DESIRE (CTF) Skylark Films, 1991

RON ORIEUX

ANYTHING TO SURVIVE (TF) B.C. Films/ATL
    Productions, 1990
BURNING BRIDGES (TF) Lorimar TV/Andrea
    Baynes Productions, 1990
SMALL SACRIFICES (TF) Fries Entertainment/
    Motown Productions/Louis Rudolph Films, 1990
THE LADY FORGETS (TF) Leonard Hill Films, 1990
DEADLY INTENTIONS...AGAIN? (TF) Green
    Epstein Productions, 1991

P

JERRY PANTZER

BOOK OF DAYS House Foundation for the Arts/
    Tatge-Lasseur Productions, 1990

PETER PAO

THE KILLER Circle Releasing, 1991,
    w/Wong Wing Hang

PHEDON PAPAMICHAEL

AFTER MIDNIGHT High Bar Pictures/MGM/UA, 1989
STREETS Concorde, 1990
BODY CHEMISTRY Concorde, 1990

ANDREW PARKE

THE FINAL SANCTION Action International Pictures/AIP
    Home Video, 1990

DAVID PARKER

MALCOLM Vestron, 1986
RIKKY AND PETE MGM/United Artists, 1988

PHIL PARMET

SREET HUNTER Street Hunter Production/21st Century
    Films/DGP Video, 1990
FATAL MISSION Funahara, 1990

ROBERT PAYNTER, BSC

THE BIG SLEEP United Artists, 1978
FIREPOWER AFD, 1979
SUPERMAN II Warner Bros., 1980,
    w/Geoffrey Unsworth
AN AMERICAN WEREWOLF IN LONDON
    Universal, 1981
THE FINAL CONFLICT 20th Century Fox, 1981,
    w/Phil Meheux
SUPERMAN III Warner Bros., 1983
TRADING PLACES Paramount, 1983
CURTAINS Jensen Farley Pictures, 1983, w/Fred Guthe
THE MUPPETS TAKE MANHATTAN Tri-Star, 1984
SCREAM FOR HELP Lorimar, 1984
NATIONAL LAMPOON'S EUROPEAN VACATION
    Warner Bros., 1985
INTO THE NIGHT Universal, 1985
SPIES LIKE US Warner Bros., 1985
LITTLE SHOP OF HORRORS The Geffen Company/
    Warner Bros., 1986
WHEN THE WHALES CAME 20th Century Fox, 1989
STRIKE IT RICH Millimeter Films, 1990

DANIEL PEARL

ZAPPED! Embassy, 1982
INVADERS FROM MARS Cannon, 1986
FULL MOON HIGH Orion, 1986
IT'S ALIVE III: ISLAND OF THE ALIVE Warner
    Bros., 1987
AMAZON WOMEN ON THE MOON Universal, 1987
HIDING OUT DEG, 1987
DEADLY ILLUSION CineTel Films, 1988

Pe

CINEMATOGRAPHERS
PRODUCTION
DESIGNERS,
COSTUME
DESIGNERS AND
FILM EDITORS
GUIDE

C
I
N
E
M
A
T
O
G
R
A
P
H
E
R
S

Pe

CINEMATOGRAPHERS
PRODUCTION
DESIGNERS,
COSTUME
DESIGNERS AND
FILM EDITORS
GUIDE

C
I
N
E
M
A
T
O
G
R
A
P
H
E
R
S

70

EDWARD J. PEI
MASTERS OF MENACE   CineTel Films/New
Line Cinema, 1990
WATCHERS II   Concorde, 1990

JOE PENNELLA
TO MY DAUGHTER   Zacs Productions/Nugget
Entertainment/Warner Bros. TV, 1990
HAPPY TOGETHER   Apollo Pictures/Borde
Releasing, 1990

JULIAN PENNEY
TRAVELLING NORTH   Cineplex Odeon, 1987
THE EVERLASTING SECRET FAMILY   International
Film Exchange, 1990

JEAN PENZER
GET OUT YOUR HANDKERCHIEFS   New Line
Cinema, 1978
BUFFET FROID   Parafrance, 1979
MY BEST FRIEND'S GIRL   European
International, 1984
THE AFRICAN   AMFC, 1986
MENAGE   Cinecom, 1986

PEPIN
LIVING TO DIE   PM Entertainment, 1990
REPO JAKE   PM Home Video, 1991

JAMES PERGOLA, ASC
THUNDER AND LIGHTNING   20th Century Fox, 1977
HOT STUFF   Columbia, 1979
HARDLY WORKING   20th Century Fox, 1981
NOBODY'S PERFEKT   Columbia, 1981
LOVE CHILD   The Ladd Company/Warner Bros., 1982
SMOKEY AND THE BANDIT - PART 3
Universal, 1983
WET GOLD (TF)   Telepictures Productions, 1984
THE TOUGHEST MAN IN THE WORLD (TF)
Guber-Peters Productions/Centerpoint
Productions, 1984
ON OUR WAY (Pilot)   1985
WHAT COMES AROUND   W.O. Associates, 1986
POLICE ACADEMY 5: ASSIGNMENT MIAMI BEACH
Warner Bros., 1988
HOW TO MURDER A MILLIONAIRE (TF)   Robert
Greenwald Films, 1990
GUESS WHO'S COMING FOR CHRISTMAS (TF)
The Poison Company/Fox Unicorn Inc./Corapeake
Productions, 1990

MARK PERRY
DEAD SPACE   Concorde, 1991

JORGEN PERSSON
MY LIFE AS A DOG   Skouras Pictures, 1987

DONALD PETERMAN, ASC
Agent: The Gersh Agency, Inc., Beverly Hills -
213/274-6611, New York - 212/997-1818

WHEN A STRANGER CALLS   Columbia, 1979
KING OF THE MOUNTAIN   Universal, 1981
RICH AND FAMOUS   MGM/United Artists, 1981
YOUNG DOCTORS IN LOVE   20th Century Fox, 1982
KISS ME GOODBYE   20th Century Fox, 1982
FLASHDANCE ★   Paramount, 1983
SPLASH   Buena Vista, 1984

MASS APPEAL   Universal, 1984
BEST DEFENSE   Paramount, 1984
COCOON   20th Century Fox, 1985
AMERICAN FLYERS   Warner Bros., 1985
GUNG HO   Paramount, 1986
STAR TREK IV: THE VOYAGE HOME ★
Paramount, 1986
PLANES, TRAINS & AUTOMOBILES   Paramount, 1987
SHE'S HAVING A BABY   Paramount, 1988
SHE'S OUT OF CONTROL   Columbia, 1989

ALEX PHILLIPS, ASC
THE FOOL KILLER   Allied Artists, 1965
BUCK AND THE PREACHER   Columbia, 1972
THE SAVAGE IS LOOSE   Campbell Devon, 1974
BRING ME THE HEAD OF ALFREDO GARCIA
United Artists, 1974
MAN FRIDAY   Avco Embassy, 1975
THE DEVIL'S RAIN   Bryanston, 1975
FOXTROT   New World, 1976
THE GREAT SCOUT & CATHOUSE THURSDAY
American International, 1976
LOS ALBANILES   *THE BRICKLAYERS*   1977
GOOD LUCK, MISS WYCKOFF   Bel Air/Gradison, 1979
SUNBURN   Paramount, 1979
SURVIVAL RUN   Film Ventures International, 1980
FADE TO BLACK   American Cinema, 1980
WOLF LAKE   Filmcorp Distribution, 1981
CABOBLANCO   Avco Embassy, 1981
HIGH RISK   American Cinema, 1981
DEMONOID   American Playhouse, 1981
SURF II   Arista, 1983
SORCERESS   New World, 1983
TORCHLIGHT   International Film Marketing, 1984
BLAME IT ON THE NIGHT   Tri-Star, 1984
LITTLE TREASURE   Tri-Star, 1985
LA CHEVRE   European Classics, 1985
TO KILL A STRANGER   1985
KING SOLOMON'S MINES   Cannon, 1985
FIREWALKER   Cannon, 1986
MURPHY'S LAW   Cannon, 1986
ALLAN QUATERMAIN AND THE LOST CITY OF GOLD,
Cannon, 1987, w/Fred Elmes
NUMBER ONE WITH A BULLET   Cannon, 1987
BORN IN EAST L.A.   Universal, 1987
THE TROUBLE WITH SPIES   DEG, 1987

FRANK PHILLIPS, ASC
ESCAPE TO WITCH MOUNTAIN   Buena Vista, 1975
THE APPLE DUMPLING GANG   Buena Vista, 1975
NO DEPOSIT, NO RETURN   Buena Vista, 1976
GUS   Buena Vista, 1976
TREASURE OF MATECUMBE   Buena Vista, 1976
THE SHAGGY D.A.   Buena Vista, 1976
PETE'S DRAGON   Buena Vista, 1977
RETURN FROM WITCH MOUNTAIN   Buena Vista, 1978
HOT LEAD AND COLD FEET   Buena Vista, 1978
GOIN' COCONUTS   Osmond Distribution, 1978
THE APPLE DUMPLING GANG RIDES AGAIN
Buena Vista, 1979
THE BLACK HOLE ★   Buena Vista, 1979
MIDNIGHT MADNESS   Buena Vista, 1980
HERBIE GOES BANANAS   Buena Vista, 1980
GOING APE!   Paramount, 1981

ROBERTO D'ETTORRE PIAZZOLI
SONNY BOY   Triumph Releasing, 1990
LAMBADA   Cannon Pictures/Warner Bros., 1990

TONY PIERCE-ROBERTS
MOONLIGHTING   Universal Classics, 1982
KIPPERBANG   MGM/UA Classics, 1984
THE COLD ROOM (TF)   Jethro Films/Mark Forstater
    Productions, 1984
A PRIVATE FUNCTION   Island Alive, 1985
A ROOM WITH A VIEW ★   Cinecom, 1986
TINKER, TAILOR, SOLDIER, SPY (TF)   BBC/
    Paramount TV, 1979
CAUGHT ON A TRAIN (TF)   BBC, 1980
THE GOOD SOLDIER (TF)   Granada TV, 1983
A VOYAGE ROUND MY FATHER (TF)   Thames TV/
    D.L. Taffner Ltd., 1983
A TIGER'S TALE   Atlantic Releasing
    Corporation, 1988
OUT COLD   Hemdale, 1989
SLAVES OF NEW YORK   Tri-Star, 1989
MR. & MRS. BRIDGE   Cineplex Odeon/
    Miramax Films, 1990
WHITE FANG   Buena Vista, 1991

KELVIN PIKE
Agent: London Management, 235/241 Regent Street -
    London, W1R 7AG, 01-493-1610

THE DRESSER   Columbia, 1983
BAD MEDICINE   20th Century Fox, 1985
GULAG (CTF)   Lorimar Productions/HBO Premiere
    Films, 1985
ANNA KARENINA (TF)   Rastar Productions/Colgems
    Productions, 1985
A NEW LIFE   Paramount, 1988
APPRENTICE TO MURDER   New World, 1988
A DRY WHITE SEASON   MGM/UA, 1989,
    w/Pierre-William Glenn
BETSY'S WEDDING   Silver Screen Partners IV/
    Touchstone/Buena Vista, 1990

TOMISLAV (TOM) PINTER
THE WIDOWHOOD OF KAROLINA ZASTER
    Yugoslav Film Releasing, 1976
MONTENEGRO   Atlantic Releasing Corporation, 1981
PETRIA'S WREATH   New Yorker, 1983
TWILIGHT TIME   MGM/UA, 1983
TRANSYLVANIA 6-5000   New World, 1985
IN THE JAWS OF LIFE   1987
THE GIRL   Shapiro Entertainment, 1987
CRUSOE   Island Pictures/Virgin Vision, 1988
MANIFESTO   Cannon, 1989
THAT SUMMER OF WHITE ROSES   Amy
    International/Jadram Film, 1989

LARRY PIZER
Phone: 212/246-8484

MORGAN!   *MORGAN: A SUITABLE CASE FOR
    TREATMENT*   Cinema 5, 1966
OUR MOTHER'S HOUSE   MGM, 1967
ISADORA   Universal, 1969
THE OPTIMISTS   *THE OPTIMISTS OF NINE ELMS*
    Paramount, 1973
PHANTOM OF THE PARADISE   20th
    Century Fox, 1974
WELCOME TO MY NIGHTMARE (FD)   Warner
    Bros., 1976
THE FURY   20th Century Fox, 1978
THE EUROPEANS   Levitt-Pickman, 1979
STONE (TF)   Stephen J. Cannell Productions/
    Universal TV, 1979

MY OLD MAN (TF)   Zeitman-McNichol-Halmi
    Productions, 1979
PAUL'S CASE (TF)   Learning in Focus, 1979
THE SKY IS GREY (TF)   Learning in Focus, 1980
A PRIVATE BATTLE (TF)   Procter & Gamble
    Productions/Robert Halmi, Inc., 1980
CATTLE ANNIE AND LITTLE BRITCHES
    Universal, 1981
THE GIFT OF LOVE (TF)   CBS Entertainment, 1982
DENMARK VESSEY'S REBELLION (TF)
    WPBT-Miami, 1982
TIMERIDER   Jensen Farley Pictures, 1983
THE CLAIRVOYANT   *THE KILLING HOUR*   Jensen
    Farley Pictures, 1983
FOUND MONEY (TF)   Cypress Point Productions/
    Warner Bros. TV, 1983
MURDER IN COWETA COUNTY (TF)   Telecom
    Entertainment/The International Picture
    Show Co., 1983
PHANTOM OF THE OPERA (TF)   Robert Halmi
    Productions, 1983
SVENGALI (TF)   Robert Halmi Productions, 1983
GRACE QUIGLEY   Cannon, 1984
TOO SCARED TO SCREAM   The Movie Store, 1984
THREE SOVEREIGNS FOR SARAH (TF)   Night
    Owl Productions, 1985
WHERE ARE THE CHILDREN   Columbia, 1986
DARK HOLIDAY (TF)   1989
MY BOYFRIEND'S BACK (TF)   1989
BLIND WITNESS (TF)   Victoria Principal Productions/
    King Phoenix Productions, 1990
SPARKS: THE PRICE OF PASSION (TF)   King Phoenix
    Entertainment/Victoria Principal Productions/
    Shadowplay Films, 1990

MARK PLUMMER
TWO MOON JUNCTION   Lorimar, 1988
AFTER DARK, MY SWEET   Avenue, 1990

CRISTIANO POGANY
JUST ANOTHER SECRET (CTF)   Blair Communications/
    Taurusfilm/F.F.S. Productions, 1990
A CASUALTY OF WAR (CTF)   Blair Communications/
    Taurusfilm/F.F.S. Productions, 1990

GABOR POGANY
JUDGMENT IN BERLIN   New Line Cinema, 1988
THE BIG BLUE   Columbia, 1988

GENE POLITO, ASC
TRACKDOWN   United Artists, 1976
UP IN SMOKE   Paramount, 1978
THE BAD NEWS BEARS GO TO JAPAN
    Paramount, 1978

BILL POPE
DARKMAN   Darkman Productions/Universal, 1990

DICK POPE
THE GIRL IN THE PICTURE   Samuel Goldwyn
    Company, 1986
COMING UP ROSES   Skouras Pictures, 1987
WONDERLAND   Vestron, 1989

GIDEON PORATH
HARRY'S MACHINE   Cannon, 1986
AVENGING FORCE   Cannon, 1986
DEATHWISH 4: THE CRACKDOWN   Cannon, 1987

Po

CINEMATOGRAPHERS
PRODUCTION
DESIGNERS,
COSTUME
DESIGNERS AND
FILM EDITORS
GUIDE

C
I
N
E
M
A
T
O
G
R
A
P
H
E
R
S

Po

CINEMATOGRAPHERS
PRODUCTION
DESIGNERS,
COSTUME
DESIGNERS AND
FILM EDITORS
GUIDE

C
I
N
E
M
A
T
O
G
R
A
P
H
E
R
S

AMERICAN NINJA 2: THE CONFRONTATION
Cannon, 1987
MESSENGER OF DEATH   Cannon, 1988
SHE WAS MARKED FOR MURDER (TF)   Litke/Jack
Grossbart Prods., 1988
KINJITE: FORBIDDEN SUBJECTS   Cannon, 1989
83 HOURS 'TIL DAWN (TF)   Consolidated
Entertainment, 1990
THE FIFTH MONKEY   Columbia, 1990

STEPHEN L. POSEY

EMMA MAE   Pro-International, 1976
PENITENTIARY II   MGM/UA, 1982
THE HOUSE WHERE DEATH LIVES   New
American, 1982
THE SLUMBER PARTY MASSACRE   Santa
Fe, 1982
MODERN DAY HOUDINI   Mid America
Promotions, 1983
SAVAGE STREETS   MPM, 1984
HELLHOLE   Arkoff International, 1985
FRIDAY THE 13TH - A NEW BEGINNING
Paramount, 1985
BLOODY BIRTHDAY   Judica Productions, 1986
WELCOME TO 18   American Distribution Group, 1986
THREE FOR THE ROAD   New Century/Vista, 1987

STEVEN B. POSTER, ASC*

West Coast, MidWest & Canadian Cards
Agent: Smith Gosnell Nicholson & Associates - Pacific
Palisades, 213/459-0307

THE GRASS IS ALWAYS GREENER OVER THE
SEPTIC TANK (TF)   Joe Hamilton
Productions, 1978
THE NIGHT RIDER (TF)   Stephen J. Cannell
Productions/Universal TV, 1979
BEGGERMAN, THIEF (TF)   Universal TV, 1980
COWARD OF THE COUNTY (TF)   Kraco
Productions, 1981
BLOOD BEACH   Jensen Farley Pictures, 1981
DEAD AND BURIED   Avco Embassy, 1981
THE CRADLE WILL FALL (TF)   Cates Films Inc./
Procter & Gamble Productions, 1983
SPRING BREAK   Columbia, 1983
STRANGE BREW   MGM/UA, 1983
TESTAMENT   Paramount, 1983
THE NEW KIDS   Columbia, 1985
THE HEAVENLY KID   Orion, 1985
BLUE CITY   Paramount, 1986
THE BOY WHO COULD FLY   20th Century Fox,
1986, w/Adam Holender
SOMEONE TO WATCH OVER ME   Columbia, 1987
I'LL TAKE MANHATTAN (MS)   Steve Krantz
Productions, 1987
ALOHA SUMMER   Spectrafilm, 1988
BIG TOP PEE-WEE   Paramount, 1988
NEXT OF KIN   Warner Bros., 1989
OPPORTUNITY KNOCKS   Universal, 1990
ROCKY V   Chartoff-Winkler/MGM/UA, 1990
LIFE STINKS   MGM, 1991

ROGER PRATT

THE SENDER   Paramount, 1982
MEANTIME   Central Pictures, 1983
BRAZIL   Universal, 1985
MONA LISA   Island Pictures, 1986
CONSUMING PASSIONS   Samuel Goldwyn Co., 1988
HIGH HOPES   Skouras Pictures, 1989

BATMAN   Warner Bros., 1989
PARIS BY NIGHT   Cineplex Odeon, 1989
SCOOP (TF)   London Weekend TV, 1990

JEFF PREISS

BROKEN NOSES (FD)   Weber/Bush, 1987

JACK PRIESTLEY, ASC

Agent: The Miller Agency - Santa Clarita, 818/843-7335

NO WAY TO TREAT A LADY   Paramount, 1968
THE SUBJECT WAS ROSES   MGM, 1968
STILETTO   Avco Embassy, 1969
WHERE'S POPPA?   United Artists, 1970
BORN TO WIN   United Artists, 1971
ACROSS 110TH ST.   1972
THE MIDNIGHT MAN   Universal, 1974
THE FIRST DEADLY SIN   Filmways, 1980
ROCKSHOW (FD)   Miramax, 1980
LADY BLUE (TF)   David Gerber Productions/
MGM-UA TV, 1985
A MAN CALLED HAWK (Pilot)   1989

TOM PRIESTLEY, JR.*

East Coast Card
Agent: Smith Gosnell Nicholson & Associates -
Pacific Palisades, 213/459-0307

BEAT STREET   Orion, 1984
WISEGUY (TF)   Stephen J. Cannell Productions, 1990

ROBERT PRIMES*

West Coast Card
Agent: Smith Gosnell Nicholson & Associates -
Pacific Palisades, 213/459-0307

DR. HECKYL AND MR. HYPE   Cannon, 1980
THEY CALL ME BRUCE?   Artists Releasing Corporation/
Film Ventures International, 1982
16 DAYS OF GLORY (FD)   Paramount, 1986, w/others
CRIMEWAVE   Columbia, 1985
A GREAT WALL   Orion Classics, 1986, w/Peter Stein
BIRD ON A WIRE   Badham-Cohen/Interscope/
Universal, 1990
THE HARD WAY   Badham-Cohen/Universal, 1991

FRANK PRINZI

Agent: The Gersh Agency, Inc., Beverly Hills -
213/274-6611, New York - 212/997-1818

SLEEPWALK   First Run Features, 1987,
w/Jim Jarmusch
THE PRINCE OF PENNSYLVANIA   New Line
Cinema, 1988
ASK ME AGAIN (TF)   DBR Films Ltd., 1989
GIDEON OLIVER (Pilot)   1989
APPOINTMENTS OF DENNIS JENNINGS   HBO
Productions, 1989
RICH BOYS *CHIEF ZABU*   International Film
Marketing, 1990
NIGHT OF THE LIVING DEAD   21st Century/
Columbia, 1990

FRANCOIS PROTAT

JACOB TWO-TWO MEETS THE HOODED FANG
Cinema Shares International, 1978
TOMORROW NEVER COMES   Rank, 1978
TULIPS   Avco Embassy, 1981

DIRTY DISHES   Quartet, 1983
RUNNING BRAVE   Buena Vista, 1983
JOSHUA THEN AND NOW   20th Century
    Fox, 1985
SEPARATE VACATIONS   RSK Entertainment, 1986
SWITCHING CHANNELS   Tri-Star, 1988
THE KISS   Tri-Star, 1988
WINTER PEOPLE   Columbia, 1989
SPEED ZONE   Orion, 1989
WEEKEND AT BERNIE'S   20th Century Fox, 1989
IN DEFENSE OF A MARRIED MAN   The Landsburg
    Company, 1990
BEAUTIFUL DREAMERS   Cinexus/Famous
    Players, 1990

ALAN PUDNEY
DON'T OPEN TIL CHRISTMAS   21st
    Century, 1984
SCREAMTIME   Rugged Films, 1985
SLAUGHTER HIGH   Vestron, 1987

IAN PUNTER
ORANGES ARE NOT THE ONLY FRUIT (CTF)
    BBC-TV, 1990

Q

DAVID QUAID, ASC
I AM THE CHEESE   Libra Cinema 5, 1983
A NIGHT IN HEAVEN   20th Century Fox, 1983
CONCEALED ENEMIES (TF)   WGBH-Boston/
    Goldcrest Films and Television/Comworld
    Productions, 1984

DICK QUINLAN
IN THE SPIRIT   Running River/Castle Hill
    Productions, 1990

DECLAN QUINN
Agent: Dattner & Associates - Los Angeles,
    213/447-5986

BLOOD AND CONCRETE   I.R.S. Media, 1991

R

JEAN-PAUL RABIE
NIGHT OF THE FOX (MS)   ITC Entertainment/
    Tribune Entertainment/Dove Inc./TF1/Canal Plus/
    Societe Francaise de Broduction/Channel 60
    (Germany)/Group Media TV, 1990

JEAN RABIER
QUIET DAYS IN CLICHY   Pathe-Europa, 1990

HERBERT RADITSCHING
THE OUTING   *THE LAMP*   TMS Pictures, 1987

KEVIN RAFFERTY
BLOOD IN THE FACE   First Run Features, 1991, w/
    Sandi Sissel

ELEMER RAGALYI
BRADY'S ESCAPE   Satori, 1984
SINGING ON THE TREADMILL   Hungarofilm, 1987
HANNA'S WAR   Cannon, 1988
MURDERERS AMONG US: THE SIMON WIESENTHAL
    STORY (CTF)   Citadel Entertainment, 1989
MACK THE KNIFE   21st Century, 1989
THE PHANTOM OF THE OPERA   21st Century
    Films, 1989
MAX AND HELEN (CTF)   Citadel Entertainment, 1990
RED KNIGHT, WHITE KNIGHT (CTF)   Zenith/John
    Kemeny Citdale Entertainment Productions, 1990
JUDGMENT (CTF)   Tisch/Wigutow/Hershman
    Productions, 1990

CLAUDIO RAGANO
MACARONI   Paramount, 1985

STEPHEN RAMSEY*
West Coast Commercial Card
Agent: Smith Gosnell Nicholson & Associates -
    Pacific Palisades, 213/459-0307

NOMADS   Atlantic Releasing Corporation, 1985

OUSAMA RAWI, CSC, BSC
Address: Rawfilm Inc., 567 Queen St. West, Toronto,
    Ontario M5V 2B6, 416/366-7881

ZULU DAWN   Orion/Warner Bros., 1979

RICHARD RAWLINGS, JR.
CASEY'S GIFT: FOR LOVE OF A CHILD (TF)   American
    First Run Studios, 1990

DON REDDY*
Local 666
Agent: Grace Lyons Management - Los Angeles,
    213/655-5100

BENJI   Mulberry Square, 1974
HAWPS   Mulberry Square, 1976
FOR THE LOVE OF BENJI   Mulberry Square, 1977

Re

CINEMATOGRAPHERS
PRODUCTION
DESIGNERS,
COSTUME
DESIGNERS AND
FILM EDITORS
GUIDE

C
I
N
E
M
A
T
O
G
R
A
P
H
E
R
S

Re

CINEMATOGRAPHERS
PRODUCTION
DESIGNERS,
COSTUME
DESIGNERS AND
FILM EDITORS
GUIDE

C
I
N
E
M
A
T
O
G
R
A
P
H
E
R
S

THE DOUBLE McGUFFIN   Mulberry Square, 1979
OH HEAVENLY DOG   20th Century Fox, 1980
TIME BOMB (TF)   Barry Weitz Films/
   Universal TV, 1984
ONE TERRIFIC GUY (TF)   CBS Entertainment, 1986
BENJI THE HUNTED   Buena Vista, 1987

LEE REDMOND
FLIGHT OF BLACK ANGEL (CTF)   Hess-Kallberg
   Productions, 1991

MICHAEL REED
GALILEO   Fenice Cinematografica/Rizzoli Film/
   Kinozenter, 1968
ON HER MAJESTY'S SECRET SERVICE   United
   Artists, 1969
THE HIDING PLACE   World Wide, 1975
SHOUT AT THE DEVIL   American International, 1976
NO LONGER ALONE   World Wide, 1978
THE STICK UP   Trident-Barber, 1978
THE PASSAGE   United Artists, 1979
LOOPHOLE   MGM/United Artists, 1981
KIM (TF)   London Films, 1984
WILD GEESE II   Universal, 1985

CLAUDE RENOIR
FRENCH CONNECTION II   20th Century Fox, 1975
THE SPY WHO LOVED ME   United Artists, 1977

GAYNE RESCHER, ASC
Agent: Tobias-Skouras & Associates - Los Angeles,
   213/277-6211

SEVEN WONDERS OF THE WORLD   Stanley
   Warner Cinema Corporation, 1956
A FACE IN THE CROWD   Warner Bros., 1957
THE TROUBLEMAKER   Janus, 1964
RACHEL, RACHEL   Warner Bros., 1968
JOHN AND MARY   20th Century Fox, 1969
A NEW LEAF   Paramount, 1971
SUCH GOOD FRIENDS   Paramount, 1971
BOOK OF NUMBERS   Avco Embassy, 1973
CLAUDINE   20th Century Fox, 1974
SHELL GAME (TF)   Thoroughbred Productions, 1975
NORMAN IS THAT YOU?   MGM/United Artists, 1976
OLLY, OLLY, OXEN FREE   Sanrio, 1978
MOVIOLA (MS)   David L. Wolper-Stan
   Margulies Productions/Warner Bros. TV, 1980
STAR TREK II: THE WRATH OF KHAN
   Paramount, 1982
THE DAY AFTER (TF)   ABC Circle Films, 1983
A BUNNY'S TALE (TF)   Stan Margulies Company/
   ABC Circle Films, 1985
RIGHT TO KILL? (TF)   Wrye-Konigsberg
   Productions/Taper Media Enterprises/Telepictures
   Productions, 1985
TOUGHLOVE (TF)   Fries Entertainment, 1985
SPACE (MS)   Stonehenge Productions, 1985
UNFINISHED BUSINESS (TF)   BBC, 1986
DRESS GRAY (TF)   Frank von Zerneck Productions/
   Warner Bros. TV, 1986
THERE MUST BE A PONY (TF)   R.J. Productions/
   Columbia TV, 1986
IN LOVE AND WAR (TF)   Carol Schreder
   Productions/Tisch-Avnet Productions, 1987
SIDNEY SHELDON'S WINDMILLS OF THE
   GODS (TF)   Dove Productions/ITC
   Productions, 1988
SHOOTER (TF) ☆   UBU Productions/
   Paramount TV, 1988

GET SMART, AGAIN! (TF)   IndieProd/Phoenix
   Entertainment Group, 1989
JACKIE COLLINS' 'LUCKY/CHANCES' - PARTS I-III (MS)
   NBC Productions, 1990
FOLLOW YOUR HEART (TF)   NBC Productions/
   Danson-Fauci Producions/Force Ten
   Productions, 1990
SINGLE WOMEN, MARRIED MEN (TF)   CBS
   Entertainment/Michele Lee Productions, 1990

LARRY REVENE
PREPPIES   Platinum Pictures, 1984
DELIVERY BOYS   New World, 1985
SEX APPEAL   Platinum Pictures, 1986
SLAMMER GIRLS   Lightning Pictures, 1987
WIMPS   Platinum Pictures, 1987
HEAVEN BECOMES HELL   Taurus Entertainment, 1989
WILDEST DREAMS   Platinum Pictures, 1989

JAIME REYES
DANCE OF HOPE   First Run Features, 1989

BRIAN REYNOLDS
Agent: Dattner & Associates - Los Angeles, 213/447-5986

JEZEBEL'S KISS   Film Warriors/Shapiro
   Glickenhaus, 1990

BUSTER REYNOLDS
THE GODS MUST BE CRAZY   20th Century Fox, 1984
THE GODS MUST BE CRAZY II   WEG, 1990
SCHWEITZER   Concorde Films/Sugar
   Entertainment, 1990

JACK L. RICHARDS, ASC *
MidWest Card
Agent: Smith Gosnell Nicholson & Associates -
   Pacific Palisades, 213/459-0307

THE MONKEY HUSTLE   American International, 1976
ON THE RIGHT TRACK   20th Century Fox, 1981
THE CHICAGO STORY (TF)   Eric Bercovici Productions/
   MGM TV, 1981
THE BEAST WITHIN   MGM/UA, 1982
THROUGH NAKED EYES (TF)   Charles Fries
   Productions, 1983
LISTEN TO YOUR HEART (TF)   CBS
   Entertainment, 1983
FIRST STEPS (TF)   CBS Entertainment, 1985
WHEN DREAMS COME TRUE (TF)   1985
VITAL SIGNS (TF)   CBS Entertainment, 1986
NIGHT OF COURAGE (TF)   Titus Productions/The
   Eugene O'Neill Memorial Theater Center, 1987
OPEN ADMISSIONS (TF)   CBS Entertainment, 1987

ROBERT RICHARDSON
Agent: Sanford-Skouras & Gross - Los Angeles,
   213/208-2100

SALVADOR   Hemdale, 1986
PLATOON ★   Orion, 1986
WALL STREET   20th Century Fox, 1987
DUDES   New Century/Vista, 1988
EIGHT MEN OUT   Orion, 1988
TALK RADIO   Universal, 1988
BORN ON THE FOURTH OF JULY ★   Universal, 1989
CITY OF HOPE   Esperanza, 1991
THE DOORS   Tri-Star, 1991

ANTHONY B. RICHMOND, BSC

Agent: Paul Gerard Agency - Newport Beach, 714/644-7950

LET IT BE (FD)   United Artists, 1970
WALK ABOUT   20th Century Fox, 1971
DON'T LOOK NOW   Paramount, 1974
OLD DRACULA *VAMPIRA*   American
    International, 1975
THE MAN WHO FELL TO EARTH   Cinema 5, 1976
THE EAGLE HAS LANDED   Columbia, 1977
SILVER BEARS   Columbia, 1977
THE GREEK TYCOON   Universal, 1978
LOVE AND BULLETS   ITC, 1979,
    w/Fred J. Koenekamp
THE KIDS ARE ALRIGHT (FD)   New World, 1979,
    w/Peter Nevard & Norman Wexler
THE AMERICAN SUCCESS CO.   Columbia, 1979
FATAL ATTRACTION   Greentree Productions, 1980
BAD TIMING/A SENSUAL OBSESSION   World
    Northal, 1980
IMPROPER CHANNELS   Crown International 1981
SLAPSTICK OF ANOTHER KIND   Entertainment
    Releasing Corporation/International Film
    Marketing, 1984
THAT'S LIFE!   Columbia, 1986
SUNSET   Tri-Star, 1988
THE IN-CROWD   Orion, 1988
THE ROAD RAIDERS (TF)   New East
    Entertainment, 1989
SETTLE THE SCORE (TF)   ITC Entertainment/
    Steve Sohmer Productions, 1990
CAT CHASER   Vestron, 1990

TOM RICHMOND

Agent: The Gersh Agency, Inc., Beverly Hills -
    213/274-6611, New York - 212/997-1818

RUNNING HOT   New Line Cinema, 1984
HARDBODIES   Columbia, 1984
HARD ROCK ZOMBIES   Cannon, 1985
STAND ALONE   New World, 1985, w/Tim Suhrstedt
CHOPPING MALL *KILLBOTS*   Concorde, 1986
HARDBODIES 2   CineTel, 1986
THE BIKINI SHOP   International Film
    Marketing, 1987
STRAIGHT TO HELL   Island Pictures, 1987
STAND AND DELIVER   Warner Bros., 1988
THE CHOCOLATE WAR   MCEG, 1988
I'M GONNA GIT YOU SUCKA   MGM/UA, 1988
AMITYVILLE: THE EVIL ESCAPES (TF)   1989
NIGHTMARE ON THE 13TH FLOOR (CTF)   Wilshire
    Court Productions/G.C. Group Ltd., 1990
ONE CUP OF COFFEE   Bullpen/Open Road, 1991

LISA RINZLER

Agent: The Gersh Agency, Inc., Beverly Hills -
    213/274-6611, New York - 212/997-1818

FOREVER, LULU   Tri-Star, 1987
I WAS A TEENAGE T.V. TERRORIST   Troma, 1987
JOHN HUSTON (FD)   Point Blank, 1988
TRUE LOVE   MGM/UA, 1989

RAY RIVAS

HEART OF MIDNIGHT   Samuel Goldwyn Co., 1988

NEIL ROACH

Agent: The Miller Agency - Santa Clarita, 818/843-7335

THE WILD AND THE FREE (TF)   BSR Productions/
    Marble Arch Productions, 1980
OF MICE AND MEN (TF)   Of Mice and Men
    Productions, 1981
SILENT RAGE   Columbia, 1982, w/Robert Jessup
RED HEADED STRANGER   Alive Films, 1986
MY NAME IS BILL W. (TF)   1989
DECORATION DAY (TF)   Marion Rees Associates, 1990
DONOR (TF)   Peter Frankovich-Daniel A. Sherkow
    Productions/CBS Entertainment Productions, 1990
THE IMAGE (CTF)   Citadel Entertainment
    Productions, 1990
HIROSHIMA: OUT OF THE ASHES (TF)   Robert
    Greenwald Productions, 1990

JAMES W. ROBERSON

BACK TO HANNIBAL: THE RETURN OF TOM SAWYER
    AND HUCKLEBERRY FINN (CTF)   WonderWorks/
    The Disney Channel/Gay-Jay Productions, 1990

JEAN-FRANCOIS ROBIN

LE PLEIN DE SUPPER   UGC, 1976
LE COMMUNION SOLENNELLE *SOLEMN
    COMMUNION*   Planfilm, 1977
LE COEUR FROID *THE COLD HEART*   Films
    Moliere, 1977
LE COUP DE SIROCCO *THE SIROCCO BLOW*
    Gaumont, 1979
LIGHT YEARS AWAY   New Yorker, 1983
BETTY BLUE   Alive Films, 1986
MALADIE D'AMOUR   AMLF, 1987
A FEW DAYS WITH ME   Galaxy Films, 1989
THE LOOKALIKE (CTF)   Gallo Entertainment, 1990

MIGUEL RODRIGUEZ

MISS MARY   New World, 1986
APARTMENT ZERO   Skouras Pictures, 1989

RICHARD P. ROGERS

THE POWER OF THE PAST WITH BILL MOYERS:
    FLORENCE (CTF)   David Grubin Productions/
    WETA, 1990

OWEN ROIZMAN, ASC

THE FRENCH CONNECTION ★   20th Century Fox, 1971
THE GANG THAT COULDN'T SHOOT STRAIGHT
    MGM, 1972
PLAY IT AGAIN, SAM   Paramount, 1972
THE HEARTBREAK KID   20th Century Fox, 1972
THE EXORCIST ★   Warner Bros., 1973
THE STEPFORD WIVES   Columbia, 1975
3 DAYS OF THE CONDOR   Paramount, 1975
THE RETURN OF A MAN CALLED HORSE   United
    Artists, 1976
NETWORK ★   MGM/United Artists, 1976
INDEPENDENCE   20th Century Fox, 1976
STRAIGHT TIME   Warner Bros., 1978
SGT. PEPPER'S LONELY HEARTS CLUB BAND
    Universal, 1978
THE ELECTRIC HORSEMAN   Columbia, 1979
THE BLACK MARBLE   Avco Embassy, 1980
TRUE CONFESSIONS   United Artists, 1981
ABSENCE OF MALICE   Columbia, 1981
TAPS   20th Century Fox, 1981
TOOTSIE ★   Columbia, 1982
VISION QUEST   Warner Bros., 1985
I LOVE YOU TO DEATH   Tri-Star, 1990
HAVANA   Mirage/Universal, 1990

CINEMATOGRAPHERS
PRODUCTION
DESIGNERS,
COSTUME
DESIGNERS AND
FILM EDITORS
GUIDE

CINEMATOGRAPHERS

Ro

CINEMATOGRAPHERS
PRODUCTION
DESIGNERS,
COSTUME
DESIGNERS AND
FILM EDITORS
GUIDE

C
I
N
E
M
A
T
O
G
R
A
P
H
E
R
S

MIMI ROJAS
EYES OF A STRANGER   Warner Bros., 1981
TO BEGIN AGAIN   20th Century Fox International
   Classics, 1982

ERICH ROLAND
ELLIOT FAUMAN, PH.D.   Ventcap Film Partners/
   Taurus Entertainment, 1990

GERNOT ROLL
THE KING'S WHORE   J & M Entertainment, 1990

HOWARD ROSENBERG
CIRCUITRY MAN   I.R.S. Media/Skouras, 1990

JAMES A. ROSENTHAL
SOULTAKER   Pacific West Entertainment Group/
   Taurus Entertainment, 1990

CHARLES ROSHER, JR., ASC *
West Coast Card
Agent: The Gersh Agency, Inc., Beverly Hills -
   213/274-6611, New York - 212/997-1818

ADAM AT SIX A.M.   National General, 1970
THE BABY MAKER   National General, 1970
PRETTY MAIDS ALL IN A ROW   MGM, 1971
3 WOMEN   20th Century Fox, 1977
SEMI-TOUGH   United Artists, 1977
THE LATE SHOW   Warner Bros., 1977
A WEDDING   20th Century Fox, 1978
MOVIE MOVIE ("Dynamite Hands")   Warner
   Bros.,1978
NIGHTWING   Columbia, 1979
THE ONION FIELD   Avco Embassy, 1979
HEARTBEEPS   Universal, 1981
INDEPENDENCE DAY   Warner Bros., 1983
PRINCESS DAISY (MS)   NBC Productions/Steve
   Krantz Productions, 1983
ELYSIAN FIELDS (TF)   Sarabande Productions, 1989
POLICE ACADEMY 6: CITY UNDER SEIGE   Warner
   Bros., 1989

JOHN ROSNELL
STRAIGHT OUT OF BROOKLYN   American
   Playhouse Theatrical Films, 1991

EDWARD ROSSON
LOVE AT FIRST BITE   American International, 1979

GIUSEPPE ROTUNNO, ASC
Agent: The Gersh Agency, Inc., Beverly Hills -
   213/274-6611, New York - 212/997-1818

STORMTROOPERS   CIDIF, 1977
ALL THAT JAZZ ★   20th Century Fox, 1979
POPEYE   Paramount, 1980
CITY OF WOMEN   New Yorker, 1981
ROLLOVER   Orion/Warner Bros., 1981
FIVE DAYS ONE SUMMER   The Ladd Company/
   Warner Bros., 1984
AND THE SHIP SAILS ON   Triumph, 1984
CHINA 9, LIBERTY 37   Lorimar, 1984
AMERICAN DREAMER   Warner Bros., 1984
THE ASSISI UNDERGROUND   Cannon, 1985
RED SONJA   MGM/UA, 1985
HOTEL COLONIAL   Orion, 1987

JULIA AND JULIA   Cinecom, 1988
RENT-A-COP   Kings Road Productions, 1988
HAUNTED SUMMER   Cannon, 1988
THE ADVENTURES OF BARON MUNCHAUSEN
   Columbia, 1989

PHILIPPE ROUSSELOT
Agent: The Gersh Agency, Inc., Beverly Hills -
   213/274-6611, New York - 212/997-1818

LE COUPLE TEMOIN   Planfilm, 1977
PEPPERMINT SODA   New Yorker, 1977
LES CHEMINS DE L'EXIT DU LES DERNIERESANNEES
   DE JEAN JACQUES ROUSSEAU (MS)   TRI/SSR/
   Telecip/BBC/RTB/SRC/TV60, 1978
LA DROLESSE   New Yorker, 1979
LA PROVINCIALE   Citel, 1980
COCKTAIL MOLOTOV   Putnam Square, 1980
THE ROADS OF EXILE   Corinth, 1981
DIVA   United Artists Classics, 1982
THE GIRL FROM LORRAINE   New Yorker, 1983
THE MOON IN THE GUTTER   Triumph, 1983
THIEVES AFTER DARK   Parafrance, 1983
DREAM ONE   Columbia, 1984
THE EMERALD FOREST   20th Century Fox, 1985
HOPE AND GLORY ★   Columbia, 1987
DANGEROUS LIAISONS   Warner Bros., 1988
THE BEAR   Tri-Star, 1989
WE'RE NO ANGELS   Paramount, 1989
HENRY & JUNE ★   Walrus & Associates/Universal, 1990

AL RUBAN
LOVE STREAMS   Cannon, 1984

JUAN RUIZ-ANCHIA
Agent: Sanford-Skouras & Gross - Los Angeles,
   213/208-2100

REBORN   Diseno y Producion de Films/Dianant/
   Laurel, 1982
MISS LONELY HEARTS   H. Jay Holman Productions/
   American Film Institute, 1983
VALENTINA   Frank Moreno, 1983
THE STONE BOY   TLC Films/20th Century Fox, 1984
MARIA'S LOVERS   Cannon, 1984
SINGLE BARS, SINGLE WOMEN (TF)   Carsey-Werner
   Productions/Sunn Classic Pictures, 1984
NOON WINE (TF)   Noon Wine Company, 1985
THAT WAS THEN...THIS IS NOW   Paramount, 1985
IN'N'OUT   Peliculas Mexicanas, 1986
AT CLOSE RANGE   Orion, 1986
WHERE THE RIVER RUNS BLACK   MGM/UA, 1986
SURRENDER   Warner Bros., 1987
HOUSE OF GAMES   Orion, 1987
THE SEVENTH SIGN   Tri-Star, 1988
THINGS CHANGE   Columbia, 1988
LOST ANGELS   Orion, 1989
THE LAST OF THE FINEST   Davis Entertainment/
   Orion, 1990
NAKED TANGO   Grupo Baires/Praesens-Film AG/
   Towa Production Company/Sugarloaf-Gotan/Scotia
   International, 1990

MARVIN RUSH
DOWN HOME (Pilot)   Paramount Network Television/
   Jabberwocky Productions/Savage Cake
   Productions, 1989
MEET THE HOLLOWHEADS   Linden Productions/
   Moviestore Entertainment, 1989

WARD RUSSELL
DAYS OF THUNDER   Simpson-Bruckheimer/
   Paramount, 1990

GIUSEPPE RUZZOLINI
TREASURE OF THE FOUR CROWNS   Cannon,
   1983, w/Marcello Masciocchi
FIRESTARTER   Universal, 1984
OEDIPUS REX   Horizon Films, 1984
BYE BYE BABY   Seymour Borde & Associates, 1989
VOYAGE OF TERROR: THE ACHILLE LAURO
   AFFAIR-PARTS 1 & 2 (TF)   TF1/Filmalpha
   Productions/Beta Taurus Group/Tribune
   Entertainment Company/RAIDUE, 1990

DOUG RYAN
BEST OF THE BEST   SVS/The Movie Group/Kuys
   Entertainment/Taurus Entertainment, 1989

ELLERY RYAN
WHICH WAY HOME (CTF)   McElroy & McElroy, 1991

PAUL G. RYAN
West Coast card, Local 659
Agent: The Doug Apatow Agency, 10559 Blythe
   Ave. - Los Angeles, LA 90064, 213/202-6888

FOXES   United Artists, 1980 (as Leon Bijou)
HOT DOG - THE MOVIE   MGM/UA, 1984
FRATERNITY VACATION   New World, 1985
YOU TALKIN' TO ME?   MGM/UA, 1987
A MATTER OF DEGREES   Backbeat, 1989

S

ROBERT SAAD
THE HOUSE BY THE LAKE   American
   International, 1976
THEY CAME FROM WITHIN SHIVERS
   Trans-America, 1976
THE RETURN OF BILLY JACK   Billy Jack
   Productions, 1986
POLICE ACADEMY 3: BACK IN TRAINING   Warner
   Bros., 1986
POLICE ACADEMY 4: CITIZENS ON PATROL
   Warner Bros., 1987

ERIC SAARINEN
SUMMER SCHOOL TEACHERS   New World, 1975
EAT MY DUST   New World, 1976
YOU LIGHT UP MY LIFE   Columbia, 1977
THE HILLS HAVE EYES   Vanguard, 1977
STARHOPS   First American, 1978
REAL LIFE   Paramount, 1979
HEADIN' FOR BROADWAY   20th Century Fox, 1980
MODERN ROMANCE   Columbia, 1981
BOX OFFICE   1982
THE GOLDEN SEAL   Samuel Goldwyn
   Company , 1983
LOST IN AMERICA   The Geffen Company/Warner
   Bros., 1985

MORIO SAEGUSA
IRON MAZE   Iron Maze Productions, 1991

TAKAO SAITO
RAN ★   Orion Classics, 1985, w/Asakazu Nakai &
   Masaharu Ueda
AKIRA KUROSAWA'S DREAMS   Warner Bros., 1990,
   w/Masaharu Ueda

VINCENT SAIZIS, ASC
Agent: The Miller Agency - Santa Clarita, 818/843-7335

THE FLIM-FLAM MAN   20th Century Fox, 1967
IN LIKE FLYNT   20th Century Fox, 1967
BONNIE AND CLYDE   Warner Bros., 1967
HELLFIGHTERS   Universal, 1969
GAILY, GAILY   United Artists, 1969
SKULLDUGGERY   Universal, 1970
THE DELTA FACTOR   1970
YOU'LL LIKE MY MOTHER   Universal, 1972
RAVAGERS   Columbia, 1979
THE CONCRETE COWBOYS (TF)   Frankel Films, 1979

MIKAEL SALOMON
Agent: Sanford-Skouras & Gross - Los Angeles,
   213/208-2100

WELCOME TO THE CLUB   Athena Films/
   Columbia, 1971
THE PHANTASTS   1972
Z.P.G.   Paramount, 1972
THREE FROM HAPARANDA   1973
THE FIVE *DE FEN*   Panorama Films, 1974
ME AND MY KID BROTHER   Palladium Films, 1974
THE OWLFARM BROTHERS   1975
FIVE ON THE RUN   1975
NOTHING BUT THE TRUTH   1975
MY SISTERS CHILDREN GO TO TOWN   Saga
   Films, 1976
24 HOURS WITH ILSE   1976
WHY?   1977
BEDSIDE FREEWAY   Palladium Films, 1977
MY SISTERS CHILDREN GO ASTRAY   1978
AROUND THE WORLD   1978
BEHIND CLOSED DOORS   1979
THREESOME   1979
SONIA, 16 YEARS   Athena Films, 1979
VIOLETS ARE BLUE   1980
TINTOMARE   Athena Films/Columbia, 1982
TELL IT LIKE IT IS, BOYS   Athena Films, 1982
COPPER   Crone Films, 1982
ELVIS, ELVIS   Moviemakers, 1982
HEARTS ARE TRUMP   Panorama Films, 1983
THE MARKSMAN   Steen Herdel Productions, 1983
THE BARON   Panorama Films, 1984
THE FLYING DEVILS   Crone Films, 1984
PETER VON SCHOLTEN   Crone Films, 1985
ONCE A COP...   1985
EARLY SPRING   Metronome Films, 1986
GOODBYE NEW YORK   Castle Hill Productions, 1985
THE WOLF AT THE DOOR   International Film
   Marketing, 1986
THE MAN WHO BROKE 1,000 CHAINS (CTF)   HBO
   Pictures/Journey Entertainment, 1987
UNSETTLED LAND   *ONCE WE WERE DREAMERS*
   Hemdale, 1987
ZELLY AND ME   Columbia, 1988
TORCH SONG TRILOGY   New Line Cinema, 1988
STEALING HEAVEN   Scotti Bros., 1989

Sa

**CINEMATOGRAPHERS
PRODUCTION
DESIGNERS,
COSTUME
DESIGNERS** AND
**FILM EDITORS
GUIDE**

C
I
N
E
M
A
T
O
G
R
A
P
H
E
R
S

Sa

CINEMATOGRAPHERS
PRODUCTION
DESIGNERS,
COSTUME
DESIGNERS AND
FILM EDITORS
GUIDE

C
I
N
E
M
A
T
O
G
R
A
P
H
E
R
S

THE ABYSS ★   20th Century Fox, 1989
ALWAYS   Universal, 1989
ARACHNOPHOBIA   Buena Vista, 1990
BACKDRAFT   Universal, 1991

SERGIO SALVATI
1990: THE BRONX WARRIORS   United Film
    Distribution, 1983
CATACOMBS   Empire Pictures, 1985
CRAWLSPACE   Empire Pictures, 1986
PUPPET MASTER   Full Moon, 1989

BERNARD SALZMANN
Agent: Camera Masters - Venice, 213/306-0810

BORN TO RACE   MGM/UA, 1988
RIDING THE EDGE   Kodiak Films/Trans World
    Entertainment, 1989

RODOLFO SANCHEZ
PIXOTE   Unifilm, 1981
KISS OF THE SPIDER WOMAN   Island Alive, 1985
THE BLUE IGUANA   Paramount, 1988
ONE DOWN, FOUR UP (Pilot)   Patrick Hasburgh
    Productions, 1989

VIC SARIN
HEARTACHES   MPM, 1982
DANCING IN THE DARK   New World, 1986
NOWHERE TO HIDE   New Century/Vista, 1987
LOYALTIES   Cinema Group, 1987
NORMAN'S AWSOME EXPERIENCE   Norstar
    Entertainment, 1989
BYE BYE BLUES   Circle Releasing, 1990

PAUL SAROSSY
WHITE ROOM   Vos Productions/Alliance
    Releasing, 1990
SPEAKING PARTS   Cinephile, 1990

GEOFFREY SCHAAF
THE CHINA LAKE MURDERS (CTF)   MCA TV
    Entertainment/Papazian Hirsch Entertainment, 1990
FATAL EXPOSURE (CTF)   G.C. Group/Wilshire
    Court Productions, 1991

RONN SCHMIDT
CATH ME IF YOU CAN   MCEG, 1989
BRAIN DEAD   Concorde, 1989

DANIEL SCHNEOR
MERCENERY FIGHTERS   Cannon, 1988

FRED SCHULER, ASC *
West & East Coast Cards
Agent: Smith Gosnell Nicholson & Associates -
    Pacific Palisades, 213/459-0307

GLORIA   Columbia, 1980
STIR CRAZY   Columbia, 1980
ARTHUR   Orion/Warner Bros., 1981
LOVE AND MONEY   Paramount, 1982
SOUP FOR ONE   Warner Bros., 1982
THE KING OF COMEDY   20th Century Fox, 1983
EASY MONEY   Orion, 1983
AMITYVILLE 3-D   Orion, 1983
NOTHING LASTS FOREVER   MGM/UA
    Classics, 1984

A GOOD SPORT (TF)   Ralph Waite Productions/Warner
    Bros. TV, 1984
THE WOMAN IN RED   Orion, 1984
THE STREETS (Pilot)   1984
FLETCH   Universal, 1985
MAXIE   Orion, 1985
HAUNTED HONEYMOON   Orion, 1986
WISE GUYS   MGM/UA, 1986
ARMED AND DANGEROUS   Columbia, 1986

HOWARD SCHWARTZ, ASC
FUTUREWORLD   American International, 1976
THE DEVIL AND MAX DEVLIN   Buena Vista, 1981
RIGHT OF WAY (CTF)   HBO Premiere Films/
    Schaefer-Karpf Productions/Post-Newsweek
    Video, 1983

JOHN SCHWARTZMAN
YOU CAN'T HURRY LOVE   MCEG, 1988,
    w/Peter Lyons Collister

XAVER SCHWARZENBERGER
LILI MARLEEN   United Artists Classics, 1981
LOLA   United Artists Classics, 1982
VERONIKA VOSS   United Artists Classics, 1982
QUERELLE   Triumph, 1983
BERLIN ALEXANDERPLATZ   Teleculture, 1983
KAMIKAZE '89   Teleculture, 1983

MICHAEL SCOTT
FRANKENSTEIN UNBOUND   Mount Company/20th
    Century Fox, 1990, w/Armando Nannuzzi

JOHN SEALE, ACS *
West & East Coast Cards
Agent: Smith Gosnell Nicholson & Associates -
    Pacific Palisades, 213/459-0307

DEATHCHEATERS   Roadshow, 1976
FATTY FINN   Hoyts, 1980
THE SURVIVOR   Hemdale, 1981
GOODBYE PARADISE   New South Wales
    Film Corp., 1982
FIGHTING BACK   Paramount, 1982
CAREFUL HE MIGHT HEAR YOU   TLC Films/20th
    Century Fox, 1983
SILVER CITY   Samuel Goldwyn Company, 1985
BMX BANDITS   Nilsen Premiere, 1985
WITNESS ★   Paramount, 1985
TOP KID (TF)   Australian Children's
    Television Foundation/Australian Film Commission/Film
    Victoria/New South Wales Film Corporation, 1985
THE HITCHER   Tri-Star, 1986
THE MOSQUITO COAST   Warner Bros., 1986
CHILDREN OF A LESSER GOD   Paramount, 1986
STAKEOUT   Buena Vista, 1987
GORILLAS IN THE MIST   Universal, 1988
RAIN MAN ★   MGM/UA, 1988
DEAD POETS SOCIETY   Buena Vista, 1989

ROBERT SEAMAN
PERRY MASON: THE CASE OF THE MALIGNED
    MOBSTER (TF)   Viacom, 1991

CHRISTIAN SEBALDT
MORTAL PASSIONS   Gibraltar Releasing, 1989

FERD SEBASTIAN
THE AMERICAN ANGELS: BAPTISM OF BLOOD
  Sebastian International Pictures/Paramount,
  1990 (also edited)

DEAN SEMLER, ASC, ACS
Agent: Smith Gosnell Nicholson & Associates -
  Pacific Palisades, 213/459-0307

LET THE BALLOON GO   1976
HOODWINK   CB Films, 1982
THE ROAD WARRIOR   Warner Bros., 1982
KITTY AND THE BAGMAN   Quartet, 1983
RAZORBACK   Warner Bros., 1984
RETURN TO EDEN - PARTS 1 & 2 (TF)   1985
THE COCA-COLA KID   Cinecom/Film Gallery, 1985
MAD MAX BEYOND THUNDERDOME   Warner
  Bros., 1985
THE LIGHTHORSEMEN   Cinecom, 1988
COCKTAIL   Buena Vista, 1988
YOUNG GUNS   20th Century Fox, 1988
FAREWELL TO THE KING   Orion, 1989
DEAD CALM   Warner Bros., 1989
K-9   Universal, 1989
IMPULSE   Warner Bros., 1990
YOUNG GUNS II   Morgan Creek/20th Century
  Fox, 1990
DANCES WITH WOLVES ★★   Tig/Orion, 1990
CITY SLICKERS   Columbia, 1991

MICHAEL SERESIN
BUGSY MALONE   Paramount, 1976, w/Peter Biziou
SLEEPING DOGS   Aardvark Films, 1977
MIDNIGHT EXPRESS   Columbia, 1978
FAME   MGM/United Artists, 1980
SHOOT THE MOON   MGM/United Artists, 1982
BIRDY   Tri-Star, 1984
ANGEL HEART   Tri-Star, 1987
COME SEE THE PARADISE   Touchstone/Buene
  Vista, 1990

STEVEN SHAW
Agent: Sanford-Skouras & Gross - Los Angeles,
  213/208-2100

FOXTRAP   Snizzlefritz Distribution, 1985,
  w/John Stephens
THE ZERO BOYS   Omega Pictures, 1986
LIGHTNING: THE WHITE STALLION   Cannon, 1986
FORGOTTEN PRISONERS: THE AMNESTY
  FILE (CTF)   Robert Greenwald Productions, 1990
DANGEROUS PASSION (TF)   Davis Entertainment/
  Stormy Weathers, 1990

WILLIAM STEVEN SHAW
HER WICKED WAYS (TF)   ITC Entertainment
  Group/Freyda Rothstein Productions/Lois Luger
  Productions, 1990

MIKE SHEA
BODY SLAM   DEG, 1987

ROGER SHEARMAN
A FORCE OF ONE   American Cinema, 1979
STEEL   World Northal, 1980
AN EYE FOR AN EYE   Avco Embassy, 1981
LONE WOLF McQUADE   Orion, 1983

RICHARD SHORE, ASC
Agent: The Miller Agency - Santa Clarita, 818/843-7335

NIGHT OF DARK SHADOWS   MGM, 1971
BANG THE DRUM SLOWLY   Paramount, 1973

TOM SIGEL
LATINO   Cinecom, 1986
ROE VS. WADE (TF)   The Manheim Co./NBC
  Productions, 1989
RUDE AWAKENING   Orion, 1989
A PROMISE TO KEEP (TF)   Warner Bros. TV/
  Sacret, 1990
ROCK HUDSON (TF)   The Konigsberg-Sanitsky
  Company, 1990
CHALLENGER (TF)   George Englund Productions/King
  Phoenix Entertainment/The IndieProd Company, 1990

AMANDA SILVER
TALES OF THE UNKOWN   AIP Home Video/Pacific
  West Entertainment, 1990

GEOFFREY SIMPSON, ACS
Agent: Jill Nicholas, Top Technicians Pty. Ltd.,
  P. O. Box 1035, DEE WHY N.S.W., 2099 Australia,
  612/981-1622 or fax - 612/971-2880
Agent: Smith Gosnell Nicholson & Associates -
  Pacific Palisades, 213/454-7987

THE NAVIGATOR   Circle Releasing, 1989
GREEN CARD   Touchstone/Buena Vista

PETER SINCLAIR
SPACED OUT   Miramax, 1981, w/John Metcalfe
GOOD TO GO   Island Pictures, 1986
SIGN 'O' THE TIMES   Cineplex Odeon, 1987
DEALERS   Rank, 1989
LENNY LIVE AND UNLEASHED   Miramax, 1989

GEZA SINKOVICS
DELUSION   I.R.S. Media, 1991

ARNIE SIRLIN
Agent: Paul Gerard Agency - Newport Beach,
  714/644-7950

DOUBLE REVENGE   Smart Egg Releasing, 1988

SANDI SISSEL
Agent: The Gersh Agency, Inc., Beverly Hills -
  213/274-6611, New York - 212/997-1818

RISING SON (CTF)   Sarabande Productions, 1990
DRUG WARS: THE CAMARENA STORY (MS)   World
  International Network/ZZY Productions, 1990
THE FLASH (TF)   Warner Bros. TV/Pet Fly
  Productions, 1990
BLOOD IN THE FACE   First Run Features, 1991,
  w/Kevin Rafferty

DOUGLAS SLOCOMBE
Agent: London Management, 235/241 Regent Street -
  London, W1R 7AG, 01-493-1610

THE MUSIC LOVERS   United Artists, 1971
MURPHY'S WAR   Paramount, 1971
TRAVELS WITH MY AUNT ★   MGM, 1972

SI

CINEMATOGRAPHERS
PRODUCTION
DESIGNERS,
COSTUME
DESIGNERS AND
FILM EDITORS
GUIDE

CINEMATOGRAPHERS

CINEMATOGRAPHERS
PRODUCTION
DESIGNERS,
COSTUME
DESIGNERS AND
FILM EDITORS
GUIDE

**C
I
N
E
M
A
T
O
G
R
A
P
H
E
R
S**

JESUS CHRIST SUPERSTAR   Universal, 1973
THE DESTRUCTORS   *THE MARSEILLES CONTRACT*
    American International, 1974
THE GREAT GATSBY   Paramount, 1974
THE MAIDS   American Film Theatre, 1975
ROLLERBALL   United Artists, 1975
HEDDA   Brut Productions, 1975
THE BAWDY ADVENTURES OF TOM JONES
    Universal, 1975
THE SAILOR WHO FELL FROM GRACE WITH
    THE SEA   Avco Embassy, 1976
NASTY HABITS   Brut Productions, 1977
JULIA ★   20th Century Fox, 1977
CARAVANS   Universal, 1979
THE LADY VANISHES   Rank, 1979
LOST AND FOUND   Columbia, 1979
NIJINSKY   Paramount, 1980
RAIDERS OF THE LOST ARK ★   Paramount, 1981
THE PIRATES OF PENZANCE   Universal, 1983
NEVER SAY NEVER AGAIN   Warner Bros., 1983
INDIANA JONES AND THE TEMPLE OF DOOM
    Paramount 1984
WATER   Atlantic Releasing Corporation, 1984
LADY JANE   Paramount, 1986
INDIANA JONES AND THE LAST CRUSADE
    Paramount, 1989

FEDERIKO SLONISKO

QUEST FOR THE MIGHTY SWORD   Filmirage/RCA
    Columbia Pictures Home Video, 1990

DOYLE SMITH

THE LOVELESS   Atlantic Releasing Corporation, 1984

GREGORY SMITH

TERMINAL BLISS   Distant Horizon, 1990

ROLAND "OZZIE" SMITH

Agent: The Miller Agency - Santa Clarita, 818/843-7335

CHEAPER TO KEEP HER   American Cinema, 1980
LOVE THY NEIGHBOR (TF)   Patricia Nardo
    Productions/20th Century Fox TV, 1984
UPHILL ALL THE WAY   New World, 1986
THE NEW ADVENTURES OF PIPPI LONGSTOCKING
    Columbia, 1988
STREET JUSTICE   Lorimar, 1989
KEATON'S COP   Third Coast/Cannon, 1990

STEPHEN SMITH

SLAYGROUND   Universal, 1984

PETER SMOKLER

THE SECRET LIFE OF PLANTS   Paramount, 1978,
    w/Ghislain Cloquet & David Myers
THIS IS SPINAL TAP   Embassy, 1984
SCORNED AND SWINDLED (TF)   Cypress
    Point Productions, 1984
NORTH SHORE   Universal, 1987
CAMP CUCAMONGA (TF)   NBC Productions/
    Richmel, 1990

REED SMOOT

THE GREAT BRAIN   Osmond Distribution
    Company,1978
TAKE DOWN   Buena Vista, 1979
WINDWALKER   Pacific International, 1980
HARRY'S WAR   Taft International, 1981

WHEN YOUR LOVER LEAVES (TF)   Major H
    Productions, 1983
DOOR TO DOOR   Castle Hill Productions, 1985
THE LONG HOT SUMMER (TF)   Leonard Hill
    Productions, 1985
LOTS OF LUCK (CTF)   Tomorrow Entertainment, 1985
THE WRAITH   New Century/Vista, 1986
DOWN THE LONG HILLS (TF)   The Finnegan Company/
    Walt Disney TV, 1987
RUSSKIES   New Century/Vista, 1987
GLEAMING THE CUBE   20th Century Fox, 1989
DON'T TELL HER IT'S ME   Hemdale, 1990
LUCI & DESI (TF)   Larry Thompson
    Entertainment, 1991

WITOLD SOBOCINSKI

Agent: Paul Gerard Talent Agency - Newport Beach,
    714/644-7950

THE SANDGLASS   Polish Corp., 1983
PIRATES   Cannon, 1986
FRANTIC   Warner Bros., 1988
TORRENTS OF SPRING   Erne/Reteitalia, 1989,
    w/Dante Spinotti

YURI SOKOL, ACS

Agent: Jill Nicholas, Top Technicians Pty. Ltd.,
    P. O. Box 1035, DEE WHY N.S.W., 2099 Australia,
    612/981-1622 or fax - 612/971-2880

LONELY HEARTS   Samuel Goldwyn Company, 1983
MAN OF FLOWERS   Spectrafilm, 1984
MY FIRST WIFE   Spectrafilm, 1985
CACTUS   Spectrafilm, 1986
WARM NIGHTS ON A SLOW MOVING TRAIN
    Miramax, 1987

LEONARDO SOLIS

DEATHSTALKER   New World, 1984
THE WARRIOR AND THE SORCERESS   New
    World, 1984
WIZARDS OF THE LOST KINGDOM   Concorde, 1985
FUNNY DIRTY LITTLE WAR   Cinevista, 1986
DEATHSTALKER II   Concorde, 1986
NIGHT OF THE PENCILS   Marquis Pictures, 1987

BARRY SONNENFELD

Agent: The Gersh Agency, Inc., Beverly Hills -
    213/274-6611, New York - 212/997-1818

BLOOD SIMPLE   Circle Releasing Corporation, 1984
COMPROMISING POSITIONS   Paramount, 1985
THREE O'CLOCK HIGH   Universal, 1987
RAISING ARIZONA   20th Century Fox, 1987
THROW MOMMA FROM THE TRAIN   Orion, 1987
BIG   20th Century Fox, 1988
WHEN HARRY MET SALLY...   Columbia, 1989
MILLER'S CROSSING   Circle Films/20th Century
    Fox, 1990
MISERY   Castle Rock Entertainment/Nelson
    Entertainment/Columbia, 1990

JERI SOPANEN

MY DINNER WITH ANDRE   New Yorker, 1981
THE GIG   Castle Hill Productions, 1985
THE LUCKIEST MAN IN THE WORLD   Second
    Effort Co., 1989

LEONARD J. SOUTH, ASC *
West Coast Card
Agent: Smith Gosnell Nicholson & Associates - Pacific Palisades, 213/459-0307

SCREAM, PRETTY PEGGY (TF)   Universal TV, 1973
THE ROCKFORD FILES (TF)   Universal TV, 1974
FAMILY PLOT   Universal, 1976
HERBIE GOES TO MONTE CARLO   Buena Vista, 1977
THREE SISTERS (TF)   NTA, 1977
THE NORTH AVENUE IRREGULARS   Buena Vista, 1979
AMY   Buena Vista, 1981
FATHER MURPHY (TF)   NBC Productions, 1981

MIKE SOUTHON
BURROUGHS (FD)   Citifilmworks, 1984, shared credit
GOTHIC   Vestron, 1987
PAPERHOUSE   Vestron, 1989
QUEEN OF HEARTS   Cinecom, 1989
CHICAGO JOE AND THE SHOWGIRL   New Line Cinema, 1990
THE SECRET LIFE OF IAN FLEMING (CTF)   Saban Scherick Productions, 1990
A KISS BEFORE DYING   Universal, 1991

PETER SOVA
Agent: Lawrence A. Mirsich, Triad Artists, Inc. - Los Angeles, 213/556-2727

SUMMER OF MY GERMAN SOLDIER (TF)   Highgate Productions, 1978
SHORT EYES   The Film League, 1978
ROCKERS   New Yorker, 1979
DINER   MGM/United Artists, 1982
A SOLDIER'S STORY (TF)   Columbia, 1984
TIN MEN   Buena Vista, 1987
GOOD MORNING, VIETNAM   Buena Vista, 1987
SING   Tri-Star, 1989

ALBERTO SPAGNOLI
KILLER FISH   Associated Film Distribution, 1978
HERCULES   Cannon, 1983
HERCULES II   Cannon, 1985
CUT AND RUN   New World, 1986

BRENTON SPENCER
HIGHER EDUCATION   Norstar Releasing, 1987
CHRISTMAS COMES TO WILLOW CREEK (TF)   Blue Andre Productions/ITC Productions, 1987
BLUE MONKEY   Spectrafilm, 1987

DAVID SPERLING
REACHING OUT   Par Films, 1983
COOL RUNNINGS: THE REGGAE MOVIE (FD)   R5/S8, 1986, shared credit
STREET TRASH   Lightning Pictures, 1987
THE DRIFTER   Concorde, 1988
OVEREXPOSED   Concorde, 1990

MICHAEL SPILLER
TRUST   True Fiction Pictures/Zenith Productions, 1991

DANTE SPINOTTI
Agent: Smith Gosnell Nicholson & Associates - Pacific Palisades, 213/459-0307

SOTTO, SOTTO   Triumph/Columbia, 1984
THE BERLIN AFFAIR   Cannon, 1985
CHOKE CANYON   United Film Distribution, 1986
MANHUNTER   DEG, 1986
FROM THE HIP   DEG, 1987
CRIMES OF THE HEART   DEG, 1987
ILLEGALLY YOURS   DEG, 1988
BEACHES   Buena Vista, 1988
MAMBA   Eidoscope/Reteitelia, 1988
TORRENTS OF SPRING   Erre/Reteitalia, 1989, w/Witold Sobocinski
THE COMFORT OF STRANGERS   Reteitalia s.p.a./Erre Produzioni/Sovereign Pictures, 1990
TRUE COLORS   Paramount, 1991

TONY SPRATLING
EDGE OF SANITY   Millimeter Films, 1989

BUDDY SQUIRES
THE CIVIL WAR I-IX   WETA-Washington, D.C./Florentine Films, 1990, w/Ken Burns and Allen Moore

JORGE STAHL
MISSING IN ACTION 2: THE BEGINNING   Cannon, 1985

JOHN STANIER, BSC
Agent: Dattner & Associates - Los Angeles, 213/447-5986

OXFORD BLUES   MGM/UA, 1984
DEATH WISH 3   Cannon, 1985
RAMBO III   Tri-Star, 1988

FRANK STANLEY, ASC
MR. RICCO   MGM, 1975
THE EIGER SANCTION   Universal, 1975
CAR WASH   Universal, 1976
HEROES   Universal, 1977
A HERO AIN'T NOTHIN' BUT A SANDWICH   New World, 1977
CORVETTE SUMMER   MGM/United Artists, 1978
THE BIG FIX   Universal, 1978
10   Orion/Warner Bros., 1979
THE FISH THAT SAVED PITTSBURGH   United Artists, 1979
WHOLLY MOSES!   Columbia, 1980
UNDER THE RAINBOW   Orion/Warner Bros., 1981
GREASE 2   Paramount, 1982
THE PRODIGAL   World Wide, 1984
THE THREE WISHES OF BILLY GRIER (TF)   I & C Productions, 1984
CONSENTING ADULT (TF)   Starger Company/David Lawrence and Ray Aghayan Productions, 1985

OLIVER STAPLETON
THE SECRET POLICEMAN'S OTHER BALL (FD)   Miramax, 1982
MY BEAUTIFUL LAUNDRETTE   Orion Classics, 1986
RESTLESS NATIVES   Orion Classics, 1985
ABSOLUTE BEGINNERS   Orion, 1986
SAMMY AND ROSIE GET LAID   Cinecom, 1987
PRICK UP YOUR EARS   Samuel Goldwyn Company, 1987

St

CINEMATOGRAPHERS
PRODUCTION
DESIGNERS,
COSTUME
DESIGNERS AND
FILM EDITORS
GUIDE

C
I
N
E
M
A
T
O
G
R
A
P
H
E
R
S

CHUCK BERRY: HAIL! HAIL! ROCK'N'ROLL (FD)
Universal, 1987
DANNY, THE CHAMPION OF THE WORLD (CTF)
The Disney Channel, 1989
EARTH GIRLS ARE EASY   Vestron, 1989
COOKIE   Warner Bros., 1989
SHE-DEVIL   Orion, 1989
THE GRIFTERS   Cineplex Odeon Films/Miramax
Films, 1990

R O B E R T   S T E A D M A N *
West Coast Card
Agent: The Gersh Agency, Inc., Beverly Hills -
213/274-6611, New York - 212/997-1818

THE VICTIMS (TF)   Hajeno Productions/Warner
Bros. TV, 1982
WOMEN OF SAN QUENTIN (TF)   David Gerber
Company/MGM-UA TV, 1983
THE CALENDAR GIRL MURDERS (TF)   Tisch-Avnet
Productions, 1984
SECRETS OF A MARRIED MAN (TF)   ITC
Productions, 1984
MUSSOLINI: THE UNTOLD STORY (MS)   Trian
Productions, 1985
ON WINGS OF EAGLES (MS)   Edgar J.
ScherickProductions/Taft Entertainment TV, 1986
FRESNO (MS)   MTM Productions, 1986
POLICE STORY II: THE FREEWAY KILLINGS (TF)
David Gerber Company/MGM-UA TV/Columbia
TV, 1987
ABOVE THE LAW   Warner Bros., 1988
SUPERCARRIER (TF)   Fries Entertainment, 1988
THOSE SHE LEFT BEHIND (TF)   NBC
Productions, 1989
TREASURE ISLAND (CTF)   British Lion/Agamemnon
Films Productions, 1990

U E L I   S T E I G E R
Agent: Sandra Marsh Management - Sherman Oaks,
818/905-6961

PRIVILEGED   New Yorker, 1982
PROMISED LAND   Vestron, 1988, w/Alexander
Gruszynski
SOME GIRLS   MGM/UA, 1988
THE HOT SPOT   Orion, 1990

P E T E R   S T E I N
NABET
Agent: Smith Gosnell Nicholson & Associates -
Pacific Palisades, 213/459-0307

JUST CRAZY ABOUT HORSES   Fred Baker, 1978
FRIDAY THE 13TH PART 2   Paramount, 1981
BEACH HOUSE   New Line Cinema, 1982
PRIVATE CONTENTMENT (TF)   WNET-13/
South Carolina Educational TV, 1982
REUBEN, REUBEN   20th Century Fox, 1983
C.H.U.D.   New World, 1984
WILDROSE   Troma, 1985
A BILLION FOR BORIS   Comworld, 1985
IZZY & MOE (TF)   Robert Halmi, Inc., 1985
A GREAT WALL   Orion Classics, 1986,
w/Robert Primes
UNDER SIEGE (TF)   Ohlmeyer Communications
Company/Telepictures Productions, 1986
THE LAST FLING (TF)   Leonard Hill Films, 1987
PARENT TRAP II (TF)   The Landsburg Company/
Walt Disney TV, 1987

THE WILD PAIR   Trans World Entertainment, 1987
ELVIS AND ME (MS)   Navarone Productions/New
World TV, 1988
ERNEST SAVES CHRISTMAS   Buena Vista, 1988
THE PASSAGE   Spectrum Films, 1988
PET SEMATARY   Paramount, 1989
NIGHT VISIONS (TF)   MGM/UA TV/Wes Craven
Films, 1990
ERNEST GOES TO JAIL   Buena Vista, 1990
GRAVEYARD SHIFT   Paramount, 1990
BRENDA STARR   New World, 1991, w/Freddie Fields

C H A R L Y   S T E I N B E R G E R
JUST A GIGOLO   United Artists Classics, 1981

J O H N   M .   S T E P H E N S
Agent: The Miller Agency - Santa Clarita, 818/843-7335

BLACULA   American International, 1972
BOXCAR BERTHA   American International, 1972
BILLY JACK   Warner Bros., 1973, w/Fred Koenekamp
SORCERER   Universal/Paramount, 1977, w/Dick Bush
THE HIGHWAYMAN (TF)   Glen A. Larson Productions/
20th Century Fox TV, 1987
FOXTRAP   Snizzlefritz Distribution, 1985, w/Steve Shaw
STEELE JUSTICE   Atlantic Releasing Corporation, 1987
CRYSTALSTONE   TMS Pictures/The Movie Store, 1988
SKI PATROL   Triumph, 1990
THE MARLA HANSON STORY (TF)   Citadel
Entertainment, 1991

G E O F F R E Y   S T E P H E N S O N
A BREED APART   Orion, 1984
HOWLING II...YOUR SISTER IS A WEREWOLF
Thorn-EMI, 1986

R O B E R T   M .   S T E V E N S *
West Coast Card
Agent: Smith Gosnell Nicholson & Associates -
Pacific Palisades, 213/459-0307

MAX HEADROOM (Pilot)   1988
EARTH*STAR VOYAGER (TF)   Walt Disney TV/Marstar
Productions, 1988
THE NAKED GUN: FROM THE FILES OF POLICE
SQUAD   Paramount, 1988
THE 'BURBS   Universal, 1989
FEAR   Vestron, 1990
TUNE IN TOMORROW...   Polar Films/Cinecom, 1990

C H A R L E S   S T E W A R T
PLEASURE AT HER MAJESTY'S (FD)   1976
THE GAMEKEEPER   ATV, 1980, w/Chris Menges
DEEP IN THE HEART   *HANDGUN*   Warner Bros., 1981

J A C Q U E S   S T E Y N *
German & French Union
Agent: Smith Gosnell Nicholson & Associates -
Pacific Palisades, 213/459-0307

OUT OF ORDER   Sandstar Releasing Company, 1985
BAY COVEN (TF)   Guber-Peters Company/
Phoenix Entertainment Group, 1987
NIGHTMARE AT BITTER CREEK (TF)   Swanton Films/
Guber-Peters Entertainment Company/
Phoenix Entertainment Group, 1988
THE MIGHTY QUINN   MGM/UA, 1988
KILL ME AGAIN   MGM/UA, 1990

WITOLD STOK
HIDDEN CITY   Hidden City Films/Channel Four, 1987
EAT THE RICH   New Line Cinema, 1987
ECHOES   Working Title Productions/
   Channel Four, 1988
STAR TRAP   Zenith Productions, 1989
TAILSPIN: BEHIND THE KOREAN AIRLINE
   TRAGEDY (CTF)   HBO/Granada/Darlow Smithson
   Productions, 1990
BACK HOME (CTF)   Citadel Entertainment/TVS
   Films-Verronmead Productions, 1990

VITTORIO STORARO, AIC, ASC
THE BIRD WITH THE CRYSTAL PLUMAGE
   UMC, 1970
THE CONFORMIST   Paramount, 1971
LAST TANGO IN PARIS   United Artists, 1973
1900   Paramount, 1976
SCANDALO *SUBMISSION*   Brenner, 1977
AGATHA   Warner Bros., 1979
APOCALYPSE NOW HH   United Artists, 1979
LUNA   20th Century Fox, 1979
REDS ★★   Paramount, 1981
ONE FROM THE HEART   Columbia, 1982
WAGNER (MS)   London Trust Productions/Richard
   Wagner Productions/Ladbroke Productions/
   Hungarofilm, 1983
LADYHAWKE   Warner Bros./20th Century Fox, 1985
THE LAST EMPEROR ★★   Columbua, 1987
ISHTAR   Columbia, 1987
TUCKER: THE MAN AND HIS DREAM
   Paramount, 1988
NEW YORK STORIES ("Life Without Zoe")   Buena
   Vista, 1989
DICK TRACY ★   Buena Vista, 1990
THE SHELTERING SKY   Warner Bros, 1990

HARRY STRADLING, JR., ASC
Agent: Sanford-Skouras & Gross - Los Angeles,
   213/208-2100

THE GOOD GUYS AND THE BAD GUYS   Warner
   Bros., 1969
SUPPORT YOUR LOCAL SHERIFF   United
   Artists, 1969
THERE WAS A CROOKED MAN   Warner Bros., 1970
LITTLE BIG MAN   National General, 1970
DIRTY DINGUS MAGEE   MGM, 1970
SUPPORT YOUR LOCAL GUNFIGHTER   United
   Artists, 1971
SOMETHING BIG   National General, 1971
SKYJACKED   MGM, 1972
1776 H   Columbia, 1972
THE WAY WE WERE ★   Columbia, 1973
THE MAN WHO LOVED CAT DANCING   MGM, 1973
THUMB TRIPPING   Avco Embassy, 1973
McQ   Warner Bros., 1974
BITE THE BULLET   Columbia, 1975
MITCHELL   Allied Artists, 1975
ROOSTER COGBURN   Universal, 1975
MIDWAY   Universal, 1976
THE BIG BUS   Paramount, 1976
SPECIAL DELIVERY   American International, 1976
THE GREATEST   Columbia, 1977
DAMNATION ALLEY   20th Century Fox, 1977
GO TELL THE SPARTANS   Avco Embassy, 1978
CONVOY   United Artists, 1978
BORN AGAIN   Avco Embassy, 1978
PROPHECY   Paramount, 1979

CARNY   United Artists, 1980
MAD MAGAZINE PRESENTS UP THE ACADEMY
   Warner Bros., 1980
S.O.B.   Lorimar/Paramount, 1981
THE PURSUIT OF D.B. COOPER   Universal, 1981
BUDDY BUDDY   MGM/UA, 1981
O'HARA'S WIFE   Davis-Panzer Productions, 1982
GEORGE WASHINGTON (MS)   David GerberCompany/
   MGM-UA TV, 1984
MICKI AND MAUDE   Columbia, 1984
A FINE MESS   Columbia, 1986
BLIND DATE   Tri-Star, 1987
CADDYSHACK II   Warner Bros., 1988

IVAN STRASBURG
BACKSTAGE AT THE KIROV (FD)   Armand Hammer
   Productions, 1983
FLANAGAN   United Film Distribution, 1985
NINETEEN NINETEEN   Spectrafilm, 1986

R. MICHAEL STRINGER
DOUBLE EXPOSURE   Crown International, 1983
AMERICANA   Crown International, 1983
DEMONWARP   Vidmark, 1988
THE FORBIDDEN DANCE   21st Century/Columbia, 1990

IGOR SUNARA
Agent: The Gersh Agency, Inc., Beverly Hills -
   213/274-6611, New York - 212/997-1818

LOVE OR MONEY   Hemdale, 1989
MISPLACED   Original Cinema, 1991

JENS STURUP
WITCHCRAFT PART II: THE TEMPTRESS   Vista Street
   Entertainment, 1990

TIM SUHRSTEDT
Agent: The Gersh Agency, Inc., Beverly Hills -
   213/274-6611, New York - 212/997-1818

FORBIDDEN WORLD   New World, 1982
ANDROID   New World, 1982
THE HOUSE ON SORORITY ROW   Artists
   Releasing Corporation/Film Ventures
   International, 1983
THE RATINGS GAME (CTF)   Imagination-New Street
   Productions, 1984
SUBURBIA   New Horizons, 1984
STAND ALONE   New World, 1985, w/Tom Richmond
TEEN WOLF   Atlantic Releasing Corporation, 1985
CITY LIMITS   Atlantic Releasing Corporation, 1985
SPACE RAGE   Vestron, 1985
AND THE CHILDREN SHALL LEAD (TF)   Rainbow TV
   Workshop, 1985
CRITTERS   New Line Cinema, 1986,
   w/Christopher Tufty
MANNEQUIN   20th Century Fox, 1987
MYSTIC PIZZA   Samuel Goldwyn Company, 1988
SPLIT DECISIONS   New Century/Vista, 1988
FEDS   Warner Bros., 1988
DEAD SOLID PERFECT (CTF)   HBO Pictures/
   David Merrick Productions, 1988
BILL & TED'S EXCELLENT ADVENTURE
   Orion, 1989
THE COVER GIRL AND THE COP (TF)   Barry & Enright
   Prods., 1989
SHE KNOWS TOO MUCH (TF)   Finnegun/Pinchuk
   Company/Fred Silverman Co., MGM/UA, 1989

Su

CINEMATOGRAPHERS
PRODUCTION
DESIGNERS,
COSTUME
DESIGNERS AND
FILM EDITORS
GUIDE

CINEMATOGRAPHERS

Su

CINEMATOGRAPHERS
PRODUCTION
DESIGNERS,
COSTUME
DESIGNERS AND
FILM EDITORS
GUIDE

C
I
N
E
M
A
T
O
G
R
A
P
H
E
R
S

THE REVENGE OF AL CAPONE (TF)   Unity
    Productions/River City Productions, 1989
DOIN' TIME ON PLANET EARTH   Cannon, 1989
PAIR OF ACES (TF)   Once Apon A Time Films/
    Pedernales Films, 1990
MAN AGAINST THE MOB: THE CHINATOWN
    MURDERS (TF)   von Zerneck-Sertner
    Productions, 1990
MEN AT WORK   Epic-Elwes-Euphoria/
    Triumph, 1990

BRUCE SURTEES
Agent: The Gersh Agency, Inc., Beverly Hills -
    213/274-6611, New York - 212/997-1818

THE BEGUILED   Universal, 1971
PLAY MISTY FOR ME   Universal, 1971
DIRTY HARRY   Warner Bros., 1972
BLUME IN LOVE   Warner Bros., 1973
HIGH PLAINS DRIFTER   Universal, 1972
LENNY ★   United Artists, 1974
NIGHT MOVES   Warner Bros., 1975
LEADBELLY   Paramount, 1976
SPARKLE   Warner Bros., 1976
THE OUTLAW JOSEY WALES   Warner Bros., 1976
THE SHOOTIST   Paramount, 1976
THREE WARRIORS   United Artists, 1978
BIG WEDNESDAY   Warner Bros., 1978
MOVIE MOVIE ("Baxters Beauties of 1933")   Warner
    Bros., 1978
DREAMER   20th Century Fox, 1979
ESCAPE FROM ALCATRAZ   Paramount, 1979
INCHON!   MGM/UA, 1982
FIREFOX   Warner Bros., 1982
WHITE DOG   Paramount, 1982
LADIES AND GENTLEMEN...THE FABULOUS
    STAINS   Paramount, 1982
HONKYTONK MAN   Warner Bros., 1982
BAD BOYS   Universal/AFD, 1983, w/Donald Thorin
RISKY BUSINESS   The Geffen Co./
    Warner Bros.,1983
SUDDEN IMPACT   Warner Bros., 1983
TIGHTROPE   Warner Bros., 1984
BEVERLY HILLS COP   Paramount, 1984
PALE RIDER   Warner Bros., 1985
OUT OF BOUNDS   Columbia, 1986
PSYCHO III   Universal, 1986
RATBOY   Warner Bros., 1986
BACK TO THE BEACH   Paramount, 1987
LICENSE TO DRIVE   20th Century Fox, 1988
MEN DON'T LEAVE   The Geffen Company/Warner
    Bros., 1990
RUN   Buena Vista, 1991

ROBERT SURTEES†
MUTINY ON THE BOUNTY ★   MGM, 1962
DOCTOR DOLITTLE ★   20th Century Fox, 1967
THE GRADUATE ★   Embassy, 1967
THE LAST PICTURE SHOW ★   Columbia, 1971
THE STING ★   Universal, 1973
THE HINDENBURG ★   Universal, 1975
THE GREAT WALDO PEPPER   Universal, 1975
A STAR IS BORN ★   Warner Bros., 1976
TURNING POINT ★   20th Century Fox, 1977
SAME TIME, NEXT YEAR ★   Universal, 1978
BLOODBROTHERS   Warner Bros., 1979

PETER SUSCHITZKY*
IATSE 644
Agent: Sandra Marsh Management - Sherman Oaks,
    818/905-6961

THE WAR GAME   Pathe Contemporary, 1966
IT HAPPENED HERE   United Artists, 1966
PRIVILEGE   Universal, 1967
CHARLIE BUBBLES   Regional, 1968
A MIDSUMMER NIGHT'S DREAM   Eagle, 1968
LEO THE LAST   United Artists, 1970
MELODY/SWALK   1971
THE PIED PIPER   1972
HENRY VIII & HIS SIX WIVES   Levitt-Pickman, 1973
THAT'LL BE THE DAY   EMI, 1974
ALL CREATURES GREAT AND SMALL
    Talent Associates/EMI TV, 1975
LISZTOMANIA   Warner Bros., 1975
THE ROCKY HORROR PICTURE SHOW   20th Century
    Fox, 1976
VALENTINO   United Artists 1977
THE EMPIRE STRIKES BACK   20th Century
    Fox, 1980
KRULL   Columbia, 1983
FALLING IN LOVE   Paramount, 1984
DEAD RINGERS   20th Century Fox, 1988
WHERE THE HEART IS   Buena Vista, 1990

MIKHAIL SUSLOV
Agent: Lawrence A. Mirisch, Triad Artists, Inc. -
    Los Angeles, 213/556-2727

STRANGER'S KISS   Orion Classics, 1984
SHATTERED VOWS (TF)   Bertinelli-Pequod
    Productions, 1984
THE JOY THAT KILLS (TF)   Cypress Point
    Productions, 1985
3:15   Dakota Entertainment, 1986
BLACK MOON RISING   New World, 1986
NOBODY'S FOOL   Island Pictures, 1986
ROANOAK (TF)   South Carolina ETV Network/
    First Contract Films/National Video
    Corporation, 1986
VERNE MILLER   Alive Films, 1987
STEAL THE SKY (CTF)   HBO Pictures/Yoram BenAmi
    Productions/Paramount TV ,1988
PRANCER   Orion, 1989

TOBIAS SWANEPOEL
BRUTAL GLORY   Quest Entertainment, 1991

T

FRED TAMMES
THE SHOOTING PARTY   European Classics, 1984
THE WHISTLE BLOWER   Hemdale, 1987
SOUVENIR (CTF)   Fancy Free productions Ltd., 1988
OUT OF TIME   Motion Picture International, 1989

MASAKI TAMURA
TAMPOPO   New Yorker Films, 1987

CARLO TAPANI
SATURDAY, SUNDAY, MONDAY   Silvio Berlusconi
    Communications, 1990

GALE TATTERSALL
Agent: Camera Masters - Venice, 213/306-0810

COMRADES   British Film Institute, 1986
VROOM   Motion Pictures, 1988
HOMEBOY   Redbury Ltd./Elliott Kastner Prods., 1988
WILD ORCHID   Vision International/Triumph, 1990

ALFRED TAYLOR
Agent: Selwyn - Los Angeles, 213/463-3700

THE TERROR   American International, 1963
SPIDER BABY   *CANNIBAL ORGY*   1968
THE GREAT WALTZ   MGM, 1972
SLITHER   MGM, 1973
THE MAN WHO LOVED CAT DANCING   MGM, 1973
THE SWINGING CHEERLEADERS   Centaur, 1974
FANNY HILL   Playboy Enterprises, 1983
NIGHTSHADOWS *MUTANT*   Artists Releasing
    Corporation/Film Ventures International, 1984

DYANNA TAYLOR
EAT AND RUN   New World, 1987

GIL TAYLOR, BSC
A HARD DAY'S NIGHT   United Artists, 1964
THE OMEN   20th Century Fox, 1976
STAR WARS   20th Century Fox, 1977
DRACULA   Universal, 1979
ESCAPE TO ATHENA   AFD, 1979
FLASH GORDON   Universal, 1980
VENOM   Paramount, 1982, w/Denys Coop
LOSIN' IT   Embassy, 1982
LASSITER   Warner Bros., 1984
THE BEDROOM WINDOW   DEG, 1987

STAN TAYLOR
Agent: The Production Agency - Los Angeles,
    213/651-1858
MURDER AT THE PTA LUNCHEON (TF)
    von Zerneck-Sertner Films/Patricia K. Meyers
    Productions, 1990
THE LAKER GIRLS (TF)   Viacom, 1990
MANHUNT: SEARCH FOR THE NIGHT STALKER (TF)
    Leonard Hill Films, 1990

RONNIE TAYLOR, BSC
Agent: London Management, 235/241 Regent St. -
    London, W1R 7AG, 071-493-1610

CIRCLE OF IRON   Avco Embassy, 1979
SAVAGE HARVEST   20th Century Fox, 1981
GANDHI ★★   Columbia, 1982, w/Billy Williams
HIGH ROAD TO CHINA   Warner Bros., 1983
SPLITZ   Film Ventures, 1984
A CHORUS LINE   Columbia, 1985
FOREIGN BODY   Orion, 1986
OPERA   Dacfilm/RAI, 1987
CRY FREEDOM   Universal, 1987
THE EXPERTS   Paramount, 1990
SEA OF LOVE   Universal, 1990
POPCORN   Studio Three, 1991

GARY THIELTGES
Agent: Creative Technique, 413/466-4173

EATING RAOUL   20th Century Fox International
    Classics, 1982
SNO-LINE   Vandom International Pictures, 1986
VASECTOMY: A DELICATE MATTER   Vandom
    International Pictures, 1986
THE BOSS' WIFE   Tri-Star, 1986
STICKY FINGERS   Spectrafilm, 1988
RETRIBUTION   United Film Distribution, 1988
UNDER THE GUN   Marquis Pictures, 1989

JOHN THOMAS
METROPOLITAN   Westerly Film-Video, 1990

JAMIE THOMPSON
Manager: Matt Harvey, 213/662-0107
Home: 232 S. New Hampshire Ave., #4, Los Angeles,
    213/387-7515

RED HERRING   Red Herring Productions, 1989
GRAVE SECRETS   Planet Productions, 1990
CIRCUITRY MAN   Skouras, 1990
DESIRE & HELL AT SUNSET MOTEL   Planet
    Productions, 1991
HIGHLANDER II   DDM Film Corporation, 1991
    (N. American unit)

ALEX THOMSON, BSC
THE CLASS OF MISS MacMICHAEL   Brut
    Productions, 1978
EXCALIBUR ★   Orion/Warner Bros., 1981
THE CAT AND THE CANARY   Quartet, 1982
THE KEEP   Paramount, 1983
ELECTRIC DREAMS   MGM/UA, 1984
EUREKA   United Artists Classics, 1984
BULLSHOT   Island Alive, 1985
YEAR OF THE DRAGON   MGM/UA, 1985
LEGEND   Universal, 1986
LABYRINTH   Tri-Star, 1986
RAW DEAL   DEG, 1986
DUET FOR ONE   Cannon, 1987
THE SICILIAN   20th Century Fox, 1987
DATE WITH AN ANGEL   DEG, 1987
TRACK 29   Island Pictures, 1988
HIGH SPIRITS   Tri-Star, 1988
LEVIATHAN   MGM/UA, 1989
THE RACHEL PAPERS   MGM/UA, 1989
MR. DESTINY   Silver Screen Partners IV/Touchstone/
    Buena Vista, 1990
THE KRAYS (uncredited)   Parkfield Entertainment/
    Fugitive Features/Rank, 1990

Th

CINEMATOGRAPHERS
PRODUCTION
DESIGNERS,
COSTUME
DESIGNERS AND
FILM EDITORS
GUIDE

CINEMATOGRAPHERS

Th

CINEMATOGRAPHERS
PRODUCTION
DESIGNERS,
COSTUME
DESIGNERS AND
FILM EDITORS
GUIDE

C
I
N
E
M
A
T
O
G
R
A
P
H
E
R
S

DONALD E. THORIN, ASC *

Agent: Larry Mirisch, Triad Artists - Los Angeles,
    213/556-2727

THIEF   United Artists, 1981
AN OFFICER AND A GENTLEMAN   Paramount, 1982
BAD BOYS   Universal/AFD, 1983, w/Bruce Surtees
AGAINST ALL ODDS   Columbia, 1984
PURPLE RAIN   Warner Bros., 1984
MISCHIEF   20th Century Fox, 1985
AMERICAN ANTHEM   Columbia, 1986
WILDCATS   Warner Bros., 1986
THE GOLDEN CHILD   Paramount, 1986
COLLISION COURSE   DEG, 1988
THE COUCH TRIP   Orion, 1988
MIDNIGHT RUN   Universal, 1988
TROOP BEVERLY HILLS   WEG, 1989
LOCK UP   Tri-Star, 1989
TANGO & CASH   Guber-Peters/Warner Bros., 1989
THE MARRYING MAN   Buena Vista, 1991

ERLING THURMANN-ANDERSON

ISTANBUL: KEEP YOUR EYES OPEN   Omegafilm/
    Cori Films, 1990

CLIVE TICKNER

THE PLOUGHMAN'S LUNCH   Samuel Goldwyn
    Company, 1984
SHE'LL BE WEARING PINK PAJAMAS   Film
    Forum, 1986
FRENCH LESSONS   Warner Bros., 1986
GETTING IT RIGHT   MCEG, 1989
HIDDEN AGENDA   Hemdale, 1990
TRAFFICK: PARTS I-V (MS)   Channel 4/Picture
    Partnership Productions, 1990

FRANK TIDY

Agent: London Management, 235/241 Regent St. -
    London, W1R 7AG, 071-493-1610

THE DUELLISTS   Paramount, 1978
THE LUCKY STAR   Pickman Films, 1981
THE GREY FOX   United Artists Classics, 1983
SPACEHUNTER: ADVENTURES IN THE
    FORBIDDEN ZONE   Columbia, 1983
ONE MAGIC CHRISTMAS   Buena Vista, 1985
THE MEAN SEASON   Orion, 1985
CODE OF SILENCE   Orion, 1985
SWEET LIBERTY   Universal, 1986
HOT PURSUIT   Paramount, 1987
JOHN AND THE MISSUS   Cinema Group, 1987
SLIPSTREAM   Entertainment Film, 1989
THE PACKAGE   Orion, 1989
THE RAGGEDY RAWNEY   Four Seasons
    Entertainment, 1989
HITLER'S DAUGHTER (CTF)   Wilshire Court
    Productions/OTML Films, 1990
THE LAST BEST YEAR OF MY LIFE (TF)   World
    International Network/David W. Rintels
    Productions, 1990
PERSONALS (CTF)   Wilshire Court Productions/
    Sharmill Productions, 1990
THE KISSING PLACE (CTF)   Wilshire Court
    Productions/Cynthia Cherbak Productions, 1990
THE BUTCHER'S WIFE   Paramount, 1991

GEORGE TIRL

NOT FOR PUBLICATION   Samuel Goldwyn
    Company, 1984
ELLIE   Film Ventures, 1984
1918   Cinecom, 1985
ON VALENTINE'S DAY   Angelika Films, 1986
STEEL DAWN   Vestron, 1987
END OF THE LINE   Orion Classics, 1987
THE HEIST (CTF)   HBO Pictures, 1989
DAMNED RIVER   Silver Lion/MGM/UA, 1990

JOHN TOLL

GOOD NIGHT, SWEET WIFE: A MURDER IN
    BOSTON (TF)   Arnold Shapiro Productions/CBS
    Entertainment Productions, 1990

HERNAN TORO

Management: Esteban Films, 250 W. Fisk Bldg., 57th St.,
    New York, NY 10017, 212/948-1491

AGONIA   Joel Films, 1984
EL ESCANDALO   Yekuana Films, 1986
OPERACION BILLETE   Cine Arte, 1987
SENORA BOLERO   Cinematografica Macuto, 1989
UN SUENO EN EL ABISMO   Lucien Films, 1990
VISUAL   Casablanco Producies, 1990

MARIO TOSI, ASC

FROGS   American International, 1972
SOME CALL IT LOVING   Cine Globe, 1973
KILLING KIND   Media Trend, 1974
BUSTER AND BILLIE   Columbia, 1974
REPORT TO THE COMMISSIONER   United
    Artists, 1975
HEARTS OF THE WEST   MGM/United Artists, 1975
CARRIE   United Artists, 1976
MACARTHUR   Universal, 1977
THE BETSY   Allied Artists, 1978
THE MAIN EVENT   Warner Bros., 1979
THE STUNT MAN   20th Century Fox, 1980
RESURRECTION   Universal, 1980
COAST TO COAST   Paramount, 1980
WHOSE LIFE IS IT ANYWAY?   MGM/UA, 1981
SIX PACK   20th Century Fox, 1982

JEAN TOURNIER

MOONRAKER   United Artists, 1979
THE FIENDISH PLOT OF DR. FU MANCHU
    United Artists, 1980
CAMILLE (TF)   Rosemont Productions, 1984
TARGET   Warner Bros., 1985
FEMMES DE PERSONNE   European
    Classics, 1986

LUCIANO TOVOLI

Agent: Smith Gosnell Nicholson & Associates -
    Pacific Palisades, 213/459-0307

ADOPTION   Studio Hunnai, 1975
LEONOR   CIC, 1975
SUNDAY WOMAN   *LA DONNA DELLA DOMENICA*
    20th Century Fox, 1976
THE LAST WOMAN   *LA DERNIERE FEMME*
    Columbia, 1976
LE DESERT DES TARTARES   Gaumont, 1976
SUSPIRIA   International Classics, 1977
BREAD AND CHOCOLATE   World Northal, 1978

WHERE ARE YOU GOING ON HOLIDAY? *DORE VAIIN VACANZA?* Cineriz, 1979
UNSANE Bedford Entertainment/Film Fallery, 1982
BIANCA FasoFilm/Reteitalia, 1985
POLICE Island Pictures, 1985
LA CAGE AU FOLLES 3: THE WEDDING Tri-Star, 1986
REVERSAL OF FORTUNE Shochiku Fuji-Sovereign Pictures/Warner Bros., 1990

WOLFGANG TREU
THE LITTLE DRUMMER GIRL Warner Bros., 1984
QUICKER THAN THE EYE Eural Films/FR3/Condor Film, 1988

HAL TRUSSELL
Agent: Smith Gosnell Nicholson & Associates - Pacific Palisades, 213/459-0307

ONE DARK NIGHT Comworld, 1983
BACHELOR PARTY 20th Century Fox, 1984
THE NAKED CAGE Cannon, 1986
ORDINARY HEROES Crow Productions/Ira Barmak Productions, 1986
THE FOURTH MAN (TF) Rosebud Productions, 1990

BRIAN TUFANO
Agent: The Gersh Agency, Inc. - Beverly Hills, 213/274-6611

THE SAILOR'S RETURN Euston Films Ltd., 1978
QUADROPHENIA World Northal, 1979
THE LORDS OF DISCIPLINE Paramount, 1983
DREAMSCAPE 20th Century Fox, 1984
WAR PARTY Tri-Star, 1989
THE ENDLESS GAME (CTF) Pixit/Reteitalia/TVS Films Productions, 1990

CHRISTOPHER G. TUFTY
Agent: Tom Turley - New York, 212/874-6842
Address: 3957 Albright Ave., Los Angeles, CA 90066, 213/391-2611

LAS VEGAS WEEKEND Pygmalion Company, 1985
CRITTERS New Line Cinema, 1986, w/Tim Suhrstedt
STOOGEMANIA Atlantic Releasing Corporation, 1986
WEST IS WEST Rathod Partners, 1987
SMASH, CRASH, AND BURN Commercial Pictures Corp., 1988
DAREDREAMER The Lensmen Company, 1989
MODERN LOVE Lyric Films/SVS/Skouras, 1990

MASAHARU UEDA
RAN ★ Orion Classics, 1985, w/Takao Saito & Asakazu Nakai
AKIRA KUROSAWA'S DREAMS Warner Bros., 1990, w/Takao Saito

ALEXANDER ULLOA
CRYSTAL HEART New World, 1987

JOSEPH URBANCZYK
THE ALLNIGHTER Universal, 1987

JOST VACANO
Agent: The Gersh Agency, Inc., Beverly Hills - 213/274-6611, New York - 212/997-1818

SOLDIER OF ORANGE Samuel Goldwyn Co., 1977
SPETTERS Samuel Goldwyn Co., 1980
DAS BOOT ★ Columbia ,1982
THE NEVERENDING STORY Warner Bros., 1984
52 PICK-UP Cannon, 1986
ROBOCOP Orion, 1987
ROCKET GIBRALTAR Columbia, 1988
TOTAL RECALL Tri-Star, 1990

THOMAS VAMOS
THE GATE New Century/Vista, 1987
CAPTIVE HEARTS MGM/UA, 1987

REYNALDO VILLALOBOS
COUPE DE VILLE Morgan Creek Productions/ Universal, 1990
SIBLING RIVALRY Nelson Entertainment/Castle Rock Entertainment/Columbia, 1990

THEO VAN DE SANDE
Agent: Smith Gosnell Nicholson & Associates - Pacific Palisades, 213/459-0307

THE GIRL WITH THE RED HAIR United Artists Classics, 1983
THE ILLUSIONIST Film Forum, 1985
THE ASSAULT Cannon, 1986
CROSSING DELANCEY Warner Bros., 1988
ROOFTOPS New Visions, 1989
MIRACLE MILE Tri-Star, 1989
THE FIRST POWER Interscope Communications/ Nelson Entertainment/Orion, 1990
ONCE AROUND Universal, 1991
THE TENDER Trans World Entertainment, 1991

Va

CINEMATOGRAPHERS
PRODUCTION
DESIGNERS,
COSTUME
DESIGNERS AND
FILM EDITORS
GUIDE

CINEMATOGRAPHERS

Va

CINEMATOGRAPHERS
PRODUCTION
DESIGNERS,
COSTUME
DESIGNERS and
FILM EDITORS
GUIDE

C
I
N
E
M
A
T
O
G
R
A
P
H
E
R
S

EDDY VAN DER ENDEN
BUTTERFLY   Analysis, 1982
A TIME TO DIE   Almi Pictures, 1983
FAKE OUT   Analysis, 1983
GRUNT! THE WRESTLING MOVIE   New World, 1985
CAUGHT   World Wide, 1987

ERIC VAN HAREN NORMAN
PLAYING FOR KEEPS   Universal, 1986
HERO AND THE TERROR   Cannon, 1988
GO TOWARD THE LIGHT (TF)   Corapeake
    Productions, 1988
LENA: MY HUNDRED CHILDREN (TF)   1988
I KNOW MY FIRST NAME IS STEVEN (TF)   Andrew
    Adelson Company/Lorimar TV, 1989
OVER MY DEAD BODY (TF)   Universal
    Television, 1990
TOO YOUNG TO DIE? (TF)   von Zerneck-Sertner
    Films, 1990
A CRY FOR HELP: THE TRACEY THURMAN
    STORY (TF)   AUTL Productions, 1990

DEREK VANLINT
ALIEN   20th Century Fox, 1979
DRAGONSLAYER   Paramount, 1981

KEES VAN OOSTRUM
BLUE HEAVEN   Vetron/Shapiro Entertainment, 1984
HER LIFE AS A MAN (TF)   LS Entertainment, 1984
CERTAIN FURY   New World, 1985
THE GIFTED ONE (TF)   Richard Rothstein
    Productions/NBC Productions, 1989
A SON'S PROMISE (TF)   Marian Rees
    Associates, 1990
THE INCIDENT (TF)   Qintex Entertainment, 1990
LONG ROAD HOME (TF)   Rosemont
    Productions, 1991
SON OF THE MORNING STAR-PARTS I & II (MS)
    The Mount Company, 1991

KENNETH VAN SICKLE
BETWEEN THE LINES   Midwest Film
    Productions, 1977

MICK VAN VORNEMANN
A TEST OF LOVE   Universal, 1985

HENRY VARGAS
Agent: Paul Gerard Agency - Newport Beach,
    714/644-7950

THE UNHOLY   Vestron, 1988
MIDNIGHT CROSSING   Vestron, 1988
THE TAKE (CTF)   MCA TV Entertainment/
    Cine-Nevada, 1990

RON VARGAS
DINNER AT EIGHT (CTF)   Think Entertainment, 1990
BROTHER FUTURE (TF)   Laneauville/Morris
    Entertainment, 1991

CARLO VARINI
SUBWAY   Island Alive, 1985
ONE WOMAN OR TWO   Orion Classics, 1987

RENE VERZIER
THE LITTLE GIRL WHO LIVES DOWN THE LANE
    American International, 1977
RABID   New World, 1977

TWO SOLITUDES   New World-Mutual, 1978
RITUALS   Day and Date International, 1978
HIGH-BALLIN'   American International, 1978
SEARCH AND DESTROY   1978
CITY ON FIRE   Avco Embassy, 1979
DEATH SHIP   Avco Embassy, 1980
DOUBLE NEGATIVE   Best Film and Video, 1980
HOG WILD   Avco Embassy, 1980
FISH HAWK   Avco Embassy, 1981
GAS   Paramount, 1981
VISITING HOURS   20th Century Fox, 1982
NIGHT EYES   Warner Bros. 1983
THE FUNNY FARM   New World, 1983
CROSS COUNTRY   New World, 1983
OF UNKNOWN ORIGIN   New World, 1983
COVERGIRL   New World, 1984
TOBY McTEAGUE   Spectrafilm, 1985
RECKLESS DISREGARD (CTF)   Telecom Entertainment/
    Polar Film Corporation/Fremantle of Canada Ltd., 1985
BREAKING ALL THE RULES   New World, 1985
IN LIKE FLYNN (TF)   Glen A. Larson Productions/20th
    Century Fox TV/Astral Film Productions, 1985
BULLIES   Universal, 1986
WILD THING   Atlantic Releasing Corporation, 1987
RED EARTH, WHITE EARTH (TF)   Chris/Rose
    Prods., 1989
THE PENTHOUSE (TF)   Greene-White Productions/
    Spectacor Films, 1989
EDDIE AND THE CRUISERS II: EDDIE LIVES   Scotti
    Bros., 1989

ROBIN VIDGEON, BSC
Agent: London Management, 235/241 Regent St. -
    London, W1R 7AG, 071-493-1610

HELLRAISER   New World, 1987
MR. NORTH   Samuel Goldwyn Co., 1988
THE PENITENT   Cineworld, 1988
HELLBOUND: HELLRAISER 2   New World, 1988
PARENTS   Vestron, 1989, w/Ernest Day
THE FLY II   20th Century Fox, 1989
NIGHTBREED   20th Century Fox, 1990
HIGHWAY TO HELL   Highway Productions, 1991

SACHA VIERNY
BEAU PERE   New Line Cinema, 1981
A ZED AND TWO NOUGHTS   Skouras Pictures, 1985
THE COOK, THE THIEF, HIS WIFE & HER LOVER
    Miramax, 1990
DROWNING BY NUMBERS   Galaxy International, 1991

REYNALDO VILLALOBOS
Agent: Candace Lake, Lake & Douroux Agency - Los
    Angeles, 213/557-0700

URBAN COWBOY   Paramount, 1980
NINE TO FIVE   20th Century Fox, 1980
THE BALLAD OF GREGORIO CORTEZ   Embassy, 1983
BLAME IT ON RIO   20th Century Fox, 1984
GRANDVIEW, U.S.A.   Warner Bros., 1984
WINDY CITY   Warner Bros., 1984
MIKE'S MURDER   The Ladd Co./Warner Bros., 1984
SAVING GRACE   Embassy, 1986
BAND OF THE HAND   Tri-Star, 1986
DESERT BLOOM   Columbia, 1986
LUCAS   20th Century Fox, 1986
PUNCHLINE   Columbia, 1988
MAJOR LEAGUE   Paramount, 1989
COUP DE VILLE   Universal, 1990

ERNEST VINCZE
ROSELAND   Cinema Shares International, 1977
JANE AUSTEN IN MANHATTAN
   Contemporary, 1980
SHARMA AND BEYOND   Cinecom, 1983
SCRUBBERS   Orion Classics, 1984
SHANGHAI SURPRISE   MGM/UA, 1986
THE NIGHTMARE YEARS (CTF)   Consolidated
   Artists, 1989
CREAM IN MY COFFEE (TF)   Pennies From Heaven/
   London Weekend TV, 1990

PAUL VON BRACK
Agent: The Miller Agency - Santa Clarita,
   818/843-7335

THREE TOUGH GUYS   1974
COOLEY HIGH   American International, 1975
AMERICAN DREAM (TF)   Mace Neufeld Productions/
   Viacom, 1981
COACH   Crown International, 1978

NICHOLAS VON STERNBERG
THE TOURIST TRAP   Compass International, 1979
GAS PUMP GIRLS   Cannon, 1979
X-RAY   Cannon, 1981
PINK MOTEL   New Image, 1982
HOSPITAL MASSACRE   Cannon, 1982
WACKO   Jensen Farley Pictures, 1983
JOYSTICKS   Jensen Farley Pictures, 1983
JUNGLE WARRIORS   Aquarius, 1984
FINAL JUSTICE   Arista Films, 1985
APPOINTMENT WITH FEAR   Galaxy, 1985
VALET GIRLS   Empire Pictures, 1987
SLAUGHTERHOUSE ROCK   Artists Entertainment
   Group, 1988
DANGEROUS LOVE   Concorde, 1988
NO RETREAT, NO SURRENDER II   Shapiro
   Glickenhaus, 1989
DR. ALIEN   Phantom Productions, 1989
TEXASVILLE   Cine-Source/Nelson Entertainment/
   Columbia, 1990
OUT OF SIGHT, OUT OF MIND   Spectrum
   Entertainment, 1990
THE CLOSER   Ion Pictures, 1991

MARIO VULPIANI
AN AVERAGE MAN   Cineric, 1977
THE KEY TO REBECCA (TF)   Taft Entertainment TV/
   Castle Combe Productions, 1985

WILLIAM WAGES
Agent: Smith Gosnell Nicholson & Associates -
   Pacific Palisades, 213/459-0307

SHOOTDOWN (TF)   Leonard Hill Films, 1985
RESTING PLACE (TF)   Marian Rees
   Associates, 1986
VENGEANCE: THE STORY OF TONY CIMO (TF)
   Nederlander TV and Films Productions/Robirdie
   Pictures, 1986
EYE ON THE SPARROW (TF)   Sarabande Productions/
   Republic Pictures, 1987
BABY GIRL SCOTT (TF)   Polson Company Productions/
   The Finnegan-Pinchuk Company, 1987
MAN OUTSIDE   Stouffer Enterprise Film Partners, 1987
DIXIE LANES   SC Entertainment, 1987
GORE VIDAL'S LINCOLN (TF)   Chris-Rose Productions/
   Finnegan-Pinchuk Company, 1988
PANCHO BARNES (TF)   Blue Andre Productions/
   Orion TV, 1988
DESPERATE FOR LOVE (TF)   Vishudda Productions/
   Andrew Adelson Productions/Lorimar
   Telepictures, 1989
THE TRAVELING MAN (CTF)   Irvin Kershner
   Films, 1989
VOICES WITHIN: THE LIVES OF TRUDDI CHASE (MS)
   New World TV/P.A. Productions/Itzbinzo Long
   Productions, 1990
WHEN WILL I BE LOVED? (TF)   Nederlander Television
   and Film Productions, 1990
CAROLINE? (TF)   Barry & Enright Productions, 1990

ROY H. WAGNER, ASC
Agent: Scott Harris, Harris & Goldberg Talent Agency -
   Los Angeles, 213/553-5200

PRAY FOR DEATH   American Distribution
   Group, 1985
9 DEATHS OF THE NINJA   Crown
   International, 1985
RETURN TO HORROR HIGH   New World, 1987
WITCHBOARD   Cinema Group, 1987
A NIGHTMARE ON ELM STREET PART 3:
   DREAM WARRIORS   New Line Cinema, 1987
BEAUTY AND THE BEAST (Pilot) ☆☆   1987
MORTUARY ACADEMY   Landmark Releasing, 1987
DAKOTA'S WAY (Pilot)   1988
SOME KINDA WOMAN (Pilot)   1988
JUAREZ (Pilot)   1988
HOUSTON KNIGHTS (Pilot)   1988
DISASTER AT SILO 7 (TF) ☆   Mark Carliner
   Prods., 1988
QUANTUM LEAP (Pilot) ☆   1989

DAVID WAGREICH
JUST LIFE (TF)   Aaron Spelling Productions/Victoria
   Principal Productions, 1990

Wa

CINEMATOGRAPHERS
PRODUCTION
DESIGNERS,
COSTUME
DESIGNERS AND
FILM EDITORS
GUIDE

C
I
N
E
M
A
T
O
G
R
A
P
H
E
R
S

Wa

CINEMATOGRAPHERS
PRODUCTION
DESIGNERS,
COSTUME
DESIGNERS AND
FILM EDITORS
GUIDE

C
I
N
E
M
A
T
O
G
R
A
P
H
E
R
S

KEITH WAGSTAFF
Agent: Smith Gosnell Nicholson & Associates -
     Pacific Palisades, 213/459-0307

THE MAN FROM SNOWY RIVER   20th Century
     Fox, 1983
THE COOLANGATTA GOLD   Film Gallery, 1984
WILD HORSES (TF)   WIld Horses Productions/
     Telepictures Productions, 1985
BACKSTAGE   Skouras Pictures, 1989
RETURN TO SNOWY RIVER   Buena Vista, 1989

RIC WAITE, ASC
RED ALERT (TF)   The Jozak Company/
     Paramount TV, 1976
TAIL GUNNER JOE (TF)   Universal TV, 1977
A QUESTION OF GUILT (TF)   Lorimar
     Productions, 1978
THE INITIATION OF SARAH (TF)   Charles Fries
     Productions, 1978
A GUIDE FOR THE MARRIED WOMAN (TF)   20th
     Century Fox TV, 1978
THE OTHER SIDE OF THE MOUNTAIN - PART 2
     Universal, 1978
LEAVE YESTERDAY BEHIND (TF)   ABC Circle
     Films, 1978
DEAR DETECTIVE (TF)   CBS, 1979
CHARLESTON (TF)   Robert Stigwood Productions/
     RSO, Inc., 1979
AMATEUR NIGHT AT THE DIXIE BAR & GRILL (TF)
     Motown/Universal TV, 1979
AND BABY MAKES SIX (TF)   Alan Landsburg
     Productions, 1979
DEFIANCE   American International, 1980
ON THE NICKEL   Rose's Park, 1980
THE LONG RIDERS   United Artists, 1980
REVENGE OF THE STEPFORD WIVES (TF)   Edgar J.
     Scherick Productions, 1980
A PERFECT MATCH (TF)   Lorimar Productions, 1980
THE BORDER   Universal, 1982
TEX   Buena Vista, 1982
48HRS.   Paramount, 1982
DEMPSEY (TF)   Charles Fries Productions, 1983
CLASS   Orion, 1983
UNCOMMON VALOR   Paramount, 1983,
     w/Stephen Burum
FOOTLOOSE   Paramount, 1984
RED DAWN   MGM/UA, 1984
BREWSTER'S MILLIONS   Universal, 1985
MIDAS VALLEY (MS)   Edward S. Feldman Company/
     Warner Bros. TV, 1985
SUMMER RENTAL   Paramount, 1985
VOLUNTEERS   Tri-Star, 1985
COBRA   Warner Bros., 1986
ADVENTURES IN BABYSITTING   Buena Vista, 1987
YOU RUINED MY LIFE (TF)   Lantana-Kosberg
     Productions/Mark H. Ovitz Productions/Walt
     Disney TV, 1987
THE GREAT OUTDOORS   Universal, 1988
MARKED FOR DEATH   Steamroller Productions/20th
     Century Fox, 1990
OUT FOR JUSTICE   Warner Bros., 1991

KENT WAKEFORD
MEAN STREETS   Warner Bros., 1973
THE PRINCESS ACADEMY   Empire Pictures, 1987
THE WOMEN'S CLUB   Lightning Pictures, 1987

JOHN WALKER
A WINTER TAN   1989

JACK WALLNER
INSIDE OUT   Hemdale, 1986

DAVID M. WALSH*
West Coast Card
Agent: The Gersh Agency, Inc., Beverly Hills -
     213/274-6611, New York - 212/997-1818

MONTE WALSH   Natioanl General, 1970
I WALK THE LINE   Columbia 1970
EVERYTHING YOU ALWAYS WANTED TO
     KNOW ABOUT SEX* (*BUT WERE AFRAID TO ASK)
     United Artists, 1972
SLEEPER   United Artists, 1973
THE LAUGHING POLICEMAN   20th Century Fox, 1973
THE OTHER SIDE OF THE MOUNTAIN   Universal, 1975
THE SUNSHINE BOYS   MGM/United Artists, 1975
W.C. FIELDS AND ME   Universal, 1976
MURDER BY DEATH   Columbia, 1976
SILVER STREAK   20th Century Fox, 1976
ROLLERCOASTER   Universal, 1977
THE GOODBYE GIRL   Warner Bros., 1977
SCOTT JOPLIN   Universal, 1977
FOUL PLAY   Paramount, 1978
HOUSE CALLS   Universal, 1978
CALIFORNIA SUITE   Columbia, 1978
THE IN-LAWS   Warner Bros., 1979
JUST YOU AND ME, KID   Columbia, 1979
CHAPTER TWO   Columbia, 1979
HERO AT LARGE   MGM/United Artists, 1980
SEEMS LIKE OLD TIMES   Columbia, 1980
PRIVATE BENJAMIN   Warner Bros., 1980
ONLY WHEN I LAUGH   Columbia, 1981
MAKING LOVE   20th Century Fox, 1982
I OUGHT TO BE IN PICTURES   20th Century Fox 1982
MAX DUGAN RETURNS   20th Century Fox, 1983
ROMANTIC COMEDY   MGM/UA, 1983
UNFAITHFULLY YOURS   20th Century Fox, 1984
JOHNNY DANGEROUSLY   20th Century Fox, 1984
COUNTRY   Buena Vista, 1984
TEACHERS   MGM/UA, 1984
MY SCIENCE PROJECT   Buena Vista, 1985
OUTRAGEOUS FORTUNE   Buena Vista, 1987
SUMMER SCHOOL   Paramount, 1987
FATAL BEAUTY   MGM/UA, 1987
SECOND SIGHT   Warner Bros., 1989
TAKING CARE OF BUSINESS   Hollywood Pictures/
     Buena Vista, 1990

NIGEL WALTERS
MOTHER LOVE-PARTS I-III (MS)   WGBH Boston/BBC
     TV Productions, 1990, w/Simon Maggs

JURG WALTHERS
NIGHT PATROL   New World, 1984, w/Hanania Baer
BLOOD DINER   Lightning Pictures, 1987

BURLEIGH WARTES
SUPERSTAR (Andy Warhol documentary)   Marilyn Lewis
     Entertainment, 1991

NORMAN WARWICK
THE GODSEND   Cannon, 1980
THE DOCTOR AND THE DEVILS   20th Century Fox,
     1985, w/Gerry Turpin

PHILIP ALAN WATERS
CYBORG Cannon, 1989

PETE WARRILOW, BSC
Agent: Smith Gosnell Nicholson & Associates -
   Pacific Palisades, 213/459-0307

13 O'CLOCK Third Coast Entertainment, 1988

MAKOTO WATANABE
LITTLE NOISES Monument Pictures, 1991

DAVID WATKIN
HELP! United Artists, 1965
THE CHARGE OF THE LIGHT BRIGADE United
   Artists, 1968, British
THE BOY FRIEND MGM, 1971
THE THREE MUSKETEERS 20th Century Fox, 1974
THE FOUR MUSKETEERS 20th Century Fox, 1975
MAHOGANY Paramount, 1975
ROBIN AND MARIAN Columbia, 1976
TO THE DEVIL A DAUGHTER EMI, 1976
JOSEPH ANDREWS Paramount, 1977
HANOVER STREET Columbia, 1979
THAT SUMMER Columbia, 1979
CUBA United Artists, 1979
CHARIOTS OF FIRE The Ladd Company/Warner
   Bros., 1981
ENDLESS LOVE Universal, 1981
YENTL MGM/UA, 1983
THE HOTEL NEW HAMPSHIRE Orion, 1984
WHITE NIGHTS Columbia, 1985
RETURN TO OZ Buena Vista, 1985
OUT OF AFRICA ★★ Univeral, 1985
SKY BANDITS Galaxy International, 1986
MOONSTRUCK MGM/UA, 1987
MASQUERADE MGM/UA, 1988
THE GOOD MOTHER Buena Vista, 1988
LAST RITES MGM/United Artists, 1988
JOURNEY TO THE CENTER OF THE EARTH
   Cannon, 1989, w/Tom Fraser
MURDER BY MOONLIGHT (TF) 1989
MEMPHIS BELLE Enigma/Warner Bros., 1990
HAMLET Icon/Nelson Entertainment/Warner
   Bros., 1990

MICHAEL WATKINS
Home: 93 Bell Canyon Road, Bell Canyon,
   818/347-8636

FIGHTING MAD 20th Century Fox, 1976
THE LAST WALTZ United Artists, 1978
   (Additional DP w/Bobby Byrne, Laszlo Kovaks,
   David Myers, Hiro Narita & Vilmos Zsigmond)
THE GLITTER DOME (CTF) HBO Premiere Films/
   Telepictures Productions/Trincomali
   Productions, 1984
PARAMEDICS Vestron, 1988
COLD SASSY TREE (CTF) Faye Dunaway and Don
   Ohlmeyer Productions, 1990

FRANK WATTS
Agent: Smith Gosnell Nicholson & Associates -
   Pacific Palisades, 213/459-0307

RISING DAMP ITC, 1980
THE SHILLINGBURY BLOWERS ...AND THE BAND
   PLAYED ON Inner Circle, 1980

DANGEROUS DAVIES - THE LAST DETECTIVE 1980
THE MANIONS OF AMERICA (MS) Roger Gimbel
   Productions/EMI TV/Argonaut Films Ltd., 1981
EDUCATING RITA Columbia, 1983
HELEN KELLER - THE MIRACLE CONTINUES (TF)
   Castle Combe Productions/20th Century Fox TV, 1984
REARVIEW MIRROR (TF) Simon-Asher Entertainment/
   Sunn Classic Pictures, 1984
DEADLY INTENTIONS (TF) Green-Epstein
   Productions, 1985
THE GIRL WHO COULDN'T LOSE (TF) Filmways, 1985
THE CORSICAN BROTHERS (TF)
   Rosemont Productions, 1985
MARTIN'S DAY MGM/UA, 1985
D.A.R.Y.L. Paramount, 1985
HOUSTON: THE LEGEND OF TEXAS (TF) Taft
   Entertainment TV/J.D. Feigelson Productions, 1987

HARRY WAXMAN †
Agent: London Management - London, 011/441/493-1610

SWISS FAMILY ROBINSON Buena Vista, 1960
THE ROMAN SPRING OF MRS. STONE Warner
   Bros., 1961
THE DAY THE EARTH CAUGHT FIRE Universal, 1962
LANCELOT AND GUINEVERE Universal, 1963
STOLEN HOURS United Artists, 1963
CROOKS IN CLOISTERS Warner-Pathe, 1964
SHE MGM, 1965
KHARTOUM United Artists, 1966
THE FAMILY WAY Warner Bros., 1967
DANGER ROUTE United Artsts, 1968
THE ANNIVERSARY 20th Century Fox, 1968
TWISTED NERVE National General, 1969
THERE'S A GIRL IN MY SOUP Columbia, 1970
FLIGHT OF THE DOVES Columbia, 1971
DIGBY, THE BIGGEST DOG IN THE WORLD Cinerama
   Releasing Corporation, 1974
THE WICKER MAN Warner Bros., 1975
BLUE BLOOD Mallard Poductions, 1975
FIND THE LADY Danton, 1975
JOURNEY INTO FEAR Stirling Gold, 1976
THE PINK PANTHER STRIKES AGAIN United
   Artists, 1976
A BRIDGE TOO FAR United Artists, 1977
THE 39 STEPS International Picture Show
   Company, 1978
FORCE 10 FROM NAVARONE American
   International, 1978
FLASH GORDON Universal, 1980

JOSSI WEIN
THE HOUSE OF USHER RCA/Columbia Pictures Home
   Video, 1991

JAN WEINCKE
THE TREE OF KNOWLEDGE Scandinavia Today, 1982
ZAPPA Spectrafilm, 1984
TWIST AND SHOUT Miramax, 1986
DEAD OF WINTER MGM/UA, 1987
HELLO AGAIN Buena Vista, 1987
WEEDS DEG, 1987
PENN & TELLER GET KILLED Warner Bros., 1989

HELGE WEINDLER, BUK
MEN New Yorker Films, 1986
ME AND HIM Columbia, 1989

We

CINEMATOGRAPHERS
PRODUCTION
DESIGNERS,
COSTUME
DESIGNERS AND
FILM EDITORS
GUIDE

C
I
N
E
M
A
T
O
G
R
A
P
H
E
R
S

We

CINEMATOGRAPHERS
PRODUCTION
DESIGNERS,
COSTUME
DESIGNERS and
FILM EDITORS
GUIDE

C
I
N
E
M
A
T
O
G
R
A
P
H
E
R
S

PHILIPPE WELT
UNTIL SEPTEMBER   MGM/UA, 1984

BRIAN WEST
Agent: London Management, 235/241 Regent St. -
London, W1R 7AG, 071-493-1610

OUTBACK   United Artists, 1971
THE SPIKES GANG   United Artists, 1974
THE APPRENTICESHIP OF DUDDY KRAVITZ
Paramount, 1974
RUSSIAN ROULETTE   Avco Embassy, 1975
HOLOCAUST (MS)   Titus Productions, 1978
YESTERDAY'S HERO   EMI, 1979
STORIES FROM A FLYING TRUNK   EMI, 1979
THE DAY THE WOMEN GOT EVEN (TF)   Otto
Salaman Productions/PKO, 1980
A QUESTION OF HONOUR (TF)   Roger Gimbel
Productions/EMI TV/Sonny Grosso
Productions, 1982
BENNY'S PLACE (TF)   Titus Productions, 1982
THE LONELY LADY   Universal, 1983
MARVIN AND TIGE   20th Century Fox International
Classics, 1983
FINDERS KEEPERS   Warner Bros., 1984
MURDER WITH MIRRORS (TF)   1985
OUT OF THE DARKNESS (TF)   Grosso-Jacobson
Productions/Centerpoint Productions, 1985
84 CHARING CROSS ROAD   Columbia, 1987
THE CHRISTMAS WIFE (CTF)   HBO Showcase, 1988
TERROR ON HIGHWAY 91 (TF)   Katy Film
Productions Inc., 1989
JACKNIFE   Cineplex Odeon, 1989
FORBIDDEN NIGHTS (TF)   Warner Bros. TV/Tristine
Rainer Productions, 1990

JONATHAN WEST
MUNCHIES   Concorde, 1987
FINISH LINE (TF)   Guber-Peters Entertainment
Prods., 1989
A SINFUL LIFE   New Line Cinema, 1989
THE WHEREABOUTS OF JENNY (TF)   Katie Face
Productions, 1991

KEN WESTBURY, BSC
Agent: Grace Lyons Management - Los Angeles,
213/655-5100

THE VANISHING ARMY (TF)   1978, British
TO THE LIGHTHOUSE (TF)   BBC/Colin Gregg
Films, 1978
DOCTOR FISCHER OF GENEVA (TF)   Consolidated
Productions/BBC, 1985
TENDER IS THE NIGHT (CMS)   Showtime/BBC/
Seven Network, 1985
BELLMAN AND TRUE   Island Pictures, 1987
THE SINGING DETECTIVE (TF)   BBC/ABC
Australia, 1987
MAGIC MOMENTS (TF)   Arena Films/Yorkshire TV/
Atlantic Videoventures, 1988, British
TEARS IN THE RAIN (CTF)   British Lion/Yorkshire TV/
Atlantic Videoventures, 1988
AMERICAN ROULETTE   Film Four International/British
Screen/Mandemar Group, 1988
THE TRAGEDY OF FLIGHT 103: THE INSIDE STORY
(CTF)   Granada Film/HBO Showcase, 1990
HANDS OF A MURDERER (TF)   Yorkshire Television/
Storke-Fuisz Productions, 1990

HASKELL WEXLER, ASC
Agent: Sanford-Skouras & Gross - Los Angeles,
213/208-2100

THE LIVING CITY   1953
THE SAVAGE EYE   Trans-Lux, 1959
ANGEL BABY   Allied Artists, 1961
THE HOODLUM PRIEST   United Artists, 1961
A FACE IN THE RAIN   Embassy, 1963
AMERICA AMERICA   Warner Bros., 1963
THE BEST MAN   United Artists, 1964
THE LOVED ONE   1965
THE BUS (FD)   1965
WHO'S AFRAID OF VIRGINIA WOOLF? ★★   Warner
Bros., 1966
IN THE HEAT OF THE NIGHT   United Artists, 1967
THE THOMAS CROWN AFFAIR   United Artists, 1968
MEDIUM COOL   Paramount, 1969
BRAZIL: A REPORT ON TORTURE (FD)   1971
INTERVIEWS WITH MY LAI VETERANS (FD)   1971
THE TRIAL OF THE CATONSVILLE NINE
Cinema 5, 1972
AMERICAN GRAFFITI   Universal, 1973,
Visual Consultant
INTRODUCTION TO THE ENEMY   1974
ONE FLEW OVER THE CUCKOO'S NEST ★   United
Artists, 1975, w/Bill Butler
UNDER GROUND   New Yorker, 1976
BOUND FOR GLORY ★★   United Artists, 1976
COMING HOME   United Artists, 1978
CIA: A CASE OFFICER (FD)   1978
NO NUKES (FD)   Warner Bros., 1980
SECOND HAND HEARTS   Paramount, 1981
RICHARD PRYOR LIVE ON THE SUNSET STRIP (FD)
Columbia, 1982
LOOKIN' TO GET OUT   Paramount, 1982
THE MAN WHO LOVED WOMEN   Columbia, 1983
THE BUS II (FD)   1983
LATINO   Cinecom, 1985
MATEWAN ★   Cinecom, 1987
COLORS   Orion, 1988
THREE FUGITIVES   Buena Vista, 1989
BLAZE ★   Buena Vista, 1989

HOWARD WEXLER
REFORM SCHOOL GIRLS   New World, 1986
BANZAI RUNNER   Montage Films, 1987
HARD TICKET TO HAWAII   Malibu Bay Films, 1987
PICASSO TRIGGER   Malibu Bay Films, 1988
ANGEL III: THE FINAL CHAPTER   New World, 1988
SAVAGE BEACH   Malibu Bay Films, 1989

CHARLES F. WHEELER, ASC *
West Coast Card
Agent: Smith Gosnell Nicholson & Associates -
Pacific Palisades, 213/459-0307

YOURS, MINE AND OURS   United Artists, 1968
TORA! TORA! TORA! ★   20th Century Fox, 1970
C.C. AND COMPANY   Avco Embassy, 1970
SILENT RUNNING   Universal, 1972
PURSUIT (TF)   ABC Circle Films, 1972
TRUCK TURNER   American International, 1974
THE RED BADGE OF COURAGE (TF)   20th Century
Fox TV, 1974
A TREE GROWS IN BROOKLYN (TF)   20th Century
Fox TV, 1974
POSSE   Paramount, 1975
BABE (TF)   MGM TV, 1975

THE LINDBERGH KIDNAPPING CASE (TF)
Columbia TV, 1976
FREAKY FRIDAY   Buena Vista, 1976
THE GIFT OF LOVE (TF)   Osmond Productions, 1987
THE CAT FROM OUTER SPACE   Buena Vista, 1978
C.H.O.M.P.S.   American International, 1979
THE LAST FLIGHT OF NOAH'S ARK   Buena
Vista, 1980
CONDORMAN   Buena Vista, 1981
THE RENEGADES (TF)   Lawrence Gordon
Productions/Paramount TV, 1982
THURSDAY'S CHILD (TF)   The Catalina Production
Group/Viacom, 1983
I WANT TO LIVE (TF)   United Artists
Corporation, 1983
FOR LOVE AND HONOR (TF)   David Gerber
Company/MGM-UA TV, 1983
THE BEST OF TIMES   Universal, 1986

PAUL WHITE
JOBMAN   Blue Rock Films, 1990

JOSEPH M. WILCOTS
THE WHITE GIRL   Tony Brown Productions, 1990

DON WILDER
MEATBALLS   Paramount, 1979

BILLY WILLIAMS, BSC *
East Coast Card
Agent: Smith Gosnell Nicholson & Associates -
PacificPalisades, 213/459-0307

BILLION DOLLAR BRAIN   United Artists, 1967
THE MAGUS   20th Century Fox, 1968
TWO GENTLEMEN SHARING   American
International, 1969
WOMEN IN LOVE ★   United Artists, 1970
THE MIND OF MR. SOAMES   Columbia, 1970
SUNDAY BLOODY SUNDAY   United Artists, 1970
TAM LIN   Americna International, 1971
X, Y & ZEE   *ZEE & CO.*   Columbia, 1972
KID BLUE   20th Century Fox, 1973
NIGHT WATCH   Avco Embassy, 1973
THE GLASS MENAGERIE (TF)   Talent
Associates, 1973
THE WIND AND THE LION   MGM/United Artists, 1975
VOYAGE OF THE DAMNED   Avco Embassy, 1976
THE DEVIL'S ADVOCATE   Film World
Distributions, 1978
THE SILENT PARTNER   EMC Film/Aurora, 1979
EAGLE'S WING   International Picture Show, 1979
BOARDWALK   Atlantic Releasing Corporation, 1979
GOING IN STYLE   Warner Bros., 1979
SATURN 3   AFD, 1980
ON GOLDEN POND ★   Universal/AFD, 1981
MONSIGNOR   20th Century Fox, 1982
GANDHI ★★   Columbia, 1982, w/Ronnie Taylor
THE SURVIVORS   Columbia, 1983
ORDEAL BY INNOCENCE   MGM/UA, 1984
DREAMCHILD   Universal, 1985
ELENI   Warner Bros., 1985
THE MANHATTAN PROJECT   20th Century
Fox, 1986
SUSPECT   Tri-Star, 1987
THE RAINBOW   Vestron, 1989
STELLA   Buena Vista, 1990
DIAMOND'S EDGE   Castle Hill, 1990

GERALD M. WILLIAMS
GETTING LUCKY   Feifer-Miller/Vista St. Productions/
Raedon Home Video, 1990

GORDON WILLIS, ASC
END OF THE ROAD   Allied Artists, 1970
LOVING   Columbia, 1970
LITTLE MURDERS   20th Century Fox, 1970
KLUTE   Warner Bros., 1971
UP THE SANDBOX   National General, 1972
THE GODFATHER   Paramount, 1972
BAD COMPANY   Paramount, 1972
THE PAPER CHASE   20th Century Fox, 1973
THE PARALLAX VIEW   Paramount, 1974
THE GODFATHER PART II   Paramount, 1974
THE DROWNING POOL   Warner Bros., 1975
ALL THE PRESIDENT'S MEN   Warner Bros., 1976
ANNIE HALL   United Artists, 1977
9/30/55   Universal, 1977
INTERIORS   United Artists, 1978
COMES A HORSEMAN   United Artists, 1978
MANHATTAN   United Artists, 1979
WINDOWS   United Artists, 1980
STARDUST MEMORIES   United Artists, 1980
PENNIES FROM HEAVEN   MGM/United Artists, 1981
A MIDSUMMER NIGHT'S SEX COMEDY   Orion/Warner
Bros., 1982
ZELIG ★   Orion/Warner Bros., 1983
BROADWAY DANNY ROSE   Orion, 1984
THE PURPLE ROSE OF CAIRO   Orion, 1985
PERFECT   Columbia, 1985
THE MONEY PIT   Universal, 1986
THE PICK-UP ARTIST   20th Century Fox, 1987
BRIGHT LIGHTS, BIG CITY   MGM/UA, 1988
PRESUMED INNOCENT   Mirage/Warner Bros., 1990
THE GODFATHER PART III ★   Zoetrope Studios/
Paramount, 1990

IAN WILSON
PRIVATES ON PARADE   Orion Classics, 1984
WISH YOU WERE HERE   Atlantic Releasing
Corporation, 1987
DREAM DEMON   Palace Pictures, 1988
CHECKING OUT   Warner Bros., 1989
ERIK THE VIKING   Orion, 1989

PAUL WITTE
PLACE OF WEEPING   New World, 1986
A WHISPER TO A SCREAM   Lighthouse
Communications/Distant Horizon, 1989

DARIUSZ (DEREK) ADAMS WOLSKI
Agent: Smith Gosnell Nicholson & Associates -
Pacific Palisades, 213/459-0307

HEART   New World, 1987, w/Jacek Laskus
THE LAND OF LITTLE RAIN   Denver Center for
the Performing Arts/Mayport Productions, 1988
NIGHTFALL   Concorde, 1988

OLIVER WOOD
Agent: The Gersh Agency, Inc., Beverly Hills -
213/274-6611, New York - 212/997-1818

MAYA   Claridge, 1982
IN OUR HANDS   Almi Pictures, 1983 w/others
ALPHABET CITY   Atlantic Releasing Corporation, 1984

Wo

CINEMATOGRAPHERS
PRODUCTION
DESIGNERS,
COSTUME
DESIGNERS AND
FILM EDITORS
GUIDE

CINEMATOGRAPHERS

Wo

**CINEMATOGRAPHERS
PRODUCTION
DESIGNERS,
COSTUME
DESIGNERS** AND
**FILM EDITORS
GUIDE**

C
I
N
E
M
A
T
O
G
R
A
P
H
E
R
S

JOEY   Satori, 1985
NEON MANIACS   Bedford Entertainment, 1986,
   w/Joseph Mangine
THE ADVENTURES OF FORD FAIRLANE   Silver
   Pictures/20th Century Fox, 1990
DIE HARD 2: DIE HARDER   Gordon Company-Silver
   Pictures/20th Century Fox, 1990

JON WOODS
AFTER THE WAR-PARTS I - III (MS)   Granada
   TV, 1990

MARK WOODS
Agent Production Agency - Los Angeles,
   213/651-1858
LESS THAN PERFECT DAUGHTER (TF)   Hallinan
   Plus Productions, 1991

RALPH WOOLSEY, ASC
Agent: The Gersh Agency, Inc. - Beverly Hills,
   213/274-6611

LITTLE FAUSS AND BIG HALSY   Paramount, 1970
THE STRAWBERRY STATEMENT   MGM, 1970
DEADHEAD MILES   Paramount, 1971
THE NEW CENTURIONS   Columbia, 1972
THE ICEMAN COMETH   American Film
   Theatre, 1973
RAFFERTY & THE GOLD DUST TWINS   Warner
   Bros., 1975
MOTHER, JUGS & SPEED   20th Century Fox, 1976
LIFEGUARD   Paramount, 1976
FIRE SALE   20th Century Fox, 1977
THE PACK   Warner Bros., 1977
THE PROMISE   Universal, 1979
THE GREAT SANTINI   Orion/Warner Bros., 1979
THE LAST MARRIED COUPLE IN AMERICA
   Universal, 1980
OH GOD! BOOK II   Warner Bros., 1980

ARTHUR WOOSTER, BSC
Agent: London Management, 235/241 Regent St. -
   London, W1R 7AG, 071-493-1610

WHITE ROCK   EMI, 1977
EAT THE PEACH   Skouras Pictures, 1987
PLATOON LEADER   Cannon, 1988

DAVID WORLEY
HELLRAISER   New World, 1987

DAVID WORTH
Agent: The Miller Agency - Santa Clarita,
   818/843-7335

DEATH GAME   Levitt-Pickman, 1977
A GREAT RIDE   Manson International, 1978
BRONCO BILLY   Warner Bros., 1980
ANY WHICH WAY YOU CAN   Warner Bros., 1980
THE HOLLYWOOD KNIGHTS   Columbia, 1980
THE NIGHT THEY SAVED CHRISTMAS (TF)   Robert
   Halmi, Inc., 1984
NEVER TOO YOUNG TO DIE   Paul Releasing, 1986
TRAXX   DEG, 1988
BLOODSPORT   Cannon, 1988
CHINA CRY   Parakletos/TBN Films/Penland, 1990

ERIC WOSTER
FAR OUT MAN   New Line Cinema, 1990

JIM WRENN
DAKOTA   Miramax, 1988

JOSEPH YACOE
WITHOUT YOU I'M NOTHING   M.C.E.G., 1990

STEVE YACONELLI
Agent: The Gersh Agency, Inc., Beverly Hills -
   213/274-6611, New York - 212/997-1818

AMERICAN JUSTICE   The Movie Store, 1986
THE KARATE KID PART III   Columbia, 1989
GROSS ANATOMY   Buena Vista, 1989
PHANTOM OF THE OPERA (TF)   Saban-Scherick
   Productions, 1990

DANIEL YARUSSI
Agent: The Miller Agency - Santa Clarita, 818/843-7335

AND BABY MAKES SIX (TF)   Alan Landsburg
   Productions, 1979
THE COMING   1981
GRADUATION DAY   IFI/Scope III, 1981
STINGRAY (TF)   Stephen J. Cannell Productions, 1985
TOMBOY   Crown International, 1985
DEADLY INTENT   Fries Distribution, 1988
DANGER ZONE II: REAPERS' REVENGE   Skouras
   Pictures, 1989
DANGER ZONE III: STEEL HORSE WAR   Danger Zone
   Company, 1990

ROBERT D. YEOMAN
Agent: Smith Gosnell Nicholson & Associates -
   Pacific Palisades, 213/459-0307

HERO   Mirror Flims, 1985
C.A.T. SQUAD (TF)   NBC Productions, 1986
RAMPAGE   DEG, 1987, unreleased
RENTED LIPS   New Century/Vista, 1988
DEAD HEAT   New World, 1988
JOHNNY BE GOOD   Orion, 1988
DRUGSTORE COWBOY   Avenue Pictures, 1989
THE WIZARD   Universal, 1989
TOO MUCH SUN   CineTel/New Line Cinema, 1990

FREDDIE YOUNG, OBE
Agent: London Management, 235/241 Regent St. -
   London, W1R 7AG, 071-493-1610

BHOWANI JUNCTION   MGM, 1956
INDISCREET   Warner Bros., 1958
THE INN OF THE SIXTH HAPPINESS   20th Century
   Fox, 1958
THE GREENGAGE SUMMER   Columbia, 1961
LAWRENCE OF ARABIA ★★   Columbia, 1962
CHARADE   Universal, 1964

LORD JIM   Columbia, 1964
ROTTEN TO THE CORE   Cinema 5, 1965
DOCTOR ZHIVAGO ★★   MGM, 1965
THE DEADLY AFFAIR   Columbia, 1967
YOU ONLY LIVE TWICE   United Artists, 1967
BATTLE OF BRITAIN   United Artists, 1969
RYAN'S DAUGHTER ★★   MGM, 1970
NICHOLAS AND ALEXANDRA ★   Columbia, 1971
LUTHER   American Film Theatre, 1974
THE TAMARIND SEED   Avco Embassy, 1974
THE BLUE BIRD   20th Century Fox, 1976,
   w/Lonas Gritzus
THE MAN IN THE IRON MASK (TF)   Norman
   Rosemont Productions/ITC, 1977
STEVIE   First Artists, 1978
IKE (MS)   ABC Circle Films, 1979
SIDNEY SHELDON'S BLOODLINE   Paramount, 1979
ROUGH CUT   Paramount, 1980
RICHARD'S THINGS   New World, 1981
SWORD OF THE VALIANT   Cannon, 1984,
   w/Peter Hurst
INVITATION TO THE WEDDING   Chancery Line
   Films, 1984

LES YOUNG
TERROR   Crown International, 1979
SWEET WILLIAM   Kendon Films, 1980

RICHARD YURICICH, ASC
BRAINSTORM   MGM/UA, 1983

Z

STEFAN ZAPASNIK
MIXED BLOOD   Sara Films, 1985

FRED ZIEGLER
HAPPILY EVER AFTER   Filmation/First National
   Film/Kel-Air Entertainment, 1990

JERZY ZIELINSKI
Agent: Smith Gosnell Nicholson & Associates -
   Pacific Palisades, 213/459-0307

ARIA FOR AN ATHLETE   New Yorker Films, 1983
CAL   Warner Bros., 1984
SHIVERS   New Yorker Films, 1985
FLIGHT OF THE SPRUCE GOOSE   Filmhaus, 1986
STARS AND BARS   Columbia, 1988
IN A SHALLOW GRAVE   Skouras Pictures, 1988
THE JANUARY MAN   MGM/UA, 1989
VALENTINO RETURNS   Skouras Pictures, 1989
FOOLS OF FORTUNE   Palace Picture/New
   Line Cinema, 1990

JEFF ZIMMERMAN
THE DECLINE OF WESTERN CIVILIZATION PART II:
   THE METAL YEARS (FD)   New Line Cinema, 1988

BERNARD ZITZERMANN
MOLIERE   United Artists, 1978
MY FIRST LOVE   Greater Union Film Distributors, 1978
I MARRIED A SHADOW   International Spectrafilm, 1983
LA BALANCE   Spectrafilm, 1983
THE MYSTERY OF ALEXINA   European Classics, 1985
A MAN IN LOVE   Cinecom, 1987

LEONIDAS ZOURDOUMIS
POWAQQATSI   Cannon, 1988, w/Graham Berry

VILMOS ZSIGMOND, ASC *
West Coast Card
Agent: Smith Gosnell Nicholson & Associates -
   Pacific Palisades, 213/459-0307

THE HIRED HAND   Universal, 1971
McCABE AND MRS. MILLER   Warner Bros., 1971
IMAGES   Columbia, 1972
DELIVERANCE   Warner Bros., 1972
THE LONG GOODBYE   United Artists, 1973
SCARECROW   Warner Bros., 1973
CINDERELLA LIBERTY   20th Century Fox, 1974
SUGARLAND EXPRESS   Universal, 1974
SWEET REVENGE   MGM/United Artists, 1976
OBSESSION   Columbia, 1976
CLOSE ENCOUNTERS OF THE THIRD KIND ★★
   Columbia, 1977
THE LAST WALTZ   United Artists, 1978, Additional DP
   w/Bobby Byrne, Laszlo Kovacs, David Myers, Hiro
   Narita & Michael Watkins
THE DEER HUNTER ★   Universal, 1978
WINTER KILLS   Avco Embassy, 1979
THE ROSE   20th Century Fox, 1979
FLESH AND BLOOD (TF)   The Jozak Company/Cypress
   Point Productions/Paramount TV, 1979
HEAVEN'S GATE   United Artists, 1980
BLOW OUT   Filmways, 1981
JINXED   MGM/UA, 1982
TABLE FOR FIVE   Warner Bros., 1983
THE RIVER ★   Universal, 1984
NO SMALL AFFAIR   Columbia, 1984
REAL GENIUS   Tri-Star, 1985
THE WITCHES OF EASTWICK   Warner Bros., 1987
FAT MAN AND LITTLE BOY   Paramount, 1989
THE TWO JAKES   Paramount, 1990
THE BONFIRE OF THE VANITIES   Warner Bros., 1990

★ ★ ★ ★

Zs

**CINEMATOGRAPHERS
PRODUCTION
DESIGNERS,
COSTUME
DESIGNERS** AND
**FILM EDITORS
GUIDE**

C
I
N
E
M
A
T
O
G
R
A
P
H
E
R
S

You can make a difference

People who want to make a difference in the community give their best to United Way--whether it's their time, talent or financial support. They know that through United Way they help address critical community issues such as AIDS, drug abuse, homelessness, child care and gangs. And because of their generosity, millions of people receive help each year from United Way's human care network.

If you want to make a difference, call (213) 736-1300, x290. You'll be surprised at the difference you can make.

United Way
It brings out the best in all of us.

PRODUCTION DESIGNERS

LISTINGS

CINEMATOGRAPHERS
PRODUCTION
DESIGNERS,
COSTUME
DESIGNERS AND
FILM EDITORS
GUIDE

P
R
O
D
U
C
T
I
O
N

D
E
S
I
G
N
E
R
S

PRODUCTION DESIGNERS
ACADEMY AWARDS AND NOMINATIONS
1977-1990

★★ = denotes winner in the category
(SD) indicates Set Decorator

1977
AIRPORT '77 .... George C. Webb & Mickey Michaels
CLOSE ENCOUNTERS OF THE
    THIRD KIND .... Joe Alves & Dan Lomino; Phil Abramson (SD)
STAR WARS .... John Barry, Norman Reynolds
    & Leslie Dilley; Roger Christian (SD) ★★
THE SPY WHO
    LOVED ME .... Ken Adam & Peter Lamont; Hugh Scaife (SD)
THE TURNING POINT .... Albert Brenner; Marvin March (SD)

1978
CALIFORNIA SUITE .... Albert Brenner; Marvin March (SD)
HEAVEN CAN WAIT .... Paul Sylbert & Edwin O'Donovan;
    George Gaines (SD) ★★
INTERIORS .... Mel Bourne; Daniel Robert (SD)
THE BRINK'S JOB .... Dean Tavoularis & Angelo Graham;
    George R. Nelson (SD) & Bruce Kay (SD)
THE WIZ .... Tony Walton & Philip Rosenberg;
    Edward Stewart (SD) & Robert Drumheller (SD)

1979
ALIEN .... Michael Seymour, Leslie Dilley
    & Roger Christian; Ian Whittaker (SD)
ALL THAT JAZZ .... Philip Rosenberg & Tony Walton;
    Edward Stewart (SD) & Gary Brink (SD) ★★
APOCALYPSE NOW .... Dean Tavoularis &
    Angelo Graham; George R. Nelson (SD)
STAR TREK—THE MOTION
    PICTURE .... Harold Michelson, Joe Jennings, Leon Harris
    & John Vallone; Linda DeScenna (SD)
THE CHINA
    SYNDROME .... George Jenkins; Arthur Jeph Parker (SD)

1980
COAL MINER'S
    DAUGHTER .... John W. Corso; John M. Dwyer (SD)
KAGEMUSHA: THE SHADOW
    WARRIOR .... Yoshiro Muraki
TESS .... Pierre Guffroy & Jack Stephens ★★
THE ELEPHANT
    MAN .... Stuart Craig & Bob Cartwright; Hugh Scaife (SD)
THE EMPIRE STRIKES
    BACK .... Noman Reynolds, Leslie Dilley, Harry Lange
    & Alan Tomkins; Michael Ford (SD)

1981
HEAVEN'S GATE .... Tambi Larsen; Jim Berkey (SD)
RAGTIME .... John Graysmark, Patrizia Von Brandenstein,
    & Anthony Reading; George de Titta, Sr. (SD)
    George de Titta, Jr., (SD) & Peter Howitt (SD)
RAIDERS OF THE
    LOST ARK .... Norman Reynolds & Leslie Dilley ★★
REDS .... Richard Sylbert; Michael Seirton (SD)
THE FRENCH LIEUTENANT'S
    WOMAN .... Assheton Gorton; Ann Mollo (SD)

1982
ANNIE .... Dale Hennessy; Marvin March (SD)
BLADE RUNNER .... Lawrence G. Paull &
    David L. Snyder; Linda DeScenna (SD)
GANDHI .... Stuart Craig & Bob Laing; Michael Seirton (SD) ★★
LA TRAVIATA .... Franco Zeffirelli; Gianni Quaranta (SD)
VICTOR/VICTORIA .... Rodger Maus, Tim Hutchinson
    & William Craig Smith; Harry Cordwell (SD)

1983
FANNY AND ALEXANDER .... Anna Asp ★★
RETURN OF THE JEDI .... Norman Reynolds, Fred Hole
    & James Schoppe; Michael Ford (SD)
TERMS OF ENDEARMENT .... Polly Platt & Harold Michelson;
    Tom Pedigo (SD) & Anthony Mendello (SD)
THE RIGHT STUFF .... Geoffrey Kirkland, Richard J. Lawrence,
    W. Stewart Campbell & Peter Romero;
    Pat Pending (SD) & George R. Nelson (SD)
YENTL .... Roy Walker & Leslie Tomkins; Tessa Davies (SD)
2010 .... Albert Brenner; Rick Simpson (SD)

1984
A PASSAGE
    TO INDIA .... John Box & Leslie Tomkins; Hugh Scaife (SD)
AMADEUS .... Patrizia Von Brandenstein; Karel Cerny (SD) ★★
THE COTTON
    CLUB ...... Richard Sylbert; George Gaines (SD) & Les Bloom (SD)
THE NATURAL .... Angelo Graham, Mel Bourne, James J.
    Murakami & Speed Hopkins; Bruce Weintraub (SD)
2010 .... Albert Brenner; Rick Simpson (SD)

1985
BRAZIL .... Norman Garwood; Maggie Gray (SD)
OUT OF AFRICA .... Stephen Grimes; Josie MacAvin (SD) ★★
RAN .... Yoshiro Muraki & Shinobu Muraki
THE COLOR PURPLE .... J. Michael Riva & Robert W. Welch;
    Linda DeScenna (SD)
WITNESS .... Stan Jolley; John Anderson (SD)

1986
A ROOM WITH A VIEW .... Gianni Quaranta & Brian Ackland-Snow
    Brian Savegar (SD) & Elio Altramura (SD) ★★
ALIENS .... Peter Lamont; Crispian Sallis
HANNAH AND HER SISTERS .... Stuart Wurtzel; Carol Joffe (SD)
THE COLOR OF MONEY .... Boris Leven; Karen A. O'Hara (SD)
THE MISSION .... Stuart Craig; Jack Stephens (SD)

1987
EMPIRE OF THE SUN .... Norman Reynolds; Harry Cordwell (SD)
HOPE AND GLORY .... Anthony Pratt; Joan Woolard (SD)
RADIO DAYS .... Santo Loquasto; Carol Joffe (SD),
    Les Bloom (SD) & George DeTitta, Jr (SD)
THE LAST EMPEROR .... Ferdinando Scarfiotti;
    Bruno Cesari (SD) & Osvaldo Desideri (SD) ★★
THE UNTOUCHABLES .... Patrizia Von Brandenstein
    & William A. Elliott; Hal Gausman (SD)

1988
BEACHES .... Albert Brenner; Garrett Lewis (SD)
DANGEROUS LIAISONS ...... Stuart Craig ; Gerard James (SD) ★★
RAINMAN .... Ida Random; Linda De Scenna (SD)
TUCKER: A MAN AND
    HIS DREAMS .... Dean Tavoularis; Armin Ganz (SD)
WHO FRAMED ROGER RABBIT .... Elliot Scott; Peter Howitt (SD)

1989
THE ABYSS .... Leslie Dilley; Anne Kuljian (SD)
THE ADVENTURES OF BARON
    MUNCHHAUSEN .... Dante Ferretti; Francesca Lo Schiavo (SD)
BATMAN .... Anton Furst; Peter Young (SD) ★★
DRIVING MISS DAISY .... Bruno Rubeo; Crispian Sallis (SD)
GLORY .... Norman Garwood; Garrett Lewis (SD)

1990
CYRANO DE BERGERAC .... Ezio Frigerio; Jacques Rouxel (SD)
DANCES WITH WOLVES .... Jeffrey Beecroft; Lisa Dean (SD)
DICK TRACY .... Richard Sylbert; Rick Simpson (SD) ★★
THE GODFATHER PART III .... Dean Tavoularis; Gary Fettis (SD)
HAMLET .... Dante Ferretti; Francesca Lo Schiavo (SD)

★ ★ ★ ★

A

GENE ABEL
WICKED STEPMOTHER   MGM/UA, 1989, AD
RELENTLESS   New Line Cinema, 1989
MANIAC COP 2   Movie House Sales Company,
   1990, w/Charles LaGola

WERNER ACHMAN
WHO IS KILLING THE GREAT CHEFS OF EUROPE?
   Warner Bros., 1978, AD
ENEMY MINE   20th Century Fox, 1985, AD

BRIAN ACKLAND-SNOW
THE SAILOR WHO FELL FROM GRACE WITH
   THE SEA   Avco Embassy, 1976, AD
DEATH ON THE NILE   Paramount, 1978,
   AD w/Terry Ackland-Snow
DRACULA   Universal, 1979, AD
McVICAR   Crown International, 1981, AD
SUPERMAN III   Warner Bros., 1983, AD w/Terry
   Ackland-Snow & Charles Bishop
SCANDALOUS   Orion, 1984, AD w/John Sidall
LASSITER   Warner Bros., 1984,
   AD w/Alan Tompkins
THE HOLCROFT COVENANT   Universal,
   1985, AD
THE DOCTOR AND THE DEVILS   20th Century
   Fox, 1985, AD
A ROOM WITH A VIEW ★★   Cinecom, 1986, AD
MAURICE   Cinecom, 1987
WITHOUT A CLUE   Orion, 1988,
   w/Martyn Hebert
THE MAN IN THE BROWN SUIT (TF)   Alan Shayne
   Productions Inc./Warner Bros. TV, 1989

TERRY ACKLAND-SNOW
Agent: London Management, 235/241 Regent St. -
   London W1R 7AG, 071-493-1610

SKY RIDERS   20th Century Fox, 1976, AD
DEATH ON THE NILE   Paramount, 1978,
   AD w/Brian Ackland-Snow
THE GREAT MUPPET CAPER   Universal/AFD,
   1981, AD w/Charles Bishop
THE DARK CRYSTAL   Universal/AFD, 1982, AD
SUPERMAN III   Warner Bros., 1983, AD w/Brian
   Ackland-Snow & Charles Bishop
SUPERGIRL   Warner Bros., 1984, AD
KING DAVID   Paramount, 1985, AD
SPIES LIKE US   Warner Bros., 1985, AD
ALIENS   20th Century Fox, 1986,
   AD, shared credit
LABYRINTH   Tri-Star, 1986, AD, shared credit
THE LIVING DAYLIGHTS   MGM/UA, 1987, AD
WITHOUT A CLUE   Orion, 1988, AD
CONSUMING PASSIONS   Samuel Goldwyn
   Company, 1988, AD
BATMAN   Warner Bros., 1989, AD

KEN ADAM*
NY Local 829
Agent: Lawrence A. Mirisch, Triad Artists, Inc. -
   Los Angeles, 213/556-2727

AROUND THE WORLD IN 80 DAYS ★   United
   Artists, 1956
THE TRIALS OF OSCAR WILDE   Kingsley
   International, 1960
DR. NO   United Arists, 1962
IN THE COOL OF THE DAY   1963
DR. STRANGELOVE OR: HOW I LEARNED TO STOP
   WORRYING AND LOVE THE BOMB   Columbia, 1964
GOLDFINGER   United Artists, 1964
THE IPCRESS FILE   Universal, 1965
THUNDERBALL   United Artists, 1965
FUNERAL IN BERLIN   Paramount, 1966
YOU ONLY LIVE TWICE   United Artists, 1967
CHITTY CHITTY BANG BANG   United Artists, 1968
GOODBYE, MR. CHIPS   MGM, 1969
THE OWL AND THE PUSSYCAT   Columbia, 1970
DIAMONDS ARE FOREVER   United Artists, 1971
SLEUTH   20th Century Fox, 1972
THE LAST OF SHEILA   Warner Bros., 1973
BARRY LYNDON ★★   Warner Bros., 1975
THE SEVEN-PER-CENT SOLUTION   Universal, 1976
THE SPY WHO LOVED ME ★   United Artists, 1977
MOONRAKER   Untied Artists, 1979
PENNIES FROM HEAVEN   MGM/United Artists, 1981
KING DAVID   Paramount, 1985
AGNES OF GOD   Columbia, 1985
CRIMES OF THE HEART   DEG, 1986
THE DECEIVERS   Cinecom, 1988
DEAD BANG   Warner Bros., 1989
THE FRESHMAN   Tri-Star, 1990

CHARMIAN ADAMS
STORMY MONDAY   Atlantic Releasing Corporation,
   1988, AD
FOR QUEEN AND COUNTRY   Atlantic Releasing
   Corporation, 1989, AD

JAMES J. AGAZZI
DANIELLE STEEL'S FINE THINGS (TF)   The Cramer
   Company, 1990

MAHER AHMAD
CODE OF SILENCE   Orion, 1985
ONE MORE SATURDAY NIGHT   Columbia, 1986, AD
RAW DEAL   DEG, 1986, AD
ABOVE THE LAW   Warner Bros., 1988
MARRIED TO THE MOB   Orion, 1988, AD
MISS FIRECRACKER   Corsair Pictures, 1989, AD
MIAMI BLUES   Orion, 1990
GOODFELLAS   Warner Bros., 1990, AD

JOSE MARIA ALARCON
CONAN THE DESTROYER   Universal, 1984,
   AD w/Kevin Phipps
SOLARBABIES   MGM/UA, 1986, AD, w/others

THEONI V. ALDREDGE
Agent: Joan Hyler, William Morris Agency - Beverly Hills,
   213/274-7451

THE CHAMP   MGM/UA, 1979

ARLENE ALEN
SATURDAY THE 14TH   New World, 1981

AI

CINEMATOGRAPHERS
PRODUCTION
DESIGNERS,
COSTUME
DESIGNERS AND
FILM EDITORS
GUIDE

P
R
O
D
U
C
T
I
O
N

D
E
S
I
G
N
E
R
S

AI

CINEMATOGRAPHERS
PRODUCTION
DESIGNERS,
COSTUME
DESIGNERS and
FILM EDITORS
GUIDE

**P
R
O
D
U
C
T
I
O
N
D
E
S
I
G
N
E
R
S**

100

VITO ALEOTORI
GETTING LUCKY   Raedon Home Video, 1990

WILLIAM ALEXANDER
JEKYLL & HYDE (TF)   David Wickes TV, 1990

CHET ALLEN
P.K. AND THE KID   Castle Hill Productions, 1987

JAMES ALLEN*
IATSE Local 876
Agent: Jay Gilbert Talent Agency - Los Angeles,
   213/656-8090

THE TOURIST TRAP   Compass International,
   1979, AD
ROAR   1981
THE STING II   Universal, 1983, AD
PSYCHO II   Universal, 1983, AD
STREETS OF FIRE   Universal, 1984, AD
FATAL VISION (TF)   NBC Productions, 1984, AD
WEIRD SCIENCE   Universal, 1985 , AD
SHADOW CHASERS (TF)   Kenneth Johnson
   Productions/Brian Grazer Productions/Warner
   Bros. TV, 1985, AD
STREET HAWK (TF)   Limekin and Templar Productions/
   Universal TV, 1985, AD
REAL MEN   MGM/UA, 1987, AD w/William J. Cassidy
SWEET HEARTS DANCE   Tri-Star, 1988

LINDA ALLEN*
IATSE Local 876

THREE FOR THE ROAD   New Century/Vista, 1987

JOSEPH ALTADONNA*
IATSE Local 876
Agent: Grace Lyons Management - Los Angeles,
   213/655-5100

WALKING TALL   Cinerama Releasing
   Corporation, 1973
THEY WENT THAT-A-WAY & THAT-A-WAY
   International Picture Show Company, 1978, AD
DIARY OF A TEENAGE HITCHHIKER (TF)   The
   Shpetner Company, 1979
THE DEATH OF OCEAN VIEW PARK (TF)   Furia-
   Oringer Productions/Playboy Productions, 1979
THE BIG BRAWL   Warner Bros., 1980
MOTEL HELL   United Artists, 1980
THE OTHER VICTIM (TF)   Shpetner Company, 1981
LOTTERY! (TF)   Rosner TV Productions/
   Orion TV, 1983
LADY BLUE (TF)   David Gerber Productions/
   MGM-UA TV, 1985
THE LONGSHOT   Orion, 1986, Consultant
HARD TIMES ON PLANET EARTH (Pilot)   1989
CAGE   New Century/Vista, 1989

KATE ALTMAN
PARIS, TEXAS   TLC Films/20th Century Fox,
   1984, AD

STEPHEN ALTMAN
Agent: The Gersh Agency, Inc., Beverly Hills -
   213/274-6611, New York - 212/997-1818

STREAMERS   United Artists Classics, 1983, AD
FOOL FOR LOVE   Cannon, 1985

BEYOND THERAPY   New World, 1987, AD
NEAR DARK   DEG, 1987
VINCENT & THEO   Hemdale, 1990

JOE ALVES*
IATSE Local 876
Agent: Shapiro-Lichtman, Inc. - Los Angeles,
   213/859-8877

JAWS   Universal, 1975
EMBRYO   Cine Artists, 1976, AD
CLOSE ENCOUNTERS OF THE THIRD KIND ★
   Columbia, 1977, w/Dan Lomino
JAWS 2   Universal, 1978
ESCAPE FROM NEW YORK   Avco Embassy, 1981
EVERYBODY'S ALL-AMERICAN   Warner Bros., 1988

ROY ALAN AMARAL
THE FINAL DAYS (TF)   The Samuels Films
   Company, 1990
DREAM DATE (TF)   Frederic Golchan/Robert Kosberg
   Productions, 1990
MAN AGAINST THE MOB: THE CHINATOWN
   MURDERS (TF)   von Zerneck-Sertner Films, 1990
MURDER AT THE PTL LUNCHEON (TF)   Patricia K.
   Meyers Productions, 1990
THE COURT-MARTIAL OF JACKIE ROBINSON (CTF)
   von Zerneck-Sertner Films, 1990

RICHARD AMEND
Agent: Camera Masters - Venice, 213/306-0810

MANNEQUIN   20th Century Fox, 1986, AD
D.O.A.   Buena Vista, 1988

PRESTON AMES
AIRPORT ★   Universal, 1970, w/Alexander Golitzen
EARTHQUAKE ★   Universal, 1974,
   w/Alexander Golitzen
DAMNATION ALLEY   20th Century Fox, 1977
BEYOND THE POSEIDON ADVENTURE   Warner
   Bros., 1979
THE LAST FLIGHT OF NOAH'S ARK   Buena Vista, 1980
OH, GOD! BOOK II   Warner Bros., 1980
THE PURSUIT OF D.B. COOPER   Universal, 1981

CAROLINE AMIES
NINETEEN NINETEEN   Spectrafilm, 1986, AD
EAT THE RICH   New Line Cinema, 1987, AD
WISH YOU WERE HERE   Atlantic Releasing
   Corporation, 1987
THE DRESSMAKER   Euro-American, 1988
GETTING IT RIGHT   MCEG, 1989

RUTH AMMON
TALES FROM THE DARKSIDE: THE MOVIE
   Paramount, 1990

CARL ANDERSON
LADY SINGS THE BLUES ★   Paramount, 1972
THE VILLAIN   Columbia, 1979, AD
...ALL THE MARBLES   MGM/United Artists, 1981
THE PAPER CHASE (TVS)   1984

CLETUS ANDERSON
KNIGHTRIDERS   United Film Distribution, 1981
CREEPSHOW   Warner Bros., 1982
THE BOY WHO LOVED TROLLS (TF)
   Q Productions, 1984

DAY OF THE DEAD   United Film Distribution
    Company, 1985
SILENCE AT BETHANY   Keener Productions/
    American Playhouse Theatrical Films, 1988
MONKEY SHINES   Orion, 1988
NIGHT OF THE LIVING DEAD   Columbia, 1990

NEIL ANGWIN
LONELY HEARTS   Samuel Goldwyn Company,
    1983, AD

LYNN RUTH APPEL
ICE HOUSE   Upfront Films, 1989

WILLIAM APPERSON
PLAIN CLOTHES   Paramount, 1988, AD

REGINA ARGENTINE
GIRLFRIEND FROM HELL   IVE, 1990

LUCIANA ARRIGHI
MY BRILLIANT CAREER   Analysis, 1980
PRIVATES ON PARADE   Orion Classics, 1984
THE PLOUGHMAN'S LUNCH   Samuel Goldwyn
    Company, 1984
MRS. SOFFEL   MGM/UA, 1984
THE RETURN OF THE SOLDIER   European
    Classics, 1985
MADAME SOUSATZKA   Universal, 1988
THE RAINBOW   Vestron, 1989

ANNA ASP
FANNY AND ALEXANDER ★★   Embassy, 1983
AFTER THE REHEARSAL   Triumph, 1984, AD

ADRIENNE ATKINSON
THAT SINKING FEELING   Samuel Goldwyn
    Company, 1979
GREGORY'S GIRL   Samuel Goldwyn
    Company, 1982
LOCAL HERO   Warner Bros., 1983, AD
COMFORT AND JOY   Universal, 1984
WINTER FLIGHT   Cinecom, 1984, AD
RESTLESS NATIVES   Orion Classics, 1985
MR. LOVE   Warner Bros., 1986
HOUSEKEEPING   Columbia, 1987
BREAKING IN   Samuel Goldwyn Company, 1989,
    w/John Willett
KILLING DAD   Scottish Television/British
    Screen, 1989

PETER ATTENDER
JUDGMENT IN BERLIN   New Line Cinema, 1988,
    AD w/Jan Schlubach

JOE AUBEL*
IATSE Local 876

DEAD AND BURIED   Avco Embassy, 1981,
    AD w/Bill Sandell
STAR TREK IV: THE VOYAGE HOME   Paramount,
    1986, AD w/Pete Smith
THE MILAGRO BEANFIELD WAR   Universal, 1988, AD

CHRIS AUGUST
ERNEST GOES TO JAIL   Buena Vista, 1990

LEO AUSTIN
Agent: London Management, 235/241 Regent St. -
    London W1R 7AG, 071-493-1610

THE BOSTONIANS   Almi Pictures, 1984
TURTLE DIARY   Samuel Goldwyn Company, 1985
A MONTH IN THE COUNTRY   Orion Classics, 1987
A SUMMER STORY   Atlantic/ITC
    Entertainment, 1988
WILT   LWT, 1990

SHAY AUSTIN
BILLY GALVIN   Vestron, 1986
A TIGER'S TALE   Atlantic Releasing
    Corporation, 1988
THE WOMEN OF BREWSTER PLACE (Pilot)   Harpo
    Productions/Phoenix Entertainment, 1989
KICKBOXER   Pathe Entertainment, 1989
REPOSSESSED   Seven Arts, 1990

ALAN AVCHEN
CEASE FIRE   Cineworld Enterprises, 1985

KIRK AXTELL*
IATSE Local 876
Agent: Sanford-Skouras & Gross - Los Angeles,
    213/08-2100

EXECUTIVE ACTION   National General,
    1973, AD
THE TAKE   1974, AD
THE PHOTOGRAPHER   Avco Embassy,
    1974, AD
GATOR   United Artists, 1976, AD
MYSTERIOUS ISLAND OF BEAUTIFUL WOMEN (TF)
    Alan Landsburg Productions, 1977, AD
RAGING BULL   United Artists, 1978, AD
FRIENDLY FIRE (TF)   Marble Arch Productions,
    1979, AD
THE SOLITARY MAN (TF)   Universal TV, 1979, AD
WHEN SHE WAS BAD... (TF)   Ladd Productions/
    Henry Jaffe Enterprises, 1979, AD
CHEAPER TO KEEP HER   American Cinema,
    1980, AD

B

DANIEL BADIN
CHEECH & CHONG'S THE CORSICAN BROTHERS
    Orion, 1984

ROBB BACON
BACK TO HANNIBAL: THE RETURN OF TOM
    SAWYER AND HUCKLEBERRY FINN (CTF)
    Gay-Jay Productions, 1990

TED BAFALOUKOS
DINER   MGM/UA, 1982, Creative Consultant
THE THIN BLUE LINE   Miramax, 1988

Ba

CINEMATOGRAPHERS
PRODUCTION
DESIGNERS,
COSTUME
DESIGNERS AND
FILM EDITORS
GUIDE

PRODUCTION DESIGNERS

Ba

CINEMATOGRAPHERS
PRODUCTION
DESIGNERS,
COSTUME
DESIGNERS AND
FILM EDITORS
GUIDE

**P
R
O
D
U
C
T
I
O
N

D
E
S
I
G
N
E
R
S**

CHARLES BAILEY
SERPICO   Paramount, 1973
THE FRONT   Columbia, 1976
SATURDAY NIGHT FEVER   Paramount, 1977

MARK BALET
NORTH SHORE   Universal, 1987

JOHN BALLOWE
MUNCHIES   Concorde, 1987, AD

VICKI BARAL
THE WICKEDEST WITCH (TF)   Boo You
    Productions, 1990, w/Gerry Hariton

JIM BARBALEY
DEADLY DANCER   AIP Home Video, 1990

WILLIAM BARCLAY
Agent: Cyd Levin, C.N.A. & Associates - Los Angeles,
    213/556-4343
Phone: 212/222-8122

A BREED APART   Orion, 1984, AD
BERRY GORDY'S THE LAST DRAGON   Tri-Star,
    1985, AD
POWER   20th Century Fox, 1986, AD
THE SECRET OF MY SUCCESS   Universal,
    1987, AD
HELLO AGAIN   Buena Vista, 1987, AD
BIG BUSINESS   Buena Vista, 1988, AD
BEACHES   Buena Vista, 1988, AD (New York)
JACKNIFE   Cineplex Odeon, 1989, AD
MEN OF RESPECT   Columbia, 1991
TRUE COLORS   Paramount, 1991, AD

HOWARD BARKER
CLINTON AND NADINE   HBO Pictures/ITC, 1988

DAVE BARKHAM
PLACE OF WEEPING   New World, 1986

GUY BARNES
IN THE LINE OF DUTY: A COP FOR THE KILLING (TF)
    Patchett-Kaufman Entertainment, 1990

NORM BARON*
IATSE Local 876
Agent: Sanford-Skouras & Gross - Los Angeles,
    213/208-2100

FAST BREAK   Columbia, 1979, AD
A FORCE OF ONE   American Cinema, 1979
HERO AT LARGE   MGM/United Artists, 1980
THE COMEBACK KID (TF)   ABC Circle Films, 1980
TERROR AMONG US (TF)   David Gerber
    Company, 1981
LOIS GIBBS AND THE LOVE CANAL (TF)   Moonlight
    Productions/Warner Bros. TV, 1982
IN THE CUSTODY OF STRANGERS (TF)   Moonlight
    Productions/Filmways, 1982
THE FIRST TIME (TF)   Moonlight Productions, 1982
NIGHT PARTNERS (TF)   Moonlight Productions II, 1983
HAPPY (TF)   Bacchus Films Inc., 1983
LONE WOLF McQUADE   Orion, 1983
CHILDREN OF THE NIGHT (TF)   Robert Guenette
    Productions, 1985
DO YOU REMEMBER LOVE (TF)   Dave Bell
    Productions, 1985

THE LITTLE SISTER (TF)   Shefida Features/American
    Playhouse/Christina Associates, 1986
JAKE SPEED   New World, 1986
NUMBER ONE WITH A BULLET   Cannon, 1987
A STONING IN FULLHAM COUNTY (TF)   The Landsburg
    Company, 1988
THE RYAN WHITE STORY (TF)   The Landsburg
    Company, 1989
WAR AND REMEMBRANCE (MS)   Dan Curtis
    Productions, 1989, AD, US, w/William Cruise
CHINA CRY   Penland, 1990
THE LOOKALIKE (CTF)   Gallo Entertainment, 1990

KEITH BARRETT
CRACK HOUSE   Cannon Pictures, 1990

PENNY BARRETT
TO SLEEP WITH ANGER   SVS, 1990

PIERLUIGI BASILE
NIJINSKY   Paramount, 1980, AD
INCHON!   MGM/UA, 1982, AD
CONAN THE BARBARIAN   Universal, 1982, AD
AMITYVILLE II: THE POSSESSION   Orion, 1982
CONAN THE DESTROYER   Universal, 1984
DUNE   Universal, 1984, AD w/Benjamin Fernandez
TAI-PAN   DEG, 1986, AD w/Benjamin Fernandez

LINDA BASS
STACKING   Spectrafilm, 1987

MICHAEL BAUGH*
IATSE Local 876
Agent: Steve England, Paul Gerard Agency - Newport
    Beach, 714/644-7950

SHADOW OF A GUNMAN (TF)   Hollywood TV Theatre/
    PBS, 1974
WINEBURGH (TF)   Hollywood TV Theatre/PBS, 1974
ME (TF)   Hollywood TV Theatre/PBS, 1974
MAN OF DESSTINY (TF)   Hollywood TV Theatre/
    PBS, 1974
LET'S SWITCH (TF)   Universal, 1975
TWIN DETECTIVES (TF)   Charles Fries
    Productions, 1976
FREEMAN (TF)   Visions, 1977
THREE ON A DATE (TF)   ABC Circle Films, 1978
THE NEW ADVENTURES OF HEIDI (TF)   Pierre
    Cossette Enterprises, 1978
LEAVE YESTERDAY BEHIND (TF)   ABC Circle
    Films, 1978
BLIND AMBITION (TF) ☆   Time-Life
    Productions, 1978
HOT ROD (TF)   ABC Circle Films, 1979
MOVIOLA (MS) ☆   David L. Wolper-Stan Margulies
    Productions/Warner Bros. TV, 1980
ELVIS AND THE BEAUTY QUEEN (TF)   David
    Gerber Company/Columbia TV, 1981
JACQUELINE BOUVIER KENNEDY (TF)   ABC Circle
    Films, 1981
TAKE YOUR BEST SHOT (TF)   Levinson-Link
    Productions/Robert Papazian Productions, 1982
RICHARD PRYOR LIVE ON THE SUNSET STRIP (FD)
    Columbia, 1982
WHERE THE BOYS ARE   Tri-Star, 1984
CRAZY LIKE A FOX (TVS)   Columbia, 1985
THE LATE CHRISTOPHER BEAN (TF)   Schaefer/
    Karpf, 1985
THIS BABY IS MINE (TF)   Finnegan
    Associates, 1985

THIS WIFE FOR HIRE (TF)   The Belle Company/
    Guillaume-Margo Productions/Comworld
    Productions, 1985
FAST FORWARD   Columbia, 1985
MISSING IN ACTION II: THE BEGINNING
    Cannon, 1985
DOLLY PARTON'S SMOKEY MOUNTAIN
    CHRISTMAS (TF)   Sandollar, 1986
ON WINGS OF EAGLES (MS)   Edgar J. Scherick
    Productions/Taft Entertainment TV, 1986
POLICE STORY II (TF)   David Gerber, 1987
FATAL JUDGMENT (TF)   Jack Farren Productions/
    Group W Productions, 1988
STRANGER ON MY LAND (TF)   Edgar
    Scherick, 1989
LADYKILLERS (TF)   ABC Circle Films, 1989
SEMESTER AT SEA CLASS CRUISE (TF)
    Portoangelo Productions, 1990
THE BIG ONE: THE GREAT LOS ANGELES
    EARTHQUAKES-PARTS I & II (MS)
    von Zerneck-Sertner Films, 1990
PLYMOUTH (TF)   Walt Disney, 1991
FOUR EYES (TF)   Edgar Scherick, 1991

JOHN BEARD
BRAZIL   Universal, 1985, AD w/Keith Pain
ABSOLUTE BEGINNERS   Orion, 1986
SIESTA   Lorimar, 1987
THE LAST TEMPTATION OF CHRIST
    Universal, 1988
ERIK THE VIKING   Orion, 1989

JEFFREY BEECROFT
Agent: Smith Gosnell Nicholson & Associates -
    Pacific Palisades, 213/459-0307

STOP MAKING SENSE (FD)   Cinecom International/
    Island Alive, 1984
KOJAK: THE PRICE OF JUSTICE (TF)   MCA/
    Universal TV, 1987
SOMEONE TO WATCH OVER ME   Columbia,
    1987, AD
THE WIZARD OF LONELINESS   Skouras
    Pictures, 1988
MIDNIGHT CALLER (Pilot)   1988
DANCES WITH WOLVES ★   Tig/Orion, 1990

WILLIAM BEETON
UTILITIES   New World, 1983
THE BOY IN BLUE   20th Century Fox, 1985
THE GATE   New Century/Vista, 1987

JULIE BELLE
SECRET WEAPON (CTF)   Griffin-Elysian Films, 1990
    w/Martyn Herbert

BRUCE BELLAMY
BOYZ N THE HOOD   Columbia, 1991 AD

CHARLES BENNETT
BEYOND AND BACK   Schick Sunn Classics, 1978
THE BERMUDA TRIANGLE   Schick Sunn Classics,
    1979, AD
EVERGREEN (MS) ☆☆   Edgar J. Scherick Associates/
    Metromedia Producers Corporation, 1985
MORGAN STEWART'S COMING HOME   New Century/
    Vista, 1987
SHAKEDOWN   Universal, 1988
HOME FIRES BURNING (TF)   Marian Rees Associates,
    1989, AD

THE LITTLEST VICTIMS (TF)   CBS
    Entertainment, 1989
ROXANNE: THE PRIZE PULITZER (TF)   Qintex
    Entertainment, 1990
MURDER IN MISSISSIPPI (TF)   David L. Wolper
    Productions, 1990
THE ROSE AND THE JACKAL (CTF)   Steve White
    Productions, 1990
NEW JACK CITY   Warner Bros., 1991

LAURENCE BENNETT
THE MEN'S CLUB   Atlantic Releasing Corporation,
    1986, AD
MODERN GIRLS   Atlantic Releasing Corporation, 1986

LEROY BENNETT
SIGN O' THE TIMES   Cineplex Odeon, 1987

JOSEPH BENNETT
HARDWARE   Millimeter Films, 1990

FRANCOISE BENOIT-FRESCO
SWEET REVENGE (CTF)   Turner Pictures, 1990

ROBERT R. BENTON
ODD JOBS   Tri-Star, 1986

MARTY BERCAW
DIVING IN   Skouras Pictures, 1991, AD

RICHARD BERGER*
IATSE Local 876

MR. BILLION   20th Century Fox, 1976, AD
HARRY AND WALTER GO TO NEW YORK   Columbia,
    1976, AD
NICKELODEON   Columbia, 1976, AD
ROCKY II   United Artists, 1979, AD
SCAVENGER HUNT   20th Century Fox, 1979, AD
INDIANA JONES AND THE LAST CRUSADE
    Paramount, 1989, AD w/Stephen Scott

STEPHEN M. BERGER*
IATSE Local 876
Agent: The Miller Agency - Santa Clarita, 818/843-7335

THE MASTER GUNFIGHTER   Taylor-Laughlin,
    1975, AD
THE SUNSHINE BOYS   MGM/United Artists,
    1975, AD
THE MISSOURI BREAKS   United Artists, 1976, AD
NORMAN...IS THAT YOU?   MGM/United Artists,
    1976, AD
SILENT MOVIE   20th Century Fox, 1976, AD
ROLLING THUNDER   American International, 1977
BAD NEWS BEARS IN BREAKING TRAINING
    Paramount, 1977, AD
THE JERICHO MILE (TF)   ABC Circle Films, 1979
SWAN SONG (TF)   Renee Valente Productions/
    Topanga Services Ltd./20th Century Fox, 1980
TENSPEED AND BROWN SHOE (TF)   Stephen
    J.Cannell Productions, 1980
LOTTERY! (TF)   Rosner TV Productions/
    Orion TV, 1983
VIOLATED   1984
THE LADIES CLUB   New Line Cinema, 1985
THE LAST FLING (TF)   Leonard Hill
    Productions, 1985

Be

CINEMATOGRAPHERS
PRODUCTION
DESIGNERS,
COSTUME
DESIGNERS AND
FILM EDITORS
GUIDE

P
R
O
D
U
C
T
I
O
N

D
E
S
I
G
N
E
R
S

Be

CINEMATOGRAPHERS
PRODUCTION
DESIGNERS,
COSTUME
DESIGNERS AND
FILM EDITORS
GUIDE

P
R
O
D
U
C
T
I
O
N

D
E
S
I
G
N
E
R
S

WILDCATS   Warner Bros., 1986, AD
SINS OF INNOCENCE (TF)   20th Century
   Fox TV, 1986
THE WILD PAIR   Trans World Entertainment, 1987
THE NEW ADVENTURE OF PIPPI LONGSTOCKING
   Columbia, 1988, AD
THE PRICE OF OUR BLOOD   *OUT FOR JUSTICE*
   SAH Rocco Productions, 1991, AD

CHRIS BERKWOLDT
E.A.R.T.H. FORCE (TF)   Paramount
   Network TV, 1990

TIVADAR BERTALAN
MACK THE KNIFE   21st Century, 1990
THE PHANTOM OF THE OPERA   21st Century, 1990

MAX BERTO
MR. FROST   Triumph Releasing, 1990

MARY ANN BIDDLE*
IATSE Local 876

ALL THE RIGHT MOVES   20th Century Fox,
   1983, AD

MARK BILLERMAN
THE PRINCIPAL   Tri-Star, 1987, AD

ASHER BILU
MY FIRST WIFE   Spectrafilm, 1985
CACTUS   Spectrafilm, 1986

JAMES R. BILZ
TRADING HEARTS   New Century/Vista, 1988, AD

MICHAEL BINGHAM
NIGHTFLYERS   New Century/Vista, 1987, AD
WAR PARTY   Hemdale, 1989
CAMERON'S CLOSET   SVS Films, 1989

LESLIE BINNS
PATRICK   Cinema Shares International, 1978
THE MAN FROM SNOWY RIVER   20th Century Fox,
   1983, AD
RETURN TO SNOWY RIVER   20th Century Fox, 1988

CAMERON BIRNIE*
IATSE Local 876

FLETCH LIVES   Universal, 1989, AD w/Jimmy
   Bly, Cameron Birnie, W. Steven Graham &
   Donald B. Woodruff
COLUMBO (Pilot)   1989

CHARLES BISHOP
MOONRAKER   United Artists, 1979, AD w/Max Douy
THE GREAT MUPPET CAPER   Universal/AFD,
   1981, AD
THE SENDER   Paramount, 1982, AD
THE DARK CRYSTAL   Universal/AFD, 1982, AD
SUPERMAN III   Warner Bros., 1983, AD w/Brian
   Ackland-Snow & Terry Ackland-Snow
RETURN TO OZ   Buena Vista, 1985, AD
SKY BANDITS   Galaxy International, 1986, AD
EMPIRE OF THE SUN ★   Warner Bros., 1987,
   Supervising AD

DAN BISHOP
Address: 73-74 E. 3rd St., #3-B - New York, NY 10003,
   212/598-9156

MATEWAN   Cinecomn, 1987, AD
EIGHT MEN OUT   Orion, 1988, AD
CONVICTS   MCEG, 1989
MYSTERY TRAIN   Orion, 1989
CRIMINAL JUSTICE (CTF)   Elysian Films, 1990,
   w/Dianna Freas
CITY OF HOPE   Esperanza, 1991, w/Dianna Freas

JAMES D. BISSELL*
IATSE Local 876
Agent: Sanford-Skouras & Gross - Los Angeles,
   213/208-2100

GOOD LUCK, MISS WYCKOFF   Bel Air/Gradison, 1979
FLATBED ANNIE & SWEETIEPIE: LADY
   TRUCKERS (TF)   Moonlight Productions/
   Filmways, 1979
VALENTINE (TF)   Malloy-Phillips Productions/Edward S.
   Feldman Company, 1979
ANATOMY OF A SEDUCTION (TF)   Moonlight Produc-
   tions/Filmways, 1979
PALMERSTOWN, U.S.A. (TF) ☆☆   Haley-TAT Produc-
   tions, 1980
DON'T LOOK BACK (TF)   TBA Productions/Satie
   Productions/TRISEME, 1981
E.T.: THE EXTRATERRESTRIAL   Universal, 1982
TWILIGHT ZONE - THE MOVIE   Warner Bros., 1983
THE LAST STARFIGHTER   Universal, 1984
THE FALCON AND THE SNOWMAN   Orion, 1985
ST. ELMO'S FIRE   Columbia, 1985
THE BOY WHO COULD FLY   20th Century Fox, 1986
SOMEONE TO WATCH OVER ME   Columbia, 1987
HARRY AND THE HENDERSONS   Universal, 1987
TWINS   Universal, 1988
ALWAYS   Universal, 1989
ARACHNOPHOBIA   Buena Vista, 1990

JOHN BLACKIE
LAST TRAIN HOME (CTF)   Atlantis Films, 1990

JACK BLACKMAN
MANHUNTER   DEG, 1986, AD
MAKING MR. RIGHT   Orion, 1987, AD
FATAL ATTRACTION   Paramount, 1987, AD

STUART BLATT
CATCH ME IF YOU CAN   MCEG, 1990, AD
FLIGHT OF BLACK ANGEL (CTF)   Hess-Kallberg
   Productions, 1991

JOHN BLEZARD
FIREPOWER   AFD, 1979, w/Robert Gundlach &
   John Stoll
NIJINSKY   Paramount, 1980
THE WICKED LADY   MGM/UA/Cannon, 1983, AD
APPOINTMENT WITH DEATH   Cannon, 1988
JACK THE RIPPER (MS)   Euston Films, 1988

BECKY BLOCK
Phone: 213/466-7454

NOT FOR PUBLICATION   Samuel Goldwyn
   Company, 1984, AD
1918   Cinecom, 1985, AD
THE DIRT BIKE KID   Concorde, 1985,
   w/J. Grey Smith

REFORM SCHOOL GIRLS   New World, 1986, AD
THE DIRT BIKE KID   Concorde/Cinema Group, 1986
THE KINDRED   FM Entertainment, 1987, AD
UNDER COVER   Cannon, 1987
STARS AND BARS   Columbia, 1988, AD

HERMAN A. BLUMENTHAL
Phone: 213/552-1948

CLEOPATRA ★★   20th Century Fox, 1963,
    AD w/others
HELLO, DOLLY ! ★★   20th Century Fox, 1969,
    AD w/Jack Martin Smith
TWO-MINUTE WARNING   Universal, 1976, AD
THE BETSY   Allied Artists, 1978
THE CHAMP   MGM/United Artists, 1979, AD
THE BALTIMORE BULLET   Avco Embassy, 1980
THE FORMULA   MGM/UA, 1980
ZORRO, THE GAY BLADE   20th Century Fox, 1981

JIMMIE BLY*
IATSE Local 876

THE COUCH TRIP   Orion, 1988
FLETCH LIVES   Universal, 1989, AD w/Cameron
    Birnie, W. Steven Graham & Donald B. Woodruff

EVA ANNA BOHN*
IATSE Local 876

VICE VERSA   Columbia, 1988, AD

GREGORY BOLTON
WITHOUT A TRACE   20th Century Fox, 1983, AD
THE COTTON CLUB   Orion, 1984,
    AD w/David Chapman
BAND OF THE HAND   Tri-Star, 1986
APPRENTICE TO MURDER   New World, 1988
TERROR ON HIGHWAY 91 (TF)   Katy Film
    Productions, 1989
DREAM STREET (Pilot)   1989

MICHAEL S. BOLTON*
Canada IATSE Local 891
Agent: Spyros Skouras, Sanford-Skouras & Gross -
    Los Angeles, 213/208-2100

HARRY TRACY   Desperado Productions, 1980, AD
MOTHER LODE   Agmemnon Films, 1982,
    AD w/James H. Chow
STAR 80   The Ladd Company/Warner Bros., 1983,
    AD w/Jack G. Taylor
RUNAWAY   Tri-Star, 1984, AD
THE GLITTER DOME (CTF)   HBO Premiere Films/
    Telepictures Productions/Trincomali Productions,
    1984, AD
THE JOURNEY OF NATTY GANN   Buena Vista,
    1985, AD
FIRE WITH FIRE   Paramount, 1986, AD
I-MAN (TF)   Disney, 1986
STRANGER IN MY BED (TF)   Edgar J. Scherick
    Productions, 1986
A HERO IN THE FAMILY (TF)   Disney, 1986
A CHRISTMAS STAR (TF)   Disney, 1986
HANDS OF A STRANGER (MS)   1987
ASSAULT AND MATRIMONY (TF)   1987
THE RED SPIDER (TF)   1987
THE FLY II   20th Century Fox, 1989
SHORT TIME   Gladden Entertainment/20th
    Century Fox, 1989
WHITE FANG   Buena Vista, 1991

JODY BORLAND
DOGS IN SPACE   Skouras Films, 1987, AD

MEL BOURNE
ANNIE HALL   United Artists, 1977, AD
THE GREEK TYCOON   Universal, 1978, AD w/Gene
    Gurlitz & Tony Reading
INTERIORS ★   United Artists, 1978
NUNZIO   Universal, 1978
MANHATTAN   United Artists, 1979
WINDOWS   United Artists, 1980
STARDUST MEMORIES   United Artists, 1980
THIEF   United Artists, 1981
A MIDSUMMER NIGHT'S SEX COMEDY   Orion/Warner
    Bros., 1982
STILL OF THE NIGHT   MGM/UA, 1982
ZELIG   Orion/Warner Bros., 1983
BROADWAY DANNY ROSE   Orion, 1984
THE NATURAL ★   Tri-Star, 1984
F/X   Orion, 1986
MANHUNTER   DEG, 1986
FATAL ATTRACTION   Paramount, 1987
COCKTAIL   Buena Vista, 1988
RUDE AWAKENING   Orion, 1989
REVERSAL OF FORTUNE   Warner Bros., 1990

TRACY BOUSMAN*
IATSE Local 876

SIDEWINDER 1   Avco Embassy, 1977,
    AD w/Liz Bousman
NORMA RAE   20th Century Fox, 1979, AD
YOUNG DOCTORS IN LOVE   20th Century Fox,
    1982, AD
PROTOCOL   Warner Bros., 1984, AD
PRIZZI'S HONOR   20th Century Fox, 1985, AD
THOSE SHE LEFT BEHIND (MS)   NBC
    Productions, 1988
A MAN CALLED HAWK (Pilot)   1989

JOHN BOX
LAWRENCE OF ARABIA ★   Columbia, 1962
DOCTOR ZHIVAGO ★   MGM, 1965
OLIVER! ★★   Columbia, 1968
NICHOLAS AND ALEXANDRA ★★   Columbia, 1971
TRAVELS WITH MY AUNT ★   MGM, 1972
THE GREAT GATSBY   Paramount, 1974
SORCERER   Universal/Paramount, 1977
THE KEEP   Paramount, 1983
A PASSAGE TO INDIA ★   Columbia, 1984
MURDER BY THE BOOK (CTF)   TVS
    International, 1990

ROBERT F. BOYLE*
IATSE Local 876
Agent: The Gersh Agency, Inc., Beverly Hills -
    213/274-6611, New York - 212/997-1818

THE BIRDS   Universal, 1963
GAILY, GAILY ★   United Artists, 1969
FIDDLER ON THE ROOF ★   United Artists, 1971
LEADBELLY   Paramount, 1976
THE SHOOTIST ★   Paramount, 1976
W.C. FIELDS AND ME   Universal, 1976
THE BIG FIX   Universal, 1978
WINTER KILLS   Avco Embassy, 1979
PRIVATE BENJAMIN   Warner Bros., 1980
THE BEST LITTLE WHOREHOUSE IN TEXAS
    Universal, 1982

CINEMATOGRAPHERS
PRODUCTION
DESIGNERS,
COSTUME
DESIGNERS AND
FILM EDITORS
GUIDE

P
R
O
D
U
C
T
I
O
N

D
E
S
I
G
N
E
R
S

Br

CINEMATOGRAPHERS
PRODUCTION
DESIGNERS,
COSTUME
DESIGNERS AND
FILM EDITORS
GUIDE

P
R
O
D
U
C
T
I
O
N

D
E
S
I
G
N
E
R
S

LOOKIN' TO GET OUT   Paramount, 1982
TABLE FOR FIVE   Warner Bros., 1983
STAYING ALIVE   Paramount, 1983
RHINESTONE   20th Century Fox, 1984
NO SMALL AFFAIR   Columbia, 1984
EXPLORERS   Paramount, 1985
JUMPIN' JACK FLASH   20th Century Fox, 1986
DRAGNET   Universal, 1987
TROOP BEVERLY HILLS   WEG, 1989

HUB BRADEN*
IATSE Local 876

MIKE'S MURDER   The Ladd Company/Warner
   Bros., 1984, AD
LITTLE NIKITA   Columbia, 1988, AD
ARTHUR 2 ON THE ROCKS   Warner Bros.,
   1988, AD

JACQUES BRADETTE
MRS. SOFFEL   MGM/UA, 1984

CHRISTOPHER J. BRADSHAW
IN THE HEAT OF THE DAY (TF)   Granada
   Television, 1990

RAYMOND A. BRANDT
THE INCREDIBLE SHRINKING WOMAN
   Universal, 1981

ALBERT BRENNER*
IATSE Local 876, NY Local 829
Agent: Lawrence A. Mirisch, Triad Artists, Inc. -
   Los Angeles, 213/556-2727

THE HUSTLER   20th Century Fox, 1961
THE PAWNBROKER   Landau/Allied Artists, 1965
POINT BLANK   MGM, 1967
BULLITT   Warner Bros., 1968
MONTE WALSH   National General, 1970
SUMMER OF '42   Warner Bros., 1971
THE OTHER   20th Century Fox, 1972
SCARECROW   Warner Bros., 1973
ZANDY'S BRIDE   Warner Bros., 1974
THE SUNSHINE BOYS ★   MGM/United Artists, 1975
THE MISSOURI BREAKS   United Artists, 1976
SILENT MOVIE   20th Century Fox, 1976
THE GOODBYE GIRL   Warner Bros., 1977
THE TURNING POINT ★   20th Century Fox, 1977
CAPRICORN ONE   Warner Bros., 1978
CALIFORNIA SUITE ★   Columbia, 1978
COMA   MGM/UA, 1978
HERO AT LARGE   MGM/United Artists, 1980
DIVINE MADNESS (FD)   The Ladd Company/Warner
   Bros., 1980
ONLY WHEN I LAUGH   Columbia, 1981
THE LEGEND OF THE LONE RANGER   Universal/
   AFD, 1981
I OUGHT TO BE IN PICTURES   20th Century Fox, 1982
MAX DUGAN RETURNS   20th Century Fox, 1983
TWO OF A KIND   20th Century Fox, 1983
UNFAITHFULLY YOURS   20th Century Fox, 1984
2010 ★   MGM/United Artists, 1984
SWEET DREAMS   Tri-Star, 1985
RUNNING SCARED   MGM/UA, 1986
THE MORNING AFTER   20th Century Fox, 1986
MONSTER SQUAD   Tri-Star, 1987

THE PRESIDIO   Paramount, 1988
BAJA OKLAHOMA   HBO Pictures, 1988
BEACHES ★   Buena Vista, l988
PRETTY WOMAN   *3000*   Buena Vista, 1990
BACKDRAFT   Universal, 1991

KEN BRIDGEMAN
ORDEAL BY INNOCENCE   MGM/UA/Cannon, 1984

DAVID BRISBIN
LOVE LETTERS   New World, 1982, AD
DESERT HEARTS   D.H. Productions, 1984, AD
MARIA'S LOVERS   Cannon, 1984, AD
THE SERPENT AND THE RAINBOW   Universal,
   1988, AD
DRUGSTORE COWBOY   Avenue, 1989
THE INCIDENT (TF)   Qintex Entertainment, 1990
AFTER DARK, MY SWEET   Avenue Pictures, 1990
CROOKED HEARTS   MGM/UA, 1991
THE TENDER   Trans World Entertainment, 1991

BILL BRODIE
Agent: The Gersh Agency, Inc., Beverly Hills -
   213/274-6611, New York - 212/997-1818

AGENCY   Jensen Farley Pictures, 1981
SILENCE OF THE NORTH   Universal, 1982
THE GREY FOX   United Artists Classics, 1983
ONE MAGIC CHRISTMAS   Buena Vista, 1985
DEAD OF WINTER   MGM/UA, 1987
SHORT CIRCUIT 2   Tri-Star, 1988

DAVID BROCKHURST
BAD TIMING/A SEXUAL OBSESSION   World
   Northal, 1980
PRIEST OF LOVE   Filmways, 1981, w/Ted Tester
INSIGNIFICANCE   Island Alive, 1985
THE FRUIT MACHINE   Ideal Communications, 1988
WONDERLAND   Vestron, 1989

ANTHONY BROCKLISS*
IATSE Locak 876
Agent: The Production Agency - Los Angeles,
   213/651-1858

THE BEST OF TIMES   Universal, 1986
NO WAY OUT   Orion, 1987, AD
THE GREGORY HARRISON SHOW (Pilot)   1989

KAREN BROMLEY
Agent: London Management, 011/44/493-1610

HOMER   National General, 1970
DORIAN GRAY   1970
WHEN MICHAEL CALLS (TF)   Palomar
   International, 1972
WEDDING IN WHITE   Avco Embassy, 1973
BLACK CHRISTMAS   Warner Bros., 1975
SECOND WIND   Health and Entertainment
   Corporation of America, 1976
WHY SHOOT THE TEACHER?   Quartet, 1977
STARSHIP INVASIONS   Warner Bros., 1977, AD
OUTRAGEOUS!   Cinema 5, 1977, AD
RITUALS   Day and Date International, 1978
POWER PLAY   Magnum International Pictures/
   Cowry Film Productions, 1978
SEPARATION (TF)   CFTO-TV, 1978
TITLE SHOT   Arista, 1979

BEAR ISLAND   Taft International, 1980
MIDDLE AGE CRAZY   20th Century Fox, 1980, AD
THE OSTERMAN WEEKEND   20th Century Fox, 1983
HARRY TRACY   Quartet/Films Inc., 1983
WILL THERE REALLY BE A MORNING? (TF)
   Jaffe-Blakely Films/Sama Productions/
   Orion TV, 1983

LEZ BROTHERSTON
LETTER TO BREZHNEV   Circle Releasing
   Corporation, 1985, w/Nick Englefield &
   Jonathan Swain

HILYARD BROWN*
IATSE Local 876

THE NIGHT OF THE HUNTER   UA, 1965, AD
CLEOPATRA ★★   20th Century Fox, 1963,
   AD, shared credit
BILLY JACK GOES TO WASHINGTON
   Taylor-Laughlin, 1978, AD
HOOPER   Warner Bros., 1978, AD
COAST TO COAST   Paramount, 1980, AD
SIX WEEKS   Unviersal, 1982, AD

MICHAEL BUCHANAN
GOTHIC   Vestron, 1987, AD
HELLRAISER   New World, 1987
HELLBOUND: HELLRAISER 2   New World, 1988
SALOME'S LAST DANCE   Vestron, 1988, AD

CLOVIS BUENO
KISS OF THE SPIDER WOMAN   New Yorker Films,
   1985, AD
HOUR OF THE STAR   Kino International, 1987, AD

JACQUES BUFNOIR
PHANTOM OF THE OPERA (TF)   Saban-Scherick
   Productions, 1990

HENRY BUMSTEAD*
IATSE Local 876
Agent: Smith Gosnell Nicholson & Associates -
   Pacific Palisades, 213/459-0307

VERTIGO ★★   Paramount, 1958
COME SEPTEMBER   Universal, 1961
TO KILL A MOCKINGBIRD ★   Universal, 1962
FATHER GOOSE   Universal, 1964
THE WAR LORD   Universal, 1965
TOPAZ   Universal, 1969
SLAUGHTERHOUSE FIVE   Universal, 1971
HIGH PLAINS DRIFTER   Universal, 1972
THE STING ★★   Universal, 1973
THE FRONT PAGE   Universal, 1974
THE GREAT WALDO PEPPER   Universal, 1975, AD
FAMILY PLOT   Universal, 1976
ROLLER COASTER   Universal, 1977
SLAP SHOT   Universal, 1977
SAME TIME, NEXT YEAR   Universal, 1978
HOUSE CALLS   Universal, 1978
A LITTLE ROMANCE   Orion/Warner Bros., 1979
THE CONCORDE - AIRPORT '79   Universal, 1979
SMOKEY AND THE BANDIT, PART II   Universal, 1980
THE WORLD ACCORDING TO GARP   Warner
   Bros.,1982
HARRY & SON   Orion, 1984

THE LITTLE DRUMMER GIRL   Warner Bros., 1984
WARNING SIGN   20th Century Fox, 1985
PSYCHO III   Universal, 1986
FUNNY FARM   Warner Bros., 1988
A TIME OF DESTINY   Columbia, 1988
HER ALIBI   Warner Bros., 1989
GHOST DAD   Universal, 1990
ALMOST AN ANGEL   Ironbark Films/Paramount, 1990

JON BUNKER
REVOLUTION   Warner Bros., 1985, AD
BELLMAN AND TRUE   Island Pictures, 1989

LYNDA BURBANK
REPO MAN   Universal, 1984, AD w/J. Rae Fox
BLOODY BIRTHDAY   Judica Productions, 1986,
   AD w/J. Rae Fox
QUIET COOL   New Line Cinema, 1986,
   AD w/J. Rae Fox
SID & NANCY   Samuel Goldwyn Company, 1986,
   AD w/J. Rae Fox
BORN IN EAST L.A.   Universal, 1987, AD w/J. Rae Fox

GIANTITO BURCHIELLARO
MAN ON FIRE   Tri-Star, 1987, AD

SARAH BURDICK
WITCHBOARD   Cinema Group, 1987, AD

MILLY BURNS
JABBERWOCKY   Cinema 5, 1977, AD
YANKS   Universal, 1979, AD
TIME BANDITS   Avco Embassy, 1981
JOSHUA THEN AND NOW   20th Century Fox, 1985, AD

ROBERT BURNS
THE HILLS HAVE EYES   Vanguard, 1977, AD
THE TOURIST TRAP   Compass International, 1979, AD
THE HOWLING   Avco Embassy, 1980, AD
MAUSOLEUM   MPM, 1983, AD
RE-ANIMATOR   Empire Pictures, 1985, AD
PLAY DEAD   Troma, 1986, AD
THE OUTING   TMS Pictures/The Movie Store, 1988

SCOTT BUSHNELL
O.C. AND STIGGS   MGM/UA, 1987

CHAS. BUTCHER*
IATSE Local 876

COLORS   Orion, 1988, AD
WINTER PEOPLE   Columbia, 1989, AD

Bu

CINEMATOGRAPHERS
PRODUCTION
DESIGNERS,
COSTUME
DESIGNERS AND
FILM EDITORS
GUIDE

P
R
O
D
U
C
T
I
O
N

D
E
S
I
G
N
E
R
S

Ca

CINEMATOGRAPHERS
PRODUCTION
DESIGNERS,
COSTUME
DESIGNERS AND
FILM EDITORS
GUIDE

P
R
O
D
U
C
T
I
O
N

D
E
S
I
G
N
E
R
S

C

KATHY CURTIS CAHILL
DON'T ANSWER THE PHONE   Crown
    International, 1980, AD
SCHIZOID   Cannon, 1980, AD
THE BOSS' WIFE   Tri-Star, 1986,
    AD w/Albert J. Locatelli

MAURICE CAIN
ACTT
Agent: Sandra Marsh Management - Sherman Oaks,
    818/905-6961

THE SEA WOLVES   United Artists, 1980, AD
LOOPHOLE   MGM/United Artists, 1981, AD
LION OF THE DESERT   United Film Distribution,
    1981, AD
THE FINAL OPTION   *WHO DARES WINS*   MGM/UA,
    1983, AD
NATE AND HAYES   *SAVAGE ISLANDS*
    Paramount, 1983
THOSE GLORY, GLORY DAYS   Cinecom, 1983, AD
SHARMA AND BEYOND   Cinecom, 1984
THE LAST PLACE ON EARTH (MS)   Central
    Productions/Renegade Films, 1985
HEART OF THE HIGH COUNTRY (MS)   Philips/
    Whitehouse, 1985
INTIMATE CONTACT (MS)   Zenith Productions/
    Central TV, 1987
THE RESCUE   Buena Vista, 1988
THE ENDLESS GAME (CTF)   TVS Films/Reteitalia/Pixit,
    1989

ROGER CAIN
LABYRINTH   Tri-Star, 1986, AD w/others
INDIANA JONES AND THE TEMPLE OF DOOM
    Paramount, 1984, AD w/Alan Cassie
WHO FRAMED ROGER RABBIT   Buena Vista, 1988

SYD CAIN
FROM RUSSIA WITH LOVE   United Artists, 1963
FAHRENHEIT 451   Universal, 1967, AD
ON HER MAJESTY'S SECRET SERVICE   United
    Artists, 1969
LIVE AND LET DIE   United Artists, 1973, AD
SHOUT AT THE DEVIL   American International, 1976
THE SEA WOLVES   United Artists, 1980
THE FINAL OPTION   *WHO DARES WINS*
    MGM/UA, 1983
WILD GEESE II   Universal, 1986

LEONARDO COEN CALGI
BURIED ALIVE   RCA/Columbia Pictures Home
    Video, 1990
THE HOUSE OF USHER   RCA/Columbia Pictures
    Home Video, 1991

GENE CALLAHAN*
IATSE Local 876
Agent: The Gersh Agency, Inc. - Beverly Hills,
    213/274-6611

AMERICA AMERICA ★★   Warner Bros., 1963
THE GROUP   United Artists, 1965
THE CANDIDATE   Warner Bros., 1972
THE LAST TYCOON ★   Paramount, 1976
THE NEXT MAN   Allied Artists, 1976
JULIA   20th Century Fox, 1977, w/Carmen Dillon &
    Willy Holt
KING OF THE GYPSIES   Paramount, 1978
EYES OF LAURA MARS   Columbia, 1978
BLOODBROTHERS   Warner Bros., 1979
CHAPTER TWO   Columbia, 1979
THE LAST MARRIED COUPLE IN AMERICA
    Universal, 1980
SEEMS LIKE OLD TIMES   Columbia, 1980
WHOSE LIFE IS IT, ANYWAY?   MGM/UA, 1981
GREASE II   Paramount, 1982
THE SURVIVORS   Columbia, 1983
PLACES IN THE HEART   Columbia, 1984
JAGGED EDGE   Columbia, 1985
BIG TROUBLE   Columbia, 1986
CHILDREN OF A LESSER GOD   Paramount, 1986
BLACK WIDOW   20th Century Fox, 1987
LITTLE NIKITA   Columbia, 1988
ARTHUR 2 ON THE ROCKS   Warner Bros., 1988
STEEL MAGNOLIAS   Tri-Star, 1989, w/Edward Pisoni

ALLAN CAMERON
Agent: Grace Lyons Management - Los Angeles,
    213/655-5100

THE FRENCH LIEUTENANT'S WOMAN   United Artists,
    1981, AD w/Norman Dorme & Terry Pritchard
BEYOND THE LIMIT   *THE HONORARY CONSUL*
    Paramount, 1983
1984   Atlantic Releasing Corporation, 1984
HIGHLANDER   20th Century Fox, 1986
LADY JANE   Paramount, 1986
THE FOURTH PROTOCOL   Lorimar, 1987
WILLOW   MGM/UA, 1988
AIR AMERICA   Carolco/Tri-Star, 1990

JUDY CAMMER
IN THE BEST INTEREST OF THE CHILD (TF)
    Papazian-Hirsch Entertainment, 1990
THE ROOKIE   Malpaso/Warner Bros., 1990

CHRIS CAMPBELL
THE PHILADELPHIA EXPERIMENT   New World,
    1984, AD

SALLY CAMPBELL
THE GOOD WIFE   Atlantic Releasing Corporation, 1986
HIGH TIDE   Tri-Star, 1987
THE NAVIGATOR: AN ODYSSEY ACROSS TIME
    Circle Releasing, 1989

W. STEWART CAMPBELL*
IATSE Local 876
Phone: 818/782-6789

CHINATOWN ★   Paramount, 1974, AD
SHAMPOO ★   Columbia, 1975, AD

THE RETURN OF A MAN CALLED HORSE   United
    Artists, 1976
JAWS 2   Universal, 1978, AD w/Gene Johnson
URBAN COWBOY   Paramount, 1980, AD
TRUE CONFESSIONS   United Artists, 1981, AD
SHOOT THE MOON   MGM/UA, 1982, AD
INDEPENDENCE DAY   Warner Bros., 1983
THE RIGHT STUFF ★   The Ladd Company/
    Warner Bros., 1983, AD w/Richard J. Lawrence &
    Peter Romero
SPRAGGUE (TF)   MF Productions/Lorimar
    Productions, 1984
BIRDY   Tri-Star, 1984, AD w/Armin Ganz
PEYTON PLACE: NEXT GENERATION (TF)   Michael
    Filerman Productions/20th Century Fox TV, 1985
APRIL FOOL'S DAY   Parmount, 1986, AD
THE ROSARY MURDERS   New Line Cinema, 1987,
    Visual Consultant
MAC AND ME   Orion, 1988
I KNOW MY FIRST NAME IS STEVEN (TF)   Andrew
    Adelson Company/Lorimar TV, 1989
MURDER IN PARADISE (TF)   Bill McCutchen
    Productions, 1990
ANGEL OF DEATH (TF)   Once Upon A Time
    Productions, 1990
THE CHASE (TF)   Steve White Productions, 1991

BERNT AMADEUS CAPRA
ECHO PARK   Atlantic Releasing Corporation,
    1985, AD
THE KILLING TIME   New World, 1987
BAGDAD CAFE   Island Pictures, 1988, AD
COLD FEET   Avenue Pictures, 1989
SETTLE THE SCORE (TF)   Steve Sohmer
    Productions, 1990, w/Bernadette di Santo

EDWARD C. CARFAGNO*
IATSE Local 876
Agent: The Gersh Agency, Inc. - Beverly Hills,
    213/274-6611

BEN HUR ★★   MGM, 1959
THE SHOES OF THE FISHERMAN ★   Columbia,
    1968, AD
SOYLENT GREEN   MGM, 1972
THE HINDENBURG ★   Universal, 1975
THE LAST HARD MEN   20th Century Fox, 1976
GABLE AND LOMBARD   Universal, 1976
LOOKING FOR MR. GOODBAR   Paramount, 1977
DEMON SEED   MGM/UA, 1977
THE ONE AND ONLY   Paramount, 1978
METEOR   American International, 1979
TIME AFTER TIME   Orion/Warner Bros., 1979
LITTLE MISS MARKER   Universal, 1980
WRONG IS RIGHT   Columbia, 1982
HONKYTONK MAN   Warner Bros., 1982
THE STING II   Universal, 1983
SUDDEN IMPACT   Warner Bros., 1983
ALL OF ME   Universal, 1984
TIGHTROPE   Warner Bros., 1984
CITY HEAT   Warner Bros., 1984
PALE RIDER   Warner Bros., 1985
RATBOY   Warner Bros., 1986
HEARTBREAK RIDGE   Warner Bros., 1986
THE DEAD POOL   Warner Bros., 1988
BIRD   Warner Bros., 1988
PINK CADILLAC   Warner Bros., 1989

THAD CARR
SOULTAKER   Taurus Entertainment, 1990, AD

FERNANDO CARRERE
CAMELOT ★★   Warner Bros., 1967, AD
I WILL, I WILL...FOR NOW   20th Century Fox, 1976
FOOLIN' AROUND   Columbia, 1980
THE FINAL COUNTDOWN   United Artists, 1980

MAURICE CARTER
THE PEOPLE THAT TIME FORGOT   American
    International, 1977
THE GREAT TRAIN ROBBERY   United Artists, 1979
ffolkes   Universal, 1980

RICHARD (RICK) CARTER*
IATSE Local 876
Agent: Sanford-Skouras & Gross - Los Angeles,
    213/208-2100

BOUND FOR GLORY   United Artists, 1976, AD
THE CHINA SYNDROME   Columbia, 1979, AD
SECOND-HAND HEARTS   Paramount, 1981, AD
THE POSTMAN ALWAYS RINGS TWICE   Paramount,
    1981, AD
PERSONAL BEST   The Geffen Company/Warner Bros.,
    1982, AD
THE ADVENTURES OF BUCKAROO BANZAI: ACROSS
    THE 8TH DIMENSION   20th Century Fox, 1984,
    AD w/Stephen Dane
THE SLUGGER'S WIFE   Columbia, 1985, AD
THE GOONIES   Warner Bros., 1985, AD
TALKING WALLS   Drummond Productions, 1987
EMPIRE OF THE SUN   Warner Bros., 1987
THREE FUGITIVES   Buena Vista, 1989, AD w/Marjorie
    Stone McShirley
BACK TO THE FUTURE II   Universal, 1989
BACK TO THE FUTURE III   Universal, 1990
GHOST DAD   Universal, 1990

JOHN CARTWRIGHT*
IATSE Local 876

FIRST MONDAY IN OCTOBER   Paramount, 1981, AD
AN OFFICER AND A GENTLEMAN   Paramount,
    1982, AD
KISS ME GOODBYE   20th Century Fox, 1982, AD
KIDS DON'T TELL (TF)   Chris-Rose Productions/
    Viacom Productions, 1985

ROBERT CARTWRIGHT
SCROOGE ★   National General, 1970, AD
MARY, QUEEN OF SCOTS ★   Universal, 1971, AD
HANOVER STREET   Columbia, 1979,
    AD w/Malcolm Middleton
THE ELEPHANT MAN ★   Paramount, 1980, AD
SECRET PLACES   TLC Films/20th Century Fox,
    1984, AD
LIFEFORCE   Tri-Star, 1985, AD
NATIONAL LAMPOON'S EUROPEAN VACATION
    Warner Bros., 1985
BEJEWELLED (CTF)   TVS Productions, 1991

WILLIAM J. CASSIDY*
IATSE Local 876
Agent: The Gersh Agency, Inc., Beverly Hills -
    213/274-6611, New York - 212/997-1818

ROCKY   United Artists, 1976
SLOW DANCING IN THE BIG CITY   United
    Artists, 1978

Ca

CINEMATOGRAPHERS
PRODUCTION
DESIGNERS,
COSTUME
DESIGNERS AND
FILM EDITORS
GUIDE

P
R
O
D
U
C
T
I
O
N

D
E
S
I
G
N
E
R
S

DUMMY (TF)   The Konigsberg Company/Warner
    Bros. TV, 1979
CARNY   United Artists, 1980
ROCKY III ★★   United Artists, 1982
RISKY BUSINESS   The Geffen Company/Warner
    Bros., 1983
A NIGHT IN HEAVEN   20th Century Fox, 1983
THE KARATE KID   Columbia, 1984
FIRESTARTER   Universal, 1984
SECRET ADMIRER   Orion, 1985
THE KARATE KID PART II   Columbia, 1986
HAPPY NEW YEAR   Columbia, 1987
REAL MEN   MGM/UA, 1987, AD w/James Allen
FOR KEEPS   Tri-Star, 1988
MEMORIES OF ME   MGM/UA, 1988
A SHOW OF FORCE   Paramount, 1989,
    w/Sonya Polansky
ROCKY V   MGM/UA, 1990

ALAN CASSIE
THE WATCHER IN THE WOODS   Buena Vista,
    1980, AD
DRAGONSLAYER   Paramount, 1981, AD
EVIL UNDER THE SUN   Universal/AFD, 1982, AD
THE LORDS OF DISCIPLINE   Paramount, 1983, AD
THE PIRATES OF PENZANCE   Universal, 1983,
    AD w/Ernest Archer
INDIANA JONES AND THE TEMPLE OF DOOM
    Paramount, 1984, AD w/Roger Cain
D.A.R.Y.L.   Paramount, 1985

SUZANNE CAVEDON
Agent: The Gersh Agency, Inc., Beverly Hills -
    213/274-6611, New York - 212/997-1818

ME AND HIM   Columbia, 1990
AGAINST THE LAW (Pilot)   Sarabande
    Productions, 1990
BED AND BREAKFAST   Schwartzman Pictures, 1991

CLINTON CAVERS
PINK FLOYD - THE WALL   MGM/United Artists,
    1982, AD
QUEST FOR FIRE   20th Century Fox, 1982, AD
THE HUNGER   MGM/UA, 1983, AD
ANOTHER COUNTRY   Orion Classics, 1984, AD
NUNS ON THE RUN   20th Century Fox, 1990, AD

EVE CAULEY
THE HEIST (CTF)   HBO Pictures, 1990

ELAYNE CEDER*
Phone: 213/656-8272

PONY EXPRESS RIDER   Doyt-Dayton, 1976
A SMALL TOWN IN TEXAS   American
    International, 1976
AMERICAN HOT WAX   Paramount, 1978
MURDER AT THE WORLD SERIES (TF)   ABC Circle
    Films, 1977
PORTRAIT OF A HIT MAN   Shapiro Entertainment, 1977
A SENSITIVE, PASSIONATE MAN (TF)   Factor-Newland
    Production Corporation, 1977
EVERY WHICH WAY BUT LOOSE   Warner Bros., 1978
THE SUICIDE'S WIFE (TF)   Factor-Newland Production
    Corporation, 1979
A SHINING SEASON (TF)   Green-Epstein Productions/
    T-M Productions/Columbia TV, 1979
WHEN A STRANGER CALLS   Columbia, 1979

THE LOVE TAPES (TF)   Christiana Productions/
    MGM TV, 1980
THE JAYNE MANSFIELD STORY (TF)   Alan Landsburg
    Productions, 1980
THE FIVE OF ME (TF)   Jack Farren Productions/
    Factor-Newland Production Corporation, 1981
MYSTERIOUS TWO (TF)   Alan Landsburg
    Productions, 1982
FIREFOX   Warner Bros., 1982, AD w/John Graysmark
SECRETS OF A MOTHER AND DAUGHTER (TF)
    The Shpetner Company, 1983
GET CRAZY   Embassy, 1983
MARVIN AND TIGE   20th Century Fox International
    Classics, 1983
GETTING PHYSICAL (TF)   CBS Entertainment, 1984
HEAD OFFICE   Tri-Star, 1985
SISTER MARGARET AND THE SATURDAY NIGHT
    LADIES (TF)   Poolhouse Productions, 1986
R.E.L.A.X. (TF)   CBS Entertainment, 1986
NOT QUITE HUMAN (TF)   Sharmhill Productions/Walt
    Disney TV, 1987
THE SECRET LIFE OF KATHY McCORMICK (TF)   1989
CHARLIE (Pilot)   MGM Television, 1990
SAIL AWAY   *BARE ESSENTIALS*   Republic
    Pictures, 1991
RESCUE ME   Cannon, 1991

KAREL CERNY
AMADEUS ★   Orion, 1984, AD

PAUL CHADWICK
AFTER MIDNIGHT   MGM/UA, 1990

DAVID CHAPMAN
Agent: The Gersh Agency, Inc., Beverly Hills -
    213/274-6611, New York - 212/997-1818

SOMEBODY KILLED HER HUSBAND   Columbia,
    1978, AD
THE SEDUCTION OF JOE TYNAN   Universal, 1979, AD
WOLFEN   Orion/Warner Bros., 1981, AD
FOUR FRIENDS   Filmways, 1981, AD
THE COTTON CLUB   Orion, 1984, AD w/Gregory Bolton
DIRTY DANCING   Vestron, 1987
MYSTIC PIZZA   Samuel Goldwyn Company, 1988
OPPORTUNITY KNOCKS   Universal, 1990

DIANA CHARNLEY
CLOCKWISE   Universal, 1986, AD
DEFENSE OF THE REALM   Hemdale, 1987, AD
HIGH HOPES   Skouras Pictures, 1989

CYNTHIA CHARETTE
RACE FOR GLORY   New Century/Vista, 1990

NORA CHAVOOSHIAN
THE BROTHER FROM ANOTHER PLANET
    Cinecom, 1984
ALMOST YOU   TLC Films/20th Century Fox, 1984, AD
MATEWAN   Cinecom, 1987
EIGHT MEN OUT   Orion, 1988

ROBERT CHECCHI
CHALLENGER (TF)   The IndieProd Company, 1990

MAY LING CHENG
83 HOURS 'TIL DAWN (TF)   Consolidated
    Entertainment, 1990

KATHY EMILY CHERRY
ERNEST GOES TO CAMP   Buena Vista, 1987, AD

JOHN E. CHILBERG
STAR TREK III: THE SEARCH FOR SPOCK
    Paramount, 1984, AD
THE JESSE OWENS STORY (TF)   Harve Bennett
    Productions/Paramount TV, 1984

PETER CHILDS
THE ABYSS ★   20th Century Fox, 1989, Supv AD

JO ANNE CHORNEY
Agent: The Gersh Agency, Inc., Beverly Hills -
    213/274-6611, New York - 212/997-1818

MURDER C.O.D. (TF)   Perry Lafferty
    Productions, 1990

ROGER CHRISTIAN
STAR WARS ★★   20th Century Fox, 1977, AD
ALIEN ★   20th Century Fox, 1979, AD w/Les Dilley
MONTY PYTHON'S LIFE OF BRIAN   Orion/
    Warner Bros., 1979, AD

RUSSELL CHRISTIAN
52 PICK-UP   Cannon, 1986
THE ABYSS ★   20th Century Fox, 1989,
    AD w/Joseph Nemec III

GEO CLARKE
MURDER ON LINE ONE   Academy
    Entertainment, 1990

JIM CLAY
TUNE IN TOMORROW...   Cinecom, 1990
A KISS BEFORE DYING   Universal, 1991

NIGEL CLINKER
WHEELS OF TERROR (CTF)   Once Upon A Time
    Productions, 1990, AD

RON COBB*
IATSE Local 876

CONAN THE BARBARIAN   Universal, 1982
THE LAST STARFIGHTER   Universal, 1984
LEVIATHAN   MGM/UA, 1989

LESTER W. COHEN
Agent: The Doug Apatow Agency - Los Angeles,
    213/202-6888

SALVATION!   Circle Films, 1987
ANNA   Vestron, 1987
THE LASER MAN   1989
TRUE LOVE   MGM/UA, 1989

LEE COLE*
IATSE Local 876
Phone: 213/398-1897

THE MAN WHO SAW TOMORROW   Warner Bros.,
    1981, AD
SPACESHIP *THE CREATURE WASN'T NICE*   Almi
    Cinema 5, 1982, AD

JACK T. COLLIS*
IATSE Local 876
Agent: The Gersh Agency, Inc., Beverly Hills - 213/274-
    6611, New York - 212/997-1818

DARKER THAN AMBER   National General, 1970
THE DELTA FACTOR   American International, 1971
SAVE THE TIGER   Paramount, 1973
MAGNUM FORCE   Warner Bros., 1973
THE LAST TYCOON ★   Paramount, 1976, AD
EXORCIST II: THE HERETIC   Warner Bros., 1977
THE JERK   Universal, 1979
THE NORTH AVENUE IRREGULARS   Buena Vista,
    1979, AD w/John B. Mansbridge
THE LAST WORD   Samuel Goldwyn Company, 1979
THE LONG RIDERS   United Artists, 1980
THE FOUR SEASONS   Universal, 1981
PATERNITY   Paramount, 1981
NIGHT SHIFT   The Ladd Company/Warner Bros., 1982
TEX   Buena Vista, 1982
NATIONAL LAMPOON'S VACATION   Warner
    Bros., 1983
SPLASH   Buena Vista, 1984
IMPULSE   20th Century Fox, 1984
COCOON   20th Century Fox, 1985
CROSSROADS   Columbia, 1986
STAR TREK IV: THE VOYAGE HOME
    Paramount, 1986
THE RUNNING MAN   Tri-Star, 1987
ALIEN NATION   20th Century Fox, 1988
NEXT OF KIN   Warner Bros., 1989
FLIGHT OF THE INTRUDER   Paramount, 1991

SHARON COMPTON
Phone: 213/393-7891

DEATHSPORT   New World, 1978
BATTLE BEYOND THE STARS   New World, 1979
AVALANCHE   New World, 1979

FRANÇOIS COMTET
ENIGMA   Embassy, 1983, AD w/Marc Frederix
THE BLOOD OF OTHERS (CMS)   HBO Premiere Films/
    ICC/Filmax Productions, 1984

GUY J. COMTOIS
IATSE Local 876
Agent: The Gersh Agency, Inc., Beverly Hills -
    213/274-6611, New York - 212/997-1818

QUEST FOR FIRE   20th Century Fox, 1982,
    w/Brian Morris
TERROR TRAIN   20th Century Fox, 1980, AD
BODY ROCK   New World, 1984
CUJO   Warner Bros., 1984
THE CLAN OF THE CAVE BEAR   Warner Bros.,
    1986, AD
WAR AND REMEMBRANCE (MS) ☆   Dan Curtis
    Productions, 1989
NAVY SEALS   Orion, 1990
IF LOOKS COULD KILL   Warner Bros., 1991

BUDDY CONE
TO LIVE AND DIE IN L.A.   MGM/UA, 1985
RAMPAGE   DEG, 1987
SHAG: THE MOVIE   Hemdale, 1989

KEVIN CONSTANT
HARD TRAVELING   New World, 1986, AD

Co

CINEMATOGRAPHERS
PRODUCTION
DESIGNERS,
COSTUME
DESIGNERS AND
FILM EDITORS
GUIDE

P
R
O
D
U
C
T
I
O
N

D
E
S
I
G
N
E
R
S

CINEMATOGRAPHERS
PRODUCTION
DESIGNERS,
COSTUME
DESIGNERS AND
FILM EDITORS
GUIDE

FRANK CONWAY
THE FIELD   Avenue Pictures, 1990

JEREMY CONWAY
"CROCODILE" DUNDEE II   Paramount, 1988, AD

KATHLEEN B. COOPER
THE TERROR WITHIN   Concorde, 1989

DAVID COPPING
Agent: The Gersh Agency, Inc. - Beverly Hills,
    213/274-6611

MAN FROM HONG KONG   The Movie Company/
    Golden Harvest, 1975, AD
PICNIC AT HANGING ROCK   Atlantic Releasing
    Corporation, 1975, AD
STORM BOY   South Australian Film
    Corporation, 1976
LET THE BALLOON GO   Film Australia, 1976, AD
THE PICTURE SHOW MAN   Roadshow
    Distributors, 1977, AD
THE EARTHLING   Roadshow Distributors, 1980
BREAKER MORANT   New World/Quartet, 1980, AD
MONEY MOVERS   South Australian Film
    Corporation, 1981, AD
THE CLUB   South Australian Film Corporation,
    1981, AD
THE RETURN OF CAPTAIN INVINCIBLE   New
    World, 1983
PUBERTY BLUES   Universal Classics, 1983, AD
BROTHERHOOD OF THE ROSE (TF)   CBS
    Entertainment, 1989

TOBY CORBETT
East Coast card
Agent: The Doug Apatow Agency - Los Angeles,
    213/202-6888

THE PRINCE OF PENNSYLVANIA   New Line
    Cinema, 1988
BLUE STEEL   MGM/UA, 1990
IRON MAZE   1991

MICHAEL CORENBLITH*
IATSE Local 876
Phone: 213/876-8634

PRINCE JACK   Castle Hill Productions, 1984
THE RATINGS GAME (CTF)   Imagination - New
    Street Productions, 1984
PRIVATE RESORT   Tri-Star, 1985
HOLLYWOOD VICE SQUAD   Concorde/Cinema
    Group, 1986, AD
BURGLAR   Warner Bros., 1987, AD
RED HEAT   Tri-Star, 1988, AD
SAN BERDOO (Pilot)   1989
LITTLE WHITE LIES (TF)   Larry A. Thompson
    Organization, 1990
HE SAID, SHE SAID   Paramount, 1991

BILL CORNFORD
VESTIGE OF HONOR (TF)   Desperado Pictures, 1990
LAMBADA   Warner Bros., 1990

DORA CORONA
GHOST FEVER   Miramax, 1987

JOHN W. CORSO*
IATSE Local 876

PARADISE ALLEY   Universal, 1978
COAL MINER'S DAUGHTER ★   Universal, 1980
XANADU   Universal, 1980
BUSTIN' LOOSE   Universal, 1981, w/Charles Davis
HEARTBEEPS   Universal, 1981
TALES OF THE GOLD MONKEY II (Pilot)   1982,
    w/Frank Grieco Jr.
PSYCHO II   Universal, 1983
SIXTEEN CANDLES   Universal, 1984
THE BREAKFAST CLUB   Universal, 1985
WEIRD SCIENCE   Universal, 1985
PRETTY IN PINK   Paramount, 1986
FERRIS BUELLER'S DAY OFF   Paramount, 1986
PLANES, TRAINS AND AUTOMOBILES
    Paramount, 1987
SHE'S HAVING A BABY   Paramount, 1988
THE GREAT OUTDOORS   Universal, 1988
UNCLE BUCK   Universal, 1989

GEORGE COSTELLO
Agent: Grace Lyons Management - Los Angeles,
    213/655-5100
Phone: 818/784-0813

THE SWORD AND THE SORCERER   Group 1,
    1982, AD
LIAR'S MOON   Crown International, 1982, AD
THE BEAR   Embassy, 1984
THE TERMINATOR   Orion, 1984, AD
HOT MOVES   Cardinal Releasing, 1984
THE NIGHT THEY SAVED CHRISTMAS (TF)   Robert
    Halmi Inc., 1984
HAMBURGER...THE MOTION PICTURE   FM Entertain-
    ment, 1986
NIGHT OF THE CREEPS   Tri-Star, 1986
DISORDERLIES   Warner Bros., 1987
RENTED LIPS   New Century/Vista, 1988
THE WRONG GUYS   New World, 1988
CRYSTALSTONE   TMS Pictures/The Movie Store, 1988
K-9   Universal, 1989
BEVERLY HILLS BRATS   Taurus Entertainment, 1990
PROBLEM CHILD   Imagine/Universal, 1990
BACKSTREET DREAMS   Vidmark Entertainment, 1990

KEN COURT
LADYHAWKE   Warner Bros., 1985, AD
ALIENS   20th Century Fox, 1986, AD w/Bert Davey,
    Fred Hole & Michael Lamont
GORILLAS IN THE MIST   Universal, 1988, AD

ANTHONY COWLEY
REVEALING EVIDENCE (TF)   T.W.S. Productions, 1990
DARK SHADOWS-PARTS I & II (Pilot)   Dan Curtis
    Television Productions, 1991 (Part two only)

STUART CRAIG
SATURN 3   AFD, 1980
THE ELEPHANT MAN ★   Paramount, 1980
GANDHI ★★   Columbia, 1982
GREYSTOKE: THE LEGEND OF TARZAN, LORD OF
    THE APES   Warner Bros., 1984
CAL   Warner Bros., 1984
THE MISSION ★   Warner Bros., 1986
CRY FREEDOM   Universal, 1987
STARS AND BARS   Columbia, 1988, w/Les Dilley
DANGEROUS LIAISONS ★★   Warner Bros., 1988

CHAPLIN   ✳

SHADOWLANDS.
MARY RILEY . TRISTAR

WILLIAM J. CREBER*
IATSE Local 876, SA Local 829
Agent: The Gersh Agency, Inc., Beverly Hills -
  213/274-6611, New York - 212/997-1818

RIO CONCHOS   20th Century Fox, 1964
THE GREATEST STORY EVER TOLD   United
  Artists, 1965
PLANET OF THE APES   20th Century Fox, 1968
THE DETECTIVE   20th Century Fox, 1968
THREE IN THE ATTIC   American International, 1968
JUSTINE   20th Century Fox, 1969
ALONG CAME A SPIDER (TF)   20th Century
  Fox TV, 1970
SUPERDAD   Buena Vista, 1972
THE POSEIDON ADVENTURE ★   20th Century
  Fox, 1972
THE TOWERING INFERNO ★   20th Century
  Fox, 1974
ISLANDS IN THE STREAM   Paramount, 1977
THE DOMINO PRINCIPLE   Avco Embassy, 1977
ANY WHICH WAY YOU CAN   Warner Bros., 1980
HOPSCOTCH   Avco Embassy, 1980
YES, GIORGIO   MGM/UA, 1982
SIX PACK   20th Century Fox, 1982
THE PRODIGAL   World Wide, 1984
CHILDREN IN THE CROSSFIRE (TF)   Schaefer-Karp
  Prodcutions/Prendergast-Brittcadia Productions/
  Gaylord Production Company, 1984
TWICE IN A LIFETIME   The Yorkin Company, 1985
FLIGHT OF THE NAVIGATOR   Buena Vista, 1986
HOT PURSUIT   Paramount, 1987
REMEMBERING CAPRI   *CAPRICCIO*   DEG, 1987

FELIPE CRESCENTI
KISS OF THE SPIDER WOMAN   Island Alive, 1985

VINCENT M. CRESCIMAN*
IATSE Local 876
Agent: Sanford-Skouras & Gross - Los Angeles,
  213/208-2100

FUTZ   Commonwealth United, 1969
COUNT YORGA, VAMPIRE   1970
THE LAST MOVIE   Universal, 1971
THE LAST PICTURE SHOW   Columbia, 1971
SKYJACKED   MGM, 1972
STEELYARD BLUES   Warner Bros., 1973
LEPKE   Warner Bros., 1975
BITTERSWEET LOVE   Avco Embassy, 1976, AD
TRACKDOWN   United Artists, 1976, AD
BROTHERS   Warner Bros., 1977, AD
A SMALL KILLING (TF)   Orgolini-Nelson Productions/
  Motown Productions, 1982
OFF THE MINNESOTA STRIP (TF)   Cherokee
  Productions/Universal TV, 1980
HAPPY ENDINGS (TF)   Blinn-Thorpe Productions/
  Viacom, 1980
A WHALE FOR THE KILLING (TF)   Play Productions/
  Beowulf Productions, 1981
MURDER IN TEXAS (TF)   Dick Clark Productions/Billy
  Hale Films, 1981
THE AMBUSH MURDERS (TF)   David Goldsmith
  Productions/Charles Fries Productions, 1982
DANGEROUS COMPANY (TF)   The Dangerous
  Company/Finnegan Associates, 1982
RED DAWN   MGM/UA, 1984
DEADLY INTENTIONS (TF)   Green-Epstein
  Productions, 1985

FEAR CITY   Chevy Chase Distribution, 1985
YOUNGBLOOD   MGM/UA, 1986, Visual Consultant
LA BAMBA   Columbia, 1987
BAT 21   Tri-Star, 1988
FLASHBACK   Paramount, 1990
EL DIABLO (CTF)   Wizan/Black Films Productions, 1990
NIGHT VISION (TF)   Wes Craven Films, 1990

ROSALIND CREW
BAD DREAMS   20th Century Fox, 1988, AD

ANDREA CRISANTI
CINEMA PARADISO   Miramax Films, 1989

IVO G. CRISTANTE
Agent: Sanford-Skouras & Gross - Los Angeles,
  213/277-6211

THEY CALL ME BRUCE?   Artists Releasing Corporation/
  Film Ventures International, 1982
THE VICTIMS (TF)   Hajeno Productions/Warner
  Bros. TV, 1982
REVENGE OF THE NINJA   MGM/UA/Cannon, 1983
PRIVATE SCHOOL   Universal, 1983
LOUISIANA (CTF)   ICC/Antenne-2/Superchannel/CTV/
  Societe de Development de L'Industrie
  Cinematographique Canadienne, 1983
WEEKEND PASS   Crown International, 1984
SINGLE BARS, SINGLE WOMEN (TF)   Carsey-Werner
  Productions/Sunn Classic Pictures, 1984
AMAZON WOMEN IN THE MOON   Universal, 1987
BAD DREAMS   20th Century Fox, 1988
TREMORS   Universal, 1989
CHILD'S PLAY 2   Universal, 1990

WOODY CROCKER
WHY ME?   Triumph, 1990

AURELIO CRUGNOLA
THE EIGER SANCTION   Universal, 1974, AD, US,
  w/Norm Baron
STARCRASH   New World, 1979
THE BLACK STALLION   United Artists, 1979, AD
THE BLACK STALLION RETURNS   MGM/UA, 1983, AD
RENT-A-COP   Kings Road, 1988, AD

WILLIAM CRUISE*
IATSE Local 876

MURPHY'S LAW   Cannon, 1986
ASSASSINATION   Cannon, 1987
WAR AND REMEMBRANCE (MS) ☆   Dan Curtis
  Productions, 1989, AD, shared credit
HIROSHIMA: OUT OF THE ASHES (TF)   Robert
  Greenwald Productions, 1990
THE HUNT FOR RED OCTOBER   Paramount, 1990, AD

ZSOLT CSENGERY
THE NIGHTMARE YEARS (CTF)   Consolidated
  Artists, 1990

HOWARD CUMMINGS
BLUE HEAVEN   Vestron/Shapiro Entertainment,
  1984, AD
ON VALENTINE'S DAY   Angelika Films, 1986, AD
SIGNS OF LIFE   Avenue Pictures, 1989
MORTAL THOUGHTS   Columbia Pictures, 1991

Cu

CINEMATOGRAPHERS
PRODUCTION
DESIGNERS,
COSTUME
DESIGNERS AND
FILM EDITORS
GUIDE

P
R
O
D
U
C
T
I
O
N

D
E
S
I
G
N
E
R
S

ANTHONY CURTIS
THE ODD JOB   Columbia, 1978
THE WORLD IS FULL OF MARRIED MEN   New Realm, 1979, AD
VENOM   Paramount, 1982, AD
KRULL   Columbia, 1983, AD w/Norman Dorme, Colin Grimes & Tony Reading
HALF MOON STREET   20th Century Fox, 1986
A GHOST IN MONTE CARLO (CTF)   The Grade Company, 1990

BERNIE CUTLER*
IATSE Local 876

SMOKEY AND THE BANDIT, PART II   Universal, 1980, AD
PENNIES FROM HEAVEN   MGM/UA, 1981, AD w/Fred Tuch
D.C. CAB   Universal, 1983, AD
RIPTIDE (TVS)   1984
FAVORITE SON (MS)   Steve Sohmer Inc./NBC Productions, 1989, AD
GHOST DAD   Universal, 1990, AD

D

PHIL DAGORT
Phone: 213/656-5218

CONSPIRACY: THE TRIAL OF THE CHICAGO EIGHT (CTF)   Jeremy Kagan/Inter Planetary Productions, 1987, AD
DUTCH TREAT   Cannon, 1987, AD
CASUAL SEX?   Universal, 1988, AD
FEDS   Warner Bros., 1988, AD
DARKMAN   Universal, 1990, AD

DINS DANIELSON
VALET GIRLS   Empire Pictures, 1987, AD
IN THE MOOD   Lorimar, 1987, AD
MEN AT WORK   Triumph Releasing, 1990
GERARD DAOUDAL
IMPROMPTU   Hemdale, 1991, AD

BERT DAVEY
THE GREAT TRAIN ROBBERY   United Artists, 1979, AD
ffolkes   Universal, 1980, AD
EYE OF THE NEEDLE   United Artists, 1981, AD w/John Hoesli
THE DOGS OF WAR   United Artists, 1981, AD
SUPERMAN III   Warner Bros., 1983 , AD
MORONS FROM OUTER SPACE   Universal, 1985, AD
ALIENS   20th Century Fox, 1986, AD w/Ken Court, Fred Hole & Michael Lamont

GAVIN DAVIES
FELLOW TRAVELLER (CTF)   British Film Institute/BBC TV/HBO Showcase, 1990

DAN DAVIS
MOONSTRUCK   MGM/UA, 1987, AD w/Barbara Matis
COCKTAIL   Buena Vista, 1988, AD
MASQUERADE   MGM/UA, 1988, AD
THE FRESHMAN   Tri-Star, 1990, AD w/Alice Keywan

JAMES DAVIS
THE PRINCIPAL   Tri-Star, 1987

KEN DAVIS*
IATSE Local 876

THE CONCRETE COWBOYS (TF)   Frankel Films, 1979
MURDER BY DECREE   Avco Embassy, 1979
CIRCLE OF POWER   *MYSTIQUE*   Televicine, 1983
9 1/2 WEEKS   Paramount, 1986
THE MEN'S CLUB   Atlantic Releasing Corporation, 1986
BEVERLY HILLS COP II   Paramount, 1987

RICHARD DAWKING
MONTY PYTHON'S THE MEANING OF LIFE   Universal, 1983, AD
ELECTRIC DREAMS   MGM/UA, 1984, AD
THE JEWEL OF THE NILE   20th Century Fox, 1985, w/Terry Knight
WHITE NIGHTS   Columbia, 1985, AD

DON DAY
MARTIANS GO HOME   Taurus Entertainment, 1990, w/Catherine Hardwicke
THE FORBIDDEN DANCE   Columbia, 1990

JOHN DE CUIR*
IATSE Local 876
Agent: Smith Gosnell Nicholson & Associates - Los Angeles, 213/459-0307

THE HOUSE ON TELEGRAPH HILL ★★   20th Century Fox, 1951
DIPLOMATIC COURIER   20th Century Fox, 1952
THE SNOWS OF KILIMANJARO ★   20th Century Fox, 1952
MY COUSIN RACHEL ★   20th Century Fox, 1953
CALL ME MADAM   20th Century Fox, 1953
THREE COINS IN THE FOUNTAIN   20th Century Fox, 1954
THERE'S NO BUSINESS LIKE SHOW BUSINESS   20th Century Fox, 1954
DADDY LONG LEGS   20th Century Fox, 1955
THE KING AND I ★   20th Century Fox, 1956
ISLAND IN THE SUN   20th Century Fox, 1957
A CERTAIN SMILE   20th Century Fox, 1958
THE BIG FISHERMAN ★   Buena Vista, 1959
SEVEN THIEVES   20th Century Fox, 1960
CLEOPATRA ★★   20th Century Fox, 1963
THE AGONY AND THE ECSTASY ★   20th Century Fox, 1965
THE HONEY POT   United Artists, 1967
THE TAMING OF THE SHREW ★   Columbia, 1967
DR. FAUSTUS   1968
CHARLY   Cinerama Releasing Corporation, 1968
HELLO, DOLLY! ★★   20th Century Fox, 1969
THE GREAT WHITE HOPE   20th Century Fox, 1970
ON A CLEAR DAY YOU CAN SEE FOREVER   Paramount, 1970
JACQUELINE SUSANN'S ONCE IS NOT ENOUGH   Paramount, 1975
THAT'S ENTERTAINMENT, PART 2   MGM/United Artists, 1976

THE OTHER SIDE OF MIDNIGHT   20th Century
   Fox, 1977
ZIEGFELD: THE MAN AND HIS WOMEN (TF) ☆☆
   Frankovich Productions/Columbia TV, 1978
LOVE AND BULLETS   ITC, 1979
DEAD MEN DON'T WEAR PLAID   Universal, 1979
RAISE THE TITANIC   AFD, 1980
MONSIGNOR   20th Century Fox, 1982
GHOSTBUSTERS   Columbia, 1984
JO JO DANCER, YOUR LIFE IS CALLING
   Columbia, 1986
LEGAL EAGLES   Universal, 1986

JOHN DE CUIR JR.*
IATSE Local 876

RAISE THE TITANIC   AFD, 1980, AD
GHOSTBUSTERS   Columbia, 1984, AD
FRIGHT NIGHT   Columbia, 1985
TOP GUN   Paramount, 1986
ELVIRA: MISTRESS OF THE DARK   New
   World, 1988
TURNER & HOOCH   Buena Vista, 1989
APT PUPIL   New Century/Vista, 1990

DON DE FINA*
IATSE Local 876
Agent: The Irv Schechter Company - Beverly Hills,
   213/278-8070

STREET MUSIC   Specialty, 1982, AD
HOT DOG...THE MOVIE   MGM/UA, 1984, AD
ON THE EDGE   Skouras Pictures, 1986
GHOST TOWN   Trans World Entertainment, 1989

JACKSON DE GOVIA*
IATSE Local 876

THE PEOPLE (TF)   Metromedia Productions/
   American Zoetrope, 1972
PRISONERS   1973
THIEVES LIKE US   United Artists, 1974
THE FOUR DEUCES   Avco Embassy, 1974
LEPKE   Warner Bros., 1975
BUTCH AND SUNDANCE: THE EARLY DAYS
   20th Century Fox, 1979
BOULEVARD NIGHTS   Warner Bros., 1979
NO OTHER LOVE (TF)   Tisch-Avnet
   Productions, 1979
IT'S MY TURN   Columbia, 1980
MY BODYGUARD   20th Century Fox, 1980
THE WINDS OF WAR (MS)   Paramount TV/Dan
   Curtis Productions, 1983
SPACEHUNTER: ADVENTURES IN THE
   FORBIDDEN ZONE   Columbia, 1983
RED DAWN   MGM/UA, 1984
REMO WILLIAMS: THE ADVENTURE BEGINS
   Orion, 1985
'NIGHT, MOTHER   Universal, 1986
NOBODY'S FOOL   Island Pictures, 1986
ROXANNE   Columbia, 1987
PUNCHLINE   Columbia, 1988
DIE HARD   20th Century Fox, 1988
IN COUNTRY   Warner Bros., 1989
DAD   Universal, 1989

FRANCOIS DE LAMOTHE
A LITTLE ROMANCE   Orion/Warner Bros., 1979, AD
JUST THE WAY YOU ARE   MGM/UA, 1984, AD

LINDA DEL ROSARIO
SPEAKING PARTS   Cinephile, 1990

WENDELL DENNIS
THE GUNRUNNER   New World, 1989

BRIAN DENSMORE
ANGEL TOWN   Taurus Entertainment, 1990

COLIN DE ROVIN
MOB BOSS   Vidmark Entertainment, 1990, AD

WILLIAM F. DE SETA
SOMETHING SHORT OF PARADISE   American
   International, 1979, AD
THE PROTECTOR   Warner Bros., 1985

JACK DE SHIELDS*
IATSE Local 876

MARATHON MAN   Paramount, 1976
PANDEMONIUM   MGM/United Artists, 1982
ERNIE KOVACS: BETWEEN THE LAUGHTER (TF)
   ABC Circle Films, 1984
SPACE (MS)   Stonehenge Productions/
   Paramount TV, 1985
MICKEY SPILLANE'S MIKE HAMMER: MURDER TAKES
   ALL (TF)   Jay Bernstein Productions, 1989, AD

FERNANDO VASQUES DE VELASCO
FULL FATHOM FIVE   Concorde, 1990

SPENCER DEVERILL
THE FISH THAT SAVED PITTSBURGH   United Artists,
   1979 , AD
HEAVEN'S GATE   United Artists, 1980, AD
THE JAZZ SINGER   AFD, 1980, AD
TWO OF A KIND   20th Century Fox, 1983, AD

DOUGLAS DICK
MY DEMON LOVER   New Line Cinema, 1987, AD
HERO AND THE TERROR   Cannon, 1988,
   AD w/Mark Haskins
84 CHARLIE MOPIC   New Century/Vista, 1989, AD

WENDY DICKSON
BREAK OF DAY   Greater Union Film Distributors, 1977
A CRY IN THE DARK   Warner Bros., 1988,
   w/George Liddle

DON DIERS
SOUL MAN   New World, 1986, AD w/John Reinhart
TAPEHEADS   Avenue Pictures, 1988, AD
RACHEL RIVER   American Playhouse, 1989, AD

LESLIE (LES) DILLEY
Agent: The Gersh Agency, Inc., Beverly Hills -
   213/274-6611, New York - 212/997-1818

THE LAST REMAKE OF BEAU GESTE   Universal,
   1977, AD
STAR WARS ★★   20th Century Fox, 1977, AD w/John
   Barry & Norman Reynolds
SUPERMAN   Warner Bros., 1978, AD
ALIEN ★   20th Century Fox, 1979,
   AD w/Roger Christian

Di

CINEMATOGRAPHERS
PRODUCTION
DESIGNERS,
COSTUME
DESIGNERS AND
FILM EDITORS
GUIDE

P
R
O
D
U
C
T
I
O
N

D
E
S
I
G
N
E
R
S

Di

CINEMATOGRAPHERS
PRODUCTION
DESIGNERS,
COSTUME
DESIGNERS AND
FILM EDITORS
GUIDE

P
R
O
D
U
C
T
I
O
N

D
E
S
I
G
N
E
R
S

THE EMPIRE STRIKES BACK ★   20th Century Fox,
   1980, AD w/Harry Lange & Alan Tomkins
AN AMERICAN WEREWOLF IN LONDON
   Universal, 1981, AD
RAIDERS OF THE LOST ARK ★★   Paramount,
   1981, AD
NEVER SAY NEVER AGAIN   Warner Bros., 1983,
   AD w/Roy Stannard & Michael White
EUREKA   MGM/UA Classics, 1984, AD
BAD MEDICINE   20th Century Fox, 1985
INVADERS FROM MARS   Cannon, 1986
LEGEND   Universal, 1986, AD
ALLAN QUATERMAIN AND THE LOST CITY OF GOLD
   Cannon, 1987
STARS AND BARS   Columbia, 1988, w/Stuart Craig
THE ABYSS ★   20th Century Fox, 1989
THE EXORCIST III   20th Century Fox, 1990
GUILTY BY SUSPICION   Warner Bros., 1991
WHAT ABOUT BOB?   Buena Vista, 1991

CARMEN DILLON
THE OMEN   20th Century Fox, 1976
JULIA   20th Century Fox , 1977, w/Gene Callahan &
   Willy Holt

BERNADETTE DI SANTO
SETTLE THE SCORE (TF)   Steve Sohmer
   Productions, 1990, w/Berndt Amadeus Capra
STEPFATHER II   Millimeter Films, 1990

EILEEN DISS
SWEET WILLIAM   Kendon Films, 1980
BETRAYAL   20th Century Fox, 1983
SECRET PLACES   TLC Films/20th
   Century Fox, 1984
HITLER'S S.S.: PORTRAIT IN EVIL (TF)   Colason Ltd.
   Productions/Edgar J. Scherick Associates, 1985
84 CHARING CROSS ROAD   Columbia, 1987,
   w/Edward Pisoni
A HANDFUL OF DUST   New Line Cinema, 1988
JEEVES AND WOOSTER (MS)   Granada/Picture
   Partnership, 1990

MAREK DOBROWOLSKI
Local 829
Agent: The Gersh Agency, Inc., Beverly Hills -
   213/274-6611, New York - 212/997-1818

FEAR, ANXIETY AND DEPRESSION   Propaganda
   Films/Samuel Goldwyn Company, 1988
RUMPELSTILTSKIN   Cannon, 1987
BEAUTY AND THE BEAST   Cannon, 1987
JUST LIKE IN THE MOVIES   Just Like in the Movies
   Productions, 1988
PUSS IN BOOTS   Cannon, 1989
DISTURBED   Live Entertainment/Odyssey
   Distribution, 1990
MIND GAME   Miramax, 1990
BLOOD IN...BLOOD OUT   New Visions, 1991, AD

MARY DODSON*
IATSE Local 876

THIEF   United Artists, 1981, AD

DANILO DONATI
HURRICANE   Paramount, 1979
FLASH GORDON   Universal, 1980

RED SONJA   MGM/UA, 1985
FRANCESCO   Karol Film/RAI/Royal Film, 1989, AD

NORMAN DORME
SATURN 3   AFD, 1980, AD
THE FRENCH LIEUTENANT'S WOMAN   United Artists,
   1981, AD w/Allan Cameron & Terry Pritchard
GANDHI   Columbia, 1982, AD, w/Ram Yedeker
KRULL   Columbia, 1983, AD w/Tony Curtis, Colin
   Grimes & Tony Reading
GREYSTOKE: THE LEGEND OF TARZAN, LORD
   OF THE APES   Warner Bros., 1984,
   AD w/Simon Holland
LEGEND   Universal, 1986, AD
CRY FREEDOM   Universal, 1987, AD w/John King &
   George Richardson
EMPIRE OF THE SUN   Warner Bros., 1987,
   Supervising AD, Spain

SERGE DOUY
THE FATAL IMAGE (TF)   Ellipse Programming,
   1990, AD

JON DOWDING
RAW DEAL   Greater Union Film Distributors, 1977, AD
MAD MAX   American International, 1979, AD
THE DAY AFTER HALLOWEEN   *SNAP-SHOT*   Group 1,
   1979, AD w/Jill Eden
THIRST   Greater Union Film Distributors, 1979,
   AD w/Jill Eden
BLUE LAGOON   Columbia, 1980, AD
ROAD GAMES   Avco Embassy, 1981

STUART DRAIG
MEMPHIS BELLE   Enigma/Warner Bros., 1990

GEOFFREY DRAKE
YOUNG WINSTON ★   Columbia, 1972, w/John
   Graysmark & William Hutchinson
SINBAD AND THE EYE OF THE TIGER   Columbia, 1977
FORCE 10 FROM NAVARONE   American
   International, 1978
ALL THINGS BRIGHT AND BEAUTIFUL   World
   Northal, 1978

TOM DUFFIELD*
IATSE Local 876

THE LOST BOYS   Warner Bros., 1987, AD
BEETLEJUICE   Warner Bros., 1988, AD
THE ACCIDENTAL TOURIST   Warner Bros., 1988, AD
GHOSTBUSTERS II   Columbia, 1989, AD
JOE VERSUS THE VOLCANO   Warner Bros., 1990, AD

PHILIP J.C. DUFFIN
KGB - THE SECRET WAR   *LETHAL*   Cinema Group,
   1986, AD
CLUB LIFE   Troma, 1986, AD w/Cynthia Sowder
EVIL DEAD 2   Rosebud Releasing Corporation, 1987,
   AD w/Randy Bennett
SOUTH OF RENO   Open Road Productions/Pendulum
   Productions, 1987
PHANTASM II   Universal, 1988
PRISON   Empire Pictures, 1988
VIETNAM, TEXAS   Epic Productions, 1990, AD
BRIDE OF RE-ANIMATOR   Wildstreet Pictures/50th St.
   Films, 1991

JIM DULTZ*
IATSE Local 876

YOUNGBLOOD American International, 1978, AD
TAKE THIS JOB AND SHOVE IT Avco Embassy, 1981, AD
THE LAST AMERICAN VIRGIN Cannon, 1982, AD
BAD MANNERS New World, 1984
GOING UNDERCOVER Miramax Films, 1985
OVERBOARD MGM/UA, 1987, AD w/James Shanahan
PROMISED LAND Vestron, 1988, AD

CHARLES DUNLOP
MEATBALLS III TMS Pictures, 1986
SWITCHING CHANNELS Tri-Star, 1988, AD
WHISPERS Live Home Video, 1990
MILLENNIUM 20th Century Fox, 1989, AD

BARBARA DUNPHY
Agent: The Gersh Agency, Inc., Beverly Hills - 213/274-6611, New York - 212/997-1818

RUNNING BRAVE Buena Vista, 1983, AD
THE DEAD ZONE Paramount, 1983, AD
HEARTS OF FIRE Lorimar, 1987, AD w/Kit Surrey
ADVENTURES IN BABYSITTING Buena Vista, 1987, AD
A NEW LIFE Paramount, 1988
MANHUNT: THE SEARCH FOR THE NIGHT STALKER (TF) Leonard Hill Films, 1990
THE STORY OF THE BEACH BOYS: SUMMER DREAMS (TF) Leonard Hill Films, 1990
GOOD COPS, BAD COPS (TF) Kushner-Locke Company, 1990

WILLIAM J. DURRELL, JR.*
IATSE Local 876
Agent: The Jay Gilbert Talent Agency, Los Angeles, 213/656-8090
Home: 28832 N. Oakspring Canyon Rd. - Canyon Country, 805/251-3011

COLLISION COURSE DEG, 1988
STARMAN Columbia, 1984
THEY LIVE Universal, 1988, w/Dan Lomino
ROAD HOUSE MGM/UA, 1988
SHOW OF FORCE Paramount, 1989
LOOSE CANNONS Tri-Star, 1990, AD

E

PAUL EADS
SO FINE Warner Bros., 1981, AD
THE FAN Paramount, 1981, AD
TEMPEST Columbia, 1982, AD
JAWS 3-D Universal, 1983, AD w/Chris Horner
THE MUPPETS TAKE MANHATTAN Tri-Star, 1984, AD w/W. Stephen Graham
TURK 182 20th Century Fox, 1985, AD
WANTED DEAD OR ALIVE New World, 1986
WISE GUYS MGM/UA, 1986, AD
BRIGHTON BEACH MEMOIRS Universal, 1986, AD
POLTERGEIST III MGM/UA, 1988

LAWRENCE EASTWOOD
PHAR LAP 20th Century Fox, 1984
DEAD END DRIVE-IN New World, 1986
"CROCODILE" DUNDEE II Paramount, 1988
WEEKEND WITH KATE Phillip Emanuel, 1990
THE DELINQUENTS Greater Union Distributors, 1990

BRIAN EATWELL*
IATSE Local 876
Agent: The Gersh Agency, Inc., Beverly Hills - 213/274-6611, New York - 212/997-1818

WALKABOUT 20th Century Fox, 1971
GODSPELL Columbia, 1973
THE THREE MUSKETEERS 20th Century Fox, 1974
THE FOUR MUSKETEERS 20th Century Fox, 1975
THE LAST REMAKE OF BEAU GESTE Universal, 1977
SGT. PEPPER'S LONELY HEARTS CLUB BAND Universal, 1978
THE ONION FIELD Avco Embassy, 1979
BUTCH AND SUNDANCE: THE EARLY DAYS 20th Century Fox, 1979
SAVAGE HARVEST 20th Century Fox, 1981
WHITE DOG Paramount, 1982
EXPOSED MGM/United Artists, 1983
AMERICAN DREAMER Warner Bros., 1984
MORONS FROM OUTER SPACE Universal, 1985
WIRED Taurus Entertainment, 1989
CAPITAL NEWS (Pilot) 1989

BEN EDWARDS
Phone: 212/922-2931

LOVERS AND OTHER STRANGERS Cinerama Releasing Corporation, 1970
LAST OF THE RED HOT LOVERS Paramount, 1972
THE CLASS OF '44 Warner Bros., 1973
BLIND AMBITION (TF) Time-Life Productions, 1979
FORT APACHE, THE BRONX 20th Century Fox, 1981
PHOBIA Paramount, 1981
HANKY PANKY Columbia, 1982
KENNEDY (MS) Central Independent TV Productions/ Alan Landsburg Productions, 1983
FAST FORWARD Columbia, 1985
SWEET LIBERTY Universal, 1986
APOLOGY (CTF) Roger Gimbel Productions/Peregrine Entertainment/ASAP Productions/HBO, 1986

Ed

CINEMATOGRAPHERS
PRODUCTION
DESIGNERS,
COSTUME
DESIGNERS AND
FILM EDITORS
GUIDE

P R O D U C T I O N   D E S I G N E R S

Ed

CINEMATOGRAPHERS
PRODUCTION
DESIGNERS,
COSTUME
DESIGNERS AND
FILM EDITORS
GUIDE

**P
R
O
D
U
C
T
I
O
N**

**D
E
S
I
G
N
E
R
S**

A SPECIAL FRIENDSHIP (TF)   Entertainment
   Partners, 1987
EVERYBODY'S BABY: THE RESCUE OF
   JESSICA McCLURE (TF)   Dick Berg/Stonehenge
   Productions, 1989

CHRIS EDWARDS
WE THINK THE WORLD OF YOU   Cinecom,
   1988, AD

GEORGE EDWARDS
INSTANT KARMA   Rosenbloom Entertainment,
   1990, w/Michele Seffman

VAUGHAN EDWARDS
SEVEN MINUTES IN HEAVEN   Warner Bros., 1986
END OF THE LINE   Orion Classics, 1988, AD
STEALING HOME   Warner Bros., 1988, AD

WILLIAM A. ELLIOTT
BODY DOUBLE   Columbia, 1984, AD
SILVERADO   Columbia, 1985, AD
ABOUT LAST NIGHT   Tri-Star, 1986, AD
CROSS MY HEART   Universal, 1987, AD
THE UNTOUCHABLES   Paramount, 1987, AD
THROW MOMMA FROM THE TRAIN   Orion,
   1987, AD
RAIN MAN   MGM/UA, 1988, AD
FLYING BLIND   Columbia, 1988
IMPULSE   Warner Bros., 1990

DAVID ENSLEY
THE CHOCOLATE WAR   MCEG, 1988
LONG ROAD HOME (TF)   Rosemont
   Productions, 1991

JOHN EMERY
CREAM IN MY COFFEE (TF)   London
   Weekend TV, 1990

LEON ERICKSON
McCABE & MRS. MILLER   Warner Bros., 1971
UP IN SMOKE   Paramount, 1978
QUINTET   20th Century Fox, 1979
LADIES AND GENTLEMAN...THE FABULOUS
   STAINS   Paramount, 1982
HAMMETT   Orion/Warner Bros., 1982, AD
ICEMAN   20th Century Fox, 1984,
   AD w/Josan Russo

ENRIQUE ESTEVEZ
SANDINO   RTVE-Miguel Littin Productions, 1990

F

ABEL FACELLO
THE STRANGER   Columbia, 1987

MELBA FARQUHAR
HOLLYWOOD SHUFFLE   Samuel Goldwyn Company,
   1987, AD
I'M GONNA GIT YOU SUCKA   MGM/UA, 1987,
   w/Catherine Hardwicke

JIM FENG
MONKEY SHINES   Orion, 1988,
   AD w/J. Mark Herrington

ALLAN FELLOWS
FRIENDS, LOVERS & LUNATICS   Fries
   Entertainment, 1990

JOHN FENNER
FOR YOUR EYES ONLY   United Artists, 1981, AD
OCTOPUSSY   MGM/UA, 1983, AD
TOP SECRET!   Paramount, 1984, AD w/Michael Lamont
A VIEW TO A KILL   MGM/UA, 1985, AD
LITTLE SHOP OF HORRORS   The Geffen Company/
   Warner Bros., 1986, AD w/Stephen Spence
SUPERMAN IV: THE QUEST FOR PEACE   Warner
   Bros., 1987, AD w/Leslie Tomkins
A DRY WHITE SEASON   MGM/UA, 1989

BENJAMIN FERNANDEZ
CONAN THE BARBARIAN   Universal, 1982, AD
DUNE   Universal, 1984, AD w/Pierluigi Basile
TAI-PAN   DEG, 1986, AD w/Pierluigi Basile
REVENGE   Columbia, 1990, w/Michael Seymour
DAYS OF THUNDER   Paramount, 1990,
   AD w/Thomas E. Sanders

DANTE FERRETTI
Agent: Sandra Marsh Management - Sherman Oaks,
   818/905-6961

MEDEA   New Line Cinema, 1970
THE DECAMERON   United Artists, 1971
THE WORKING CLASS GOES TO HEAVEN   1971
THE CANTERBURY TALES   United Artists, 1972
SBATTI IL MOSTRO IN PRIMA PAGINA   1972
STORIE SCELLERATE   1973
THE NIGHTPORTER   1974
THE ARABIAN NIGHTS   United Artists, 1974
CRIME OF LOVE   *DELITTO D'AMORE*   Documento
   Film, 1974
MIO DIO COME SONO CADUTA IN BASSO
   Dean Film, 1974
SALO, 120 DAYS OF SODOM   Zebra, 1975
TODO MODO   1976
BYE BYE MONKEY   Fida, 1978
ORCHESTRA REHEARSAL   New Yorker, 1979
CITY OF WOMEN   New Yorker, 1981, AD
LA PELLE   Triumph/Columbia, 1981
TALES OF ORDINARY MADNESS   Fred Baker
   Films, 1983

LA NUIT DE VARENNES   Triumph/Columbia, 1983
AND THE SHIP SAILS ON   Triumph/Columbia, 1984
DESIRE   Hemisphere, 1983
GINGER & FRED   MGM/UA, 1986
THE NAME OF THE ROSE   20th Century Fox, 1986
IL SECRETO DEL SAHARA (MS)   RAI/TFI/TVE/
   BetaFilm/Racing Pictures, 1987
THE ADVENTURES OF BARON MUNCHAUSEN ★
   Columbia, 1989
THE VOICE OF THE MOON   1989
THE SLEAZY UNCLE   Penta Distribuzione, 1990
HAMLET ★   Warner Bros., 1990

VIRGINIA FIELD
FRIDAY THE 13TH   Paramount, 1980, AD
FRIDAY THE 13TH PART 2   Paramount, 1981
A STRANGER IS WATCHING   MGM/United Artists,
   1982, AD
SPRING BREAK   Columbia, 1983
EXTERMINATOR 2   Cannon, 1984, AD
GOODBYE NEW YORK   Castle Hill Productions, 1985
MOVING VIOLATIONS   20th Century Fox, 1985,
   w/Gregory Pickrell

STEPHEN FINEREN
AFTER THE WAR-PARTS I-III (MS)   Granada TV,
   1990, w/Chris Wilkinson
CROSSING TO FREEDOM (TF)   Procter & Gamble
   Productions, 1990

DAVID FISCHER
DEADLY INTENTIONS...AGAIN? (TF)   Green/Epstein
   Productions, 1991

LEE FISCHER*
IATSE Local 876

THE HOLLYWOOD KNIGHTS   Columbia, 1980, AD
LOVE AND MONEY   Paramount, 1982, AD
VICE SQUAD   Avco Embassy, 1982

JACK FISK
Agent: Creative Artists Agency - Beverly Hills,
   213/288-4545

VIGILANTE FORCE   United Artists, 1976, AD
MOVIE MOVIE   Warner Bros., 1978, AD
DAYS OF HEAVEN   Paramount, 1978, AD
HEART BEAT   Orion/Warner Bros., 1979

MARCOS FLAKSMAN
Agent: The Gersh Agency, Inc., Beverly Hills -
   213/274-6611, New York - 212/997-1818

BLAME IT ON RIO   20th Century Fox, 1984, AD
THE EMERALD FOREST   Embassy, 1985, AD
STREETS OF GOLD   20th Century Fox, 1986
WHERE THE RIVER RUNS BLACK   MGM/UA, 1986
MOON OVER PARADOR   Universal, 1988, AD

SEAMUS FLANNERY
Agent: The Miller Agency - Santa Clarita, 818/843-7335

JACOB TWO-TWO MEETS THE HOODED FANG
   Cinema Shares International, 1978
ANGELA   1978
THE SHAPE OF THINGS TO COME   Film Ventures
   International, 1979
HIGHPOINT   1980
THE COURAGE OF KAVIK THE WOLF DOG (TF)   1980

KLONDIKE FEVER (TF)   1980
MURDER BY PHONE   *BELLS*   New World, 1983
HEAVENLY BODIES   MGM/UA, 1985
NIGHT HEAT (TVS)   1985
BEAUTIFUL DREAMERS   Cinexus/Famous Players/CF/P
   Distribution, 1990

GREGG FONSECA
Agent: Grace Lyons Management - Los Angeles,
   213/655-5100

EYES OF FIRE   Aquarius/Clark Films, 1984
HARDBODIES   Columbia, 1984
MISSING IN ACTION 2: THE BEGINNING
   Cannon, 1984
A NIGHTMARE ON ELM STREET   New Line
   Cinema, 1984
CRITTERS   New Line Cinema, 1985
HOUSE   New World, 1986
SOUL MAN   New World, 1986
SAMARITAN (TF)   Levine-Robins Productions/Fries
   Entertainment, 1986
DREAM WEST (MS)   Sunn Classic Pictures, 1986
THE STEPFORD CHILDREN (TF)   Edgar J. Scherick
   Productions/Taft Entertainment TV, 1987
HOUSE II: THE SECOND STORY   New World, 1987
JOHNNY BE GOOD   Orion, 1988
HONEY, I SHRUNK THE KIDS   Buena Vista, 1989
THE GUARDIAN   Universal, 1989
FAT MAN AND LITTLE BOY   Paramount, 1989

JOSEPHINE FORD
NATE AND HAYES   *SAVAGE ISLANDS*   Paramount,
   1983, AD w/Dan Hennah & Rick Koford
WE OF THE NEVER NEVER   Triumph, 1983
HOT TARGET   Crown International, 1985
THE QUIET EARTH   Skouras Pictures, 1985
RIKKY AND PETE   MGM/UA, 1988

PHILIP DEAN FOREMAN
Agent: Grace Lyons Management - Los Angeles,
   213/655-5100

CITY LIMITS   Atlantic Releasing Corporation, 1985
ZONE TROOPER   Empire Pictures, 1985
CRITTERS   New Line Cinema, 1985, AD
ELIMINATORS   Empire Pictures, 1986
KILLER CLOWNS FROM OUTER SPACE   Trans World
   Entertainment, 1987, AD
SLAM DANCE   Island Pictures, 1987, AD
THE JUDAS PROJECT   1988
CRITTERS 2: THE MAIN COURSE   New Line
   Cinema, 1988
THE DAVE THOMAS SHOW (Pilot)   1989
HIGHWAY TO HELL   Hemdale, 1990
BORIS & NATASHA   MCEG, 1991

RONALD KENT FOREMAN*
IATSE Local 876

ROCKY III   MGM/UA, 1982, AD
THE ICE PIRATES   MGM/UA, 1984
MARIE   MGM/UA, 1985, AD
IN THE SHADOW OF KILIMANJARO   Scotti Bros.,
   1986, AD
THE BEDROOM WINDOW   DEG, 1987
COLORS   Orion, 1988
WINTER PEOPLE   Columbia, 1989
BAD INFLUENCE   Epic/Triumph, 1990
SHE SAID NO (TF)   Steve White Productions, 1990

CINEMATOGRAPHERS
PRODUCTION
DESIGNERS,
COSTUME
DESIGNERS AND
FILM EDITORS
GUIDE

P
R
O
D
U
C
T
I
O
N

D
E
S
I
G
N
E
R
S

Fo

CINEMATOGRAPHERS
PRODUCTION
DESIGNERS,
COSTUME
DESIGNERS AND
FILM EDITORS
GUIDE

P
R
O
D
U
C
T
I
O
N

D
E
S
I
G
N
E
R
S

WILLIAM FOSSER
ON THE RIGHT TRACK   20th Century Fox, 1981, AD
THE NAKED FACE   MGM/UA, 1984

MAURICE FOWLER
Agent: London Management - London,
    011/441/493-1610

THE VICTORS   Columbia, 1963, AD
THE LAST SAFARI   Paramount, 1967, AD
GOODBYE, MR. CHIPS   MGM, 1969, AD
WELCOME TO THE CLUB   1971, AD
MOHAMMED, MESSENGER OF GOD
    THE MESSAGE   Tarik, 1977
CROSSED SWORDS   *THE PRINCE AND
    THE PAUPER*   Warner Bros., 1978, AD
HEAVEN'S GATE   United Artists, 1980, AD
SUPERMAN II   Warner Bros., 1980, Supv AD
EDUCATING RITA   Columbia, 1983, AD
HEAT AND DUST   Universal Classics, 1983,
    AD w/Ram Yedeker
SWORD OF THE VALIANT   Cannon, 1984,
    w/Derek Nice
STEAMING   New World, 1984
EMPIRE OF THE SUN   Warner Bros., 1987,
    Supv AD, China

J. RAE FOX
Phone: 213/623-6609

SEED OF INNOCENCE   Cannon, 1981, AD
FOLLOW THAT CAR   New World, 1981, AD
X-RAY   Cannon, 1981, AD
REPO MAN   Universal, 1984, AD w/Lynda Burbank
QUIET COOL   New Line Cinema, 1986,
    AD w/Lynda Burbank
BLOODY BIRTHDAY   Judica Productions, 1986,
    w/Lynda Burbank
SID & NANCY   Samuel Goldwyn Company, 1986,
    AD w/Lynda Burbank
BORN IN EAST L.A.   Universal, 1987,
    AD w/Lynda Burbank
WALKER   Universal, 1987, Tucson
JUDGMENT (CTF)   Tisch/Wigutow/Hershman
    Productions, 1990

K. C. FOX
CHILD IN THE NIGHT (TF)   Mike Robe
    Productions, 1990

GUY-CLAUDE FRANCOIS
HENRY & JUNE   Universal, 1990

JEREMIE FRANK
THE RETURN OF SUPERFLY   Triton Pictures, 1990

DIANNA FREAS
Address: 72-74 E. 3rd Street, #3-B - New York, NY
    10003, 212/598-9156

ZELLY AND ME   Columbia, 1988, AD
LEMON SKY (TF)   American Playhouse, 1988, AD
CONVICTS   MCEG, 1989, AD
CRIMINAL JUSTICE (CTF)   Elysian Films, 1990,
    w/Dan Bishop
CITY OF HOPE   Esperanza, 1991, w/Dan Bishop

MARK S. FREEBORN
DISTANT THUNDER   Paramount, 1988, AD
COUSINS   Paramount, 1989
IMMEDIATE FAMILY   Columbia, 1989
THE LADY FORGETS (TF)   Leonard Hill Films, 1990

JIM FRENCH
DAN TURNER (TF)   Fries Entertainment, 1990, AD

REUBEN FREED
Agent: The Gersh Agency, Inc., Beverly Hills -
    213/274-6611, New York - 212/997-1818

THE CHANGELING   AFD, 1980, AD
PROM NIGHT   Avco Embassy, 1980, AD
TRIBUTE   20th Century Fox, 1980, AD
THE HIGH COUNTRY   Crown International, 1981, AD
BY DESIGN   Atlantic Releasing Corporation, 1982, AD
A CHRISTMAS STORY   MGM/UA, 1983
PORKY'S   20th Century Fox, 1982
KILLER PARTY   MGM/UA, 1986
BLUE MONKEY   Spectrafilm, 1987, AD
NIGHTSTICK   Production Distribution Company,
    1987, AD
CRACK IN THE MIRROR   Paul International, 1988
PROM NIGHT III: THE LAST KISS   Norstar
    Entertainment, 1990
LOOK WHO'S TALKING TOO   Tri-Star, 1990

JOHN FRICK
IN BROAD DAYLIGHT (TF)   Force Ten
    Productions, 1991

EZIO FRIGERIO
CYRANO DE BERGERAC ★   Orion Classics, 1990

FRANCESCO FRIGGERI
VOYAGE OF TERROR: THE ACHILLE LAURO
    AFFAIR-PARTS I & II (TF)   RAIDUE, 1990

ANTON FURST
Agent: Creative Artists Agency - Beverly Hills,
    213/288-4545

MOONRAKER   United Artists, 1979
ALIEN   20th Century Fox, 1979
LADY CHATTERLEY'S LOVER   Cannon, 1982
AN UNSUITABLE JOB FOR A WOMAN   Boyd's
    Company, 1982
DOWN IN THE VALLEY (TF)   The Moving Picture
    Company, 1983
THE COMPANY OF WOLVES   Cannon, 1984
FRENCH LESSON   *THE FROG PRINCE*   Warner
    Bros., 1984
FULL METAL JACKET   Warner Bros., 1987
HIGH SPIRITS   Tri-Star, 1988
BATMAN ★★   Warner Bros., 1989
AWAKENINGS   Columbia, 1990

Gi

CINEMATOGRAPHERS
PRODUCTION
DESIGNERS,
COSTUME
DESIGNERS AND
FILM EDITORS
GUIDE

G

CARMI GALLO

AGE-OLD FRIENDS (CTF)   Granger Productions, 1990, AD
I'LL TAKE ROMANCE (TF)   New World TV, 1990

GLENDA GANIS

Agent: The Gersh Agency, Inc., Beverly Hills -
   213/274-6611, New York - 212/997-1818

THE LORDS OF FLATBUSH   Columbia, 1974, AD
PIPE DREAMS   Avco Embassy, 1976
BOARDWALK   Atlantic Releasing Corporation, 1979
LONG GONE (CTF)   HBO/The Landsburg
   Company, 1987
A PLACE AT THE TABLE (TF)   1989
HEART OF DIXIE   Orion, 1989
LOVE AND LIES (TF)   Freyda Rothstein
   Productions, 1990
A MOM FOR CHRISTMAS (CTF)   Walt Disney
   Company, 1990
HER WICKED WAYS (TF)   Lois Luger
   Productions, 1991
HELD HOSTAGE: THE SIS AND JERRY LEVIN
   STORY (TF)   Paragon Entertainment, 1991
   (U.S. sequences)

ARMIN GANZ

Agent: Spyros Skouras, Sanford-Skouras & Gross -
   Los Angeles, 213/208-2100

BIRDY   Tri-Star, 1984, AD w/W. Stewart Campbell
A VIEW TO A KILL   MGM/UA, 1985, AD
ANGEL HEART   Tri-Star, 1987, AD w/Kristi Zea
TOUGH GUYS DON'T DANCE   Cannon, 1987
BULL DURHAM   Orion, 1988
THE APPOINTMENTS OF DENNIS JENNINGS
   HBO Pictures, 1989
LOVE HURTS   Vestron, 1989
BLAZE   Buena Vista, 1989

JOSEPH T. GARRITY

Agent: Sandra Marsh Management - Sherman Oaks,
   818/905-6961
Phone: 213/650-2268

FORBIDDEN WORLD   New World, 1982
MAKING THE GRADE   Cannon, 1984, AD
BREAKIN' 2 ELECTRIC BOOGALOO   Tri-Star/
   Cannon, 1984
THUNDER ALLEY   Cannon, 1985
TWO FATHERS' JUSTICE (TF)   A. Shane
   Company, 1985
RUNAWAY TRAIN   Cannon, 1986, AD
FRIDAY THE 13TH, PART VI: JASON LIVES
   Paramount, 1986
UNCLE TOM'S CABIN (CTF)   Edgar J. Scherick
   Productions/Taft Entertainment TV, 1987
LAGUNA HEAT (CTF)   HBO Pictures/Jay Weston
   Productions, 1987
WEEDS   DEG, 1987

THE IN CROWD   Orion, 1988
THE BIG PICTURE   Columbia, 1989
CHATTAHOOCHEE   Hemdale, 1990
THE FIRST POWER   Orion, 1990
FIRE BIRDS   Buena Vista, 1990
DROP DEAD FRED   New Line Cinema, 1991

NORMAN GARWOOD

ACTT
Agent: Sandra Marsh Management - Sherman Oaks,
   818/905-6961

TIME BANDITS   Avco Embassy, 1981, AD
BRIMSTONE AND TREACLE   United Artists Classics,
   1982, AD
THE MISSIONARY   Columbia, 1982, AD
RED MONARCH   Enigma Films/Goldcrest Films &
   Television Ltd., 1983
BULLSHOT!   Island Alive, 1983
WATER   Atlantic Releasing Corporation, 1984
BRAZIL ★   Universal, 1985
LINK   Thorn EMI/Cannon, 1986
SHADEY   Skouras Pictures, 1986
THE PRINCESS BRIDE   20th Century Fox, 1987
GLORY ★   Tri-Star, 1989
MISERY   Columbia, 1990

DENNIS GASSNER

Agent: The Gersh Agency, Inc., Beverly Hills -
   213/274-6611, New York - 212/997-1818

WET GOLD (TF)   Telepictures Productions, 1984, AD
THE HITCHER   Tri-Star, 1986
IN THE MOOD   Lorimar, 1987
WISDOM   20th Century Fox, 1987
LIKE FATHER LIKE SON   Tri-Star, 1987
FIELD OF DREAMS   Universal, 1989
EARTH GIRLS ARE EASY   Vestron, 1989
MILLER'S CROSSING   Orion, 1990
BARTON FINK   20th Century Fox, 1991

STEPHEN GEAGHAN

BETRAYED   MGM/UA, 1988, AD
UNSUB (Pilot)   1989, AD

ANTONELLO GELENG

AFTER THE FALL OF NEW YORK   Almi Pictures, 1985
WARRIOR OF THE LOST WORLD   Visto
   International, 1985
DETECTIVE SCHOOL DROPOUTS   Cannon, 1986
MONSTER SHARK   Cinema Shares International, 1986

DON GIBBIN

LIBERTY & BASH   Fries Home Video, 1990

JEFFREY S. GINN

Directors Guild Canada
Home: RR#1, Orangeville, Ontario, Canada L9W-2Y8,
   519/941-9283

A BREED APART   Orion, 1983
STEPHEN KING'S CAT'S EYE   MGM/UA, 1985, AD
DATE WITH AN ANGEL   DEG, 1987, AD
THE BLOB   Tri-Star, 1988, AD
STELLA   Buena Vista, 1990, AD
THE LAST BEST YEAR OF MY LIFE (TF)   ABC
   Television, 1990, AD
MARRIED TO IT   Orion, 1991, AD

CINEMATOGRAPHERS
PRODUCTION
DESIGNERS,
COSTUME
DESIGNERS AND
FILM EDITORS
GUIDE

BOB GLASER
THE LONE RUNNER   Trans World Entertainment, 1988, AD

LES GOBRUEGGE*
IATSE Local 876

THE MUPPET MOVIE   AFD, 1979, AD
BIG TROUBLE IN LITTLE CHINA   20th Century Fox, 1986, AD
A TIME OF DESTINY   Columbia, 1988, AD

LINDSEY GODDARD
HEAVENLY BODIES   MGM/UA, 1985

JEFFREY L. GOLDSTEIN*
IATSE Local 876
Agent: Smith Gosnell Nicholson & Associates - Los Angeles, 213/459-0307

HILL STREET BLUES (TVS) I   1981-82
CALL TO GLORY (TF)   Tisch-Avnet Productions/ Paramount TV, 1984
NOT MY KID (TF)   Beth Polson Productions/Finnegan Associates, 1985
L.A. LAW (TVS) ☆☆   1987
DOWNPAYMENT ON MURDER (TF)   Adam Productions/20th Century Fox TV, 1987
WHITE WATER SUMMER   *RITES OF SUMMER* Columbia, 1987, AD

GEORGE GOODRIDGE
TRADING HEARTS   New Century/Vista, 1988

PERRI GORRARA
LANTERN HILL (CTF)   Sullivan Films, 1989

ADRIAN H. GORTON*
IATSE Local 876

THE BALTIMORE BULLET   Avco Embassy, 1980, AD
ZORRO, THE GAY BLADE   20th Century Fox, 1981, AD
PRAY FOR DEATH   American Distribution Group, 1985, AD
AMERICAN NINJA   Cannon, 1987
COBRA   Warner Bros., 1986, AD
RAGE OF HONOR   American Distribution Group, 1986
BULLETPROOF   CineTel Films, 1988

ASSHETON GORTON   ✦
ACTT
Agent: Sandra Marsh Management - Sherman Oaks, 818/905-6961

THE KNACK...AND HOW TO GET IT   Lopert, 1965
BLOW UP   MGM, 1966
THE BLISS OF MISS BLOSSOM   Paramount, 1969
THE BED SITTING ROOM   United Artists, 1969
THE MAGIC CHRISTIAN   Commonwealth United, 1970
ZACHARIAH   Cinerama Releasing Corporation, 1970
GET CARTER   MGM, 1971
THE PIED PIPER   Paramount, 1972
THE MARTIAN CHRONICLES (TF)   Charles Fries Productions/Stonehenge Productions, 1980
THE FRENCH LIEUTENANT'S WOMAN ★   United Artists, 1981
LEGEND   Universal, 1985
REVOLUTION   Warner Bros., 1985

COBRA   Warner Bros., 1986, AD w/William Skinner
LOST ANGELS   Orion, 1989
BOB ROY • 101 DALMATIONS

ANGELO GRAHAM*
IATSE Local 876
Agent: Sanford-Skouras & Gross - Los Angeles, 213/208-2100

LITTLE BIG MAN   National General, 1970, AD
THE DAY OF THE DOLPHIN   Avco Embassy, 1973, AD
THE GODFATHER, PART II ★★   Paramount, 1974, AD
FAREWELL, MY LOVELY   Avco Embassy, 1975, AD
F.I.S.T.   United Artists, 1978, AD
OUR WINNING SEASON   American International, 1978, AD
THE BRINKS JOB ★   Universal, 1978, AD
APOCALPYSE NOW ★   United Artists, 1979, AD
HAMMETT   Orion/Warner Bros., 1982, AD
THE ESCAPE ARTIST   Orion/Warner Bros., 1982
WARGAMES   MGM/UA, 1983
THE NATURAL ★   Tri-Star, 1984, AD
BEVERLY HILLS COP   Paramount, 1984
ONE FROM THE HEART   Columbia, 1982, AD
BATTERIES NOT INCLUDED   Universal, 1987, AD
MIDNIGHT RUN   Universal, 1988
COUP DE VILLE   Universal, 1990

WRAY STEVEN GRAHAM
THE MUPPETS TAKE MANHATTAN   Tri-Star, 1984, AD w/Paul Eads
THE MONEY PIT   Universal, 1986, AD
THE HOUSE ON CARROLL STREET   Orion, 1987, AD
NEW YORK STORIES ("Life Lessons")   Buena Vista, 1989, AD
FLETCH LIVES   Universal, 1989, AD w/Jimmy Bly, Cameron Birnie & Donald B. Woodruff
STAYING TOGETHER   Hemdale, 1990, AD

JOSE RODRIGUEZ GRANADA
CAVEMAN   United Artists, 1981, AD
UNDER THE VOLCANO   Universal, 1984, AD
VOLUNTEERS   Tri-Star, 1985, AD
FIREWALKER   Cannon, 1986
TOTAL RECALL   Tri-Star, 1990, AD w/James Tocci

GREG J. GRANDE
A KILLER AMONG US (TF)   Dave Bell Associates, 1990
SILHOUETTE (CTF)   Dutch Productions, 1990, AD

JOHN GRAYSMARK
ACTT
Agent: Sandra Marsh Management - Sherman Oaks, 818/905-6961

YOUNG WINSTON ★   Columbia, 1972, AD w/Geoffrey Drake & William Hutchinson
THE BIG SLEEP   United Artists, 1978, AD
ESCAPE TO ATHENA   AFD, 1979, AD
FLASH GORDON   Universal, 1980, AD
RAGTIME ★   Paramount, 1981
FIREFOX   Warner Bros., 1981, AD w/Elayne Ceder
THE LORDS OF DISCIPLINE   Paramount, 1983
THE BOUNTY   Orion, 1984
LIFEFORCE   Tri-Star, 1985
CLUB PARADISE   Warner Bros., 1986
DUET FOR ONE   Cannon, 1987
SUPERMAN IV: THE QUEST FOR PEACE   Warner Bros., 1987
GORILLAS IN THE MIST   Universal, 1988

HONOR BOUND   MGM/UA, 1989
WHITE HUNTER, BLACK HEART   Warner
   Bros., 1990

STEPHEN GREENBERG
ARCHIE: TO RIVERDALE AND BACK AGAIN (TF)
   Patchett-Kaufman Entertainment Productions, 1990
HANGFIRE   Motion Picture Corporation
   of America, 1991

ALEXIS GREY
THE TOXIC AVENGER, PART III: THE LAST
   TEMPTATION OF TOXIE   Troma, 1990

HAYDEN GRIFFIN
WEATHERBY   MGM/UA Classics, 1985

BRUCE GRIMES
WHEN THE WHALES CAME   20th Century Fox, 1990

COLIN GRIMES
THE DRESSER   Columbia, 1983, AD
KRULL   Columbia, 1983, AD w/Tony Curtis, Norman
   Dorme & Tony Reading

BILL GROOM
ISHTAR   Columbia, 1987, AD w/Vicki Paul
THE PICK-UP ARTIST   20th Century Fox, 1987, AD
ROCKET GIBRALTAR   Columbia, 1988
COOKIE   Warner Bros., 1989, AD
LOCK UP   Tri-Star, 1989, AD, NY
PRISONERS OF INERTIA   Northwinds
   Entertainment, 1989
THE TEDDY BEAR HABIT   Advocate
   Productions, 1990

DAVID GROPMAN*
Local 829
Agent: Sandra Marsh Management - Sherman Oaks,
   818/905-6961

COME BACK TO THE 5 & DIME JIMMY DEAN,
   JIMMY DEAN   Cinecom, 1982
KEY EXCHANGE   20th Century Fox, 1985
THE LAUNDROMAT (CTF)   Byck-Lancaster
   Productions/Sancastle 5 Productions, 1985
HOME OF THE BRAVE   Cinecom International, 1986
THE LAST DAYS OF FRANK AND JESSE JAMES (TF)
   Joseph Cates Productions, 1986
SWEET LORRAINE   Angelika Films, 1987
O.C. AND STIGGS   MGM/UA, 1987, AD
CAMPUS MAN   Paramount, 1987
MILES FROM HOME   Cinecom, 1988
BABYCAKES (TF)   The Konigsberg/Sanitsky
   Company, 1989
SLAVES OF NEW YORK   Tri-Star, 1989
LIFE UNDER WATER (TF)   American Playhouse/
   PBS, 1989
QUICK CHANGE   Warner Bros., 1990
MR. & MRS. BRIDGE   Miramax Films, 1990
ONCE AROUND   Universal, 1991

HOLGER GROSS
POSSESSION   Limelight International, 1983, AD
A WALK ON THE MOON   Benenson/Midwest Film
   Productions, 1987
AMERICAN NINJA 2: THE CONFRONTATION
   Cannon, 1987
HERO AND THE TERROR   Cannon, 1988
PULSE   Columbia, 1988

ANDRÉ GUERIN
THE WOLF AT THE DOOR   International Film Marketing,
   1986, w/Karl-Otto Hedal

ROBERT GUERRA
ANNIE   Columbia, 1982, AD w/Diane Wager
THE MANHATTAN PROJECT   20th Century Fox,
   1986, AD
IRONWEED   Tri-Star, 1987, AD
RUNNING ON EMPTY   Warner Bros., 1988, AD
SEE YOU IN THE MORNING   Warner Bros., 1989, AD
FAMILY BUSINESS   Tri-Star, 1989, AD

PIERRE GUFFROY
THE BRIDE WORE BLACK   Lopert, 1968
THE DISCREET CHARM OF THE BOURGEOUISIE
   20th Century Fox, 1972
HANNA K.   Universal Classics, 1983
TESS ★★   Columbia, 1980
PIRATES   Cannon, 1986
THE UNBEARABLE LIGHTNESS OF BEING
   Orion, 1988
FRANTIC   Warner Bros., 1988
VALMONT   Orion, 1989

ROBERT GUNDLACH
BANG THE DRUM SLOWLY   Paramount, 1973
KING KONG   Paramount, 1976, AD w/Archie J.
   Bacon & David A. Constable
THIEVES   Paramount, 1977, AD
OLIVER'S STORY   Paramount, 1978, AD
EYES OF LAURA MARS   Columbia, 1978, AD
FIREPOWER   AFD, 1979
TRIBUTE   20th Century Fox, 1980, AD
HERO AT LARGE   MGM/United Artists, 1980, AD
FIGHTING BACK   Paramount, 1982, AD
I, THE JURY   20th Century Fox, 1982
THE TOUGHEST MAN IN THE WORLD (TF)   Guber-
   Peters Productions/Centerpoint Productions, 1984
SEE NO EVIL, HEAR NO EVIL   Tri-Star, 1989

CLAUDIO GUZMAN
NIGHT OF THE FOX-PARTS I & II (MS)   ITC
   Entertainment, 1990

PATO GUZMAN*
IATSE Local 876
Agent: The Gersh Agency, Inc. - Beverly Hills,
   213/274-6611

THE PRESIDENT'S ANALYST   Janus, 1964
I LOVE YOU, ALICE B. TOKLAS   Warner Bros., 1968
BOB & CAROL & TED & ALICE   Columbia, 1969
ALEX IN WONDERLAND   MGM, 1970
MARRIAGE OF A YOUNG STOCKBROKER   20th
   Century Fox, 1971
PLAY IT AS IT LAYS   Universal, 1972
BLUME IN LOVE   Warner Bros., 1973
AN UNMARRIED WOMAN   20th Century Fox, 1978
THE IN-LAWS   Warner Bros., 1979
HIDE IN PLAIN SIGHT   MGM/United Artists, 1980
WILLIE AND PHIL   20th Century Fox, 1980
TEMPEST   Columbia, 1982
MOSCOW ON THE HUDSON   Columbia, 1984
DOWN AND OUT IN BEVERLY HILLS   Buena
   Vista, 1986
MOON OVER PARADOR   Universal, 1988
ENEMIES, A LOVE STORY   20th Century Fox, 1989
SCENES FROM A MALL   Buena Vista, 1991

Gu

CINEMATOGRAPHERS
PRODUCTION
DESIGNERS,
COSTUME
DESIGNERS AND
FILM EDITORS
GUIDE

P
R
O
D
U
C
T
I
O
N

D
E
S
I
G
N
E
R
S

Ha

CINEMATOGRAPHERS
PRODUCTION
DESIGNERS,
COSTUME
DESIGNERS AND
FILM EDITORS
GUIDE

H

MARK HAACK
DIRTY DANCING   Vestron, 1987, AD w/Stephen
     Lineweaver
MYSTIC PIZZA   Samuel Goldwyn Company,
     1988, AD

DAVID M. HABER*
IATSE Local 876
Phone: 213/883-6886

CORNBREAD, EARL AND ME   American International,
     1975, AD
THE DRIVER   20th Century Fox, 1978, AD
CAPRICORN ONE   Warner Bros., 1978, AD
MOMENT BY MOMENT   Universal, 1978, AD
THE LEGEND OF THE LONE RANGER   Universal/
     AFD, 1981, AD
NEIL SIMON'S ONLY WHEN I LAUGH   Columbia,
     1981, AD
THE BEAST WITHIN   United Artists, 1982
MAX DUGAN RETURNS   20th Century Fox, 1983, AD
THE ICE PIRATES   MGM/UA, 1984
SWEET DREAMS   Tri-Star, 1985, AD
THE MONSTER SQUAD   Tri-Star, 1987, AD
BAJA OKLAHOMA   HBO Pictures, 1988, AD
FAVORITE SON (MS)   Steve Sohmer Inc./NBC
     Productions, 1988
COHEN AND TATE   Nelson Entertainment, 1989
PRETTY WOMAN   Buena Vista, 1990, AD

JIMMY HADDER
SAVAGE BEACH   Malibu Bay Films, 1990

PENNY HADFIELD
Agent: The Gersh Agency, Inc., Beverly Hills -
     213/274-6611, New York - 212/997-1818

TENNESSE WILLIAMS' SWEET BIRD OF YOUTH (TF)
     Atlantic/Kushner-Locke Productions, 1990

ROGER HALL
ACTT
Agent: Sandra Marsh Management - Sherman Oaks,
     818/905-6961

CHARIOTS OF FIRE   20th Century Fox, 1981
COMING OUT OF THE ICE (TF)   The Konigsberg
     Company, 1982
HELEN KELLER - THE MIRACLE CONTINUES (TF)
     1984
REILLY ACE OF SPIES (MS)   Euston Films Ltd., 1984
KIM (TF)   London Films, 1984
DREAMCHILD   Universal, 1985
UPSTAIRS, DOWNSTAIRS (TVS)   3rd & 4th Series
THE STORYTELLER (Pilot)   1987
WHITE MISCHIEF   Columbia, 1987
TILL WE MEET AGAIN (TF)   1989
JUDITH KRANTZ'S TILL WE MEET AGAIN-
     PARTS I & II (MS)   Steve Krantz Productions, 1990
STRAPLESS   Miramax, 1990

TONY HALL
LOVE & MURDER   Norstar Entertainment, 1989
PERSONALS (CTF)   Sharmill Productions, 1990
HITLER'S DAUGHTER (CTF)   OTML Films, 1990, AD
ON THIN ICE: THE TAI BABILONIA STORY (TF)
     Bernard Rothman Productions, 1990

MICHAEL D. HALLER*
IATSE Local 876
Agent: Lawrence A. Mirisch, Triad Artists, Inc. -
     Los Angeles, 213/556-2727

THX 1138   Warner Bros., 1971
HAROLD AND MAUDE   Paramount, 1971
THE LAST DETAIL   Columbia, 1973
THE AUTOBIOGRAPHY OF MISS JANE PITTMAN (TF)
     Tomorrow Entertainment, 1974
RANCHO DELUXE   United Artists, 1975
BOUND FOR GLORY   United Artists, 1976
COMING HOME   United Artists, 1978
BEING THERE   United Artists, 1979
PERFECT   Columbia, 1985
8 MILLION WAYS TO DIE   Tri-Star, 1986
COOKIE   Warner Bros., 1989

TODD HALLOWELL*
IATSE Local 876

MIAMI VICE (TVS)   1984
CLOAK AND DAGGER   Universal, 1984, AD
BACK TO THE FUTURE   Universal, 1985, AD
FLETCH   Universal, 1985, AD
TOUGH GUYS   Buena Vista, 1986
DOWN AND OUT IN BEVERLY HILLS   Buena Vista,
     1986, AD
ADVENTURES IN BABYSITTING   Buena Vista, 1987
BURGLAR   Warner Bros., 1987
THE DREAM TEAM   Universal, 1989
PARENTHOOD   Universal, 1989
VITAL SIGNS   20th Century Fox, 1990
CLASS ACTION   20th Century Fox, 1991

RICHARD Y. HAMAN*
IATSE Local 876

SUNSET   Tri-Star, 1988, AD
PETER GUNN - ROGUE COPS (TF)   B.E.C.O./New
     World TV, 1989, AD

PETER J. HAMPTON
THE DUELLISTS   Paramount, 1978
DEALERS   Rank, 1989

MICHAEL Z. HANAN
Agent: Smith Gosnell Nicholson & Associates -
     Los Angeles, 213/459-0307

THE NIGHT THEY SAVED CHRISTMAS (TF)   Robert
     Halmi Inc., 1984
MIAMI VICE (TVS)   1985-86
HEARTBEAT (HVD)   1986
SIGN O' THE TIMES   Cineplex Odeon, 1987
SPLIT DECISIONS   New Century/Vista, 1988, AD
PET SEMATARY   Paramount, 1989
THREE'S A MATCH (TF)   1989
DRUG WARS: THE CAMARENA STORY (MS)   ZZY
     Productions, 1990

SOMEBODY HAS TO SHOOT THE PICTURE (CTF)
    Alan Barnette Productions, 1990
PSYCHO IV: THE BEGINNING (CTF)   Smart Money
    Productions, 1990

GARY HANSEN
SYLVIA   MGM/UA Classics, 1985

STEVE HARDIE
NIGHTBREED   20th Century Fox, 1990

CATHERINE HARDWICKE
Agent: Camera Masters - Venice, 213/06-0810

THRASHIN'   Fries Entertainment, 1986
HUNK   Crown International, 1987, AD
I'M GONNA GIT YOU SUCKA   MGM/UA, 1987,
    w/Melba Farquhar
TAPEHEADS   Avenue Pictures, 1988
BRAIN DEAD   Concorde, 1989
MARTIANS GO HOME   Taurus Entertainment,
    1990, w/Don Day

KENNETH A. HARDY
AFTER DARK, MY SWEET   Avenue Pictures,
    1990, AD

GERRY HARITON
THE WICKEDEST WITCH (TF)   Boo You
    Productions, 1990, w/Vicki Baral

FRANZ HARLAND
SMITHEREENS   New Line Cinema, 1982

FRED HARPMAN*
IATSE Local 876

TAKE THE MONEY AND RUN   Cinerama Releasing
    Corporation, 1969, AD
MYRA BRECKENRIDGE   20th Century Fox,
    1970, AD
DELIVERANCE   Warner Bros., 1972, AD
THE TERMINAL MAN   Warner Bros., 1974, AD
DOC SAVAGE, THE MAN OF BRONZE   Warner
    Bros., 1975
DAMIEN - OMEN II   20th Century Fox, 1978,
    AD w/Philip M. Jeffries
CHEECH AND CHONG'S NEXT MOVIE
    Universal, 1980
RICH AND FAMOUS   MGM/United Artists, 1981, AD
MY NAME IS BILL W. (TF)   1989
DARK SHADOWS-PARTS I & II (Pilot)   Dan Curtis
    Television Productions, 1991 (Part one only)

MARK HARRINGTON
WISEGUY (TF)   Stephen J. Cannell Productions, 1990

ANDY HARRIS
COMFORT AND JOY   Universal, 1984, AD

LEON HARRIS*
IATSE Local 876

ON THE YARD   Midwest Film Productions,
    1979, AD
STAR TREK - THE MOTION PICTURE ★
    Paramount, 1979, AD w/Joe Jennings &
    John Vallone

THE DEVIL AND MAX DEVLIN   Buena Vista, 1981,
    AD w/John B. Mansbridge
DINER   MGM/UA, 1982, AD
SPACECAMP   20th Century Fox, 1986,
    AD w/Richard J. Lawrence

PHILIP HARRISON
Agent: The Gersh Agency, Inc., Beverly Hills -
    213/274-6611, New York - 212/997-1818

VALENTINO   United Artists, 1977, AD
HANOVER STREET   Columbia, 1979, AD
OUTLAND   The Ladd Company/Warner Bros., 1981
NEVER SAY NEVER AGAIN   Warner Bros., 1983,
    w/Stephen Grimes
BLUE THUNDER   Columbia, 1983
THE RAZOR'S EDGE   Columbia, 1984
WHITE NIGHTS   Columbia, 1985
SHORT CIRCUIT   Tri-Star, 1986
52 PICK-UP   Cannon, 1986
STAKEOUT   Buena Vista, 1987
MISSISSIPPI BURNING   Orion, 1988,
    w/Geoffrey Kirkland
BIRD ON A WIRE   Universal, 1990
THE HARD WAY   Universal, 1991

RICHARD HARRISON
THE BAY BOY   Orion, 1984, AD
THE GOOD MOTHER   Buena Vista, 1988,
    AD w/Hilton Rosemarin
WE'RE NO ANGELS   Paramount, 1989, AD

MICHAEL HARTOG
LITTLE VEGAS   I.R.S. Releasing, 1990

TIM HARVEY
HENRY V   Renaissance Films, 1989
THE SECRET LIFE OF IAN FLEMING (CTF)   Saban
    Scherick Productions, 1990
VOICE OF THE HEART (CTF)   Worldvision, 1990
COINS IN THE FOUNTAIN (TF)   Michael Filerman
    Productions, 1990

SHUNA HARWOOD
TRACK 29   Island Pictures, 1988

MARK HASKINS
SALSA   Cannon, 1988
HERO AND THE TERROR   Cannon, 1988,
    AD w/Douglas Dick
PICASSO TRIGGER   Malibu Bay Films, 1988, AD
MY BOYFRIEND'S BACK (TF)   Interscope
    Productions, 1990
LINE OF FIRE (TF)   BoJames Entertainment, 1991

SHAWN HAUSMAN
TOO MUCH SUN   New Line Cinema, 1990

ANDRIS HAUSMANIS
PRETTYKILL   Spectrafilm, 1987,
    AD w/Jimmy Williams
TOO OUTRAGEOUS!   Spectrafilm, 1987, AD
ALMOST GROWN (Pilot)   1988, AD
GLORY! GLORY! (CTF)   Atlantis Films Ltd./
    Orion TV, 1989
PARENTS   Vestron, 1989, AD

Ha

**CINEMATOGRAPHERS
PRODUCTION
DESIGNERS,
COSTUME
DESIGNERS AND
FILM EDITORS
GUIDE**

**P
R
O
D
U
C
T
I
O
N

D
E
S
I
G
N
E
R
S**

Ha

CINEMATOGRAPHERS
PRODUCTION
DESIGNERS,
COSTUME
DESIGNERS and
FILM EDITORS
GUIDE

P
R
O
D
U
C
T
I
O
N

D
E
S
I
G
N
E
R
S

TED HAWORTH*
IATSE Local 876

STRANGERS ON A TRAIN   Warner Bros., 1951
I CONFESS   Warner Bros., 1953
INVASION OF THE BODY SNATCHERS   Allied
   Artists, 1956
SAYONARA ★★   Warner Bros., 1957
I WANT TO LIVE!   United Artists, 1958
SOME LIKE IT HOT ★   United Artists, 1959
WHO WAS THAT LADY?   Columbia, 1960
PEPE ★   Columbia, 1960
THE OUTSIDER   Universal, 1961
THE LONGEST DAY ★   20th Century Fox, 1962
WHAT A WAY TO GO! ★   20th Century Fox, 1964
MARTY ★   United Artists, 1965
THE PROFESSIONALS   Columbia, 1966
HALF A SIXPENCE   Paramount, 1968
THE WAY WEST   United Artists, 1967
THE KREMLIN LETTER   20th Century Fox, 1970
THE BEGUILED   Universal, 1971
JEREMIAH JOHNSON   Warner Bros., 1972
THE GETAWAY   National General, 1972
JUNIOR BONNER   Cinerama Releasing
   Corporation, 1973
PAT GARRETT & BILLY THE KID   MGM, 1973
CLAUDINE   20th Century Fox, 1974
HARRY AND TONTO   20th Century Fox, 1974
THE KILLER ELITE   United Artists, 1975
THE SAILOR WHO FELL FROM GRACE WITH
   THE SEA   Avco Embassy, 1976
TELEFON   MGM/United Artists, 1977
CROSS OF IRON   Avco Embassy, 1977
SOMEBODY KILLED HER HUSBAND
   Columbia, 1978
WHEN YOU COMIN' BACK, RED RYDER?
   Columbia, 1979
SIDNEY SHELDON'S BLOODLINE   Paramount, 1979
ROUGH CUT   Paramount, 1980
CARBON COPY   Avco Embassy, 1981
DEATH HUNT   20th Century Fox, 1981
JINXED   MGM/United Artist, 1982
THE OSTERMAN WEEKEND   20th Century Fox, 1983
   (refused screen credit)
BLAME IT ON THE NIGHT   Tri-Star, 1984
THE LEGEND OF BILLIE JEAN   Tri-Star, 1985
POLTERGEIST II: THE OTHER SIDE   MGM/UA, 1986
BATTERIES NOT INCLUDED   Universal, 1987
MOTHERS, DAUGHTERS AND LOVERS (TF)
   Katz/Huyck/Films Productions, 1990

MARTYN HEBERT
Agent: London Management, 235/241 Regent St. -
   London W1R 7AG, 071-493-1610

1984   Atlantic Releasing Corporation, 1984,
   AD w/Grant Hicks
LADY JANE   Paramount, 1986, AD w/Fred Carter &
   Mark Raggett
A PRAYER FOR THE DYING   1988, AD
WITHOUT A CLUE   Orion, 1988,
   w/Brian Ackland-Snow

MICHAEL HELMY*
IATSE Local 876
Address: 9348 Civic Center Drive, Suite 101,
   Beverly Hills 90210, 213/278-4700

PRIZZI'S HONOR   20th Century Fox, 1985, AD
BACK TO THE BEACH   Paramount, 1987

TALES FROM THE HOLLYWOOD HILLS (TVS)   1987
ELYSIAN FIELDS (TF)   Sarabande Productions, 1989
THE HEAT (Pilot)   1989
GINGER ALE AFTERNOON   Skouras Pictures, 1989
THE TAKE (CTF)   Cine-Nevada Productions, 1990

STEPHEN HENDRICKSON
Agent: The Gurian Agency - Los Angeles, 213/550-0400
Address: 280 Riverside Drive, New York, New York
   10025, 212/864-2161

GOING IN STYLE   Warner Bros., 1979
CAN'T STOP THE MUSIC   AFD, 1980
ARTHUR   Orion/Warner Bros., 1981
A LITTLE SEX   Universal, 1982
THE MUPPETS TAKE MANHATTAN   Tri-Star, 1984
WALL STREET   20th Century Fox, 1987
FLETCH LIVES   Universal, 1989

CHRISTOPHER HENRY
SILENT SCREAM   American Cinema, 1980
GRADUATION DAY   IFI-Scope III, 1981, AD
LIES   International Film Marketing, 1983, AD
PRIME RISK   Almi Pictures, 1985

JOCELYN HERBERT
THE WHALES OF AUGUST   Alive Films, 1987

MARTYN HERBERT
SECRET WEAPON (CTF)   Griffin-Elysian Films, 1990,
   w/Julie Belle

EVAN HERCULES
MIDNIGHT EXPRESS   Columbia, 1978, AD
BREAKING GLASS   Paramount, 1980
A PRAYER FOR THE DYING   Samuel Goldwyn
   Company, 1987

J. MARK HERRINGTON
MONKEY SHINES   Orion, 1988, AD w/Jim Feng

ALBERT HESCHONG*
IATSE Local 876
Agent: Grace Lyons Management - Los Angeles,
   213/655-5100

LIKE MOTHER, LIKE ME (TF)   CBS Entertainment, 1978
THADDEUS ROSE AND EDDIE (TF)   CBS, Inc., 1978
FIRST YOU CRY (TF)   MTM Enterprises, 1978
THE WILD, WILD WEST REVISITED (TF)   CBS
   Entertainment, 1979
MORE WILD, WILD WEST (TF)   CBS
   Entertainment, 1980
RASCALS AND ROBBERS: THE SECRET
   ADVENTURES OF TOM SAWYER AND
   HUCKLEBERRY FINN (TF)   CBS
   Entertainment, 1982
GAMES MOTHER NEVER TAUGHT YOU (TF)   CBS
   Entertainment, 1982
THE OTHER WOMAN (TF)   CBS Entertainment, 1983
CALAMITYJANE (TF)   CBS Entertainment, 1983
FIRST STEPS (TF)   CBS Entertainment, 1985
MY WICKED, WICKED WAYS: THE LEGEND OF ERROL
   FLYNN (TF)   CBS Entertainment, 1985
GUNSMOKE: THE RETURN TO DODGE (TF)   CBS
   Entertainment, 1987
EISENHOWER & LUTZ (TVS)   1987
EXTREME PREJUDICE   Tri-Star, 1987

BERNARD HIDES
THE ODD ANGRY SHOT   Roadshow
    Distributors, 1979
HARLEQUIN   Greater Union Film Distributors, 1980
THE LIGHTHORSEMEN   Cinecom, 1988
CASUALTIES OF WAR   Columbia, 1989, AD

DOUGLAS HIGGINS*
Canadian Union
Agent: Smith Gosnell Nicholson & Associates -
    Los Angeles, 213/459-0307

THE BABYSITTER (TF)   Moonlight Productions/
    Filmways, 1980
THE KIDNAPPING OF THE PRESIDENT   Crown
    International, 1980
STIR CRAZY   Columbia, 1980
CAGNEY & LACEY (TF)   Mace Neufield Productions/
    Filmways, 1981
MOTHER LODE   Agamemnon Films, 1982
THE GOLDEN SEAL   Samuel Goldwyn
    Company, 1983
THE GLITTER DOME (CTF)   HBO Premiere Films/
    Telepictures Productions/Trincomali
    Productions, 1984
RUNAWAY   Tri-Star, 1984
THE VINDICATOR *FRANKENSTEIN '88* 20th
    Century Fox, 1985
THE HITCHHIKER (TVS)   1986
MRS. DELAFIELD WANTS TO MARRY (TF)
    Schaefer-Karpf Productions/Gaylord Prodution
    Company, 1986
C.A.T. SQUAD (TF)   NBC Productions, 1986
EASY PREY (TF)   New World TV/Rene Malo
    Productions, 1987
STRANGE COMPANIONS (TF)   Walt Disney TV, 1987
ALMOST GROWN (Pilot)   1988
THE TRIAL OF THE INCREDIBLE HULK (TF)
    Bixby-Brandon Productions/New World TV, 1989
LADY IN A CORNER (TF)   Pantheon Pictures, 1990
STEPHEN KING'S IT (TF)   Konigsberg/Sanitsky
    Productions, 1990
THE DEATH OF THE INCREDIBLE HULK (TF)
    Bixby-Brandon Productions/New World TV, 1990
HANG TOUGH   Moviestore Entertainment, 1990

RON HIGHFIELD
CAME A HOT FRIDAY   Orion Classics, 1985

VIRGINIA E. HILDRETH
APPEARANCES (TF)   Echo Cove Productions, 1990

MARCIA HINDS
Agent: Sanford-Skouras & Gross - Los Angeles,
    213/208-2100

BODY ROCK   New World, 1984
NOMADS   Atlantic Releasing Corporation, 1985
BEHIND ENEMY LINES (TF)   TVS Productions/MTM
    Enterprises, 1985
DANGEROUSLY CLOSE   Cannon, 1986
AVENGING FORCE   Cannon, 1986
P.O.W. THE ESCAPE   Cannon, 1986
SUMMER HEAT   Atlantic Releasing Corporation, 1987
1969   Atlantic Releasing Corporation, 1988
HAPPY TOGETHER   MGM/UA, 1989
THE MYSTERY OF FLIGHT 1501 (TF)   Schaefer-Karpf
    Productions, 1990

WILLIAM HINEY*
IATSE Local 876
Agent: Sanford-Skouras & Gross - Los Angeles,
    213/208-2100
Phone: 213/457-3969

A STAR IS BORN   Warner Bros., 1976, AD
SCOTT JOPLIN   Universal, 1977, AD
ALMOST SUMMER   Universal, 1978
CALIFORNIA DREAMING   American International, 1979
FIRST FAMILY   Warner Bros., 1980, AD
LITTLE DARLINGS   Paramount, 1980
DEATH WISH II   Filmways, 1982
UP THE CREEK   Orion, 1984
A CASE OF RAPE (TF)   Universal TV, 1974
RICH MAN, POOR MAN (MS)   Universal TV, 1976
THE DEFECTION OF SIMAS KUDIRKA (TF)   The Jozak
    Company/Paramount TV, 1978
FLESH AND BLOOD (TF)   The Jozak Company/
    Cypress Point Productions/Paramount TV, 1979
HOMEWARD BOUND (TF)   Tisch-Avnet
    Productions, 1980
BREWSTER'S MILLIONS   Universal, 1985
DAUGHTER OF THE STREETS (TF)   Adam
    Productions, 1990

JIMMY JAY HINKLE
PARKER KANE (TF)   Parker Kane Productions, 1990

CHRISTOPHER HOBBS
CARAVAGGIO   Cinevista, 1986
GOTHIC   Vestron, 1987
STRIKE IT RICH   Millimeter Films, 1990

RON HOBBS
Agent: Creative Technique - Toronto, Ontario, Canada,
    416/466-4173

THE DOMINO PRINCIPLE   Avco Embassy, 1977, AD
THE DEERHUNTER   Universal, 1978,
    AD w/Kim Swados
JUST YOU AND ME KID   Columbia, 1979
RAVAGERS   Columbia, 1979
TOM HORN   Warner Bros., 1980, AD
THE HUNTER   Paramount, 1980
THE DIARY OF ANNE FRANK (TF)   Katz-Gallin/Half-Pint
    Productions/20th Century Fox TV, 1980
DIAL M FOR MURDER (TF)   Freyda Rothstein
    Productions/Time-Life TV, 1981
THE VICTIMS (TF)   Hajeno Productions/Warner
    Bros. TV, 1982
JOHNNY BELINDA (TF)   Dick Berg-Stonehenge
    Productions/Lorimar Productions, 1982
PERSONAL BEST   Warner Bros., 1982
SMOKEY AND THE BANDIT PART 3   Universal,
    1983, AD
FOOTLOOSE   Paramount, 1984
COUNTRY   Buena Vista, 1984
STINGRAY(TVS)   1985
THE HEAVENLY KID   Tri-Star, 1985
LEGAL EAGLES   Universal, 1986, AD

FRED HOLE
RETURN OF THE JEDI ★   20th Century Fox, 1983,
    AD w/James Schoppe
ALIENS   20th Century Fox, 1986, AD w/Ken Court,
    Bert Davey & Michael Lamont
EMPIRE OF THE SUN   Warner Bros., 1987,
    AD w/Charles Bishop

Hi

CINEMATOGRAPHERS
PRODUCTION
DESIGNERS,
COSTUME
DESIGNERS AND
FILM EDITORS
GUIDE

**P
R
O
D
U
C
T
I
O
N

D
E
S
I
G
N
E
R
S**

Ho

CINEMATOGRAPHERS
PRODUCTION
DESIGNERS,
COSTUME
DESIGNERS and
FILM EDITORS
GUIDE

P
R
O
D
U
C
T
I
O
N

D
E
S
I
G
N
E
R
S

SIMON HOLLAND
ACTT
Agent: Sandra Marsh Management - Sherman Oaks, 818/905-6961

THE BOY FRIEND   MGM, 1971, AD
A WAR OF CHILDREN (TF)   Tomorrow Entertainment, 1972, AD
MURDER ON THE ORIENT EXPRESS   Paramount, 1974, AD
IN THIS HOUSE OF BREDE (TF)   Tomorrow Entertainment, 1975, AD
ROSEBUD   United Artists, 1975, AD
EQUUS   United Artists, 1977, AD
SWALLOWS AND AMAZONS   LDS, 1977, AD
THE SHOUT   Films Inc., 1979, AD
AGATHA   Warner Bros., 1979, AD
QUADROPHENIA   World Northal, 1979
REDS   Paramount, 1981, AD
GREYSTOKE: THE LEGEND OF TARZAN, LORD OF THE APES   Warner Bros., 1984, AD w/Norman Dorme
THE EMERALD FOREST   20th Century Fox, 1985
HAREM (TF)   Highgate Pictures, 1986
THE BELIEVERS   Orion, 1987
BUSTER   Tri-Star, 1988
SCANDAL   Miramax, 1989
NUNS ON THE RUN   HandMade Films/20th Century Fox, 1990
KING RALPH   Universal, 1991

C. ROBERT HOLLOWAY
FALSE WITNESS (TF)   Valente/Kritzer/EPI Productions, 1990
THIS GUN FOR HIRE (CTF)   BBK Productions, 1991

WILLY HOLT
JULIA   20th Century Fox, 1977, w/Gene Callahan & Carmen Dillon
FIVE DAYS ONE SUMMER   The Ladd Company/WarnerBros., 1982
TARGET   Warner Bros., 1985
AU REVOIR LES ENFANTS   Orion Classics, 1987, AD

RICHARD HOOVER
IT TAKES TWO   MGM/UA, 1988
TORCH SONG TRILOGY   New Line Cinema, 1988
CHECKING OUT   Warner Bros., 1989, AD
FAMILY OF SPIES-PARTS I & II (MS)   King Phoenix Entertainment, 1990
HEAT WAVE (CTF)   Avnet/Kerner Company, 1990
TWIN PEAKS (TF)   Propaganda Films, 1990

CHRIS HOPKINS
THE POWER   Film Ventures, 1984
TORMENT   New World, 1986, AD
THE KINDRED   FM Entertainment, 1987

SPEED HOPKINS
A MIDSUMMER NIGHT'S SEX COMEDY   Orion/Warner Bros., 1982, AD
ZELIG   Orion/Warner Bros., 1983, AD
FALLING IN LOVE   Paramount, 1984, AD
THE NATURAL ★   Tri-Star, 1984, AD
DESPERATELY SEEKING SUSAN   Orion, 1985, AD
F/X   Orion, 1986, AD
SEPTEMBER   Orion, 1987, AD
BIG   20th Century Fox, 1988, AD w/Tom Warren

NEW YORK STORIES ("Life Without Zoe" & "Oedipus Wrecks")   Buena Vista, 1989, AD,
QUICK CHANGE   Warner Bros., 1990, AD

MARYBETH HORIARI
LIVING TO DIE   PM Entertainment, 1990, AD

CHRISTOPHER HORNER
MURDEROUS VISION (CTF)   Wilshire Court Productions, 1991

HARRY HORNER*
IATSE Local 876
Agent: The Gersh Agency, Inc. - Beverly Hills, 213/274-6611

THE HUSTLER ★★   20th Century Fox, 1961
FAHRENHEIT 451   Universal, 1967
THEY SHOOT HORSES, DON'T THEY?   Cinerama Releasing Corporation, 1969
WHO IS HARRY KELLERMAN AND WHY IS HE SAYING ALL THOSE TERRIBLE THINGS ABOUT ME?   National General, 1971
UP THE SANDBOX   National General, 1972
HARRY AND WALTER GO TO NEW YORK   Columbia, 1976
AUDREY ROSE   United Artists, 1977
MOMENT BY MOMENT   Universal, 1978
THE JAZZ SINGER   AFD, 1980

TAMAS HORNYANSZKY
DAUGHTER OF DARKNESS (TF)   King Phoenix Entertainment, 1990, AD

JEFFREY HOWARD*
IATSE Local 876

PRIVATE BENJAMIN   Warner Bros., 1980, AD
BABY BOOM   Warner Bros., 1987
CLARA'S HEART   Warner Bros., 1988
MAJOR LEAGUE   Paramount, 1989

PETER HOWITT
CLASH OF THE TITANS   United Artists, 1981, AD w/Giorgio Desideri, Fernando Gonzalez & Don Picton
LABYRINTH   Tri-Star, 1986, AD w/others
HAWKS   Skouras Pictures, 1989

ROBERT HOWLAND
FRIDAY THE 13TH PART V - A NEW BEGINNING   Paramount, 1985
THE RETURN OF THE LIVING DEAD   Orion, 1985, AD
ONCE BITTEN   Samuel Goldwyn Company, 1985, AD
GHOST WARRIOR *SWORDKILL*   Empire Pictures, 1986, w/Pamela B. Warner
MASTERS OF THE UNIVERSE   Cannon, 1987, AD
BEST SELLER   Orion, 1987, AD

RICHARD HUDOLIN
IATSE Canada card
Agent: The Doug Apatow Agency - Los Angeles, 213/202-6888

HYPER SAPHIEN   Tri-Star, 1986, AD
STAKEOUT   Buena Vista, 1987, AD
LOYALTIES   Cinema Group, 1987, AD
SPEED ZONE   Orion, 1989
DEAD BANG   Warner Bros., 1989, AD
BIRD ON A WIRE   Universal, 1989, AD

MIKE HUDSON
A TEST OF LOVE   Universal, 1985, w/Robbie Perkins

DIANE HUGHES
DEADLY DESIRE (CTF)   Skylark Films/Wilshire Court
   Productions, 1991 w/Phillip Vasels

JAMES G. HULSEY*
IATSE Local 876
Agent: Smith Gosnell Nicholson & Associates -
   Pacific Palisades, 213/459-0307

PAINT YOUR WAGON   Paramount, 1969, AD
VIVA MAX!   Commonwealth United, 1969, AD
THE MAN   Paramount, 1972, AD
THE PRESIDENT'S PLANE IS MISSING (TF)
   ABC Circle Films, 1973, AD
THE RED PONY (TF)   Universal TV/Omnibus
   Productions, 1973, AD
BREAKOUT 1975
WHO IS THE BLACK DAHLIA? (TF)   Douglas S.
   Cramer Productions, 1975, AD
CHRISTMAS MIRACLE IN CAUFIELD, USA (TF)
   20th Century Fox TV, 1977, AD
THE DEATH OF RICHIE (TF)   Henry Jaffe
   Enterprises, 1977
FUN WITH DICK AND JANE   Columbia, 1977
AUNT MARY (TF)   Henry Jaffe Enterprises, 1979, AD
THE WOMEN'S ROOM (TF)   Philip Mandelker
   Productions/Warner Bros. TV, 1980, AD
FREEDOM (TF)   Hill-Mandelker Films, 1981, AD
THE LETTER (TF) ☆☆   Hajeno Productions/Warner
   Bros. TV, 1982, AD
WHO WILL LOVE MY CHILDREN? (TF)   ABC Circle
   Films, 1983
THE DUCK FACTORY (Pilot) ☆☆   1984
A STREETCAR NAMED DESIRE (TF) ☆☆   Keith
   Barish Productions, 1984
PAPER DOLLS (TVS)   1984
THE ATLANTA CHILD MURDERS (TF)   Mann-
   Rafshoon Productions/Finnegan Associates, 1985
RIGHT TO KILL? (TF)   Wrye-Konigsberg Productions/
   Taper Media Enterprises/Telepictures
   Productions, 1985
AN EARLY FROST (TF)   NBC Productions, 1985
STRANDED (TF)   Tim Flack Productions/
   Columbia TV, 1986
ACCEPTABLE RISKS (TF)   ABC Circle Films, 1986
WHEN THE TIME COMES (TF)   Jaffe Lansing
   Productions/Republic Pictures, 1987
I SAW WHAT YOU DID (TF)   Universal TV, 1987
LOVEMAKING (TF)   1988
DAVID (TF)   Tough Boys Inc./Donald March
   Productions/ITC Entertainment Group, 1988
THE FULFILLMENT OF MARY GRAY (TF)   Lee
   Caplin Productions/Indian Neck Entertainment, 1989
STELLA   Buena Vista, 1990
THE DREAMER OF OZ (TF)   Bedrock
   Productions, 1990
THE LAST BEST YEAR (TF)   David W. Rintels
   Productions, 1990

RICHARD K. HUMMEL
DOWN TWISTED   Cannon, 1987,
   AD w/Douglas K. Leonard
LADY IN WHITE   New Century/Vista, 1988
MASTERS OF MENACE   New Line Cinema, 1990

LEN HUNTINGFORD
DREAMCHILD   Universal, 1985, AD
RAWHEAD REX   Empire Pictures, 1987, AD
RITA, SUE AND BOB TOO   Orion Classics, 1987, AD
WHITE MISCHIEF   Columbia, 1987, AD

TIM HUTCHINSON
THAT SUMMER   Columbia, 1979, AD
ROUGH CUT   Paramount, 1980, AD
EXCALIBUR   Orion/Warner Bros., 1981, AD
VICTOR/VICTORIA ★   MGM/UA, 1982, AD w/William
   Craig Smith
TRAIL OF THE PINK PANTHER   MGM/UA, 1982, AD
CURSE OF THE PINK PANTHER   MGM/UA, 1983,
   AD w/John Sidall & Alan Tomkins
SANTA CLAUS: THE MOVIE   Tri-Star, 1985, AD
HIGHLANDER   20th Century Fox, 1986, AD w/Martin
   Atkinson & Mark Roggett
THE FOURTH PROTOCOL   Lorimar, 1987, AD
WILLOW   MGM/UA, 1988, w/Tony Reading &
   Malcolm Stone
GREAT BALLS OF FIRE   Orion, 1989, AD, London
BACK HOME (CTF)   TVS Films/Verronmead
   Productions, 1990

JON HUTMAN*
IATSE Local 876
Agent: The Gersh Agency, Inc., Beverly Hills -
   213/274-6611, New York - 212/997-1818

SURRENDER   Warner Bros., 1987, AD
HEATHERS   New World, 1989
I LOVE YOU TO DEATH   Tri-Star, 1990, AD
TAKING CARE OF BUSINESS   Buena Vista, 1990

I

JOHN IACOVELLI
HONEY, I SHRUNK THE KIDS   Buena Vista, 1989,
   AD w/Dorree Cooper

SHIRLEY INGET
RAD   Tri-Star, 1986, AD

GUIDO IOSIA
ONLY ONE SURVIVED (TF)   CBS Entertainment,
   1990, AD

COLIN D. IRWIN
TRICK OR TREAT   DEG, 1986, AD
LAST RESORT   Concorde, 1986, AD
DOIN' TIME ON PLANET EARTH   Cannon, 1988, AD

AUGUSTIN ITUARTE
SUNBURN   Paramount, 1979, AD
EAGLE'S WING   International Picture Show, 1979, AD
WOLF LAKE   Filmcorp Distribution, 1981
HIGH RISK   American Cinema, 1981
MISSING   Universal, 1982, AD w/Lucero Isaac
UNDER FIRE   Orion, 1983, AD w/Toby Rafelson

It

CINEMATOGRAPHERS
PRODUCTION
DESIGNERS,
COSTUME
DESIGNERS AND
FILM EDITORS
GUIDE

P
R
O
D
U
C
T
I
O
N

D
E
S
I
G
N
E
R
S

Iv

CINEMATOGRAPHERS
PRODUCTION
DESIGNERS,
COSTUME
DESIGNERS AND
FILM EDITORS
GUIDE

P
R
O
D
U
C
T
I
O
N

D
E
S
I
G
N
E
R
S

ROMANCING THE STONE   20th Century Fox, 1984, AD
REMO WILLIAMS: THE ADVENTURE BEGINS   Orion, 1985, AD
LET'S GET HARRY   Tri-Star, 1986, AD

DON K. IVEY

HARDLY WORKING   20th Century Fox, 1981, AD
NOBODY'S PERFEKT   Columbia, 1981, AD
LOVE CHILD   The Ladd Company/Warner Bros., 1982, AD
BLUE SKIES AGAIN   Warner Bros., 1983, AD
WHAT COMES AROUND   W.O. Associates, 1986

J

GEMMA JACKSON

THE GIRL IN THE PICTURE   Samuel Goldwyn Company, 1986
MONA LISA   Island Pictures, 1986, AD
PAPERHOUSE   Vestron, 1989
CHICAGO JOE AND THE SHOWGIRL   New Line Cinema, 1990

MATTHEW JACOBS

KANSAS   Trans World Entertainment, 1988
I, MADMAN   Trans World Entertainment, 1989, w/Ron Wilson
DREAM A LITTLE DREAM   Vestron, 1989
NAKED LIE (TF)   Shadowplay Films/Phoenix Entertainment, 1989

JOCELYN JAMES

HELLRAISER   New World, 1987, AD
DISTANT VOICES, STILL LIVES   Alive Films, 1989, AD
DIAMOND SKULLS   Film Four/British Screen, 1989

RICHARD JAMES

IATSE Local 876
Agent: Miller Agency - Santa Clarita, 818/843-1511

BATTLESTAR GALACTICA (TF)   Universal, 1979
LOCAL HERO   Warner Bros., 1983, AD
SILKWOOD   20th Century Fox, 1983, AD
PEYTON PLACE: THE NEXT GENERATION (TF)   Michael Filerman Productions/20th Century Fox TV, 1985
STORMIN' HOME (TF)   CBS Entertainment, 1985
GETTING EVEN HOSTAGE: DALLAS   American Distribution Group, 1986, AD
THE BEAST   Columbia, 1988, AD

PETER JAMISON*

IATSE Local 876
Agent: The Gersh Agency, Inc., Beverly Hills - 213/274-6611, New York - 212/997-1818

EAT MY DUST   New World, 1976, AD
MOONSHINE COUNTY EXPRESS   New World, 1977, AD

THE EVIL   New World, 1978, AD
I WANNA HOLD YOUR HAND   Universal, 1978, AD
OLD BOYFRIENDS   Avco Embassy, 1979, AD
HEAD OVER HEELS CHILLY SCENES OF WINTER   United Artists, 1979
THE BIG RED ONE   United Artists, 1980, AD
USED CARS   Columbia, 1980
ALL NIGHT LONG   Universal, 1981
CONTINENTAL DIVIDE   Universal, 1981
MISSING   Universal, 1982
HALLOWEEN III: SEASON OF THE WITCH   Universal, 1982
SWING SHIFT   Warner Bros., 1983
MIKE'S MURDER   The Ladd Company/Warner Bros., 1984
BEST DEFENSE   Paramount, 1984
HOWARD THE DUCK   Universal, 1986
VIOLETS ARE BLUE   Columbia, 1986
AT CLOSE RANGE   Orion, 1986
TIN MEN   Buena Vista, 1987
FAR NORTH   Alive Films, 1988
TALK RADIO   Universal, 1988
WEEKEND AT BERNIE'S   20th Century Fox, 1989
COLD SASSY TREE (CTF)   Faye Dunaway and Don Ohlmeyer Productions, 1989
ROBOCOP 2   Orion, 1990

MARYA DELIA JAVIER

VALLEY GIRL   Atlantic Releasing Corporation, 1983

PHILIP M. JEFFERIES

Agent: Grace Lyons Management - Los Angeles, 213/655-5100

THIS PROPERTY IS CONDEMNED   Paramount, 1966
OH DAD, POOR DAD, MOMMA'S HUNG YOU IN THE CLOSET AND I'M FEELING SO SAD   Paramount, 1967
VALLEY OF THE DOLLS   20th Century Fox, 1967
SOMETIMES A GREAT NOTION   Universal, 1971
CONQUEST OF THE PLANET OF THE APES   20th Century Fox, 1972
THE COWBOYS   Warner Bros., 1972
TOM SAWYER ★   United Artists, 1973
WALKING TALL   Cinerama Releasing Corporation, 1973
ODE TO BILLY JOE   Warner Bros., 1976
ST. IVES   Warner Bros., 1976
THE ISLAND OF DR. MOREAU   American International, 1977
GREASE   Paramount, 1978
DAMIEN - OMEN II   20th Century Fox, 1978, w/Fred Harpman
WHEN TIME RAN OUT   Warner Bros., 1980
CAVEMAN   United Artists, 1981
FIRST MONDAY IN OCTOBER   Paramount, 1981
AN OFFICER AND A GENTLEMAN   Paramount, 1982
KISS ME GOODBYE   20th Century Fox, 1982
MASS APPEAL   Universal, 1984
THE MEAN SEASON   Orion, 1985

DAVID JENKINS

I'M DANCING AS FAST AS I CAN   Paramount, 1982
CAT ON A HOT TIN ROOF (CTF)   1984

GEORGE JENKINS*

IATSE Local 876

FUNNY LADY   Columbia, 1975
NIGHT MOVES   Warner Bros., 1975
ALL THE PRESIDENT'S MEN ★★   Warner Bros., 1976

COMES A HORSEMAN   United Artists, 1978
THE CHINA SYNDROME ★   Columbia, 1979
STARTING OVER   Paramount, 1979
THE POSTMAN ALWAYS RINGS TWICE
     Paramount, 1981
ROLLOVER   Orion/Warner Bros., 1981
SOPHIE'S CHOICE   Universal/AFD, 1982
THE DOLLMAKER (TF)   Finnegan Associates/IPC
     Films, Inc./Dollmaker Productions, 1984
DREAM LOVER   MGM/UA, 1986
ORPHANS   Lorimar, 1987
SEE YOU IN THE MORNING   Warner Bros., 1989
PRESUMED INNOCENT   Warner Bros., 1990

ROBERT JENKINSON
AMERICAN NINJA 2   Cannon, 1987, AD

JOSEPH R. JENNINGS*
IATSE Local 876
Agent: Grace Lyons Management - Los Angeles,
     213/655-5100

KANSAS CITY BOMBER   MGM, 1972
GOODNIGHT MY LOVE (TF)   ABC Circle Films, 1972
YESTERDAY'S CHILD (TF)   Paramount TV, 1977
ROOTS (MS) ☆   Wolper Productions, 1977
STAR TREK - THE MOTION PICTURE ★
     20th Century Fox, 1979, AD w/Leon Harris &
     John Vallone
SHOGUN (MS)   Paramount TV/NBC
     Entertainment, 1980
STAR TREK II: THE WRATH OF KHAN
     Paramount, 1982
THE DAY THE BUBBLE BURST (TF)   Tamara
     Productions/20th Century Fox TV/The Production
     Company, 1982
YELLOWBEARD   Orion, 1983
THE BOYS IN BLUE   MAM Ltd./Apollo Leisure
     Group, 1983
JOHNNY DANGEROUSLY   20th Century Fox, 1984
SPACE (MS)   Stonehenge Productions/
     Paramount TV, 1985
GEORGE WASHINGTON: THE FORGING OF A
     NATION (TF)   David Gerber Company, 1986
NORTH AND SOUTH, BOOK II (MS)   Wolper
     Productions/Robert A. Papazian Productions/
     Warner Bros. TV, 1986
MOVING TARGET (TF)   Lewis B. Chesler Productions/
     Bateman Company Productions/Finnegan-Pinchuk
     Company/MGM-UA TV, 1988
GUNSMOKE: THE LAST APACHE (TF)   CBS
     Entertainment Productions, 1990

GEORGE JENSEN*
IATSE Local 876

EVERYBODY'S ALL-AMERICAN   Warner Bros.,
     1988, AD
SOLAR CRISIS   Shochiku-Fuji, 1990

JOHN R. JENSEN*
IATSE Local 876

SPACEHUNTER: ADVENTURES IN THE
     FORBIDDEN ZONE   Columbia, 1983,
     AD w/Michael Neminsky & Brent Swift
NOBODY'S FOOL   Island Pictures, 1986, AD
DIE HARD   20th Century Fox, 1988, AD
A NIGHT IN THE LIFE OF JIMMY REARDON
     20th Century Fox, 1988, AD

PUNCHLINE   Columbia, 1988, AD
IN COUNTRY   Warner Bros., 1989, AD

DUSKO JERICEVIC
THE AVIATOR   MGM/UA, 1985
ARTHUR THE KING (TF)   Martin Poll Productions/
     Comworld Productions/Jadran Film, 1985

ROBERT I. JILLSON*
IATSE Local 876

THE GARBAGE PAIL KIDS MOVIE   Atlantic Releasing
     Corporation, 1987

ENRICO JOB
CAMORRA   Cannon, 1985

TOM H. JOHN*
IATSE Local 876

THANK GOT IT'S FRIDAY   Columbia, 1978
ZOOT SUIT   Universal, 1982
AMERICAN PLAYHOUSE THEATER: THE ROPE (CTF)
     Nederlander Television and Film Productions, 1989
MONEY, POWER, MURDER (TF)   SKids
     Productions, 1990
ORPHEUS DESCENDING (CTF)   Nederlander TV and
     Film Productions, 1990

BO JOHNSON
NOMADS   Atlantic Releasing Corporation, 1985, AD
DANGEROUSLY CLOSE   Cannon, 1986, AD
AVENGING FORCE   Cannon, 1986, AD
P.O.W. THE ESCAPE   Cannon, 1986, AD
SUMMER HEAT   Atlantic Releasing Corporation,
     1987, AD

DOUGLAS G. JOHNSON
TAKE DOWN   Buena Vista, 1979, AD
HARRY'S WAR   Taft International, 1981
SNOW KILL (CTF)   Wilshire Court Productions, 1990

MARTIN JOHNSON
HIDDEN AGENDA   Hemdale, 1990

ROBERT JOHNSON
SINGING THE BLUES IN RED   Angelika Films, 1988

STAN JOLLEY*
IATSE Local 876
Phone: 213/243-8652

DRUM   United Artists, 1976
THE SWARM   Warner Bros., 1978
AMERICATHON   United Artists, 1979
CADDYSHACK   Orion/Warner Bros., 1980
CATTLE ANNIE AND LITTLE BRITCHES
     Universal, 1981
TAPS   20th Century Fox, 1981, AD w/Alfred Sweeney
WITNESS ★   Paramount, 1985
THE GOOD MOTHER   Buena Vista, 1988

JOCELYN JOLY
MARIA CHAPDELAINE   The Movie Store, 1986, AD
TOBY McTEAGUE   Spectrafilm, 1986

Jo

CINEMATOGRAPHERS
PRODUCTION
DESIGNERS,
COSTUME
DESIGNERS AND
FILM EDITORS
GUIDE

P
R
O
D
U
C
T
I
O
N

D
E
S
I
G
N
E
R
S

Jo

CINEMATOGRAPHERS
PRODUCTION
DESIGNERS,
COSTUME
DESIGNERS AND
FILM EDITORS
GUIDE

P
R
O
D
U
C
T
I
O
N

D
E
S
I
G
N
E
R
S

BRYAN JONES
Agent: The Gersh Agency, Inc., Beverly Hills -
213/274-6611, New York - 212/997-1818

THIS IS SPINAL TAP   Embassy, 1984
HOUSE PARTY   New Line Cinema, 1990

K

CHESTER KACZENSKI
Agent: Sandra Marsh Management - Sherman Oaks,
818/905-6961

PINK MOTEL   New Image, 1982
ROADHOUSE 66   Atlantic Releasing
Corporation, 1984
THE KID WITH THE 200 I.Q. (TF)   Guillame-Margo
Productions/Zephyr Productions, 1983
TEEN WOLF   Atlantic Releasing Corporation,
1985, AD
THAT WAS THEN, THIS IS NOW   Paramount,
1985, AD
RADIOACTIVE DREAMS   DEG, 1986
EXTREMITIES   Atlantic Releasing Corporation, 1986
WEEKEND WARRIORS   The Movie Store, 1986
DOWN TWISTED   Cannon, 1987
THE QUICK AND THE DEAD (CTF)   HBO Pictures/
Joseph Cates Company, 1987
CIRCUS (TF)   1989
SAVE THE DOG (CTF)   1989
THIRD DEGREE BURN (CTF)   HBO Pictures, 1989
TIME FLIES WHEN YOU'RE ALIVE   Kings Road, 1989
PRANCER   Orion, 1989
THE GIRL WHO CAME BETWEEN THEM (TF)
Saban-Scherick Productions, 1990
TOY SOLDIERS   Tri-Star, 1991

WALDEMAR KALINOWSKI
Agent: The Doug Apatow Agency - Los Angeles,
213/202-6888

FINNEGAN BEGIN AGAIN (CTF)   HBO Premiere
Films/Zenith Productions/Jennie & Company Film
Productions, 1985
PLAYING FOR KEEPS   Universal, 1986
THE BOOST   Hemdale, 1988
DISORGANIZED CRIME   Buena Vista, 1989
INTERNAL AFFAIRS   Paramount, 1990
LIEBESTRAUM   1991

COREY KAPLAN
COMMANDO SQUAD   Trans World Entertainment,
1987, AD
COLD FEET   Avenue Pictures, 1989, AD

STEVEN KARATZAS†
SHADOW PLAY   New World, 1986, AD
PERMANENT RECORD   Paramount, 1988, AD
FORBIDDEN NIGHTS (TF)   Tristine Rainer
Productions, 1990
FOURTH STORY (CTF)   Viacom Pictures, 1991
FATAL EXPOSURE (CTF)   Wilshire Court
Productions, 1991

JOHN KASARDA *
SA 829
Agent: Smith Gosnell Nicholson & Associates -
Pacific Palisades, 213/459-0307

THE VERDICT   20th Century Fox, 1982, AD
DEATH OF A SALESMAN (TF) ☆☆   Roxbury and Punch
Productions, 1985, AD
THE PURPLE ROSE OF CAIRO   Orion, 1985, AD
HEARTBURN   Paramount, 1986, AD
THE GLASS MENAGERIE   Cineplex Odeon, 1987, AD
THE BELIEVERS   Orion, 1987, AD
MASQUERADE   MGM/UA, 1988

GREGORY KEEN
THE KISSING PLACE (CTF)   Cynthia Cherbak
Productions, 1990, AD

CHRISTIAN KELLY
FACE TO FACE (TF)   Robert Halmi Productions, 1990

ERROLL KELLY
THE FURTHER ADVENTURES OF TENNESSEE BUCK
Trans World Entertainment, 1988
THE IRON TRIANGLE   Scotti Bros., 1989

VICTOR KEMPSTER
AND GOD CREATED WOMAN   Vestron, 1988
LAST RITES   MGM/UA, 1988, AD
BORN ON THE FOURTH OF JULY   Universal, 1989, AD
DRIVING MISS DAISY ★   Warner Bros., 1989,
AD w/Richard L. Johnson

WILLIAM KENNEY*
IATSE Local 876
Agent: The Gersh Agency, Inc. - Beverly Hills,
213/274-6611
Address: 4074 Kraft Ave., Studio City, CA 91604,
818/985-9455

DIAMONDS ARE FOREVER   United Artists, 1971, AD
ATTACK ON TERROR: THE FBI VS. THE KU KLUX
KLAN (TF)   QM Productions, 1975
DRUM   United Artists, 1976, AD
CARRIE   United Artists, 1976, AD
BAKER'S HAWK   Doyt-Dayton, 1976
SWEET REVENGE   MGM/UA, 1976, AD
THE CHOIRBOYS   Universal, 1977
BORN AGAIN   Avco Embassy, 1978
UNCLE JOE SHANNON   United Artists, 1978
RAGING BULL   United Artists, 1978, AD
A CHANGE OF SEASONS   20th Century Fox, 1980
THE MOUNTAIN MEN   Columbia, 1980
BODY HEAT   The Ladd Company/Warner Bros., 1981
EDDIE MACON'S RUN   Universal, 1983
TOUGH ENOUGH   20th Century Fox, 1983
TANK   Universal, 1984
WINDY CITY   Warner Bros. 1984
ROBERT KENNEDY AND HIS TIMES (MS)   Chris-Rose
Productions/Columbia TV, 1985
RAMBO: FIRST BLOOD PART II   Tri-Star, 1985
ROCKY IV   MGM/UA, 1985
COBRA   Warner Bros., 1986
HARRY'S HONG KONG (TF)   Aaron Spelling
Productions, 1987
EXTREME PREJUDICE   Tri-Star, 1987
THE BIG TOWN   Columbia, 1987
RAMBO III   Tri-Star, 1988
LOCK-UP   Tri-Star, 1989
OSCAR   Buena Vista, 1991

BOB KENSINGER
SCENES FROM THE CLASS STRUGGLE IN
    BEVERLY HILLS   Cinecom, 1989, AD

ALICIA KEYWAN
YOUNGBLOOD   MGM/UA, 1986,
    AD w/Alta Louise Doyle
DEAD OF WINTER   MGM/UA, 1987, AD
SHORT CIRCUIT 2   Tri-Star, 1988, AD
STANLEY & IRIS   MGM/UA, 1990, AD
THE FRESHMAN   Tri-Star, 1990, AD w/Dan Davis

MARINA KIESER
FACE OF THE ENEMY   Tri-Culture Pictures, 1990

LILLY KILVERT
IATSE Local 876
Agent: Smith Gosnell Nicholson & Associates -
    Pacific Palisades, 213/459-0307

ALAMBRISTA!   Bobwin/Films Haus, 1977, AD
ROCKERS   New Yorker, 1979, AD
DEEP IN THE HEART   HANDGUN   Warner
    Bros., 1984, AD
THE LOVELESS   Atlantic Releasing Corporation, 1981
SMITHEREENS   New Line Cinema, 1982, AD
TOO SCARED TO SCREAM   The Movie Store, 1984
TO LIVE AND DIE IN L.A.   MGM/UA, 1985
THE SURE THING   Embassy, 1985
RUTHLESS PEOPLE   Buena Vista, 1986
SURRENDER   Warner Bros., 1987
I LOVE YOU TO DEATH   Tri-Star, 1990
WORTH WINNING   20th Century Fox, 1989

JOHN KING
THE MISSION   Warner Bros., 1986, AD
CRY FREEDOM   Universal, 1987, AD w/Norman
    Dorme & George Richardson

ROBB WILSON KING
Agent: Grace Lyons Management - Los Angeles,
    213/655-5100

LONGSHOT   GG Productions, 1981
SWAMP THING   Avco Embassy, 1982,
    w/David Nichols
FRIDAY THE 13TH PART 3   Paramount, 1982
LOSIN' IT   Embassy, 1983
THE OSTERMAN WEEKEND   20th Century Fox,
    1983, AD
THE MAN WHO WASN'T THERE   Paramount, 1983
SPECIAL BULLETIN (TF)   1983
THE SKY'S THE LIMIT (TF)   Palance-Levy
    Productions, 1984
THE NEW KIDS   Columbia, 1985
SAVAGE DAWN   MAG Enterprises/Gregory Earls
    Productions, 1985
THE HILLS HAVE EYES PART II   Castle Hill
    Productions, 1986
WHERE ARE THE CHILDREN?   Columbia, 1986
DREAMS OF GOLD: THE MEL FISHER STORY (TF)
    Inter Planetary Productions, 1986
IRON EAGLE   Tri-Star, 1986
A DIFFERENT AFFAIR (TF)   Rogers-Samuels
    Productions, 1987
BATES MOTEL (TVS)   1987
RETRIBUTION   United Film Distribution, 1987
IRON EAGLE II: THE BATTLE BEYOND THE FLAG
    Tri-Star, 1988

THE RETURN OF SWAMP THING   Lightyear
    Entertainment, 1989
HARD TO KILL   SEVEN YEAR STORM   Warner
    Bros., 1990
PUMP UP THE VOLUME   New Line Cinema, 1990
FOLLOW YOUR HEART (TF)   Force Ten
    Productions, 1990
OPPOSITES ATTRACT (TF)   Bar-Gene
    Productions, 1990
MARKED FOR DEATH   SCREWFACE   20th Century
    Fox, 1990

ROBERT KINOSHITA*
IATSE Local 876
Agent: The Miller Agency - Santa Clarita, 818/843-1511

THE BLACK SHEEP   United Artists, 1956
REBEL IN TOWN   1956
PHARAOH'S CURSE   1957
BOP GIRL   United Artists, 1957
ROCK ALL NIGHT   American International, 1957
TEENAGE DOLL   Allied Artists, 1957
CARNIVAL ROCK   Howco, 1957
THE VIKING WOMEN AND THE SEA SERPENT
    American International, 1957
TOKYO AFTER DARK   1959
THE NUN AND THE SERGEANT   1962
THE PRIVATE NAVY OF SGT. O'FARRELL
    United Artists, 1968
HELL'S BLOODY DEVILS   THE FAKERS
    Independent-International, 1970
FAREWELL TO MANZANAR (TF)   Korty Films/
    Universal TV, 1976
MAYDAY AT 40,000 FEET (TF)   Andrew J. Fenady
    Associates/Warner Bros. TV, 1976
RABBIT TEST   Avco Embassy, 1978, AD
THE MAN WITH BOGART'S FACE   20th Century
    Fox, 1980
THE GONG SHOW MOVIE   Unviersal, 1980
BELLE STAR (TF)   Entheos Unlimited Productions/
    Hanna-Barbera Productions, 1980
GOING APE!   Paramount, 1981, AD
GIRLS OF THE WHITE ORCHID   DEATH RIDE TO
    OSAKA (TF)   Hill-Mandelker Films, 1983
LOVELINES   Tri-Star, 1984

GEOFFREY KIRKLAND*
IATSE Local 876

MIDNIGHT EXPRESS   Columbia, 1978
BUGSY MALONE   Paramount, 1978
FAME   MGM/UA, 1980
SHOOT THE MOON   MGM/UA, 1982
THE RIGHT STUFF ★   The Ladd Company/Warner
    Bros., 1983
BIRDY   Tri-Star, 1984
LEONARD PART 6   Columbia, 1987
MISSISSIPPI BURNING   Orion, 1988, w/Philip Harrison
WILDFIRE   Zupnick Cinema Group, 1989
JOURNEY TO THE CENTER OF THE EARTH
    Cannon, 1989
COME SEE THE PARADISE   20th Century Fox, 1990

ROBERT P. KRACIK
LOVE OR MONEY   Hemdale, 1989

DOUGLAS KRANER
NO MERCY   Tri-Star, 1986, AD
DOMINICK AND EUGENE   Orion, 1988
WORKING GIRL   20th Century Fox, 1988, AD

Kr

CINEMATOGRAPHERS
PRODUCTION
DESIGNERS,
COSTUME
DESIGNERS AND
FILM EDITORS
GUIDE

P
R
O
D
U
C
T
I
O
N

D
E
S
I
G
N
E
R
S

Kr

CINEMATOGRAPHERS
PRODUCTION
DESIGNERS,
COSTUME
DESIGNERS AND
FILM EDITORS
GUIDE

P
R
O
D
U
C
T
I
O
N

D
E
S
I
G
N
E
R
S

LEAN ON ME   Warner Bros., 1989
UNCLE BUCK   Universal, 1989 (visual consultant)
SLEEPING WITH THE ENEMY   20th Century
   Fox, 1991

WOLF KROEGER
Agent: The Gersh Agency, Inc., Beverly Hills -
   213/274-6611, New York - 212/997-1818

SPLIT IMAGE   Orion, 1982
BREAKING POINT   20th Century Fox, 1976
IN PRAISE OF OLDER WOMEN   Avco Embassy,
   1978, AD
QUINTET   20th Century Fox, 1979, AD
POPEYE   Paramount, 1980
SPLIT IMAGE   Orion, 1982
FIRST BLOOD   Orion, 1982
STREAMERS   United Artists Classics, 1983
THE BAY BOY   Orion, 1984
LADYHAWKE   Warner Bros., 1985
YEAR OF THE DRAGON   MGM/UA, 1985
THE SICILIAN   20th Century Fox, 1987
CASUALTIES OF WAR   Columbia, 1989
WE'RE NO ANGELS   Paramount, 1989
LET IT RIDE   Paramount, 1990

NATASHA KROLL
ABSOLUTION   Trans World Entertainment, 1988

SANDY KYBARTAS
HELLO MARY LOU: PROM NIGHT II   Samuel
   Goldwyn Company, 1987

L

RANDALL LaBRY
BELIZAIRE THE CAJUN   Skouras Pictures, 1986

CHARLES LAGOLA
MANIAC COP 2   Movie House Sales Company,
   1990, w/Gene Abel
LITTLE NOISES   Monument Pictures, 1991

ROBERT LAING
TRAVELS WITH MY AUNT ★   MGM, 1972,
   AD w/Gil Parrondo
THE GREAT GATSBY   Paramount, 1974,
   AD w/Eugene Rudolf
NIGHT GAMES   Avco Embassy, 1980
GANDHI ★★   Columbia, 1982, Supv AD
HIGH ROAD TO CHINA   Warner Bros., 1983
THE FAR PAVILIONS (CMS)   Geoff Reeve &
   Associates/Goldcrest, 1984
ELLIS ISLAND (MS)   Pantheon Pictures/Telepictures
   Productions, 1984
THE DOCTOR AND THE DEVILS   20th Century
   Fox, 1985
THE NEVERENDING STORY II: THE NEXT CHAPTER
   Warner Bros., 1990, w/Goetz Weidner

GUY LaLONDE
CRAZY MOON   Miramax Films, 1987, AD

MICHAEL LAMONT
TOP SECRET!   Paramount, 1984, AD w/John Fenner
ALIENS ★   20th Century Fox, 1986, AD w/Ken Court,
   Bert Davey, Peter Lamont & Fred Hole

PETER LAMONT
Agent: Grace Lyons Management - Los Angeles,
   213/655-5100

THE SEVEN-PER CENT SOLUTION   Universal,
   1976, AD
THE SPY WHO LOVED ME ★   United Artists, 1977, AD
THE BOYS FROM BRAZIL   20th Century Fox, 1978, AD
FOR YOUR EYES ONLY   United Artists, 1981
OCTOPUSSY   MGM/UA, 1983
TOP SECRET!   Paramount, 1984
A VIEW TO A KILL   MGM/UA, 1985
ALIENS ★   20th Century Fox, 1986, AD w/Ken Court,
   Bert Davey, Michael Lamont & Fred Hole
THE LIVING DAYLIGHTS   MGM/UA, 1987
CONSUMING PASSIONS   Samuel Goldwyn
   Company, 1988
LICENCE TO KILL   MGM/UA, 1989
EVE OF DESTRUCTION   Orion, 1991
THE TAKING OF BEVERLY HILLS   Columbia, 1991

HARRY LANGE
THE EMPIRE STRIKES BACK ★   20th Century Fox,
   1980, AD w/Les Dilley & Alan Tompkins
THE GREAT MUPPET CAPER   Universal/AFD, 1981
THE DARK CRYSTAL   Universal/AFD, 1982
MONTY PYTHON'S THE MEANING OF LIFE
   Universal, 1983
HYPER SAPIEN   Taliafilm II, 1986

RANDY LAPIN
SHOCK 'EM DEAD   Academy Entertainment, 1991

PETER S. LARKIN
Agent: The Gersh Agency, Inc., Beverly Hills -
   213/274-6611, New York - 212/997-1818

NIGHTHAWKS   Universal, 1981
NEIGHBORS   Columbia, 1981
TOOTSIE   Columbia, 1982
REUBEN, REUBEN   20th Century Fox International
   Classics, 1983
THE LOST HONOR OF KATHRYN BECK (TF)   Open
   Road Productions, 1984
BERRY GORDY'S THE LAST DRAGON   Tri-Star, 1985
COMPROMISING POSITIONS   Paramount, 1985
POWER   20th Century Fox, 1986
THE SECRET OF MY SUCCESS   Universal, 1987,
   w/Edward Pisoni
THREE MEN AND A BABY   Buena Vista, 1987
LAST RITES   MGM/UA, 1988
EVERYBODY WINS   Orion, 1990
LIFE STINKS   MGM, 1991

TAMBI LARSEN
THE MOLLY MAGUIRES ★   Paramount, 1970
THE OUTLAW JOSEY WALES   Warner Bros., 1976
THE WHITE BUFFALO   United Artists, 1977
HEAVEN'S GATE ★   United Artists, 1980, AD

DARRELL LASS
THE WILD DUCK   Orion, 1983

JOHN LAWLESS
OVER THE BROOKLYN BRIDGE   Cannon, 1984

RICHARD J. LAWRENCE*
IATSE Local 876

FROM NOON TIL THREE   United Artists, 1976, AD
EXORCIST II: THE HERETIC   Warner Bros.,
   1977, AD
THE FURY   20th Century Fox, 1978, AD
MAGIC   20th Century Fox, 1978, AD
STRAIGHT TIME   Warner Bros., 1978, AD
THE LAST FLIGHT OF NOAH'S ARK   Buena Vista,
   1980, AD
MIDNIGHT MADNESS   Buena Vista, 1980,
   AD w/John B. Mansbridge
FORCE: FIVE   American Cinema, 1981, AD
THE RIGHT STUFF ★   The Ladd Company/Warner
   Bros., 1983, AD w/W. Stewart Campbell &
   Peter Romero
SOMETHING WICKED THIS WAY COMES   Buena
   Vista, 1983, AD w/John B. Mansbridge
AGAINST ALL ODDS   Columbia, 1984, AD
BLUE CITY   Paramount, 1986, AD
SPACECAMP   20th Century Fox, 1986,
   AD w/Leon Harris
FRIDAY THE 13th PART VII: THE NEW BLOOD
   Paramount, 1988

PETA LAWSON
THE EVERLASTING SECRET FAMILY   International
   Film Exchange, 1990, AD

KEN LEDSHAM
MOTHER LOVE-PARTS I-III (MS)   BBC TV
   Productions, 1990, w/Lawrence Williams

EUGENE LEE
MR. MIKE'S MONDO VIDEO   New Line Cinema,
   1979, w/Franne Lee
GILDA LIVE (FD)   Warner Bros., 1980
EASY MONEY   Orion, 1983
MR. NORTH   Samuel Goldwyn Company, 1988

STEVEN LEGLER*
IATSE Local 876
Agent: Sanford-Skouras & Gross - Los Angeles,
   213/208-2100

THE HOWLING   Avco Embassy, 1980
HELL NIGHT   Compass International, 1981
THE HOUSE WHERE DEATH LIVES   New World,
   1982, AD
CHOOSE ME   Island Alive/New Cinema, 1984
THE ZOO GANG   New World, 1985
TROUBLE IN MIND   Alive Films, 1985
WELCOME TO 18   American Distribution Group, 1986
MADE IN HEAVEN   Lorimar, 1987, AD
THE LAST INNOCENT MAN (CTF)   HBO Pictures/
   Maurice Singer Productions, 1987
THE MODERNS   Alive Films, 1988
LOVE AT LARGE   Orion, 1989
PAINT IT BLACK   Vestron, 1989
A RAGE IN HARLEM   Miramax, 1991

DAN LEIGH*
IATSE Local 876

CHINA GIRL   Vestron, 1987
STREET SMART   Cannon, 1987
HIDING OUT   DEG, 1987
MY LITTLE GIRL   Hendale, 1988
CROSSING DELANCEY   Warner Bros., 1988
LOVERBOY   Tri-Star, 1989
CAT CHASER   Vestron, 1990
MADHOUSE   Orion, 1990
RISING SON (CTF)   Sarabande Productions, 1990

JOHN LEIMANIS
CHAMELEONS (TF)   NBC Productions, 1990
GUESS WHO'S COMING FOR CHRISTMAS (TF)
   Corapeake Productions, 1990
SINS OF THE MOTHER (TF)   Corapeake
   Productions, 1991

MASSIMO LENTINI
QUEST FOR THE MIGHTY SWORD   RCA/Columbia
   Pictures Home Video, 1990, AD

JAMIE LEONARD
WETHERBY   MGM/UA Classics, 1985, AD
MONA LISA   Island Pictures, 1986
THE KITCHEN TOTO   Cannon, 1988
WE THINK THE WORLD OF YOU   Cinecom, 1988
LORD OF THE FLIES   Castle Rock Entertainment/
   Columbia, 1990

PHILLIP M. LEONARD
I COME IN PEACE   Triumph Releasing, 1990
NOT OF THIS WORLD (TF)   Barry & Enright
   Productions, 1991

JOHAN LeTENOUX
CORPORATE AFFAIRS   Concorde-New Horizons,
   1990, AD
THE RAIN KILLER   Concorde, 1990, AD

ADAM LEVENTHAL
DECEPTIONS   Republic Pictures, 1990
DEAD WOMEN IN LINGERIE   Monarch Home
   Video, 1990

MICHAEL LEVESQUE*
IATSE Local 876
Phone: 818/994-2207

CANNONBALL   New World, 1976, AD
BOBBI JO AND THE OUTLAW   American International,
   1976, AD
THE INCREDIBLE MELTING MAN   American Interna-
   tional, 1978, AD
BORDERLINE   AFD, 1980, AD
FOXES   United Artists, 1980, AD
BARBAROSA   Universal/AFD, 1982
PERMANENT RECORD   Paramount, 1988
PLAIN CLOTHES   Paramount, 1988
HOMER AND EDDIE   Cineplex Odeon, 1989
THE PACKAGE   Orion, 1989

MARINA LEVIKOVA
LIQUID SKY   Cinevista, 1983 (Costume Designer0

Le

CINEMATOGRAPHERS
PRODUCTION
DESIGNERS,
COSTUME
DESIGNERS AND
FILM EDITORS
GUIDE

P
R
O
D
U
C
T
I
O
N

D
E
S
I
G
N
E
R
S

Le

CINEMATOGRAPHERS
PRODUCTION
DESIGNERS,
COSTUME
DESIGNERS AND
FILM EDITORS
GUIDE

**P
R
O
D
U
C
T
I
O
N

D
E
S
I
G
N
E
R
S**

RICHARD B. LEWIS*
IATSE Local 876
Agent: Smith Gosnell Nicholson & Associates -
   Pacific Palisades, 213/459-0307
Phone: 213/661-8641

COACH OF THE YEAR (TF)   A. Shane
   Company, 1980
THE MARVA COLLINS STORY (TF)   NRW
   Features, 1981
MEMORIES NEVER DIE (TF)   Groverton Productions/
   Scholastic Productions/Universal TV, 1982
VOYAGERS (TVS)   1983
THE JERK, TOO (TF)   40 Share Productions/
   Universal TV, 1984
WHIZ KIDS (TVS)   1984
OTHERWORLD (TVS)   1984
TIME BOMB (TF)   Barry Weitz Films/Universal
   TV, 1984
AMAZING STORIES (TVS)   1985-86
MAX HEADROOM II (TVS)   1987
DEAR JOHN (TVS)   1988-89
COMING TO AMERICA   Paramount, 1988, AD
WHORE   Trimark, 1991

GEORGE LIDDLE
THE TIME GUARDIAN   Hemdale, 1987
A CRY IN THE DARK   Warner Bros., 1988,
   w/Wendy Dickson
WHICH WAY HOME (CTF)   McElroy & McElroy, 1991

DONALD LIGHT-HARRIS*
IATSE Local 876

MOVERS & SHAKERS   MGM/UA, 1985, AD
CAN'T BUY ME LOVE   Buena Vista, 1987
ALOHA SUMMER   Spectrafilm, 1988, AD
WORLD GONE WILD   Lorimar, 1988
THE COVER GIRL AND THE COP (TF)   Barry &
   Enright Productions, 1988
THE SEX TAPES (TF)   von Zerneck-Sertner, 1989
GORE VIDAL'S BILLY THE KID (TF)   von
   Zerneck-Sertner, 1989
MONTANA (CTF)   HBO Productions, 1990
TOO YOUNG TO DIE? (TF)   von Zerneck-Sertner
   Films, 1990
SHATTERED DREAMS (TF)   Roger Gimbel
   Productions, 1990
A QUIET LITTLE NEIGHBORHOOD, A PERFECT
   LITTLE MURDER (TF)   Neal and Gary
   Productions, 1990
LOVE, LIES AND MURDER-PARTS I & II (TF)
   Republic Pictures, 1991

STEPHEN J. LINEWEAVER
Agent: The Gersh Agency, Inc., Beverly Hills -
   213/274-6611, New York - 212/997-1818

ROSALIE GOES SHOPPING   1990
SINGLES   Warner Bros., 1991

BARBARA LING
Agent: The Gersh Agency, Inc., Beverly Hills -
   213/274-6611, New York - 212/997-1818

TRUE STORIES   Warner Bros., 1986
HEAVEN (FD)   Island Pictures, 1987, AD
MAKING MR. RIGHT   Orion, 1987
LESS THAN ZERO   20th Century Fox, 1987
CHECKING OUT   Warner Bros., 1989

MEN DON'T LEAVE   Warner Bros., 1990
DECORATION DAY (TF)   Marion Rees Associates, 1990
THE DOORS   Tri-Star, 1991

SYDNEY Z. LITWACK*
IATSE Local 876
Agent: The Miller Agency - Santa Clarita, 818/843-7335

WATERMELON MAN   Columbia, 1970, AD
BUCK AND THE PREACHER   Columbia, 1972, AD
WHITE LINE FEVER   Columbia, 1975, AD
LADY OF THE HOUSE (TF)   Metromedia
   Productions, 1978
THE WINDS OF KITTY HAWK (TF)   Charles Fries
   Productions, 1978
SHE'S DRESSED TO KILL (TF)   Grant-Case-McGrath
   Enterprises/Barry Weitz Associates, 1979
MIND OVER MURDER (TF)   Paramount, 1979
GOLDENGIRL   Avco Embassy, 1979, AD
IF THINGS WERE DIFFERENT (TF)   Bob Banner
   Associates, 1980
MARILYN: THE UNTOLD STORY (TF)   Lawrence
   Schiller Productions, 1980
WHOSE LIFE IS IT ANYWAY?   MGM/United Artists,
   1981, AD
BLUE THUNDER   Columbia, 1983, AD
BLOOD FEUD (TF)   20th Century Fox TV/Glickman-
   Selznick Productions, 1983
PLACES IN THE HEART   Tri-Star, 1984, AD
SOMETHING IN COMMON (TF)   New World TV/Freyda
   Rothstein Productions/Litke-Grossbart Productions,
   1986, AD
JUST BETWEEN FRIENDS   Orion, 1986
PLEASURES (TF)   Catalina Production Group/
   Columbia TV, 1986
BRONX ZOO (TVS)   1988

JOHN J. LLOYD*
IATSE Local 876
Agent: The Gersh Agency, Inc., Beverly Hills -
   213/274-6611, New York - 212/997-1818

NATIONAL LAMPOON'S ANIMAL HOUSE
   Universal, 1978, AD
THE PRISONER OF ZENDA   Universal, 1979, AD
THE BLUES BROTHERS   Universal, 1980
RAGGEDY MAN   Universal, 1981
THE THING   Universal, 1982
D.C. CAB   Universal, 1983
CRACKERS   Universal, 1984
THE RIVER RAT   Paramount, 1984
MAXIE   Orion, 1985
CLUE   Paramount, 1985
INTO THE NIGHT   Universal, 1985
SPIES LIKE US   Warner Bros., 1985, AD
BIG TROUBLE IN LITTLE CHINA   20th Century
   Fox, 1986
CRITICAL CONDITION   Paramount, 1987
JAWS THE REVENGE   Universal, 1987
THE NAKED GUN: FROM THE FILES OF POLICE
   SQUAD!   Paramount, 1988
CRAZY PEOPLE   Paramount, 1990
BRENDA STARR   New World, 1991

JOHN ROBERT LLOYD
MIDNIGHT COWBOY   United Artists, 1969
THE DAY OF THE LOCUST   Paramount, 1975, AD
SWASHBUCKLER   Unviersal, 1976
THIEVES   Paramount, 1977
THE BELL JAR   Avco Embassy, 1979

ADRIANNE LOBEL
FIVE CORNERS   Cineplex Odeon, 1987

JOHN LOGGIA
PARTING GLANCES   Cinecom, 1986

DANIEL LOMINO*
IATSE Local 876
Agent: Creative Technique - Toronto, Ontario, Canada,
    416/466-4173

CLOSE ENCOUNTERS OF THE THIRD KIND ★
    Columbia, 1977, w/Joe Alves
YOUNG JOE, THE FORGOTTEN KENNEDY (TF)
    ABC Circle Films, 1977
SHARON: PORTRAIT OF A MISTRESS (TF)
    Moonlight Productions/Paramount TV, 1977
THE GHOST OF FLIGHT 401 (TF)   Paramount
    TV, 1978
GETTING MARRIED (TF)   Paramount TV, 1978
THE CLONE MASTER (TF)   Mel Ferber Productions/
    Paramount TV, 1978
PORTRAIT OF A STRIPPER (TF)   Moonlight
    Productions/Filmways, 1979
BATTERED (TF)   Henry Jaffe Enterprises, 1979
FREEDOM ROAD (TF)   Zev Braun Productions/
    Freedom Road Films, 1979
BABY COMES HOME (TF)   Alan Landsburg
    Productions, 1979
MAKE ME AN OFFER (TF)   ABC Circle Films, 1980
FUN AND GAMES (TF)   Kanin-Gallo Productions/
    Warner Bros. TV, 1980
UNDERGROUND ACES   Filmways, 1981
CHU CHU AND THE PHILLY FLASH   20th Century
    Fox, 1981
BUDDY BUDDY   MGM/United Artists, 1981
FAST TIMES AT RIDGEMONT HIGH
    Universal, 1982
CHRISTINE   Columbia, 1983
LOVE IS FOREVER *COMEBACK* (TF)   Michael
    Landon-Hal Bartlett Films/NBC-TV/20th Century
    Fox TV, 1983
CONCRETE BEAT (TF)   Picturemaker Productions/
    Viacom, 1984
STARMAN   Columbia, 1984
DEADLY FRIEND   Warner Bros., 1986
STEWARDESS SCHOOL   Columbia, 1986
BACKFIRE   New Century/Vista, 1987
PRINCE OF DARKNESS   Universal, 1987
CHILD'S PLAY   MGM/UA, 1988
THEY LIVE   Universal, 1988,
    w/William J. Durrell Jr.
SIDE OUT   Tri-Star, 1990

SUSAN LONGMIRE
TICKET TO HEAVEN   UA Classics, 1981

SANTO LOQUASTO
Agent: Roberta Kent, STE Representation -
    Beverly Hills, 213/550-3982

RANCHO DELUXE   United Artists, 1975
STARDUST MEMORIES   United Artists, 1980
THE FAN   Paramount, 1981
SO FINE   Warner Bros., 1981
FALLING IN LOVE   Paramount, 1984
DESPERATELY SEEKING SUSAN   Orion, 1985
RADIO DAYS ★   Orion, 1987

SEPTEMBER   Orion, 1987
BRIGHT LIGHTS, BIG CITY   MGM/UA, 1988
BIG   20th Century Fox, 1988
ANOTHER WOMAN   Orion, 1988
NEW YORK STORIES ("Oedipus Wrecks")   Buena
    Vista, 1989
CRIMES AND MISDEMEANORS   Orion, 1989
SHE-DEVIL   Orion, 1989
ALICE   Orion, 1990

VANCE LORENZINI
GRAFFITI BRIDGE   Paisley Park/Warner
    Bros., 1990

EUGENE LOURIE
BURNT OFFERINGS   United Artists, 1976
AN ENEMY OF THE PEOPLE   Warner Bros., 1978
BRONCO BILLY   Warner Bros., 1980, AD

ROBERT LOVY
CIRCUITRY MAN   Skouras, 1990

DAVID LUBIN
HOOSIERS   Orion, 1986, AD
BULL DURHAM   Orion, 1988, AD
DISORGANIZED CRIME   Buena Vista, 1989, AD

JOHN LUCAS
DANNY BOY   Triumph, 1984
THE LOVE SHE SOUGHT (TF)   Arnold
    Productions, 1990

TONI LUDI
THE BEAR   Tri-Star, 1989

GERRY LUHMAN
AMONG THE CINDERS   New World, 1985

ALEJANDRO LUNA
GABY - A TRUE STORY   Tri-Star, 1987, AD

ROBERT LUTHARDT
LIPSTICK   Paramount, 1976
FIRST LOVE   Paramount, 1977
9/30/55   Universal, 1977, AD
THE CHEAP DETECTIVE   Columbia, 1978
CASEY'S SHADOW   Columbia, 1978

Lu

CINEMATOGRAPHERS
PRODUCTION
DESIGNERS,
COSTUME
DESIGNERS AND
FILM EDITORS
GUIDE

P
R
O
D
U
C
T
I
O
N

D
E
S
I
G
N
E
R
S

Ma

CINEMATOGRAPHERS
PRODUCTION
DESIGNERS,
COSTUME
DESIGNERS AND
FILM EDITORS
GUIDE

P
R
O
D
U
C
T
I
O
N

D
E
S
I
G
N
E
R
S

M

RICHARD MACDONALD*
IATSE Local 876
Agent: The Gersh Agency, Inc. - Beverly Hills,
213/274-6611

EVA   Times, 1962
THE SERVANT   Landau, 1964
KING AND COUNTRY   Allied Artists, 1965
MODESTY BLAISE   20th Century Fox, 1966
FAR FROM THE MADDING CROWD   MGM, 1967
SECRET CEREMONY   Universal, 1968
BOOM!   Universal, 1968
A SEVERED HEAD   Columbia, 1971
THE ASSASSINATION OF TROTSKY   Cinerama
   Releasing Corporation, 1972
JESUS CHRIST SUPERSTAR   Universal, 1973
GALILEO   American Film Theatre, 1975
THE ROMANTIC ENGLISHWOMAN   New
   World, 1975
THE DAY OF THE LOCUST   Paramount, 1975
MARATHON MAN   Paramount, 1976
EXORCIST II: THE HERETIC   Warner Bros., 1977
F.I.S.T.   United Artists, 1978
THE ROSE   20th Century Fox, 1979
...AND JUSTICE FOR ALL   Columbia, 1979
ALTERED STATES   Warner Bros., 1980
CANNERY ROW   MGM/UA, 1982
SOMETHING WICKED THIS WAY COMES   Buena
   Vista, 1983
SUPERGIRL   Warner Bros., 1984
ELECTRIC DREAMS   MGM/UA, 1984
TEACHERS   MGM/UA, 1984
PLENTY   20th Century Fox, 1985
SPACECAMP   20th Century Fox, 1986
COMING TO AMERICA   Paramount, 1988
THE RUSSIA HOUSE   MGM/UA, 1990

WOODS MacINTOSH
THE FIRST DEADLY SIN   Filmways, 1980
ONE TRICK PONY   Warner Bros., 1980,
   AD w/David Mitchell
THE WORLD ACCORDING TO GARP   Warner Bros.,
   1982, AD
JAWS 3-D   Universal, 1983
REMO WILLIAMS: THE ADVENTURE BEGINS
   Orion, 1985, AD
OFF BEAT   Buena Vista, 1986
MURDER IN BLACK AND WHITE (TF)   Titus
   Productions, 1990

ROSS MAJOR
HEATWAVE   New Line Cinema, 1983
HOWLING III   Square Pictures, 1987
THE HIJACKING OF THE ACHILLE LAURO (TF)
   Tamara Asseyec Productions/Spectacor Films/
   New World Television, 1989
QUIGLEY DOWN UNDER   Pathe Entertainment/
   MGM/UA, 1990

WILLIAM MALLEY*
IATSE Local 876
Agent: Smith Gosnell Nicholson & Associates -
   Pacific Palisades, 213/459-0307

PRIME CUT   National General, 1972
THE EXORCIST ★   Warner Bros., 1973
HUCKLEBERRY FINN   United Artists, 1974
THE RED BADGE OF COURAGE (TF)   20th Century
   Fox TV, 1974
THE GREAT ICE RIP-OFF (TF)   ABC Circle Films, 1974
PRAY FOR THE WILDCATS (TF)   ABC Circle
   Films, 1974
ALEX & THE GYPSY   20th Century Fox, 1976
GRIFFIN AND PHOENIX (TF)   ABC Circle Films, 1976
CITIZEN'S BAND   Paramount, 1977
THE FURY   20th Century Fox, 1978
THE NINTH CONFIGURATION   Warner Bros., 1980,
   w/J. Dennis Washington
DEFIANCE   American International, 1980
THE HOUSE OF GOD   United Artists, 1981
MOMMIE DEAREST   Paramount, 1981
WORLD WAR III (TF)   Finnegan Associates/David
   Greene Productions, 1982
THE STAR CHAMBER   20th Century Fox, 1983
DEAL OF THE CENTURY   Warner Bros., 1983
SOMETHING ABOUT AMELIA (TF)   Leonard Goldberg
   Productions, 1984
PROTOCOL   Warner Bros., 1984
VISION QUEST   Warner Bros., 1985
UFORIA   Universal, 1985
ALFRED HITCHCOCK PRESENTS (TVS)   1986
WALK LIKE A MAN   MGM/UA, 1987
BIG SHOTS   20th Century Fox, 1987
MARGARET BOURKE-WHITE (TF)   1989
COMMON GROUND-PARTS I & II (TF)   Daniel H. Blatt
   Productions, 1990
DARK AVENGER (TF)   Columbia Pictures
   Television, 1990
THE WHEREABOUTS OF JENNY (TF)   Katie Face
   Productions, 1991

MICHAEL MANAN
CURIOSITY KILLS (CTF)   Dutch Productions, 1990

MATT MANIA
AMERICAN BORN   PM Home Video, 1990

JOHN B. MANSBRIDGE*
IATSE Local 876
Agent: Smith Gosnell Nicholson & Associates -
   Pacific Palisades, 213/459-0307

THE LOVE BUG   Buena Vista, 1969
BEDKNOBS AND BROOMSTICKS ★   Buena Vista, 1971
DELIVERANCE   Warner Bros., 1972
THE ISLAND AT THE TOP OF THE WORLD ★   Buena
   Vista, 1974, AD w/others
FREAKY FRIDAY   Buena Vista, 1976, AD
TREASURE OF MATECUMBE   Buena Vista, 1976, AD
NO DEPOSIT, NO RETURN   Buena Vista, 1976,
   AD w/Jack Senter
THE SHAGGY D.A.   Buena Vista, 1976,
   AD w/Perry Ferguson
HERBIE GOES TO MONTE CARLO   Buena Vista,
   1977, AD w/Perry Ferguson
PETE'S DRAGON   Buena Vista, 1977,
   AD w/Jack Martin Smith

RETURN FROM WITCH MOUNTAIN   Buena Vista,
    1978, AD w/Jack Senter
HOT LEAD AND COLD FEET   Buena Vista, 1978,
    AD w/Frank T. Smith
THE NORTH AVENUE IRREGULARS   Buena Vista,
    1979, AD w/Jack Collis
HERBIE GOES BANANAS   Buena Vista, 1980,
    AD w/Rodger Maus
THE LAST FLIGHT OF NOAH'S ARK   Buena Vista,
    1980, AD
MIDNIGHT MADNESS   Buena Vista, 1980,
    AD w/Richard Lawrence
THE DEVIL AND MAX DEVLIN   Buena Vista, 1981,
    w/Leon R. Harris
AMY   Buena Vista, 1981, w/Mark Mansbridge
TEX   Buena Vista, 1982, AD
TRON   Buena Vista, 1982, AD w/Al Roberts
TRENCHCOAT   Buena Vista, 1983, AD
SOMETHING WICKED THIS WAY COMES   Buena
    Vista, 1983, AD w/Richard J. Lawrence
SPLASH   Buena Vista, 1984, AD
COUNTRY   Buena Vista, 1984, AD
BABY - SECRET OF THE LOST LEGEND   Buena
    Vista, 1985
TWILIGHT ZONE (TVS)   1986
THE MAN WHO FELL TO EARTH (TF)   David
    Gerber Productions/MGM TV, 1987
BEAUTY AND THE BEAST (TVS) ☆☆   1988
STONE COLD   Columbia Pictures, 1991

MARK MANSBRIDGE*
IATSE Local 876

SMOKEY AND THE BANDIT   Universal, 1977, AD
AMY   Buena Vista, 1981, AD w/John B. Mansbridge
THE MAN WITH TWO BRAINS   Warner Bros.,
    1983, AD
8 MILLION WAYS TO DIE   Tri-Star, 1986, AD
THE WITCHES OF EASTWICK   Warner Bros.,
    1987, AD
SAY ANYTHING   20th Century Fox, 1989
DREAM BREAKERS (TF)   CBS Entertainment, 1989
THE WAR OF THE ROSES   20th Century Fox,
    1989, AD
GHOST   Paramount, 1990, AD

ALAN MANZER
THE FOURTH WAR   New Age Releasing, 1990

STEPHEN MARSH*
IATSE Local 876
Agent: Sanford-Skouras & Gross - Los Angeles,
    213/208-2100

UP THE CREEK   Orion, 1983, AD
ANGEL   New World, 1984, AD
CRIMES OF PASSION   New World, 1984, AD
AVENGING ANGEL   New World, 1985, AD
RUNAWAY TRAIN   Cannon, 1985
NATIVE SON   Cinecom International, 1985
UNDER SIEGE (TF)   Ohlmeyer Communications
    Company/Telepicture Productions, 1986
CRIMES OF THE HEART   DEG, 1986
SHY PEOPLE   Cannon, 1987
THE SEVENTH SIGN   Tri-Star, 1988
BIG TOP PEE-WEE   Paramount, 1988
NATIONAL LAMPOON'S CHRISTMAS VACATION
    Warner Bros., 1989

TERENCE MARSH*
IATSE Local 876, ACTT
Agent: Sandra Marsh Management - Sherman Oaks,
    818/905-6961

DR. ZHIVAGO ★   MGM, 1965, AD
A MAN FOR ALL SEASONS   Columbia, 1966
OLIVER! ★★   Columbia, 1968, AD
THE LOOKING GLASS WAR   Columbia, 1970
PERFECT FRIDAY   Chevron, 1970
SCROOGE ★   National General, 1970
MARY, QUEEN OF SCOTS ★   Universal, 1971
A TOUCH OF CLASS   Embassy, 1973
THE MACKINTOSH MAN   Warner Bros., 1973
THE GLASS MENAGERIE (TF)   Talent
    Associates, 1973
JUGGERNAUT   United Artists, 1974
THE ADVENTURE OF SHERLOCK HOLMES' SMARTER
    BROTHER   20th Century Fox, 1975
ROYAL FLASH   20th Century Fox, 1976
A BRIDGE TOO FAR   United Artists, 1977
THE WORLD'S GREATEST LOVER   20th Century
    Fox, 1977
MAGIC   20th Century Fox, 1978
THE FRISCO KID   Warner Bros., 1979
ABSENCE OF MALICE   Columbia, 1981
SPHINX   Orion/Warner Bros., 1981
TO BE OR NOT TO BE   20th Century Fox, 1983
HAUNTED HONEYMOON   Orion, 1986
SPACEBALLS   MGM/UA, 1987
BERT RIGBY, YOU'RE A FOOL   Warner Bros., 1989
THE HUNT FOR RED OCTOBER   Paramount, 1990
HAVANA   Universal, 1990

KERRY MARSHALL
DAUGHTERS OF THE DUST   American
    Playhouse, 1991

BLAIR MARTIN
STEEL & LACE   Fries Distribution, 1990

JANE MARTIN
EXPERIENCE PREFERRED BUT NOT ESSENTIAL
    Samuel Goldwyn Company, 1983

JACK MARTY
OUTLAW BLUES   Warner Bros., 1977, AD
DEADLY BLESSING   United Artists, 1981
SPLIT IMAGE   Orion, 1982, AD
SILENT RAGE   Columbia, 1982, AD
KILLING IN A SMALL TOWN (TF)   The IndieProd
    Company, 1990

ANTHONY (TONY) MASTERS*
IATSE Local 876

LAWRENCE OF ARABIA   Columbia, 1962
2001: A SPACE ODYSSEY ★   MGM, 1968
PAPILLON   Allied Artists, 1973
BUFFALO BILL AND THE INDIANS   United
    Artists, 1976
THE DEEP   Columbia, 1977
DUNE   Universal, 1984
TAI-PAN   DEG, 1986
THE CLAN OF THE CAVE BEAR   Warner
    Bros., 1986
RENT-A-COP   Kings Road, 1988

CINEMATOGRAPHERS
PRODUCTION
DESIGNERS,
COSTUME
DESIGNERS AND
FILM EDITORS
GUIDE

**P
R
O
D
U
C
T
I
O
N

D
E
S
I
G
N
E
R
S**

Ma

CINEMATOGRAPHERS
PRODUCTION
DESIGNERS,
COSTUME
DESIGNERS AND
FILM EDITORS
GUIDE

P
R
O
D
U
C
T
I
O
N

D
E
S
I
G
N
E
R
S

WILLIAM F. MATTHEWS*
IATSE Local 876
Agent: Smith Gosnell Nicholson & Associates - Pacific Palisades, 213/459-0307

THE KARATE KID   Columbia, 1984, AD
CLUB PARADISE   Warner Bros., 1986
THE KARATE KID PART II   Columbia, 1986, AD
HARRY AND THE HENDERSONS   Universal, 1987, AD
HAPPY NEW YEAR   Columbia, 1987, AD
INNERSPACE   Warner Bros., 1987, AD
THREE O'CLOCK HIGH   Universal, 1987
HOT TO TROT   Warner Bros., 1988 , AD
CADDYSHACK II   Warner Bros., 1988, AD
THE KARATE KID PART III   Columbia, 1989
GROSS ANATOMY   Buena Vista, 1989
THE MARRYING MAN   Buena Vista, 1991

JIRI MATOLIN
THE RAGGEDY RAWNEY   Island Pictures, 1989

RODGER MAUS*
IATSE Local 876
Agent: Paul Gerard Agency - Newport Beach, 714/644-7950

10   Orion/Warner Bros., 1979
HERBIE GOES BANANAS   Buena Vista, 1980, AD w/John B. Mansbridge
S.O.B.   Paramount, 1981
VICTOR/VICTORIA ★   MGM/United Artists, 1982
THE MAN WHO LOVED WOMEN   Columbia, 1983
TRENCHCOAT   Buena Vista, 1983
THE BUDDY SYSTEM   20th Century Fox, 1984
MICKI & MAUDE   Columbia, 1984
A FINE MESS   Columbia, 1986
BLIND DATE   Tri-Star, 1987
SUNSET   Tri-Star, 1988
SPELLBINDER   MGM/United Artists, 1988
SKIN DEEP   20th Century Fox, 1989
FIRE! TRAPPED ON THE 37TH FLOOR (TF) Papazian-Hirsch Productions, 1991
SWITCH   Warner Bros., 1991

YVAN MAUSSION
3 MEN AND A CRADLE   Samuel Goldwyn Company, 1986

LEONARD MAZZOLA
I'M DANGEROUS TONIGHT (CTF)   BBK Productions, 1990

JACK McADAM*
IATSE Local 876

DOIN' TIME   The Ladd Company/Warner Bros., 1984
BULLIES   Universal, 1986

WILLIAM McALLISTER*
IATSE Local 876
Agent: The Gersh Agency, Inc., Beverly Hills - 213/274-6611, New York - 212/997-1818

MADAME X (TF)   Levenback-Riche Productions/ Universal TV, 1981
THE PRINCESS AND THE CABBIE (TF)   Freyda Rothstein Productions/Time-Life Productions, 1981

THE FACTS OF LIFE GOES TO PARIS (TF) Embassy, 1982
WILL THERE REALLY BE A MORNING? (TF) Orion, 1983
SQUARE PEGS (TVS)   1983
MIAMI VICE (TVS)   1984
BEER   Orion, 1985
BRIDGE ACROSS TIME (TF)   Fries Entertainment, 1985
CRIME OF INNOCENCE (TF)   Ohlmeyer Communications Company, 1985
WHO FRAMED ROGER RABBIT   Buena Vista, 1988, AD

ANDREW McALPINE
Agent: Sandra Marsh Management - Sherman Oaks, 818/905-6961

SID & NANCY   Samuel Goldwyn Company, 1986
STRAIGHT TO HELL   Island Pictures, 1987
ARIA   RCA VP/Virgion Vision, 1987, Bruce Beresford & Charles Sturridge Segments
STORMY MONDAY   Atlantic Releasing Corporation, 1988
HIGH SEASON   Hemdale, 1988
FOR QUEEN AND COUNTRY   Atlantic Releasing Corporation, 1989
SLIPSTREAM   Entertainment Film, 1989
THE RACHEL PAPERS   MGM/UA, 1989

BRIAN McCABE
DANGER ZONE III: STEEL HORSE WAR   Danger Zone Company, 1990, AD
LAST CALL   Prism Entertainment, 1990

STEPHEN McCABE
MY DINNER WITH ANDRE   New Yorker, 1981, AD
MIXED BLOOD   Sara Films, 1984, AD
FOREVER, LULU   Tri-Star, 1987, AD
CALL ME   Vestron, 1988
SPIKE OF BENSONHURST   Film Dallas, 1988
VOODOO DAWN   Academy Entertainment, 1990

DANIEL McCAULEY
UP THE CREEK   Orion, 1984

PEG McCLELLAN
TEEN WOLF, TOO   Atlantic Releasing Corporation, 1987, AD

HILTON McCONNICO
DIVA   United Artists Classics, 1982
THE MOON IN THE GUTTER   Triumph/Columbia, 1983
UNTIL SEPTEMBER   MGM/UA, 1984

LESLIE McDONALD
THE GRIFTERS   Miramax Films, 1990

RODNEY McDONALD
CHOPPER CHICKS IN ZOMBIE TOWN   Troma, 1991

JEANNE McDONNELL
LIANNA   United Artists Classics, 1983, AD

RICHARD McGUIRE
SUMMER CAMP NIGHTMARE   Concorde, 1987
STEELE JUSTICE   Atlantic Releasing Corporation, 1987

STEWART McGUIRE
STOLEN: ONE HUSBAND (TF)

RITA McGURN
GOSPEL ACCORDING TO VIC   Skouras
   Pictures, 1987

ANDY McLEOD
SWIMMING TO CAMBODIA   Cinecom, 1987

MARJORIE STONE McSHIRLEY*
IATSE Local 876

PEE-WEE'S BIG ADVENTURE   Warner Bros.,
   1985, AD
BACK TO SCHOOL   Orion, 1986, AD
THREE FUGITIVES   Buena Vista, 1989,
   AD w/Rick Carter
BACK TO THE FUTURE II   Universal, 1989, AD
BACK TO THE FUTURE III   Universal, 1990,
   AD w/Jim Teegarden

JOHN MEIGHEN
THE HOTEL NEW HAMPSHIRE   Orion, 1984, AD
WILD THING   Atlantic Releasing Corporation, 1987

GILBERT MERCIER
INITIATION: SILENT NIGHT, DEADLY NIGHT 4
   Live Home Video, 1990

PATRICE MERCIER
A SUNDAY IN THE COUNTRY   MGM/UA
   Classics, 1984
SINCERELY CHARLOTTE   New Line Cinema, 1986
WAITING FOR THE MOON   Skouras Pictures, 1987

MICHAEL MERRITT
HOUSE OF GAMES   Orion, 1987
THINGS CHANGE   Columbia, 1988
A MOTHER'S COURAGE: THE MARY THOMAS
   STORY (TF)   Interscope Communications,
   1990, AD
HOWARD BEACH: MAKING A CASE FOR
   MURDER (TF)   Patchett-Kaufman Entertainment
   Productions, 1990, AD
HOMICIDE   Triumph, 1991

HAROLD MICHELSON*
IATSE Local 876

PRETTY POISON   20th Century Fox, 1968, AD
JOHNNY GOT HIS GUN   1971, AD
TWO PEOPLE   Universal, 1973, AD
MAME   Warner Bros., 1974, AD
STAR TREK - THE MOTION PICTURE ★
   Paramount, 1979
FATSO   20th Century Fox, 1980, AD
CAN'T STOP THE MUSIC   AFD, 1980, AD
HISTORY OF THE WORLD, PART 1   20th Century
   Fox, 1981, AD
MOMMIE DEAREST   Paramount, 1981, AD
TERMS OF ENDEARMENT ★   Paramount, 1983, AD
SPACEBALLS   MGM/UA, 1987, AD
PLANES, TRAINS AND AUTOMOBILES   Paramount,
   1987, AD
MURDER BY MOONLIGHT (TF)   Tamara Asseyev
   Productions, 1989, Supv AD
DICK TRACY ★   Buena Vista, 1990, AD

MALCOLM MIDDLETON
HANOVER STREET   Columbia, 1979,
   AD w/Robert Cartwright
SILVER DREAM RACER   Almi Cinema 5, 1980, AD
OUTLAND   The Ladd Company/Warner Bros., 1981, AD
THE SENDER   Paramount, 1982
THE RAZOR'S EDGE   Columbia, 1984, AD
SHEENA   Columbia, 1984, AD
WHITE NIGHTS   Columbia, 1985, AD
THE TWO MRS. GRENVILLES (TF) ☆☆
   Lorimar-Telepictures, 1987, AD
THE OLD MAN AND THE SEA (TF)   Storke
   Enterprises, 1990
DANIELLE STEEL'S KALEIDOSCOPE (TF)   The Cramer
   Company, 1990

DAVID BRIAN MILLER
976-EVIL   New Line Cinema, 1989
SUNDOWN: THE VAMPIRE IN RETREAT
   Vestron, 1989
FAR OUT MAN!   New Line Pictures, 1990

LAWRENCE MILLER*
IATSE Local 876, SA Local 829
Agent: Smith Gosnell Nicholson & Associates -
   Pacific Palisades, 213/459-0307
Address: 2257 Chelan Drive, Los Angeles, CA 90068,
   213/850-7678 or 212/247-1989

THE JILTING OF GRANNY WEATHERALL (TF)
   Learning in Focus/American Short Story, 1980
THE ELECTRIC GRANDMOTHER (TF)   Highgate
   Pictures, 1982
THE KING OF COMEDY   20th Century Fox, 1983,
   AD w/Edward Pisoni
THE FLAMINGO KID   20th Century Fox, 1984
COURAGE (TF)   Highgate Pictures/New World TV, 1986
DESERT BLOOM   Columbia, 1986, AD
OVERBOARD   MGM/UA, 1987, Visual Consultant
CONSPIRACY: TRIAL OF THE CHICAGO 8 (CTF)
   Jeremy Kagan Productions/Inter Planetary
   Productions, 1987
TRUE BELIEVER   Columbia, 1989
L.A. STORY   Carolco/Tri-Star, 1991

STEVE MILLER
RAPPIN'   Cannon, 1985
PLAYING FOR KEEPS   Universal, 1986, AD

MILO
STAND AND DELIVER   Warner Bros., 1988, AD
TALK RADIO   Universal, 1988

MICHELLE MINCH
Address: 1921 North Avenue 66, Los Angeles, CA 90042,
   213/258-2255

TWO MOON JUNCTION   Lorimar, 1988
KILL ME AGAIN   MGM/UA, 1989
SOMETHING IS WAITING   Wildstreet Productions, 1990
DADDY'S DYIN'...WHO'S GOT THE WILL?
   MGM/UA, 1990

DAVID MINTY
DEATHWISH 3   Cannon, 1985, AD
SHANGHAI SURPRISE   MGM/UA, 1986,
   AD w/John Siddall

Mi

CINEMATOGRAPHERS
PRODUCTION
DESIGNERS,
COSTUME
DESIGNERS AND
FILM EDITORS
GUIDE

P
R
O
D
U
C
T
I
O
N

D
E
S
I
G
N
E
R
S

CINEMATOGRAPHERS
PRODUCTION
DESIGNERS,
COSTUME
DESIGNERS AND
FILM EDITORS
GUIDE

DAVID MITCHELL
RICH KIDS   United Artists, 1979, AD
ONE TRICK PONY   Warner Bros., 1980,
   AD w/Woods MacIntosh
MY DINNER WITH ANDRE   New Yorker, 1981

GAVIN MITCHELL
A CHRISTMAS STORY   MGM/UA, 1983, AD
THE TERRY FOX STORY   20th Century Fox,
   1983, AD

DEAN E. MITZNER*
IATSE Local 876
Agent: Creative Technique - Toronto, Ontario, Canada,
   416/466-4173

REPORT TO THE COMMISSIONER   United Artists,
   1975, AD
THE DAY OF THE LOCUST   Paramount, 1975, AD
BIG WEDNESDAY   Warner Bros., 1978, AD
1941   Universal, 1979
NINE TO FIVE   20th Century Fox, 1980
LOOKER   The Ladd Company/Warner Bros., 1981
TRON   Buena Vista, 1982
NATIONAL LAMPOON'S CLASS REUNION   20th
   Century Fox, 1982
MAN, WOMAN AND CHILD   Paramount, 1983
NIGHTMARES   Universal, 1983
THE MAN WITH ONE RED SHOE   20th Century
   Fox, 1985
B.L. STRYKER (Pilot)   1989
THE FLASH (Pilot)   Pet Fly Productions, 1990
TAGGET (CTF)   Mirisch Films, 1991

ANDREW MOLLO
XTRO   New Line Cinema, 1983, AD w/Peter Body
INVITATION TO THE WEDDING   Chancery Lane
   Films, 1984
THE INNOCENT   TVS Ltd./Tempest Films, 1985
DANCE WITH A STRANGER   Samuel Goldwyn
   Company, 1985
NO SURRENDER   Circle Releasing Corporation, 1986

MICHAEL MOLLY
Phone: 212/242-2980

STARTING OVER   Paramount, 1979, AD
NIGHT OF THE JUGGLER   Columbia, 1980, AD
STARDUST MEMORIES   United Artists, 1980, AD
THIEF   United Artists, 1981, AD
STILL OF THE NIGHT   MGM/UA, 1982, AD
A QUESTION OF HONOR (TF)   Roger Gimbel
   Productions/EMI TV/Sonny Gross Productions,
   1982, AD
TRACKDOWN: FINDING THE GOODBAR KILLER (TF)
   Grosso-Jacobson Productions, 1983, AD
ZELIG   Orion/Warner Bros., 1983, AD
MOSCOW ON THE HUDSON   Columbia, 1984,
   AD w/Peter Rothe
SENTIMENTAL JOURNEY (TF)   Lucille Ball
   Productions/Smith-Richmond Productions/20th
   Century Fox TV, 1984
HEAVEN HELP US   Tri-Star, 1985
MY BEST FRIEND IS A VAMPIRE   Kings Road, 1988
THE COMEBACK (TF)   CBS Entertainment, 1989

GENEVIEVE MOORE
SATAN'S PRINCESS   Paramount Home video, 1991

JOHN JAY MOORE
KING OF THE GYPSIES   Paramount, 1978, AD
THE WANDERERS   Orion/Warner Bros., 1979, AD
JUST TELL ME WHAT YOU WANT   Warner Bros.,
   1980, AD
SOPHIE'S CHOICE   Universal/AFD, 1982, AD
THE SURVIVORS   Columbia, 1983, AD
DREAM LOVER   MGM/UA, 1986, AD
ORPHANS   Lorimar, 1987, AD
SOMEONE TO WATCH OVER ME   Columbia, 1987,
   AD w/Chris Burian-Mohr
WALL STREET   20th Century Fox, 1987,
   AD w/Hilda Stark
A KILLING AFFAIR   Hemdale, 1988
SEA OF LOVE   Universal, 1989
BETSY'S WEDDING   Buena Vista, 1990
FX 2: THE DEADLY ART OF ILLUSION   Orion, 1991

RANDY MOORE
SUBURBIA   New Horizons, 1984
C.H.U.D. II: BUD THE CHUD, Vestron, 1989

SUSANNA MOORE
STRANGE INVADERS   Orion, 1983

NORMA MORICEAU
SOMETHING WILD   Orion, 1986

DAVID MORONG
ZELLY AND ME   Columbia, 1988, AD w/Diana Freas

BRIAN MORRIS
THE HAUNTING OF JULIA   Discovery Films, 1977, AD
YANKS   Universal, 1979
QUEST FOR FIRE   20th Century Fox, 1982,
   w/Guy Comtois
PINK FLOYD - THE WALL   MGM/UA, 1982
THE HUNGER   MGM/UA, 1983
ANOTHER COUNTRY   Orion Classics, 1984
ANGEL HEART   Tri-Star, 1987
A WORLD APART   Atlantic Releasing Corporation, 1988
HOMEBOY   Redbury Ltd./Elliott Kastner
   Productions, 1989
JABOB'S LADDER   Tri-Star, 1990

DIANA MORRIS
IATSE Local 876

SURVIVAL GAME   Trans World Entertainment, 1987

DOUGLAS MOWAT
YOU CAN'T HURRY LOVE   MCEG, 1987, AD

PETER MULLINS
Agent: Creative Technique - Toronto, Ontario, Canada,
   413/466-4173

KING AND COUNTRY   Allied Artists, 1965
ALFIE   Paramount, 1966
THE SPY WITH A COLD NOSE   Embassy, 1966
A MATTER OF INNOCENCE   *PRETTY POLLY*
   Universal, 1968
THE MAN OUTSIDE   1968
WHERE EAGLES DARE   MGM, 1969
THE LAST VALLEY   Cinerama Releasing
   Corporation, 1971
PUPPET ON A CHAIN   Cinerama Releasing
   Corporation, 1972

STEPTOE AND SON MGM-EMI, 1972
X Y & ZEE *ZEE & CO.* Columbia, 1972
THE HUMAN FACTOR Bryanston, 1974
11 HARROWHOUSE 20th Century Fox, 1974
LUTHER American Film Theatre, 1974
THE PINK PANTHER STRIKES AGAIN United
    Artists, 1976
THE MEDUSA TOUCH Warner Bros., 1978, AD
REVENGE OF THE PINK PANTHER United
    Artists, 1979
GOLDENGIRL Avco Embassy, 1979
THERE GOES THE BRIDE Vanguard, 1980
THE DOGS OF WAR United Artists, 1980
TRAIL OF THE PINK PANTHER MGM/UA, 1982
DEATHWISH II Filmways, 1982
CURSE OF THE PINK PANTHER MGM/UA, 1983
LASSITER Warner Bros., 1984
SCANDALOUS Orion, 1984
THE HOLCROFT COVENANT Universal, 1985
DEATHWISH 3 Cannon, 1986
SHANGHAI SURPRISE MGM/UA, 1986
A CASUALTY OF WAR (CTF) F.F.S.
    Productions, 1990

PETER MUNNEKE
PICASSO TRIGGER Malibu Bay Films, 1988

CHRISTA MUNRO
HEART OF MIDNIGHT Samuel Goldwyn Company,
    1988, AD

PAUL MUNTING
CAMPION-SWEET DANGER (TF) BBC TV, 1990

JAMES J. MURAKAMI
THE ESCAPE ARTIST Orion/Warner Bros.,
    1982, AD
WARGAMES MGM/UA, 1983, AD
JOY OF SEX Paramount, 1984, AD
BEVERLY HILLS COP Paramount, 1984, AD
THE NATURAL Tri-Star, 1984, AD
LUCAS 20th Century Fox, 1986, AD
BEVERLY HILLS COP II Paramount, 1987, AD
MIDNIGHT RUN Universal, 1988, AD
COUPE DE VILLE Universal, 1990, AD

SHINOBU MURAKI
SANSHIRO SUGATA Toho, 1943, AD
THE MOST BEAUTIFUL Toho, 1944, AD
THOSE WHO TREAD ON THE TIGER'S TAIL
    Toho, 1945, AD
SANSHIRO SUGATA - PART TWO Toho, 1945, AD
NO REGRETS FOR OUR YOUTH Toho, 1946, AD
THOSE WHO MAKE TOMORROW Toho, 1946, AD
ONE WONDERFUL SUNDAY Toho, 1947, AD
DRUNKEN ANGEL Toho, 1948, AD
THE QUIET DUEL Daiei, 1949, AD
STRAY DOG Toho, 1949, AD
SCANDAL Shochiku, 1959, AD
RASHOMON RKO Radio, 1950, AD
THE IDIOT Shochiku, 1951, AD
IKIRU Brandon, 1952, AD
SEVEN SAMURAI Landmark Releasing, 1954, AD
I LIVE IN FEAR Brandon, 1955, AD
THE LOWER DEPTHS Brandon, 1957, AD
THRONE OF BLOOD *THE CASTLE OF THE
    SPIDER'S WEB* Brandon, 1957, AD
THE HIDDEN FORTRESS *THREE BAD MEN IN A
    HIDDEN FORTRESS* Toho, 1958, AD

THE BAD SLEEP WELL Toho, 1960, AD
YOJIMBO Seneca International, 1961, AD
SANJURO Toho, 1962, AD
HIGH AND LOW East West Classics, 1963, AD
RED BEARD Toho, 1965, AD
DODES'KA'DEN Janus, 1970, AD
DERSU UZALA New World, 1975, AD
KAGEMUSHA: THE SHADOW WARRIOR 20th
    Century Fox, 1980, AD
RAN ★ Orion Classics, 1985, AD
AKIRA KUROSAWA'S DREAMS Warner Bros.,
    1989, AD

YOSHIRO MURAKI
SANSHIRO SUGATA Toho, 1943
THE MOST BEAUTIFUL Toho, 1944
THOSE WHO TREAD ON THE TIGER'S TAIL
    Toho, 1945
SANSHIRO SUGATA - PART TWO Toho, 1945
NO REGRETS FOR OUR YOUTH Toho, 1946
THOSE WHO MAKE TOMORROW Toho, 1946
ONE WONDERFUL SUNDAY Toho, 1947
DRUNKEN ANGEL Toho, 1948
THE QUIET DUEL Daiei, 1949
STRAY DOG Toho, 1949
SCANDAL Shochiku, 1959
RASHOMON RKO Radio, 1950
THE IDIOT Shochiku, 1951
IKIRU Brandon, 1952
SEVEN SAMURAI Landmark Releasing, 1954
I LIVE IN FEAR Brandon, 1955
THE LOWER DEPTHS Brandon, 1957
THRONE OF BLOOD *THE CASTLE OF THE
    SPIDER'S WEB* Brandon, 1957
THE HIDDEN FORTRESS *THREE BAD MEN IN A
    HIDDEN FORTRESS* Toho, 1958
THE BAD SLEEP WELL Toho, 1960
YOJIMBO Seneca International, 1961
SANJURO Toho, 1962
HIGH AND LOW East West Classics, 1963
RED BEARD Toho, 1965
DODES'KA'DEN Janus, 1970
DERSU UZALA New World, 1975
KAGEMUSHA: THE SHADOW WARRIOR 20th
    Century Fox, 1980
RAN ★ Orion Classics, 1985
DREAMS Warner Bros., 1989

GRAEME MURRAY
LADIES AND GENTLEMEN...THE FABULOUS STAINS
    Paramount, 1982, AD
NEVER CRY WOLF Buena Vista, 1983, AD
THE BOY WHO COULD FLY 20th Century Fox,
    1986, AD
MALONE Orion, 1987

ROGER MURRAY-LEACH
Agent: London Management, 235/241 Regent St. -
    London W1R 7AG, 071-493-1610

LOCAL HERO Warner Bros., 1983
THE KILLING FIELDS Warner Bros., 1984, AD
DEFENSE OF THE REALM Hemdale, 1985
CLOCKWISE Universal, 1986
HEARTS OF FIRE Lorimar, 1987
A FISH CALLED WANDA MGM/UA, 1988
THE MIGHTY QUINN MGM/UA, 1989
TWENTY-ONE Anglo International, 1991

Mu

CINEMATOGRAPHERS
PRODUCTION
DESIGNERS,
COSTUME
DESIGNERS AND
FILM EDITORS
GUIDE

P
R
O
D
U
C
T
I
O
N
D
E
S
I
G
N
E
R
S

CINEMATOGRAPHERS
PRODUCTION
DESIGNERS,
COSTUME
DESIGNERS and
FILM EDITORS
GUIDE

PETER MURTON
ACTT
Agent: Sandra Marsh Management - Sherman Oaks,
    818/905-6961

BILLY BUDD   Anglo-Allied, 1962
IN THE COOL OF THE DAY   MGM, 1963, AD
DR. STRANGELOVE   Columbia, 1964, AD
GOLDFINGER   United Artists, 1964, AD
THE IPCRESS FILE   Universal, 1965, AD
THUNDERBALL   United Artists, 1965, AD
FUNERAL IN BERLIN   Paramount, 1966, AD
HALF A SIXPENCE   Paramount, 1968, AD
THE LION IN WINTER   Avco Embassy, 1968
THE POSSESSION OF JOEL DELANEY
    Paramount, 1972
THE RULING CLASS   Avco Embassy, 1972
NIGHT WATCH   Avco Embassy, 1973
THE BLACK WINDMILL   Universal, 1974
THE MAN WITH THE GOLDEN GUN   United
    Artists, 1974
MAN FRIDAY   Avco Embassy, 1975
THE EAGLE HAS LANDED   Columbia, 1977
DEATH ON THE NILE   Paramount, 1978
DRACULA   Universal, 1979
IKE (MS)   ABC Circle Films, 1979
SUPERMAN II   Warner Bros., 1980, w/John Barry
SUPERMAN III   Warner Bros., 1983
SHEENA   Columbia, 1984
THE CHAIN   Rank, 1985
SPIES LIKE US   Warner Bros., 1985
KING KONG LIVES   DEG, 1986
BLIND FURY   Tri-Star, 1989
JUST ASK FOR DIAMOND   Kings Road
    Entertainment, 1989
DIAMOND'S EDGE   Castle Hill, 1990
POPCORN   Studio Three Films, 1991

JANE MUSKY*
IATSE Local 876
Agent: The Gersh Agency, Inc., Beverly Hills -
    213/274-6611, New York - 212/997-1818

BLOOD SIMPLE   Circle Releasing Corporation, 1984
UNDER THE BILTMORE CLOCK (TF)   Rubicon Film
    Productions/KTCA/American Playhouse, 1985
THE LITTLE SISTER   American Playhouse, 1985
RAISING ARIZONA   20th Century Fox, 1987
ILLEGALLY YOURS   DEG, 1987
YOUNG GUNS   20th Century Fox, 1988
PATTY HEARST   Atlantic Releasing
    Corporation, 1988
WHEN HARRY MET SALLY...   Columbia, 1989
GHOST   Paramount, 1990

JOHN MUTO
Agent: The Gersh Agency, Inc., Beverly Hills -
    213/274-6611, New York - 212/997-1818

NIGHT OF THE COMET   Atlantic Releasing
    Corporation, 1984
FLOWERS IN THE ATTIC   New World, 1987
RIVER'S EDGE   Hemdale, 1987
NIGHTFLYERS   New Century/Vista, 1987
HEARTBREAK HOTEL   Buena Vista, 1988
GLEAMING THE CUBE   20th Century Fox, 1989
HEART CONDITION   New Line Cinema, 1990
HOME ALONE   20th Century Fox, 1990
ONLY THE LONELY   20th Century Fox, 1991

DIDIER NAERT
THE MAN INSIDE   New Line Cinema, 1990

GIOVANNI NATALUCCI
LADYHAWKE   Warner Bros., 1985, AD
CRAWLSPACE   Empire Pictures, 1986, AD
FROM BEYOND   Empire Pictures, 1986
TROLL   Empire Pictures, 1986
TERRORVISION   Empire Pictures, 1986
SAVING GRACE   Embassy, 1986
THE CALLER   Empire Pictures, 1987
DOLLS   Empire Pictures, 1987
BUY AND CELL   Empire Pictures, 1988
CATACOMBS   Empire Pictures, 1988

IGOR NAY
THE WILD DUCK   Orion, 1983, AD
SILVER CITY   Samuel Goldwyn Company, 1985
REBEL   Vestron, 1986, AD

BEALA B. NEEL*
IATSE Local 876
Agent: Smith Gosnell Nicholson & Associates -
    Pacific Palisades, 213/459-0307

SWITCHBLADE SISTERS   Centaur, 1975
DEATH RACE 2000   New World, 1975, AD
I WONDER WHO'S KILLING HER NOW?   1976
THE HAPPY HOOKER GOES TO WASHINGTON
    Cannon, 1977, AD
GOOD GUYS WEAR BLACK   American
    Cinema, 1978
WILD TIMES (TF)   Metromedia Producers Corp./
    Rattlesnake Productions, 1980
ROUGHNECKS (TF)   Douglas Netter Productions/
    Metromedia Producers Corp., 1980
...ALL THE MARBLES   MGM/United Artists, 1981, AD
FIREFOX   Warner Bros., 1982, AD
FIRE ON THE MOUNTAIN (TF)   Bonnard
    Productions, 1982
CERTAIN FURY   New World, 1985
THE DEFIANT ONES (TF)   MGM-UA TV, 1986
THE FIFTH MISSILE (TF)   Bercovici-St.
    Johns Productions/MGM-UA TV, 1986
BEVERLY HILLS MADAM (TF)   NLS Productions/
    Orion TV, 1986
WHEN THE BOUGH BREAKS (TF)   Taft Entertainment
    TV/TDF Productions, 1987
DENNIS THE MENACE (TF)   DIC
    Enterprises Productions, 1987
BABY BOOM   MGM/UA, 1987, AD
ROOTS: THE GIFT (TF)   David L. Wolper Productions/
    Warner Bros. TV, 1988
BIG TOP PEE-WEE   Paramount, 1988, AD

ROBERTA NEIMAN
FRATERNITY VACATION   New World, 1985

JOSEPH C. NEMEC III*

IATSE Local 876
Phone: 818/787-8199
Agent: Marty Barkin, C.N.A. & Associates -
    Los Angeles, 213/556-4343

SPIES (TF)   Lorimar Telepictures, 1986
BLIND JUSTICE (TF)   CBS Entertainment, 1986, AD
AMERIKA (MS)   ABC Circle Films, 1987, AD
FATAL BEAUTY   MGM/UA, 1987, AD
EXTREME PREJUDICE   Tri-Star, 1987, AD
ALIEN NATION   20th Century Fox, 1987, AD
THE ABYSS ★   20th Century Fox, 1989,
    AD w/Russell Christian
FEAR   Vestron, 1989
ANOTHER 48 HRS.   Paramount, 1990

GARY T. NEW

PHANTOM OF THE MALL: ERIC'S REVENGE   Fries
    Entertainment, 1989
A CRY FOR HELP: THE TRACEY THURMAN
    STORY (TF)   AUTL Productions, 1990
RETURN TO GREEN ACRES (TF)   Jaygee
    Productions, 1990

NORMAN NEWBERRY*

IATSE Local 876
Agent: Jay Gilbert Talent Agency - Los Angeles,
    213/656-5906

WINTER KILLS   Avco Embassy, 1979, AD
GHOST STORY   Universal, 1981, AD
HISTORY OF THE WORLD, PART 1   20th Century
    Fox, 1981, AD
THE BEST LITTLE WHOREHOUSE IN TEXAS
    Universal, 1982, AD
STAYING ALIVE   Paramount, 1983, AD
TABLE FOR FIVE   Warner Bros., 1983, AD
THE RIVER   Universal, 1984, AD
MASK   Universal, 1985, AD
GOTCHA!   Universal, 1985, AD
FIRE WITH FIRE   Paramount, 1986
OUT OF BOUNDS   Columbia, 1986
A NIGHT IN THE LIFE OF JIMMY REARDON   20th
    Century Fox, 1988

JAMES WILLIAM NEWPORT*

IATSE Local 876
Agent: The Gersh Agency, Inc., Beverly Hills -
    213/274-6611, New York - 212/997-1818

THE NIGHT GOD SCREAMED   Cinemation, 1973
THE STUDENT TEACHERS   New World, 1973
WHITE LINE FEVER   Columbia, 1975,
    Visual Consultant
LAS VEGAS LADY   Crown International, 1976
MR. BILLION   20th Century Fox, 1976,
    Visual Consultant
ZERO TO SIXTY   First Artists, 1978
STRAIGHT TIME   Warner Bros., 1978,
    Visual Consultant
11TH VICTIM (TF)   Marty Katz Productions/
    Paramount, 1979
ELVIS (TF)   Dick Clark Productions, 1979
OVER THE EDGE   Orion/Warner Bros., 1979
CHEECH AND CHONG'S NICE DREAMS
    Columbia, 1981
HEART LIKE A WHEEL   20th Century Fox, 1983

MEATBALLS PART II   Tri-Star, 1984
SYLVESTER   Columbia, 1985
MADE IN USA   DEG, 1986
THE STEPFATHER   New Century/Vista, 1987
FATAL BEAUTY   MGM/UA, 1987
CHINA BEACH (TVS)   1988
I LOVE YOU PERFECT (TF)   Stephen Cannell
    Productions, 1990
NIGHTBREAKER (CTF)   Symphony Pictures, 1990
UNDER COVER (TF)   Sacret/Paint Rock
    Productions, 1991
TOKYO DIAMOND   Universal, 1991

DAVID NICHOLS*

IATSE Local 876
Agent: Sanford-Skouras & Gross - Los Angeles,
    213/208-2100

BOX CAR BERTHA   American International, 1972
MEAN STREETS   Warner Bros., 1973,
    Visual Consultant
THE WILD PARTY   American International, 1975
SWAMP THING   Avco Embassy, 1982,
    w/Robb Wilson King
RECKLESS   MGM/UA, 1984
TESTAMENT   Paramount, 1983
HEARTBREAKER   Monarex/Emerson Film
    Enterprises, 1983
FINNEGAN BEGIN AGAIN (CTF)   HBO Premiere
    Films/Zenith Productions/Jennie & Company Film
    Productions, 1985
THE BEST OF TIMES   Universal, 1986
HOOSIERS   Orion, 1986
THE SERPENT AND THE RAINBOW   Universal, 1988
GREAT BALLS OF FIRE!   Orion, 1989

BRIAN NICKLES

THE MOSQUITO COAST   Warner Bros., 1986,
    w/John Wingrove

PATRICIA NORRIS

Agent: Smith Gosnell Nicholson & Associates - Pacific
    Palisades, 213/459-0307

BLUE VELVET   DEG, 1986
TAP   Tri-Star, 1989
WILD AT HEART   The Samuel Goldwyn Company, 1990

TORI NOURAFCHAN

SILENT NIGHT, DEADLY NIGHT III: BETTER WATCH
    OUT!   Quiet Films, 1990

MICHAEL NOVOTNY

Agent: Jay Gilbert Talent Agency, 8400 Sunset Blvd.,
    Suite 3-A - Hollywood, 213/656-5906

CREATURE   Cardinal Releasing, 1985, AD
PRISON SHIP: THE ADVENTURES OF TAURA, PART 1
    Worldwide Entertainment, 1987, AD
FLIGHT OF THE NAVIGATOR   Buena Vista, 1986, AD
INVASION EARTH: THE ALIENS ARE HERE   New
    World, 1987
WEEKEND AT BERNIE'S   20th Century Fox, 1989, AD
BY DAWN'S EARLY LIGHT (CTF)   HBO, 1990
THE GRAND TOUR   Wildstreet Pictures, 1991
THE TAPES OF DEXTER JACKSON   Samuel Goldwyn
    Company, 1991

No

CINEMATOGRAPHERS
PRODUCTION
DESIGNERS,
COSTUME
DESIGNERS AND
FILM EDITORS
GUIDE

P
R
O
D
U
C
T
I
O
N

D
E
S
I
G
N
E
R
S

No

CINEMATOGRAPHERS
PRODUCTION
DESIGNERS,
COSTUME
DESIGNERS AND
FILM EDITORS
GUIDE

P
R
O
D
U
C
T
I
O
N

D
E
S
I
G
N
E
R
S

CHRISTOPHER NOWAK
FORT APACHE, THE BRONX   20th Century
   Fox, 1981, AD
HANKY PANKY   Columbia, 1982, AD
SWEET LIBERTY   Universal, 1986, AD
THE SQUEEZE   Tri-Star, 1987, AD
VAMPIRE'S KISS   Hemdale, 1989
PARENTHOOD   Universal, 1989, AD

O

WILLIAM F. O'BRIEN*
IATSE Local 876

TELEFON   MGM/United Artists, 1977, AD
1941   Universal, 1979, AD
CANNERY ROW   MGM/United Artists, 1981, AD

THOMAS A. O'CONNOR
A NIGHTMARE ON ELM STREET 4: THE DREAM
   MASTER   New Line Cinema, 1988
LUCKY STIFF   New Line Cinema, 1989, AD

EDWIN O'DONOVAN
Phone: 213/842-2889

HEAVEN CAN WAIT ★★   Paramount, 1978, AD
HARDCORE   Columbia, 1979, AD
RESURRECTION   Universal, 1980, AD
HONKY TONK FREEWAY   Universal/AFD, 1981, AD

JANET O'LEARY
DANNY BOY   Triumph, 1984

**JEANNINE CLAUDIA
OPPEWALL**
Agent: The Gersh Agency, Inc., Beverly Hills -
   213/274-6611, New York - 212/997-1818

TENDER MERCIES   Universal/AFD, 1983, AD
LOVE LETTERS   New World, 1983, AD
MARIA'S LOVERS   Cannon, 1984
DESERT HEARTS   Samuel Goldwyn Company, 1985
LIGHT OF DAY   Tri-Star, 1987
IRONWEED   Tri-Star, 1987
THE BIG EASY   Columbia, 1987
ROOFTOPS   New Visions, 1989
MUSIC BOX   Tri-Star, 1989
ANIMAL BEHAVIOR   Millimeter Films, 1989
SIBLING RIVALRY   Columbia, 1990
WHITE PALACE   Universal, 1990

ERIC W. ORBOM*
IATSE Local 876

NUTS   Warner Bros., 1987, AD
CLEAN AND SOBER   Warner Bros., 1987, AD

JANE OSMANN
DINNER AT EIGHT (CTF)   Think Entertainment, 1989

KURT OSSENFORT
WORKING GIRLS   Miramax, 1986

MICHAEL O'SULLIVAN
ELLIE   Shapiro Entertainment, 1984
NOT FOR PUBLICATION   Samuel Goldwyn Company,
   1984, AD
1918   Cinecom International, 1985, AD

DANIEL OUELLETTE
TRUST   True Fiction Pictures/Zenith Productions, 1991

P

JOSEPH G. PACELLI
THE STONE BOY   TLC Films/20th Century Fox, 1984
HARD TO HOLD   Universal, 1984

KEITH PAIN
BULLSHOT!   Island Alive, 1983, AD
WATER   Atlantic Releasing Corporation, 1984, AD
BRAZIL   Universal, 1985, AD, w/John Beard
LINK   Thorn EMI/Cannon, 1986, AD
FULL METAL JACKET   Warner Bros., 1987,
   AD w/Rod Stratford & Les Tomkins
THE PRINCESS BRIDE   20th Century Fox, 1987,
   Supervising AD

JOHN PAINO
STREET HUNTER   21st Century/DGP, 1990

RON PALEY
SHE'S GOTTA HAVE IT   Island Pictures, 1986, AD

PHEDON PAPAMICHAEL
Agent: Paul Gerard Talent Agency - Newport Beach,
   714/644-7950

LOVE STREAMS   Cannon, 1984, AD
SEVEN HOURS TO JUDGMENT   Trans World
   Entertainment, 1988
TEXASVILLE   Columbia, 1990

LYNDA PARADISE*
IATSE Local 876

WANDA NEVADA   United Artists, 1979, AD
PERFECT!   Columbia, 1985, AD
THE GOLDEN CHILD   Paramount, 1986, AD
SATISFACTION   20th Century Fox, 1988
STUDIO 5B (Pilot)   1989, AD
JUST LIFE (CTF)   Victoria Principal Productions,
   1990, AD

GIL PARRONDO
PATTON ★★   20th Century Fox, 1970, AD
NICHOLAS AND ALEXANDRA ★★   Columbia, 1971,
   AD w/Ernest Archer & Jack Maxted
TRAVELS WITH MY AUNT ★   MGM, 1972,
   AD w/Robert Laing

ROBIN AND MARIAN   Columbia, 1976, AD
MARCH OR DIE   Columbia, 1977
THE BOYS FROM BRAZIL   20th Century Fox, 1978
CUBA   United Artists, 1979
SPHINX   Orion/Warner Bros., 1981, AD
RUSTLER'S RHAPSODY   Paramount, 1985
LIONHEART   Orion, 1987
FAREWELL TO THE KING   Orion, 1989
THE RETURN OF THE MUSKETEERS
   Universal, 1989

L E S L I E   P A R S O N S
SINGLE WOMEN, MARRIED MEN (TF)   Michele Lee
   Productions, 1990

O W E N   P A T E R S O N
BLISS   New World, 1986

A L A S T A I R   P A T O N
TAILSPIN: BEHIND THE KOREAN AIRLINE
   TRAGEDY (CTF)   Darlow Smithson
   Productions, 1989

W A L T E R   P A T R I A R C A
YOR, THE HUNTER FROM THE FUTURE   Columbia,
   1983, AD

V I C T O R I A   (V I C K I)   P A U L
Agent: Sandra Marsh Management - Sherman Oaks,
   818/905-6961

YEAR OF THE DRAGON   MGM/UA, 1985, AD
VERNE MILLER   Alive Films, 1987
PRICELESS BEAUTY   Bema Productions, 1987
RED RIVER (TF)   Catalina Production Group, 1988
HEART   New World, 1987
ISHTAR   Columbia, 1987, AD
MY SISTER MELBA (Pilot)   AD
CAMPUS COMEDY (CBL)   AD
FAR FROM HOME   Vestron, 1989
HIDER IN THE HOUSE   Vestron, 1989
IT WILL STAND (TF)   1989
DESPERATE HOURS   MGM/UA, 1990

L A W R E N C E   G .   P A U L L *
IATSE Local 876
Contact: Craig Jacobson, Esq. - Hansen, Jacobson &
   Teller, 213/271-8777

LITTLE FAUSS AND BIG HALSY   Paramount, 1970
STAR-SPANGLED GIRL   Paramount, 1971
THE HIRED HAND   Universal, 1971
CHANDLER   1972
THEY ONLY KILL THEIR MASTERS   1972
THE NICKEL RIDE   20th Century Fox, 1975
THE NAKED APE   1973
THE LAST AMERICAN HERO   20th Century
   Fox, 1973
W.W. AND THE DIXIE DANCEKINGS   20th Century
   Fox, 1975
THE BINGO LONG TRAVELING ALL-STARS AND
   MOTOR KINGS   Universal, 1976
WHICH WAY IS UP?   Universal, 1977
BLUE COLLAR   Universal, 1978
FM   Universal, 1978
HOW TO BEAT THE HIGH COST OF LIVING
   American International, 1980
IN GOD WE TRUST   Universal, 1980

BLADE RUNNER ★   Warner Bros., 1982
DOCTOR DETROIT   Universal, 1983
ROMANCING THE STONE   20th Century Fox, 1984
BACK TO THE FUTURE   Universal, 1985
AMERICAN FLYERS   Warner Bros., 1985
PROJECT X   20th Century Fox, 1987
CROSS MY HEART   Universal, 1987
LICENSE TO DRIVE   20th Century Fox, 1988
COCOON: THE RETURN   20th Century Fox, 1988
HARLEM NIGHTS   Paramount, 1989
THE LAST OF THE FINEST   Orion, 1990
PREDATOR 2   20th Century Fox, 1990
CITY SLICKERS   Columbia., 1991

L I N D A   P E A R L
Agent: Smith Gosnell Nicholson & Associates -
   Los Angeles, 213/459-0307
Address: 2047 High Tower Drive, Los Angeles, CA 90068,
   213/874-8013

ROLLER BOOGIE   United Aritsts, 1979, AD
LEO AND LOREE   United Artists, 1980
PRIVATE LESSONS   Jensen Farley Pictures, 1981
TESTAMENT   Paramount, 1983, AD
WAVELENGTH   New World, 1983
TIMERIDER   Jensen Farley Pictures, 1983, AD
MY TUTOR   Crown International, 1983, AD
THE CHECK IS IN THE MAIL   Ascot Entertainment
   Group, 1984
BREACH OF CONTRACT   Atlantic Releasing
   Corporation, 1984
DEATH OF AN ANGEL   20th Century Fox, 1985
WILD HORSES (TF)   Wild Horses Productions/
   Telepictures Productions, 1985
RUSSKIES   New Century/Vista, 1987
DREAM WEST (MS)   Sunn Classic Pictures, 1988
OUT COLD   Hemdale, 1989
COMMUNION   MCEG, 1989
A SON'S PROMISE (TF)   Marian Rees Associates, 1990
DON'T TELL HER IT'S ME   *THE BOYFRIEND SCHOOL*
   Hemdale, 1990

N E N O   P E C U R
THE PLOT TO KILL HITLER (TF)   David L. Wolper
   Productions, 1990

V I N C E N T   P E R A N I O
THE PRIZE FIGHTER   New World, 1979, AD
THE PRIVATE EYES   New World, 1980, AD
POLYESTER   New Line Cinema, 1981
HOUSE ON SORORITY ROW   Artists
   Releasing Corporation/Film Ventures International,
   1983, AD
TWO FOR THE MONEY   Bonner Films, 1985
ADVENTURE OF THE ACTION HUNTERS   Troma,
   1987, AD
HAIRSPRAY   New Line Cinema, 1988, AD
CRY-BABY   Universal, 1990

M I C H A E L   P E R R Y
BLUE DESERT   Neo Films, 1991

D I A N   P E R R Y M A N
SILENT NIGHT, LONELY NIGHT   Tri-Star, 1984
NEAR DARK   DEG, 1987, AD

CINEMATOGRAPHERS
PRODUCTION
DESIGNERS,
COSTUME
DESIGNERS AND
FILM EDITORS
GUIDE

P
R
O
D
U
C
T
I
O
N

D
E
S
I
G
N
E
R
S

Pe

CINEMATOGRAPHERS
PRODUCTION
DESIGNERS,
COSTUME
DESIGNERS AND
FILM EDITORS
GUIDE

P
R
O
D
U
C
T
I
O
N

D
E
S
I
G
N
E
R
S

PAUL PETERS*

IATSE Local 876
Agent: Harris & Goldberg, 2121 Avenue of the Stars,
    Suite 950 - Los Angeles, 213/553-5200
Home: 130 Lighthouse Mall - Marina Del Ray,
    213/827-0900

BUCK ROGERS   Universal, 1979, AD
SAMURAI (TF)   Danny Thomas Productions/
    Universal TV, 1979, AD
ROADIE   United Artists, 1980
SECOND THOUGHTS   Universal, 1983
STROKER ACE   Universal/AFD, 1983
DEMPSEY (TF)   Charles Fries Productions, 1983
JEALOUSY (TF)   Charles Fries Productions/Alan
    Sacks Productions, 1983
FAMILY BUSINESS (TF)   Screenscope Inc./South
    Carolina Educational TV Network, 1983, AD
MISCHIEF   20th Century Fox, 1985
JUST ONE OF THE BOYS   Columbia, 1985
MURDER AMONG FRIENDS (TF)   Tisch-Avnet
    Productions/ABC Circle Films, 1986, AD
NO MAN'S LAND   Orion, 1987
MADE IN HEAVEN   Lorimar, 1987
LINCOLN I (TF)   1987
LITTLE MONSTERS   MGM/UA, 1989
VOICES WITHIN: THE LIVES OF TRUDDI CHASE-
    PARTS I & II (MS)   Itzbinzo Long
    Productions, 1990
ENID IS SLEEPING   Vestron, 1991

PHIL PETERS

WAITING FOR THE LIGHT   Epic Productions, 1990

BEAU PETERSON

PRETTY SMART   New World, 1987

LAWRENCE PEVEC

ALWAYS REMEMBER I LOVE YOU (TF)
    Gross-Weston Productions, 1990, AD

MIKE PHILLIPS

A WORLD APART   Atlantic Releasing Corporation,
    1988, AD

WALTER PICKETTE

LUST IN THE DUST   New World, 1984, AD

GREGORY PICKRELL*

IATSE Local 876

MOVING VIOLATIONS   20th Century Fox, 1985,
    w/Virginia Field
SOME KIND OF WONDERFUL   Paramount, 1987, AD
LISTEN TO ME   WEG, 1989
DOWNTOWN   20th Century Fox, 1990

MICHAEL PICKWOAD

HAWK THE SLAYER   ITC, 1980, AD
STEAMING   New World, 1984, AD
THE PLOUGHMAN'S LUNCH   Samuel
    Goldwyn Company, 1984, AD
COMRADES   British Film Institute, 1986
THE LONELY PASSION OF JUDITH HEARNE
    Island Films, 1987
JANE AND THE LOST CITY   New World, 1987
WITHNAIL AND I   Cineplex Odeon, 1987

HOW TO GET AHEAD IN ADVERTISING   Warner
    Bros., 1989
THE KRAYS   Rank, 1990

COLIN PIGOTT

PING PONG   Samuel Goldwyn Company, 1987

LYN PINEZICH

SIDEWALK STORIES   Island Pictures, 1990

HERBERT PINTER

THE YEAR OF LIVING DANGEROUSLY   MGM/UA,
    1983, AD
THE FRINGE DWELLERS   Atlantic Releasing
    Corporation, 1987
MR. JOHNSON   Avenue Pictures, 1991

EDWARD PISONI

Agent: The Gersh Agency, Inc., Beverly Hills -
    213/274-6611, New York - 212/997-1818

CRUISING   United Artists, 1980, AD
PRINCE OF THE CITY   Orion/Warner Bros., 1981, AD
ENDLESS LOVE   Universal, 1981, AD
DEATHTRAP   Warner Bros., 1982, AD
THE VERDICT   20th Century Fox, 1982
THE KING OF COMEDY   20th Century Fox, 1983,
    AD w/Lawrence Miller
SLAYGROUND   Universal, 1984, AD w/Dennis Bosher
THE PURPLE ROSE OF CAIRO   Orion, 1985, AD
WISE GUYS   MGM/UA, 1986
THE IMAGEMAKER   Castle Hill Productions, 1986
84 CHARING CROSS ROAD   Columbia, 1987,
    w/Eileen Diss
HELLO AGAIN   Buena Vista, 1987
THE SECRET OF MY SUCCESS   Universal, 1987,
    w/Peter Larkin
THE CHRISTMAS WIFE (CTF)   HBO Showcase, 1988
JACKNIFE   Cineplex Odeon, 1989
STEEL MAGNOLIAS   Tri-Star, 1989, w/Gene Callahan
QUEENS LOGIC   New Visions, 1991
TRUE COLORS   Paramount, 1991

POLLY PLATT*

IATSE Local 876
Agent: Rhonda Gomez, Triad Artists, Inc. - Los Angeles,
    213/556-2727

TARGETS   Paramount, 1968
THE LAST PICTURE SHOW   Columbia, 1971
WHAT'S UP, DOC?   Warner Bros., 1972
PAPER MOON   Paramount, 1973
THE THIEF WHO CAME TO DINNER   Warner Bros.,
    1972
THE FORTUNE   Columbia, 1975
THE BAD NEWS BEARS   Paramount, 1976
A STAR IS BORN   Warner Bros., 1976
YOUNG DOCTORS IN LOVE   20th Century Fox, 1982
THE MAN WITH TWO BRAINS   Warner Bros., 1983
TERMS OF ENDEARMENT ★   Paramount, 1983
BETWEEN TWO WOMEN (TF)   The Jon Avnet
    Company, 1986
THE WITCHES OF EASTWICK   Warner Bros., 1987

PIERS PLOWDEN

PRIVATE INVESTIGATIONS   MGM/UA, 1987
JACK'S BACK   Cinema Group, 1988

JIM POHL
THE TELEPHONE   New World, 1988, AD
TRUE BELIEVER   Columbia, 1989, AD

SONYA POLANSKY
A SHOW OF FORCE   Paramount, 1989,
   w/William J. Cassidy

PETER POLITANOFF
TOO LATE THE HERO (TF)   Premiere Limited
   Productions, 1990

JACK POPLIN
Agent: The Miller Agency - Santa Clarita, 818/843-7335

PORTRAIT OF A MOBSTER   Warner Bros., 1961
LAD: A DOG   Warner Bros., 1961
THE FAMILY JEWELS   Paramount, 1965
THE SLENDER THREAD   Paramount, 1965
A FINE MADNESS   Warner Bros., 1966
COUNTDOWN   Warner Bros., 1968
CHANGES   Cinerama Releasing Corporation, 1969
THE STALKING MOON   National General, 1969
THE GREAT BANK ROBBERY   Warner Bros., 1969
SUPPOSE THEY GAVE A WAR AND NOBODY
   CAME?   Cinerama Releasing Corporation, 1970
MRS. POLLIFAX - SPY   United Artists, 1971
KOTCH   Cinerama Releasing Corporation, 1971
THE WRATH OF GOD   1972
CHARLEY AND THE ANGEL   Buena Vista, 1972
THE KLANSMAN   Paramount, 1974
SPECIAL DELIVERY   American International,
   1976, AD
MEAN DOG BLUES   American International,
   1976, AD
THE GREAT SANTINI   Orion/Warner Bros., 1980
CLASS   Orion, 1983, AD
TRAXX   DEG, 1987

HUBERT POPP
THE NASTY GIRL   Miramax Films, 1990

GIORGIO POSTIGLIONE
AMITYVILLE 3-D   Orion, 1983, AD
FIRESTARTER   Universal, 1984, AD
STEPHEN KING'S CAT'S EYE   MGM/UA, 1985
SILVER BULLET   Paramount, 1985
RAW DEAL   DEG, 1986
MAXIMUM OVERDRIVE   DEG, 1986

HARRY POTTLE
STAND UP VIRGIN SOLDIERS   Warner Bros., 1977
THE 39 STEPS   International Picture Show
   Company, 1978
THE BIG SLEEP   United Artists, 1978
MURDER BY DECREE   Avco Embassy, 1979
TURK 182   20th Century Fox, 1985
COLLISION COURSE   DEG, 1988
LOOSE CANNONS   Tri-Star, 1990

ANTHONY POWELL
TESS   Columbia, 1980
INDIANA JONES AND THE TEMPLE OF
   DOOM   Paramount, 1984

MICHAEL PRATHER
CREATOR   Universal, 1985, w/Richard Prather

ANTHONY PRATT
ACTT
Agent: Sandra Marsh Management - Sherman Oaks,
   818/905-6961

HELL IN THE PACIFIC   Cinerama Releasing
   Corporation, 1968, AD
DEEP END   Paramount, 1971, AD
LOOT   Cinevision, 1972, AD
BILLY TWO HATS   United Artists, 1972
BAXTER!   National General, 1973, AD
ZARDOZ   20th Century Fox, 1974
CROSSED SWORDS   *THE PRINCE AND THE PAUPER*
   20th Century Fox, 1978
LEOPARD IN THE SNOW   New World, 1978
THE CAT AND THE CANARY   Quartet, 1978, AD
DEATH WATCH   Quartet, 1980, AD
EXCALIBUR   Orion/Warner Bros., 1981
GIVE MY REGARDS TO BROAD STREET   20th Century
   Fox, 1984
SANTA CLAUS: THE MOVIE   Tri-Star, 1985
SOLARBABIES   MGM/UA, 1986
HOPE AND GLORY ★   Columbia, 1987
PARIS BY NIGHT   Cineplex Odeon, 1990
NAKED TANGO   Scotia International, 1990
NOT WITHOUT MY DAUGHTER   Pathe Entertainment/
   MGM/UA, 1991

EARL PRESTON
SHOOT   Avco Embassy, 1976
HAPPY BIRTHDAY TO ME   Columbia, 1981
JOHN AND THE MISSUS   Cinema Group, 1987

WARD PRESTON*
IATSE Local 876
Agent: Smith Gosnell Nicholson & Associates -
   Pacific Palisades, 213/459-0307

THE STONE KILLER   Columbia, 1973
THE TOWERING INFERNO ★   20th Century Fox,
   1974, AD
CAPONE   20th Century Fox, 1975
WON TON TON, THE DOG WHO SAVED HOLLYWOOD
   Paramount, 1976, AD
FIRE! (TF)   Irwin Allen Productions/20th Century
   Fox TV, 1977
MARY WHITE (TF)   Radnitz/Mattel Productions, 1977
TO KILL A COP (TF)   David Gerber Company/
   Columbia TV, 1978
VIVA KNIEVEL!   Warner Bros., 1978
IKE (MS)   ABC Circle Films, 1979
STEEL   *LOOK DOWN AND DIE*   World Northal, 1980
AIRPLANE!   Paramount, 1980
SOGGY BOTTOM, U.S.A.   Cinemax Marketing &
   Distribution, 1981
BODY AND SOUL   Cannon, 1982
THAT CHAMPIONSHIP SEASON   Cannon, 1982
PURPLE RAIN   Warner Bros., 1984
AMERICAN ANTHEM   Columbia, 1986
J. EDGAR HOOVER (CTF)   RLC Productions/The
   Finnegan Company/Showtime, 1987
THE THREE KINGS (TF)   Aaron Spelling
   Productions, 1987
UHF   Orion, 1989
OVER MY DEAD BODY (TF)   Universal Television, 1990

FRED PRICE
GOING IN STYLE   Warner Bros., 1979, AD w/Gary Weist
PORKY'S II: THE NEXT DAY   20th Century Fox,
   1983, AD
KIDCO   20th Century Fox, 1984, AD

Pr

CINEMATOGRAPHERS
PRODUCTION
DESIGNERS,
COSTUME
DESIGNERS AND
FILM EDITORS
GUIDE

PRODUCTION DESIGNERS

Pr

CINEMATOGRAPHERS
PRODUCTION
DESIGNERS,
COSTUME
DESIGNERS AND
FILM EDITORS
GUIDE

P
R
O
D
U
C
T
I
O
N

D
E
S
I
G
N
E
R
S

MARTIN PRICE
BACHELOR PARTY   20th Century Fox, 1984,
   AD w/Kevin Conlin

ANNE PRITCHARD
WHO HAS SEEN THE WIND?   Astral Bellevue, 1977
A MAN, A WOMAN AND A BANK   Avco
   Embassy, 1979
ATLANTIC CITY   Paramount, 1981
OF UNKNOWN ORIGIN   Warner Bros., 1983
THRESHOLD   20th Century Fox International
   Classics, 1983
JOSHUA THEN AND NOW   20th Century Fox, 1985
SWITCHING CHANNELS   Tri-Star, 1988
DEAD MEN OUT (CTF)   Citadel Entertainment, 1989
DESCENDING ANGEL (CTF)   Freyda Rothstein
   Productions, 1990

TERRY PRITCHARD
THE RIDDLE OF THE SANDS   Satori, 1979, AD
THE FRENCH LIEUTENANT'S WOMAN   United Artists,
   1981, AD w/Allan Cameron & Norman Dorme
BEYOND THE LIMIT   Paramount, 1983, AD
OXFORD BLUES   MGM/UA, 1984, AD
RETURN TO WATERLOO   New Line Cinema, 1985

MICHEL PROULX
TOMORROW NEVER COMES   Rank, 1978, AD
LES BONS DEBARRAS   *GOOD RIDDANCE*
   International Film Exchange, 1981
VISITING HOURS   20th Century Fox, 1982, AD
CROSS COUNTRY   New World, 1983
COVERGIRL   New World, 1984, AD

GIANNI QUARANTA
BROTHER SUN, SISTER MOON ★   Paramount,
   1973, AD
LA TRAVIATA   Universal Classics, 1983, AD
A ROOM WITH A VIEW ★★   Cinecom
   International, 1986
OTELLO   Cannon, 1986
DANCERS   Cannon, 1987

MORT RABINOWITZ
THE MYSTIC WARRIOR (MS)   David L. Wolper-Stan
   Margulies Productions/Warner Bros. TV, 1984
V: THE FINAL BATTLE (TF)   Blatt-Singer Productions/
   Warner Bros. TV, 1984

TOBY CARR RAFELSON*
IATSE Local 876

THE KING OF MARVIN GARDENS   Columbia, 1972
STAY HUNGRY   United Artists, 1976
I NEVER PROMISED YOU A ROSE GARDEN   New
   World, 1977, AD
GOIN' SOUTH   Paramount, 1979
MELVIN AND HOWARD   Universal, 1980
THE BORDER   Universal, 1982
UNDER FIRE   Orion, 1983, AD

NICK RAFTER
Agent: Smith Gosnell Nicholson & Associates -
   Pacific Palisades, 213/459-0307

PRIVATE INVESTIGATIONS   MGM/UA, 1987, AD
MIAMI VICE (TVS)   1988-89

JEREMY RAILTON
THE TWO JAKES   Paramount, 1990, w/Richard Sawyer

JOE RAINEY
THE LAKER GIRLS (TF)   Viacom Productions, 1990

GARY RANDALL
BODY CHEMISTRY   Concorde, 1990
DEAD SPACE   Concorde, 1991

VIRGINIA RANDOLPH*
IATSE Local 876

THE HAND   Orion/Warner Bros., 1981
ACTION JACKSON   Lorimar, 1988, AD

IDA RANDOM*
IATSE Local 876

ON GOLDEN POND   Universal/AFD, 1981, AD
PARTNERS   Paramount, 1982, AD
FRANCES   Universal/AFD, 1982, AD
THE KID FROM NOWHERE (TF)   Cates-Bridges
   Company, 1982
THE BIG CHILL   Columbia, 1983
IRRECONCILABLE DIFFERENCES   Warner Bros., 1984
BODY DOUBLE   Columbia, 1984
SILVERADO   Columbia, 1985
ABOUT LAST NIGHT   Tri-Star, 1986
WHO'S THAT GIRL   Warner Bros., 1987
THROW MOMMA FROM THE TRAIN   Orion, 1987
RAIN MAN ★   MGM/UA, 1988
HOW I GOT INTO COLLEGE   20th Century Fox, 1989

FIRST FLIGHT (TF) 1989
THE WAR OF THE ROSES 20th Century Fox, 1989
DEFENDING YOUR LIFE Warner Bros., 1991

ANTHONY (TONY) READING
RAGTIME ★ Paramount, 1981,
    AD w/Patrizia Von Brandenstein
KRULL Columbia, 1983, AD w/Tony Curtis,
    Norman Dorme & Colin Grimes
THE BOUNTY Orion, 1984, AD
SCREAM FOR HELP Lorimar Distribution
    International, 1984, AD
PLENTY 20th Century Fox, 1985, AD
LIFEFORCE Tri-Star, 1985, AD
KING KONG LIVES DEG, 1986, AD w/Fred
    Carter & John Wood
CLUB PARADISE Warner Bros., 1986, AD
WILLOW MGM/UA, 1988, AD w/Tim Hutchinson &
    Malcolm Stone
JACK THE RIPPER (MS) Euston Films, 1988, AD
WHITE HUNTER, BLACK HEART Warner Bros.,
    1990, AD

RAY RECHT
DANGEROUS OBSESSION Panorama
    Entertainment, 1991

KIM REES
BEST OF THE BEST Taurus Entertainment, 1990

STEPHANE REICHEL
FIRST BLOOD Orion, 1982

JOHN REINHART
SOUL MAN New World, 1986, AD w/Don Diers
DEEPSTAR SIX Tri-Star, 1989
BURIED ALIVE (CTF) MCA Entertainment, 1990

NORMAN REYNOLDS
THE LITTLE PRINCE Paramount, 1974
MR. QUILP Avco Embassy, 1975
THE INCREDIBLE SARAH ★ Avco Embassy,
    1976, AD
STAR WARS ★★ 20th Century Fox, 1977,
    w/Les Dilley & John Barry
THE EMPIRE STRIKES BACK ★ 20th Century
    Fox, 1980
RAIDERS OF THE LOST ARK ★★ Paramount, 1981
RETURN OF THE JEDI ★ 20th Century Fox, 1983
RETURN TO OZ Buena Vista, 1985
YOUNG SHERLOCK HOLMES Paramount, 1985
EMPIRE OF THE SUN ★ Warner Bros., 1987
MOUNTAINS OF THE MOON Tri-Star, 1990
AVALON Tri-Star, 1990

LUCIANO RICCERI
LE BAL Almi Classics, 1984
THE BERLIN AFFAIR Cannon, 1985
MACARONI Paramount, 1985

STEPHEN RICE
LESS THAN ZERO 20th Century Fox, 1987, AD
TWICE DEAD Concorde, 1988
TEEN WITCH Trans World Entertainment, 1989
ONE MAN FORCE Shapiro Glickenhaus, 1989

EDWARD RICHARDSON*
IATSE Local 876

THE DOUBLE McGUFFIN Mulberry Square, 1979, AD
AMERICAN GIGOLO Paramount, 1980, AD
MODERN ROMANCE Columbia, 1981, AD
HARD COUNTRY Universal/AFD, 1981, AD
CAT PEOPLE Universal, 1982, AD
SCARFACE Universal, 1983
THIEF OF HEARTS Paramount, 1984, AD
BLAZE Buena Vista, 1989, AD

GEORGE RICHARDSON
OH, HEAVENLY DOG! 20th Century Fox, 1980, AD
NIJINSKY Paramount, 1980, AD
HIGH ROAD TO CHINA Warner Bros., 1983, AD
THE MISSION Warner Bros., 1986, AD
CRY FREEDOM Universal, 1987, AD w/Norman Dorme
    & John King

FRANK RICHWOOD*
IATSE Local 876

THE BEST LITTLE WHOREHOUSE IN TEXAS
    Universal, 1982, AD
RHINESTONE 20th Century Fox, 1984, AD
NO SMALL AFFAIR Columbia, 1984, AD
EXPLORERS Paramount, 1985, AD
JUMPIN' JACK FLASH 20th Century Fox, 1986, AD
PREDATOR 20th Century Fox, 1987, AD w/John
    Reinhart & Jorge Saenz
DRAGNET Universal, 1987, AD
BEACHES Buena Vista, 1988, AD

VALANNE RIDGEWAY
I'VE HEARD THE MERMAIDS SINGING Miramax, 1987
WHITE ROOM Alliance Releasing, 1990

J. MICHAEL RIVA*
IATSE Local 876
Agent: Lawrence A. Mirisch, Triad Artists, Inc. -
    Los Angeles, 213/556-2727

I NEVER PROMISED YOU A ROSE GARDEN
    New World, 1977
BARE KNUCKLES Intercontinental, 1978
FAST CHARLIE...THE MOONBEAM RIDER
    Universal, 1979
BRUBAKER 20th Century Fox, 1980, AD
ORDINARY PEOPLE Paramount, 1980,
    AD w/Phillip Bennett
THE HAND Orion/Warner Bros., 1981
CALLIE & SON (TF) Rosilyn Heller Productions/
    Herndale Presentations/City Films/Motown Pictures
    Company, 1981
HALLOWEEN II Universal, 1981
BAD BOYS Universal/AFD, 1983
THE ADVENTURES OF BUCKAROO BANZAI: ACROSS
    THE 8th DIMENSION 20th Century Fox, 1984
STRANGER'S KISS Orion Classics, 1984,
    Visual Consultant
THE SLUGGER'S WIFE Columbia, 1985
THE GOONIES Warner Bros., 1985
THE COLOR PURPLE ★ Warner Bros., 1985
THE GOLDEN CHILD Paramount, 1986
LETHAL WEAPON Warner Bros., 1987
SCROOGED Paramount, 1988
LETHAL WEAPON 2 Warner Bros., 1989
TANGO & CASH Warner Bros., 1989

Ri

CINEMATOGRAPHERS
PRODUCTION
DESIGNERS,
COSTUME
DESIGNERS AND
FILM EDITORS
GUIDE

P
R
O
D
U
C
T
I
O
N

D
E
S
I
G
N
E
R
S

Ro

CINEMATOGRAPHERS
PRODUCTION
DESIGNERS,
COSTUME
DESIGNERS AND
FILM EDITORS
GUIDE

P
R
O
D
U
C
T
I
O
N

D
E
S
I
G
N
E
R
S

CLIFFORD ROBINSON
A PASSAGE TO INDIA   Columbia, 1984, AD w/Leslie
    Tomkins, Herbert Westbrook & Ram Yedeker
OUT OF AFRICA   Universal, 1985, AD

BARRY ROBISON
RUNNING AGAINST TIME (CTF)   Finnegan-Pinchuk
    Productions, 1990

ALAN RODERICK-JONES
TARZAN, THE APE MAN   MGM/United Artists,
    1981, AD
SAVAGE HARVEST   20th Century Fox, 1981, AD
BOLERO   Cannon, 1984
TRIUMPHS OF A MAN CALLED HORSE   Jensen
    Farley Pictures, 1984
VAMP   New World, 1986

LESLIE E. ROLLINS
CROSSING DELANCEY   Warner Bros., 1988, AD

NICHOLAS ROMANAC
SPRING BREAK   Columbia, 1983, AD
MILES FROM HOME   Cinecom, 1988

PETER ROMERO
THE LONG RIDERS   United Artists, 1980, AD
THE RIGHT STUFF ★   The Ladd Company/Warner
    Bros., 1983, AD w/W. Stewart Campbell &
    Richard J. Lawrence

WOODY ROMINE
VALENTINO RETURNS   Skouras Pictures, 1989, AD

JOZSEF ROMVARI
MAX AND HELEN (CTF)   Citadel Entertainment, 1989
RED KING, WHITE KNIGHT (CTF)   John Kemeny
    Citadel Entertainment Productions, 1989

HILTON ROSEMARIN
THE GOOD MOTHER   Buena Vista, 1988,
    AD w/Richard Harrison

CHARLES ROSEN*
IATSE Local 876, SA Local 829
Agent: Smith Gosnell Nicholson & Associates -
    Pacific Palisades, 213/459-0307

CHARLY   Cinerama Releasing Corporation, 1968
THE PRODUCERS   Avco Embassy, 1968
A SEPARATE PEACE   Paramount, 1972
TAXI DRIVER   Columbia, 1976, AD
EMPIRE OF THE ANTS   American International, 1977
HEROES   Universal, 1977
INVASION OF THE BODY SNATCHERS   United
    Artists, 1978
BIG WEDNESDAY   Warner Bros., 1978
LAST EMBRACE   United Artists, 1979
THE MAIN EVENT   Warner Bros., 1979
INSIDE MOVES   AFD, 1980
CITY IN FEAR (TF)   Trans World International, 1981
MY FAVORITE YEAR   MGM/UA, 1982
THE TOY   Columbia, 1982
THE ENTITY   20th Century Fox, 1983
FLASHDANCE   Paramount, 1983
THE RIVER   Universal, 1984
THE WHOOPEE BOYS   Paramount, 1986

QUICKSILVER   Columbia, 1986
NOTHING IN COMMON   Tri-Star, 1986
TOUCH & GO   Tri-Star, 1987
BROADCAST NEWS   20th Century Fox, 1987
MY STEPMOTHER IS AN ALIEN   WEG, 1988
DOWNTOWN   20th Century Fox, 1990
MY BLUE HEAVEN   Warner Bros., 1990

PHILIP ROSENBERG
THE OWL AND THE PUSSYCAT   Columbia, 1970
THE ANDERSON TAPES   Columbia, 1971
THE POSSESSION OF JOEL DELANEY
    Paramount, 1972
CHILD'S PLAY   Paramount, 1972
FROM THE MIXED-UP FILES OF MRS. BASIL
    E. FRANKWEILER   Cinema 5, 1973
THE GAMBLER   Paramount, 1974
NEXT STOP, GREENWICH VILLAGE   20th Century
    Fox, 1976
NETWORK   MGM/United Artists, 1976
THE SENTINEL   Universal, 1977
FOREVER YOUNG, FOREVER FREE   Universal, 1976,
    AD w/Wendy Malan
THE WIZ ★   Universal, 1978, w/Tony Walton
ALL THAT JAZZ ★★   20th Century Fox, 1979,
    w/Tony Walton
EYEWITNESS   20th Century Fox, 1981
SOUP FOR ONE   Warner Bros., 1982
LOVESICK   The Ladd Company/Warner Bros., 1983
DANIEL   Paramount, 1983
GARBO TALKS   MGM/UA, 1984
THE MANHATTAN PROJECT   20th Century
    Fox, 1986
MOONSTRUCK   MGM/UA, 1987
RUNNING ON EMPTY   Warner Bros., 1988
THE JANUARY MAN   MGM/UA, 1989
FAMILY BUSINESS   Tri-Star, 1989
Q & A   Tri-Star, 1990

JOHN ROSEWARNE
RIVER OF DEATH   Cannon, 1990

ARIEL ROSHKO
HELD HOSTAGE: THE SIS AND JERRY LEVIN
    STORY (TF)   Paragon Entertainment, 1991
    (Israel sequences)

BILL ROSS
COLUMBO GOES TO COLLEGE (TF)   Universal
    TV, 1990
COLUMBO: MURDER CAN BE HAZARDOUS TO
    YOUR HEALTH (TF)   Universal City Studios, 1991

DENA ROTH
Phone: 213/466-3534

THE HAPPY HOOKER GOES HOLLYWOOD
    Cannon, 1980
THE UNSEEN   World Northal, 1981, AD
EVILSPEAK   The Frank Moreno Company, 1982
LIAR'S MOON   Crown International, 1982
DEATH OF AN ANGEL   20th Centuryf Fox, 1985, AD
AMAZING GRACE AND CHUCK   Tri-Star, 1987
18 AGAIN   New World, 1988
COMMUNION   MCEG, 1989, AD
WELCOME HOME, ROXY CARMICHAEL
    Paramount, 1990

PETER ROTHE

JUST A GIGOLO   United Artists, 1981
MOSCOW ON THE HUDSON   Columbia, 1984,
    AD w/Michael Molly

SARINA ROTSTEIN

Agent: Sanford-Skouras & Gross - Los Angeles,
    213/208-2100

GIRLS JUST WANT TO HAVE FUN   New World, 1985
BLACK MOON RISING   New World, 1986
NICE GIRLS DON'T EXPLODE   New World, 1987

BRUNO RUBEO

Agent: Sandra Marsh Management - Sherman Oaks,
    818/905-6961

SPRING FEVER   Comworld, 1983, AD w/Carmi Gallo
SALVADOR   Hemdale, 1986
PLATOON   Orion, 1986
WALKER   Universal, 1987
BLOOD RED   Hemdale, 1988
TALK RADIO   Universal, 1988
OLD GRINGO   Columbia, 1989, w/Stuart Wurtzel
DRIVING MISS DAISY ★   Warner Bros., 1989
BORN ON THE FOURTH OF JULY   Universal, 1989
KINDERGARTEN COP   Universal, 1990

GENE RUDOLF

Agent: The Gersh Agency, Inc., Beverly Hills -
    213/274-6611, New York - 212/997-1818

LITTLE MURDERS   20th Century Fox, 1970
THE HOSPITAL   United Artists, 1971
COPS & ROBBERS   United Artists, 1973
LAW AND DISORDER   Columbia, 1974
THE SOUL OF NIGGER CHARLEY   Paramount, 1973
THE TAKING OF PELHAM 1-2-3   United
    Artists, 1974
THE GREAT GATSBY   Paramount, 1974,
    AD w/Robert Laing
AARON LOVES ANGELA   1975
3 DAYS OF THE CONDOR   Paramount, 1975, AD
MARATHON MAN   Paramount, 1976, AD, New York
ANDY WARHOL'S BAD   New World, 1977
EXORCIST II: THE HERETIC   Warner Bros.,
    1977, AD, New York
SUPERMAN   Warner Bros., 1978, AD, New York
FINGERS   Brut Productions, 1978
RAGING BULL   United Artists, 1980
THE NIGHT THE LIGHTS WENT OUT IN GEORGIA
    Avco Embassy, 1981
DINER   MGM/UA, 1982, Visual Consultant
AUTHOR! AUTHOR!   20th Century Fox, 1982
THE RIGHT STUFF   The Ladd Company/Warner
    Bros., 1983, Visual Consultant
TRADING PLACES   Paramount, 1983
AGAINST ALL ODDS   Columbia, 1984
ONCE BITTEN   Samuel Goldwyn Company, 1985
BEST SELLER   Orion, 1987
COP   Atlantic Releasing Corporation, 1988
HEART OF MIDNIGHT   Samuel Goldwyn
    Company, 1988
MILLENNIUM   20th Century Fox, 1989
JOHNNY HANDSOME   Tri-Star, 1989
CADILLAC MAN   Orion, 1990
YOUNG GUNS II   20th Century Fox, 1990
OUT FOR JUSTICE   Warner Bros., 1991

ROY RUDOLPHE

BRUTAL GLORY   Quest Entertainment, 1991

BLAKE RUSSELL*

IATSE Local 876
Agent: The Gersh Agency, Inc. - Beverly Hills,
    213/274-6611

THOSE LIPS, THOSE EYES   United Artists, 1980, AD
HOWARD THE DUCK   Universal, 1986,
    AD w/Mark Billerman
LEONARD PART 6   Columbia, 1987, AD
THE LONG WALK HOME   Miramax Films, 1990

JOSAN F. RUSSO*

IATSE Local 876
Agent: The Gersh Agency, Inc., Beverly Hills -
    213/274-6611, New York - 212/997-1818

THE FRISCO KID   Warner Bros., 1979, AD
CARNY   United Artists, 1980, AD
RAPE AND MARRIAGE: THE RIDEOUT CASE (TF)
    Stonehenge Productions/Blue Greene Productions/
    Lorimar Productions, 1980, AD
CUTTER'S WAY   United Artists, 1981, AD
BEST FRIENDS   Warner Bros., 1982, AD
ICEMAN   Universal, 1984, AD w/Leon Erickson
CREATOR   Universal, 1985, AD
REAL GENIUS   Tri-Star, 1985
SOME KIND OF WONDERFUL   Paramount, 1987, AD
MANNEQUIN   20th Century Fox, 1987
WINNIE (TF)   All Girl Productions/NBC
    Productions, 1989
CAST THE FIRST STONE (TF)   Mench
    Productions, 1990
BURNING BRIDGES (TF)   Andrea Baynes
    Productions, 1990

BRYAN RYMAN*

IATSE Local 876
Agent: Smith Gosnell Nicholson & Associates -
    Pacific Palisades, 213/459-0307

TRACKS   Castle Hill Productions, 1976
THE KILLING OF A CHINESE BOOKIE   Faces
    International, 1976
OPENING NIGHT   Faces International, 1979, AD
BITTER HARVEST (TF)   Charles Fries
    Productions, 1981
SOMETHING SO RIGHT (TF)   List-Estrin Productions/
    Tsich-Avnet Television, 1982
THE EXECUTIONER'S SONG (TF)   Film
    Communications Inc., 1982
THE KID WITH THE BROKEN HALO (TF)   Satellite
    Productions, 1982
COCAINE: ONE MAN'S SEDUCTION (TF)   Charles Fries
    Productions/David Goldsmith Productions, 1983
THE FANTASTIC WORLD OF D.C. COLLINS (TF)
    Guillaume-Margo Productions/Zephyr
    Productions, 1984
CITY KILLER (TF)   Stan Shpetner Productions, 1984
PLAYING WITH FIRE (TF)   Zephyr Productions, 1985
PRINCE OF BEL AIR (TF)   Leonard Hill Films, 1986
BLACK MOON RISING   New World, 1986
THE CHILDREN OF TIMES SQUARE (TF)
    Gross-Weston Productions, 1986
SOMETHING IN COMMON (TF)   New World TV/
    Freyda Rothstein Productions/Litke-Grossbart
    Productions, 1986

Ry

CINEMATOGRAPHERS
PRODUCTION
DESIGNERS,
COSTUME
DESIGNERS AND
FILM EDITORS
GUIDE

PRODUCTION DESIGNERS

WARM HANDS, COLD FEET (TF)
Lorimar-Telepictures, 1987
POOR LITTLE RICH GIRL: THE BARBARA HUTTON
STORY (MS)   Lester Persky Productions/
ITC Productions, 1987
PROMISED A MIRACLE (TF)   Dick Clark Productions/
Republic Pictures, 1988
ELVIS AND ME (TF)   Navarone Productions/New
World TV, 1988
WHEN WE WERE YOUNG (TF)   Richard & Esther
Shapiro Productions, 1989
CALL ME ANNA (TF)   Finnegan-Pinchuk
Productions, 1990

KEVIN RYAN
FALSE IDENTITY (TF)   RKO Pictures, 1990

S

WILLIAM SANDELL*
IATSE Local 876
Agent: The Gersh Agency, Inc., Beverly Hills -
213/274-6611, New York - 212/997-1818

THE CLONES   Premiere International, 1977
THE PACK   Warner Bros., 1978
FAST CHARLIE...THE MOONBEAM RIDER
Universal, 1979, AD
PIRANHA   New World, 1978
THE PROMISE   Universal, 1979
SERIAL   Paramount, 1980
BLOOD BEACH   Jerry Gross Organization, 1981
DEAD AND BURIED   Avco Embassy, 1981,
w/Joe Aubel
YOUNG LUST   RSO Films, 1982
AIRPLANE II: THE SEQUEL   Paramount, 1982
THE WILD LIFE   Universal, 1984
ST. ELMO'S FIRE   Columbia, 1985
ROBOCOP   Orion, 1987
BIG BUSINESS   Buena Vista, 1988
TOTAL RECALL   Tri-Star, 1990
NOTHING BUT TROUBLE   Warner Bros., 1991

ANDREW SANDERS
SHOCK TREATMENT   20th Century Fox, 1981, AD
MERRY CHRISTMAS, MR. LAWRENCE   Universal,
1983, AD
THE HIT   Island Alive, 1984
CASTAWAY   Cannon, 1987
THE LAST TEMPTATION OF CHRIST   Universal,
1988, AD
THE WITCHES   Warner Bros., 1990

THOMAS E. SANDERS
DAYS OF THUNDER   Paramount, 1990,
AD w/Benjamin Fernandez

BRUNO SANTINI
THE BALLAD OF THE SAD CAFE   Angelika
Films, 1991

STEVE SARDANIS*
IATSE 876

THE WORLD'S GREATEST LOVER   20th Century
Fox, 1977, AD
CAPTIVE HEARTS   MGM/UA, 1987,
AD w/Francois DeLucy
SUSPECT   Tri-Star, 1987, AD

GAUDELINE SAURIOL
THE DECLINE OF THE AMERICAN EMPIRE   Cineplex
Odeon, 1986, AD

RICHARD SAWYER*
IATSE Local 876
Agent: Smith Gosnell Nicholson & Associates -
Pacific Palisades, 213/459-0307

IN SEARCH OF NOAH'S ARK   Sunn Classic, 1977, AD
FM   Universal, 1978, AD
MELVIN AND HOWARD   Universal, 1980, AD
WHERE THE BUFFALO ROAM   Universal, 1980
MOTHER AND DAUGHTER - THE LOVING WAR (TF)
Edgar J. Scherick Associates, 1980
COWARD OF THE COUNTY (TF)   Kraco
Productions, 1981
THE HAND   Orion/Warner Bros., 1981, AD
THINGS ARE TOUGH ALL OVER   Columbia, 1982
THE BORDER   Universal, 1982, AD
THE GAMBLER (TF)   Lion Share Productions, 1983
LOTTERY! (TF)   Rosner TV Productions/Orion TV, 1983
OFF THE WALL   Jensen Farley Pictures, 1983
SHATTERED VOWS (TF)   1984
BACHELOR PARTY   20th Century Fox, 1984
LOST IN AMERICA   The Geffen Company/Warner
Bros., 1985
MOVING VIOLATIONS   20th Century Fox, 1985
TWILIGHT ZONE - THE MOVIE (Segment 1)   Warner
Bros., 1985
THREE AMIGOS   Orion, 1986
C.A.T. SQUAD (TF)   NBC Productions, 1986
VIBES   Columbia, 1988
BIG MAN ON CAMPUS   Vestron, 1989
RICH MEN, SINGLE WOMEN (TF)   Aaron Spelling
Productions, 1990, AD
THE TWO JAKES   Paramount, 1990, w/Jeremy Railton

GIANNI SBARRA
GOOD MORNING, BABYLON   Vestron, 1987, AD

FERDINANDO SCARFIOTTI*
IATSE Local 876
Phone: 213/456-6641

THE CONFORMIST   Paramount, 1971
DEATH IN VENICE   Warner Bros., 1971
AVANTI!   United Artists, 1972
LAST TANGO IN PARIS   United Artists, 1973
DAISY MILLER   Paramount, 1974
FLASH GORDON   Universal, 1980
AMERICAN GIGOLO   Paramount, 1980
HONKY TONK FREEWAY   Universal/AFD, 1981
CAT PEOPLE   Universal, 1982
BRING ON THE NIGHT (FD)   Samuel Goldwyn
Company, 1985
THE LAST EMPEROR ★★   Columbia, 1987
MAMBA   Eidoscope/Reteitalia, 1988

GERLINDE SCHARINGER
COMIC BOOK CONFIDENTIAL   Cinecom, 1989

JOEL SCHILLER*
IATSE Local 876
Agent: The Gersh Agency, Inc. - Beverly Hills,
   213/274-6611

THE REIVERS   National General, 1969
THE ILLUSTRATED MAN   Warner Bros., 1969
THE McMASTERS   Chevron, 1970
VALDEZ IS COMING   1971
THE SPORTING CLUB   Avco Embassy, 1971
LADY ICE   National General, 1973
ACE ELI AND RODGER OF THE SKIES   20th
   Century Fox, 1973
A REFLECTION OF FEAR   Columbia, 1973
KID BLUE   20th Century Fox, 1973
LENNY   United Artists, 1974
THE MAN IN THE GLASS BOOTH   American Film
   Theatre, 1975
THE BIG BUS   Paramount, 1976
THE BUDDY HOLLY STORY   Columbia, 1978
THE MUPPET MOVIE   AFD, 1979
ICE CASTLES   Columbia, 1979
A SMALL CIRCLE OF FRIENDS   United Artists, 1980
CHARLIE CHAN AND THE CURSE OF THE
   DRAGON QUEEN   American Cinema, 1980
HONEYSUCKLE ROSE   Warner Bros., 1980
UNDER THE RAINBOW   Orion/Warner Bros., 1981
MEGAFORCE   20th Century Fox, 1982
SLAPSTICK OF ANOTHER KIND   Entertainment
   Releasing Corporation/International Film
   Marketing, 1983
SONGWRITER   Tri-Star, 1984
MISUNDERSTOOD   MGM/UA, 1984
MURPHY'S ROMANCE   Columbia, 1985
SEDUCED (TF)   Catalina Production Group/
   Comworld Productions, 1985
NUTS   Warner Bros., 1987
CLEAN AND SOBER   Warner Bros., 1988
STANLEY & IRIS   MGM/UA, 1989
NARROW MARGIN   Carolco/Tri-Star, 1990

JAN SCHLUBACH
THE UNAPPROACHABLE   Teleculture, 1984,
   w/Albrecht Konrad
JUDGMENT IN BERLIN   New Line Cinema, 1988,
   AD w/Peter Atteneder
THE ROSE GARDEN   Pathe Entertainment, 1989

JOANNE SCHMIDT
sex, lies, and videotape   Miramax, 1989, AD

CURTIS A. SCHNELL
Agent: Grace Lyons Management - Los Angeles,
   213/655-5100

LAST RESORT   Concorde, 1986
TRICK OR TREAT   DEG, 1986
PERFECT PEOPLE (TF)   1988
REMOTE CONTROL   Vista Organization, 1988
DAY ONE (TF)   Aaron Spelling Productions, 1989
CRIMINAL LAW   Hemdale, 1989
DOIN' TIME ON PLANET EARTH   Cannon, 1989
DEFENSELESS   New Century/Vista, 1990
FIRE AND RAIN (CTF)   Wilshire Court Productions, 1990
DEATH WARRANT   MGM/UA, 1990
THE PERFECT WEAPON   Paramount, 1991

JAMES SCHOPPE*
IATSE Local 876
Agent: Smith Gosnell Nicholson & Associates -
   Pacific Palisades, 213/459-0307

CORVETTE SUMMER   MGM/United Artists,
   1978, AD
COMING HOME   United Artists, 1978, AD
BEING THERE   United Artists, 1979, AD
THE ROSE   20th Century Fox, 1979, AD
THE STUNT MAN   20th Century Fox, 1980, AD
WHY WOULD I LIE?   MGM/United Artists, 1980, AD
THE OCTAGON   American Cinema, 1980
LOOKIN' TO GET OUT   Paramount, 1982, AD
SOME KIND OF HERO   Paramount, 1982
UNCOMMON VALOR   Paramount, 1983
RETURN OF THE JEDI ★   20th Century Fox, 1983,
   AD w/Fred Hole
REVENGE OF THE NERDS   20th Century
   Fox, 1984
VOLUNTEERS   Tri-Star, 1985
GUNG HO   Paramount, 1986
OVER THE TOP   Cannon, 1987
VICE VERSA   Columbia, 1988
WHAT'S ALAN WATCHING? (Pilot)   1989
SECOND SIGHT   Warner Bros., 1989

ROBERT SCHULLENBERG
NOT FOR PUBLICATION   Samuel Goldwyn
   Company, 1984
THINK BIG   Concorde, 1990

ELISABETH A. SCOTT
GENUINE RISK   I.R.S. Releasing, 1990

ELLIOT SCOTT
THE INCREDIBLE SARAH ★   Avco Embassy, 1976
WARLORDS OF ATLANTIS   Columbia, 1978
THE 5th MUSKETEER   Columbia, 1979
ARABIAN ADVENTURE   AFD, 1979
THE WATCHER IN THE WOODS   Buena Vista, 1980
DRAGONSLAYER   Paramount, 1981
EVIL UNDER THE SUN   Universal/AFD, 1982
THE PIRATES OF PENZANCE   Universal, 1983
LABYRINTH   Tri-Star, 1986
WHO FRAMED ROGER RABBIT ★   Buena Vista, 1988,
   w/Roger Cain
INDIANA JONES AND THE LAST CRUSADE
   Paramount, 1989

JAN SCOTT*
IATSE Local 876
Agent: Jerry Goldstein, The Goldstein Company -
   Los Angeles, 213/557-2507

STILETTO   Avco Embassy, 1969, AD
THE LEGEND OF LYLAH CLARE   MGM,
   1968, AD
SACCO AND VANZETTI   UMC, 1971
THE MAN WITHOUT A COUNTRY (TF)   Norman
   Rosemont Productions, 1973, AD
A GIRL NAMED SOONER (TF)   Frederick Brogger
   Associates/20th Century Fox TV, 1975, AD
TRILOGY OF TERROR (TF)   ABC Circle Films,
   1975, AD
JOURNEY FROM DARKNESS (TF)   Bob Banner
   Associates, 1975, AD
YOUNG PIONEERS (TF)   ABC Circle Films,
   1976, AD

Sc
CINEMATOGRAPHERS
PRODUCTION
DESIGNERS,
COSTUME
DESIGNERS AND
FILM EDITORS
GUIDE

P
R
O
D
U
C
T
I
O
N

D
E
S
I
G
N
E
R
S

Sc

CINEMATOGRAPHERS
PRODUCTION
DESIGNERS,
COSTUME
DESIGNERS AND
FILM EDITORS
GUIDE

P
R
O
D
U
C
T
I
O
N

D
E
S
I
G
N
E
R
S

NIGHTMARE IN BADHAM COUNTY (TF)   ABC Circle
    Films, 1976, AD
ELEANOR AND FRANKLIN (TF) ☆☆   Talent
    Associates, 1976, AD
ELEANOR AND FRANKLIN: THE WHITE HOUSE
    YEARS (TF)   Talent Associates, 1977, AD
THE GATHERING (TF)   Hanna-Barbera
    Productions, 1977, AD
ROOTS (TF)   Wolper Productions, 1977, AD
THE END   United Artists, 1978, AD
STUDS LONIGAN (Part III) (MS) ☆☆   Lorimar
    Productions, 1979, AD
LOVING COUPLES   20th Century Fox, 1980, AD
MARILYN: THE UNTOLD STORY (TF)   Lawrence J.
    Schiller Productions, 1980, AD
RICH AND FAMOUS   MGM/UA, 1981, AD
JACQUELINE SUSANN'S VALLEY OF THE
    DOLLS (TF)   20th Century Fox TV, 1981, AD
RITA HAYWORTH: THE LOVE GODDESS (TF)
    The Susskind Company, 1983, AD
GRANDVIEW, U.S.A.   Warner Bros., 1984, AD
EVERGREEN (MS) ☆☆   Edgar J. Scherick Associates/
    Metromedia Producers Corporation, 1984
THE DOLLMAKER (TF)   Finnegan Associates/
    IPC Films, Inc./Dollmaker Productions, 1984, AD
SQUARE DANCE   Island Pictures, 1986
I'LL BE HOME FOR CHRISTMAS (TF)   NBC
    Productions, 1988
THE KENNEDYS OF MASSACHUSETTS (MS)
    Edgar J. Scherick Associates Productions, 1990
BLIND FAITH-PARTS I & II (TF)   NBC
    Productions, 1990
CAROLINE? (TF)   Barry & Enright Productions, 1990
JACKIE COLLINS' LUCKY CHANCES-
    PARTS I-III (MS)   NBC Productions, 1990

JILL SCOTT
HOME IS WHERE THE HART IS   Atlantic Releasing
    Corporation, 1987, AD

JESSICA SCOTT-JUSTICE
STICKY FINGERS   Spectrafilm, 1988

R. CLIFFORD SEARCY
THE HANOI HILTON   Cannon, 1987
CASEY'S GIFT: FOR LOVE OF A CHILD (TF)
    American First Run Studios, 1990
SYNGENOR   South Gate Entertainment, 1990
RUSH WEEK   RCA/Columbia Pictures Home
    Video, 1991

DAVID SEARL
BLOODSPORT   Cannon, 1988

MICHELE SEFFMAN
INSTANT KARMA   Rosenbloom Entertainment,
    1990, w/George Edwards

MAURICE SENDAK
NUTCRACKER   Atlantic Releasing Corporation, 1986

ZELJKO SENECIC
TRANSYLVANIA 6-5000   New World, 1985

ANNA SENIOR
PHAR LAP   20th Century Fox, 1984

JACK SENTER*
IATSE Local 876
Agent: The Miller Agency - Santa Clarita,
    818/843-7335
Phone: 213/654-2797

KUNG FU (TF)   Warner Bros., 1972, AD
FREAKY FRIDAY   Buena Vista, 1976,
    AD w/John B. Mansbridge
NO DEPOSIT, NO RETURN   Buena Vista, 1976,
    AD w/John B. Mansbridge
OBSESSION   Columbia, 1976, AD
OH, GOD!   Warner Bros., 1977, AD
GREASED LIGHTNING   Warner Bros., 1977, AD
RETURN FROM WITCH MOUNTAIN   Buena Vista,
    1978, AD w/John B. Mansbridge
GO TELL THE SPARTANS   Avco Embassy,
    1978, AD
LOVE AND BULLETS   AFD, 1979, AD
MODERN PROBLEMS   20th Century Fox, 1981
THE MAN WHO LOVED WOMAN   Columbia,
    1983, AD
MICKI AND MAUDE   Columbia, 1984, AD
THE EXECUTION (TF)   Newland-Raynor Productions/
    Comworld Productions , 1985, AD
NUTCRACKER: MONEY, MADNESS AND
    MURDER (MS)   Green Arrow Productions/Warner
    Bros. TV, 1987, AD
DESPERATE (TF)   Toots Productions/Warner
    Bros. TV, 1987, AD
THE NEW ADVENTURES OF PIPPI LONGSTOCKING
    Columbia, 1988

RANDY SER
Agent: Grace Lyons Management - Los Angeles,
    213/655-5100
Phone: 213/661-7012

MORTUARY   Artists Releasing Corporation/Film
    Ventures International, 1983, AD
TOMBOY   Crown International, 1985, AD
JOCKS   Crown International, 1987, AD
DUTCH TREAT   Cannon, 1987
CASUAL SEX?   Universal, 1988
FEDS   Warner Bros., 1988
DARKMAN   Universal, 1990

MICHAEL SEYMOUR
Agent: Camera Masters - Venice, 213/306-0810

GUMSHOE   Columbia, 1971
THEATRE OF BLOOD   United Artists, 1973
ROSEBUD   United Artists, 1975
ALIEN ★   20th Century Fox, 1979
EUREKA   United Artists Classics, 1984
THE BRIDE   Columbia, 1985
REVENGE   Columbia, 1990, w/Benjamin Fernandez
MR. DESTINY   Buena Vista, 1990

SHARON SEYMOUR
STACKING   Spectrafilm, 1987, AD
JOHNNY BE GOOD   Orion, 1988, AD
IN A SHALLOW GRAVE   Skouras Pictures, 1988, AD
HEART OF DIXIE   Orion, 1989, AD
BROTHER FUTURE (TF)   Laneauville/Morris
    Entertainment, 1991

JAMES SHANAHAN*
IATSE Local 876

THE INCREDIBLE SHRINKING WOMAN
Universal, 1981
THE ORDEAL OF BILL CARNEY (TF)   Belle
Company/Comworld Productions, 1981
M.A.D.D.: MOTHERS AGAINST DRUNK
DRIVERS (TF)   Universal TV, 1983
GOING BESERK   Universal, 1983, AD
CHANDLERTOWN *PHILIP MARLOWE -
PRIVATE EYE* (CMS)   HBO/David Wickes
Television Ltd./London Weekend Television, 1983
POISON IVY (TF)   NBC Productions, 1985
STICK   Universal, 1985
SUNDAY DRIVE (TF)   Walt Disney TV, 1986
THE LEFTOVERS (TF)   Walt Disney TV, 1986
THE LAST ELECTRIC KNIGHT (TF)   Walt
Disney TV, 1986
QUICKSILVER   Columbia, 1986, AD
BRIDE OF BOOGEDY (TF)   Walt Disney TV, 1987
YOUNG HARRY HOUDINI (TF)   Walt Disney TV, 1987
OVERBOARD   MGM/UA, 1987, AD w/Jim Dultz
DISASTER AT SILO 7 (TF)   Mark Carliner
Productions, 1988
NO HOLDS BARRED   New Line Cinema, 1989
RIDING THE EDGE   Trans World Entertainment, 1989
THE OPERATION (TF)   Moress, Nanas, Golden
Entertainment, 1990

GEOFFREY SHARPE
TANK MALLING   Pointlane Films, 1989

MAXINE SHEPARD
Agent: The Irv Schechter Company - Beverly Hills,
213/278-8070

THE TOMB   Trans World Entertainment, 1986, AD
COLD STEEL   CineTel, 1987, AD
CYCLONE   CineTel, 1987
PULSE   Columbia, 1988, AD
UNDER THE BOARDWALK   New World, 1988

RICHARD SHERMAN
Agent: Sanford-Skouras & Gross - Los Angeles,
213/208-2100
Home: 6804 Oakwood Ave. - Los Angeles,
213/938-1175

SISTER SISTER   New World, 1988
DARK HOLIDAY (TF)   Peter Nelson/Lou Antonio
Productions, 1989
ORIGINAL SIN (TF)   Larry A. Thompson
Organization/New World TV, 1989
ROCK (TF)   The Konigsberg/Sanitsky
Company, 1990
PEOPLE LIKE US-PARTS I & II (TF)   CM Two
Productions, 1990
TOUCH OF A STRANGER   Raven-Star
Pictures, 1990
TIPPERARY   MGM/UA, 1990
PARIS TROUT   Viacom, 1991

WILFRED SHINGLETON
VOYAGE OF THE DAMNED   Avco Embassy, 1976
THE LADY VANISHES   Rank, 1979
EYE OF THE NEEDLE   United Artists, 1981
HEAT AND DUST   Universal Classics, 1983

WALTER SHIPLEY
Agent: The Miller Agency - Santa Clarita, 818/843-7335

TAKE TWO   TBJ Films, 1987, AD
LONER   International Film Entertainment, 1987, AD
SCANDAL IN A SMALL TOWN (TF)   1988, AD

NAOMI SHOHAN
FRAMED (CTF)   HBO Pictures, 1990, AD

JAMES R. SHUMAKER
9 1/2 NINJAS   Republic Pictures Home Video, 1991

JOHN SIDDALL
THE PINK PANTHER STRIKES AGAIN   United Artists,
1976, AD
REVENGE OF THE PINK PANTHER   United Artists,
1978, AD
THERE GOES THE BRIDE   Vanguard, 1980, AD
THE DOGS OF WAR   United Artists, 1980, AD
CURSE OF THE PINK PANTHER   MGM/UA, 1983,
AD w/Tim Hutchinson & Alan Tomkins
SCANDALOUS   Orion, 1984, AD w/Brian Ackland-Snow
D.A.R.Y.L.   Paramount, 1985, AD
SHANGHAI SURPRISE   MGM/UA, 1986,
AD w/David Minty

ANDREW SIEGEL
SURVIVAL QUEST   MGM/UA, 1990

GIANNI SILVESTRI
THE SHELTERING SKY   Warner Bros., 1990

CARLO SIMI
ONCE UPON A TIME IN AMERICA   The Ladd Company/
Warner Bros., 1984, AD w/James Singelis

RAYMOND SIMM
Agent: London Management - London W1 England,
011/441/493-1610

SAINT JOAN   United Artists, 1957
BONJOUR TRISTESSE   Columbia, 1958
THE ANGRY SILENCE   Valiant, 1960
ALL NIGHT LONG   Continental, 1961
THE MARK   Continental, 1961
WHISTLE DOWN THE WIND   Pathe-America, 1962
A KIND OF LOVING   Contintal, 1962
THE L-SHAPED ROOM   Columbia, 1963
BILLY LIAR   Continental, 1963
SEANCE ON A WET AFTERNOON   Artixo, 1964
A HARD DAY'S NIGHT   United Artists, 1964, AD
HELP!   United Artists, 1965, AD
DARLING   Embassy, 1965
THE WRONG BOX   Columbia, 1966
THE WHISPERERS   United Artists, 1967
DEADFALL   20th Century Fox, 1968
THE MADWOMAN OF CHAILLOT   Warner Bros., 1969
THE RECKONING   Columbia, 1969
FRAGMENT OF FEAR   Columbia, 1971
BREAKING OF BUMBO   Timon/ABPC, 1971
DULCIMA   1971
STRAW DOGS   Cinerama Releasing Corporation, 1972
NO SEX PLEASE - WE'RE BRITISH
Columbia-Warner, 1973
HENNESSY   American International, 1975
THE SLIPPER AND THE ROSE: THE STORY OF
CINDERELLA   Universal, 1976

Si

CINEMATOGRAPHERS
PRODUCTION
DESIGNERS,
COSTUME
DESIGNERS AND
FILM EDITORS
GUIDE

PRODUCTION DESIGNERS

Si

CINEMATOGRAPHERS
PRODUCTION
DESIGNERS,
COSTUME
DESIGNERS AND
FILM EDITORS
GUIDE

P
R
O
D
U
C
T
I
O
N

D
E
S
I
G
N
E
R
S

MARK SIMON
KILL CRAZY   Media Home Entertainment, 1991, AD

JAMES SINGELIS
ONCE UPON A TIME IN AMERICA   The Ladd
    Company/Warner Bros., 1984, AD
SEE NO EVIL, HEAR NO EVIL   Tri-Star, 1989, AD

ROBERT SISSMAN
PEACEMAKER   Fries Entertainment, 1990
BLOOD SALVAGE   Paragon Arts, 1990

DIAN SKINNER
TWISTED JUSTICE   Seymour Borde &
    Associates, 1990

ADRIAN SMITH
DANCE WITH A STRANGER   Samuel Goldwyn
    Company, 1985, AD
PLENTY   20th Century Fox, 1985, AD
EMPIRE STATE   Virgin/Miracle, 1987
THE GOOD FATHER   Skouras Pictures, 1987
DECEMBER BRIDE   Film Four International, 1991

JACK MARTIN SMITH*
IATSE Local 876

FANTASTIC VOYAGE ★★   20th Century Fox, 1966
DOCTOR DOLITTLE ★   20th Century Fox, 1967,
    AD w/Ed Graves
THE DETECTIVE   1968, AD
PLANET OF THE APES   20th Century Fox, 1968, AD
THE SWEET RIDE   20th Century Fox, 1968, AD
HELLO, DOLLY! ★★   20th Century Fox, 1969,
    AD w/Herman Blumenthal
TORA! TORA! TORA! ★   20th Century Fox, 1970
MYRA BRECKENRIDGE   20th Century Fox, 1970, AD
THE GREAT WHITE HOPE   20th Century Fox,
    1970, AD
COVER ME BABE   20th Century Fox, 1970, AD
BEYOND THE VALLEY OF THE DOLLS   20th
    Century Fox, 1970, AD
M*A*S*H   20th Century Fox, 1970, AD
MOVE   20th Century Fox, 1970, AD
ESCAPE FROM THE PLANET OF THE APES
    20th Century Fox, 1971, AD
THE CULPEPPER CATTLE CO.   20th Century Fox,
    1972, AD
ACE ELI AND RODGER OF THE SKIES   20th
    Century Fox, 1973, AD
EMPEROR OF THE NORTH   20th Century Fox,
    1973, AD
THE ICEMAN COMETH   American Film Theatre,
    1973, AD
RHINOCEROS   American Film Theatre, 1974, AD
LOST IN THE STARS   American Film Theatre,
    1974, AD
THE REINCARNATION OF PETER PROUD   American
    International, 1975, AD
THE GREAT SCOUT AND CATHOUSE THURSDAY
    American International, 1976, AD
GUS   Buena Vista, 1976, AD
PETE'S DRAGON   Buena Vista, 1977, AD

MICHAEL C. SMITH
IN THE SPIRIT   Castle Hill Productions, 1990

MORLEY SMITH
THE SHOOTING PARTY   European Classics, 1984
THE WHISTLE BLOWER   Hemdale, 1987
MURDER STORY   Contracts International/Elsevier
    Vendex Film, 1989

PETER LANSDOWN SMITH*
IATSE Local 876

CHAPTER TWO   Columbia, 1979, AD
THE LAST MARRIED COUPLE IN AMERICA   Universal,
    1980, AD
SEEMS LIKE OLD TIMES   Columbia, 1980, AD
PATERNITY   Paramount, 1981, AD
NIGHT SHIFT   The Ladd Company/Warner Bros.,
    1982, AD
GOING BESERK   Universal, 1983
FANDANGO   Warner Bros., 1985, AD
JAGGED EDGE   Columbia, 1985, AD
THE NEW KIDS   Columbia, 1986
BIG TROUBLE   Columbia, 1986, AD
STAR TREK IV: THE VOYAGE HOME   Paramount,
    1986, AD w/Joe Aubel
BLIND DATE   Tri-Star, 1987, AD
NADINE   Tri-Star, 1987, AD w/Cary White
TEQUILA SUNRISE   Warner Bros., 1988, AD
FAT MAN AND LITTLE BOY   Paramount, 1989,
    AD w/Larry E. Fulton

ROBERT L. SMITH
DICE RULES   Seven Arts, 1991

ROY FORGE SMITH
Agent: Sandra Marsh Management - Sherman Oaks,
    818/905-6961

FAR FROM THE MADDING CROWD   MGM, 1967, AD
THE ASSASSINATION BUREAU   Paramount, 1969, AD
THE AMAZING MR. BLUNDEN   Goldstone, 1972, AD
MONTY PYTHON AND THE HOLY GRAIL
    Cinema 5, 1974
THE HOUSE BY THE LAKE   American
    International, 1976
JABBERWOCKY   Cinema 5, 1977
THE HOUND OF THE BASKERVILLES   Atlantic
    Releasing Corporation, 1979
RUNNING   Columbia, 1979
YESTERDAY   Cinepix, 1980, AD
CLOWN WHITE (TF)   Martin-Paul Productions, 1980
FUNERAL HOME   *CRIES IN THE NIGHT*   MPM, 1981
THE LAST CHASE   Crown International, 1981, AD
MELANIE   Jensen Farley Pictures, 1983
CURTAINS   Jensen Farley Pictures, 1983
S.C.T.V. (TVS)   1984
MRS. SOFFEL   MGM/UA, 1984, AD
A DEADLY BUSINESS (TF)   Thebaut-Frey Productions/
    Taft Entertainment TV, 1986
BURNIN' LOVE   Hemdale, 1987
HAUNTED BY HER PAST (TF)   Norton Wright
    Productions/ITC Productions, 1987
THE KISS   Tri-Star, 1988
BILL & TED'S EXCELLENT ADVENTURE   Orion, 1989
TEENAGE MUTANT NINJA TURTLES   Golden Harvest/
    New Line Cinema, 1990
WARLOCK   Trimark, 1991

WILLIAM CRAIG SMITH
PROPHECY   Paramount, 1979
S.O.B.   Paramount, 1981, AD
VICTOR/VICTORIA ★   MGM/United Artists, 1982,
    AD w/Tim Hutchinson

DAVID L. SNYDER*
IATSE Local 876
Agent: The Gersh Agency, Inc. - Beverly Hills,
213/274-6611

CAPTAIN AMERICA (TF)   Universal TV, 1979
IN GOD WE TRUST   Universal, 1980, AD
THE IDOLMAKER   United Artists, 1980, AD
BLADE RUNNER ★   Warner Bros., 1982,
w/Lawrence G. Paull
STRANGE BREW   MGM/UA, 1983
BRAINSTORM   MGM/UA, 1983, AD
RACING WITH THE MOON   Paramount, 1984, AD
SINS OF THE PAST (TF)   Sinpast
Entertainment Company Productions, 1984, AD
THE WOMAN IN RED   Orion, 1984, AD
PEE-WEE'S BIG ADVENTURE   Warner Bros., 1985
MY SCIENCE PROJECT   Buena Vista, 1985, AD
ARMED AND DANGEROUS   Columbia, 1986
BACK TO SCHOOL   Orion, 1986
SUMMER SCHOOL   Paramount, 1987
MOVING   Warner Bros., 1988
SHE'S OUT OF CONTROL   Columbia, 1989
COLD DOG SOUP   HandMade Films, 1990

CYNTHIA SOWDER
HARD ROCK ZOMBIES   Cannon, 1985, AD
KING OF THE CITY   *CLUB LIFE*   Troma, 1986,
AD w/Philip J.C. Duffin
THE ALLNIGHTER   Universal, 1987
THE BLUE IGUANA   Paramount, 1988
POWWOW HIGHWAY   HandMade Films, 1988
STATIC   Sandstar Releasing Company, 1988

LUCIANO SPADONI
SAHARA   MGM/UA, 1984
KING SOLOMON'S MINES   Cannon, 1985
THE ASSISI UNDERGROUND   Cannon, 1985
THE DELTA FORCE   Cannon, 1986

STEPHEN SPENCE
Agent: The Gersh Agency, Inc., Beverly Hills -
213/274-6611, New York - 212/997-1818

THE SENDER   Paramount, 1982, AD
THE KILLING FIELDS   Warner Bros., 1984, AD
ELENI   Warner Bros., 1985, AD
BABY - SECRET OF THE LOST LEGEND   Buena
Vista, 1985, AD
LITTLE SHOP OF HORRORS   The Geffen
Company/Warner Bros., 1986, AD w/John Fenner
GOOD MORNING, VIETNAM   Buena Vista,
1987, AD

JAMES H. SPENCER*
IATSE Local 876
Agent: Smith Gosnell Nicholson & Associates - Pacific
Palisades, 213/459-0307

FRIENDLY PERSUASION (TF)   International
TV Productions/Allied Artists, 1975
ROCKY   United Artists, 1976, AD
BOUND FOR GLORY   United Artists, 1976,
AD w/William Sully
RED ALERT (TF)   The Jozak Company/
Paramount TV, 1977
KING (MS)   Abby Mann Productions/Filmways, 1978
SOME KIND OF MIRACLE (TF)   Lorimar
Productions, 1979

SON RISE: A MIRACLE OF LOVE (TF)   Rothman-Wohl
Productions/Filmways, 1979
FIRE SALE   20th Century Fox, 1979
DIE LAUGHING   Orion/Warner Bros., 1980
KING OF THE MOUNTAIN   Universal, 1981
STRIPES   Columbia, 1981
NOT IN FRONT OF THE CHILDREN (TF)
Tamtco Productions/The Edward S. Feldman
Company, 1982
THE SENDER   Paramount, 1982
POLTERGEIST   MGM/UA, 1982
GREMLINS   Warner Bros., 1984
TWILIGHT ZONE - THE MOVIE (Segment 4)   Warner
Bros., 1985, AD
INNERSPACE   Warner Bros., 1987
THE 'BURBS   Universal, 1989
GREMLINS 2: THE NEW BATCH   Warner
Bros., 1990

NORRIS SPENCER
THELMA & LOUISE   Pathe/MGM, 1991

CAROL SPIER
Agent: Sandra Marsh Management - Sherman Oaks,
818/905-6961

SEARCH AND DESTROY   Film Ventures
International, 1979
FAST COMPANY   Topar, 1979, AD
THE BROOD   New World, 1979, AD
HOG WILD   Avco Embassy, 1980, AD
SCANNERS   Avco Embassy, 1981, AD
GAS   Paramount, 1981
ESCAPE FROM IRAN, THE CANADIAN CAPER (TF)
Canamedia Productions, 1981
HUMONGOUS   Avco Embassy, 1982
VIDEODROME   Universal, 1983, AD
RUNNING BRAVE   Buena Vista, 1983
THE FUNNY FARM   New World, 1983
THE DEAD ZONE   Paramount, 1983
ANNE OF GREEN GABLES (MS)   Sullivan
Films, 1985
AGNES OF GOD   Columbia, 1985, AD
SESAME STREET PRESENTS FOLLOW THAT BIRD
Warner Bros., 1985, AD
THE FLY   20th Century Fox, 1986
THE BELIEVERS   Orion, 1987, AD
GOTHAM (CTF)   Jerior Productions, 1988
DEAD RINGERS   20th Century Fox, 1988
SING   Tri-Star, 1989
LAKOTA   Interscope, 1989
RENEGADES   Universal, 1989
WHERE THE HEART IS   Buena Vista, 1990

JON SPIRSON
GREAT BALLS OF FIRE!   Orion, 1989, AD

NEIL SPISAK
TIGER TOWN   Buena Vista, 1984
THE TRIP TO BOUNTIFUL   Island Pictures/Film
Dallas, 1985
END OF THE LINE   Orion Classics, 1988
FULL MOON IN BLUE WATER   Trans World
Entertainment, 1988
NIGHT GAME   Trans World Entertainment, 1989
PACIFIC HEIGHTS   Morgan Creek/20th Century
Fox., 1990

Sp

CINEMATOGRAPHERS
PRODUCTION
DESIGNERS,
COSTUME
DESIGNERS AND
FILM EDITORS
GUIDE

P
R
O
D
U
C
T
I
O
N

D
E
S
I
G
N
E
R
S

Sp

CINEMATOGRAPHERS
PRODUCTION
DESIGNERS,
COSTUME
DESIGNERS AND
FILM EDITORS
GUIDE

P R O D U C T I O N D E S I G N E R S

AUSTEN SPRIGGS

WHITE NIGHTS   Columbia, 1985, AD
HAMBURGER HILL   Paramount, 1987
MY LEFT FOOT   Miramax, 1989, AD

WAYNE SPRINGFIELD

THE LOST EMPIRE   JGM Enterprises, 1985
EYE OF THE TIGER   Scotti Bros., 1986, AD

JEFF STAGGS

DREAMSCAPE   20th Century Fox, 1984, AD
GIRLS JUST WANT TO HAVE FUN   New World, 1985

ROY STANNARD

FOREIGN BODY   Orion, 1986

HILDA STARK*

IATSE Local 876
Agent: The Gersh Agency, Inc., Beverly Hills -
    213/274-6611, New York - 212/997-1818

WALL STREET   20th Century Fox, 1987,
    AD w/John J. Moore
DEAD SOLID PERFECT (CTF)   HBO Pictures/
    David Merrick Productions, 1988
ROE VS. WADE (TF)   The Manheim Company/
    NBC Productions, 1989
THE IMAGE (CTF)   Citadel Entertainment
    Productions, 1990

CRAIG STEARNS

HALLOWEEN   Compass International, 1978, AD
THE FOG   Avco Embassy, 1981, AD
ONE DARK NIGHT   Comworld, 1983,
    AD w/Randy Moore
CHILDREN OF THE CORN   New World, 1984, AD
BODY ROCK   New World, 1984, AD
TORCHLIGHT   International Film Marketing, 1984, AD
TUFF TURF   New World, 1985
INVADERS FROM MARS   Cannon, 1986, AD
DATE WITH AN ANGEL   DEG, 1987
DEAD HEAT   New World, 1988
THE BLOB   Tri-Star, 1988
JURY DUTY: THE COMEDY (TF)   Steve White
    Productions, 1990

KIM STEER

THE OUTSIDE CHANCE OF MAXIMILIAN GLICK
    South Gate Entertainment, 1989

JACK STEPHENS

ONE MORE TIME   United Artists, 1970, AD
THE NELSON AFFAIR   Universal, 1973, AD
MURDER ON THE ORIENT EXPRESS   Paramount,
    1974, AD
VOYAGE OF THE DAMNED   Avco Embassy,
    1976, AD
TESS ★★   Columbia, 1980, AD
THE MISSION ★   Columbia, 1986, AD

KANDY STERN*

IATSE Local 876

THE MORNING AFTER   20th Century Fox, 1986, AD
THE PRESIDIO   Paramount, 1988, AD
THE MARLA HANSON STORY (TF)   Citadel
    Entertainment, 1991

JANE ANN STEWART

Address: 6246 Seadrift Cove - Malibu, 213/457-1535

TONIGHT'S THE NIGHT (TF)   IndieProd/Phoenix
    Entertainment, 1987, AD
ROCKULA   Cannon, 1989

WENDY STITES

GALLIPOLI   Paramount, 1981
THE YEAR OF LIVING DANGEROUSLY   MGM/UA,
    1983, Design Coordinator
DEAD POETS SOCIETY   Buena Vista, 1989
GREEN CARD   Buena Vista, 1990

JOHN STODDART

THE GETTING OF WISDOM   Atlantic Releasing
    Corporation, 1977
CAREFUL, HE MIGHT HEAR YOU   TLC Films/20th
    Century Fox, 1983
BARRY McKENZIE HOLDS HIS OWN   Satori, 1985
THE MOSQUITO COAST   Warner Bros., 1986
THE BLOOD OF HEROES   *THE SALUTE OF THE
    JUGGER*   New Line Cinema, 1990

JOHN STOLL †

Agent: London Management - London W1 England,
    011/441/493-1610

FERRY TO HONG KONG   20th Century Fox, 1959
LOSS OF INNOCENCE   *THE GREENGAGE SUMMER*
    Columbia, 1961
LAWRENCE OF ARABIA ★★   Columbia, 1962
THE RUNNING MAN   Columbia, 1963
THE SEVENTH DAWN   United Artists, 1964
PSYCHE 59   Royal Films International, 1964
THE COLLECTOR   Columbia, 1965
BORN FREE   Columbia, 1966
KHARTOUM   United Artists, 1966
CROMWELL   Columbia, 1970
CREATURES THE WORLD FORGOT   Columbia, 1971
YOUNG WINSTON   Columbia, 1972
LIVING FREE   Columbia, 1972
THE DARWIN ADVENTURE   20th Century Fox, 1972
THE ASPHYX   1972
SHAFT IN AFRICA   MGM, 1973
THE GOLDEN VOYAGE OF SINBAD   Columbia, 1974
HENNESSY   American International, 1975
SEVEN NIGHTS IN JAPAN   EMI, 1976
THE MAN IN THE IRON MASK (TF)   Norman Rosemont
    Productions/ITC, 1977
FIREPOWER   AFD, 1979, w/John Blezard &
    Robert Gundlach
ALL QUIET ON THE WESTERN FRONT (TF)   Norman
    Rosemont Productions/Marble Arch Productions, 1979
A TALE OF TWO CITIES (TF)   Norman Rosemont
    Productions/Marble Arch Productions, 1980
LITTLE LORD FAUNTLEROY (TF)   Norman Rosemont
    Productions, 1980
THE HUNCHBACK OF NOTRE DAME (TF)
    Norman Rosemont Productions/Columbia TV, 1982
NOT QUITE PARADISE   New World, 1985
SHIRLEY VALENTINE   Paramount, 1989

SARAH STOLLMAN

POISON   Zeitgeist Films, 1991

MALCOLM STONE

THE DARK CRYSTAL   Universal/AFD, 1982, AD

SANTA CLAUS: THE MOVIE   Tri-Star, 1985, AD
WILLOW   MGM/UA, 1988, AD w/Tim Hutchinson &
    Tony Reading
SLIPSTREAM   Entertainment Film, 1989, AD

STEPHEN PAUL STORER
Agent: The Gersh Agency, Inc., Beverly Hills -
    213/274-6611, New York - 212/997-1818

BREAKING POINT (CTF)   Avnet/Kerner
    Company, 1989
FUNNY ABOUT LOVE   Paramount, 1990

RAYMOND G. STOREY*
IATSE Local 876

MORE AMERICAN GRAFFITI   Universal, 1979, AD
JOHN STEINBECK'S EAST OF
    EDEN (Episode 3) (MS) ☆☆   Mace Neufield
    Productions, 1981
BABY - SECRET OF THE LOST LEGEND   Buena
    Vista, 1985
FEVER PITCH   MGM/UA, 1985
A VERY BRADY CHRISTMAS (TF)   Sherwood/
    Schwartz Company, 1988
PARENT TRAP III (TF)   Walt Disney Television, 1989
TO MY DAUGHTER (TF)   Zacs Productions, 1990
THE STRANGER WITHIN (TF)   Goodman-Rosen
    Productions, 1990

WILLIAM STOUT
THE RETURN OF THE LIVING DEAD   Orion, 1985
MASTERS OF THE UNIVERSE   Cannon, 1987

GARRETH STOVER
EXTREME CLOSE-UP (TF)   Bedford Falls
    Productions, 1990

C. J. STRAWN
Address: 6626 Franklin Ave., #306, Los Angeles, CA
    90028, 213/465-6790

MY CHAUFFEUR   Crown International, 1985
AMERICA   ASA Communications, 1986
THE HIDDEN   New Line Cinema,
    1987, w/Mick Strawn
A NIGHTMARE ON ELM STREET PART 3:
    DREAM WARRIORS   New Line Cinema, 1987,
    AD w/Mick Strawn
A NIGHTMARE ON ELM STREET PART 4:
    THE DREAM MASTER   New Line Cinema,
    1988, w/Mick Strawn
LUCKY STIFF   New Line Cinema, 1989
A NIGHTMARE ON ELM STREET PART 5: THE
    DREAM CHILD   New Line Cinema, 1989
BOOK OF LOVE   New Line Cinema, 1990

MICK STRAWN
Phone: 805/251-6637

THE HIDDEN   New Line Cinema, 1987, w/C.J. Strawn
A NIGHTMARE ON ELM STREET PART 3:
    DREAM WARRIORS   New Line Cinema, 1987,
    w/C.J. Strawn
A NIGHTMARE ON ELM STREET PART 4:
    THE DREAM MASTER   New Line Cinema,
    1988, w/C.J. Strawn
LEATHERFACE: TEXAS CHAINSAW MASSACRE III
    New Line Cinema, 1989

MICHAEL STRINGER
FIDDLER ON THE ROOF ★   20th Century Fox,
    1971, AD
ESCAPE TO ATHENA   AFD, 1979
ROBIN AND MARIAN   Columbia, 1976
THE GREEK TYCOON   Universal, 1978
THE MIRROR CRACK'D   AFD, 1980
THE AWAKENING   Orion/Warner Bros., 1980
GULLIVER'S TRAVELS   Sunn Classic, 1981
THE JIGSAW MAN   United Film Distribution, 1984
FROM THE HIP   DEG, 1987
THE TENTH MAN (TF)   William Self Productions/
    Rosemont Productions, 1988
ANYTHING TO SURVIVE (TF)   ATL
    Productions, 1990

WILLIAM STROM
STUCK WITH EACH OTHER (TF)   Nexus
    Productions, 1990

ALFRED SWEENEY
ANY WEDNESDAY   Warner Bros., 1966
THE DEVIL'S BRIGADE   United Artists, 1968
BANDOLERO!   20th Century Fox, 1968
THE BRIDGE AT REMAGEN   United Artists, 1969
RABBIT, RUN   Warner Bros., 1970
CISCO PIKE   Columbia, 1971
FOOL'S PARADE   Columbia, 1971
SOMETHING BIG   National General, 1971
THE CAREY TREATMENT   MGM, 1972
THE TRAIN ROBBERS   Warner Bros., 1973
UPTOWN SATURDAY NIGHT   Warner
    Bros., 1974
BREAKOUT   Columbia, 1975
LET'S DO IT AGAIN   Warner Bros., 1975
SILVER STREAK   20th Century Fox, 1976
A PIECE OF THE ACTION   Warner Bros., 1977
FOUL PLAY   Paramount, 1978
NORTH DALLAS FORTY   Paramount, 1979
THE RUNNER STUMBLES   20th Century Fox, 1979
STIR CRAZY   Columbia, 1980
THE BLACK MARBLE   Avco Embassy, 1980
TAPS   20th Century Fox, 1981, AD w/Stan Jolley
ROMANTIC COMEDY   MGM/UA, 1983
MR. MOM   20th Century Fox, 1983

BRENTON SWIFT
Address: 11642 Margate St., North Hollywood CA,
    818/509-0614

SEED OF INNOCENCE   Cannon, 1981
SPACEHUNTER: ADVENTURES IN THE FORBIDDEN
    ZONE   Columbia, 1983, AD w/John R. Jensen &
    Michael Nemirsky
SCORNED AND SWINDLED (TF)   Cypress Point
    Productions, 1984
THE AVIATOR   MGM/UA, 1985
THE BOSS'S WIFE   Tri-Star, 1987
MY DEMON LOVER   New Line Cinema, 1987
THE PRINCIPAL   Tri-Star, 1987
BONANZA: THE NEXT GENERATION (TF)   Gaylord
    Production Company/LBS Communications/Bonanza
    Ventures, 1988
HOW TO MURDER A MILLIONAIRE (TF)   Robert
    Greenwald Films, 1990
WEB OF DECEIT (CTF)   Sankan Productions, 1990

Sw

CINEMATOGRAPHERS
PRODUCTION
DESIGNERS,
COSTUME
DESIGNERS AND
FILM EDITORS
GUIDE

P
R
O
D
U
C
T
I
O
N

D
E
S
I
G
N
E
R
S

161

Sy

CINEMATOGRAPHERS
PRODUCTION
DESIGNERS,
COSTUME
DESIGNERS and
FILM EDITORS
GUIDE

P
R
O
D
U
C
T
I
O
N

D
E
S
I
G
N
E
R
S

PAUL SYLBERT*
IATSE Local 876

RIOT   Paramount, 1969
BAD COMPANY   Paramount, 1972
THE DROWNING POOL   Warner Bros., 1975
ONE FLEW OVER THE CUCKOO'S NEST   United
    Artists, 1976
MIKEY AND NICKY   Paramount, 1976
HARDCORE   Columbia, 1979
KRAMER VS. KRAMER   Columbia, 1979
RESURRECTION   Universal, 1980
HEAVEN CAN WAIT ★★   Paramount, 1981
WOLFEN   Orion/Warner Bros., 1981
BLOW OUT   Filmways, 1981
WITHOUT A TRACE   20th Century Fox, 1983
GORKY PARK   Orion, 1983
THE POPE OF GREENWICH VILLAGE
    MGM/UA, 1984
FIRSTBORN   Paramount, 1984
THE JOURNEY OF NATTY GANN   Buena Vista, 1985
ISHTAR   Columbia, 1987
NADINE   Tri-Star, 1987
THE PICK-UP ARTIST, 1987
BILOXI BLUES   Universal, 1988
FRESH HORSES   WEG, 1988
CAREER OPPORTUNITIES   Universal, 1991

RICHARD SYLBERT*
IATSE Local 876

BABY DOLL   Warner Bros., 1956
A FACE IN THE CROWD   Warner Bros., 1957
SPLENDOR IN THE GRASS   Warner Bros., 1961
THE MANCHURIAN CANDIDATE   United
    Artists, 1962
THE PAWNBROKER   Landau/Allied Artists, 1965
HOW TO MURDER YOUR WIFE   United Artists, 1965
WHO'S AFRAID OF VIRGINIA WOOLF? ★★
    Warner Bros., 1966
PARTNERS   Astral Films, 1967
THE GRADUATE   Avco Embassy, 1967
ROSEMARY'S BABY   Paramount, 1968
CATCH-22   Paramount, 1970
CARNAL KNOWLEDGE   Avco Embassy, 1971
THE HEARTBREAK KID   20th Century Fox, 1972
FAT CITY   Columbia, 1972
THE DAY OF THE DOLPHIN   Avco Embassy, 1973
CHINATOWN ★   Paramount, 1974
THE FORTUNE   Columbia, 1975
SHAMPOO ★   Columbia, 1975
PLAYERS   Paramount, 1979
REDS ★   Paramount, 1981
FRANCES   Universal/AFD, 1982
PARTNERS   Paramount, 1982
BREATHLESS   Orion, 1983
THE COTTON CLUB ★   Orion, 1984
UNDER THE CHERRY MOON   Warner Bros., 1986
SHOOT TO KILL   Buena Vista, 1988
TEQUILA SUNRISE   Warner Bros., 1988
THE BONFIRE OF THE VANITIES   Warner
    Bros., 1990
DICK TRACY ★★   Buena Vista, 1990

VIC SYMONDS
SCOOP (TF)   London Weekend TV, 1990

T

PATRICK TAGLIAFERRO
BREAKIN' 2 ELECTRIC BOOGALOO   Tri-Star/
    Cannon, 1984, AD
THUNDER ALLEY   Cannon, 1985, AD
FRIDAY THE13TH, PART VI: JASON LIVES
    Paramount, 1986, AD
WEEDS   DEG, 1987, AD
CHATTAHOOCHEE   Hemdale, 1990, AD
THE FIRST POWER   Orion, 1990, AD

DANIEL TALPERS
THE SPIRIT OF '76   Columbia, 1990

JEFF TANDY
ALLIGATOR EYES   Castle Hill, 1990

PETER TANNER
HAMBURGER HILL   Paramount, 1987

JOSE MARIA TAPIADOR
MARCH OR DIE   Columbia, 1977, AD
SIESTA   Lorimar, 1987, AD
THE TROUBLE WITH SPIES   DEG, 1987
THE MAN IN THE BROWN SUIT (TF)   Alan Shayne
    Productions/Warner Bros. TV, 1989, AD

DEAN TAUCHER
THE BRIDE IN BLACK (TF)   Barry Weitz
    Productions, 1990

ALEX TAVOULARIS*
IATSE Local 876

PEGGY SUE GOT MARRIED   Tri-Star, 1986, AD
GARDENS OF STONE   Tri-Star, 1987, AD
STEEL DAWN   Vestron, 1987
TUCKER: THE MAN AND HIS DREAM
    Paramount, 1988, AD
LOST ANGELS   Orion, 1989, AD
SCENES FROM THE CLASS STRUGGLE IN BEVERLY
    HILLS   Cinecom, 1989
KING OF NEW YORK   Reteitalia and Scena Film, 1990

DEAN TAVOULARIS*
IATSE Local 876
Agent: The Gersh Agency, Inc., Beverly Hills -
    213/274-6611, New York - 212/997-1818

BONNE AND CLYDE   Warner Bros., 1967
ZABRISKIE POINT   MGM, 1970
LITTLE BIG MAN   National General, 1970
THE GODFATHER   Paramount, 1972
THE GODFATHER, PART II ★★   Paramount, 1974
THE CONVERSATION   Paramount, 1974
THE BRINK'S JOB ★   Universal, 1978
APOCALYPSE NOW ★   United Artists, 1979
HAMMETT   Orion/Warner Bros., 1982
ONE FROM THE HEART   Columbia, 1982
THE ESCAPE ARTIST   Orion/Warner Bros., 1982

THE OUTSIDERS   Warner Bros., 1983
RUMBLE FISH   Universal, 1983
PEGGY SUE GOT MARRIED   Tri-Star, 1986
A MAN IN LOVE   Cinecom, 1987, AD
GARDENS OF STONE   Tri-Star, 1987
TUCKER: THE MAN AND HIS DREAM ★
   Paramount, 1988
NEW YORK STORIES ("Life Without Zoe")   Buena
   Vista, 1989
THE GODFATHER PART III ★   Zoetrope Studios/
   Paramount, 1990

DON TAYLOR
NOT A PENNY MORE, NOT A PENNY LESS-
   PARTS I & II (CTF)   BBC, 1990

JACK G. TAYLOR JR. *
IATSE Local 876
Phone: 213/246-8025

NINE TO FIVE   20th Century Fox, 1980, AD
LOOKER   The Ladd Company/Warner Bros.,
   1981, AD
UNCOMMON VALOR   Paramount, 1983, AD
NIGHTMARES   Universal, 1983, AD
STAR 80   The Ladd Company/Warner Bros., 1983,
   AD w/Michael Bolton
REAL GENIUS   Tri-Star, 1985, AD
GUNG HO   Paramount, 1986, AD
MILLION DOLLAR MYSTERY   DEG, 1987

PIERRE-LOUIS THEVENET
TWISTED OBSESSION   IVE, 1990

BRENT THOMAS
SMALL SACRIFICES (TF)   Louis Rudolph Films, 1990

IAN THOMAS
CADENCE   New Line Cinema, 1990

PHILIP THOMAS
McCABE & MRS. MILLER   Warner Bros., 1971,
   AD w/Al Locatelli
ON THE LINE   Miramax, 1987, AD

WYNN P. THOMAS
BEAT STREET   Orion, 1984, AD
SHE'S GOTTA HAVE IT   Island Pictures, 1986, AD
EDDIE MURPHY RAW   Paramount, 1987
SCHOOL DAZE   Columbia, 1988
DO THE RIGHT THING   Universal, 1989
MO' BETTER BLUES   Universal, 1990
JUNGLE FEVER   Universal, 1991
THE FIVE HEARTBEATS   20th Century Fox, 1991

BRIAN THOMSON
SHOCK TREATMENT   20th Century Fox, 1981
REBEL   Vestron, 1986
GROUND ZERO   Avenue Pictures, 1988
DADAH IS DEATH (MS)   Steve Krantz Productions/
   Roadshow, Coote & Carroll Productions/Samuel
   Goldwyn TV, 1988

HAROLD THRASHER
JOSHUA THEN AND NOW   20th Century Fox,
   1985, AD
RAISING ARIZONA   20th Century Fox, 1987, AD
YOUNG GUNS   20th Century Fox, 1988, AD

PATTY HEARST   Atlantic Releasing Corporation,
   1988, AD
WHEN HARRY MET SALLY...   Columbia, 1989,
   Art Dept Coordinator
YOUNG CATHERINE-PARTS I & II (CMS)   Consolidated
   Entertainment, 1991, w/Natalia Vasilieva

SIG TINGLOF*
IATSE Local 876

TURNER & HOOCH   Buena Vista, 1989, AD

CATHERINE TIRR
TERMINAL BLISS   Distant Horizon, 1990

BERTALAN TIVIDAR
FORGOTTEN PRISONERS: THE AMNESTY FILE (CTF)
   Robert Greenwald Productions, 1990

ALAN TOMKINS
EMPIRE STRIKES BACK ★   20th Century Fox, 1980,
   AD w/Les Dilley & Harry Lange
THE KEEP   Paramount, 1983,
   AD w/Brian Ackland-Snow
CURSE OF THE PINK PANTHER   MGM/UA, 1983,
   AD w/Tim Hutchinson & John SidDall
LASSITER   Warner Bros., 1984,
   AD w/Herbert Westbrook
LIFEFORCE   Tri-Star, 1985, AD
HAUNTED HONEYMOON   Orion, 1986, AD
HIGH SPIRITS   Tri-Star, 1988, AD, Ireland
A DRY WHITE SEASON   MGM/UA, 1989, AD
WAR AND REMEMBRANCE (MS)   Dan Curtis
   Productions, 1989, AD, England

LESLIE TOMKINS
THE SHINING   Warner Bros., 1980, AD
YENTL ★   MGM/UA , 1983, AD
A PASSAGE TO INDIA ★   Columbia, 1984,
   AD w/Clifford Robinson, Herbert Westbrook &
   Ram Yedeker
THE JEWEL OF THE NILE   20th Century Fox,
   1985, AD
SOLARBABIES   MGM/UA, 1986, AD w/others
SUPERMAN IV: THE QUEST FOR PEACE   Warner
   Bros., 1987, AD w/John Fenner
FULL METAL JACKET   Warner Bros., 1987,
   AD w/Keith Pain & Rod Stratford
HIGH SPIRITS   Tri-Star, 1988, Supv AD

CHARLES D. TOMLINSON*
IATSE Local 876

STOOGEMANIA   Atlantic Releasing Corporation,
   1986, AD

MARSHALL TOOMEY
PENITENTIARY III   Cannon, 1987

ENRICO TOVAGLIERI
FRANKENSTEIN UNBOUND   20th Century Fox, 1990

JEFFREY TOWNSEND
Agent: The Gersh Agency, Inc., Beverly Hills -
   213/274-6611, New York - 212/997-1818

BABY, IT'S YOU   Paramount, 1983
RECKLESS   MGM/UA, 1984

To

CINEMATOGRAPHERS
PRODUCTION
DESIGNERS,
COSTUME
DESIGNERS AND
FILM EDITORS
GUIDE

P
R
O
D
U
C
T
I
O
N

D
E
S
I
G
N
E
R
S

CINEMATOGRAPHERS
PRODUCTION
DESIGNERS,
COSTUME
DESIGNERS AND
FILM EDITORS
GUIDE

P
R
O
D
U
C
T
I
O
N

D
E
S
I
G
N
E
R
S

OLD ENOUGH   Orion Classics, 1984
AFTER HOURS   The Geffen Company/Warner
    Bros., 1985
MAID TO ORDER   New Century/Vista, 1987
THE FABULOUS BAKER BOYS   20th Century
    Fox, 1989

ALEXANDER TRAUNER
THE APARTMENT ★★   United Artists, 1960
THE MAN WHO WOULD BE KING ★   Columbia, 1975
THE FIENDISH PLOT OF DR. FU MANCHU   United
    Artists, 1980
SUBWAY   Island Alive, 1985
ROUND MIDNIGHT   Warner Bros., 1986
REUNION   Ariane Films/Burning Secret
    Productions, 1989

ANTHONY (TONY) TREMBLAY
Home: 10836 Hesby St. - North Hollywood,
    818/508-6210

THE BLACK FOREST   C.E.G., 1989
SPACED INVADERS   *MARTIANS!!!*   Buena
    Vista, 1990
MIRACLE LANDING (TF) ☆☆   CBS
    Entertainment, 1990

DEAN TSCHETTER
NEVER TOO YOUNG TO DIE   Paul Releasing
    Company, 1986, AD w/Michelle Starbuck
PASS THE AMMO   New Century/Vista, 1988
FRIGHT NIGHT PART II   New Century/Vista, 1988

FRED TUCH*
IATSE Local 876

AVALANCHE EXPRESS   20th Century Fox, 1979
PENNIES FROM HEAVEN   MGM/UA, 1981,
    AD w/Bernie Cutler

TED TUNNEY
TERMINAL FORCE   New World Video, 1990

WILLIAM H. TUNTKE*
IATSE Local 876

THE ANDROMEDA STRAIN ★   Universal, 1972, AD
GRAY LADY DOWN   Universal, 1978
THE NUDE BOMB   Universal, 1980
CLOAK AND DAGGER   Universal, 1984

KAREL VACEK
HOWLING II...YOUR SISTER IS A WEREWOLF
    Thorn-EMI, 1986
ROSA LUXEMBURG   New Yorker, 1987,
    AD w/Bernd Lepel

KATHERINE G. VALLIN
NEON MANIACS   Bedford Entertainment, 1986, AD
CLUB LIFE   Troma, 1986
BORN TO RACE   MGM/UA, 1988

JOHN VALLONE*
IATSE Local 876
Agent: The Gersh Agency, Inc., Beverly Hills -
    213/274-6611, New York - 212/997-1818

STAR TREK: THE MOTION PICTURE H
    Paramount, 1979, AD, w/Leon Harris & Joe Jennings
SOUTHERN COMFORT   20th Century Fox, 1981
48HRS. Paramount, 1982
BRAINSTORM   MGM/UA, 1983
STREETS OF FIRE   Universal, 1984
BREWSTER'S MILLIONS   Universal, 1985
COMMANDO   20th Century Fox, 1985
PREDATOR   20th Century Fox, 1987
RED HEAT   Tri-Star, 1988
SHANNON'S DEAL (TF)   Stan Rogow Productions/NBC
    Productions, 1989
DIE HARD 2   20th Century Fox., 1990
THE ADVENTURES OF FORD FAIRLANE   20th Century
    Fox, 1990

JAMES D. VANCE
Agent: The Gersh Agency, Inc., Beverly Hills -
    213/274-6611, New York - 212/997-1818

HUNTERS ARE FOR KILLING (TF)   Cinema
    Center, 1970
TOO LATE THE HERO   Cinerama Releasing
    Corporation, 1970
THE MIDNIGHT MAN   Universal, 1974
THE LONGEST YARD   Paramount, 1974
THE F.B.I. STORY: THE FBI VERSUS ALVIN KARPIS,
    PUBLIC ENEMY NUMBER ONE (TF)   QM
    Productions/Warner Bros. TV, 1974
LIVE A LITTLE, STEAL A LOT   *MURPH THE SURF*
    American International, 1975
3 WOMEN   20th Century Fox, 1977, AD
CINDY (TF)   John Charles Walters Productions, 1978
NIGHTWING   Columbia, 1979
MAKING LOVE   20th Century Fox, 1981
THE LONELY GUY   Universal, 1984
OUTRAGEOUS FORTUNE   Buena Vista, 1987

FRANK VANORIO
CHOKE CANYON   United Film Distribution, 1986
THE CURSE   Trans World Entertainment, 1987

PATRICIA VAN RYKER
LISA   MGM/UA, 1990

JIM VAN WYCK
ONLY WHEN I LAUGH   Columbia, 1981

PHILLIP VASELS
DEAD MEN DON'T DIE   Trans Atlantic Pictures, 1990
DEADLY DESIRE (CTF)   Skylark Films/Wilshire
   Court Productions, 1991, w/Diane Hughes

NATALIA VASILIEVA
YOUNG CATHERINE-PARTS I & II (CMS)   Consolidated
   Entertainment, 1991, w/Harold Thrasher

TAMAS VAYER
LILY IN LOVE   New Line Cinema, 1985

SANDY VENEZIANO*
IATSE Local 876
Agent: The Gersh Agency, Inc., Beverly Hills -
   213/274-6611, New York - 212/997-1818

AN EYE FOR AN EYE   Avco Embassy, 1981
SIX WEEKS   Universal, 1982
OUTRAGEOUS FORTUNE   Buena Vista, 1987, AD
DEAD POETS SOCIETY   Buena Vista, 1989, AD
FALL FROM GRACE (TF)   NBC Productions, 1990
ONE GOOD COP   Buena Vista, 1991

BERNARD VEZAT
JEAN DE FLORETTE   Orion Classics, 1987
MANON OF THE SPRING   Orion Classics, 1987

GERARD VIARD
CODE NAME: EMERALD   MGM/UA, 1985

PATRIZIA VON BRANDENSTEIN*
IATSE Local 876
Agent: Marion Rosenberg - Los Angeles, 213/653-7383

THE GARDENER'S SON (TF)   RIP/Filmhaus, 1977
GIRLFRIENDS   Warner Bros., 1978, AD
THE LAST TENANT (TF)   Titus Productions, 1978
SUMMER OF MY GERMAN SOLDIER (TF)
   Highgate Productions, 1978
HEARTLAND   Levitt-Pickman, 1979
BREAKING AWAY   20th Century Fox, 1979, AD
MY OLD MAN (TF)   Zeitman-McNichol-Halmi
   Productions, 1979
HARDHAT AND LEGS (TF)   Syzgy Productions, 1980
TELL ME A RIDDLE   Filmways, 1980
RAGTIME ★   Paramount, 1981, AD w/Tony Reading
SILKWOOD   20th Century Fox, 1983
TOUCHED   Lorimar Productions/Wildwood
   Partners, 1983
BEAT STREET   Orion, 1984
AMADEUS ★★   Orion, 1984
A CHORUS LINE   Columbia, 1985
THE MONEY PIT   Universal, 1986
NO MERCY   Tri-Star, 1987
THE UNTOUCHABLES ★   Paramount, 1987
BETRAYED   MGM/UA, 1988
WORKING GIRL   20th Century Fox, 1988
THE LEMON SISTERS   Miramax, 1990
STATE OF GRACE   Orion, 1990
POSTCARDS FROM THE EDGE   Columbia, 1990

W

DIANNE WAGER
SHORT CIRCUIT   Tri-Star, 1986, AD
THE HUNT FOR RED OCTOBER   Paramount, 1990,
   AD w/William Chuse & Donald Woodruff

LUK MAN WAH
THE KILLER   Circle Releasing, 1991, AD

GRAHAM "GRACE" WALKER
SUMMERFIELD   Greater Union Film Distributors, 1977
THE IRISHMAN   Greater Union Film Distributors, 1978
CHAIN REACTION   Hoyt, 1980
THE ROAD WARRIOR   Warner Bros., 1982, AD
THE COCA COLA KID   Cinecom/Film Gallery, 1985
MAD MAX BEYOND THUNDERDOME   Warner
   Bros., 1985
"CROCODILE" DUNDEE   Paramount, 1986
PATTERSON SAVES THE WORLD   Hoyts
   Distribution, 1987
DEAD CALM   Warner Bros., 1989

ROY WALKER
BARRY LYNDON ★★   Warner Bros., 1975, AD
SORCERER   Universal/Paramount, 1977
THE SHINING   Warner Bros., 1980
YENTL ★   MGM/UA, 1983
THE KILLING FIELDS   Warner Bros., 1984
ELENI   Warner Bros., 1985
LITTLE SHOP OF HORRORS   The Geffen Company/
   Warner Bros., 1986
GOOD MORNING, VIETNAM   Buena Vista, 1987
DIRTY ROTTEN SCOUNDRELS   Orion, 1988
   - FAT MAN - LITTLE BOY -

STEVE WALKER
HER ALIBI   Warner Bros., 1989, AD

STUART WALKER
A PRIVATE FUNCTION   Island Alive, 1984

FRANK WALSH
LOCAL HERO   Warner Bros., 1983
PAPERHOUSE   Vestron, 1988, AD w/Ann Tilby
GETTING IT RIGHT   MCEG, 1989, AD

TOM WALSH
THE HANDMAID'S TALE   Cinecom, 1990

TONY WALTON
Agent: Paul Martino, ICM - Los Angeles, 213/550-4000

FAHRENHEIT 451   Universal, 1967
MURDER ON THE ORIENT EXPRESS
   Paramount, 1974
EQUUS   United Artists, 1977
THE WIZ ★   Universal, 1978, w/Philip Rosenberg
ALL THAT JAZZ ★★   20th Century Fox, 1979,
   w/Philip Rosenberg
JUST TELL ME WHAT YOU WANT   Warner Bros., 1980
PRINCE OF THE CITY   Orion/Warner Bros., 1981

- CITY OF JOY -

**CINEMATOGRAPHERS
PRODUCTION
DESIGNERS,
COSTUME
DESIGNERS AND
FILM EDITORS
GUIDE**

P
R
O
D
U
C
T
I
O
N

D
E
S
I
G
N
E
R
S

Wa

CINEMATOGRAPHERS
PRODUCTION
DESIGNERS,
COSTUME
DESIGNERS and
FILM EDITORS
GUIDE

P
R
O
D
U
C
T
I
O
N

D
E
S
I
G
N
E
R
S

DEATHTRAP   Warner Bros., 1982
THE GOODBYE PEOPLE   Embassy, 1984
DEATH OF A SALESMAN II (TF)   Roxbury and
   Punch Productions, 1985
HEARTBURN   Paramount, 1986
THE GLASS MENAGERIE   Cineplex Odeon, 1987

PAMELA B. WARNER
METALSTORM: THE DESTRUCTION OF JARED-SYN
   Universal, 1983, AD
STAND ALONE   New World, 1985
GHOSTWARRIORS *SWORDKILL*   Empire Pictures,
   1986, w/Robert Howland
BODY SLAM   DEG, 1987, AD
NIGHT WALK (TF)   CBS Entertainment
   Productions, 1990

THOMAS C. WARREN
BIG   20th Century Fox, 1988, AD w/Speed Hopkins
BRIGHT LIGHTS BIG CITY   MGM/UA, 1988, AD

DAVID WASCO
Agent: The Doug Apatow Agency - Los Angeles,
   213-202-6888

SMOOTH TALK   Spectrafilm, 1985
STACKING   Spectrafilm, 1987
STUDENT CONFIDENTIAL   Troma, 1987
IN A SHALLOW GRAVE   Skouras Pictures, 1988
THE WASH   Skouras Pictures, 1988
RACHEL RIVER   Taurus Entertainment, 1989

J. DENNIS WASHINGTON*
IATSE Local 876
Agent: Smith Gosnell Nicholson & Associates -
   Pacific Palisades, 213/459-0307

CONVOY   United Artists, 1978, AD
THE ELECTRIC HORSEMAN   Columbia, 1979
THE NINTH CONFIGURATION   Warner Bros.,
   1980, AD w/Bill Malley
VICTORY   Paramount, 1981
TO BE OR NOT TO BE   20th Century Fox, 1983, AD
HYSTERICAL   Embassy, 1983
FINDERS KEEPERS   Warner Bros., 1984, AD
PRIZZI'S HONOR   20th Century Fox, 1985
STAND BY ME   Columbia, 1986
NO WAY OUT   Orion, 1987
THE DEAD   Vestron, 1987, w/Stephen Grimes
OFF LIMITS   20th Century Fox, 1988
CHANCES ARE   Tri-Star, 1989

SIMON WATERS
ARTHUR'S HALLOWED GROUND   Cinecom, 1983
KIPPERBANG   MGM/UA Classics, 1983
EXPERIENCE PREFERRED BUT NOT ESSENTIAL
   Samuel Goldwyn Company, 1983
THE SQUEEZE   Tri-Star, 1987

TED WATKINS
STONE COLD DEAD   Dimension, 1980, AD
TULIPS   Avco Embassy, 1981, AD

TRACY WATT
KANGAROO   Cineplex Odeon, 1987
WARM NIGHTS ON A SLOW MOVING TRAIN
   Miramax, 1989

DAN WEBSTER
IATSE Local 876

FREE RIDE   Galaxy, 1986
HEARTBREAK HOTEL   Buena Vista, 1988, AD
HEART CONDITION   New Line Cinema, 1989, AD
GLEAMING THE CUBE   20th Century Fox, 1989, AD
GLORY ★   Tri-Star, 1989, AD
HOME ALONE   20th Century Fox, 1990, AD
ONLY THE LONELY   20th Century Fox, 1991, AD

GOETZ WEIDNER
THE NEVERENDING STORY II: THE NEXT CHAPTER
   Warner Bros., 1990, w/Robert Laing

DAN WEIL
THE BIG BLUE   WEG, 1988, AD
NIKITA   Gaumont, 1989

FRED WEILER
SKI PATROL   Triumph, 1990

BRUCE WEINTRAUB
CRUISING   United Artists, 1980
SUMMER LOVERS   Filmways, 1982

GARY WEIST
Agent: The Gersh Agency, Inc., Beverly Hills -
   213/274-6611, New York - 212/997-1818

GOING IN STYLE   Warner Bros., 1979,
   AD w/Fred C. Price
DRESSED TO KILL   Filmways, 1980, AD
DROP-OUT FATHER (TF)   CBS Entertainment,
   1982, AD
MUGGABLE MARY: STREET COP (TF)   CBS
   Entertainment, 1982, AD
EDDIE AND THE CRUISERS   Embassy, 1983, AD
GRACE QUIGLEY   Cannon, 1984
GIDEON OLIVER (Pilot)   1989

ROBERT W. (BO) WELCH*
IATSE Local 876
Agent: Lawrence A. Mirisch, Triad Artists, Inc. -
   Los Angeles, 213/556-2727

HEART OF STEEL (TF)   Beowulf Productions, 1983
DEAL OF THE CENTURY   Warner Bros., 1983, AD
THE STAR CHAMBER   20th Century Fox, 1983, AD
SWING SHIFT   Warner Bros., 1984, AD
BEST DEFENSE   Paramount, 1984, AD
THE COLOR PURPLE ★   Warner Bros., 1985, AD
SLOW BURN (CTF)   Joel Schumacher Productions/
   Universal Pay TV, 1986
VIOLETS ARE BLUE   Columbia, 1986, AD
STARK: MIRROR IMAGE (TF)   CBS
   Entertainment, 1986
THE LOST BOYS   Warner Bros., 1987
BEETLEJUICE   Warner Bros., 1988
THE ACCIDENTAL TOURIST   Warner Bros., 1988
GHOSTBUSTERS II   Columbia, 1989
JOE VERSUS THE VOLCANO   Warner Bros., 1990
EDWARD SCISSORHANDS   20th Century Fox, 1990

TOM WELLS
THE GIRL OF LIMBERLOST (TF)   Sascha Schneider
   Productions, 1990

CAROL WENGER
THE CANNONBALL RUN   20th Century Fox, 1981

HERBERT WESTBROOK
EAGLE'S WING   International Picture Show, 1980
THE FINAL CONFLICT   20th Century Fox, 1981
GOOD AND BAD AT GAMES (TF)   Portman Quintet
    Productions, 1983
THE KEEP   Paramount, 1983, AD w/Alan Tomkins
SAKHAROV (CTF)   HBO Premiere Films/Titus
    Productions, 1984
A PASSAGE TO INDIA   Columbia, 1984, AD
OUT OF AFRICA   Universal, 1985, AD
THE TWO MRS. GRENVILLES (TF) ☆☆
    Lorimar-Telepictures, 1987

WHITNEY BROOKE WHEELER
DEATHWISH 4: THE CRACKDOWN   Cannon,
    1987, AD
MESSENGER OF DEATH   Cannon, 1988
KINJITE: FORBIDDEN SUBJECTS   Cannon,
    1989, AD

CARY WHITE
THE TEXAS CHAINSAW MASSACRE PART 2
    Cannon, 1986
RED HEADED STRANGER   Alive Films, 1986
LONESOME DOVE (MS) ☆   Motown Productions/
    Qintex Entertainment, 1989
PAIR OF ACES (TF)   Pedernales Films, 1990
THE HOT SPOT   Orion, 1990
SON OF THE MORNING STAR-PARTS I & II (TF)
    The Mount Company, 1991

FRANK WHITE
CLASH OF THE TITANS   United Artists, 1981

ARNOLD WHYLER
MATTERS OF THE HEART (CTF)   Tahse-Bergman
    Productions, 1990

SVEN WICHMAN
BABETTE'S FEAST   Orion Classics, 1987

RICHARD WILCOX
THE AMATEUR   20th Century Fox, 1982, AD
WATCHERS   Universal, 1988
THE ACCUSED   Paramount, 1988
PERFECT WITNESS (CTF)   HBO Pictures, 1989
LAST FLIGHT OUT (TF)   The Mannheim
    Company, 1990
DEAD RECKONING (CTF)   Houston Lady Production
    Company, 1990

LADISLAV WILHEIM
INVASION U.S.A.   Cannon, 1985
RED SCORPION   Shapiro Glickenhaus, 1989

CHRIS WILKINSON
AFTER THE WAR-PARTS I-III (MS)   Granada TV,
    1990, w/Stephen Fineren

BOYD WILLAT
ZAPPED!   Embassy, 1982

JOHN WILLETT
RUN   Buena Vista, 1991

LAWRENCE WILLIAMS
MOTHER LOVE-PARTS I-III (MS)   BBC TV Productions,
    1990, w/Ken Ledsham

OWEN WILLIAMS
BANGKOK HILTON (CTF)   Kennedy-Miller, 1990

PETER WILLIAMS
ZULU DAWN   Orion/Warner Bros., 1979, AD
HALF MOON STREET   20th Century Fox, 1986, AD
WILD GEESE II   Universal, 1986, AD

TREVOR WILLIAMS*
IATSE 876, IATSE Toronto & Vancouver, ACTT
Agent: Grace Lyons Management - Los Angeles,
    213/655-5100

JENNY   Cinerama Releasing Corporation, 1970
NIGHT OF DARK SHADOWS   MGM, 1971
FRANKENSTEIN (TF)   Dan Curtis Productions, 1973
THE PICTURE OF DORIAN GRAY (TF)   DC
    Productions, 1973
THE NIGHT STRANGLER (TF)   ABC Circle Films, 1973
DILLINGER   American International, 1973
MELVIN PURVIS: G-MAN (TF)   American International
    TV, 1974
DRACULA (TF)   Universal TV/Dan Curtis
    Productions, 1974
HARD TIMES   Columbia, 1975
THE DUCHESS AND THE DIRTWATER FOX   20th
    Century Fox, 1976, AD w/Robert Emmet Smith
FUTUREWORLD   American International, 1976, AD
PRETTY BABY   Paramount, 1978
LOST AND FOUND   Columbia, 1979
THE SILENT PARTNER   EMC Film/Aurora, 1979
MR. PATMAN   Film Consortium, 1980
THE CHANGELING   AFD, 1980
TRIBUTE   20th Century Fox, 1980
ENDANGERED SPECIES   MGM/UA, 1982
THE AMATEUR   20th Century Fox, 1982
POLICE ACADEMY   Warner Bros., 1984
REVENGE OF THE NERDS   20th Century Fox, 1984
THE GUARDIAN (CTF)   HBO Premiere Films/
    Robert Cooper Productions/Stanley Chase
    Productions, 1985
ALAMO BAY   Tri-Star, 1985
MARTIN'S DAY   MGM/UA, 1985
POLICE ACADEMY 2: THEIR FIRST ASSIGNMENT
    Warner Bros., 1985
SWORD OF GIDEON (CTF)   Alliance Entertainment/Les
    Films Ariane/HBO Premiere Films/CTV/Telefilm
    Canada/Rogers Cablesystems/Radio-Canada, 1986
POLICE ACADEMY 3: BACK IN TRAINING   Warner
    Bros., 1986
REVENGE OF THE NERDS II: NERDS IN PARADISE
    20th Century Fox, 1987
ALLAN QUATERMAIN AND THE LOST CITY OF GOLD
    Cannon, 1987
POLICE ACADEMY 4: CITIZENS ON PATROL   Warner
    Bros., 1987
POLICE ACADEMY 5: ASSIGNMENT MIAMI BEACH
    Warner Bros., 1988
WHO'S HARRY CRUMB?   Tri-Star, 1989
WHERE PIGEONS GO TO DIE (TF)   Michael Landon
    Productions, 1990, AD
LUCI & DESI (TF)   Larry Thompson
    Entertainment, 1991

CINEMATOGRAPHERS
PRODUCTION
DESIGNERS,
COSTUME
DESIGNERS AND
FILM EDITORS
GUIDE

P R O D U C T I O N   D E S I G N E R S

Wi

CINEMATOGRAPHERS
PRODUCTION
DESIGNERS,
COSTUME
DESIGNERS and
FILM EDITORS
GUIDE

P
R
O
D
U
C
T
I
O
N

D
E
S
I
G
N
E
R
S

DAVID WILSON
EAT THE PEACH   Skouras Pictures, 1986
THE STEPFATHER   New Century/Vista, 1987, AD
IMMEDIATE FAMILY   Columbia, 1989, AD

KEITH WILSON
INTERNATIONAL VELVET   MGM/United Artists, 1978
YESTERDAY'S HERO   EMI, 1979
GULAG (CTF)   Lorimar Productions/HBO Premiere
    Films, 1985
STEAL THE SKY (CTF)   HBO Pictures/Yoram BenAmi
    Productions/Paramount TV, 1988, w/Bob Zilliox
THE LADY AND THE HIGHWAYMAN (TF)   Lord
    Grade Productions/Gainsborough Pictures, 1989
GREAT EXPECTATIONS (CMS)   Disney Channel/
    Harlech TV/Primetime TV, 1989

RON WILSON
I, MADMAN   Trans World Entertainment, 1989,
    w/Matthew Jacobs

GARY WISSNER
GRAVEYARD SHIFT   Paramount, 1990

ED WITTSTEIN
FAME   MGM/UA, 1980, AD
ENDLESS LOVE   Universal, 1981
SARAH, PLAIN AND TALL (TF)   Self Help
    Productions, 1991

STEPHEN WOLF
IT HAD TO BE YOU   Limelite Studios, 1990

TONY WOLLARD
MOONLIGHTING   Universal Classics, 1982
DEJA VU   Cannon, 1985
SKY BANDITS   Galaxy International, 1986
TREASURE ISLAND (CTF)   Agamemnon Films
    Productions, 1989

CAROL WOOD
HIDING OUT   DEG, 1987, AD
B.L. STRYKER (Pilot)   1989, AD

JOE WOOD*
IATSE Local 876

SUMMER SCHOOL   Paramount, 1987, AD
MOVING   Warner Bros., 1988, AD
SHE'S OUT OF CONTROL   Columbia, 1989, AD
A PROMISE TO KEEP (TF)   Sacret, 1990

JOHN WOOD
KING KONG LIVES   DEG, 1986, AD w/Fred
    Carter & Tony Reading
A FISH CALLED WANDA   MGM/UA, 1988, AD

JEFFREY WOODBRIDGE
SECRETS   Samuel Goldwyn Company, 1984
KIPPERBANG   MGM/UA Classics, 1984, AD
FOREVER YOUNG   Cinecom, 1986, AD

PAMELA WOODBRIDGE
BLOOD AND CONCRETE   I.R.S. Media, 1991

DONALD B. WOODRUFF
IATSE Local 876

BARBAROSA   Universal/AFD, 1982
RUTHLESS PEOPLE   Buena Vista, 1986, AD
HARRY AND THE HENDERSONS   Universal, 1987, AD
JAWS THE REVENGE   Universal, 1987, AD
WHO'S THAT GIRL?   Warner Bros., 1987, AD
NAKED GUN: FROM THE FILES OF POLICE SQUAD
    Paramount, 1988, AD
FLETCH LIVES   Universal, 1989, AD w/Jimmy Bly,
    Cameron Birnie & W. Steven Graham
THE HUNT FOR RED OCTOBER   Paramount, 1990,
    AD w/Dianne Wager & William Chuse

PETER W. WOOLEY
IATSE Local 876
Agent: Smith Gosnell Nicholson & Associates -
    Pacific Palisades, 213/459-0307

GOING HOME   MGM, 1971
SOUNDER   20th Century Fox, 1972
CLEOPATRA JONES   Warner Bros., 1973
BLAZING SADDLES   Warner Bros., 1973
OUR TIME   Warner Bros., 1974
SPARKLE   Warner Bros., 1976
HIGH ANXIETY   20th Century Fox, 1977
OLLY, OLLY, OXEN FREE   Sanrio, 1978
SURVIVAL OF DANA (TF)   EMI TV, 1979
MAD MAGAZINE PRESENTS UP THE ACADEMY
    Warner Bros., 1980
FATSO   20th Century Fox, 1980
FUGITIVE FAMILY (TF)   Aubrey-Hamner
    Productions, 1980
SECOND HAND HEARTS   Paramount, 1981
UNDER THE RAINBOW   Orion/Warner Bros., 1981
JEKYLL AND HYDE...TOGETHER AGAIN
    Paramount, 1982
THE DAY AFTER (TF)   ABC Circle Films, 1983
HARD TO HOLD   Paramount, 1984
OH, GOD! YOU DEVIL   Warner Bros., 1984
PORKY'S REVENGE   20th Century Fox, 1985
SUMMER RENTAL   Paramount, 1985
LONG TIME GONE (TF)   Picturemaker Productions/ABC
    Circle Films, 1987
BLIND WITNESS (TF)   King Phoenix
    Entertainment, 1990
SPARKS: THE PRICE OF PASSION (TF)   Shadowplay
    Films, 1990
GOOD NIGHT, SWEET WIFE: A MURDER IN
    BOSTON (TF)   CBS Entertainment Productions, 1990
DONOR (TF)   CBS Entertainment Productions, 1990

JACK WRIGHT III
INSIDE OUT   Hemdale, 1986

GAYLE WURTHNER
LADY BEWARE   Scotti Bros., 1987

STUART WURTZEL
Agent: Roberta Kent, STE Representation, Ltd. -
    Beverly Hills, 213/550-3982

BETWEEN THE LINES   Midwest Film Productions, 1977
HAIR   United Artists, 1979
SIMON   Orion/Warner Bros., 1980
NIGHT OF THE JUGGLER   Columbia, 1980
TIMES SQUARE   AFD, 1980
TATTOO   20th Century Fox, 1981

THE CHOSEN   20th Century Fox International
    Classics, 1982
THE BALLAD OF GREGORIO CORTEZ
    Embassy, 1983
THE PURPLE ROSE OF CAIRO   Orion, 1985
HANNAH AND HER SISTERS ★   Orion, 1986
BRIGHTON BEACH MEMOIRS   Universal, 1986
SUSPECT   Tri-Star, 1987
THE HOUSE ON CARROLL STREET   Orion, 1988
AN INNOCENT MAN   Buena Vista, 1989
OLD GRINGO   Columbia, 1989, w/Bruno Rubeo
STAYING TOGETHER   Hemdale, 1989
MERMAIDS   Orion, 1990
THREE MEN AND A LITTLE LADY   Buena Vista, 1990

HUGO LUCZYC WYHOWSKI

MY BEAUTIFUL LAUNDRETTE   Orion Classics, 1985
PRICK UP YOUR EARS   Samuel Goldwyn
    Company, 1987
PERSONAL SERVICES   Vestron, 1987
SAMMY AND ROSIE GET LAID   Cinecom, 1987

Y

DAN YARHI

THE BIG TOWN   Columbia, 1987, AD
THREE MEN AND A BABY   Buena Vista, 1987, AD
PHYSICAL EVIDENCE   Columbia, 1989
WELCOME HOME   Columbia, 1989

HAYDEN YATES

NOT OF THIS EARTH   Concorde, 1988

RAM YEDEKAR

GANDHI   Columbia, 1982, AD w/Norman Dorme
HEAT AND DUST   Universal Classics, 1983,
    AD w/Maurice Fowler
A PASSAGE TO INDIA   Columbia, 1984, AD

Z

MICKEY ZAHAR

EVERY TIME WE SAY GOODBYE   Tri-Star, 1986, AD

LUCINDA ZAK

A NEW LIFE   Paramount, 1988, AD

EUGENIO ZANETTI

Agent: Sandra Marsh Management - Sherman Oaks,
    818/905-6961

CAMILA   European Classics, 1985
SLAM DANCE   Island Pictures, 1987
PROMISED LAND   Vestron, 1988

SOME GIRLS   MGM/UA, 1989
FLATLINERS   Columbia, 1990

MARTIN ZBORIL

ETERNITY   *THE AVATOR*   Paul Entertainment, 1990

KRISTI ZEA

LUCAS   20th Century Fox, 1986, AD
ANGEL HEART   Tri-Star, 1987, AD w/Armin Ganz
MARRIED TO THE MOB   Orion, 1988
NEW YORK STORIES ("Life Lessons")   Buena
    Vista, 1989
MISS FIRECRACKER   Corsair, 1989
GOODFELLAS   Warner Bros., 1990
THE SILENCE OF THE LAMBS   Orion, 1991

ROLF ZEHETBAUER

CABARET ★★   Allied Artists, 1972
THE SERPENT'S EGG   United Artists, 1977
TWILIGHT'S LAST GLEAMING   Allied Artists, 1977
BRASS TARGET   MGM/UA, 1978
THE AMERICAN SUCCESS CO.   Columbia, 1979
FROM THE LIFE OF THE MARIONETTES   Universal/
    AFD, 1980
DAS BOOT   *THE BOAT*   Triumph/Columbia, 1981
LILI MARLEEN   United Artists Classics, 1981
LOLA   United Artists Classics, 1982, AD
NIGHT CROSSING   Buena Vista, 1982
THE NEVERENDING STORY   Warner Bros., 1984
ENEMY MINE   20th Century Fox, 1985

ROBERT ZENTIS*
IATSE Local 876

O'HARA'S WIFE   Davis-Panzer Productions, 1982, AD
A SINFUL LIFE   New Line Cinema, 1989

ROBERT ZIEMBICKI

BODY AND SOUL   Cannon, 1982, AD
CHAINED HEAT   Jensen Farley Pictures, 1983, AD
BARFLY   Cannon, 1987
DUDES   New Century/Vista, 1988
EAT A BOWL OF TEA   Columbia, 1989

HERMAN ZIMMERMAN*
IATSE Local 876

THE BURNING BED (TF)   Tisch-Avnet
    Productions, 1984
BETTER OFF DEAD   Warner Bros., 1985
ONE CRAZY SUMMER   Warner Bros., 1986
STAR TREK V: THE FINAL FRONTIER
    Paramount, 1989
ADVENTURES IN BABYSITTING (Pilot)   1989, AD
SO PROUDLY WE HAIL (TF)   Lionel Chetwynd
    Productions, 1990

MARINA ZURKOW

BREEDERS   Empire Pictures, 1986, AD
DEADLY ILLUSION   CineTel, 1987,
    AD w/Ruth Lounsbury
ENEMY TERRITORY   Empire Pictures, 1987, AD
NECROPOLIS   Empire Pictures, 1987,
    AD w/Ruth Lounsbury

★ ★ ★ ★

Zu

CINEMATOGRAPHERS
PRODUCTION
DESIGNERS,
COSTUME
DESIGNERS AND
FILM EDITORS
GUIDE

P
R
O
D
U
C
T
I
O
N

D
E
S
I
G
N
E
R
S

C O S T U M E

D E S I G N E R S

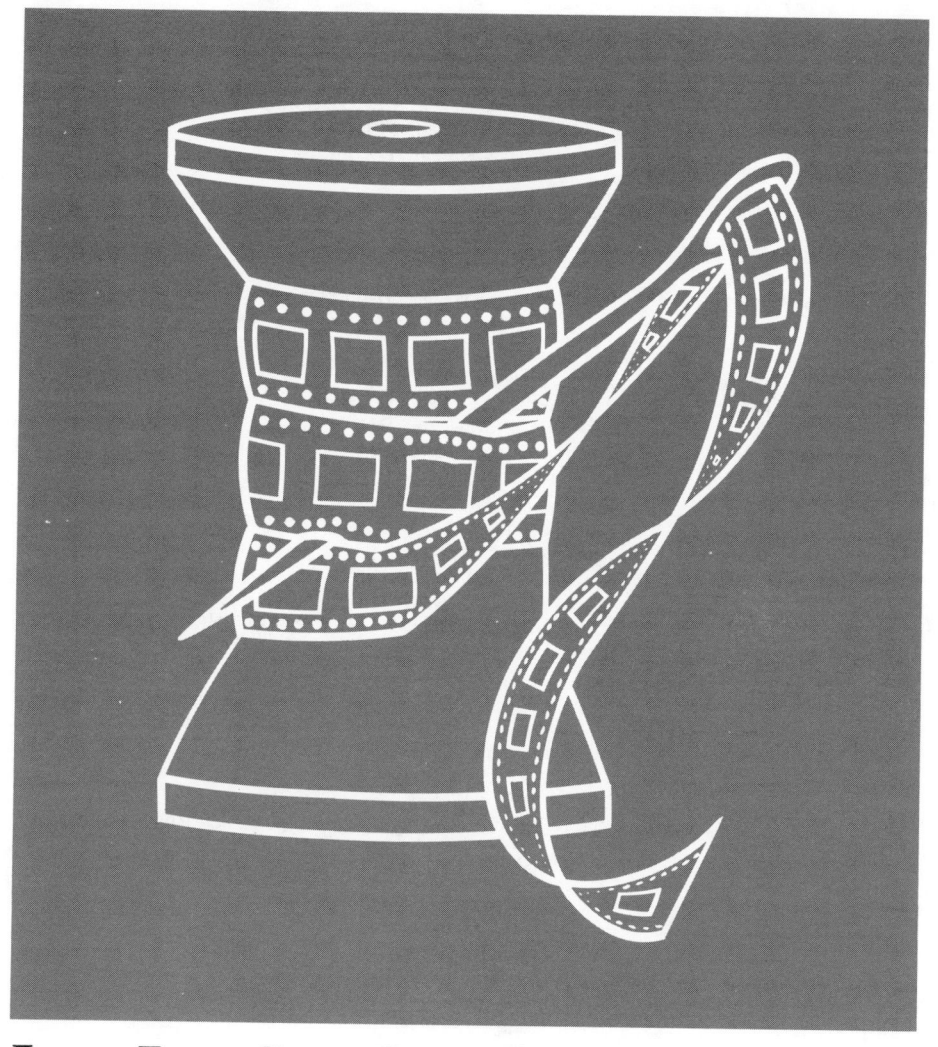

L I S T I N G S

CINEMATOGRAPHERS
PRODUCTION
DESIGNERS,
COSTUME
DESIGNERS AND
FILM EDITORS
GUIDE

C
O
S
T
U
M
E

D
E
S
I
G
N
E
R
S

COSTUME DESIGNERS
ACADEMY AWARDS AND NOMINATIONS
1977-1990

★★ = denotes winner in the category

1977
A LITTLE NIGHT MUSIC .... Florence Klotz
AIRPORT '77 .... Edith Head & Burton Miller
JULIA .... Anthea Sylbert
STAR WARS .... John Mollo ★★
THE OTHER SIDE OF MIDNIGHT .... Irene Sharaff

1978
CARAVANS .... Renie Conley
DAYS OF HEAVEN .... Patricia Norris
DEATH ON THE NILE .... Anthony Powell ★★
THE SWARM .... Paul Zastupnevich
THE WIZ .... Tony Walton

1979
AGATHA .... Shirley Russell
ALL THAT JAZZ .... Albert Wolsky ★★
BUTCH AND SUNDANCE:
    THE EARLY YEARS .... William Ware Theiss

1980
MY BRILLIANT CAREER .... Anna Senior
SOMEWHERE IN TIME .... Jean-Pierre Dorleac
TESS .... Anthony Powell ★★
THE ELEPHANT MAN .... Patricia Norris
WHEN TIME RAN OUT .... Paul Zastupnevich

1981
CHARIOTS OF FIRE .... Milena Canonera ★★
PENNIES FROM HEAVEN .... Bob Mackie
RAGTIME .... Anna Hill Johnstone
REDS .... Shirley Russell
THE FRENCH
    LIEUTENANT'S WOMAN .... Tom Rand

1982
GANDHI .... John Mollo & Bhanu Athaiya ★★
LA TRAVIATA .... Piero Tosi
SOPHIE'S CHOICE .... Albert Wolsky
TRON .... Elois Jenssen & Rosanna Norton
VICTOR/VICTORIA .... Patrica Norris

1983
CROSS CREEK .... Joe I. Tompkins
FANNY AND ALEXANDER .... Marik Vos ★★
HEART LIKE A WHEEL .... William Ware Theiss
THE RETURN OF MARTIN
    GUERRE .... Anne-Marie Marchand
ZELIG .... Santo Loquasto

1984
2010 .... Patricia Norris
A PASSAGE TO INDIA .... Judy Moorcroft
AMADEUS .... Theodor Pistek ★★
PLACES IN THE HEART .... Ann Roth
THE BOSTONIANS .... Jenny Beavan & John Bright

1985
OUT OF AFRICA .... Milena Canonero
PRIZZI'S HONOR .... Donfeld
RAN .... Emi Wada ★★
THE COLOR PURPLE .... Aggie Guerard Rodgers
THE JOUURNEY OF NATTY GANN .... Albert Wolsky

1986
A ROOM WITH A VIEW .... Jenny Beavan & John Bright ★★
OTELLO .... Anna Anni & Maurizio Millenotti
PEGGY SUE GOT MARRIED .... Theadora Van Runkle
PIRATES .... Anthony Powell
THE MISSION .... Enrico Sabbatini

1987
EMPIRE OF THE SUN .... Bob Ringwood
MAURICE .... Jenny Beavan & John Bright
THE DEAD .... Dorothy Jeakins
THE LAST EMPEROR .... James Acheson ★★
THE UNTOUCHABLES .... Marilyn Vance-Straker

1988
COMING TO AMERICA .... Deborah Nadoolman
DANGEROUS LIAISONS .... James Acheson ★★
A HANDFUL OF DUST .... Jane Robinson
SUNSET .... Patricia Norris
TUCKER: A MAN AND
    HIS DREAMS .... Milena Canonero

1989
THE ADVENTURES OF
    BARON MUNCHAUSEN .... Gabriella Pescucci
DRIVING MISS DAISY .... Elizabeth McBride
HENRY V .... Phyllis Dalton ★★
HARLEM NIGHTS .... Joe I. Tompkins
VALMONT .... Theodor Pistek

1990
AVALON .... Gloria Gresham
CYRANO DE BERGERAC .... Franca Squarciapino ★★
DANCES WITH WOLVES .... Elsa Amparelli
DICK TRACY .... Milena Canonero
HAMLET .... Maurizio Millenotti

★★★★

A

MICHAEL ABBOTT
Address: 3805 Los Feliz Blvd., #9, Los Angeles, CA
90027, 213/661-7613

ASSASINATION   Cannon, 1986
ANGEL III: THE LAST CHAPTER   New World
Entertainment, 1988
SAN BERDOO (Pilot)   Aaron Spelling
Productions, 1989
A DEADLY SILENCE (TF)   Robert Greenwald
Productions, 1989
MANNEQUIN ON THE MOVE   Gladden Entertainment/
Windstar Productions, 1990
PUMP UP THE VOLUME   New Line Cinema/Katja
Motion Pictures, 1990

JAMES ACHESON
ACTT
Agent: Sandra Marsh Management - Sherman Oaks,
818/905-6961

TIME BANDITS   Avco Embassy, 1981
MONTY PYTHON'S THE MEANING OF LIFE
Universal, 1983
BULLSHOT!   Island Alive, 1983
WATER   Atlantic Releasing Corporation, 1984
BRAZIL   Universal, 1985
BIGGLES   Compact Yellowbill/Tambarle, 1986
HIGHLANDER   20th Century Fox, 1986,
w/Gilly Hebden
THE LAST EMPEROR ★★   Columbia, 1987
DANGEROUS LIAISONS ★★   Warner Bros., 1988
THE SHELTERING SKY   Warner Bros., 1990

KEVIN ACKERMAN
TWISTED JUSTICE   Seymour Borde &
Associates, 1990

RAY AGHAYAN*
Manager: Phyllis Rab, 213/477-2075
Phone: 213/657-7377

GAILY, GAILY ★   United Artists, 1969
LADY SINGS THE BLUES ★   Paramount, 1972,
w/Norma Koch & Bob Mackie
FUNNY LADY ★   Columbia, 1975, w/Bob Mackie

MARIA AGUILAR
STEEL & LACE   Fries Distribution, 1990

IRENE ALBRIGHT
VAMPIRE'S KISS   Hemdale, 1989

THEONI V. ALDREDGE*
Agent: Joan Hyler, William Morris Agency -
Beverly Hills, 213/274-7451

THE GREAT GATSBY ★★   Paramount, 1974
SEMI-TOUGH   United Artists, 1977

THE CHEAP DETECTIVE   Columbia, 1978
EYES OF LAURA MARS   Columbia, 1978
THE FURY   Columbia, 1978
LOVING COUPLES   20th Century Fox, 1980,
w/Arnold Scaasi
RICH AND FAMOUS   MGM/United Artists, 1981
ANNIE   Columbia, 1982
MONSIGNOR   20th Century Fox, 1982
GHOSTBUSTERS   Columbia, 1984
MOONSTRUCK   MGM/UA, 1987
WE'RE NO ANGELS   Paramount, 1989
STANLEY & IRIS   MGM/UA, 1990

JERRY R. ALLEN
RAD   Tri-Star, 1986
WHO'S HARRY CRUMB?   Tri-Star, 1989

ANDRE ALLEN
HOLLYWOOD SHUFFLE   Samuel Goldwyn
Company, 1987

GAELLE ALLEN
PRETTY SMART   New World, 1987

MARIT ALLEN
Agent: Sandra Marsh Management - Sherman Oaks,
818/905-6961

DON'T LOOK NOW   Paramount, 1974
BAD TIMING/A SENSUAL OBSESSION   World
Northal, 1980
RICHARD'S THINGS   New World, 1981
AN UNSUITABLE JOB FOR A WOMAN   Boyd's
Company, 1982
EUREKA   MGM/UA Classics, 1984
THE HIT   Island Alive, 1984
DEJA VU   Cannon, 1985
FLORENCE NIGHTINGALE (TF)   Cypress Point
Productions, 1985
DREAM LOVER   MGM/UA, 1986
LITTLE SHOP OF HORRORS   The Geffen Company/
Warner Bros., 1986
WHITE MISCHIEF   Columbia, 1987
DIRTY ROTTEN SCOUNDRELS   Orion, 1988
MANIFESTO   Cannon, 1989
THE WITCHES   Warner Bros., 1989
THE RACHEL PAPERS   MGM/UA, 1989
EAT A BOWL OF TEA   Columbia, 1989
MERMAIDS   Orion, 1990
A KISS BEFORE DYING   Universal Pictures, 1991

BARBARA ANDERSON
CREEPSHOW   Warner Bros., 1982
DAY OF THE DEAD   United Film Distribution
Company, 1985
NIGHT OF THE LIVING DEAD   Columbia, 1990

JANE ANDERSON
HOOSIERS   Orion, 1986

ANNA ANNI
OTELLO ★   Cannon, 1986
DANCERS   Cannon, 1987, w/Enrico Serafiini &
Adriana Spadaro

ARLENE ANSEL
INSIDE OUT   Hemdale, 1986

An

CINEMATOGRAPHERS
PRODUCTION
DESIGNERS,
COSTUME
DESIGNERS AND
FILM EDITORS
GUIDE

C
O
S
T
U
M
E

D
E
S
I
G
N
E
R
S

Ap

CINEMATOGRAPHERS
PRODUCTION
DESIGNERS,
COSTUME
DESIGNERS AND
FILM EDITORS
GUIDE

C
O
S
T
U
M
E

D
E
S
I
G
N
E
R
S

DEENA APPEL
HE SAID, SHE SAID   Paramount, 1991

RENÉE APRIL
THE BAY BOY   Orion, 1984
AGNES OF GOD   Columbia, 1985
NOWHERE TO HIDE   New Century/Vista, 1987
THE MODERNS   Alive Films, 1988
THE KISS   Tri-Star, 1988

JAQUELINE ARONSON
SHOCK 'EM DEAD   Academy Entertainment, 1991

MICHAEL ARRALS
SALOME'S LAST DANCE   Vestron, 1988

LUCIANA ARRIGHI
PRIVATES ON PARADE   Orion Classics, 1984
THE PLOUGHMAN'S LUNCH   Samuel Goldwyn
    Company, 1984

COLLEEN C. ATWOOD*
Agent: The Lantz Office - Los Angeles, 213/858-1144
Phone: 212/787-1813

FIRSTBORN   Paramount, 1984
BRING ON THE NIGHT (FD)   Samuel Goldwyn
    Company, 1985
MANHUNTER   DEG, 1986
CRITICAL CONDITION   Paramount, 1987
THE PICK-UP ARTIST   20th Century Fox, 1987
SOMEONE TO WATCH OVER ME   Columbia, 1987
FOR KEEPS   Tri-Star, 1988
FRESH HORSES   WEG, 1988
MARRIED TO THE MOB   Orion, 1988
TORCH SONG TRILOGY   New Line Cinema, 1988
THE HANDMAID'S TALE   Cinecom, 1990
JOE VERSUS THE VOLCANO   Warner Bros., 1990
EDWARD SCISSORHANDS   20th Century Fox, 1990
THE SILENCE OF THE LAMBS   Orion, 1991

JOSEPH G. AULISI*
Address: 802 Lexington Ave., New York, NY
    10021, 212/759-6950

THE NIGHT THE LIGHTS WENT OUT IN GEORGIA
    Avco Embassy, 1981
MAN, WOMAN AND CHILD   Paramount, 1983
EASY MONEY   Orion, 1983
THE BUDDY SYSTEM   20th Century Fox, 1984
HEAVEN HELP US   Tri-Star, 1985
COMPROMISING POSITIONS   Paramount, 1985
OFF BEAT   Buena Vista, 1986
BRIGHTON BEACH MEMOIRS   Universal, 1986
THE SECRET OF MY SUCCESS   Universal, 1987
IRONWEED   Tri-Star, 1987
LINCOLN (TF)   Finnegan Associates, 1988
    (Mary Tyler Moore & Sam Waterson only)
LAST RITES   MGM/UA, 1988
MY BLUE HEAVEN   Warner Bros., 1990
TRUE COLORS   Paramount Pictures, 1991

B

DOROTHY BACA*
Address: 5608 Monte Vista, Los Angeles, CA 90042,
    213/258-1073

BREAKIN' 2 ELECTRIC BOOGALOO   Tri-Star/
    Cannon, 1984
NADIA (TF)   Dave Bell Productions/Tribune
    Entertainment Company/Jadran Film, 1984
THUNDER ALLEY   Cannon, 1985, w/David Baca
GODDESS OF LOVE (TF)   Phil Margo Enterprises/
    New World TV/Phoenix Entertainment Group, 1988

EUGENIE BAFALOUKAS
ROCKERS   New Yorker, 1979
SOMETHING WILD   Orion, 1986
SATISFACTION   20th Century Fox, 1988
ME AND HIM   Columbia, 1989
MIAMI BLUES   Orion, 1990

SWANIE R. BALDRIDGE
THE DIRT BIKE KID   Concorde, 1985
ON THE LINE   Miramax, 1987

CYNTHIA BALES*
Phone: 213/392-6916

LOST IN AMERICA   The Geffen Company/
    Warner Bros., 1985
JUST BETWEEN FRIENDS   Orion, 1986
MIRACLES   Orion, 1986
WHO GETS THE FRIENDS (TF)   CBS
    Entertainment, 1987
SECOND SIGHT   Warner Bros., 1989

LESLIE BALLARD
CLASS OF 1999   Taurus Entertainent, 1990

ANGELA BALOGH-CALIN
GENUINE RISK   I.R.S., 1990
CIRCUITRY MAN   Skouras, 1990

BETTYLEE BALSAM
FRIGHT NIGHT   Columbia, 1985

AUDREY BANSMER
P.O.W. THE ESCAPE   Cannon, 1986
AVENGING FORCE   Cannon, 1986
AMERICAN NINJA 2   Cannon, 1987
BAT 21   Tri-Star, 1988

ALBERT BARSACQ
MAN ON FIRE   Tri-Star, 1987

DENNIS MICHAEL BANSMER
FAR OUT MAN!   New Line Cinema, 1990,
    w/James Gutierrez

FRANCOIS BARBEAU
ATLANTIC CITY   Paramount, 1981

KERRI BARNETT
THE FRINGE DWELLERS   Atlantic Releasing
   Corporation, 1987

ALAN BARRETT
SEVEN PERCENT SOLUTION ★   Universal, 1976
NIJINSKY   Paramount, 1980

SHAWN BARRY
ERNEST GOES TO JAIL   Buena Vista, 1990

COLBY BART
YOU CAN'T HURRY LOVE   MCEG, 1988

LINDA BASS
ONE DARK NIGHT   Comworld, 1983
DREAMSCAPE   20th Century Fox, 1984
EXTREMITIES   Atlantic Releasing Corporation, 1986
IN THE MOOD   Lorimar, 1987
OUT COLD   Hemdale, 1989
FIELD OF DREAMS   Universal, 1989

MONIKA BAUERT
ENEMY MINE   20th Century Fox, 1985

BARBARA BAUM
LOLA   United Artists Classics, 1982
QUERELLE   Triumph, 1983
BERLIN ALEXANDERPLATZ   Teleculture, 1983
BURNING SECRET   Vestron, 1988,
   w/Monica Jacobs

LUSTER BAYLESS*
Phone: 818/764-2239

TELEFON   MGM/United Artists, 1977,
   w/Jane Robinson
COMES A HORSEMAN   United Artists, 1978
TOM HORN   Warner Bros., 1980

CATHERINE BEAUMONT
DEAD WOMEN IN LINGERIE   Monarch Home
   Video, 1990

JENNY BEAVAN
THE BOSTONIANS ★   Almi Pictures, 1984,
   w/John Bright
A ROOM WITH A VIEW ★★   Cinecom, 1986,
   w/John Bright
MAURICE ★   Cinecom, 1987, w/John Bright
A SUMMER STORY   Atlantic/ITC, 1988
THE DECEIVERS   Cinecom, 1988, w/John Bright
MOUNTAINS OF THE MOON   Tri-Star, 1990
IMPROMPTU   Hemdale Films, 1991

SUSAN BECKER*
Phone: 213/851-6195

THE BLACK MARBLE   Avco Embassy, 1980
KING OF THE MOUNTAIN   Universal, 1981
VISION QUEST   Warner Bros., 1985
ST. ELMO'S FIRE   Columbia, 1985
JUMPIN' JACK FLASH   20th Century Fox, 1986
THE LOST BOYS   Warner Bros., 1987
BURGLAR   Warner Bros., 1987

BABY BOOM   MGM/UA, 1987
THE GOOD MOTHER   Buena Vista, 1988
THE BOOST   Hemdale, 1988
FLATLINERS   Columbia, 1990
DAYS OF THUNDER   Paramount, 1990

ANGEE BECKETT
SKI PATROL   Triumph, 1990

LINDA BENEDICT
SMOKEY AND THE BANDIT PART 3   Universal, 1983,
   w/Andre Lavery
THE GIG   Castle Hill Productions, 1985

JOAN BERGIN
THE FIELD   Avenue Pictures, 1990

CYNTHIA BERGSTROM
BEST OF THE BEST   Taurus Entertainment, 1989

MARY BERTRAM
THE WARRIOR AND THE SORCERESS   New
   World, 1984

SUSAN BERTRAM
THE FORBIDDEN DANCE   21st Century/
   Columbia, 1990

CAROL BETERA
DA   FilmDallas, 1988, w/Jill Spaulding

JEF BILLINGS*
Manager: Phyllis Rab, 213/477-2075

CHATTANOOGA CHOO-CHOO   April Fools, 1984
I DREAM OF JEANNIE: 15 YEARS LATER (TF)   Can't
   Sing Can't Dance Productions/Columbia TV, 1985

PATRICIO BISSO
KISS OF THE SPIDER WOMAN   Island Alive, 1985
NAKED TANGO   Scotia International, 1990

BIRGITTA BJERKE
PARIS, TEXAS   TLC Films/20th Century Fox, 1984

TICIA BLACKBURN
HEART   New World, 1987

ROBERT BLACKMAN*
West & East Coast Cards
Agent: Smith Gosnell Nicholson & Associates -
   Pacific Palisades, 213/459-0307
Phone: 213/662-8549

'NIGHT MOTHER   Universal, 1986
THE RUNNING MAN   Tri-Star, 1987
STONES FOR IBARRA (TF)   Titus Productions, 1988
WORTH WINNING   20th Century Fox, 1989

YVONNE BLAKE
NICHOLAS AND ALEXANDRA ★★   Columbia, 1971,
   w/Antonio Castillo
THE FOUR MUSKETEERS ★   20th Century Fox, 1975,
   w/Ron Talsky
SUPERMAN II   Warner Bros., 1981, w/Susan Yelland
FLESH + BLOOD   Orion, 1985
THE RETURN OF THE MUSKETEERS   Universal, 1990

BI

CINEMATOGRAPHERS
PRODUCTION
DESIGNERS,
COSTUME
DESIGNERS AND
FILM EDITORS
GUIDE

C
O
S
T
U
M
E

D
E
S
I
G
N
E
R
S

BI

**CINEMATOGRAPHERS
PRODUCTION
DESIGNERS,
COSTUME
DESIGNERS** AND
**FILM EDITORS
GUIDE**

C
O
S
T
U
M
E

D
E
S
I
G
N
E
R
S

SUE BLANE
SHOCK TREATMENT   20th Century Fox, 1981
THE DRAUGHTSMAN'S CONTRACT   United Artists
   Classics, 1983
LADY JANE   Paramount, 1986
ABSOLUTE BEGINNERS   Orion, 1986, w/David Perry

MARIE BLOM
INITIATION: SILENT NIGHT, DEADLY NIGHT 4
   Live Home Video, 1990

JOHN BLOOMFIELD
THE FIENDISH PLOT OF DR. FU MANCHU
   United Artists, 1980
EYE OF THE NEEDLE   United Artists, 1981
CONAN THE BARBARIAN   Universal, 1982
THE WICKED LADY   MGM/UA, 1983
CONAN THE DESTROYER   Universal, 1984
THE BOUNTY   Orion, 1984
TAI-PAN   DEG, 1986
SUPERMAN IV: THE QUEST FOR PEACE
   Warner Bros., 1987
APPOINTMENT WITH DEATH   Cannon, 1988
THE PHANTOM OF THE OPERA   21st Century
   Film Corp., 1989
MACK THE KNIFE   21st Century Film Corp., 1989

MARIOLINA BONO
THE COMFORT OF STRANGERS   Erre Produzioni/
   Sovereign Pictures, 1991

BEATRICE BORDONE
CINEMA PARADISO   Miramax, 1989

GWEN CAPETANOS BOUZON*
Phone: 818/985-5064

SIXTH AND MAIN   National Cinema, 1977
THE MUPPET MOVIE   AFD, 1979

MARJORIE BOWERS*
Address: 1150 Linda Flora Dr., Los Angeles, CA
   90049, 213/472-7441

THE OUTSIDERS   Warner Bros., 1983
RUMBLE FISH   Universal, 1983
DEFENSE PLAY   Kodak Films, 1987
DENNIS THE MENACE (TF)   DIC Enterprises
   Productions, 1987
ALMOST GROWN (Pilot)   1988

JOHN BOXER
STARTING OVER   Paramount, 1979
FORT APACHE, THE BRONX   20th Century
   Fox, 1981
WOLFEN   Orion/Warner Bros., 1981
NEIGHBORS   Columbia, 1981
FIGHTING BACK   Paramount, 1982
REUBEN, REUBEN   20th Century Fox, 1983
ORPHANS   Lorimar, 1987
MASQUERADE   MGM/UA, 1988
SEE YOU IN THE MORNING   Warner Bros., 1989
PRESUMED INNOCENT   Warner Bros., 1990

CONSOLATA BOYLE
DECEMBER BRIDE   Film Four International, 1991

BAMBI BREAKSTONE*
West Coast Card
Agent: Smith Gosnell Nicholson & Associates -
   Pacific Palisades, 213/459-0307
Phone: 213/935-2113

INFIDELITY (TF)   Mark-Jett Productions/ABC
   Circle Films, 1987
TONIGHT'S THE NIGHT (TF)   IndieProd Productions/
   Phoenix Entertainment Gorup, 1987
CLARA'S HEART   Warner Bros., 1988
MINDWALK   Mindwalk Productions, 1990

HALI BREINDEL
ANNA   Vestron, 1987

JOAN BRIDGE
FIDDLER ON THE ROOF   United Artists, 1971,
   w/Elizabeth Haffenden
HANOVER STREET   Columbia, 1979

JOHN BRIGHT
THE BOSTONIANS ★   Almi Pictures, 1984,
   w/Jenny Beavan
A ROOM WITH A VIEW ★★   Cinecom, 1986,
   w/Jenny Beavan
MAURICE ★   Cinecom, 1987, w/Jenny Beavan
THE DECEIVERS   Cinecom, 1988,
   w/Jenny Beavan

CAROL BROLASKI
HONEY, I SHRUNK THE KIDS   Buena Vista, 1989

AUDE BRONSON-HOWARD
RAPPIN'   Cannon, 1985
9 1/2 WEEKS   MGM/UA, 1986,
   (Asst. to Bobbie Read)
PLAYING FOR KEEPS   Universal, 1986
ANGEL HEART   Tri-Star, 1987
MISSISSIPPI BURNING   Orion, 1988
REVENGE   Columbia, 1990

THOMAS M. BRONSON*
Phone: 818/840-1230

THE EXECUTION OF PRIVATE SLOVIK (TF) ☆
   Universal TV, 1974
FEAR ON TRIAL (TF) ☆   Alan Landsburg
   Productions, 1975
THE DEEP   Columbia, 1977, w/Ron Talsky
SLAP SHOT   Universal, 1977
RUBY AND OSWALD (TF) ☆   Alan Landsburg
   Productions, 1978
THE LONG RIDERS   United Artists,
   1980, supervisor
THE NINTH CONFIGURATION   New World, 1980
VICTORY   Paramount, 1981
FIRST BLOOD   Orion, 1982
STAYING ALIVE   Paramount, 1983, w/Bob Mackie
BEVERLY HILLS COP   Paramount, 1984
RHINESTONE   20th Century Fox, 1984, except
   Dolly Parton
ROCKY IV   MGM/UA, 1985
RAMBO: FIRST BLOOD PART II   Tri-Star, 1985
COBRA   Warner Bros., 1986
OVER THE TOP   Cannon, 1987

DONALD BROOKS*
Agent: Phil Gersh, The Gersh Agency, Inc. -
    Beverly Hills, 213/274-6611

THE CARDINAL ★   Columbia, 1963
STAR! ★   20th Century Fox, 1968
DARLING LILI ★   Paramount, 1970, w/Jack Bear
THE DROWNING POOL   Warner Bros., 1975
THE BELL JAR   Avco Embassy, 1979
SCRUPLES (TF)   Lou-Step Productions/Warner
    Bros. TV, 1980
THE LETTER (TF) ☆☆   Najeno Productions/
    Warner Bros. TV, 1982
THE TWO MRS. GRENVILLES (TF) ☆   Lorimar-
    Telepictures, 1987, w/Nolan Miller & Sue Yelland

CLAUDIA BROWN
RIVER'S EDGE   Hemdale, 1987

KRISTINE BROWN
DREAM A LITTLE DREAM   Vestron, 1989
ONE CUP OF COFFEE   Bullpen/Open Road, 1991

WINNIE D. BROWN
GHOST DAD   Universal, 1990

RICHARD BRUNO*
Phone: 818/781-6531 or 206/385-7149

THE LAST TYCOON   Paramount, 1976, shared credit
HEAVEN CAN WAIT   Paramount, 1978
RAGING BULL   United Artists, 1978
ICE CASTLES   Columbia, 1979
PLAYERS   Paramount, 1979
STRIPES   Columbia, 1981
THE KING OF COMEDY   20th Century Fox, 1983
GORKY PARK   Orion, 1983
THE KARATE KID   Columbia, 1984, Mens
FALLING IN LOVE   Paramount, 1984
WISE GUYS   MGM/UA, 1986
THE COLOR OF MONEY   Buena Vista, 1986
BIG SHOTS   20th Century Fox, 1987
THE UNTOUCHABLES   Paramount, 1987,
    Robert DeNiro only
ROXANNE   Columbia, 1987, U.S.
SHOOT TO KILL   Buena Vista, 1988
CASUALTIES OF WAR   Columbia, 1989
GOODFELLAS   Warner Bros., 1990
GUILTY BY SUSPICION   Warner Bros., 1991
OUT FOR JUSTICE   Warner Bros., 1991

CELIA BRYANT
I, THE JURY   20th Century Fox, 1982
KNIGHTS OF THE CITY   New World, 1986,
    w/Beverly Safier

JOHN (JACK) BUEHLER
DEATH OF AN ANGEL   20th Century Fox, 1985
BLACK MOON RISING   New World, 1986
AMAZING GRACE AND CHUCK   Tri-Star, 1987
18 AGAIN   New World, 1988

CLOVIS BUENO
THE EMERALD FOREST   20th Century Fox, 1985,
    w/Christel Boorman

ARLINE BURKS
DAUGHTERS OF THE DUST   American
    Playhouse, 1991

ROSEMARY BURROWS
MR. JOHNSON   Avenue Pictures, 1990

DENNY BURT
PRANCER   Orion, 1989

SCOTT BUSHNELL
QUINTET   20th Century Fox, 1979
POPEYE   Paramount, 1980
STREAMERS   United Artists Classics, 1983
VINCENT & THEO   Hemdale, 1990

MIKE BUTLER
UNDER THE RAINBOW   Orion/Warner Bros., 1981

RICHARD BUTZ
WEEKEND AT BERNIE'S   20th Century Fox, 1989,
    (costume supervisor)

SUSANNAH BUXTON
TWENTY-ONE   Anglo International Films, 1991

MARY LOU BYRD
THE HEAVENLY KID   Orion, 1985
FLIGHT OF THE NAVIGATOR   Buena Vista, 1986
HAPPY NEW YEAR   Columbia, 1987, Wardrobe

JEANIE CAMERON
SLATE, WYN & ME   Hemdale, 1987

POPPY CANNON
MISSING IN ACTION 2: THE BEGINNING
    Cannon, 1985
FIREWALKER   Cannon, 1986
STEEL DAWN   Vestron, 1987

MILENA CANONERO
BARRY LYNDON ★★   Warner Bros., 1975,
    w/Ulla-Britt Soderlund
MIDNIGHT EXPRESS   Columbia, 1978
THE SHINING   Warner Bros., 1980
CHARIOTS OF FIRE ★★   The Ladd Company/
    Warner Bros., 1981
THE HUNGER   MGM/UA, 1983
GIVE MY REGARDS TO BROAD STREET
    20th Century Fox, 1984
THE COTTON CLUB   Orion, 1984
OUT OF AFRICA ★   Universal, 1985
BARFLY   Cannon, 1987
TUCKER: THE MAN AND HIS DREAM ★
    Paramount, 1988
LOST ANGELS   Orion, 1989, Consultant
DICK TRACY ★   Buena Vista, 1990
REVERSAL OF FORTUNE   Warner Bros.,
    1990, (consultant only)
THE GODFATHER PART III   Zoetrope Studios/
    Paramount, 1990

Ca

CINEMATOGRAPHERS
PRODUCTION
DESIGNERS,
COSTUME
DESIGNERS AND
FILM EDITORS
GUIDE

C
O
S
T
U
M
E

D
E
S
I
G
N
E
R
S

Ca

CINEMATOGRAPHERS
PRODUCTION
DESIGNERS,
COSTUME
DESIGNERS AND
FILM EDITORS
GUIDE

C
O
S
T
U
M
E

D
E
S
I
G
N
E
R
S

CLIFFORD CAPONE
TOUGH ENOUGH 20th Century Fox, 1983
AMITYVILLE 3-D Orion, 1983
LILY IN LOVE New Line Cinema, 1985
STEPHEN KING'S CAT'S EYE MGM/UA, 1985
SILVER BULLET Paramount, 1985
RAW DEAL DEG, 1986
MAXIMUM OVERDRIVE DEG, 1986
KING KONG LIVES DEG, 1986
THE BEDROOM WINDOW DEG, 1987
MILLION DOLLAR MYSTERY DEG, 1987
FROM THE HIP DEG, 1987
BLACK RAINBOW Goldcrest Films, 1989

JULIE CARNAHAN
STEPFATHER II Millimeter Films, 1989

RUTH E. CARTER*
Agent: The Gersh Agency, Inc., Beverly Hills -
    213/274-6611, New York - 212/997-1818

SCHOOL DAZE Columbia, 1988
I'M GONNA GET YOU SUCKA MGM/UA, 1988
THE SEINFELD CHRONICLES (Pilot) 1989
HOME ROOM (Pilot) 1989
DO THE RIGHT THING Universal, 1989
MO' BETTER BLUES Universal, 1990
JUNGLE FEVER Universal/40 Acrea and a Mule
    Filmworks, 1991
THE FIVE HEARTBEATS 20th Century
    Fox, 1991

NANA CECCHI
LADYHAWKE Warner Bros., 1985
LIONHEART Orion, 1987

JUDIE CHAMPION
THE GARBAGE PAIL KIDS MOVIE Atlantic
    Releasing Corporation, 1987

DIANE FINN CHAPMAN
ROSELAND Cinema Shares International, 1977
SEVEN MINUTES IN HEAVEN Warner Bros., 1986

SUSAN CHEVALIER
GHOST FEVER Miramax, 1987, w/Leslie Levin

GIGI CHOA
CHINA CRY Penland, 1990

STEPHEN CHUDEJ
PRISON Empire Pictures, 1988
ANGEL TOWN Taurus Entertainment, 1990

NAN CIBULA
THINGS CHANGE Columbia, 1987
OPPORTUNITY KNOCKS Universal, 1990
HOMICIDE Triumph/Edward J. Pressman/
    Cinehaus, 1991

DIANNA CILLIERS
JAKE SPEED New World, 1986
A PRIVATE LIFE Totem Productions, 1989
THE HOUSE OF USHER RCA/Columbia
    Pictures Home Video, 1991

MARIETTA CIRIELLO
YEAR OF THE DRAGON MGM/UA, 1985

KATHIE CLARK
Phone: 213/456-2990

METALSTORM: THE DESTRUCTION OF JARED-SYN
    Universal, 1983
ANGEL New World, 1984
TUFF TURF New World, 1985
GHOULIES Empire Pictures, 1985
TERRORVISION Empire Pictures, 1986
VALET GIRLS Empire Pictues, 1987

CHARLOTTE CLASON
THE WOLF AT THE DOOR International Film
    Marketing, 1986

CANDA CLEMENTS
FOREVER, LULU Tri-Star, 1987

ELLIS COHEN
SAVAGE HARVEST 20th Century Fox, 1981
THE MAN WITH TWO BRAINS Warner Bros.,
    1983, Mens
FIRE BIRDS Buena Vista, 1990

NANCY CONE
MISSING IN ACTION Cannon, 1984
NINJA III: THE DOMINATION Cannon, 1984
RUSSKIES New Century/Vista, 1987
D.O.A. Buena Vista, 1987

RENIE CONLEY*
Agent: Randy Clark, 213/465-7140 or 465-7198
Address: 1080 Ravoli Dr., Pacific Palisades, CA 90272,
    213/454-5227

CLEOPATRA ★★ 20th Century Fox, 1963,
    w/Vittorio Nino Novarese & Irene Sharaff
THE GREAT SCOUT AND CATHOUSE THURSDAY
    American International, 1976
CARAVANS ★ Universal, 1978
HAYWIRE (TF) Pando Productions/Warner
    Bros. TV, 1980
BODY HEAT The Ladd Company/Warner Bros., 1981
THE WOMEN'S ROOM (TF) Philip Mandelker
    Productions/Warner Bros. TV, 1984
SPACE (MS) Stonehenge Productions/
    Paramount TV, 1986

JILL CONNER
TERMINAL FORCE New World Video, 1990
MOB BOSS Vidmark Entertainment, 1990

CATHERINE COOKE
SID & NANCY Samuel Goldwyn Company, 1986,
    w/Theda Deramus
RITA, SUE AND BOB TOO Orion Classics, 1987
SLIPSTREAM Entertainment Films, 1989
HAWKS Skouras Pictures, 1989
KING RALPH Universal, 1991

SOFIA COPPOLA
NEW YORK STORIES ("Life Without Zoe")
    Buena Vista, 1989
THE SPIRIT OF '76 Columbia, 1990

JOSE MARIA COSSIO
ATAME *TIE ME UP! TIE ME DOWN!* Miramax, 1990

BETSY COX*
Agent: Scott Harris, Harris & Goldberg -
Los Angeles, 213/553-5200
Phone: 818/763-1721

SEEMS LIKE OLD TIMES Columbia, 1980
PRIVATE BENJAMIN Warner Bros., 1980
LOOKER The Ladd Company/Warner Bros., 1981
BEST FRIENDS Warner Bros., 1982
YES, GIORGIO MGM/UA, 1982
ENDANGERED SPECIES MGM/UA, 1982
DOCTOR DETROIT Universal, 1983
RUNAWAY Tri-Star, 1984
THE LONELY GUY Universal, 1984
GUNG HO Paramount, 1986
QUICKSILVER Columbia, 1986
PHYSICAL EVIDENCE Columbia, 1989
ROE VS. WADE (TF) The Manheim Company/ NBC
Productions, 1989
SEA OF LOVE Universal, 1989
TOY SOLDIERS Tri-Star Pictures, 1991
CAREER OPPORTUNITIES Universal/Hughes
Entertainment, 1991

DENISE CRONENBERG
THE FLY 20th Century Fox, 1986
DEAD RINGERS 20th Century Fox, 1988
THE GUARDIAN Universal, 1990

SANDRA CULOTTA
THE LONGSHOT Orion, 1986
CAGE New Century/Vista, 1989

PATRICK CUMMINGS
Agent: Miles Kuhn, Associated Talent International -
Los Angeles, 213/271-4662
Phone: 818/882-8657

DOC SAVAGE, THE MAN OF BRONZE Warner
Bros., 1975
HEARTS OF THE WEST MGM/United
Artists, 1975
DEATH OF A CENTERFOLD: THE DOROTHY
STRATTEN STORY (TF) Wilcox Productions/
MGM TV, 1981
I WANT TO LIVE (TF) United Artists Corp., 1983

SHAY CUNLIFFE
Local 829
Agent: Sandra Marsh Management - Sherman Oaks,
818/905-6961

MRS. SOFFEL MGM/UA, 1984
D.A.R.Y.L. Paramount, 1985
THE LONG HOT SUMMER (TF) Leonard Hill
Productions, 1985
THE MANHATTAN PROJECT 20th Century
Fox, 1986
THE LAND OF LITTLE RAIN (TF) American
Playhouse, 1988
THE BELIEVERS Orion, 1987
MILES FROM HOME Cinecom, 1988
MIRACLE MILE Tri-Star, 1988
THE LONG WALK HOME Miramax, 1990

HARRY CURTIS*
Phone: 213/876-6362

CRAZY TIMES (TF) ☆ Kayden-Gleason Productions/
George Reeves Productions/Warner Bros. TV, 1981
GOING BERSERK Universal, 1983
BRIGHTON BEACH MEMOIRS Universal, 1986,
(Asst. to Joe Aulisi)
NADINE Tri-Star, 1987, (Asst. to Albert Wolsky)
MOON OVER PARADOR Universal, 1988,
(Asst. to Albert Wolsky)

JUDITH BREWER CURTIS*
Address: 2616 Purdue Ave., Los Angeles, CA 90064,
213/478-4139

HOLLYWOOD ZAP Troma, 1986
JUST YOU AND ME (Pilot) 1989

D

LIZ DA COSTA
TANK MALLING Pointlane Films, 1990

PHYLLIS DALTON
VOYAGE OF THE DAMNED Avco Embassy, 1976
THE AWAKENING Orion/Warner Bros., 1980
A PRIVATE FUNCTION Island Alive, 1985
THE PRINCESS BRIDE 20th Century Fox, 1987
HENRY V ★ Renaissance Films, 1989
DEAD AGAIN Paramount, 1991

MALISSA DANIEL
THE HIDDEN New Line Cinema, 1987
SLAM DANCE Island Pictures, 1987
COMMUNION MCEG, 1989

TIM D'ARCY
Contact: 213/663-3231

Q United Film Distribution, 1982
THE STUFF New World, 1985
THE FIRST POWER Orion, 1989
REPOSSESSED Seven Arts, 1990
SHE SAID NO (TF) Steve White Productions, 1990
PERFECT HARMONY (CTF) Joe Wizan
Productions, 1991
LOVE POTION NO. 9 20th Century Fox, 1991

DAPHNE DARE
HIDDEN AGENDA Hemdale, 1990

BARBARA DARRAGH
CAME A HOT FRIDAY Orion Classics, 1985

SANDRA DAVIDSON*
Phone: 213/659-6178

ALMOST SUMMER Universal, 1978
COAST TO COAST Paramount, 1980

Da

CINEMATOGRAPHERS
PRODUCTION
DESIGNERS,
COSTUME
DESIGNERS AND
FILM EDITORS
GUIDE

C
O
S
T
U
M
E

D
E
S
I
G
N
E
R
S

Da

CINEMATOGRAPHERS
PRODUCTION
DESIGNERS,
COSTUME
DESIGNERS and
FILM EDITORS
GUIDE

HERO AT LARGE   MGM/United Artists, 1980
EDDIE AND THE CRUISERS   Embassy, 1983
WALTZ ACROSS TEXAS   Atlantic Releasing
    Corporation, 1983
THE NAKED FACE   MGM/UA/Cannon, 1984,
    w/Jay Hurley
LONG GONE (CTF)   HBO Pictures/The Landsburg
    Company, 1987
HEART OF DIXIE   Orion, 1989

RONDI HILLSTROM DAVIS
NOT FOR PUBLICATION   Samuel Goldwyn
    Company, 1984
FULL MOON IN BLUE WATER   Trans World
    Entertainment, 1988
DAKOTA   Miramax, 1988

TOM DAWSON*
Agent: Judy Coppage, The Coppage Company -
    North Hollywood, 818/980-1106
Phone: 818/713-8676

THE CHOIRBOYS   Universal, 1977
TWILIGHT'S LAST GLEAMING   Allied Artists, 1977
CREATOR   Universal, 1985, w/Jennifer Parson

SHARON DAY-NYE*
Agent: Robert Littman - Los Angeles, 213/278-1572
Address: 937 19th St., #4, Santa Monica, CA 90403,
    213/829-4033

CHEECH & CHONG'S NICE DREAMS
    Columbia, 1981
ZAPPED!   Embassy, 1982
SYLVESTER   Columbia, 1985

CHARLES DE CARO
DESPERATE HOURS   MGM/UA, 1990

TARYN De CHELLIS*
Agent: Paul Gerard Agency - Newport Beach,
    714/644-7950

DRAGNET   Universal, 1987
AMAZON WOMEN ON THE MOON   Universal, 1987
HOT PURSUIT   Paramount, 1987
HOW I GOT INTO COLLEGE   20th Century Fox, 1989

MARIANNA ASTROM DEFINA*
Agent: The Irv Schechter Company - Beverly Hills,
    213/278-8070
Address: 123 Union St., San Rafael, CA 94901,
    415/454-2040

NORTHERN LIGHTS   Cine Manifest/New Front
    Films, 1978
A CHRISTMAS WITHOUT SNOW (TF)   Korty Films/
    The Konigsberg Company, 1980
MOTHER AND DAUGHTER - THE LOVING WAR (TF)
    Edgar J. Scherick Associates, 1980
STREET MUSIC   Specialty, 1982
PRIME SUSPECT (TF)   Tisch-Avnet Television, 1982
THE PRINCIPAL   Tri-Star, 1987

EUGENIE DEL GRECO
ALMOST YOU   TLC Films/20th Century Fox, 1984

JEAN-PIERRE DELIFER
THE LAST TEMPTATION OF CHRIST   Universal, 1988

ROBERT de MORA*
Phone: 212/691-9379

MARATHON MAN   Paramount, 1976
EXORCIST II: THE HERETIC   Warner Bros., 1977
AMERICAN HOT WAX   Paramount, 1978
THE AMERICAN SUCCESS CO.   Columbia, 1979
THE WANDERERS   Orion/Warner Bros., 1979
WINTER KILLS   Avco Embassy, 1979
TIMES SQUARE   AFD, 1980
NIGHTHAWKS   Universal, 1981, w/John Falabella
GREASE 2   Paramount, 1982
JINXED   MGM/UA, 1982
RISKY BUSINESS   The Geffen Company/Warner
    Bros., 1983
BERRY GORDY'S THE LAST DRAGON   Tri-Star, 1985
BAND OF THE HAND   Tri-Star, 1986
A NIGHT IN THE LIFE OF JIMMY REARDON   20th
    Century Fox, 1988
STEALING HOME   Warner Bros., 1988
BEACHES   Buena Vista, 1988

YVONNE SASSINOTDE NESLE
HENRY & JUNE   Universal, 1990

SUSAN DENISON
SPRING BREAK   Columbia, 1983, w/Sara Denning

KEITH DENNY
FULL METAL JACKET   Warner Bros., 1987
GOOD MORNING, VIETNAM   Buena Vista, 1987

THEDA DERAMUS
REPO MAN   Universal, 1984
MODERN GIRLS   Atlantic Releasing Corporation, 1986
SID & NANCY   Samuel Goldwyn Company, 1986,
    w/Cathy Cooke
WALKER   Universal, 1987, Tucson

SUSIE De SANTO
DISORDERLIES   Warner Bros., 1987
JOHNNY BE GOOD   Orion, 1988
BOOK OF LOVE   New Line Cinema, 1990

KATHLEEN DETORO*
Agent: The Gersh Agency, Inc., Beverly Hills -
    213/274-6611, New York - 212/997-1818

ZELLY AND ME   Columbia, 1988
ROOFTOPS   New Century/Vista, 1989

RUDY DILLON
MAKING MR. RIGHT   Orion, 1987, w/Adelle Lutz
THE WHALES OF AUGUST   Alive Films, 1987,
    (except Bette Davis)
HEATHERS   New World, 1989
INTERNAL AFFAIRS   Paramount, 1990
L.A. STORY   Carolco/Tri-Star, 1991

OLGA DIMITROV
CLOSELY WATCHED TRAINS   Sigma III, 1966
IN PRAISE OF OLDER WOMEN   Avco Embassy, 1978
AGENCY   Taft International, 1980
DEATH HUNT   20th Century Fox, 1981

SILENCE OF THE NORTH   Universal, 1982
HARRY TRACY   Quartet/Films Inc., 1983
THE DEAD ZONE   Paramount, 1983
ONE MAGIC CHRISTMAS   Buena Vista, 1985
JOHN AND THE MISSUS   Cinema Group, 1987
MILLENNIUM   20th Century Fox, 1989

ANGELA DODSON
UNDER THE VOLCANO   Universal, 1984

JUDY DOLAN
THE OUTSIDER   Paramount, 1979
THE ROSARY MURDERS   New Line Cinema, 1987

PIA DOMINIQUEZ
SILENT NIGHT, DEADLY NIGHT III: BETTER
   WATCH OUT!   Quiet Films, 1989
DISTURBED   Live Entertainment/Odyssey, 1990

DANILO DONATI
FELLINI'S CASANOVA ★★   Universal, 1976
HURRICANE   Paramount, 1979
RED SONJA   MGM/UA, 1985
GINGER & FRED   MGM/UA, 1986

LUCILE DONAY
GABY - A TRUE STORY   Tri-Star, 1987,
   w/Tolita Figueroa

DONFELD
Agent: The Gersh Agency, Inc., Beverly Hills -
   213/274-6611, New York - 212/997-1818

DAYS OF WINE AND ROSES ★   Warner Bros., 1962
THEY SHOOT HORSES, DON'T THEY? ★
   Cinerama Releasing Corporation, 1969
TOM SAWYER ★   United Artists, 1973
FIRST LOVE   Paramount, 1977
ONE ON ONE   Warner Bros., 1977
FUN WITH DICK AND JANE   Columbia, 1977
THE CHINA SYNDROME   Columbia, 1979
BRAINSTORM   MGM/UA, 1983
THE CARTIER AFFAIR (TF)   Hill-Mandelker
   Productions, 1984
PRIZZI'S HONOR ★   20th Century Fox, 1985
SPACEBALLS   MGM/UA, 1987
NEXT OF KIN   Warner Bros., 1989

JEAN-PIERRE DORLEAC*
Agent: Richard Sindell, The Lantz Office,
   213/858-1144
Phone: 213/874-9812

A DOLL'S HOUSE   Tomorrow Entertainment, 1973
THE GREAT SMOKEY ROADBLOCK
   Dimension, 1977
GOOD GUYS WEAR BLACK   American
   Cinema, 1978
THE BASTARD (TF) ☆☆   Universal TV, 1978
BUCK ROGERS IN THE 21ST CENTURY
   Universal, 1979
BLUE LAGOON   Columbia, 1980
SOMEWHERE IN TIME ★   Universal, 1980
ROSIE: THE ROSEMARY CLOONEY STORY (TF)
   Charles Fries Productions/Alan Sacks
   Productions, 1982
MAE WEST (TF) ☆☆   Hill-Mandelker Films, 1982

THE TALES OF THE GOLD MONKEY (TVS) ☆☆   1982
NATIONAL LAMPOON'S CLASS REUNION   20th
   Century Fox, 1983
THE BOSS' WIFE   Tri-Star, 1987
THE KILLING TIME   New World, 1987
JAKE AND THE FATMAN (Pilot)   1987

RONA DORON
EVERY TIME WE SAY GOODBYE   Tri-Star, 1986

SUSAN DOUGLAS
THE TOXIC AVENGER PART III: THE LAST
   TEMPTATION OF TOXIE   Troma, 1989

KATHY DOVER (KATHERINE)
RUNAWAY TRAIN   Cannon, 1985
SHY PEOPLE   Cannon, 1987
DELTA FORCE 2   MGM/UA, 1990
BLIND FURY   Tri-Star, 1990

EMILY DRAPER*
Phone: 213/479-2673

THE AMBASSADOR   Noah Films, 1976, w/Tami Moore,
   (Rock Hudson & Robert Mitchum only)
MAKING THE GRADE   MGM/UA/Cannon, 1984
STRANGE VOICES (TF)   Forrest Hills Productions/
   Dacks-Geller Productions/TLC, 1987

TERRY DRESBACH
PURPLE PEOPLE EATERS   Concorde, 1988
MINISTRY OF VENGEANCE   Concorde, 1989

LAURIE DREW
BREAKING ALL THE RULES   New World, 1985

JOHN DUNN
NEW YORK STORIES ("Life Lessons")   Buena
   Vista, 1989

NIC EDE
Agent: Grace Lyons Management - Los Angeles,
   213/655-5100

CASTAWAY   Cannon, 1987
PAPERHOUSE   Vestron, 1988
A WORLD APART   Atlantic Releasing Corporation, 1988
FAT MAN AND LITTLE BOY   Paramount, 1989
NOT WITHOUT MY DAUGHTER   Pathe Entertainment/
   MGM/UA, 1991

PATRICIA EDWARDS
10   Orion/Warner Bros., 1979
TARZAN, THE APE MAN   MGM/United Artists, 1981
CURSE OF THE PINK PANTHER   MGM/UA, 1983

Ed

CINEMATOGRAPHERS
PRODUCTION
DESIGNERS,
COSTUME
DESIGNERS AND
FILM EDITORS
GUIDE

CINEMATOGRAPHERS
PRODUCTION
DESIGNERS,
COSTUME
DESIGNERS AND
FILM EDITORS
GUIDE

MARIANNA ELLIOTT*
Agent: David Gersh, The Gersh Agency, Inc. -
   Beverly Hills, 213/274-6611
Phone: 213/277-3028

THE BIG BUS   Paramount, 1976
WHEN HELL WAS IN SESSION (TF)
   Aubrey-Hamner Productions, 1979
WHOSE LIFE IS IT, ANYWAY?   MGM/United
   Artists, 1981
BLUE THUNDER   Columbia, 1983, w/Norman Burza
AMERICAN FLYERS   Warner Bros., 1985
THE MEN'S CLUB   Atlantic Releasing Corporation,
   1986, w/Peter Mitchell
THE BALLAD OF THE SAD CAFE   Angelika
   Films, 1991

AMY ENDRIES
DEEPSTAR SIX   Tri-Star, 1989

CHARMIN ESPINOZA
PRIVATE INVESTIGATIONS   MGM/UA, 1987

GWENDA EVANS
ORDEAL BY INNOCENCE   MGM/UA/Cannon, 1984

HAROLD EVANS
HOUSE PARTY   New Line Cinema, 1990
HANGFIRE   Motion Picture Corporation of
   America, 1991

DEBORAH EVERTON
BAD DREAMS   20th Century Fox, 1988
THE ABYSS   20th Century Fox, 1989
VITAL SIGNS   20th Century Fox, 1990

F

PEGGY FARRELL-SALTEN
THE SENTINEL   Universal, 1977
DEATH WISH 3   Cannon, 1985
SHAKEDOWN   Universal, 1988
RUDE AWAKENING   Orion, 1989
BRENDA STARR   New World, 1991
   (except Brooke Shields)

TONY FASO
THE TURNING POINT   20th Century Fox, 1977,
   w/Jennifer Parsons & Albert Wolsky
OLD BOYFRIENDS   Avco Embassy, 1979

MARIANNE FASSLER
ALLAN QUATERMAIN AND THE LOST CITY
   OF GOLD   Cannon, 1987

SHARI FELDMAN
THE SENDER   Paramount, 1982
WITNESS   Paramount, 1985
HAMBURGER...THE MOTION PICTURE
   FM Entertainment, 1986

WIRED   Taurus Entertainment, 1989
LISA   MGM/UA, 1990

ELSA FENNELL
THE SEA WOLVES   Paramount, 1981

INGRID FERRIN
LOVE AT LARGE   Orion, 1990

APRIL FERRY*
Agent: Randy Clark, 213/465-7140
Address: 1615 Shell Ave., Venice, CA 90291,
   213/821-0379

GOTCHA!   Univesal, 1985
MASK   Universal, 1985, Cher only, selected
POLTERGEIST II: THE OTHER SIDE
   MGM/UA, 1986
BIG TROUBLE IN LITTLE CHINA   20th Century
   Fox, 1986
PLANES, TRAINS AND AUTOMOBILES
   Paramount, 1987
MADE IN HEAVEN   Lorimar, 1987
SHE'S HAVING A BABY   Paramount, 1988
CHILD'S PLAY   MGM/UA, 1988
THREE FUGITIVES   Buena Vista, 1989
LEVIATHAN   MGM/UA, 1989
MY NAME IS BILL W. (TF) ☆   1989
IMMEDIATE FAMILY   Columbia, 1989
ALMOST AN ANGEL   Ironbark Films/Paramount, 1990

PATRICIA FIELD*
Address: 10 E. 8th St., New York, NY 10003,
   212/254-2164

LADY BEWARE   Scotti Brothers, 1987
HE'S MY GIRL   Scotti Brothers, 1987
DREAM STREET (Pilot)   1988

TOLITA FIGUEROA
GABY - A TRUE STORY   Tri-Star, 1987,
   w/Lucile Donay

WAYNE FINKELMAN*
Agent: Susan Grode, 213/203-8410
Phone: 213/273-3372

PARTNERS   Paramount, 1982
GRANDVIEW, U.S.A.   Warner Bros., 1984
PROTOCOL   Warner Bros., 1984
RUSTLERS' RHAPSODY   Paramount, 1985
WILDCATS   Warner Bros., 1986
THE GOLDEN CHILD   Paramount, 1986
THE SICILIAN   20th Century Fox, 1987
OVERBOARD   MGM/UA, 1987
SCROOGED   Paramount, 1988
THE TWO JAKES   Paramount, 1990
BIRD ON A WIRE   Universal, 1990
QUIGLEY DOWN UNDER   Pathe/MGM/UA, 1990

BRUCE FINLAYSON
CAREFUL HE MIGHT HEAR YOU   TLC Films/20th
   Century Fox, 1984
SISTER, SISTER   New World, 1988
A CRY IN THE DARK   Warner Bros., 1988
THE DELINQUENTS   Warner Bros., 1990

LINDA FISHER*
Agent: Tom Turley, Gersh Agency, Inc. - New York, 212/997-1818
Address: 139 West 82nd St., New York, NY 10024, 212/799-4506

THE PRIVATE HISTORY OF A CAMPAIGN THAT FAILED (TF)   The Great Amwell Company/Nebraska ETV Network/WNET-13, 1981
PUDD'NHEAD WILSON (TF)   The Great Amwell Company/Nebraska ETV Network/Taurus Film, 1984
HEART OF MIDIGHT   Samuel Goldwyn Company, 1988
RACHAEL RIVER   Taurus Entertainment, 1989

PETER FLAHERTY*
Phone: 818/841-6241

POLICE ACADEMY 6: CITY UNDER SIEGE   Warner Bros., 1989

ROBERT FLETCHER
Agent: Randy Clark, 213/465-7140
Address: 645 N. Sierra Bonita, Los Angeles, CA 90036, 213/658-5158

STAR TREK: THE MOTION PICTURE   Paramount, 1979
CAVEMAN   United Artists, 1981
STAR TREK II: THE WRATH OF KHAN   Paramount, 1982
STAR TREK III: THE SEARCH FOR SPOCK   Paramount, 1984
THE LAST STARFIGHTER   Universal, 1984
SPACE (MS)   Stonehenge Productions/Paramount TV, 1985
FRIGHT NIGHT   Columbia, 1985
NORTH AND SOUTH, BOOK II (MS)   Wolper Productions/Robert A. Papazian Productions/Warner Bros. TV, 1986
STAR TREK IV: THE VOYAGE HOME   Paramount, 1986

CYNTHIA FLYNT
Agent: Camera Masters - Venice, 213/306-0810

MATEWAN   Cinecom, 1987
SWEET LORRAINE   Angelika Films, 1987
EIGHT MEN OUT   Orion, 1988
SAM'S SPA   1990
LITTLE VEGAS   I.R.S. Releasing, 1990
AWAKENINGS   Columbia, 1990

ELLIS FLYTE
LABYRINTH   Tri-Star, 1986, w/Brian Froud

SHARMAN FORMAN-HYDE
AND GOD CREATED WOMAN   Vestron, 1988

MARY JANE FORT
HANGIN' WITH THE HOMEBOYS   New Line Cinema, 1991

NANCY G. FOX
ILLEGALLY YOURS   DEG, 1988
KANSAS   Trans World Entertainment, 1988

SARA FOX
BELIZAIRE THE CAJUN   Skouras Pictures, 1986

MARIE FRANCE*
Agent: David Gersh, The Gersh Agency, Inc. - Beverly Hills, 213/274-6611
Phone: 213/851-7868

PURPLE RAIN   Warner Bros., 1984, w/Louis & Vaughn
UNDER THE CHERRY MOON   Warner Bros., 1986
SHE'S OUT OF CONTROL   Columbia, 1989
NIGHTBREED   20th Century Fox, 1990, w/Ann Hollowood

IVETTE FRANK
TWISTED OBSESSION   IVE, 1990

LOUISE FROGLEY
ACTT
Agent: Sandra Marsh Management - Sherman Oaks, 818/905-6961

CHARIOTS OF FIRE   The Ladd Company/Warner Bros., 1981, (Asst.)
ANOTHER TIME, ANOTHER PLACE   Samuel Goldwyn Company, 1983
THE COLD ROOM (CTF)   Jethro Films/Mark Forstater Productions, 1984
THE LAST PLACE ON EARTH (MS)   Central Productions/Renegade Films, 1985
HALF MOON STREET   20th Century Fox, 1986
MONA LISA   Island Pictures, 1986
DEFENSE OF THE REALM   Hemdale, 1987
NOBLE HOUSE (MS)   De Laurentis Entertainment Corporation, 1988
BULL DURHAM   Orion, 1988
BREAKING IN   Samuel Goldwyn Company, 1989
HEART CONDITION   New Line Cinema, 1990
THREE MEN AND A LITTLE LADY   Buena Vista, 1990
WARLOCK   Trimark Pictures, 1991

G

JAI ALEXANDRA GALATI
STREET DREAMS   Pathe, 1989
POLICE ACADEMY 4   Warner Bros., 1989
POLICE ACADEMY 5   Warner Bros., 1989
THE ROSE AND THE JACKAL   TNT Circa 1861, 1990
COUNTDOWN (TF)   1990
WHATEVER HAPPENED TO BABY JANE   ABC Entertainment, 1990
A MOM FOR CHRISTMAS   Disney, 1990
THE NIGHT OF THE HUNTER   ABC Entertainment, 1991

ANDREA GALER
WITH NAIL AND I   Cineplex Odeon, 1987

SUSAN GAMMIE
HIDING OUT   DEG, 1987
MY LITTLE GIRL   Hemdale, 1987

Ga

CINEMATOGRAPHERS
PRODUCTION
DESIGNERS,
COSTUME
DESIGNERS AND
FILM EDITORS
GUIDE

C
O
S
T
U
M
E

D
E
S
I
G
N
E
R
S

Ga

CINEMATOGRAPHERS
PRODUCTION
DESIGNERS,
COSTUME
DESIGNERS AND
FILM EDITORS
GUIDE

C
O
S
T
U
M
E

D
E
S
I
G
N
E
R
S

JULIE GANTON
HEAVENLY BODIES   MGM/UA, 1985

SYLVIE GAUTRELET
MANON OF THE SPRING   Orion Classics, 1987

IDA GEARON
TALES FROM THE DARKSIDE: THE MOVIE
   Paramount, 1990
THE RETURN OF SUPERFLY   Triton Pictures,
   1990, w/Vacra Russal

JUDITH R. GELLMAN
Canadian IA
Agent: Smith Gosnell Nicholson & Associates -
   Pacific Palisades, 213/459-0307

POWER PLAY   Magnum International Pictures/Cowry
   Film Productions, 1978
MEATBALLS   Paramount, 1979
THE FAMILY MAN (TF)   Time-Life Productions, 1979
TORN BETWEEN TWO LOVERS (TF)   Alan
   Landsburg Productions, 1979
THE PLUTONIUM INCIDENT (TF)   Time-Life
   Productions, 1980
BETWEEN FRIENDS (CTF)   HBO Premiere Films/
   Marian Rees Associates/Robert Cooper Films III/
   List-Estrin Productions, 1983
COUGAR! (TF)   ABC Circle Films, 1984
HEARTSOUNDS (TF)   Embassy TV, 1984
HEAD OFFICE   Tri-Star, 1985
JOSEPH WAMBAUGH'S ECHOES IN THE
   DARKNESS (TF)   Litke-Grossbart Productions/
   New Word TV, 1987
ADVENTURES IN BABYSITTING   Buena Vista, 1987

LAURA GEMSER
QUEST FOR THE MIGHTY SWORD   RCA/Columbia
   Pictures Home Video, 1990

TUDOR GEORGE
THOSE GLORY, GLORY DAYS   Cinecom, 1983
ARTHUR'S HALLOWED GROUND   Cinecom, 1986
SHADEY   Skouras Pictures, 1986
FOREVER YOUNG   Cinecom, 1986

CARLA GIBBONS
PHANTASM II   Universal, 1988
SURVIVAL QUEST   MGM/UA, 1990

EDI GIGUERE
Agent: The Gersh Agency, Inc., Beverly Hills -
   213/274-6611, New York - 212/997-1818

THE SUNSET GANG   Ceclia Roque
COLD FEET   Cinecom International, 1989

CHRISTINE GLAZIER
TRANSYLVANIA 6-5000   New World, 1985,
   w/Latica Ivanisevic

JULIE GOMBERT
THE TEXAS CHAINSAW MASSACRE PART 2
   Cannon, 1986
LAST RESORT   Concorde, 1986

MEG GOODWIN
FROM HOLLYWOOD TO DEADWOOD   Island
   Pictures, 1990

CHRISTINE GOULDING
THE PRIVATE EYES   New World, 1981

SUZANNE GRACE
THE AMATEUR   20th Century Fox, 1982

VICKI GRAEF*
Phone: 818/449-2568

BIG BAD MAMA II   Concorde, 1987
INVASION EARTH: THE ALIENS ARE HERE
   New World, 1987
KANDYLAND   New World, 1987
PROGRAMMED TO KILL   Trans World Entertainment,
   1987, w/Lennie Barin
WAR OF THE WORLDS (Pilot)   1988
THE RETURN OF SWAMP THING   Lightyear
   Entertainment, 1989

DONA GRANATA
Agent: Walter Wood, Curtis Brown, Ltd. - Los Angeles,
   213/461-0148

THE GOODBYE PEOPLE   Embassy, 1984
LUST IN THE DUST   New World, 1984
WORLD GONE WILD   Lorimar, 1988
HAPPY TOGETHER   Apollo Pictures, 1989
SCENES FROM THE CLASS STRUGGLE IN BEVERLY
   HILLS   Cinecom, 1989

MADELINE ANN GRANETO*
Address: 968 Sidonia St., Encinitas, CA 92024,
   619/943-1607 or 818/957-3964

HEARTBEEPS   Universal, 1981
O'HARA'S WIFE   Davis-Panzer Productions, 1982
SAMSON & DELILAH (TF)   Catalina Production
   Group/Comworld Productions, 1984
RED RIVER (TF)   Catalina Production Group/
   MGM-UA TV, 1988
HOT PAINT (TF)   Catalina Production Group/
   MGM-UA TV, 1988

MERRILL GREENE
WITCHBOARD   Cinema Group, 1987

JANE GREENWOOD*
Phone: 212/929-2931

LAST EMBRACE   United Artists, 1979
CAN'T STOP THE MUSIC   AFD, 1980
ARTHUR   Warner Bros., 1981
THE FOUR SEASONS   Universal, 1981
KENNEDY (MS)   Central Independent Television
   Productions/Alan Landsburg Productions, 1983
WETHERBY   MGM/UA Classics, 1985,
   w/Lindy Hemming
SWEET LIBERTY   Universal, 1986
84 CHARING CROSS ROAD   Columbia, 1987,
   w/Lindy Hemming
THE SQUEEZE   Tri-Star, 1987
MR. DESTINY   Buena Vista, 1990

GLORIA GRESHAM*
Agent: The Gersh Agency, Inc., Beverly Hills -
    213/274-6611, New York - 212/997-1818

ZORRO, THE GAY BLADE   20th Century Fox, 1981
THE ESCAPE ARTIST   Orion/Warner Bros., 1982
AUTHOR! AUTHOR!   20th Century Fox, 1982
DINER   MGM/UA, 1982
WITHOUT A TRACE   20th Century Fox, 1983
BODY DOUBLE   Columbia, 1984
THE NATURAL   Tri-Star, 1984, w/Bernie Pollack
FOOTLOOSE   Paramount, 1984
FLETCH   Universal, 1985
8 MILLION WAYS TO DIE   Tri-Star, 1986
TIN MEN   Buena Vista, 1987
OUTRAGEOUS FORTUNE   Buena Vista, 1987
MIDNIGHT RUN   Universal, 1988
TWINS   Universal, 1988
GHOSTBUSTERS II   Columbia, 1989
WHEN HARRY MET SALLY...   Columbia, 1989
THE WAR OF THE ROSES   20th Century
    Fox, 1989
AVALON ★   Tri-Star, 1990
MISERY   Castle Rock Entertainment/Nelson
    Entertainment/Columbia, 1990
KINDERGARTEN COP   Universal, 1990

PAUL-ANDRE GUERIN
OF UNKNOWN ORIGIN   Warner Bros., 1983
WILD THING   Atlantic Releasing
    Corporation, 1987
SPEED ZONE   Orion, 1989

JAMES GUTIERREZ
FAR OUT MAN!   New Line Cinema, 1990

H

ELIZABETH HAAS
VAMPING   Atlantic Releasing Corporation, 1984

DRAGO HABANZIAN
GYMKATA   MGM/UA, 1985

NORD HAGGERTY
ROCKET GIBRALTAR   Columbia, 1988
HEARTBREAK HOTEL   Buena Vista, 1988

ROBIN HALL
THE MAN FROM SNOWY RIVER   20th Century
    Fox, 1983

MICHELE HAMEL
MARIA CHAPDELAINE   The Movie Store, 1986
TOBY McTEAGUE   Spectrafilm, 1986

HOPE HANAFIN
MORTAL THOUGHTS   Columbia Pictures, 1991

ENID HARRIS*
Agent: Ken Gross, Robinson, Weintraub, Gross, Inc. -
    Los Angeles, 213/653-5802
Address: 124 Palisades Ave., Santa Monica, CA 90402,
    213/395-6008

COMMANDO   20th Century Fox, 1985, w/Bob Harris
FIRE WITH FIRE   *CAPTIVE HEART*S   20th Century Fox,
    1986, w/Andrew Brown
APOLOGY (CTF)   Roger Gimbel Productions/Peregrine
    Entertainment/ASAP Productions/HBO, 1986

JULIE HARRIS
THE SLIPPER AND THE ROSE: THE STORY OF
    CINDERELLA   Universal, 1976
DRACULA   Universal, 1979
THE GREAT MUPPET CAPER   Universal/AFD, 1981

ROBERT HARRIS, JR.
GOING APE!   Paramount, 1981
COMMANDO   20th Century Fox, 1985, w/Enid Harris

EVANGELINE HARRISON
THE OFFENCE   United Artists, 1973
SUPERMAN III   Warner Bros., 1983
WHITE NIGHTS   Columbia, 1985
DUET FOR ONE   Cannon, 1987
A PRAYER FOR THE DYING   Samuel Goldwyn
    Company, 1987
BUSTER   Hemdale, 1988

SHUNA HARWOOD
THE ODD JOB   Columbia, 1978
THE MISSIONARY   Columbia, 1982
SWORD OF THE VALIANT   Cannon, 1984
INSIGNIFICANCE   Island Alive, 1985
PERSONAL SERVICES   Vestron, 1987
WISH YOU WERE HERE   Atlantic Releasing
    Corporation, 1987

JESSICA HASTON
POISON   Zeitgeist Films, 1991

JOHN M. HAY
THE BOY IN BLUE   20th Century Fox, 1985
BEYOND THERAPY   New World, 1987
SING   Tri-Star, 1989
TEENAGE MUTANT NINJA TURTLES   Golden Harvest/
    New Line Cinema, 1990

GILLY HEBDEN
YELLOWBEARD   Orion, 1983, w/T. Stephen Miles
HIGHLANDER   20th Century Fox, 1986,
    w/James Acheson

BETSY HEIMANN*
Agent: Randy Clark - Los Angeles, 213/465-7140
Phone: 213/653-5477

SKATETOWN, U.S.A.   Columbia, 1979, w/Bob Labansat
HIGH ROAD TO CHINA   Warner Bros., 1983
THIS GIRL FOR HIRE (TF)   Barney Rosenzwieg
    Productions/Orion TV, 1983
UFORIA   Universal, 1984, w/Thomas Ed Sunly
THE DIRTY DOZEN: THE NEXT MISSION (TF)
    MGM-UA TV, 1985

He

CINEMATOGRAPHERS
PRODUCTION
DESIGNERS,
COSTUME
DESIGNERS AND
FILM EDITORS
GUIDE

C
O
S
T
U
M
E

D
E
S
I
G
N
E
R
S

CINEMATOGRAPHERS
PRODUCTION
DESIGNERS,
COSTUME
DESIGNERS and
FILM EDITORS
GUIDE

SKY BANDITS   Galaxy International, 1986,
   w/Karen Landsdown
THE PEE-WEE HERMAN SHOW (TVS)   1987
SURRENDER   Warner Bros., 1987
STRANGER ON MY LAND (TF)   Edgar J. Scherick
   Associates/Taft Entertainment TV, 1988
ELVIRA: MISTRESS OF THE DARK   New
   World, 1988
WELCOME HOME, ROXY CARMICHAEL
   Paramount, 1990
ONE GOOD COP   Hollywood Pictures/Silver Screen
   Partners IV, 1991

SYLVIA HEISEL
PARTING GLANCES   Cinecom, 1986

LINDY HEMMING
WETHERBY   MGM/UA Classics, 1985,
   w/Jane Greenwood
MY BEAUTIFUL LAUNDRETTE   Orion
   Classics, 1986
84 CHARING CROSS ROAD   Columbia, 1987,
   w/Jane Greenwood
GOSPEL ACCORDING TO VIC   Skouras
   Pictures, 1987
QUEEN OF HEARTS   Cinecom, 1989
WHEN THE WHALES CAME   20th Century Fox, 1989
THE KRAYS   Rank, 1990

LESLIE HERMAN
IT HAD TO BE YOU   Limelight Studios, 1990

D. JEAN HESTER
BLOOD SALVAGE   Paragon Arts, 1990

HELEN HIATT
GRAFFITI BRIDGE   Warner Bros., 1990
   w/Jim Shearon

WALKER HICKLIN
USA Local 829
Agent: Margi Rountree, c/o Bret Adams, Ltd., 448 W.
   44th St., New York, NY 10036, 212/765-5630

BLUE WINDOW (TF)   American Playhouse, 1986
LONGTIME COMPANION   American Playhouse/
   Samuel Goldwyn Company, 1990

J. ALLEN HIGHFILL
MEN DON'T LEAVE   Warner Bros., 1990

SUSAN HILFERTY
HOME OF THE BRAVE   Cinecom, 1986

MICHAEL HOFFMAN
FEVER PITCH   MGM/UA, 1985, w/Aggie Lyon
THE MONSTER SQUAD   Tri-Star, 1987
DEATH WISH 4: THE CRACKDOWN   Cannon,
   1987, Supervisor

VICTORIA HOLLOWAY
PROMISED LAND   Vestron, 1988

ANN HOLLOWOOD
MR. LOVE   Warner Bros., 1984
KNIGHTS AND EMERALDS   Warner Bros., 1985
TEARS IN THE RAIN   T R Films, 1988

THE OLD MAN AND THE SEA   Tomats Company, 1989
NIGHTBREED   20th Century Fox, 1990 w/Marie France
KAPPATOO   World Wide International, 1990

DIANE HOLMES
WILD GEESE II   Universal, 1986

LYNNE A. HOLMES
THE KINDRED   FM Entertainment, 1987

CARIN HOOPER
LIFEFORCE   Tri-Star, 1985
INVADERS FROM MARS   Cannon, 1986
SALSA   Cannon, 1988

HELEN HOOPER
BLISS   New World, 1986

RICHARD HORNUNG
Agent: The Gersh Agency, Inc., Beverly Hills -
   213/274-6611, New York - 212/997-1818

CHINA GIRL   Vestron, 1987
RAISING ARIZONA   Orion, 1987
LESS THAN ZERO   20th Century Fox, 1987
YOUNG GUNS   20th Century Fox, 1988
PATTY HEARST   Atlantic Releasing Corporation, 1988
MILLER'S CROSSING   20th Century Fox, 1990
SLEEPING WITH THE ENEMY   20th Century Fox, 1991
BARTON FINK   20th Century Fox, 1991

MONICA HOWE
BUGSY MALONE   Paramount, 1978
DISTANT VOICES, STILL LIVES   Alive Films, 1989

RAYMOND HUGHES
YOUNG SHERLOCK HOLMES   Paramount, 1985
RETURN TO OZ   Buena Vista, 1985,
   w/William R. McPhail
THE WHISTLE BLOWER   Hemdale, 1987

JOAN HUNTER
LEATHERFACE: TEXAS CHAINSAW MASSACRE III
   New Line Cinema, 1989

JAN HURLEY
SILVER CITY   Samuel Goldwyn Company, 1985
CODE OF SILENCE   Orion, 1985, w/Mickey Antonetti &
   Jennifer Jobst
THE NAKED FACE   MGM/UA/Cannon, 1984,
   w/Sandra Davidson
ONE MORE SATURDAY NIGHT   Columbia, 1986,
   w/Mickey Antonetti
VICE VERSA   Columbia, 1988
COCOON: THE RETURN   20th Century Fox, 1988
HOME ALONE   20th Century Fox, 1990

DEREK HYDE
THE HOLCROFT COVENANT   Universal, 1985
WATCHING   Granada Television
BRASS   Granada Television

J

LIBBY JACOBS
NOT OF THIS EARTH   Concorde, 1988
GIRLFRIEND FROM HELL   Live Entertainment, 1990

MONICA JACOBS
BURNING SECRET   Vestron, 1988,
   w/Barbara Baum
THE ROSE GARDEN   Pathe Entertainment, 1989

BARTON "KENT" JAMES
CONVOY   United Artists, 1978
AMERICAN JUSTICE   The Movie Store, 1986
DEADLY FRIEND   Warner Bros., 1986,
   w/Carol Brown-James

CHARLES JAMES
APOCALYPSE NOW   United Artists,
   1979, Supervisor

KATHE JAMES
NORTH SHORE   Universal, 1987

DOROTHY JEAKINS
THE SOUND OF MUSIC   20th Century Fox, 1965
THE WAY WE WERE ★   Columbia, 1973,
   w/Moss Mabry
THE YAKUZA   Warner Bros., 1975
THE BETSY   Allied Artists, 1978
NORTH DALLAS FORTY   Paramount, 1979
LOVE AND BULLETS   ITC, 1979
ON GOLDEN POND   Universal/AFD, 1981
THE POSTMAN ALWAYS RINGS TWICE
   Paramount, 1981
THE DEAD ★   Vestron, 1987

MICHAEL JEFFREY
THE LAIR OF THE WHITE WORM   Vestron, 1988
BEARSKIN: AN URBAN FAIRY TALE
   Film Four, 1989

LISA JENSEN
MANNEQUIN   20th Century Fox, 1987
DEAD HEAT   New World, 1988
WHITE PALACE   Universal, 1990
ENID IS SLEEPING   Vestron, 1991

ELOIS JENSSEN*
Agent: Chris Shiffren - Los Angeles, 213/937-3937
Address: 9330 Beverly Crest Dr., Beverly Hills, CA
   90210, 213/271-7077

TRON ★   Buena Vista, 1982, w/Rosanna Norton
LEAVING HOME   Hall Bartlett Films, 1986

LOUISE JOBIN
JOSHUA THEN AND NOW   20th Century Fox, 1985

BERNARD JOHNSON*
Agent: Bruce V. Bordelon - New York,
   212/867-9595
Phone: 212/580-1874 or 212/580-1888

SHOOT-OUT   Universal, 1971
CLAUDINE   20th Century Fox, 1974
WILLIE DYNAMITE   Universal, 1974
SCOTT JOPLIN   Universal, 1977
HANKY PANKY   Columbia, 1982
GO TELL IT ON THE MOUNTAIN (TF)   Learning in
   Focus, 1984
BEAT STREET   Orion, 1984
FAST FOWARD   Columbia, 1985
NEW JACK CITY   Warner Bros., 1991

JACQUELINE JOHNSON
HUNTER'S BLOOD   Concorde, 1987
FRIDAY THE 13TH PART VII: THE NEW BLOOD
   Paramount, 1988

RONDI JOHNSON
ICEMAN   Universal, 1984

JOANNA JOHNSTON
INDIANA JONES AND THE TEMPLE OF DOOM
   Paramount, 1985, (Asst.)
PIRATES   Cannon, 1985, (Asst.)
HELLRAISER   New World, 1987
WHO FRAMED ROGER RABBIT   Buena
   Vista, 1988
INDIANA JONES AND THE LAST CRUSADE
   Paramount, 1989, w/Anthony Powell
BACK TO THE FUTURE II   Universal, 1989
BACK TO THE FUTURE III   Universal, 1989

RENEE JOHNSTON
THIS IS SPINAL TAP   Embassy, 1984
DOWN TWISTED   Cannon, 1987

ANNA HILL JOHNSTONE
THE GROUP   United Artists, 1965
THE GODFATHER ★   Paramount, 1972
SERPICO   Paramount, 1973
THE LAST TYCOON   Paramount,
   1976, w/others
THE NEXT MAN   Allied Artists, 1976
KING OF THE GYPSIES   Paramount, 1978
RAGTIME ★   Paramount, 1981
PRINCE OF THE CITY   Orion/Warner Bros., 1981
A NIGHT IN HEAVEN   20th Century Fox, 1983
DANIEL   Paramount, 1983
GARBO TALKS   MGM/UA, 1984
POWER   20th Century Fox, 1986
RUNNING ON EMPTY   Warner Bros., 1988
ARTHUR 2 ON THE ROCKS   Warner Bros., 1988
FLETCH LIVES   Universal, 1989

BETSY JONES*
Phone: 213/273-9449

MY SCIENCE PROJECT   Buena Vista, 1985
THE CALENDAR GIRL MURDERS (TF)   Tisch-Avnet
   Productions, 1984
HEARTBREAKERS   Orion, 1984

Jo

CINEMATOGRAPHERS
PRODUCTION
DESIGNERS,
COSTUME
DESIGNERS AND
FILM EDITORS
GUIDE

C
O
S
T
U
M
E

D
E
S
I
G
N
E
R
S

Jo

CINEMATOGRAPHERS
PRODUCTION
DESIGNERS,
COSTUME
DESIGNERS AND
FILM EDITORS
GUIDE

C
O
S
T
U
M
E

D
E
S
I
G
N
E
R
S

GARY JONES
THE FIRST DEADLY SIN   Filmways, 1980
TIGER TOWN   Buena Vista, 1985
THE TRIP TO BOUNTIFUL   Island Pictures/Film
    Dallas, 1985
HEARTBURN   Paramount, 1986, (Asst. to Ann Roth)
THE MOSQUITO COAST   Warner Bros., 1986

CORINNE JORRY
AU REVOIR, LES ENFANTS   Orion Classics, 1987
DOCTEUR PETIOT   *DR. PETIOT*   Aries Film
    Releasing, 1990

K

HEIDI M. KACZENSKI*
Phone: 818/361-2599

TEEN WOLF TOO   Atlantic Releasing
    Company, 1987
CYBORG   Cannon, 1989

RENEE KALFUS
ONCE AROUND   Universal, 1991

TERI KANE
OLD ENOUGH   Orion Classics, 1984

MICHAEL KAPLAN*
Agent: Sandra Marsh Management - Sherman Oaks,
    818/905-6961
Phone: 213/656-1809

BLADE RUNNER   Warner Bros., 1982,
    w/Charles Knode
FLASHDANCE   Paramount, 1983
AGAINST ALL ODDS   Columbia, 1984
THIEF OF HEARTS   Paramount, 1984
PERFECT   Columbia, 1985
AMERICAN DREAMER   Columbia, 1985
CLUE   Paramount, 1985
TOUGH GUYS DON'T DANCE   Cannon, 1987
BIG BUSINESS   Buena Vista, 1988
COUSINS   Paramount, 1989
NATIONAL LAMPOON'S CHRISTMAS VACATION
    Warner Bros., 1989
CAT CHASER   Vestron, 1990

TRUDY KAPNER*
Address: 2121 Paseo Del Mar, Palos Verdes Estates,
    CA 90274, 213/377-3076

BLACKOUT   Ambient Light Entertainment, 1988

ELIZABETH KAYE
THE CHOCOLATE WAR   MCEG, 1988

TRISH KEATING
THE ACCUSED   Paramount, 1988

COLEEN KELSO
BLUE DESERT   Neo Films, 1991

LYNDA KEMP
TICKET TO HEAVEN   United Artists Classics, 1981
CERTAIN FURY   New World, 1985

EILEEN KENNEDY
YOUNGBLOOD   MGM/UA, 1986
NIGHT OF THE CREEPS   Tri-Star, 1986
K-9   Universal, 1989
FLASHBACK   Paramount, 1990
PROBLEM CHILD   Universal, 1990

BARBARA KIDD
SAMMY AND ROSIE GET LAID   Cinecom, 1987
CONSUMING PASSIONS   Samuel Goldwyn
    Company, 1988
THE KITCHEN TOTO   Cannon, 1988

GEORGE W. KIEL
LIBERTY & BASH   Fries Home Video, 1990

GINA KIELLERMAN
KILLER PARTY   MGM/UA, 1986
BLUE MONKEY   Spectrafilm, 1987
RENEGADES   Universal, 1989

WILLA KIM*
Phone: 212/877-9420

GARDENS OF STONE   Tri-Star, 1987,
    w/Judianna Makovsky

KELLY KIMBALL*
Phone: 213/684-1898

RAIDERS OF THE LOST ARK   Paramount, 1981,
    (Asst. to Deborah Nadoolman)
THE CLAN OF THE CAVE BEAR   Warner Bros., 1986
COMING TO AMERICA   Paramount, 1988,
    (Asst. to Deborah Nadoolman)

ROGER KIRK
REBEL   Vestron, 1986

CHARLES KNODE*
Address: 38 Werter Rd., London, SW15 2 LJ,
    England, 01/789-2970

JABBERWOCKY   Cinema 5, 1977
THE HOUND OF THE BASKERVILLES   Atlantic
    Releasing Corporation, 1979
MONTY PYTHON'S LIFE OF BRIAN   Orion/Warner
    Bros., 1979
BLADE RUNNER   Warner Bros., 1982,
    w/Michael Kaplan
NEVER SAY NEVER AGAIN   Warner Bros., 1983
LEGEND   Universal, 1986

SHELLEY KOMAROV*
Agent: The Gersh Agency, Inc., Beverly Hills -
    213/274-6611, New York - 212/997-1818

MURDER: BY REASON OF INSANITY (TF)   LS
    Entertainment, 1985
PETER THE GREAT (MS)   PTG Productions/NBC
    Productions, 1986

MURPHY'S LAW   Cannon, 1986
CHRISTMAS EVE (TF)   NBC Productions, 1986
THE NAKED CAGE   Cannon, 1986, Wardrobe
ASSASSINATION   Cannon, 1987
ROSES ARE FOR THE RICH (TF)   Phoenix
    Entertainment Group, 1987
THE CHILD SAVER (TF)   Michael Filerman
    Productions/NBC Productions, 1988,
    w/Aleida MacDonald
MESSENGER OF DEATH   Cannon, 1988
TAKE MY DAUGHTERS, PLEASE (TF)   Michael
    Filerman Productions/NBC Productions, 1989

**DEBORAH
LA GORCE KRAMER***
West Coast Card
Agent: Smith Gosnell Nicholson & Associates -
    Pacific Palisades, 213/459-0307
Phone: 213/662-9459

OFF LIMITS   20th Century Fox, 1987
IN LOVE AND WAR (TF)   Carol Schreder Productions/
    Tisch-Avnet Productions, 1987
CADILLAC MAN   Orion, 1990

SYLVIE KRASKER
IRON EAGLE II   Tri-Star, 1988

JEFFREY KURLAND
THE FAN   Paramount, 1981, w/Tom McKinley
BROADWAY DANNY ROSE   Orion, 1984
THE PURPLE ROSE OF CAIRO   Orion, 1985
STREETS OF GOLD   20th Century Fox, 1986
HANNAH AND HER SISTERS   Orion, 1986
REVENGE OF THE NERDS II: NERDS IN PARADISE
    20th Century Fox, 1987
RADIO DAYS   Orion, 1987
SEPTEMBER   Orion, 1987
ANOTHER WOMAN   Orion, 1988
NEW YORK STORIES ("Oedipus Wrecks")   Buena
    Vista, 1989
CRIMES AND MISDEMEANORS   Orion, 1989
QUICK CHANGE   Warner Bros., 1990
ALICE   Orion, 1990

ANN LAMBERT
Phone: 213/439-9535

ENTER THE DRAGON   Warner Bros., 1973
SHELL GAME (TF)   Thoroughbred Productions, 1975
BIG WEDNESDAY   Warner Bros., 1978
A VACATION IN HELL (TF)   David Greene
    Productions/Finnegan Associations, 1979
DON'T CRY, IT'S ONLY THUNDER   Sanrio, 1981
ELVIS AND THE BEAUTY QUEEN (TF)   David Gerber
    Company/Columbia TV, 1981
POLTERGEIST   MGM/UA, 1982
HIS MISTRESS (TF)   David L. Wolper Productions/
    Warner Bros. TV, 1984

TANK   Universal, 1984
BLISS   New World, 1985
THE DEFIANT ONES (TF)   MGM-UA TV, 1986
SIDNEY SHELDON'S WINDMILLS OF THE GODS (TF)
    Dove Productions/ITC Productions, 1988

RONA LAMONT
MY BEST FRIEND IS A VAMPIRE   Kings
    Road, 1988

RICHARD E. LA MOTTE*
Phone: 805/255-9928

A MAN CALLED HORSE   United Artists, 1970
THE WIND AND THE LION   MGM/United
    Artists, 1975
THE RETURN OF A MAN CALLED HORSE   United
    Artists, 1976
THE ISLAND OF DR. MOREAU   American International,
    1977, w/Emma Porteus & Rita Woods
MARCH OR DIE   Columbia, 1977
THE GOONIES   Warner Bros., 1985
STITCHES   International Film Marketing, 1985
THE HANOI HILTON   Cannon, 1987
RAMBO III   Tri-Star, 1988

NATASHA LANDAU
VOODOO DAWN   Academy Entertainment, 1990
DANGEROUS OBSESSION   Panorama
    Entertainment, 1991

BARBARA LANE
HEAT AND DUST   Universal Classics, 1983
BEYOND THE LIMIT   Paramount, 1983
LASSITER   Warner Bros., 1984
WILLOW   MGM/UA, 1988

GREG LAVOI
THE RAIN KILLER   Concorde, 1990
DEAD SPACE   Concorde, 1991

JANET LAWLER
DEEP IN THE HEART   Warner Bros., 1984

MERRIE LAWSON
LAST CALL   Prism Entertainment, 1990

FRANNE LEE
BABY, IT'S YOU   Pararmount, 1983

ETTA LEFF
CRYSTAL HEART   New World, 1987

LARRY LEFLER
SEVEN HOURS TO JUDGMENT   Trans World
    Entertainment, 1988

SARAH LEMIRE
GRAVEYARD SHIFT   Paramount, 1990

DANIEL J. LESTER
GUNG HO   Paramount, 1986
HOT TO TROT   Warner Bros., 1988,
    Mens wardrobe

Le

CINEMATOGRAPHERS
PRODUCTION
DESIGNERS,
COSTUME
DESIGNERS AND
FILM EDITORS
GUIDE

C
O
S
T
U
M
E

D
E
S
I
G
N
E
R
S

Le

CINEMATOGRAPHERS
PRODUCTION
DESIGNERS,
COSTUME
DESIGNERS AND
FILM EDITORS
GUIDE

C
O
S
T
U
M
E

D
E
S
I
G
N
E
R
S

CATHERINE LETERRIER
FRENCH POSTCARDS   Paramount, 1979
MY AMERICAN UNCLE   New World, 1980
L'ETOILE DU NORD   United Artists Classics, 1983
LIFE IS A BOWL OF ROSES   Spectrafilm, 1984
ONE WOMAN OR TWO   Orion Classics, 1987
GORILLAS IN THE MIST   Universal, 1988

DARRYL LeVINE
THE HOLLYWOOD KNIGHTS   Columbia, 1981
MOVING VIOLATIONS   20th Century Fox, 1985
FAVORITE SON (MS)   Steve Sohmer Inc./NBC
    Productions, 1989, Supv. w/Diana Reynolds

KEITH LEWIS
MEN AT WORK   Triumph Releasing, 1990

MARGOT LINDSAY
GROUND ZERO   Avenue Picture, 1988, Wardrobe

DONNA LINSON*
Address: 9648 Yoakum Dr., Beverly Hills, CA 90210,
    213/271-3084

STREETS OF FIRE   Universal, 1984,
    (Asst. to Marilyn Vance)
THE LEGEND OF BILLIE JEAN   Tri-Star, 1985
OUT OF BOUNDS   Columbia, 1986
FAR FROM HOME   Vestron, 1989

BRAD R. LOMAN*
Address: 12304 Hillslope St., Studio City, CA 91604,
    213/877-8985

BETTER OFF DEAD   Warner Bros., 1985
ONE CRAZY SUMMER   Warner Bros., 1986
LBJ: THE EARLY YEARS (TF)   Louis Randolph
    Films/Fries Entertainment, 1987
BILLIONAIRE BOYS CLUB (TF)   Donald March/
    Gross-Weston Productions/ITC Productions, 1987
NIGHTFLYERS   New Century/Vista, 1987
CLINTON AND NADINE   HBO Pictures/ITC, 1988
I'LL BE HOME FOR CHRISTMAS (TF)   NBC
    Productions, 1988
BROTHERHOOD OF THE ROSE (TF)   NBC
    Productions, 1989
NAVY SEALS   Orion, 1990

FRED LONG
INVASION U.S.A.   Cannon, 1985

STEPHEN LOOMIS*
ESCAPE FROM NEW YORK   Avco Embassy, 1981
BUSTIN' LOOSE   Universal, 1981, w/Bill Whitten
SEPARATE WAYS   Crown International, 1981
THE FOG   Avco Embassy, 1981

SANTO LOQUASTO
Agent: Roberta Kent, STE Representation, Ltd. -
    Beverly Hills, 213/550-3982

SAMMY STOPS THE WORLD (FD)   Elkins, 1979
SIMON   Orion/Warner Bros., 1980
A MIDSUMMER NIGHT'S SEX COMEDY   Orion/
    Warner Bros., 1982
ZELIG ★   Warner Bros., 1983
DESPERATELY SEEKING SUSAN   Orion, 1985

SANDI LOVE*
Address: 8306 Wilshire Blvd., Suite 438, Beverly Hills, CA
    90211, 213/650-8306

FRIDAY THE 13TH PART 3   Paramount, 1982
THE MAN WHO WASN'T THERE   Paramount, 1983
MEATBALLS PART II   Tri-Star, 1984

ELLEN LUTTER
FRIDAY THE 13TH PART 2   Paramount, 1981
WHEN NATURE CALLS   Troma, 1984

ADELLE LUTZ
TRUE STORIES   Warner Bros., 1986,
    Fashion Show only
MAKING MR. RIGHT   Orion, 1987, w/Rudy Dillon
CHECKING OUT   Warner Bros., 1989

ENRICO LUZZI
YOR, THE HUNTER FROM THE FUTURE
    Columbia, 1983

SUSAN LYALL
EIGHT MEN OUT   1988
MEN OF RESPECT   Columbia, 1991
LITTLE MAN TATE   1991
MISSISSIPPI MASALA   1991

DANA LYMAN
THE MIGHTY QUINN   MGM/UA, 1989
THE EXORCIST III   20th Century Fox, 1990

SHARON LYNCH
TOUCH OF A STRANGER   Raven-Star Pictures, 1990

MOSS MABRY
THE WAY WE WERE ★   Columbia, 1973,
    w/Dorothy Jeakins
CASEY'S SHADOW   Columbia, 1978
TOUCHED BY LOVE   Columbia, 1980
CONTINENTAL DIVIDE   Universal, 1981
THE TOY   Columbia, 1982
RENT-A-COP   Kings Road, 1988

ALEIDA MACDONALD*
Agent: Gerald Smith - Los Angeles, 213/849-5388
Phone: 416/963-4974

TOM SAWYER   United Artists, 1973
SECOND WIND   Health and Entertainment Corporation
    of America, 1976
FALCON'S GOLD (TF)   1982
PHOBIA   Paramount, 1981
THE CHILD SAVER (TF)   Michael Filerman Productions/
    NBC Productions, 1988, w/Shelley Komarov
POLICE ACADEMY 3: BACK IN TRAINING   Warner
    Bros., 1986
POLICE ACADEMY 4: CITIZENS ON PATROL   Warner
    Bros., 1987

LYNNE MacKAY
MARTIN'S DAY MGM/UA, 1985

BOB MACKIE*
Manager: Phyllis Rab - Los Angeles, 213/477-2075

*(Note: The following is an incomplete list of
Mr. Mackie's credits. Over the years, he has also
designed costumes for numerous performers and
their variety shows and specials.)*

DIVORCE, AMERICAN STYLE Columbia, 1967
LADY SINGS THE BLUES ★ Paramount, 1972,
  w/Ray Aghayan & Norma Koch
FUNNY LADY ★ Columbia, 1976, w/Ray Aghayan
...ALL THE MARBLES MGM/United Artists, 1981
PENNIES FROM HEAVEN ★ MGM/UA, 1981
STAYING ALIVE Paramount, 1983, w/Tom Bronson
MAX DUGAN RETURNS 20th Century Fox, 1983
FRESNO (MS) MTM Productions, 1986

BETTY PECHA MADDEN*
Phone: 213/681-9394

HER LIFE AS A MAN (TF) LS Entertainment, 1984
GIRLS JUST WANT TO HAVE FUN New World, 1985
VAMP New World, 1986
CAPTAIN EO (Disneyland/Disney World) 1986
ODD JOBS Tri-Star, 1986
MOONWALKER Warner Bros., 1988

MOLLY MAGINNIS*
West Coast Card
Agent: Smith Gosnell Nicholson & Associates -
  Pacific Palisades, 213/459-0307
Address: 933 17th Street, #14, Santa Monica, CA
  90403, 213/829-1768

THE NEW KIDS Columbia, 1985
LUCAS 20th Century Fox, 1986
WHATEVER IT TAKES Aquarius, 1986
COMBAT HIGH (TF) Frank von Zerneck Productions/
  Lynch-Biller Productions, 1986
BROADCAST NEWS 20th Century Fox, 1987
MORGAN STEWART'S COMING HOME New
  Century/Vista, 1987
IN A SHALLOW GRAVE Skouras Pictures, 1988
PERFECT PEOPLE (TF) Robert Greenwald
  Productions, 1988
MISS FIRECRACKER Corsair, 1989
LOOK WHO'S TALKING Tri-Star, 1989
DAD Universal, 1989
LOOK WHO'S TALKING TOO Tri-Star, 1990
COME SEE THE PARADISE 20th Century Fox, 1990

PATRICIA MAGUILL
CRIME ZONE Concorde, 1989

ANN SOMERS MAJOR*
Address: 1024 Chautauqua Blvd., Pacific Palisades,
  CA 90272, 213/459-8949

AMAZONS (TF) ABC Circle Films, 1984
SINS OF THE PAST (TF) Sinpast Entertainment
  Company Productions, 1984
SINGLE BARS, SINGLE WOMEN (TF) Carsey-
  Werner Productions/Sunn Classic Pictures, 1984
GENERAL HOSPITAL (TVS) 1984-85

FLOWERS IN THE ATTIC New World, 1987
DOWNPAYMENT ON MURDER (TF) Adam
  Productions/20th Century Fox TV, 1987
MURPHY'S LAW (Pilot) 1988, George Segal &
  Maggie Han only
GLEAMING THE CUBE 20th Century Fox, 1989

JUDIANNA MAKOVSKY*
Attorney: Mark Glick, 212/944-1501
Address: 345 Southend Ave. #3M, New York, NY 10280,
  212/912-0918

COTTON CLUB Orion, 1984,
  (Asst. to Milena Canonero)
GARDENS OF STONE Tri-Star, 1987, w/Willa Kim
TUCKER: A MAN AND HIS DREAM Paramount, 1988,
  (Asst. to Milena Canonero)
BIG 20th Century Fox, 1988
MARGARET BOURKE-WHITE (TF) Turner Network
  Television, 1989
LOST ANGELS Orion, 1989
REVERSAL OF FORTUNE Warner Bros., 1990

MARY MALIN*
Agent: Mark Glick, 212/944-1501
Address: 2410 Horseshoe Canyon Rd., Los Angeles, CA
  90046, 213/656-3032

ROLLOVER Orion/Warner Bros., 1981
THE WORLD ACCORDING TO GARP Warner
  Bros., 1982
PLACES IN THE HEART Tri-Star, 1984
THE KARATE KID PART II Columbia, 1986
LETHAL WEAPON Warner Bros., 1987
THE RESCUE Buena Vista, 1988
DEAD SOLID PERFECT (CTF) HBO Pictures/David
  Merrick Productions, 1988
BETSY'S WEDDING Buena Vista, 1990
LIFE STINKS MGM, 1991

MARIA MANCUSO
FRIDAY THE 13TH, PART VI: JASON LIVES
  Paramount, 1986
TWO MOON JUNCTION Lorimar, 1988

MAYA MANI
BULLIES Universal, 1986

BOBBIE MANNIX*
Agent: Abby Greshler/Lil Micelli, Diamond Artist,
  213/278-8146
Address: 1111 Tamarind Ave., Hollywood, CA 90038,
  213/871-2533

AT LONG LAST LOVE 20th Century Fox, 1975
UNCLE JOE SHANNON United Artists, 1978
THE WARRIORS Paramount, 1979
XANADU Universal, 1980
THE LONG RIDERS United Artists, 1980
PRINCE JACK Castle Hill Productions, 1984

ANTHONY MARANDO
SUMMER HEAT Atlantic Releasing Corporation, 1987

ANNE-MARIE MARCHAND
THE RETURN OF MARTIN GUERRE ★ European
  International, 1983

Ma

CINEMATOGRAPHERS
PRODUCTION
DESIGNERS,
COSTUME
DESIGNERS AND
FILM EDITORS
GUIDE

C
O
S
T
U
M
E

D
E
S
I
G
N
E
R
S

Ma

CINEMATOGRAPHERS
PRODUCTION
DESIGNERS,
COSTUME
DESIGNERS AND
FILM EDITORS
GUIDE

C
O
S
T
U
M
E

D
E
S
I
G
N
E
R
S

KATHY MARSHALL
HYPER SAPHIEN   Tri-Star, 1986

LOUISE MARTINEZ
LIANNA   United Artists Classics, 1983, Wardrobe

STEPHANIE MASLANSKY
THE WIZARD OF LONELINESS   Skouras
   Pictures, 1988
DISORGANIZED CRIME   Buena Vista, 1989

NICOLETTA MASSONE
CAPTIVE HEARTS   MGM/UA, 1987

LINDA MATHESON
IATSE Local 676
Agent: Sandra Marsh Management - Sherman Oaks,
   818/905-6961

TITLE SHOT   Arista, 1979
MIDDLE AGE CRAZY   20th Century Fox, 1980
FISH HAWK   Avco Embassy, 1981
LOVE   Velvet Films, 1982
HUMONGOUS   Avco Embassy, 1982
STRANGE INVADERS   Orion, 1983
THE SINS OF DORIAN GRAY (TF)   Rankin-Bass
   Productions, 1983
THE HOUSEKEEPER   *A JUDGMENT IN STONE*
   Castle Hill Productions, 1986
BURNIN' LOVE   DEG, 1987
GOTHAM (CTF)   Showtime/Phoenix Entertainment
   Group/Keith Addis & Associates, 1988
WHERE THE HEART IS   Buena Vista, 1990
FX 2 — THE DEADLY ART OF ILLUSION
   Orion, 1991

LINDA MATTHEWS
JUST ONE OF THE GUYS   Columbia, 1985,
   w/George Little

MARILYN MATTHEWS*
Phone: 213/396-1743

DEAD POETS SOCIETY   Buena Vista,
   1989, Supervisor
TAKING CARE OF BUSINESS   Buena Vista, 1990

ELIZABETH McBRIDE
Agent: The Doug Apatow Agency, 10559 Blythe Ave.,
   Los Angeles, CA 90064, 213/202-6888

TRUE STORIES   Warner Bros., 1986,
   except Fashion Show
SQUARE DANCE   Island Pictures, 1986
TAPEHEADS   Avenue Pictures, 1988
DRIVING MISS DAISY ★   Warner Bros., 1989
THELMA AND LOUISE   1991
THELMA & LOUISE   Pathe Entertainment, 1991

SUSIE S. McEVEETY
BABY - SECRET OF THE LOST LEGEND   Buena
   Vista, 1985

ANNE McKAY
SYLVIA   MGM/UA Classics, 1985

TOM McKINLEY
Agent: The Irv Schechter Company - Beverly Hills,
   213/278-8070

MY DEMON LOVER   New Line Cinema, 1987
UHF   Orion, 1989

MARY E. McLEOD
PORKY'S   20th Century Fox, 1982, w/Larry Wells
PORKY'S II: THE NEXT DAY   20th Century
   Fox, 1983
A CHRISTMAS STORY   MGM/UA, 1983
MEATBALLS III   TMS Pictures, 1986
A NEW LIFE   Paramount, 1988
SWITCHING CHANNELS   Tri-Star, 1988
WHISPERS   Live Home Video, 1990
IF LOOKS COULD KILL   Warner Bros., 1991

HEIDI MELINC
DEATH OF A SCHOOLBOY   Neue Film
   GMBH, 1991

ILEANE MELTZER
LOVE OR MONEY   Hemdale, 1990

LINDA MELTZER
9 1/2 NINJAS   Republic Pictures Home Video, 1991

ANTHONY MENDLESON
YOUNG WINSTON ★   Columbia, 1972
THE INCREDIBLE SARAH ★   Reader's Digest, 1976
GULLIVER'S TRAVELS   EMI, 1977
THE BOYS FROM BRAZIL   20th Century Fox, 1978
THE GREAT TRAIN ROBBERY   United
   Artists, 1979
DRAGONSLAYER   Paramount, 1981
KRULL   Columbia, 1983
THE KEEP   Paramount, 1983

JENNIFER MICHAUD
DEADLY DANCER   AIP Home Video, 1990

MAURIZIO MILLENOTTI
HAMLET ★   Warner Bros., 1990

BURTON MILLER
AIRPORT '77 ★   Universal, 1977, w/Edith Head
ROLLERCOASTER   Universal, 1977
THE CONCORDE - AIRPORT '79   Universal, 1979
THE NUDE BOMB   Universal, 1980
THE STING II   Universal, 1983

NOLAN MILLER*
Address: 241 S. Robertson Blvd., Beverly Hills, CA
   90211, 213/655-7110

MR. MOM   20th Century Fox, 1983
CROSSINGS (MS)   Aaron Spelling
   Productions, 1986
THERE MUST BE A PONY (TF)   R.J. Productions/
   Columbia TV, 1986
THE TWO MRS. GRENVILLES (TF)   Lorimar-
   Telepictures, 1987, w/Donald Brooks & Sue Yelland
SKIN DEEP   20th Century Fox, 1989

ELLEN MIROJNICK*
East Coast Card
Agent: Smith Gosnell Nicholson & Associates -
Pacific Palisades, 213/459-0307
Phone: 212/744-5859 or 213/851-0850

FRENCH QUARTER   1977
FAME   MGM/United Artists, 1980, (Asst.)
ENDLESS LOVE   Universal, 1981, (Asst.)
RIVKIN: BOUNTY HUNTER (TF)   Chiarascurio
    Productions/Ten-Four Productions, 1981
RECKLESS   MGM/UA, 1984
THE FLAMINGO KID   20th Century Fox, 1984
REMO WILLIAMS: THE ADVENTURE BEGINS...
    Orion, 1985
NOBODY'S FOOL   Island Pictures, 1986
WALL STREET   20th Century Fox, 1987
FATAL ATTRACTION   Paramount, 1987
COCKTAIL   Buena Vista, 1988
TALK RADIO   Universal, 1988
BLACK RAIN   Paramount, 1989
ALWAYS   Universal, 1989
JACOB'S LADDER   Carolco/Tri-Star, 1990
SWITCH   Warner Bros., 1991

ERNEST MISKO*
Address: 14821 Septo St., Mission Hills, CA,
    818/893-7624

UP IN SMOKE   Paramount, 1978
CALIFORNIA DREAMING   American
    International, 1979
THE HAND   Orion/Warner Bros., 1981
SUMMER LOVERS   Filmways, 1982
UNDER COVER   Paramount, 1987

KAREN MITCHELL
HARD TRAVELING   New World, 1986

PETER MITCHELL*
Phone: 213/851-3650

THE MEN'S CLUB   Atlantic Releasing Corporation,
    1986, Marianna Elliot
THE SERPENT AND THE RAINBOW   Universal, 1988
THE IN CROWD   Orion, 1988
ERNEST SAVES CHRISTMAS   Buena Vista, 1988

MINA MITTELMAN*
Address: 4128 Vantage Ave., Studio City, CA 91604,
    213/877-2366

PRETTY BABY   Paramount, 1978
KENNY ROGERS AS THE GAMBLER - THE
    ADVENTURE CONTINUES (TF)   Lion Share
    Productions, 1983
DEMPSEY (TF) ☆   Charles Fries Productions, 1983
THE MAN WITH TWO BRAINS   Warner Bros.,
    1983, Women
WET GOLD (TF)   Telepictures Productions, 1984
MALICE IN WONDERLAND (TF) ☆☆   ITC
    Productions, 1985, except Elizabeth Taylor
MISCHIEF   20th Century Fox, 1985
PICKING UP THE PIECES (TF)   CBS
    Entertainment, 1985
THE EXECUTION (TF)   Newland-Raynor
    Productions/Comworld Productions, 1985
THE LITTLE MATCH GIRL (TF)   NBC
    Productions, 1987

THE STEPFATHER   New Century/Vista, 1987
THE TAKING OF FLIGHT 847: THE ULI DERICKSON
    STORY (TF)   Columbia TV, 1988

JOHN MOLLO
Agent: The William Morris Agency, U.K.
Address: New Hayward House, NR. Hungerford, Berkshire,
    RQ 17, OP2, England

STAR WARS ★★   20th Century Fox, 1977
ALIEN   20th Century Fox, 1979
THE EMPIRE STRIKES BACK   20th Century Fox, 1980
OUTLAND   The Ladd Company/Warner Bros., 1981
GANDHI ★★   Columbia, 1982, w/Bhana Athaiya
THE LORDS OF DISCIPLINE   Paramount, 1983
GREYSTOKE: THE LEGEND OF TARZAN, LORD
    OFTHE APES   Warner Bros., 1984
KING DAVID   Paramount, 1985
REVOLUTION   Warner Bros., 1985
CRY FREEDOM   Universal, 1987
HANNA'S WAR   Cannon, 1988
AIR AMERICA   Carolco/Tri-Star, 1990
WHITE HUNTER, BLACK HEART   Warner Bros., 1990

TISH MONAGHAN
ROXANNE   Columbia, 1987, Canada
DISTANT THUNDER   Paramount, 1988

JUDY MOORCROFT
CROSSED SWORDS   *THE PRINCE AND THE PAUPER*
    20th Century Fox, 1977, w/Ulla Britt Soderland
WHO IS KILLING THE GREAT CHEFS OF EUROPE?
    Warner Bros., 1978
MURDER BY DECREE   Avco Embassy, 1979
THE EUROPEANS ★   Levitt-Pickman, 1979
SILVER DREAM RACER   Almi Cinema 5, 1980
SPHINX   Orion/Warner Bros., 1981
YENTL   MGM/UA, 1983
A PASSAGE TO INDIA ★   Columbia, 1984
FRENCH LESSON   *THE FROG PRINCE*   Warner
    Bros., 1984
THE KILLING FIELDS   Warner Bros., 1984
SHANGHAI SURPRISE   MGM/UA, 1986
CLOCKWISE   Universal, 1986
WITHOUT A CLUE   Orion, 1988

DAN MOORE*
Address: 4416 Finley Ave., Los Angeles, CA 90027,
    213/666-3561

BLUE CITY   Paramount, 1986
EXTREME PREJUDICE   Tri-Star, 1987
RED HEAT   Tri-Star, 1988
ANOTHER 48 HRS.   Paramount, 1990

SUE MOORE
STAND BY ME   Columbia, 1986, Supervisor

SUSANNA MOORE
STRANGE INVADERS   Orion, 1983

TAMI MOR
THE DELTA FORCE   Cannon, 1986

JACQUELINE MOREAU
ROUND MIDNIGHT   Warner Bros., 1986

Mo

CINEMATOGRAPHERS
PRODUCTION
DESIGNERS,
COSTUME
DESIGNERS AND
FILM EDITORS
GUIDE

C
O
S
T
U
M
E

D
E
S
I
G
N
E
R
S

Mo

CINEMATOGRAPHERS
PRODUCTION
DESIGNERS,
COSTUME
DESIGNERS AND
FILM EDITORS
GUIDE

C
O
S
T
U
M
E

D
E
S
I
G
N
E
R
S

NORMA MORICEAU
THE ROAD WARRIOR   Warner Bros., 1982
NATE AND HAYES   *SAVAGE ISLAND*S
    Paramount, 1983
MAD MAX BEYOND THUNDERDOME   Warner
    Bros., 1985
"CROCODILE" DUNDEE   Paramount, 1986
"CROCODILE" DUNDEE II   Paramount, 1988
DEAD CALM   Warner Bros., 1989

RUTH MORLEY*
Agent: The Gersh Agency, Inc., Beverly Hills -
    213/274-6611, New York - 212/997-1818

ANNIE HALL   United Artists, 1977
THE GARDENER'S SON (TF) ☆☆   RIP/
    Filmhaus, 1977
SLOW DANCING IN THE BIG CITY   United
    Artists, 1978
THE MIRACLE WORKER (TF) ☆   Katz-Gallin
    Productions/Half-Pint Productions, 1979
KRAMER VS. KRAMER   Columbia, 1979
PLAYING FOR TIME (TF)   Syzgy Productions, 1980
LITTLE MISS MARKER   Universal, 1980
I OUGHT TO BE IN PICTURES   20th Century
    Fox, 1982
THE CHOSEN   20th Century Fox International
    Classics, 1982
ONE FROM THE HEART   Columbia, 1982
TOOTSIE   Columbia, 1982
GRACE QUIGLEY   MGM/UA/Cannon, 1984
KEY EXCHANGE   20th Century Fox, 1985
DEATH OF A SALESMAN (TF)   Roxbury and Punch
    Productions, 1985
THE MONEY PIT   Universal, 1986
HELLO AGAIN   Buena Vista, 1987
WINTER PEOPLE   Columbia, 1989
THE DREAM TEAM   Universal, 1989
SEE NO EVIL, HEAR NO EVIL   Tri-Star, 1989
PARENTHOOD   Universal, 1989
GHOST   Paramount, 1990

KAY MORRIS
THE CLOSER   Ion Pictures, 1991

KATHRYN MORRISON-PAHOA
SALVADOR   Hemdale, 1986
STAND AND DELIVER   Warner Bros., 1988
WAR PARTY   Hemdale, 1989
A SHOW OF FORCE   Paramount, 1990

SYLVIA MOSS
A SINFUL LIFE   New Line Cinema, 1989

ABIGAIL MURRAY
Local 829
Agent: The Doug Apatow Agency, 10559 Blythe Ave.,
    Los Angeles, CA 90064, 213/202-6888

THE MANHATTAN PROJECT   20th Century Fox,
    1985, (Asst.)
MRS. SOFFEL   MGM/UA, 1986, (Asst.)
THE BELIEVERS   Orion, 1987, (Asst.)
BLOODHOUNDS OF BROADWAY   Columbia, 1989
TREMORS   Universal, 1989
STRANGER IN THE HOUSE   Pressman Films, 1990

ROBERT MUSCO
POLICE ACADEMY 5: ASSIGNMENT MIAMI BEACH
    Warner Bros., 1988

ISIS MUSSENDEN
THE ALLNIGHTER   Universal, 1987
THE BLUE IGUANA   Paramount, 1988
POWWOW HIGHWAY   HandMade Films, 1988
SHOCKER   Universal, 1989

GLORIA MUSSETTA
TRENCHCOAT   Buena Vista, 1983

RUTH MYERS*
IATSE Local 892, ACTT
Agent: Sandra Marsh Management - Sherman Oaks,
    818/905-6961
Phone: 213/851-1495

SMASHING TIME   Paramount, 1967
WORK IS A FOUR LETTER WORD   Universal, 1968
THREE INTO TWO WON'T GO   1969
ISADORA   Universal, 1969
A NICE GIRL LIKE ME   Avco Embassy, 1969
THE VIRGIN SOLDIERS   Columbia, 1970
THE TWELVE CHAIRS   UMC, 1970
THE RULING CLASS   Avco Embassy, 1972
A TOUCH OF CLASS   Avco Embassy, 1973
LITTLE MALCOLM AND HIS STRUGGLE AGAINST THE
    EUNUCHS   Multicetera Investments, 1974
THAT'LL BE THE DAY   EMI, 1974
GALILEO   American Film Theatre, 1975
STARDUST   Columbia, 1975
THE ROMANTIC ENGLISHWOMAN   New World, 1975
THE ADVENTURE OF SHERLOCK HOLMES' SMARTER
    BROTHER   20th Century Fox, 1975
THE WORLD'S GREATEST LOVER   20th Century
    Fox, 1977
MAGIC   20th Century Fox, 1978
THE MAIN EVENT   First Artists, 1979
...AND JUSTICE FOR ALL   Columbia, 1979
ALTERED STATES   Warner Bros., 1980
IT'S MY TURN   Columbia, 1980
THE COMPETITION   Columbia, 1980
IN GOD WE TRUST   Universal, 1980
THE FIRST MONDAY IN OCTOBER   Paramount, 1981
CANNERY ROW   MGM/UA, 1982
SOMETHING WICKED THIS WAY COMES   Buena
    Vista, 1983
ELECTRIC DREAMS   MGM/UA, 1984
THE WOMAN IN RED   Orion, 1984
TEACHERS   MGM/UA, 1984
PLENTY   20th Century Fox, 1985
HAUNTED HONEYMOON   Orion, 1986
BAJA OKLAHOMA   HBO Pictures, 1988
VIBES   Columbia, 1988
THE ACCIDENTAL TOURIST   Warner Bros., 1988
BERT RIGBY, YOU'RE A FOOL   Warner Bros., 1989
BLAZE   Buena Vista, 1989
THE RUSSIA HOUSE   Pathe/MGM/UA, 1990
THE MARRYING MAN   Buena Vista, 1991

N

DEBORAH NADOOLMAN*
THE KENTUCKY FRIED MOVIE   United Film
   Distributors, 1977
NATIONAL LAMPOON'S ANIMAL HOUSE
   Universal, 1978
1941   Universal, 1979
THE BLUES BROTHERS   Universal, 1980
RAIDERS OF THE LOST ARK   Paramount, 1981
TRADING PLACES   Paramount, 1983
TWILIGHT ZONE - THE MOVIE   Warner Bros., 1985
SPIES LIKE US   Warner Bros., 1985
INTO THE NIGHT   Universal, 1986
THREE AMIGOS   Orion, 1986
COMING TO AMERICA ★   Paramount, 1988
NOTHING BUT TROUBLE   Warner Bros., 1991
OSCAR   Beuna Vista, 1991

ELIZABETH WARNER NANKIN
DADDY'S DYIN'...WHO'S GOT THE WILL?
   MGM/UA, 1990

ANNALISA NASALLI-ROCCA
SHEENA   Columbia, 1984

MICHELE NEELY
FANDANGO   Warner Bros., 1985, w/Art Brouillard

KRISTIN NELSON
MY TUTOR   Crown International, 1983
TOMBOY   Crown International, 1985

LANA NELSON
RED HEADED STRANGER   Alive Films, 1986

PIP NEWBERY
DANCE WITH A STRANGER   Samuel Goldwyn
   Company, 1985
HEARTS OF FIRE   Lorimar, 1987

LESLEY LYNN NICHOLSON
CRITTERS 2: THE MAIN COURSE   New Line
   Cinema, 1988

BRIGITTE NIERHAUS
A MAN IN LOVE   Cinecom, 1987
THE MAN INSIDE   New Line Cinema, 1990

DAVID NORBURY
STICKY FINGERS   Spectrafilm, 1988,
   w/Cynthia Schumacher

PATRICIA NORRIS*
West Coast Card
Agent: Smith Gosnell Nicholson & Associates -
   Pacific Palisades, 213/459-0307

THE CANDIDATE   Warner Bros., 1972
ZANDY'S BRIDE   Warner Bros., 1974

THE SUNSHINE BOYS   MGM/United Artists, 1975
SMILE   United Artists, 1975
THE MISSOURI BREAKS   United Artists, 1976
SILENT MOVIE   20th Century Fox, 1976
HIGH ANXIETY   20th Century Fox, 1977
CALIFORNIA SUITE   Columbia, 1978
CAPRICORN ONE   Warner Bros., 1978
DAYS OF HEAVEN ★   Paramount, 1978
MOVIE MOVIE   Warner Bros., 1978
THE FISH THAT SAVED PITTSBURGH   United
   Artists, 1979
THE BALTIMORE BULLET   Avco Embassy, 1980
ON THE NICKEL   Rose's Park, 1980
HEART BEAT   Orion/Warner Bros., 1980
FATSO   20th Century Fox, 1980
THE ELEPHANT MAN ★   Paramount, 1980
FOUR FRIENDS   Filmways, 1981
HISTORY OF THE WORLD, PART 1   20th Century
   Fox, 1981
VICTOR/VICTORIA ★   MGM/United Artists, 1982
FRANCES   Universal/AFD, 1982
THE STAR CHAMBER   20th Century Fox, 1983
SCARFACE   Universal, 1983
2010 ★   MGM/UA, 1984
JOHNNY DANGEROUSLY   20th Century Fox, 1984
RACING WITH THE MOON   Paramount, 1984
MICKI AND MAUDE   Columbia, 1984
THE BEST OF TIMES   Universal, 1986
SPACECAMP   20th Century Fox, 1986
A FINE MESS   Columbia, 1986
THE WHOOPEE BOYS   Paramount, 1986
BLUE VELVET   DEG, 1986
BLACK WIDOW   20th Century Fox, 1987
LITTLE NIKITA   Columbia, 1988
SUNSET ★   Tri-Star, 1988
TAP   Tri-Star, 1989

ROSANNA NORTON*
Phone: 213/396-2393

CARRIE   United Artists, 1976
OUTLAW BLUES   Warner Bros., 1977, w/Pam Scrape
I WANNA HOLD YOUR HAND   Universal, 1978
HEAD OVER HEELS   *CHILLY SCENES OF WINTER*
   United Artists, 1979
THE STUNT MAN   20th Century Fox, 1980
AIRPLANE!   Paramount, 1980
RASCALS AND ROBBERS: THE SECRET
   ADVENTURES OF TOM SAWYER AND
   HUCKLEBERRY FINN (TF) ☆   CBS
   Entertainment, 1982
TRON ★   Buena Vista, 1982, w/Elois Jenssen
HARD TO HOLD   Universal, 1984
EXPLORERS   Paramount, 1985
NOTHING IN COMMON   Tri-Star, 1986
INNERSPACE   Warner Bros., 1987
RUTHLESS PEOPLE   Buena Vista, 1986
THE 'BURBS   Universal, 1989
LOVERBOY   Tri-Star, 1989
GREMLINS 2: THE NEW BATCH   Warner Bros., 1990
ROBOCOP 2   Orion, 1990

NINO NOVARESE
CROMWELL ★★   Columbia, 1970
THE TERMINAL MAN   Warner Bros., 1974

No

CINEMATOGRAPHERS
PRODUCTION
DESIGNERS,
COSTUME
DESIGNERS AND
FILM EDITORS
GUIDE

COSTUME DESIGNERS

CINEMATOGRAPHERS
PRODUCTION
DESIGNERS,
COSTUME
DESIGNERS AND
FILM EDITORS
GUIDE

C
O
S
T
U
M
E

D
E
S
I
G
N
E
R
S

O

BERNADETTE O'BRIEN
PRIME RISK   Almi Pictures, 1985
HOUSE   New World, 1986
HUNK   Crown International, 1987

CAROL ODITZ*
Agent: The Gersh Agency, Inc., Beverly Hills -
    213/274-6611, New York - 212/997-1818

SMOOTH TALK   Spectrafilm, 1985
NOBODY'S CHILD (TF)   Joseph Feury Productions/
    Gaylord Productions Company, 1986
STAYING TOGETHER   Hemdale, 1989

JILL OHANNESON
STACY'S KNIGHTS   Crown International, 1983
ONCE BITTEN   Samuel Goldwyn Company, 1985
ELIMINATORS   Empire Pictures, 1986
HOLLYWOOD VICE SQUAD   Concorde/Cine
    Group, 1986
ZONE TROOPERS   Empire Pictures, 1986
TRICK OR TREAT   DEG, 1986
THE WRONG GUYS   New World, 1988
DUDES   New Century/Vista, 1988
BILL & TED'S EXCELLENT ADVENTURE
    Orion, 1989

DONNA O'NEAL
DATE WITH AN ANGEL   DEG, 1987

P

PETER PABST
COLONEL REDL   Orion Classics, 1985

ELIZABETH P. PALMER*
Address: 6231 Buffalo Ave., Van Nuys, CA 91401,
    818/904-0645

CONCEALED ENEMIES (TF)   WGBH-Boston/
    Goldcrest Films and Television/Comworld
    Productions, 1984
PERSONAL FOUL   1987
A TIGER'S TALE   Atlantic Releasing
    Corporation, 1988

DANIEL PAREDES*
Phone: 213/652-1781

SPARKLE   Warner Bros., 1976
SCRUPLES (TF)   Lou-Step Productions/Warner
    Bros. TV, 1981

CAT PEOPLE   Universal, 1982
THE ICE PIRATES   MGM/UA, 1983
THE WOMEN OF BREWSTER PLACE (TF)   Harpo
    Productions/Phoenix Entertainment, 1989
DOWNTOWN   20th Century Fox, 1990

GALE PARKER-SMITH*
Address: 844 19th St., Santa Monica, CA 90403,
    213/828-1510

PROMISE (TF)   Garner-Duchow Productions/Warner
    Bros. TV, 1986
SLOW BURN (CTF)   Joel Schumacher Productions/
    Universal Pay TV, 1986
COP   Atlantic Releasing Corporation, 1988
GROSS ANATOMY   Buena Vista, 1989

JENNIFER L. PARSONS
ARACHNOPHOBIA   Buena Vista, 1990

WENDY PARTRIDGE
THE HIGH COUNTRY   Crown International, 1981
LOYALTIES   Cinema Group, 1987
THE BIG TOWN   Columbia, 1987

BETH PASTERNAK
FRIENDS, LOVERS & LUNATICS   Fries
    Entertainment, 1990

CINDY PATERSON
NOT QUITE PARADISE   New World, 1985

ANN PAYNE
ERNEST GOES TO CAMP   Buena Vista, 1987

MARIE-FRANCOISE PEROCHEN
TARGET   Warner Bros., 1985

DAVID PERRY
ABSOLUTE BEGINNERS   Orion, 1986, w/Sue Blane

KAREN PERRY
THE BROTHER FROM ANOTHER PLANET
    Cinecom, 1984
STREETWALKIN'   Concorde, 1985

BENITO PERSICO
SATURDAY, SUNDAY, MONDAY   Silvio Berlusconi
    Communications, 1990

GABRIELLA PESCUCCI
PASSIONE D'AMORE   Putnam Square, 1982
THREE MOTHERS   New World, 1982
LA NUIT DE VARENNES   Triumph/Columbia, 1983
ONCE UPON A TIME IN AMERICA   The Ladd Company/
    Warner Bros., 1984
THE NAME OF THE ROSE   20th Century Fox, 1986
HAUNTED SUMMER   Cannon, 1988
THE ADVENTURES OF BARON MUNCHAUSEN ★
    Columbia, 1989

HAZEL PETHIG
MONTY PYTHON'S LIFE OF BRIAN   Orion/Warner
    Bros., 1979
A FISH CALLED WANDA   MGM/UA, 1988
GETTING IT RIGHT   MCEG, 1989

ERICA EDELL PHILLIPS*
IATSE Local 892
Agent: Sandra Marsh Management - Sherman Oaks,
   818/905-6961
Address: 149 S. Bedford Dr., Beverly Hills, CA 90212,
   213/276-1511

HOW TO BEAT THE HIGH COST OF LIVING
   American International, 1980
DEAD AND BURIED   Avco Embassy, 1981
A LONG WAY HOME (TF)   Alan Landsburg
   Productions, 1981
PRAY TV (TF)   ABC Circle Films, 1982
M.A.D.D.: MOTHERS AGAINST DRUNK
   DRIVERS (TF)   Universal TV, 1983
COCAINE AND BLUE EYES (TF)   Orenthal
   Productions/Columbia TV, 1983
PRINCESS DAISY (MS)   NBC Productions/Steve
   Krantz Productions, 1983
ONE COOKS, THE OTHER DOESN'T (TF)
   Kaleidoscope Films Ltd./Lorimar Productions, 1983
HADLEY'S REBELLION   American Film
   Distributors, 1984
PEYTON PLACE: THE NEXT GENERATION (TF)
   Michael Filerman Productions/20th Century
   Fox TV, 1985
A LETTER TO THREE WIVES (TF)   20th Century
   Fox TV, 1985
TWICE IN A LIFETIME   The Yorkin Company, 1985
TOUGH GUYS   Buena Vista, 1986
UNDER THE INFLUENCE (TF)   CBS
   Entertainment, 1986
ROBOCOP   Orion, 1987, except RoboCop
ALIEN NATION   20th Century Fox, 1988
TRUE BELIEVER   Columbia, 1989
MAJOR LEAGUE   Paramount, 1989
TOTAL RECALL   Tri-Star, 1990

LYNN A. PICKWELL
Agent: The Gersh Agency, 130 W. 42nd St.,
   Suite 2400 - New York, NY 10036, 212/997-1818

THE APPOINTMENT   Elsboy Entertainment, 1989
AN URBAN FAIRYTALE   MGM Productions, 1989
NIGHT WARRIOR   Kodiak Films, 1990

THEODOR PISTEK
AMADEUS ★★   Orion, 1984
THE RAGGEDY RAWNEY   Island Pictures, 1989
VALMONT ★   Orion, 1989

GREGORY POE
CAN'T BUY ME LOVE   Buena Vista, 1987

FAYE POLIAKIN
A CHORUS LINE   Columbia, 1985

BERNIE POLLACK*
Phone: 818/783-6362

BOBBY DEERFIELD   Columbia, 1977
STRAIGHT TIME   Warner Bros., 1978
THE ELECTRIC HORSEMAN   Columbia, 1979
ORDINARY PEOPLE   Paramount, 1980
ABSENCE OF MALICE   Columbia, 1981
THE NATURAL   Tri-Star, 1984, w/Gloria Gresham
TWICE IN A LIFETIME   The Yorkin Company, 1985
POLICE ACADEMY 2: THEIR FIRST ASSIGNMENT
   Warner Bros., 1985

LEGAL EAGLES   Universal, 1986, w/Gail Bixby &
   Albert Wolsky
TOUCH & GO   Tri-Star, 1987
THE MILAGRO BEANFIELD WAR   Universal, 1988
BRIGHT LIGHTS, BIG CITY   MGM/UA, 1988
RAIN MAN   MGM/UA, 1988
LOCK-UP   Tri-Star, 1989
TANGO & CASH   Warner Bros., 1990
HAVANA   Mirage/Universal, 1990
WHAT ABOUT BOB?   Buena Vista/Touchtone, 1991

LEONARD POLLACK
Address: 1425 Talmadge St., Los Angeles, CA 90027,
   213/661-4302

WAXWORK   Vestron, 1988
PAINT IT BLACK   Vestron, 1990
SUNDOWN: THE VAMPIRE IN RETREAT
   Vestron, 1990
WHORE   Trimark Pictures, 1991

ROSEMARY PONZO*
Agent: Stuart G. Shestack - New York, 212/267-6115
Address: 181 7th Ave., Suite 3B, New York, NY 10011,
   212/463-7971

SUDDEN DEATH   Marvin Films, 1985
CRACK IN THE MIRROR   Rebo Productions, 1987

JOSEPH PORRO
Agent: Grace Lyons Management - Los Angeles,
   213/655-5100

NEON MANIACS   Bedford Entertainment, 1986
NEAR DARK   DEG, 1987
FRIGHT NIGHT II   Columbia, 1988
THE BLOB   Tri-Star, 1988
MEET THE APPLEGATES   Triton Pictures, 1990
I COME IN PEACE   Triumph Releasing, 1990
DEATH WARRANT   MGM/UA, 1990
THE PERFECT WEAPON   Paramount Pictures, 1991

EMMA PORTEUS
THE ISLAND OF DR. MOREAU   American International,
   1977, w/Richard La Motte & Rita Woods
THE DOGS OF WAR   United Artists, 1980
CLASH OF THE TITANS   United Artists, 1981
FIVE DAYS ONE SUMMER   The Ladd Company/Warner
   Bros., 1982
TOP SECRET!   Paramount, 1984
1984   Atlantic Entertainment Corporation, 1984
A VIEW TO A KILL   MGM/UA, 1985
THE JEWEL OF THE NILE   20th Century Fox, 1985
ALIENS   20th Century Fox, 1986
THE LIVING DAYLIGHTS   MGM/UA, 1987
HIGH SPIRITS   Tri-Star, 1988
AROUND THE WORLD IN 80 DAYS (MS) ☆   Harmony
   Gold/Rete Europa/Valente-Baerwald Productions, 1989

ANTHONY POWELL*
Agent: Andrew Glynne - London, 01/935-5541

TRAVELS WITH MY AUNT ★★   MGM, 1972
PAPILLON   Allied Artists, 1973
BUFFALO BILL AND THE INDIANS or SITTING BULL'S
   HISTORY LESSON   United Artists, 1976
DEATH ON THE NILE ★★   Paramount, 1978
TESS ★★   Columbia, 1980
PRIEST OF LOVE   Filmways, 1981

CINEMATOGRAPHERS
PRODUCTION
DESIGNERS,
COSTUME
DESIGNERS AND
FILM EDITORS
GUIDE

C
O
S
T
U
M
E

D
E
S
I
G
N
E
R
S

Po

CINEMATOGRAPHERS
PRODUCTION
DESIGNERS,
COSTUME
DESIGNERS AND
FILM EDITORS
GUIDE

C O S T U M E · D E S I G N E R S

EVIL UNDER THE SUN   Universal/AFD, 1982
INDIANA JONES & THE TEMPLE OF DOOM
    Paramount, 1984
PIRATES ★   Cannon, 1986
ISHTAR   Columbia, 1987
FRANTIC   Warner Bros., 1988
INDIANA JONES AND THE LAST CRUSADE
    Paramount, 1989, w/Joanna Johnston

S A N D Y   P O W E L L
CARAVAGGIO   Cinevista, 1986
STORMY MONDAY   Atlantic Releasing
    Corporation, 1988

G R A N I A   P R E S T O N
CASUAL SEX?   Universal, 1988
DARKMAN   Universal, 1990

M A R I A   P R I C E
DIAMOND'S EDGE   Castle Hill, 1990

T O N Y   P U E O
KING SOLOMON'S MINES   Cannon, 1985

R

C A R O L   R A M S E Y
SLAVES OF NEW YORK   Tri-Star, 1989
KING OF NEW YORK   Reteitalia and Scena
    Film, 1990
MR. & MRS. BRIDGE   Miramax, 1990

V A N   B R O U G H T O N   R A M S E Y *
Agent: Grace Lyons Management - Los Angeles,
    213/655-5100
Address: Sharon Valley Rd., Sharon, CT 06069,
    203/364-0620

1918   Cinecom, 1985
ON VALENTINE'S DAY   Angelika Films, 1986
STORY OF A MARRIAGE (TF)   Indian Falls
    Corporation/American Playhouse/
    WGBH-Boston, 1987
END OF THE LINE   Orion Classics, 1988
LONESOME DOVE (MS) ☆ Motown Productions/
    Pangea/Qintex Entertainment, 1989

T O M   R A N D
ACTT
Agent: Sandra Marsh Management - Sherman Oaks,
    818/905-6961

THE DUELLISTS   Paramount, 1978
THE FRENCH LIEUTENANT'S WOMAN ★   United
    Artists, 1981
THE PIRATES OF PENZANCE   Universal, 1983
THE SHOOTING PARTY   European Classics, 1984
ELENI   Warner Bros., 1985
YOUNG TOSCANINI   Carthago Films/Canal Plus/
    FR3/La Sept/Italian International Pictures/RAI, 1988
STRIKE IT RICH   Millimeter Films, 1990

B O B B I E   R E A D *
Phone: 213/650-7879

TOP GUN   Paramount, 1986, Women's
9 1/2 WEEKS   Paramount, 1986
SWEET HEARTS DANCE   Tri-Star, 1988

J O H N   M I C H A E L   R E E F E R
CLASS OF NUKE 'EM HIGH   Troma, 1986,
    w/Ivy Rosovsky
SHE'S GOTTA HAVE IT   Island Pictures, 1986

R O B Y N   R E I C H E K
MARTIANS GO HOME   Taurus Entertainment, 1990

M A R Y - J A N E   R E Y N E R
RESTLESS NATIVES   Orion Classics, 1986
THE GIRL IN THE PICTURE   Samuel Goldwyn
    Company, 1986
HOUSEKEEPING   Columbia, 1987

M A R K   R E Y N O L D S
LETTER TO BREZHNEV   Circle Releasing, 1985

R E V E   R I C H A R D S
PASS THE AMMO   New Century/Vista, 1988
IT TAKES TWO   MGM/UA, 1988
DOIN' TIME ON PLANET EARTH   Cannon, 1989

I M O G E N E   R I C H A R D S O N
THE DOCTOR AND THE DEVILS   20th Century
    Fox, 1985

R I T A   R I G G S *
Agent: The Lantz Office - Los Angeles, 213/858-1144
Address: The Loft: Costume Studio, 5917 W. 3rd St.,
    Los Angeles, CA 90036

NIGHT MOVES   Warner Bros., 1975, Supervisor
THE DOMINO PRINCIPLE   Avco Embassy, 1977,
    w/Laurie Riley
THE IDOLMAKER   United Artists, 1980
CATTLE ANNIE AND LITTLE BRITCHES
    Universal, 1981
YES, GIORGIO   MGM/UA, 1982
AN OFFICER AND A GENTLEMAN   Paramount, 1982
DEAL OF THE CENTURY   Warner Bros., 1983
BAD MEDICINE   20th Century Fox, 1985
MR. NORTH   Samuel Goldwyn Company, 1988
TEXASVILLE   Columbia, 1990

B O B   R I N G W O O D
THE CORN IS GREEN (TF)   Warner Bros. TV, 1979
EXCALIBUR   Orion/Warner Bros., 1981
THE DRAUGHTMAN'S CONTRACT   United Artists
    Classics, 1983
DUNE   Universal, 1984
SANTA CLAUS: THE MOVIE   Tri-Star, 1985
SOLARBABIES   MGM/UA, 1986
PRICK UP YOUR EARS   Samuel Goldwyn
    Company, 1987
EMPIRE OF THE SUN ★   Warner Bros., 1987
BATMAN   Warner Bros., 1989, w/Linda Henrikson
CHICAGO JOE AND THE SHOWGIRL   New Line
    Cinema, 1990

ALIENS 4

PIERRO RIZZO
THE SEVEN MAGNIFICENT GLADIATORS
    Cannon, 1985

CARRIE ROBBINS
IN THE SPIRIT   Castle Hill, 1990

AMY ROBERTS
MADAME SOUSATZKA   Universal, 1988

JANE ROBINSON
ACTT
Agent: Sandra Marsh Management - Sherman Oaks,
    818/905-6961

CAESAR AND CLEOPATRA (TF)   NBC-TV, 1976
TELEFON   MGM/United Artists, 1977,
    w/Luster Bayless
BRIDESHEAD REVISITED (MS)   Granada TV/
    WNET-13/NDR Hamburg, 1982
MOONLIGHTING   Universal Classics, 1982
PHILLIP MARLOWE - PRIVATE EYE
    CHANDLERTOWN (CTF)   HBO/David Wickes
    Televion Ltd./London Weekend Television, 1983
BETRAYAL   20th Cenutry Fox International
    Classics, 1983
SAHARA   MGM/UA/Cannon, 1984
SECRET PLACES   TLC Films/20th Century Fox, 1984
A WOMAN OF SUBSTANCE (MS)   Artemis Portman
    Productions, 1984
AGATHA CHRISTIE'S "MURDER WITH MIRRORS"(TF)
    Hajeno Productions/Warner Bros. TV, 1985
DREAMCHILD   Universal, 1985
NAZI HUNTER: THE BEATE KLARSFELDSTORY(TF)
    William Kayden Productions/Orion TV/Silver Chalice/
    Revcom/George Walker TV/TF1/SFP, 1986
ANASTASIA: THE MYSTERY OF ANNA (TF) ☆☆
    Telecom Entertainment/Consolidated
    Productions/Reteitalia, 1986
NINETEEN NINETEEN   Spectrafilm, 1986
POOR LITTLE RICH GIRL: THE BARBARA HUTTON
    STORY (MS) ☆☆   Lester Persky Productions/ITC
    Productions, 1987
A HANDFUL OF DUST ★   New Line Cinema, 1988
SCANDAL   Miramax, 1989
MEMPHIS BELLE   Enigma/Warner Bros., 1990

AGGIE GUERARD RODGERS*
Agent: Larry Mirisch, Triad Artists, Inc. - Los Angeles,
    213/556-2727
Address: 4405 24th St., San Francisco, CA 94114,
    415/821-7977

AMERICAN GRAFFITI   Universal, 1973
THE CONVERSATION   Paramount, 1974
ONE FLEW OVER THE CUCKOO'S NEST   United
    Artists, 1975
CORVETTE SUMMER   MGM/United Artists, 1978
MORE AMERICAN GRAFFITI   Universal, 1979
THE ADVENTURES OF BUCKAROO BANZAI:
    ACROSS THE 8TH DIMENSION   20th Century
    Fox, 1983
THE RETURN OF THE JEDI   20th Century Fox,
    1984, w/Nilo Rodis-Jomero
WARNING SIGN   20th Century Fox, 1985
COCOON   20th Century Fox, 1985
THE COLOR PURPLE ★   Universal, 1985
PEE-WEE'S BIG ADVENTURE   Warner Bros., 1986
THE WITCHES OF EASTWICK   Warner Bros., 1987

BATTERIES NOT INCLUDED   Universal, 1987
FATAL BEAUTY   MGM/UA, 1987
LEONARD PART 6   Columbia, 1987
BEETLEJUICE   Warner Bros., 1988
MY STEPMOTHER IS AN ALIEN   WEG, 1988
IN COUNTRY   Warner Bros., 1989
I LOVE YOU TO DEATH   Tri-Star, 1989

NILO RODIS-JAMERO*
RETURN OF THE JEDI   20th Century Fox, 1983,
    w/Aggie Guerard Rodgers
STAR TREK V: THE FINAL FRONTIER
    Paramount, 1989

ELISABETTA ROGIANI
CAMPUS MAN   Paramount, 1987

MARY ROSE
PARIS TROUT   Viacom Pictures, 1991

PENNY ROSE
CAL   Warner Bros., 1984
STRAPLESS   Miramax, 1990, w/Rebecca Hale

HILARY ROSENFELD
ONE TRICK PONY   Warner Bros., 1980
EYEWITNESS   20th Century Fox, 1981
DESERT BLOOM   Columbia, 1986
NO MERCY   Tri-Star, 1986
DIRTY DANCING   Vestron, 1987
DOMINICK AND EUGENE   Orion, 1989
TRIUMPH OF THE SPIRIT   Nova International, 1989

KAREN ROSTON
THE MUPPETS TAKE MANHATTAN   Tri-Star, 1984,
    w/Calista Hendrickson & Polly Smith

ANN ROTH*
Address: Rd. 3, Box 3124, Bangor, PA 18013,
    215/588-7752 or 212/255-5502

MIDNIGHT COWBOY   United Artists, 1969
THE DAY OF THE LOCUST   Paramount, 1975
BURNT OFFERINGS   United Artists, 1976
INDEPENDENCE   20th Century Fox, 1976
THE GOODBYE GIRL   Warner Bros., 1977
COMING HOME   United Artists, 1978
NUNZIO   Universal, 1978
PROMISES IN THE DARK   Orion/Warner Bros., 1979
HAIR   United Artists, 1979
THE ISLAND   Universal, 1980
DRESSED TO KILL   Filmways, 1980
NINE TO FIVE   20th Century Fox, 1980
ROLLOVER   Orion/Warner Bros., 1981
HONKY TONK FREEWAY   Universal/AFD, 1981
ONLY WHEN I LAUGH   Columbia, 1981
THE WORLD ACCORDING TO GARP   Warner
    Bros., 1982
THE MAN WHO LOVED WOMEN   Columbia, 1983
SILKWOOD   20th Century Fox, 1983
THE SURVIVORS   Columbia, 1983
PLACES IN THE HEART ★   Tri-Star, 1984
SWEET DREAMS   Tri-Star, 1985
THE SLUGGER'S WIFE   Columbia, 1985
MAXIE   Orion, 1985
JAGGED EDGE   Columbia, 1985
HEARTBURN   Paramount, 1986
THE MORNING AFTER   20th Century Fox, 1986

Ro

CINEMATOGRAPHERS
PRODUCTION
DESIGNERS,
COSTUME
DESIGNERS AND
FILM EDITORS
GUIDE

C
O
S
T
U
M
E

D
E
S
I
G
N
E
R
S

Ro

CINEMATOGRAPHERS
PRODUCTION
DESIGNERS,
COSTUME
DESIGNERS AND
FILM EDITORS
GUIDE

C O S T U M E   D E S I G N E R S

BILOXI BLUES   Universal, 1988
FUNNY FARM   Warner Bros., 1988
THE UNBEARABLE LIGHTNESS OF BEING
    Orion, 1988
STARS AND BARS   Columbia, 1988
WORKING GIRL   20th Century Fox, 1988
THE JANUARY MAN   MGM/UA, 1989, w/Neil Spisak
HER ALIBI   Warner Bros., 1989
FAMILY BUSINESS   Tri-Star, 1989
EVERYBODY WINS   Orion, 1990
Q & A   Tri-Star, 1990, w/Neil Spisak
PACIFIC HEIGHTS   20th Century Fox, 1990
POSTCARDS FROM THE EDGE   Columbia, 1990
THE BONFIRE OF THE VANITIES   Warner
    Bros., 1990

IDA MAY ROUTH*

Agent: The Gersh Agency, Inc., Beverly Hills -
    213/274-6611, New York - 212/997-1818

THE MAN WHO FELL TO EARTH   Cinema 5, 1976
THE LAST REMAKE OF BEAU GESTE   Universal,
    1977, w/Ron Beck
SGT. PEPPER'S LONELY HEARTS CLUB BAND
    Universal, 1978
BEING THERE   United Artists, 1979
GHOST STORY   Universal, 1981
MY FAVORITE YEAR   MGM/UA, 1982
SPLASH   Buena Vista, 1984
MORONS FROM OUTER SPACE   Universal, 1985
CADDYSHACK II   Warner Bros., 1988
CAPITAL NEWS (Pilot)   1990

DAVID ROWE

THE WILD DUCK   Orion, 1983
FAREWELL TO THE KING   Orion, 1989

ARTHUR ROWSELL

CHILDREN OF A LESSER GOD   Paramount, 1986,
    w/Fabienne April
DEAD OF WINTER   MGM/UA, 1987
PARENTS   Vestron, 1989

JANE RUHM*

Phone: 213/939-6011

I NEVER PROMISED YOU A ROSE GARDEN
    New World, 1977
FINNEGAN BEGIN AGAIN (CTF)   HBO Premiere
    Films/Zenith Productions/Jennie & Company Film
    Productions, 1985
THREE O'CLOCK HIGH   Universal, 1987
SAY ANYTHING   20th Century Fox, 1989

JUDY RUSKIN

YOUNG GUNS II   20th Century Fox, 1990
CITY SLICKERS   Columbia, 1991

VACRA RUSSAL

THE RETURN OF SUPERFLY   Triton Pictures, 1990,
    w/Ida Gearon

SHIRLEY RUSSELL

YANKS   Universal, 1979
AGATHA ★   Warner Bros., 1979
REDS ★   Paramount, 1981
WAGNER (MS)   London Trust Productions/Richard
    Wagner Productions/Ladbroke Productions/
    Hungarofilm, 1983

THE RAZOR'S EDGE   Columbia, 1984
THE RETURN OF THE SOLDIER   European
    Classics, 1985
THE BRIDE   Columbia, 1985
HOPE AND GLORY   Columbia, 1987

VICTORIA RUSSELL

GOTHIC   Vestron, 1987

RITA RYACK

Agent: The Gersh Agency, Inc., Beverly Hills -
    213/274-6611, New York - 212/997-1818

AFTER HOURS   The Geffen Company/Warner
    Bros., 1985
SUSPECT   Tri-Star, 1987
THE HOUSE ON CARROLL STREET   Orion, 1988
CROSSING DELANCEY   Warner Bros., 1988
AN INNOCENT MAN   Buena Vista, 1989
PENN & TELLER GET KILLED   Warner Bros., 1989
CLASS ACTION   20th Century Fox, 1991

CHRISTOPHER RYAN

POLICE ACADEMY   The Ladd Company/Warner
    Bros., 1984
THE FLY II   20th Century Fox, 1989
SHORT TIME   20th Century Fox, 1990

TERRY RYAN

THE YEAR OF LIVING DANGEROUSLY   MGM/UA,
    1983
HEATWAVE   New Line Cinema, 1983
THE COCA COLA KID   Cinecom/Film Gallery, 1985
KANGAROO   Cineplex Odeon, 1987
HIGH TIDE   Tri-Star, 1987

S

ENRICO SABBATINI

Agent: Sandra Marsh Management - Sherman Oaks,
    818/905-6961

A PLACE FOR LOVERS   MGM, 1968
SUNFLOWERS   Avco Embassy, 1969
SACCO AND VANZETTI   UMC, 1971
GIORDANO BRUNO   Champion/Les Films
    Concordia, 1973
MOSES   Avco Embassy, 1976
A SPECIAL DAY   Cinema 5, 1977
JESUS OF NAZARETH (MS)   Sir Lew Grade
    Productions/ITC, 1978
SIDNEY SHELDON'S BLOODLINE   Paramount, 1979
CHRIST STOPPED ON EBOLI   1979
MARCO POLO (MS) ☆☆   RAI/Franco Cristaldi
    Productions/Vincenzo Labella Productions, 1982
A.D. - ANNO DOMINI (MS)   Procter & Gamble
    Productions/International Film Productions, 1985
THE MISSION ★   Warner Bros., 1986
CHRONICLE OF A DEATH FORETOLD   Mediactuel/
    Italmedia/Soprofilms/Focine, 1986
OLD GRINGO   Columbia, 1989

BEVERLY SAFIER
KNIGHTS OF THE CITY   New World, 1986,
    w/Celia Bryant
THE UNHOLY   Vestron, 1988

JACQUELINE SAINT ANNE*
Agent: Susan Grant - Los Angeles, 213/552-1100
Address: 3211 Ocean Front Walk, Marina del Rey, CA
    90291, 213/828-0690

FEAR NO EVIL   Avco Embassy, 1981
CIRCLE OF POWER   Televicine, 1983
FATAL VISION (TF)   NBC Productions, 1984
DUTCH TREAT   Cannon, 1987
GUILTY CONSCIENCE (TF)   Levinson-Link
    Productions/Robert Papazian Productions, 1985
THE NEW ADVENTURES OF PIPPI LONGSTOCKING
    Columbia, 1988
PULSE   Columbia, 1988
LADY IN WHITE   New Century/Vista, 1988

RITA SALAZAR*
Phone: 213/651-5979

COUNTRY   Buena Vista, 1984, w/Tommy Walsh
FAR NORTH   Alive Films, 1989
MUSIC BOX   Carolco Pictures/Tri-Star, 1989

PETER V. SALDUTTI
THE RIVER RAT   Paramount, 1984
PSYCHO III   Universal, 1986, w/Marla Denise Schlom
HARRY AND THE HENDERSONS   Universal, 1987,
    w/Marla Denise Schlom (except "Harry")

NORMAN SALLING*
Phone: 818/769-7004

NICKELODEON   Columbia, 1976, w/Sandra Berke &
    Theodora Van Runkle
HOOPER   Warner Bros., 1978, Supervisor
THE END   United Artists, 1978
SHARKY'S MACHINE   Orion/Warner Bros., 1982
STROKER ACE   Universal, 1983
CANNONBALL RUN II   Warner Bros., 1984
CITY HEAT   Warner Bros., 1984
STICK   Universal, 1985
MALONE   Orion, 1987
HEAT   New Century/Vista, 1987

NILE SAMPLES
A RAGE IN HARLEM   Miramax, 1991

DANA SANCHEZ
DANGEROUSLY CLOSE   Cannon, 1986

VICKI SANCHEZ*
Agent: Judy Copage, The Coppage Company -
    North Hollywood, 818/980-1106

THE FARMER   Columbia, 1977
CHAPTER TWO   Columbia, 1979
OH GOD! BOOK II   Warner Bros., 1980
BLOW OUT   Filmways, 1981
THE BORDER   Universal, 1982
TABLE FOR FIVE   Warner Bros., 1983

ERIC H. SANDBERG
MEMORIES OF ME   MGM/UA, 1988
TURNER & HOOCH   Buena Vista, 1989,
    Supervisor w/Jean Rosone

ARNOLD SCAASI*
Address: 681 Fifth Ave., New York, NY 10022,
    212/755-5105

ON A CLEAR DAY YOU CAN SEE FOREVER
    Paramount, 1970, w/Cecil Beaton
LOVING COUPLES   20th Century Fox, 1980,
    w/Theoni V. Aldredge
KISS ME GOODBYE   20th Century Fox, 1982

DEAHDRA SCARANO
PRINCE OF DARKNESS   Universal, 1987

NICK SCARANO
COLORS   Orion, 1988

TONY SCARANO
MASK   Universal, 1985, Mens

RICHARD SCHISSLER
BLUE STEEL   MGM/UA, 1990

MARLA DENISE SCHLOM
MASK   Universal, 1985, Womens
PSYCHO III   Universal, 1986, w/Peter V. Saldutti
JAWS THE REVENGE   Universal, 1987, w/Hugo Pena
HARRY AND THE HENDERSONS   Universal, 1987,
    w/Peter V. Saldutti (except "Harry")

CAMILE SCHROEDER
MY CHAUFFEUR   Crown International, 1986

CYNTHIA SCHUMACHER
STICKY FINGERS   Spectrafilm, 1988, w/David Norbury

BARBARA SCOTT
Agent: Camera Masters - Venice, 213/306-0810

HUMANOIDS FROM THE DEEP   New World, 1980
TO WILL A MIRACLE (TF)   Dick Clark Productions, 1984
CHILDREN OF THE CORN   New World, 1984
CRIMES OF PASSION   New World, 1984
FREE RIDE   Galaxy International, 1986
BLOOD RED   Hemdale, 1989, Asst. Designer
THE GRAND TOUR (CTF)   HBO Pictures, 1990,
    Asst. Designer

DEBORAH L. SCOTT*
Agent: The Gersh Agency, Inc., Beverly Hills -
    213/274-6611, New York - 212/997-1818

E.T.: THE EXTRATERRESTRIAL   Universal, 1982
BACK TO THE FUTURE   Universal, 1985
ABOUT LAST NIGHT...   Tri-Star, 1986
ARMED AND DANGEROUS   Columbia, 1986
WHO'S THAT GIRL?   Warner Bros., 1987
MOVING   Warner Bros., 1988
COUP DE VILLE   Universal, 1990
EVE OF DESTRUCTION   Orion, 1991
DEFENDING YOUR LIFE   Warner Bros., 1991

ELISABETH SCOTT
BACKSTREET DREAMS   Vidmark Entertainment, 1990

RUTH SECORD
THE LITTLE KIDNAPPERS (CTF)   Resnick/Margellos
    Productions, 1990

Se

CINEMATOGRAPHERS
PRODUCTION
DESIGNERS,
COSTUME
DESIGNERS AND
FILM EDITORS
GUIDE

COSTUME DESIGNERS

Se

CINEMATOGRAPHERS
PRODUCTION
DESIGNERS,
COSTUME
DESIGNERS AND
FILM EDITORS
GUIDE

C
O
S
T
U
M
E

D
E
S
I
G
N
E
R
S

ELIZABETH ANN SELEY
APPRENTICE TO MURDER   New World, 1988
A KILLING AFFAIR   Hemdale, 1988

MAURICE SENDAK
NUTCRACKER   Atlantic Releasing Corporation, 1986

ANNA SENIOR
BREAKER MORANT   New World/Quartet, 1979
MY BRILLIANT CAREER ★   Analysis, 1980

GAYE SHANNON-BURNETT
TO SLEEP WITH ANGER   SVS, 1990

IRENE SHARAFF*
Agent: Gloria Safier - New York, 212/838-4868
Address: 116 E. 66th Street, New York, NY 10021

AN AMERICAN IN PARIS ★★   MGM, 1951,
   w/Orry-Kelly & Walter Plunkett
CALL ME MADAM ★   20th Century Fox, 1953
A STAR IS BORN ★   Warner Bros., 1954,
   w/Jean Louis & Mary Ann Nyberg
BRIGADOON ★   MGM, 1954
GUYS AND DOLLS ★   MGM, 1955
THE KING AND I ★★   20th Century Fox, 1956
PORGY AND BESS ★   Columbia, 1959
CAN-CAN ★   20th Century Fox, 1960
FLOWER DRUM SONG ★   Universal, 1961
WEST SIDE STORY ★★   United Artists, 1961
CLEOPATRA ★★   20th Century Fox, 1963,
   w/Vittorio Nino Novarese & Renie Conley
THE SANDPIPER   MGM, 1965
WHO'S AFRAID OF VIRGINIA WOOLF? ★★   Warner
   Bros., 1966
THE TAMING OF THE SHREW ★   Columbia, 1967,
   w/Danilo Donati
HELLO, DOLLY! ★   20th Century Fox, 1969
JUSTINE   20th Century Fox, 1969
THE OTHER SIDE OF MIDNIGHT ★   20th Century
   Fox, 1977
MOMMIE DEAREST   Paramount, 1981

JIM SHEARON
GRAFFITI BRIDGE   Warner Bros., 1990 w/Helen Hiatt

DODIE SHEPARD*
Address: 1018 N. Kenwood St., Burbank, CA 91505,
   818/846-4287

MARK OF THE DEVIL   Hallmark Releasing
   Corporation, 1970
STRANGE NEW WORLD (TF)   Warner
   Bros. TV, 1975
GUMBALL RALLY   Warner Bros., 1976
LOVE LEADS THE WAY (TF)   Hawkins-Permut
   Productions, 1984
TERRORIST ON TRIAL: THE UNITED STATES OF
   AMERICA VS. SALIM AJAMI (TF)   Eccolo
   Productions, 1988

JUDY SHREWSBURY
MR. FROST   Triumph Releasing, 1990

PAUL SIMMONS
THE WHITE GIRL   Tony Brown Productions, 1990

SHARON SIMONAIRE
SOUL MAN   New World, 1986

PAMELA SKAIST
CHILD'S PLAY 2   Universal, 1990

JERRY N. SKEELS*
Agent: Shapiro-Lichtman, Inc. - Los Angeles,
   213/859-8877
Address: 8411 Melrose Ave., Los Angeles, CA 90069,
   213/651-2546 or 666-4506

SMART ALEC   1986
PENITENTIARY III   Cannon, 1987

PATRICIA SMITH
THE AVIATOR   MGM/UA, 1985

ROBYN SMITH
RIVER OF DEATH   Cannon, 1990

JENNIFER SMITH-ASHLEY
LOVE STREAMS   Cannon, 1984

VAN SMITH
POLYESTER   New Line Cinema, 1981
HAIRSPRAY   New Line Cinema, 1988
CRY-BABY   Universal, 1990

ANNIKA SONEBY
RUSSIAN TERMINATOR   Arena Home Video, 1991

BARBARA SONNEX
LITTLE DORRIT   Cannon, 1988

LUCIANO SOPRANI
WILD ORCHID   Triumph, 1990

ADRIANA SPADARO
HERCULES II   Cannon, 1985
THE ASSISI UNDERGROUND   Cannon, 1985
AFTER THE FALL OF NEW YORK   Almi
   Pictures, 1985
DANCERS   Cannon, 1987, w/Anna Anni &
   Enrico Serafini

JILL SPALDING
DA   Film Dallas, 1988, w/Carol Betera

KATIE SPARKS
CHOPPING MALL   *KILLBOTS*   Concorde,
   1986, Wardrobe
REFORM SCHOOL GIRLS   New World, 1986
MUNCHIES   Concorde, 1987

DENIS SPERDOUKLIS
THE DECLINE OF THE AMERICAN EMPIRE   Cineplex
   Odeon, 1986

NEIL SPISAK
Q & A   Tri-Star, 1990, w/Ann Roth

FRANCA SQUARCIAPINO
CYRANO DE BERGERAC ★★   Orion Classics, 1990

ILENE STARGER
THE BEAST   Columbia, 1988

MARLENE STEWART*
Phone: 213/846-6975

BODY ROCK   New World, 1984
BACK TO THE BEACH   Paramount, 1987
SIESTA   Lorimar, 1987
PET SEMATARY   Paramount, 1989
THE DOORS   Tri-Star, 1991

SANDRA STEWART
Agent: David Barskin, 818/985-2992
Phone: 415/482-0460

BLACULA   American International, 1972
THE AUTOBIOGRAPHY OF MISS JANE
   PITTMAN (TF) ☆☆   Tomorrow
   Entertainment, 1974
LEADBELLY   Paramount, 1976
THE GREATEST   Columbia, 1977
MINSTREL MAN (TF)   Roger Gimbel Productions/
   EMI TV, 1977
CINDY (TF) ☆   John Charles Walters
   Productions, 1978

JANE STILL
HOME IS WHERE THE HART IS   Atlantic Releasing
   Corporation, 1987

MARY KAY STOLZ
THE BIG EASY   Columbia, 1987, Dennis Quaid only
WEEDS   DEG, 1987
GREAT BALLS OF FIRE!   Orion, 1989,
   Dennis Quaid only
THE HOT SPOT   Orion, 1990

MONIQUE STRANAN
WATCHERS   Universal, 1988

RAY SUMMERS
WRONG IS RIGHT   Columbia, 1982
PORKY'S REVENGE   20th Century Fox, 1985
52 PICK-UP   Cannon, 1986
THE FOURTH WAR   New Age Releasing, 1990

JUDY B. SWARTZ
PHANTOM OF THE MALL: ERIC'S REVENGE   Fries
   Entertainment, 1990

ANTHEA SYLBERT
ROSEMARY'S BABY   Paramount, 1968
SHAMPOO   Columbia, 1975
THE HEARTBREAK KID   20th Century Fox, 1972
THE DAY OF THE DOLPHIN   Avco Embassy, 1973
CHINATOWN ★   Paramount, 1974
KING KONG   Paramount, 1976, shared credit
JULIA ★   20th Century Fox, 1977

T

JANE TABACHNIK
STREET HUNTER   DGP Release, 1990

PAM TAIT
ACTT
Agent: Sandra Marsh Management - Sherman Oaks,
   818/905-6961

SID AND NANCY   Samuel Goldwyn Company,
   1986 (Asst.)
STRAIGHT TO HELL   Island Films, 1987
WALKER   Universal, 1987
PASCALI'S ISLAND   Avenue Pictures, 1988
ERIK THE VIKING   Orion, 1989

RON TALSKY*
Agent: Mark Lichtman, Shapiro-Lichtman, Inc. -
   Los Angeles, 213/859-8877
Address: 100 N. Kilkea Dr., Beverly Hills, CA,
   213/655-1950

THE FOUR MUSKETEERS ★   20th Century Fox,
   1975, w/Yvonne Blake
THE DEEP   Columbia, 1977, w/Tom Bronson
HOT LEAD AND COLD FEET   Buena Vista, 1978
RAVAGERS   Columbia, 1979
INSIDE MOVES   AFD, 1980
CHU CHU AND THE PHILLY FLASH   20th Century
   Fox, 1981
THAT CHAMPIONSHIP SEASON   Cannon, 1982
THE BEAR   Embassy, 1984
THAT'S DANCING! (FD)   MGM/UA, 1985
VIETNAM, TEXAS   Epic Productions, 1990

JENNIE TATE
THE GOOD WIFE   Atlantic Releasing Corporation, 1986

ELISABETH TAVERNIER
L'ADDITION   New World, 1985
WAITING FOR THE MOON   Skouras Pictures, 1987

LINA NERLI TAVIANI
DEVIL IN THE FLESH   Orion Classics, 1987
GOOD MORNING, BABYLON   Vestron, 1987

GILDA TEXTER
LET'S GET HARRY   Tri-Star, 1986

WILLIAM WARE THEISS*
West Coast Card
Agent: Smith Gosnell Nicholson & Associates -
   Pacific Palisades, 213/459-0307
Phone: 213/467-5191

THE PINK PANTHER   United Artists, 1964
PRETTY MAIDS ALL IN A ROW   MGM, 1971
HAROLD AND MAUDE   Paramount, 1971
HICKEY AND BOGGS   United Artists, 1972
BOUND FOR GLORY ★   United Artists, 1976

Th

CINEMATOGRAPHERS
PRODUCTION
DESIGNERS,
COSTUME
DESIGNERS AND
FILM EDITORS
GUIDE

C
O
S
T
U
M
E

D
E
S
I
G
N
E
R
S

Th

CINEMATOGRAPHERS
PRODUCTION
DESIGNERS,
COSTUME
DESIGNERS and
FILM EDITORS
GUIDE

**C
O
S
T
U
M
E**

**D
E
S
I
G
N
E
R
S**

WHO'LL STOP THE RAIN   United Artists, 1978
BUTCH AND SUNDANCE: THE EARLY DAYS ★
   20th Century Fox, 1979
GOIN' SOUTH   Paramount, 1979
MR. PATMAN   Film Consortium, 1980
KIDCO   20th Century Fox, 1983
HEART LIKE A WHEEL ★   20th Century Fox, 1983
THE MAN WITH ONE RED SHOE   20th Century
   Fox, 1985

BILL THOMAS
SEVEN THIEVES   20th Century Fox, 1960
THE HAWAIIANS ★   United Artists, 1970
BEDKNOBS AND BROOMSTICKS ★   Buena
   Vista, 1971
THE DEVIL AND MAX DEVLIN   Buena Vista, 1981

JODIE TILLEN*
Agent: Scott Harris, Harris & Goldberg - Los Angeles,
   213/553-5200

LOOKING FOR MR. GOODBAR   Paramount, 1977
CITIZENS BAND   Paramount, 1977
AMERICAN ANTHEM   Columbia, 1986
HAPPY NEW YEAR   Columbia, 1987
NO MAN'S LAND   Orion, 1987
LIGHT OF DAY   Tri-Star, 1987
REAL MEN   MGM/UA, 1987
DEAD BANG   Warner Bros., 1989
LICENCE TO KILL   MGM/UA, 1989
BACKDRAFT   Universal/Imagine Films/Trilogy/Brian
   Grazer, 1991

JOE I. TOMPKINS*
Agent: Larry Mirisch, Triad Artists, Inc. - Los Angeles,
   213/556-2727
Phone: 619/324-7782

ELEANOR AND FRANKLIN (TF)☆☆   ABC Circle
   Films, 1976
ELEANOR AND FRANKLIN: THE WHITE HOUSE
   YEARS (TF) ☆☆   ABC Circle Films, 1977
WHEN YOU COMIN' BACK, RED RYDER?
   Columbia, 1979
COAL MINER'S DAUGHTER   Universal, 1980
FOOLIN' AROUND   Columbia, 1980
TRUE CONFESSIONS   United Artists, 1981
RAGGEDY MAN   Universal, 1981
MISSING   Unviersal, 1982
ROMANTIC COMEDY   MGM/UA, 1983
CROSS CREEK ★   Universal/AFD, 1983
SWING SHIFT   Warner Bros., 1983
THE RIVER   Universal, 1984
IRRECONCILABLE DIFFERENCES   Warner
   Bros., 1984
MURPHY'S ROMANCE   Columbia, 1985
MARIE   MGM/UA, 1985
BIG TROUBLE   Columbia, 1986
HOWARD THE DUCK   Universal, 1986
VIOLETS ARE BLUE   Columbia, 1986
NUTS   Warner Bros., 1987
BETRAYED   MGM/UA, 1988
WEEKEND AT BERNIE'S   20th Century Fox, 1989,
   Costume Consultant
HARLEM NIGHTS ★   Paramount, 1989

PIERO TOSI
DEATH IN VENICE ★   Warner Bros., 1971
LUDWIG ★   MGM, 1973

LA CAGE AUX FOLLES ★   United Artists, 1979
LA TRAVIATA ★   Universal Classics, 1982
LA CAGE AUX FOLLES 3: THE WEDDING   Tri-Star,
   1986, Michel Serrault & Ugo Tognazzi only

TRAVILLA†
(Bill Travilla)
THE ADVENTURES OF DON JUAN ★★   Warner Bros.,
   1949, w/Marjorie Brest & Leah Rhodes
THERE'S NO BUSINESS LIKE SHOW BUSINESS ★
   20th Century Fox, 1954, w/Charles LeMaire &
   Miles White
HOW TO MARRY A MILLIONAIRE ★   20th Century Fox,
   1953, w/Charles LeMaire
THE STRIPPER ★   20th Century Fox, 1963
MOVIOLA (MS) ☆☆   David L. Wolper-Stan Margulies
   Productions/Warner Bros. TV, 1980
EVITA PERON (TF) ☆☆   Hartwest Productions/Zephyr
   Productions, 1981
JACQUELINE BOUVIER KENNEDY (TF) ☆☆   ABC Circle
   Films, 1981
THE THORN BIRDS (MS) ☆   David L. Wolper-Stan
   Margulies Productions/Edward Lewis Productions/
   Warner Bros. TV, 1983
MY WICKED, WICKED WAYS: THE LEGEND OF ERROL
   FLYNN (TF)   CBS Entertainment, 1984
A STREETCAR NAMED DESIRE (TF) ☆   Keith Barish
   Productions, 1984

UTE TRUTHMANN
THE NASTY GIRL   Miramax Films, 1990

ROBERT TURTURICE*
Agent: Judy Coppage, The Coppage Company - North
   Hollywood, 818/980-1106

UP THE CREEK   Orion, 1983
BLOOD FEUD (TF)   20th Century Fox TV/Glickman-
   Selznick Productions, 1983
MY MOTHER'S SECRET LIFE (TF)   Furia-Oringer
   Productions/ABC Circle Films, 1984
COPACABANA (TF)   Dick Clark Cinema Productions/
   Stiletto Ltd., 1985
LIKE FATHER LIKE SON   Tri-Star, 1987
CLEAN AND SOBER   Warner Bros., 1988
BIG TOP PEE-WEE   Paramount, 1988
SOLAR CRISIS   Shochiku-Fuji, 1990

ALEXANDRA TYNAN
DEATH OF A SOLDIER   Scotti Bros., 1986

TRACY TYNAN*
Agent: Lawrence A. Mirisch, Triad Artists, Inc. -
   Los Angeles, 213/556-2727

SHATTERED VOWS (TF)   Bertinelli-Pequod
   Productions, 1984
CHOOSE ME   Island/Alive, 1984
STRANGER'S KISS   Orion Classics, 1984
FRATERNITY VACATION   New World, 1985
THAT'S LIFE   Columbia, 1986
BLIND DATE   Tri-Star, 1987
THE BIG EASY   Columbia, 1987
TROUBLE IN MIND   Island/Alive, 1987
SLEDEHAMMER (Pilot)   1987

GLORY DAYS   Paramount, 1988
PLAIN CLOTHES   Paramount, 1988
PERMANENT RECORD   Paramount, 1988
GREAT BALLS OF FIRE!   Orion, 1989
WARM NIGHTS ON A SLOW MOVING TRAIN
     Miramax Fims, 1989

JAMES W. TYSON
TOP GUN   Paramount, 1986
THE HUNT FOR RED OCTOBER   Paramount, 1990

U

JEFFREY ULLMAN
MY DINNER WITH ANDRE   New Yorker, 1981
SIGNS OF LIFE   Avenue Pictures, 1989

PATTI UNGER
EQUUS   United Artists, 1977, w/Brenda Dabbs &
     Tony Walton
HIGHPOINT   New World, 1984
TERMINAL CHOICE   Almi Pictures, 1985

V

MARILYN VANCE-STRAKER
Phone: 213/464-5232

FAST TIMES AT RIDGEMONT HIGH   Universal, 1982
48HRS.   Paramount, 1982
JEKYLL AND HYDE...TOGETHER AGAIN
     Paramount, 1982
STREETS OF FIRE   Universal, 1984
THE WILD LIFE   Universal, 1984
ROMANCING THE STONE   20th Century Fox, 1984
WEIRD SCIENCE   Universal, 1985
BREWSTER'S MILLIONS   Universal, 1985
THE BREAKFAST CLUB   Universal, 1985
PRETTY IN PINK   Paramount, 1986
FERRIS BUELLER'S DAY OFF   Paramount, 1986
JO JO DANCER, YOUR LIFE IS CALLING
     Columbia, 1986
PREDATOR   20th Century Fox, 1987
SOME KIND OF WONDERFUL   Paramount, 1987
THE UNTOUCHABLES ★★   Paramount, 1987,
     except Robert De Niro
THROW MOMMA FROM THE TRAIN   Orion, 1987
CROSS MY HEART   Universal, 1987
DIE HARD   20th Century Fox, 1988
THE GREAT OUTDOORS   Universal, 1988
ACTION JACKSON   Lorimar, 1988
ROAD HOUSE   MGM/UA, 1989
UNCLE BUCK   Universal, 1989
THE PACKAGE   Orion, 1989
LITTLE MONSTERS   MGM/UA, 1989

PRETTY WOMAN   *3000*   Buena Vista, 1990
THE LAST OF THE FINEST   Orion, 1990
THE FIRST POWER   Orion, 1990, Wardrobe Consultant
THE ADVENTURES OF FORD FAIRLANE   20th
     Century Fox, 1990
DIE HARD 2   20th Century Fox, 1990
PREDATOR 2   20th Century Fox, 1990

THEADORA VAN RUNKLE*
Agent: Randy Clark, 213/465-7140
Address: 8805 Lookout Mountain Rd., Los Angeles, CA
     90046, 213/654-5523

BONNIE AND CLYDE ★   Warner Bros., 1967
THE THOMAS CROWN AFFAIR   United Artists, 1968
THE REIVERS   National General, 1969
MAME   Warner Bros., 1974
THE GODFATHER - PART II ★   Paramount, 1974
NICKELODEON   Columbia, 1976, w/Sandra Berke &
     Norman Salling
NEW YORK, NEW YORK   United Artists, 1977
SAME TIME, NEXT YEAR   Universal, 1978
THE JERK   Universal, 1979
S.O.B.   Paramount, 1981
THE BEST LITTLE WHOREHOUSE IN TEXAS
     Universal, 1982
RHINESTONE   20th Century Fox, 1984,
     Dolly Parton only
PEGGY SUE GOT MARRIED ★   Tri-Star, 1986
EVERYBODY'S ALL-AMERICAN   Warner Bros., 1988
TROOP BEVERLY HILLS   WEG, 1989
STELLA   Buena Vista, 1990

ISABELLA VAN SOEST CHUBB
BORN IN EAST L.A.   Universal, 1987
FEDS   Warner Bros., 1988
WAITING FOR THE LIGHT   Epic, 1990

SYLVIA VEGA-VASQUEZ
LA BAMBA   Columbia, 1987
FACE OF THE ENEMY   Tri-Culture Pictures, 1990

EDITH VESPERINI
HANNA K.   Universal, 1983

GAIL VIOLA*
Phone: 213/851-1402

THE STONE BOY   TLC Films/20th Century Fox, 1984
THE BOYS NEXT DOOR   New World, 1985
THE SUPERNATURALS   Republic Entertainment/
     Sandy Howard Productions, 1985
FLYING BLIND   Columbia, 1988

MARY E. VOGT*
Agent: The Gersh Agency, Inc., Beverly Hills -
     213/274-6611, New York - 212/997-1818

SECRET ADMIRER   Orion, 1985
SHORT CIRCUIT   Tri-Star, 1986
STAKEOUT   Buena Vista, 1987
PROJECT X   20th Century Fox, 1987
THE NAKED GUN   Paramount, 1988
SHAG: THE MOVIE   Hemdale, 1989
CRAZY PEOPLE   Paramount, 1990
THE HARD WAY   Universal, 1991
ONLY THE LONELY   20th Century Fox, 1991
ONLY THE LONELY   29th Century Fox, 1991
THE HARD WAY   Universal Pictures, 1991

Vo

CINEMATOGRAPHERS
PRODUCTION
DESIGNERS,
COSTUME
DESIGNERS AND
FILM EDITORS
GUIDE

COSTUME DESIGNERS

CINEMATOGRAPHERS
PRODUCTION
DESIGNERS,
COSTUME
DESIGNERS AND
FILM EDITORS
GUIDE

PATRIZIA VON BRANDENSTEIN
SATURDAY NIGHT FEVER   Paramount, 1977
A LITTLE SEX   Universal, 1982

RICHARD VON ERNST
Agent: The Doug Apatow Agency, 10559 Blythe Ave.,
   Los Angeles, CA 90064, 213/202-6888

COCKTAIL   Buena Vista, 1988 (Asst.)
YOUNG GUNS   20th Century Fox, 1988 (Asst.)
BLACK RAIN   Paramount, 1989 (Asst.)
THE LINGUINI INCIDENT   1991

JENNIFER VON MAYRHAUSER
Agent: The Gersh Agency, Inc., Beverly Hills -
   213/274-6611, New York - 212/997-1818

MYSTIC PIZZA   Samuel Goldwyn Company, 1988
LEAN ON ME   Warner Bros., 1989

ISABELLA VON SOEST CHUBB
MARKED FOR DEATH   20th Century Fox, 1990

MARIK VOS
CRIES AND WHISPERS ★   New World, 1973
FANNY AND ALEXANDER ★★   Embassy, 1983

EMI WADA
RAN ★★   Orion Classics, 1985
AKIRA KUROSAWA'S DREAMS   Warner Bros., 1990

ANN WALLACE
THAT WAS THEN, THIS IS NOW   Paramount, 1985

ROSALIE WALLACE
NUMBER ONE WITH A BULLET   Cannon, 1987

ELIZABETH WALLER
ACTT
Agent: Sandra Marsh Management - Sherman Oaks,
   818/905-6961

FOR YOUR EYES ONLY   United Artists, 1981
THE COMPANY OF WOLVES   Cannon, 1984
REILLY - ACE OF SPIES (MS)   Euston Films
   Ltd., 1984
HITLER'S S.S.: PORTRAIT IN EVIL (TF)   Colason
   Limited Productions/Edgar J. Scherick
   Associates, 1985
JOHN & YOKO - A LOVE STORY (TF)   Carson
   Production Group, 1985
TURTLE DIARY   Samuel Goldwyn Company, 1986
THE LONELY PASSION OF JUDITH HEARNE   Island
   Pictures, 1987

INTIMATE CONTACT (MS)   Zenith Productions/
   Central TV, 1987
WILT   LWT/Talkback, 1989
PARIS BY NIGHT   Cineplex Odeon, 1990

TONY WALTON
FARENHEIT 451   Universal, 1967, Consultant
MURDER ON THE ORIENT EXPRESS ★
   Paramount, 1974
EQUUS   United Artists, 1977, w/Brenda Dabbs &
   Patti Unger
THE WIZ ★   Universal, 1978
DEATHTRAP   Warner Bros., 1982
THE GLASS MENAGERIE   Cineplex Odeon, 1987

LINDA WAYNE*
Agent: Kevin Huvane - New York, 212/903-1182
Address: 10 W. 66th St., New York, NY 10023,
   212/362-3133

TURK 182   20th Century Fox, 1985

HEIDI WEBER
THE NEVERENDING STORY II: THE NEXT CHAPTER
   Warner Bros., 1990

ROBERTA WEINER*
THE INCREDIBLE SHRINKING WOMAN
   Universal, 1981
PANDEMONIUM   MGM/UA, 1982
D.C. CAB   Universal, 1983

BARBARA WEISS*
Agent: Pat Little, Camera Masters - Los Angeles,
   213/306-0810
Address: 299 Riverside Dr., New York, NY 10025,
   212/666-5532

THE QUICK AND THE DEAD (CTF)   Ace Nomination/
   HBO Pictures/Joseph Cates Company, 1987
LEMON SKY (TF)   American Playhouse, 1988
NORMAN'S CORNER   (Pilot)
HEART   New World, 1987
THE LASER MAN   1990

JULIE WEISS*
Agent: The Gersh Agency, Inc., Beverly Hills -
   213/274-6611, New York - 212/997-1818

THE GANGSTER CHRONICLES (TF)   Universal
   TV, 1981
THE ELEPHANT MAN (TF) ☆   1981
LITTLE GLORIA...HAPPY AT LAST (TF) ☆☆
   Edgar J. Scherick Associates/Metromedia
   Producers Corporation, 1982
I'M DANCING AS FAST AS I CAN   Paramount, 1982
INDEPENDENCE DAY   Warner Bros., 1983
TESTAMENT   Paramount, 1983
SECOND THOUGHTS   Universal, 1983
SPACEHUNTER: ADVENTURES IN THE FORBIDDEN
   ZONE   Columbia, 1983
THE DOLLMAKER (TF) ☆☆   Finnegan Associates/IPC
   Films, Inc./Dollmaker Productions, 1984
DO YOU REMEMBER LOVE (TF)   CBS
   Entertainment, 1985
EVERGREEN (MS) ☆   Edgar J. Scherick Associates/
   Metromedia Producers Corporation, 1985
F/X   Orion, 1986

CONSPIRACY OF LOVE (TF)   New World TV, 1987
THE WHALES OF AUGUST   Alive Films, 1987,
    Bette Davis only
MASTERS OF THE UNIVERSE   Cannon, 1987
CHERRY 2000   Orion, 1988, Consultant
1969   Atlantic Releasing Corporation, 1988
TEQUILA SUNRISE   Warner Bros., 1988
WICKED STEPMOTHER   MGM/UA, 1989,
    Bette Davis only
STEEL MAGNOLIAS   Tri-Star, 1989
THE FRESHMAN   Tri-Star, 1990

BELINDA WELLS
NICE GIRLS DON'T EXPLODE   New World, 1987

LARRY WELLS
PORKY'S   20th Century Fox, 1982, w/Mary McLeod
STRANGE BREW   MGM/UA, 1983
THREE MEN AND A BABY   Buena Vista, 1987
SHORT CIRCUIT 2   Tri-Star, 1988

SUE WHALL
MURDER ON LINE ONE   Academy
    Entertainment, 1990

DELPHINE WHITE
VIDEODROME   Universal, 1983

DEIRDRE WILLIAMS
ALAMO BAY   Tri-Star, 1985

GRAHAM WILLIAMS
NATIONAL LAMPOON'S EUROPEAN VACATION
    Warner Bros., 1985

LESLIE WILSHIRE
STEELE JUSTICE   Atlantic Releasing
    Corporation, 1987

MARY ELLEN WINSTON
WHERE ARE THE CHILDREN?   Columbia, 1986
HERO AND THE TERROR   Cannon, 1988

PAKI WOLFE*
Address: 113 31st St., Manhattan Beach, CA
    90266, 213/546-2704

THE KARATE KID PART II   Columbia, 1986,
    (Asst. to Mary Malin)
LETHAL WEAPON   Warner Bros., 1987,
    (Asst. to Mary Malin)
THE RESCUE   Buena Vista, 1988,
    (Asst. to Mary Malin)

ALBERT WOLSKY*
Address: 11444 Decente Court, Studio City, CA
    91604, 818/766-5058 or 212/362-3103

THE TURNING POINT   20th Century Fox, 1977,
    w/Tony Faso & Jennifer Parsons
THIEVES   Paramount, 1977
AN UNMARRIED WOMAN   20th Century Fox, 1978
MOMENT BY MOMENT   Universal, 1978
FINGERS   Brut Productions, 1978
GREASE   Paramount, 1978
ALL THAT JAZZ ★★   20th Century Fox, 1979
MANHATTAN   United Artists, 1979

THE JAZZ SINGER   AFD, 1980
PATERNITY   Paramount, 1981
TEMPEST   Columbia, 1982
STILL OF THE NIGHT   MGM/UA, 1982
SOPHIE'S CHOICE ★   Universal/AFD, 1982
STAR 80   The Ladd Company/Warner Bros., 1983
TO BE OR NOT TO BE   20th Century Fox, 1983
MOSCOW ON THE HUDSON   Columbia, 1984
THE FALCON AND THE SNOWMAN   Orion, 1985
THE JOURNEY OF NATTY GANN ★   Buena Vista, 1985
LEGAL EAGLES   Universal, 1986, w/Gail Bixby &
    Bernie Pollack
DOWN AND OUT IN BEVERLY HILLS   Buena
    Vista, 1986
CRIMES OF THE HEART   DEG, 1986
NADINE   Tri-Star, 1987
MOON OVER PARADOR   Universal, 1988
CHANCES ARE   Tri-Star, 1989
COOKIE   Warner Bros., 1989
SHE-DEVIL   Orion, 1989
ENEMIES, A LOVE STORY   20th Century Fox, 1989
SCENES FROM A MALL   Buena Vista, 1991
BUGSY ·1992   ✗ ✗

CAROL WOOD
Phone: 212/777-4103

DOWN BY LAW   Island Pictures, 1986
THE PRINCE OF PENNSYLVANIA   New Line
    Cinema, 1988
TWISTER   Vestron, 1989
COLD FEET   Avenue Pictures, 1989
MYSTERY TRAIN   1990
DON'T TELL HER IT'S ME   THE BOYFRIEND SCHOOL
    Hemdale, 1990
DROP DEAD FRED   New Line Cinema, 1991

DURINDA RICE WOOD*
East & West Coast Cards
Agent: Smith Gosnell Nicholson & Associates -
    Pacific Palisades, 213/459-0307

BATTLE BEYOND THE STARS   New World, 1979
TAKE THIS JOB AND SHOVE IT   Avco Embassy, 1981
THE KID FROM NOT-SO-BIG   1982
MARIA'S LOVERS   Cannon, 1984
THE SURE THING   Embassy, 1985
BACK TO SCHOOL   Orion, 1986
MY FATHER, MY SON (TF)   Fred Weintraub
    Productions, 1988
THE SEVENTH SIGN   Tri-Star, 1988
A TIME OF DESTINY   Columbia, 1988
LISTEN TO ME   WEG, 1989
ANIMAL BEHAVIOR   Millimeter Films, 1989
SIBLING RIVALRY   Columbia, 1990

YVONNE WOOD
ZOOT SUIT   Universal, 1982

CATHERINE WOOTEN
EXPLORERS   Paramount, 1985

GLENN WRIGHT
THE EIGER SANCTION   Universal, 1974, Supervisor
THE ENFORCER   Warner Bros., 1976
THE GAUNTLET   Warner Bros., 1977
EVERY WHICH WAY BUT LOOSE   Warner Bros., 1978
ANY WHICH WAY YOU CAN   Warner Bros., 1980
TIGHTROPE   Warner Bros., 1984
PALE RIDER   Warner Bros., 1985

Wr

CINEMATOGRAPHERS
PRODUCTION
DESIGNERS,
COSTUME
DESIGNERS AND
FILM EDITORS
GUIDE

C
O
S
T
U
M
E

D
E
S
I
G
N
E
R
S

Wr

CINEMATOGRAPHERS
PRODUCTION
DESIGNERS,
COSTUME
DESIGNERS and
FILM EDITORS
GUIDE

C
O
S
T
U
M
E

D
E
S
I
G
N
E
R
S

HEARTBREAK RIDGE   Warner Bros.,
   1986, Supervisor
RATBOY   Warner Bros., 1986, w/Darryl Athons &
   Deborah Ann Hopper
THE DEAD POOL   Warner Bros., 1988
BIRD   Warner Bros., 1988

HILARY WRIGHT*

Agent: Scott Harris/Steve Lovitt, Harris & Goldberg -
   Los Angeles, 213/553-5200
Phone: 213/469-3667

THE TERMINATOR   Orion, 1984
EL NORTE   Cinecom/Island Alive, 1984
CRITTERS   New Line Cinema, 1985
NATIVE SON   Cinecom, 1986
THREE FOR THE ROAD   New Century/Vista, 1987
LICENSE TO DRIVE   20th Century Fox, 1988
SPLIT DECISIONS   New Century/Vista, 1988

Y

SUSAN YELLAND

THE PRISONER OF ZENDA   Universal, 1979
SUPERMAN II   Warner Bros., 1981, w/Yvonne Blake
KIPPERBANG   MGM/UA Classics, 1984
WINTER FLIGHT   Cinecom, 1984
THE TWO MRS. GRENVILLES (TF) ☆   Lorimar-
   Telepictures, 1987, w/Donald Brooks & Nolan Miller
NUNS ON THE RUN   20th Century Fox, 1990

JO YNOCENCIO*

Address: 302 E. 88th St., New York, NY 10128,
   212/348-5332

PANIC IN NEEDLE PARK   20th Century Fox, 1971
SCARECROW   Warner Bros., 1973
THE SEDUCTION OF JOE TYNAN   Universal, 1979
HONEYSUCKLE ROSE   Warner Bros., 1980
FIRST AFFAIR (TF)   CBS Entertainment, 1983
NO SMALL AFFAIR   Columbia, 1984
MISUNDERSTOOD   MGM/UA, 1984
AS SUMMERS DIE (CTF)   HBO Premiere Films/
   Chris-Rose Productions/Baldwin/Aldrich
   Productions/Lorimar-Telepictures
   Productions, 1986
STREET SMART   Cannon, 1987

Z

ARLENE J. ZAMIARA

Phone: 818/985-5943

DOIN' TIME   The Ladd Company/Warner Bros., 1984

ELSA ZAMPARELLI

DANCES WITH WOLVES ★   Orion, 1990

PAUL ZASTUPNEVICH*

Address: Penthouse, 4237-39 Dixie Canyon Ave.,
   Sherman Oaks, CA 91423, 818/954-1321 or
   818/784-4195

THE POSEIDON ADVENTURE ★   20th Century
   Fox, 1972
THE TOWERING INFERNO   20th Century Fox, 1974
THE SWARM ★   Warner Bros., 1978
BEYOND THE POSEIDON ADVENTURE   Warner
   Bros., 1979
WHEN TIME RAN OUT ★   Warner Bros., 1980
THE MEMORY OF EVA RYKER (TF)   Irwin Allen
   Productions, 1980
CODE RED (TF)   Irwin Allen Productions/Columbia
   TV, 1981
OUTRAGE! (TF)   Irwin Allen Productions/Columbia
   TV, 1986

JEAN ZAY

CODE NAME: EMERALD   MGM/UA, 1985

KRISTI ZEA*

Agent: Judy Scott-Fox, William Morris Agency -
   Beverly Hills, 213/274-7451

FAME   MGM/United Artists, 1980
ENDLESS LOVE   Universal, 1981
SHOOT THE MOON   MGM/United Artists, 1982
EXPOSED   MGM/UA, 1983
TERMS OF ENDEARMENT   20th Century Fox, 1983
LOVESICK   Warner Bros., 1983
UNFAITHFULLY YOURS   20th Century Fox, 1983
BEST DEFENSE   Paramount, 1984
BIRDY   Tri-Star, 1984
SILVERADO   Columbia, 1985

PATRICIA ZIPPRODT*

Address: 29 King St. PH-C, New York, NY 10014

THE GRADUATE   Avco Embassy, 1967
1776   Columbia, 1972
THE GLASS MENAGERIE (TF)   Talent Associates, 1973

INGRID ZORE

JUDGMENT IN BERLIN   New Line Cinema, 1988

FRANCA ZUCHELLI

FRANKENSTEIN UNBOUND   20th Century Fox, 1990

★ ★ ★ ★

FILM EDITORS

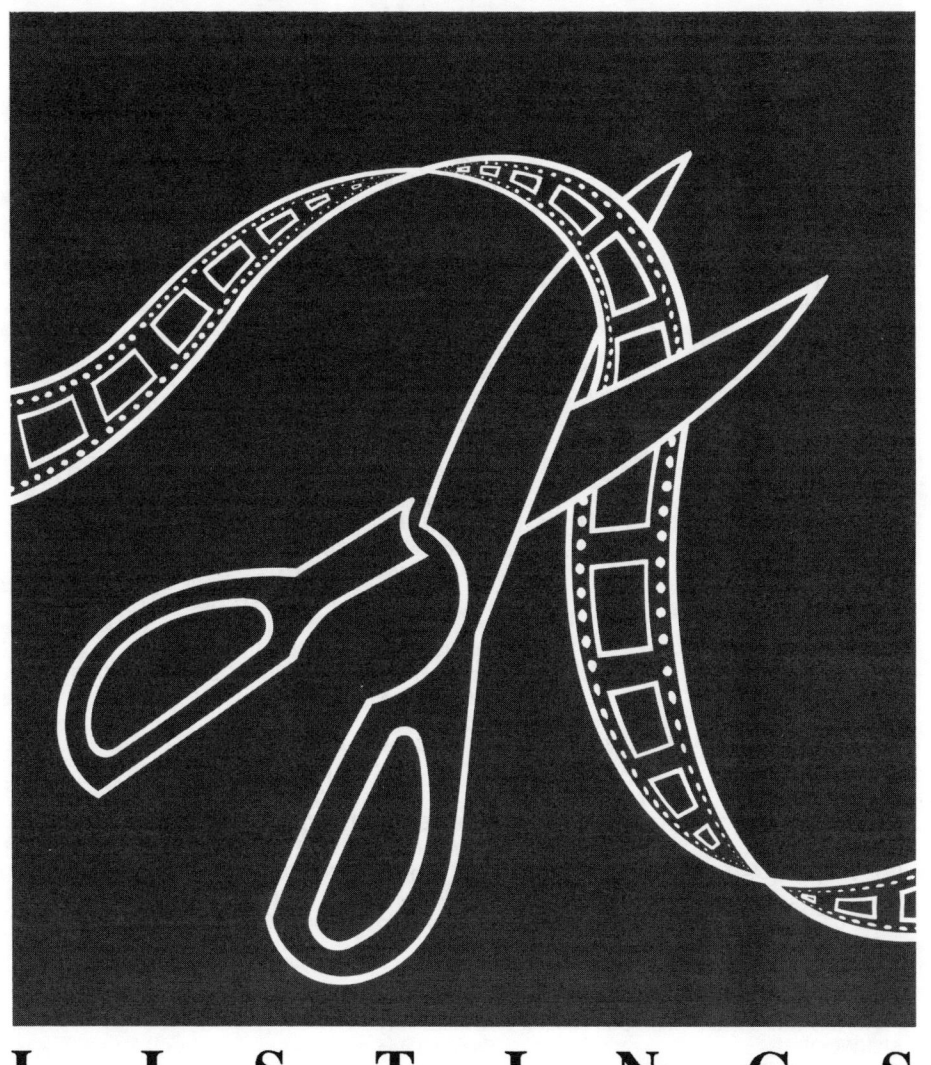

LISTINGS

CINEMATOGRAPHERS
PRODUCTION
DESIGNERS,
COSTUME
DESIGNERS AND
FILM EDITORS
GUIDE

F
I
L
M

E
D
I
T
O
R
S

FILM EDITORS
ACADEMY AWARDS AND NOMINATIONS
1977-1990

★★ = denotes winner in the category

1977
CLOSE ENCOUNTERS OF
  THE THIRD KIND .... Michael Kahn
JULIA .... Walter Murch & Marcel Durham
SMOKEY AND THE
  BANDIT .... Walter Hannemann & Angelo Ross
STAR WARS .... Paul Hirsch, Marcia Lucas &
                                        Richard Chew ★★
THE TURNING POINT .... William Reynolds

1978
COMING HOME .... Don Zimmerman
MIDNIGHT EXPRESS .... Gerry Hambling
SUPERMAN .... Stuart Baird
THE BOYS FROM BRAZIL .... Robert W. Swink
THE DEER HUNTER .... Peter Zinner ★★

1979
ALL THAT JAZZ .... Alan Heim ★★
APOCALYPSE NOW .... Richard Marks, Walter Murch,
              Gerald B. Greenberg & Lisa Fruchtman
KRAMER VS. KRAMER .... Jerry Greenberg
THE BLACK STALLION .... Robert Dalva
THE ROSE .... Robert L. Wolfe & C.Timothy O'Meara

1980
COAL MINER'S DAUGHTER .... Arthur Schmidt
FAME .... Gerry Hambling
RAGING BULL .... Thelma Schoonmaker ★★
THE COMPETITION .... David Blewitt
THE ELEPHANT MAN .... Anne V. Coates

1981
CHARIOTS OF FIRE .... Terry Rawlings
ON GOLDEN POND .... Robert L. Wolfe
RAIDERS OF THE LOST ARK .... Michael Kahn ★★
REDS .... Dede Allen & Craig McKay
THE FRENCH LIEUTENANT'S WOMAN .... John Bloom

1982
AN OFFICER AND A GENTLEMAN .... Peter Zinner
DAS BOOT .... Hannes Nikel
E.T. THE EXTRA-TERRESTRIAL .... Carol Littelton
GANDHI .... John Bloom ★★
TOOTSIE .... Frederic Steinkamp & William Steinkamp

1983
BLUE THUNDER .... Frank Morriss & Edward Abroms
FLASHDANCE .... Bud Smith & Walt Mulconery
SILKWOOD .... Sam O'Steen
TERMS OF ENDEARMENT .... Richard Marks
THE RIGHT STUFF .... Glenn Farr, Lisa Fruchtman,
              Stephen A. Rotter, Douglas Stewart & Tom Rolf ★★

1984
A PASSAGE TO INDIA .... David Lean
AMADEUS .... Nena Danevic & Michael Chandler
ROMANCING
  THE STONE .... Donn Cambern & Frank Morriss
THE COTTON CLUB .... Barry Malkin & Robert Q. Lovett
THE KILLING FIELDS .... Jim Clark ★★

1985
A CHORUS LINE .... John Bloom
OUT OF AFRICA .... Fredric Steinkamp, William
              Steinkamp, Pembroke Herring & Sheldon Kahn
PRIZZI'S HONOR .... Rudi Fehr & Kaja Fehr
RUNAWAY TRAIN .... Henry Richardson
WITNESS .... Thom Noble ★★

1986
ALIENS .... Ray Lovejoy
HANNAH AND HER SISTERS .... Susan E. Morse
PLATOON .... Claire Simpson ★★
THE MISSION .... Jim Clark
TOP GUN .... Billy Weber & Chris Lebenzon

1987
BROADCAST NEWS .... Richard Marks
EMPIRE OF THE SUN .... Michael Kahn
FATAL ATTRACTION .... Michael Kahn & Peter E. Berger
ROBOCOP .... Frank J. Urioste
THE LAST EMPEROR .... Gabriella Cristiani ★★

1988
DIE HARD .... Frank J. Urioste and John F. Link
MISSISSIPPI BURNING .... Gerry Hambling
RAINMAN .... Stu Linder
WHO FRAMED ROGER RABBIT? .... Arthur Schmidt ★★
GORILLAS IN THE MIST .... Stuart Baird

1989
THE BEAR .... Noelle Boisson
BORN ON THE FOURTH
  OF JULY .... David Brenner & Joe Hutshing ★★
DRIVING MISS DAISY .... Mark Roy Warner
THE FABULOUS BAKER BOYS .... William Steinkamp
GLORY .... Steven J. Rosenblum

1990
DANCES WITH WOLVES .... Neil Travis ★★
GHOST .... Walter Murch
THE GODFATHER
  PART III ...... Lisa Fruchtman, Barry Malkin & Walter Murch
GOODFELLAS .... Thelma Schoonmaker
THE HUNT FOR RED
  OCTOBER .... Dennis M. Virkler & John Wright

★★★★

A

EDWARD M. ABROMS, ACE
Agent: Triad Artists, Inc. - Los Angeles, 213/556-2727
Address: 866 Marlowe Street, Thousand Oaks, CA 91360

THE GROUNDSTAR CONSPIRACY   Universal, 1972
YOU'LL LIKE MY MOTHER   Universal, 1972
THE SUGARLAND EXPRESS   Universal, 1974
BLUE THUNDER ★   Columbia, 1983, w/Frank Morriss
THE OSTERMAN WEEKEND   20th Century Fox,
   1983, w/David Rawlins
CHERRY 2000   Orion, 1988, w/Duwayne Dunham
PLAIN CLOTHES   Paramount, 1988,
   w/Patrick Kennedy
GLORY DAYS   Paramount, 1988
COHEN & TATE   Nelson Entertainment, 1989
CRASH: THE MYSTERY OF FLIGHT 1501 (TF)
   Schaefer-Karpf Productions, 1990

SANDRA ADAIR
THE TELEPHONE   New World, 1988

JOHN ADAMS
DEATHSTALKER   New World, 1984, w/Silvia Ripoli

DIANE ADLER
FORBIDDEN NIGHTS (TF)   Tristine Rainer
   Productions, 1989, w/Parke Singh

STEPHEN ADRIANSON
FROM HOLLYWOOD TO DEADWOOD   Island,
   1989 w/Robert Erickson
THE BIG ONE: THE GREAT LOS ANGELES
   EARTHQUAKES-PARTS I & II (MS)   von
   Zerneck-Sertner Films, 1990, w/Gregory Prange

GEORGE AKERS
Agent: London Management, 235/241 Regent St. -
   London W1R 7AG, 071-493-1610

CARAVAGGIO   Cinevista, 1986
WISH YOU WERE HERE   Atlantic Releasing
   Corporation, 1987
PERSONAL SERVICES   Vestron, 1987
ERIK THE VIKING   Orion, 1989
PARIS BY NIGHT   Cineplex Odeon, 1990
THE BIG MAN   1991

CAROLLE ALAIN
WATCHERS   Universal, 1988, w/Bill Freda

ROSS ALBERT
Agent: Jay Gilbert Talent Agency - Los Angeles,
   213/656-5906

SUBURBIA   New Horizons, 1984
WANTED DEAD OR ALIVE   New World, 1986
BLUE CITY   Paramount, 1986
POLTERGEIST III   MGM/UA, 1988

LISA   MGM/UA, 1990
AFTER THE SHOCK (CTF)   Wilshire Court
   Productions, 1990
MURDEROUS VISION (CTF)   Wilshire Court
   Productions, 1991

ERIC ALBERTSON
INDEPENDENCE   20th Century Fox, 1976
SUNNYSIDE   American International, 1979, SE
THE FIRST DEADLY SIN   Filmways, 1980
TOO FAR TO GO   Zoetrope, 1982
KILLER PARTY   MGM/UA, 1986
CHEETAH   Buena Vista, 1989

MAURO ALICE
KISS OF THE SPIDER WOMAN   Island Alive, 1985

DEDE ALLEN, ACE
Agent: Bauer Benedek Agency - Los Angeles,
   212/275-2421

AMERICA AMERICA   Warner Bros., 1963
BONNIE AND CLYDE   Warner Bros., 1967
RACHEL, RACHEL   Warner Bros., 1968
ALICE'S RESTAURANT   United Artists, 1969
LITTLE BIG MAN   National General, 1970
SERPICO   Paramount, 1973
DOG DAY AFTERNOON ★   Warner Bros., 1975
NIGHT MOVES   Warner Bros., 1975
THE MISSOURI BREAKS   United Artists, 1976,
   w/Jerry Greenberg & Stephen A. Rotter
SLAP SHOT   Universal, 1977
THE WIZ   Universal, 1978
REDS ★   Paramount, 1981, w/Craig McKay
HARRY & SON   Orion, 1984
MIKE'S MURDER   The Ladd Company/Warner Bros.,
   1984, w/Jeff Gourson
THE BREAKFAST CLUB   Universal, 1985
OFF BEAT   Buena Vista, 1986, w/Angelo Corrao
THE MILAGRO BEANFIELD WAR   Universal, 1988,
   w/Jim Miller
LET IT RIDE   Paramount, 1989, w/Jim Miller
HENRY & JUNE   Universal, 1990, w/Vivien Hillgrove
   Gilliam & William Scharf

STANFORD C. ALLEN
TAKE A HARD RIDE   20th Century Fox, 1974
ZARDOZ   20th Century Fox, 1974
THE BLUE BIRD   20th Century Fox, 1976,
   w/Tatyana Shapiro & Ernest Walter
SILENT MOVIE   20th Century Fox, 1976,
   w/John C. Howard
RABBIT TEST   Avco Embassy, 1978
THE HOLLYWOOD KNIGHTS   Columbia, 1980,
   w/Scott Conrad
THE FIFTH FLOOR   Film Ventures International, 1980
MORTUARY   Film Ventures, 1983
DOIN' TIME   Warner Bros., 1986
THE NIGHT STALKER   Almi Pictures, 1987
ROOTS: THE GIFT (TF)   David L. Wolper Productions/
   Warner Bros. TV, 1988

RON AMICK
ROLLER BLADE   New World, 1986

MICHAEL F. ANDERSON, ACE
HUCKLEBERRY FINN   UA, 1973
THE REINCARNATION OF PETER PROUD   Bing Crosby
   Productions, 1974

An

CINEMATOGRAPHERS
PRODUCTION
DESIGNERS,
COSTUME
DESIGNERS AND
FILM EDITORS
GUIDE

F
I
L
M

E
D
I
T
O
R
S

An

CINEMATOGRAPHERS
PRODUCTION
DESIGNERS,
COSTUME
DESIGNERS and
FILM EDITORS
GUIDE

F
I
L
M

E
D
I
T
O
R
S

ECHOES OF A SUMMER   Sandy Howard
   Productions, 1975
ST. IVES   Warner Bros., 1976
THE WHITE BUFFALO   United Artists, 1977
LOVE AND BULLETS   AFD, 1979
CABOBLANCO   Avco Embassy, 1981
SPHINX   Orion/Warner Bros., 1981, w/Robert F. Swink
YES, GIORGIO   MGM/UA, 1982
HOSTAGE (TF)   CBS Entertainment, 1987
BROKEN ANGEL (TF)   MGM Television, 1988
THE LITTLEST VICTIMS (TF)   CBS
   Entertainment, 1989
PANCHO BARNES (TF)   Blue Andre Productions/
   Orion Television, 1989, w/Michael Eliot
TO MY DAUGHTER (TF)   Zacs Productions/Nugget
   Entertainment, 1990

WILLIAM A. ANDERSON
NEVER TOO YOUNG TO DIE   Paul Releasing,
   1986, w/Ned Humphreys & Paul Seydor
LEMON SKY (TF)   American Playhouse, 1988,
   w/Jeanne Jordan
AGAINST THE LAW (TF)   Sarabande
   Productions, 1990

WILLIAM M. ANDERSON, ACE
Agent: Lawrence A. Mirisch, Triad Artists, Inc. -
   Los Angeles, 213/556-2727
Address: 10100 Santa Monica Blvd., 16th Floor,
   Los Angeles, CA 90067, 213/393-3301

DON'S PARTY   Satori, 1976
THE GETTING OF WISDOM   Atlantic Releasing
   Corporation, 1977
MONEY MOVERS   South Australian Film
   Corporation, 1978
BREAKER MORANT   New World/Quartet, 1980
THE CLUB   Roadshow, 1980
GALLIPOLI   Paramount, 1981
PUBERTY BLUES   Universal Classics, 1983
THE YEAR OF LIVING DANGEROUSLY
   MGM/UA, 1983
TENDER MERCIES   Universal/AFD, 1983
STANLEY   1984
RAZORBACK   Warner Bros., 1984
KING DAVID   Paramount, 1985
BARRY McKENZIE HOLDS HIS OWN   Satori, 1985
A TIME TO LIVE (TF)   Blue Andre Productions/ITC
   Productions, 1985
BIG SHOTS   20th Century Fox, 1987, w/Sheldon
   Kahn & Dennis Virkler
1969   Atlantic Releasing Corporation, 1988
SIGNS OF LIFE   Avenue Pictures, 1989,
   w/Angelo Corrao
DEAD POETS SOCIETY   Buena Vista, 1989
OLD GRINGO   Columbia, 1989, w/Glenn Farr &
   Juan Carlos Macias
ROBOCOP 2   Orion, 1990
GREEN CARD   Buena Vista, 1990

GEORGE APPLEBY
PARTNERS   Astral Films, 1976
OUTRAGEOUS!   Cinema 5, 1977
WILD HORSE HANK   Film Consortium of Canada, 1979
NOTHING PERSONAL   American International, 1980
DOUGLE NEGATIVE   Best Film & Video, 1981
THE INCUBUS   Film Ventures International, 1982
TOO OUTRAGEOUS!   Spectrafilm, 1987

BRAD ARENSMAN
PARASITE   Embassy, 1982
METALSTORM: THE DESTRUCTION OF JARED-SYN
   Universal, 1983
GHOST WARRIOR   SWORDKILL   Empire
   Pictures, 1986

PAMELA S. ARNOLD
EAT AND RUN   New World, 1986
HOME REMEDY   Kino International, 1988

DONN ARON
RED HEAT   Tri-Star, 1988, w/Carmel Davies &
   Freeman Davies
ANOTHER 48 HRS.   Paramount, 1990,
   w/Freeman Davies & Carmel Davies

JANET ASHIKAGA
THE DEATH OF THE INCREDIBLE HULK (TF)
   Bixby-Brandon Productions, 1990

MICK AUDSLEY
THE HIT   Island Alive, 1985
DANCE WITH A STRANGER   Samuel Goldwyn
   Company, 1985
WALTER AND JUNE   LOVING WALTER   Film
   Forum, 1986
MY BEAUTIFUL LAUNDRETTE   Orion Classics, 1986
PRICK UP YOUR EARS   Samuel Goldwyn
   Company, 1987
SAMMY AND ROSIE GET LAID   Cinecom, 1987
DANGEROUS LIAISONS   Warner Bros., 1988
SOURSWEET   British Screen/Zenith, 1988
WE'RE NO ANGELS   Paramount, 1989,
   w/Johanna Van Wijk
THE GRIFTERS   Miramax, 1990

JENNIFER AUGE
CANDY MOUNTAIN   International Film Exchange, 1987
BEYOND THERAPY   New World, 1987

PETER AUSTIN
FEAR, ANXIETY AND DEPRESSION   Samuel Goldwyn
   Company, 1989

JOHN G. AVILDSEN
SLOW DANCING IN THE BIG CITY   United Artists, 1978
THE FORMULA   MGM/UA, 1980, w/David Bretherton &
   John Carter
A NIGHT IN HEAVEN   20th Century Fox, 1983
THE KARATE KID   Columbia, 1984, w/Walt Mulconery
   & Bud Smith
THE KARATE KID PART II   Columbia, 1985,
   w/David Garfield & Jane Kurson
FOR KEEPS   Tri-Star, 1988
LEAN ON ME   Warner Bros., 1989 , w/John Carter
THE KARATE KID PART III   Columbia, 1989,
   w/John Carter
ROCKY V   MGM/UA, 1990, w/Michael N. Knue

THOMAS AVILDSEN
CHEECH & CHONG'S NICE DREAMS   Columbia, 1981
CHEECH & CHONG'S THE CORSICAN BROTHERS
   Orion, 1984

B

DEREK BAINE
CREAM IN MY COFFEE (TF)   London
    Weekend TV, 1989
SCOOP (TF)   London Weekend TV, 1990

STUART BAIRD, ACE
LA Local 776, ACTT
Agent: Lawrence A. Mirisch, Triad Artists, Inc. -
    Los Angeles, 213/556-2727

TOMMY   Columbia, 1975
LISZTOMANIA   Warner Bros., 1975
THE OMEN   20th Century Fox, 1976
WELCOME TO MY NIGHTMARE (FD)   Warner
    Bros., 1976
VALENTINO   United Artists, 1977
SUPERMAN ★   Warner Bros., 1978
SUPERMAN II   Warner Bros., 1980
ALTERED STATES   Warner Bros., 1980
OUTLAND   The Ladd Company/Warner Bros., 1981
FIVE DAYS ONE SUMMER   The Ladd Company/
    Warner Bros., 1982
BEYOND THE LIMIT *THE HONORARY COUNSEL*
    Paramount, 1983
REVOLUTION   Warner Bros., 1985
LADYHAWKE   Warner Bros., 1985
LETHAL WEAPON   Warner Bros., 1987
GORILLAS IN THE MIST ★   Universal, 1988
LETHAL WEAPON 2   Warner Bros., 1989
DIE HARD 2   20th Century Fox, 1990,
    w/Robert A. Ferretti
TANGO & CASH   Warner Bros., 1989, Supervising
    editor w/Hubert De La Boullerie & Robert Ferretti

LORI SCOTT BALL
ROBOT JOX   Triumph Releasing, 1990,
    w/Ted Nicolaou

ALAN BALSAM
DIVINE MADNESS (FD)   The Ladd Company/
    Warner Bros., 1980
THE PRIVATE EYES   New World, 1980
LOOSE SHOES   1980
DEAD AND BURIED   Avco Embassy, 1981
DAS BOOT *THE BOAT*   Triumph/Columbia, 1981
TO BE OR NOT TO BE   20th Century Fox, 1983
REVENGE OF THE NERDS   20th Century Fox, 1984
BETTER OFF DEAD   Warner Bros., 1985
ONE CRAZY SUMMER   Warner Bros., 1986
FIRE AND ICE   Concorde, 1987
MOVING   Warner Bros., 1988
DOIN' TIME ON PLANET EARTH   Cannon, 1989,
    w/Sharyn L. Ross
WHY ME?   Epic Pictures/Triumph, 1989

MALCOLM BANTHORPE
THE SILVER CHAIR (TF)   BBC Television, 1990

DEBRA BARD
BLUE DESERT   Neo Films, 1991

NINO BARAGLI, AMC
ONCE UPON A TIME IN AMERICA   Warner Bros., 1984
OEDIPUS REX   Horizon Film, 1984
GINGER & FRED   MGM/UA, 1986, w/Ugo De Rossi &
    Ruggero Mastroianni
A BOY FROM CALABRIA   International Film
    Exchange, 1987
HOTEL COLONIAL   Orion, 1987
THE LITTLE DEVIL   Columbia, 1988
THE VOICE OF THE MOON   Penta Distribuzione, 1989

ANDREW BARKER
HANSEL AND GRETEL (TF)   BBC Television, 1990,
    w/Phil Southby

MICHAEL BARNARD
THE PREY   New World, 1984
EYES OF FIRE   Aquarius Films, 1986

PAM BARNETTA
THE EVERLASTING SECRET FAMILY   International
    Film Exchange, 1990

PAUL BARNES
WASN'T THAT A TIME!   United Artists Classics, 1982
SAY AMEN, SOMEBODY   United Artists Classics, 1983
PUMPING IRON II: THE WOMEN (FD)   Cinecom, 1985
HEAVEN (FD)   Island Pictures, 1987
THE THIN BLUE LINE   Miramax, 1988
THE CIVIL WAR I-IX (MS)   Florentine Films, 1990,
    w/Bruce Shaw & Tricia Reidy

SUZANNE BARON
PRETTY BABY   Paramount, 1978, w/Suzanne Fenn
THE TIN DRUM   New World, 1980
ATLANTIC CITY   Paramount, 1981
MY DINNER WITH ANDRE   New Yorker, 1981
CIRCLE OF DECEIT   United Artists Classics, 1982
CRACKERS   Universal, 1984
THE MAN IN THE SILK HAT   Kino International, 1986,
    w/Pierre Gilette

MARTINE BARRAQUE
THE LAST METRO   United Artists, 1981
THE WOMAN NEXT DOOR   United Artists
    Classics, 1981
CONFIDENTIALLY YOURS   Spectrafilm, 1984
REUNION   Anare Films/Burning Secret
    Productions, 1989

ROBERT BARRERE
MALIBU BEACH   Crown International, 1978
OVER THE EDGE   Orion/Warner Bros., 1979
KANSAS   Trans World Entertainment, 1988
NIGHT GAME   Trans World Entertainment, 1989
CURIOSITY KILLS (CTF)   MCA TV Entertainment, 1989

JANET BARTELS
GUESS WHO'S COMING FOR CHRISTMAS (TF)
    Corapeake Productions, 1990
ALWAYS REMEMBER I LOVE YOU (TF)   Gross-Weston
    Productions, 1990
DANGEROUS PASSION (TF)   Stormy Weathers, 1990

RAIMUND BARTHELMES, BES
MEN   New Yorker, 1986
ME AND HIM   Columbia, 1988

Ba

CINEMATOGRAPHERS
PRODUCTION
DESIGNERS,
COSTUME
DESIGNERS AND
FILM EDITORS
GUIDE

F
I
L
M

E
D
I
T
O
R
S

Ba

CINEMATOGRAPHERS
PRODUCTION
DESIGNERS,
COSTUME
DESIGNERS AND
FILM EDITORS
GUIDE

F
I
L
M

E
D
I
T
O
R
S

DAVID BARTLETT
COLD STEEL   CineTel, 1987

JOHN A. BARTON
DEATH WARRANT   MGM/UA, 1990, w/G. Gregg
   McLaughlin

SEAN BARTON
EYE OF THE NEEDLE   United Artists, 1981
RETURN OF THE JEDI   20th Century Fox, 1983,
   w/Duwayne Dunham & Marcia Lucas
UNTIL SEPTEMBER   MGM/UA, 1984
RESTLESS NATIVES   Orion Classics, 1985
JAGGED EDGE   Columbia, 1985, w/Conrad Buff
HEARTS OF FIRE   Lorimar, 1988
THE FLY II   20th Century Fox, 1989
WAR PARTY   Hemdale, 1989

SONNY BASKIN
OVERBOARD   MGM/UA, 1987, w/Dov Hoenig
LIMIT UP   MCEG, 1990

CRAIG BASSETT
MEN AT WORK   Triumph, 1990

FRANCO BATTISTA
CRAZY MOON   Miramax, 1987

MARY BAUER
SUMMER HEAT   Atlantic Releasing
   Corporation, 1987
FRANKENSTEIN UNBOUND   20th Century
   Fox, 1990

DAVID BEATTY
LADY IN A CORNER (TF)   Fries Entertainment/Allan
   Leicht Productions, 1990, w/Les Green

NICHOLAS BEAUMAN
THE SINGER AND THE DANCER   Columbia, 1977
THE PICTURE SHOW MAN   Roadshow
   Distributors, 1977
MY BRILLIANT CAREER   Analysis, 1980
STARSTRUCK   Cinecom, 1982
MRS. SOFFEL   MGM/UA, 1984
HIGH TIDE   Tri-Star, 1987

REGINALD BECK
STEAMING   New World, 1984

RICHARD BEDFORD
SHOCK TREATMENT   20th Century Fox, 1981
ABSOLUTE BEGINNERS   Orion, 1986, w/Michael
   Bradsell, Gerry Hambling & Russell Lloyd
THE FRUIT MACHINE   Ideal Communications, 1988
WONDERLAND   Vestron, 1989

DALE BELDIN
OSCAR   Buena Vista, 1991

GERAINT BELL
LIVING TO DIE   PM Entertainment, 1990

JENNIFER BEMAN
ROGER & ME   Dog Eat Dog Films, 1989,
   w/Wendeye Stanzler

MAX BENEDICT
MR. PATMAN   FIlm Consortium, 1980, w/Vince Hatherly
NUTCRACKER   Almi Pictures, 1984

TOM BENKO, ACE
LADIES AND GENTLEMAN...THE FABULOUS STAINS
   Paramount, 1982
MOVERS AND SHAKERS   MGM/UA, 1985

JIM BENSON
ZABRISKIE POINT   MGM, 1970
HONKY   Jack H. Harris Enterprises, 1972
ELECTRA GLIDE IN BLUE   United Artists, 1973
THE BOYS IN COMPANY C   Columbia, 1978

RICK BENWICK
HYPER SAPIEN   Tri-Star, 1986

MICHAEL BERENBAUM
MISPLACED   Original Cinema Release, 1991

PETER E. BERGER, ACE
Agent: The Gersh Agency, Inc., Beverly Hills -
   213/274-6611, New York - 212/997-1818

IT'S SHOWTIME   United Artists, 1976, w/Alan Holzman
HOT POTATO   Warner Bros., 1976
THE PACK   Warner Bros., 1977
THE PROMISE   Universal, 1979
OH, GOD! BOOK II   Warner Bros., 1980
THE LAST MARRIED COUPLE IN AMERICA
   Universal, 1980
MOMMIE DEAREST   Paramount, 1981
FIRST MONDAY IN OCTOBER   Paramount, 1981
MONSIGNOR   20th Century Fox, 1982
STAYING ALIVE   Paramount, 1983
STAR TREK IV: THE VOYAGE HOME
   Paramount, 1986
FIRE WITH FIRE   Paramount, 1986
LESS THAN ZERO   20th Century Fox, 1987,
   w/Michael Tronick
FATAL ATTRACTION ★   Paramount, 1987,
   w/Michael Kahn
MEMORIES OF ME   MGM/UA, 1988
THE GOOD MOTHER   Buena Vista, 1988
STAR TREK V: THE FINAL FRONTIER
   Paramount, 1989
FUNNY ABOUT LOVE   Paramount, 1990

TOM BERNER
DANCING IN THE DARK   New World, 1985

GEORGE BERNDT
ST. HELENS   Parnell, 1981
O'HARA'S WIFE   Davis-Panzer Productions, 1982
MEATBALLS PART II   Tri-Star, 1984

PETER BESTON
GIVE MY REGARDS TO BROAD STREET   20th Century
   Fox, 1984

KENT BEYDA, ACE
SATURDAY THE 14TH   New World, 1981,
   w/Joanne D'Antonio
GET CRAZY   Embassy, 1983, w/Michael Jablow
THIS IS SPINAL TAP   Embassy, 1984, w/Kim Secrist
THE UNHEARD MUSIC (FD)   Skouras Pictures,
   1985, w/others

FRIGHT NIGHT   Columbia, 1985
OUT OF BOUNDS   Columbia, 1986, w/Larry Bock
INNERSPACE   Warner Bros., 1987
ALIEN NATION   20th Century Fox, 1988
FEAR   Vestron, 1990
GREMLINS 2: THE NEW BATCH   Warner Bros., 1990

NANCY NUTTAL BEYDA
DA   Film Dallas, 1988

EDWARD BEYER
MATTERS OF THE HEART (CTF)   Tahse-Bergman
   Productions, 1990

GIRISH BHARGAVA
BOOK OF DAYS   Tatge/Lasseur Productions, 1990

EDWARD A. BIERY
Address: 2047 E. Live Oak Dr., Los Angeles, CA
   90068, 213/467-2869

SWASHBUCKLER   Universal, 1976
ROLLERCOASTER   Universal, 1977,
   w/Richard Sprague
WHEN TIME RAN OUT   Warner Bros., 1980,
   w/Freeman Davies
SENTIMENTAL JOURNEY (TF)   Lucille Ball
   Productions/Smith-Richmond Productions/20th
   Century Fox TV, 1984

CAROLINE BIGGERSTAFF
Agent: Broder Kurland Webb Uffner - Los Angeles,
   213/656-9262

JACKSON COUNTY JAIL   New World, 1976
THE STUNT MAN   20th Century Fox, 1980,
   w/Jack Hofstra
CUTTER'S WAY   United Artists Classics, 1981
A SOLDIER'S STORY   Columbia, 1984,
   w/Mark Warner
TRUE STORIES   Warner Bros., 1986
9-1/2 WEEKS   MGM/UA, 1986
THE SEVENTH SIGN   Tri-Star, 1988
RENEGADES   Universal, 1989
WILDFIRE   Zupnik Cinema Group, 1989
WITHOUT HER CONSENT (TF)   Raymond Katz
   Enterprises, 1990
EVE OF DESTRUCTION   Orion, 1991

JILL BILCOCK
DOGS IN SPACE   Skouras Pictures, 1987
A CRY IN THE DARK   Warner Bros., 1988

RON BINKOWSKI
THE SECRET LIFE OF ARCHIE'S WIFE (TF)
   Interscope Productions, 1990

JERRY BIXMAN
KRUSH GROOVE   Warner Bros., 1985,
   w/Conrad M. Gonzalez

DAVID BLANGSTED
STEPHEN KING'S 'IT' (TF)   Konigsberg/Sanitsky
   Productions, 1990, w/Robert F. Shugrue

BETSY BLANKETT
PENITENTIARY   Jerry Gross Organization, 1980
EL NORTE   Cinecom/Island Alive, 1984
A TIME OF DESTINY   Columbia, 1988

DAVID BLEWITT, ACE
Address: 4210 Woodman Ave., Sherman Oaks, CA
   91423, 818/789-2229

BUTTERFLIES ARE FREE   Columbia, 1972
REPORT TO THE COMMISSIONER   United
   Artists, 1975
THAT'S ENTERTAINMENT, PART 2   MGM/United
   Artists, 1976, w/David Bretherton, Peter C. Johnson &
   Bud Friedgen
THE BUDDY HOLLY STORY   Columbia, 1978
STEEL   World Northal, 1980
IN GOD WE TRUST   Universal, 1980
THE COMPETITION ★   Columbia, 1980
UNDER THE RAINBOW   Orion/Warner Bros., 1981
SMOKEY AND THE BANDIT PART 3   Universal, 1983,
   w/Byron Brandt & Christopher Greenbury
D.C. CAB   Universal, 1983
GHOSTBUSTERS   Columbia, 1984, w/Sheldon Kahn
PSYCHO III   Universal, 1986
MOONWALKER   Warner Bros., 1988

MICHAEL BLOECHER
THE FIRST POWER   Orion, 1990

JOHN BLOOM
Agent: Lawrence A. Mirisch, Triad Artists, Inc. -
   Los Angeles, 213/556-2727

FUNERAL IN BERLIN   Paramount, 1966
GEORGY GIRL   Columbia, 1967
THE LION IN WINTER   Avco Embassy, 1968
TRAVELS WITH MY AUNT   MGM, 1972
THE GLASS MENAGERIE (TF)   Talent Associates, 1973
THE MESSAGE   Tarik, 1976
THE RITZ   Warner Bros., 1976
ORCA   Paramount, 1977, w/Marion Rothman &
   Ralph E. Winters
WHO'LL STOP THE RAIN   United Artists, 1978
MAGIC   20th Century Fox, 1978
DRACULA   Universal, 1979
MASADA (MS) ☆   Arnon Milchan Productions/Universal
   Television, 1981
THE FRENCH LIEUTENANT'S WOMAN ★   United
   Artists, 1981
GANDHI ★★   Columbia, 1982
BETRAYAL   20th Century Fox International
   Classics, 1983
UNDER FIRE   Orion, 1983, SE
MISTRAL'S DAUGHTR (MS)   Steve Krantz Productions/
   R.T.L. Productions/Antenne-2, 1984
A CHORUS LINE ★   Columbia, 1985
BLACK WIDOW   20th Century Fox, 1987
BRIGHT LIGHTS, BIG CITY   MGM/UA, 1988
JACKNIFE   Cineplex Odeon, 1989
EVERYBODY WINS   Orion, 1990
AIR AMERICA   Carolco International/Tri-Star, 1990,
   w/Lois Freeman-Fox

JOHN BLOOMGARDEN
BEACH HOUSE   New Line Cinema, 1982, w/Victor
   Kanefsky
CHORDS OF FAME   Pretty Smart, 1984

ANDY BLUMENTHAL
RUNNING HOT   New Line Cinema, 1984
HARDBODIES   Columbia, 1984
HARDBODIES 2   CineTel, 1986
FIVE CORNERS   Cineplex Odeon, 1988
SHOCKER   Universal, 1989

BI

CINEMATOGRAPHERS
PRODUCTION
DESIGNERS,
COSTUME
DESIGNERS AND
FILM EDITORS
GUIDE

F
I
L
M

E
D
I
T
O
R
S

BI

CINEMATOGRAPHERS
PRODUCTION
DESIGNERS,
COSTUME
DESIGNERS AND
FILM EDITORS
GUIDE

F
I
L
M

E
D
I
T
O
R
S

BILL BLUNDEN
THE BAWDY ADVENTURES OF TOM JONES
   Universal, 1975
WARLORDS OF ATLANTIS   Columbia, 1978
HUSSY   Watchgrove Ltd., 1980
A CASUALTY OF WAR (CTF)   F.F.S.
   Productions, 1990
JUST ANOTHER SECRET (CTF)   F.F.S.
   Productions, 1990
DARK SHADOWS-PARTS I-II (Pilot)   Dan Curtis
   Television Productions, 1991,
   (part one; supervising editor, part two)

CHRIS BLUNDEN
WILT   LWT, 1989
THE NEVERENDING STORY II: THE NEXT CHAPTER
   Warner Bros., 1990

TERRY BLYTHE
SHOCK 'EM DEAD   Academy Entertainment, 1991

LARRY BOCK
DEATHSPORT   New World, 1978
ROCK 'N' ROLL HIGH SCHOOL   New World, 1979,
   w/Gail Werbin
THE LADY IN RED   New World, 1979, w/Ron
   Medico & Lewis Teague
SMOKEY BITES THE DUST   New World, 1981
GALAXY OF TERROR   New World, 1981,
   w/Robert J. Kizer & Barry Zetlin
SORCERESS   New World, 1983, w/Barry Zetlin
JOYSTICKS   Jensen Farley Pictures, 1983
HEARTBREAKER   Monorex, 1983
BREAKIN'   MGM/UA/Cannon, 1984, w/Gib Jaffe &
   Vincent Sklena
THE LOST EMPIRE   JGM Enterprises, 1985
BASIC TRAINING   The Movie Store, 1985
THE GIFTED ONE (TF)   Richard Rothstein
   Productions/NBC Productions, 1985
OUT OF BOUNDS   Columbia, 1986, w/Kent Beyda
CRITTERS   New Line Cinema, 1986
BILL & TED'S EXCELLENT ADVENTURE   Orion,
   1989, w/Patrick Rand

MICHAEL BOCKMAN
THE HAUNTING OF M   Nu-Image, 1981,
   w/Trevor Black & Anna Thomas

MICHELE BOEHM
STORMY SUMMER   Slay Productions, 1990

BARBARA BOGUSKI
SATAN'S PRINCESS   Paramount Home
   Video, 1991

ANNE BOISSEL
SINCERELY CHARLOTTE   New Line
   Cinema, 1986

NOELLE BOISSON
LOVE SONGS   Spectrafilm, 1986
MAN ON FIRE   Tri-Star, 1987
JEAN DE FLORETTE   Orion Classics, 1987,
   w/Herve de Luze & Arlette Longmann
THE BEAR ★   Tri-Star, 1989
CYRANO DE BERGERAC   Orion Classics, 1990

PETER BOITA
LUCKY LADY   20th Century Fox, 1975
MOSES   Avco Embassy, 1976, w/Gerry Hambling, John
   Guthridge, Alberto Gallitti & Freddie Wilson
CANDLESHOE   Buena Vista, 1977
CARRY ON EMMANNUELLE   Rank, 1978
THE UNIDENTIFIED FLYING ODDBALL   Buena
   Vista, 1979
HEARTACHES   MPM, 1982, w/Gerry Hambling
THE FAR PAVILIONS (CMS)   Geoff Reeve & Associates/
   Goldcrest, 1984
LACE 2 (MS)   Lorimar Productions, 1985
THE JEWEL OF THE NILE   20th Century Fox, 1985,
   w/Michael Ellis

FRANÇOISE BONNOT
Agent: Triad Artists, Inc. - Los Angeles, 213/556-2727

Z   Cinema 5, 1969
THE CONFESSION   Paramount, 1970
MASSACRE IN ROME   National General, 1973
STATE OF SIEGE   Cinema 5, 1973
SPECIAL SECTION   Universal, 1975
THE TENANT   Paramount, 1976
THE CASSANDRA CROSSING   Avco Embassy, 1977,
   w/Roberto Silvi
BLACK AND WHITE IN COLOR   Allied Artists, 1978
CLAIR DE FEMME   Atlantic Releasing Corporation, 1979
I SENT A LETTER TO MY LOVE   Atlantic Releasing
   Corporation, 1980
MISSING   Universal, 1982
HANNAH K.   Universal Classics, 1983
SWANN IN LOVE   Orion Classics, 1984
YEAR OF THE DRAGON   MGM/UA, 1985
THE SICILIAN   20th Century Fox, 1987
FAT MAN AND LITTLE BOY   Paramount, 1989

MARGARET BOOTH
MURDER BY DEATH   Columbia, 1976,
   w/John F. Burnett
THE GOODBYE GIRL   Warner Bros., 1977,
   w/John F. Burnett
CALIFORNIA SUITE   Columbia, 1978, SE
ANNIE   Columbia, 1982
CAMILLE (TF)   Rosemont Productions, 1984

CHARLES BORNSTEIN
Agent: The Gersh Agency, Inc., Beverly Hills -
   213/274-6611, New York - 212/997-1818

HALLOWEEN   Compass International, 1978,
   w/Tommy Wallace
THE FOG   Avco Embassy, 1980, w/Tommy Wallace
ANGEL   New World, 1984, w/Will Henderson
GETTING EVEN   American Distribution Group, 1986
CRITTERS 2: THE MAIN COURSE   New Line
   Cinema, 1988
RETURN OF THE LIVING DEAD PART II   Lorimar, 1988
PSYCHO IV: THE BEGINNING (CTF)   Smart Money
   Productions, 1990
THE PHANTOM OF THE OPERA   21st Century, 1989

KEN BORNSTEIN
LIGHTNING: THE WHITE STALLION   Cannon, 1986
THE ARROGANT   Cannon, 1989
RIVER OF DEATH   Cannon, 1989

ANDREW BOULTON
WHEN THE WHALES CAME   20th Century Fox, 1990

TOM BOUTROSS
WINTERHAWK   Howco International, 1975
THE TOWN THAT DREADED SUNDOWN   American
   International, 1977
DARK BEFORE DAWN   Prism Entertainment, 1988,
   w/Ron Honthaner

GEORGE BOWERS
THE POM-POM GIRLS   Crown International, 1976
VAN NUYS BLVD.   Crown International, 1979
BEACH GIRLS   Crown International, 1982
THE ADVENTURES OF BUCKAROO BANZAI:
   ACROSS THE 8TH DIMENSION   20th Century
   Fox, 1984, w/Richard Marks
THE STEPFATHER   New Century/Vista, 1987
SHOOT TO KILL   Buena Vista, 1988, w/Garth Craven
TRUE BELIEVER   Columbia, 1989
HARLEM NIGHTS   Paramount, 1989
SLEEPING WITH THE ENEMY   20th Century
   Fox, 1991

JOHN BOWEY
AVENGING ANGEL   New World, 1985
HOLLYWOOD VICE SQUAD   Cinema Group, 1986

ERIC BOYD-PERKINS, ACE
NO BLADE OF GRASS   MGM, 1970
JULIUS CAESAR   American International, 1971
A WAR OF CHILDREN (TF)   Tomorrow
   Entertainment, 1972
ANTONY AND CLEOPATRA   Rank, 1973
HENNESSY   American International, 1975
THE TERRORISTS   *RANSOM*   20th Century
   Fox, 1975
THE WICKER MAN   Warner Bros., 1975
THE DISAPPEARANCE   Levitt-Pickman, 1977
THE FOUR FEATHERS (TF)   Norman Rosemont
   Productions/Trident Films Ltd., 1978
THE 39 STEPS   International Picture Show
   Company, 1978
HAWK THE SLAYER   ITC, 1980
BREAKING GLASS   Paramount, 1980
BEAR ISLAND   Taft International, 1980
MOTHER LODE   Agamemnon Films, 1982
THE SLAYER   21st Century Distribution, 1982
SECRETS   Samuel Goldwyn Company, 1984
GOING UNDERCOVER   Miramax Films, 1985,
   w/Danny Retz
TREASURE ISLAND (CTF)   Agamemnon Film
   Productions, 1990

PETER BOYLE
McVICAR   Crown International, 1982
HORROR PLANET   *INSEMINOID*   Almi Pictures, 1982
THE RAZOR'S EDGE   Columbia, 1984
MORONS FROM OUTER SPACE   Universal, 1985
CLOCKWISE   Universal, 1986
A PRAYER FOR THE DYING   Samuel Goldwyn
   Company, 1987
THE BEAST   Columbia, 1988
QUEEN OF HEARTS   Cinecom, 1989
TUNE IN TOMORROW...   Cinecom, 1990

FRANK BRACHT
THE ODD COUPLE ★   Paramount, 1968
THE MOLLY MAGUIRES   Paramount, 1970
PLAZA SUITE   Paramount, 1971
PETE N' TILLIE   Universal, 1972

THE DUCHESS & THE DIRTWATER FOX   20th
   Century Fox, 1976, w/William Butler
GOIN' COCONUTS   Osmond Distribution, 1978
SOMETHING SHORT OF PARADISE   American
   International, 1979

RICHARD BRACKEN
DEADLY BESSING   United Artists/Polygram, 1981
SWAMP THING   Embassy, 1982
BRIDESMAIDS (TF)   Motown/Qintex
   Entertainment, 1989
THE KAREN CARPENTER STORY (TF)   Weintraub
   Entertainment Productions, 1989
A KILLER AMONG US (TF)   Dave Bell Associates, 1990
COLUMBO: MURDER CAN BE HAZARDOUS TO YOUR
   HEALTH (TF)   Universal City Studios, 1991

MICHAEL BRADSELL, GBFE
FLAME   Goodtime Enterprises, 1975
INSERTS   United Artists, 1976
JABBERWOCKY   Cinema 5, 1977
THE DUELLISTS   Paramount, 1978, SE
SCUM   Berwick Street Films, 1979
THAT SUMMER   Columbia, 1979
I'M DANCING AS FAST AS I CAN   Paramount, 1982
VENOM   Paramount, 1982
LOCAL HERO   Warner Bros., 1983
SCANDALOUS   Orion, 1984
CAL   Warner Bros., 1984
ABSOLUTE BEGINNERS   Orion, 1986, w/Richard
   Bedford, Gerry Hambling & Russell Loyd
DEFENSE OF THE REALM   Hemdale, 1987
GOTHIC   Vestron, 1987
STARS AND BARS   Columbia, 1988
HIGH SPIRITS   Tri-Star, 1988
HENRY V   Renaissance Films, 1989
A KISS BEFORE DYING   Universal Pictures, 1991

BOB BRADY
QUIET COOL   New Line Cinema, 1986

MARTIN BRAM
EXECUTIVE ACTION   National General, 1973
WIN, PLACE OR STEAL   1975
YOU CAN'T GO HOME AGAIN (TF)   CBS
   Entertainment, 1979
WOLFEN   Orion/Warner Bros., 1981, w/Dennis Dolan,
   Christopher Lebenzon & Marshall M. Borden
THE BEING   BFV Films, 1983

BILL BRAME
RED LINE 7000   Paramount, 1965
JOURNEY TO THE CENTER OF TIME   1967
HANG 'EM HIGH   United Artists, 1968
PRETTY MAIDS ALL IN A ROW   MGM, 1971
THE HARRAD EXPERIMENT   Cinerama Releasing
   Corporation, 1973
THE HARRAD SUMMER   Cinerama Releasing
   Corporation, 1974
BEYOND THE POSEIDON ADVENTURE   Warner
   Bros., 1979
STAR TREK - THE MOTION PICTURE
   Paramount, 1979
THE PRODIGAL   World Wide, 1984

MARYANN BRANDON
RACE FOR GLORY   New Century/Vista, 1989

Br

**CINEMATOGRAPHERS
PRODUCTION
DESIGNERS,
COSTUME
DESIGNERS** AND
**FILM EDITORS
GUIDE**

F
I
L
M

E
D
I
T
O
R
S

CINEMATOGRAPHERS
PRODUCTION
DESIGNERS,
COSTUME
DESIGNERS AND
FILM EDITORS
GUIDE

F
I
L
M

E
D
I
T
O
R
S

BYRON "BUZZ" BRANDT, ACE

BREAKHEART PASS   United Artists, 1976
THE GREATEST   Columbia, 1977
THE PRISONER OF ZENDA   Universal, 1979
ROLLER BOOGIE   United Artists, 1979,
   w/Ediberto Cruz & Edward Salier
IT'S MY TURN   Columbia, 1980, w/James
   Coblentz & Marjorie Fowler
A TIME TO DIE   Almi Pictures, 1983, w/Fred Chulack
SMOKEY AND THE BANDIT PART 3   Universal,
   1983, w/David Blewitt & Christopher Greenbury
HARD TIME ON PLANET EARTH (Pilot)   1989,
   w/Anita Brandt-Burgoyne
UNCONQUERED (TF)   Alexandra Film Productions
   Inc./Double Helix/Dick Lowry Productions, 1989,
   w/Anita Brandt-Burgoyne
ARCHIE: TO RIVERDALE AND BACK AGAIN (TF)
   Patchett-Kaufman Entertainment Productions, 1989,
   w/Anita Brandt-Burgoyne
HOWARD BEACH: MAKING THE CASE FOR
   MURDER (TF)   Patchett-Kaufman Entertainment
   Productions, 1990
MIRACLE LANDING (TF)   CBS Entertainment
   Productions, 1990
IN THE LINE OF DUTY: A COP FOR THE
   KILLING (TF)   Patchett-Kaufman Entertainment,
   1990, w/Anita Brandt-Burgoyne

ANITA BRANDT-BURGOYNE

ARCHIE: TO RIVERDALE AND BACK AGAIN (TF)
   Patchett-Kaufman Entertainment Productions,
   1989, w/Byron "Buzz" Brandt
IN THE LINE OF DUTY: A COP FOR THE
   KILLING (TF)   Patchett-Kaufman Entertainment,
   1990, w/Byron "Buzz" Brandt

JONATHAN BRAUN

THE UNSEEN   World Northal, 1981

ROBERT BREEN

STOLEN: ONE HUSBAND (TF)   King Phoenix
   Entertainment, 1990, w/Michael J. Sheridan

DAVID BRENNER

Agent: Sanford-Skouras & Gross - Los Angeles,
   213/208-2100

TALK RADIO   Universal, 1988
BORN ON THE FOURTH OF JULY   Universal, 1989
THE DOORS   Tri-Star, 1991, w/Joe Hutshing

GORDON D. BRENNER

PETE'S DRAGON (AF)   Buena Vista, 1977
THE NORTH AVENUE IRREGULARS   Buena
   Vista, 1979
HERBIE GOES BANANAS   Buena Vista, 1980
THE LAST FLIGHT OF NOAH'S ARK   Buena
   Vista, 1980
CONDORMAN   Buena Vista, 1981
NIGHT CROSSING   Buena Vista, 1982

DAVID BRETHERTON, ACE

Home: 1375 Londonderry Place, Hollywood, CA 90069,
   213/657-3337

THE SANDPIPER   MGM, 1965
LOVERS AND OTHER STRANGERS   Cinerama
   Releasing Corporation, 1970

ON A CLEAR DAY YOU CAN SEE FOREVER
   Paramount, 1970
SLITHER   MGM, 1972
CABARET ★★   Allied Artists, 1972
THE MAN IN THE GLASS BOOTH   American
   Film Theatre, 1975
THAT'S ENTERTAINMENT, PART 2   MGM/United
   Artists, 1976, w/David Blewitt, Bud Friedgen &
   Peter C. Johnson
HARRY AND WALTER GO TO NEW YORK   Columbia,
   1976, w/Don Guidice & Fredric Steinkamp
SILVER STREAK   20th Century Fox, 1976
COMA   MGM/United Artists, 1978
THE GREAT TRAIN ROBBERY   United Artists, 1979
WINTER KILLS   Avco Embassy, 1979
THE FORMULA   MGM/United Artists, 1980,
   w/John G. Avildsen & John Carter
CADDYSHACK   Orion/Warner Bros., 1980, SE
CANNERY ROW   MGM/United Artists, 1982
THE BEST LITTLE WHOREHOUSE IN TEXAS
   Universal, 1982, w/Nicholas Elipoulos, Pembroke
   Herring & Jack Hofstra
MAN, WOMAN AND CHILD   Paramount, 1983
LOVELINES   Tri-Star, 1984, w/Fred Chulack
BABY - SECRET OF THE LOST LEGEND   Buena Vista,
   1985, w/Howard Smith
CLUE   Paramount, 1985, w/Richard Haines
THE PICK-UP ARTIST   20th Century Fox, 1987,
   w/Angelo Corrao
LIONHEART   Orion, 1987
SEA OF LOVE   Universal, 1989

WENDY BRICMONT

LA Local 776, NY Local 771
Agent: Lawrence A. Mirisch, Triad Artists, Inc. -
   Los Angeles, 213/556-2727

ANNIE HALL   United Artists, 1977
ON THE NICKEL   Rose's Park, 1980
THE SLUMBER PARTY MASSACRE   Santa Fe, 1982
LOVE LETTERS   New World, 1983
ALL THE RIGHT MOVES   20th Century Fox, 1983,
   w/David Garfield
GIMME AN F   20th Century Fox, 1984, w/Todd Ramsay
   & Tom Walls
THE CLAN OF THE CAVE BEAR   Warner Bros., 1986
SURRENDER   Warner Bros., 1987
LICENSE TO DRIVE   20th Century Fox, 1988
PERFECT WITNESS (CTF)   HBO Pictures, 1990
KINDERGARTEN COP   Universal, 1990,
   w/Sheldon Kahn

BOB BRING, ACE

Representation: Bruce Fritzberg - Los Angeles,
   213/651-1858

WHERE THE RED FERN GROWS
   DOTY-DAYTON, 1972
CHARLEY AND THE ANGEL   Buena Vista, 1972
WHERE THE RED FERN GROWS   1974
THE SHAGGY D.A.   Buena Vista, 1976,
   w/Norman Palmer
RETURN FROM WITCH MOUNTAIN   Buena Vista, 1978
THE SKY TRAP (TF)   Disney Productions, 1979
MARK, I LOVE YOU (TF)   Aubrey Company, 1980
FORCE FIVE   American Cinema, 1981
ZAPPED!   Embassy, 1982, w/Robert Ferretti
DARK MIRROR (TF) ☆   Aaron Spelling
   Productions, 1983

HOLLYWOOD BEAT (TF)   Aaron Spelling
    Productions, 1985
THE THREE KINGS (TF)   Aaron Spelling
    Productions, 1986
TAX SEASON   Movidex/Paramount Home Video, 1988
DANGEROUS CURVES   Allmar Productions, 1988
STOLEN: ONE HUSBAND (TF)   Hearst
    Entertainment, 1990
JAILBIRDS (TF)   JBS Productions, 1990

DON BROCHU
THE SLUGGER'S WIFE   Columbia, 1985,
    w/George C. Villashar
LA BAMBA   Columbia, 1987, w/Sheldon Kahn
BORN IN EAST L.A.   Universal, 1987
MYSTIC PIZZA   Samuel Goldwyn Company, 1988,
    w/Marion Rothman
MARGARET BOURKE-WHITE (TF)   Turner Network
    Television, 1989
LOCK UP   Tri-Star, 1989, w/Michael N. Knue
OUT FOR JUSTICE   Warner Bros., 1991,
    w/Robert A. Ferretti

SCOTT BROCK
THE MODERNS   Alive Films, 1988, w/Debra T. Smith

SUSAN B. BROWDY
VOICES WITHIN: THE LIVES OF TRUDDI
    CHASE-PARTS I & II (MS)   Itzbinzo Long
    Productions, 1989
THE KENNEDYS OF MASSACHUSETTS (TF)
    Orion TV/Edgar J. Scherick Associates
    Productions, 1990
THE BRIDE IN BLACK (TF)   Barry Weitz Films, 1990

BARRY ALEXANDER BROWN
SCHOOL DAZE   Columbia, 1988
DO THE RIGHT THING   Universal, 1989

MacDONALD BROWN
THY KINGDOM COME...THY WILL BE DONE (FD)
    Roxie Films Releasing, 1988

MICHAEL BROWN
NIGHTMARES   Universal, 1983, w/Rod Stephens
JAWS THE REVENGE   Universal, 1987
ABOVE THE LAW   Warner Bros., 1988
DADAH IS DEATH (MS)   Steve Krantz Productions/
    Roadshow Coote & Carroll/Samuel Goldwyn
    Television, 1988
KISS SHOT (TF)   London Productions/
    Whoop Inc., 1989
SHATTERED DREAMS (TF)   Roger Gimbel
    Productions, 1989
JUDITH KRANTZ'S TILL WE MEET AGAIN-
    PARTS I & II (MS)   Steve Krantz Productions, 1990
VESTIGE OF HONOR (TF)   Desperado Pictures, 1990

O. NICHOLAS (NICK) BROWN
MR. BILLION   20th Century Fox, 1976
SHADOW OF THE HAWK   Columbia, 1976
MARCH OR DIE   Columbia, 1977
HEART LIKE A WHEEL   20th Century Fox, 1983
BAD MEDICINE   20th Century Fox, 1985, w/John
    Jympson & Keith Palmer
THE MAN WITH ONE RED SHOE   20th Century Fox,
    1985, w/Bud Molin

MISCHIEF   20th Century Fox, 1985
PROJECT X   20th Century Fox, 1987
RAMBO III   Tri-Star, 1988, w/Andrew London, James
    Symons & Edward Warschilka
THE ACCUSED   Paramount, 1988, w/Jerry Greenberg
TREMORS   Universal, 1990
HAPPY TOGETHER   Borde Releasing, 1990
MARKED FOR DEATH   20th Century Fox, 1990

ROBERT N. "TOBY" BROWN, ACE
West Coast Card
Agent: Smith Gosnell Nicholson & Associates -
    Pacific Palisades, 213/459-0307

THE MACK   Cinerama Releasing Corporation, 1973
THE ADVENTURES OF THE WILDERNESS FAMILY
    Pacific International, 1975
ACROSS THE GREAT DIVIDE   Pacific
    International, 1976
THE SEA GYPSIES   Warner Bros., 1978, w/Dan Greer
DAMIEN: OMEN II   20th Century Fox, 1978
THE AMITYVILLE HORROR   American
    International, 1979
BRUBAKER   20th Century Fox, 1980
HIGH RISK   American Cinema, 1981
THE BEAST WITHIN   MGM/United Artists, 1982,
    w/Bert Lovitt
THE POPE OF GREENWICH VILLAGE   MGM/UA, 1984
POLICE ACADEMY   The Ladd Company/Warner Bros.,
    1984, w/Zach Staenberg
LET'S GET HARRY   Tri-Star, 1986
THE LOST BOYS   Warner Bros., 1987
PERMANENT RECORD   Paramount, 1988
COUSINS   Paramount, 1989
FACE OF THE ENEMY   Tri-Culture Pictures, 1989
VITAL SIGNS   20th Century Fox, 1990
FLATLINERS   Columbia, 1990

STEVE BROWN
WILD STYLE   First Run Features, 1983
TOUGHER THAN LEATHER   New Line Cinema, 1988

JAMES BRUCE
ALAMO BAY   Tri-Star, 1985
BAIL JUMPER   Angelika Films, 1990

RICHARD FRANCIS BRUCE
(See Richard FRANCIS-BRUCE)

RALPH BRUNJES
LAST TRAIN HOME (CTF)   Atlantis Films, 1990
IN DEFENSE OF A MARRIED MAN (TF)   The Landsburg
    Company, 1990

RICHARD S. BRUMMER
LOVELY BUT DEADLY   Juniper, 1983
BRAINWAVES   MPM, 1983
THE DEVONSVILLE TERROR   MPM, 1983
SPIKER   Seymour Borde & Associates, 1986

PASQUALE BUBA
Agent: The Gersh Agency, Inc., Beverly Hills -
    213/274-6611, New York - 212/997-1818

EFFECTS   Harmony Vision, 1980
KNIGHTRIDERS   United Film Distribution, 1981,
    w/George A. Romero

Bu

CINEMATOGRAPHERS
PRODUCTION
DESIGNERS,
COSTUME
DESIGNERS AND
FILM EDITORS
GUIDE

F
I
L
M

E
D
I
T
O
R
S

Bu

CINEMATOGRAPHERS
PRODUCTION
DESIGNERS,
COSTUME
DESIGNERS AND
FILM EDITORS
GUIDE

F
I
L
M

E
D
I
T
O
R
S

CREEPSHOW   Warner Bros., 1982, w/George A.
    Romero, Paul Hirsch & Michael Spolan
DAY OF THE DEAD   United Film Distribution, 1985
THE SILENCE AT BETHANY (TF)   American
    Playhouse, 1988
MONKEY SHINES   Orion, 1988
STEPFATHER II   Millimeter Films, 1989
TWO EVIL EYES   1989
THE DARK HALF   Orion, 1991

NORMAN BUCKLEY
FIRE BIRDS   Buena Vista, 1990, w/Jon Poll &
    Dennis O'Connor

CONRAD BUFF IV
Agent: Broder Kurland Webb Uffner - Los Angeles,
    213/656-9262

JAGGED EDGE   Columbia, 1985, w/Sean Barton
SOLARBABIES   MGM/UA, 1986
SPACEBALLS   MGM/UA, 1987
SHORT CIRCUIT 2   Tri-Star, 1988
SIDE OUT   Tri-Star, 1990

LEE BURCH
CALL ME ANNA (TF)   Gilbert Cates/Mianna Pearce/
    Finnegan-Pinchuk Productions, 1990

PETER BURGESS
QUIGLEY DOWN UNDER   Pathe Entertainment/
    MGM/UA, 1990, w/Adrian Carr

JOHN F. BURNETT, ACE
Agent: Lawrence A. Mirisch, Triad Artists, Inc. -
    Los Angeles, 213/556-2727
Address: 18326 Kinzie Street, Northridge, CA 91325,
    818/349-9312

THE HEART IS A LONELY HUNTER   Warner
    Bros., 1968
THE OWL AND THE PUSSYCAT   Columbia, 1970
SUPPOSE THEY GAVE A WAR AND NOBODY CAME?
    Cinerama Releasing Corporation, 1970
WILD ROVERS   MGM, 1971
THE CULPEPPER CATTLE COMPANY   20th Century
    Fox, 1972
THE WAY WE WERE   Columbia, 1973
THE SUNSHINE BOYS   MGM/United Artists, 1975
LOVE AMONG THE RUINS (TF)   ABC Circle
    Films, 1975
MURDER BY DEATH   Columbia, 1976,
    w/Margaret Booth
THE DOMINO PRINCIPLE   Avco Embassy, 1977
THE GOODBYE GIRL   Warner Bros., 1977,
    w/Margaret Booth
GREASE   Paramount, 1978
MOMENT BY MOMENT   Universal, 1978
...AND JUSTICE FOR ALL   Columbia, 1979
CAN'T STOP THE MUSIC   AFD, 1980
DEATH HUNT   20th Century Fox, 1981,
    w/Allan Jacobs
RICH AND FAMOUS   MGM/United Artists, 1981
GREASE 2   Paramount, 1982
THE WINDS OF WAR (MS)   Paramount TV/Dan Curtis
    Productions, 1983, w/Peter Zinner
IRRECONCILABLE DIFFERENCES   Warner
    Bros., 1984
SURVIVING (TF)   Telepictures Productions, 1985
A FINE MESS   Columbia, 1986, w/Robert Pergament

WAR AND REMEMBRANCE (MS) ☆   Dan Curtis
    Productions, 1988, w/Peter Zinner
LEVIATHAN   MGM/UA, 1989, w/Roberto Silvi
FOURTH STORY (CTF)   Viacom Pictures, 1991

MARK BURNS
ALMOST YOU   TLC Films/20th Century Fox, 1984
OLD ENOUGH   Orion Classics, 1984
EVERY TIME WE SAY GOODBYE   Tri-Star, 1986

JOSEPH BURTON
DAUGHTERS OF THE PAST   American Playhouse,
    1991, w/Amy Carey

RAYMOND BUSH
RICHARD PRYOR HERE AND NOW (FD)
    Columbia, 1983

WILLIAM (BILL) BUTLER
A CLOCKWORK ORANGE ★   Warner Bros., 1971
OLD DRACULA   American International, 1975
THE DUCHESS & THE DIRTWATER FOX   20th Century
    Fox, 1976, w/Frank Bracht
BITTERSWEET LOVE   Avco Embassy, 1976
JOYRIDE   American International, 1977
OUR WINNING SEASON   American International, 1978
LOST AND FOUND   Columbia, 1979
GORP   American International, 1980
HOW TO BEAT THE HIGH COST OF LIVING   American
    International, 1980
ON THE RIGHT TRACK   20th Century Fox, 1981
A LITTLE SEX   Universal, 1982
UP THE CREEK   Orion, 1984
PRAY FOR DEATH   American Distribution
    Group, 1985
THE MEN'S CLUB   Atlantic Releasing Corporation,
    1986, w/David Dresher & Cynthia Scheider
WALK LIKE A MAN   MGM/UA, 1987, w/Steve Butler
SEVEN HOURS TO JUDGMENT   Trans World
    Entertainment, 1988
FATAL CHARM   MCEG, 1990

STEPHEN BUTLER
DARK SHADOWS-PARTS I-II (Pilot)   Dan Curtis
    Television Productions, 1991   (part two only)

C

DANN (DANIEL TODD) CAHN, ACE

Address: 856 Leonard Road, Los Angeles, CA 90049

THE OCTAGON   American Cinema, 1980
TOUGH ENOUGH   20th Century Fox, 1983
THE LONG HOT SUMMER (TF)   Leonard Hill
   Productions, 1985
TARZAN IN MANHATTAN (TF)   American First Run
   Studios, 1989
FALL FROM GRACE (MS)   NBC Productions, 1989
THE LADY FORGETS (TF)   Leonard Hill Films, 1990
E.A.R.T.H. FORCE (TF)   Paramount Network TV,
   1990, w/George Potter

IRIS CAHN

POWAQQATSI   Cannon, 1988, w/Alton Walpole

JACQUELINE CAMBAS

FALLING IN LOVE AGAIN   International Pictures Show
   Company, 1980, w/Doug Jackson & Bud Smith
ZOOT SUIT   Universal, 1982
CAT PEOPLE   Universal, 1982, w/Bud Smith
SURF II   Arista, 1983
RACING WITH THE MOON   Paramount, 1984
CITY HEAT   Warner Bros., 1984
THE MONEY PIT   Universal, 1986
LIGHT OF DAY   Tri-Star, 1987
LITTLE NIKITA   Columbia, 1988
MY STEPMOTHER IS AN ALIEN   WEG, 1988
DOWNTOWN   20th Century Fox, 1990
MERMAIDS   Orion, 1990

DONN CAMBERN, ACE

Home: 11611 Amanda Drive, Studio City, CA 91604,
   818/761-9874

2000 YEARS LATER   Warner Bros., 1969
EASY RIDER   Columbia, 1969
DRIVE, HE SAID   Columbia, 1970, w/Christopher
   Holems, Pat Somerset & Robert Wolfe
THE LAST PICTURE SHOW   Columbia, 1971
STEELYARD BLUES   Warner Bros., 1972
BLUME IN LOVE   Warner Bros., 1973
CINDERELLA LIBERTY   20th Century Fox, 1974
THE HINDENBURG   Universal, 1975
ALEX & THE GYPSY   20th Century Fox, 1976
THE OTHER SIDE OF MIDNIGHT   20th Century
   Fox, 1977, w/Harold F. Kress
HOOPER   Warner Bros., 1978
THE END   United Artists, 1978
TIME AFTER TIME   Orion/Warner Bros., 1979
WILLIE AND PHIL   20th Century Fox, 1980
SMOKEY AND THE BANDIT PART II   Universal,
   1980, w/William Gordean
THE CANNONBALL RUN   20th Century Fox, 1981,
   w/William Gordean
PATERNITY   Paramount, 1981
TEMPEST   Columbia, 1982
GOING BERSERK   Universal, 1983

ROMANCING THE STONE ★   20th Century Fox, 1984,
   w/Frank Morriss
BIG TROUBLE   Columbia, 1986, w/Ralph Winters
JO JO DANCER, YOUR LIFE IS CALLING
   Columbia, 1986
HARRY AND THE HENDERSONS   Universal, 1987
CASUAL SEX?   Universal, 1988, w/Sheldon Kahn
FEDS   Universal, 1988
TWINS   Universal, 1988, w/Sheldon Kahn
GHOSTBUSTERS II   Columbia, 1989, w/Sheldon Kahn

M. KATHRYN CAMPBELL

MARTIANS GO HOME   Taurus Entertainment, 1990

MALCOLM CAMPBELL

AN AMERICAN WEREWOLF IN LONDON
   Universal, 1981
TWILIGHT ZONE - THE MOVIE (Prologue & Segment 1)
   Warner Bros., 1983
TRADING PLACES   Paramount, 1983
INTO THE NIGHT   Universal, 1985
SPIES LIKE US   Warner Bros., 1985
THREE AMIGOS   Orion, 1986
AMAZON WOMEN ON THE MOON   Universal, 1987,
   w/Marshall Harvey & Bert Lovitt
REAL MEN   MGM/UA, 1987, w/Glenn Farr
COMING TO AMERICA   Paramount, 1988, w/George
   Folsey Jr.
ENID IS SLEEPING   Vestron, 1990
NOTHING BUT TROUBLE   Warner Bros., 1991,
   w/James Symons

MICHAEL CAMPBELL

DEATH SHIP   Avco Embassy, 1980
MERCENARY FIGHTERS   Cannon, 1988,
   w/Dean Goodhill

DAVID CAMPLING

WHEN WILL I BE LOVED (TF)   Nederlander Television
   and Film Productions, 1990

RICHARD CANDIB

YOU CAN'T HURRY LOVE   MCEG, 1988
EAT A BOWL OF TEA   Columbia, 1989

BRUCE CANNON

BOYZ N THE HOOD   Columbia, 1991

BERNARD F. CAPUTO

Mid-West Card
Agent: Smith Gosnell Nicholson & Associates -
   Pacific Palisades, 213/459-0307

DRIVE-IN   Columbia, 1976, w/Guy Scarpitta
TOWING   UIP, 1978
DEADLY DREAMS   Concorde, 1988
THE LAWLESS LAND   Concorde, 1989, w/Steven Kane
SATURDAY THE 14TH STRIKES BACK
   Concorde, 1989

AMY CAREY

DAUGHTERS OF THE DUST   American Playhouse,
   1991, w/Joseph Burton

JOHN CARNOCHEN

INDEPENDENCE DAY   Unifilm, 1977
THE BOSS'S SON   Circle Associates, 1978
HEARTBREAKERS   Orion, 1984

Ca

CINEMATOGRAPHERS
PRODUCTION
DESIGNERS,
COSTUME
DESIGNERS AND
FILM EDITORS
GUIDE

FILM EDITORS

Ca

CINEMATOGRAPHERS
PRODUCTION
DESIGNERS,
COSTUME
DESIGNERS AND
FILM EDITORS
GUIDE

F
I
L
M

E
D
I
T
O
R
S

BAJA OKLAHOMA (CTF)   HBO Pictures, 1988,
    w/Gail Yasunaga
ELYSIAN FIELDS (TF)   Sarabande Productions, 1989
THE LITTLE MERMAID (AF)   Buena Vista, 1989, SE

STEPHEN CARPENTER
PRANKS   New Image, 1982, w/Jeffrey Obrow
THE POWER   Film Ventures International, 1984,
    w/Jeffrey Obrow

ADRIAN CARR
HARLEQUIN   Greater Union Film Distributors, 1980
THE MAN FROM SNOWY RIVER   20th Century
    Fox, 1983
D.A.R.Y.L.   Paramount, 1985
THE LIGHTHORSEMEN   Cinecom, 1988
QUIGLEY DOWN UNDER   Pathe Entertainment/
    MGM/UA, 1990, w/Peter Burgess

LEON CARRERE
THE GARBAGE PAIL KIDS MOVIE   Atlantic
    Releasing Corporation, 1987

WILLIAM CARRUTH
NICKELODEON   Columbia, 1976
SAINT JACK   New World, 1979
CADDYSHACK   Orion/Warner Bros., 1980
STRANGERS KISS   Orion Classics, 1984,
    Editorial Consultant
WHAT COMES AROUND   W.O. Associates, 1986

JOHN CARTER, ACE
Home: 300 W. 55th Street, #10V, New York, NY
    10019, 212/541-7006

MIKEY AND NICKY   Paramount, 1976
BETWEEN THE LINES   Midwest Film
    Productions, 1977
THE FORMULA   MGM/United Artists, 1980,
    w/John G. Avildsen & David Bretherton
COLD RIVER   Pacific International 1982
SOLOMON NORTHUP'S ODYSSEY (CTF)   Past
    America, Inc., 1985
LEAN ON ME   Warner Bros., 1989, w/John Avildsen
THE KARATE KID PART III   Columbia, 1989,
    w/John Avildsen
THE FIVE HEARTBEATS   20th Century Fox, 1991

JAY CASSIDY
THE END OF AUGUST   Quartet, 1982
ROAD HOUSE 66   Atlantic Releasing
    Corporation, 1984
FRIGHT NIGHT PART II   New Century/Vista, 1988
ALOHA SUMMER   Spectrafilm, 1988, w/James
    Coblentz & Jack Hofstra
FRANKENSTEIN UNBOUND   20th Century Fox, 1990,
    w/Mary Bauer

ROBERT J. CASTALDO
POSITIVE I.D.   Universal, 1987, w/Andy Anderson

EMMANUELLE CASTRO
AU REVOIR, LES ENFANTS   Orion Classics, 1987

WARREN CHADWICK
HOLLYWOOD HIGH PART II   Lone Star, 1981
JUNGLE WARRIORS   Aquarius, 1984,
    w/Juan Jose Marino

WALKING THE EDGE   Empire Pictures, 1985
SWORD OF HEAVEN   Trans World Entertainment, 1985
ANGEL III: THE FINAL CHAPTER   New World, 1988

MICHAEL CHANDLER
Agent: The Gersh Agency, Inc., Beverly Hills -
    213/274-6611, New York - 212/997-1818

NEVER CRY WOLF   Buena Vista, 1983,
    w/Peter Parasheles
AMADEUS ★   Orion, 1984, w/Nena Danevic
MISHIMA: A LIFE IN FOUR CHAPTERS   Warner Bros.,
    1985, w/Tomaya Oshima
HOWARD THE DUCK   Universal, 1986,
    w/Sidney Wolinsky
JULIA AND JULIA   Cinecom, 1988

JOAN E. CHAPMAN
WEEKEND AT BERNIE'S   20th Century Fox, 1989

YVES CHAROY
NIGHT OF THE FOX-PARTS I & II (MS)   ITC
    Entertainment, 1990

ANNICK CHARVEIN
BERNADETTE   Cannon France, 1988

JULIO CHAVES
CEASE FIRE   Cineworld, 1985

SCOTT CHESTNUT
PRIVATE INVESTIGATIONS   MGM/UA, 1987
THE BLUE IGUANA   Paramount, 1988

RICHARD CHEW
West Coast Card
Agent: Smith Gosnell Nicholson & Associates -
    Pacific Palisades, 213/459-0307

THE CONVERSATION   Paramount, 1974, CE
ONE FLEW OVER THE CUCKOO'S NEST ★   United
    Artists, 1976, SE
STAR WARS ★★   20th Century Fox, 1977,
    w/Paul Hirsch & Marcia Lucas
GOIN' SOUTH   Paramount, 1978,
    w/John Fitzgerald Beck
WHEN YOU COMIN' BACK, RED RYDER?
    Columbia, 1979
MY FAVORITE YEAR   MGM/UA, 1982
RISKY BUSINESS   The Geffen Company/Warner
    Bros., 1983
REAL GENIUS   Tri-Star, 1985
CREATOR   Universal, 1985
WHERE THE RIVER RUNS BLACK   MGM/UA, 1986
STREETS OF GOLD   20th Century Fox, 1986
REVENGE OF THE NERDS II: NERDS IN PARADISE
    20th Century Fox, 1987
CLEAN AND SOBER   Warner Bros., 1988
MEN DON'T LEAVE   The Geffen Company/Warner
    Bros., 1990

DEBRA CHIATE
Agent: The Gersh Agency, Inc., Beverly Hills -
    213/274-6611, New York - 212/997-1818

LOOK WHO'S TALKING TOO   Tri-Star, 1990

Co

CINEMATOGRAPHERS
PRODUCTION
DESIGNERS,
COSTUME
DESIGNERS AND
FILM EDITORS
GUIDE

**F
I
L
M

E
D
I
T
O
R
S**

FRED A. CHULACK, ACE
THE LAST HARD MEN   20th Century Fox, 1976
A HERO AIN'T NOTHIN BUT A SANDWICH   1978
DREAMER   20th Century Fox, 1979
TOUCHED BY LOVE   Columbia, 1980
PRIVATE LESSONS   Jensen Farley Pictures, 1981
PRIVATE SCHOOL   Universal, 1983
A TIME TO DIE   Almi Pictures, 1983, w/Byron Brandt
LOVELINES   Tri-Star, 1984, w/David Bretherton
THOSE SHE LEFT BEHIND (TF)   NBC
    Productions, 1988
THE SHRIMP ON THE BARBIE   Unity Pictures, 1990

J. BENJAMIN CHULAY
COINS IN THE FOUNTAIN (TF)   Michael Filerman
    Productions, 1990

LISA CHURGIN
LOVE AT LARGE   Orion, 1990

CHRIS CIBELLI
THE UNHOLY   Vestron, 1988
WAXWORK   Vestron, 1988
SUNDOWN: THE VAMPIRE IN RETREAT
    Vestron, 1989

RICHARD P. CIRINCIONE
TARGET   Warner Bros., 1985, w/Stephen A. Rotter
ISHTAR   Columbia, 1987, w/William Reynolds &
    Stephen A. Rotter
Q & A   Tri-Star, 1990

JIM CLARK
THE ADVENTURE OF SHERLOCK HOLMES'
    SMARTER BROTHER   20th Century Fox, 1975
THE DAY OF THE LOCUST   Paramount, 1975
MARATHON MAN   Paramount, 1976
THE LAST REMAKE OF BEAU GESTE   Universal,
    1977, w/Arthur Schmidt
AGATHA   Warner Bros., 1979
YANKS   Universal, 1979
HONKY TONK FREEWAY   Universal/AFD, 1981
PRIVATES ON PARADE   Orion Classics, 1984
THE KILLING FIELDS ★★   Warner Bros., 1984
FRENCH LESSON   *THE FROG PRINCE*   Warner
    Bros., 1984
THE MISSION ★   Warner Bros., 1986
YOUNG TOSCANINI   Carthago Films/Canal Plus/
    FR3/La Sept/Italian International Pictures/RAI,
    1988, w/Brian Oats
MEMPHIS BELLE   Enigma/Warner Bros., 1990

LAURENCE MÉRY CLARK
Agent: Sandra Marsh Management - Sherman Oaks,
    818/905-6961

RED MONARCH   Enigma Films/Goldcrest Films &
    Television Ltd., 1983
GOOD AND BAD AT GAMES (TF)   Portman Quintet
    Productions, 1983
SECRET PLACES   TLC Films/20th Century Fox, 1984
THE RETURN OF THE SOLDIER   European
    Classics, 1985
THE DOCTOR AND THE DEVILS   20th Century
    Fox, 1985
INTIMATE CONTACT (MS)   Zenith Productions/
    Central TV, 1987
SHAG: THE MOVIE   Hemdale, 1989
INSPECTOR MORSE   Zenith Productions, 1990

CURTISS CLAYTON
THE UNHEARD MUSIC (FD)   Skouras Pictures,
    1986, w/others
ON THE LINE   Miramax, 1987, w/Cari Coughlin
HALLOWEEN 4: THE RETURN OF MICHAEL MYERS
    Galaxy International, 1988
DRUGSTORE COWBOY   Avenue Pictures, 1989
A MATTER OF DEGREES   Backbeat Productions, 1989
A RAGE IN HARLEM   Miramax, 1991

GRAEME CLIFFORD
Agent: Lou Pitt, ICM - Los Angeles, 213/550-4000

DON'T LOOK NOW   Paramount, 1974
THE ROCKY HORROR PICTURE SHOW   20th Century
    Fox, 1976
THE MAN WHO FELL TO EARTH   Cinema 5, 1976
F.I.S.T.   United Artists, 1978, w/Antony Gibbs
CONVOY   United Artists, 1978, w/Garth Craven &
    John Wright
THE POSTMAN ALWAYS RINGS TWICE
    Paramount, 1981

ANNE V. COATES, ACE
Agent: The Gersh Agency, Inc., Beverly Hills -
    213/274-6611, New York - 212/997-1818

LAWRENCE OF ARABIA ★★   Columbia, 1962
BECKET ★   Paramount, 1964
THE ADVENTURERS   Paramount, 1970
THE PUBLIC EYE   Universal, 1972
FRIENDS   Paramount, 1971
THE NELSON AFFAIR   Universal, 1973
MURDER ON THE ORIENT EXPRESS
    Paramount, 1974
11 HARROWHOUSE   20th Century Fox, 1974
MAN FRIDAY   Avco Embassy, 1975
ACES HIGH   Cinema Shares International, 1976
THE EAGLE HAS LANDED   Columbia, 1977
THE MEDUSA TOUCH   Warner Bros., 1978
THE LEGACY   Universal, 1979
THE ELEPHANT MAN ★   Paramount, 1980
RAGTIME   Paramount, 1981, w/Antony Gibbs &
    Stanley Warnow
THE BUSHIDO BLADE   Aquarius, 1982
THE PIRATES OF PENZANCE   Universal, 1983
GREYSTROKE: THE LEGEND OF TARZAN, LORD OF
    THE APES   Warner Bros., 1984
RAW DEAL   DEG, 1986
LADY JANE   Paramount, 1986
MASTERS OF THE UNIVERSE   Cannon, 1987
FAREWELL TO THE KING   Orion, 1989
LISTEN TO ME   WEG, 1989
I LOVE YOU TO DEATH   Tri-Star, 1990
WHAT ABOUT BOB?   Buena Vista, 1991

JAMES COBLENTZ
FOXES   United Artists, 1980
IT'S MY TURN   Columbia, 1980 , w/Byron Brandt &
    Marjorie Fowler
NATIONAL LAMPOON'S MOVIE MADNESS
    United Artists, 1981
CHEECH & CHONG: STILL SMOKIN'   Paramount, 1983
ALOHA SUMMER   Spectrafilm, 1988, w/Jay Cassidy &
    Jack Hofstra
MURDER IN PARADISE (TF)   Bill McCutchen
    Productions, 1990
NIGHT VISION (TF)   Wes Craven Films, 1990,
    w/Mark Melnick

223

Co

CINEMATOGRAPHERS
PRODUCTION
DESIGNERS,
COSTUME
DESIGNERS and
FILM EDITORS
GUIDE

F
I
L
M

E
D
I
T
O
R
S

ARTHUR COBURN

THE BALLAD OF GREGORIO CORTEZ   Embassy,
    1983, w/John Bertucci
BEVERLY HILLS COP   Paramount, 1984,
    w/Billy Weber
WILDROSE   Troma, 1985
EXTREMITIES   Atlantic Releasing Corporation, 1986
REAL GENIUS   Tri-Star, 1987
DOMINICK AND EUGENE   Orion, 1988
TRIUMPH OF THE SPIRIT   Nova International, 1989

ANDREW COHEN

FOLLOW YOUR HEART (TF)   Force Ten
    Productions, 1990
LEONA HELMSLEY: THE QUEEN OF MEAN (TF)
    Fries Entertainment, 1990
HER WICKED WAYS (TF)   Lois Luger
    Productions, 1990

MARTIN COHEN

THE PRINCESS ACADEMY   Empire Pictures, 1987
THE WOMEN'S CLUB   Lightning Pictures, 1987

STEVE COHEN

NO MAN'S LAND   Orion, 1987
FROM THE DEAD OF NIGHT (TF)   Shadowplay
    Films/Phoenix Entertainment Group, 1989,
    w/Christopher Cooke
WHEELS OF TERROR (CTF)   Once Upon A Time
    Productions, 1989
THE IMAGE (CTF)   Citadel Entertainment
    Productions, 1990
BARE ESSENTIALS (TF)   Republic Pictures TV, 1991

FRANCOISE COISPEAU

VINCENT & THEO   Hemdale, 1990,
    w/Geraldine Peroni

STAN COLE

BREAKING POINT   20th Century Fox, 1976
JACOB TWO-TWO MEETS THE HOODED FANG
    Cinema Shares International, 1978
MURDER BY DECREE   Avco Embassy, 1979
PHOBIA   Paramount, 1981
PORKY'S   20th Century Fox, 1982
PORKY'S II: THE NEXT DAY   20th Century Fox, 1983
A CHRISTMAS STORY   MGM/UA, 1983
RHINESTONE   20th Century Fox, 1984,
    w/John Wheeler
TURK 182!   20th Century Fox, 1985
FROM THE HIP   DEG, 1987
THE HOUSEKEEPER   Castle Hill Productions, 1987
COLLISION COURSE   DEG, 1988
THE KISS   Tri-Star, 1988
LOOSE CANNONS   Tri-Star, 1990
POPCORN   Studio Three, 1991

JASON COLEMAN

SOULTAKER   Taurus Entertainment, 1990,
    w/Michael Rissi

ALAN COLLINS

THE BROOD   New World, 1979
DIRTY TRICKS   Avco Embassy, 1981
TULIPS   Avco Embassy, 1981, w/Yuri Lohovy

JIM CONNOCK

SLAUGHTER HIGH   Vestron, 1987

SCOTT CONRAD, ACE

Agent: The Gersh Agency, Inc. - Beverly Hills,
    213/274-6611
Home: 10880 Wilshire Blvd., Suite 908, Los Angeles, CA
    90024, 213/456-1618

A BOY AND HIS DOG   Pacific Film Enterprises, 1975
MESSIAH OF EVIL   International Cinefilm, 1975
ALOHA, BOBBY AND ROSE   Columbia, 1975
A STAR IS BORN   Warner Bros., 1976
ROCKY ★★   United Artists, 1976, w/Richard Halsey
OUTLAW BLUES   Warner Bros., 1977,
    w/Danford B. Greene
UP IN SMOKE   Paramount, 1978
WANDA NEVADA   United Artists, 1979
CHEECH & CHONG'S NEXT MOVIE   Universal, 1980
THE HOLLYWOOD KNIGHTS   Columbia, 1980,
    w/Stan Allen
CHEECH & CHONG'S NICE DREAMS   Columbia, 1981
SPACEHUNTER: ADVENTURES IN THE FORBIDDEN
    ZONE   Columbia, 1983
ERNIE KOVACS: BETWEEN THE LAUGHTER (TF)
    ABC Circle Films, 1984
HEY BABE!   Rafal, 1984, w/Afte Chinaeff
STEPHEN KING'S CAT'S EYE   MGM/UA, 1985
RIGHT TO KILL? (TF)   Wrye-Konigsberg Productions/
    Taper Media Enterprises/Telepictures
    Productions, 1985
LUCAS   20th Century Fox, 1986
THE WRAITH   New Century/Vista, 1986,
    w/Gary Rocklen
THE BEDROOM WINDOW   DEG, 1987
MASQUERADE   MGM/UA, 1988
CLASS OF 1999   Taurus Entertainment, 1990
THE STRANGER WITHIN (TF)   Goodman-Rosen
    Productions, 1990
THE LAST TO GO (TF)   Freyda Rothstein
    Productions, 1991

MARK CONTE

East & West Coast Cards
Agent: The Doug Apatow Agency, 10559 Blythe Ave. -
    Los Angeles, CA 90064, 213/202-6888

UNDER FIRE   Orion, 1983
MISSING IN ACTION 2: THE BEGINNING
    Cannon, 1984
OPPOSING FORCE   Orion, 1986
KNIGHTS OF THE CITY   New World, 1986, CE
STEEL DAWN   Vestron, 1987
MONSTER IN THE CLOSET   Troma, 1987, CE
TURNER + HOOCH   Buena Vista, 1989, CE

BETH CONWELL

SNO-LINE   Vandom International, 1986
VASECTOMY: A DELICATE MATTER   Vandom
    International Pictures, 1986
GIRLFRIEND FROM HELL   IVE, 1990

CHRISTOPHER COOKE

BLIND FAITH-PARTS I & II (TF)   NBC Productions,
    1990, w/James Galloway
GOOD COPS, BAD COPS (TF)   Kushner-Locke
    Company, 1990
OVER MY DEAD BODY (TF)   Universal TV, 1990,
    w/Tom Finnen
THE CHASE (TF)   Steve White Productions, 1991

MALCOLM COOKE
Agent: Sandra Marsh Management - Sherman Oaks,
    818/905-6961

FAR FROM THE MADDING CROWD   MGM, 1967
CASTLE KEEP   Columbia, 1969
FRAGMENT OF FEAR   Columbia, 1971
PHILADELPHIA HERE I COME   1972, Irish
ENGLAND MADE ME   Cine Globe, 1973
THEATRE OF BLOOD   United Artists, 1973
LUTHER   American Film Theatre, 1974
BUTLEY   American Film Theatre, 1974
BRANNIGAN   United Artists, 1975
SKY RIDERS   20th Century Fox, 1976
DEATH ON THE NILE   Paramount, 1978
THE 5TH MUSKETEER   Columbia, 1979
ZULU DAWN   Orion/Warner Bros., 1979
FLASH GORDON   Universal, 1980
COMING OUT OF THE ICE (TF)   The Konigsberg
    Company, 1982
LITTLE GLORIA...HAPPY AT LAST (TF)   Edgar J.
    Scherick Associates/Metromedia Producers
    Corp., 1982
HOUND OF THE BASKERVILLES   Mapleton Films
    Ltd., 1983
SUPERGIRL   Tri-Star, 1984
SWEET DREAMS   Tri-Star, 1985
ACT OF VENGEANCE (CTF)   HBO Premiere Films/
    Telepix Canada Corp., 1986
KING KONG LIVES   DEG, 1986
EDGE OF SANITY   Millimeter Films, 1989
HAWKS   Skouras Pictures, 1989
BLACK RAINBOW   Goldcrest, 1989

ANGELO CORRAO
DREAM LOVER   MGM/UA, 1986
OFF BEAT   Buena Vista, 1986, w/Dede Allen
THE PICK-UP ARTIST   20th Century Fox, 1987,
    w/David Bretherton
LET'S GET LOST (FD)   Zeitgeist Films, 1988
SIGNS OF LIFE   Avenue Pictures, 1989,
    w/William M. Anderson
BETHUNE: THE MAKING OF A HERO   Filmline
    International, 1990, w/Yves Langlois

DON COSCARELLI
SURVIVAL QUEST   MGM/UA, 1989

JON COSTELLOE
DEALERS   Skouras, 1990

PAVIENDA COTT
MURDER ON LINE ONE   Academy
    Entertainment, 1990

BELINDA COTTRELL
BEJEWELLED (CTF)   TVS Productions, 1991

CARI COUGHLIN
THE UNHEARD MUSIC (FD)   Skouras Pictures,
    1986, w/others
DESERT BLOOM   Columbia, 1986, w/John Currin &
    David Garfield
PURPLE PEOPLE EATERS   Concorde, 1988

PETER COULSON
SWEET WILLIAM   Kendon Films, 1980
A HANDFUL OF DUST   New Line Cinema, 1988

BACK HOME (CTF)   TVS Films, 1989
PAPER MASK   Film Four International, 1991

STUART COURTNEY
TALES OF THE UNKNOWN   AIP Home Video, 1990,
    w/Jeff Parkin

ALEX COX
Agent: Stephanie Mann & Associates - Los Angeles,
    213/653-7130

WALKER   Universal, 1987, w/Carlos Puente

JOEL COX
Agent: The Gersh Agency, Inc. - Beverly Hills,
    213/274-6611

FAREWELL, MY LOVELY   Avco Embassy, 1975
THE ENFORCER   Warner Bros., 1976, w/Ferris Webster
THE GAUNTLET   Warner Bros., 1977, w/Ferris Webster
EVERY WHICH WAY BUT LOOSE   Warner Bros., 1978,
    w/Ferris Webster
BRONCO BILLY   Warner Bros., 1980, w/Ferris Webster
DEATH VALLEY   Universal, 1982
HONKYTONK MAN   Warner Bros., 1982, w/Michael
    Kelly & Ferris Webster
SUDDEN IMPACT   Warner Bros., 1983
TIGHTROPE   Warner Bros, 1984
PALE RIDER   Warner Bros., 1985
HEARTBREAK RIDGE   Warner Bros., 1986
RATBOY   Warner Bros., 1986
BIRD   Warner Bros., 1988
PINK CADILLAC   Warner Bros., 1989
WHITE HUNTER, BLACK HEART   Rastar/Malpaso/
    Warner Bros., 1990
THE ROOKIE   Malpaso/Warner Bros., 1990

IAN CRAFFORD
ACTT
Agent: Grace Lyons Management - Los Angeles,
    213/655-5100

LEGACY   Kino International, 1976
THE MEDUSA TOUCH   Warner Bros., 1978
BEYOND THE REEF   Universal, 1981
THE BUSHIDO BLADE   Aquarius, 1982
NEVER SAY NEVER AGAIN   Warner Bros., 1983
THE EMERALD FOREST   20th Century Fox, 1985
HOPE AND GLORY   Columbia, 1987
DREAM DEMON   Spectrafilm, 1988, w/David Martin
FIELD OF DREAMS   Universal, 1989
WHERE THE HEART IS   Buena Vista, 1990
CLASS ACTION   20th Century Fox, 1991

TONY CRANSTOUN
CROSSING TO FREEDOM (TF)   Procter & Gamble
    Productions, 1989, w/Edward Mansell

GARTH CRAVEN
Agent: The Gersh Agency, Inc., Beverly Hills -
    213/274-6611, New York - 212/997-1818

STRAW DOGS   Cinerama Releasing Corporation, 1972
PAT GARRETT & BILLY THE KID   MGM, 1973
BRING ME THE HEAD OF ALFREDO GARCIA
    United Artists, 1974
THE KILLER ELITE   United Artists, 1975
I NEVER PROMISED YOU A ROSE GARDEN   New
    World, 1977

Cr

CINEMATOGRAPHERS
PRODUCTION
DESIGNERS,
COSTUME
DESIGNERS AND
FILM EDITORS
GUIDE

F
I
L
M

E
D
I
T
O
R
S

Cr

CINEMATOGRAPHERS
PRODUCTION
DESIGNERS,
COSTUME
DESIGNERS AND
FILM EDITORS
GUIDE

F
I
L
M

E
D
I
T
O
R
S

CONVOY   United Artists, 1978, w/Graeme Clifford &
    John Wright
AVALANCHE EXPRESS   20th Century Fox, 1979
I, THE JURY   20th Century Fox, 1982
EDUCATING RITA   Columbia, 1983
LITTLE TREASURE   Tri-Star, 1985
THE BEST OF TIMES   Universal, 1986
GABY - A TRUE STORY   Tri-Star, 1987
SHOOT TO KILL   Buena Vista, 1988,
    w/George Bowers
TURNER + HOOCH   Buena Vista, 1989

PATRICK M. CRAWFORD
THE PRIVATE EYES   New World, 1981
ON ANY SUNDAY II   International Film Marketing/
    Arista, 1981, w/Ed Forsyth

GABRIELLA CRISTIANI, ACE
Agent: The Gersh Agency, Inc., Beverly Hills -
    213/274-6611, New York - 212/997-1818

LUNA   20th Century Fox, 1979
THE TRAGEDY OF A RIDICULOUS MAN   Warner
    Bros., 1982
THE LAST EMPEROR ★★   Columbia, 1987
HIGH SEASON   Hemdale, 1988
FRANCESCO   Istituto Luce/Italnoleggio, 1989
THE SHELTERING SKY   Warner Bros., 1990

RAIMONDO CROCIANI
THE NIGHT OF THE SHOOTING STARS   United
    Artists Classics, 1981
MYSTERE   Tris Films, 1983
LE BAL   Almi Classics, 1984
BYE BYE BABY   Seymour Brode & Associates, 1989

ARNOLD CRUST
FIREPOWER   AFD, 1979
DEATHWISH II   Filmways, 1982, w/Julian Semilian
THE WICKED LADY   MGM/UA, 1983
DEATHWISH 3   Cannon, 1985
APPOINTMENT WITH DEATH   Cannon, 1988

SUSAN CRUTCHER
RACHEL RIVER   Taurus Entertainment, 1989

ALAN J. CUMNER-PRICE
MR. LOVE   Warner Bros., 1986

SUSAN E. CUNNINGHAM
FRIDAY THE 13TH PART 2   Paramount, 1981
A STRANGER IS WATCHING   MGM/UA, 1982
SPRING BREAK   Columbia, 1983

JOHN K. CURRIN
DICE RULES   Seven Arts, 1991

CLAUDIO CUTRY
(Claude Kutry)
THE SALAMANDER   ITC, 1983
YELLOW HAIR AND THE FORTRESS OF GOLD
    Crown International, 1984
THE OUTING   TMS Pictures/The Movie Store, 1987
THE CURSE   Trans World Entertainment, 1987
SONNY BOY   Triumph Releasing, 1989
THE CURSE II: THE BITE   Trans World
    Entertainment, 1989

D

JOHN DAVID DAGNEN
TERMINAL FORCE   PM Home Video, 1990, w/Paul Volk
REPO JAKE   PM Home Video, 1991

ROBERT DALVA
Agent: The Agency - Los Angeles, 213/551-3000

THE BLACK STALLION ★   United Artists, 1979
LATINO   Cinecom, 1986

CESARE D'AMICO
CHINA 9, LIBERTY 37   Lorimar, 1984
WARRIORS OF THE LOST WORLD   Vista
    International, 1985
DETECTIVE SCHOOL DROP OUTS   Cannon, 1986
HAUNTED SUMMER   Cannon, 1988, w/Richard Fields
TORRENTS OF SPRING   Erre/Reteitalia, 1989

MERCEDES DANEVIC
END OF THE LINE   Orion Classics, 1988

NENA DANEVIC
AMADEUS ★   Orion, 1984, w/Michael Chandler
VALMONT   Orion, 1989, w/Alan Heim

HENRY DANGAR
STIR   Hoyts, 1980
WINTER OF OUR DREAMS   Satori, 1982
THE BOY WHO HAD EVERYTHING   1984
WHICH WAY HOME (CTF)   McElroy & McElroy, 1991,
    w/David Huggett

LUIS CESAR D'ANGIOLILLO
MISS MARY   New World, 1986
MAN FACING SOUTHEAST   Film Dallas, 1987

RAY DANIELS
GUNSMOKE: THE LAST APACHE (TF)   CBS
    Entertainment Productions, 1990
NIGHT WALK (TF)   CBS Entertainment
    Productions, 1990

ROBERT A. DANIELS
THE TAKE (CTF)   Cine-Nevada, 1990

JOANNE D'ANTONIO
Address: 3267 Deronda Dr., Los Angeles, CA 90068,
    213/469-0988

SATURDAY THE 14TH   New World, 1981
SUMMERSPELL   Summerspell Productions, 1984
BROKEN RAINBOW   Earthworks Productions, 1986
MURDER BY THE BOOK (TF)   Nelson Productions/
    Orion TV, 1987
RENO'S KIDS: 87 DAYS + 11   Go For It
    Productions, 1987
WHO GETS THE FRIENDS? (TF)   CBS
    Entertainment, 1988
ESCAPE   Tri-Star, 1990
VOICE OF THE PLANET (MS)   GAIA Productions, 1990

MARCUS D'ARCY
BANGKOK HILTON   Kennedy-Miller, 1990,
w/Frans Vandenburg

HUGUES DARMOIS
A MAN AND A WOMAN: 20 YEARS LATER   Warner
Bros., 1986

TEDDY DARVAS
JUDGMENT IN BERLIN   New Line Cinema, 1988

JOE D'AUGUSTINE
TOO MUCH SUN   New Line Pictures, 1990

BRURIA DAVIDSON
THE LAST AMERICAN VIRGIN   Cannon, 1982
DUTCH TREAT   Cannon, 1987

CARMEL DAVIES
RED HEAT   Tri-Star, 1988, w/Donn Aron &
Freeman Davies
ANOTHER 48 HRS.   Paramount, 1990,
w/Freeman Davies & Donn Aron

FREEMAN DAVIES
WHEN TIME RAN OUT   Warner Bros., 1980,
w/Edward A. Biery
THE LONG RIDERS   United Artists, 1980,
w/David Holden
SOUTHERN COMFORT   20th Century Fox, 1981
48HRS.   Paramount, 1982, w/Mark Warner &
Billy Weber
BRAINSTORM   MGM/UA, 1983,
w/Edward Warschilka
STREETS OF FIRE   Universal, 1984,
w/Michael Ripps
BREWSTER'S MILLIONS   Universal, 1985,
w/Michael Ripps
CROSSROADS   Columbia, 1986
EXTREME PREJUDICE   Tri-Star, 1987
RED HEAT   Tri-Star, 1988, w/Donn Aron &
Carmel Davies
JOHNNY HANDSOME   Tri-Star, 1989
ANOTHER 48 HRS.   Paramount, 1990, w/Carmel
Davies & Donn Aron

PETER DAVIES
Agent: Grace Lyons Management - Los Angeles,
213/655-5100

THE FINAL OPTION   *WHO DARES WINS*
MGM/UA, 1983
OCTOPUSSY   MGM/UA, 1983, w/Henry Richardson
THE SHOOTING PARTY   European Classics, 1984
A VIEW TO A KILL   MGM/UA, 1985
THE LIVING DAYLIGHTS   MGM/UA, 1987,
w/John Grover
THE LAIR OF THE WHITE WORM   Vestron, 1988
THE RAINBOW   Vestron, 1989
RED KING, WHITE KNIGHT (CTF)   John Kemeny
Citdale Entertainment Productions, 1990

T. BATTLE DAVIS
THE NINTH CONFIGURATION   Warner Bros.,
1980, w/Peter Lee Thompson
WILD THING   Atlantic Releasing Corporation,
1987, w/Steven Rosenblum

ELVIRA: MISTRESS OF THE DARK   New
World, 1988
AWAKENINGS   Columbia, 1990, w/Gerald B. Greenberg

FREEMAN DAVIS
JOHNNY HANDSOME   Carolco/Tri-Star, 1989

KAYE DAVIS
EVIL DEAD 2   Rosebud Releasing Corporation, 1987

ZACK DAVIS
KILL CRAZY   Media Home Entertainment, 1991

LISA DAY
Agent: Jay Gilbert Talent Agency - Los Angeles,
213/656-5906

LET'S SPEND THE NIGHT TOGETHER (FD)
Embassy, 1983
STOP MAKING SENSE (FD)   Cinecom International/
Island Alive, 1984
HOME OF THE BRAVE   Cinecom International, 1986
CHUCK BERRY: HAIL! HAIL! ROCK N' ROLL! (FD)
Universal, 1987
EDDIE MURPHY RAW   Paramount, 1987
THE WIZARD OF LONELINESS   Skouras Pictures, 1988
GREAT BALLS OF FIRE   Orion, 1989, w/Pembroke
Herring & Bert Lovitt
WHITE FANG   Buena Vista, 1991

ROBERT DEARBERG
HOUSE OF THE LONG SHADOWS   Cannon, 1984
THREE KINDS OF HEAT   Cannon, 1987

JOHN DE BELLO
HAPPY HOUR   The Movie Store, 1987

CARTER DE HAVEN IV
PERRY MASON: THE CASE OF THE POISONED
PEN (TF)   Viacom Productions, 1990
PERRY MASON: THE CASE OF THE DESPERATE
DECEPTION (TF)   Viacom Productions, 1990
PERRY MASON: THE CASE OF THE DEFIANT
DAUGHTER (TF)   Viacom Productions, 1990
PERRY MASON: THE CASE OF THE MALIGNED
MOBSTER (TF)   Viacom Productions, 1991

HUBERT C. DE LA BOUILLERIE
THE WITCHES OF EASTWICK   Warner Bros., 1987,
w/Richard Francis-Bruce
POLICE ACADEMY 5: ASSIGNMENT MIAMI BEACH
Warner Bros., 1988
POLICE ACADEMY 6: CITY UNDER SIEGE   Warner
Bros., 1989
TANGO & CASH   Warner Bros., 1989, w/Stuart Baird &
Robert Ferretti

PABLO G. DEL AMO
AY, CARMELA!   Prestige Films, 1991

PETER DELFGOU
LAMB   Film Forum, 1986
WE THINK THE WORLD OF YOU   Cinecom, 1988

De

**CINEMATOGRAPHERS
PRODUCTION
DESIGNERS,
COSTUME
DESIGNERS** AND
**FILM EDITORS
GUIDE**

**F
I
L
M

E
D
I
T
O
R
S**

De

CINEMATOGRAPHERS
PRODUCTION
DESIGNERS,
COSTUME
DESIGNERS AND
FILM EDITORS
GUIDE

F
I
L
M

E
D
I
T
O
R
S

PEDRO DEL REY
SANDINO   RTVE-Miguel Littin Productions, 1990

HERVE de LUZE
PIRATES   Cannon, 1986, w/William Reynolds
JEAN DE FLORETTE   Orion Classics, 1987,
   w/Noelle Boisson & Arlette Langmann
MANON OF THE SPRING   Orion Classics, 1987,
   w/Genevieve Louveau
TO KILL A PRIEST   Columbia, 1988

LESLIE DENNIS-BRACKEN
DREAM DATE (TF)   Frederic Golchan/Robert
   Kosberg Productions, 1990

FRANK DE PALMA
CAMERON'S CLOSET   Cinema Group, 1987

LORENZO DE STEFANO
GIRLS JUST WANT TO HAVE FUN   New
   World, 1985
THE KILLING TIME   New World, 1987
GINGER ALE AFTERNOON   Skouras Pictures, 1989

DAVID DE WILDE
MARTIN'S DAY   MGM/UA, 1985

TONY DI MARCO
HELL NIGHT   Aquarius, 1981
THE SEDUCTION   Avco Embassy, 1982

WILLIAM DIVER
DISTANT VOICES, STILL LIVES   Alive Films, 1989

HUMPHREY DIXON
Agent: London Management, 235/241 Regent St. -
   London W1R 7AG, 071-493-1610

ROSELAND   Cinema Shares International, 1977,
   w/Richard Schiechen
HULLABALOO OVER GEORGIE & BONNIE'S
   PICTURES   Corinth, 1979
QUARTET   New World, 1981
HEAT AND DUST   Universal Classics, 1983
MARIA'S LOVERS   Cannon, 1984
A ROOM WITH A VIEW   Cinecom, 1986
CRUSOE   Island Pictures, 1988
MR. & MRS. BRIDGE   Miramax, 1990
MR. JOHNSON   Avenue, 1990
STEPPING OUT   1991

PAUL DIXON
WHAT EVER HAPPENED TO BABY JANE? (TF)
   Steve White Productions, 1991

PATRICK DODD
THEY CAME FROM WITHIN   *SHIVERS*
   TransAmerica, 1976

GAS   Paramount, 1981
SMOOTH TALK   Spectrafilm, 1985
STACKING   Spectrafilm, 1987
PIN   Malofilm Distribution, 1988

DENNIS DOLAN
BOULEVARD NIGHTS   Warner Bros., 1979
CARNY   United Artists, 1980

WOLFEN   Orion/Warner Bros., 1981, w/Marshall
   M.Borden, Martin Bram & Christopher Lebenzon
THINGS ARE TOUGH ALL OVER   Columbia, 1982
REPO MAN   Universal, 1984

WILLIAM DORNISCH
Agent: Jay Gilbert Talent Agency - Los Angeles,
   213/656-5906

THE PICASSO SUMMER   Warner Bros., 1969
JOHNNY GOT HIS GUN   1971
BROTHERS   Warner Bros., 1977
STAR TREK II: THE WRATH OF KHAN
   Paramount, 1982

KATHLEEN DOUGHERTY
NOTHING LASTS FOREVER   MGM/UA, 1984,
   w/Margot Francis

JULIAN DOYLE
MONTY PYTHON'S LIFE OF BRIAN   Orion/Warner
   Bros., 1979
TIME BANDITS   Avco Embassy, 1981
MONTY PYTHON LIVE AT THE HOLLYWOOD
   BOWL (FD)   Columbia, 1982, w/Jimmy B. Frazier
MONTY PYTHON'S THE MEANING OF LIFE
   Universal, 1983
BRAZIL   Universal, 1985

LEE DRAGU
LIBERTY & BASH   Fries Home Video, 1990

MILLER DRAKE
DAN TURNER (TF)   Fries Entertainment, 1990

TOM DUBENSKY
NIGHT OF THE LIVING DEAD   Columbia, 1990

VICTOR DU BOIS
EXTREME CLOSE-UP (TF)   Bedford Falls
   Productions, 1990

MARIE-SOPHIE DUBUS
SWEET REVENGE (CTF)   Turner Pictures, 1989

BOB DUCSAY
CATCH ME IF YOU CAN   MCEG, 1990

J. PATRICK DUFFNER
DANNY BOY   Triumph, 1984
EAT THE PEACH   Skouras Pictures, 1987
MY LEFT FOOT   Miramax, 1989
THE FIELD   Avenue, 1990

JOHN DUFFY
THE WOMAN INSIDE   20th Century Fox, 1981
STITCHES   International Film Marketing, 1985
ANGEL OF DEATH (TF)   Once Upon A Time Films, 1990

DANIEL DUNCAN
WITCHBOARD   Cinema Group, 1987,
   w/Stephen J. Waller

DAVID DUNCAN
PEACEMAKER   Fries Entertainment, 1990

DUWAYNE DUNHAM
RETURN OF THE JEDI   20th Century Fox, 1983, w/
  Sean Barton & Marcia Lucas
THE MEAN SEASON   Orion, 1985
BLUE VELVET   DEG, 1986
CHERRY 2000   Orion, 1988, w/Edward Abroms
MAD HOUSE   Orion, 1990
WILD AT HEART   Samuel Goldwyn Company, 1990
TWIN PEAKS (TF)   Propaganda Films, 1990

STEPHEN DUNN
THE NORSEMAN   American International, 1978, w/
  Robert Bell, Aladar Klein, Shirak Kojayan & Sarah
  Legor
BEYOND THERAPY   New World, 1987
FOOL FOR LOVE   Cannon, 1987, w/Luce Grunenwaldt
LIP SERVICE (CTF)   Cinehaus, 1988

MICHAEL J. DUTHIE
SHOUT AT THE DEVIL   American International, 1976
REVENGE OF THE NINJA   MGM/UA/Cannon, 1983, w/
  Mark Helfrich
NINJA III: THE DOMINATION   Cannon, 1984
AMERICAN NINJA   Cannon, 1985
THE ASSISI UNDERGROUND   Cannon, 1985
AVENGING FORCE   Cannon, 1986
NUMBER ONE WITH A BULLET   Cannon, 1987
AMERICAN NINJA 2   Cannon, 1987
BRADDOCK: MISSING IN ACTION III   Cannon, 1988
PLATOON LEADER   Cannon, 1988
AMERICAN NINJA 3: BLOOD HUNT   Cannon, 1989
THE HOUSE OF USHER   RCA/Columbia Pictures Home
  Video, 1991

E

CAROL EASTMAN
SCREEN TEST   CineTel Films, 1986   .

MICHAEL ECONOMOU
MINNIE AND MOSKOWITZ   Universal, 1971
FIVE ON THE BLACK HAND SIDE   United Artists, 1973
THE DEADLY TRACKERS   1973
THE TRIAL OF LEE HARVEY OSWALD (TF)   Charles
  Fries Productions, 1977
THE DEATH OF RICHIE (TF)   Henry Jaffe Enterprises,
  1977
A SENSITIVE, PASSIONATE MAN (TF)   Factor-Newland
  Productions Corp., 1978
OFF THE EDGE   Pentacle, 1977
HARPER VALLEY P.T.A.   April Fools, 1978
FRIENDLY FIRE (TF)   Marble Arch Productions, 1979
S*H*E (TF)   Martin Bregman Productions, 1980
CHILD BRIDE OF SHORT CREEK (TF)   Lawrence
  Schiller Paul Monash Productions, 1981
THE FOUR SEASONS   Universal, 1981
THE EXECUTIONER'S SONG (TF)   Film Communica-
  tions Inc., 1982
TOO SCARED TO SCREAM   The Movie Store, 1984
EMBASSY (TF)   Stan Margulies Company/ABC Circle
  Films, 1985

COURAGE (TF)   Highgate Pictures/New World TV, 1986
SWEET LIBERTY   Universal, 1986
SPEED ZONE   Orion, 1989

ROBERT EDWARDS
THE FORBIDDEN DANCE   21st Century/Columbia,
  1990, w/Earl Watson

BERT EELES
THE GIRL IN THE PICTURE   Samuel Goldwyn Company,
  1985

CORKY EHLERS
REVEALING EVIDENCE (TF)   T.W.S. Productions, 1989
A SON'S PROMISE (TF)   Marian Rees Associates, 1990
MONTANA (CTF)   HBO Productions, 1990
CASEY'S GIFT: FOR LOVE OF A CHILD (TF)   American
  First Run Studios, 1990

MICHAEL ELIOT, ACE
DEADLY FRIEND   Warner Bros., 1986
PANCHO BARNES (TF)   Blue Andre Productions/Orion
  Television, 1988, w/Michael F. Anderson

CHRISTOPHER ELLIS
NOT OF THIS WORLD (TF)   Barry & Enright Productions,
  1991, w/Richard C. Leeman

MICHAEL ELLIS
Agent: London Management, 235/241 Regent St. - London
  W1R 7AG, 071-493-1610

CROSS OF IRON   Avco Embassy, 1977, w/Tony
  Lawson & Albert Taschner
DEATH WATCH   Quartet, 1980 , w/Armand Psenny
THE GODSEND   Cannon, 1980
BRITANNIA HOSPITAL   United Artists Classics, 1982
THE LORDS OF DISCIPLINE   Paramount, 1983
COMFORT AND JOY   Universal, 1984
DEATHWATCH   Quartet, 1984, w/Armand Psenny
THE JEWEL OF THE NILE   20th Century Fox, 1985, w/
  Peter Boita
THE BRIDE   Columbia, 1985
HOUSEKEEPING   Columbia, 1987
STEALING HEAVEN   FilmDallas, 1989
BREAKING IN   Samuel Goldwyn Company, 1989
IMPROMPTU   Hemdale Films, 1991

KEN ELUTO
Phone: 212/222-7438

KING OF AMERICA (TF)   Center for Television in the
  Humanities, 1982
FORTY-DEUCE   Island Alive, 1982
THAT RHYTHM, THOSE BLUES (FD)   1989

RENEE ENGELBRECHT
THE GODS MUST BE CRAZY II   Columbia, 1990, w/
  Ivan Hall

ROBERT ERICKSON
FROM HOLLYWOOD TO DEADWOOD   Island, 1989, w/
  Stephen Adrianson

DONALD W. ERNST, ACE
WIZARDS (AF)   20th Century Fox, 1977
THE LORD OF THE RINGS (AF)   United Artists, 1978

CINEMATOGRAPHERS
PRODUCTION
DESIGNERS,
COSTUME
DESIGNERS AND
FILM EDITORS
GUIDE

F
I
L
M

E
D
I
T
O
R
S

Er

CINEMATOGRAPHERS
PRODUCTION
DESIGNERS,
COSTUME
DESIGNERS AND
FILM EDITORS
GUIDE

F
I
L
M

E
D
I
T
O
R
S

HEY GOOD LOOKIN' (AF)   Warner Bros., 1982
STARCHASER: THE LEGEND OF ORION (AF)
   Atlantic Releasing Corporation, 1985
TUMMY TROUBLE (animated short)   Buena
   Vista, 1989

ROBERT ERNST
ALLEY CAT   Film Ventures International, 1984
HELL SQUAD   Cannon, 1987

ROBERT L. ESTRIN, ACE
THE CANDIDATE   Warner Bros., 1972,
   w/Richard A. Harris
PIPE DREAMS   Avco Embassy, 1976
BREATHLESS   Orion, 1983
MIRRORS   First American, 1984
DESERT HEARTS   Samuel Goldwyn Company, 1985
WHAT HAPPENED TO KEROUAC?   New Yorker,
   1986, w/Nathanial Dorsky
COLORS   Orion, 1988
INTERNAL AFFAIRS   Paramount, 1989

BRIAN EVANS
LAST CALL   Prism Entertainment, 1990

SCOTT EYLER
THE FATAL IMAGE (TF)   Ellipse Programme,
   1990, w/Karen Sharp

PHYLLIS FAMIGLIETTI
BROKEN NOSES (FD)   Weber/Bush, 1987

STEPHEN FANFARA
HAPPY BIRTHDAY, GEMINI   United Artists, 1980
THE AMATEUR   20th Century Fox, 1981
LOOSE SCREWS   Concorde, 1985
RECRUITS   Concorde, 1986, w/Christie Wilson
NORMAN'S AWESOME EXPERIENCE   Norstar, 1989

SUSAN FANSHEL
THE POWER OF THE PAST WITH BILL MOYERS:
   FLORENCE (TF)   David Grubin Productions, 1990

GLENN FARR
Agent: Jay Gilbert Talent Agency - Los Angeles,
   213/656-5906

HEROES OF ROCK AND ROLL (FD)   ABC, 1979
FATSO   20th Century Fox, 1980
DIVINE MADNESS (FD)   The Ladd Company/Warner
   Bros., 1980
THIS IS ELVIS (FD)   Warner Bros., 1981 CE
THE RIGHT STUFF ★   The Ladd Company/
   Warner Bros., 1983, w/Lisa Fruchtman, Tom Rolf,
   Stephen A. Rotter & Douglas Stewart
GOSPEL (FD)   20th Century Fox, 1984
RUNAWAY   Tri-Star, 1984
COMMANDO   20th Century Fox, 1985

NOTHING IN COMMON   Tri-Star, 1986
THE SERPENT AND THE RAINBOW   Universal, 1988
REAL MEN   MGM/UA, 1987, w/Malcolm Campbell
PHYSICAL EVIDENCE   Columbia, 1989
OLD GRINGO   Columbia, 1989, w/William Anderson &
   Juan Carlos Macias
MOTHERS, DAUGHTERS AND LOVERS (TF)   Katz-
   Huyck Films, 1990, w/Michael Tronick & Fred Roth
CAREER OPPORTUNITIES   Universal, 1991,
   w/Peck Prior

IAN FARR
NOT A PENNY MORE, NOT A PENNY LESS -
   PARTS I & II (MS)   Paramount-Revcom/BBC, 1989

KAJA FEHR
Agent: The Gersh Agency, Inc., Beverly Hills -
   213/274-6611, New York - 212/997-1818

PRIZZI'S HONOR ★   20th Century Fox, 1985,
   w/Rudi Fehr
TOUGH GUYS   Buena Vista, 1986
HOW I GOT INTO COLLEGE   20th Century Fox, 1989,
   w/Sonya Sones Tramer

RUDI FEHR, ACE
Address: 3410 La Sombra Drive, Hollywood, CA 90068,
   213/851-3441

ONE FROM THE HEART   Columbia, 1982,
   w/Anne Goursaud & Randy Roberts
HARD KNOX (TF)   A. Shane Company, 1984
PRIZZI'S HONOR ★   20th Century Fox, 1985,
   w/Kaja Fehr

NINA FEINBERG
SIMON   Orion/Warner Bros., 1980
LOVESICK   Warner Bros., 1983
THE MANHATTAN PROJECT   20th Century Fox, 1986

JOHN FELDMAN
ALLIGATOR EYES   Castle Hill, 1990, w/Cynthia
   Rogers & Mike Frisino

SUZANNE FENN
PRETTY BABY   Paramount, 1978, w/Suzanne Baron
THE TWO WORLDS OF ANGELITA   First-Run
   Features, 1983
HOTEL NEW YORK   World Artists, 1985
A NIGHT IN THE LIFE OF JIMMY REARDON   20th
   Century Fox, 1988

ANITA FERNANDEZ
DOCTEUR PETIOT   *DR. PETIOT*   Aries Film
   Releasing, 1990

ROBERT A. FERRETTI, ACE
GYMKATA   MGM/UA, 1985
OUT OF CONTROL   New World, 1985,
   w/Allan Holzman
TANGO & CASH   Warner Bros., 1989, w/Stuart Baird &
   Hubert De La Boullerie
DIE HARD 2   20th Century Fox, 1990, w/Stuart Baird
OUT FOR JUSTICE   Warner Bros., 1991,
   w/Donald Brochu

RICHARD FETTERMAN
Address: 1691 Oakdale Street, Pasadena, CA 91106,
818/793-8638

SWEET REVENGE   MGM/United Artists, 1976,
w/Evan Lottman
TAKE DOWN   Buena Vista, 1979
BEATLEMANIA   American Cinema, 1981
THE BURNING BED (TF)   Tisch-Avnet
Productions, 1984

TOD FEUERMAN
THE BLOB   Tri-Star, 1988, w/Terry Stokes
SAN BERDOO (Pilot)   1989

RICHARD FIELDS
ILLEGALLY YOURS   DEG, 1987, w/Ronald Krehel
HAUNTED SUMMER   Cannon, 1988,
w/Cesare D'Amico
TEXASVILLE   Columbia, 1990

DAVID FINFER
Agent: The Gersh Agency, Inc., Beverly Hills -
213/274-6611, New York - 212/997-1818

REAL LIFE   Paramount, 1979
DEFIANCE   American International, 1980
MODERN ROMANCE   Columbia, 1981
THE SKY'S THE LIMIT (TF)   Palance-Levy
Productions, 1984
LOST IN AMERICA   The Geffen Company/Warner
Bros., 1985
SOUL MAN   New World, 1986
BACK TO THE BEACH   Paramount, 1987
INSIDE OUT   Hemdale, 1987
HEART CONDITION   New Line Cinema, 1990
WARLOCK   Trimark Pictures, 1991
DEFENDING YOUR LIFE   Warner Bros., 1991

CLAUDIA FINKLE
HOWLING IV...THE ORIGINAL NIGHTMARE   Allied
Entertainment, 1988, w/Malcolm Burns-Errlington
CRACK HOUSE   Cannon, 1989

TOM FINNEN
IT HAD TO BE YOU   Limelight Studios, 1989
THE WIZARD   Universal, 1989
OVER MY DEAD BODY (TF)   Universal TV, 1990,
w/Chris Cooke

ARDAN FISHER
SHE'S BEEN AWAY   BBC, 1990

ROBERT FITZGERALD
SCHIZOID   Cannon, 1980, w/Dick Brummer
THE GLOVE   Pro International, 1981

JOHN J. FITZSTEPHENS
JUST TELL ME WHAT YOU WANT   Warner
Bros., 1980
PRINCE OF THE CITY   Orion/Warner Bros., 1981
DEATHTRAP   Warner Bros., 1982
FIGHTING BACK   Paramount, 1982,
w/Nicholas Smith

SETH FLAUM
THE GREAT OUTDOORS   Universal, 1988,
w/William Gordean & Tom Rolf

THE GUARDIAN   Universal, 1990
THANKSGIVING DAY (TF)   Zacharias-Buhai
Productions, 1990

WILLIAM FLICKER
HOUR OF THE ASSASSIN   Concorde, 1987
SLUMBER PARTY MASSACRE II   Concorde, 1987
CRIME ZONE   Concorde, 1988

ROBERT FLORIO, ACE
THE BEAR   Embassy, 1984
SWEET HEARTS DANCE   Tri-Star, 1988
A DEADLY SILENCE (TF)   Robert Greenwald
Productions, 1989
THE RYAN WHITE STORY (TF)   The Landsburg
Company, 1989
HOW TO MURDER A MILLIONAIRE (TF)   Robert
Greenwald Films, 1989
FORGOTTEN PRISONERS: THE AMNESTY FILE (CTF)
Robert Greenwald Productions, 1990
HIROSHIMA: OUT OF THE ASHES (TF)   Robert
Greenwald Productions, 1990
FIRE! TRAPPED ON THE 37TH FLOOR (TF)   Papazian/
Hirsch Productions, 1991
THE MARLA HANSON STORY (TF)   Citadel
Entertainment, 1991

JOE ANN FOGLE, ACE
THREE O'CLOCK HIGH   Universal, 1987
FAVORITE SON (MS)   NBC Productions, 1988, SE
ROE VS. WADE (TF) ☆   Manheim Company/NBC
Productions, 1989, w/Elodie Keene

GEOFFREY FOOT
STAND UP VIRGIN SOLDIERS   Warner Bros., 1977
SUNBURN   Paramount, 1979
THE WATCHER IN THE WOODS   Buena Vista, 1980

NANCY FORNER
RETURN TO HORROR HIGH   New World, 1987

MONIQUE FORTIER
THE DECLINE OF THE AMERICAN EMPIRE   Cineplex
Odeon, 1986

GENE FOWLER JR.
IT'S A MAD, MAD, MAD, MAD WORLD ★   United Artists,
1963, w/Frederic Knudtson & Robert C. Jones
SKATEBOARD, U.S.A.   Columbia, 1979
CAVEMAN   United Artists, 1981
SMORGASBORD   Warner Bros., 1985

LOIS FREEMAN FOX
(See Lois FREEMAN-FOX)

RICHARD FRANCIS-BRUCE
Agent: Smith Gosnell Nicholson & Associates -
Pacific Palisades, 213/459-0307

GOODBYE PARADISE   New South Wales Film
Corporation, 1982
THE DISMISSAL (MS)   1983
CAREFUL, HE MIGHT HEAR YOU   TLC Films/20th
Century Fox, 1984
MAD MAX BEYOND THUNDERDOME   Warner
Bros., 1985
SHORT CHANGED   Greater Union, 1985

Fr

CINEMATOGRAPHERS
PRODUCTION
DESIGNERS,
COSTUME
DESIGNERS AND
FILM EDITORS
GUIDE

F
I
L
M

E
D
I
T
O
R
S

Fr

CINEMATOGRAPHERS
PRODUCTION
DESIGNERS,
COSTUME
DESIGNERS AND
FILM EDITORS
GUIDE

F
I
L
M

E
D
I
T
O
R
S

THE COWRA BREAKOUT (MS)   Kennedy-Miller
    Productions, 1985
BULLSEYE   Cinema Group, 1986
THE MOSQUITO COAST   Warner Bros., 1986
THE WITCHES OF EASTWICK   Warner Bros.,
    1987, w/Hubert De La Bouillerie
DEAD CALM   Warner Bros., 1989
THE BLOOD OF HEROES *THE SALUTE OF THE
    JUGGER*   Kings Road, 1990
CADILLAC MAN   Orion, 1990

PETER C. FRANK
THE VERDICT   20th Century Fox, 1982
DANIEL   Paramount, 1983
COMPROMISING POSITIONS   Paramount, 1985
DIRTY DANCING   Vestron, 1987
HELLO AGAIN   Buena Vista, 1987, w/Trudy Ship
THE APPOINTMENTS OF DENNIS JENNINGS
    HBO Pictures, 1989
MISS FIRECRACKER   Corsair Pictures, 1989

FRANCO FRATICELLI
TREASURE OF THE FOUR CROWNS   Cannon, 1983
INFERNO   20th Century Fox, 1986
UNSANE   Bedford Entertainment/Film Gallery, 1987

NANCY FRAZEN, ACE
FALSE IDENTITY (TF)   RKO Pictures, 1990

LINDSAY FRAZER
A TEST OF LOVE   Universal, 1985

STANLEY FRAZER
HYSTERICAL   Embassy, 1983

BILL FREDA
AGENT ON ICE   Shapiro Entertainment, 1986
WATCHERS   Universal, 1988, w/Carolle Alain

JEFF FREEMAN
Agent: The Gersh Agency, Inc., Beverly Hills -
    213/274-6611, New York - 212/997-1818

THE DIRT BIKE KID   Concorde, 1985
BULLETPROOF   CineTel Films, 1987
BAD DREAMS   20th Century Fox, 1988
SPLIT DECISIONS   New Century/Vista, 1988,
    w/Thomas Stanford & John W. Wheeler
THE REVENGE OF AL CAPONE (TF)   Unity
    Productions/River City Productions, 1989
FAVORITE SON (MS)   Steve Sohmer Inc./NBC
    Productions, 1989
REPOSSESSED   Seven Arts, 1990

LOIS FREEMAN-FOX, ACE
Agent: Grace Lyons Management - Los Angeles,
    213/655-5100

TEEN WOLF   Atlantic Releasing Corporation, 1985
STRANDED (TF)   Tim Flack Productions/Columbia
    TV, 1986
WELCOME TO 18   American Distribution Group, 1986
THE LAST INNOCENT MAN (CTF)   HBO Pictures/
    Maurice Singer Productions, 1987, w/Paul Seydor
LIKE FATHER LIKE SON   Tri-Star, 1987
K-9   Universal, 1989
AIR AMERICA   Carolco International/Tri-Star, 1990,
    w/John Bloom

CURTIS FREILICH
83 HOURS TILL DAWN (TF)   Consolidated
    Entertainment, 1990

JAY FREUND
DREAMLAND   First-Run Features, 1983, w/Nancy Baker
GO TELL IT ON THE MOUNTAIN (TF)
    Learning in Focus, 1984
THE TRIP TO BOUNTIFUL   Island Pictures/Film
    Dallas, 1985
FOREVER, LULU   Tri-Star, 1987
THE WASH   Skouras Pictures, 1988
SONS   Pacific Pictures, 1989

CARMEN FRIAS
TWISTED OBSESSION   IVE, 1990

PAUL FRIED
Agent: The Gersh Agency, Inc., Beverly Hills -
    213/274-6611, New York - 212/997-1818

SHAKEDOWN   Universal, 1988
CALL ME   Vestron, 1988
RUDE AWAKENING   Orion, 1989

BUD FRIEDGEN, ACE
HOORAY FOR HOLLYWOOD   American Vitagraph
    Productions, 1975, w/Michael J. Sheridan
THAT'S ENTERTAINMENT, PART 2 (FD)   MGM/United
    Artists, 1976, w/David Blewitt, David Bretherton &
    Peter C. Johnson
THIS IS ELVIS   Warner Bros., 1981
THAT'S DANCING! (FD)   MGM/UA, 1985,
    w/Michael J. Sheridan

RICHARD FRIEDMAN
MONDO NEW YORK   Island Pictures, 1988

PETER FRIEDRICH
SLATE, WYN & ME   Hemdale, 1987

MIKE FRISINO
ALLIGATOR EYES   Castle Hill, 1990, w/John Feldman &
    Cynthia Rogers

ERNIE FRITZ
LITTLE NOISES   Monument Pictures, 1991

JERRY FRIZELL
BEVERLY HILLS BRATS   Taurus Entertainment, 1990

LISA FRUCHTMAN
Agent: Lawrence A. Mirisch, Triad Artists, Inc. -
    Los Angeles, 213/556-2727

APOCALYPSE NOW ★   United Artists, 1979, w/Jerry
    Greenberg & Walter Murch
HEAVEN'S GATE   United Artists, 1980, w/Jerry
    Greenberg, William Reynolds & Tom Rolf
STREET MUSIC   Specialty, 1982, w/Diana Pelligrini
THE RIGHT STUFF ★   The Ladd Company/Warner Bros.,
    1983, w/Glenn Farr, Tom Rolf, Stephen A. Rotter &
    Douglas Stewart
CAPTAIN EO   Disneyland, 1986
CHILDREN OF A LESSER GOD   Paramount, 1987
THE GODFATHER PART III ★   Zoetrope Studios/
    Paramount, 1990, w/Barry Malkin & Walter Murch

MICHAEL FRUET
BLUE MONKEY   Spectrafilm, 1987

BRAD FULLER
IN THE SPIRIT   Castle Hill Productions, 1990

CHRISTER FURUBRAND
MY LIFE AS A DOG   Skouras Pictures, 1987,
   w/Susanne Linnman

G

JAMES GALLOWAY
BLIND FAITH-PARTS I & II (TF)   NBC Productions,
   1990, w/Christopher Cooke
SINGLE WOMEN, MARRIED MEN (TF)   Michele
   Lee Productions, 1990
JACKIE COLLINS' LUCKY CHANCES -
   PARTS I-III (MS)   NBC Productions, 1990,
   w/Les Green & Susan Heick

MARIA-LUISA GARCIA
SUMMER   Orion Classics, 1986
FOUR ADVENTURES OF REINETTE AND
   MIRABELLE   New Yorker, 1989

EVA GARDOS
Agent: The Gersh Agency, Inc., Beverly Hills -
   213/274-6611, New York - 212/997-1818

LOOKIN' TO GET OUT   Paramount, 1982
VALLEY GIRL   Atlantic Releasing Corporation, 1983
JOY OF SEX   Paramount, 1984, w/Wlilliam Elias,
   Ned Humphreys & Allan Jacobs
THE CITY GIRL   Moon Pictures, 1984
MASK   Universal, 1985, SE
UNDER THE CHERRY MOON   Warner Bros., 1986
BARFLY   Cannon, 1987
MURDERERS AMONG US: THE SIMON
   WIESENTHAL STORY (CTF)   Citadel
   Entertainment, 1989, w/Chris Wimble
WAITING FOR THE LIGHT   Triumph Releasing, 1990

DAVID GARFIELD
Agent: The Gersh Agency, Inc. - Los Angeles,
   213/274-6611

HERO AT LARGE   MGM/United Artists, 1980
THE BIG BRAWL   Warner Bros., 1980
TULIPS   Avco Embassy, 1981
THE CHOSEN   20th Century Fox International
   Classics, 1982
SILENT RAGE   Columbia, 1982
THE STING II   Universal, 1983
ALL THE RIGHT MOVES   20th Century Fox, 1983,
   w/Wendy Bricmont
FLASHPOINT   Tri-Star, 1984
SYLVESTER   Columbia, 1985, w/Suzanne Petit &
   Howard Smith
DESERT BLOOM   Columbia, 1986,
   w/CariCoughlin & John Currin

THE KARATE KID PART II   Columbia, 1986
VICE VERSA   Columbia, 1988
IT TAKES TWO   MGM/UA, 1988

W. O. GARRETT
HOLLYWOOD SHUFFLE   Samuel Goldwyn
   Company, 1987
THE OFFSPRING   TMS Pictures, 1987
CHOPPER CHICKS IN ZOMBIE TOWN   Troma, 1991

MIRCO GARRONE
HENRY IV   Orion Classics, 1985
DEVIL IN THE FLESH   Orion Classics, 1987

ARLINE GARSON
ALONE IN THE DARK   New Line Cinema, 1982
A NIGHTMARE ON ELM STREET PART 2: FREDDY'S
   REVENGE   New Line Cinema, 1985

MICHAEL GARVEY
TORN APART   Castle Hill, 1990

NICOLAS GASTER
XTRO   New Line Cinema, 1983, w/Jo Ann Kaplan
SLAYGROUND   Universal, 1984
THE WHALES OF AUGUST   Alive Films, 1987
A WORLD APART   Atlantic Releasing
   Corporation, 1988
THE MAHABHARATA   Les Productions du Seme
   Etage, 1989
ROSENCRANTZ & GUILDENSTERN ARE DEAD
   Cinecom, 1991

SETH GAVEN
SPACED INVADERS   Buena Vista, 1990,
   w/Daniel Gross

NORMAN GAY
THE EXORCIST H   Warner Bros., 1973, w/others
SHOCK WAVES   Joseph Brenner Associates, 1977
HONEYSUCKLE ROSE   Warner Bros., 1980,
   w/Aram Avakian, Marc Laub & Evan Lottman
BRADY'S ESCAPE   Satori, 1984
LILY IN LOVE   New Line Cinema, 1985
MURDER TIMES SEVEN (TF)   Titus Productions, 1990

TIMOTHY GEE
Agent: London Management, 235/241 Regent St. -
   London W1R 7AG, 071-493-1610

THE SLIPPER AND THE ROSE: THE STORY OF
   CINDERELLA   Universal, 1976
INTERNATIONAL VELVET   MGM/United Artists, 1978
CLASH OF THE TITANS   United Artists, 1981
ORDEAL BY INNOCENCE   MGM/UA, 1984
SALOME'S LAST DANCE   Vestron, 1988

HELENA GERBER
ALPINE FIRE   Vestron, 1987

EARL GHAFFARI
THE KINDRED   FM Entertainment, 1987,
   w/John Penny
THE DECLINE OF WESTERN CIVILIZATION PART II:
   THE METAL YEARS (FD)   New Line Cinema, 1988

Gh

CINEMATOGRAPHERS
PRODUCTION
DESIGNERS,
COSTUME
DESIGNERS AND
FILM EDITORS
GUIDE

F
I
L
M

E
D
I
T
O
R
S

Gi

CINEMATOGRAPHERS
PRODUCTION
DESIGNERS,
COSTUME
DESIGNERS AND
FILM EDITORS
GUIDE

F
I
L
M

E
D
I
T
O
R
S

ANTONY GIBBS, ACE

Agent: The Gersh Agency, Inc., Beverly Hills -
213/274-6611, New York - 212/997-1818

A TASTE OF HONEY   Continental, 1962
THE LONELINESS OF THE LONG DISTANCE
    RUNNER   Continental, 1962
TOM JONES   Lopert, 1963
THE LOVED ONE   MGM, 1965
THE KNACK...AND HOW TO GET IT   Lopert, 1965
PETULIA   Warner Bros., 1968
PERFORMANCE   Warner Bros., 1970
WALKABOUT   20th Century Fox, 1971
FIDDLER ON THE ROOF   United Artists, 1971,
    w/Robert Lawrence
JESUS CHRIST SUPERSTAR   Universal, 1973,
    w/Robert Lawrence
ROLLERBALL   United Artists, 1975
THE SAILOR WHO FELL FROM GRACE WITH
    THE SEA   Avco Embassy, 1976
A BRIDGE TOO FAR   United Artists, 1977
F.I.S.T.   United Artists, 1978, w/Graeme Clifford
BUTCH AND SUNDANCE: THE EARLY DAYS   20th
    Century Fox, 1979, w/George Trirogoff
YESTERDAY'S HERO   EMI, 1979
THE DOGS OF WAR   United Artists, 1981
RAGTIME   Paramount, 1981, w/Anne V. Coates &
    Stanley Warnow
BAD BOYS   Universal/AFD, 1983
DUNE   Universal, 1984
AGNES OF GOD   Columbia, 1985
TAI-PAN   DEG, 1986
RUSSKIES   New Century/Vista, 1987
STEALING HOME   Warner Bros., 1988
IN COUNTRY   Warner Bros., 1989, w/Lou Lombardo

GABRIELLE GILBERT

THE INVISIBLE KID   Taurus Entertainment, 1988
ACTION U.S.A.   Stewart & Berger Inc., 1989

NINA GILBERTI

BODY CHEMISTRY   Concorde, 1990
TAILSPIN: BEHIND THE KOREAN AIRLINE
    TREGEDY (CTF)   Darlow Smithson
    Productions, 1990

PIERRE GILLETTE

MY FATHER'S GLORY   Gaumont, 1991

VIVIEN HILLGROVE GILLIAM

THE UNBEARABLE LIGHTNESS OF BEING   Orion,
    1988, w/Stephen A. Rotter & B.J. Sears
HENRY & JUNE   Universal, 1990, w/William S.
    Scharf & Dede Allen

HELENE GIRARD

TADPOLE AND THE WHALE   New World, 1988

DAVID GLADWELL

NINETEEN NINETEEN   Spectrafilm, 1986
LOST ANGELS   Orion, 1989

BERT GLATSTEIN

BREAKIN' 2: ELECTRIC BOOGALOO   Tri-Star,
    1984, w/Barry Zetlin
RAPPIN'   Cannon, 1984, w/Andy Horvitch &
    Marcus Manton
THE CALLER   Empire Pictures, 1987

BUY AND CELL   Empire Pictures, 1988
A FRIENDSHIP IN VIENNA (CTF)   Finnegan-Pinchuk
    Productions, 1988
FALSE WITNESS (TF)   Valente/Kritzer/EPI
    Productions, 1990
THE KID WHO LOVED CHRISTMAS (TF)   Paramount
    TV/Eddie Murphy TV Enterprises, 1990

JOHN GLEN

Agent: Sanford-Skouras & Gross - Los Angeles,
    213/208-2100

SEVEN NIGHTS IN JAPAN   EMI, 1976
THE SPY WHO LOVED ME   United Artists, 1977
THE WILD GEESE   Rank, 1978
MOONRAKER   United Artists, 1979
THE SEA WOLVES   Paramount, 1981

BARRY GOLD

DARK AVENGER (TF)   Columbia Pictures
    Television, 1990

MARK GOLDBLATT

Agent: The Gersh Agency, Inc., Beverly Hills -
    213/274-6611, New York - 212/997-1818

PIRANHA   New World, 1978, w/Joe Dante
SPIRIT OF THE WIND   Raven-Doyon, 1979
HUMANOIDS OF THE DEEP   New World, 1980
HALLOWEEN II   Universal, 1980
THE HOWLING   Avco Embassy, 1981, w/Joe Dante
ENTER THE NINJA   Cannon, 1981
WAVELENGTH   New World, 1983, w/Robert Leighton
OVER THE BROOKLYN BRIDGE   MGM/UA/
    Cannon, 1984
THE TERMINATOR   Orion, 1984
THE AMBASSADOR   MGM/UA/Cannon, 1985,
    w/Thierry J. Couturier & Peter Lee Thompson
RAMBO: FIRST BLOOD PART II   Tri-Star, 1985,
    w/Mark Helfrich
COMMANDO   20th Century Fox, 1985
JUMPIN' JACK FLASH   20th Century Fox, 1986
NIGHTBREED   20th Century Fox, 1989
PREDATOR 2   20th Century Fox, 1990

WILLIAM GOLDENBERG

TOUCH OF A STRANGER   Raven-Star Pictures, 1990

DEREK GOLDMAN

PRIVILEGED   New Yorker Films, 1983

MIA GOLDMAN

Agent: Christine Cuddy, Esq., Mitchell, Silberberg &
    Knupp - Los Angeles, 213/312-3246

CHOOSE ME   Island Alive, 1984
2010   MGM, 1984, CE
THE BIG EASY   Columbia, 1987
CROSS MY HEART   Universal, 1987
DEAD MEN OUT (CTF)   Citadel Entertainment, 1989
CRAZY PEOPLE   Paramount, 1990

NICK GOMEZ

TRUST   True Fiction Pictures/Zenith Productions, 1991

DEAN GOODHILL

MERCENARY FIGHTERS   Cannon, 1988,
    w/Michael Campbell

JOEL GOODMAN
FRIDAY THE 13TH   Paramount, 1980
MISSING IN ACTION   Cannon, 1984
THE MORNING AFTER   20th Century Fox, 1986
SATISFACTION   20th Century Fox, 1988
THE ABYSS   20th Century Fox, 1989

WILLIAM GORDEAN, ACE
SMOKEY AND THE BANDIT, PART II   Universal,
   1980, w/Donn Cambern
THE CANNONBALL RUN   20th Century Fox, 1981,
   w/Donn Cambern
SHARKEY'S MACHINE   Orion/Warner Bros., 1981
STROKER ACE   Universal, 1983, w/Carl Kress
CANNONBALL RUN II   Warner Bros., 1984,
   w/Carl Kress
STICK   Universal, 1985
LEGEND   Universal, 1986
LEGAL EAGLES   Universal, 1986, w/Pembroke
   Herring & Sheldon Kahn
DRAGNET   Universal, 1987, w/Richard Halsey
THE GREAT OUTDOORS   Universal, 1988, w/Seth
   Flaum & Tom Rolf
TEENAGE MUTANT NINJA TURTLES   Golden
   Harvest/New Line Cinema, 1990, w/Sally Menke &
   James Symons

ROBERT GORDON
Agent: The Production Agency - Los Angeles,
   213/651-1858

LAS VEGAS LADY   Crown International, 1976
COACH   Crown International, 1978
BLUE LAGOON   Columbia, 1980
SUMMER LOVERS   Filmways, 1982
GRANDVIEW, U.S.A.   Warner Bros., 1984
THE RETURN OF THE LIVING DEAD   Orion, 1985
THE NORTH SHORE   Universal, 1987
RAGE OF HONOR   Trans World Entertainment, 1987
THE GIRL IN A SWING   Millimeter Films, 1989
BACKSTREET DREAMS   Vidmark
   Entertainment, 1990

RAJA GOSNELL
West Coast Card
Agent: Smith Gosnell Nicholson & Associates -
   Pacific Palisades, 213/459-0307

THE SILENCE (TF)   Palomar Pictures
   International, 1975
HEALTH   20th Century Fox, 1980
POPEYE   Paramount, 1980, CE
THE LONELY GUY   Universal, 1984, w/William
   Reynolds
WEEKEND WARRIORS   The Movie Store, 1986
THE RETURN OF BILLY JACK   Billy Jack Productions,
   1986, unfinished
MONSTER IN THE CLOSET   Troma, 1986,
   w/Stephanie Palewski
TEEN WOLF TOO   Atlantic Releasing Corporation,
   1987, w/Steven Polivka, Harvey Rosenstock &
   Kim Secrist
HEARTBREAK HOTEL   Buena Vista, 1988
D.O.A.   Buena Vista, 1988
JURY DUTY: THE COMEDY (TF)   Steve White
   Productions, 1990
HOME ALONE   20th Century Fox, 1990
ONLY THE LONELY   20th Century Fox, 1991

ANNE GOURSAUD, ACE
LA Local 776, NY Local 771
Agent: Lawrence A. Mirisch, Triad Artists, Inc. -
   Los Angeles, 213/556-2727

FREEDOM ROAD (TF)   Zev Braun Productions/Freedom
   Road Films, 1979
THE NIGHT THE LIGHTS WENT OUT IN GEORGIA
   Avco Embassy, 1981
ONE FROM THE HEART   Columbia, 1982, w/Rudi Fehr
   & Randy Roberts
THE OUTSIDERS   Warner Bros., 1983
AMERICAN DREAMER   Warner Bros., 1984
DALTON (TVS)   1985
JUST BETWEEN FRIENDS   Orion, 1986
CRIMES OF THE HEART   DEG, 1986
IRONWEED   Tri-Star, 1987
HER ALIBI   Warner Bros., 1989
THE TWO JAKES   Paramount, 1990

JEFF S. GOURSON
Agent: The Gersh Agency, Inc., Beverly Hills -
   213/274-6611, New York - 212/997-1818

9/30/55   Universal, 1977
FM   Universal, 1978
SOMEWHERE IN TIME   Universal, 1980
THE INCREDIBLE SHRINKING WOMAN   Universal,
   1981, w/Anthony Redman
TRON   Buena Vista, 1982
MIKE'S MURDER   The Ladd Company/Warner Bros.,
   1984, w/Dede Allen
PERFECT   Columbia, 1985
MY MAN ADAM   Tri-Star, 1985
FLIGHT OF THE NAVIGATOR   Buena Vista, 1986
CAN'T BUY ME LOVE   Buena Vista, 1987
BIG TOP PEE-WEE   Paramount, 1988

JOHN GOW
THAT SINKING FEELING   Samuel Goldwyn
   Company, 1979
GREGORY'S GIRL   Samuel Goldwyn Company, 1981
GOSPEL ACCORDING TO VIC   Skouras Pictures, 1987

TRACEY S. GRANGER
THE CLOSER   Ion Pictures, 1991

BRUCE GREEN
Agent: The Gorfaine/Schwartz Agency - Los Angeles,
   213/969-1011

POLTERGEIST   MGM/UA, 1982
TABLE FOR FIVE   Warner Bros., 1983
PRIME RISK   Almi Pictures, 1985
APRIL FOOL'S DAY   Paramount, 1986
FRIDAY THE 13TH PART VI: JASON LIVES
   Paramount, 1986
SQUARE DANCE   Island Pictures, 1986
PUNCHLINE   Columbia, 1988
THREE FUGITIVES   Buena Vista, 1989
WELCOME HOME, ROXY CARMICHAEL
   Paramount, 1990
YOUNG GUNS II   Morgan Creek/20th Century
   Fox, 1990
THE DOCTORS   Touchtone Pictures, 1991

CINEMATOGRAPHERS
PRODUCTION
DESIGNERS,
COSTUME
DESIGNERS AND
FILM EDITORS
GUIDE

F
I
L
M

E
D
I
T
O
R
S

CINEMATOGRAPHERS
PRODUCTION
DESIGNERS,
COSTUME
DESIGNERS and
FILM EDITORS
GUIDE

F
I
L
M

E
D
I
T
O
R
S

LES GREEN

DEAD RECKONING (CTF)   Houston Lady Production
   Company, 1989
LADY IN A CORNER (TF)   Fries Entertainment/Allan
   Leicht Productions, 1990, w/David Beatty
A MOM FOR CHRISTMAS (TF)   Walt Disney
   Company, 1990
JACKIE COLLINS' LUCKY CHANCES-PARTS I-III (MS)
   NBC Productions, 1990, w/James Galloway &
   Susan Heick

PAUL GREEN

THE MISSIONARY   Columbia, 1982
BRIMSTONE AND TREACLE   United Artists
   Classics, 1982
BELLMAN AND TRUE   Island Pictures, 1988
BURNING SECRET   Vestron, 1988

GERALD B. GREENBERG, ACE

Agent: Bauer Benedek Agency - Los Angeles,
   213/275-2421

THE SUBJECT WAS ROSES   MGM/UA, 1968
THE BOYS IN THE BAND   National General, 1970
THE FRENCH CONNECTION ★★   20th Century
   Fox, 1971
THEY MIGHT BE GIANTS   Universal, 1971
THE STOOLIE   Jama, 1972
COME BACK CHARLESTON BLUE   Warner
   Bros., 1972
THE SEVEN UPS   20th Century Fox, 1973
THE HAPPY HOOKER   Cannon, 1975
THE MISSOURI BREAKS   United Artists, 1976,
   w/Dede Allen & Stephen Rotter
KRAMER VS. KRAMER ★   Columbia, 1979
APOCALYPSE NOW ★   United Artists, 1979,
   w/Lisa Fruchtman & Walter Murch
DRESSED TO KILL   Filmways, 1980
HEAVEN'S GATE   United Artists, 1980, w/Lisa
   Fruchtman, William Reynolds & Tom Rolf
STILL OF THE NIGHT   MGM/UA, 1982
SCARFACE   Universal, 1983, w/David Ray
BODY DOUBLE   Columbia, 1984, w/Bill Pankow
SAVAGE DAWN   MAG Enterprises/Gregory Earls
   Productions, 1985
WISE GUYS   MGM/UA, 1986
NO MERCY   Tri-Star, 1986, w/Bill Yahraus
THE UNTOUCHABLES   Paramount, 1987,
   w/Bill Pankow
COLLISION COURSE   DEG, 1988
THE ACCUSED   Paramount, 1988,
   w/O. Nicholas Brown
NATIONAL LAMPOON'S CHRISTMAS VACATION
   Warner Bros., 1989
AWAKENINGS   Columbia, 1990, w/Battle Davis

CHRISTOPHER GREENBURY

THE WORLD'S GREATEST LOVER   20th Century
   Fox, 1977
THE MUPPET MOVIE   AFD, 1979
SURVIVAL RUN   Film Ventures International, 1980
WHERE THE BUFFALO ROAM   Universal, 1980
SOME KIND OF HERO   Paramount, 1982
LIAR'S MOON   Crown International, 1982
DOCTOR DETROIT   Universal, 1983
SMOKEY AND THE BANDIT PART 3   Universal,
   1983, w/David Blewitt & Byron Brandt
THE WOMAN IN RED   Orion, 1984
THE HEAVENLY KID   Orion, 1985

HAUNTED HONEYMOON   Orion, 1986
THREE FOR THE ROAD   New Century/Vista, 1987
RENTED LIPS   New Century/Vista, 1988
OPTIONS   Vestron, 1990
ETERNITY   *THE AVATAR*   Paul Entertainment, 1990,
   w/Peter Zinner & Michael Sheridan

DANFORD B. GREENE

Agent: The Gersh Agency, Inc., Beverly Hills -
   213/274-6611, New York - 212/997-1818

M*A*S*H ★   20th Century Fox, 1970
MYRA BRECKENRIDGE   20th Century Fox, 1970
BLAZING SADDLES ★   Warner Bros., 1974,
   w/John C. Howard
ALOHA, BOBBY AND ROSE   Columbia, 1975
THE MASTER GUNFIGHTER   Taylor-Laughlin, 1975
THE KILLER INSIDE ME   Warner Bros., 1976,
   w/Aaron Stell
FUN WITH DICK AND JANE   Columbia, 1977
OUTLAW BLUES   Warner Bros., 1977, w/Scott Conrad
WHICH WAY IS UP?   Universal, 1977
AMERICAN HOT WAX   Paramount, 1978
VOICES   MGM/Untied Artists, 1979
ROCKY II   United Artists, 1979
THE HOLLYWOOD KNIGHTS   Columbia, 1980, SE
PARTNERS   Paramount, 1982
BLUE SKIES AGAIN   Warner Bros., 1983
HEAD OFFICE   Tri-Star, 1985, w/Bob Lederman
BURNIN' LOVE   DEG, 1987
18 AGAIN   New World, 1988
WHO'S HARRY CRUMB?   Tri-Star, 1989
VITAL SIGNS   20th Century Fox, 1990, w/Robert Brown

JON GREGORY

HIGH HOPES   Skouras Pictures, 1989

PATRICK GREGSTON

LESS THAN PERFECT DAUGHTER (TF)   Hallinan Plus
   Productions, 1991

GEORGE GRENVILLE, ACE

Agent: The Gersh Agency, Inc., Beverly Hills -
   213/274-6611, New York - 212/997-1818

THE HAPPY ENDING   United Artists, 1969
$ *DOLLARS*   Columbia, 1971
EXECUTIVE ACTION   National General, 1973
HAPPY MOTHER'S DAY - LOVE GEORGE
   Cinema 5, 1973
TRIAL OF BILLY JACK   Taylor-Laughlin, 1974
BITE THE BULLET   Columbia, 1975
LOOKING FOR MR. GOODBAR   Paramount, 1977
BILLY JACK GOES TO WASHINGTON
   Taylor-Laughlin, 1978
THE LAST WORD   Samuel Goldwyn Company, 1979
TOM HORN   Warner Bros., 1980
THE BIG BRAWL   Warner Bros., 1980
WRONG IS RIGHT   Columbia, 1982
PURPLE HEARTS   The Ladd Company/Warner
   Bros., 1984
IRON EAGLE   Tri-Star, 1986

BERNARD GRIBBLE, ACE

CRIME AND PASSION   American International, 1976,
   w/John Jympson
WON TON TON, THE DOG WHO SAVED HOLLYWOOD
   Paramount, 1976

Ha

CINEMATOGRAPHERS
PRODUCTION
DESIGNERS,
COSTUME
DESIGNERS AND
FILM EDITORS
GUIDE

F
I
L
M

E
D
I
T
O
R
S

THE SENTINEL   Universal, 1977, w/Terence Rawlings
SILVER BEARS   Columbia, 1977
MOTEL HELL   United Artists, 1980
TOP SECRET!   Paramount, 1984
CADDYSHACK II   Warner Bros., 1988
THE HAUNTING OF SARAH HARDY (TF)   1989
THE PLOT TO KILL HITLER (TF)   David L. Wolper
    Productions, 1990

GARY A. GRIFFEN
BLOOD BEACH   Jerry Gross Organization, 1981
WORLD GONE WILD   Lorimar, 1988
DARK HOLIDAY (TF)   Peter Nelson/Lou Antonio
    Productions/The Finnegun-Pinchuk Company/
    Orion Television, 1989
RETURN TO GREEN ACRES (TF)   Orion Television,
    1989, w/Michael Renaud
FACE TO FACE (TF)   Robert Halmi Productions, 1990
THIS GUN FOR HIRE (CTF)   BBK Productions, 1991

DANIEL GROSS
THE ANNIHILATORS   New World, 1985
PRETTY SMART   New World, 1987
UNDER THE BOARDWALK   New World, 1989
SPACED INVADERS   *MARTIANS!!!*   Buena Vista,
    1990, w/Seth Gaven

JIM GROSS
CHAMELEONS (TF)   NBC Productions, 1990
GRAVEYARD SHIFT   Paramount, 1990,
    w/Randy Jon Morgan

MARC GROSSMAN
Home: 1016 Nowita Place, Venice, CA 90291

TUFF TURF   New World, 1985
ONCE BITTEN   Samuel Goldwyn Company, 1985
VAMP   New World, 1985
SOUTH OF RENO   Open Road Productions/
    Pendulum, 1988
TWO MOON JUNCTION   Lorimar, 1988
FAR FROM HOME   Vestron, 1989

JOHN GROVER
FOR YOUR EYES ONLY   United Artists, 1981
OCTOPUSSY   Untied Artists, 1983, SE
THE FINAL OPTION   MGM/UA, 1983
LIFEFORCE   Tri-Star, 1985
LABYRINTH   Tri-Star, 1985
THE LIVING DAYLIGHTS   MGM/UA, 1987,
    w/Peter Davies
CONSUMING PASSIONS   Samuel Goldwyn
    Company, 1988
LICENCE TO KILL   MGM/UA, 1989

LUCE GRUNENWALDT
FOOL FOR LOVE   Cannon, 1987, w/Stephen Dunn
THE MAN INSIDE   New Line Cinema, 1990

DON GUIDICE
3 DAYS OF THE CONDOR ★   Paramount, 1975,
    w/Fredric Stenkamp
HARRY AND WALTER GO TO NEW YORK   Columbia,
    1976, w/David Bretherton & Fredric Steinkamp
TILT   Warner Bros., 1979, w/Robert Wyman

ELIZABETH GUIDO
TAXI BLUES   Lenfilm Leningrad, 1991

H

MICHAEL HACKING
TEARAWAY   Spectrafilm, 1987

JOHN HACKNEY
THE SECRET POLICEMAN'S THIRD BALL (FD)
    Virgin, 1987

DAVE HAGGERTY
WHAT'S UP, DOC? (CTF)   Communications Inc.,
    1990, w/Karl Woitach

MICHAEL HAIGHT
HARD TICKET TO HAWAII   Malibu Bay Films, 1987
PICASSO TRIGGER   Malibu Bay Films, 1988
SAVAGE BEACH   Malibu Bay Films, 1989
MINISTRY OF VENGEANCE   Concorde, 1989

JACK HAIGIS
STRAIGHT OUT OF BROOKLYN   American
    Playhouse, 1991

RICHARD HAINES
STUCK ON YOU   Troma, 1983, w/Darren Kloomok &
    Ralph Rosenblum
THE FIRST TURN-ON!   Troma, 1983, w/Adam
    Fredericks & Richard King
THE TOXIC AVENGER   Troma, 1985,
    w/Alan J. Polyniak
CLUE   Paramount, 1985, w/David Bretherton
CLASS OF NUKE 'EM HIGH   Troma, 1986
BURIED ALIVE (CTF)   MCA Entertainment, 1989

IVAN HALL
THE GODS MUST BE CRAZY II   Columbia, 1990,
    w/Renee Engelbrecht

RICHARD HALSEY, ACE
Home: 3263 Primera, Los Angeles, CA 90068,
    213/876-8315

HARRY AND TONTO   20th Century Fox, 1974
W.W. AND THE DIXIE DANCEKINGS   20th Century
    Fox, 1975
NEXT STOP, GREENWICH VILLAGE   20th Century
    Fox, 1976
ROCKY ★★   United Artists, 1976, w/Scott Conrad
FIRE SALE   20th Century Fox, 1977
THANK GOD IT'S FRIDAY   Columbia, 1978
BOULEVARD NIGHTS   Warner Bros., 1979
AMERICAN GIGOLO   Paramount, 1980
TRIBUTE   20th Century Fox, 1980
THE AMATEUR   20th Century Fox, 1981
THAT CHAMPIONSHIP SEASON   Cannon, 1982
LOSIN' IT   Embassy, 1983
MOSCOW ON THE HUDSON   Columbia, 1984
DREAMSCAPE   20th Century Fox, 1984
BODY ROCK   New World, 1984
HEATED VENGEANCE   Media Home Entertainment/
    Jungle Production Corporation, 1985

Ha

CINEMATOGRAPHERS
PRODUCTION
DESIGNERS,
COSTUME
DESIGNERS AND
FILM EDITORS
GUIDE

F
I
L
M

E
D
I
T
O
R
S

DOWN AND OUT IN BEVERLY HILLS   Buena
   Vista, 1986
JOCKS   Crown International, 1987
DRAGNET   Universal, 1987, w/William Gordean
MANNEQUIN   20th Century Fox, 1987
BEACHES   Buena Vista, 1988
EARTH GIRLS ARE EASY   Vestron, 1989
JOE VERSUS THE VOLCANO   Warner Bros., 1990
EDWARD SCISSORHANDS   20th Century Fox, 1990

GERRY HAMBLING, ACE
MOSES   Avco Embassy, 1976, w/Peter Boita, Albert
   Gallitti, John Guthridge & Freddie Wilson
BUGSY MALONE   Paramount, 1976
MIDNIGHT EXPRESS ★   Columbia, 1978
FAME ★   MGM/United Artists, 1980
HEARTACHES   MGM, 1982, w/Peter Boita
SHOOT THE MOON   MGM/United Artists, 1982
PINK FLOYD - THE WALL   MGM/UA, 1982
ANOTHER COUNTRY   Orion Classics, 1984
BIRDY   Tri-Star, 1984
INVITATION TO THE WEDDING   Chancery Lane
   Films, 1985
ABSOLUTE BEGINNERS   Orion, 1986, w/Richard
   Bedford, Michael Bradsell & Russell Lloyd
LEONARD PART 6   Columbia, 1987
ANGEL HEART   Tri-Star, 1987
MISSISSIPPI BURNING ★   Orion, 1988
LENNY: LIVE AND UNLEASHED   Miramax
   Films, 1989
COME SEE THE PARADISE   20th Century Fox, 1990

MARCY HAMILTON
DIVING IN   Skouras Pictures, 1990

JANICE HAMPTON
ROCKY II   UA, 1979
METEOR   AIP, 1979
WINDWALKER   Pacific International, 1980,
   w/Stephen J. Johnson & Peter L. McCrea
IT CAME FROM HOLLYWOOD (FD)   Paramount,
   1982, w/Bert Lovitt
LOOKIN' TO GET OUT   Paramount, 1982
HAMMETT   Zoetrope Studios, 1982
PRINCE JACK   Castle Hill Productions, 1984
JUMPIN' JACK FLASH   20th Century Fox, 1986
NOTHING IN COMMON   Tri-Star, 1986
MY BEST FRIEND IS A VAMPIRE   Kings Road,
   1988, w/Gail Yasunaga
HAIRSPRAY   New Line Cinema, 1988
CRY-BABY   Universal, 1990
PUMP UP THE VOLUME   New Line Cinema, 1990

DAVID HANDMAN
YOU TALKIN' TO ME?   MGM/UA, 1987
WEEDS   DEG, 1987, w/Chris Lebenzon & Jon Poll
DEEPSTAR SIX   Tri-Star, 1989
DISTURBED   Live Entertainment, 1990

DANIEL P. HANLEY
Agent: Lawrence A. Mirisch, Triad Artists, Inc. -
   Los Angeles, 213/556-2727

NIGHT SHIFT   The Ladd Company/Warner Bros.,
   1982, w/Michael Hill & Robert J. Kern
SPLASH   Buena Vista, 1984, w/Michael Hill
OBSESSIVE LOVE (TF)   Onza Inc./Moonlight
   Productions, 1984, w/Michael Hill
COCOON   20th Century Fox, 1985, w/Michael Hill

GUNG HO   Paramount, 1986, w/Michael Hill
ARMED AND DANGEROUS   Columbia, 1986,
   w/Michael Hill & Gregory Prange
WILLOW   MGM/UA, 1988, w/Michael Hill
PET SEMATARY   Paramount, 1989, w/Michael Hill
PARENTHOOD   Universal, 1989, w/Michael Hill
PROBLEM CHILD   Imagine Entertainment/Universal,
   1990, w/Michael Hill
BACKDRAFT   Universal/Imagine Films/Trilogy/Brian
   Grazer, 1991, w/ Michael Hill

WALTER HANNEMANN
TWO-MINUTE WARNING ★   Universal, 1976,
   w/Eve Newman
SMOKEY & THE BANDIT ★   Universal, 1977,
   w/Angelo Ross
THE OTHER SIDE OF THE MOUNTAIN - PART 2
   Universal, 1978, w/Eve Newman
THE VILLAIN   Columbia, 1979
THE NUDE BOMB   Universal, 1980, w/Phil Tucker
CHARLIE CHAN AND THE CURSE OF THE DRAGON
   QUEEN   American Cinema, 1981, w/Phil Tucker

ROBERT HARGREAVES
ZINA   Film Forum, 1986
BORN OF FIRE   Vidmark Entertainment, 1987

ED HARKER
PENITENTIARY III   Cannon, 1987

RICHARD A. HARRIS
Agent: The Gersh Agency, Inc. - Beverly Hills,
   213/274-6611

DOWNHILL RACER   Paramount, 1969
DUSTY AND SWEETS McGEE   Warner Bros., 1971
THE CHRISTIAN LICORICE STORE   National
   General, 1971
THE CANDIDATE   Warner Bros., 1972, w/Robert Estrin
CHANDLER   1972
CATCH MY SOUL   Cinerama Releasing
   Corporation, 1974
SMILE   United Artists, 1975
THE BAD NEWS BEARS   Paramount, 1976
SEMI-TOUGH   United Artists, 1977
THE BAD NEWS BEARS GO TO JAPAN
   Paramount, 1978
AN ALMOST PERFECT AFFAIR   Paramount, 1979
THE ISLAND   Universal, 1980
MOMMIE DEAREST   Paramount, 1981
THE CHOSEN   20th Century Fox International
   Classics, 1981
THE TOY   Columbia, 1982, w/Michael A. Stevenson
THE SURVIVORS   Columbia, 1983
TIGER TOWN   Buena Vista, 1984, w/John F. Link
FLETCH   Universal, 1985
WILDCATS   Warner Bros., 1986
THE GOLDEN CHILD   Paramount, 1986
THE COUCH TRIP   Orion, 1988
FLETCH LIVES   Universal, 1989
A MOTHER'S COURAGE: THE MARY THOMAS
   STORY (TF)   Interscope Communications, 1990
MY BOYFRIEND'S BACK (TF)   Interscope
   Productions, 1990
L.A. STORY   Carolco/Tri-Star, 1991

DORIAN HARRIS
DANGEROUS OBSESSION   Panorama
   Entertainment, 1991

LARRY HARRIS
CAMP CUCAMONGA (TF)   Richmel, 1990

BURTON LEE HARRY
THUNDER RUN   Cannon, 1986

MICHELLE HART
EATING   International Rainbow Pictures, 1990,
   w/Mary Pritchard

DUANE HARTZELL, ACE
Phone: 213/390-4315

BLACK SAMSON   Warner Bros., 1974
JENNIFER   American International, 1978
JONI   World Wide, 1980
BEYOND THE NEXT MOUNTAIN   Cornerstone
   Pictures/Inspirational Films, 1981
THE AVIATOR   MGM/UA, 1985
CHILLER (TF)   Polar Film Corporation/D. Feigleson
   Productions, 1985
CASEBUSTERS (TF)   Walt Disney Productions, 1986
MR. BOOGEDY (TF)   Walt Disney Productions, 1986
SUNDAY DRIVE (TF)   Walt Disney Productions, 1986
BRIDE OF BOOGEDY (TF)   Walt Disney
   Productions, 1987
THE ANN JILLIAN STORY (TF)   ITC Productions, 1988
APT PUPIL   New Century/Vista, 1988
CHANCES ARE   Tri-Star, 1989, w/Harry Keramidas
THE FINAL ALLIANCE   Kingsway/Trans World, 1989
PARENT TRAP III (TF)   Walt Disney Television,
   1989, w/Howard Kunin
ANGEL TOWN   Taurus Entertainment, 1990
CHINA CRY   Penland, 1990

MARSHALL HARVEY
Agent: Paul Gerard Agency - Newport Beach,
   714/644-7950
Address: 515 N. Harper Avenue, Los Angeles,
   CA 90048

THE SWORD AND THE SORCERER   Group 1, 1982
THE RATINGS GAME (CTF)   Imagination-New Street
   Productions, 1984
ERNEST GOES TO CAMP   Buena Vista, 1987
AMAZON WOMEN ON THE MOON   Universal,
   1987, w/Malcolm Campbell & Bert Lovitt
DATE WITH AN ANGEL   DEG, 1987
THE 'BURBS   Universal, 1989
DON'T TELL HER IT'S ME   THE BOYFRIEND
   SCHOOL   Hemdale, 1990
DROP DEAD FRED   New Line Cinema, 1991

WILLIAM HAUGSE
CATTLE ANNIE AND LITTLE BRITCHES
   Universal, 1981

VERONIKA HAUSSLER
AN ANGEL AT MY TABLE   Circle Releasing, 1990

CLIFFORD HAYES
MAD MAX   American International, 1977,
   w/Tony Paterson
WE OF THE NEVER NEVER   Triumph, 1983

TODD HAYNES
POISON   Zeitgeist Films, 1991, w/James Lyons

JAMES HECKERT
ASSASSINATION   Cannon, 1987

SUSAN HEICK
HARD TRAVELING   New World, 1986
JACKIE COLLINS' LUCKY CHANCES-PARTS I-III (MS)
   NBC Productions, 1990, w/Les Green &
   James Galloway

ALAN HEIM, ACE
Address: 441 W. End Avenue, New York, NY 10024,
   212/874-5422

THE SEA GULL   Warner Bros., 1968
THE TWELVE CHAIRS   UMC, 1970
GODSPELL   Columbia, 1983
LENNY   United Artists, 1974
NETWORK ★   MGM/United Artists, 1976
ALL THAT JAZZ ★★   20th Century Fox, 1979
THE FAN   Paramount, 1981
SO FINE   Warner Bros., 1981
STAR 80   The Ladd Company/Warner Bros., 1983
GOODBYE, NEW YORK   Castle Hill Productions, 1985
BEER   Orion, 1985
SHE'S HAVING A BABY   Paramount, 1988
FUNNY FARM   Warner Bros., 1988
VALMONT   Orion, 1989, w/Nena Danevic
QUICK CHANGE   Warner Bros., 1990

DAVID HEITNER
PLACE OF WEEPING   New World, 1986

MARK HELFRICH
Phone: 213/666-0320

REVENGE OF THE NINJA   MGM/UA/Cannon, 1983,
   w/Michael J. Duthie
BABY LOVE   Cannon, 1983
BREAKIN'   MGM/UA/Cannon, 1984
RAMBO: FIRST BLOOD PART II   Tri-Star, 1985,
   w/Marc Goldblatt
PREDATOR   20th Century Fox, 1987, w/John F. Link
ACTION JACKSON   Lorimar, 1988
LICENSE TO DRIVE   20th Century Fox, 1988,
   w/Wendy Bricmont & Stephen Semel
PARKER KANE (TF)   Parker Kane Productions, 1990
I COME IN PEACE   Triumph Releasing, 1990
THE BROTHERHOOD   Columbia, 1991
STONE COLD   Columbia Pictures, 1991

BARBARA HENNINGS
THE NASTY GIRL   Miramax, 1990

FIN HENRICKSEN
BABETTE'S FEAST   Orion Classics, 1987

PEMBROKE J. HERRING
Agent: Broder Kurland Webb Uffner - Los Angeles,
   213/656-9262

TORA! TORA! TORA! ★   20th Century Fox, 1970,
   w/Inoue Chikaya & James E. Newcom
BUCK AND THE PREACHER   Columbia, 1972
A WARM DECEMBER   National General, 1973
LET'S DO IT AGAIN   Warner Bros., 1975
BOUND FOR GLORY ★   United Artists, 1976,
   w/Robert Jones
A PIECE OF THE ACTION   Warner Bros., 1977

CINEMATOGRAPHERS
PRODUCTION
DESIGNERS,
COSTUME
DESIGNERS AND
FILM EDITORS
GUIDE

FILM EDITORS

He

CINEMATOGRAPHERS
PRODUCTION
DESIGNERS,
COSTUME
DESIGNERS AND
FILM EDITORS
GUIDE

F
I
L
M

E
D
I
T
O
R
S

FOUL PLAY   Paramount, 1978
THE RUNNER STUMBLES   20th Century Fox, 1979
LITTLE DARLINGS   Paramount, 1980
NINE TO FIVE   20th Century Fox, 1980
ZORRO, THE GAY BLADE   20th Century Fox, 1981
THE BEST LITTLE WHOREHOUSE IN TEXAS
    1982, w/David Bretherton, Nicholas Eliopoulos &
    Jack Hofstra
NATIONAL LAMPOON'S VACATION   Warner
    Bros., 1983
JOHNNY DANGEROUSLY   20th Century Fox, 1984
NATIONAL LAMPOON'S EUROPEAN VACATION
    Warner Bros., 1985
OUT OF AFRICA ★   Universal, 1985, w/Sheldon
    Kahn & Fredric Steinkamp & William Steinkamp
LEGAL EAGLES   Universal, 1986, w/William
    Gordean & Sheldon Kahn
WHO'S THAT GIRL   Warner Bros., 1987
LAST RITES   MGM/UA, 1988
GREAT BALLS OF FIRE!   Orion, 1989, w/Lisa Day &
    Bert Lovitt
GHOST DAD   Universal, 1990

NORBERT HERZNER
OUT OF ORDER   Sandstar Releasing Company, 1985
BAGDAD CAFE   Island Pictures, 1988
SILENCE LIKE GLASS   Bavaria/Lisa/Roxy, 1989

MARY HICKEY
Address: 60 W. 10th St., New York, NY 10011,
    212/260-5917

ONE LIFE IS NOT ENOUGH (FD)   Theatre Lab
    Productions, 1985
SHE'S BACK   Vestron, 1989
STREET HUNTER   21st Century/DGP, 1989

DENNIS M. HILL
NASHVILLE   Paramount, 1976
BUFFALO BILL AND THE INDIANS   United Artists,
    1976, w/Peter Appleton
3 WOMEN   20th Century Fox, 1977
UP IN SMOKE   Paramount, 1978
QUINTET   20th Century Fox, 1979
LOVE AND MONEY   Paramount, 1982
LIES   International Film Marketing, 1983
UFORIA   Universal, 1984
ODD JOBS   Tri-Star, 1986
ALIEN PREDATOR   Trans World Entertainment,
    1987, w/Peter Teschner
MAJOR LEAGUE   Warner Bros., 1989
OUT COLD   Hemdale, 1989
MY HEROES HAVE ALWAYS BEEN COWBOYS
    Samuel Goldwyn Company, 1991

MICHAEL J. HILL
Agent: Lawrence A. Mirisch, Triad Artists, Inc. -
    Los Angeles, 213/556-2727

BERLIN TUNNEL 21 (TF)   Cypress Point
    Productions/Filmways, 1981
CAGNEY & LACEY (TF)   Mace Neufeld
    Productions/Filmways, 1981
THE FIRST TIME (TF)   Moonlight Productions, 1982
NIGHT SHIFT   The Ladd Company/Warner Bros.,
    1982, w/Daniel P. Hanley & Robert J. Kern
BABY SISTER (TF)   Moonlight Productions II, 1983
SPLASH   Buena Vista, 1984, w/Daniel P. Hanley
OBSESSIVE LOVE (TF)   Onza Inc./Moonlight
    Productions, 1984, w/Daniel P. Hanley

COCOON   20th Century Fox, 1985, w/Daniel P. Hanley
GUNG HO   Paramount, 1986, w/Daniel P. Hanley
ARMED AND DANGEROUS   Columbia, 1986,
    w/Daniel P. Hanley & Gregory Prange
COMBAT HIGH (TF)   Frank von Zerneck Productions/
    Lynch-Biller Productions, 1986
WILLOW   MGM/UA, 1988, w/Daniel P. Hanley
PET SEMATARY   Paramount, 1989, w/Daniel P. Hanley
PARENTHOOD   Universal, 1989, w/Daniel P. Hanley
PROBLEM CHILD   Imagine Entertainment/Universal,
    1990, w/Daniel P. Hanley
BACKDRAFT   Universal/Imagine Films/Trilogy/Brian
    Grazer, 1991, w/Daniel P. Hanley

PAUL HIRSCH, ACE
Agent: The Gersh Agency, Inc., Beverly Hills -
    213/274-6611, New York - 212/997-1818

PHANTOM OF THE PARADISE   20th Century Fox, 1974
OBSESSION   Columbia, 1976
STAR WARS ★★   20th Century Fox, 1977, w/Richard
    Chew & Marcia Lucas
CARRIE   United Artists, 1976
THE FURY   20th Century Fox, 1978
KING OF THE GYPSIES   Paramount, 1978
THE EMPIRE STRIKES BACK   20th Century Fox, 1980
BLOW OUT   Filmways, 1981
CREEPSHOW   Warner Bros., 1982, w/Pasquale Buba,
    George A. Romero & Michael Spolan
THE BLACK STALLION RETURNS   MGM/UA, 1983
FOOTLOOSE   Paramount, 1984
PROTOCOL   Warner Bros., 1984
FERRIS BUELLER'S DAY OFF   Paramount, 1986
THE SECRET OF MY SUCCESS   Universal, 1987
PLANES, TRAINS & AUTOMOBILES   Paramount, 1987
STEEL MAGNOLIAS   Tri-Star, 1989
COUP DE VILLE   Universal, 1990

TINA HIRSCH, ACE
Agent: The Gersh Agency, Inc., Beverly Hills -
    213/274-6611, New York - 212/997-1818

DEATH RACE 2000   New World, 1975
EAT MY DUST   New World, 1976
THE DRIVER   20th Century Fox, 1978,
    w/Robert K. Lambert
MORE AMERICAN GRAFFITI   Universal, 1979
HEARTBEEPS   Universal, 1981
INDEPENDENCE DAY   Warner Bros., 1983
TWILIGHT ZONE - THE MOVIE (Segment 3)
    Warner Bros., 1983
GREMLINS   Warner Bros., 1984
EXPLORERS   Paramount, 1985

DAGMAR HIRTZ
SHEER MADNESS   R5/S8, 1983
MARLENE (FD)   Zev Braun Pictures, 1986,
    w/Heidi Genee

GEORGE HIVELY, ACE
THE LITTLE PRINCE   Paramount, 1974
LUCKY LADY   20th Century Fox, 1975
MOVIE MOVIE   Warner Bros., 1978
FRIDAY THE 13TH PART 3   Paramount, 1982
OFF THE WALL   Jensen Farley Pictures, 1983
HOT DOG...THE MOVIE   MGM/UA, 1984
BLAME IT ON RIO   20th Century Fox, 1984,
    w/Richard Marden

LESLIE HODGSON
RETURN TO OZ   Buena Vista, 1985

DOV HOENIG, ACE
Agent: The Gersh Agency, Inc., Beverly Hills -
   213/274-6611, New York - 212/997-1818

GOOD TIMES, WONDERFUL TIMES (FD)
   Rogosin, 1966
LES STANCES A SOPHIE   Prodis, 1971
I LOVE YOU, ROSA   Leisure Media, 1973
THE HOUSE ON CHELOUCHE STREET
   Productions Unlimited, 1974
LEPKE   Warner Bros., 1975
DIAMONDS   Avco Embassy, 1975
THE PASSOVER PLOT   Atlas, 1977
OPERATION THUNDERBOLT   GS Films
   Productions, 1977
THE MAGICIAN OF LUBLIN   International Picture
   Show, 1978
THE URANIUM CONSPIRACY   Noah Films, 1978
STONY ISLAND   World Northal, 1980
THIEF   United Artists, 1981
YOUNG DOCTORS IN LOVE   20th Century Fox, 1982
THE KEEP   Paramount, 1983
ONE MORE CHANCE   Cannon, 1983
BEAT STREET   Orion, 1984
MANHUNTER   DEG, 1986
OVERBOARD   MGM/UA, 1987, w/Sonny Baskin
SHE'S OUT OF CONTROL   Columbia, 1989

JACK HOFSTRA
West Coast Card
Agent: Smith Gosnell Nicholson & Associates -
   Pacific Palisades, 213/459-0307

CHALLENGE   1974
DEATH DRIVER   Omni, 1977
DARK SUNDAY   Intercontinental, 1978
VEGA$ (TF)   Aaron Spelling Productions, 1978
THE STUNT MAN   20th Century Fox, 1980,
   w/Caroline Biggerstaff
THE FUNHOUSE   Universal, 1981
THE BEST LITTLE WHOREHOUSE IN TEXAS
   Universal, 1982, w/David Bretherton, Nicholas
   Eliopoulos & Pembroke J. Herring
TWO OF A KIND   20th Century Fox, 1983
HAUNTED (TF)   Post Mills Productions/
   WGBH-Boston, 1984
BAND OF THE HAND   Tri-Star, 1986
YOUNGBLOOD   MGM/UA, 1986, w/Stephen E. Rivkin
CRIME STORY (TF)   Michael Mann Company/New
   World TV, 1986
THE PRINCIPAL   Tri-Star, 1987
ALOHA SUMMER   Spectrafilm, 1988, w/Jay
   Cassidy & Richard Coblentz
YOUNG GUNS   20th Century Fox, 1988
RUN   Buena Vista, 1991, w/Stephen E. Rivkin

DAVID HOLDEN
THE WARRIORS   Paramount, 1979
THE LONG RIDERS   United Artists, 1980,
   w/Freeman Davies
BUSTIN' LOOSE   Universal, 1981
IMPULSE   20th Century Fox, 1984
THE JOURNEY OF NATTY GANN   Buena Vista, 1985
THE RESCUE   Buena Vista, 1988,
   w/C. Timothy O'Meara
DESCENDING ANGEL (CTF)   Freyda Rothstein
   Productions, 1990

RODNEY HOLLAND
SCRUBBERS   Orion Classics, 1984
THE COMPANY OF WOLVES   Cannon, 1985
NO SURRENDER   Circle Releasing Corporation, 1986,
   w/Kevin Brownlow
DIAMOND SKULLS   Film Four International/British
   Screen, 1989
MURDER STORY   Contracts International, 1989
DECEMBER BRIDE   Film Four International, 1991

NORMAN HOLLYN
Agent: The Gersh Agency, Inc., Beverly Hills -
   213/274-6611, New York - 212/997-1818
Messages: 213/281-8916

LEFTOVERS (TF)   Walt Disney Television, 1986
YOUNG HARRY HOUDINI (TF)   Walt Disney
   Television, 1987
SILENCE AT BETHANY   American Playhouse Theatical
   Films, 1987
DADDY'S BOYS   Concorde, 1987
SAVE THE DOG (CTF)   The Disney Channel, 1988
HEATHERS   New World, 1989
HELL STREET HIGH (Pilot)   Walt Disney
   Television, 1990
MR. DESTINY   Touchtone Films, 1990
THOSE SECRETS (TF)   MGM Television, 1991
MEET THE APPLEGATES   Triton Pictures, 1991
JERSEY GIRLS   Triumph Films/Columbia, 1992

PETER HOLLYWOOD
Agent: Sandra Marsh Management - Sherman Oaks,
   818/905-6961

THE RIDDLE OF THE SANDS   Satori, 1979
FOXES   United Artists, 1980
SILVER DREAM RACER   Almi Cinema 5, 1980
SREDNI VASHTAR (short film) ★   Laurentic Film
   Productions, 1982
BAD BLOOD   Southern Pictures/New Zealand Film
   Commission, 1983
SUPERMAN III   Warner Bros., 1983
WHERE IS PARSIFAL?   Tri-Star, 1984
SUPERGIRL - THE MAKING OF THE MOVIE (TF)
   ABC TV, 1985
SANTA CLAUS - THE MOVIE   Tri-Star, 1985
THE GOOD FATHER   Skouras Pictures, 1987
AMAZING GRACE AND CHUCK   Tri-Star, 1987
THE ADVENTURES OF BARON MUNCHAUSEN
   Columbia, 1989
THE NEVERENDING STORY II: THE NEXT CHAPTER
   Warner Bros., 1990, w/Chris Blunden

CHRISTOPHER HOLMES
West Coast Card
Agent: Smith Gosnell Nicholson & Associates -
   Pacific Palisades, 213/459-0307

PADDY   Allied Artists, 1970
THE DUNWICH HORROR   American International, 1970
FIVE EASY PIECES   Columbia, 1970
DRIVE, HE SAID   Columbia, 1971
A WAR OF CHILDREN (TF)   Tomorrow
   Entertainment, 1972
THE ALL-AMERICAN BOY   Warner Bros., 1973
DIRTY MARY CRAZY LARRY   20th Century Fox, 1974
IT COULDN'T HAPPEN TO A NICER GUY (TF)   The
   Jozak Company, 1974
COOLEY HIGH   American International, 1975
CAR WASH   Universal, 1976

Ho

CINEMATOGRAPHERS
PRODUCTION
DESIGNERS,
COSTUME
DESIGNERS AND
FILM EDITORS
GUIDE

F
I
L
M

E
D
I
T
O
R
S

Ho

**CINEMATOGRAPHERS
PRODUCTION
DESIGNERS,
COSTUME
DESIGNERS** AND
**FILM EDITORS
GUIDE**

F
I
L
M

E
D
I
T
O
R
S

GREASED LIGHTNING   Warner Bros., 1977,
    w/Randy Roberts & Robert Wyman
SGT. PEPPER'S LONELY HEARTS CLUB BAND
    Universal, 1978
SCAVENGER HUNT   20th Century Fox, 1979
NIGHTHAWKS   Universal, 1981
COVERGIRL   New World, 1984
BERRY GORDY'S THE LAST DRAGON
    Tri-Star, 1985
CODE OF SILENCE   Orion, 1985
FLAGRANT DESIRE   Hemdale, 1986
CATCH THE HEAT   Trans World Entertainment,
    1987, w/Darren Holmes
THE WILD PAIR   Trans World Entertainment, 1987

JOHN W. HOLMES

THE STORY OF RUTH   20th Century Fox, 1960
THE MARRIAGE-GO-ROUND   20th Century
    Fox, 1961
SNOW WHITE AND THE THREE STOOGES   20th
    Century Fox, 1961
GOODBYE, CHARLIE   20th Century Fox, 1964
THE ONLY GAME IN TOWN   20th Century
    Fox, 1971
DIAMONDS ARE FOREVER   United Artists, 1971,
    w/Bert Bates
THE ANDROMEDA STRAIN ★   Universal, 1971,
    w/Stuart Gilmore
JUST YOU AND ME, KID   Columbia, 1979
POPEYE   Paramount, 1980, w/David Simmons
INCHON!   MGM/UA, 1982 , w/Michael J. Sheridan
JOURNEY TO THE CENTER OF THE EARTH
    Cannon, 1987
WARLOCK   Trimark, 1991

ALLAN HOLZMAN

Agent: Frank Wuliger, The Agency - Los Angeles,
    213/551-3000

FORBIDDEN WORLD   New World, 1982
OUT OF CONTROL   New World, 1985,
    w/Robert Ferretti
GRUNT! THE WRESTLING MOVIE   New World,
    1985, w/Barry Zetlin

PETER HONESS

Agent: Sandra Marsh Management - Sherman Oaks,
    818/905-6961

CHAMPIONS   Embassy, 1984
ELECTRIC DREAMS   MGM/UA, 1984
MEMED, MY HAWK   Filmworld Distribution, 1984
PLENTY   20th Century Fox, 1985
HIGHLANDER   20th Century Fox, 1986
THE BELIEVERS   Orion, 1987
MADAME SOUSATZKA   Universal, 1988
NEXT OF KIN   Warner Bros., 1989
THE RUSSIA HOUSE   Pathe Entertainment/
    MGM/UA, 1990

MICHAEL HONEY

REBEL   Vestron, 1986

RON HONTHANER

FREE RIDE   Galaxy, 1986
DARK BEFORE DAWN   PSM Entertainment, 1988,
    w/Tom Boutross

KATHRYN RUTH HOPE

STUDENT BODIES   Paramount, 1981

JOHN C. HORGER, ACE

LA Local 776
Agent: Smith Gosnell Nicholson & Associates -
    Pacific Palisades, 213/459-0307

START THE REVOLUTION WITHOUT ME   Warner
    Bros., 1970, shared credit
COLD TURKEY   United Artists, 1971
THE THIEF WHO CAME TO DINNER   Warner
    Bros., 1972
KUNG FU (TF)   Warner Bros. TV, 1972
GRAVY TRAIN   Columbia, 1974
NEVADA SMITH (TF)   Rackin-Hayes Productions/
    Paramount TV, 1975
DR. BLACK, MR. HYDE   Dimension, 1976
A SMALL TOWN IN TEXAS   American
    International, 1976
THE MAGIC OF LASSIE   International Picture
    Show, 1978
THE GIFT OF LOVE (TF)   Osmond Productions, 1978
THE FRISCO KID   Warner Bros., 1979
THE FACTS OF LIFE GOES TO PARIS (TF)
    Embassy TV, 1982
BILL: ON HIS OWN (TF)   Alan Landsburg
    Productions, 1983
GRACE KELLY (TF)   The Kota Company/
    Embassy TV, 1983
MIAMI VICE (TVS)   1984
MURDER BY REASON OF INSANITY (TF)   LS
    Entertainment, 1985
SECOND SERVE (TF)   Linda Yellen Productions/
    Lorimar-Telepictures, 1986
LOVE HURTS   Vestron, 1990

KAREN HORN

BLOODFIST   Concorde, 1990
FULL FATHOM FIVE   Concorde, 1990
CORPORATE AFFAIRS   Concorde, 1990

MICHAEL HORTON

MIDDLE AGE SPREAD   Embrafilms, 1979
GOODBYE PORK PIE   Samuel Goldwyn
    Company, 1980
SMASH PALACE   Atlantic Releasing
    Corporation, 1982
WARLORDS OF THE 21ST CENTURY
    BATTLE - TRUCK   New World, 1982
BEYOND REASONABLE DOUBT   Satori, 1983
HEART OF THE STAG   New World, 1984
HOT TARGET   Crown International, 1985
SYLVIA   MGM/UA Classics, 1985
THE QUIET EARTH   Skouras Pictures, 1985
A SOLDIER'S TALE   Atlantic Releasing
    Corporation, 1988

ANDY HORVITCH

ANDROID   New World, 1982
THE BOYS NEXT DOOR   New World, 1985
RAPPIN'   Cannon, 1985, w/Bert Glatstein &
    Marcus Manton
ELIMINATORS   Empire Pictures, 1986
RAWHEAD REX   Empire Pictures 1987
DUDES   New Century/Vista, 1988

JOHN C. HOWARD
BUTCH CASSIDY AND THE SUNDANCE KID   20th
    Century Fox, 1969
BELIEVE IN ME   MGM, 1971
A SEPARATE PEACE   Paramount, 1972
SCALAWAG   Paramount, 1973
BLAZING SADDLES ★   Warner Bros., 1974,
    w/Danford B. Greene
YOUNG FRANKENSTEIN   20th Century Fox, 1974
THE DROWNING POOL   Warner Bros., 1975
W.C. FIELDS AND ME   Universal, 1976
SILENT MOVIE   20th Century Fox, 1976,
    w/Stanford C. Allen
HIGH ANXIETY   20th Century Fox, 1977
NIGHTWING   Columbia, 1979
AMERICATHON   United Artists, 1979
WHY WOULD I LIE?   MGM/United Artists, 1980
HISTORY OF THE WORLD, PART I   20th Century
    Fox, 1981
ROMANTIC COMEDY   MGM/UA, 1983

WILLIAM HOY
BEST OF THE BEST   Taurus Entertainment, 1990

RAY HUBLEY
LOVE OR MONEY   Hemdale, 1989

DAVID HUGGETT
FAST TALKING   Cinecom, 1985
WHICH WAY HOME (CTF)   McElroy & McElroy,
    1991, w/Henry Dangar

JERE HUGGINS
DEAL OF THE CENTURY   Warner Bros., 1983,
    w/Ned Humphreys & Bud Smith
SING   Tri-Star, 1989, w/Bud Smith & Scott Smith

NED HUMPHREYS
DEAL OF THE CENTURY   Warner Bros., 1983,
    w/Jere Huggins & Bud Smith
JOY OF SEX   Paramount, 1984, w/William Elias,
    Eva Gardos & Allan Jacobs
NEVER TOO YOUNG TO DIE   Paul Releasing,
    1986, w/William A. Anderson & Paul Seydor
DISORDERLIES   Warner Bros., 1987

PETER HUNT
DESPERATE HOURS   MGM/UA, 1990

MARTIN HUNTER
Agent: Sandra Marsh Management - Sherman Oaks,
    818/905-6961

FULL METAL JACKET   Warner Bros., 1987
COLD FRONT   Cold Front Productions, 1989
CADENCE   New Line Cinema, 1990

RUSSELL HURLEY
GOLDEN BRAID   1990

JOE HUTSHING
TALK RADIO   Universal, 1988, CE
BORN ON THE FOURTH OF JULY ★★   Universal,
    1989, CE
THE DOORS   Tri-Star, 1991, w/David Brenner

MICHOU HUTTER
DEATH OF A SCHOOLBOY   Neue Studio Film
    GMBH, 1991

ROBERT HYAMS
TAGGET (CTF)   Papazian/Hirsch Productions,
    1991, w/Ralph E. Winters

GLENN HYDE
THE HOUND OF THE BASKERVILLES   Atlantic
    Releasing Corporation, 1980, w/Richard Marden

I

DOUGLAS IBOLD, ACE
OFF LIMITS   20th Century Fox, 1988
FINISH LINE (TF)   Guber/Peters/Barris
    Productions, 1989
B.L. STRYKER (Pilot)   1989, w/Carl Kress &
    Stephen Lovejoy
SILHOUETTE (CTF)   MCA Television
    Entertainment, 1990

SYLVIA INGEMARSSON
MONTENEGRO   Atlantic Releasing Corporation, 1981
SALLY AND FREEDOM   Scandinavia Today, 1982,
    w/Siv Lundgren
THE FAREWELL   Scandinavia Today, 1982
FANNY AND ALEXANDER   Embassy, 1983
AFTER THE REHEARSAL   Triumph, 1984

FRANK IRVINE
THE GREY FOX   United Artists Classics, 1983

STEPHEN A. ISAACS
OMEGA SYNDROME   New World, 1987

Is

CINEMATOGRAPHERS
PRODUCTION
DESIGNERS,
COSTUME
DESIGNERS AND
FILM EDITORS
GUIDE

F
I
L
M

E
D
I
T
O
R
S

CINEMATOGRAPHERS
PRODUCTION
DESIGNERS,
COSTUME
DESIGNERS AND
FILM EDITORS
GUIDE

F
I
L
M

E
D
I
T
O
R
S

J

MICHAEL JABLOW
LA Local 776, NY Local 771
Agent: Lawrence A. Mirisch, Triad Artists, Inc. -
   Los Angeles, 213/556-2727

MODERN PROBLEMS   20th Century Fox, 1981
GET CRAZY   Embassy, 1983, w/Kent Beyda
THE WILD LIFE   Universal, 1984
COPACABANA (TF)   Dick Clark Cinema Productions/
   Stiletto Ltd., 1985
CALIFORNIA GIRLS (TF)   ABC Circle Films, 1985
THE GIRL WHO SPELLED FREEDOM (TF)
   Knopf-Simons Productions/ITC Productions/Walt
   Disney Productions, 1986
ACCEPTABLE RISKS (TF)   ABC Circle Films, 1986
WHEN THE BOUGH BREAKS (TF)   Taft Entertainment
   TV/TDF Productions, 1986
TONIGHT'S THE NIGHT (TF)   IndieProd Productions/
   Phoenix Entertainment Group, 1987
THROW MOMMA FROM THE TRAIN   Orion, 1987
CONSPIRACY - THE TRIAL OF THE CHICAGO 8 (CTF)
   HBO Premiere Films, 1988
THE NAKED GUN: FROM THE FILES OF POLICE
   SQUAD!   Paramount, 1988
FAMILY OF SPIES-PARTS I & II (MS)   King Phoenix
   Entertainment, 1990
MADHOUSE   Orion, 1990
THE MARRYING MAN   Buena Vista, 1991

DOUG JACKSON
FALLING IN LOVE AGAIN   International Picture Show
   Company, 1980, w/Jacqueline Cambas & Bud Smith
SLAPSTICK OF ANOTHER KIND   Entertainment
   Releasing Corporation/International Film
   Marketing, 1983

ALLAN JACOBS
MAKING IT   20th Century Fox, 1971
BLACULA   American International, 1971
CLEOPATRA JONES   Warner Bros., 1973
THE LONGEST YARD   Paramount, 1974
RACE WITH THE DEVIL   20th Century Fox, 1975
MATILDA   American International, 1978
THE FRENCH ATLANTIC AFFAIR (TF)   Aaron
   Spelling Productions/MGM TV, 1978
LOVE AT FIRST BITE   American International,
   1979, w/Mort Fallick
THE SHADOW BOX (TF)   The Shadow Box Film
   Company, 1980
DEATH HUNT   20th Century Fox, 1981,
   w/John F. Burnett
THE PURSUIT OF D.B. COOPER   Universal, 1982,
   w/Robbe Roberts
LASSITER   Warner Bros., 1984, SE
JOY OF SEX   Paramount, 1984, w/William Elias,
   Eva Gardos & Ned Humphreys
THE GLITTER DOME (CTF)   HBO Premiere Films/
   Telepicture Productions/Trincomali
   Productions, 1984

SUSAN JAEGER
JUST A GIGOLO   United Artists Classics, 1981,
   w/Fred Srp & Maxine Julius

GIB JAFFE
Agent: Sandra Marsh Management - Sherman Oaks,
   818/905-6961

BREAKIN'   MGM/UA Cannon, 1984, w/Larry Bock &
   Vincent Sklena
THE GIFTED ONE (TF)   Richard Rothstein Productions/
   NBC Productions, 1985
GOOD TO GO   Island Pictures, 1986, w/Kimberly Logan
   & D.C. Stringer
RUTHLESS PEOPLE   Buena Vista, 1986,
   w/Arthur Schmidt
LONG GONE (CTF)   HBO Pictures/The Landsburg
   Company, 1987
PULSE   Columbia, 1988
THEY LIVE   Universal, 1988, w/Frank Jiminez
BLESSED (TF)   1989

JANE SCHWARTZ JAFFE
TRICK OR TREAT   DEG, 1986
MILES FROM HOME   Cinecom, 1988

ALAIN JAKUBOWICZ
IT'S A FUNNY, FUNNY WORLD   Noah Film, 1978
THE DELTA FORCE   Cannon, 1986
AMERICA 3000   Cannon, 1986
INVADERS FROM MARS   Cannon, 1986
THE TEXAS CHAINSAW MASSACRE PART 2
   Cannon, 1986
ALLAN QUATERMAIN AND THE LOST CITY OF GOLD
   Cannon, 1987
SHY PEOPLE   Cannon, 1987
TOO MUCH   Cannon, 1987
SALSA   Cannon, 1988
HANNA'S WAR   Cannon, 1988
MACK THE KNIFE   21st Century, 1989
THE FIFTH MONKEY   Columbia, 1990,
   w/Fabien D. Tordjmann

JANUS BILLESKOV JANSEN
THE TREE OF KNOWLEDGE   Scandinavia Today, 1982,
   w/Merete Brusendorff & Hannah Lowy
ZAPPA   Spectrafilm, 1984
THE WOLF AT THE DOOR   International Film
   Marketing, 1986
TWIST AND SHOUT   Miramax, 1986
PELLE THE CONQUEROR   Miramax, 1988

JIM JARMUSCH
Business: Black Snake Productions, Inc., 24 Prince Street,
   Suite 7, New York, NY 10012, 212/226-1341

PERMANENT VACATION   Cinesthesia, 1981
STRANGER THAN PARADISE   Samuel Goldwyn
   Company, 1984, w/Melody London

RODERICK JAYNES
BLOOD SIMPLE   Circle Releasing Corporation, 1985,
   w/Don Wiegmann
BARTON FINK   20th Century Fox, 1991

JACQUES JEAN
WHISPERS   ITC Entertainment, 1990

ERIC JENKINS
HEART BEAT   Warner Bros./Orion, 1979
ALTERED STATES   Warner Bros., 1980
FAST TIMES AT RIDGEMONT HIGH   Universal, 1982
PANDEMONIUM   MGM/UA, 1982
THE WHOOPEE BOYS   Paramount, 1986

MONDO JENKINS
TAPEHEADS   Avenue Pictures, 1988

FRANK JIMENEZ
THE WRONG GUYS   New World, 1988
THEY LIVE   Universal, 1988, w/Gib Jaffe
KILL ME AGAIN   Polygram Pictures, 1989
THE FLASH (Pilot)   Pet Fly Productions, 1990

PHIL JOANOU
Agent: Creative Artists Agency - Beverly Hills,
   213/288-4545

U2 RATTLE AND HUM   Paramount, 1988,
   also directed

MARY E. JOCHEM
KINJITE: FORBIDDEN SUBJECTS   Cannon, 1989,
   w/Peter Lee Thompson

KEN JOHNSON
SIXTH AND MAIN   National Cinema, 1977
THAT WAS THEN...THIS IS NOW   Paramount, 1985

ALAN JONES
THE PINK PANTHER STRIKES AGAIN   United
   Artists, 1976
PORRIDGE   ITC, 1979
REVENGE OF THE PINK PANTHER   United
   Artists, 1979
THERE GOES THE BRIDE   Vanguard, 1980
TRAIL OF THE PINK PANTHER   MGM/United
   Artists, 1982
BULLSHOT   Island Alive, 1985
JANE AND THE LOST CITY   New World, 1987
THE RAGGEDY RAWNEY   Four Seasons
   Entertainment, 1989

AMY JONES
Agent: David Gersh, The Gersh Agency, Inc. -
   Beverly Hills, 213/274-6611

HOLLYWOOD BOULEVARD   New World, 1976,
   w/Allan Arkush
CORVETTE SUMMER   MGM/UA, 1978
SECOND HAND HEARTS   Paramount, 1981

CLIFFORD JONES
WINDY CITY   Warner Bros., 1984

JEFF JONES
FEVER PITCH   MGM/UA, 1985

KIRK JONES
AGENCY   Jensen Farley Pictures, 1981
SPRING FEVER   Comworld, 1983, w/Tony Lower

ROBERT C. JONES
INVITATION TO A GUNFIGHTER   United Artists, 1964
I LOVE YOU, ALICE B. TOKLAS   Warner Bros., 1968
GUESS WHO'S COMING TO DINNER ★
   Columbia, 1969
PAINT YOUR WAGON   Paramount, 1969
LOVE STORY   Paramount, 1970
CISCO PIKE   Columbia, 1971
THE NEW CENTURIONS   Columbia, 1972
MAN OF LA MANCHA   United Artists, 1972
THE LAST DETAIL   Columbia, 1973
THE CRAZY WORLD OF JULIUS VROODER   20th
   Century Fox, 1974
SHAMPOO   Columbia, 1975
BOUND FOR GLORY ★   United Artists, 1976,
   w/Pembroke Herring
HEAVEN CAN WAIT   Paramount, 1978,
   w/Don Zimmerman
LOOKIN' TO GET OUT   Paramount, 1982
TWICE IN A LIFETIME   The Yorkin Company, 1985
SEE NO EVIL, HEAR NO EVIL   Tri-Star, 1989

LAWRENCE JORDAN
DEAD SPACE   Concorde, 1991

ALBERT JURGENSON
MON ONCLE D'AMERIQUE   New World, 1980
UNDER SUSPICION   Fred Baker, 1982
L'ADOLESCENTE   Landmark Films, 1982
LIFE IS A BED OF ROSES   Spectrafilm, 1984,
   w/Jean-Pierre Besnard
LA CHEVRE   European Clasics, 1985
HOTEL TERMINUS: KLAUS BARBIE, HIS LIFE AND
   TIMES (FD)   Samuel Goldwyn Company, 1988,
   w/Catherine Zina
THE LITTLE THIEF   Miramax, 1990

JOHN JYMPSON, ACE
Agent: Sandra Marsh Management - Sherman Oaks,
   818/905-6961

A HARD DAY'S NIGHT   United Artists, 1964
ZULU   Paramount, 1964
THE BEDFORD INCIDENT   Columbia, 1965
KALEIDOSCOPE   Warner Bros., 1966
WHERE EAGLES DARE   MGM, 1969
KELLY'S HEROES   MGM, 1970
FRENZY   Universal, 1972
THE OPTIMISTS   Paramount, 1973
THE DOVE   Paramount, 1974
MR. QUILP   Avco Embassy, 1975
CRIME AND PASSION   American International, 1976,
   w/Bernard Gribble
THE INCREDIBLE SARAH   Avco Embassy, 1976
A LITTLE NIGHT MUSIC   New World, 1977
MEETINGS WITH REMARKABLE MEN   Libra, 1979
GREEN ICE   Universal/AFD, 1981
HIGH ROAD TO CHINA   20th Century Fox, 1983
THE FAR PAVILIONS (CMS)   Geoff Reeve & Associates/
   Goldcrest, 1984
BAD MEDICINE   20th Century Fox, 1985, w/O. Nicholas
   Brown & Keith Palmer
GULAG (CTF)   Lorimar Productions/HBO Premiere
   Films, 1985
LITTLE SHOP OF HORRORS   The Geffen Company/
   Warner Bros., 1986
A FISH CALLED WANDA   MGM/UA, 1988
THE MIGHTY QUINN   MGM/UA, 1989
HONOR BOUND   MGM/UA, 1989
KING RALPH   Universal, 1991

Jy

CINEMATOGRAPHERS
PRODUCTION
DESIGNERS,
COSTUME
DESIGNERS AND
FILM EDITORS
GUIDE

F
I
L
M

E
D
I
T
O
R
S

Ka

CINEMATOGRAPHERS
PRODUCTION
DESIGNERS,
COSTUME
DESIGNERS AND
FILM EDITORS
GUIDE

F
I
L
M

E
D
I
T
O
R
S

K

BOB KAGEY
BLIND WITNESS (TF)   King-Phoenix Entertainment,
    1990, w/Robert Kimble
SPARKS: THE PRICE OF PASSION (TF)   King
    Phoenix Entertainment, 1990, w/Robert L. Kimble
ROXANNE: THE PRIZE PULITZER (TF)   Qintex
    Entertainment, 1990, w/Robert Kimble

MICHAEL KAHN, ACE
Agent: The Gersh Agency, Inc., Beverly Hills -
    213/274-6611, New York - 212/997-1818

TROUBLE MAN   20th Century Fox, 1972
THE SPOOK WHO SAT BY THE DOOR   United
    Artists, 1973
TRUCK TURNER   American International, 1974
THE SAVAGE IS LOOSE   Campbell Devon, 1974
BLACK BELT JONES   Warner Bros., 1974
GOLDEN NEEDLES   American International, 1974
BUSTER AND BILLIE   Columbia, 1974
THE DEVIL'S RAIN   Bryanston, 1975
THE RETURN OF A MAN CALLED HORSE   United
    Artists, 1976
CLOSE ENCOUNTERS OF THE THIRD KIND ★
    Columbia, 1977
EYES OF LAURA MARS   Columbia, 1978
ICE CASTLES   Columbia, 1979, w/Melvin Shapiro &
    Maury Winetrobe
1941   Universal, 1979
USED CARS   Columbia, 1980
RAIDERS OF THE LOST ARK ★★   Paramount, 1981
POLTERGEIST   MGM/UA, 1982
TABLE FOR FIVE   Warner Bros., 1983
TWILIGHT ZONE - THE MOVIE (Segment 2)
    Warner Bros., 1983
INDIANA JONES AND THE TEMPLE OF DOOM
    Paramount, 1984
FALLING IN LOVE   Paramount, 1984
THE GOONIES   Warner Bros., 1985
THE COLOR PURPLE   Warner Bros., 1986
WISDOM   20th Century Fox, 1986
EMPIRE OF THE SUN ★   Warner Bros., 1987
FATAL ATTRACTION ★   Paramount, 1987,
    w/Peter Berger
ARTHUR 2 ON THE ROCKS   Warner Bros., 1988
INDIANA JONES AND THE LAST CRUSADE
    Paramount, 1989
ALWAYS   Universal, 1989
ARACHNOPHOBIA   Amblin/Buena Vista, 1990
TOY SOLDIERS   Tri-Star Pictures, 1991

SHELDON KAHN, ACE
Phone: 818/986-2800

ONE FLEW OVER THE CUCKOO'S NEST ★   United
    Artists, 1975, w/Lynzee Klingman
THE GREAT SCOUT AND CATHOUSE THURSDAY
    American International, 1976
MIKEY AND NICKY   Paramount, 1976
AN ENEMY OF THE PEOPLE   Warner Bros., 1978

SAME TIME, NEXT YEAR   Universal, 1978
BLOODBROTHERS   Warner Bros., 1979
THE ELECTRIC HORSEMAN   Columbia, 1979
PRIVATE BENJAMIN   Warner Bros., 1980
ABSENCE OF MALICE   Columbia, 1981
RICHARD PRYOR LIVE ON THE SUNSET STRIP (FD)
    Columbia, 1982
KISS ME GOODBYE   20th Century Fox, 1982
UNFAITHFULLY YOURS   20th Century Fox, 1984
GHOSTBUSTERS   Columbia, 1984, w/David Blewitt
OUT OF AFRICA ★   1985, w/Pembroke J. Herring,
    Fredric Steinkamp & William Steinkamp
LEGAL EAGLES   Universal, 1986, w/William Gordean &
    Pembroke J. Herring
LA BAMBA   Columbia, 1987, w/Don Brochu
BIG SHOTS   20th Century Fox, 1987, w/William M.
    Anderson & Dennis Virkler
CASUAL SEX?   Universal, 1988, w/Donn Cambern
TWINS   Universal, 1988, w/Donn Cambern
GHOSTBUSTERS II   Columbia, 1989, w/Donn Cambern
KINDERGARTEN COP   Universal, 1990,
    w/Wendy Bricmont

JAY KAMEN
Address: 3233 DeWitt Drive, Hollywood, CA 90068,
    213/876-4173

NORTH DALLAS FORTY   Paramount, 1979
SPLIT IMAGE   Orion, 1982

JEFF KANEW
Agent: Jeremy Zimmer, ICM - Los Angeles, 213/550-4000

ORDINARY PEOPLE   Paramount, 1980
EDDIE MACON'S RUN   Universal, 1983

NANCY KANTER
THE LOVELESS   Atlantic Releasing Corporation, 1984

MARK ALLAN KAPLAN
DELUSION   I.R.S. Media, 1991

CINDY KAPLAN - ROONEY
Address: 492 Henry St. Apt. L, Brooklyn, NY 11231,
    718/875-1606

ZELLY AND ME   Columbia, 1988

DEBRA KAREN
MEATBALLS   Paramount, 1979
FINAL ASSIGNMENT   Almi Cinema 5, 1980
YESTERDAY   Cinepix, 1980
HAPPY BIRTHDAY TO ME   Columbia, 1981
MEATBALLS III   TMS Pictures, 1986
DAY ONE (TF)   Aaron Spelling Productions/Paragon
    Motion Pictures/David W. Rintels Productions, 1989
THE INCIDENT (TF)   Qintex Entertainment, 1990
THE LOVE SHE SOUGHT (TF)   Arnold
    Productions, 1990

GARY KARR
DELIVERY BOYS   New World, 1985

ROBIN KATZ
9 1/2 NINJAS   Republic Pictures Home Video, 1991

SIDNEY KATZ
NIGHTMARE ON THE 13TH FLOOR (CTF)
    G.C. Group, 1990

BRIAN KAVANAGH
THE ODD ANGRY SHOT   Roadshow
    Distribution, 1979
THE QUEST   Miramax, 1986

HARRY KELLER
Agent: The Gersh Agency, Inc. - Beverly Hills,
    213/274-6611

THE RED PONY (TF)   Universal TV/Omnibus
    Productions, 1973
BORDERLINE   AFD, 1980
STIR CRAZY   Columbia, 1980
STRIPES   Columbia, 1981
HANKY PANKY   Columbia, 1982
THE MAN WHO WASN'T THERE   Paramount, 1983
FAST FORWARD   Columbia, 1985
TRANSYLVANIA 6-5000   New World, 1985

CHRISTOPHER KELLY
Agent: London Management, 235/241 Regent St. -
    London W1R 7AG, 071-493-1610

SHADEY   Skouras Pictures, 1986
GETTING IT RIGHT   MCEG, 1989

JOHN KELLY
MIDDLE AGE CRAZY   20th Century Fox, 1980
UTILITIES   New World, 1983

MICHAEL KELLY
PROGRAMMED TO KILL   Trans World
    Entertainment, 1987
THE RESCUERS DOWN UNDER   Buena Vista, 1990

STEVEN KEMPER
Agent: The Gersh Agency, Inc., Beverly Hills -
    213/274-6611, New York - 212/997-1818

3:15   Dakota Entertainment, 1986
NEW JACK CITY   Warner Bros., 1991

RALPH KEMPLEN
THE GREAT MUPPET CAPER   Universal/AFD, 1981
THE DARK CRYSTAL   Universa/AFD, 1982

ELLEN KENESHEA
MORTUARY ACADEMY   Landmark Films, 1988
SYNGENOR   South Gate Entertainment, 1990

KIM KENNEDY
CAT CHASER   Vestron, 1990

PATRICK KENNEDY
Agent: Grace Lyons Management - Los Angeles,
    213/655-5100

TRIBES (TF)   20th Century Fox, 1970
CINDERELLA LIBERTY   20th Century Fox, 1974, CE
SERPICO: THE DEADLY GAME (TF)   Dino De
    Laurentiis Productions/Paramount TV, 1976
KATHERINE (TF)   The Jozak Company, 1975
SCOTT JOPLIN   Universal, 1977
HEROES   Universal, 1977
THE BIG FIX   Universal, 1978
AIRPLANE!   Paramount, 1980
SAVAGE HARVEST   20th Century Fox, 1981,
    w/Scott Wallace

MR. MOM   20th Century Fox, 1983
BRAINSTORM   MGM/UA, 1983
SPACE (MS)   Stonehenge Productions/
    Paramount TV, 1985
THE BOY WHO COULD FLY   20th Century Fox, 1986
J. EDGAR HOOVER (CTF)   RLC Productions/The
    Finnegan Company/Showtime, 1987
IN THE MOOD   Lorimar, 1987
PLAIN CLOTHES   Paramount, 1988, w/Edward Abroms
TAP   Tri-Star, 1989
QUEENS LOGIC   New Visions, 1991

ROBERT KENNEDY
COMIC BOOK CONFIDENTIAL   Cinecom, 1990,
    w/Ron Mann

HARRY KERAMIDAS
Agent: The Gersh Agency, Inc., Beverly Hills -
    213/274-6611, New York - 212/997-1818

MASSACRE AT CENTRAL HIGH   Brian
    Distributing, 1976
MANSION OF THE DOOMED   1977
CRASH   Group 1, 1977
DRACULA'S DOG   Crown International, 1978
NANCY DREW MYSTERIES (TVS)
THE HARDY BOYS MYSTERIES (TVS)
HOMEWARD BOUND (TF)   Tisch-Avnet
    Productions, 1980
SCARED STRAIGHT! ANOTHER STORY (TF)   Golden
    West Television, 1980
THE CHILDREN NOBODY WANTED (TF)   Blatt-Singer
    Productions, 1981
BUSTIN' LOOSE   Universal, 1981
FOR US, THE LIVING (TF)   Charles Fries
    Productions, 1983
TOUCHED   Lorimar Productions/Wildwood
    Partners, 1983
THE JERK, TOO (TF)   40 Share Productions/Universal
    Television, 1984
CHILDREN OF THE CORN   New World, 1984
BACK TO THE FUTURE   Universal, 1985,
    w/Arthur Schmidt
ABOUT LAST NIGHT...   Tri-Star, 1986
THE SQUEEZE   Tri-Star, 1987
BIG BUSINESS   Buena Vista, 1988
CHANCES ARE   Tri-Star, 1989
BACK TO THE FUTURE II   Universal, 1989,
    w/Arthur Schmidt
BACK TO THE FUTURE III   Universal, 1990,
    w/Arthur Schmidt

DAVID KERN
Local 776
Address: 880 Camino Colibri, Calabasas, CA 91302,
    818/704-7146

AMERICANA   Crown International, 1983, w/David
    Carradine
THE BLACK ROOM   CI Films, 1984
LAS VEGAS WEEKEND   New World, 1985
KING OF THE CITY *CLUB LIFE*   Troma, 1986
IT'S ALIVE III: ISLAND OF THE ALIVE   Warner
    Bros., 1987
MANIAC COP   Shapiro-Glickenhaus, 1987
HIT LIST   New Line Cinema, 1989
WICKED STEPMOTHER   MGM/UA, 1989
SPONTANEOUS COMBUSTION   Taurus
    Entertainment, 1989

Ke

CINEMATOGRAPHERS
PRODUCTION
DESIGNERS,
COSTUME
DESIGNERS AND
FILM EDITORS
GUIDE

F
I
L
M

E
D
I
T
O
R
S

Ki

CINEMATOGRAPHERS
PRODUCTION
DESIGNERS,
COSTUME
DESIGNERS AND
FILM EDITORS
GUIDE

F
I
L
M

E
D
I
T
O
R
S

RELENTLESS   New Line Cinema, 1989
MANIAC COP 2   Movie House Sales Company, 1990
FAST GETAWAY   CineTel, 1990

GILBERT KIKONE
BURIED ALIVE   RCA/Columbia Home Video

ROBERT KIMBLE
BLIND WITNESS (TF)   King-Phoenix Entertainment,
   1990, w/Bob Kagey
SPARKS: THE PRICE OF PASSION (TF)   King
   Phoenix Entertainment, 1990, w/Bob Kagey
ROXANNE: THE PRIZE PULITZER (TF)   Qintex
   Entertainment, 1990, w/Bob Kagey
STORM AND SORROW (CTF)   Accent Entertainment,
   1990, w/Marianna Miklos & Zsuzsa Posan

ROBERT KIZER
SPACE RAIDERS   New World, 1983
HAMBONE AND HILLIE   New World, 1984

LOU KLEINMAN
BILLY GALVIN   Vestron, 1986

ELIZABETH KLING
O.C. AND STIGGS   MGM/UA, 1987
SALVATION!   Circle Releasing Corporation, 1987
LIFE UNDER WATER (TF)   American
   Playhouse, 1989
MEN OF RESPECT   Columbia, 1991

LYNZEE KLINGMAN, ACE
Agent: Lawrence A. Mirisch, Triad Artists, Inc. -
   Los Angeles, 213/556-2727
Home: 526 Spoleto Drive, Pacific Palisades, CA 90272,
   213/459-7526

IN THE YEAR OF THE PIG (FD) ★   Pathe
   Contemporary, 1969
HEARTS AND MINDS (FD) ★★   Warner Bros., 1975
ONE FLEW OVER THE CUCKOO'S NEST ★   United
   Artists, 1975, w/Sheldon Kahn
YOU LIGHT UP MY LIFE   Columbia, 1977
ALMOST SUMMER   Universal, 1978
HAIR   United Artists, 1979
GILDA LIVE (FD)   Warner Bros., 1980, w/Ellen
   Hivde & Muffie Meyer
TRUE CONFESSIONS   United Artists, 1981
MAXIE   Orion, 1985
BABY BOOM   MGM/UA, 1987
THE WAR OF THE ROSES   20th Century Fox, 1989

DARREN KLOOMOK
STUCK ON YOU   Troma, 1983, w/Richard Haines &
   Ralph Rosenblum
VAMPING   Atlantic Releasing Corporation, 1984
MY DARK LADY   Film Gallery, 1987
PRISONERS OF INERTIA   Northwinds Entertainment,
   1989, w/Chip Cronkite & Juliet Weber

GEORGES KLOTZ
JUST THE WAY YOU ARE   MGM/UA, 1984,
   w/Claudio Ventura
PETIT CON   Samuel Goldwyn Company, 1985
WAITING FOR THE MOON   Skouras Pictures, 1987

MICHAEL KNUE
HOUSE   New World, 1986
NIGHT OF THE CREEPS   Tri-Star, 1986

THE HIDDEN   New Line Cinema, 1987
A NIGHTMARE ON ELM STREET 4: THE DREAM
   MASTER   New Line Cinema, 1988, w/Chuck Weiss
LUCKY STIFF   New Line Cinema, 1989, w/Tom Walls
LOCK UP   Tri-Star, 1989, w/Don Brochu
ROCKY V   MGM/UA, 1990, w/John G. Avildsen

CHRISTOPHER KOEFOED
GENUINE RISK   I.R.S., 1990

BONNIE KOEHLER
Agent: Smith Gosnell Nicholson & Associates -
   Pacific Palisades, 213/459-0307

THREE WARRIORS   United Artists, 1978
STACY'S KNIGHTS   Crown International, 1983
RESTING PLACE (TF)   Marian Rees Associates, 1986
HEART OF DIXIE   Orion, 1989
BAD INFLUENCE   Epic/Triumph, 1990
IRON MAZE   Iron Maze Productions, 1991

JACKIE KONG
NIGHT PATROL   New World, 1985

INGRID KOOLER
ECHO PARK   Atlantic Releasing Corporation, 1985

KEVIN KRASNY
DRUG WARS: THE CAMARENA STORY (MS)
   ZZY Productions, 1990, w/Skip Schollnik

RONALD KREHEL
ILLEGALLY YOURS   DEG, 1987, w/Richard Fields

CARL KRESS
ALVAREZ KELLY   Columbia, 1966
LUV   Columbia, 1967
WATERMELON MAN   Columbia, 1970
RAPE SQUAD   1970
THE LIBERATION OF L.B. JONES   Columbia, 1970
DOCTOR'S WIVES   Columbia, 1971
THE TOWERING INFERNO ★★   20th Century Fox,
   1974, w/Harold F. Kress
SUGAR HILL   American International, 1974
DRUM   United Artists, 1976
GATOR   United Artists, 1976
AUDREY ROSE   United Artists, 1977
A MAN, A WOMAN AND A BANK   Avco Embassy, 1979
METEOR   American International, 1979
HOPSCOTCH   Avco Embassy, 1980
LOOKER   The Ladd Company/Warner Bros., 1981
STROKER ACE   Universal, 1983, w/William Gordean
CANNONBALL RUN II   Warner Bros., 1984,
   w/William Gordean
HAWAIIAN HEAT (TF)   James D. Parriott Productions/
   Universal TV, 1984
RAD   Tri-Star, 1986
BLOODSPORT   Cannon, 1988
B.L. STRYKER (Pilot)   1989, w/Doug Ibold &
   Stephen Lovejoy
MEET THE HOLLOWHEADS   Moviestore
   Entertainment, 1990
I'M DANGEROUS TONIGHT (CTF)   BBK
   Productions, 1990

HAROLD F. KRESS, ACE
HOW THE WEST WAS WON ★★   MGM, 1982
I WALK THE LINE   Columbia, 1970
THE HORSEMAN   Columbia, 1971

STAND UP AND BE COUNTED   Columbia, 1971
THE POSEIDON ADVENTURE   20th Century
     Fox, 1972
THE ICEMAN COMETH   American Film Theatre, 1973
99 AND 44/100% DEAD   20th Century Fox, 1974
THE TOWERING INFERNO ★★   20th Century Fox,
     1974, w/Carl Kress
GATOR   United Artists, 1976
THE OTHER SIDE OF MIDNIGHT   20th Century Fox,
     1977, w/Donn Cambern
VIVA KNIEVEL!   Warner Bros., 1977
THE SWARM   Warner Bros., 1978

HOWARD KUNIN, ACE
ROLLER BOOGIE   United Artists, 1979, SE
FADE TO BLACK   American Cinema, 1980
CLASS OF 1984   United Film Distribution, 1982
FIRESTARTER   Universal, 1984
PARENT TRAP III (TF)   Walt Disney Television,
     1989, w/Duane Hartzell

JANE KURSON, ACE
Agent: Smith Gosnell Nicholson & Associates -
     Pacific Palisades, 213/459-0307

DON'T GO INTO THE HOUSE   Film Ventures
     International, 1980
NEIGHBORS   Columbia, 1982
THE KILLING FLOOR (TF)   Public Forum
     Productions/KERA-Dallas-Ft. Worth, 1984
PUMPING IRON II: THE WOMEN (FD)   Cinecom, 1985
THE KARATE KID PART II   Columbia, 1985,
     w/John G. Avildsen & David Garfield
HAPPY NEW YEAR   Columbia, 1987
BEETLEJUICE   Warner Bros., 1988
IMMEDIATE FAMILY   Columbia, 1989

L

RICHARD LaBRIE
BLOOD AND CONCRETE   I.R.S. Media, 1991,
     w/Jeffrey Reiner

JEAN LaFLEUR
RABID   New World, 1977
MY BLOODY VALENTINE   Paramount, 1981

ALAN LAKE
ESCAPE 2000   New World, 1983
DEAD END DRIVE-IN   New World, 1986, w/Lee Smith

PAUL LA MASTRA
CAROLINE? (TF)   Barry & Enright Productions, 1989
THE LAST BEST YEAR (TF)   David W. Rintels
     Productions, 1990

ROBERT K. LAMBERT, ACE
Agent: The Gersh Agency, Inc. - Beverly Hills,
     213/274-6611

THE MYSTERIOUS MONSTERS   Sunn Classic, 1976,
     w/Earle Herdan

THE DRIVER   20th Century Fox, 1978, w/Tina Hirsch
THE BRINK'S JOB   Universal, 1978, w/Bud Smith
THE SECRET LIFE OF PLANTS (FD)   Paramount, 1978,
     w/Christopher Lebenzon & Ian Masters
THE FINAL COUNTDOWN   United Artists, 1980
THE BORDER   Universal, 1982
THE HOTEL NEW HAMPSHIRE   Orion, 1984
HEAVENLY BODIES   MGM/UA, 1985
BRING ON THE NIGHT (FD)   Samuel Goldwyn
     Company, 1985
CRITICAL CONDITION   Paramount, 1987
SHADOW OF THE SUN - PART II (MS)   New World TV,
     1988, w/David Simmons & Fabien Tordjmann
MURDER BY MOONLIGHT (TF)   Tamara Asseyev
     Productions/London Weekend Television, 1989 , SE
THE HIJACKING OF THE ACHILLE LAURO (TF) ☆
     Tamara Asseyev Productions/Spectacor Films/New
     World Television, 1989
THE PHANTOM OF THE OPERA (TF)   Saban/Scherick
     Productions, 1990

CHARLES LANE
SIDEWALK STORIES   Island Pictures, 1989,
     w/Anne Stein

BRUCE LANGE
CLARENCE (CTF)   Atlantis Films, 1990

YVES LANGLOIS
THE LITTLE GIRL WHO LIVES DOWN THE LANE
     American International, 1977
QUEST FOR FIRE   20th Century Fox, 1982
ANGELA   Embassy, 1984
TOBY McTEAGUE   Spectrafilm, 1985
BETHUNE: THE MAKING OF A HERO   Filmline
     International, 1990, w/Angelo Corrao

SUZANNE LANG-WILLAR
FIRST NAME: CARMEN   Spectrafilm, 1984

TONY LANZA
DANGEROUS LOVE   Concorde, 1988

MARC LAUB
HONEYSUCKLE ROSE   Warner Bros., 1980, w/Aram
     Avakian, Norman Gay & Evan Lottman
FOUR FRIENDS   Filmways, 1981, w/Barry Malkin
HAMMETT   Orion/Warner Bros., 1982, w/Robert
     Q.Lovett, Barry Malkin & Randy Roberts
MISUNDERSTOOD   MGM/UA, 1984
SEVEN MINUTES IN HEAVEN   Warner Bros., 1985

ROBERT LAWRENCE
Agent: The Gersh Agency, Inc., Beverly Hills -
     213/274-6611, New York - 212/997-1818

SPARTACUS ★   Universal, 1960
EL CID   Allied Artists, 1961
55 DAYS IN PEKING   Allied Artists, 1962
FALL OF THE ROMAN EMPIRE   Paramount, 1963
IS PARIS BURNING   Paramount, 1965
BUONA SERA, MRS. CAMPBELL   UA, 1967
UPTIGHT   Paramount, 1967
UPTIGHT   Paramount, 1968
LE CONDE   CineFrance, 1969
PROMISE AT DAWN   Avco Embassy, 1970
LOVING   Columbia, 1970
FIDDLER ON THE ROOF   United Artists, 1971,
     w/Antony Gibbs

La

CINEMATOGRAPHERS
PRODUCTION
DESIGNERS,
COSTUME
DESIGNERS AND
FILM EDITORS
GUIDE

F
I
L
M

E
D
I
T
O
R
S

La

CINEMATOGRAPHERS
PRODUCTION
DESIGNERS,
COSTUME
DESIGNERS AND
FILM EDITORS
GUIDE

F
I
L
M

E
D
I
T
O
R
S

UP THE SANDBOX   National General, 1972
S.P.Y.S.   20th Century Fox, 1974
WHIFFS   20th Century Fox, 1975
I WILL, I WILL...FOR NOW   20th Century Fox, 1976
HUGO THE HIPPO (AF)   20th Century Fox, 1976
FINGERS   Brut Productions, 1978
EXPOSED   MGM/UA, 1983
NEVER SAY NEVER AGAIN   Warner Bros., 1983
WARNING SIGN   20th Century Fox, 1985
8 MILLION WAYS TO DIE   Tri-Star, 1986,
   w/Stuart Pappe
RENT-A-COP   Kings Road, 1988

TONY LAWSON
BARRY LYNDON   Warner Bros., 1975
CROSS OF IRON   Avco Embassy, 1977,
   w/Michel Ellis & Herbert Taschner
BAD TIMING/A SENSUAL OBSESSION   World
   Northal, 1980
DRAGONSLAYER   Paramount, 1981
EUREKA   United Artists Classics, 1984
THE BOUNTY   Orion, 1984
INSIGNIFICANCE   Island Alive, 1985
CASTAWAY   Cannon, 1987
THE AMERICAN WAY   Miramax, 1987
TRACK 29   Island Pictures, 1988
MANIFESTO   Cannon, 1989
THE WITCHES   Warner Bros., 1990

DAVID LEAN
Contact: Film Producers Association, 162 Wardour
   Street, London W1, England

A PASSAGE TO INDIA ★   Columbia, 1984

CHRIS LEBENZON
Phone: 213/454-3342

DEMON   New World, 1977
THE PRIVATE FILES OF J. EDGAR HOOVER
   American International, 1978
THE SECRET LIFE OF PLANTS (FD)   Paramount,
   1978, w/Robert K. Lambert & Ian Masters
WOLFEN   Orion/Warner Bros., 1981, w/Marshall M.
   Borden, Martin Bram & Dennis Dolan
A BREED APART   Orion, 1984
WEIRD SCIENCE   Universal, 1985, w/Scott Wallace &
   Mark Warner
DEATH OF AN ANGEL   20th Century Fox, 1985
TOP GUN H   Paramount, 1986, w/Billy Weber
BEVERLY HILLS COP II   Paramount, 1987,
   w/Michael Tronick & Billy Weber
WEEDS   DEG, 1987, w/David Handman & Jon Poll
MIDNIGHT RUN   Universal, 1988, w/Michael
   Tronick & Billy Weber
DAYS OF THUNDER   Paramount, 1990,
   w/Billy Weber
REVENGE   Columbia, 1990

ARMOND LEBOWITZ
Q   United Film Distribution, 1982
PERFECT STRANGERS   ITC, 1984
THE STUFF   New World, 1985
SPECIAL EFFECTS   New Line Cinema, 1986

WAYNE LeCLOS
BLISS   New World, 1986

SPIKE LEE
Business: Forty Acres & A Mule Productions - Brooklyn,
   718/624-3703

SHE'S GOTTA HAVE IT   Island Pictures, 1985
   (also directed)

RICHARD C. LEEMAN
NOT OF THIS WORLD (TF)   Barry & Enright Productions,
   1991, w/Christopher Ellis

ROBERT LEIGHTON
DELUSION   New Line Cinema, 1981
KILL AND KILL AGAIN   Film Ventures International,
   1981, w/Peter Thornton
BLOOD TIDE   21st Century, 1982
THE HOUSE WHERE DEATH LIVES   New
   American, 1982
THE BEING   BFV Films, 1983
WAVELENGTH   New World, 1983, w/Mark Goldblatt
THIS IS SPINAL TAP   Embassy, 1984, SE
THE SURE THING   Embassy, 1985
STAND BY ME   Columbia, 1986
THE PRINCESS BRIDE   20th Century Fox, 1987
BULL DURHAM   Orion, 1988, w/Adam Weiss
WHEN HARRY MET SALLY...   Castle Rock/
   Columbia, 1989
BLAZE   Buena Vista, 1989
MISERY   Castle Rock/Nelson Entertainment/
   Columbia, 1990

WARNER E. LEIGHTON
THE JUNKMAN   H.B. Halicki International, 1982
THE TROUBLE WITH SPIES   DEG, 1987

MAX LEMON
THE LAST WAVE   World Northal, 1978
THOSE GLORY, GLORY DAYS   Cinecom, 1983
SHARMA AND BEYOND   Cinecom, 1984
BETWEEN WARS   Satori, 1985
FOREVER YOUNG   Cinecom, 1986

JERRY LEON
CAMPION-SWEET DANGER (TF)   BBC TV, 1990

LARRY D. LESTER
BROKEN BADGES (TF)   Stephen J. Cannell Productions,
   1990, w/Argyle Coe Nelson & Casey O. Rohrs

BOB LETTERMAN
MORGAN STEWART'S COMING HOME   New Century/
   Vista, 1987

SIDNEY LEVIN, ACE
West Coast Card
Agent: Smith Gosnell Nicholson & Associates -
   Pacific Palisades, 213/459-0307

SOUNDER   20th Century Fox, 1972
MEAN STREETS   Warner Bros., 1973
THE AUTOBIOGRAPHY OF MISS JANE PITTMAN (TF)
   Tomorrow Entertainment, 1974
NASHVILLE   Paramount, 1976
THE FRONT   Columbia, 1976
PART 2 SOUNDER   Gamma III, 1976
CASEY'S SHADOW   Columbia, 1978
THE CHEAP DETECTIVE   Columbia, 1978,
   w/Michael Stevenson

NORMA RAE   20th Century Fox, 1979
CALIFORNIA DREAMING   American International,
   1979, w/Herb Dow & Roy Peterson
HERO AT LARGE   MGM/United Artists, 1980
WHOLLY MOSES!   Columbia, 1980
BACK ROADS   Warner Bros., 1981
I OUGHT TO BE IN PICTURES   20th Century
   Fox, 1982
CROSS CREEK   Universal/AFD, 1983
THE RIVER   Universal, 1984
MURPHY'S ROMANCE   Columbia, 1985
NUTS   Warner Bros., 1987
CLARA'S HEART   Warner Bros., 1988
STANLEY & IRIS   MGM/UA, 1990
HE SAID, SHE SAID   Paramount, 1991

FARREL LEVY (DUFFY)
Agent: Bruce E. Fritzberg, The Production Agency, 8489
   W. 3rd St., Los Angeles, CA 90048, 213/651/1858

DIRTY DANCING   Vestron, 1987, CE
HELLO AGAIN   Buena Vista, 1987, CE
PRIVATE DEBTS   Columbia, 1989
ERNEST GOES TO JAIL   Buena Vista, 1990,
   w/Sharyn L. Ross
ACROSS THE TRACKS   Rosenbloom
   Entertainment, 1991

TIM LEWIS
MAN ON FLOWERS   Spectrafilmm, 1983
LONELY HEARTS   Samuel Goldwyn Company, 1983
MY FIRST WIFE   Spectrafilm, 1985, w/Peter McBolin
CACTUS   Spectrafilm, 1986
WARM NIGHTS ON A SLOW MOVING TRAIN
   Miramax Films, 1989

STU LINDER
THE FORTUNE   Columbia, 1975
MY BODYGUARD   20th Century Fox, 1980
FIRST FAMILY   Warner Bros., 1980, w/Susan Martin
DINER   MGM/United Artists, 1982
SIX WEEKS   Universal, 1982
THE NATURAL   Tri-Star, 1984
YOUNG SHERLOCK HOLMES   Paramount, 1985
CODE NAME: EMERALD   MGM/UA, 1985
TIN MEN   Buena Vista, 1987
GOOD MORNING, VIETNAM   Buena Vista, 1987
RAIN MAN ★   MGM/UA, 1988
AVALON   Baltimore Pictures/Tri-Star, 1990

KEES LINDHORST
THE ROSE GARDEN   Pathe International, 1990

JAMES B. LING
TARZAN, THE APE MAN   MGM/United Artists, 1981

JOHN F. LINK
THE KING OF MARVIN GARDENS   Columbia, 1972
ELECTRA GLIDE IN BLUE   United Artists, 1973
RACE WITH THE DEVIL   20th Century Fox, 1975
STAY HUNGRY   United Artists, 1976
CITIZENS BAND   Paramount, 1977
BORDERLINE   AFD, 1980
TIGER TOWN   Buena Vista, 1984,
   w/Richard A. Harris
PREDATOR   20th Century Fox, 1987, w/Mark Helfrich
DIE HARD ★★   20th Century Fox, 1988,
   w/Frank J. Urioste

ROAD HOUSE   MGM/UA, 1989, w/Frank J. Urioste
HARD TO KILL *SEVEN YEAR STORM*   Warner
   Bros., 1990
IF LOOKS COULD KILL   Warner Bros., 1991

PHILLIP LINSON
AFTER MIDNIGHT   MGM/UA, 1989,
   w/Quinnie Martin Jr.

KEES LINTHORST
THE ASSAULT   Cannon, 1986

CAROL LITTLETON, ACE
Agent: Bauer Benedek Agency - Los Angeles,
   213/275-2421

THE MAFU CAGE   Clouds Productions, 1978
FRENCH POSTCARDS   Paramount, 1979
ROADIE   United Artists, 1980, SE
BODY HEAT   The Ladd Company/Warner Bros., 1981
E.T.: THE EXTRATERRESTRIAL ★   Universal, 1982
THE BIG CHILL   Columbia, 1983
PLACES IN THE HEART   Tri-Star, 1984
SILVERADO   Columbia, 1985
BRIGHTON BEACH MEMOIRS   Universal, 1986
SWIMMING TO CAMBODIA   Cinecom, 1987
VIBES   Columbia, 1988
THE ACCIDENTAL TOURIST   Warner Bros., 1988
WHITE PALACE   Universal, 1990

VICTOR LIVINGSTON
JOURNEY TO THE CENTER OF THE EARTH   Cannon,
   1989, w/Roxanne Zingale

RUSSELL LIVINGSTONE
DREAM A LITTLE DREAM   Vestron, 1989
ONLY ONE SURVIVED (TF)   CBS Entertainment, 1990

DAVID LLOYD
HIDDEN VIEW (TF)   LBS Communications, 1990

RUSSELL LLOYD, ACE, GBFE
THE MAN WHO WOULD BE KING ★   Columbia/Allied
   Artists, 1975
THE LADY VANISHES   Rank, 1979
ABSOLUTE BEGINNERS   Orion, 1986, w/Richard
   Bedford, Michael Bradsell & Gerry Hambling
BLOOD LINK   Zadar Films, 1986

DANIEL LOEWENTHAL
Agent: Paul Gerard Agency - Newport Beach,
   714/644-7950

WAITRESS *SOUP TO NUTS*   Troma, 1982
THE BIG SCORE   Almi Pictures, 1983
HOME FREE ALL   Almi Pictures, 1984
THE ROSEBUD BEACH HOTEL   Almi Pictures, 1984
MISSING IN ACTION   Cannon, 1984, w/Joel Goodman
INVASION U.S.A.   Cannon, 1985, w/Scott Vickrey
STEPHEN KING'S SILVER BULLET   Paramount, 1985
HARD CHOICES   Lorimar, 1986
ALIEN FROM L.A.   Cannon, 1988
RED SCORPION   Shapiro Glickenhaus, 1989

J. ANTHONY LOMA
COUNTEFORCE (TF)   Golden Sun/ESME, 1991,
   w/Nicholas Wentworth

Lo

CINEMATOGRAPHERS
PRODUCTION
DESIGNERS,
COSTUME
DESIGNERS AND
FILM EDITORS
GUIDE

F
I
L
M

E
D
I
T
O
R
S

Lo

CINEMATOGRAPHERS
PRODUCTION
DESIGNERS,
COSTUME
DESIGNERS and
FILM EDITORS
GUIDE

F
I
L
M

E
D
I
T
O
R
S

LOU LOMBARDO

THE WILD BUNCH   Warner Bros., 1969
THE BALLAD OF CABLE HOGUE   Warner Bros., 1970
BREWSTER McCLOUD   MGM, 1970
McCABE & MRS. MILLER   Warner Bros., 1971
THE LONG GOODBYE   United Artists, 1973
THIEVES LIKE US   United Artists, 1974
CALIFORNIA SPLIT   Columbia, 1974
THE BLACK BIRD   Columbia, 1975
THE LATE SHOW   Warner Bros., 1977
UP IN SMOKE   Paramount, 1978, SE
THE CHANGELING   AFD, 1980
JUST ONE OF THE GUYS   Columbia, 1985
STEWARDESS SCHOOL   Columbia, 1987,
    w/Kenneth C. Paonessa
MOONSTRUCK   MGM/UA, 1987
THE JANUARY MAN   MGM/UA, 1989
UNCLE BUCK   Universal, 1989
IN COUNTRY   Warner Bros., 1989, w/Antony Gibbs

TONY LOMBARDO

Agent: The Gersh Agency, Inc., Beverly Hills -
    213/274-6611, New York - 212/997-1818

A PERFECT COUPLE   20th Century Fox, 1979
CHEECH & CHONG'S NICE DREAMS
    Columbia, 1981
A WEDDING   20th Century Fox, 1978
RECKLESS   MGM/UA, 1984
BLAME IT ON THE NIGHT   Tri-Star, 1984
P.K. AND THE KID   Castle Hill Productions, 1987
BORN TO RACE   MGM/UA, 1988, w/Thomas Stanford
MAN OUTSIDE   Virgin Vision, 1988
UNCLE BUCK   Universal, 1989, CE
BY DAWN'S EARLY LIGHT (CTF)   HBO, 1989
THE HARD WAY   Universal, 1991, w/Frank Morriss

ANDREW LONDON

IATSE 776
Home: 3642 Cadman Dr., Los Angeles, CA 90027,
    213/662-3879

PSYCHO II   Universal, 1983
CLOAK AND DAGGER   Universal, 1984
THE CHRISTMAS STAR (TF)   Walt Disney, 1986
LINK   Thorn EMI/Cannon, 1986
BEAUTY AND THE BEAST (Pilot)   CBS
    Entertainment, 1987
RAMBO III   Tri-Star, 1988, w/O. Nicholas Brown,
    James Symons & Edward Warschilka
F/X 2 — THE DEADLY ART OF ILLUSION
    Orion, 1991

MELODY LONDON

East & West Coast cards
Agent: The Doug Apatow Agency, 10559 Blythe Ave. -
    Los Angeles, CA 90064

STRANGER THAN PARADISE   Samuel Goldwyn
    Company, 1984, w/Jim Jarmusch
DOWN BY LAW   Island Pictures, 1986
ROCKET GIBRALTAR   Columbia, 1988
MYSTERY TRAIN   Orion, 1989

EDUARDO LOPEZ

FUNNY DIRTY LITTLE WAR   Cinevista, 1986
THE STRANGER   Columbia, 1987

MIGUEL MARIO LOPEZ

NIGHT OF THE PENCILS   Marquis Pictures, 1987

JULIANE LORENZ

LOLA   United Artists Classics, 1982
VERONIKA VOSS   United Artists Classics, 1982
BERLIN ALEXANDERPLATZ   Teleculture, 1983
THE ROSE KING   Film Verlag, 1987

EVAN LOTTMAN, ACE

Home: 15 W. 72nd Street, New York, NY 10023,
    212/873-0448

PUZZLE OF A DOWNFALL CHILD   Universal, 1970
PANIC IN NEEDLE PARK   20th Century Fox, 1971
SCARECROW   Warner Bros., 1973
THE EFFECT OF GAMMA RAYS ON MAN-IN-THE-MOON
    MARIGOLDS   20th Century Fox, 1973
THE EXORCIST ★   Warner Bros., 1973, w/others
SWEET REVENGE   MGM/UA, 1976,
    w/Richard Fetterman
THE SEDUCTION OF JOE TYNAN   Universal, 1979
HONEYSUCKLE ROSE   Warner Bros., 1980, w/Aram
    Avakian, Norman Gay & Marc Laub
ROLLOVER   Orion/Warner Bros., 1981
THE PILOT   Summit, 1981
SOPHIE'S CHOICE   Universal/AFD, 1982
THE MUPPETS TAKE MANHATTAN   Tri-Star, 1984
THE PROTECTOR   Warner Bros., 1985
MAXIMUM OVERDRIVE   DEG, 1986
ON THE YARD   Midwest Film Productions, 1987
ORPHANS   Lorimar, 1987
GOTHAM (CTF)   Showtime/Phoenix EntertainmentGroup/
    Keith Addis & Associates, 1988
SEE YOU IN THE MORNING   Warner Bros., 1989
PRESUMED INNOCENT   Mirage/Warner Bros., 1990

RAY LOVEJOY

Agent: Grace Lyons Management - Los Angeles,
    213/655-5100

2001: A SPACE ODYSSEY   MGM, 1968
A DAY IN THE DEATH OF JOE EGG   Columbia, 1972
THE RULING CLASS   Avco Embassy, 1972
FEAR IS THE KEY   Paramount, 1973
LITTLE MALCOLM AND HIS STRUGGLE AGAINST THE
    EUNUCHS   Multicetera Investments, 1974
GHOST IN THE NOONDAY SUN   Columbia, 1974
THE SHINING   Warner Bros., 1980
KRULL   Columbia, 1983
THE DRESSER   Columbia, 1983
SHEENA   Columbia, 1984
ALIENS ★   20th Century Fox, 1986
ELENI   Warner Bros., 1985
SUSPECT   Tri-Star, 1987
THE HOUSE ON CARROLL STREET   Orion, 1988
BATMAN   Warner Bros., 1989
HOMEBOY   Redbury Ltd./Elliott Kastner
    Productions, 1989
MR. FROST   Triumph Releasing, 1990

STEPHEN LOVEJOY

DEADLY DESIRE (CTF)   Skylark Films, 1991

ROBERT Q. LOVETT

THE NEXT MAN   Allied Artists, 1976, w/Aram Avakian
ONCE IN PARIS...   Atlantic Releasing Corporation, 1978
HAMMETT   Orion/Warner Bros., 1982, w/Marc Laub,
    Barry Malkin & Randy Roberts

THE GOLDEN SEAL   Samuel Goldwyn
    Company, 1983
THE COTTON CLUB ★   Orion, 1984

B E R T   L O V I T T
Home: 8427 Kirkwood Dr., Los Angeles, CA 90046,
    213/650-1044

ELVIS ON TOUR   MGM/UA, 1972
BIRDS DO IT, BEES DO IT   Columbia, 1973
A FORCE OF ONE   American Cinema, 1979
HARRY'S WAR   Taft International, 1981,
    w/Peter L. McCrea
IT CAME FROM HOLLYWOOD (FD)   Paramount,
    1982, w/Janice Hampton
THE BEAST WITHIN   MGM/United Artists, 1982,
    w/Robert A. Brown
ON THE EDGE   Skouras Pictures, 1986,
    w/Rich Harkness
AMAZON WOMEN ON THE MOON   Universal, 1987,
    w/Malcolm Campbell & Marshall Harvey
IMAGINE: JOHN LENNON (FD)   Warner Bros., 1988
GREAT BALLS OF FIRE!   Orion, 1989, w/Lisa Day &
    Pembroke Herring

E D W A R D   L O W E
COCAINE WARS   Concorde, 1985

T O N Y   L O W E R
BEAR ISLAND   Taft International, 1980
HARD FEELINGS   Astral Bellevue, 1981
RUNNING BRAVE   Buena Vista, 1983,
    w/Earl Herdan
SPRING FEVER   Comworld, 1983, w/Kirk Jones
BEDROOM EYES   Film Gallery/Aquarius, 1984
RECKLESS DISREGARD (CTF)   Telecom
    Entertainment/Polar Film Corp./Freemantla of
    Canada Ltd., 1985
HANG TOUGH   Moviestore Entertainment, 1990

N I C O L E   L U B T C H A N S K Y
LOVE ON THE GROUND   Spectrafilm, 1986

M A R C I A   L U C A S
AMERICAN GRAFFITI ★   Universal, 1973,
    w/Verna Fields
ALICE DOESN'T LIVE HERE ANYMORE   Warner
    Bros., 1974
TAXI DRIVER   Columbia, 1976, w/Tom Rolf &
    Melvin Shapiro
NEW YORK, NEW YORK   United Artists, 1977,
    w/Irving Lerner
STAR WARS ★★   20th Century Fox, 1977,
    w/Richard Chew & Paul Hirsch
RETURN OF THE JEDI   20th Century Fox, 1983,
    w/Sean Barton & Duwayne Dunham

M I C H A E L   L U C I A N O ,   A C E
HUSH...HUSH, SWEET CHARLOTTE ★   20th Century
    Fox, 1964
THE FLIGHT OF THE PHOENIX ★   20th Century
    Fox, 1965
THE DIRTY DOZEN ★   MGM, 1967
THE LONGEST YARD ★   Paramount, 1974
BOBBIE JO & THE OUTLAW   American
    International, 1976
SCORCHY   American International, 1976
EMPIRE OF THE ANTS   American International, 1977

TWILIGHT'S LAST GLEAMING   Allied Artists,
    1977, Supervisor
HARDLY WORKING   20th Century Fox, 1981
STRIPES   Columbia, 1981, w/Eva Ruggero

J E R R O L D   L .   L U D W I G
STELLA   Buena Vista, 1990
THE DREAMER OF OZ (TF)   Bedrock Productions, 1990
LOVE, LIES AND MURDER-PARTS I & II (TF)   Republic
    Pictures, 1991

Y U R I J   L U H O V Y
TULIPS   Avco Embassy, 1981, w/Alan Collins
CAPTIVE HEARTS   MGM/UA, 1987

S K I P   L U S K
REUBEN, REUBEN   20th Century Fox, 1983

M I C H A E L   L Y N C H
MY DAD CAN'T BE CRAZY...CAN HE? (TF)   Rosebud
    Productions, 1990

J A M E S   L Y O N S
POISON   Zeitgeist Films, 1991, w/Todd Haynes

H E A T H E R   M a c D O U G A L L
RUNNING AGAINST TIME (CTF)   Finnegan-Pinchuk
    Productions, 1990

J U A N   C A R L O S   M A C I A S
THE OFFICIAL STORY   Historias Cinematografias, 1985
OLD GRINGO   Columbia, 1989, w/William Anderson &
    Glenn Farr

S T E P H E N   M A C K
BREATHLESS   Orion, 1983

G U Y   M A G A R
RETRIBUTION   United Film Distribution, 1987,
    w/Alan Shefland

A L B E R T   M A G N O L I
RECKLESS   MGM/UA, 1984
PURPLE RAIN   Warner Bros., 1984, w/Ken Robinson

B A R R Y   M A L K I N
THE RAIN PEOPLE   Warner Bros., 1969
WHO IS HARRY KELLERMAN AND WHY IS HE SAYING
    ALL THOSE TERRIBLE THINGS ABOUT ME?
    National General, 1971
THEY MIGHT BE GIANTS   Univeral, 1971
COPS AND ROBBERS   United Artists, 1973
ONE SUMMER LOVE   American International, 1976
SOMEBODY KILLED HER HUSBAND   Columbia, 1978
LAST EMBRACE   United Artists, 1979
WINDOWS   United Artists, 1980
ONE TRICK PONY   Warner Bros., 1980, w/Edward
    Beyer & David Ray

Ma

CINEMATOGRAPHERS
PRODUCTION
DESIGNERS,
COSTUME
DESIGNERS AND
FILM EDITORS
GUIDE

F
I
L
M

E
D
I
T
O
R
S

CINEMATOGRAPHERS
PRODUCTION
DESIGNERS,
COSTUME
DESIGNERS AND
FILM EDITORS
GUIDE

FOUR FRIENDS   Filmways, 1981, w/Marc Laub
HAMMETT   Orion/Warner Bros., 1982, w/Marc Laub,
    Robert Q. Lovett & Randy Roberts
RUMBLE FISH   Universal, 1983
THE COTTON CLUB ★   Orion, 1984, SE
PEGGY SUE GOT MARRIED   Tri-Star, 1986
GARDENS OF STONE   Tri-Star, 1987
BIG   20th Century Fox, 1988
NEW YORK STORIES ("Life Without Zoe")   Buena
    Vista, 1989
THE FRESHMAN   Tri-Star, 1990
THE GODFATHER PART III ★   Zoetrope Studios/
    Paramount, 1990, w/Lisa Fruchtman &
    Walter Murch

PAMELA MALOUF-CUNDY
TENNESSEE WILLIAMS' SWEET BIRD OF
    YOUTH (TF)   Atlantic/Kushner-Locke
    Productions, 1990
MURDER C.O.D. (TF)   Perry Lafferty
    Productions, 1990
I'LL TAKE ROMANCE (TF)   New World
    Television, 1990

NEIL MANDELBERG
WEB OF DECEIT (CTF)   Wilshire Court
    Productions, 1990

RON MANN
COMIC BOOK CONFIDENTIAL   Cinecom, 1990,
    w/Robert Kennedy

STEVE MANN
LUST FOR FREEDOM   Troma, 1987, w/David
    Khachatorian & Thomas R. Rondinella
LADY IN WHITE   New Century/Vista, 1988

EDWARD MANSELL
CROSSING TO FREEDOM (TF)   Procter & Gamble
    Productions, 1989, w/Tony Cranstoun
THE TRAGEDY OF FLIGHT 103: THE INSIDE
    STORY (CTF)   HBO Showcase, 1990

MARCUS MANTON
THE FUNNY FARM   New World, 1983
EXTERMINATOR 2   Cannon, 1984, w/George Norris
MISSING IN ACTION 2: THE BEGINNING   Cannon,
    1985, w/Marck Conte
RAPPIN'   Cannon, 1985, w/Bert Glatstein &
    Andy Horvitch
P.O.W. THE ESCAPE   Cannon, 1986
BERSERKER   Shapiro Entertainment, 1987
PUMPKINHEAD   MGM/UA, 1988
I, MADMAN   Trans World Entertainment, 1989
RIVERBEND   International Releasing, 1989
LAMBADA   Cannon/Warner Bros., 1990

ANDREW MARCUS
THE BALLAD OF THE SAD CAFE   Angelika
    Films, 1991

RICHARD MARDEN
RUSSIAN ROULETTE   Avco Embassy, 1975
ESCAPE FROM THE DARK   Buena Vista, 1976
CARRY ON ENGLAND   20th Century Fox-Rank, 1976
CARAVANS   Universal, 1978
THE HOUND OF THE BASKERVILLES   Atlantic
    Releasing Corporation, 1979, w/Glenn Hyde

SATURN 3   AFD, 1980
THE MIRROR CRACK'D   AFD, 1980
EVIL UNDER THE SUN   Universal/AFD, 1982
SWORD OF THE VALIANT   Cannon, 1984,
    w/Barry Peters
BLAME IT ON RIO   20th Century Fox, 1984,
    w/George Hively
THE FALCON AND THE SNOWMAN   Orion, 1985
HALF MOON STREET   20th Century Fox, 1986
HELLRAISER   New World, 1987
NIGHTBREED   20th Century Fox, 1990,
    w/Mark Goldblatt
HAMLET   Warner Bros., 1990

LORENZO MARINELLI
HEART   New World, 1987

PETER MARIS
HANGFIRE   Motion Picture Corporation of America, 1991

EDWARD MARNIER
STRAPLESS   Film Four International, 1990
ORPHEUS DESCENDING (CMS)   Nederlander TV and
    Film Productions, 1990

STEPHEN MARK
THE DRIFTER   Concorde, 1988
STRIPPED TO KILL 2   Concorde, 1989
MASQUE OF THE RED DEATH   Concorde, 1989
STREETS   Concorde, 1990

RICHARD MARKS, ACE
Address: 648 Ashland Avenue, Santa Monica, CA
    90405, 213/369-3011

LITTLE BIG MAN   National General, 1970, CE
BANG THE DRUM SLOWLY   Paramount, 1973
SERPICO   Paramount, 1973, CE
THE GODFATHER, PART II   Paramount, 1974
LIES MY FATHER TOLD ME   Columbia, 1975
THE LAST TYCOON   Paramount, 1976
APOCALYPSE NOW ★   United Artists, 1979, SE
THE HAND   Orion/Warner Bros., 1981
PENNIES FROM HEAVEN   MGM/United Artists, 1981
MAX DUGAN RETURNS   20th Century Fox, 1983
TERMS OF ENDEARMENT ★   Paramount, 1983
THE ADVENTURES OF BUCKAROO BANZAI: ACROSS
    THE 8TH DIMENSION   20th Century Fox, 1984,
    w/George Bowers
ST. ELMO'S FIRE   Columbia, 1985
PRETTY IN PINK   Paramount, 1986
FIREWALKER   Cannon, 1986
BROADCAST NEWS ★   20th Century Fox, 1987
SAY ANYTHING   20th Century Fox, 1989
DICK TRACY   Buena Vista, 1990
ONE GOOD COP   Hollywood Pictures, 1991

EDWARD MARNIER
PASCALI'S ISLAND   Avenue Pictures, 1988
KILLING DAD   Scottish Television, 1989
STRAPLESS   Miramax, 1990
BEARSKIN: AN URBAN FAIRY TALE   Film Four, 1989

DAVID MARTIN
THE PLOUGHMAN'S LUNCH   Samuel Goldwyn
    Company, 1984
SID & NANCY   Samuel Goldwyn Company, 1986
STRAIGHT TO HELL   Island Pictures, 1987

STORMY MONDAY   Atlantic Releasing
    Corporation, 1987
DREAM DEMON   Spectrafilm, 1988, w/Ian Crafford
THE RACHEL PAPERS   MGM/UA, 1989
NUNS ON THE RUN   20th Century Fox, 1990

QUINNIE MARTIN JR.
AFTER MIDNIGHT   MGM/UA, 1989, w/Phillip Linson

RICHARD MARTIN
THE OUTSIDE CHANCE OF MAXIMILIAN GLICK
    South Gate Entertainment, 1989

RICK MARTIN
ANYTHING TO SURVIVE (TF)   ATL Productions, 1990

ROBERT MARTIN
MOVING OUT   Satori, 1985

SUSAN MARTIN
THRESHOLD   20th Century Fox International
    Classics, 1983
PALAIS ROYALE   Spectrafilm, 1988
A WINTER TAN   1989, w/Alan Lee

JOHN A. MARTINELLI, ACE
HARD COUNTRY   AFD, 1981
THE BOSS' WIFE   Tri-Star, 1986
COLUMBO (Pilot)   1989

RUGGERO MASTROIANNI
TRAVELS WITH ANITA   United Artists, 1979
CITY OF WOMEN   New Yorker Films, 1981
ILLUSTRIOUS CORPSES   1981, Italian
THREE BROTHERS   New World, 1982
TALES OF ORDINARY MADNESS   Fred Baker
    Films, 1983
AND THE SHIP SAILS ON   Triumph, 1984
CARMEN   Triumph, 1984, w/Colette Semprun
THE BERLIN AFFAIR   Cannon, 1985
GINGER & FRED   MGM/UA, 1986, w/Nino Baragli &
    Ugo De Rossi

WENDY PHIFER MATE
NICE GIRLS DON'T EXPLODE   New World, 1987
THE HOT SPOT   Orion, 1990

OLIVIER MAUFFROY
THE BIG BLUE   WEG, 1988
NIKITA   Gaumont, 1990

FRANK MAZZOLA
INSTANT KARMA   Rosenbloom Entertainment, 1990

DEBRA McDERMOTT
TOUGH GUYS DON'T DANCE   Cannon, 1987
COLD FEET   Avenue Pictures, 1989, w/David Rawlins
NAKED TANGO   Scotia International, 1990,
    w/Lee Percy

BRUCE McDONALD
SPEAKING PARTS   Cinephile, 1990

JIM McELROY
APPEARANCES (TF)   Echo Cove Productions,
    1989, w/Kelly Snyder

ROSS McELWEE
SHERMAN'S MARCH   First Run Features, 1986

JOSEPH McGIRR
THE TOXIC AVENGER PART III: THE LAST
    TEMPTATION OF TOXIE   Troma, 1989

CRAIG McKAY, ACE
Home: 345 W. 58th Street, New York, NY 10019,
    212/765-1083

SCARECROW   Warner Bros., 1973
THIEVES   Paramount, 1977
MELVIN AND HOWARD   Universal, 1980
REDS ★   Paramount, 1981, w/Dede Allen
SWING SHIFT   Warner Bros., 1983
PRIVATE SESSIONS (TF)   The Belle Company/Seltzer-
    Gimbel Productions/Raven's Claw Productions/
    Comworld Productions, 1985
SOMETHING WILD   Orion, 1987
MARRIED TO THE MOB   Orion, 1988
CRACK IN THE MIRROR   Rebo Productions, 1988,
    w/Alan Miller
SHE-DEVIL   Orion, 1989
MIAMI BLUES   Orion, 1990
THE SILENCE OF THE LAMBS   Orion, 1991

DAVID E. McKENNA
JANE AUSTEN IN MANHATTAN   Contemporary, 1980

G. GREGG McLAUGHLIN
DEATH WARRANT   MGM/UA, 1990, w/John A. Barton

MICHAEL S. McLEAN
DANIELLE STEEL'S FINE THINGS (TF)   The Cramer
    Company, 1990, w/Wayne Wahrman

MICHAEL McMAHON
MURDER ONE   Miramax, 1988
FRIENDS, LOVERS & LUNATICS   Fries
    Entertainment, 1989

PATRICK McMAHON
STRANGE BREW   MGM/UA, 1983
APPRENTICE TO MURDER   New World, 1988
A KILLING AFFAIR   Hemdale, 1988
PERSONAL CHOICE   The MovieStore, 1989
LITTLE MONSTERS   MGM/UA, 1989

EDWARD McQUEEN-MASON
ROAD GAMES   Avco Embassy, 1981
THE CLINIC   Satori, 1985
KANGAROO   Cineplex Odeon, 1987

MARK MELNICK, ACE
Agent: Sandra Marsh Management - Sherman Oaks,
    818/905-6961

STAYING ALIVE   Paramount, 1983
UNCOMMON VALOR   Paramount, 1983
LOTS OF LUCK (CTF)   Tomorrow Entertainment, 1985
REMO WILLIAMS: THE ADVENTURE BEGINS
    Orion, 1985
THE KING OF LOVE (TF)   Sarabande Productions/
    MGM-UA TV, 1986
MOVING TARGET (TF)   NBC TV, 1988
THE UNHOLY   Vestron, 1988

Me

CINEMATOGRAPHERS
PRODUCTION
DESIGNERS,
COSTUME
DESIGNERS AND
FILM EDITORS
GUIDE

F
I
L
M

E
D
I
T
O
R
S

Me

CINEMATOGRAPHERS
PRODUCTION
DESIGNERS,
COSTUME
DESIGNERS and
FILM EDITORS
GUIDE

F
I
L
M

E
D
I
T
O
R
S

DIRTY DANCING (Pilot)   1989
TROOP BEVERLY HILLS   WEG, 1989
NIGHT VISION (TF)   Wes Craven Films, 1990,
    w/James Cablentz
BRENDA STARR   New World, 1991

JAMES MELTON
THE RESCUERS (AF)   Buena Vista, 1977,
    w/Jim Koford
THE FOX AND THE HOUND (AF)   Buena Vista,
    1981, w/Jim Koford
THE BLACK CAULDRON (AF)   Buena Vista, 1985
THE GREAT MOUSE DETECTIVE (AF)   Buena Vista,
    1986, w/Ray M. Brewer Jr.

ENZO MENICONI
DARK EYES   Island Pictures, 1987

SALLY MENKE
Agent: Dattner & Associates - Los Angeles,
    213/447-5986

COLD FEET   Cinecom, 1984
TEENAGE MUTANT NINJA TURTLES   Golden
    Harvest/New Line Cinema, 1990, w/William
    Gordean & James Symons

TOM MERCHANT
PRETTYKILL   Spectrafilm, 1987
DARK TOWER   Spectrafilm, 1989

CLAUDINE MERLIN
MENAGE   Cinecom, 1986
BUFFET FROID   Interama, 1987

JOHN MERRITT
EXCALIBUR   Orion/Warner Bros., 1981

TOM MESHELSKI
TERRORVISION   Empire Pictures, 1986
NECROPOLIS   Empire Pictures, 1987, w/Barry Zetlin
BLOOD DINER   Lightning Pictures, 1987
SORORITY BABES IN THE SLIMEBALL
    BOWL-A-RAMA   Urban Classics, 1988,
    w/Barry Zetlin
CATACOMBS   Empire Pictures, 1988
PUPPETMASTER   Full Moon, 1989

RICHARD C. MEYER
SILENT RAGE   Columbia, 1982
NATIONAL LAMPOON'S CLASS REUNION   20th
    Century Fox, 1982
JIMMY THE KID   New World, 1983
HARRY'S MACHINE   Cannon, 1986

PIERRE MIGNOT
BEYOND THERAPY   New World, 1987, SE

MARIANNA MIKLOS
STORM AND SORROW (CTF)   Accent Entertainment,
    1990, w/Robert Kimble and Zsuzsa Posan

ALAN MILLER
MR. MIKE'S MONDO VIDEO   New Line Cinema,
    1979, w/Bob Tischler
CRACK IN THE MIRROR   Rebo Productions, 1988,
    w/Craig McKay

GREG MILLER
FELLOW TRAVELLER (CTF)   British Film Institute/BBC
    Television/HBO Showcase, 1990

HARRY B. MILLER, III
WEEKEND PASS   Crown International, 1984
JACK'S BACK   Palisades Entertainment, 1988
TALES FROM THE DARKSIDE: THE MOVIE
    Paramount, 1990

JIM MILLER
Business Manager: Joan Marie, Cinevideo Arts, Inc.,
    4219 W. Olive St., Suite 141, Burbank, CA 91505,
    805/529-3986
Address: 3926 Corte Cancion, Thousand Oaks, CA
    91360, 805/529-3986

FEEL THE HEAT (Pilot)   1983
ALICE IN WONDERLAND (TF)   CBS/Columbia/
    Irwin Allen, 1985
THE WIZARD (Pilot)   1986
BLUE CITY   Paramount, 1986
THE MILAGRO BEANFIELD WAR   Universal, 1988,
    w/Dede Allen
LET IT RIDE   Paramount, 1989, w/Dede Allen

KENNETH MILLER
RICH MEN, SINGLE WOMEN (TF)   Aaron Spelling
    Productions, 1990

MICHAEL R. MILLER
NIGHTMARE AT SHADOW WOODS   Film Concept
    Group, 1987
RAISING ARIZONA   20th Century Fox, 1987
D.O.A.   Buena Vista, 1988
PATTY HEARST   Atlantic Releasing Corporation, 1988
I'M GONNA GIT YOU SUCKA   MGM/UA, 1988
THE LEMON SISTERS   Miramax, 1990
MILLER'S CROSSING   Circle Films/20th Century
    Fox, 1990
THE LEMON SISTERS   Miramax, 1990,
    w/Joseph Weintraub
MR. DESTINY   Buena Vista, 1990

ANN MILLGATE
MONEY, POWER, MURDER (TF)   SKids
    Productions, 1990

ANN E. MILLS
HAMBURGER...THE MOTION PICUTRE   FM
    Entertainment, 1986, w/Steven Schoenberg
BLOODY BIRTHDAY   Judica Productions, 1986

FAN KUNG MING
THE KILLER   Circle Releasing, 1991

DAVID MINGAY
RETURN TO WATERLOO   New Line Cinema, 1985
SOPHISTICATED LADY (FD)   Channel 4, 1989

STEVE MIRKOVICH, ACE
BIG TROUBLE IN LITTLE CHINA   20th Century Fox,
    1986, w/Mark Roy Warner & Edward A. Warschilka
AMERICAN JUSTICE   The Movie Store, 1986
DEATH BEFORE DISHONOR   New World, 1987
PRINCE OF DARKNESS   Universal, 1987
DEADLY ILLULSION   CineTel Films, 1987,
    w/Ronald G. Spang

SPELLBINDER   MGM/UA, 1988
FRIDAY THE 13TH PART VIII: JASON TAKES
    MANHATTAN   Paramount, 1989
FLIGHT OF THE INTRUDER   Paramount, 1991,
    w/C. Timothy O'Meara & Peck Prior

ANNA MISONI
THE ICICLE THIEF   Aries Releasing, 1990,
    w/Rita Rossi

JAMES MITCHELL
Agent: Broder Kurland Webb Uffner - Los Angeles,
    213/656-9262

BUSTING   United Artists, 1974
OUR TIME   Warner Bros., 1974
PEEPER   20th Century Fox, 1976
FUTUREWORLD   American International, 1976
CAPRICORN ONE   Warner Bros., 1978
HANOVER STREET   Columbia, 1979
THE GONG SHOW MOVIE   Universal, 1980
THE STAR CHAMBER   20th Century Fox, 1983,
    w/Charles Tetoni
2010   MGM/UA, 1984
RUNNING SCARED   MGM/UA, 1986
THE MONSTER SQUAD   Tri-Star, 1987
THE PRESIDIO   Paramount, 1988
NARROW MARGIN   Carolco Pictures/Tri-Star, 1990

BUD MOLIN
Agent: Lawrence A. Mirisch, Triad Artists, Inc. -
    Los Angeles, 213/556-2727

A GLOBAL AFFAIR   MGM, 1964
HOW SWEET IT IS!   Buena Vista, 1968
VIVA MAX!   Commonwealth United, 1969
THE FIRST TIME   United Artists, 1969
THE LAST ESCAPE   United Artists, 1970
HALLS OF ANGER   United Artists, 1970
THEY CALL ME MR. TIBBS   United Artists, 1970
WHERE'S POPPA?   United Artists, 1970
THE BROTHERS O'TOOLE   1973
OH, GOD!   Warner Bros., 1977
THE ONE AND ONLY   Paramount, 1978
SIDNEY SHELDON'S BLOODLINE   Paramount, 1979
THE JERK   Universal, 1979
DEAD MEN DON'T WEAR PLAID   Universal, 1979
MAD MAGAZINE PRESENTS UP THE ACADEMY
    Warner Bros., 1980
THE MAN WITH TWO BRAINS   Warner Bros., 1983
ALL OF ME   Universal, 1984
THE MAN WITH ONE RED SHOE   20th Century Fox,
    1985, w/O. Nicholas Brown
SUMMER RENTAL   Paramount, 1985
POLICE ACADEMY 3: BACK IN TRAINING   Warner
    Bros., 1986
SUMMER SCHOOL   Paramount, 1987
THE EXPERTS   Paramount, 1989
BERT RIGBY, YOU'RE A FOOL   Warner Bros., 1989
SIBLING RIVALRY   Castle Rock Entertainment/
    Columbia, 1990

DAN MOLINA
AN AMERICAN TAIL (AF)   Universal, 1986
THE LAND BEFORE TIME (AF)   Universal, 1988

ANDREW MONDSHEIN
GARBO TALKS   MGM/UA, 1984
DESPERATELY SEEKING SUSAN   Orion, 1985

POWER   20th Century Fox, 1986
MAKING MR. RIGHT   Orion, 1987
RUNNING ON EMPTY   Warner Bros., 1988
COOKIE   Warner Bros., 1989
FAMILY BUSINESS   Tri-Star, 1989
ONCE AROUND   Universal, 1991

SERGIO MONTANARI
STARCRASH   New World, 1979
HERCULES   Cannon, 1983
SWEE' PEA   Summit, 1983
VICTORY MARCH   Summit, 1983
HERCULES II   Cannon, 1985

MILLIE MOORE, ACE
THE GREAT TEXAS DYNAMITE CHASE   New
    World, 1976
JOE PANTHER   Artists Creation & Associates, 1976
STARSHIP INVASIONS   Warner Bros., 1977,
    w/Ruth Hope
GO TELL THE SPARTANS   Avco Embasy, 1978
THOSE LIPS, THOSE EYES   United Artists, 1980
HALLOWEEN III: SEASON OF THE WITCH
    Universal, 1982
VICTIMS FOR VICTIMS (TF)   Daniel L. Paulson -Loehr
    Spivey Productions/Orion TV, 1984
THE IMPOSTER (TF)   Warner Bros. TV, 1985
A BUNNY'S TALE (TF)   Stan Margulies Company/ABC
    Circle Films, 1985
THE TENTH MAN (TF)   William Self Productions/
    Rosemont Productions Ltd., 1988
THE FULFILLMENT OF MARY GRAY (TF)   Les Caplin
    Productions/Indian Neck Entertainment, 1989
JOSHUA'S HEART (TF)   Spectacor, 1990

PATRICK MOORE
OXFORD BLUES   MGM/UA, 1984

MARIO MORA
CINEMA PARADISO   Miramax, 1989

BOB MORGAN
THE WHISTLE BLOWER   Hemdale, 1987
SOUVENIR (CTF)   Fancyfree Productions Ltd., 1988

GLENN A. MORGAN
Agent: Susan Grant, Artists Group - Los Angeles,
    213/552-1100
Address: 12325 Gorham Ave., Los Angeles, CA 90049,
    213/820-0310

VENDETTA   Concorde, 1986
SIESTA   Lorimar, 1987

RANDY JON MORGAN
GRAVEYARD SHIFT   Paramount, 1990, w/Jim Gross

ALBERTO MORIANI
YOR, THE HUNTER FROM THE FUTURE
    Columbia, 1983
HUNTERS OF THE GOLDEN COBRA   World
    Northal, 1984

MARIO MORRA
CUT AND RUN   New World, 1986

Mo

CINEMATOGRAPHERS
PRODUCTION
DESIGNERS,
COSTUME
DESIGNERS AND
FILM EDITORS
GUIDE

F
I
L
M

E
D
I
T
O
R
S

Mo

CINEMATOGRAPHERS
PRODUCTION
DESIGNERS,
COSTUME
DESIGNERS AND
FILM EDITORS
GUIDE

F
I
L
M

E
D
I
T
O
R
S

JONATHAN MORRIS
SINGING THE BLUES IN RED   Angelika Films, 1988
HIDDEN AGENDA   Hemdale, 1990

MARGARET MORRISON
"SAY YES"   CineTel, 1986

FRANK MORRISS
Agent: Lawrence A. Mirisch, Triad Artists, Inc. -
   Los Angeles, 213/556-2727

DUEL (TF)   Universal TV, 1971
CHARLEY VARRICK   Universal, 1973
THE LAW (TF)   Universal TV, 1974
THE EXECUTION OF PRIVATE SLOVIK (TF)
   Universal TV, 1974
ODE TO BILLY JOE   Warner Bros., 1976
FIRST LOVE   Paramount, 1977
I WANNA HOLD YOUR HAND   Universal, 1978
YOUNGBLOOD   American International, 1978
HOMETOWN, U.S.A.   Film Ventures
   International, 1979
INSIDE MOVES   AFD, 1980
THE EARTHLING   Filmways, 1981
WHOSE LIFE IS IT ANYWAY?   MGM/United
   Artists, 1981
BLUE THUNDER ★   Columbia, 1983,
   w/Edward Abroms
ROMANCING THE STONE ★   20th Century Fox,
   1984, w/Donn Cambern
AMERICAN FLYERS   Warner Bros., 1985
SHORT CIRCUIT   Tri-Star, 1986
HOT TO TROT   Warner Bros., 1988
DISORGANIZED CRIME   Buena Vista, 1989,
   w/Dallas Puett
BIRD ON A WIRE   Universal, 1990, w/Dallas Puett
SHORT TIME   20th Century Fox, 1990
THE HARD WAY   Universal, 1991, w/Tony Lombardo

SUSAN E. MORSE, ACE
MANHATTAN   United Artists, 1979
STARDUST MEMORIES   United Artists, 1980
ARTHUR   Orion/Warner Bros., 1981
A MIDSUMMER NIGHT'S SEX COMEDY   Orion/
   Warner Bros., 1982
ZELIG   Orion/Warner Bros., 1983
BROADWAY DANNY ROSE   Orion, 1984
THE PURPLE ROSE OF CAIRO   Orion, 1985
HANNAH AND HER SISTERS ★   Orion, 1986
RADIO DAYS   Orion, 1987
SEPTEMBER   Orion, 1987
ANOTHER WOMAN   Orion, 1988
NEW YORK STORIES ("Oedipus Wrecks")   Buena
   Vista, 1989
CRIMES AND MISDEMEANORS   Orion, 1989
ALICE   Orion, 1990

DENNIS MOSHER
BLIND VENGEANCE (CTF)   Spanish Trail/MCA TV
   Entertainment, 1990

MICHAEL MULCONERY
LIFE STINKS   MGM, 1991

WALT MULCONERY
FLASHDANCE ★   Paramount, 1983, w/Bud Smith
THE KARATE KID   Columbia, 1984,
   w/John G. Avildsen & Bud Smith
TOUCH AND GO   Tri-Star, 1987

JOHN MULLEN
THE RETURN OF SUPERFLY   Triton Pictures, 1990

BOB MURAWSKI
DANGER ZONE III: STEEL HORSE WAR   Danger Zone
   Company, 1990

WALTER MURCH
Agent: Lawrence A. Mirisch, Triad Artists, Inc. -
   Los Angeles, 213/556-2727

JULIA ★   20th Century Fox, 1977
APOCALYPSE NOW ★   United Artists, 1980, w/Lisa
   Fruchtman & Jerry Greenberg
CAPTAIN EO   Disneyland/Walt Disney World, 1986
THE UNBEARABLE LIGHTNESS OF BEING   Orion,
   1988, SE
GHOST ★   Paramount, 1990
THE GODFATHER PART III ★   Zoetrope Studios/
   Paramount, 1990, w/Barry Malkin & Lisa Fruchtman

MICHAEL S. MURPHY
SWEET REVENGE   Concorde, 1987
TAKE MY DAUGHTERS, PLEASE! (TF)   Michael
   Filerman Productions/NBC Productions, 1989
DANIELLE STEEL'S KALEIDOSCOPE (TF)   The Cramer
   Company, 1990

JOHN MURRAY
ICEHOUSE   Upfront Films, 1989

STEPHEN MYERS
976-EVIL   New Line Cinema, 1989
FAR OUT MAN!   New Line Cinema, 1990,
   w/Gilberto Costa Nunes
MASTERS OF MENACE   New Line Cinema, 1990

MARCELO NAVARRO
DANCE OF HOPE   First Run Features, 1990

PRISCILLA ANNE NEDD, ACE
Agent: Harris & Goldberg - Los Angeles, 213/553-5200

EDDIE AND THE CRUISERS   Embassy, 1983
NO SMALL AFFAIR   Columbia, 1984, w/Eve Newman &
   Melvin Shapiro
THE FLAMINGO KID   20th Century Fox, 1984
LUCAS   20th Century Fox, 1986
STREET SMART   Cannon, 1987
TUCKER: THE MAN AND HIS DREAM
   Paramount, 1988
DEAD POETS SOCIETY   Buena Vista, 1989
PRETTY WOMAN   *3000*   Buena Vista, 1990
GUILTY BY SUSPICION   Warner Bros., 1991
DOC HOLLYWOOD   Warner Bros., 1991
GUILTY BY SUSPICION   Warner Bros., 1991

TOVA NEEMAN
RUMPELSTILTSKIN   Cannon, 1987

JOEL NEGRON
Address: 9325 Oak St., Bellflower, CA 90706

WARBIRDS   Vidmark Entertainment, 1989
HEAVEN AND EARTH   Hausberg Productions, 1989

DEBRA NEIL
THE GIRL WHO CAME BETWEEN THEM (TF)
   Saban/Scherick Productions, 1990
BREAKING POINT (CTF)   Avnet/Kerner
   Company, 1990
HEAT WAVE (CTF)   Avnet/Kerner Company, 1990

ANDREW NELSON
FOREIGN BODY   Orion, 1986

ARGYLE NELSON, ACE
Agent: The Gersh Agency, Inc. - Beverly Hills,
   213/274-6611

THE GREATEST STORY EVER TOLD   United
   Artists, 1965
THE LAWYER   Paramount, 1970
LITTLE FAUSS AND BIG HALSY   Paramount, 1970
LADY SINGS THE BLUES   Paramount, 1972
HIT!   Paramount, 1973
SHEILA LEVINE IS DEAD AND LIVING IN NEW YORK
   Paramount, 1975
GABLE AND LOMBARD   Universal, 1976
LIFEGUARD   Paramount, 1976
SEXTETTE   Crown International, 1978
NIGHT OF THE JUGGLER   Columbia, 1980
UNDERGROUND ACES   Filmways, 1981
BUDDY BUDDY   MGM/United Artists, 1981
CHU CHU AND THE PHILLY FLASH   20th Century
   Fox, 1981
SOMETHING WICKED THIS WAY COMES   Buena
   Vista, 1983
BROKEN BADGES (TF)   Stephen J. Cannell
   Productions, 1990, w/Larry D. Lester &
   Casey O. Rohrs

CHRISTOPHER NELSON
BURNING BRIDGES (TF)   Anfrea Baynes
   Productions, 1989
A PROMISE TO KEEP (TF)   Sacret/Warner
   Bros. TV, 1990

SANDY NERVIG
LIFE IS CHEAP...BUT TOILET PAPER IS EXPENSIVE
   Silverlight Entertainment, 1990, w/Chris Sanderson

EVE NEWMAN
Agent: Grace Lyons Management - Los Angeles,
   213/655-5100

WILD IN THE STREETS ★   American International,
   1968, w/Fred Feitshans
BLOODY MAMA   American International, 1970
THE OTHER SIDE OF THE MOUNTAIN
   Universal, 1975
TWO-MINUTE WARNING ★   Universal, 1976,
   w/Walter Hannemann
THE OTHER SIDE OF THE MOUNTAIN - PART 2
   Universal, 1978, w/Walter Hannemann
PARADISE ALLEY   Universal, 1978
LITTLE MISS MARKER   Universal, 1980
NO SMALL AFFAIR   Columbia, 1984, w/Priscilla
   Nedd & Melvin Shapiro
INTO THE HOMELAND (CTF)   HBO Pictures/Capistrano
   Pictures, 1987

ANGUS NEWTON
Agent: Grace Lyons Management - Los Angeles,
   213/655-5100

THE WEATHER IN THE STREETS (TF)   Rediffusion
   Films/BBC/Brittania Television, 1983
UNFAIR EXCHANGES (TF)   BBC, 1984
THE GHOST WRITER (TF)   WGBH-Boston/Malone-Gill
   Productions/BBC, 1984
DREAMCHILD   Universal, 1985
DANNY, THE CHAMPION OF THE WORLD (CTF)
   Disney Channel, 1989, w/Peter Tanner
SCANDAL   Miramax, 1989
VAMPIRE'S KISS   Hemdale, 1989

GEORGE JAY NICHOLSON
THE MAN   Paramount, 1972
WHITE LIGHTNING   United Artists, 1973
MACARTHUR   Universal, 1977
GOLDENGIRL   Avco Embassy, 1979
COAST TO COAST   Paramount, 1980

MARTY NICHOLSON
HOUSE II: THE SECOND STORY   New World, 1987

TED NICOLAOU
THE TOURIST TRAP   Compass International, 1979
THE DAY TIME ENDED   Compass International, 1979
YOUNG WARRIORS   Cannon, 1983
THE DUNGEONMASTER   Empire Pictures, 1985,
   w/Marc Leif
ZONE TROOPERS   Empire Pictures, 1986
PRISON   Empire Pictures, 1988
ROBOT JOX   Triumph Releasing, 1990, w/Lori Scott Ball

STEVE NIELSON
DEADLY DANCER   AIP Home Video, 1990

HANNES NIKEL
DAS BOOT ★   Columbia, 1982
ENEMY MINE   20th Century Fox, 1985

THOM NOBLE
Agent: The Gersh Agency, Inc., Beverly Hills -
   213/274-6611, New York - 212/997-1818

FARENHEIT 451   Universal, 1967
ROSEBUD   United Artists, 1975
INSIDE OUT   Warner Bros., 1976
JOSEPH ANDREWS   Paramount, 1977
BLACK JOY   Hemdale, 1977
ALL THINGS BRIGHT AND BEAUTFIUL   World
   Northal, 1978
WHO IS KILLING THE GREAT CHEFS OF EUROPE?
   Warner Bros., 1978
NORTH DALLAS FORTY   Paramount, 1979
BOARDWALK   Atlantic Releasing Corporation, 1979
IMPROPER CHANNELS   Crown International, 1981
TATTOO   20th Century Fox, 1981
RED DAWN   MGM/UA, 1984
WITNESS ★★   Paramount, 1985
POLTERGEIST II: THE OTHER SIDE   MGM/UA, 1986
THE MOSQUITO COAST   Warner Bros., 1986
SWITCHING CHANNELS   Tri-Star, 1988
WINTER PEOPLE   Columbia, 1989
MOUNTAINS OF THE MOON   Tri-Star, 1990
THELMA & LOUISE   Pathe Entertainment, 1991

No

CINEMATOGRAPHERS
PRODUCTION
DESIGNERS,
COSTUME
DESIGNERS AND
FILM EDITORS
GUIDE

FILM EDITORS

No

CINEMATOGRAPHERS
PRODUCTION
DESIGNERS,
COSTUME
DESIGNERS AND
FILM EDITORS
GUIDE

F
I
L
M

E
D
I
T
O
R
S

JAMES E. NOWNES
PENITENTIARY II   MGM/UA, 1982

JOHN NUTT
NUTCRACKER   Atlantic Releasing Corporation,
   1986, w/Michael Silvers
BREAK OF DAWN   Cinewest, 1988

CAROL OBLATH
BRAIN DEAD   *PARANOID*   Concorde, 1989

DENNIS O'CONNOR
Agent: Smith Gosnell Nicholson & Associates -
   Pacific Palisades, 213/459-0307

NO NUKES (FD)   Warner Bros., 1980
THE MATING SEASON (TF)   Highgate Pictures, 1980
THE ELECTRIC GRANDMOTHER (TF)   Highgate
   Pictures, 1982
THE CRADLE WILL FALL (TF)   Cates Films Inc./
   Procter & Gamble Productions, 1983
C.H.U.D.   New World, 1984
WHEN DREAMS COMES TRUE (TF)   I & C
   Productions, 1985
RADIOACTIVE DREAMS   DEG, 1986
DANGEROUSLY CLOSE   Cannon, 1986
DOWN TWISTED   Cannon, 1987
STEAL THE SKY (CTF)   HBO Pictures/Yoram Ben Ami
   Productions/Paramount Television, 1988, w/Jon Poll
WEEDS   DEG, 1987, SE
UHF   Orion, 1989
PRANCER   Orion, 1989
FIRE BIRDS   Buena Vista, 1990, w/Jon Poll &
   Norman Buckley

JOHN O'CONNOR
SAVAGE STREETS   MPM, 1984,
   w/Bruce Stubblefield
KNIGHTS OF THE CITY   New World, 1986, w/Paul
   Lamon & Nicholas Smith
STEELE JUSTICE   Atlantic Releasing Corporation,
   1987, w/Steve Rosenblum

CORKY O'HARA
THE EXTERMINATOR   Avco Embassy, 1980
YOU BETTER WATCH OUT   Edward R. Pressman
   Productions, 1980, w/Linda Leeds
FLIGHT OF THE SPRUCE GOOSE   Filmhaus, 1986

JAMES OLIVER
AMERICAN ANTHEM   Columbia, 1986
WINNIE (MS)   All Girl Productions/NBC
   Productions, 1988
THE ROSE AND THE JACKAL (CTF)   Steve White
   Productions, 1989
THE LAKER GIRLS (TF)   Viacom, 1990
THE HEIST (CTF)   HBO Pictures, 1990
CAST THE FIRST STONE (TF)   Columbia Pictures
   TV/Mench Productions, 1990

LONG ROAD HOME (TF)   Rosemont Productions, 1991
SINS OF THE MOTHER (TF)   Corapeake
   Productions, 1991
LINE OF FIRE: THE MORRIS DEES STORY (TF)
   BoJames Entertainment, 1991

**CARROLL TIMOTHY
O'MEARA, ACE**
Agent: Jay Gilbert Talent Agency - Los Angeles,
   213/656-5906

BIG WEDNESDAY   Warner Bros., 1978,
   w/Robert L. Wolfe
GOING IN STYLE   Warner Bros., 1979, w/Robert Swink
THE ROSE ★   20th Century Fox, 1979,
   w/Robert L. Wolfe
CONAN THE BARBARIAN   Universal, 1982,
   w/Fred Stafford
THE LAST STARFIGHTER   Universal, 1984
MY SCIENCE PROJECT   Buena Vista, 1985
HOOSIERS   Orion, 1986
THE RESCUE   Buena Vista, 1988, w/David Holden
THE DREAM TEAM   Universal, 1989
FLASHBACK   Paramount, 1990
FLIGHT OF THE INTRUDER   Paramount, 1991,
   w/Steve Mirkovich & Peck Prior

MICHAEL ORNSTEIN
PAIR OF ACES (TF)   Pedernales Films, 1990
DEAD MEN DON'T DIE   Trans Atlantic Pictures, 1990

ROBERT ORTIZ
MINGUS' EPITAPH (FD)   Dennis Woolf
   Productions, 1991

SAM O'STEEN
Business Manager: Robert Morgan, Tucker, Morgan &
   Martindale - Los Angeles, 213/274-0891

WHO'S AFRAID OF VIRGINIA WOOLF? ★   Warner
   Bros., 1966
THE GRADUATE   Avco Embassy, 1967
COOL HAND LUKE   Warner Bros., 1967
HOTEL   Warner Bros., 1967
ROSEMARY'S BABY   Paramount, 1968
THE STERILE CUCKOO   Paramount, 1969
CATCH-22   Paramount, 1970
CARNAL KNOWLEDGE   Avco Embassy, 1971
PORTNOY'S COMPLAINT   Warner Bros., 1972
THE DAY OF THE DOLPHIN   Avco Embassy, 1973
CHINATOWN ★   Paramount, 1974
STRAIGHT TIME   Warner Bros., 1978, w/Randy Roberts
HURRICANE   Paramount, 1979
AMITYVILLE II: THE POSSESSION   Orion, 1982
SILKWOOD ★   20th Century Fox, 1983
HEARTBURN   Paramount, 1986
NADINE   Tri-Star, 1987
BILOXI BLUES   Universal, 1988
FRANTIC   Warner Bros., 1988
WORKING GIRL   20th Century Fox, 1988
A DRY WHITE SEASON   MGM/UA, 1989,
   w/Glenn Cunningham
POSTCARDS FROM THE EDGE   Columbia, 1990

P

EMILY PAINE
STATIC   Sandstar Releasing Company, 1988

KEITH PALMER
THE DEVIL WITHIN HER   American
   International, 1976
WELCOME TO BLOOD CITY   EMI, 1977
AMIN: THE RISE AND FALL   Twin
   Continental, 1983
THE LONELY LADY   Universal, 1983
SAKHAROV (CTF)   HBO Premiere Films/ Titus
   Productions, 1984
WILD GEESE II   Universal, 1985
BAD MEDICINE   20th Century Fox, 1985,
   w/O. Nicholas Brown & John Jympson
JACK THE RIPPER (MS)   Euston Films, 1988
HANDS OF A MURDERER (TF)   Stork/Fuisz
   Productions, 1989
SECRET WEAPON (CTF)   Griffin-Elysian
   Films, 1990
THE NIGHTMARE YEARS (CTF)   Consolidated
   Atrists, 1990

BILL PANKOW
Attorney: Karen Levinson, Paul, Weiss, Wharton &
   Garrison, 1285 Avenue of the Americas, New York,
   New York, 10019, 212/373-3000

BOBY DOUBLE   Columbia, 1984,
   w/Jerry Greenberg
THE UNTOUCHABLES   Paramount, 1987
PARENTS   Vestron, 1989
CASUALTIES OF WAR   Columbia, 1989
THE BONFIRE OF THE VANITIES   Warner Bros.,
   1990, w/David Ray
THE COMFORT OF STRANGERS   Erre Produzioni/
   Sovereign Pictures, 1991

STUART H. PAPPE
THE KILLERS   Universal, 1964
THE LOVED ONE   MGM, 1965
THE PRESIDENT'S ANALYST   Paramount, 1967
BOB & CAROL & TED & ALICE   Columbia, 1969
ALEX IN WONDERLAND   MGM, 1970
THE GUMBALL RALLY   Warner Bros., 1976,
   w/Gordon Scott & Maury Winetrobe
UNMARRIED WOMAN   20th Century Fox, 1978
OLIVER'S STORY   Paramount, 1978
THE WANDERERS   Orion, 1979, w/Ronald Roose
CARNY   United Artists, 1980
CLASS   Orion, 1983
SONGWRITER   Tri-Star, 1984
8 MILLION WAYS TO DIE   Tri-Star, 1986,
   w/Robert Lawrence
THE BIG TOWN   Columbia, 1987
MOON OVER PARADOR   Universal, 1988
ENEMIES, A LOVE STORY   20th Century Fox, 1989
SCENES FROM A MALL   Buena Vista, 1991

PETER PARASHELES
Address: 13489 Rand Drive, Sherman Oaks, CA
   91423, 818/784-4276

NEVER CRY WOLF   Buena Vista, 1983,
   w/Michael Chandler
CODE OF SILENCE   Orion, 1985 ,
   w/Christopher Holmes
AROUND THE WORLD IN 80 DAYS (MS)   Harmony Gold
   Productions, 1989, w/David Beatty & Les Green
ROCK HUDSON (TF)   The Konigsberg/Sanitsky
   Company, 1990

BILL PARKER
COLUMBO GOES TO COLLEGE (TF)   Universal
   TV, 1990

JEFF PARKIN
TALES OF THE UNKNOWN   AIP Home Video, 1990,
   w/Stuart Courtney

SALLY PATERSON
ON THIN ICE: THE TAI BABILONIA STORY (TF)
   Bernard Rothman Productions, 1990

TONY PATERSON
MAD MAX   American International, 1979, w/Cliff Hayes
PHAR LAP   20th Century Fox, 1984
DRIVING FORCE   J&M Entertainment, 1990

ALAN PATTILLO
Agent: Grace Lyons Management - Los Angeles,
   213/655-5100

THE BOYS IN COMPANY C   Columbia, 1978,
   w/Michael Berman, James Benson & Frank J. Urioste
THE MUSIC MACHINE   Norfolk International Pictures/
   Target International Pictures, 1979, w/Brian
   Smedley-Aston
GAME OF DEATH   Columbia, 1979
ALL QUIET ON THE WESTERN FRONT (TF)   Norman
   Rosemont Productions/Marble Arch Productions, 1979
MASTER OF THE GAME (MS)   Rosemont
   Productions, 1984
THE CORSICAN BROTHERS (TF)   Rosemont
   Productions, 1985
THE TED KENNEDY, JR. STORY (TF)   Entertainment
   Partners, 1986
POOR LITTLE RICH GIRL: THE BARBARA HUTTON
   STORY (MS)   Lester Persky Productions/ITC
   Productions, 1987

EDNA RUTH PAUL
FEAR NO EVIL   Avco Embassy, 1981
THE EVIL DEAD   New Line Cinema, 1983

HAIDA PAUL
MY AMERICAN COUSIN   Spectrafilm, 1985

BRIAN PEACHEY
TANK MALLING   Pointlane Films, 1990

KENOUT PELTIER
TEA IN THE HAREM   Cinecom, 1985

Pe

CINEMATOGRAPHERS
PRODUCTION
DESIGNERS,
COSTUME
DESIGNERS AND
FILM EDITORS
GUIDE

F
I
L
M

E
D
I
T
O
R
S

Pe

CINEMATOGRAPHERS
PRODUCTION
DESIGNERS,
COSTUME
DESIGNERS AND
FILM EDITORS
GUIDE

**F
I
L
M

E
D
I
T
O
R
S**

LEE PERCY, ACE
Agent: The Gersh Agency, Inc., Beverly Hills -
213/274-6611, New York - 212/997-1818

RE-ANIMATOR Empire Pictures, 1985
FROM BEYOND Empire Pictures, 1986
SLAM DANCE Island Pictures, 1987
DOLLS Empire Pictures, 1987
THE STICK Distant Horizon International, 1987
CHECKING OUT Warner Bros., 1989
BLUE STEEL MGM/UA, 1990
NAKED TANGO Scotia International, 1990,
w/Debra McDermott
REVERSAL OF FORTUNE Warner Bros., 1990

ROBERT PERGAMENT
Agent: Grace Lyons Management - Los Angeles,
213/655-5100

A FINE MESS Columbia, 1986, w/John F. Burnett
BLIND DATE Tri-Star, 1987
SUNSET Tri-Star, 1988
PETER GUNN (Pilot) 1989
JUSTIN CASE (Pilot) 1989
SKIN DEEP 20th Century Fox, 1989
LITTLE WHITE LIES (TF) The Larry A. Thompson
Organization, 1990
SWITCH Warner Bros., 1991

ERIC BOYD PERKINS
(See Eric BOYD-PERKINS)

GERALDINE PERONI
VINCENT & THEO Hemdale, 1990,
w/Francoise Coispeau

ROBERTO PERPIGNANI
GOOD MORNING, BABYLON Vestron, 1987

BARRY PETERS
THE PEOPLE THAT TIME FORGOT American
International, 1977, w/John Ireland
THE HOUSE WHERE EVIL DWELLS MGM/UA, 1982
SWORD OF THE VALIANT Cannon, 1984,
w/Richard Marden
GREAT EXPECTATIONS (CMS) The Disney
Channel/Harlech Television/Primetime TV, 1989
GREAT EXPECTATIONS (CTF) HTV Limited/
Tesauro Television, 1990

ROY E. PETERSON
CALIFORNIA DREAMING American International,
1979, w/Herb Dow & Sidney Levin
CHILD'S PLAY MGM/UA, 1988,
w/Edward Warschilka

SUZANNE PETTIT
Agent: Smith Gosnell Nicholson & Associates -
Pacific Palisades, 213/459-0307

GIRLFRIENDS Warner Bros., 1978
TELL ME A RIDDLE Filmways, 1980
THE WILLMAR 8 (FD) California Newsreel, 1981
TIMERIDER Jensen Farley Pictures, 1983, CE
TESTAMENT Paramount, 1983
SYLVESTER Columbia, 1985, w/David Garfield &
Howard Smith
IN HER OWN TIME (FD) Direct Cinema, 1985

'NIGHT MOTHER Universal, 1986
AND GOD CREATED WOMAN Vestron, 1988
FRAMED (CTF) HBO Pictures, 1989

JEAN CLAUDE PIROUE
MINDWALK Mindwalk Productions, 1990

GREGORY F. PLOTTS
FLOWERS IN THE ATTIC New World, 1987
PHANTOM OF THE MALL: ERIC'S REVENGE Fries
Entertainment, 1990, w/Amy Tompkins

BARBARA POKRAS
WOMEN IN CAGES New World, 1972
UNHOLY ROLLERS American International, 1972
BOX CAR BERTHA American International, 1972
THE GIANT SPIDER INVASION 1975
TNT JACKSON New World, 1975
CRAZY MAMA New World, 1975
TOO HOT TO HANDLE Derio Productions, 1978
H.O.T.S. Derio Productions, 1979
HUMAN EXPERIMENTS 1980
FADE TO BLACK American Cinema, 1980
DON'T CRY, IT'S ONLY THUNDER Sanrio, 1981,
w/Jack Woods
SLIPPING INTO DARKNESS MCEG, 1990
C.H.U.D. III: BUD THE CHUD Vestron, 1989

MICHAEL POLAKOW
Agent: The Gersh Agency, Inc., Beverly Hills -
213/274-6611, New York - 212/997-1818

SEA OF LOVE Universal, 1989, CE
A NEW LIFE Paramount, 1990, CE
BETSY'S WEDDING Buena Vista, 1990

STEVEN POLIVKA
COURAGE New World, 1984
VOLUNTEERS Tri-Star, 1985, w/Ronald Roose
TEEN WOLF TOO Atlantic Releasing Corporation, 1987,
w/Raja Gosnell, Harvey Rosenstock & Kim Secrist
CAMPUS MAN Paramount, 1987

JON POLL
Agent: The Gersh Agency, Inc., Beverly Hills -
213/274-6611, New York - 212/997-1818

WEEDS DEG, 1987, w/David Handman &
Chris Lebenson
STEAL THE SKY (CTF) HBO Pictures/Yoramben Ami
Productions/Paramount Television, 1988,
w/Dennis O'Connor
FIRE BIRDS Buena Vista, 1990, w/Norman Buckley &
Dennis O'Connor
CAPTAIN AMERICA 21st Century/Columbia, 1991
WILD HEARTS CAN'T BE BROKEN Buena Vista, 1991

SAM POLLARD
MO' BETTER BLUES 40 Acres and a Mule Filmworks/
Universal, 1990
JUNGLE FEVER Universal/40 Acres and a Mule
Filmworks, 1991

SONYA POLONSKY
BABY, IT'S YOU Paramount, 1983
THE LITTLE SISTER American Playhouse, 1985
MATEWAN Cinecom, 1987

ALAN POON
NO RETREAT, NO SURRENDER New World, 1986,
    w/Dane Davis, James Melkonian & Mark Pierce

ZSUZSA POSAN
STORM AND SORROW (CTF) Accent Entertainment,
    1990, w/Robert Kimble and Marianna Miklos

GEORGE POTTER
E.A.R.T.H. FORCE (TF) Paramount Network TV,
    1990, w/Dann Cahn

RAYMOND POULTON
FORCE 10 FROM NAVARONE American
    International, 1978
BREAKTHROUGH Maverick Pictures
    International, 1981

PAMELA POWER
THE DUELLISTS Paramount, 1978
THE HUNGER MGM/UA, 1983

GREGORY PRANGE
ARMED AND DANGEROUS Columbia, 1986,
    w/Daniel Hanley & Michael Hill
ONE MORE SATURDAY NIGHT Columbia, 1986
EYE OF THE TIGER Scotti Bros., 1986
MAYBE BABY (TF) Perry Lafferty Productions/von
    Zerneck/Samuels Productions, 1988
THE SEX TAPES (TF) von Zerneck/Sertner
    Films, 1989
DAUGHTER OF THE STREETS (TF) Adam
    Productions, 1990
THE BIG ONE: THE GREAT LOS ANGELES
    EARTHQUAKES-PARTS I & II (MS) von
    Zerneck-Sertner Films, 1990, w/Stephen Adrianson

MIRIAM PREISSEL
Contact: 818/763-0956

BIOHAZARD 21st Century Productions, 1984
THE TOMB Trans World Entertainment, 1985
STARSLAMMER - PRISON SHIP Worldwide
    Films, 1985
ARMED RESPONSE CineTel Films, 1986
CREEPOZOIDS Empire Films, 1987
LADY AVENGER Cinema Home Video, 1987
TRAPPER COUNTY WAR Noble Entertainment, 1988

JOHN PRICE
MURDER BY THE BOOK (CTF) TVS
    International, 1989

TOM PRIESTLEY
DELIVERANCE ★ Warner Bros., 1972
THE GREAT GATSBY Paramount, 1974
THE RETURN OF THE PINK PANTHER United
    Artists, 1975
ALPHA BETA Cine III, 1976
VOYAGE OF THE DAMNED Avco Embassy, 1976
EXORCIST II: THE HERETIC Warner Bros., 1977
TIMES SQUARE AFD, 1980
ANOTHER TIME, ANOTHER PLACE Samuel
    Goldwyn Company, 1984
DREAM ONE Columbia, 1984
1984 Atlantic Releasing Corporation, 1984
THE KITCHEN TOTO Cannon, 1988
WHITE MISCHIEF Columbia, 1988
LORD OF THE FLIES Castle Rock/Columbia, 1990

MONIQUE PRIM
BETTY BLUE Alive Films, 1986

PECK PRIOR
FLIGHT OF THE INTRUDER Paramount, 1991,
    w/C. Timothy O'Meara & Steve Mirkovich
CAREER OPPORTUNITIES Universal, 1991,
    w/Glenn Farr

MARY PRITCHARD
EATING International Rainbow Pictures, 1990,
    w/Mary Pritchard

TOM PRYOR
NO HOLDS BARRED New Line Cinema, 1989
THE OPERATION (TF) Viacom, 1990
SNOW KILL (CTF) Wilshire Court Productions, 1990

PETER PRZYGODDA
THE AMERICAN FRIEND New Yorker, 1977
LIGHTNING OVER WATER Pari Films, 1980
THE GLASS CELL Roxy/Solaris, 1981
SLOW ATTACK New Yorker, 1983, w/Barbara
    von Weiterhausen
FLIGHT TO BERLIN Road Movies/British Film Institute/
    Channel Four, 1984
PARIS, TEXAS TLC Films/20th Century Fox, 1984
DEADLINE Skouras Pictures, 1987

ARMAND PSENNY
DEATHWATCH Quartet, 1982, w/Michael Ellis
COUP DE TORCHON Biograph/Quartet/Frank
    Moreno, 1982
A WEEK'S VACATION Biograph International, 1982
A SUNDAY IN THE COUNTRY MGM/UA Classics, 1984
ROUND MIDNIGHT Warner Bros., 1986
LIFE AND NOTHING BUT AB Films/Little Bear, 1989

DALLAS PUETT
DISORGANIZED CRIME Buena Vista, 1989,
    w/Frank Morriss
BIRD ON A WIRE Universal, 1990, w/Frank Morris

CARLOS PUENTE
WALKER Universal, 1987, w/Alex Cox

DAVID PULBROCK
GROUND ZERO Avenue Pictures, 1988

STEVE PURCELL
SIGN O' THE TIMES Cineplex Odeon, 1987

STEPHEN PURVIS
Agent: Paul Gerard Agency - Newport Beach,
    714/644-7950

84 CHARLIE MOPIC New Century/Vista, 1989

Pu

CINEMATOGRAPHERS
PRODUCTION
DESIGNERS,
COSTUME
DESIGNERS AND
FILM EDITORS
GUIDE

F
I
L
M

E
D
I
T
O
R
S

Ra

CINEMATOGRAPHERS
PRODUCTION
DESIGNERS,
COSTUME
DESIGNERS AND
FILM EDITORS
GUIDE

F
I
L
M

E
D
I
T
O
R
S

R

RICHARD E. RABJOHN
SLUGS   New World, 1988
THE HEAT (Pilot)   1989, w/Geoffrey Rowland
VOYAGE OF TERROR: THE ACHILLE LAURO
    AFFAIR-PARTS I & II (MS)   RAIDUE, 1989
BACK TO HANNIBAL: THE RETURN OF TOM
    SAWYER AND HUCKLEBERRY FINN (CTF)
    Gay-Jay Productions, 1990

DAN RAE
PAPERHOUSE   Vestron, 1989
THE TALL GUY   Miramax, 1989
CHICAGO JOE AND THE SHOWGIRL   New Line
    Cinema, 1990

KEVIN RAFFERTY
BLOOD IN THE FACE   First Run Features, 1991

DAVID RAMIREZ
AMERICAN POP (AF)   Paramount, 1981
BARBAROSA   Universal/AFD, 1982,
    w/Don Zimmerman
CHEECH & CHONG: STILL SMOKIN
    Paramount, 1983
I KNOW MY FIRST NAME IS STEVEN (TF)   1989,
    w/Peter V. White

TODD RAMSAY
Agent: Lawrence A. Mirisch, Triad Artists, Inc. -
    Los Angeles, 213/556-2727

STAR TREK - THE MOTION PICTURE
    Paramount, 1979
ESCAPE FROM NEW YORK   Avco Embassy, 1981
THE THING   Universal, 1982
CERTAIN FURY   New World, 1985
DEF-CON 4   New World, 1985, w/Michael Spence
GIMME AN F   20th Century Fox, 1984, w/Wendy
    Bricmont & Tom Walls
BLACK MOON RISING   New World, 1986
MALONE   Orion, 1987
THE EXORCIST III   20th Century Fox, 1990,
    w/Peter Lee Thompson

PATRICK RAND
STREETWALKIN'   Concorde, 1985
BILL & TED'S EXCELLENT ADVENTURE   Orion,
    1989, w/Larry Bock
THE RAIN KILLER   Concorde, 1990

GENE RANNEY
WISEGUY (TF)   Stephen J. Cannell Productions,
    1990, w/Howard Terrill

TERENCE RAWLINGS
THE SENTINEL   Universal, 1977, w/Bernard Gribble
WATERSHIP DOWN   Avco Embassy, 1978
ALIEN   20th Century Fox, 1979
THE AWAKENING   Orion/Warner Bros., 1980

CHARIOTS OF FIRE ★   The Ladd Company/Warner
    Bros., 1981
BLADE RUNNER   The Ladd Company/Warner
    Bros., 1982
YENTL   MGM/UA, 1983
LEGEND   Universal, 1986
F/X   Orion, 1986
THE LONELY PASSION OF JUDITH HEARNE   Island
    Films, 1987
WHITE OF THE EYE   Palisades Entertainment, 1988
SLIPSTREAM   Entertainment Film, 1989
NOT WITHOUT MY DAUGHTER   Pathe Entertainment,
    MGM/UA, 1991

DAVID RAWLINS
West Coast Card
Agent: Smith Gosnell Nicholson & Associates -
    Pacific Palisades, 213/459-0307

NIGHT GALLERY (TF)   Universal TV, 1969
KUNG FU (TF)   Warner Bros. TV, 1972
REFLECTIONS OF MURDER (TF)   ABC Circle
    Films, 1974
A SHADOW IN THE STREETS (TF)   Playboy
    Productions, 1975
THE BINGO LONG TRAVELING ALL-STARS &
    MOTOR KINGS   Universal, 1976
SATURDAY NIGHT FEVER   Paramount, 1977
THE CHINA SYNDROME   Columbia, 1979
URBAN COWBOY   Paramount, 1980
SOUP FOR ONE   Warner Bros., 1982
THE OSTERMAN WEEKEND   20th Century Fox, 1983,
    w/Edward Abroms
FIRESTARTER   Universal, 1984, w/Ron Sanders
GIRLS JUST WANT TO HAVE FUN   New World, 1985
BACK TO SCHOOL   Orion, 1986
POLICE ACADEMY 4: CITIZENS ON PATROL   Warner
    Bros., 1987
COLD FEET   Avenue Pictures, 1989,
    w/Debra McDermott
LIFE STINKS   MGM, 1991

DAVID RAY
ONE TRICK PONY   Warner Bros., 1980, w/Edward
    Beyer & Barry Malkin
SCARFACE   Universal, 1983, w/Jerry Greenberg
THE GLASS MENAGERIE   Cineplex Odeon, 1987
WHITE WATER SUMMER   Columbia, 1987
CLINTON AND NADINE (CTF)   HBO Pictures/ ITC
    Entertainment, 1988
SECOND SIGHT   Warner Bros., 1989
THE HANDMAID'S TALE   Cinecom, 1990
THE BONFIRE OF THE VANITIES   Warner Bros., 1990,
    w/Bill Pankow

KEITH L. REAMER
Address: 173 Union Street, Ridgewood, NJ 07450,
    201/447-9005

PRIMAL SCREAM   Magnum Entertainment, 1986
PLUTONIUM BABY   Trans World Entertainment, 1987
KIDS AT RISK: NOBODY LISTENS (Pilot)   1988
UNDERGROUND TERROR   SVS Releasing, 1988
VOODOO DAWN   *STRANGE TURF*   Academy
    Entertainment, 1990

ANTHONY REDMAN
THUNDER AND LIGHTNING   20th Century Fox, 1977
THE INCREDIBLE SHRINKING WOMAN   Universal,
    1981, w/Jeff Gourson

AN EYE FOR AN EYE   Avco Embassy, 1981
LONE WOLF McQUADE   Orion, 1983
FEAR CITY   Chevy Chase Distribution, 1985,
   w/Jack Holmes
SEDUCED   (TF)   Catalina Production Group/
   Comworld Productions, 1985
CHINA GIRL   Vestron, 1987
SACRIFICE   Trans World Entertainment, 1988
THE FURTHER ADVENTURES OF TENNESSEE
   BUCK   Trans World Entertainment, 1988
THE COMEBACK (TF)   CBS Entertainment, 1989
GOOD NIGHT, SWEET WIFE: A MURDER IN
   BOSTON (TF)   CBS Entertainment
   Productions, 1990
KING OF NEW YORK   New Line Cinema, 1990
LIFE STINKS   MGM, 1991

SIMON REECE

DARK OF THE NIGHT   Castle Hill Productions, 1986

DAVID REES

AFTER THE WAR-PARTS I-III (MS)   Granada
   TV, 1990

TRICIA REIDY

THE CIVIL WAR I-IX (MS)   Florentine Films, 1990,
   w/Paul Barnes & Bruce Shaw

JEFFREY REINER

KANDYLAND   New World, 1988
A SINFUL LIFE   New Line Cinema, 1989
THINK BIG   Concorde, 1990
RUSH WEEK   RCA/Columbia Pictures Home
   Video, 1991
BLOOD AND CONCRETE   I.R.S. Media, 1991,
   w/Richard LaBrie (also directed)

ROBERT REITANO

NIGHT SCHOOL   Paramount, 1981
GRACE QUIGLEY   MGM/UA/Cannon, 1984
STICKY FINGERS   Spectrafilm, 1988
ASK ME AGAIN (TF)   American Playhouse, 1989
MURDER IN BLACK AND WHITE (TF)   Titus
   Productions, 1990
TRUE COLORS   Paramount Pictures, 1991,
   w/Stephen A. Rotter

MICHAEL RENAUD

RETURN TO GREEN ACRES (TF)   Orion Television,
   1989, w/Gary Griffen

CATHERINE RENAULT

THREE MEN AND A CRADLE   Samuel Goldwyn
   Company, 1986
"MAMA, THERE'S A MAN IN YOUR BED"   Miramax
   Films, 1990

CHRISTOPHER REYNOLDS

THE FINAL SANCTION   AIP Home Video, 1990

WILLIAM H. REYNOLDS, ACE

Agent: The Gersh Agency, Inc., Beverly Hills -
   213/274-6611, New York - 212/997-1818

FANNY ★   Warner Bros., 1961
THE SOUND OF MUSIC ★★   20th Century Fox, 1965
THE SAND PEBBLES ★   20th Century Fox, 1966

STAR!   20th Century Fox, 1968
HELLO, DOLLY! ★   20th Century Fox, 1969
THE GREAT WHITE HOPE   20th Century Fox, 1970
WHAT'S THE MATTER WITH HELEN?   United
   Artists, 1971
THE GODFATHER ★   Paramount, 1972, w/Peter Zinner
THE STING ★★   Universal, 1973
THE GREAT WALDO PEPPER   Universal, 1975
THE MASTER GUNFIGHTER, 1975
THE SEVEN-PERCENT SOLUTION   Universal, 1976,
   w/Chris Barnes
THE TURNING POINT ★   20th Century Fox, 1977
OLD BOYFRIENDS   Avco Embassy, 1979
A LITTLE ROMANCE   Orion/Warner Bros., 1979
HEAVEN'S GATE   United Artists, 1980, w/Lisa
   Fruchtman, Jerry Greenberg & Tom Rolf
NIJINSKY   Paramount, 1980
MAKING LOVE   20th Century Fox, 1982
AUTHOR! AUTHOR!   20th Century Fox, 1982
YELLOWBEARD   Orion, 1983
THE LONELY GUY   Universal, 1984, w/Raja Gosnell
THE LITTLE DRUMMER GIRL   Warner Bros., 1984
PIRATES   Cannon, 1986, w/Herve De Luze
DANCERS   Cannon, 1987
ISHTAR   Columbia, 1987, w/Richard A. Cirincione &
   Stephen A. Rotter
A NEW LIFE   Paramount, 1988
ROOFTOPS   New Visions, 1989
TAKING CARE OF BUSINESS   Buena Vista, 1990

LEE RHOADS

THAT'S LIFE!   Columbia, 1986

DAN M. RICH

THE ALLNIGHTER   Universal, 1987

HENRY RICHARDSON, ACE

Agent: The Gersh Agency, Inc., Beverly Hills -
   213/274-6611, New York - 212/997-1818

BEYOND THE FOG   Independent-International, 1981
OCTOPUSSY   MGM/UA, 1983, w/Peter Davies
MATA HARI   Cannon, 1985
RUNAWAY TRAIN ★   Cannon, 1985
DUET FOR ONE   Cannon, 1987
HOMER AND EDDIE   Kings Road Entertainment, 1989
A SHOW OF FORCE   Paramount, 1990

NANCY RICHARDSON

STAND AND DELIVER   Warner Bros., 1988
TO SLEEP WITH ANGER   SVS, 1990

SILVIA RIPOLL

THE WARRIOR AND THE SORCERESS   New
   World, 1984

MICHAEL RIPPS

Agent: Broder Kurland Webb Uffner - Los Angeles,
   213/656-9262

WARGAMES   MGM/UA, 1983
PORTRAIT OF A HIT MAN   Wildfire, 1984
STREETS OF FIRE   Universal, 1984, w/Freeman Davies
BREWSTER'S MILLIONS   Universal, 1985,
   w/Freeman Daviies
JAKE SPEED   New World, 1986, w/Fred Stafford
QUEENIE (TF)   New World Televison, 1987
STAKEOUT   Buena Vista, 1987, w/Tom Rolf
ELVIS AND ME (TF)   New World Television, 1988

Ri

CINEMATOGRAPHERS
PRODUCTION
DESIGNERS,
COSTUME
DESIGNERS AND
FILM EDITORS
GUIDE

F
I
L
M

E
D
I
T
O
R
S

Ri

CINEMATOGRAPHERS
PRODUCTION
DESIGNERS,
COSTUME
DESIGNERS AND
FILM EDITORS
GUIDE

F
I
L
M

E
D
I
T
O
R
S

CHRIS RISDALE
ARTHUR'S HALLOWED GROUND   Cinecom, 1986
EAT THE RICH   New Line Cinema, 1987

MICHAEL RISSI
SOULTAKER   Taurus Entertainment, 1990,
   w/Jason Coleman

FRANCESCA RIVIERE
ALWAYS   Samuel Goldwyn Company, 1985

STEPHEN E. RIVKIN
THE PERSONALS   New World, 1982
HOT DOG - THE MOVIE   MGM/UA, 1984
YOUNGBLOOD   MGM/UA, 1986, w/Jack Hofstra
STRANDED   New Line Cinema, 1987
BAT 21   Tri-Star, 1988
EL DIABLO (CTF)   Wizan/Black Films
   Productions, 1989
NIGHTBREAKER (TF)   Turner Network
   Television, 1989
RUN   Buena Vista, 1991, w/Jack Hofstra

PATRICK ROARK
MEGAFORCE   20th Century Fox, 1982,
   w/Skip Schoolnik

RANDY ROBERTS
GREASED LIGHTNING   Warner Bros., 1977,
   w/Christopher Holmes & Robert Wyman
STRAIGHT TIME   Warner Bros., 1978,
   w/Sam O'Steen
PLAYERS   Paramount, 1979
A SMALL CIRCLE OF FRIENDS   United Artists, 1980
ONE FROM THE HEART   Columbia, 1982,
   w/Rudi Fehr & Anne Goursaud
HAMMETT   Orion/Warner Bros., 1982, w/Marc Laub,
   Robert Q. Lovett & Barry Malkin
JAWS 3-D   Universal, 1983
OH, GOD! YOU DEVIL   Warner Bros., 1984,
   w/Andy Zall
KID'S DON'T TELL (TF)   Chris-Rose Productions/
   Viacom Productions, 1985

KEN ROBINSON
PURPLE RAIN   Warner Bros., 1984,
   w/Albert Magnoli

GARY ROCKLIN
THE WRAITH   New Century/Vista, 1986,
   w/Scott Conrad

DONALD R. RODE
Agent: Writers & Artists Agency - Los Angeles,
   213/820-2240

DUMMY (TF)   The Konigsberg Company/Warner
   Bros. TV, 1979
TANK   Universal, 1984
SPACE (MS)   Paramount TV, 1985
GET SMART, AGAIN! (TF)   IndieProd Company/
   Phoenix Entertainment Group, 1989
THE MAN IN THE BROWN SUIT (TF)   Alan Shayne
   Productions/ITC/Warner Bros. Television, 1989
THE LOOKALIKE (CTF)   Gallo Entertainment, 1990

CYNTHIA ROGERS
ALLIGATOR EYES   Castle Hill, 1990, w/John Feldman &
   Mike Frisino

CHARLES ROGGERO
DESPERATE LIVING   New Line Cinema, 1977
POLYESTER   New Line Cinema, 1981

CASEY O. ROHRS
BROKEN BADGES (TF)   Stephen J. Cannell Productions,
   1990, w/Larry D. Lester & Argyle Coe Nelson

RITA ROLAND
Agent: Don Schwartz & Associate - Los Angeles,
   213/657-8910

GIRL HAPPY   MGM, 1965
A PATCH OF BLUE   MGM, 1965
SPINOUT   MGM, 1966
THE SINGING NUN   MGM, 1966
PENELOPE   MGM, 1966
DON'T MAKE WAVES   MGM, 1967
WHERE WERE YOU WHEN THE LIGHTS WENT OUT?
   MGM, 1968
THE SPLIT   MGM, 1968
JUSTINE   20th Century Fox, 1969
MOVE   Cinema 5, 1969
TO FIND A MAN   Columbia, 1972
JACQUELINE SUSANN'S ONCE IS NOT ENOUGH
   Paramount, 1975
THE BETSY   Allied Artists, 1978
GOOD LUCK, MISS WYCKOFF   Bel Air/Gradison, 1979
RESURRECTION   Universal, 1980
FORT APACHE, THE BRONX   20th Century Fox, 1981
SIX PACK   20th Century Fox, 1982
THE DOLLMAKER (TF)   Finnegan Associates/IPC Films,
   Inc./Dollmaker Productions, 1984
THE NEW KIDS   Columbia, 1985

TOM ROLF, ACE
Address: 12417 Mulholland Drive, Beverly Hills, CA
   90210, 818/506-8229

FRENCH CONNECTION II   20th Century Fox, 1975
LUCKY LADY   20th Century Fox, 1975
BLACK SUNDAY   Paramount, 1976
TAXI DRIVER   Columbia, 1976, w/Marcia Lucas &
   Melvin Shapiro
BLUE COLLAR   Universal, 1978
HARD CORE   Columbia, 1979
PROPHECY   Paramount, 1979
HEAVEN'S GATE   United Artists, 1980, w/Lisa
   Fruchtman, Jerry Greenberg & William Reynolds
GHOST STORY   Universal, 1981
WARGAMES   MGM/UA, 1983
THE RIGHT STUFF ★   The Ladd Company/Warner Bros.,
   1983, w/Glenn Farr, Lisa Fruchtman, Stephen A. Rotter
   & Douglas Stewert
THIEF OF HEARTS   Paramount, 1984
QUICKSILVER   Columbia, 1986
9 1/2 WEEKS   MGM/UA, 1986
OUTRAGEOUS FORTUNE   Buena Vista, 1987
STAKEOUT   Buena Vista, 1987, w/Michael Ripps
THE GREAT OUTDOORS   Universal, 1988, w/Seth
   Flaum & William Gordean
BLACK RAIN   Paramount, 1989
JACOB'S LADDER   Carolco Pictures/Tri-Star, 1990

RONALD ROOSE

Agent: Sanford Skouras & Gross - Los Angeles, 213/208-2100

THE LAST TYCOON   Paramount, 1975
THE WANDERERS   Orion/Warner Bros., 1979,
    w/Stewart H. Pappe
THE WORLD ACCORDING TO GARP   Warner Bros.,
    1982, w/Stephen A. Rotter
EASY MONEY   Orion, 1983
VOLUNTEERS   Tri-Star, 1985, w/Steven Polivka
MY DEMON LOVER   New Line Cinema, 1987
LAST FLIGHT OUT (TF)   The Mannheim
    Company, 1990

RONALD ROSE

MAN AGAINST THE MOB: THE CHINATOWN
    MURDERS (TF)   von Zerneck-Sertner
Productions, 1990

MARK W. ROSENBAUM

THE STORY OF THE BEACH BOYS: SUMMER
    DREAMS (TF)   Leonard Hill Films, 1989
MANHUNT: SEARCH FOR THE NIGHT STALKER (TF)
    Leonard Hill Films, 1990
CHILDREN OF THE BRIDE (TF)   Leonard Hill
    Films, 1990

GEORGE ROSENBERG

BLIND DATE   New Line Cinema, 1984
GLITCH   Omega, 1988, w/Nico Mastorakis

DAVID ROSENBLOOM, ACE

Agent: Bauer Benedek - Los Angeles, 213/275-2421

BEST SELLER   Orion, 1987
FRESH HORSES   WEG, 1988
SWIMSUIT (TF)   Musifilm/American First Run
    Studios, 1989

IRVING C. ROSENBLUM

Agent: Triad Artists - Los Angeles, 213/556-2727
Address: 12314 Moorpark Street, Studio City, CA
    91604, 818/509-8197

THE CHOIRBOYS   Universal, 1977, w/William
    Martin & Maury Winetrobe
TWILIGHT'S LAST GLEAMING   Allied Artists, 1977
THE FRISCO KID   Warner Bros., 1979, w/Jack
    Harger & Maury Winetrobe
...ALL THE MARBLES   MGM/United Artists, 1981
FORCED VENGEANCE   MGM/United Artists, 1982

RALPH ROSENBLUM

THE GROUP   United Artists, 1965
BYE BYE BRAVERMAN   Warner Bros., 1968
GOODBYE COLUMBUS   Paramount, 1969
DON'T DRINK THE WATER   Avco Embassy, 1969
SOMETHING FOR EVERYONE   National
    General, 1970
BORN TO WIN   United Artists, 1971
BAD COMPANY   Paramount, 1972
SLEEPER   United Artists, 1973
LOVE AND DEATH   United Artists, 1975
ANNIE HALL   United Artists, 1977
THE GREAT BANK HOAX   SHENANIGANS   Warner
    Bros., 1978
INTERIORS   United Artists, 1978

STUCK ON YOU   Troma, 1983, w/Richard Haines &
    Darren Kloomok
FOREVER, LULU   Tri-Star, 1987, Consultant

STEVEN J. ROSENBLUM

Agent: Sanford Skouras & Gross - Los Angeles,
    213/208-2100

WILD THING   Atlantic Releasing Corporation, 1987,
    w/Battle Davis
STEEL JUSTICE   Atlantic Releasing Corporation, 1987,
    w/John O'Connor
DREAM STREET (Pilot)   1989, w/Harvey Rosenstock
GLORY ★   Tri-Star, 1989

JASON ROSENFIELD

COME BACK TO THE 5 & DIME, JIMMY DEAN,
    JIMMY DEAN   Cinecom, 1982

HARVEY ROSENSTOCK, ACE

Address: 3313 Colby Avenue, Los Angeles, CA 90066,
    213/390-0592

NIGHT OF THE JUGGLER   Jay Weston Prod., 1978
CLOSING NIGHT   Stuart Berton Productions, 1983
NO REGRETS   Sara Banks Productions, 1984
TEEN WOLF TOO   Atlantic Releasing Corporation, 1987,
    w/Raja Gosnell, Steven Polivka & Kim Secrist
DEAD HEAT   New World, 1988
STUDIO 5B (Pilot)   1989
DREAM STREET (Pilot)   1989, w/Steven Rosenblum
KILLING IN A SMALL TOWN (TF)   IndieProd
    Company, 1989
TOO YOUNG TO DIE? (TF)   von Zerneck-Sertner Films,
    1990, w/Eric Sears
A CRY FOR HELP: THE TRACEY THURMAN
    STORY (TF)   AUTL Productions, 1990
DECORATION DAY (TF)   Marion Rees Associates, 1990
PARIS TROUT   Viacom Pictures, 1991

LESLIE ROSENTHAL

BARBARIAN QUEEN   Concorde, 1985,
    w/Sylvia Roberts
CHOPPING MALL   KILLBOTS   Concorde, 1986
THE RETURN OF SWAMP THING   Lightyear
    Entertainment, 1989

JACQUIE FREEMAN ROSS

BLOOD SALVAGE   Paragon Arts, 1990

REBECCA ROSS

GRAFFITI BRIDGE   Paisley Park/Warner Bros., 1990

SHARYN LESLIE ROSS

LA Local 776, NY Local 771
Agent: Lawrence A. Mirisch, Triad Artists - Los Angeles,
    213/556-2727

SLEEPAWAY CAMP   United Film Distribution, 1983,
    w/Ron Kalish
LIQUID SKY   Cinevista, 1983
PLAYING FOR KEEPS   Universal, 1986, w/Gary Karr
UNDER COVER   Cannon, 1987
DOIN' TIME ON PLANET EARTH   Cannon, 1988,
    w/Alan Balsam
ERNEST SAVES CHRISTMAS   Buena Vista, 1988
WORKING TRASH (TF)   Westgate Productions, 1990
ERNEST GOES TO JAIL   Buena Vista, 1990,
    w/Farrel Levy

Ro

CINEMATOGRAPHERS
PRODUCTION
DESIGNERS,
COSTUME
DESIGNERS AND
FILM EDITORS
GUIDE

F
I
L
M

E
D
I
T
O
R
S

Ro

CINEMATOGRAPHERS
PRODUCTION
DESIGNERS,
COSTUME
DESIGNERS AND
FILM EDITORS
GUIDE

F
I
L
M

E
D
I
T
O
R
S

RITA ROSSI
THE ICICLE THIEF   Aries Releasing, 1990,
    w/Anna Misoni

CHRIS ROTH
MOB BOSS   American Independent Productions/
    Vidmark Entertainment, 1990
STEEL & LACE   Fries, 1990

FRED ROTH
MOTHERS, DAUGHTERS AND LOVERS (TF)
    Katz-Huyck Films, 1990, w/Glenn Farr &
    Michael Tronick

ED ROTHKOWITZ
SILENT NIGHT, DEADLY NIGHT III: BETTER
    WATCH OUT!   Quiet Films, 1989

MARION ROTHMAN
Agent: The Gersh Agency, Inc., Beverly Hills -
    213/274-6611, New York - 212/997-1818

THE BOSTON STRANGLER   20th Century Fox, 1968
CHE!   20th Century Fox, 1969
BENEATH THE PLANET OF THE APES   20th
    Century Fox, 1970
PLAY IT AGAIN, SAM   Paramount, 1972
BILLY JACK   Warner Bros., 1973, w/Larry Heath
TOM SAWYER   United Artists, 1973
ASH WEDNESDAY   Paramount, 1973
FUNNY LADY   Columbia, 1975
BABY BLUE MARINE   Columbia, 1976
LIPSTICK   Paramount, 1977
THE ISLAND OF DR. MOREAU   American
    International, 1977
ORCA   Paramount, 1977, w/John Bloom &
    Ralph E. Winters
COMES A HORSEMAN   United Artists, 1978
STARTING OVER   Paramount, 1979
ALL NIGHT LONG   Universal, 1981
HYSTERICAL   Embassy, 1983
CHRISTINE   Columbia, 1983
STARMAN   Columbia, 1984
CLUB PARADISE   Warner Bros., 1986
SISTER, SISTER   New World, 1988
MYSTIC PIZZA   Samuel Goldwyn Company, 1988,
    w/Don Brochu
OPPORTUNITY KNOCKS   Imagine/Universal, 1990

STEPHEN A. ROTTER
NIGHT MOVES   Warner Bros., 1975, CE
THE MISSOURI BREAKS   United Artists, 1976,
    w/Dede Allen & Jerry Greenberg
THE WORLD ACCORDING TO GARP   Warner Bros.,
    1982, w/Ronald Roose
THE RIGHT STUFF ★   The Ladd Company/Warner
    Bros., 1983, w/Glenn Farr, Lisa Fruchtman,
    Douglas Stewart & Tom Rolf
HEAVEN HELP US   Tri-Star, 1985
TARGET   Warner Bros., 1985, w/Richard P. Cirincone
ISHTAR   Columbia, 1987, w/Richard P. Cirincione &
    William Reynolds
THE UNBEARABLE LIGHTNESS OF BEING   Orion,
    1988, w/Vivien Hollgrove Gilliam & B.J. Sears
DIRTY ROTTEN SCOUNDRELS   Orion, 1988,
    w/William Scharf
AN INNOCENT MAN   Buena Vista, 1989,
    w/William Scharf

MY BLUE HEAVEN   Warner Bros., 1990
TRUE COLORS   Paramount Pictures, 1991,
    w/Robert Reitano

NICK ROTUNDO
HUMONGOUS   Embassy, 1982
CROSS COUNTRY   New World, 1983
BREAKING ALL THE RULES   New World, 1985,
    w/Janet Lazare
BULLIES   Universal, 1986
HELLO MARY LOU: PROM NIGHT II   Samuel Goldwyn
    Company, 1987
PROM NIGHT III: THE LAST KISS   Norstar
    Entertainment, 1990

DENINE ROWAN
VALENTINO RETURNS   Skouras Pictures, 1989

GEOFFREY ROWLAND, ACE
TOY SOLDIERS   New World, 1984
THE HEAT (Pilot)   1989, w/Richard E. Rabjohn
THE KISSING PLACE (CTF)   Cynthia Cherbak
    Productions, 1989

RITA ROY
FALLING OVER BACKWARDS   Astral Films, 1990

PATRICIA ROZEMA
Address: 785 Queen Street, Apt. 1, Toronto, Ontario
    M4M 1H5, Canada, 416/461-8874

I'VE HEARD THE MERMAIDS SINGING   Miramax, 1987

PAUL RUBELL, ACE
Agent: Smith Gosnell Nicholson & Associates -
    Pacific Palisades, 213/459-0307

THE FINAL TERROR   Comworld, 1983, w/Erica Flaum
    & Hannah Washonig
THE STONE BOY   TLC Films/20th Century Fox, 1984
MIRRORS (TF)   Leonard Hill Films, 1985
TOUGH LOVE (TF)   Fries Entertainment, 1985
DRESS GRAY (TF)   Frank von Zerneck Productions/
    Warner Bros. TV, 1986
IN THE SHADOW OF KILIMANJARO   Scotti Bros.,
    1986, SE
BLUE SKIES (Pilot)   1986
PROMISE (TF)   Garner-Duchow Productions/Warner
    Bros. TV, 1986
SOMETHING IN COMMON (TF)   New World TV/
    Freyda Rothstein Productions/Littke-Grossbart
    Productions, 1986
JOSEPH WAMBAUGH'S ECHOES IN THE
    DARKNESS (MS)   Littke-Grossbart Productions/
    New World TV, 1987
MURPHY'S LAW (Pilot)   1988
MY NAME IS BILL W. (TF) ☆   1989, w/John Wright
HOME FIRES BURNING (TF)   Marian Rees
    Associates, 1989
CHALLENGER (TF)   King Phoenix Entertainment/
    IndieProd Company, 1990

EVA RUGGIERO
ADIOS AMIGO   Atlas, 1976, w/Gene Ruggiero
THE MOUNTAIN MEN   Columbia, 1980
STRIPES   Columbia, 1981, w/Michael Luciano
SAVANNAH SMILES   Embassy, 1983

GENE RUGGIERO
MARLOWE   MGM, 1969
THE MAD BOMBER   Cinemation, 1973
BLACK EYE   Warner Bros., 1974
BOSS NIGGER   Dimension, 1975
ADIOS AMIGO   Atlas, 1976, w/Eva Ruggiero
MOONSHINE COUNTY EXPRESS   New World, 1977
LITTLE SISTER   Columbia, 1988

JAMES RUXIN
Address: 12140 W. Olympic Blvd., #21, Los
   Angeles, CA 90064, 213/826-3666

FADE TO BLACK   American Cineman, 1980
STOOGEMANIA   Atlantic Releasing Corporation, 1986
GHOST FEVER   Miramax, 1987
DEFENSE PLAY   Kodiak Films, 1987
BLACK ROSES   Shapiro Entertainment, 1988
RIDING THE EDGE   Kodiak Films/Trans World
   Entertainment, 1989

S

MARTIN JAY SADOFF
THE WORD (MS)   Charles Fries Productions/
   Stonehenge Productions, 1978
GRADUATION DAY   IFI-Scope III, 1981
FRIDAY THE 13TH PART VII - THE NEW BREED
   Paramount, 1988, w/Maureen O'Connell &
   Barry Zetlin

JOSE SALCEDO
DEMONS IN THE GARDEN   Spectrafilm, 1984
LAW OF DESIRE   Cinevista, 1987
WOMEN ON THE VERGE OF A NERVOUS
   BREAKDOWN   Orion Classics, 1988
ATAME   *TIE ME UP! TIE ME DOWN!*
   Miramax, 1990

STAN SALFAS
METROPOLITAN AVENUE   New Day, 1986
SPIKE OF BENSONHURST   FilmDallas, 1988

EDWARD SALIER
ROLLER BOOGIE   United Artists, 1979,
   w/Buzz Brandt & Ediberto Cruz
SILENT SCREAM   American Cinema, 1980
LUNCH WAGON   Seymour Borde Associates, 1981
THE KIRLIAN WITNESS   Sarno, 1981,
   w/Len Dell'Amico
BOXOFFICE   1982, w/Bonnie Kozck
THE SLAYER   21st Century, 1982
THE LAST HORROR FILM   Twin Continental, 1982
THE FACE OF FEAR (TF)   Lee Rich Productions/
   Papazian-Hirsch Productions, 1990

KEN SALLOWS
MALCOLM   Vestron, 1986
RIKKY AND PETE   MGM/UA, 1988

KEITH SANBORN
FUN DOWN THERE   Frameline, 1990,
   w/Roger Stigliano

RONALD SANDERS
Canadian Card
Agent: Smith Gosnell Nicholson & Associates -
   Pacific Palisades, 213/459-0307

BLOOD AND GUTS   Ambassador, 1978
FAST COMPANY   Topar, 1979
TITLE SHOT   Arista, 1979
SCANNERS   Avco Embassy, 1981
VIDEODROME   Universal, 1983
THE DEAD ZONE   Paramount, 1983
CHANDLERTOWN   *PHILIP MARLOWE -
   PRIVATE EYE* (CMS)   HBO/David Wickes Television
   Ltd./London Weekend Television, 1983
FIRESTARTER   Universal, 1984, w/David Rawlins
ALFRED HITCHCOCK PRESENTS (TVS)   1985
THE FLY   20th Century Fox, 1986
DEAD RINGERS   20th Century Fox, 1988
AGE-OLD FRIENDS (CTF)   Granger Productions, 1990

CHRIS SANDERSON
LIFE IS CHEAP...BUT TOILET PAPER IS EXPENSIVE
   Silverlight Entertainment, 1990, w/Sandy Nervig

CARLA SANTARELLI
MACARONI   Paramount, 1985

DON SAUNDERS
THE WILD DUCK   Orion, 1983
SILVER CITY   Samuel Goldwyn Company, 1985
THE RIGHT HAND MAN   FilmDallas, 1987

JILL SAVITT
KEY EXCHANGE   20th Century Fox, 1985
FULL MOON IN BLUE WATER   Trans World
   Entertainment, 1988

DAVID SAXON
THE GIRL OF THE LIMBERLOST (TF)   Sascha
   Schneider Productions, 1990

JOHN SAYLES
Contact: Writers Guild of America, West - Los Angeles,
   213/550-1000

RETURN OF THE SECAUCUS SEVEN   Libra/Specialty
   Films, 1980 (also directed)
LIANNA   United Artists Classics, 1983 (also directed)
THE BROTHER FROM ANOTHER PLANET   Cinecom,
   1984 (also directed)
CITY OF HOPE   Esperanza, 1991 (also directed)

GLENN SCANTLEBURY
BIG TIME   Island Pictures, 1988
THE SPIRIT OF '76   Black Diamond/Columbia, 1990

WILLIAM SCHARF
THE PRINCE OF PENNSYLVANIA   New Line
   Cinema, 1988
DIRTY ROTTEN SCOUNDRELS   Orion, 1988,
   w/Stephen A. Rotter
AN INNOCENT MAN   Buena Vista, 1989,
   w/Stephen A. Rotter
HENRY & JUNE   Universal, 1990, w/Vivien Hillgrove
   Gilliam & Dede Allen

Sc

CINEMATOGRAPHERS
PRODUCTION
DESIGNERS,
COSTUME
DESIGNERS AND
FILM EDITORS
GUIDE

F
I
L
M

E
D
I
T
O
R
S

Sc

**CINEMATOGRAPHERS
PRODUCTION
DESIGNERS,
COSTUME
DESIGNERS** and
**FILM EDITORS
GUIDE**

**F
I
L
M

E
D
I
T
O
R
S**

CYNTHIA SCHEIDER
BREAKING AWAY 20th Century Fox, 1979
HEAD OVER HEELS *CHILLY SCENES OF WINTER*
    United Artists, 1979
EYEWITNESS 20th Century Fox, 1981
WITHOUT A TRACE 20th Century Fox, 1983
THE LEGEND OF BILLIE JEAN Tri-Star, 1985
BATTERIES NOT INCLUDED Universal, 1987
THE MEN'S CLUB Atlantic Releasing Corporation,
    1986, w/Bill Butler & David Dresher
JUDGMENT (CTF) Tisch/Wigutow/Hershman
    Productions, 1990
WILD ORCHID 1990
THE TEDDY BEAR HABIT 1990

INE SCHENKKAN
FLESH + BLOOD Orion, 1985

PETER SCHINK
Contact: Peter Schink Film Productions, 11954 Goshen
    Ave., #106, Los Angeles, CA 90049, 213/473-7298

LETHAL PURSUIT Shapiro Glickenhaus, 1988
THE DARK BACKWARD RCA Columbia, 1990

ARTHUR SCHMIDT
THE LAST REMAKE OF BEAU GESTE Universal,
    1977, w/Jim Clark
COAL MINER'S DAUGHTER ★ Universal, 1980
THE ESCAPE ARTIST Orion/Warner Bros., 1982
THE BUDDY SYSTEM 20th Century Fox, 1984
FIRSTBORN Paramount, 1984
FANDANGO Warner Bros., 1985
BACK TO THE FUTURE Universal, 1985,
    w/Harry Keramidas
RUTHLESS PEOPLE Buena Vista, 1986, w/Gib Jaffe
WHO FRAMED ROGER RABBIT ★★ Buena
    Vista, 1988
BACK TO THE FUTURE II Universal, 1989,
    w/Harry Keramidas
BACK TO THE FUTURE III Universal, 1990,
    w/Harry Keramidas

NATE SCHMIDT
THE FOURTH MAN (TF) Rosebud Productions, 1990

SOPHIE SCHMIT
SUBWAY Island Alive, 1985

STEVEN SCHOENBERG
HAMBURGER...THE MOTION PICTURE FM
    Entertainment, 1986, w/Ann E. Mills

BRENT SCHOENFELD
BUTTERFLY Analysis, 1982
HOT RESORT Cannon, 1985, w/Dom Lubliner
THE TERROR WITHIN Concorde, 1989
A NIGHTMARE ON ELM STREET 5: THE DREAM
    CHILD New Line Cinema, 1989, w/Chuck Weiss
LEATHERFACE: TEXAS CHAINSAW MASSACRE III
    New Line Cinema, 1989
THE TERROR WITHIN II Concorde, 1991

SKIP SCHOLLNIK
MAX AND HELEN (CTF) Citadel Entertainment, 1990
DRUG WARS: THE CAMARENA STORY (MS)
    ZZY Productions, 1990, w/Kevin Krasny
THE WHEREABOUTS OF JENNY (TF) Katie Face
    Productions, 1991

THELMA SCHOONMAKER-POWELL
WOODSTOCK (FD) ★ Warner Bros., 1970
RAGING BULL ★★ United Artists, 1980
THE KING OF COMEDY 20th Century Fox, 1983
AFTER HOURS The Geffen Company/Warner
    Bros., 1985
THE COLOR OF MONEY Buena Vista, 1986
THE LAST TEMPTATION OF CHRIST Universal, 1988
NEW YORK STORIES ("Life Lessons") Buena
    Vista, 1989
GOODFELLAS ★ Warner Bros., 1990
CAPE FEAR Universal, 1991

GREGORY SCHORER
TWISTED JUSTICE Seymour Borde & Associates, 1990

THOMAS SCHWALM
STRIKE IT RICH Millimeter Films, 1990

MICHAEL SCHWEITZER
Address: 31-36 32nd St., Astoria, NY 11106,
    718/204-8995

THE TOXIC AVENGER, PART II Troma, 1989
THE BRONX WAR Filmworld International, 1990
HANGIN' WITH THE HOMEBOYS New Line
    Cinema, 1991

JOHN SCOTT
ACT
Agent: Smith Gosnell Nicholson & Associates -
    Pacific Palisades, 213/459-0307

THE ADVENTURES OF BARRY McKENZIE Double
    Head Productions, 1972
BOESMAN AND LENA Bluewater, 1974
THE GREAT MACARTHY 1975
MAD DOG Cinema Shares International, 1976
THE MANGO TREE Greater Union Film
    Distributors, 1977
JOURNEY AMONG WOMEN Greater Union Film
    Distributors, 1978
NEWSFRONT New Yorker, 1979
KOSTAS Illumination Film Productions, 1979
HEATWAVE New Line Cinema, 1983
WRONG SIDE OF THE ROAD 1983
DEAD EASY 1983
THE RETURN OF CAPTAIN INVINCIBLE New
    World, 1983
BULLAMAKANKA Bullamakanka Film
    Productions, 1984
ONE NIGHT STAND Astra Film Productions/
    Hoyts-Edgely, 1984
THE COCA COLA KID Cinecom/Film Gallery, 1985
DEATH OF A SOLDIER Scotti Brothers, 1986
HARD TO HANDLE: BOB DYLAN WITH TOM PETTY
    AND THE HEARTBREAKERS (HVD) CBS/Fox
    Video Music, 1986
WINDRIDER MGM/UA, 1987
THE UMBRELLA WOMAN 1987
THE GOOD WIFE Atlantic Releasing Corporation, 1987
ROXANNE Columbia, 1987
THE NAVIGATOR: AN ODYSSEY ACROSS TIME Circle
    Releasing, 1989
THE DELINQUENTS Warner Bros., 1990

B. J. SEARS

HUNGRY REUNION   Cinema Ventures, 1981
MASSIVE RETALIATION   One-Pass
   Hammermak, 1984
THE UNBEARABLE LIGHTNESS OF BEING
   Orion, 1988, w/Vivien Hillgrove Gilliam &
   Stephen A. Rotter

ERIC SEARS, ACE

Agent: Grace Lyons Management - Los Angeles,
   213/655-5100

CELEBRITY (MS)   NBC Productions, 1984
A REASON TO LIVE (TF)   Rastar Productions/
   Robert Papazian Productions, 1985
LOVE LIVES ON (TF)   Script-Song Productions/
   ABC Circle Films, 1985
INTO THIN AIR (TF)   Tony Ganz Productions/Major H
   Productions, 1985
NORTH AND SOUTH, BOOK II (MS)   Wolper
   Productions/Robert A. Papazian Productions/
   Warner Bros. TV, 1986
QUEENIE (MS)   von Zerneck-Samuels Productions/
   Highgate Pictures, 1987
PRISON FOR CHILDREN (TF)   Knopf-Simons
   Productions/Viacom Productions, 1987
TERRORIST ON TRIAL: THE UNITED STATES VS.
   SALIM AJAMI (TF)   George Englund Productions/
   Robert Papazian Productions, 1988
ELVIS AND ME (MS)   Navarone Productions/New
   World TV, 1988
BABY M (TF)   ABC Circle Films, 1988
WIRED   Taurus Entertainment, 1989
DAD   Universal, 1989
IN THE BEST INTEREST OF THE CHILD (TF)
   Papazian-Hirsch Entertainment, 1990
TOO YOUNG TO DIE? (TF)   von Zerneck-Sertner
   Films, 1990, w/Harvey Rosenstock
THE COURT-MARTIAL OF JACKIE ROBINSON (CTF)
   von Zerneck-Sertner Films, 1990, w/Bob Wyman

KIM SECRIST

TIMERIDER   Jensen Farley Pictures, 1983,
   w/R.J. Kizer
THIS IS SPINAL TAP   Embassy, 1984, w/Kent Beyda
QUICKSILVER   Columbia, 1986
TEEN WOLF, TOO   Atlantic Releasing Corporation,
   1987, w/Raja Gosnell, Steven Polivka &
   Harvey Rosenstock

MARION SEGAL

CARBON COPY   Avco Embassy, 1981
THE LUCKY STAR   Pickman Films, 1981
THE LADIES CLUB   New Line Cinema, 1983,
   w/Randall Torno

SUSAN SEIDELMAN

Agent: Sam Cohn, ICM - New York, 212/556-6810

SMITHEREENS   New Line Cinema, 1982
   (also directed)

LEON SEITH

HAWMPS   Mulberry Square, 1976
FOR THE LOVE OF BENJI   Mulberry Square, 1977
THE DOUBLE McGUFFIN   Mulberry Square, 1979
OH HEAVENLY DOG   20th Century Fox, 1980
1918   Cinecom, 1985
FUTURE-KILL   International Film Marketing, 1985
DAKOTA   Miramax, 1988

JANE SEITZ

CHRISTIANE F.   New World, 1982
THE NEVERENDING STORY   Warner Bros., 1984
THE NAME OF THE ROSE   20th Century Fox, 1986
THE BLIND DIRECTOR   Spectrafilm, 1986

VERONICA SELVER

BERKELEY IN THE SIXTIES   P.O.V. Theatrical
   Films, 1990

LIONEL SELWYN

MARIGOLDS IN AUGUST   RM Productions, 1984
THE GUEST   RM Productions, 1984

STEPHEN SEMEL

MIRACLE MILE   Hemdale, 1989

ROBERT P. SEPPEY

COLD SASSY TREE (CTF)   Faye Dunaway/Don
   Ohlmeyer Productions, 1990
SUDIE AND SIMPSON (CTF)   Freed/Laufer
   Productions, 1990

PAUL SEYDOR

West Coast Card
Agent: Smith Gosnell Nicholson & Associates -
   Pacific Palisades, 213/459-0307

NEVER TOO YOUNG TO DIE   Paul Releasing, 1986,
   w/William A. Anderson & Ned Humphreys
THE LAST INNOCENT MAN (CTF)   HBO Pictures/
   Maurice Singer Productions, 1987, w/Lois
   Freeman-Fox
TIME FLIES WHEN YOU'RE ALIVE (CTF)   HBO
   Showcase/Kings Road Entertainment, 1989

PHILIP J. SGRICCIA

STUCK WITH EACH OTHER (TF)   Nexus
   Productions, 1990

WILLIAM SHAFFER

TERMINAL FORCE   New World Video, 1990

RICK SHAINE

Agent: The Gersh Agency, Inc., Beverly Hills -
   213/274-6611, New York - 212/997-1818

IF EVER I SEE YOU AGAIN   Columbia, 1978
EYES OF A STRANGER   Warner Bros., 1981
THE GOODBYE PEOPLE   Embassy, 1984
A NIGHTMARE ON ELM STREET   New Line
   Cinema, 1984
THE GIG   Castle Hill Productions, 1985
DEAD OF WINTER   MGM/UA, 1987
CROSSING DELANCEY   Warner Bros., 1988
TRADING HEARTS   New Century/Vista, 1988
LOVERBOY   Tri-Star, 1989

SUSAN SHANKS

THE BAY BOY   Orion, 1985

MELVIN SHAPIRO

TAXI DRIVER   Columbia, 1976, w/Marcia Lucas &
   Tom Rolf
AMERICAN HOT WAX   Paramount, 1978
   w/Ronald J. Fagan
ICE CASTLES   Columbia, 1979, w/Michael Kahn &
   Maury Winetrobe

Sh

CINEMATOGRAPHERS
PRODUCTION
DESIGNERS,
COSTUME
DESIGNERS AND
FILM EDITORS
GUIDE

F I L M   E D I T O R S

Sh

CINEMATOGRAPHERS
PRODUCTION
DESIGNERS,
COSTUME
DESIGNERS AND
FILM EDITORS
GUIDE

F
I
L
M

E
D
I
T
O
R
S

WHERE THE BOYS ARE   Tri-Star, 1984,
    w/Bobby Shapiro
NO SMALL AFFAIR   Columbia, 1984, w/Priscilla
    Nedd & Eve Newman
BRING ON THE NIGHT (FD)   Samuel Goldwyn
    Company, 1985
CONSENTING ADULT (TF)   Starger Company/David
    Lawrence and Ray Aghayan Productions, 1985
BACKFIRE   New Century/Vista, 1987

WILLIAM SHAPTER
DEEP IN THE HEART   Warner Bros., 1984

ROY SHARMAN
CLOSE RELATIONS (CTF)   Lionheart Television, 1990

KAREN SHARP
THE FATAL IMAGE (TF)   Ellipse Programme, 1990

BRUCE SHAW
THE CIVIL WAR I-IX (MS)   Florentine Films, 1990,
    w/Paul Barnes & Tricia Reidy

PENELOPE SHAW
MAXIMUM OVERDRIVE   DEG, 1986
THE HANOI HILTON   Cannon, 1987
HEART OF MIDNIGHT   Samuel Goldwyn
    Company, 1988
MOTHER, MOTHER   1990
SO PROUDLY WE HAIL (TF)   Lionel Chetwynd
    Productions, 1990

PHILIP SHAW
SUNDAY LOVERS   United Artists, 1981
BETTER LATE THAN NEVER   Warner Bros., 1983
THE NAKED FACE   MGM/UA, 1984
THE ENDLESS GAME (CTF)   TVS Films
    Productions, 1990

ALAN SHEFLAND
RETRIBUTION   United Film Distribution, 1987,
    w/Guy Magar

RALPH SHELDON
Agent: London Management, 235/241 Regent St. -
    London W1R 7AG, 071-493-1610

THE HOLCROFT COVENANT   Universal, 1985
SHANGHAI SURPRISE   MGM/UA, 1986
LOOPHOLE   Almi Pictures, 1986
A SUMMER STORY   Atlantic Releasing
    Corporation/ITC, 1988
MURDER BY MOONLIGHT (TF)   Tamara Asseyev
    Productions/London Weekend Television, 1989

GERALD S. SHEPARD
FIVE EASY PIECES   Columbia, 1970, CE

MICHAEL J. SHERIDAN, ACE
LA Local 776
Phone: 818/884-8328

HOORAY FOR HOLLYWOOD   American Vitagraph
    Productions, 1975, w/Bud Friedgen
THE CHAMP   MGM/United Artists, 1979
ENDLESS LOVE   Universal, 1981
INCHON!   MGM/UA, 1982 , w/John Holmes
WILDSIDE (TVS)   1984

THAT'S DANCING! (FD)   MGM/UA, 1985,
    w/Bud Friedgen
CHALLENGE OF A LIFETIME (TF)   Moonlight
    Productions, 1985
MARATHON   Fontana Films Ltd., 1987
BORN IN EAST L.A.   Universal, 1987, CE
LENA: MY 100 CHILDREN (TF)   Robert Greenwald
    Productions, 1987, CE
PAINT IT BLACK   Vestron, 1989
CLASS CRUISE (TF)   Portoangelo Productions, 1990
STOLEN: ONE HUSBAND (TF)   King Phoenix
    Entertainment, 1990, w/Robert Breen
ETERNITY *THE AVATAR*   Paul Entertainment, 1990,
    w/Christopher Greenbury & Peter Zinner

BILL SHERWOOD
Agent: Creative Artists Agency - Beverly Hills,
    213/288-4545

PARTING GLANCES   Cinecom, 1985

TRUDY SHIP
Address: 9644 1/2 W. Olympic Blvd., Beverly Hills,
    CA 90212

HOUSE OF GAMES   Orion, 1987
HELLO AGAIN   Buena Vista, 1987, w/Peter C. Frank
THINGS CHANGE   Columbia, 1988
RISING SUN (CTF)   Sarabande Productions, 1990

JOHN SHIRLEY
THE SQUEEZE   Warner Bros., 1977
TOMORROW NEVER COMES   Rank, 1978
LION OF THE DESERT   United Film Distribution, 1981
EXPERIENCE PREFERRED BUT NOT ESSENTIAL
    Samuel Goldwyn Company, 1983
NATE AND HAYES   Paramount, 1983
KIPPERBANG   MGM/UA Classics, 1984
KIM (TF)   London Films, 1984
HITLER'S S.S.: PORTRAIT IN EVIL (TF)   Colasan
    Limited Productions/Edgar J. Scherick Assoc., 1985
KING SOLOMON'S MINES   Cannon, 1985
SUPERMAN IV: THE QUEST FOR PEACE   Warner
    Bros., 1987
OUT OF TIME   Alexander's Treasure Projects/Tamido
    Film Productions, 1989
VOICE OF THE HEART (CTF)   Portman
    Productions, 1989
JEKYLL & HYDE (TF)   David Wickes TV, 1990

TIM SHOEMAKER
DEATHROW GAMESHOW   Crown International,
    1987, SE

ROBERT F. SHUGRUE
Agent: The Bennett Agency - Los Angeles, 213/471-2251

TWO MULES FOR SISTER SARA   Universal, 1970
RAISE THE TITANIC   AFD, 1980, w/J. Terry Williams
A WOMAN CALLED GOLDA (TF)   1982
PRINCESS DAISY (MS)   NBC Productions/Steve Krantz
    Producitons, 1983
THE THORN BIRDS (MS)   David L. Wolper-Stan
    Margulies Productions/Edward Lewis Productions/
    Warner Bros. TV, 1983
STAR TREK III: THE SEARCH FOR SPOCK
    Paramount, 1984
THE JESSE OWENS STORY (TF)   Harve Bennett
    Productions/Paramount TV, 1984

POISON IVY (TF)   NBC Productions, 1985
52 PICK-UP   Cannon, 1986
DEAD BANG   Warner Bros., 1989
THE FOURTH WAR   New Age Releasing, 1990
STEPHEN KING'S IT (TF)   Konigsberg/Sanitsky
    Productions, 1990, w/David Blangsted

TOM SIITER
Agent: Carl Bressler, Camera Masters, 213/306-0810

JOCKS   Crown, 1986
NIGHTFLYERS   New Century/Vista, 1987
DRACULA'S WIDOW   Dino De Laurentiis
    Productions, 1988
UP YOUR ALLEY   Carolco/IVE, 1989
THE GREAT BAR 20   Commercial Pictures, 1989

ROBERTO SILVI
THE CASSANDRA CROSSING   Avco Embassy,
    1977, w/Francois Bonnot
WISE BLOOD   New Line Cinema, 1979
VICTORY   Paramount, 1981
OF UNKNOWN ORIGIN   Warner Bros., 1983
PIRANHA II - THE SPAWNING   Saturn
    International, 1983
UNDER THE VOLCANO   Universal, 1984
CHOKE CANYON   United Film Distribution, 1986
THE DEAD   Vestron, 1987
MR. NORTH   Samuel Goldwyn Company, 1988
TWISTER   Vestron, 1989
LEVIATHAN   MGM/UA, 1989, w/John F. Burnett

CHARLES SIMMONS
SURVIVAL GAME   Trans World Entertainment,
    1987, w/Karen Gebura

DAVID SIMMONS, ACE
POPEYE   Paramount, 1980, w/John W. Holmes
BLIND FURY   Tri-Star, 1990
UNDER COVER (TF)   Sacret/Paint Rock
    Productions, 1991

MARK SIMON
BEGINNER'S LUCK   New World, 1986

CLAIRE SIMPSON-CROZIER
C.H.U.D.   New World, 1984
SALVADOR   Hemdale, 1986
PLATOON ★★   Orion, 1986
WALL STREET   20th Century Fox, 1987
SOMEONE TO WATCH OVER ME   Columbia, 1987
TEQUILA SUNRISE   Warner Bros., 1988
HELL HIGH   MGM Enterprises, 1989, CE
STATE OF GRACE   Cinehaus/Orion, 1990

STANFORD SINGER
TUNNEL UNDER THE WALL   NBC News
    Productions, 1990

PARKIE SINGH
FORBIDDEN NIGHTS (TF)   Tristine Rainer
    Productions, 1989, w/Diane Adler
SMALL SACRIFICES (TF)   Louis Rudolph Films, 1990

STEPHEN SINGLETON
RITA, SUE AND BOB TOO   Orion Classics, 1987
VROOM   Film Four, 1988
FOR QUEEN AND COUNTRY   Atlantic Releasing
    Corporation, 1989

BRUCE SINOFSKY
TERMINAL BLISS   Distant Horizon, 1990

MITCHELL SINOWAY
MODERN GIRLS   Atlantic Releasing Corporation, 1986
HOT PURSUIT   Paramount, 1987

JULIE SLOANE
ANNA   Vestron, 1987

BRIAN SMEDLEY-ASTON
SQUIRM   American International, 1976
THE MUSIC MACHINE   Norfolk International Pictures/
    Target International Pictures, 1979, w/Alan Patillo
TIGER WARSAW   Sony Pictures, 1988

BUD SMITH
Agent: Bauer Benedek Agency - Los Angeles,
    213/275-2421

PUTNEY SWOPE   Cinema 5, 1969
THE EXORCIST ★   Warner Bros., 1973, w/others
RHINOCEROS   American Film Theatre, 1974
SORCERER   Universal/Paramount, 1977
THE BRINK'S JOB   Universal, 1978,
    w/Robert K. Lambert
CRUISING   United Artists, 1980
FALLING IN LOVE AGAIN   International Picture Show
    Company, 1980, w/Jacqueline Cambas &
    Doug Jackson
PERSONAL BEST   The Geffen Compay/Warner
    Bros., 1982
CAT PEOPLE   Universal, 1982, w/Jacqueline Cambas
FLASHDANCE ★   Paramount, 1983, w/Walt Mulconery
DEAL OF THE CENTURY   Warner Bros., 1983, w/Jere
    Huggins & Ned Humphreys
THE KARATE KID   Columbia, 1984, w/John G. Avildsen
    & Walt Mulconery
TO LIVE AND DIE IN L.A.   MGM/UA, 1985
SOME KIND OF WONDERFUL   Paramount, 1987,
    w/Scott Smith
SING   Tri-Star, 1989, w/Jere Huggins & Scott Smith
GROSS ANATOMY   Buena Vista, 1989, w/Scott Smith
DARKMAN   Universal, 1990, w/Scott Smith &
    David Stiven

DEBRA T. SMITH
THE MODERNS   Alive Films, 1988, w/Scott Brock
HIDER IN THE HOUSE   Vestron, 1990

HOWARD SMITH
West Coast Card
Agent: Smith Gosnell Nicholson & Associates -
    Pacific Palisades, 213/459-0307

LIVE A LITTLE, STEAL A LOT   *MURPH THE SURF*
    American International, 1975
MACKINTOSH & T.J.   Penland, 1975
TEX   Buena Vista, 1982
TWILIGHT ZONE - THE MOVIE   Warner Bros.,
    1983, Segment 4
SYLVESTER   Columbia, 1985, w/David Garfield &
    Suzanne Petit
BABY - SECRET OF THE LOST LEGEND   Buena Vista,
    1985, w/David Bretherton
AT CLOSE RANGE   Orion, 1986
NEAR DARK   DEG, 1987
RIVER'S EDGE   Hemdale, 1987,
    w/Sonya Sones Tramer

**CINEMATOGRAPHERS
PRODUCTION
DESIGNERS,
COSTUME
DESIGNERS** AND
**FILM EDITORS
GUIDE**

CINEMATOGRAPHERS
PRODUCTION
DESIGNERS,
COSTUME
DESIGNERS AND
FILM EDITORS
GUIDE

F
I
L
M

E
D
I
T
O
R
S

BIG MAN ON CAMPUS   Vestron, 1989
AFTER DARK, MY SWEET   Avenue Pictures, 1990
FLYING BLIND (TF)   NBC Productions, 1990

JOHN VICTOR SMITH
Agent: London Management, 235/241 Regent St. -
    London W1R 7AG, 071-493-1610

HELP!   United Artists, 1965
THE OFFENCE   United Artists, 1973
THE FOUR MUSKETEERS   20th Century Fox, 1975
ROYAL FLASH   20th Century Fox, 1975
ROBIN AND MARIAN   Columbia, 1976
EQUUS   United Artists, 1977
POWER PLAY   Magnum International Pictures/
    Cowry Film Productions, 1978
CUBA   United Artists, 1979
SUPERMAN II   Warner Bros., 1981
ABSOLUTION   Transworld, 1981
SUPERMAN III   Warner Bros., 1983
FINDERS KEEPERS   Warner Bros., 1984
WATER   Atlantic Releasing Corporation, 1984
RUSTLER'S RHAPSODY   Paramount, 1985
KNIGHTS AND EMERALDS   Warner Bros., 1986
AMERICAN GOTHIC   Vidmark, 1988
THE RETURN OF THE MUSKETEERS
    Universal, 1990

LEE SMITH
DEAD END DRIVE-IN   New World, 1986,
    w/Alan Lake
HOWLING III   Square Pictures, 1987
COMMUNION   MCEG, 1989

NICHOLAS C. SMITH
East & West Coast Cards
Agent: The Doug Apatow Agency, 10559 Blythe Ave. -
    Los Angeles, CA 90064

FIGHTING BACK   Paramount, 1982,
    w/John J. Fitzstephens
I AM THE CHEESE   Libra Cinema 5, 1983
COOK & PEARY: THE RACE TO THE POLE (TF)
    Robert Halmi, Inc., 1983
THE ROOMMATE   Rubicon Film Productions, 1985
KNIGHTS OF THE CITY   New World, 1986,
    w/Paul Lamori & John O'Connor
THRASHIN'   Fries Entertainment, 1986
THE RETURN OF BILLY JACK   Billy Jack
    Productions, 1986
HOME FIRES (CTF)   Edgar J. Scherick
    Productions, 1987
SPACEBALLS   20th Century Fox, 1987, CE
TORCH SONG TRILOGY   New Line Cinema, 1988
IN A SHALLOW GRAVE   Skouras Pictures, 1988
WHAT'S ALAN WATCHING? (Pilot)   1989,
    w/Peter V. White
THE WAR OF THE ROSES   20th Century Fox, 1989
SHE SAID NO (TF)   Steve White Productions, 1990
LOVE CRIMES   1991

NORMAN SMITH
STREAMERS   United Artists Classics, 1983
GRAVEYARD SHIFT   Shapiro Entertainment, 1987,
    w/Robert Bergman

PAUL MARTIN SMITH
BORN AMERICAN   Cinema Group, 1986

SCOTT SMITH
SOME KIND OF WONDERFUL   Paramount, 1987,
    w/Bud Smith
JOHNNY BE GOOD   Orion, 1988
SING   Tri-Star, 1988, w/Jere Huggins & Bud Smith
GROSS ANATOMY   Buena Vista, 1989, w/ Bud Smith
DARKMAN   Universal, 1990, w/Bud Smith &
    David Stiven
HITLER'S DAUGHTER (CTF)   OTML Films, 1990

KELLY SNYDER
APPEARANCES (TF)   Echo Cove Productions, 1989,
    w/Jim McElroy

LAURENCE SOLOMON
SWEET LORRAINE   Angelika Films, 1987

PHIL SOUTHBY
HANSEL AND GRETEL (TF)   BBC Television, 1990,
    w/Andrew Barker

RONALD G. SPANG
ANY WHICH WAY YOU CAN   Warner Bros., 1980,
    w/Ferris Webster
FIREFOX   Warner Bros., 1982, w/Ferris Webster
DEADLY ILLUSION   CineTel Films, 1987,
    w/Steve Mirkovich
THE DEAD POOL   Warner Bros., 1988

ANTHONY SPANO
COP   Atlantic Releasing Corporation, 1988

MICHAEL SPENCE
HANGAR 18   Sunn Classic, 1980
THE BOOGENS   Jensen Farley Pictures, 1981
LEGEND OF THE WILD   Jensen Farley Pictures, 1981
ONE DARK NIGHT   Comworld, 1983, w/Charles Tetoni
SILENT NIGHT, DEADLY NIGHT   Tri-Star, 1984
DEF-CON 4   New World, 1985, w/Todd Ramsay
REFORM SCHOOL GIRLS   New World, 1986
SUMMER CAMP NIGHTMARE   Concorde, 1987

DOROTHY SPENCER
CLEOPATRA ★   20th Century Fox, 1963
EARTHQUAKE ★   Universal, 1974
THE CONCORDE - AIRPORT '79   Universal, 1979

DAVID SPIERS
Agent: London Management, 235/241 Regent St. -
    London W1R 7AG, 071-493-1610

PING PONG   Samuel Goldwyn Company, 1987
PROMISED LAND   Vestron, 1988
SOME GIRLS   MGM/UA, 1989
VENUS PETER   Atlantic Releasing Corporation, 1989
TWENTY-ONE   Anglo International Films, 1991

ZACH STAENBERG
East & West Coast cards
Agent: The Doug Apatow Agency, 10559 Blythe Ave. -
    Los Angeles, CA 90064, 213/202-6888

RUSTLER'S RHAPSODY   1985 CE
POLICE ACADEMY   The Ladd Company/Warner Bros.,
    1984, w/Robert Brown
STRIPPED TO KILL   Concorde, 1987
BLACKOUT   Ambient Light Entertainment, 1989
THE TENDER   1991, CE

FRED STAFFORD
THE NIGHT OF THE COMET   Atlantic Releasing
    Corporation, 1984
JAKE SPEED   New World, 1986, w/Michael Ripps

THOMAS STANFORD
THE LEGEND OF THE LONE RANGER   Universal/
    AFD, 1981
SPLIT DECISIONS   New Century/Vista, 1988,
    w/Jeff Freeman & John W. Wheeler
BORN TO RACE   MGM/UA, 1988, w/Tony Lombardo

WENDEYE STANZLER
ROGER & ME   Dog Eat Dog Films, 1989,
    w/Jennifer Beman

ANNE STEIN
SIDEWALK STORIES   Island Pictures, 1989,
    w/Charles Lane

FREDRIC STEINKAMP
Agent: Lawrence A. Mirisch, Triad Artists, Inc. -
    Los Angeles, 213/556-2727
Phone: 213/837-0448

THE UNSINKABLE MOLLY BROWN   MGM, 1964
GRAND PRIX ★   MGM, 1966, w/Henry Berman,
    Stewart Linder & Frank Santillo
CHARLY   Cinerama Releasing Corporation, 1968
THEY SHOOT HORSES, DON'T THEY? ★
    MGM, 1969
A NEW LEAF   Paramount, 1971
FREEBIE AND THE BEAN   Warner Bros., 1974
THE YAKUZA   Warner Brothers, 1975, SE
3 DAYS OF THE CONDOR ★   Paramount, 1975,
    w/Don Guidice
HARRY AND WALTER GO TO NEW YORK   Columbia,
    1976, w/David Bretherton & Don Guidice
BOBBY DEERFIELD   Columbia, 1977
FEDORA   United Artists, 1979
HIDE IN PLAIN SIGHT   MGM/United Artists, 1980,
    w/William Steinkamp
TOOTSIE ★   Columbia, 1982, w/William Steinkamp
AGAINST ALL ODDS   Columbia, 1984,
    w/William Steinkamp
WHITE NIGHTS   Columbia, 1985,
    w/William Steinkamp
OUT OF AFRICA ★   Universal, 1985, w/William
    Steinkamp, Pembroke J. Herring & Sheldon Kahn
ADVENTURES IN BABYSITTING   Buena Vista, 1987,
    w/William Steinkamp
BURGLAR   Warner Bros., 1987, w/William Steinkamp
SCROOGED   Paramount, 1988, w/William Steinkamp
HAVANA   Mirage/Universal, 1990,
    w/William Steinkamp

FRITZ STEINKAMP
THE OLD MAN AND THE SEA (TF)   Storke
    Enterprises, 1990

WILLIAM STEINKAMP
HIDE IN PLAIN SIGHT   MGM/United Artists, 1980,
    w/Frederic Steinkamp
KING OF THE MOUNTAIN   Universal, 1981
TOOTSIE ★   Columbia, 1982, w/Fredric Steinkamp
AGAINST ALL ODDS   Columbia, 1984,
    w/Fredric Steinkamp

WHITE NIGHTS   Columbia, 1985,
    w/Fredric Steinkamp
OUT OF AFRICA ★   Universal, 1985, w/Fredric
    Steinkamp, Pembroke J. Herring & Sheldon Kahn
ADVENTURES IN BABYSITTING   Buena Vista, 1987,
    w/Fredric Steinkamp
BURGLAR   Warner Bros., 1987, w/FredricSteinkamp
SCROOGED   Paramount, 1988, w/Fredric Steinkamp
THE FABULOUS BAKER BOYS ★   20th Century
    Fox, 1989
HAVANA   Mirage/Universal, 1990, w/Fredric Steinkamp

AARON STELL
FEAR STRIKES OUT   Paramount, 1957
TOUCH OF EVIL   Universal, 1958
TO KILL A MOCKINGBIRD   Universal, 1962
LOVE WITH THE PROPER STRANGER
    Paramount, 1964
BABY, THE RAIN MUST FALL   Columbia, 1966
INSIDE DAISY CLOVER   Warner Bros., 1966
THE STALKING MOON   National General, 1969
THE GRASSHOPPER   National General, 1969
SILENT RUNNING   Universal, 1972
WILLIE DYNAMITE   Universal, 1974
THE KILLER INSIDE ME   Warner Bros., 1976, w/
    Danford B. Greene
NATIVE SON   Cinecom, 1986

ROD STEPHENS
A CONNECTICUT YANKEE IN KING ARTHUR'S
    COURT (TF)   Schaefer/Karpf Productions, 1990

STEPHEN STEPT
DEAR AMERICA (FD)   HBO Pictures, 1987

KAREN STERN
THE LOST CAPONE (CTF)   Patchett-Kaufman
    Entertainment, 1990

TOM STEVENS
FIRE AND RAIN (CTF)   Wilshire Court Productions, 1990
LUCY & DESI (TF)   Larry Thompson Entertainment, 1991

HOUSELEY STEVENSON
SPECIAL DELIVERY   American International, 1976
MEAN DOG BLUES   American Internationl, 1978
THE MAN WITH BOGART'S FACE   20th Century
    Fox, 1980
THE GREAT SANTINI   Orion/Warner Bros., 1980

MICHAEL A. STEVENSON, ACE
THE CHEAP DETECTIVE   Columbia, 1978,
    w/Sidney Levin
CALIFORNIA SUITE   Columbia, 1978
CHAPTER TWO   Columbia, 1979
SEEMS LIKE OLD TIMES   Columbia, 1980
THE TOY   Columbia, 1982, w/Richard Harris
THE BURNING BED (TF) ☆   Tisch-Avnet Productions,
    1984, CE
GOTCHA!   Universal, 1985
A WINNER NEVER QUITS (TF)   Blatt-Singer
    Productions/Columbia TV, 1985
SPOT MARKS THE X (CTF)   Catalina Production
    Group, 1986
THREE MEN AND A BABY   Buena Vista, 1987
HONEY, I SHRUNK THE KIDS   Buena Vista, 1989
THREE MEN AND A LITTLE LADY   Buena Vista, 1990

St

CINEMATOGRAPHERS
PRODUCTION
DESIGNERS,
COSTUME
DESIGNERS AND
FILM EDITORS
GUIDE

F
I
L
M

E
D
I
T
O
R
S

CINEMATOGRAPHERS
PRODUCTION
DESIGNERS,
COSTUME
DESIGNERS AND
FILM EDITORS
GUIDE

SCOTT STEVENSON
CYBORG   Cannon, 1989, w/Rozanne Zingale

DOUGLAS STEWART
THE WHITE DAWN   Paramount, 1974
THE SHOOTIST   Paramount, 1976
TELEFON   MGM/United Artists, 1977
INVASION OF THE BODY SNATCHERS   United
   Artists, 1978
WALK PROUD   Universal, 1979
ROUGH CUT   Paramount, 1980
FAST-WALKING   Pickman Films, 1982
JINXED   MGM/UA, 1982
THE RIGHT STUFF ★   The Ladd Company/Warner
   Bros., 1983, w/Glenn Farr, Lisa Fruchtman,
   Stephen A. Rotter & Tom Rolf

JAMES AUSTIN STEWART
POWWOW HIGHWAY   Warner Bros., 1989

ROGER STIGLIANO
FUN DOWN THERE   Frameline, 1990, w/Keith Sanborn

WILLIAM B. STITCH
SETTLE THE SCORE (TF)   Steve Sohmer
   Productions, 1990

DAVID STIVEN
Agent: The Gersh Agency, Inc., Beverly Hills -
   213/274-6611, New York - 212/997-1818

TIM   Satori, 1979
THE ROAD WARRIOR   Warner Bros., 1982,
   w/Michael Balson & Tim Wellburn
"CROCODILE" DUNDEE   Paramount, 1986
"CROCODILE" DUNDEE II   Paramount, 1988
DARKMAN   Universal, 1990, w/Bud Smith &
   Scott Smith
ALMOST AN ANGEL   Ironbark Films/Paramount, 1990

OLIVIER STOCKMAN
LITTLE DORRIT   Cannon, 1988

TERRY STOKES
A NIGHTMARE ON ELM STREET, PART 3: THE
   DREAM WARRIORS   New Line Cinema, 1987
THE BLOB   Tri-Star, 1988, w/Tod Feuerman
BOOK OF LOVE   New Line Cinema, 1990

ALAN STRACHAN
THE HUMAN FACTOR   Bryanston, 1974
THE GREEK TYCOON   Universal, 1978
THE PASSAGE   United Artists, 1979
ffolkes   Universal, 1980
THE FINAL CONFLICT   20th Century Fox, 1981
THE SENDER   Paramount, 1982
THE JIGSAW MAN   United Film Distribution, 1984,
   w/Peter Hunt
THE DIRTY DOZEN: THE NEXT MISSION (TF)
   MGM-UA TV, 1985
NOT QUITE PARADISE   *NOT QUITE JERUSALEM*
   New World, 1985
WITHNAIL AND I   Cineplex Odeon, 1987
HOW TO GET AHEAD IN ADVERTISING   Warner
   Bros., 1989

KATHLEEN STRATTON
QUEST FOR THE MIGHTY SWORD   RCA/Columbia
   Home Video, 1990

MARK STRATTON
DEAD WOMEN IN LINGERIE   Monarch Home Video,
   1990, w/Stacia Thompson

JOHN STRICKLAND
ORANGES ARE NOT THE ONLY FRUIT (CTF)
   BBC-TV, 1990

BRUCE STUBBLEFIELD
SAVAGE STREETS   MPM, 1984, w/John O'Connor
STRIPPED TO KILL   Concorde, 1987
SLAVE GIRLS FROM BEYOND INFINITY   Urban
   Classics, 1987

ANDREW SUMNER
THE HEAT OF THE DAY (TF)   Granada Television, 1990

AKIRA SUZUKI
TAMPOPO   New Yorker, 1987
THE FUNERAL   New Yorker, 1987
A TAXING WOMAN'S RETURN   New Yorker, 1989

ROBERT E. SWINK
Agent: The Gersh Agency, Inc. - Beverly Hills,
   213/274-6611

FUNNY GIRL ★   Columbia, 1968, w/William Sands &
   Maury Winetrobe
SKYJACKED   MGM, 1972
PAPILLON   Allied Artists, 1973
LADY ICE   1973
THREE THE HARD WAY   1974
ROOSTER COGBURN   Universal, 1975
MIDWAY   Universal, 1976, w/Frank J. Urioste
ISLANDS IN THE STREAM   Paramount, 1977
THE BOYS FROM BRAZIL ★   20th Century Fox, 1978
GRAY LADY DOWN   Universal, 1978
GOING IN STYLE   Warner Bros., 1979,
   w/C. Timothy O'Meara
THE IN-LAWS   Warner Bros., 1979
SPHINX   Orion/Warner Bros., 1981,
   w/Michael F. Anderson
WELCOME HOME   Columbia, 1989

JAMES SYMONS
Agent: The Gersh Agency, Inc., Beverly Hills -
   213/274-6611, New York - 212/997-1818

THE ZOO GANG   New World, 1985
COBRA   Warner Bros., 1986, w/Don Zimmerman
OVER THE TOP   Cannon, 1987, w/Don Zimmerman
RAMBO III   Tri-Star, 1988, w/O. Nicholas Brown, Andrew
   London & Edward Warschilka
TEENAGE MUTANT NINJA TURTLES   Golden Harvest/
   New Line Cinema, 1990, w/William Gordean &
   Sally Menke
NOTHING BUT TROUBLE   Warner Bros., 1991,
   w/Malcolm Campbell

T

BRIAN TAGG
CRIMES OF PASSION   New World, 1984

PETER TANNER, ACE
Agent: London Management, 235/241 Regent St. -
   London W1R 7AG, 071-493-1610

HEDDA   Brut Productions, 1975
THE MAIDS   American Film Theatre, 1975
NASTY HABITS   Brut Productions, 1977
STEVIE   First Artists, 1978
WOMBLING FREE   Satori, 1979
THE MONSTER CLUB   ITC, 1981
TO CATCH A KING (CTF)   HBO Premiere Films/
   Entertainment Partners/Gaylord Productions, 1984
A CHRISTMAS CAROL (TF)   Entertainment
   Partners Ltd., 1984
ARTHUR THE KING (TF)   Martin Poll Productions/
   Comworld Productions/Jadran Film, 1985
TURTLE DIARY   Samuel Goldwyn Company, 1985
SKY BANDITS   Galaxy International, 1986
HAMBURGER HILL   Paramount, 1987
WITHOUT A CLUE   Orion, 1988
DANNY, CHAMPION OF THE WORLD (CTF)   Disney
   Channel, 1989, w/Angus Newton

CHRISTOPHER TATE
BYE BYE BLUES   Circle Releasing, 1990

BARRETT TAYLOR
PERSONALS (CTF)   Sharmill Productions, 1990
OPPOSITES ATTRACT (TF)   Rastar Productions/
   Bar-Gene Productions, 1990

JERRY TAYLOR
WHERE PIGEONS GO TO DIE (TF)   Michael Landon
   Productions, 1990

MIKE TAYLOR
QUADROPHENIA   World Northal, 1979
THE LONG GOOD FRIDAY   Embassy, 1982

PETER TAYLOR
LA TRAVIATA   Universal Classics, 1983,
   w/Franca Silvi
OTELLO   Cannon, 1985, w/Franca Sylvi
THE PENITENT   Cineworld, 1988

KEVIN TENT
NOT OF THIS EARTH   Concorde, 1988
FRANKENHOOKER   Shapiro Glickenhaus, 1990
BASKET CASE 2   Shapiro Glickenhaus, 1990

HOWARD TERRILL
WISEGUY (TF)   Stephen J. Cannell Productions,
   1990, w/Gene Ranney

PETER TESCHNER
ALIEN PREDATOR   Trans World Entertainment, 1987,
   w/Dennis Hill
ENEMY TERRITORY   Empire Pictures, 1987
PHANTASM II   Universal, 1988
GHOST TOWN   Trans World Entertainment, 1988,
   w/King Wilder
DEADLY WEAPON   Empire Picutres, 1989
BRIDE OF RE-ANIMATOR   Wildstreet Pictures/50 St.
   Films, 1991

JONAS THALER
CIRCUITRY MAN   Skouras, 1990

MICHAEL THIBAULT
HEROES STAND ALONE   Concorde, 1990

JACQUELINE THIEDOT
A FEW DAYS WITH ME   Galaxy Films, 1989

SCOTT THOMAS
DIAMOND'S EDGE   Castle Hill, 1990

PETER LEE THOMPSON
THE NINTH CONFIGURATION   Warner Bros., 1980,
   w/Battle Davis
10 TO MIDNIGHT   Cannon, 1983
THE AMBASSADOR   MGM/UA/Cannon, 1985,
   w/Thierry J. Couturier & Mark Goldblatt
MURPHY'S LAW   Cannon, 1985
DEATHWISH 4: THE CRACKDOWN   Cannon, 1987
MESSENGER OF DEATH   Cannon, 1988
KINJITE: FORBIDDEN SUBJECTS   Cannon, 1989,
   w/Mary E. Jochem
THE EXORCIST III   20th Century Fox, 1990,
   w/Todd Ramsay

STACIA THOMPSON
DEAD WOMEN IN LINGERIE   Monarch Home Video,
   1990, w/Mark Stratton

NEIL THOMSON
AND NOTHING BUT THE TRUTH   Cannon, 1984

KAREN THORNDIKE
BENJI THE HUNTED   Buena Vista, 1987
DAREDREAMER   Lensmen Company, 1989

RANDY THORNTON
BODY SLAM   DEG, 1987

JOHN TINTORI
East Coast card, ,Local 776
Agent: The Doug Apatow Agency, 10559 Blythe Ave. -
   Los Angeles, CA 90064, 213/202-6888

SUDDEN DEATH   Marvin Films, 1985
EIGHT MEN OUT   Orion, 1988
TRUE LOVE   MGM/UA, 1989
LITTLE VEGAS   I.R.S., 1990

MICHAEL TODD
HOME IS WHERE THE HART IS   Atlantic Releasing
   Corporation, 1987
NIGHT FRIEND   Cineplex Odeon, 1988

To

CINEMATOGRAPHERS
PRODUCTION
DESIGNERS,
COSTUME
DESIGNERS AND
FILM EDITORS
GUIDE

F
I
L
M

E
D
I
T
O
R
S

To

CINEMATOGRAPHERS
PRODUCTION
DESIGNERS,
COSTUME
DESIGNERS AND
FILM EDITORS
GUIDE

F I L M   E D I T O R S

AMY TOMPKINS
PHANTOM OF THE MALL: ERIC'S REVENGE   Fries
    Entertainment, 1990, w/Gregory F. Plotts

CAMILLA TONIOLO
TOKYO POP   Spectrafilm, 1988
BLOODHOUNDS OF BROADWAY   Columbia, 1989

ALAN TOOMAYAN
EATING RAOUL   20th Century Fox International
    Classics, 1982
NOT FOR PUBLICATION   Samuel Goldwyn
    Company, 1984
LUST IN THE DUST   New World, 1984
THE LONG SHOT   Orion, 1986
SCENES FROM THE CLASS STRUGGLE IN
    BEVERLY HILLS   Cinecom, 1989

FABIEN TORDJMANN, ACE
THEY WENT THAT-A-WAY & THAT-A-WAY
    International Picture Show, 1978
THE PRIZE FIGHTER   New World, 1979
THE PRIVATE EYES   New World, 1980
MARVIN AND TIGE   20th Century Fox International
    Classics, 1983
STAND ALONE   New World, 1985
SHADOW ON THE SUN - PART II (MS)   New World
    TV, 1988, w/Robert K. Lambert & David Simmons
TH FIFTH MONKEY   Columbia, 1990,
    w/Alain Jakubowicz

SONYA SONES TRAMER
FLESHBURN   Crown International, 1984
SCHOOL SPIRIT   Concorde, 1985
RIVER'S EDGE   Hemdale, 1987, w/Howard Smith
HOW I GOT INTO COLLEGE   20th Century Fox,
    1989, w/Kaja Fehr

NEIL TRAVIS, ACE
Contact: 818/342-9895

ROOTS (MS) ☆☆   Wolper Productions, 1977
JAWS II   Universal, 1978
DIE LAUGHING   Orion/Warner Bros., 1980
THE IDOLMAKER   United Artists, 1980
NOBODY'S PERFEKT   Columbia, 1981
SECOND THOUGHTS   Universal, 1983
CUJO   Warner Bros., 1983
THE PHILADELPHIA EXPERIMENT   New World, 1984
THE ATLANTA CHILD MURDERS (TF)   Mann-
    Rafshoon Productions/Finnegan Associates, 1985
MARIE   MGM/UA, 1985
NO WAY OUT   Orion, 1987
COCKTAIL   Buena Vista, 1988
SHANNON'S DEAL (TF)   Stan Rogow Productions/
    NBC Productions, 1989
DANCES WITH WOLVES ★★   Tig/Orion, 1990

PAUL TREJO
BELIZAIRE THE CAJUN   Skouras Pictures, 1986

RICHARD TREVOR
THE HUMAN FACTOR   United Artists, 1979
DEJA VU   Cannon, 1985
THE DECEIVERS   Cinecom, 1988

DEREK TRIGG
THE GIRL   Shapiro Entertainment, 1987
HARDWARE   Millimeter Films, 1990

MICHAEL TRONICK
LESS THAN ZERO   1987, w/Peter E. Berger
MIDNIGHT RUN   Universal, 1988, w/Chris Lebenzon &
    Billy Weber
THE ADVENTURES OF FORD FAIRLANE   20th Century
    Fox, 1990
MOTHERS, DAUGHTERS AND LOVERS (TF)
    Katz-Huyck Films, 1990, w/Glenn Farr & Fred Roth

JACK TUCKER, ACE
THEY'RE PLAYING WITH FIRE   New World, 1984

BARBARA TULLIVER
HOMICIDE   Triumph Pictures/Edward R. Pressman/
    Cinehaus, 1991

U

FRANK J. URIOSTE, ACE
Agent: Lawrence A. Mirisch, Triad Artists, Inc. -
    Los Angeles, 213/556-2727
Address: 1610 Highland Avenue, Glendale, CA 91202,
    818/246-0208

WHAT EVER HAPPENED TO AUNT ALICE?   Cinerama
    Releasing Corporation, 1969
THE GRISSOM GANG   Cinerama Releasing
    Corporation, 1971
MIDWAY   Universal, 1976, w/Robert Swink
DAMNATION ALLEY   20th Century Fox, 1977
THE BOYS IN COMPANY C   Columbia, 1978,
    w/Michael Berman, James Benson & Alan Pattillo
FAST BREAK   Columbia, 1979
LOVING COUPLES   20th Century Fox, 1980,
    w/Grey Fox
THE JAZZ SINGER   AFD, 1980, SE
THE ENTITY   20th Century Fox, 1983
TRENCHCOAT   Buena Vista, 1983
AMITYVILLE 3-D   Orion, 1983
CONAN THE DESTROYER   Universal, 1984
RED SONJA   MGM/UA, 1985
THE HITCHER   Tri-Star, 1986
ROBOCOP ★   Orion, 1987
DIE HARD ★★   20th Century Fox, 1988, w/John F. Link
ROAD HOUSE   MGM/UA, 1989, w/John Link
TOTAL RECALL   Tri-Star, 1990

JAMIE UYS
Contact: Department of Interior, Civitas Building, Struben
    Street, Pretoria 0002, South Africa, 12/48-2551

THE GODS MUST BE CRAZY   TLC Films/20th Century
    Fox, 1984 (also directed)

V

FRANS VANDENBURG
BANGKOK HILTON   Kennedy-Miller, 1990,
    w/Marcus D'Arcy

JOËLE VAN EFFENTERRE
COCKTAIL MOLOTOV   Putnam Square, 1980
THE ROADS OF EXILE   Corinth, 1981
LIKE A TURTLE ON ITS BACK   New Line
    Cinema, 1981
ENTRE NOUS   United Artists Classics, 1983
HEAT OF DESIRE   Triumph, 1984
BURROUGHS   Citifilmworks, 1984
FLANAGAN   United Film Distribution, 1985
THE DEATH OF MARIO RICCI   New Line
    Cinema, 1985
A MAN IN LOVE   Cinecom, 1987
BETRAYED   MGM/UA, 1988
MUSIC BOX   Carolco/Tri-Star, 1989

AGNES VARDA
Contact: French Film Office, 745 Fifth Avenue,
    New York, NY 10151, 212/832-8860

VAGABOND   International Film Exchange, 1986,
    w/Patricia Mazuy

SCOTT VICKREY
THEY ALL LAUGHED   20th Century Fox, 1981
MIXED BLOOD   Sara Films, 1985
INVASION U.S.A.   Cannon, 1985,
    w/Daniel Loewenthal
DEADLY INTENTIONS...AGAIN? (TF)   Green/Epstein
    Productions, 1991
IN BROAD DAYLIGHT (TF)   Force Ten
    Productions, 1991

TONY VIGNA
THE WHITE GIRL   Tony Brown Productions, 1990

GEORGE C. VILLASENOR
GLORIA   Columbia, 1980
LOVE STREAMS   Cannon, 1984
THE SLUGGER'S WIFE   Columbia, 1985,
    w/Don Brochu

BARRIE VINCE
THE LAST DAYS OF MAN ON EARTH   New
    World, 1974
THE ODD JOB   Columbia, 1978
THE SHOUT   Films Inc., 1979
MOONLIGHTING   Universal, 1982
THE BOUNTY   Orion, 1984
SUCCESS IS THE BEST REVENGE   Triumph/
    Columbia, 1984
A PRIVATE FUNCTION   Island Alive, 1985
THE LIGHT SHIP   Castle Hill Productions, 1986

DENNIS M. VIRKLER
West Coast Card
Agent: Smith Gosnell Nicholson & Associates -
    Pacific Palisades, 213/459-0307

BURNT OFFERINGS   United Artists, 1976
XANADU   Universal, 1980
CONTINENTAL DIVIDE   Universal, 1981
AIRPLANE II: THE SEQUEL   Paramount, 1982
INDEPENDENCE DAY   Warner Bros., 1983
GORKY PARK   Orion, 1983
THE RIVER RAT   Paramount, 1984
SECRET ADMIRER   Orion, 1985
NOBODY'S FOOL   Island Pictures, 1986
BIG SHOTS   20th Century Fox, 1987, w/William M.
    Anderson & Sheldon Kahn
DISTANT THUNDER   Paramount, 1988
THE HUNT FOR RED OCTOBER ★   Paramount, 1990,
    w/John Wright

SAM VITALE
WHEN A STRANGER CALLS   Columbia, 1979
THE ROSARY MURDERS   New Line Cinema, 1987

STANLEY VOGEL
THE FIRST TIME   New Line Cinema, 1983

PAUL VOLK
AMERICAN BORN   PM Home Video, 1990,
    w/John David Dagnen

ILA VON HASPERG
END OF THE NIGHT   In Absentia Productions, 1991

PETRA VON OELFFEN
Agent: Sandra Marsh Management - Sherman Oaks,
    818/905-6961

SERPENT'S EGG   United Artists, 1978
FROM THE LIFE OF THE MARIONETTES   Universal/
    AFD, 1980
STRANGE BEHAVIOR   World Northal, 1981
YOUTH   1983
MESMERIZED   RKO/Challenge Corp. Services, 1984
ANASTASIA: THE MYSTERY OF ANNA (TF)
    Telecom Entertainment/Consolidated Productions/
    Reteitalia, 1986
FIRE AND ICE   Concorde, 1987, w/Claudia Travnecek
DEAD SOLID PERFECT (CTF)   HBO Premiere
    Films, 1988

CINEMATOGRAPHERS
PRODUCTION
DESIGNERS,
COSTUME
DESIGNERS AND
FILM EDITORS
GUIDE

F
I
L
M

E
D
I
T
O
R
S

Wa

CINEMATOGRAPHERS
PRODUCTION
DESIGNERS,
COSTUME
DESIGNERS AND
FILM EDITORS
GUIDE

F
I
L
M

E
D
I
T
O
R
S

W

CHRISTIAN WAGNER
HERO AND THE TERROR   Cannon, 1988

WAYNE WAHRMAN
KICKBOXER   Kings Road/Pathe, 1989
DANIELLE STEEL'S FINE THINGS (TF)   The Cramer
     Company, 1990, w/Michael S. McLean
JUST LIFE (TF)   Aaron Spelling Productions/Victoria
     Principal Productions, 1990
THE PERFECT WEAPON   Paramount Pictures, 1991

GRAHAM WALKER
THE FOURTH PROTOCOL   Lorimar, 1987
THE LAST OF THE FINEST   Orion, 1990

LESLEY WALKER
Agent: Sandra Marsh Management - Sherman Oaks,
     818/905-6961

PORTRAIT OF AN ARTIST AS A YOUNG MAN
     Howard Mahler Films, 1979
EAGLE'S WING   International Picture Show
     Company, 1980
THE TEMPEST   World Northal, 1980
RICHARD'S THINGS   New World, 1981
ILL FARES THE LAND   Channel Four Pictures, 1982
WINSTON CHURCHILL - THE WILDERNESS
     YEARS (MS)   Southern Pictures
     Productions, 1983
MEANTIME   Central Pictures, 1983
WINTER'S FLIGHT   Cinecom, 1984
LETTER TO BREZHNEV   Circle Releasing, 1985
MONA LISA   Island Pictures, 1986
CRY FREEDOM   Universal, 1987
BUSTER   Hemdale, 1988
SHIRLEY VALENTINE   Paramount, 1989
THE SECRET LIFE OF IAN FLEMING (CTF)   Saban/
     Scherick Productions, 1990

SCOTT WALLACE
Agent: Grace Lyons Management - Los Angeles,
     213/655-5100

SAVAGE HARVEST   20th Century Fox, 1981,
     w/Patrick Kennedy
WEIRD SCIENCE   Universal, 1985 , w/Christopher
     Lebenzon & Mark Warner
ALL THE NEWS (Pilot)
REMOTE CONTROL   Vista Organization, 1988
STREETS OF MALICE (TF)   1989
SKI PATROL   Triumph, 1990

NORM WALLERSTEIN, ACE
THAT'S NOT ALL FOLKS   1972
THE TEACHER   Crown International, 1974
DR. MINX   Dimension, 1975
THE SPECIALIST   Crown International, 1975
THE PRICELESS GIFT   1983

RIT WALLIS
THE BOY IN BLUE   20th Century Fox, 1985
THE GATE   New Century/Vista, 1987
NOWHERE TO HIDE   New Century/Vista, 1987
IRON EAGLE II   Tri-Star, 1988

TOM WALLS
Agent: Grace Lyons Management - Los Angeles,
     213/655-5100

WELCOME TO L.A.   United Artists/Lions Gate, 1976,
     w/William A. Sawyer
REMEMBER MY NAME   Columbia/Lagoon
     Associates, 1979
ROADIE   Untied Artists, 1980, CE
HIGH RISK   American Cinema, 1981
TAG   New World, 1982
RETURN ENGAGEMENT (FD)   Island Alive, 1983
SONGWRITER   Tri-Star, 1984
ENDANGERED SPECIES   MGM/UA, 1982
THE ICE PIRATES   MGM/UA, 1984
BACHELOR PARTY   20th Century Fox, 1984
GIMME AN F   20th Century Fox, 1984, w/Wendy
     Bricmont & Todd Ramsay
TROUBLE IN MIND   Alive Films, 1985,
     w/Sally Coryn Allen
MOVING VIOLATIONS   20th Century Fox, 1985
MADE IN HEAVEN   Lorimar, 1987
MAC AND ME   Orion, 1988
LUCKY STIFF   New Line Cinema, 1989,
     w/Michael N. Knue
THE COVER GIRL AND THE COP (TF)   Barry & Enright
     Productions, 1989
SKETCHES   MCEG, 1990
MORTAL THOUGHTS   Columbia Pictures, 1991

ALTON WALPOLE
KOYAANISQATSI   New Line Cinema, 1983,
     w/Ron Fricke
POWAQQATSI   Cannon, 1988, w/Iris Cahn

MARTIN WALSH
THE KRAYS   Rank, 1990

MARK ROY WARNER
ROCKY III   MGM/UA, 1982, w/Don Zimmerman
48HRS.   Paramount, 1982, w/Freeman Davies &
     Billy Weber
STAYING ALIVE   Paramount, 1983, w/Don Zimmerman
A SOLDIER'S STORY   Columbia, 1984,
     w/Caroline Biggerstaff
WEIRD SCIENCE   Universal, 1985, w/Christopher
     Lebenzon & Scott Wallace
BIG TROUBLE IN LITTLE CHINA   20th Century Fox,
     1986, w/Steve Mirkovich & Edward A. Warschilka
THE RUNNING MAN   Tri-Star, 1987, w/Edward A.
     Warschilka & John Wright
COCOON: THE RETURN   20th Century Fox, 1988
DRIVING MISS DAISY ★   Warner Bros., 1989
PACIFIC HEIGHTS   20th Century Fox, 1990

STANLEY WARNOW
Agent: The Gersh Agency, Inc., Beverly Hills -
     213/274-6611, New York - 212/997-1818

MOMENT TO MOMENT   Universal, 1966
WOODSTOCK (FD)   Warner Bros., 1970
THE HONEYMOON KILLERS   1970

HURRY UP OR I'LL BE THIRTY   Avco Embassy, 1973
HAIR   United Artists, 1979
NO NUKES (FD)   Warner Bros., 1980
RAGTIME   Paramount, 1981, w/Anne V. Coates &
    Antony Gibbs
IN OUR HANDS (FD)   Libra Cinema 5, 1984 ,
    shared credit
SESAME STREET PRESENTS: FOLLOW THAT BIRD
    Warner Bros., 1985
TAKEN AWAY (TF)   Hart, Thomas & Berlin
    Productions, 1990
HELD HOSTAGE: THE SIS AND JERRY LEVIN
    STORY (TF)   Paragon Entertainment, 1991

EDWARD A. WARSCHILKA
Agent: Broder Kurland Webb Uffner - Los Angeles,
    213/656-9262

THE LANDLORD   1970 w/William Sawyer
HAROLD AND MAUDE   1972 w/William Sawyer
HEARTS OF THE WEST   MGM/United Artists, 1975
THE BIG BUS   Paramount, 1976
HOUSE CALLS   Universal, 1978
THE MAIN EVENT   Warner Bros., 1979
CHEAPER TO KEEP HER   American Cinema, 1980
RAGGEDY MAN   Universal, 1981
BRAINSTORM   MGM/United Artists, 1983,
    w/Freeman Davies
SIXTEEN CANDLES   Universal, 1984
TWICE IN A LIFETIME   The Yorkin Company, 1985
VIOLETS ARE BLUE   Columbia, 1986
BIG TROUBLE IN LITTLE CHINA   20th Century Fox,
    1986, w/Steve Mirkovich & Mark Roy Warner
HIDING OUT   DEG, 1987
THE RUNNING MAN   Tri-Star, 1987, w/Mark Roy
    Warner & John Wright
RAMBO III   Tri-Star, 1988, w/O. Nicholas Brown,
    Andrew London & James Symons
CHILD'S PLAY   MGM/UA, 1988, w/Roy E. Peterson
CHILD'S PLAY 2   Universal, 1990
DADDY'S DYIN'...WHO'S GOT THE WILL?
    MGM/UA, 1990

EARL WATSON
PINK MOTEL   New Image, 1982
WACKO   Jensen Farley Pictures, 1983, w/Chris Burch
THE FORBIDDEN DANCE   21st Century/Columbia,
    1990, w/Robert Edwards
HOUSE PARTY   New Line Cinema, 1990

ERIC WATSON
MIDNIGHT CROSSING   Vestron, 1988

ROY WATTS
SINBAD AND THE EYE OF THE TIGER
    Columbia, 1977
IT'S NOT THE SIZE THAT COUNTS   Joseph Brenner
    Associates, 1979
GENOCIDE (FD)   Simon Wiesenthal Center, 1981,
    w/Robert Jenkis & Richard Zukaitis
VICE SQUAD   Avco Embassy, 1982
THE BEASTMASTER   MGM/UA, 1982
DEADLY FORCE   Embassy, 1983
TRIUMPHS OF A MAN CALLED HORSE   Jensen
    Farley Pictures, 1983
P.O.W. THE ESCAPE   Cannon, 1986
WHERE ARE THE CHILDREN   Columbia, 1986
THEY STILL CALL ME BRUCE   Shapiro
    Entertainment, 1987
HE'S MY GIRL   Scotti Bros., 1987

LADY BEWARE   Scotti Bros., 1987
THE IRON TRIANGLE   Scotti Bros., 1989
DINNER AT EIGHT (CTF)   Think Entertainment, 1990

PETER WEATHERLEY
THE WATER BABIES   Pethurst International/
    Film Polski, 1978
RISING DAMP   ITC, 1980
ENIGMA   Embassys, 1983, w/Peter Culverwell
CREEPSHOW 2   New World, 1987
THE LADY AND THE HIGHWAYMAN (TF)   Lord Grade
    Productions/Gainsborough Productions, 1989
A GHOST IN MONTE CARLO (CTF)   The Grade
    Company, 1990

KATHIE WEAVER
CRIMEWAVE   Embassy, 1986
FAT GUY GOES NUTZOID   Troma, 1986, w/Krissy
    Boden & Jeffrey Wolfe
COMMANDO SQUAD   Trans World Entertainment, 1987

TONY WEBB
CHANDLER (TF)   R.M. Associates, 1991

BILLY WEBER
DAYS OF HEAVEN   Paramount, 1978
JEKYLL AND HYDE...TOGETHER AGAIN
    Paramount, 1982
48HRS.   Paramount, 1982, w/Freeman Davies &
    Mark Warner
ICEMAN   Universal, 1984
BEVERLY HILLS COP   Paramount, 1984,
    w/Arthur Coburn
THE HOUSE OF GOD   United Artists, 1984,
    w/Robert Wyman
PEE-WEE'S BIG ADVENTURE   Warner Bros., 1985
TOP GUN ★   Paramount, 1986, w/Christopher Lebenzon
BEVERLY HILLS COP II   Paramount, 1987,
    w/Christopher Lebenzon & Michael Tronick
MIDNIGHT RUN   Universal, 1988, w/Chris Lebenzon &
    Michael Tronick
THE PACKAGE   Orion, 1989, w/ Don Zimmerman
DAYS OF THUNDER   Paramount, 1990,
    w/Chris Lebenzon

JULIET WEBER
SECRET HONOR   Cinecom, 1985

FERRIS WEBSTER
THE MAGNIFICENT SEVEN   Unitd Artists, 1960
THE MANCHURIAN CANDIDATE ★   Untied Artists, 1962
THE GREAT ESCAPE ★   United Artists, 1963
SEVEN DAYS IN MAY   Paramount, 1964
SECONDS   Paramount, 1966
THE PICTURE OF DORIAN GRAY (TF)   Dan Curtis
    Productions, 1973
THUNDERBOLT AND LIGHTFOOT   United Artists, 1974
THE EIGER SANCTION   Universal, 1974
THE ENFORCER   Warner Bros., 1976, w/Joel Cox
THE OUTLAW JOSEY WALES   Warner Bros., 1976
THE GAUNTLET   Warner Bros., 1977, w/Joel Cox
EVERY WHICH WAY BUT LOOSE   Warner Bros., 1978,
    w/Joel Cox
ESCAPE FROM ALCATRAZ   Paramount, 1979
BRONCO BILLY   Warner Bros., 1980, w/Joel Cox
ANY WHICH WAY YOU CAN   Warner Bros., 1980,
    w/Ronald G. Spang
HONKYTONK MAN   Warner Bros., 1982,
    w/Joel Cox & Michael Kelly
FIREFOX   Warner Bros., 1982, w/Ronald G. Spang

We

CINEMATOGRAPHERS
PRODUCTION
DESIGNERS,
COSTUME
DESIGNERS AND
FILM EDITORS
GUIDE

F
I
L
M

E
D
I
T
O
R
S

We

CINEMATOGRAPHERS
PRODUCTION
DESIGNERS,
COSTUME
DESIGNERS AND
FILM EDITORS
GUIDE

F
I
L
M

E
D
I
T
O
R
S

GRAHAME WEINBREN
ALPHABET CITY   Atlantic Releasing
 Corporation, 1984
A GREAT WALL   Orion Classics, 1985

JOSEPH WEINTRAUB
THE LEMON SISTERS   Miramax, 1990,
 w/Michael Miller

STEVEN WEISBERG
East & West Coast cards
Agent: The Doug Apatow Agency, 10559 Blythe Ave. -
 Los Angeles, CA 90064, 213/202-6888

GABY, A TRUE STORY   1987, CE
THE WICKEDEST WITCH (FT)   Boo You
 Productions, 1990
THE COLOR OF EVENING   1991, CE

ADAM WEISS
BULL DURHAM   Orion, 1988, w/Robert Leighton

CHUCK WEISS
UPHILL ALL THE WAY   New World, 1986
A NIGHTMARE ON ELM STREET 4: THE
 DREAM MASTER   New Line Cinema, 1988,
 w/Michael Knue
A NIGHTMARE ON ELM STREET 5: THE
 DREAM CHILD   New Line Cinema, 1989,
 w/Brent Schoenfeld

BENJAMIN A. WEISSMAN, ACE
LASSITER   Warner Bros., 1984
NICK KNIGHT (Pilot)   1989
CHILD IN THE NIGHT (TF)   Mike Robe
 Productions, 1989
LOVE AND LIES (TF)   Freyda Rothstein
 Productions, 1990
MURDER IN MISSISSIPPI (TF)   David L. Wolper
 Productions, 1990
SON OF THE MORNING STAR (MS)   The Mount
 Company, 1991

TIM WELLBURN
THE IRISHMAN   Forest Home Films, 1978
CATHY'S CHILD   Roadshow, 1979
CHAIN REACTION   Hoyt, 1980
CADDIE   Atlantic Releasing Corporation, 1981
THE ROAD WARRIOR   Warner Bros., 1982,
 w/Michael Balson & David Stiven
THE KILLING OF ANGEL STREET   Satori, 1983
THE COOLANGATTA GOLD   Film Gallery, 1984
BURKE AND WILLS   Hemdale, 1985
THE FRINGE DWELLERS   Atlantic Releasing
 Corporation, 1987
DANGEROUS GAME   Quantum, 1988

KATHERINE WENNING
Agent: Triad Artists, Inc. - Los Angeles, 213/556-2727

HESTER STREET   Midwest Film Productions, 1975
GIRLFRIENDS   Warner Bros., 1978
THE BOSTONIANS   Almi Pictures, 1984,
 w/Mark Potter
MY LITTLE GIRL   Hemdale, 1987
MAURICE   Cinecom, 1987
SLAVES OF NEW YORK   Tri-Star, 1989

STAYING TOGETHER   Hemdale, 1989
LONGTIME COMPANION   Samuel Goldwyn
 Company, 1990
CRIMINAL JUSTICE (CTF)   Elysian Films, 1990

NICHOLAS WENTWORTH
CRYSTAL HEART   Trans World Entertainment, 1987
COUNTERFORCE (TF)   Golden Sun/ESME, 1991,
 w/J. Anthony Loma

HARRY WERKMEISTER
THE MAGIC SEASON OF ROBERTSON DAVIES
 Canadian Broadcasting Corporation, 1990

DENNIS WERNER
STREET TRASH   Lightning Pictures, 1987

MARK S. WESTMORE
DONOR (TF)   CBS Entertainment Productions, 1990
ONE CUP OF COFFEE   Bullpen/Open Road, 1991

RICHARD E. WESTOVER
TOMBOY   Crown International, 1985
MY CHAUFFEUR   Crown International, 1985
THE PATRIOT   Crown International, 1986
HOLLYWOOD ZAP   Troma, 1986
BEACH FEVER   Crown International, 1987
HUNK   Crown International, 1987

DAN WETHERBEE
MAKING THE GRADE   MGM/UA/Cannon, 1984
THUNDER ALLEY   Cannon, 1985

JOHN W. WHEELER, ACE
Agent: The Gersh Agency, Inc., Beverly Hills -
 213/274-6611, New York - 212/997-1818

FADE-IN   Paramount, 1968
THE STERILE CUCKOO   Paramount, 1969
JENNIFER ON MY MIND   United Artists, 1971
THE PARALLAX VIEW   Paramount, 1974
POSSE   Paramount, 1975
THE BAD NEWS BEARS IN BREAKING TRAINING
 Paramount, 1977
THE ONION FIELD   Avco Embassy, 1979
SERIAL   Paramount, 1980
GOING APE!   Paramount, 1981
THE CHALLENGE   Embassy, 1982
STRANGE INVADERS   Orion, 1983
RHINESTONE   20th Century Fox, 1984, w/Stan Cole
PORKY'S REVENGE   20th Century Fox, 1985
ROCKY IV   MGM/UA, 1985, w/Don Zimmerman
SPACECAMP   20th Century Fox, 1986,
 w/Timothy Board
MILLION DOLLAR MYSTERY   DEG, 1987
SPLIT DECISIONS   New Century/Vista, 1988,
 w/Jeff Freeman & Thomas Stanford
IMPULSE   Warner Bros., 1990

PETER V. WHITE
COMMON GROUND-PARTS I & II (TF)   Daniel H. Blatt
 Productions, 1990
A QUIET LITTLE NEIGHBORHOOD, A PERFECT LITTLE
 MURDER (TF)   Neal and Gary Productions, 1990

RALPHE WIKKE
DIM SUM: A LITTLE BIT OF HEART   Orion
 Classics, 1985

KING WILDER
GHOST TOWN   Trans World Entertainment, 1988,
     w/Peter Teschner

MAIRIN WILKINSON
LANTERN HILL (CTF)   Sullivan Films, 1990

ERIC AUSTIN WILLIAMS
RED HEADED STRANGER   Alive Films, 1986

JOHN WILSON
THE DRAUGHTMAN'S CONTRACT   United Artists
     Classics, 1983
A ZED AND TWO NAUGHTS   Skouras Pictures, 1985
DROWNING BY NUMBERS   Galaxy
     International, 1989
THE COOK, THE THIEF, HIS WIFE & HER LOVER
     Miramax, 1990

ROBIN WILSON
BROTHER FUTURE (TF)   Laneauville/Morris
     Entertainment, 1991

CHRISTOPHER WIMBLE
WETHERBY   MGM/UA Classics, 1985
84 CHARING CROSS ROAD   Columbia, 1987
CRIMINAL LAW   Hemdale, 1989
MURDERERS AMONG US: THE SIMON
     WIESENTHAL STORY (CTF)   Citadel
     Entertainment, 1989, w/Eva Gardos

MAURY WINETROBE, ACE
Agent: Broder Kurland Webb Uffner - Los Angeles, 2
     13/656-9262
Address: 23358 Agnes Avenue, Studio City, CA
     91604, 818/716-1544

THE WRECKING CREW   Columbia, 1966
FUNNY GIRL ★   Columbia, 1968, w/William
     Sands & Robert Swink
CACTUS FLOWER   Columbia, 1969
GETTING STRAIGHT   Columbia, 1970
SUMMERTREE   Columbia, 1971
T.R. BASKIN   Paramount, 1971
LAST OF THE RED HOT LOVERS   Paramount, 1972
LOST HORIZON   Columbia, 1972
MAME   Warner Bros., 1974
FUNNY LADY   Columbia, 1975
FROM NOON TILL THREE   United Artists, 1976
TWILIGHT'S LAST GLEAMING   Allied Artists, 1977
THE CHOIRBOYS   Universal, 1977, w/William
     Martin & Irving Rosenblum
ICE CASTLES   Columbia, 1979, w/Michael Kahn &
     Melvin Shapiro
THE FRISCO KID   Warner Bros., 1979, w/Jack
     Horger & Irving Rosenblum
THE RAVAGERS   Columbia, 1979
THE BLACK MARBLE   Avco Embassy, 1980
THE JAZZ SINGER   AFD, 1980
TAPS   20th Century Fox, 1981
VISION QUEST   Warner Bros., 1985
THE BOOST   Hemdale, 1988

RAY WINGROVE
MOTHER LOVE-PARTS I & II (MS)   BBC TV, 1990

RALPH E. WINTERS, ACE
Agent: Broder Kurland Webb Uffner - Los Angeles,
     213/656-9262
Address: 4454 Ventura Canyon Avenue, Sherman Oaks,
     CA 91423, 818/995-3104

THE PINK PANTHER   United Artists, 1964
THE GREAT RACE   Warner Bros., 1965
FITZWILLY   United Artists, 1967
HOW TO SUCCEED IN BUSINESS WITHOUT REALLY
     TRYING   United Artists, 1967
THE THOMAS CROWN AFFAIR   United Artists, 1968
THE PARTY   United Artists, 1968
GAILY, GAILY   United Artists, 1969
THE HAWAIIANS   United Artists, 1970
KOTCH ★   Cinerama Releasing Corporation, 1971
THE CAREY TREATMENT   MGM, 1972
THE OUTFIT   MGM, 1974
THE ALL-AMERICAN BOY   Warner Bros., 1973
THE FRONT PAGE   Universal, 1974
THE SPIKES GANG   United Artists, 1974
MR. MAJESTYK   United Artists, 1974
KING KONG   Paramount, 1976
ORCA   Paramount, 1977, w/John Bloom &
     Marion Rothman
10   Orion/Warner Bros., 1979
THE AMERICAN SUCCESS CO.   Columbia, 1979
S.O.B.   Paramount, 1981
VICTOR/VICTORIA   MGM/United Artists, 1982
THE CURSE OF THE PINK PANTHER   MGM/UA, 1983
THE MAN WHO LOVED WOMEN   Columbia, 1983
MICKI AND MAUDE   Columbia, 1984
BIG TROUBLE   Columbia, 1986, w/Donn Cambern
LET'S GET HARRY   Tri-Star, 1986, w/Robert Hyams &
     Rick R. Sparr
TAGGET (CTF)   Mirisch Films, 1991, w/Robert Hyams

JEFF WISHENGRAD
THE CHOCOLATE WAR   MCEG, 1988

RON WISMAN
SHOOT   Avco Embassy, 1976, w/Peter Shatalow
THE HAUNTING OF JULIA   Discovery Films, 1977
FISH HAWK   Avco Embassy, 1981
THE HIGH COUNTRY   Crown International, 1981
TICKET TO HEAVEN   United Artists Classics, 1981
THE TERRY FOX STORY   20th Century Fox, 1983
NIGHT EYES *THE RATS*   Warner Bros., 1983
HARRY TRACY   Quartet/Films Inc., 1983
DRAW! (CTF)   HBO Premiere Films/Astral Film
     Productions/ICC, 1984
SPECIAL PEOPLE: BASED ON A TRUE STORY (TF)
     Joe Cates Productions/CTV Broadcasting
     Corporation, 1984
JOSHUA THEN AND NOW   20th Century Fox, 1985
THE UNDERGRADS (CTF)   Sharmhill Productions/Walt
     Disney Productions, 1986
SEPARATE VACATIONS   RSK Entertainment, 1986
ROLLING VENGEANCE   Apollo Pictures, 1987
MILLENNIUM   Fox, 1989
LOVE AND MURDER   Norstar Entertainment, 1989
BEAUTIFUL DREAMERS   Cinexus/Famous
     Players, 1990
THE LITTLE KIDNAPPERS (CTF)   Resnick/Margellos
     Productions, 1990
YOUNG CATHERINE-PARTS I & II (CMS)   Consolidated
     Entertainment, 1991

JACQUES WITTA
ONE DEADLY SUMMER   Universal Classics, 1984

Wi

CINEMATOGRAPHERS
PRODUCTION
DESIGNERS,
COSTUME
DESIGNERS AND
FILM EDITORS
GUIDE

F
I
L
M

E
D
I
T
O
R
S

CINEMATOGRAPHERS
PRODUCTION
DESIGNERS,
COSTUME
DESIGNERS and
FILM EDITORS
GUIDE

F
I
L
M

E
D
I
T
O
R
S

KARL WOITACH
WHAT'S UP, DOC? (CTF)   Communications Inc.,
   1990, w/Dave Haggerty

JEFFREY WOLF
East and West Coast Cards
Agent: Writers & Artists Agency - Los Angeles,
   213/820-2240

FAT GUY GOES NUTZOID   Troma, 1986
HEAT   New Century/Vista, 1987
THE IN CROWD   Orion, 1988
PENN & TELLER GET KILLED   Warner Bros., 1989
ANDRE'S MOTHER   American Playhouse, 1990

ADAM WOLFE
PENNY ANTE   Andrew Solt Productions, 1990

ROBERT L. WOLFE
STRAW DOGS   Cinerama Releasing
   Corporation, 1972
THE GETAWAY   National General, 1972
JUNIOR BONNER   Cinerama Releasing
   Corporation, 1973
PAT GARRETT & BILLY THE KID   MGM, 1973
THE NAKED APE   1974
THE TERMINAL MAN   Warner Bros., 1974
THE WIND AND THE LION   MGM/United Artists, 1975
ALL THE PRESIDENT'S MEN ★   Warner Bros., 1976
THE DEEP   Columbia, 1977, SE
BIG WEDNESDAY   Warner Bros., 1978,
   w/C. Timothy O'Meara
THE ROSE ★   20th Century Fox, 1979,
   w/C. Timothy O'Meara
THE HUNTER   Paramount, 1980
ON GOLDEN POND ★   Universal, 1981

SYDNEY WOLINSKY
Agent: The Gersh Agency, Inc., Beverly Hills -
   213/274-6611, New York - 212/997-1818

YOUNG DOCTORS IN LOVE   20th Century Fox, 1982
MY TUTOR   Crown International, 1983
BEST DEFENSE   Paramount, 1984
ONE MAGIC CHRISTMAS   Buena Vista, 1985
HOWARD THE DUCK   Universal, 1986,
   w/Michael Chandler
MAID TO ORDER   New Century/Vista, 1987
ALMOST GROWN (Pilot)   1988
WORTH WINNING   20th Century Fox, 1989
THE CHINA LAKE MURDERS (CTF)   Papazian-
   Hirsch Entertainment, 1990

GARY WOODYARD
RETURN TO SNOWY RIVER   Buena Vista, 1988

ERIC WRATE
HIGH-BALLIN'   American International, 1978
HIGHPOINT   New World, 1984

JOHN WRIGHT
Agent: Broder Kurland Webb Uffner - Los Angeles,
   213/656-9262

CONVOY   United Artists, 1978, w/Graeme Clifford &
   Garth Craven
ONLY WHEN I LAUGH   Columbia, 1981
FRANCES   Universal/AFD, 1982
SEPARATE WAYS   Crown International, 1983

HEARTSOUNDS (TF)   Embassy TV, 1984
MASS APPEAL   Universal, 1984
EXPLORERS   Paramount, 1985
THE RUNNING MAN   Tri-Star, 1987, w/Mark Roy
   Warner & Edward A. Warschilka
GLEAMING THE CUBE   20th Century Fox, 1989
MY NAME IS BILL W. (TF) ☆   1989, w/Paul Rubell
THE HUNT FOR RED OCTOBER ★   Paramount, 1990,
   w/Dennis Virkler
SARAH, PLAIN AND TALL (TF)   Self Help
   Productions, 1991

ROBERT WYMAN
AN EYE FOR AN EYE   Creative Film Enterprises, 1966
ROSEMARY'S BABY   Paramount, 1968
THE APRIL FOOLS   National General, 1969
WUSA   Paramount, 1970
SOMETIMES A GREAT NOTION   Universal, 1971
POCKET MONEY   National General, 1972
THE LAUGHING POLICEMAN   20th Century Fox, 1973
THE PRISONER OF SECOND AVENUE   Warner
   Bros., 1975
LOGAN'S RUN   MGM/United Artists, 1976
GREASED LIGHTNING   Warner Bros., 1977,
   w/Christopher Holmes & Randy Roberts
TILT   Warner Bros., 1979, w/Don Guidice
PROMISES IN THE DARK   Orion/Warner Bros., 1979
LOVE CHILD   The Ladd Company/Warner Bros., 1982
THE HOUSE OF GOD   United Artists, 1984,
   w/Billy Weber
HARD TO HOLD   Universal, 1984
POLICE ACADEMY 2: THEIR FIRST ASSIGNMENT
   Warner Bros., 1985
MUDER AT THE PTL LUNCHEON (TF)   Patrick K.
   Meyers Productions, 1990
THE COURT-MARTIAL OF JACKIE ROBINSON (CTF)
   von Zerneck-Sertner Films, 1990, w/Eric Sears

Y

BILL YAHRAUS
HEARTLAND   Levitt-Pickman, 1979
SAMMY STOPS THE WORLD (FD)   Elkins, 1979
COUNTRY   Buena Vista, 1984
NO MERCY   Tri-Star, 1986, w/Jerry Greenberg
PASS THE AMMO   New Century/Vista, 1987
FAR NORTH   Alive Films, 1988
THE FINAL DAYS (TF)   The Samuels Film
   Company, 1990
THE LONG WALK HOME   Miramax, 1990

GAIL YASUNAGA
CIRCLE OF POWER   Televicine, 1983
BAJA OKLAHOMA (CTF)   HBO Pictures, 1988,
   w/John Carnochen
MY BEST FRIEND IS A VAMPIRE   Kings Road, 1988,
   w/Janice Hampton

MARIE-JOSEPHE YOYOTTE
NEXT SUMMER   European Classics, 1986
ONE WOMAN OR TWO   Orion Classics, 1987

Z

KEN ZEMKE
THE PIRATE MOVIE   20th Century Fox, 1982
CAME A HOT FRIDAY   Orion Classics, 1985
THE NEW ADVENTURES OF PIPPI LONGSTOCKING
    Columbia, 1988

BARRY ZETLIN
GALAXY OF TERROR   New World, 1981,
    w/Larry Bock
ANGEL OF H.E.A.T.   Summa Vista, 1982
SORCERESS   New World, 1983, w/Larry Bock
BAD MANNERS   New World, 1984
BREAKIN 2: ELECTRIC BOOGALOO   Tri-Star,
    1984, w/Sally Allen, Bert Glatstein & Bob Jenkis
GRUNT! THE WRESTLING MOVIE   New World,
    1985, w/Allan Holzman
BREEDERS   Empire Pictures, 1986
HUNTER'S BLOOD   Concorde, 1987
NECROPOLIS   Empire Pictures, 1987,
    w/Tom Meshelski
ASSAULT OF THE KILLER BIMBOS   Empire
    Pictures, 1988
FRIDAY THE 13TH PART VII - THE NEW BLOOD
    Paramount, 1988, w/Maureen O'Connell &
    Martin Jay Sadoff
SORORITY BABES IN THE SLIMEBALL BOWL-A-RAMA
    Urban Classics, 1988, w/Tom Meshelski
TRUST ME   Cinecom, 1989
FLIGHT OF BLACK ANGEL (CTF)   Hess-Kallberg
    Productions, 1991

DON ZIMMERMAN, ACE
Agent: The Gersh Agency, Inc., Beverly Hills -
    213/274-6611, New York - 212/997-1818

COMING HOME ★   United Artists, 1978
HEAVEN CAN WAIT   Paramount, 1978,
    w/Robert C. Jones
UNCLE JOE SHANNON   United Artists, 1978
BEING THERE   United Artists, 1979
A CHANGE OF SEASONS   20th Century Fox, 1980
BARBAROSA   Universal/AFD, 1982, w/David Ramirez
ROCKY III   MGM/UA, 1982, w/Mark Warner
BEST FRIENDS   Warner Bros., 1982
STAYING ALIVE   Paramount, 1983, w/Mark Warner
TEACHERS   MGM/UA, 1984
ROCKY IV   MGM/UA, 1985, w/John W. Wheeler
COBRA   Warner Bros., 1986, w/James Symons
OVER THE TOP   Cannon, 1986, w/James Symons
FATAL BEAUTY   MGM/UA, 1987
EVERYBODY'S ALL-AMERICAN   Warner Bros., 1988
THE PACKAGE   Orion, 1989, w/Billy Weber
NAVY SEALS   Orion, 1990

CATHERINE ZINA
HOTEL TERMINUS: KLAUS BARBIE, HIS LIFE AND
    TIMES (FD)   Samuel Goldwyn Company, 1988,
    w/Albert Jurgenson

ROZANNE ZINGALE
DECEPTIONS (CTF)   Republic Pictures, 1989

PETER ZINNER, ACE
Agent: Broder Kurland Webb Uffner - Los Angeles,
    213/656-9262
Address: 334 Arno Way, Pacific Palisades, CA 90272,
    213/454-6691

THE PROFESSIONALS   American International, 1960
KING KONG VS. GODZILLA   Universal, 1963
GUNN   Warner Bros., 1967
IN COLD BLOOD   Columbia, 1967
CHANGES   Cinerama Releasing Corporation, 1969
DARLING LILI   Paramount, 1970
THE RED TENT   1971
THE GODFATHER ★   Paramount, 1972,
    w/William Reynolds
THE GODFATHER, PART II   Paramount, 1974
MAHOGANY   Paramount, 1975
FOXTROT   New World, 1976
A STAR IS BORN   Warner Bros., 1976
THE DEER HUNTER ★★   Universal, 1978
THE FISH THAT SAVED PITTSBURGH   United
    Artists, 1979
FOOLIN' AROUND   Columbia, 1980
AN OFFICER AND A GENTLEMAN ★   Paramount, 1982
WAR AND LOVE   Cannon, 1985
SAVING GRACE   Columbia, 1986, Supervisor
WAR AND REMEMBRANCE (MS) ☆   Dan Curtis
    Productions, 1988, w/John F. Burnett
THE HUNT FOR RED OCTOBER ★   Paramount, 1990
ETERNITY   THE AVATAR   Paul Entertainment, 1990,
    w/Christopher Greenbury & Michael Sheridan
SOMEBODY HAS TO SHOOT THE PICTURE (CTF)
    Alan Barnette Productions, 1990

LUIGI ZITA
CAMORRA   Cannon, 1985
SOTTO, SOTTO   Triumph, 1985

★ ★ ★ ★

Zi

CINEMATOGRAPHERS
PRODUCTION
DESIGNERS,
COSTUME
DESIGNERS AND
FILM EDITORS
GUIDE

F
I
L
M

E
D
I
T
O
R
S

I N D I C E S

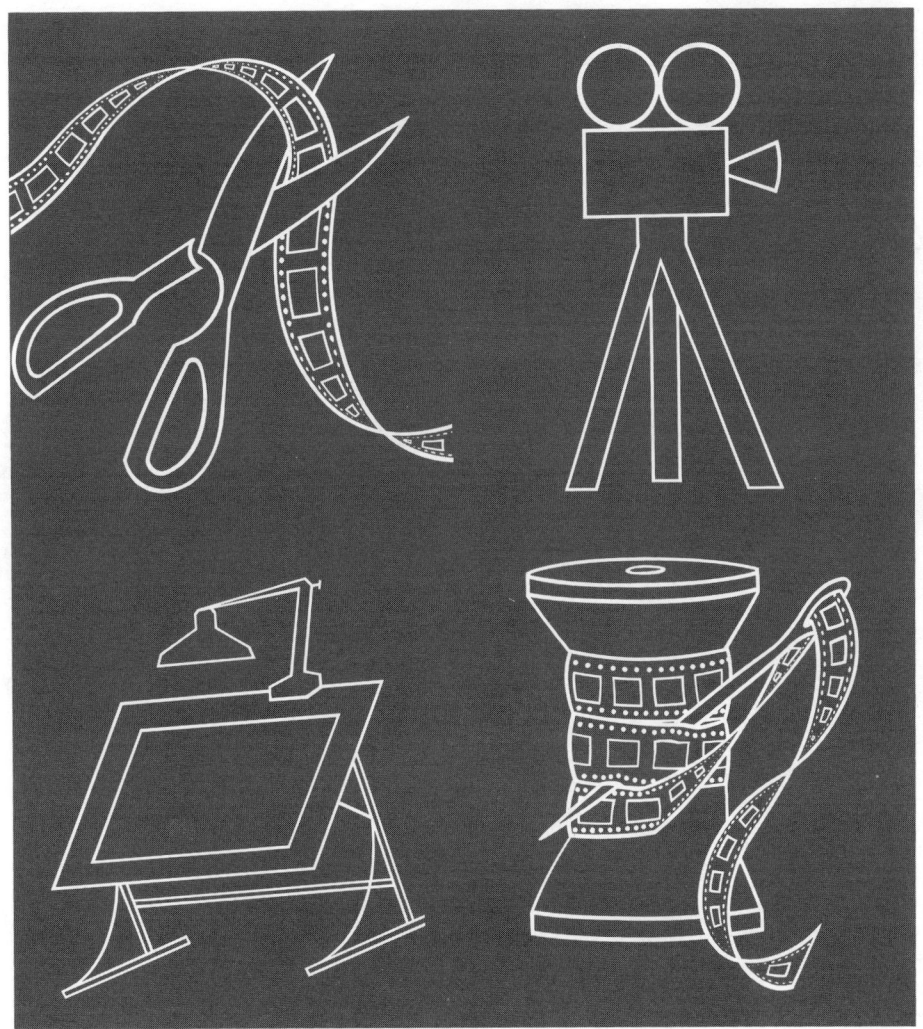

F I L M   T I T L E S
AGENTS & MANAGERS · ADVERTISERS

TAKE A FEW MINUTES TO GO THROUGH YOUR GARBAGE.

Every Sunday, more than 500,000 trees are used to produce the 88% of newspapers that are never recycled.

We throw away enough glass bottles and jars to fill the 1,350-foot twin towers of New York's World Trade Center *every two weeks.*

Americans go through 2.5 million plastic bottles *every hour,* only a small percentage of which are now recycled.

American consumers and industry throw away enough aluminum to rebuild our entire commercial airfleet *every three months.*

Every year we dispose of *24 million tons* of leaves and grass clippings, which could be composted to conserve landfill space.

We throw away enough iron and steel to *continuously* supply all the nation's automakers.

The ordinary bag of trash you throw away is slowly becoming a serious problem for everybody.

Because the fact is, not only are we running out of resources to make the products we need, we're running out of places to put what's left over.

Write the Environmental Defense Fund at: 257 Park Avenue South, New York, NY 10010, for a free brochure that will tell you virtually everything you'll need to know about recycling.

One thing's for certain, the few minutes you take to learn how to recycle will spare us all a lot of garbage later.

IF YOU'RE NOT RECYCLING SM **YOU'RE THROWING IT ALL AWAY.**

© 1988 EDF

INDEX OF FILM TITLES

$-1918

CINEMATOGRAPHERS
PRODUCTION
DESIGNERS,
COSTUME
DESIGNERS AND
FILM EDITORS
GUIDE

Note: This is not a listing of all films, only those listed in this book.

† = deceased

CINEMATOGRAPHERS
PRODUCTION
DESIGNERS,
COSTUME
DESIGNERS and
FILM EDITORS
GUIDE

I
N
D
E
X

O
F

F
I
L
M

T
I
T
L
E
S

1919
IVAN STRASSBURG .... CINEMATOGRAPHER

1941
WILLIAM A. FRAKER .... CINEMATOGRAPHER
DEAN E. MITZNER .... PRODUCTION DESIGNER
WILLIAM F. O'BRIEN .... PRODUCTION DESIGNER
DEBORAH NADOOLMAN .... COSTUME DESIGNER
MICHAEL KAHN .... FILM EDITOR

1969
JULES BRENNER .... CINEMATOGRAPHER
MARCIA HINDS .... PRODUCTION DESIGNER
JULIE WEISS .... COSTUME DESIGNER
WILLIAM M. ANDERSON .... FILM EDITOR

1984
ROGER DEAKINS .... CINEMATOGRAPHER
ALLAN CAMERON .... PRODUCTION DESIGNER
MARTYN HEBERT .... PRODUCTION DESIGNER
EMMA PORTEUS .... COSTUME DESIGNER
TOM PRIESTLEY .... FILM EDITOR

2000 YEARS LATER
DONN CAMBERN .... FILM EDITOR

2001: A SPACE ODYSSEY
JOHN ALCOTT† .... CINEMATOGRAPHER
ANTHONY MASTERS .... PRODUCTION DESIGNER
RAY LOVEJOY .... FILM EDITOR

2010
PETER HYAMS .... CINEMATOGRAPHER
ALBERT BRENNER .... PRODUCTION DESIGNER
PATRICIA NORRIS .... COSTUME DESIGNER
JAMES MITCHELL .... FILM EDITOR
MIA GOLDMAN .... FILM EDITOR

3000
CHARLES D. (CHUCK) MINSKY .... CINEMATOGRAPHER
ALBERT BRENNER .... PRODUCTION DESIGNER
PRISCILLA ANNE NEDD .... FILM EDITOR1990: THE BRONX WARRIORS
SERGIO SALVATI .... CINEMATOGRAPHER

A

A.D. ANNO DOMINI (MS)
ENRICO SABBATINI .... COSTUME DESIGNER

AARON LOVES ANGELA
GENE RUDOLF .... PRODUCTION DESIGNER

AARON'S WAY: THE HARVEST
RON HAGEN .... CINEMATOGRAPHER

ABBA - THE MOVIE
PAUL ONORATO .... CINEMATOGRAPHER
PAUL ONORATO .... PRODUCTION DESIGNER

ABDICATION, THE
GEOFFREY UNSWORTH† .... CINEMATOGRAPHER

ABOUT LAST NIGHT
ANDREW DINTENFASS .... CINEMATOGRAPHER
IDA RANDOM .... PRODUCTION DESIGNER
WILLIAM A. ELLIOT .... PRODUCTION DESIGNER
DEBORAH L. SCOTT .... COSTUME DESIGNER
HARRY KERAMIDAS .... FILM EDITOR

ABOVE THE LAW
ROBERT STEADMAN .... CINEMATOGRAPHER
MAHER AHMAD .... PRODUCTION DESIGNER
MICHAEL BROWN .... FILM EDITOR

ABSENCE OF MALICE
OWEN ROIZMAN .... CINEMATOGRAPHER
TERENCE MARSH .... PRODUCTION DESIGNER
BERNIE POLLACK .... COSTUME DESIGNER
SHELDON KAHN .... FILM EDITOR

ABSOLUTE BEGINNERS
OLIVER STAPLETON .... CINEMATOGRAPHER
JOHN BEARD .... PRODUCTION DESIGNER
DAVID PERRY .... COSTUME DESIGNER
SUE BLANE .... COSTUME DESIGNER
GERRY HAMBLING .... FILM EDITOR
MICHAEL BRADSELL .... FILM EDITOR
RICHARD BEDFORD .... FILM EDITOR
RUSSELL LLOYD .... FILM EDITOR

ABSOLUTION
JOHN COQUILLON .... CINEMATOGRAPHER
NATASHA KROLL .... PRODUCTION DESIGNER
JOHN VICTOR SMITH .... FILM EDITOR

ABYSS, THE
MIKAEL SALOMON .... CINEMATOGRAPHER
JOSEPH C. NEMEC III .... PRODUCTION DESIGNER
LESLIE DILLEY .... PRODUCTION DESIGNER
PETER CHILDS .... PRODUCTION DESIGNER
RUSSELL CHRISTIAN .... PRODUCTION DESIGNER
DEBORAH EVERTON .... COSTUME DESIGNER
JOEL GOODMAN .... FILM EDITOR

ACADEMY AWARDS TELECAST (TV)
BOB MACKIE .... COSTUME DESIGNER

ACCEPTABLE RISKS (TF)
JAMES G. HULSEY .... PRODUCTION DESIGNER
MICHAEL JABLOW .... FILM EDITOR

ACCIDENTAL TOURIST
JOHN BAILEY .... CINEMATOGRAPHER
ROBERT W. (BO) WELCH .... PRODUCTION DESIGNER
TOM DUFFIELD .... PRODUCTION DESIGNER
RUTH MYERS .... COSTUME DESIGNER
CAROL LITTLETON .... FILM EDITOR

ACCUSED, THE
RALF D. BODE .... CINEMATOGRAPHER
RICHARD WILCOX .... PRODUCTION DESIGNER
TRISH KEETING .... COSTUME DESIGNER
GERALD B. GREENBERG .... FILM EDITOR
O. NICHOLAS BROWN .... FILM EDITOR

ACE EIL AND RODGER OF THE SKIES
JACK MARTIN SMITH .... PRODUCTION DESIGNER
JOEL SCHILLER .... PRODUCTION DESIGNER

ACES HIGH
GERRY FISHER .... CINEMATOGRAPHER
ANNE V. COATES .... FILM EDITOR

ACROSS 110TH ST.
JACK PRIESTLEY .... CINEMATOGRAPHER
ACROSS THE GREAT DIVIDE
ROBERT BROWN .... FILM EDITOR

ACROSS THE TRACKS
FARREL LEVY .... FILM EDITOR

ACT OF VENGEANCE
MALCOLM COOKE .... FILM EDITOR

ACTION JACKSON
MATTHEW F. LEONETTI .... CINEMATOGRAPHER
VIRGINIA RANDOLPH .... PRODUCTION DESIGNER
MARILYN VANCE-STRAKER .... COSTUME DESIGNER
MARK HELFRICH .... FILM EDITOR

ACTION U.S.A.
THOMAS L. CALLAWAY .... CINEMATOGRAPHER
GABRIELLE GILBERT .... FILM EDITOR

ADAM AT SIX A.M.
CHARLES ROSHER, JR. .... CINEMATOGRAPHER

ADIOS AMIGO
EVA RUGGIERO .... FILM EDITOR
GENE RUGGIERO .... FILM EDITOR

ADOPTION
LAJOS KOLTAI .... CINEMATOGRAPHER
LUCIANO TOVOLI .... CINEMATOGRAPHER

ADVENTURE CONTINUES, THE (TF)
MINA MITTELMAN .... COSTUME DESIGNER

ADVENTURE OF SHERLOCK HOLMES' SMARTER BROTHER, THE
GERRY FISHER .... CINEMATOGRAPHER
TERENCE MARSH .... PRODUCTION DESIGNER
RUTH MYERS .... COSTUME DESIGNER
JIM CLARK .... FILM EDITOR

ADVENTURE OF THE ACTION HUNTERS
DAVID INSLEY .... CINEMATOGRAPHER
VINCENT PERANIO .... PRODUCTION DESIGNER

ADVENTURERS, THE
ANNE V. COATES .... FILM EDITOR

Ad-Al

CINEMATOGRAPHERS
PRODUCTION
DESIGNERS,
COSTUME
DESIGNERS AND
FILM EDITORS
GUIDE

I
N
D
E
X

O
F

F
I
L
M

T
I
T
L
E
S

AI-AI

CINEMATOGRAPHERS
PRODUCTION
DESIGNERS,
COSTUME
DESIGNERS and
FILM EDITORS
GUIDE

I
N
D
E
X

O
F

F
I
L
M

T
I
T
L
E
S

Al-Am

CINEMATOGRAPHERS
PRODUCTION
DESIGNERS,
COSTUME
DESIGNERS AND
FILM EDITORS
GUIDE

Am-An

CINEMATOGRAPHERS
PRODUCTION
DESIGNERS,
COSTUME
DESIGNERS AND
FILM EDITORS
GUIDE

I
N
D
E
X

O
F

F
I
L
M

T
I
T
L
E
S

ANGEL BABY
HASKELL WEXLER .... CINEMATOGRAPHER

ANGEL HEART
MICHAEL SERESIN .... CINEMATOGRAPHER
ARMIN GANZ .... PRODUCTION DESIGNER
BRIAN MORRIS .... PRODUCTION DESIGNER
KRISTI ZEA .... PRODUCTION DESIGNER
AUDE BRONSON-HOWARD .... COSTUME DESIGNER
GERRY HAMBLING .... FILM EDITOR

ANGEL III: THE FINAL CHAPTER
HOWARD WEXLER .... CINEMATOGRAPHER
WARREN CHADWICK .... FILM EDITOR

ANGEL OF DEATH (TF)
SHELLY JOHNSON .... CINEMATOGRAPHER
STEWART CAMPBELL .... PRODUCTION DESIGNER
JOHN DUFFY .... FILM EDITOR

ANGEL OF H.E.A.T.
JACQUES HAITKIN .... CINEMATOGRAPHER
BARRY ZETLIN .... FILM EDITOR

ANGEL TOWN
JOHN LEBLANC .... CINEMATOGRAPHER
BRIAN DENSMORE .... PRODUCTION DESIGNER
STEPHEN CHUDEJ .... COSTUME DESIGNER
DUANE HARTZELL .... FILM EDITOR

ANGELA
MARC CHAMPION ....: CINEMATOGRAPHER
YVES LANGLOIS .... FILM EDITOR

ANGELA
SEAMUS FLANNERY .... PRODUCTION DESIGNER

ANGELO MY LOVE
JOSEPH FRIEDMAN .... CINEMATOGRAPHER

ANGELS BRIGADE
DEAN CUNDEY .... CINEMATOGRAPHER

ANGELS HARD AS THEY COME
STEPHEN M. KATZ .... CINEMATOGRAPHER

ANGRY SILENCE, THE
RAYMOND SIMM .... PRODUCTION DESIGNER

ANIMAL BEHAVIOR
RICHARD BOWEN .... CINEMATOGRAPHER
DAVID SPELLVIN .... CINEMATOGRAPHER
J.ENNINE CLAUDIA OPPEWALL .... PRODUCTION DESIGNER
DURINDA RICE WOOD .... COSTUME DESIGNER
JOSEPH WEINTRAUB .... FILM EDITOR

ANIMAL HOUSE
GEORGE FOLSEY JR.* .... FILM EDITOR

ANN-MARGRET - HOLLYWOOD MOVIE GIRLS (TV)
BOB MACKIE .... COSTUME DESIGNER

ANNA
BOBBY BUKOWSKI .... CINEMATOGRAPHER
LESTER COHEN .... PRODUCTION DESIGNER
HALI BREINDEL .... COSTUME DESIGNER
JULIE SLOANE .... FILM EDITOR

ANNA KARENINA (TF)
KELVIN PIKE .... CINEMATOGRAPHER

ANNE OF GREEN GABLES (MS)
CAROL SPIER .... PRODUCTION DESIGNER

ANNE OF THE THOUSAND DAYS
ARTHUR IBBETSON .... CINEMATOGRAPHER

ANNIE
RICHARD MOORE .... CINEMATOGRAPHER
DALE HENNESY† .... PRODUCTION DESIGNER
ROBERT GUERRA .... PRODUCTION DESIGNER
THEONI V. ALDREDGE .... COSTUME DESIGNER
MARGARET BOOTH .... FILM EDITOR

ANNIE HALL
GORDON WILLIS .... CINEMATOGRAPHER
MEL BOURNE .... PRODUCTION DESIGNER
RUTH MORLEY .... COSTUME DESIGNER
RALPH ROSENBLUM .... FILM EDITOR
WENDY BRICMONT .... FILM EDITOR

ANNIHILATORS, THE
DANIEL GROSS .... FILM EDITOR

ANNIVERSARY, THE
HARRY WAXMAN .... CINEMATOGRAPHER

ANOTHER 48 HRS
MATTHEW F. LEONETTI .... CINEMATOGRAPHER
JOSEPH C. NEMEC III .... PRODUCTION DESIGNER
DAN MOORE .... COSTUME DESIGNER
CARMEL DAVIES .... FILM EDITOR
DONN ARON .... FILM EDITOR
FREEMAN DAVIES .... FILM EDITOR

ANOTHER CHANCE
RICHARD C. GLOUNER .... CINEMATOGRAPHER

ANOTHER COUNTRY
PETER BIZIOU .... CINEMATOGRAPHER
BRIAN MORRIS .... PRODUCTION DESIGNER
CLINTON CAVERS .... PRODUCTION DESIGNER
GERRY HAMBLING .... FILM EDITOR

ANOTHER TIME, ANOTHER PLACE
ROGER DEAKINS .... CINEMATOGRAPHER
LOUISE FROGLEY .... COSTUME DESIGNER
TOM PRIESTLEY .... FILM EDITOR

ANOTHER WOMAN
SVEN NYKVIST .... CINEMATOGRAPHER
SANTO LOQUASTO .... PRODUCTION DESIGNER
JEFFREY KURLAND .... COSTUME DESIGNER
SUSAN E. MORSE .... FILM EDITOR

ANTONY AND CLEOPATRA
ERIC BOYD-PERKINS .... FILM EDITOR

ANY WEDNESDAY
ALFRED SWEENEY .... PRODUCTION DESIGNER

ANY WHICH WAY YOU CAN
DAVID WORTH .... CINEMATOGRAPHER
WILLIAM J. CREBER .... PRODUCTION DESIGNER
GLENN WRIGHT .... COSTUME DESIGNER
FERRIS WEBSTER .... FILM EDITOR
RONALD G. SPANG .... FILM EDITOR

ANYTHING BUT LOVE (PILOT)
RONALD W. BROWNE .... CINEMATOGRAPHER

APARTMENT ZERO
MIGUEL RODRIGUEZ .... CINEMATOGRAPHER

APARTMENT, THE
ALEXANDER TRAUNER .... PRODUCTION DESIGNER

APOCALYPSE NOW
VITTORIO STORARO .... CINEMATOGRAPHER
ANGELO GRAHAM .... PRODUCTION DESIGNER
DEAN TAVOULARIS .... PRODUCTION DESIGNER
CHARLES JAMES .... COSTUME DESIGNER
GERALD B. GREENBERG .... FILM EDITOR
LISA FRUCHTMAN .... FILM EDITOR
RICHARD MARKS .... FILM EDITOR
WALTER MURCH .... FILM EDITOR

APOLOGY (CTF)
BEN EDWARDS .... PRODUCTION DESIGNER
ENID HARRIS .... COSTUME DESIGNER

APPLE DUMPLING GANG RIDES AGAIN,THE
FRANK PHILLIPS .... CINEMATOGRAPHER

APPLE DUMPLING GANG,THE
FRANK PHILLIPS .... CINEMATOGRAPHER

APPOINTMENT WITH DEATH
DAVID GURFINKEL .... CINEMATOGRAPHER
JOHN BLEZARD .... PRODUCTION DESIGNER
JOHN BLOOMFIELD .... COSTUME DESIGNER
ARNOLD CRUST .... FILM EDITOR

APPOINTMENTS OF DENNIS JENNINGS, THE
FRANK PRINZI .... CINEMATOGRAPHER
ARMIN GANZ .... PRODUCTION DESIGNER
PETER C. FRANK .... FILM EDITOR

APPRENTICE TO MURDER
KELVIN PIKE .... CINEMATOGRAPHER
GREGORY BOLTON .... PRODUCTION DESIGNER
ELIZABETH ANN SELEY .... COSTUME DESIGNER
PATRICK MCMAHON .... FILM EDITOR

An-Ap

CINEMATOGRAPHERS
PRODUCTION
DESIGNERS,
COSTUME
DESIGNERS AND
FILM EDITORS
GUIDE

I
N
D
E
X

O
F

F
I
L
M

T
I
T
L
E
S

Ap-Au

CINEMATOGRAPHERS
PRODUCTION
DESIGNERS,
COSTUME
DESIGNERS and
FILM EDITORS
GUIDE

I
N
D
E
X

O
F

F
I
L
M

T
I
T
L
E
S

AUTHOR! AUTHOR!
VICTOR J. KEMPER .... CINEMATOGRAPHER
GENE RUDOLF .... PRODUCTION DESIGNER
GLORIA GRESHAM .... COSTUME DESIGNER
WILLIAM REYNOLDS .... FILM EDITOR

AUTOBIOGRAPHY OF A PRINCESS
WALTER LASSALLY .... CINEMATOGRAPHER

AUTOBIOGRAPHY OF MISS JANE PITTMAN, THE (TF)
MICHAEL D. HALLER .... PRODUCTION DESIGNER
SANDRA STEWART .... COSTUME DESIGNER
SIDNEY LEVIN .... FILM EDITOR

AUTOGRAPH, THE
MICHAEL BALLHAUS .... CINEMATOGRAPHER

AUTUMN SONATA
SVEN NYKVIST .... CINEMATOGRAPHER

AVALANCHE
PIERRE WILLIAM GLENN .... CINEMATOGRAPHER
SHARON COMPTON .... PRODUCTION DESIGNER

AVALANCHE EXPRESS
JACK CARDIFF .... CINEMATOGRAPHER
FRED TUCH .... PRODUCTION DESIGNER
GARTH CRAVEN .... FILM EDITOR

AVALON
ALLEN DAVIAU .... CINEMATOGRAPHER
NORMAN REYNOLDS .... PRODUCTION DESIGNER
GLORIA GRESHAM .... COSTUME DESIGNER
STU LINDER .... FILM EDITOR

AVANTI!
FERDINANDO SCARFIOTTI .... PRODUCTION DESIGNER

AVENGERS OF THE REEF
PETER JAMES .... CINEMATOGRAPHER

AVENGING ANGEL
PETER LYONS COLLISTER .... CINEMATOGRAPHER
STEPHEN MARSH .... PRODUCTION DESIGNER
JOHN BOWEY .... FILM EDITOR

AVENGING FORCE
GIDEON PORATH .... CINEMATOGRAPHER
BO JOHNSON .... PRODUCTION DESIGNER
MARCIA HINDS .... PRODUCTION DESIGNER
AUDREY BANSMER .... COSTUME DESIGNER
MICHAEL J. DUTHIE .... FILM EDITOR

AVERAGE MAN, AN
MARIO VULPIANI .... CINEMATOGRAPHER

AVIATOR'S WIFE, THE
BERNARD LUTIC .... CINEMATOGRAPHER

AVIATOR, THE
DAVID CONNELL .... CINEMATOGRAPHER
BRENTON SWIFT .... PRODUCTION DESIGNER
DUSKO JERICEVIC .... PRODUCTION DESIGNER
PATRICIA SMITH .... COSTUME DESIGNER
DUANE HARTZELL .... FILM EDITOR

AWAKENING, THE
JACK CARDIFF .... CINEMATOGRAPHER
MICHAEL STRINGER .... PRODUCTION DESIGNER
PHYLLIS DALTON .... COSTUME DESIGNER
TERRY RAWLINGS .... FILM EDITOR

AWAKENINGS
MIROSLAV ONDRICEK .... CINEMATOGRAPHER
ANTON FURST .... PRODUCTION DESIGNER
CYNTHIA FLYNT .... COSTUME DESIGNER
BATTLE DAVIS .... FILM EDITOR
JERRY GREENBERG .... FILM EDITOR

AY, CARMELA!
JOSE LUIS ALCAINE .... CINEMATOGRAPHER
PABLO G. DEL AMO .... FILM EDITOR

B

B.L. STRYKER (PILOT)
CAROL WOOD .... PRODUCTION DESIGNER
DEAN E. MITZNER .... PRODUCTION DESIGNER
CARL KRESS .... FILM EDITOR
DOUGLAS IBOLD .... FILM EDITOR

BABE (TF)
CHARLES F. WHEELER .... CINEMATOGRAPHER

BABETTE'S FEAST
HENNING KRISTIANSEN .... CINEMATOGRAPHER
SVEN WICHMAN .... PRODUCTION DESIGNER
FIN HENRICKSON .... FILM EDITOR

BABY
JOHN ALCOTT† .... CINEMATOGRAPHER
RAYMOND G. STOREY .... PRODUCTION DESIGNER
STEVE SPENCE .... PRODUCTION DESIGNER

BABY - SECRET OF THE LOST LEGEND
JOHN B. MANSBRIDGE .... PRODUCTION DESIGNER
SUSIE S. MCVEETY .... COSTUME DESIGNER
DAVID BRETHERTON .... FILM EDITOR
HOWARD SMITH .... FILM EDITOR

BABY BLUE MARINE
LASZLO KOVACS .... CINEMATOGRAPHER
MARION ROTHMAN .... FILM EDITOR

BABY BOOM
WILLIAM A. FRAKER .... CINEMATOGRAPHER
BEALA B. NEEL .... PRODUCTION DESIGNER
JEFFREY HOWARD .... PRODUCTION DESIGNER
SUSAN BECKER .... COSTUME DESIGNER
LYNZEE KLINGMAN .... FILM EDITOR

BABY COMES HOME (TF)
DANIEL LOMINO .... PRODUCTION DESIGNER

BABY DOLL
RICHARD SYLBERT .... PRODUCTION DESIGNER

BABY GIRL SCOTT (TF)
WILLIAM WAGES .... CINEMATOGRAPHER

BABY M (MS)
JAMES A. CRABE† .... CINEMATOGRAPHER
ERIC SEARS .... FILM EDITOR

BABY MAKER, THE
CHARLES ROSHER, JR. .... CINEMATOGRAPHER

BABY SISTER (TF)
MICHAEL J. HILL .... FILM EDITOR

BABY, IT'S YOU
MICHAEL BALLHAUS .... CINEMATOGRAPHER
JEFFREY TOWNSEND .... PRODUCTION DESIGNER
FRANNE LEE .... COSTUME DESIGNER
SONYA POLONSKY .... FILM EDITOR

BABY, THE
MICHAEL D. MARGULIES .... CINEMATOGRAPHER

BABY, THE RAIN MUST FALL
AARON STELL .... FILM EDITOR

BABYCAKES (TF)
TONY IMI .... CINEMATOGRAPHER
DAVID GROPMAN .... PRODUCTION DESIGNER

BABYSITTER, THE (TF)
DOUGLAS HIGGINS .... PRODUCTION DESIGNER

BACHELOR PARTY
HAL TRUSSELL .... CINEMATOGRAPHER
MARTIN PRICE .... PRODUCTION DESIGNER
RICHARD SAWYER .... PRODUCTION DESIGNER
TOM WALLS .... FILM EDITOR

BACK ROADS
JOHN A. ALONZO .... CINEMATOGRAPHER
WALTER SCOTT HERNDON† .... PRODUCTION DESIGNER
SIDNEY LEVIN .... FILM EDITOR

Au-Ba

CINEMATOGRAPHERS
PRODUCTION
DESIGNERS,
COSTUME
DESIGNERS AND
FILM EDITORS
GUIDE

I
N
D
E
X

O
F

F
I
L
M

T
I
T
L
E
S

Ba-Ba

CINEMATOGRAPHERS
PRODUCTION
DESIGNERS,
COSTUME
DESIGNERS AND
FILM EDITORS
GUIDE

I
N
D
E
X

O
F

F
I
L
M

T
I
T
L
E
S

BALLERINA & THE BLUES (TF)
PETER BENISON .... CINEMATOGRAPHER

BALTIMORE BULLET, THE
JAMES A. CRABE .... CINEMATOGRAPHER
ADRIAN H. GORTON .... PRODUCTION DESIGNER
HERMAN A. BLUMENTHAL .... PRODUCTION DESIGNER
PATRICIA NORRIS .... COSTUME DESIGNER

BAND OF THE HAND
REYNALDO VILLALOBOS .... CINEMATOGRAPHER
GREGORY BOLTON .... PRODUCTION DESIGNER
ROBERT DE MORA .... COSTUME DESIGNER
JACK HOFSTRA .... FILM EDITOR

BANDOLERO!
ALFRED SWEENEY .... PRODUCTION DESIGNER

BANG THE DRUM SLOWLY
RICHARD SHORE .... CINEMATOGRAPHER
ROBERT GUNDLACH .... PRODUCTION DESIGNER
RICHARD MARKS .... FILM EDITOR

BANGKOK HILTON (CTF)
GEOFF BURTON .... CINEMATOGRAPHER
OWEN WILLIAMS .... PRODUCTION DESIGNER
FRANS VANDENBURG .... FILM EDITOR
MARCUS D'ARCY .... FILM EDITOR

BANZAI RUNNERS
HOWARD WEXLER .... CINEMATOGRAPHER

BARBARIAN QUEEN
LESLIE ROSENTHAL .... FILM EDITOR

BARBARIANS, THE
LORENZO BATTAGLIA .... CINEMATOGRAPHER
EUGENE ALABISO .... FILM EDITOR

BARBAROSA
IAN BAKER .... CINEMATOGRAPHER
DONALD B. WOODRUFF .... PRODUCTION DESIGNER
MICHAEL LEVESQUE .... PRODUCTION DESIGNER
DAVID RAMIREZ .... FILM EDITOR
DON ZIMMERMAN .... FILM EDITOR

BARE ESSENTIALS (TF)
JOHNNY E. JENSEN .... CINEMATOGRAPHER
ELAYNE CEDER .... PRODUCTION DESIGNER
STEVEN COHEN .... FILM EDITOR

BARE KNUCKLES
DEAN CUNDEY .... CINEMATOGRAPHER
J. MICHAEL RIVA .... PRODUCTION DESIGNER

BARFLY
ROBBY MULLER .... CINEMATOGRAPHER
ROBERT ZIEMBICKI .... PRODUCTION DESIGNER
MILENA CANONERO .... COSTUME DESIGNER
EVA GARDOS .... FILM EDITOR

BARON, THE
MIKAEL SALOMON .... CINEMATOGRAPHER

BARRY LYNDON
JOHN ALCOTT† .... CINEMATOGRAPHER
KEN ADAM .... PRODUCTION DESIGNER
ROY WALKER .... PRODUCTION DESIGNER
MILENA CANONERO .... COSTUME DESIGNER
TONY LAWSON .... FILM EDITOR

BARRY MCKENZIE HOLDS HIS OWN
JOHN STODDART .... PRODUCTION DESIGNER
WILLIAM M. ANDERSON .... FILM EDITOR

BARTON FINK
ROGER DEAKINS .... CINEMATOGRAPHER
DENNIS GASSNER .... PRODUCTION DESIGNER
RICHARD HORNUNG .... COSTUME DESIGNER
RODERICK JAYNES .... FILM EDITOR

BASIC TRAINING
STEPHEN W. GRAY .... CINEMATOGRAPHER
LARRY BOCK .... FILM EDITOR

BASTARD, THE (TF)
JEAN-PIERRE DORLEAC .... COSTUME DESIGNER

BAT 21
MARK IRWIN .... CINEMATOGRAPHER
VINCENT M. CRESCIMAN .... PRODUCTION DESIGNER
AUDREY BANSMER .... COSTUME DESIGNER
STEPHEN E. RIVKIN .... FILM EDITOR

BATMAN
ROGER PRATT .... CINEMATOGRAPHER
ANTON FURST .... PRODUCTION DESIGNER
RAY LOVEJOY .... FILM EDITOR

BATTERED (TF)
DANIEL LOMINO .... PRODUCTION DESIGNER

BATTERIES NOT INCLUDED
JOHN MCPHERSON .... CINEMATOGRAPHER
ANGELO GRAHAM .... PRODUCTION DESIGNER
TED HAWORTH .... PRODUCTION DESIGNER
AGGIE GUERARD RODGERS .... COSTUME DESIGNER
CYNTHIA SCHEIDER .... FILM EDITOR

BATTLE BEYOND THE STARS
DANIEL LACAMBRE .... CINEMATOGRAPHER
SHARON COMPTON .... PRODUCTION DESIGNER
DURINDA RICE WOOD .... COSTUME DESIGNER

BATTLE GROUND
STEPHEN ASHLEY BLAKE .... CINEMATOGRAPHER

BATTLE OF BRITAIN, THE
FREDDIE YOUNG .... CINEMATOGRAPHER

BATTLESTAR GALACTICA (TF)
RICHARD JAMES .... PRODUCTION DESIGNER

BATTLESTAR GALACTICA (TVS)
JEAN-PIERRE DORLEAC .... COSTUME DESIGNER

BATTLETRUCK
CHRIS MENGES .... CINEMATOGRAPHER
MICHAEL HORTON .... FILM EDITOR

BAWDY ADVENTURES OF TOM JONES, THE
DOUGLAS SLOCOMBE .... CINEMATOGRAPHER
BILL BLUNDEN .... FILM EDITOR

BAXTER!
GEOFFREY UNSWORTH† .... CINEMATOGRAPHER
ANTHONY PRATT .... PRODUCTION DESIGNER

BAY BOY, THE
CLAUDE AGOSTINI .... CINEMATOGRAPHER
RICHARD HARRISON .... PRODUCTION DESIGNER
WOLF KROEGER .... PRODUCTION DESIGNER
RENEE APRIL .... COSTUME DESIGNER
SUSAN SHANKS .... FILM EDITOR

BAY COVEN (TF)
JACQUES STEYN .... CINEMATOGRAPHER

BEACH FEVER
RICHARD E. WESTOVER .... FILM EDITOR

BEACH GIRLS, THE
MICHAEL D. MURPHY .... CINEMATOGRAPHER
GEORGE BOWERS .... FILM EDITOR

BEACH HOUSE
PETER STEIN .... CINEMATOGRAPHER
JOHN BLOOMGARDEN .... FILM EDITOR

BEACHES
DANTE SPINOTTI .... CINEMATOGRAPHER
ALBERT BRENNER .... PRODUCTION DESIGNER
FRANK RICHWOOD .... PRODUCTION DESIGNER
ROBERT DE MORA .... COSTUME DESIGNER
RICHARD HALSEY .... FILM EDITOR

BEAR ISLAND
ALAN HUME .... CINEMATOGRAPHER
KAREN BROMLEY .... PRODUCTION DESIGNER
ERIC BOYD-PERKINS .... FILM EDITOR
TONY LOWER .... FILM EDITOR

BEAR, THE
ASZLO GEORGE .... CINEMATOGRAPHER
PHILIPPE ROUSSELOT .... CINEMATOGRAPHER
TONI LUDI .... PRODUCTION DESIGNER
GEORGE COSTELLO .... PRODUCTION DESIGNER
RON TALSKY .... COSTUME DESIGNER
NOELLE BOISSON .... FILM EDITOR
ROBERT FLORIO .... FILM EDITOR

Ba-Be

CINEMATOGRAPHERS
PRODUCTION
DESIGNERS,
COSTUME
DESIGNERS AND
FILM EDITORS
GUIDE

I N D E X   O F   F I L M   T I T L E S

299

Be-Be

CINEMATOGRAPHERS
PRODUCTION
DESIGNERS,
COSTUME
DESIGNERS AND
FILM EDITORS
GUIDE

I
N
D
E
X

O
F

F
I
L
M

T
I
T
L
E
S

Be-Be

CINEMATOGRAPHERS
PRODUCTION
DESIGNERS,
COSTUME
DESIGNERS AND
FILM EDITORS
GUIDE

BERLIN ALEXANDERPLATZ
XAVIER SCHWARZENBERGER ..................................CINEMATOGRAPHER
BARBARA BAUM ....COSTUME DESIGNER
JULIANE LORENZ ....FILM EDITOR

BERLIN BLUES
TEO ESCAMILLA ....CINEMATOGRAPHER
TEO ESCAMILLA ....COSTUME DESIGNER

BERLIN TUNNEL 21 (TF)
MICHAEL J. HILL ....FILM EDITOR

BERMUDA TRIANGLE, THE
CHARLES BENNETT ....PRODUCTION DESIGNER

BERNADETTE
ANNICK CHARVAIN ....FILM EDITOR

BERRY GORDY'S THE LAST DRAGON
ROBERT DE MORA ....COSTUME DESIGNER
CHRISTOPHER HOLMES ....FILM EDITOR

BERSERKER
MARCUS MANTON ....FILM EDITOR

BERT RIBGY, YOU'RE A FOOL
JAN DE BONT ....CINEMATOGRAPHER
TERENCE MARSH ....PRODUCTION DESIGNER
RUTH MYERS ....COSTUME DESIGNER
BUD MOLIN ....FILM EDITOR

BEST DEFENSE
DONALD PETERMAN ....CINEMATOGRAPHER
PETER JAMISON ....PRODUCTION DESIGNER
ROBERT W. (BO) WELCH ....PRODUCTION DESIGNER
KRISTI ZEA ....COSTUME DESIGNER
SIDNEY WOLINSKY ....FILM EDITOR

BEST FRIENDS
JORDAN CRONENWETH ....CINEMATOGRAPHER
STEPHEN M. KATZ ....CINEMATOGRAPHER
JOSAN F. RUSSO ....PRODUCTION DESIGNER
BETSY COX ....COSTUME DESIGNER
DON ZIMMERMAN ....FILM EDITOR

BEST LITTLE WHOREHOUSE IN TEXAS, THE
WILLIAM A. FRAKER ....CINEMATOGRAPHER
ROBERT F. BOYLE ....PRODUCTION DESIGNER
FRANK RICHWOOD ....PRODUCTION DESIGNER
NORMAN NEWBERRY ....PRODUCTION DESIGNER
THEADORA VAN RUNKLE ....COSTUME DESIGNER
JACK HOFSTRA ....FILM EDITOR
PEMBROKE J. HERRING ....FILM EDITOR
DAVID BRETHERTON ....FILM EDITOR

BEST MAN, THE
HASKELL WEXLER ....CINEMATOGRAPHER

BEST OF FRIENDS, THE
DAVID GRIBBLE ....CINEMATOGRAPHER

BEST OF THE BEST
DOUG RYAN ....CINEMATOGRAPHER
KIM REES ....PRODUCTION DESIGNER
CYNTHIA BERGSTROM ....COSTUME DESIGNER
WILLIAM HOY ....FILM EDITOR

BEST OF TIMES, THE
BRUCE SURTEES ....CINEMATOGRAPHER
CHARLES F. WHEELER ....CINEMATOGRAPHER
ANTHONY BROCKLISS ....PRODUCTION DESIGNER
DAVID NICHOLS ....PRODUCTION DESIGNER
PATRICIA NORRIS ....COSTUME DESIGNER
GARTH CRAVEN ....FILM EDITOR

BEST SELLER
FRED MURPHY ....CINEMATOGRAPHER
GENE RUDOLF ....PRODUCTION DESIGNER
ROBERT HOWLAND ....PRODUCTION DESIGNER
DAVID ROSENBLOOM ....FILM EDITOR

BETHUNE: THE MAKING OF A HERO
MIKE MOLLOY ....CINEMATOGRAPHER
RAOUL COUTARD ....CINEMATOGRAPHER
ANGELO CORRAO ....FILM EDITOR
YVES LANGLOIS ....FILM EDITOR

BETRAYAL
MIKE FASH ....CINEMATOGRAPHER
EILEEN DISS ....PRODUCTION DESIGNER
JANE ROBINSON ....COSTUME DESIGNER
JOHN BLOOM ....FILM EDITOR

BETRAYED
PATRICK BLOSSIER ....CINEMATOGRAPHER
PATRIZIA VON BRANDENSTEIN ....PRODUCTION DESIGNER
STEPHEN GEAGHAN ....PRODUCTION DESIGNER
JOE I. TOMPKINS ....COSTUME DESIGNER
JOELE VAN EFFENTERRE ....FILM EDITOR

BETSY'S WEDDING
KELVIN PIKE ....CINEMATOGRAPHER
JOHN JAY MOORE ....PRODUCTION DESIGNER
MARY MALIN ....COSTUME DESIGNER
MICHAEL POLAKOW ....FILM EDITOR

BETSY, THE
HERMAN A. BLUMENTHAL ....PRODUCTION DESIGNER
DOROTHY JEAKINS ....COSTUME DESIGNER
RITA ROLAND ....FILM EDITOR

BETTER LATE THAN NEVER
CLAUDE LECOMTE ....CINEMATOGRAPHER
PHILIP SHAW ....FILM EDITOR

BETTER OFF DEAD
ISIDORE MANKOFSKY ....CINEMATOGRAPHER
HERMAN ZIMMERMAN ....PRODUCTION DESIGNER
BRAD R. LOMAN ....COSTUME DESIGNER
ALAN BALSAM ....FILM EDITOR

BETTY BLUE
JEAN-FRANÇOIS ROBIN ....CINEMATOGRAPHER
MONIQUE PRIM ....FILM EDITOR

BETWEEN FRIENDS (CTF)
JUDITH R. GELLMAN ....COSTUME DESIGNER

BETWEEN THE LINES
KENNETH VAN SICKLE ....CINEMATOGRAPHER
STUART WURTZEL ....PRODUCTION DESIGNER
JOHN CARTER ....FILM EDITOR

BETWEEN TWO WOMEN (TF)
POLLY PLATT ....PRODUCTION DESIGNER

BETWEEN WARS
MAX LEMON ....FILM EDITOR

BEVERLY HILLS BRATS
HARRY MATHIAS ....CINEMATOGRAPHER
GEORGE COSTELLO ....PRODUCTION DESIGNER

BEVERLY HILLS BUNTZ (PILOT)
FREDERICK MOORE ....CINEMATOGRAPHER

BEVERLY HILLS COP
BRUCE SURTEES ....CINEMATOGRAPHER
ANGELO GRAHAM ....PRODUCTION DESIGNER
JAMES J. MURAKAMI ....PRODUCTION DESIGNER
THOMAS M. BRONSON ....COSTUME DESIGNER
ARTHUR COBURN ....FILM EDITOR
BILLY WEBER ....FILM EDITOR

BEVERLY HILLS COP II
JEFFREY L. KIMBALL ....CINEMATOGRAPHER
JAMES J. MURAKAMI ....PRODUCTION DESIGNER
KEN DAVIS ....PRODUCTION DESIGNER
BILLY WEBER ....FILM EDITOR
CHRIS LEBENZON ....FILM EDITOR

BEVERLY HILLS MADAM (TF)
BEALA B. NEEL ....PRODUCTION DESIGNER

BEVERLY HILLS VAMP
STEPHEN ASHLEY BLAKE ....CINEMATOGRAPHER

BEYOND AND BACK
CHARLES BENNETT ....PRODUCTION DESIGNER

BEYOND GOOD AND EVIL
ARMANDO NANNUZZI ....CINEMATOGRAPHER

BEYOND REASON
JOHN A. ALONZO ....CINEMATOGRAPHER

BEYOND REASONABLE DOUBT
ALAN BOLLINGER ....CINEMATOGRAPHER
MICHAEL HORTON ....FILM EDITOR

BEYOND THE FOG
HENRY RICHARDSON ....FILM EDITOR

Be-Bi

CINEMATOGRAPHERS
PRODUCTION
DESIGNERS,
COSTUME
DESIGNERS AND
FILM EDITORS
GUIDE

I
N
D
E
X

O
F

F
I
L
M

T
I
T
L
E
S

302

BILL JOHNSON STORY, THE (TF)
ROBERT JESSUP .... CINEMATOGRAPHER

BILL: ON HIS OWN (TF)
JOHN C. HORGER .... FILM EDITOR

BILLION DOLLAR BRAIN
BILLY WILLIAMS .... CINEMATOGRAPHER

BILLION FOR BORIS, A
PETER STEIN .... CINEMATOGRAPHER

BILLIONAIRE BOYS CLUB (MS)
ISIDORE MANKOFSKY .... CINEMATOGRAPHER
BRAD R. LOMAN .... COSTUME DESIGNER

BILLY BUDD
PETER MURTON .... PRODUCTION DESIGNER

BILLY GALVIN
SHAY AUSTIN .... PRODUCTION DESIGNER
LOU KLEINMAN .... FILM EDITOR

BILLY JACK
FRED J. KOENEKAMP .... CINEMATOGRAPHER
JOHN M. STEPHENS .... CINEMATOGRAPHER
MARION ROTHMAN .... FILM EDITOR

BILLY JACK GOES TO WASHINGTON
HILYARD BROWN .... PRODUCTION DESIGNER
GEORGE GRENVILLE .... FILM EDITOR

BILLY LIAR
RAYMOND SIMM .... PRODUCTION DESIGNER

BILLY TWO HATS
ANTHONY PRATT .... PRODUCTION DESIGNER

BILOXI BLUES
BILL BUTLER .... CINEMATOGRAPHER
PAUL SYLBERT .... PRODUCTION DESIGNER
ANN ROTH .... COSTUME DESIGNER
SAM O'STEEN .... FILM EDITOR

**BINGO LONG TRAVELING ALL STARS & MOTOR
KINGS, THE**
BILL BUTLER .... CINEMATOGRAPHER
LAWRENCE G. PAULL .... PRODUCTION DESIGNER
DAVID RAWLINS .... FILM EDITOR

BIOHAZARD
PAUL ELLIOTT .... CINEMATOGRAPHER
MIRIAM PREISSEL .... FILM EDITOR

BIRD
JACK N. GREEN .... CINEMATOGRAPHER
EDWARD C. CARFAGNO .... PRODUCTION DESIGNER
GLENN WRIGHT .... COSTUME DESIGNER
JOEL COX .... FILM EDITOR

BIRD ON A WIRE
ROBERT PRIMES .... CINEMATOGRAPHER
PHILIP HARRISON .... PRODUCTION DESIGNER
WAYNE FINKELMAN .... COSTUME DESIGNER
EDUARDO CASTRO .... COSTUME DESIGNER
MONIQUE STRANAN .... COSTUME DESIGNER
DALLAS PUETT .... FILM EDITOR
FRANK MORRISS .... FILM EDITOR

BIRD WITH THE CRYSTAL PLUMMAGE, THE
VITTORIO STORARO .... CINEMATOGRAPHER

BIRDS OF PREY (TF)
JORDAN CRONENWETH .... CINEMATOGRAPHER

BIRDS, THE
ROBERT F. BOYLE .... PRODUCTION DESIGNER

BIRDY
MICHAEL SERESIN .... CINEMATOGRAPHER
ARMIN GANZ .... PRODUCTION DESIGNER
GEOFFREY KIRKLAND .... PRODUCTION DESIGNER
W. STEWART CAMPBELL .... PRODUCTION DESIGNER
KRISTI ZEA .... COSTUME DESIGNER
GERRY HAMBLING .... FILM EDITOR

BISHOP'S BEDROOM
FRANCO DI GIACOMO .... CINEMATOGRAPHER

BITE THE BULLET
HARRY STRADLING, JR. .... CINEMATOGRAPHER
GEORGE GRENVILLE .... FILM EDITOR

BITTER HARVEST (TF)
BRYAN RYMAN .... PRODUCTION DESIGNER

BITTERSWEET LOVE
STEPHEN M. KATZ .... CINEMATOGRAPHER
VINCENT M. CRESCIMAN .... PRODUCTION DESIGNER
WILLIAM BUTLER .... FILM EDITOR

BLACK AND WHITE IN COLOR
FRANÇOISE BONNOT .... FILM EDITOR

BLACK ARROW (CTF)
JOHN CABRERA .... CINEMATOGRAPHER

BLACK BELT JONES
MICHAEL KAHN .... FILM EDITOR

BLACK BIRD, THE
PHILIP LATHROP .... CINEMATOGRAPHER
LOU LOMBARDO .... FILM EDITOR

BLACK CAESAR
GEORGE FOLSEY JR.* .... FILM EDITOR

BLACK CAULDRON, THE (AF)
JAMES MELTON .... FILM EDITOR

BLACK CHRISTMAS
REGINALD H. MORRIS .... CINEMATOGRAPHER
KAREN BROMLEY .... PRODUCTION DESIGNER

BLACK EYE
GENE RUGGIERO .... FILM EDITOR

BLACK FOREST, THE
ANTHONY TREMBLAY .... PRODUCTION DESIGNER

BLACK HOLE, THE
FRANK PHILLIPS .... CINEMATOGRAPHER

BLACK JACK
CHRIS MENGES .... CINEMATOGRAPHER

BLACK JOY
PHIL MEHEUX .... CINEMATOGRAPHER
THOM NOBLE .... FILM EDITOR

BLACK MARBLE, THE
OWEN ROIZMAN .... CINEMATOGRAPHER
ALFRED SWEENEY .... PRODUCTION DESIGNER
SUSAN BECKER .... COSTUME DESIGNER
MAURY WINETROBE .... FILM EDITOR

BLACK MOON
SVEN NYKVIST .... CINEMATOGRAPHER

BLACK MOON RISING
MIKHAIL SUSLOV .... CINEMATOGRAPHER
BRYAN RYMAN .... PRODUCTION DESIGNER
SARINA ROTSTEIN .... PRODUCTION DESIGNER
JOHN BUEHLER .... COSTUME DESIGNER
TODD RAMSAY .... FILM EDITOR

BLACK NARCISSUS
JACK CARDIFF .... CINEMATOGRAPHER

BLACK RAIN
JAN DE BONT .... CINEMATOGRAPHER
ELLEN MIROJNICK .... COSTUME DESIGNER
TOM ROLF .... FILM EDITOR

BLACK RAINBOW
GERRY FISHER .... CINEMATOGRAPHER
MALCOLM COOKE .... FILM EDITOR

BLACK ROOM, THE
DAVID KERN .... FILM EDITOR

BLACK ROSE, THE
JACK CARDIFF .... CINEMATOGRAPHER

BLACK ROSES
JAMES RUXIN .... FILM EDITOR

Bi-Bl

CINEMATOGRAPHERS
PRODUCTION
DESIGNERS,
COSTUME
DESIGNERS AND
FILM EDITORS
GUIDE

I
N
D
E
X

O
F

F
I
L
M

T
I
T
L
E
S

BI-BI

CINEMATOGRAPHERS
PRODUCTION
DESIGNERS,
COSTUME
DESIGNERS AND
FILM EDITORS
GUIDE

INDEX

OF

FILM

TITLES

BLACK SHEEP, THE
ROBERT KINOSHITA .... PRODUCTION DESIGNER

BLACK STALLION, THE
CALEB DESCHANEL .... CINEMATOGRAPHER
AURELIO CRUGNOLA .... PRODUCTION DESIGNER
ROBERT DALVA .... FILM EDITOR

BLACK STALLION RETURNS, THE
CARLO DI PALMA .... CINEMATOGRAPHER
AURELIO CRUGNOLA .... PRODUCTION DESIGNER
PAUL HIRSCH .... FILM EDITOR

BLACK SUNDAY
JOHN A. ALONZO .... CINEMATOGRAPHER
TOM ROLF .... FILM EDITOR

BLACK WIDOW
CONRAD HALL .... CINEMATOGRAPHER
GENE CALLAHAN .... PRODUCTION DESIGNER
PATRICIA NORRIS .... COSTUME DESIGNER
JOHN BLOOM .... FILM EDITOR

BLACK WINDMILL, THE
PETER MURTON .... PRODUCTION DESIGNER

BLACKEYES
ANDREW DUNN .... CINEMATOGRAPHER

BLACKOUT
ARLEDGE ARMENAKI .... CINEMATOGRAPHER
TRUDY KAPNER .... COSTUME DESIGNER
ZACH STAENBERG .... FILM EDITOR

BLACULA
JOHN M. STEPHENS .... CINEMATOGRAPHER
SANDRA STEWART .... COSTUME DESIGNER
ALLAN JACOBS .... FILM EDITOR

BLADE IN HONG KONG (TF)
WOODY OMENS .... CINEMATOGRAPHER

BLADE RUNNER
JORDAN CRONENWETH .... CINEMATOGRAPHER
DAVID L. SNYDER .... PRODUCTION DESIGNER
LAWRENCE G. PAULL .... PRODUCTION DESIGNER
CHARLES KNODE .... COSTUME DESIGNER
MICHAEL KAPLAN .... COSTUME DESIGNER
TERRY RAWLINGS .... FILM EDITOR

BLAME IT ON RIO
REYNALDO VILLALOBOS .... CINEMATOGRAPHER
MARCOS FLAKSMAN .... PRODUCTION DESIGNER
GEORGE HIVELY .... FILM EDITOR
RICHARD MARDEN .... FILM EDITOR

BLAME IT ON THE NIGHT
ALEX PHILLIPS .... CINEMATOGRAPHER
TED HAWORTH .... PRODUCTION DESIGNER
TONY LOMBARDO .... FILM EDITOR

BLAZE
HASKELL WEXLER .... CINEMATOGRAPHER
ARMIN GANZ .... PRODUCTION DESIGNER
ED RICHARDSON .... PRODUCTION DESIGNER
RUTH MYERS .... COSTUME DESIGNER
ROBERT LEIGHTON .... FILM EDITOR

BLAZING SADDLES
PETER W. WOOLEY .... PRODUCTION DESIGNER
DANFORD B. GREENE .... FILM EDITOR
JOHN C. HOWARD .... FILM EDITOR

BLEAK HOUSE (MS)
KENNETH MACMILLAN .... CINEMATOGRAPHER

BLESS THE BEASTS AND THE CHILDREN
MICHEL HUGO .... CINEMATOGRAPHER

BLESSED (TF)
GIB JAFFE .... FILM EDITOR

BLIND ALLEY
PAUL GLICKMAN .... CINEMATOGRAPHER

BLIND AMBITION (TF)
BEN EDWARDS .... PRODUCTION DESIGNER
MICHAEL BAUGH .... PRODUCTION DESIGNER

BLIND DATE
HARRY STRADLING, JR. .... CINEMATOGRAPHER
PETER LANDSDOWN SMITH .... PRODUCTION DESIGNER
RODGER MAUS .... PRODUCTION DESIGNER
TRACY TYNAN .... COSTUME DESIGNER
ROBERT PERGAMENT .... FILM EDITOR

BLIND DATE (1984)
GEORGE ROSENBERG .... FILM EDITOR

BLIND DIRECTOR, THE
THOMAS MAUCH .... CINEMATOGRAPHER
JANE SEITZ .... FILM EDITOR

BLIND FURY
DON BURGESS .... CINEMATOGRAPHER
PETER MURTON .... PRODUCTION DESIGNER
KATHERINE DOVER .... COSTUME DESIGNER
DAVID SIMMONS .... FILM EDITOR

BLIND JUSTICE (TF)
JOSEPH C. NEMEC III .... PRODUCTION DESIGNER

BLIND RAGE
LARRY PIZER .... CINEMATOGRAPHER

BLIND TRUST
GUY DUFAUX .... CINEMATOGRAPHER

BLIND VENGEANCE (CTF)
DARYN OKADA .... CINEMATOGRAPHER
DENNIS MOSHER .... FILM EDITOR

BLISS
PAUL MURPHY .... CINEMATOGRAPHER
OWEN PATERSON .... PRODUCTION DESIGNER
ANN LAMBERT .... COSTUME DESIGNER
HELEN HOOPER .... COSTUME DESIGNER
WAYNE LECLOS .... FILM EDITOR

BLISS OF MISS BLOSSOM, THE
ASSHETON GORTON .... PRODUCTION DESIGNER

BLOB, THE
MARK IRWIN .... CINEMATOGRAPHER
CRAIG STEARNS .... PRODUCTION DESIGNER
JEFFREY S. GINN .... PRODUCTION DESIGNER
JOSEPH PORRO .... COSTUME DESIGNER
TERRY STOKES .... FILM EDITOR
TOD FEUERMAN .... FILM EDITOR

BLOOD AND CONCRETE
DECLAN QUINN .... CINEMATOGRAPHER
PAMELA WOODBRIDGE .... PRODUCTION DESIGNER

BLOOD AND GUTS
MARK IRWIN .... CINEMATOGRAPHER
RONALD SANDERS .... FILM EDITOR

BLOOD BEACH
STEVEN B. POSTER .... CINEMATOGRAPHER
WILLIAM SANDELL .... PRODUCTION DESIGNER
GARY A. GRIFFEN .... FILM EDITOR

BLOOD DINER
JURG WALTHERS .... CINEMATOGRAPHER
TOM MASHELSKI .... FILM EDITOR

BLOOD FEUD (TF)
SYDNEY Z. LITWAK .... PRODUCTION DESIGNER
ROBERT TURTURICE .... COSTUME DESIGNER

BLOOD IN THE FACE (FD)
SANDI SISSEL .... CINEMATOGRAPHER
KEVIN RAFFERTY .... CINEMATOGRAPHER
KEVIN RAFFERTY .... FILM EDITOR

BLOOD LINK
ROMANO ALBANI .... CINEMATOGRAPHER
RUSSELL LLOYD .... FILM EDITOR

BLOOD OF HEROES, THE
DAVID EGGBY .... CINEMATOGRAPHER
JOHN SOTDDART .... PRODUCTION DESIGNER
RICHARD FRANCIS-BRUCE .... FILM EDITOR

BLOOD OF OTHERS, THE (CMS)
RICHARD CIUPKA .... CINEMATOGRAPHER
FRANÇOIS COMTET .... PRODUCTION DESIGNER

BLOOD ON SATAN'S CLAW, THE
DICK BUSH .... CINEMATOGRAPHER

BLOOD RED
BRUNO RUBEO .... PRODUCTION DESIGNER
BARBARA SCOTT .... COSTUME DESIGNER

BLOOD SALVAGE
MICHAEL KARP .... CINEMATOGRAPHER
ROBERT SISSMAN .... PRODUCTION DESIGNER
D. JEAN HESTER .... COSTUME DESIGNER
JACQUI FREEMAN ROSS .... FILM EDITOR

BLOOD SIMPLE
BARRY SONNENFELD .... CINEMATOGRAPHER
JANE MUSKY .... PRODUCTION DESIGNER
RODERICK JAYNES .... FILM EDITOR

BLOOD TIDE
ROBERT LEIGHTON .... FILM EDITOR

BLOOD WEDDING
TEO ESCAMILLA .... CINEMATOGRAPHER

BLOOD...BLOOD OUT
MAREK DOBROWOLSKI .... PRODUCTION DESIGNER

BLOODBROTHERS
ROBERT SURTEES† .... CINEMATOGRAPHER
GENE CALLAHAN .... PRODUCTION DESIGNER
SHELDON KAHN .... FILM EDITOR

BLOODFIST
RICARDO JACQUES GALE .... CINEMATOGRAPHER
KAREN HORN .... FILM EDITOR

BLOODHOUNDS OF BROADWAY
ELLIOT DAVIS .... CINEMATOGRAPHER
CAMILLA TONIOLO .... FILM EDITOR

BLOODLINE
BUD MOLIN .... FILM EDITOR

BLOODRUSH
SOL NEGRIN .... CINEMATOGRAPHER

BLOODSPORT
DAVID WORTH .... CINEMATOGRAPHER
DAVID SEARL .... PRODUCTION DESIGNER
CARL KRESS .... FILM EDITOR

BLOODY BIRTHDAY
STEPHEN L. POSEY .... CINEMATOGRAPHER
J. RAE FOX .... PRODUCTION DESIGNER
LYNDA BURBANK .... PRODUCTION DESIGNER
ANN E. MILLS .... FILM EDITOR

BLOODY MAMA
JOHN A. ALONZO .... CINEMATOGRAPHER
EVE NEWMAN .... FILM EDITOR

BLOW OUT
VILMOS ZSIGMOND .... CINEMATOGRAPHER
PAUL SYLBERT .... PRODUCTION DESIGNER
VICKI SANCHEZ .... COSTUME DESIGNER
PAUL HIRSCH .... FILM EDITOR

BLOW UP
ASSHETON GORTON .... PRODUCTION DESIGNER

BLUE BIRD, THE
FREDDIE YOUNG .... CINEMATOGRAPHER
STANFORD C. ALLEN .... FILM EDITOR

BLUE BLOOD
HARRY WAXMAN .... CINEMATOGRAPHER

BLUE CITY
STEVEN B. POSTER .... CINEMATOGRAPHER
RICHARD J. LAWRENCE .... PRODUCTION DESIGNER
DAN MOORE .... COSTUME DESIGNER
JIM MILLER .... FILM EDITOR
ROSS ALBERT .... FILM EDITOR

BLUE COLLAR
BOBBY BYRNE .... CINEMATOGRAPHER
LAWRENCE G. PAULL .... PRODUCTION DESIGNER
TOM ROLF .... FILM EDITOR

BLUE DESERT
PAUL MURPHY .... CINEMATOGRAPHER
MICHAEL PERRY .... PRODUCTION DESIGNER
COLEEN KELSO .... COSTUME DESIGNER
DEBRA BARD .... FILM EDITOR

BLUE FUN
GEOFF BURTON .... CINEMATOGRAPHER

BLUE HEAVEN
KEES VAN OOSTRUM .... CINEMATOGRAPHER
HOWARD CUMMINGS .... PRODUCTION DESIGNER

BLUE IGUANA, THE
RODOLFO SANCHEZ .... CINEMATOGRAPHER
CYNTHIA SOWDER .... PRODUCTION DESIGNER
ISIS MUSSENDEN .... COSTUME DESIGNER
SCOTT CHESTNUT .... FILM EDITOR

BLUE LAGOON, THE
NESTOR ALMENDROS .... CINEMATOGRAPHER
JON DOWDING .... PRODUCTION DESIGNER
JEAN-PIERRE DORLEAC .... COSTUME DESIGNER
ROBERT GORDON .... FILM EDITOR

BLUE MONKEY
BRENTON SPENCER .... CINEMATOGRAPHER
REUBEN FREED .... PRODUCTION DESIGNER
GINA KIELLERMAN .... COSTUME DESIGNER
MICHAEL FRUET .... FILM EDITOR

BLUE SKIES (PILOT)
PAUL RUBELL .... FILM EDITOR

BLUE SKIES AGAIN
DONALD MCALPINE .... CINEMATOGRAPHER
DON K. IVEY .... PRODUCTION DESIGNER
DANFORD B. GREENE .... FILM EDITOR

BLUE STEEL
AMIR MOKRI .... CINEMATOGRAPHER
TOBY CORBETT .... PRODUCTION DESIGNER
RICHARD SCHISSLER .... COSTUME DESIGNER
LEE PERCY .... FILM EDITOR

BLUE SUEDE SHOES
ROGER DEAKINS .... CINEMATOGRAPHER

BLUE THUNDER
JOHN A. ALONZO .... CINEMATOGRAPHER
PHILIP HARRISON .... PRODUCTION DESIGNER
SYDNEY Z. LITWAK .... PRODUCTION DESIGNER
MARIANNA ELLIOTT .... COSTUME DESIGNER
EDWARD M. ABROMS .... FILM EDITOR
FRANK MORRISS .... FILM EDITOR

BLUE VELVET
FREDERICK ELMES .... CINEMATOGRAPHER
PATRICIA NORRIS .... PRODUCTION DESIGNER
PATRICIA NORRIS .... COSTUME DESIGNER
DUWAYNE DYNHAM .... FILM EDITOR

BLUE WINDOW (TF)
WALKER HICKLIN .... COSTUME DESIGNER

BLUES BROTHERS, THE
STEPHEN M. KATZ .... CINEMATOGRAPHER
JOHN J. LLOYD .... PRODUCTION DESIGNER
DEBORAH NADOOLMAN .... COSTUME DESIGNER
GEORGE FOLSEY JR.* .... FILM EDITOR

BLUME IN LOVE
PATO GUZMAN .... PRODUCTION DESIGNER
DONN CAMBERN .... FILM EDITOR

BMX BANDITS
JOHN SEALE .... CINEMATOGRAPHER

BOARDWALK
BILLY WILLIAMS .... CINEMATOGRAPHER
GLENDA GANIS .... PRODUCTION DESIGNER
THOM NOBLE .... FILM EDITOR

BOAT, THE
ROLF ZEHETBAUER .... PRODUCTION DESIGNER
ALAN BALSAM .... FILM EDITOR

BOB & CAROL & TED & ALICE
PATO GUZMAN .... PRODUCTION DESIGNER
STUART H. PAPPE .... FILM EDITOR

BI-Bo

CINEMATOGRAPHERS
PRODUCTION
DESIGNERS,
COSTUME
DESIGNERS AND
FILM EDITORS
GUIDE

I
N
D
E
X

O
F

F
I
L
M

T
I
T
L
E
S

Bo-Bo

CINEMATOGRAPHERS
PRODUCTION
DESIGNERS,
COSTUME
DESIGNERS AND
FILM EDITORS
GUIDE

I
N
D
E
X

O
F

F
I
L
M

T
I
T
L
E
S

306

BOSS' WIFE, THE
GARY THIELTGES .... CINEMATOGRAPHER
KATHY CURTIS CAHILL .... PRODUCTION DESIGNER
BRENTON SWIFT .... PRODUCTION DESIGNER
JEAN-PIERRE DORLEAC .... COSTUME DESIGNER
JOHN A. MARTINELLI .... FILM EDITOR

BOSTON STRANGLER, THE
RICHARD H. KLINE .... CINEMATOGRAPHER
MARION ROTHMAN .... FILM EDITOR

BOSTONIANS, THE
WALTER LASSALLY .... CINEMATOGRAPHER
LEO AUSTIN .... PRODUCTION DESIGNER
JENNY BEAVEN .... COSTUME DESIGNER
JOHN BRIGHT .... COSTUME DESIGNER
KATHERINE WENNING .... FILM EDITOR

BOULEVARD NIGHTS
JOHN BAILEY .... CINEMATOGRAPHER
JACKSON DE GOVIA .... PRODUCTION DESIGNER
DENNIS DOLAN .... FILM EDITOR
RICHARD HALSEY .... FILM EDITOR

BOUND FOR GLORY
HASKELL WEXLER .... CINEMATOGRAPHER
JAMES H. SPENCER .... PRODUCTION DESIGNER
MICHAEL D. HALLER .... PRODUCTION DESIGNER
RICHARD CARTER .... PRODUCTION DESIGNER
WILLIAM WARE THEISS .... COSTUME DESIGNER
PEMBROKE J. HERRING .... FILM EDITOR
ROBERT C. JONES .... FILM EDITOR

BOUNTY, THE
ARTHUR IBBETSON .... CINEMATOGRAPHER
ANTHONY READING .... PRODUCTION DESIGNER
JOHN GRAYSMARK .... PRODUCTION DESIGNER
JOHN BLOOMFIELD .... COSTUME DESIGNER
BARRIE VINCE .... FILM EDITOR
TONY LAWSON .... FILM EDITOR

BOX OFFICE
ERIC SAARINEN .... CINEMATOGRAPHER
EDWARD SALIER .... FILM EDITOR

BOXCAR BERTHA
JOHN M. STEPHENS .... CINEMATOGRAPHER
DAVID NICHOLS .... PRODUCTION DESIGNER
BARBARA POKRAS .... FILM EDITOR

BOY AND HIS DOG, A
SCOTT CONRAD .... FILM EDITOR

BOY FROM CALABRIA, A
FRANCO DI GIACOMO .... CINEMATOGRAPHER
NINO BARAGLI .... FILM EDITOR

BOY IN BLUE, THE
PIERRE MIGNOT .... CINEMATOGRAPHER
WILLIAM BEETON .... PRODUCTION DESIGNER
JOHN HAY .... COSTUME DESIGNER
RIT WALLIS .... FILM EDITOR

BOY WHO COULD FLY, THE
ADAM HOLENDER .... CINEMATOGRAPHER
STEVEN B. POSTER .... CINEMATOGRAPHER
GRAEME MURRAY .... PRODUCTION DESIGNER
JAMES D. BISSELL .... PRODUCTION DESIGNER
PATRICK KENNEDY .... FILM EDITOR

BOY WHO DRANK TOO MUCH, THE (TF)
ALLEN DAVIAU .... CINEMATOGRAPHER

BOY WHO HAD EVERYTHING, THE
HENRY DANGAR .... FILM EDITOR

BOY WHO LOVED TROLLS THE, (TF)
CLETUS ANDERSON .... PRODUCTION DESIGNER

BOY'S LIFE
DICK BUSH .... CINEMATOGRAPHER

BOYFRIEND SCHOOL, THE
REED SMOOT .... CINEMATOGRAPHER
LINDA PEARL .... PRODUCTION DESIGNER
CAROL WOOD .... COSTUME DESIGNER
MARSHALL HARVEY .... FILM EDITOR

BOYFRIEND, THE
DAVID WATKIN .... CINEMATOGRAPHER
SIMON HOLLAND .... PRODUCTION DESIGNER

BOYS FROM BRAZIL, THE
HENRI DECAE† .... CINEMATOGRAPHER
GIL PARRONDO .... PRODUCTION DESIGNER
PETER LAMONT .... PRODUCTION DESIGNER
ANTHONY MENDLESON .... COSTUME DESIGNER
ROBERT E. SWINK .... FILM EDITOR

BOYS IN BLUE, THE
JOSEPH R. JENNINGS .... PRODUCTION DESIGNER

BOYS IN COMPANY C, THE
GODFREY A. GODAR .... CINEMATOGRAPHER
FRANK J. URIOSTE .... FILM EDITOR
JIM BENSON .... FILM EDITOR

BOYS IN THE BAND, THE
GERALD B. GREENBERG .... FILM EDITOR

BOYS N THE HOOD
CHARLES MILLS .... CINEMATOGRAPHER
BRUCE BELLAMY .... PRODUCTION DESIGNER
BRUCE CANNON .... FILM EDITOR

BOYS NEXT DOOR, THE
ARTHUR ALBERT .... CINEMATOGRAPHER
GAIL VIOLA .... COSTUME DESIGNER
ANDY HORVITCH .... FILM EDITOR

BRADDOCK: MISSING IN ACTION
MICHAEL J. DUTHIE .... FILM EDITOR

BRADDOCK: MISSING IN ACTION III
JOAO FERNANDES .... CINEMATOGRAPHER

BRADY'S ESCAPE
ELMER RAGALYI .... CINEMATOGRAPHER
NORMAN GAY .... FILM EDITOR

BRAINSTORM
RICHARD YURICICH .... CINEMATOGRAPHER
DAVID L. SNYDER .... PRODUCTION DESIGNER
JOHN VALLONE .... PRODUCTION DESIGNER
DONFELD .... COSTUME DESIGNER
EDWARD A. WARSCHILKA .... FILM EDITOR
FREEMAN DAVIES .... FILM EDITOR
PATRICK KENNEDY .... FILM EDITOR

BRAINWAVES
JON KRANHOUSE .... CINEMATOGRAPHER
ULLI LOMMEL .... CINEMATOGRAPHER
RICHARD S. BRUMMER .... FILM EDITOR

BRANNIGAN
GERRY FISHER .... CINEMATOGRAPHER
MALCOLM COOKE .... FILM EDITOR

BRASS (TF)
DEREK HYDE .... COSTUME DESIGNER

BRASS TARGET
TONY IMI .... CINEMATOGRAPHER
ROLF ZEHETBAUER .... PRODUCTION DESIGNER

BRAZIL
ROGER PRATT .... CINEMATOGRAPHER
JOHN BEARD .... PRODUCTION DESIGNER
KEITH PAIN .... PRODUCTION DESIGNER
NORMAN GARWOOD .... PRODUCTION DESIGNER
JAMES ACHESON .... COSTUME DESIGNER
JULIAN DOYLE .... FILM EDITOR

BRAZIL: A REPORT ON TORTURE
HASKELL WEXLER .... CINEMATOGRAPHER

BREACH OF CONTRACT
LINDA PEARL .... PRODUCTION DESIGNER

BREAD AND CHOCOLATE
LUCIANO TOVOLI .... CINEMATOGRAPHER

BREAK OF DAWN
JOHN NUTT .... FILM EDITOR

BREAK OF DAY
RUSSELL BOYD .... CINEMATOGRAPHER
WENDY DICKSON .... PRODUCTION DESIGNER

BREAKER BREAKER
MARIO DI LEO .... CINEMATOGRAPHER

Bo-Br

CINEMATOGRAPHERS
PRODUCTION
DESIGNERS,
COSTUME
DESIGNERS AND
FILM EDITORS
GUIDE

I
N
D
E
X

O
F

F
I
L
M

T
I
T
L
E
S

Br-Br

CINEMATOGRAPHERS
PRODUCTION
DESIGNERS,
COSTUME
DESIGNERS AND
FILM EDITORS
GUIDE

I
N
D
E
X

O
F

F
I
L
M

T
I
T
L
E
S

308

BREAKER MORANT
DONALD McALPINIE .... CINEMATOGRAPHER
DAVID COPPING .... PRODUCTION DESIGNER
ANNA SENIOR .... COSTUME DESIGNER
WILLIAM M. ANDERSON .... FILM EDITOR

BREAKER BREAKER
MARIO DI LEO .... CINEMATOGRAPHER

BREAKFAST CLUB, THE
THOMAS DEL RUTH .... CINEMATOGRAPHER
JOHN W. CORSO .... PRODUCTION DESIGNER
MARILYN VANCE-STRAKER .... COSTUME DESIGNER
DEDE ALLEN .... FILM EDITOR

BREAKHEART PASS
LUCIEN BALLARD† .... CINEMATOGRAPHER
BUZZ BRANDT .... FILM EDITOR

BREAKIN'
HANANIA BAER .... CINEMATOGRAPHER
LARRY BOCK .... FILM EDITOR
MARK HELFRICH .... FILM EDITOR
GIB JAFFE .... FILM EDITOR

BREAKIN' 2: ELECTRIC BOOGALOO
HANANIA BAER .... CINEMATOGRAPHER
PATRICK TAGLIAFERRO .... PRODUCTION DESIGNER
JOSEPH T. GARRITY .... PRODUCTION DESIGNER
DOROTHY BACA .... COSTUME DESIGNER
BARRY ZETLIN .... FILM EDITOR
BERT GLATSTEIN .... FILM EDITOR

BREAKING ALL THE RULES
RENE VERZIER .... CINEMATOGRAPHER
LAURIE DREW .... COSTUME DESIGNER
NICK ROTUNDO .... FILM EDITOR

BREAKING AWAY
MATTHEW F. LEONETTI .... CINEMATOGRAPHER
PATRIZIA VON BRANDENSTEIN .... PRODUCTION DESIGNER
CYNTHIA SCHEIDER .... FILM EDITOR

BREAKING GLASS
STEPHEN GOLDBLATT .... CINEMATOGRAPHER
EVAN HERCULES .... PRODUCTION DESIGNER
ERIC BOYD-PERKINS .... FILM EDITOR

BREAKING IN
MICHAEL COULTER .... CINEMATOGRAPHER
ADRIENNE ATKINSON .... PRODUCTION DESIGNER
LOUISE FROGLEY .... COSTUME DESIGNER
MICHAEL ELLIS .... FILM EDITOR

BREAKING OF BUMBO
RAYMOND SIMM .... PRODUCTION DESIGNER

BREAKING POINT
WOLF KROEGER .... PRODUCTION DESIGNER
STAN COLE .... FILM EDITOR

BREAKOUT
ALFRED SWEENEY .... PRODUCTION DESIGNER
JAMES G. HULSEY .... PRODUCTION DESIGNER

BREAKTHROUGH
RAYMOND POULTON .... FILM EDITOR

BREATHLESS
RICHARD H. KLINE .... CINEMATOGRAPHER
RICHARD SYLBERT .... PRODUCTION DESIGNER
J. ALLEN HIGHFILL† .... COSTUME DESIGNER
ROBERT L. ESTRIN .... FILM EDITOR
STEPHEN MACK .... FILM EDITOR

BREED APART, A
GEOFFREY STEPHENSON .... CINEMATOGRAPHER
WILLIAM BARCLAY .... PRODUCTION DESIGNER
CHRIS LEBENZON .... FILM EDITOR

BREEDERS
ARTHUR D. MARKS .... CINEMATOGRAPHER
MARINA ZURKOW .... PRODUCTION DESIGNER
BARRY ZETLIN .... FILM EDITOR

BRENDA STARR
FREDDIE FRANCIS .... CINEMATOGRAPHER
PETER STEIN .... CINEMATOGRAPHER
JOHN J. LLOYD .... PRODUCTION DESIGNER
PEGGY FARRELL-SALTEN .... COSTUME DESIGNER
MARK MELNICK .... FILM EDITOR

BREWSTER McCLOUD
JORDAN CRONENWETH .... CINEMATOGRAPHER
LOU LOMBARDO .... FILM EDITOR

BREWSTER'S MILLIONS
RIC WAITE .... CINEMATOGRAPHER
JOHN VALLONE .... PRODUCTION DESIGNER
WILLIAM HINEY .... PRODUCTION DESIGNER
MARILYN VANCE-STRAKER .... COSTUME DESIGNER
FREEMAN DAVIES .... FILM EDITOR
MICHAEL RIPPS .... FILM EDITOR

BRIAN'S SONG (TF)
JOSEPH BIROC .... CINEMATOGRAPHER

BRICKLAYERS ,THE
ALEX PHILLIPS .... CINEMATOGRAPHER

BRIDE IN BLACK, THE (TF)
RON GARCIA .... CINEMATOGRAPHER
DEAN TAUCHER .... PRODUCTION DESIGNER
SUSAN B. BROWDY .... FILM EDITOR

BRIDE OF BOOGEDY (TF)
JAMES SHANAHAN .... PRODUCTION DESIGNER

BRIDE OF RE-ANIMATOR
RICK FICHTER .... CINEMATOGRAPHER
PHILIP J.C. DUFFIN .... PRODUCTION DESIGNER
PETER TESCHNER .... FILM EDITOR

BRIDE WORE BLACK, THE
PIERRE GUFFROY .... PRODUCTION DESIGNER

BRIDE, THE
STEPHEN H. BURUM .... CINEMATOGRAPHER
MICHAEL SEYMOUR .... PRODUCTION DESIGNER
SHIRLEY RUSSELL .... COSTUME DESIGNER
MICHAEL ELLIS .... FILM EDITOR

BRIDESHEAD REVISITED (MS)
JANE ROBINSON .... COSTUME DESIGNER

BRIDESMAIDS (TF)
RICHARD BRACKEN .... FILM EDITOR

BRIDGE ACROSS TIME
WILLIAM MC ALLISTER .... PRODUCTION DESIGNER

BRIDGE AT REMAGEN, THE
ALFRED SWEENEY .... PRODUCTION DESIGNER

BRIDGE TO SILENCE (TF)
TOM NEUWIRTH .... CINEMATOGRAPHER

BRIDGE TOO FAR, A
GEOFFREY UNSWORTH† .... CINEMATOGRAPHER
HARRY WAXMAN .... CINEMATOGRAPHER
TERENCE MARSH .... PRODUCTION DESIGNER
ANTONY GIBBS .... FILM EDITOR

BRIEF ENCOUNTER
ARTHUR IBBETSON .... CINEMATOGRAPHER

BRIGADOON
IRENE SHARAFF .... COSTUME DESIGNER
BOB MACKIE .... COSTUME DESIGNER

BRIGHT LIGHTS, BIG CITY
GORDON WILLIS .... CINEMATOGRAPHER
SANTO LOQUASTO .... PRODUCTION DESIGNER
THOMAS C. WARREN .... PRODUCTION DESIGNER
BERNIE POLLACK .... COSTUME DESIGNER
JOHN BLOOM .... FILM EDITOR

BRIGHTON BEACH MEMOIRS
JOHN BAILEY .... CINEMATOGRAPHER
PAUL EADS .... PRODUCTION DESIGNER
STUART WURTZEL .... PRODUCTION DESIGNER
HARRY CURTIS .... COSTUME DESIGNER
JOSEPH G. AULISI .... COSTUME DESIGNER
CAROL LITTLETON .... FILM EDITOR

BRIMSTONE AND TREACLE
PETER HANNAN .... CINEMATOGRAPHER
NORMAN GARWOOD .... PRODUCTION DESIGNER
PAUL GREEN .... FILM EDITOR

BRING ME THE HEAD OF ALFREDO GARCIA
ALEX PHILLIPS .... CINEMATOGRAPHER
GARTH CRAVEN .... FILM EDITOR

BRING ON THE NIGHT (FD)
RALF D. BODE .... CINEMATOGRAPHER
FERDINANDO SCARFIOTTI .... PRODUCTION DESIGNER
COLLEEN C. ATWOOD .... COSTUME DESIGNER
MELVIN SHAPIRO .... FILM EDITOR
ROBERT K. LAMBERT .... FILM EDITOR

BRINK'S JOB, THE
A. NORMAN LEIGH .... CINEMATOGRAPHER
ANGELO GRAHAM .... PRODUCTION DESIGNER
DEAN TAVOULARIS .... PRODUCTION DESIGNER
BUD SMITH .... FILM EDITOR
ROBERT K. LAMBERT .... FILM EDITOR

BRITANNIA HOSPITAL
MIKE FASH .... CINEMATOGRAPHER
MICHAEL ELLIS .... FILM EDITOR

BROADCAST NEWS
MICHAEL BALLHAUS .... CINEMATOGRAPHER
CHARLES ROSEN .... PRODUCTION DESIGNER
MOLLY MAGINNIS .... COSTUME DESIGNER
RICHARD MARKS .... FILM EDITOR

BROADWAY DANNY ROSE
GORDON WILLIS .... CINEMATOGRAPHER
MEL BOURNE .... PRODUCTION DESIGNER
JEFFREY KURLAND .... COSTUME DESIGNER
SUSAN E. MORSE .... FILM EDITOR

BROKEN BADGES (TF)
CYRUS BLOCK .... CINEMATOGRAPHER
GRAEME MURRAY .... PRODUCTION DESIGNER
ARGYLE COE NELSON .... FILM EDITOR
LARRY D. LESTER .... FILM EDITOR

BROKEN ENGLISH
ELLIOT DAVIS .... CINEMATOGRAPHER

BROKEN NOSES (FD)
JEFF PREISS .... CINEMATOGRAPHER
PHYLLIS FAMIGLIETTI .... FILM EDITOR

BROKEN RAINBOW
JOANNE D'ANTONIO .... FILM EDITOR

BROKEN VOWS
THOMAS BURSTYN .... CINEMATOGRAPHER

BRONCO BILLY
DAVID WORTH .... CINEMATOGRAPHER
EUGENE LOURIE .... PRODUCTION DESIGNER
FERRIS WEBSTER .... FILM EDITOR
JOEL COX .... FILM EDITOR

BRONTE SISTERS, THE
BRUNO NUYTTEN .... CINEMATOGRAPHER

BRONX WAR, THE
MICHAEL SCHWEITZER .... FILM EDITOR

BROOD, THE
MARK IRWIN .... CINEMATOGRAPHER
CAROL SPIER .... PRODUCTION DESIGNER
ALAN COLLINS .... FILM EDITOR

BROTHER FROM ANOTHER PLANET, THE
ERNEST DICKERSON .... CINEMATOGRAPHER
NORA CHAVOOSHIAN .... PRODUCTION DESIGNER
CYNTHIA FLYNT .... COSTUME DESIGNER
KAREN PERRY .... COSTUME DESIGNER
JOHN SAYLES .... FILM EDITOR

BROTHER FUTURE (TF)
RON VARGAS .... CINEMATOGRAPHER
SHARON SEYMOUR .... PRODUCTION DESIGNER
ROBIN WILSON .... FILM EDITOR

BROTHER SUN SISTER MOON
GIANNI QUARANTA .... PRODUCTION DESIGNER

BROTHERHOOD OF JUSTICE (TF)
HANANIA BAER .... CINEMATOGRAPHER

BROTHERHOOD OF THE ROSE (TF)
JAMES BARTLE .... CINEMATOGRAPHER
DAVID COPPING .... PRODUCTION DESIGNER
BRAD R. LOMAN .... COSTUME DESIGNER

BROTHERLY LOVE (TF)
BRADFORD MAY .... CINEMATOGRAPHER

BROTHERS
JOHN A. MORRILL .... CINEMATOGRAPHER
VINCENT M. CRESCIMAN .... PRODUCTION DESIGNER
WILLIAM DORNISCH .... FILM EDITOR

BROTHERS O'TOOLE, THE
BUD MOLIN .... FILM EDITOR

BROTHERS-IN-LAW (TF)
DONALD BIRNKRANT .... CINEMATOGRAPHER

BRUBAKER
BRUNO NUYTTEN .... CINEMATOGRAPHER
J. MICHAEL RIVA .... PRODUCTION DESIGNER
ROBERT BROWN .... FILM EDITOR

BRUTE CORPS
MICHAEL D. MARGULIES .... CINEMATOGRAPHER

BUCK AND THE PREACHER
ALEX PHILLIPS .... CINEMATOGRAPHER
SYDNEY Z. LITWAK .... PRODUCTION DESIGNER
PEMBROKE J. HERRING .... FILM EDITOR

BUCK ROGERS
FRANK BEASCOECHEA .... CINEMATOGRAPHER
PAUL PETERS .... PRODUCTION DESIGNER

BUCK ROGERS IN THE 21ST CENTURY
JEAN-PIERRE DORLEAC .... COSTUME DESIGNER

BUCKTOWN
GEORGE FOLSEY JR.* .... FILM EDITOR

BUDDY BUDDY
HARRY STRADLING, JR. .... CINEMATOGRAPHER

BUDDY HOLLY STORY, THE
STEVAN LARNER .... CINEMATOGRAPHER
JOEL SCHILLER .... PRODUCTION DESIGNER
DAVID BLEWITT .... FILM EDITOR

BUDDY SYSTEM, THE
MATTHEW F. LEONETTI .... CINEMATOGRAPHER
RODGER MAUS .... PRODUCTION DESIGNER
JOSEPH G. AULISI .... COSTUME DESIGNER
ARTHUR SCHMIDT .... FILM EDITOR

BUDDY BUDDY
DANIEL LOMINO .... PRODUCTION DESIGNER
ARGYLE NELSON .... FILM EDITOR

BUFFALO BILL AND THE INDIANS
ANTHONY MASTERS .... PRODUCTION DESIGNER
ANTHONY POWELL .... COSTUME DESIGNER
DENNIS M. HILL .... FILM EDITOR

BUFFALO BILL AND THE INDIANS OR SITTING BULL'S HISTORY LESSON
PAUL LOHMANN .... CINEMATOGRAPHER

BUFFET FROID
JEAN PENZER .... CINEMATOGRAPHER
CLAUDE MERLIN .... FILM EDITOR

BUG
MICHEL HUGO .... CINEMATOGRAPHER

BUGSY MALONE
MICHAEL SERESIN .... CINEMATOGRAPHER
PETER BIZIOU .... CINEMATOGRAPHER
MONICA HOWE .... COSTUME DESIGNER
GERRY HAMBLING .... FILM EDITOR

BULL DURHAM
BOBBY BYRNE .... CINEMATOGRAPHER
ARMIN GANZ .... PRODUCTION DESIGNER
DAVID LUBIN .... PRODUCTION DESIGNER
LOUISE FROGLEY .... COSTUME DESIGNER
ADAM WEISS .... FILM EDITOR
ROBERT LEIGHTON .... FILM EDITOR

BULLAMANKANKA
DAVID EGGBY .... CINEMATOGRAPHER
JOHN SCOTT .... FILM EDITOR

Br-Bu

CINEMATOGRAPHERS
PRODUCTION
DESIGNERS,
COSTUME
DESIGNERS AND
FILM EDITORS
GUIDE

INDEX OF FILM TITLES

Bu-By

CINEMATOGRAPHERS
PRODUCTION
DESIGNERS,
COSTUME
DESIGNERS AND
FILM EDITORS
GUIDE

I
N
D
E
X

O
F

F
I
L
M

T
I
T
L
E
S

BULLETPROOF
FRANCIS GRUMMAN .... CINEMATOGRAPHER
ADRIAN H. GORTON .... PRODUCTION DESIGNER
JEFF FREEMAN .... FILM EDITOR

BULLIES
RENE VERZIER .... CINEMATOGRAPHER
JACK MCADAM .... PRODUCTION DESIGNER
MAYA MANI .... COSTUME DESIGNER
NICK ROTUNDO .... FILM EDITOR

BULLITT
ALBERT BRENNER .... PRODUCTION DESIGNER

BULLSEYE
RICHARD FRANCIS-BRUCE .... FILM EDITOR

BULLSHOT
ALEX THOMSON .... CINEMATOGRAPHER
KEITH PAIN .... PRODUCTION DESIGNER
NORMAN GARWOOD .... PRODUCTION DESIGNER
JAMES ACHESON .... COSTUME DESIGNER
ALAN JONES .... FILM EDITOR

BUNNY'S TALE, A (TF)
GAYNE RESCHER .... CINEMATOGRAPHER
MILLIE MOORE .... FILM EDITOR

BURBS, THE
ROBERT M. STEVENS .... CINEMATOGRAPHER
JAMES H. SPENCER .... PRODUCTION DESIGNER
ROSANNA NORTON .... COSTUME DESIGNER
MARSHALL HARVEY .... FILM EDITOR

BURGLAR
WILLIAM A. FRAKER .... CINEMATOGRAPHER
MICHAEL CORENBLITH .... PRODUCTION DESIGNER
TODD HALLOWELL .... PRODUCTION DESIGNER
SUSAN BECKER .... COSTUME DESIGNER
WILLIAM STEINKAMP .... FILM EDITOR
FREDRIC STEINKAMP .... FILM EDITOR

BURIED ALIVE
GERARD LOUBEAU .... CINEMATOGRAPHER
LEONARDO COEN .... PRODUCTION DESIGNER
GILBERT KIKONE .... FILM EDITOR

BURKE AND WILLS
RUSSELL BOYD .... CINEMATOGRAPHER
TIM WELLBURN .... FILM EDITOR

BURNIN' LOVE
MARK IRWIN .... CINEMATOGRAPHER
LINDA MATHESON .... COSTUME DESIGNER
DANFORD B. GREENE .... FILM EDITOR

BURNING BED, THE (TF)
ISIDORE MANKOFSKY .... CINEMATOGRAPHER
HERMAN ZIMMERMAN .... PRODUCTION DESIGNER
MICHAEL A. STEVENSON .... FILM EDITOR
RICHARD FETTERMAN .... FILM EDITOR

BURNING LOVE
ROY FORGE SMITH .... PRODUCTION DESIGNER

BURNING SECRET
ERNEST DAY .... CINEMATOGRAPHER
BARBARA BAUM .... COSTUME DESIGNER
MONICA JACOBS .... COSTUME DESIGNER
PAUL GREEN .... FILM EDITOR

BURNING, THE
HARVEY HARRISON .... CINEMATOGRAPHER

BURNT OFFERINGS
JACQUES MARQUETTE .... CINEMATOGRAPHER
STEVAN LARNER .... CINEMATOGRAPHER
EUGENE LOURIE .... PRODUCTION DESIGNER
ANN ROTH .... COSTUME DESIGNER
DENNIS M. VIRKLER .... FILM EDITOR

BURROUGHS
JOELE VAN EFFENTERRE .... FILM EDITOR

BURROWS (FD)
MIKE SOUTHON .... CINEMATOGRAPHER
TOM DICILLO .... CINEMATOGRAPHER

BUS, THE
HASKELL WEXLER .... CINEMATOGRAPHER

BUS II
HASKELL WEXLER .... CINEMATOGRAPHER

BUSGY MALONE
GEOFFREY KIRKLAND .... PRODUCTION DESIGNER

BUSHIDO BLADE, THE
ANNE V. COATES .... FILM EDITOR
IAN CRAFFORD .... FILM EDITOR

BUSTED UP
LUDEK BOGNER .... CINEMATOGRAPHER

BUSTER
TONY IMI .... CINEMATOGRAPHER
SIMON HOLLAND .... PRODUCTION DESIGNER
EVANGELINE HARRISON .... COSTUME DESIGNER
LESLEY WALKER .... FILM EDITOR

BUSTER AND BILLIE
MARIO TOSI .... CINEMATOGRAPHER
MICHAEL KAHN .... FILM EDITOR

BUSTIN' LOOSE
DENNIS DALZELL .... CINEMATOGRAPHER
JOHN W. CORSO .... PRODUCTION DESIGNER
STEPHEN LOOMIS .... COSTUME DESIGNER
DAVID HOLDEN .... FILM EDITOR
HARRY KERAMIDAS .... FILM EDITOR

BUSTING
JAMES MITCHELL .... FILM EDITOR

BUTCH AND SUNDANCE: THE EARLY DAYS
LASZLO KOVACS .... CINEMATOGRAPHER
BRIAN EATWELL .... PRODUCTION DESIGNER
JACKSON DE GOVIA .... PRODUCTION DESIGNER
WILLIAM WARE THEISS .... COSTUME DESIGNER
ANTONY GIBBS .... FILM EDITOR
GEORGE TRIROGOFF .... FILM EDITOR

BUTCH CASSIDY AND THE SUNDANCE KID
CONRAD HALL .... CINEMATOGRAPHER
JOHN C. HOWARD .... FILM EDITOR

BUTCHER, BAKER, NIGHTMARE MAKER
ROBBIE GREENBERG .... CINEMATOGRAPHER

BUTLEY
GERRY FISHER .... CINEMATOGRAPHER
MALCOLM COOKE .... FILM EDITOR

BUTTERFLIES ARE FREE
DAVID BLEWITT .... FILM EDITOR

BUTTERFLY
EDDY VAN DER ENDEN .... CINEMATOGRAPHER
BRENT SCHOENFIELD .... FILM EDITOR

BUY AND CELL
DANIELE NANNUZZI .... CINEMATOGRAPHER
GIOVANNI NATALUCCI .... PRODUCTION DESIGNER
BERT GLATSTEIN .... FILM EDITOR

BY DAWN'S EARLY LIGHT (CTF)
MICHAEL NOVOTNY .... PRODUCTION DESIGNER

BY DESIGN
REUBEN FREED .... PRODUCTION DESIGNER

BYE BYE BABY
GIUSEPPE RUZZOLINI .... CINEMATOGRAPHER
RAIMONDO CROCIANI .... FILM EDITOR

BYE BYE BLUES
VIC SARIN .... CINEMATOGRAPHER
CHRISTOPHER TATE .... FILM EDITOR

BYE BYE BRAZIL
LAURO ESCOREL .... CINEMATOGRAPHER

BYE BYE MONKEY
DANTE FERRETTI .... PRODUCTION DESIGNER

BYE, BYE BRAVERMAN
RALPH ROSENBLUM .... FILM EDITOR

C

C.A.T. SQUAD (TF)
ROBERT D. YEOMAN .... CINEMATOGRAPHER
DOUGLAS HIGGINS .... PRODUCTION DESIGNER
RICHARD SAWYER .... PRODUCTION DESIGNER

C.C. & COMPANY
CHARLES F. WHEELER .... CINEMATOGRAPHER

C.H.O.M.P.S.
CHARLES F. WHEELER .... CINEMATOGRAPHER

C.H.U.D.
PETER STEIN .... CINEMATOGRAPHER
CLAIRE SIMPSON-CROZIER .... FILM EDITOR
DENNIS O'CONNOR .... FILM EDITOR

C.H.U.D II: BUD THE CHUD
RANDY MOORE .... PRODUCTION DESIGNER

CABARET
GEOFFREY UNSWORTH† .... CINEMATOGRAPHER
ROLF ZEHETBAUER .... PRODUCTION DESIGNER
DAVID BRETHERTON .... FILM EDITOR

CABOBLANCO
ALEX PHILLIPS .... CINEMATOGRAPHER
MICHAEL F. ANDERSON .... FILM EDITOR

CACTUS
YURI SOKOL .... CINEMATOGRAPHER
ASHER BILU .... PRODUCTION DESIGNER
TIM LEWIS .... FILM EDITOR

CACTUS FLOWER
MAURY WINETROBE .... FILM EDITOR

CADDIE
PETER JAMES .... CINEMATOGRAPHER
TIM WELLBURN .... FILM EDITOR

CADDYSHACK
STEVAN LARNER .... CINEMATOGRAPHER
STAN JOLLEY .... PRODUCTION DESIGNER
DAVID BRETHERTON .... FILM EDITOR
WILLIAM CARRUTH .... FILM EDITOR

CADDYSHACK II
HARRY STRADLING, JR. .... CINEMATOGRAPHER
WILLIAM F. MATTHEWS .... PRODUCTION DESIGNER
MAY ROUTH .... COSTUME DESIGNER
BERNARD GRIBBLE .... FILM EDITOR

CADENCE
RICHARD LEITERMAN .... CINEMATOGRAPHER
IAN THOMAS .... PRODUCTION DESIGNER
MARTIN HUNTER .... FILM EDITOR

CADILLAC MAN
DAVID GRIBBLE .... CINEMATOGRAPHER
GENE RUDOLF .... PRODUCTION DESIGNER
DEBORAH LA GORCE KRAMER .... COSTUME DESIGNER
RICHARD FRANCIS-BRUCE .... FILM EDITOR

CAESAR AND CLEOPATRA (TF)
JANE ROBINSON .... COSTUME DESIGNER

CAGE
JOSEPH ALTADONNA .... PRODUCTION DESIGNER
SANDRA CULOTTA .... COSTUME DESIGNER

CAGED HEAT
TAK FUJIMOTO .... CINEMATOGRAPHER

CAGNEY & LACEY (TF)
BERT DUNK .... CINEMATOGRAPHER
DOUGLAS HIGGINS .... PRODUCTION DESIGNER
MICHAEL J. HILL .... FILM EDITOR

CAINE MUTINY COURT MARTIAL, THE (TF)
JACEK LASKUS .... CINEMATOGRAPHER

CAL
JERZY ZIELINSKI .... CINEMATOGRAPHER
STUART CRAIG .... PRODUCTION DESIGNER
PENNY ROSE .... COSTUME DESIGNER
MICHAEL BRADSELL .... FILM EDITOR

CALAMITY JANE (TF)
ALBERT HESCHONG .... PRODUCTION DESIGNER

CALENDAR GIRL MURDERS, THE (TF)
ROBERT STEADMAN .... CINEMATOGRAPHER
BETSY JONES .... COSTUME DESIGNER

CALIFORNIA DREAMING
BOBBY BYRNE .... CINEMATOGRAPHER
WILLIAM HINEY .... PRODUCTION DESIGNER
ERNEST MISKO .... COSTUME DESIGNER
ROY E. PETERSON .... FILM EDITOR
SIDNEY LEVIN .... FILM EDITOR

CALIFORNIA GIRLS (TF)
GIL HUBBS .... CINEMATOGRAPHER
MICHAEL JABLOW .... FILM EDITOR

CALIFORNIA SPLIT
PAUL LOHMANN .... CINEMATOGRAPHER
LOU LOMBARDO .... FILM EDITOR

CALIFORNIA SUITE
DAVID M. WALSH .... CINEMATOGRAPHER
ALBERT BRENNER .... PRODUCTION DESIGNER
PATRICIA NORRIS .... COSTUME DESIGNER
MARGARET BOOTH .... FILM EDITOR
MICHAEL A. STEVENSON .... FILM EDITOR

CALL ME
ZOLTAN DAVID .... CINEMATOGRAPHER
STEVEN MCCABE .... PRODUCTION DESIGNER
PAUL FRIED .... FILM EDITOR

CALL ME ANNA (TF)
MARK IRWIN .... CINEMATOGRAPHER
BRYAN RYMAN .... PRODUCTION DESIGNER
LEE BURCH .... FILM EDITOR

CALL ME MADAM
JOHN DE CUIR .... PRODUCTION DESIGNER
IRENE SHARAFF .... COSTUME DESIGNER

CALL TO GLORY
WARD PRESTON .... PRODUCTION DESIGNER

CALL TO GLORY (TF)
JEFFREY L. GOLDSTEIN .... PRODUCTION DESIGNER

CALLER, THE
ARMANDO NANNUZZI .... CINEMATOGRAPHER
GIOVANNI NATALUCCI .... PRODUCTION DESIGNER
BERT GLATSTEIN .... FILM EDITOR

CALLIE & SON (TF)
J. MICHAEL RIVA .... PRODUCTION DESIGNER

CAME A HOT FRIDAY
ALAN BOLLINGER .... CINEMATOGRAPHER
RON HIGHFIELD .... PRODUCTION DESIGNER
BARBARA DARRAGH .... COSTUME DESIGNER
KEN ZEMKE .... FILM EDITOR

CAMELOT
RICHARD H. KLINE .... CINEMATOGRAPHER
FERNANDO CARRERE .... PRODUCTION DESIGNER

CAMERON'S CLOSET
RUSSELL CARPENTER .... CINEMATOGRAPHER
MICHAEL BINGHAM .... PRODUCTION DESIGNER
FRANK DE PALMA .... FILM EDITOR

CAMILA
EUGENIO ZANETTI .... PRODUCTION DESIGNER

CAMILLE (TF)
JEAN TOURNIER .... CINEMATOGRAPHER
MARGARET BOOTH .... FILM EDITOR

CAMORRA
GIUSEPPI LANCI .... CINEMATOGRAPHER
ENRICO JOB .... PRODUCTION DESIGNER
LUIGI ZITA .... FILM EDITOR

CAMP CUCAMONGA (TF)
PETER SMOKLER .... CINEMATOGRAPHER
LARRY HARRIS .... FILM EDITOR

C.-Ca

CINEMATOGRAPHERS
PRODUCTION
DESIGNERS,
COSTUME
DESIGNERS AND
FILM EDITORS
GUIDE

INDEX OF FILM TITLES

CINEMATOGRAPHERS
PRODUCTION
DESIGNERS,
COSTUME
DESIGNERS AND
FILM EDITORS
GUIDE

I
N
D
E
X

O
F

F
I
L
M

T
I
T
L
E
S

CAMPION-SWEET DANGER (TF)
JOHN BAKER .... CINEMATOGRAPHER
PAUL MUNTING .... PRODUCTION DESIGNER
JERRY LEON .... FILM EDITOR
PHILIP KLOSS .... FILM EDITOR

CAMPUS MAN
FRANCIS KENNEY .... CINEMATOGRAPHER
DAVID GROPMAN .... PRODUCTION DESIGNER
ELISABETTA ROGIANI .... COSTUME DESIGNER
STEVEN POLIVKA .... FILM EDITOR

CAN SHE BAKE A CHERRY PIE?
ROBERT FIORE .... CINEMATOGRAPHER

CAN'T BUY ME LOVE
PETER LYONS COLLISTER .... CINEMATOGRAPHER
DONALD LIGHT-HARRIS .... PRODUCTION DESIGNER
GREGORY POE .... COSTUME DESIGNER
JEFF S. GOURSON .... FILM EDITOR

CAN'T STOP THE MUSIC
BILL BUTLER .... CINEMATOGRAPHER
HAROLD MICHELSON .... PRODUCTION DESIGNER
STEPHEN HENDRICKSON .... PRODUCTION DESIGNER
JANE GREENWOOD .... COSTUME DESIGNER
JOHN F. BURNETT .... FILM EDITOR

CAN-CAN
IRENE SHARAFF .... COSTUME DESIGNER

CANDIDATE, THE
VICTOR J. KEMPER .... CINEMATOGRAPHER
GENE CALLAHAN .... PRODUCTION DESIGNER
PATRICIA NORRIS .... COSTUME DESIGNER
RICHARD A. HARRIS .... FILM EDITOR
ROBERT L. ESTRIN .... FILM EDITOR

CANDLESHOE
PETER BOITA .... FILM EDITOR

CANDY MOUNTAIN
PIO CORRADI .... CINEMATOGRAPHER
JENNIFER AUGE .... FILM EDITOR

CANNERY ROW
SVEN NYKVIST .... CINEMATOGRAPHER
RICHARD MACDONALD .... PRODUCTION DESIGNER
WILLIAM F. O'BRIEN .... PRODUCTION DESIGNER
RUTH MYERS .... COSTUME DESIGNER
DAVID BRETHERTON .... FILM EDITOR

CANNIBAL ORGY
ALFRED TAYLOR .... CINEMATOGRAPHER

CANNONBALL
TAK FUJIMOTO .... CINEMATOGRAPHER
MICHAEL LEVESQUE .... PRODUCTION DESIGNER

CANNONBALL RUN, THE
MICHAEL C. BUTLER .... CINEMATOGRAPHER
CAROL WENGER .... PRODUCTION DESIGNER
DONN CAMBERN .... FILM EDITOR
WILLIAM GORDEAN .... FILM EDITOR

CANNONBALL RUN II
NICK MCLEAN .... CINEMATOGRAPHER
NORMAN SALLING .... COSTUME DESIGNER
CARL KRESS .... FILM EDITOR
WILLIAM GORDEAN .... FILM EDITOR

CANTERBURY TALES, THE
DANTE FERRETTI .... PRODUCTION DESIGNER

CAPE FEAR
THELMA SCHOONMAKER-POWELL .... FILM EDITOR

CAPITAL NEWS (PILOT)
CHARLES D. (CHUCK) MINSKY .... CINEMATOGRAPHER
BRIAN EATWELL .... PRODUCTION DESIGNER
MAY ROUTH .... COSTUME DESIGNER

CAPRICCIO
WILLIAM J. CREBER .... PRODUCTION DESIGNER

CAPRICORN ONE
BILL BUTLER .... CINEMATOGRAPHER
ALBERT BRENNER .... PRODUCTION DESIGNER
DAVID M. HABER .... PRODUCTION DESIGNER
PATRICIA NORRIS .... COSTUME DESIGNER
JAMES MITCHELL .... FILM EDITOR

CAPTAIN & TENNILLE SONG BOOK, THE (TV)
BOB MACKIE .... COSTUME DESIGNER

CAPTAIN AMERICA (TF)
DAVID L. SNYDER .... PRODUCTION DESIGNER
VIN BURNHAM .... COSTUME DESIGNER

CAPTAIN EO
BETTY PECHA MADDEN .... COSTUME DESIGNER
LISA FRUCHTMAN .... FILM EDITOR
WALTER MURCH .... FILM EDITOR

CAPTIVE HEARTS
STEVE SARDANIS .... PRODUCTION DESIGNER
NICOLETTA MASSONE .... COSTUME DESIGNER
YURI LUHOVY .... FILM EDITOR

CAR TROUBLE
MIKE GARFATH .... CINEMATOGRAPHER

CAR WASH
FRANK STANLEY .... CINEMATOGRAPHER
CHRISTOPHER HOLMES .... FILM EDITOR

CAR, THE
GERALD HIRSCHFELD .... CINEMATOGRAPHER

CARAVAGGIO
GABRIEL BERISTAIN .... CINEMATOGRAPHER
CHRISTOPHER HOBBS .... PRODUCTION DESIGNER
SANDY POWELL .... COSTUME DESIGNER
GEORGE AKERS .... FILM EDITOR

CARAVANS
DOUGLAS SLOCOMBE .... CINEMATOGRAPHER
RENIE CONLEY .... COSTUME DESIGNER
RICHARD MARDEN .... FILM EDITOR

CARBON COPY
FRED J. KOENEKAMP .... CINEMATOGRAPHER
TED HAWORTH .... PRODUCTION DESIGNER
MARION SEGAL .... FILM EDITOR

CARDINAL, THE
DONALD BROOKS .... COSTUME DESIGNER

CAREER OPPORTUNITIES
DON MCALPINE .... CINEMATOGRAPHER
PAUL SYLBERT .... PRODUCTION DESIGNER
BETSY COX .... COSTUME DESIGNER
GLENN FARR .... FILM EDITOR
PECK PRIOR .... FILM EDITOR

CAREFUL HE MIGHT HEAR YOU
JOHN SEALE .... CINEMATOGRAPHER
JOHN STODDART .... PRODUCTION DESIGNER
BRUCE FINLAYSON .... COSTUME DESIGNER
RICHARD FRANCIS-BRUCE .... FILM EDITOR

CAREY TREATMENT, THE
ALFRED SWEENEY .... PRODUCTION DESIGNER
RALPH E. WINTERS .... FILM EDITOR

CARMEN
PASQUALINO DE SANTIS .... CINEMATOGRAPHER
TEO ESCAMILLA .... CINEMATOGRAPHER
RUGGERO MASTROIANNI .... FILM EDITOR

CARNAL KNOWLEDGE
RICHARD SYLBERT .... PRODUCTION DESIGNER
SAM O'STEEN .... FILM EDITOR

CARNIVAL ROCK
ROBERT KINOSHITA .... PRODUCTION DESIGNER

CARNY
HARRY STRADLING, JR. .... CINEMATOGRAPHER
JOSAN F. RUSSO .... PRODUCTION DESIGNER
WILLIAM J. CASSIDY .... PRODUCTION DESIGNER
DENNIS DOLAN .... FILM EDITOR
STUART H. PAPPE .... FILM EDITOR

CARO PAPA
TONINO DELLI COLLI .... CINEMATOGRAPHER

CAROL BURNETT SHOW, THE (TV)
BOB MACKIE .... COSTUME DESIGNER

CAROL CHANNING PRESENTS THE SEVEN DEADLY SINS (TV)
BOB MACKIE .... COSTUME DESIGNER

Ca-Ch

CINEMATOGRAPHERS
PRODUCTION
DESIGNERS,
COSTUME
DESIGNERS AND
FILM EDITORS
GUIDE

CAROL, CARL, WHOOPIE AND ROBIN (TV)
BOB MACKIE .... COSTUME DESIGNER

CAROUSEL (TV)
BOB MACKIE .... COSTUME DESIGNER

CARRIE
MARIO TOSI .... CINEMATOGRAPHER
WILLIAM KENNEY .... PRODUCTION DESIGNER
ROSANNA NORTON .... COSTUME DESIGNER
PAUL HIRSCH .... FILM EDITOR

CARRY ON EMMANNUELLE
ALAN HUME .... CINEMATOGRAPHER
PETER BOITA .... FILM EDITOR

CARRY ON ENGLAND
RICHARD MARDEN .... FILM EDITOR

CARTIER AFFAIR, THE (TF)
DONFELD .... COSTUME DESIGNER

CASE OF RAPE, A (TF)
WILLIAM HINEY .... PRODUCTION DESIGNER

CASEY'S GIFT: FOR LOVE OF A CHILD (TF)
RICHARD RAWLINGS JR. .... CINEMATOGRAPHER
R. CLIFFORD SEARCY .... PRODUCTION DESIGNER
CORKY EHLERS .... FILM EDITOR

CASEY'S SHADOW
JOHN A. ALONZO .... CINEMATOGRAPHER
ROBERT LUTHARDT .... PRODUCTION DESIGNER
MOSS MABRY .... COSTUME DESIGNER
SIDNEY LEVIN .... FILM EDITOR

CASSANDRA CROSSING, THE
ENNIO GUARNIERI .... CINEMATOGRAPHER
FRANÇOISE BONNOT .... FILM EDITOR
ROBERTO SILVI .... FILM EDITOR

CASTAWAY
HARVEY HARRISION .... CINEMATOGRAPHER
ANDREW SANDERS .... PRODUCTION DESIGNER
NIC EDE .... COSTUME DESIGNER
TONY LAWSON .... FILM EDITOR

CASTLE KEEP
MALCOLM COOKE .... FILM EDITOR

CASTLE OF THE SPIDER'S WEB, THE
SHINOBU MURAKI .... PRODUCTION DESIGNER
YOSHIRO MURAKI .... PRODUCTION DESIGNER

CASUAL SEX
ROLF KESTERMANN .... CINEMATOGRAPHER
RANDY SER .... PRODUCTION DESIGNER
GRANIA PRESTON .... COSTUME DESIGNER
DONN CAMBERN .... FILM EDITOR
SHELDON KAHN .... FILM EDITOR

CASUALTIES OF WAR
STEPHEN H. BURUM .... CINEMATOGRAPHER
BERNARD HIDES .... PRODUCTION DESIGNER
WOLF KROEGER .... PRODUCTION DESIGNER
RICHARD BRUNO .... COSTUME DESIGNER
BILL PANKOW .... FILM EDITOR

CAT AND THE CANARY, THE
ALEX THOMSON .... CINEMATOGRAPHER
ANTHONY PRATT .... PRODUCTION DESIGNER

CAT CHASER
ANTHONY B. RICHMOND .... CINEMATOGRAPHER
DAN LEIGH .... PRODUCTION DESIGNER
MICHAEL KAPLAN .... COSTUME DESIGNER
KIM KENNEDY .... FILM EDITOR

CAT FROM OUTER SPACE, THE
CHARLES F. WHEELER .... CINEMATOGRAPHER

CAT ON A HOT TIN ROOF (TF)
DAVID JENKINS .... PRODUCTION DESIGNER

CAT PEOPLE
JOHN BAILEY .... CINEMATOGRAPHER
ED RICHARDSON .... PRODUCTION DESIGNER
FERDINANDO SCARFIOTTI .... PRODUCTION DESIGNER
DANIEL PAREDES .... COSTUME DESIGNER
BUD SMITH .... FILM EDITOR
JACQUELINE CAMBAS .... FILM EDITOR

CAT'S EYE
JEFFREY S. GINN .... PRODUCTION DESIGNER
CLIFFORD CAPONE .... COSTUME DESIGNER
SCOTT CONRAD .... FILM EDITOR

CATACOMBS
SERGIO SALVATI .... CINEMATOGRAPHER
GIOVANNI NATALUCCI .... PRODUCTION DESIGNER
TOM MASHELSKI .... FILM EDITOR

CATCH 22
RICHARD SYLBERT .... PRODUCTION DESIGNER
SAM O'STEEN .... FILM EDITOR

CATCH A PEBBLE
PAUL LOHMANN .... CINEMATOGRAPHER

CATCH ME IF YOU CAN
RONN SCHMIDT .... CINEMATOGRAPHER
STUART BLATT .... PRODUCTION DESIGNER
BOB DUCSAY .... FILM EDITOR

CATCH MY SOUL
RICHARD A. HARRIS .... FILM EDITOR

CATCH THE HEAT
FRANK HARRIS .... CINEMATOGRAPHER
CHRISTOPHER HOLMES .... FILM EDITOR

CATCHS THE HEAT
ROBERT JESSUP .... CINEMATOGRAPHER

CATHY'S CHILD
TIM WELLBURN .... FILM EDITOR

CATTLE ANNIE AND LITTLE BRITCHES
LARRY PIZER .... CINEMATOGRAPHER
STAN JOLLEY .... PRODUCTION DESIGNER
RITA RIGGS .... COSTUME DESIGNER
WILLIAM HAUGSE .... FILM EDITOR

CAUGHT
EDDY VAN DER ENDEN .... CINEMATOGRAPHER

CAUGHT ON A TRAIN (TF)
TONY PIERCE-ROBERTS .... CINEMATOGRAPHER

CAVEMAN
ALAN HUME .... CINEMATOGRAPHER
JOSE RODRIGUEZ GRANADA .... PRODUCTION DESIGNER
PHILIP JEFFRIES .... PRODUCTION DESIGNER
ROBERT FLETCHER .... COSTUME DESIGNER
GENE FOWLER JR. .... FILM EDITOR

CEASE FIRE
ALAN AVCHEN .... PRODUCTION DESIGNER
JULIA CHAVES .... FILM EDITOR

CELEBRITY (MS)
PHILIP LATHROP .... CINEMATOGRAPHER
ERIC SEARS .... FILM EDITOR

CERTAIN FURY, A
KEES VAN OOSTRUM .... CINEMATOGRAPHER
BEALA B. NEEL .... PRODUCTION DESIGNER
LYNDA KEMP .... COSTUME DESIGNER
TODD RAMSAY .... FILM EDITOR

CERTAIN SMILE, A
JOHN DE CUIR .... PRODUCTION DESIGNER

CHAIN REACTION
RUSSELL BOYD .... CINEMATOGRAPHER
GRAHAM GRACE WALKER .... PRODUCTION DESIGNER
TIM WELLBURN .... FILM EDITOR

CHAIN, THE
PETER MURTON .... PRODUCTION DESIGNER

CHAINED HEAT
MAC AHLBERG .... CINEMATOGRAPHER
ROBERT ZIEMBICKI .... PRODUCTION DESIGNER

CHALK GARDEN, THE
ARTHUR IBBETSON .... CINEMATOGRAPHER

CHALLENGE
JACK HOFSTRA .... FILM EDITOR

CINEMATOGRAPHERS
PRODUCTION
DESIGNERS,
COSTUME
DESIGNERS AND
FILM EDITORS
GUIDE

I
N
D
E
X

O
F

F
I
L
M

T
I
T
L
E
S

Ch-Ch

CINEMATOGRAPHERS
PRODUCTION
DESIGNERS,
COSTUME
DESIGNERS AND
FILM EDITORS
GUIDE

I
N
D
E
X

O
F

F
I
L
M

T
I
T
L
E
S

CHER (TVS)
BOB MACKIE .... COSTUME DESIGNER

CHER SPECIAL, THE (TV)
BOB MACKIE .... COSTUME DESIGNER

CHER...AND OTHER FANTASIES (TV)
BOB MACKIE .... COSTUME DESIGNER

CHERRY 2000
JACQUES HAITKIN .... CINEMATOGRAPHER
JULIE WEISS .... COSTUME DESIGNER
DUWAYNE DUNHAM .... FILM EDITOR
EDWARD M. ABROMS .... FILM EDITOR

CHERYL LADD SPECIAL, THE (TV)
BOB MACKIE .... COSTUME DESIGNER

CHICAGO JOE AND THE SHOWGIRL
MIKE SOUTHON .... CINEMATOGRAPHER
GEMMA JACKSON .... PRODUCTION DESIGNER
DAN RAE .... FILM EDITOR

CHICAGO STORY, THE (TF)
JACK L. RICHARDS .... CINEMATOGRAPHER
PAUL VON BRACK .... CINEMATOGRAPHER

CHICKEN CHRONICLES, THE
MATTHEW F. LEONETTI .... CINEMATOGRAPHER
GEORGE FOLSEY JR.* .... FILM EDITOR

CHIEF ZABU
FRANK PRINZI .... CINEMATOGRAPHER

CHILD BRIDE OF SHORT CREEK (TF)
MICHAEL ECONOMOU .... FILM EDITOR

CHILD SAVER, THE (TF)
SHELLEY KOMAROV .... COSTUME DESIGNER
ALEIDA MACDONALD .... COSTUME DESIGNER

CHILD'S PLAY
BILL BUTLER .... CINEMATOGRAPHER
DANIEL LOMINO .... PRODUCTION DESIGNER
PHILIP ROSENBERG .... PRODUCTION DESIGNER
APRIL FERRY .... COSTUME DESIGNER
EDWARD A. WARSCHILKA .... FILM EDITOR
ROY E. PETERSON .... FILM EDITOR

CHILD'S PLAY 2
STEFAN CZAPSKY .... CINEMATOGRAPHER
IVO CRISTANTE .... PRODUCTION DESIGNER
PAMELA SKAIST .... COSTUME DESIGNER
EDWARD WARSCHILKA .... FILM EDITOR

CHILDREN IN THE CROSSFIRE (TF)
WALTER LASSALLY .... CINEMATOGRAPHER
WILLIAM J. CREBER .... PRODUCTION DESIGNER

CHILDREN NOBODY WANTED, THE (TF)
HARRY KERAMIDAS .... FILM EDITOR

CHILDREN OF A LESSER GOD
JOHN SEALE .... CINEMATOGRAPHER
GENE CALLAHAN .... PRODUCTION DESIGNER
ARTHUR ROWSELL .... COSTUME DESIGNER
LISA FRUCHTMAN .... FILM EDITOR

CHILDREN OF SANCHEZ, THE
GABRIEL FIGUEROA .... CINEMATOGRAPHER

CHILDREN OF THE BRIDE (TF)
RONALD M. LAUTORE .... CINEMATOGRAPHER
MARK W. ROSENBAUM .... FILM EDITOR

CHILDREN OF THE CORN
RAOUL LOMAS .... CINEMATOGRAPHER
CRAIG STEARNS .... PRODUCTION DESIGNER
BARBARA SCOTT .... COSTUME DESIGNER
HARRY KERAMIDAS .... FILM EDITOR

CHILDREN OF THE NIGHT (TF)
GIL HUBBS .... CINEMATOGRAPHER
NORM BARON .... PRODUCTION DESIGNER

CHILDREN OF TIMES SQUARE, THE (TF)
BRYAN RYMAN .... PRODUCTION DESIGNER

CHILLER (TF)
DUANE HARTZELL .... FILM EDITOR

CHILLY SCENES OF WINTER
PETER JAMISON .... PRODUCTION DESIGNER
ROSANNA NORTON .... COSTUME DESIGNER
CYNTHIA SCHEIDER .... FILM EDITOR

CHIMERA
DEREK HYDE .... COSTUME DESIGNER

CHINA 9 LIBERTY 37
GIUSEPPE ROTUNNO .... CINEMATOGRAPHER
CESARE D'AMICO .... FILM EDITOR

CHINA BEACH (PILOT)
CHARLES D. (CHUCK) MINSKY .... CINEMATOGRAPHER

CHINA CRY
DAVID WORTH .... CINEMATOGRAPHER
NORMAN BARON .... PRODUCTION DESIGNER
GIGI CHOA .... COSTUME DESIGNER
DUANE HARTZELL .... FILM EDITOR

CHINA GIRL
BOJAN BAZELLI .... CINEMATOGRAPHER
DAN LEIGH .... PRODUCTION DESIGNER
RICHARD HORNUNG .... COSTUME DESIGNER
ANTHONY REDMAN .... FILM EDITOR

CHINA SYNDROME, THE
JAMES A. CRABE .... CINEMATOGRAPHER
GEORGE JENKINS .... PRODUCTION DESIGNER
RICHARD CARTER .... PRODUCTION DESIGNER
DONFELD .... COSTUME DESIGNER
DAVID RAWLINS .... FILM EDITOR

CHINATOWN
JOHN A. ALONZO .... CINEMATOGRAPHER
RICHARD SYLBERT .... PRODUCTION DESIGNER
W. STEWART CAMPBELL .... PRODUCTION DESIGNER
ANTHEA SYLBERT .... COSTUME DESIGNER
SAM O'STEEN .... FILM EDITOR

CHITTY CHITTY BANG BANG
KEN ADAM .... PRODUCTION DESIGNER

CHLOE IN THE AFTERNOON
NESTOR ALMENDROS .... CINEMATOGRAPHER

CHOCOLATE WAR, THE
TOM RICHMOND .... CINEMATOGRAPHER
DAVID ENSLEY .... PRODUCTION DESIGNER
ELIZABETH KAYE .... COSTUME DESIGNER
JEFF WISHENDRAD .... FILM EDITOR

CHOICE OF ARMS
PIERRE WILLIAM GLENN .... CINEMATOGRAPHER

CHOIRBOYS, THE
JOSEPH BIROC .... CINEMATOGRAPHER
WILLIAM KENNEY .... PRODUCTION DESIGNER
TOM DAWSON .... COSTUME DESIGNER
IRVING C. ROSENBLUM .... FILM EDITOR
MAURY WINETROBE .... FILM EDITOR

CHOKE CANYON
DANTE SPINOTTI .... CINEMATOGRAPHER
FRANK VANORIO .... PRODUCTION DESIGNER
ROBERTO SILVI .... FILM EDITOR

CHOOSE ME
JAN KIESSER .... CINEMATOGRAPHER
STEVEN LEGLER .... PRODUCTION DESIGNER
TRACY TYNAN .... COSTUME DESIGNER
MIA GOLDMAN .... FILM EDITOR

CHOPPER CHICKS IN ZOMBIE TOWN
TOM FRASER .... CINEMATOGRAPHER
RODNEY MCDONALD .... PRODUCTION DESIGNER
W.O. GARRETT .... FILM EDITOR

CHOPPING MALL
TOM RICHMOND .... CINEMATOGRAPHER
KATIE SPARKS .... COSTUME DESIGNER
LESLIE ROSENTHAL .... FILM EDITOR

CHORDS OF FAME
JOHN BLOOMGARDEN .... FILM EDITOR

CHORUS LINE, A
RONNIE TAYLOR .... CINEMATOGRAPHER
PATRIZIA VON BRANDENSTEIN .... PRODUCTION DESIGNER
FAYE POLIAKIN .... COSTUME DESIGNER
JOHN BLOOM .... FILM EDITOR

CINEMATOGRAPHERS
PRODUCTION
DESIGNERS,
COSTUME
DESIGNERS AND
FILM EDITORS
GUIDE

I
N
D
E
X

O
F

F
I
L
M

T
I
T
L
E
S

CHOSEN, THE
ARTHUR ORNITZ† .... CINEMATOGRAPHER
STUART WURTZEL .... PRODUCTION DESIGNER
RUTH MORLEY .... COSTUME DESIGNER
DAVID GARFIELD .... FILM EDITOR

CHOSEN,THE
RICHARD A. HARRIS .... FILM EDITOR

CHRIST STOPPED ON EBOLI
ENRICO SABBATINI .... COSTUME DESIGNER

CHRISTIAN LICORICE STORE, THE
RICHARD A. HARRIS .... FILM EDITOR

CHRISTIANE F
JURGEN JURGES .... CINEMATOGRAPHER
JANE SEITZ .... FILM EDITOR

CHRISTINE
DONALD M. MORGAN .... CINEMATOGRAPHER
DANIEL LOMINO .... PRODUCTION DESIGNER
MARION ROTHMAN .... FILM EDITOR

CHRISTMAS CAROL, A (TF)
PETER TANNER .... FILM EDITOR

CHRISTMAS COMES TO WILLOW CREEK (TF)
BRENTON SPENCER .... CINEMATOGRAPHER

CHRISTMAS EVE (TF)
SHELLEY KOMAROV .... COSTUME DESIGNER

CHRISTMAS LILES OF THE FIELD (TF)
ROBERT B. HAUSER .... CINEMATOGRAPHER

CHRISTMAS MIRACLE IN CAUFIELD, USA (TF)
JAMES G. HULSEY .... PRODUCTION DESIGNER

CHRISTMAS STORY, A
REGINALD H. MORRIS .... CINEMATOGRAPHER
GAVIN MITCHELL .... PRODUCTION DESIGNER
REUBEN FREED .... PRODUCTION DESIGNER
MARY E. MCLEOD .... COSTUME DESIGNER
STAN COLE .... FILM EDITOR

CHRISTMAS WIFE, THE (CTF)
BRIAN WEST .... CINEMATOGRAPHER
EDWARD PISONI .... PRODUCTION DESIGNER

CHRISTMAS WITHOUT SNOW, A (TF)
MARIANNA ASTROM DEFINA .... COSTUME DESIGNER

CHRONICLE OF A DEATH FORETOLD
ENRICO SABBATINI .... COSTUME DESIGNER

CHU CHU AND THE PHILLY FLASH
VICTOR J. KEMPER .... CINEMATOGRAPHER
DANIEL LOMINO .... PRODUCTION DESIGNER
RON TALSKY .... COSTUME DESIGNER
ARGYLE NELSON .... FILM EDITOR

CHUCK BARRY: HAIL! HAIL! ROCK 'N' ROLL (FD)
OLIVER STAPLETON .... CINEMATOGRAPHER
LISA DAY .... FILM EDITOR

CIA: A CASE OFFICER
HASKELL WEXLER .... CINEMATOGRAPHER

CINCINNATI KID, THE
PHILIP LATHROP .... CINEMATOGRAPHER

CINDERELLA LIBERTY
VILMOS ZSIGMOND .... CINEMATOGRAPHER
DONN CAMBERN .... FILM EDITOR
PATRICK KENNEDY .... FILM EDITOR

CINDY (TF)
JAMES D. VANCE .... PRODUCTION DESIGNER
SANDRA STEWART .... COSTUME DESIGNER

CINEMA PARADISO
BLASCO GIURATO .... CINEMATOGRAPHER
ANDREA CRISANTI .... PRODUCTION DESIGNER
BEATRICE BORDONE .... COSTUME DESIGNER
MARIO MORA .... FILM EDITOR

CIRCLE OF DECEIT
SUZANNE BARON .... FILM EDITOR

CIRCLE OF IRON
RONNIE TAYLOR .... CINEMATOGRAPHER

CIRCLE OF POWER
AFFONSO BEATO .... CINEMATOGRAPHER
KEN DAVIS .... PRODUCTION DESIGNER
JACQUELINE SAINT ANNE .... COSTUME DESIGNER
GAIL YASUNAGA .... FILM EDITOR

CIRCLE OF TWO
LASZLO GEORGE .... CINEMATOGRAPHER

CIRCUS (TF)
CHESTER KACZENSKI .... PRODUCTION DESIGNER

CISCO PIKE
ALFRED SWEENEY .... PRODUCTION DESIGNER
ROBERT C. JONES .... FILM EDITOR

CITIZEN'S BAND
JORDAN CRONENWETH .... CINEMATOGRAPHER
WILLIAM MALLEY .... PRODUCTION DESIGNER
JODIE TILLEN .... COSTUME DESIGNER
JOHN F. LINK .... FILM EDITOR

CITY GIRL, THE
EVA GARDOS .... FILM EDITOR

CITY HEAT
NICK MCLEAN .... CINEMATOGRAPHER
EDWARD C. CARFAGNO .... PRODUCTION DESIGNER
NORMAN SALLING .... COSTUME DESIGNER
JACQUELINE CAMBAS .... FILM EDITOR

CITY IN FEAR (TF)
CHARLES ROSEN .... PRODUCTION DESIGNER

CITY KILLER (TF)
FRED J. KOENEKAMP .... CINEMATOGRAPHER
BRYAN RYMAN .... PRODUCTION DESIGNER

CITY LIMITS
TIM SUHRSTEDT .... CINEMATOGRAPHER
PHILIP DEAN FOREMAN .... PRODUCTION DESIGNER

CITY OF HOPE
ROBERT RICHARDSON .... CINEMATOGRAPHER
DAN BISHOP .... PRODUCTION DESIGNER
DIANNA FREAS .... PRODUCTION DESIGNER
JOHN SAYLES .... FILM EDITOR

CITY OF WOMEN
GIUSEPPE ROTUNNO .... CINEMATOGRAPHER
DANTE FERRETTI .... PRODUCTION DESIGNER
RUGGERO MASTROIANNI .... FILM EDITOR

CITY ON FIRE
RENE VERZIER .... CINEMATOGRAPHER

CIVIL WAR I-IX, THE (TD)
ALLEN MOORE .... CINEMATOGRAPHER
BUDDY SQUIRES .... CINEMATOGRAPHER
KEN BURNS .... CINEMATOGRAPHER
BRUCE SHAW .... FILM EDITOR
PAUL BARNES .... FILM EDITOR

CLAIR DE FEMME
RICARDO ARONOVITCH .... CINEMATOGRAPHER
FRANÇOISE BONNOT .... FILM EDITOR

CLAIRE'S KNEE
NESTOR ALMENDROS .... CINEMATOGRAPHER

CLAIRVOYANT, THE
LARRY PIZER .... CINEMATOGRAPHER

CLAN OF THE CAVE BEAR, THE
JAN DE BONT .... CINEMATOGRAPHER
ANTHONY MASTERS .... PRODUCTION DESIGNER
GUY COMTOIS .... PRODUCTION DESIGNER
KELLY KIMBALL .... COSTUME DESIGNER
WENDY BRICMONT .... FILM EDITOR

CLARA'S HEART
FREDDIE FRANCIS .... CINEMATOGRAPHER
JEFFREY HOWARD .... PRODUCTION DESIGNER
BAMBI BREAKSTONE .... COSTUME DESIGNER
SIDNEY LEVIN .... FILM EDITOR

CLARENCE (CTF)
GLEN MACPHERSON .... CINEMATOGRAPHER
BRUCE LANGE .... FILM EDITOR

CLASH OF THE TITANS
TED MOORE .... CINEMATOGRAPHER
FRANK WHITE .... PRODUCTION DESIGNER
PETER HOWITT .... PRODUCTION DESIGNER
EMMA PORTEUS .... COSTUME DESIGNER
TIMOTHY GEE .... FILM EDITOR

CLASS
RIC WAITE .... CINEMATOGRAPHER
JACK POPLIN .... PRODUCTION DESIGNER
STUART H. PAPPE .... FILM EDITOR

CLASS ACTION
CONRAD L. HALL .... CINEMATOGRAPHER
TODD HALLOWELL .... PRODUCTION DESIGNER
RITA RYACK .... COSTUME DESIGNER
IAN CRAFFORD .... FILM EDITOR

CLASS ENEMY
ROBBY MULLER .... CINEMATOGRAPHER

CLASS OF 1984
BERT DUNK .... CINEMATOGRAPHER
HOWARD KUNIN .... FILM EDITOR

CLASS OF 1999
MARK IRWIN .... CINEMATOGRAPHER
LESLIE BALLARD .... COSTUME DESIGNER
SCOTT CONRAD .... FILM EDITOR

CLASS OF 44
ANDREW LASZLO .... CINEMATOGRAPHER
BEN EDWARDS .... PRODUCTION DESIGNER

CLASS OF MISS MACMICHAEL, THE
ALEX THOMSON .... CINEMATOGRAPHER

CLASS OF NUKE 'EM HIGH
JOHN MICHAEL REEFER .... COSTUME DESIGNER
RICHARD HAINES .... FILM EDITOR

CLASS RELATIONS
WILLIAM LUBTCHANSKY .... CINEMATOGRAPHER

CLASS REUNION
RICHARD C. MEYER .... FILM EDITOR

CLAUDINE
GAYNE RESCHER .... CINEMATOGRAPHER
TED HAWORTH .... PRODUCTION DESIGNER
BERNARD JOHNSON .... COSTUME DESIGNER

CLEAN AND SOBER
JAN KIESSER .... CINEMATOGRAPHER
ERIC W. ORBOM .... PRODUCTION DESIGNER
JOEL SCHILLER .... PRODUCTION DESIGNER
ROBERT TURTURICE .... COSTUME DESIGNER
RICHARD CHEW .... FILM EDITOR

CLEAN SLATE
PIERRE-WILLIAM GLENN .... CINEMATOGRAPHER

CLEOPATRA
HERMAN A. BLUMENTHAL .... PRODUCTION DESIGNER
HILYARD BROWN .... PRODUCTION DESIGNER
JOHN DE CUIR .... PRODUCTION DESIGNER
IRENE SHARAFF .... COSTUME DESIGNER
RENIE CONLEY .... COSTUME DESIGNER
DOROTHY SPENCER .... FILM EDITOR

CLEOPATRA JONES
PETER W. WOOLEY .... PRODUCTION DESIGNER
ALLAN JACOBS .... FILM EDITOR

CLEOPATRA JONES AND THE CASINO OF GOLD,
ALAN HUME .... CINEMATOGRAPHER

CLINIC, THE
IAN BAKER .... CINEMATOGRAPHER
EDWARD MCQUEEN-MASON .... FILM EDITOR

CLINTON AND NADINE (CTF)
ISIDORE MANKOFSKY .... CINEMATOGRAPHER
HOWARD BARKER .... PRODUCTION DESIGNER
BRAD R. LOMAN .... COSTUME DESIGNER
DAVID RAY .... FILM EDITOR

CLOAK AND DAGGER
VICTOR J. KEMPER .... CINEMATOGRAPHER
TODD HALLOWELL .... PRODUCTION DESIGNER
WILLIAM H. TUNTKE .... PRODUCTION DESIGNER
ANDREW LONDON .... FILM EDITOR

CLOCKWISE
JOHN COQUILLON .... CINEMATOGRAPHER
DIANA CHARNLEY .... PRODUCTION DESIGNER
ROGER MURRAY-LEACH .... PRODUCTION DESIGNER
JUDY MOORCROFT .... COSTUME DESIGNER
PETER BOYLE .... FILM EDITOR

CLOCKWORK ORANGE, A
JOHN ALCOTT† .... CINEMATOGRAPHER
JOHN BARRY† .... PRODUCTION DESIGNER
WILLIAM BUTLER .... FILM EDITOR

CLONE MASTERS, THE (TF)
DANIEL LOMINO .... PRODUCTION DESIGNER

CLONE, THE
WILLIAM SANDELL .... PRODUCTION DESIGNER

CLOSE ENCOUNTERS OF THE THIRD KIND
VILMOS ZSIGMOND .... CINEMATOGRAPHER
JOE ALVES .... PRODUCTION DESIGNER
DANIEL LOMINO .... PRODUCTION DESIGNER
MICHAEL KAHN .... FILM EDITOR

CLOSE RELATIONS (CTF)
JOHN DALEY .... CINEMATOGRAPHER
ROY SHARMAN .... FILM EDITOR

CLOSELY WATCHED TRAINS
OLGA DIMITROV .... COSTUME DESIGNER

CLOSER, THE
NICHOLAS V. STERNBERG .... CINEMATOGRAPHER
KAY MORRIS .... COSTUME DESIGNER
TRACY S. GRANGER .... FILM EDITOR

CLOSING NIGHT
HARVEY ROSENSTOCK .... FILM EDITOR

CLOUDS OF GLORY: WILLIAM & DOROTHY (TF)
DICK BUSH .... CINEMATOGRAPHER

CLOWN, THE
WALTER LASSALLY .... CINEMATOGRAPHER

CLOWN WHITE
ROY FORGE SMITH .... PRODUCTION DESIGNER

CLUB LIFE
CYNTHIA SOWDER .... PRODUCTION DESIGNER
KATHERINE G. VALLIN .... PRODUCTION DESIGNER
PHILIP J.C. DUFFIN .... PRODUCTION DESIGNER
DAVID KERN .... FILM EDITOR

CLUB PARADISE
PETER HANNAN .... CINEMATOGRAPHER
ANTHONY READING .... PRODUCTION DESIGNER
JOHN GRAYSMARK .... PRODUCTION DESIGNER
WILLIAM F. MATTHEWS .... PRODUCTION DESIGNER
MARION ROTHMAN .... FILM EDITOR

CLUB, THE
DONALD MCALPINE .... CINEMATOGRAPHER
DAVID COPPING .... PRODUCTION DESIGNER
WILLIAM M. ANDERSON .... FILM EDITOR

CLUE
VICTOR J. KEMPER .... CINEMATOGRAPHER
JOHN J. LLOYD† .... PRODUCTION DESIGNER
MICHAEL KAPLAN .... COSTUME DESIGNER
DAVID BRETHERTON .... FILM EDITOR
RICHARD HAINES .... FILM EDITOR

COACH
MICHAEL D. MURPHY .... CINEMATOGRAPHER
ROBERT GORDON .... FILM EDITOR

COACH (PILOT)
RONALD W. BROWNE .... CINEMATOGRAPHER

COACH OF THE YEAR (TF)
RICHARD B. LEWIS .... PRODUCTION DESIGNER

CI-Co

CINEMATOGRAPHERS
PRODUCTION
DESIGNERS,
COSTUME
DESIGNERS AND
FILM EDITORS
GUIDE

I
N
D
E
X

O
F

F
I
L
M

T
I
T
L
E
S

Co-Co

CINEMATOGRAPHERS
PRODUCTION
DESIGNERS,
COSTUME
DESIGNERS AND
FILM EDITORS
GUIDE

I
N
D
E
X

O
F

F
I
L
M

T
I
T
L
E
S

318

COMBAT HIGH (TF)
MOLLY MAGINNIS .... COSTUME DESIGNER
MICHAEL J. HILL .... FILM EDITOR

COME BACK CHARLESTON BLUE
GERALD B. GREENBERG .... FILM EDITOR

COME BACK TO THE THE 5 & DIME, JIMMY DEAN, JIMMY DEAN
PIERRE MIGNOT .... CINEMATOGRAPHER
DAVID GROPMAN .... PRODUCTION DESIGNER
JASON ROSENFIELD .... FILM EDITOR

COME SEE THE PARADISE
MICHAEL SERESIN .... CINEMATOGRAPHER
GEOFFREY KIRKLAND .... PRODUCTION DESIGNER
MOLLY MAGINNIS .... COSTUME DESIGNER
GERRY HAMBLING .... FILM EDITOR

COME SEPTEMBER
HENRY BUMSTEAD .... PRODUCTION DESIGNER

COMEBACK (TF)
DANIEL LOMINO .... PRODUCTION DESIGNER

COMEBACK KID, THE (TF)
NORM BARON .... PRODUCTION DESIGNER

COMEBACK, THE (TF)
BOJAN BAZELLI .... CINEMATOGRAPHER
MICHAEL MOLLY .... PRODUCTION DESIGNER
ANTHONY REDMAN .... FILM EDITOR

COMES A HORSEMAN
GORDON WILLIS .... CINEMATOGRAPHER
GEORGE JENKINS .... PRODUCTION DESIGNER
LUSTER BAYLESS .... COSTUME DESIGNER
MARION ROTHMAN .... FILM EDITOR

COMFORT AND JOY
CHRIS MENGES .... CINEMATOGRAPHER
ADRIENNE ATKINSON .... PRODUCTION DESIGNER
ANDY HARRIS .... PRODUCTION DESIGNER
MICHAEL ELLIS .... FILM EDITOR

COMFORT OF STRANGERS, THE
DANTE SPINOTTI .... CINEMATOGRAPHER
MARIOLINA BONO .... COSTUME DESIGNER
BILL PANKOW .... FILM EDITOR

COMIC BOOK CONFIDENTIAL
JOAN CHURCHILL .... CINEMATOGRAPHER
ROBERT FRESCO .... CINEMATOGRAPHER
GERLINDE SCHARINGER .... PRODUCTION DESIGNER
ROBERT KENNEDY .... FILM EDITOR
RON MANN .... FILM EDITOR

COMING HOME
HASKELL WEXLER .... CINEMATOGRAPHER
GEORGE GAINES† .... PRODUCTION DESIGNER
JAMES SCHOPPE .... PRODUCTION DESIGNER
MICHAEL D. HALLER .... PRODUCTION DESIGNER
ANN ROTH .... COSTUME DESIGNER
DON ZIMMERMAN .... FILM EDITOR

COMING OUT OF THE ICE (TF)
MALCOLM COOKE .... FILM EDITOR
ROGER HALL .... PRODUCTION DESIGNER

COMING SOON (CTD)
STEPHEN M. KATZ .... CINEMATOGRAPHER

COMING TO AMERICA
WOODY OMENS .... CINEMATOGRAPHER
RICHARD B. LEWIS .... PRODUCTION DESIGNER
RICHARD MACDONALD .... PRODUCTION DESIGNER
DEBORAH NADOOLMAN .... COSTUME DESIGNER
KELLY KIMBALL .... COSTUME DESIGNER
GEORGE FOLSEY JR.* .... FILM EDITOR
MALCOLM CAMPBELL .... FILM EDITOR

COMING UP ROSES
DICK POPE .... CINEMATOGRAPHER

COMING, THE
DANIEL YARUSSI .... CINEMATOGRAPHER

COMMANDO
MATTHEW F. LEONETTI .... CINEMATOGRAPHER
JOHN VALLONE .... PRODUCTION DESIGNER
ENID HARRIS .... COSTUME DESIGNER
ROBERT HARRIS, JR. .... COSTUME DESIGNER
GLENN FARR .... FILM EDITOR
MARK GOLDBLATT .... FILM EDITOR

COMMANDO SQUAD
GARY GRAVER .... CINEMATOGRAPHER
COREY KAPLAN .... PRODUCTION DESIGNER
KATHIE WEAVER .... FILM EDITOR

COMMUNION
LOUIS IRVING .... CINEMATOGRAPHER
DENA ROTH .... PRODUCTION DESIGNER
LINDA PEARL .... PRODUCTION DESIGNER
MALISSA DANIEL .... COSTUME DESIGNER
LEE SMITH .... FILM EDITOR

COMPANY OF WOLVES, THE
BRYAN LOFTUS .... CINEMATOGRAPHER
ANTON FURST .... PRODUCTION DESIGNER
LIZ WALLER .... COSTUME DESIGNER
RODNEY HOLLAND .... FILM EDITOR

COMPETITION, THE
RICHARD H. KLINE .... CINEMATOGRAPHER
DALE HENNESY† .... PRODUCTION DESIGNER
RUTH MYERS .... COSTUME DESIGNER
DAVID BLEWITT .... FILM EDITOR

COMPROMISING POSITIONS
BARRY SONNENFELD .... CINEMATOGRAPHER
PETER S. LARKIN .... PRODUCTION DESIGNER
JOSEPH G. AULISI .... COSTUME DESIGNER
PETER C. FRANK .... FILM EDITOR

COMRADES
GALE TATTERSALL .... CINEMATOGRAPHER
MICHAEL PICKWOAD .... PRODUCTION DESIGNER

CONAN THE BARBARIAN
DUKE CALLAGHAN .... CINEMATOGRAPHER
JOHN CABRERA .... CINEMATOGRAPHER
BENJAMIN FERNANDEZ .... PRODUCTION DESIGNER
PIERLUIGI BASILE .... PRODUCTION DESIGNER
RON COBB .... PRODUCTION DESIGNER
JOHN BLOOMFIELD .... COSTUME DESIGNER
CARROLL TIMOTHY O'MEARA .... FILM EDITOR

CONAN THE DESTROYER
JACK CARDIFF .... CINEMATOGRAPHER
JOSE MARIA ALARCON .... PRODUCTION DESIGNER
PIERLUIGI BASILE .... PRODUCTION DESIGNER
JOHN BLOOMFIELD .... COSTUME DESIGNER
FRANK J. URIOSTE .... FILM EDITOR

CONCEALED ENEMIES
DAVID QUAID .... CINEMATOGRAPHER
ELIZABETH P. PALMER .... COSTUME DESIGNER

CONCORDE - AIRPORT '79, THE
PHILIP LATHROP .... CINEMATOGRAPHER
HENRY BUMSTEAD .... PRODUCTION DESIGNER
BURTON MILLER .... COSTUME DESIGNER
DOROTHY SPENCER .... FILM EDITOR

CONCRETE BEAT (TF)
DANIEL LOMINO .... PRODUCTION DESIGNER

CONCRETE COWBOYS, THE (TF)
VINCENT SAIZIS .... CINEMATOGRAPHER
KEN DAVIS .... PRODUCTION DESIGNER

CONCRETE JUNGLE
JAMES A. CRABE .... CINEMATOGRAPHER

CONDORMAN
CHARLES F. WHEELER .... CINEMATOGRAPHER
GORDON D. BRENNER .... FILM EDITOR

CONFESSION, THE
FRANÇOISE BONNOT .... FILM EDITOR

CONFIDENCE
LAJOS KOLTAI .... CINEMATOGRAPHER

CONFIDENTIALLY YOURS
NESTOR ALMENDROS .... CINEMATOGRAPHER
MARTINE BARRAQUE .... FILM EDITOR

Co-Co

CINEMATOGRAPHERS
PRODUCTION
DESIGNERS,
COSTUME
DESIGNERS AND
FILM EDITORS
GUIDE

I
N
D
E
X

O
F

F
I
L
M

T
I
T
L
E
S

319

Co-Co

CINEMATOGRAPHERS
PRODUCTION
DESIGNERS,
COSTUME
DESIGNERS and
FILM EDITORS
GUIDE

I
N
D
E
X

O
F

F
I
L
M

T
I
T
L
E
S

320

Co-Cr

CINEMATOGRAPHERS
PRODUCTION
DESIGNERS,
COSTUME
DESIGNERS AND
FILM EDITORS
GUIDE

**I
N
D
E
X

O
F

F
I
L
M

T
I
T
L
E
S**

COURAGE
LAWRENCE MILLER .... PRODUCTION DESIGNER
STEVEN POLIVKA .... FILM EDITOR

COURAGE (TF)
MICHAEL ECONOMOU .... FILM EDITOR

COURAGE OF KAVIK THE WOLF DOG, THE (TF)
SEAMUS FLANNERY .... PRODUCTION DESIGNER

COURIER, THE
GABRIEL BERISTAIN .... CINEMATOGRAPHER

COURT-MARTIAL OF JACKIE ROBINSON, THE (CTF)
DON BURGESS .... CINEMATOGRAPHER
ROY ALAN AMARAL .... PRODUCTION DESIGNER
BOB WYMAN .... FILM EDITOR
ERIC SEARS .... FILM EDITOR

COUSINS
RALF D. BODE .... CINEMATOGRAPHER
MARK S. FREEBORN .... PRODUCTION DESIGNER
MICHAEL KAPLAN .... COSTUME DESIGNER
ROBERT BROWN .... FILM EDITOR

COVER GIRL AND THE COP, THE (TF)
TIM SUHRSTEDT .... CINEMATOGRAPHER
DONALD LIGHT-HARRIS .... PRODUCTION DESIGNER
TOM WALLS .... FILM EDITOR

COVER ME BABE
JACK MARTIN SMITH .... PRODUCTION DESIGNER

COVERGIRL
RENE VERZIER .... CINEMATOGRAPHER
MICHEL PROULX .... PRODUCTION DESIGNER
CHRISTOPHER HOLMES .... FILM EDITOR

COWARD OF THE COUNTRY, THE (TF)
STEVEN B. POSTER .... CINEMATOGRAPHER
RICHARD SAWYER .... PRODUCTION DESIGNER

COWBOY
ROBERT JESSUP .... CINEMATOGRAPHER

COWBOYS DON'T CRY
BRIAN HEBB .... CINEMATOGRAPHER

COWBOYS, THE
PHILIP JEFFRIES .... PRODUCTION DESIGNER

COWRA BREAKOUT (MS)
RICHARD FRANCIS-BRUCE .... FILM EDITOR

CRACK HOUSE
ARLEDGE ARMENAKI .... CINEMATOGRAPHER
KEITH BARRETT .... PRODUCTION DESIGNER
CLAUDIA FINKLE .... FILM EDITOR

CRACK IN THE MIRROR
REUBEN FREED .... PRODUCTION DESIGNER
ROSEMARY PONZO .... COSTUME DESIGNER
ALLAN MILLER .... FILM EDITOR
CRAIG MCKAY .... FILM EDITOR

CRACKERS
LASZLO KOVACS .... CINEMATOGRAPHER
JOHN J. LLOYD .... PRODUCTION DESIGNER
SUZANNE BARON .... FILM EDITOR

CRADLE WILL FALL, THE (TF)
STEVEN B. POSTER .... CINEMATOGRAPHER
DENNIS O'CONNOR .... FILM EDITOR

CRASH
HARRY KERAMIDAS .... FILM EDITOR

CRAWLSPACE
SERGIO SALVATI .... CINEMATOGRAPHER
GIOVANNI NATALUCCI .... PRODUCTION DESIGNER

CRAZY MAMA
BRUCE LOGAN .... CINEMATOGRAPHER
BARBARA POKRAS .... FILM EDITOR

CRAZY MOON
SAVAS KALOGERAS .... CINEMATOGRAPHER
GUY LALANDE .... PRODUCTION DESIGNER
FRANCO BATTISTA .... FILM EDITOR

CRAZY PEOPLE
VICTOR J. KEMPER .... CINEMATOGRAPHER
JOHN J. LLOYD .... PRODUCTION DESIGNER
MARY E. VOGT .... COSTUME DESIGNER
MIA GOLDMAN .... FILM EDITOR

CRAZY TIMES (TF)
HARRY CURTIS .... COSTUME DESIGNER

CRAZY WORLD OF JULIUS VROODER, THE
ROBERT C. JONES .... FILM EDITOR

CREATOR
ROBBIE GREENBERG .... CINEMATOGRAPHER
JOSAN F. RUSSO .... PRODUCTION DESIGNER
MICHAEL PRATHER .... PRODUCTION DESIGNER
TOM DAWSON .... COSTUME DESIGNER
RICHARD CHEW .... FILM EDITOR

CREATURE
HARRY MATHIAS .... CINEMATOGRAPHER
MICHAEL NOVOTNY .... PRODUCTION DESIGNER

CREATURE WASN'T NICE, THE
LEE COLE .... PRODUCTION DESIGNER

CREATURES THE WORLD FORGOT
JOHN STOLL .... PRODUCTION DESIGNER

CREEPOZOIDS
MIRIAM PREISSEL .... FILM EDITOR

CREEPS, THE
ROBERT C. NEW .... CINEMATOGRAPHER

CREEPSHOW
MICHAEL GORNICK .... CINEMATOGRAPHER
CLETUS ANDERSON .... PRODUCTION DESIGNER
BARBARA ANDERSON .... COSTUME DESIGNER
PASQUALE BUBA .... FILM EDITOR
PAUL HIRSCH .... FILM EDITOR

CREEPSHOW II
TOM D. HURWITZ .... CINEMATOGRAPHER
PETER WEATHERLY .... FILM EDITOR

CRIES AND WHISPERS
MARIK VOS .... COSTUME DESIGNER

CRIES IN THE NIGHT
ROY FORGE SMITH .... PRODUCTION DESIGNER

CRIME AND PASSION
JOHN JYMPSON .... FILM EDITOR

CRIME OF INNOCENCE (TF)
WILLIAM MC ALLISTER .... PRODUCTION DESIGNER

CRIME OF LOVE
DANTE FERRETTI .... PRODUCTION DESIGNER

CRIME STORY (TF)
JACK HOFSTRA .... FILM EDITOR

CRIME ZONE
CUSI BARRIO .... CINEMATOGRAPHER
PATRICIA MAGUILL .... COSTUME DESIGNER

CRIMES AND MISDEMEANORS
SVEN NYKVIST .... CINEMATOGRAPHER
SPEED HOPKINS .... PRODUCTION DESIGNER
SANTO LOQUASTO .... PRODUCTION DESIGNER
JEFFREY KURLAND .... COSTUME DESIGNER
SUSAN E. MORSE .... FILM EDITOR

CRIMES OF PASSION
DICK BUSH .... CINEMATOGRAPHER
STEPHEN MARSH .... PRODUCTION DESIGNER
BARBARA SCOTT .... COSTUME DESIGNER
BRIAN TAGG .... FILM EDITOR

CRIMES OF THE HEART
DANTE SPINOTTI .... CINEMATOGRAPHER
KEN ADAM .... PRODUCTION DESIGNER
STEPHEN MARSH .... PRODUCTION DESIGNER
ALBERT WOLSKY .... COSTUME DESIGNER
ANNE GOURSAUD .... FILM EDITOR

CRIMEWAVE
ROBERT PRIMES .... CINEMATOGRAPHER
KATHIE WEAVER .... FILM EDITOR

Cr-Cu

CINEMATOGRAPHERS
PRODUCTION
DESIGNERS,
COSTUME
DESIGNERS AND
FILM EDITORS
GUIDE

I
N
D
E
X

O
F

F
I
L
M

T
I
T
L
E
S

CRIMINAL JUSTICE (CTF)
STEVEN FIERBERG .... CINEMATOGRAPHER
DAN BISHOP .... PRODUCTION DESIGNER
DIANNA FREAS .... PRODUCTION DESIGNER
KATHERINE WENNING .... FILM EDITOR

CRIMINAL LAW
PHIL MEHEUX .... CINEMATOGRAPHER
CURTIS A. SCHNELL .... PRODUCTION DESIGNER
CHRISTOPHER WIMBLE .... FILM EDITOR

CRISIS AT CENTRAL HIGH (TF)
DONALD M. MORGAN .... CINEMATOGRAPHER

CRITICAL CONDITION
RALF D. BODE .... CINEMATOGRAPHER
JOHN J. LLOYD .... PRODUCTION DESIGNER
COLLEEN C. ATWOOD .... COSTUME DESIGNER
ROBERT K. LAMBERT .... FILM EDITOR

CRITTERS
CHRISTOPHER G. TUFTY .... CINEMATOGRAPHER
TIM SUHRSTEDT .... CINEMATOGRAPHER
GREGG FONSECA .... PRODUCTION DESIGNER
PHILIP DEAN FOREMAN .... PRODUCTION DESIGNER
HILARY WRIGHT .... COSTUME DESIGNER
LARRY BOCK .... FILM EDITOR

CRITTERS 2: THE MAIN COURSE
RUSSELL CARPENTER .... CINEMATOGRAPHER
PHILIP DEAN FOREMAN .... PRODUCTION DESIGNER
LESLEY LYNN NICHOLSON .... COSTUME DESIGNER
CHARLES BORNSTEIN .... FILM EDITOR

CROCODILE DUNDEE
RUSSELL BOYD .... CINEMATOGRAPHER
GRAHAM GRACE WALKER .... PRODUCTION DESIGNER
NORMA MORICEAU .... COSTUME DESIGNER
DAVID STIVEN .... FILM EDITOR

CROCODILE DUNDEE II
RUSSELL BOYD .... CINEMATOGRAPHER
JEREMY CONWAY .... PRODUCTION DESIGNER
LAWRENCE EASTWOOD .... PRODUCTION DESIGNER
NORMA MORICEAU .... COSTUME DESIGNER
DAVID STIVEN .... FILM EDITOR

CROMWELL
GEOFFREY UNSWORTH† .... CINEMATOGRAPHER
JOHN STOLL .... PRODUCTION DESIGNER
NINO NOVARESSE .... COSTUME DESIGNER

CROOKS IN CLOISTERS
HARRY WAXMAN .... CINEMATOGRAPHER

CROSS COUNTRY
RENE VERZIER .... CINEMATOGRAPHER
MICHEL PROULX .... PRODUCTION DESIGNER
NICK ROTUNDO .... FILM EDITOR

CROSS CREEK
JOHN A. ALONZO .... CINEMATOGRAPHER
WALTER SCOTT HERNDON† .... PRODUCTION DESIGNER
JOE I. TOMPKINS .... COSTUME DESIGNER
SIDNEY LEVIN .... FILM EDITOR

CROSS MY HEART
THOMAS DEL RUTH .... CINEMATOGRAPHER
LAWRENCE G. PAULL .... PRODUCTION DESIGNER
WILLIAM A. ELLIOT .... PRODUCTION DESIGNER
MARILYN VANCE-STRAKER .... COSTUME DESIGNER
MIA GOLDMAN .... FILM EDITOR

CROSS OF IRON
TED HAWORTH .... PRODUCTION DESIGNER
MICHAEL ELLIS .... FILM EDITOR
TONY LAWSON .... FILM EDITOR

CROSSED SWORDS
JACK CARDIFF .... CINEMATOGRAPHER
ANTHONY PRATT .... PRODUCTION DESIGNER
MAURICE FOWLER .... PRODUCTION DESIGNER
JUDY MOORCROFT .... COSTUME DESIGNER

CROSSING DELANCEY
THEO VAN DE SANDE .... CINEMATOGRAPHER
DAN LEIGH .... PRODUCTION DESIGNER
LESLIE E. ROLLINS .... PRODUCTION DESIGNER
RITA RYACK .... COSTUME DESIGNER
RICK SHAINE .... FILM EDITOR

CROSSINGS (MS)
NOLAN MILLER .... COSTUME DESIGNER

CROSSOVER DREAMS
CLAUDIO CHEA .... CINEMATOGRAPHER

CROSSROADS
JOHN BAILEY .... CINEMATOGRAPHER
JACK T. COLLIS .... PRODUCTION DESIGNER
FREEMAN DAVIES .... FILM EDITOR

CRUISING
JAMES A. CONTNER .... CINEMATOGRAPHER
BRUCE WEINTRAUB .... PRODUCTION DESIGNER
EDWARD PISONI .... PRODUCTION DESIGNER
BUD SMITH .... FILM EDITOR

CRUSOE
TOMISLAV PINTER .... CINEMATOGRAPHER
HUMPHREY DIXON .... FILM EDITOR

CRY BABY
DAVID INSLEY .... CINEMATOGRAPHER
VINCENT PERANIO .... PRODUCTION DESIGNER

CRY FREEDOM
RONNIE TAYLOR .... CINEMATOGRAPHER
GEORGE RICHARDSON .... PRODUCTION DESIGNER
JOHN KING .... PRODUCTION DESIGNER
NORMAN DORME .... PRODUCTION DESIGNER
STUART CRAIG .... PRODUCTION DESIGNER
JOHN MOLLO .... COSTUME DESIGNER
LESLEY WALKER .... FILM EDITOR

CRY IN THE DARK, A
IAN BAKER .... CINEMATOGRAPHER
GEORGE LIDDLE .... PRODUCTION DESIGNER
WENDY DICKSON .... PRODUCTION DESIGNER
BRUCE FINLAYSON .... COSTUME DESIGNER
JILL BILLCOCK .... FILM EDITOR

CRYSTAL HEART
ALEXANDER ULLOA .... CINEMATOGRAPHER
ETTA LEFF .... COSTUME DESIGNER
NICHOLAS WENTWORTH .... FILM EDITOR

CRYSTALSTONE
JOHN M. STEPHENS .... CINEMATOGRAPHER
GEORGE COSTELLO .... PRODUCTION DESIGNER

CUBA
DAVID WATKIN .... CINEMATOGRAPHER
GIL PARRONDO .... PRODUCTION DESIGNER
JOHN VICTOR SMITH .... FILM EDITOR

CUJO
JAN DE BONT .... CINEMATOGRAPHER
GUY COMTOIS .... PRODUCTION DESIGNER
NEIL TRAVIS .... FILM EDITOR

CULLODEN
DICK BUSH .... CINEMATOGRAPHER

CULPEPPER CATTLE CO., THE
JACK MARTIN SMITH .... PRODUCTION DESIGNER
JOHN F. BURNETT .... FILM EDITOR

CURSE OF THE PINK PANTHER
DICK BUSH .... CINEMATOGRAPHER
PETER MULLINS .... PRODUCTION DESIGNER
ALAN TOMKINS .... PRODUCTION DESIGNER
JOHN SIDALL .... PRODUCTION DESIGNER
TIM HUTCHINSON .... PRODUCTION DESIGNER
PATRICIA EDWARDS .... COSTUME DESIGNER
RALPH E. WINTERS .... FILM EDITOR

CURSE, THE
ROBERT D. FORGES .... CINEMATOGRAPHER
FRANK VANORIO .... PRODUCTION DESIGNER
CLAUDIO CUTRY .... FILM EDITOR

CURTAINS
MANFRED GUTHE .... CINEMATOGRAPHER
ROBERT PAYNTER .... CINEMATOGRAPHER
ROY FORGE SMITH .... PRODUCTION DESIGNER

CUT AND RUN
ALBERTO SPAGNOLI .... CINEMATOGRAPHER
MARIO MORRA .... FILM EDITOR

CUTTER'S WAY
JORDAN CRONENWETH .... CINEMATOGRAPHER
JOSAN F. RUSSO .... PRODUCTION DESIGNER
CAROLINE BIGGERSTAFF .... FILM EDITOR

CYBORG
PHILIP ALAN WATERS .... CINEMATOGRAPHER
HEIDI M. KACZENSKI .... COSTUME DESIGNER
ROZANNE ZINGALE .... FILM EDITOR
SCOTT STEVENSON .... FILM EDITOR

CYCLONE
PAUL ELLIOTT .... CINEMATOGRAPHER
MAXINE SHEPARD .... PRODUCTION DESIGNER

CYRANO DE BERGERAC
PIERRE LHOMME .... CINEMATOGRAPHER
EZIO FRIGERIO .... PRODUCTION DESIGNER
FRANCA SQUARCIAPINO .... COSTUME DESIGNER
NOELLE BOISSON .... FILM EDITOR

D

D.A.R.Y.L.
FRANK WATTS .... CINEMATOGRAPHER
ALAN CASSIE .... PRODUCTION DESIGNER
JOHN SIDALL .... PRODUCTION DESIGNER
SHAY CUNLIFFE .... COSTUME DESIGNER
ADRIAN CARR .... FILM EDITOR

D.C. CAB
DEAN CUNDEY .... CINEMATOGRAPHER
BERNIE CUTLER .... PRODUCTION DESIGNER
JOHN J. LLOYD .... PRODUCTION DESIGNER
ROBERTA WEINER .... COSTUME DESIGNER
DAVID BLEWITT .... FILM EDITOR

D.O.A.
YURI NEYMAN .... CINEMATOGRAPHER
RICHARD AMEND .... PRODUCTION DESIGNER
NANCY CONE .... COSTUME DESIGNER
MICHAEL R. MILLER .... FILM EDITOR
RAJA GOSNELL .... FILM EDITOR

DA
ALAR KIVILO .... CINEMATOGRAPHER
CAROL BETERA .... COSTUME DESIGNER
JILL SPAULDING .... COSTUME DESIGNER
NANCY NUTTAL BEYDA .... FILM EDITOR

DAD
JAN KIESSER .... CINEMATOGRAPHER
JACKSON DE GOVIA .... PRODUCTION DESIGNER
JOHN R. JENSEN .... PRODUCTION DESIGNER
MOLLY MAGINNIS .... COSTUME DESIGNER
ERIC SEARS .... FILM EDITOR

DADAH IS DEATH (MS)
BRIAN THOMPSON .... PRODUCTION DESIGNER
MICHAEL BROWN .... FILM EDITOR

DADDY LONG LEGS
JOHN DE CUIR .... PRODUCTION DESIGNER

DADDY'S BOYS
NORMAN HOLLYN .... FILM EDITOR

DADDY'S DEADLY DARLING
IRV GOODNOFF .... CINEMATOGRAPHER

DADDY'S DYIN'...WHO'S GOT THE WILL?
PAUL ELLIOTT .... CINEMATOGRAPHER
MICHELLE MINCH .... PRODUCTION DESIGNER
ELIZABETH W. NANKIN .... COSTUME DESIGNER
EDWARD WARSCHILKA JR. .... FILM EDITOR

DAISY MILLER
FERDINANDO SCARFIOTTI .... PRODUCTION DESIGNER

DAKOTA
JIM WRENN .... CINEMATOGRAPHER
RONDI HILLSTROM DAVIS .... COSTUME DESIGNER
LEON SEITH .... FILM EDITOR

DAKOTA'S WAY (PILOT)
ROY H. WAGNER .... CINEMATOGRAPHER

DAMIEN - OMEN II
BILL BUTLER .... CINEMATOGRAPHER
FRED HARPMAN .... PRODUCTION DESIGNER
PHILIP JEFFRIES .... PRODUCTION DESIGNER
ROBERT BROWN .... FILM EDITOR

DAMNATION ALLEY
HARRY STRADLING, JR. .... CINEMATOGRAPHER
PRESTON AMES .... PRODUCTION DESIGNER
FRANK J. URIOSTE .... FILM EDITOR

DAN TURNER, THE HOLLYWOOD DETECTIVE (TF)
STEVE MCWILLIAMS .... CINEMATOGRAPHER
JIM FRENCH .... PRODUCTION DESIGNER
MILLER DRAKE .... FILM EDITOR

DANCE OF HOPE
JAIME REYES .... CINEMATOGRAPHER

DANCE OF THE DWARFS
MICHAEL C. BUTLER .... CINEMATOGRAPHER

DANCE WITH A STRANGER
PETER HANNAN .... CINEMATOGRAPHER
ADRIAN SMITH .... PRODUCTION DESIGNER
ANDREW MOLLO .... PRODUCTION DESIGNER
PIP NEWBERY .... COSTUME DESIGNER
MICK AUDSLEY .... FILM EDITOR

DANCERS
ENNIO GUARNIERI .... CINEMATOGRAPHER
GIANNI QUARANTA .... PRODUCTION DESIGNER
ADRIANA SPARADO .... COSTUME DESIGNER
ANNA ANNI .... COSTUME DESIGNER
WILLIAM REYNOLDS .... FILM EDITOR

DANCES WITH WOLVES
DEAN SEMLER .... CINEMATOGRAPHER
JEFFREY BEECROFT .... PRODUCTION DESIGNER
ELSA ZAMPARELLI .... COSTUME DESIGNER
NEIL TRAVIS .... FILM EDITOR

DANCING IN THE DARK
VIC SARIN .... CINEMATOGRAPHER
TOM BERNER .... FILM EDITOR

DANGER ROUTE
HARRY WAXMAN .... CINEMATOGRAPHER

DANGER ZONE, THE
DANIEL YARUSSI .... CINEMATOGRAPHER

DANGER ZONE III: STEEL HORSE WAR
DANIEL YARUSSI .... CINEMATOGRAPHER
BRIAN MCCABE .... PRODUCTION DESIGNER
BOB MURAWSKI .... FILM EDITOR

DANGEROUS COMPANY (TF)
VINCENT M. CRESCIMAN .... PRODUCTION DESIGNER

DANGEROUS CURVES
BOB BRING .... FILM EDITOR

DANGEROUS DAVIES - THE LAST DETECTIVE
FRANK WATTS .... CINEMATOGRAPHER

DANGEROUS GAME
PETER LEVY .... CINEMATOGRAPHER
TIM WELLBURN .... FILM EDITOR

DANGEROUS LIAISONS
PHILIPPE ROUSSELOT .... CINEMATOGRAPHER
STUART CRAIG .... PRODUCTION DESIGNER
JAMES ACHESON .... COSTUME DESIGNER
MICK AUDSLEY .... FILM EDITOR

DANGEROUS LIFE, A (CMS)
JAMES BARTLE .... CINEMATOGRAPHER

DANGEROUS LOVE
NICHOLAS VON STERNBERG .... CINEMATOGRAPHER
TONY LANZA .... FILM EDITOR

DANGEROUS MOVES
RAOUL COUTARD .... CINEMATOGRAPHER

DANGEROUS OBSESSION
BOBBY BUKOWSKI .... CINEMATOGRAPHER
RAY RECHT .... PRODUCTION DESIGNER
NATASHA LANDAU .... COSTUME DESIGNER
DORIAN HARRIS .... FILM EDITOR

Cu-Da

CINEMATOGRAPHERS
PRODUCTION
DESIGNERS,
COSTUME
DESIGNERS AND
FILM EDITORS
GUIDE

I N D E X   O F   F I L M   T I T L E S

CINEMATOGRAPHERS
PRODUCTION
DESIGNERS,
COSTUME
DESIGNERS AND
FILM EDITORS
GUIDE

I
N
D
E
X

O
F

F
I
L
M

T
I
T
L
E
S

DAY OF THE LOCUST, THE
CONRAD HALL .... CINEMATOGRAPHER
DEAN E. MITZNER .... PRODUCTION DESIGNER
JOHN ROBERT LLOYD .... PRODUCTION DESIGNER
RICHARD MACDONALD .... PRODUCTION DESIGNER
ANN ROTH .... COSTUME DESIGNER
JIM CLARK .... FILM EDITOR

DAY ONE (TF)
CURTIS A. SCHNELL .... PRODUCTION DESIGNER
DEBRA KAREN .... FILM EDITOR

DAY THE BUBBLE BURST, THE (TF)
JOSEPH R. JENNINGS .... PRODUCTION DESIGNER

DAY THE EARTH CAUGHT FIRE, THE
HARRY WAXMAN .... CINEMATOGRAPHER

DAY THE LOVING STOPPED, THE (TF)
ROBERT B. HAUSER .... CINEMATOGRAPHER

DAY THE WOMEN GOT EVEN, THE
BRIAN WEST .... CINEMATOGRAPHER

DAY TIME ENDED, THE
JOHN A. MORRILL .... CINEMATOGRAPHER
TED NICOLAOU .... FILM EDITOR

DAYS OF HEAVEN
NESTOR ALMENDROS .... CINEMATOGRAPHER
JACK FISK .... PRODUCTION DESIGNER
PATRICIA NORRIS .... COSTUME DESIGNER
BILLY WEBER .... FILM EDITOR

DAYS OF THUNDER
WARD RUSSELL .... CINEMATOGRAPHER
BENJAMIN FERNANDEZ .... PRODUCTION DESIGNER
THOMAS E. SANDERS .... PRODUCTION DESIGNER
BILLY WEBER .... FILM EDITOR
CHRIS LEBENZON .... FILM EDITOR

DAYS OF WINE AND ROSES
DONFELD .... COSTUME DESIGNER

DEAD
JAN KIESSER .... CINEMATOGRAPHER

DEAD AND BURIED
STEVEN B. POSTER .... CINEMATOGRAPHER
JOE AUBEL .... PRODUCTION DESIGNER
WILLIAM SANDELL .... PRODUCTION DESIGNER
ERICA EDELL PHILLIPS .... COSTUME DESIGNER
ALAN BALSAM .... FILM EDITOR

DEAD BANG
GERRY FISHER .... CINEMATOGRAPHER
KEN ADAM .... PRODUCTION DESIGNER
JODIE TILLEN .... COSTUME DESIGNER
ROBERT F. SHUGRUE .... FILM EDITOR

DEAD CALM
DEAN SEMLER .... CINEMATOGRAPHER
GRAHAM GRACE WALKER .... PRODUCTION DESIGNER
NORMA MORICEAU .... COSTUME DESIGNER
RICHARD FRANCIS-BRUCE .... FILM EDITOR

DEAD EASY
JOHN SCOTT .... FILM EDITOR

DEAD END DRIVE-IN
PAUL MURPHY .... CINEMATOGRAPHER
LAWRENCE EASTWOOD .... PRODUCTION DESIGNER
ALAN LAKE .... FILM EDITOR
LEE SMITH .... FILM EDITOR

DEAD HEAT
ROBERT D. YEOMAN .... CINEMATOGRAPHER
CRAIG STEARNS .... PRODUCTION DESIGNER
LISA JENSEN .... COSTUME DESIGNER
HARVEY ROSENSTOCK .... FILM EDITOR

DEAD MEN DON'T DIE
TOM FRASER .... CINEMATOGRAPHER
PHILIP VASELS .... PRODUCTION DESIGNER
MICHAEL ORNSTEIN .... FILM EDITOR

DEAD MEN DON'T WEAR PLAID
MICHAEL CHAPMAN .... CINEMATOGRAPHER
JOHN DE CUIR .... PRODUCTION DESIGNER
EDITH HEAD† .... COSTUME DESIGNER
BUD MOLIN .... FILM EDITOR

DEAD MEN OUT (CTF)
MICHEL BRAULT .... CINEMATOGRAPHER
ANNE PRITCHARD .... PRODUCTION DESIGNER
MIA GOLDMAN .... FILM EDITOR

DEAD OF WINTER
JAN WEINCKE .... CINEMATOGRAPHER
ALICIA KEYWAN .... PRODUCTION DESIGNER
BILL BRODIE .... PRODUCTION DESIGNER
ARTHUR ROWSELL .... COSTUME DESIGNER
RICK SHAINE .... FILM EDITOR

DEAD POETS SOCIETY
JOHN SEALE .... CINEMATOGRAPHER
SANDY VENEZIANO .... PRODUCTION DESIGNER
WENDY STITES .... PRODUCTION DESIGNER
MARILYN MATTHEWS .... COSTUME DESIGNER
PRISCILLA ANNE NEDD .... FILM EDITOR
WILLIAM M. ANDERSON .... FILM EDITOR

DEAD POOL, THE
JACK N. GREEN .... CINEMATOGRAPHER
EDWARD C. CARFAGNO .... PRODUCTION DESIGNER
GLENN WRIGHT .... COSTUME DESIGNER
RONALD G. SPANG .... FILM EDITOR

DEAD RINGERS
PETER SUSCHITZKY .... CINEMATOGRAPHER
CAROL SPIER .... PRODUCTION DESIGNER
DENISE CRONENBERG .... COSTUME DESIGNER
RONALD SANDERS .... FILM EDITOR

DEAD SOLID PERFECT (CTF)
TIM SUHRSTEDT .... CINEMATOGRAPHER
HILDA STARK .... PRODUCTION DESIGNER
MARY MALIN .... COSTUME DESIGNER
PETRA VON OELFFEN .... FILM EDITOR

DEAD SPACE
MARK PERRY .... CINEMATOGRAPHER
GARY RANDALL .... PRODUCTION DESIGNER
GREG LA VOI .... COSTUME DESIGNER
LAWRENCE JORDAN .... FILM EDITOR

DEAD WOMEN IN LINGERIE
JOHN C. NEWBY .... CINEMATOGRAPHER
ADAM LEVENTHAL .... PRODUCTION DESIGNER
CATHERINE BEAUMONT .... COSTUME DESIGNER
MARK STRATTON .... FILM EDITOR

DEAD ZONE, THE
MARK IRWIN .... CINEMATOGRAPHER
BARBARA DUNPHY .... PRODUCTION DESIGNER
CAROL SPIER .... PRODUCTION DESIGNER
OLGA DIMITROV .... COSTUME DESIGNER
RONALD SANDERS .... FILM EDITOR

DEAD, THE
FRED MURPHY .... CINEMATOGRAPHER
DENNIS WASHINGTON .... PRODUCTION DESIGNER
STEPHEN GRIMES† .... PRODUCTION DESIGNER
DOROTHY JEAKINS .... COSTUME DESIGNER
ROBERTO SILVI .... FILM EDITOR

DEADFALL
RAYMOND SIMM .... PRODUCTION DESIGNER

DEADHEAD MILES
RALPH WOOLSEY .... CINEMATOGRAPHER

DEADLINE
MANFRED GUTHE .... CINEMATOGRAPHER
THOMAS MAUCH .... CINEMATOGRAPHER
PETER PRZYGODDA .... FILM EDITOR

DEADLY AFFAIR, THE
FREDDIE YOUNG .... CINEMATOGRAPHER

DEADLY BLESSING
ROBERT JESSUP .... CINEMATOGRAPHER
JACK MARTY .... PRODUCTION DESIGNER
RICHARD BRACKEN .... FILM EDITOR

DEADLY BUSINESS, A
ROY FORGE SMITH .... PRODUCTION DESIGNER

DEADLY DANCER
MARSHALL ADAMS .... CINEMATOGRAPHER
VOYA MIKULIC .... CINEMATOGRAPHER
JIM BARBALEY .... PRODUCTION DESIGNER
JENNIFER MICHAUD .... COSTUME DESIGNER
STEVE NIELSON .... FILM EDITOR

Da-De

CINEMATOGRAPHERS
PRODUCTION
DESIGNERS,
COSTUME
DESIGNERS AND
FILM EDITORS
GUIDE

I
N
D
E
X

O
F

F
I
L
M

T
I
T
L
E
S

De-De

CINEMATOGRAPHERS
PRODUCTION
DESIGNERS,
COSTUME
DESIGNERS and
FILM EDITORS
GUIDE

I
N
D
E
X

O
F

F
I
L
M

T
I
T
L
E
S

326

DEATH WISH 3

JOHN STANIER .... CINEMATOGRAPHER
DAVID MINTY .... PRODUCTION DESIGNER
PETER MULLINS .... PRODUCTION DESIGNER
PEGGY FARRELL-SALTEN .... COSTUME DESIGNER
ARNOLD CRUST .... FILM EDITOR

DEATH WISH 4: THE CRACKDOWN

GIDEON PORATH .... CINEMATOGRAPHER
WHITNEY BROOKE WHEELER .... PRODUCTION DESIGNER
MICHAEL HOFFMAN .... COSTUME DESIGNER
PETER LEE THOMPSON .... FILM EDITOR

DEATHCHEATERS

JOHN SEALE .... CINEMATOGRAPHER

DEATHROW GAMESHOW

CRAIG BASSUK .... CINEMATOGRAPHER
TIM SHOEMAKER .... FILM EDITOR

DEATHSPORT

GARY GRAVER .... CINEMATOGRAPHER
SHARON COMPTON .... PRODUCTION DESIGNER
LARRY BOCK .... FILM EDITOR

DEATHSTALKER

LEONARD SOLIS .... CINEMATOGRAPHER
JOHN ADAMS .... FILM EDITOR

DEATHSTALKER II

LEONARD SOLIS .... CINEMATOGRAPHER

DEATHTRAP

ANDRZEJ BARTKOWIAK .... CINEMATOGRAPHER
EDWARD PISONI .... PRODUCTION DESIGNER
TONY WALTON .... PRODUCTION DESIGNER
TONY WALTON .... COSTUME DESIGNER
JOHN J. FITZSTEPHENS .... FILM EDITOR

DEATHWATCH

PIERRE-WILLIAM GLENN .... CINEMATOGRAPHER
ANTHONY PRATT .... PRODUCTION DESIGNER
ARMAND PSENNY .... FILM EDITOR
MICHAEL ELLIS .... FILM EDITOR

DECAMERON, THE

DANTE FERRETTI .... PRODUCTION DESIGNER

DECEIVERS, THE

WALTER LASSALLY .... CINEMATOGRAPHER
KEN ADAM .... PRODUCTION DESIGNER
JENNY BEAVEN .... COSTUME DESIGNER
JOHN BRIGHT .... COSTUME DESIGNER
RICHARD TREVOR .... FILM EDITOR

DECEMBER BRIDE

BRUNO DE KEYZER .... CINEMATOGRAPHER
ADRIAN SMITH .... PRODUCTION DESIGNER
CONSOLATA BOYLE .... COSTUME DESIGNER
RODNEY HOLLAND .... FILM EDITOR

DECEPTIONS (TF)

ERNEST DAY .... CINEMATOGRAPHER

DECLINE OF THE AMERICAN EMPIRE, THE

GUY DUFAUX .... CINEMATOGRAPHER
GUDELINE SAURIOL .... PRODUCTION DESIGNER
DENIS SPERDOUKLIS .... COSTUME DESIGNER
MONIQUE FORTIER .... FILM EDITOR

DECLINE OF WESTERN CIVILIZATION PART II: THE METAL YEARS, THE (FD)

JEFF ZIMMERMAN .... CINEMATOGRAPHER
EARL GHAFFARI .... FILM EDITOR

DECORATION DAY (TF)

NEIL ROACH .... CINEMATOGRAPHER
DONALD LIGHT-HARRIS .... PRODUCTION DESIGNER
HARVEY ROSENSTOCK .... FILM EDITOR

DEEP END

ANTHONY PRATT .... PRODUCTION DESIGNER

DEEP IN THE HEART

CHARLES STEWART .... CINEMATOGRAPHER
LILLY KILVERT .... PRODUCTION DESIGNER
JANET LAWLER .... COSTUME DESIGNER
WILLIAM SHAPTER .... FILM EDITOR

DEEP, THE

CHRISTOPHER CHALLIS .... CINEMATOGRAPHER
WILLY KURANT .... CINEMATOGRAPHER
ANTHONY MASTERS .... PRODUCTION DESIGNER
RON TALSKY .... COSTUME DESIGNER
THOMAS M. BRONSON .... COSTUME DESIGNER
ROBERT L. WOLFE .... FILM EDITOR

DEEPSTAR SIX

MAC AHLBERG .... CINEMATOGRAPHER
JOHN REINHART .... PRODUCTION DESIGNER
AMY ENDRIES .... COSTUME DESIGNER
DAVID HANDMAN .... FILM EDITOR

DEERHUNTER, THE

VILMOS ZSIGMOND .... CINEMATOGRAPHER
RON HOBBS .... PRODUCTION DESIGNER
PETER ZINNER .... FILM EDITOR

DEF-CON 4

MICHAEL SPENCE .... FILM EDITOR
TODD RAMSAY .... FILM EDITOR

DEFECTION OF SIMAS KUDIRKA, THE (TF)

WILLIAM HINEY .... PRODUCTION DESIGNER

DEFENDING YOUR LIFE

ALLEN DAVIAU .... CINEMATOGRAPHER
IDA RANDOM .... PRODUCTION DESIGNER
DEBORAH L. SCOTT .... COSTUME DESIGNER
DAVID FINFER .... FILM EDITOR

DEFENSE OF THE REALM

ROGER DEAKINS .... CINEMATOGRAPHER
DIANA CHARNLEY .... PRODUCTION DESIGNER
ROGER MURRAY-LEACH .... PRODUCTION DESIGNER
LOUISE FROGLEY .... COSTUME DESIGNER
MICHAEL BRADSELL .... FILM EDITOR

DEFENSE PLAY

TIMOTHY GALFAS .... CINEMATOGRAPHER
MARJORIE BOWERS .... COSTUME DESIGNER
JAMES RUXIN .... FILM EDITOR

DEFENSELESS

CURTIS A. SCHNELL .... PRODUCTION DESIGNER

DEFIANCE

RIC WAITE .... CINEMATOGRAPHER
WILLIAM MALLEY .... PRODUCTION DESIGNER
DAVID FINFER .... FILM EDITOR

DEFIANT ONES, THE (TF)

BEALA B. NEEL .... PRODUCTION DESIGNER

DEJA VU

TONY WOLLARD .... PRODUCTION DESIGNER
MARIT ALLEN .... COSTUME DESIGNER
RICHARD TREVOR .... FILM EDITOR

DELICATE MATTER, A

GARY THIELTGES .... CINEMATOGRAPHER

DELINQUENTS, THE

ANDREW LESNIE .... CINEMATOGRAPHER
LAURENCE EASTWOOD .... PRODUCTION DESIGNER
BRUCE FINLAYSON .... COSTUME DESIGNER
JOHN SCOTT .... FILM EDITOR

DELIVERANCE

VILMOS ZSIGMOND .... CINEMATOGRAPHER
FRED HARPMAN .... PRODUCTION DESIGNER
JOHN B. MANSBRIDGE .... PRODUCTION DESIGNER
TOM PRIESTLEY .... FILM EDITOR

DELIVERY BOYS

LARRY REVENE .... CINEMATOGRAPHER
GARY KARR .... FILM EDITOR

DELTA FACTOR, THE

VINCENT SAIZIS .... CINEMATOGRAPHER
JACK T. COLLIS .... PRODUCTION DESIGNER

DELTA FORCE, THE

AVRAHAM KARPICK .... CINEMATOGRAPHER
DAVID GURFINKEL .... CINEMATOGRAPHER
LUCIANO SPADONI .... PRODUCTION DESIGNER
TAMI MOR .... COSTUME DESIGNER
ALAIN JAKUBOWICZ .... FILM EDITOR

De-De

CINEMATOGRAPHERS
PRODUCTION
DESIGNERS,
COSTUME
DESIGNERS AND
FILM EDITORS
GUIDE

I
N
D
E
X

O
F

F
I
L
M

T
I
T
L
E
S

CINEMATOGRAPHERS
PRODUCTION
DESIGNERS,
COSTUME
DESIGNERS and
FILM EDITORS
GUIDE

I
N
D
E
X

O
F

F
I
L
M

T
I
T
L
E
S

DELTA FORCE 2
JOAO FERNANDES .... CINEMATOGRAPHER
LADISLAV WILHEIM .... PRODUCTION DESIGNER
KADY DOVER .... COSTUME DESIGNER
MICHAEL DUTHIE .... FILM EDITOR

DELTA PIE
PAUL LOHMANN .... CINEMATOGRAPHER

DELUSION
GEZA SINKOVICS .... CINEMATOGRAPHER
ROBERT LEIGHTON .... FILM EDITOR
MARK ALLAN KAPLAN .... FILM EDITOR

DEMANOID
ALEX PHILLIPS .... CINEMATOGRAPHER

DEMON
CHRIS LEBENZON .... FILM EDITOR

DEMON MURDER CASE, THE (TF)
JOHN LINDLEY .... CINEMATOGRAPHER

DEMON SEED
BILL BUTLER .... CINEMATOGRAPHER
EDWARD C. CARFAGNO .... PRODUCTION DESIGNER

DEMONS IN THE GARDEN
JOSE LUIS ALCAINE .... CINEMATOGRAPHER
JOSE SALCEDO .... FILM EDITOR

DEMONSVILLE TERROR, THE
ULLI LOMMEL .... CINEMATOGRAPHER

DEMONWARP
R. MICHAEL STRINGER .... CINEMATOGRAPHER

DEMPSEY (TF)
RIC WAITE .... CINEMATOGRAPHER
PAUL PETERS .... PRODUCTION DESIGNER
MINA MITTELMAN .... COSTUME DESIGNER

DENNIS THE MENACE (TF)
BEALA B. NEEL .... PRODUCTION DESIGNER
MARJORIE BOWERS .... COSTUME DESIGNER

DERSU UZALA
SHINOBU MURAKI .... PRODUCTION DESIGNER
YOSHIRO MURAKI .... PRODUCTION DESIGNER

DESCENDING ANGEL (CTF)
LAJOS KOLTAI .... CINEMATOGRAPHER
ANNE PRITCHARD .... PRODUCTION DESIGNER
DAVID HOLDEN .... FILM EDITOR

DESERT BLOOM
REYNALDO VILLALOBOS .... CINEMATOGRAPHER
LAWRENCE MILLER .... PRODUCTION DESIGNER
HILARY ROSENFELD .... COSTUME DESIGNER
CARI COUGHLIN .... FILM EDITOR
DAVID GARFIELD .... FILM EDITOR

DESERT HEARTS
ROBERT ELWSIT .... CINEMATOGRAPHER
JEANNINE CLAUDIA OPPEWALL .... PRODUCTION DESIGNER
ROBERT L. ESTRIN .... FILM EDITOR

DESIRE
DANTE FERRETTI .... PRODUCTION DESIGNER

DESPAIR
MICHAEL BALLHAUS .... CINEMATOGRAPHER

DESPERADO (TF)
DICK BUSH .... CINEMATOGRAPHER
ROBERT JESSUP .... CINEMATOGRAPHER

DESPERATE (TF)
JACK SENTER .... PRODUCTION DESIGNER

DESPERATE FOR LOVE (TF)
WILLIAM WAGES .... CINEMATOGRAPHER

DESPERATE HOURS
DOUG MILSOME .... CINEMATOGRAPHER
VICTORIA PAUL .... PRODUCTION DESIGNER
CHARLES DE CARLO .... COSTUME DESIGNER
PETER HUNT .... FILM EDITOR

DESPERATE LIVING
CHARLES ROGGERO .... FILM EDITOR

DESPERATELY SEEKING SUSAN
EDWARD LACHMAN .... CINEMATOGRAPHER
SANTO LOQUASTO .... PRODUCTION DESIGNER
SPEED HOPKINS .... PRODUCTION DESIGNER
SANTO LOQUASTO .... COSTUME DESIGNER
ANDREW MONDSHEIN .... FILM EDITOR

DESTRUCTORS, THE
DOUGLAS SLOCOMBE .... CINEMATOGRAPHER

DETECTIVE
BRUNO NUYTTEN .... CINEMATOGRAPHER

DETECTIVE SCHOOL DROPOUTS
GIANCARLO FERRANDO .... CINEMATOGRAPHER
ANTONELLO GELENG .... PRODUCTION DESIGNER
CESARE D'AMICO .... FILM EDITOR

DETECTIVE, THE
JACK MARTIN SMITH .... PRODUCTION DESIGNER
WILLIAM J. CREBER .... PRODUCTION DESIGNER

DEVIL AND MAX DEVLIN, THE
HOWARD SCHWARTZ .... CINEMATOGRAPHER
JOHN B. MANSBRIDGE .... PRODUCTION DESIGNER
LEON HARRIS .... PRODUCTION DESIGNER
BILL THOMAS .... COSTUME DESIGNER

DEVIL IN THE FLESH
GIUSEPPI LANCI .... CINEMATOGRAPHER
LINA NERLI TAVIANI .... COSTUME DESIGNER
MIRCO GARRONE .... FILM EDITOR

DEVIL WITHIN HER, THE
KEITH PALMER .... FILM EDITOR

DEVIL'S ADVOCATE, THE
BILLY WILLIAMS .... CINEMATOGRAPHER

DEVIL'S BRIGADE
ALFRED SWEENEY .... PRODUCTION DESIGNER

DEVIL'S PLAYGROUND, THE
IAN BAKER .... CINEMATOGRAPHER

DEVIL'S RAIN, THE
ALEX PHILLIPS .... CINEMATOGRAPHER
MICHAEL KAHN .... FILM EDITOR

DEVONSVILLE TERROR, THE
RICHARD S. BRUMMER .... FILM EDITOR

DIAHANN CARROLL SUMMER SHOW, THE (TV)
BOB MACKIE .... COSTUME DESIGNER

DIAL M FOR MURDER (TF)
RON HOBBS .... PRODUCTION DESIGNER

DIAMOND SKULLS
MICHAEL COULTER .... CINEMATOGRAPHER
JOCELYN JAMES .... PRODUCTION DESIGNER
RODNEY HOLLAND .... FILM EDITOR

DIAMOND'S EDGE
BILLY WILLIAMS .... CINEMATOGRAPHER
PETER MURTON .... PRODUCTION DESIGNER
MARIA PRICE .... COSTUME DESIGNER
SCOTT THOMAS .... FILM EDITOR

DIAMONDS
ADAM GREENBERG .... CINEMATOGRAPHER
DOV HOENIG .... FILM EDITOR

DIAMONDS ARE FOREVER
TED MOORE .... CINEMATOGRAPHER
KEN ADAM .... PRODUCTION DESIGNER
WILLIAM KENNEY .... PRODUCTION DESIGNER
JOHN W. HOLMES .... FILM EDITOR

DIANA ROSS SPECIAL, THE (TV)
BOB MACKIE .... COSTUME DESIGNER

DIARY OF A MAD HOUSEWIFE
GERALD HIRSCHFELD .... CINEMATOGRAPHER

DIARY OF A MADMAN, THE
CLAUDE LECOMTE .... CINEMATOGRAPHER

CINEMATOGRAPHERS
PRODUCTION
DESIGNERS,
COSTUME
DESIGNERS AND
FILM EDITORS
GUIDE

INDEX OF FILM TITLES

CINEMATOGRAPHERS
PRODUCTION
DESIGNERS,
COSTUME
DESIGNERS and
FILM EDITORS
GUIDE

**I
N
D
E
X

O
F

F
I
L
M

T
I
T
L
E
S**

DO THE RIGHT THING
WYNN P. THOMAS .... PRODUCTION DESIGNER
RUTH E. CARTER .... COSTUME DESIGNER
BARRY ALEXANDER BROWN .... FILM EDITOR

DO YOU REMEBER LOVE? (TF)
BRADFORD MAY .... CINEMATOGRAPHER
NORM BARON .... PRODUCTION DESIGNER
JULIE WEISS .... COSTUME DESIGNER

DOBERMAN GANG, THE
ROBERT CARAMICO .... CINEMATOGRAPHER

DOC HOLLYWOOD
PRISCILLA ANNE NEDD .... FILM EDITOR

DOC SAVAGE, THE MAN OF BRONZE
FRED J. KOENEKAMP .... CINEMATOGRAPHER
FRED HARPMAN .... PRODUCTION DESIGNER
PATRICK CUMMINGS .... COSTUME DESIGNER

DOCTEUR PETIOT
PATRICK BLOSSIER .... CINEMATOGRAPHER
CORINNE JORRY .... COSTUME DESIGNER
ANITA FERNANDEZ .... FILM EDITOR

DOCTOR AND THE DEVILS, THE
GERRY TURPIN .... CINEMATOGRAPHER
NORMAN WARWICK .... CINEMATOGRAPHER
BRIAN ACKLAND-SNOW .... PRODUCTION DESIGNER
ROBERT LAING .... PRODUCTION DESIGNER
IMOGENE RICHARDSON .... COSTUME DESIGNER
LAURENCE MÉRY CLARK .... FILM EDITOR

DOCTOR DETROIT
KING BAGGOT .... CINEMATOGRAPHER
LAWRENCE G. PAULL .... PRODUCTION DESIGNER
BETSY COX .... COSTUME DESIGNER
CHRISTOPHER GREENBURY .... FILM EDITOR

DOCTOR DOOLITTLE
ROBERT SURTEES† .... CINEMATOGRAPHER
JACK MARTIN SMITH .... PRODUCTION DESIGNER

DOCTOR ZHIVAGO
FREDDIE YOUNG .... CINEMATOGRAPHER
JOHN BOX .... PRODUCTION DESIGNER

DOCTOR'S WIVES
CARL KRESS .... FILM EDITOR

DODES'KA'DEN
SHINOBU MURAKI .... PRODUCTION DESIGNER
YOSHIRO MURAKI .... PRODUCTION DESIGNER

DOG DAY AFTERNOON
VICTOR J. KEMPER .... CINEMATOGRAPHER
DEDE ALLEN .... FILM EDITOR

DOGS IN SPACE
ANDREW DE GROOT .... CINEMATOGRAPHER
JODY BORLAND .... PRODUCTION DESIGNER
JILL BILCOCK .... FILM EDITOR

DOGS OF WAR, THE
JACK CARDIFF .... CINEMATOGRAPHER
BERT DAVEY .... PRODUCTION DESIGNER
JOHN SIDALL .... PRODUCTION DESIGNER
PETER MULLINS .... PRODUCTION DESIGNER
EMMA PORTEUS .... COSTUME DESIGNER
ANTONY GIBBS .... FILM EDITOR

DOIN' TIME
RONALD VICTOR GARCIA .... CINEMATOGRAPHER
JACK MCADAM .... PRODUCTION DESIGNER
ARLENE J. ZAMIARA .... COSTUME DESIGNER
STANFORD C. ALLEN .... FILM EDITOR

DOIN' TIME ON PLANET EARTH
COLIN D. IRWIN .... PRODUCTION DESIGNER
CURTIS A. SCHNELL .... PRODUCTION DESIGNER
REVE RICHARDS .... COSTUME DESIGNER
ALAN BALSAM .... FILM EDITOR
SHARYN L. ROSS .... FILM EDITOR

DOIN' TIME ON PLANET EARTH (PILOT)
TIM SUHRSTEDT .... CINEMATOGRAPHER

DOLEMITE
NICHOLAS VON STERNBERG .... CINEMATOGRAPHER

DOLL'S HOUSE, A
GERRY FISHER .... CINEMATOGRAPHER
JEAN-PIERRE DORLEAC .... COSTUME DESIGNER

DOLLARS
GEORGE GRENVILLE .... FILM EDITOR

DOLLMAKER, THE (TF)
PAUL LOHMANN .... CINEMATOGRAPHER
GEORGE JENKINS .... PRODUCTION DESIGNER
JAN SCOTT .... PRODUCTION DESIGNER
JULIE WEISS .... COSTUME DESIGNER
RITA ROLAND .... FILM EDITOR

DOLLS
MAC AHLBERG .... CINEMATOGRAPHER
GIOVANNI NATALUCCI .... PRODUCTION DESIGNER
LEE PERCY .... FILM EDITOR

DOMINICK AND EUGENE
CURTIS CLARK .... CINEMATOGRAPHER
DOUG KRANER .... PRODUCTION DESIGNER
HILARY ROSENFELD .... COSTUME DESIGNER
ARTHUR COBURN .... FILM EDITOR

DOMINIQUE
TED MOORE .... CINEMATOGRAPHER

DOMINO PRINCIPLE, THE
FRED J. KOENEKAMP .... CINEMATOGRAPHER
ERNEST LAZLO† .... CINEMATOGRAPHER
RON HOBBS .... PRODUCTION DESIGNER
WILLIAM J. CREBER .... PRODUCTION DESIGNER
RITA RIGGS .... COSTUME DESIGNER
JOHN F. BURNETT .... FILM EDITOR

DON GIOVANNI
GERRY FISHER .... CINEMATOGRAPHER

DON'S PARTY
WILLIAM M. ANDERSON .... FILM EDITOR

DON'T ANSWER THE PHONE
KATHY CURTIS CAHILL .... PRODUCTION DESIGNER

DON'T CRY, IT'S ONLY THUNDER
DONALD MCALPINE .... CINEMATOGRAPHER
ANN LAMBERT .... COSTUME DESIGNER
BARBARA POKRAS .... FILM EDITOR

DON'T DRINK THE WATER
RALPH ROSENBLUM .... FILM EDITOR

DON'T GO INTO THE HOUSE
JANE KURSON .... FILM EDITOR

DON'T LOOK BACK (TF)
JAMES D. BISSELL .... PRODUCTION DESIGNER

DON'T LOOK NOW
MARIT ALLEN .... COSTUME DESIGNER
GRAEME CLIFFORD .... FILM EDITOR

DON'T MAKE WAVES
RITA ROLAND .... FILM EDITOR

DON'T OPEN TIL CHRISTMAS
ALAN PUDNEY .... CINEMATOGRAPHER

DON'T TELL HER IT'S ME
REED SMOOT .... CINEMATOGRAPHER
LINDA PEARL .... PRODUCTION DESIGNER
CAROL WOOD .... COSTUME DESIGNER
MARSHALL HARVEY .... FILM EDITOR

DONNY & MARIE (TVS)
BOB MACKIE .... COSTUME DESIGNER

DONOR (TF)
NEIL ROACH .... CINEMATOGRAPHER
PETER WOOLEY .... PRODUCTION DESIGNER
MARK WESTMORE .... FILM EDITOR

DOOR TO DOOR
REED SMOOT .... CINEMATOGRAPHER

DOORMAN, THE
LARRY PIZER .... CINEMATOGRAPHER

DOORS, THE

ROBERT RICHARDSON ....CINEMATOGRAPHER
BARBARA LING ....PRODUCTION DESIGNER
MARLENE STEWART ....COSTUME DESIGNER
DAVID BRENNER ....FILM EDITOR
JOE HUTSHING ....FILM EDITOR

DORE VAI IN VACANZA

LUCIANO TOVOLI ....CINEMATOGRAPHER

DORIAN GRAY

KAREN BROMLEY ....PRODUCTION DESIGNER

DORM THAT DRIPPED BLOOD, THE

STEPHEN CARPENTER ....CINEMATOGRAPHER

DOUBLE EXPOSURE

R. MICHAEL STRINGER ....CINEMATOGRAPHER

DOUBLE MCGUFFIN, THE

DON REDDY ....CINEMATOGRAPHER
ED RICHARDSON ....PRODUCTION DESIGNER
LEON SEITH ....FILM EDITOR

DOUBLE NEGATIVE

RENE VERZIER ....CINEMATOGRAPHER
GEORGE APPLEBY ....FILM EDITOR

DOUBLE REVENGE

ARNIE SIRLIN ....CINEMATOGRAPHER

DOVE, THE

JOHN JYMPSON ....FILM EDITOR

DOWN AND OUT IN AMERICA (FD)

TOM D. HURWITZ ....CINEMATOGRAPHER

DOWN AND OUT IN BEVERLY HILLS

DONALD MCALPINE ....CINEMATOGRAPHER
PATO GUZMAN ....PRODUCTION DESIGNER
TODD HALLOWELL ....PRODUCTION DESIGNER
ALBERT WOLSKY ....COSTUME DESIGNER
RICHARD HALSEY ....FILM EDITOR

DOWN BY LAW

ROBBY MULLER ....CINEMATOGRAPHER
CAROL WOOD ....COSTUME DESIGNER
MELODY LONDON ....FILM EDITOR

DOWN IN THE VALLEY (TF)

ANTON FURST ....PRODUCTION DESIGNER

DOWN THE LONG HILLS (TF)

REED SMOOT ....CINEMATOGRAPHER

DOWN TWISTED

CHESTER KACZENSKI ....PRODUCTION DESIGNER
RICHARD K. HUMMEL ....PRODUCTION DESIGNER
RENEE JOHNSTON ....COSTUME DESIGNER
DENNIS O'CONNOR ....FILM EDITOR

DOWNHILL RACER

RICHARD A. HARRIS ....FILM EDITOR

DOWNPAYMENT ON MURDER (TF)

BRADFORD MAY ....CINEMATOGRAPHER
JEFFREY L. GOLDSTEIN ....PRODUCTION DESIGNER
ANN SOMERS MAJOR ....COSTUME DESIGNER

DOWNTOWN

RICHARD H. KLINE ....CINEMATOGRAPHER
GREGORY PICKRELL ....PRODUCTION DESIGNER
CHARLES ROSEN ....PRODUCTION DESIGNER
DANIEL PAREDES ....COSTUME DESIGNER
JACQUELINE CAMBAS ....FILM EDITOR

DOWNTWISTED

WALT LLOYD ....CINEMATOGRAPHER

DR. ALIEN

NICHOLAS VON STERNBERG ...................................CINEMATOGRAPHER

DR. BLACK, MR. HYDE

TAK FUJIMOTO ....CINEMATOGRAPHER
JOHN C. HORGER ....FILM EDITOR

DR. FAUSTUS

JOHN DE CUIR ....PRODUCTION DESIGNER

DR. FISCHER OF GENEVA (TF)

KEN WESTBURY ....CINEMATOGRAPHER

DR. HECKYL & MR. HYPE

ROBERT PRIMES ....CINEMATOGRAPHER

DR. MINX

NORM WALLERSTEIN ....FILM EDITOR

DR. NO

TED MOORE ....CINEMATOGRAPHER
KEN ADAM ....PRODUCTION DESIGNER

DR. STRANGELOVE OR: HOW I LEARNED TO STOP WORRYING AND LOVE THE BOMB

KEN ADAM ....PRODUCTION DESIGNER
PETER MURTON ....PRODUCTION DESIGNER

DR. ZHIVAGO

TERENCE MARSH ....PRODUCTION DESIGNER

DRACULA

GIL TAYLOR ....CINEMATOGRAPHER
BRIAN ACKLAND-SNOW ....PRODUCTION DESIGNER
PETER MURTON ....PRODUCTION DESIGNER
JULIE HARRIS ....COSTUME DESIGNER
JOHN BLOOM ....FILM EDITOR

DRACULA (TF)

TREVOR WILLIAMS ....PRODUCTION DESIGNER

DRACULA'S DOG

BRUCE LOGAN ....CINEMATOGRAPHER
HARRY KERAMIDAS ....FILM EDITOR

DRACULA'S WIDOW

TOM SIITER ....FILM EDITOR

DRAGNET

MATTHEW F. LEONETTI ....CINEMATOGRAPHER
FRANK RICHWOOD ....PRODUCTION DESIGNER
ROBERT F. BOYLE ....PRODUCTION DESIGNER
TARYN DECHELLIS ....COSTUME DESIGNER
RICHARD HALSEY ....FILM EDITOR
WILLIAM GORDEAN ....FILM EDITOR

DRAGONSLAYER

DEREK VANLINT ....CINEMATOGRAPHER
ALAN CASSIE ....PRODUCTION DESIGNER
ELLIOT SCOTT ....PRODUCTION DESIGNER
ANTHONY MENDLESON ....COSTUME DESIGNER
TONY LAWSON ....FILM EDITOR

DRAUGHTMAN'S CONTRACT, THE

CURTIS CLARK ....CINEMATOGRAPHER
BOB RINGWOOD ....COSTUME DESIGNER
SUE BLANE ....COSTUME DESIGNER
JOHN WILSON ....FILM EDITOR

DRAW! (TF)

LASZLO GEORGE ....CINEMATOGRAPHER
RON WISMAN ....FILM EDITOR

DREAM A LITTLE DREAM

KING BAGGOT ....CINEMATOGRAPHER
MATTHEW JACOBS ....PRODUCTION DESIGNER
KRISTINE BROWN ....COSTUME DESIGNER
RUSSELL LIVINGSTONE ....FILM EDITOR

DREAM BREAKERS

THOMAS DEL RUTH ....CINEMATOGRAPHER

DREAM BREAKERS (TF)

MARK MANSBRIDGE ....PRODUCTION DESIGNER

DREAM DEMON

IAN WILSON ....CINEMATOGRAPHER
DAVID MARTIN ....FILM EDITOR
IAN CRAFFORD ....FILM EDITOR

DREAM LOVER

GEORGE JENKINS ....PRODUCTION DESIGNER
JOHN JAY MOORE ....PRODUCTION DESIGNER
MARIT ALLEN ....COSTUME DESIGNER
ANGELO CORRAO ....FILM EDITOR

DREAM ONE

PHILIPPE ROUSSELOT ....CINEMATOGRAPHER
TOM PRIESTLEY ....FILM EDITOR

Do-Dr

CINEMATOGRAPHERS
PRODUCTION
DESIGNERS,
COSTUME
DESIGNERS AND
FILM EDITORS
GUIDE

I
N
D
E
X

O
F

F
I
L
M

T
I
T
L
E
S

Dr-Du

CINEMATOGRAPHERS
PRODUCTION
DESIGNERS,
COSTUME
DESIGNERS and
FILM EDITORS
GUIDE

I
N
D
E
X

O
F

F
I
L
M

T
I
T
L
E
S

DREAM STREET (PILOT)
GREGORY BOLTON .... PRODUCTION DESIGNER
PATRICIA FIELD .... COSTUME DESIGNER
HARVEY ROSENSTOCK .... FILM EDITOR
STEVEN J. ROSENBLUM .... FILM EDITOR

DREAM TEAM, THE
ADAM HOLENDER .... CINEMATOGRAPHER
TODD HALLOWELL .... PRODUCTION DESIGNER
RUTH MORLEY .... COSTUME DESIGNER
CARROLL TIMOTHY O'MEARA .... FILM EDITOR

DREAM WEST (MS)
DAVID EGGBY .... CINEMATOGRAPHER
GREGG FONSECA .... PRODUCTION DESIGNER
LINDA PEARL .... PRODUCTION DESIGNER

DREAMCHILD
BILLY WILLIAMS .... CINEMATOGRAPHER
LEN HUNTINGFORD .... PRODUCTION DESIGNER
ROGER HALL .... PRODUCTION DESIGNER
JANE ROBINSON .... COSTUME DESIGNER
ANGUS NEWTON .... FILM EDITOR

DREAMER
BRUCE SURTEES .... CINEMATOGRAPHER
FRED A. CHULACK .... FILM EDITOR

DREAMER OF OZ, THE (TF)
THOMAS BURSTYN .... CINEMATOGRAPHER
JAMES HULSEY .... PRODUCTION DESIGNER
JERROLD L. LUDWIG .... FILM EDITOR

DREAMERS
STEPHEN ASHLEY BLAKE .... CINEMATOGRAPHER

DREAMLAND
JOSEPH MANGINE .... CINEMATOGRAPHER
JAY FREUND .... FILM EDITOR

DREAMS
SHINOBU MURAKI .... PRODUCTION DESIGNER
YOSHIRO MURAKI .... PRODUCTION DESIGNER

DREAMS OF GOLD: THE MEL FISHER STORY (TF)
ROBB WILSON KING .... PRODUCTION DESIGNER

DREAMSCAPE
BRIAN TUFANO .... CINEMATOGRAPHER
JEFF STAGGS .... PRODUCTION DESIGNER
LINDA BASS .... COSTUME DESIGNER
RICHARD HALSEY .... FILM EDITOR

DREAMSTEET (PILOT)
ROBERT ELSWIT .... CINEMATOGRAPHER

DRESS GRAY (TF)
GAYNE RESCHER .... CINEMATOGRAPHER
PAUL RUBELL .... FILM EDITOR

DRESSED TO KILL
RALF D. BODE .... CINEMATOGRAPHER
GARY WEIST .... PRODUCTION DESIGNER
ANN ROTH .... COSTUME DESIGNER
GERALD B. GREENBERG .... FILM EDITOR

DRESSER, THE
KELVIN PIKE .... CINEMATOGRAPHER
COLIN GRIMES .... PRODUCTION DESIGNER
STEPHEN GRIMES† .... PRODUCTION DESIGNER
RAY LOVEJOY .... FILM EDITOR

DRESSMAKER, THE
MICHAEL COULTER .... CINEMATOGRAPHER
CAROLYN AMIES .... PRODUCTION DESIGNER

DRIFTER, THE
DAVID SPERLING .... CINEMATOGRAPHER
STEPHEN MARK .... FILM EDITOR

DRIVE, HE SAID
BILL BUTLER .... CINEMATOGRAPHER
CHRISTOPHER HOLMES .... FILM EDITOR
DONN CAMBERN .... FILM EDITOR

DRIVE-IN
ROBERT JESSUP .... CINEMATOGRAPHER
BERNARD F. CAPUTO .... FILM EDITOR

DRIVER, THE
PHILIP LATHROP .... CINEMATOGRAPHER
DAVID M. HABER .... PRODUCTION DESIGNER
ROBERT K. LAMBERT .... FILM EDITOR
TINA HIRSCH .... FILM EDITOR

DRIVING MISS DAISY
BRUNO RUBEO .... PRODUCTION DESIGNER
VICTOR KEMPSTER .... PRODUCTION DESIGNER
ELIZABETH MCBRIDE .... COSTUME DESIGNER
MARK ROY WARNER .... FILM EDITOR

DROP DEAD FRED
PETER DEMING .... CINEMATOGRAPHER
JOSEPH T. GARRITY .... PRODUCTION DESIGNER
CAROL WOOD .... COSTUME DESIGNER
MARSHALL HARVEY .... FILM EDITOR

DROP-OUT FATHER (TF)
GARY WEIST .... PRODUCTION DESIGNER

DROWNING BY NUMBERS
SACHA VIERNEY .... CINEMATOGRAPHER
JOHN WILSON .... FILM EDITOR

DROWNING POOL, THE
GORDON WILLIS .... CINEMATOGRAPHER
PAUL SYLBERT .... PRODUCTION DESIGNER
DONALD BROOKS .... COSTUME DESIGNER
JOHN C. HOWARD .... FILM EDITOR

DRUGSTORE COWBOY
ROBERT D. YEOMAN .... CINEMATOGRAPHER
DAVID BRISBIN .... PRODUCTION DESIGNER
CURTISS CLAYTON .... FILM EDITOR

DRUM
STAN JOLLEY .... PRODUCTION DESIGNER
WILLIAM KENNEY .... PRODUCTION DESIGNER
CARL KRESS .... FILM EDITOR

DRUNKEN ANGEL
SHINOBU MURAKI .... PRODUCTION DESIGNER
YOSHIRO MURAKI .... PRODUCTION DESIGNER

DRY WHITE SEASON, A
PIERRE-WILLIAM GLENN .... CINEMATOGRAPHER
KELVIN PIKE .... CINEMATOGRAPHER
JOHN FENNER .... PRODUCTION DESIGNER
SAM O'STEEN .... FILM EDITOR

DUCHESS & THE DIRTWATER FOX, THE
JOSEPH BIROC .... CINEMATOGRAPHER
TREVOR WILLIAMS .... PRODUCTION DESIGNER
FRANK BRACHT .... FILM EDITOR
WILLIAM BUTLER .... FILM EDITOR

DUCK FACTORY, THE (PILOT)
JAMES G. HULSEY .... PRODUCTION DESIGNER

DUDES
ROBERT RICHARDSON .... CINEMATOGRAPHER
ROBERT ZIEMBICKI .... PRODUCTION DESIGNER
JILL OHANNESON .... COSTUME DESIGNER
ANDY HORVITCH .... FILM EDITOR

DUEL
JACK A. MARTA .... CINEMATOGRAPHER

DUEL (TF)
FRANK MORRISS .... FILM EDITOR

DUELLISTS, THE
FRANK TIDY .... CINEMATOGRAPHER
PETER J. HAMPTON .... PRODUCTION DESIGNER
TOM RAND .... COSTUME DESIGNER
MICHAEL BRADSELL .... FILM EDITOR
PAMELA POWER .... FILM EDITOR

DUET FOR ONE
ALEX THOMSON .... CINEMATOGRAPHER
JOHN GRAYSMARK .... PRODUCTION DESIGNER
EVANGELINE HARRISON .... COSTUME DESIGNER
HENRY RICHARDSON .... FILM EDITOR

DULCIMA
RAYMOND SIMM .... PRODUCTION DESIGNER

DUMMY (TF)
WILLIAM J. CASSIDY .... PRODUCTION DESIGNER
DONALD R. RODE .... FILM EDITOR

DUNE
FREDDIE FRANCIS .... CINEMATOGRAPHER
ANTHONY MASTERS .... PRODUCTION DESIGNER
BENJAMIN FERNANDEZ .... PRODUCTION DESIGNER
PIERLUIGI BASILE .... PRODUCTION DESIGNER
BOB RINGWOOD .... COSTUME DESIGNER
ANTONY GIBBS .... FILM EDITOR

DUNGEONMASTER, THE
MAC AHLBERG .... CINEMATOGRAPHER
TED NICOLAOU .... FILM EDITOR

DUNWHICH HORROR, THE
CHRISTOPHER HOLMES .... FILM EDITOR

DUSTY AND SWEETS MCGEE
RICHARD A. HARRIS .... FILM EDITOR

DUTCH TREAT
RANDY SER .... PRODUCTION DESIGNER
JACQUELINE SAINT ANNE .... COSTUME DESIGNER
BRURIA DAVIDSON .... FILM EDITOR

E

E.A.R.T.H. FORCE (TF)
MARTIN MCGRATH .... CINEMATOGRAPHER
CHRIS BERKWOLDT .... PRODUCTION DESIGNER
DANNY CAHN .... FILM EDITOR
GEORGE POTTER .... FILM EDITOR

E.T.: THE EXTRATERRESTRIAL
ALLEN DAVIAU .... CINEMATOGRAPHER
JAMES D. BISSELL .... PRODUCTION DESIGNER
DEBORAH L. SCOTT .... COSTUME DESIGNER
CAROL LITTLETON .... FILM EDITOR

EAGLE HAS LANDED, THE
ANTHONY B. RICHMOND .... CINEMATOGRAPHER
PETER MURTON .... PRODUCTION DESIGNER
ANNE V. COATES .... FILM EDITOR

EAGLE'S WING
BILLY WILLIAMS .... CINEMATOGRAPHER
AUGUSTIN ITUARTE .... PRODUCTION DESIGNER
HERBERT WESTBROOK .... PRODUCTION DESIGNER
LESLEY WALKER .... FILM EDITOR

EARLY FROST, AN (TF)
WOODY OMENS .... CINEMATOGRAPHER
JAMES G. HULSEY .... PRODUCTION DESIGNER

EARLY SPRING
MIKAEL SALOMON .... CINEMATOGRAPHER

EARTH GIRLS ARE EASY
OLIVER STAPLETON .... CINEMATOGRAPHER
DENNIS GASSNER .... PRODUCTION DESIGNER
RICHARD HALSEY .... FILM EDITOR

EARTH*STAR VOYAGER (TF)
ROBERT M. STEVENS .... CINEMATOGRAPHER

EARTHLING, THE
DONALD MCALPINIE .... CINEMATOGRAPHER
DAVID COPPING .... PRODUCTION DESIGNER
FRANK MORRISS .... FILM EDITOR

EARTHQUAKE
PHILIP LATHROP .... CINEMATOGRAPHER
PRESTON AMES .... PRODUCTION DESIGNER
DOROTHY SPENCER .... FILM EDITOR

EASY MONEY
FRED SCHULER .... CINEMATOGRAPHER
EUGENE LEE .... PRODUCTION DESIGNER
JOSEPH G. AULISI .... COSTUME DESIGNER
RONALD ROOSE .... FILM EDITOR

EASY PREY (TF)
DOUGLAS HIGGINS .... PRODUCTION DESIGNER

EASY RIDER
LASZLO KOVACS .... CINEMATOGRAPHER
DONN CAMBERN .... FILM EDITOR

EAT A BOWL OF TEA
AMIR MOKRI .... CINEMATOGRAPHER
ROBERT ZIEMBICKI .... PRODUCTION DESIGNER
MARIT ALLEN .... COSTUME DESIGNER
RICHARD CANDIB .... FILM EDITOR

EAT AND RUN
DYANNA TAYLOR .... CINEMATOGRAPHER
PAMELA S. ARNOLD .... FILM EDITOR

EAT MY DUST
ERIC SAARINEN .... CINEMATOGRAPHER
PETER JAMISON .... PRODUCTION DESIGNER
TINA HIRSCH .... FILM EDITOR

EAT THE PEACH
ARTHUR WOOSTER .... CINEMATOGRAPHER
DAVID WILSON .... PRODUCTION DESIGNER
J. PATRICK DUFFNER .... FILM EDITOR

EAT THE RICH
WITOLD STOK .... CINEMATOGRAPHER
CAROLYN AMIES .... PRODUCTION DESIGNER
CHRIS RISDALE .... FILM EDITOR

EATING
HANANIA BAER .... CINEMATOGRAPHER
MARY PRITCHARD .... FILM EDITOR
MICHELLE HART .... FILM EDITOR

EATING RAOUL
GARY THIELTGES .... CINEMATOGRAPHER
ALAN TOOMAYAN .... FILM EDITOR

ECHO PARK
BERNT AMADEUS CAPRA .... PRODUCTION DESIGNER
INGRID KOOLER .... FILM EDITOR

ECHOES
HANANIA BAER .... CINEMATOGRAPHER
WITOLD STOK .... CINEMATOGRAPHER

ECHOES IN THE DARKNESS (TF)
JUDITH R. GELLMAN .... COSTUME DESIGNER
PAUL RUBELL .... FILM EDITOR

ECHOES OF A SUMMER
JOHN COQUILLON .... CINEMATOGRAPHER

ECHOES OF PARADISE
PETER JAMES .... CINEMATOGRAPHER

EDDIE AND THE CRUISERS
FRED MURPHY .... CINEMATOGRAPHER
GARY WEIST .... PRODUCTION DESIGNER
SANDRA DAVIDSON .... COSTUME DESIGNER
PRISCILLA ANNE NEDD .... FILM EDITOR

EDDIE AND THE CRUISERS II: EDDIE LIVES
RENE VERZIER .... CINEMATOGRAPHER

EDDIE MACON'S RUN
JAMES A. CONTNER .... CINEMATOGRAPHER
WILLIAM KENNEY .... PRODUCTION DESIGNER
JEFF KANEW .... FILM EDITOR

EDDIE MURPHY RAW
ERNEST DICKERSON .... CINEMATOGRAPHER
WYNN P. THOMAS .... PRODUCTION DESIGNER
LISA DAY .... FILM EDITOR

EDGE OF SANITY
TONY SPRATLING .... CINEMATOGRAPHER
MALCOLM COOKE .... FILM EDITOR

EDITH AND MARCEL
JEAN BOFFETY .... CINEMATOGRAPHER

EDUCATING RITA
FRANK WATTS .... CINEMATOGRAPHER
MAURICE FOWLER .... PRODUCTION DESIGNER
GARTH CRAVEN .... FILM EDITOR

EDWARD SCISSORHANDS
STEFAN CZAPSKY .... CINEMATOGRAPHER
BO WELSH .... PRODUCTION DESIGNER
COLLEEN ATWOOD .... COSTUME DESIGNER
RICHARD HALSEY .... FILM EDITOR

Du-Ed

CINEMATOGRAPHERS
PRODUCTION
DESIGNERS,
COSTUME
DESIGNERS AND
FILM EDITORS
GUIDE

I
N
D
E
X

O
F

F
I
L
M

T
I
T
L
E
S

Ef-Em

CINEMATOGRAPHERS
PRODUCTION
DESIGNERS,
COSTUME
DESIGNERS AND
FILM EDITORS
GUIDE

I
N
D
E
X

O
F

F
I
L
M

T
I
T
L
E
S

EFFECT OF GAMMA RAYS ON MAN-IN-THE-MOON MARIGOLDS, THE
ADAM HOLENDER .... CINEMATOGRAPHER
EVAN LOTTMAN .... FILM EDITOR

EFFECTS
PASQUALE BUBA .... FILM EDITOR

EFFI BRIEST
JURGEN JURGES .... CINEMATOGRAPHER

EIGER SANCTION, THE
FRANK STANLEY .... CINEMATOGRAPHER
AURELIO CRUGNOLA .... PRODUCTION DESIGNER
GLENN WRIGHT .... COSTUME DESIGNER
FERRIS WEBSTER .... FILM EDITOR

EIGHT MEN OUT
ROBERT RICHARDSON .... CINEMATOGRAPHER
DAN BISHOP .... PRODUCTION DESIGNER
NORA CHAVOOSHIAN .... PRODUCTION DESIGNER
CYNTHIA FLYNT .... COSTUME DESIGNER
JOHN TINTORI .... FILM EDITOR

EL AMOR BRUJO
TEO ESCAMILLA .... CINEMATOGRAPHER

EL NORTE
JAMES M. GLENNON .... CINEMATOGRAPHER
HILARY WRIGHT .... COSTUME DESIGNER
BETSY BLANKETT .... FILM EDITOR

ELEANOR AND FRANKLIN: THE WHITE HOUSE YEARS (TF)
JAMES A. CRABE† .... CINEMATOGRAPHER
JAN SCOTT .... PRODUCTION DESIGNER
JOE I. TOMPKINS .... COSTUME DESIGNER

ELEANOR ROOSEVELT: FIRST LADY OF THE WORLD (TF)
JOHN MCPHERSON .... CINEMATOGRAPHER

ELECTRA GLIDE IN BLUE
CONRAD HALL .... CINEMATOGRAPHER
JIM BENSON .... FILM EDITOR
JOHN F. LINK .... FILM EDITOR

ELECTRIC DREAMS
ALEX THOMSON .... CINEMATOGRAPHER
RICHARD DAWKING .... PRODUCTION DESIGNER
RICHARD MACDONALD .... PRODUCTION DESIGNER
RUTH MYERS .... COSTUME DESIGNER
PETER HONESS .... FILM EDITOR

ELECTRIC GRANDMOTHER, THE (TF)
LAWRENCE MILLER .... PRODUCTION DESIGNER
DENNIS O'CONNOR .... FILM EDITOR

ELECTRIC HORSEMAN, THE
OWEN ROIZMAN .... CINEMATOGRAPHER
DENNIS WASHINGTON .... PRODUCTION DESIGNER
STEPHEN GRIMES† .... PRODUCTION DESIGNER
BERNIE POLLACK .... COSTUME DESIGNER
SHELDON KAHN .... FILM EDITOR

ELENI
BILLY WILLIAMS .... CINEMATOGRAPHER
ROY WALKER .... PRODUCTION DESIGNER
STEVE SPENCE .... PRODUCTION DESIGNER
TOM RAND .... COSTUME DESIGNER
RAY LOVEJOY .... FILM EDITOR

ELEPHANT MAN, THE
FREDDIE FRANCIS .... CINEMATOGRAPHER
ROBERT CARTWRIGHT .... PRODUCTION DESIGNER
STUART CRAIG .... PRODUCTION DESIGNER
PATRICIA NORRIS .... COSTUME DESIGNER
JULIE WEISS .... COSTUME DESIGNER
ANNE V. COATES .... FILM EDITOR

ELIMINATORS
MAC AHLBERG .... CINEMATOGRAPHER
PHILIP DEAN FOREMAN .... PRODUCTION DESIGNER
JILL OHANNESON .... COSTUME DESIGNER
ANDY HORVITCH .... FILM EDITOR

ELLIE
GEORGE TIRL .... CINEMATOGRAPHER
MICHAEL O'SULLIVAN .... PRODUCTION DESIGNER

ELLIS ISLAND (MS)
JACK HILDYARD .... CINEMATOGRAPHER
ROBERT LAING .... PRODUCTION DESIGNER

ELVIRA: MISTRESS OF THE DARK
HANANIA BAER .... CINEMATOGRAPHER
JOHN DE CUIR JR. .... PRODUCTION DESIGNER
BETSY HEIMANN .... COSTUME DESIGNER
BATTLE DAVIS .... FILM EDITOR

ELVIS (TF)
DONALD M. MORGAN .... CINEMATOGRAPHER

ELVIS AND ME (MS)
PETER STEIN .... CINEMATOGRAPHER
BRYAN RYMAN .... PRODUCTION DESIGNER
MICHAEL RIPPS .... FILM EDITOR
ERIC SEARS .... FILM EDITOR

ELVIS AND THE BEAUTY QUEEN (TF)
MICHAEL BAUGH .... PRODUCTION DESIGNER
ANN LAMBERT .... COSTUME DESIGNER

ELVIS, ELVIS
MIKAEL SALOMON .... CINEMATOGRAPHER

ELYSIAN FIELDS (TF)
CHARLES ROSHER, JR. .... CINEMATOGRAPHER
MICHAEL HELMY .... PRODUCTION DESIGNER
JOHN CARNOCHEN .... FILM EDITOR

EMBRYO
FRED J. KOENEKAMP .... CINEMATOGRAPHER
JOE ALVES .... PRODUCTION DESIGNER

EMERALD CITY
PAUL MURPHY .... CINEMATOGRAPHER

EMERALD FOREST, THE
PHILIPPE ROUSSELOT .... CINEMATOGRAPHER
SIMON HOLLAND .... PRODUCTION DESIGNER
MARCOS FLAKSMAN .... PRODUCTION DESIGNER
CLOVIS BUENO .... COSTUME DESIGNER
IAN CRAFFORD .... FILM EDITOR

EMERALD POINT, N.A.S. (TVS)
ERICA EDELL PHILLIPS .... COSTUME DESIGNER

EMMA MAE
STEPHEN L. POSEY .... CINEMATOGRAPHER

EMPEROR OF THE NORTH
JACK MARTIN SMITH .... PRODUCTION DESIGNER

EMPERORS NEW CLOTHES
MAREK DOBROWOLSKI .... PRODUCTION DESIGNER

EMPIRE OF ASH III
DANNY NOWAK .... CINEMATOGRAPHER

EMPIRE OF THE ANTS
REGINALD H. MORRIS .... CINEMATOGRAPHER
CHARLES ROSEN .... PRODUCTION DESIGNER
MICHAEL LUCIANO .... FILM EDITOR

EMPIRE OF THE SUN
ALLEN DAVIAU .... CINEMATOGRAPHER
CHARLES BISHOP .... PRODUCTION DESIGNER
FRED HOLE .... PRODUCTION DESIGNER
MAURICE FOWLER .... PRODUCTION DESIGNER
NORMAN DORME .... PRODUCTION DESIGNER
NORMAN REYNOLDS .... PRODUCTION DESIGNER
RICHARD CARTER .... PRODUCTION DESIGNER
BOB RINGWOOD .... COSTUME DESIGNER
MICHAEL KAHN .... FILM EDITOR

EMPIRE STATE
TONY IMI .... CINEMATOGRAPHER
ADRIAN SMITH .... PRODUCTION DESIGNER

EMPIRE STRIKES BACK, THE
PETER SUSCHITZKY .... CINEMATOGRAPHER
NORMAN REYNOLDS .... PRODUCTION DESIGNER
HARRY LANGE .... PRODUCTION DESIGNER
ALAN TOMPKINS .... PRODUCTION DESIGNER
LESLIE DILLEY .... PRODUCTION DESIGNER
JOHN MOLLO .... COSTUME DESIGNER
PAUL HIRSCH .... FILM EDITOR

END OF AUGUST, THE
ROBERT ELWSIT .... CINEMATOGRAPHER
JAY CASSIDY .... FILM EDITOR

END OF THE LINE
GEORGE TIRL .... CINEMATOGRAPHER
NEIL SPISAK .... PRODUCTION DESIGNER
VAUGHAN EDWARDS .... PRODUCTION DESIGNER
VAN BROUGHTON RAMSEY .... COSTUME DESIGNER
MERCEDES DANEVIC .... FILM EDITOR

END OF THE NIGHT
TOM DICILLO .... CINEMATOGRAPHER
ILA VON HASPERG .... FILM EDITOR

END OF THE ROAD
GORDON WILLIS .... CINEMATOGRAPHER

END, THE
BOBBY BYRNE .... CINEMATOGRAPHER
JAN SCOTT .... PRODUCTION DESIGNER
NORMAN SALLING .... COSTUME DESIGNER
DONN CAMBERN .... FILM EDITOR

ENDANGERED SPECIES
PAUL LOHMANN .... CINEMATOGRAPHER
TREVOR WILLIAMS .... PRODUCTION DESIGNER
BETSY COX .... COSTUME DESIGNER
TOM WALLS .... FILM EDITOR

ENDLESS GAME, THE
MAURICE CAIN .... PRODUCTION DESIGNER

ENDLESS LOVE
DAVID WATKIN .... CINEMATOGRAPHER
ED WITTSTEIN .... PRODUCTION DESIGNER
EDWARD PISONI .... PRODUCTION DESIGNER
ELLEN MIROJNICK .... COSTUME DESIGNER
KRISTI ZEA .... COSTUME DESIGNER
MICHAEL J. SHERIDAN .... FILM EDITOR

ENEMIES, A LOVE STORY
FRED MURPHY .... CINEMATOGRAPHER
PATO GUZMAN .... PRODUCTION DESIGNER
ALBERT WOLSKY .... COSTUME DESIGNER
STUART H. PAPPE .... FILM EDITOR

ENEMY AMONG US, AN (TF)
HANANIA BAER .... CINEMATOGRAPHER

ENEMY MINE
TONY IMI .... CINEMATOGRAPHER
ROLF ZEHETBAUER .... PRODUCTION DESIGNER
WERNER ACHMAN .... PRODUCTION DESIGNER
MONIKA BAUERT .... COSTUME DESIGNER
HANNES NIKEL .... FILM EDITOR

ENEMY OF THE PEOPLE, AN
PAUL LOHMANN .... CINEMATOGRAPHER
EUGENE LOURIE .... PRODUCTION DESIGNER
SHELDON KAHN .... FILM EDITOR

ENEMY TERRITORY
ERNEST DICKERSON .... CINEMATOGRAPHER
MARINA ZURKOW .... PRODUCTION DESIGNER
PETER TESCHNER .... FILM EDITOR

ENFORCER, THE
GLENN WRIGHT .... COSTUME DESIGNER
FERRIS WEBSTER .... FILM EDITOR
JOEL COX .... FILM EDITOR

ENGLAND MADE ME
MALCOLM COOKE .... FILM EDITOR

ENID IS SLEEPING
AFFONSO BEATO .... CINEMATOGRAPHER
PAUL PETERS .... PRODUCTION DESIGNER
LISA JENSEN .... COSTUME DESIGNER
MALCOLM CAMPBELL .... FILM EDITOR

ENIGMA
FRANÇOIS COMTET .... PRODUCTION DESIGNER
PETER WEATHERLY .... FILM EDITOR

ENORMOUS CHANGES AT THE LAST MINUTE
TOM MCDONOUGH .... CINEMATOGRAPHER

ENTER THE DRAGON
GIL HUBBS .... CINEMATOGRAPHER
ANN LAMBERT .... COSTUME DESIGNER

ENTER THE NINJA
DAVID GURFINKEL .... CINEMATOGRAPHER
MARK GOLDBLATT .... FILM EDITOR

ENTERTAINER, THE (TF)
JAMES A. CRABE† .... CINEMATOGRAPHER

ENTITY, THE
STEPHEN H. BURUM .... CINEMATOGRAPHER
CHARLES ROSEN .... PRODUCTION DESIGNER
FRANK J. URIOSTE .... FILM EDITOR

ENTRE NOUS
BERNARD LUTIC .... CINEMATOGRAPHER
JOELE VAN EFFENTERRE .... FILM EDITOR

EPITAPH (CTF)
ROBERT ORTIZ .... FILM EDITOR

EQUAL JUSTICE (PILOT)
PAUL ELLIOTT .... CINEMATOGRAPHER

EQUUS
OSWALD MORRIS .... CINEMATOGRAPHER
SIMON HOLLAND .... PRODUCTION DESIGNER
TONY WALTON .... PRODUCTION DESIGNER
PATTI UNGER .... COSTUME DESIGNER
TONY WALTON .... COSTUME DESIGNER
JOHN VICTOR SMITH .... FILM EDITOR

ERASERHEAD
FREDERICK ELMES .... CINEMATOGRAPHER

ERIC THE VIKING
IAN WILSON .... CINEMATOGRAPHER
JOHN BEARD .... PRODUCTION DESIGNER
PAM TAIT .... COSTUME DESIGNER
GEORGE AKERS .... FILM EDITOR

ERNEST GOES TO CAMP
HARRY MATHIAS .... CINEMATOGRAPHER
KATHY EMILY CHERRY .... PRODUCTION DESIGNER
ANN PAYNE .... COSTUME DESIGNER
MARSHALL HARVEY .... FILM EDITOR

ERNEST GOES TO JAIL
PETER STEIN .... CINEMATOGRAPHER
CHRIS AUGUST .... PRODUCTION DESIGNER
SHAWN BARRY .... COSTUME DESIGNER
FARREL LEVY .... FILM EDITOR
SHARYN L. ROSS .... FILM EDITOR

ERNEST SAVES CHRISTMAS
PETER STEIN .... CINEMATOGRAPHER
PETER MITCHELL .... COSTUME DESIGNER
SHARYN L. ROSS .... FILM EDITOR

ERNIE KOVACKS: BETWEEN THE LAUGHTER (TF)
REXFORD METZ .... CINEMATOGRAPHER
SCOTT CONRAD .... FILM EDITOR
JACK DE SHEILDS .... PRODUCTION DESIGNER

ESCAPE
JOANNE D'ANTONIO .... FILM EDITOR

ESCAPE 2000
JOHN MCLEAN .... CINEMATOGRAPHER
ALAN LAKE .... FILM EDITOR

ESCAPE ARTIST, THE
STEPHEN H. BURUM .... CINEMATOGRAPHER
ANGELO GRAHAM .... PRODUCTION DESIGNER
DEAN TAVOULARIS .... PRODUCTION DESIGNER
JAMES J. MURAKAMI .... PRODUCTION DESIGNER
GLORIA GRESHAM .... COSTUME DESIGNER
ARTHUR SCHMIDT .... FILM EDITOR

ESCAPE FROM ALCATRAZ
BRUCE SURTEES .... CINEMATOGRAPHER
FERRIS WEBSTER .... FILM EDITOR

ESCAPE FROM IRAN, THE (TF)
CAROL SPIER .... PRODUCTION DESIGNER

ESCAPE FROM NEW YORK
DEAN CUNDEY .... CINEMATOGRAPHER
JOE ALVES .... PRODUCTION DESIGNER
STEPHEN LOOMIS .... COSTUME DESIGNER
TODD RAMSAY .... FILM EDITOR

En-Es

CINEMATOGRAPHERS
PRODUCTION
DESIGNERS,
COSTUME
DESIGNERS AND
FILM EDITORS
GUIDE

INDEX OF FILM TITLES

335

CINEMATOGRAPHERS
PRODUCTION
DESIGNERS,
COSTUME
DESIGNERS AND
FILM EDITORS
GUIDE

I N D E X O F F I L M T I T L E S

ESCAPE FROM THE DARK
RICHARD MARDEN .... FILM EDITOR

ESCAPE FROM THE PLANET OF THE APES
JACK MARTIN SMITH .... PRODUCTION DESIGNER

ESCAPE TO ATHENA
GIL TAYLOR .... CINEMATOGRAPHER
JOHN GRAYSMARK .... PRODUCTION DESIGNER
MICHAEL STRINGER .... PRODUCTION DESIGNER

ESCAPE TO WITCH MOUNTAIN
FRANK PHILLIPS .... CINEMATOGRAPHER

ETERNITY
JOHN LAMBERT .... CINEMATOGRAPHER
MARTIN ZBORIL .... PRODUCTION DESIGNER
MICHAEL J. SHERIDAN .... FILM EDITOR
CHRISTOPHER GREENBURY .... FILM EDITOR
PETER ZINNER .... FILM EDITOR

EUREKA
ALEX THOMSON .... CINEMATOGRAPHER
LESLIE DILLEY .... PRODUCTION DESIGNER
MICHAEL SEYMOUR .... PRODUCTION DESIGNER
MARIT ALLEN .... COSTUME DESIGNER
TONY LAWSON .... FILM EDITOR

EUROPEANS, THE
LARRY PIZER .... CINEMATOGRAPHER
JUDY MOORCROFT .... COSTUME DESIGNER

EVA
RICHARD MACDONALD .... PRODUCTION DESIGNER

EVE OF DESTRUCTION
ALAN HUME .... CINEMATOGRAPHER
PETER LAMONT .... PRODUCTION DESIGNER
DEBORAH L. SCOTT .... COSTUME DESIGNER
CAROLINE BIGGERSTAFF .... FILM EDITOR

EVERGREEN (MS)
WOODY OMENS .... CINEMATOGRAPHER
CHARLES BENNETT .... PRODUCTION DESIGNER
JAN SCOTT .... PRODUCTION DESIGNER
JULIE WEISS .... COSTUME DESIGNER

EVERLASTING SECRET FAMILY, THE
JULIAN PENNEY .... CINEMATOGRAPHER
PETA LAWSON .... PRODUCTION DESIGNER
PAM BARNETTA .... FILM EDITOR

EVERY TIME WE SAY GOODBYE
GIUSEPPI LANCI .... CINEMATOGRAPHER
MICKEY ZAHAR .... PRODUCTION DESIGNER
RONA DORON .... COSTUME DESIGNER

EVERY WHICH WAY BUT LOOSE
REXFORD METZ .... CINEMATOGRAPHER
ELAYNE CEDER .... PRODUCTION DESIGNER
GLENN WRIGHT .... COSTUME DESIGNER
FERRIS WEBSTER .... FILM EDITOR
JOEL COX .... FILM EDITOR

EVERYBODY WINS
IAN BAKER .... CINEMATOGRAPHER
PETER S. LARKIN .... PRODUCTION DESIGNER
ANN ROTH .... COSTUME DESIGNER
JOHN BLOOM .... FILM EDITOR

EVERYBODY'S ALL-AMERICAN
STEPHEN GOLDBLATT .... CINEMATOGRAPHER
GEORGE JENSEN .... PRODUCTION DESIGNER
JOE ALVES .... PRODUCTION DESIGNER
THEADORA VAN RUNKLE .... COSTUME DESIGNER
DON ZIMMERMAN .... FILM EDITOR

**EVERYBODY'S BABY: THE RESCUE OF JESSICA
MCCLURE (TF)**
SHELLY JOHNSON .... CINEMATOGRAPHER
BEN EDWARDS .... PRODUCTION DESIGNER

**EVERYTHING YOU ALWAYS WANTED TO KNOW
ABOUT SEX* (*BUT WERE AFRAID TO ASK)**
DAVID M. WALSH .... CINEMATOGRAPHER

EVERYTIME WE SAY GOODBYE
MARK BURNS .... FILM EDITOR

EVIL DEAD, THE
EDNA RUTH PAUL .... FILM EDITOR

EVIL DEAD 2
PETER DEMING .... CINEMATOGRAPHER
PHILIP J.C. DUFFIN .... PRODUCTION DESIGNER
KAYE DAVIS .... FILM EDITOR

EVIL UNDER THE SUN
CHRISTOPHER CHALLIS .... CINEMATOGRAPHER
ALAN CASSIE .... PRODUCTION DESIGNER
ELLIOT SCOTT .... PRODUCTION DESIGNER
ANTHONY POWELL .... COSTUME DESIGNER
RICHARD MARDEN .... FILM EDITOR

EVIL, THE
MARIO DI LEO .... CINEMATOGRAPHER
PETER JAMISON .... PRODUCTION DESIGNER

EVILSPEAK
DENA ROTH .... PRODUCTION DESIGNER

EVITA PERON (TF)1981
TRAVILLA .... COSTUME DESIGNER

EWOKS: THE BATTLE FOR ENDOR (TF)
ISIDORE MANKOFSKY .... CINEMATOGRAPHER

EXCALIBUR
ALEX THOMSON .... CINEMATOGRAPHER
ANTHONY PRATT .... PRODUCTION DESIGNER
TIM HUTCHINSON .... PRODUCTION DESIGNER
BOB RINGWOOD .... COSTUME DESIGNER
JOHN MERRITT .... FILM EDITOR

EXECUTION OF PRIVATE SLOVICK, THE (TF)
BILL BUTLER .... CINEMATOGRAPHER
THOMAS M. BRONSON .... COSTUME DESIGNER
FRANK MORRISS .... FILM EDITOR

EXECUTION, THE (TF)
JACK SENTER .... PRODUCTION DESIGNER
MINA MITTELMAN .... COSTUME DESIGNER

EXECUTIONER'S SONG, THE (TF)
BRYAN RYMAN .... PRODUCTION DESIGNER
MICHAEL ECONOMOU .... FILM EDITOR

EXECUTIVE ACTION
KIRK AXTELL .... PRODUCTION DESIGNER
GEORGE GRENVILLE .... FILM EDITOR
MARTIN BRAM .... FILM EDITOR

EXORCIST, THE
OWEN ROIZMAN .... CINEMATOGRAPHER
GERRY FISHER .... CINEMATOGRAPHER
WILLIAM MALLEY .... PRODUCTION DESIGNER
BUD SMITH .... FILM EDITOR
EVAN LOTTMAN .... FILM EDITOR
NORMAN GAY .... FILM EDITOR

EXORCIST II: THE HERETIC, THE
WILLIAM A. FRAKER .... CINEMATOGRAPHER
RICHARD J. LAWRENCE .... PRODUCTION DESIGNER
GENE RUDOLF .... PRODUCTION DESIGNER
JACK T. COLLIS .... PRODUCTION DESIGNER
RICHARD MACDONALD .... PRODUCTION DESIGNER
ROBERT DE MORA .... COSTUME DESIGNER
TOM PRIESTLEY .... FILM EDITOR

EXORCIST III, THE
GERRY FISHER .... CINEMATOGRAPHER
LESLIE DILLEY .... PRODUCTION DESIGNER
DANA LYMAN .... COSTUME DESIGNER
PETER LEE THOMPSON .... FILM EDITOR
TODD RAMSAY .... FILM EDITOR

EXPERIENCE PREFERRED BUT NOT ESSENTIAL
PHIL MEHEUX .... CINEMATOGRAPHER
SIMON WATERS .... PRODUCTION DESIGNER
JANE MARTIN .... PRODUCTION DESIGNER
JOHN SHIRLEY .... FILM EDITOR

EXPERIMENT IN TERROR
PHILIP LATHROP .... CINEMATOGRAPHER

EXPERTS, THE
RONNIE TAYLOR .... CINEMATOGRAPHER
BUD MOLIN .... FILM EDITOR

EXPLORER
CATHERINE WOOTEN .... COSTUME DESIGNER

EXPLORERS
JOHN HORA .... CINEMATOGRAPHER
FRANK RICHWOOD .... PRODUCTION DESIGNER
ROBERT F. BOYLE .... PRODUCTION DESIGNER
ROSANNA NORTON .... COSTUME DESIGNER
JOHN WRIGHT .... FILM EDITOR
TINA HIRSCH .... FILM EDITOR

EXPOSED
HENRI DECAE† .... CINEMATOGRAPHER
BRIAN EATWELL .... PRODUCTION DESIGNER
KRISTI ZEA .... COSTUME DESIGNER
ROBERT LAWRENCE .... FILM EDITOR

EXTERMINATOR, THE
ROBERT M. BALDWIN .... CINEMATOGRAPHER
CORKY O'HARA .... FILM EDITOR

EXTERMINATOR 2
JOSEPH MANGINE .... CINEMATOGRAPHER
ROBERT M. BALDWIN .... CINEMATOGRAPHER
VIRGINIA FIELD .... PRODUCTION DESIGNER
MARCUS MANTON .... FILM EDITOR

EXTREME CLOSE UP
PAUL LOHMANN .... CINEMATOGRAPHER

EXTREME CLOSE-UP (TF)
WALT LLOYD .... CINEMATOGRAPHER
GARRETH STOVER .... PRODUCTION DESIGNER
VICTOR DU BOIS .... FILM EDITOR

EXTREME PREJUDICE
MATTHEW F. LEONETTI .... CINEMATOGRAPHER
ALBERT HESCHONG .... PRODUCTION DESIGNER
JOSEPH C. NEMEC III .... PRODUCTION DESIGNER
WILLIAM KENNEY .... PRODUCTION DESIGNER
DAN MOORE .... COSTUME DESIGNER
FREEMAN DAVIES .... FILM EDITOR

EXTREMITIES
CURTIS CLARK .... CINEMATOGRAPHER
CHESTER KACZENSKI .... PRODUCTION DESIGNER
LINDA BASS .... COSTUME DESIGNER
ARTHUR COBURN .... FILM EDITOR

EYE FOR AN EYE, AN
ROGER SHEARMAN .... CINEMATOGRAPHER
SANDY VENEZIANO .... PRODUCTION DESIGNER
ANTHONY REDMAN .... FILM EDITOR
ROBERT WYMAN .... FILM EDITOR

EYE OF THE NEEDLE
ALAN HUME .... CINEMATOGRAPHER
BERT DAVEY .... PRODUCTION DESIGNER
WILFRED SHINGLETON .... PRODUCTION DESIGNER
JOHN BLOOMFIELD .... COSTUME DESIGNER
SEAN BARTON .... FILM EDITOR

EYE OF THE TIGER
PETER LYONS COLLISTER .... CINEMATOGRAPHER
WAYNE SPRINGFIELD .... PRODUCTION DESIGNER
GREGORY PRANGE .... FILM EDITOR
RICK SHAINE .... FILM EDITOR

EYE ON THE SPARROW (TF)
WILLIAM WAGES .... CINEMATOGRAPHER

EYES OF A STRANGER
MIMI ROJAS .... CINEMATOGRAPHER

EYES OF FIRE
GREGG FONSECA .... PRODUCTION DESIGNER
MICHAEL BARNARD .... FILM EDITOR

EYES OF LAURA MARS
VICTOR J. KEMPER .... CINEMATOGRAPHER
GENE CALLAHAN .... PRODUCTION DESIGNER
ROBERT GUNDLACH .... PRODUCTION DESIGNER
THEONI V. ALDREDGE .... COSTUME DESIGNER
MICHAEL KAHN .... FILM EDITOR

EYEWITNESS
MATTHEW F. LEONETTI .... CINEMATOGRAPHER
PHILIP ROSENBERG .... PRODUCTION DESIGNER
HILARY ROSENFELD .... COSTUME DESIGNER
CYNTHIA SCHEIDER .... FILM EDITOR

F

F.B.I. STORY: THE FBI VERSUS ALVIN KARPIS, PUBLIC ENEMY NUMBER ONE, THE (TF)
JAMES D. VANCE .... PRODUCTION DESIGNER

F.I.S.T.
LASZLO KOVACS .... CINEMATOGRAPHER
ANGELO GRAHAM .... PRODUCTION DESIGNER
RICHARD MACDONALD .... PRODUCTION DESIGNER
ANTONY GIBBS .... FILM EDITOR
GRAEME CLIFFORD .... FILM EDITOR

F/X
MIROSLAV ONDRICEK .... CINEMATOGRAPHER
MEL BOURNE .... PRODUCTION DESIGNER
SPEED HOPKINS .... PRODUCTION DESIGNER
JULIE WEISS .... COSTUME DESIGNER
TERRY RAWLINGS .... FILM EDITOR

FABULOUS BAKER BOYS, THE
MICHAEL BALLHAUS .... CINEMATOGRAPHER
JEFFREY TOWNSEND .... PRODUCTION DESIGNER
WILLIAM STEINKAMP .... FILM EDITOR

FACE IN THE CROWD, A
GAYNE RESCHER .... CINEMATOGRAPHER
RICHARD SYLBERT .... PRODUCTION DESIGNER

FACE IN THE RAIN, A
HASKELL WEXLER .... CINEMATOGRAPHER

FACE OF FEAR, THE (TF)
PETER MACKAY .... CINEMATOGRAPHER
M. EDWARD SALIER .... FILM EDITOR

FACE OF THE ENEMY
PETER INDERGAND .... CINEMATOGRAPHER
MARINA KIESER .... PRODUCTION DESIGNER
PIERLUCA DECARLO .... PRODUCTION DESIGNER
SYLVIA VASQUEZ .... COSTUME DESIGNER
TOBY BROWN .... FILM EDITOR

FACE TO FACE
SVEN NYKVIST .... CINEMATOGRAPHER

FACE TO FACE (TF)
CHARLES CORRELL .... CINEMATOGRAPHER
CHRISTIAN KELLY .... PRODUCTION DESIGNER
GARY GRIFFEN .... FILM EDITOR

FACTS OF LIFE, THE
EDITH HEAD† .... COSTUME DESIGNER

FACTS OF LIFE GOES TO PARIS, THE (TF)
WOODY OMENS .... CINEMATOGRAPHER
WILLIAM MC ALLISTER .... PRODUCTION DESIGNER
JOHN C. HORGER .... FILM EDITOR

FADE TO BLACK
ALEX PHILLIPS .... CINEMATOGRAPHER
BARBARA POKRAS .... FILM EDITOR
HOWARD KUNIN .... FILM EDITOR
JAMES RUXIN .... FILM EDITOR

FADE-IN
JOHN W. WHEELER .... FILM EDITOR

FAERIE TALE THEATRE (CTV)
J. ALLEN HIGHFILL† .... COSTUME DESIGNER

FAHRENHEIT 451
HARRY HORNER .... PRODUCTION DESIGNER
SYD CAIN .... PRODUCTION DESIGNER
TONY WALTON .... PRODUCTION DESIGNER

FAKE OUT
EDDY VAN DEN ENDEN .... CINEMATOGRAPHER

FAKERS, THE
ROBERT KINOSHITA .... PRODUCTION DESIGNER

FALCON AND THE SNOWMAN, THE
ALLEN DAVIAU .... CINEMATOGRAPHER
JAMES D. BISSELL .... PRODUCTION DESIGNER
ALBERT WOLSKY .... COSTUME DESIGNER
RICHARD MARDEN .... FILM EDITOR

Ex-Fa

CINEMATOGRAPHERS
PRODUCTION
DESIGNERS,
COSTUME
DESIGNERS AND
FILM EDITORS
GUIDE

INDEX

OF

FILM

TITLES

337

Fa-Fa

CINEMATOGRAPHERS
PRODUCTION
DESIGNERS,
COSTUME
DESIGNERS AND
FILM EDITORS
GUIDE

I
N
D
E
X

O
F

F
I
L
M

T
I
T
L
E
S

338

FALCON'S GOLD (TF)
ALEIDA MAC DONALD .... COSTUME DESIGNER

FALLING IN LOVE
PETER SUSCHITZKY .... CINEMATOGRAPHER
SANTO LOQUASTO .... PRODUCTION DESIGNER
SPEED HOPKINS .... PRODUCTION DESIGNER
RICHARD BRUNO .... COSTUME DESIGNER
MICHAEL KAHN .... FILM EDITOR

FALLING IN LOVE AGAIN
DICK BUSH .... CINEMATOGRAPHER
BUD SMITH .... FILM EDITOR
DOUG JACKSON .... FILM EDITOR
JACQUELINE CAMBAS .... FILM EDITOR

FALLING OVER BACKWARDS
SAVAS KALOGERAS .... CINEMATOGRAPHER
RITA ROY .... FILM EDITOR

FALSE IDENTITY (TF)
BERNARD AUROUX .... CINEMATOGRAPHER
KEVIN RYAN .... PRODUCTION DESIGNER
NANCY FRAZEN .... FILM EDITOR

FAME
MICHAEL SERESIN .... CINEMATOGRAPHER
ED WITTSTEIN .... PRODUCTION DESIGNER
GEOFFREY KIRKLAND .... PRODUCTION DESIGNER
ELLEN MIROJNICK .... COSTUME DESIGNER
KRISTI ZEA .... COSTUME DESIGNER
GERRY HAMBLING .... FILM EDITOR

FAMILY BUSINESS
ANDRZEJ BARTKOWIAK .... CINEMATOGRAPHER
ROBERT ALAZRAKI .... CINEMATOGRAPHER
PAUL PETERS .... PRODUCTION DESIGNER
PHILIP ROSENBERG .... PRODUCTION DESIGNER
ANDREW MONDSHEIN .... FILM EDITOR

FAMILY JEWELS, THE
JACK POPLIN .... PRODUCTION DESIGNER

FAMILY MAN, THE (TF)
JUDITH R. GELLMAN .... COSTUME DESIGNER

FAMILY PLOT
LEONARD J. SOUTH .... CINEMATOGRAPHER
HENRY BUMSTEAD .... PRODUCTION DESIGNER

FAMILY SECRETS (TF)
JAMES A. CRABE .... CINEMATOGRAPHER

FAMILY WAY, THE
HARRY WAXMAN .... CINEMATOGRAPHER

FAN, THE
DICK BUSH .... CINEMATOGRAPHER
PAUL EADS .... PRODUCTION DESIGNER
SANTO LOQUASTO .... PRODUCTION DESIGNER
JEFFREY KURLAND .... COSTUME DESIGNER
ALAN HEIM .... FILM EDITOR

FANDANGO
THOMAS DEL RUTH .... CINEMATOGRAPHER
PETER LANDSDOWN SMITH .... PRODUCTION DESIGNER
MICHELE NEELY .... COSTUME DESIGNER
ARTHUR SCHMIDT .... FILM EDITOR

FANNY
JACK CARDIFF .... CINEMATOGRAPHER
WILLIAM REYNOLDS .... FILM EDITOR

FANNY AND ALEXANDER
SVEN NYKVIST .... CINEMATOGRAPHER
ANNA ASP .... PRODUCTION DESIGNER
MARIK VOS .... COSTUME DESIGNER
SYLVIA INGEMARSSON .... FILM EDITOR

FANNY HILL
ALFRED TAYLOR .... CINEMATOGRAPHER

FANTASM COMES AGAIN
VINCENT MONTON .... CINEMATOGRAPHER

FANTASTIC VOYAGE
DALE HENNESY† .... PRODUCTION DESIGNER
JACK MARTIN SMITH .... PRODUCTION DESIGNER

FANTASTIC WORLD OF D.C. COLLINS, THE (TF)
BRYAN RYMAN .... PRODUCTION DESIGNER

FAR COUNTRY, THE
RON HAGEN .... CINEMATOGRAPHER

FAR FROM HOME
PAUL ELLIOT .... CINEMATOGRAPHER
VICTORIA PAUL .... PRODUCTION DESIGNER
DONNA LINSON .... COSTUME DESIGNER
MARC GROSSMAN .... FILM EDITOR

FAR FROM THE MADDING CROWD
ROY FORGE SMITH .... PRODUCTION DESIGNER
RICHARD MACDONALD .... PRODUCTION DESIGNER
MALCOLM COOKE .... FILM EDITOR

FAR NORTH
ROBBIE GREENBERG .... CINEMATOGRAPHER
PETER JAMISON .... PRODUCTION DESIGNER
RITA SALAZAR .... COSTUME DESIGNER
BILL YAHRAUS .... FILM EDITOR

FAR OUT MAN
ERIC WOSTER .... CINEMATOGRAPHER
GREG GARDINER .... CINEMATOGRAPHER
DAVID B. MILLER .... PRODUCTION DESIGNER
GILBERTO C. NUNES .... FILM EDITOR
STEPHEN MYER .... FILM EDITOR

FAR PAVILIONS, THE (CMS)
JACK CARDIFF .... CINEMATOGRAPHER
ROBERT LAING .... PRODUCTION DESIGNER
JOHN JYMPSON .... FILM EDITOR
PETER BOITA .... FILM EDITOR

FAR SHORE, THE
RICHARD LEITERMAN .... CINEMATOGRAPHER

FARENHEIT 451
TONY WALTON .... COSTUME DESIGNER
THOM NOBLE .... FILM EDITOR

FAREWELL TO MANZANAR (TF)
HIRO NARITA .... CINEMATOGRAPHER
ROBERT KINOSHITA .... PRODUCTION DESIGNER

FAREWELL TO THE KING
DEAN SEMLER .... CINEMATOGRAPHER
GIL PARRONDO .... PRODUCTION DESIGNER
DAVID ROWE .... COSTUME DESIGNER
ANNE V. COATES .... FILM EDITOR

FAREWELL, MY LOVELY
JOHN A. ALONZO .... CINEMATOGRAPHER
ANGELO GRAHAM .... PRODUCTION DESIGNER
JOEL COX .... FILM EDITOR

FAREWELL, THE
SYLVIA INGEMARSSON .... FILM EDITOR

FARMER, THE
VICKI SANCHEZ .... COSTUME DESIGNER

FAST BREAK
CHARLES CORRELL .... CINEMATOGRAPHER
JOHN BARRY† .... PRODUCTION DESIGNER
NORM BARON .... PRODUCTION DESIGNER
FRANK J. URIOSTE .... FILM EDITOR

FAST CHARLIE...MOONBEAM RIDER
J. MICHAEL RIVA .... PRODUCTION DESIGNER
WILLIAM SANDELL .... PRODUCTION DESIGNER

FAST COMPANY
MARK IRWIN .... CINEMATOGRAPHER
CAROL SPIER .... PRODUCTION DESIGNER
RONALD SANDERS .... FILM EDITOR

FAST FORWARD
MATTHEW F. LEONETTI .... CINEMATOGRAPHER
BEN EDWARDS .... PRODUCTION DESIGNER
MICHAEL BAUGH .... PRODUCTION DESIGNER
BERNARD JOHNSON .... COSTUME DESIGNER
HARRY KELLER .... FILM EDITOR

FAST FORWARD (TF)
FRED J. KOENEKAMP .... CINEMATOGRAPHER

FAST TALKING
DAVID HUGGETT .... FILM EDITOR

FAST TIMES AT RIDGEMONT HIGH
MATTHEW F. LEONETTI .... CINEMATOGRAPHER
DANIEL LOMINO .... PRODUCTION DESIGNER
MARILYN VANCE-STRAKER .... COSTUME DESIGNER
ERIC JENKINS .... FILM EDITOR

FAST-WALKING
KING BAGGOT .... CINEMATOGRAPHER
DOUGLAS STEWART .... FILM EDITOR

FAT CITY
RICHARD SYLBERT .... PRODUCTION DESIGNER

FAT GUY GOES NUTZOID
JEFFREY WOLF .... FILM EDITOR
KATHIE WEAVER .... FILM EDITOR

FAT MAN AND LITTLE BOY
VILMOS ZSIGMOND .... CINEMATOGRAPHER
GREGG FONSECA .... PRODUCTION DESIGNER
PETER LANDSDOWN SMITH .... PRODUCTION DESIGNER
NIC EDE .... COSTUME DESIGNER
FRANCOISE BONNOT .... FILM EDITOR

FATAL ATTRACTION
ANTHONY B. RICHMOND .... CINEMATOGRAPHER
HOWARD ATHERTON .... CINEMATOGRAPHER
JACK BLACKMAN .... PRODUCTION DESIGNER
MEL BOURNE .... PRODUCTION DESIGNER
ELLEN MIROJNICK .... COSTUME DESIGNER
MICHAEL KAHN .... FILM EDITOR
PETER E. BERGER .... FILM EDITOR

FATAL BEAUTY
DAVID M. WALSH .... CINEMATOGRAPHER
JAMES WILLIAM NEWPORT .... PRODUCTION DESIGNER
JOSEPH C. NEMEC III .... PRODUCTION DESIGNER
AGGIE GUERARD RODGERS .... COSTUME DESIGNER
DON ZIMMERMAN .... FILM EDITOR

FATAL CHARM
WILLIAM BUTLER .... FILM EDITOR

FATAL IMAGE, THE (TF)
JEAN-YVES LE MENER .... CINEMATOGRAPHER
SERGE DOUY .... PRODUCTION DESIGNER
KAREN SHARP .... FILM EDITOR
SCOTT EYLER .... FILM EDITOR

FATAL JUDGMENT (TF)
ISIDORE MANKOFSKY .... CINEMATOGRAPHER
MICHAEL BAUGH .... PRODUCTION DESIGNER

FATAL VISION (MS)
STEVAN LARNER .... CINEMATOGRAPHER
JAMES ALLEN .... PRODUCTION DESIGNER
JACQUELINE SAINT ANNE .... COSTUME DESIGNER

FATE OF A HUNTER
THOMAS VAMOS .... CINEMATOGRAPHER

FATHER GOOSE
HENRY BUMSTEAD .... PRODUCTION DESIGNER

FATHER MURPHY (TF)
LEONARD J. SOUTH .... CINEMATOGRAPHER

FATHER OF HELL TOWN (TF)
JOSEPH BIROC .... CINEMATOGRAPHER

FATHER'S HOMECOMING, A
FRANK BEASCOECHEA .... CINEMATOGRAPHER

FATSO
BRIANNE MURPHY .... CINEMATOGRAPHER
HAROLD MICHELSON .... PRODUCTION DESIGNER
PETER W. WOOLEY .... PRODUCTION DESIGNER
PATRICIA NORRIS .... COSTUME DESIGNER
GLENN FARR .... FILM EDITOR

FATTY FINN
JOHN SEALE .... CINEMATOGRAPHER

FAVORITE SON (MS)
BRADFORD MAY .... CINEMATOGRAPHER
BERNIE CUTLER .... PRODUCTION DESIGNER
DAVID M. HABER .... PRODUCTION DESIGNER
DARRYL LEVINE .... COSTUME DESIGNER
JEFF FREEMAN .... FILM EDITOR
JOE ANN FOGLE .... FILM EDITOR

FEAR
ROBERT M. STEVENS .... CINEMATOGRAPHER
JOSEPH C. NEMEC III .... PRODUCTION DESIGNER
KENT BEYDA .... FILM EDITOR

FEAR CITY
JAMES LEMMO .... CINEMATOGRAPHER
VINCENT M. CRESCIMAN .... PRODUCTION DESIGNER
ANTHONY REDMAN .... FILM EDITOR

FEAR IS THE KEY
RAY LOVEJOY .... FILM EDITOR

FEAR NO EVIL
JACQUELINE SAINT ANNE .... COSTUME DESIGNER
EDNA RUTH PAUL .... FILM EDITOR

FEAR OF FEAR
JURGEN JURGES .... CINEMATOGRAPHER

FEAR ON TRIAL (TF)
THOMAS M. BRONSON .... COSTUME DESIGNER

FEAR STRIKES OUT
AARON STELL .... FILM EDITOR

FEDORA
GERRY FISHER .... CINEMATOGRAPHER
FREDRIC STEINKAMP .... FILM EDITOR

FEDS
TIM SUHRSTEDT .... CINEMATOGRAPHER
RANDY SER .... PRODUCTION DESIGNER
ISABELLA VAN SOEST .... COSTUME DESIGNER
DONN CAMBERN .... FILM EDITOR

FEEL THE HEAT
ROBERT JESSUP .... CINEMATOGRAPHER

FEEL THE HEAT (PILOT)
JIM MILLER .... FILM EDITOR

FELLINI'S CASANOVA
DANILO DONATI .... COSTUME DESIGNER

FEMMES DE PERSONNE
JEAN TOURNIER .... CINEMATOGRAPHER

FERRIS BUELLER'S DAY OFF
TAK FUJIMOTO .... CINEMATOGRAPHER
JOHN W. CORSO .... PRODUCTION DESIGNER
MARILYN VANCE-STRAKER .... COSTUME DESIGNER
PAUL HIRSCH .... FILM EDITOR

FERRY TO HONG KONG
JOHN STOLL .... PRODUCTION DESIGNER

FEVER PITCH
RAYMOND G. STOREY .... PRODUCTION DESIGNER
MICHAEL HOFFMAN .... COSTUME DESIGNER
JEFF JONES .... FILM EDITOR

FEW DAYS WITH ME, A
JEAN-FRANÇOIS ROBIN .... CINEMATOGRAPHER
JACQUELINE THIEDOT .... FILM EDITOR

ffolkes
TONY IMI .... CINEMATOGRAPHER
BERT DAVEY .... PRODUCTION DESIGNER
MAURICE CARTER .... PRODUCTION DESIGNER
ALAN STRACHAN .... FILM EDITOR

FIDDLER ON THE ROOF
OSWALD MORRIS .... CINEMATOGRAPHER
MICHAEL STRINGER .... PRODUCTION DESIGNER
ROBERT F. BOYLE .... PRODUCTION DESIGNER
JOAN BRIDGE .... COSTUME DESIGNER
ANTONY GIBBS .... FILM EDITOR
ROBERT LAWRENCE .... FILM EDITOR

FIELD OF DREAMS
JOHN LINDLEY .... CINEMATOGRAPHER
DENNIS GASSNER .... PRODUCTION DESIGNER
LINDA BASS .... COSTUME DESIGNER
IAN CRAFFORD .... FILM EDITOR

FIELD, THE
JACK CONROY .... CINEMATOGRAPHER
FRANK CONWAY .... PRODUCTION DESIGNER
JOAN BERGIN .... COSTUME DESIGNER
J. PATRICK DUFFNER .... FILM EDITOR

Fa-Fi

CINEMATOGRAPHERS
PRODUCTION
DESIGNERS,
COSTUME
DESIGNERS AND
FILM EDITORS
GUIDE

INDEX
OF
FILM
TITLES

339

CINEMATOGRAPHERS
PRODUCTION
DESIGNERS,
COSTUME
DESIGNERS AND
FILM EDITORS
GUIDE

FIENDISH PLOT OF DR. FU MANCHU, THE
JEAN TOURNIER .... CINEMATOGRAPHER
ALEXANDER TRAUNER .... PRODUCTION DESIGNER
JOHN BLOOMFIELD .... COSTUME DESIGNER

FIFTH FLOOR, THE
STANFORD C. ALLEN .... FILM EDITOR

FIFTH MISSILE, THE (TF)
BEALA B. NEEL .... PRODUCTION DESIGNER

FIFTH MONKEY, THE
GIDEON PORATH .... CINEMATOGRAPHER
ALAIN JAKUBOWICZ .... FILM EDITOR
FABIEN D. TORDJMANN .... FILM EDITOR

FIGHTING BACK
FRANCO DI GIACOMO .... CINEMATOGRAPHER
JOHN SEALE .... CINEMATOGRAPHER
ROBERT GUNDLACH .... PRODUCTION DESIGNER
JOHN BOXER .... COSTUME DESIGNER
JOHN J. FITZSTEPHENS .... FILM EDITOR
NICHOLAS C. SMITH .... FILM EDITOR

FIGHTING MAD
MICHAEL WATKINS .... CINEMATOGRAPHER

FINAL ASSIGNMENT
JOHN COQUILLON .... CINEMATOGRAPHER
DEBRA KAREN .... FILM EDITOR

FINAL CHAPTER - WALKING TALL
ROBERT B. HAUSER .... CINEMATOGRAPHER

FINAL CONFLICT, THE
PHIL MEHEUX .... CINEMATOGRAPHER
ROBERT PAYNTER .... CINEMATOGRAPHER
HERBERT WESTBROOK .... PRODUCTION DESIGNER
ALAN STRACHAN .... FILM EDITOR

FINAL COUNTDOWN, THE
VICTOR J. KEMPER .... CINEMATOGRAPHER
FERNANDO CARRERE .... PRODUCTION DESIGNER
ROBERT K. LAMBERT .... FILM EDITOR

FINAL JUSTICE
NICHOLAS VON STERNBERG .... CINEMATOGRAPHER

FINAL OPTION, THE
PHIL MEHEUX .... CINEMATOGRAPHER
MAURICE CAIN .... PRODUCTION DESIGNER
SYD CAIN .... PRODUCTION DESIGNER
JOHN GROVER .... FILM EDITOR
PETER DAVIES .... FILM EDITOR

FINAL SANCTION, THE
ANDREW PARKE .... CINEMATOGRAPHER
CHRISTOPHER REYNOLDS .... FILM EDITOR

FINAL TERROR, THE
PAUL RUBELL .... FILM EDITOR

FIND THE LADY
HARRY WAXMAN .... CINEMATOGRAPHER

FINDERS KEEPERS
BRIAN WEST .... CINEMATOGRAPHER
DENNIS WASHINGTON .... PRODUCTION DESIGNER
JOHN VICTOR SMITH .... FILM EDITOR

FINE MADNESS, A
JACK POPLIN .... PRODUCTION DESIGNER

FINE MESS, A
HARRY STRADLING, JR. .... CINEMATOGRAPHER
RODGER MAUS .... PRODUCTION DESIGNER
PATRICIA NORRIS .... COSTUME DESIGNER
JOHN F. BURNETT .... FILM EDITOR
ROBERT PERGAMENT .... FILM EDITOR

FINGERS
MICHAEL CHAPMAN .... CINEMATOGRAPHER
GENE RUDOLF .... PRODUCTION DESIGNER
ALBERT WOLSKY .... COSTUME DESIGNER
ROBERT LAWRENCE .... FILM EDITOR

FINIAN'S RAINBOW
PHILIP LATHROP .... CINEMATOGRAPHER

FINISH LINE (TF)
JONATHAN WEST .... CINEMATOGRAPHER
DOUGLAS IBOLD .... FILM EDITOR

FINNEGAN BEGIN AGAIN (CTF)
ROBBY MULLER .... CINEMATOGRAPHER
DAVID NICHOLS .... PRODUCTION DESIGNER
WALDEMAR KALINOWSKI .... PRODUCTION DESIGNER
JANE RUHM .... COSTUME DESIGNER

FIRE AND ICE
WILLY BOGNER .... CINEMATOGRAPHER
ALAN BALSAM .... FILM EDITOR
PETRA VAN OELFFEN .... FILM EDITOR

FIRE BIRDS
TONY IMI .... CINEMATOGRAPHER
JOSEPH T. GARRITY .... PRODUCTION DESIGNER
ELLIS COHEN .... COSTUME DESIGNER
DENNIS O'CONNOR .... FILM EDITOR
JON POLL .... FILM EDITOR
NORMAN BUCKLEY .... FILM EDITOR

FIRE ON THE MOUNTAIN (TF)
WOODY OMENS .... CINEMATOGRAPHER
BEALA B. NEEL .... PRODUCTION DESIGNER

FIRE SALE
RALPH WOOLSEY .... CINEMATOGRAPHER
JAMES H. SPENCER .... PRODUCTION DESIGNER
RICHARD HALSEY .... FILM EDITOR

FIRE WITH FIRE
HIRO NARITA .... CINEMATOGRAPHER
MICHAEL S. BOLTON .... PRODUCTION DESIGNER
NORMAN NEWBERRY .... PRODUCTION DESIGNER
PETER E. BERGER .... FILM EDITOR

FIRE WITH FIRE (TV)
ENID HARRIS .... COSTUME DESIGNER

FIRE! (TF)
WARD PRESTON .... PRODUCTION DESIGNER

FIRE! TRAPPED ON THE 37TH FLOOR (TF)
ERNEST DAY .... CINEMATOGRAPHER
RODGER MAUS .... PRODUCTION DESIGNER
ROBERT FLORIA .... FILM EDITOR

FIREFOX
BRUCE SURTEES .... CINEMATOGRAPHER
BEALA B. NEEL .... PRODUCTION DESIGNER
ELAYNE CEDER .... PRODUCTION DESIGNER
JOHN GRAYSMARK .... PRODUCTION DESIGNER
FERRIS WEBSTER .... FILM EDITOR
RONALD G. SPANG .... FILM EDITOR

FIREPOWER
ROBERT PAYNTER .... CINEMATOGRAPHER
JOHN BLEZARD .... PRODUCTION DESIGNER
JOHN STOLL .... PRODUCTION DESIGNER
ROBERT GUNDLACH .... PRODUCTION DESIGNER
ARNOLD CRUST .... FILM EDITOR

FIRESTARTER
GIUSEPPE RUZZOLINI .... CINEMATOGRAPHER
GIORGIO POSTIGLIONE .... PRODUCTION DESIGNER
WILLIAM J. CASSIDY .... PRODUCTION DESIGNER
DAVID RAWLINS .... FILM EDITOR
HOWARD KUNIN .... FILM EDITOR
RONALD SANDERS .... FILM EDITOR

FIREWALKER
ALEX PHILLIPS .... CINEMATOGRAPHER
JOSE RODRIGUEZ GRANADA .... PRODUCTION DESIGNER
POPPY CANNON .... COSTUME DESIGNER
RICHARD MARKS .... FILM EDITOR

FIRST AFFAIR (TF)
JO YNOCENCIO .... COSTUME DESIGNER

FIRST BLOOD
ANDREW LASZLO .... CINEMATOGRAPHER
STEPHANIE REICHEL .... PRODUCTION DESIGNER
WOLF KROEGER .... PRODUCTION DESIGNER
THOMAS M. BRONSON .... COSTUME DESIGNER

FIRST BORN
RALF D. BODE .... CINEMATOGRAPHER
PAUL SYLBERT .... PRODUCTION DESIGNER
COLLEEN C. ATWOOD .... COSTUME DESIGNER
ARTHUR SCHMIDT .... FILM EDITOR

FIRST DEADLY SIN, THE
JACK PRIESTLEY .... CINEMATOGRAPHER
WOODS MACINTOSH .... PRODUCTION DESIGNER
GARY JONES .... COSTUME DESIGNER
ERIC ALBERTSON .... FILM EDITOR

FIRST FAMILY
FRED J. KOENEKAMP .... CINEMATOGRAPHER
WILLIAM HINEY .... PRODUCTION DESIGNER
STU LINDER .... FILM EDITOR

FIRST FLIGHT (TF)
IDA RANDOM .... PRODUCTION DESIGNER

FIRST LOVE
BOBBY BYRNE .... CINEMATOGRAPHER
ROBERT LUTHARDT .... PRODUCTION DESIGNER
DONFELD .... COSTUME DESIGNER
FRANK MORRISS .... FILM EDITOR

FIRST MONDAY IN OCTOBER
FRED J. KOENEKAMP .... CINEMATOGRAPHER
JOHN CARTWRIGHT .... PRODUCTION DESIGNER
PHILIP JEFFRIES .... PRODUCTION DESIGNER
RUTH MYERS .... COSTUME DESIGNER
PETER E. BERGER .... FILM EDITOR

FIRST NAME: CARMEN
RAOUL COUTARD .... CINEMATOGRAPHER
SUZANNE LANG-WILLAR .... FILM EDITOR

FIRST POWER, THE
THEO VAN DE SANDE .... CINEMATOGRAPHER
JOSEPH T. GARRITZ .... PRODUCTION DESIGNER
TIM D'ARCY .... COSTUME DESIGNER
MICHAEL BLOECHER .... FILM EDITOR

FIRST STEPS (TF)
JACK L. RICHARDS .... CINEMATOGRAPHER
ALBERT HESCHONG .... PRODUCTION DESIGNER

FIRST TIME, THE
STEVEN FIERBERG .... CINEMATOGRAPHER
BUD MOLIN .... FILM EDITOR
STANLEY VOGEL .... FILM EDITOR

FIRST TIME, THE (TF)
NORM BARON .... PRODUCTION DESIGNER
MICHAEL J. HILL .... FILM EDITOR

FIRST TRAIN ROBBERY, THE
DAVID BRETHERTON .... FILM EDITOR

FIRST TURN-ON, THE
LLOYD KAUFMAN .... CINEMATOGRAPHER
RICHARD HAINES .... FILM EDITOR

FIRST YOU CRY (TF)
ALBERT HESCHONG .... PRODUCTION DESIGNER

FISH CALLED WANDA, A
ALAN HUME .... CINEMATOGRAPHER
ROGER MURRAY-LEACH .... PRODUCTION DESIGNER
JOHN WOOD .... PRODUCTION DESIGNER
HAZEL PETHIG .... COSTUME DESIGNER
JOHN JYMPSON .... FILM EDITOR

FISH HAWK
RENE VERZIER .... CINEMATOGRAPHER
LINDA MATHESON .... COSTUME DESIGNER
RON WISMAN .... FILM EDITOR

FISH THAT SAVED PITTSBURGH, THE
FRANK STANLEY .... CINEMATOGRAPHER
SPENCER DEVERILL .... PRODUCTION DESIGNER
PATRICIA NORRIS .... COSTUME DESIGNER
PETER ZINNER .... FILM EDITOR

FITZCARRALDO
THOMAS MAUCH .... CINEMATOGRAPHER

FITZWILLY
RALPH E. WINTERS .... FILM EDITOR

FIVE CORNERS
FRED MURPHY .... CINEMATOGRAPHER
ADRIANNE LOBEL .... PRODUCTION DESIGNER
ANDY BLUMENTHAL .... FILM EDITOR

FIVE DAYS FROM HOME
HARVEY GENKINS .... CINEMATOGRAPHER

FIVE DAYS ONE SUMMER
GIUSEPPE ROTUNNO .... CINEMATOGRAPHER
WILLY HOLT .... PRODUCTION DESIGNER
EMMA PORTEUS .... COSTUME DESIGNER
STUART BAIRD .... FILM EDITOR

FIVE EASY PIECES
LASZLO KOVACS .... CINEMATOGRAPHER
CHRISTOPHER HOLMES .... FILM EDITOR
GERALD S. SHEPARD .... FILM EDITOR

FIVE HEARTBEATS, THE
BILL DILL .... CINEMATOGRAPHER
WYNN THOMAS .... PRODUCTION DESIGNER
RUTH CARTER .... COSTUME DESIGNER
JOHN CARTER .... FILM EDITOR

FIVE OF ME, THE (TF)
ELAYNE CEDER .... PRODUCTION DESIGNER

FIVE ON THE BLACK
MICHAEL ECONOMOU .... FILM EDITOR

FIVE ON THE RUN
MIKAEL SALOMON .... CINEMATOGRAPHER

FIVE, THE
MIKAEL SALOMON .... CINEMATOGRAPHER

FJ HOLDER, THE
DAVID GRIBBLE .... CINEMATOGRAPHER

FLAGRANT DESIRE
WILLY KURANT .... CINEMATOGRAPHER
CHRISTOPHER HOLMES .... FILM EDITOR

FLAME
PETER HANNAN .... CINEMATOGRAPHER
MICHAEL BRADSELL .... FILM EDITOR

FLAMINGO KID, THE
JAMES A. CONTNER .... CINEMATOGRAPHER
LAWRENCE MILLER .... PRODUCTION DESIGNER
ELLEN MIROJNICK .... COSTUME DESIGNER
PRISCILLA ANNE NEDD .... FILM EDITOR

FLANAGAN
IVAN STRASSBURG .... CINEMATOGRAPHER
JOELE VAN EFFENTERRE .... FILM EDITOR

FLASH GORDON
GIL TAYLOR .... CINEMATOGRAPHER
HARRY WAXMAN .... CINEMATOGRAPHER
DANILO DONATI .... PRODUCTION DESIGNER
FERDINANDO SCARFIOTTI .... PRODUCTION DESIGNER
JOHN GRAYSMARK .... PRODUCTION DESIGNER
MALCOLM COOKE .... FILM EDITOR

FLASH, THE (TF)
SANDI SISSEL .... CINEMATOGRAPHER
DEAN MITZNER .... PRODUCTION DESIGNER
FRANK JIMINEZ .... FILM EDITOR

FLASHBACK
STEFAN CZAPSKY .... CINEMATOGRAPHER
VINCENT M. CRESCIMAN .... PRODUCTION DESIGNER
EILEEN KENNEDY .... COSTUME DESIGNER
CARROLL TIMOTHY O'MEARA .... FILM EDITOR

FLASHDANCE
DONALD PETERMAN .... CINEMATOGRAPHER
CHARLES ROSEN .... PRODUCTION DESIGNER
MICHAEL KAPLAN .... COSTUME DESIGNER
BUD SMITH .... FILM EDITOR
WALT MULCONERY .... FILM EDITOR

FLASHPOINT
PETER MOSS .... CINEMATOGRAPHER
DAVID GARFIELD .... FILM EDITOR

FLATBED ANNIE & SWEETIEPIE: LADY TRUCKERS (TF)
JAMES D. BISSELL .... PRODUCTION DESIGNER

FLATLINERS
JAN DE BONT .... CINEMATOGRAPHER
EUGENIO ZANETTI .... PRODUCTION DESIGNER
SUSAN BECKER .... COSTUME DESIGNER
ROBERT BROWN .... FILM EDITOR

Fi-Fl

CINEMATOGRAPHERS
PRODUCTION
DESIGNERS,
COSTUME
DESIGNERS AND
FILM EDITORS
GUIDE

I
N
D
E
X

O
F

F
I
L
M

T
I
T
L
E
S

Fl-Fo

CINEMATOGRAPHERS
PRODUCTION
DESIGNERS,
COSTUME
DESIGNERS and
FILM EDITORS
GUIDE

I
N
D
E
X

O
F

F
I
L
M

T
I
T
L
E
S

FLESH + BLOOD
JAN DE BONT .... CINEMATOGRAPHER
YVONNE BLAKE .... COSTUME DESIGNER
INE SCHENKKAN .... FILM EDITOR

FLESH AND BLOOD (TF)
VILMOS ZSIGMOND .... CINEMATOGRAPHER
WILLIAM HINEY .... PRODUCTION DESIGNER

FLESH GORDON MEETS THE COSMIC CHEERLEADERS
DANNY NOWAK .... CINEMATOGRAPHER

FLESHBURN
SONYA SONES TRAMER .... FILM EDITOR

FLETCH
FRED SCHULER .... CINEMATOGRAPHER
BORIS LEVEN† .... PRODUCTION DESIGNER
TODD HALLOWELL .... PRODUCTION DESIGNER
GLORIA GRESHAM .... COSTUME DESIGNER
RICHARD A. HARRIS .... FILM EDITOR

FLETCH LIVES
JOHN MCPHERSON .... CINEMATOGRAPHER
CAMERON BIRNIE .... PRODUCTION DESIGNER
DONALD B. WOODRUFF .... PRODUCTION DESIGNER
JIMMY BLY .... PRODUCTION DESIGNER
STEPHEN HENDRICKSON .... PRODUCTION DESIGNER
WRAY STEVEN GRAHAM .... PRODUCTION DESIGNER
ANNA HILL JOHNSTONE .... COSTUME DESIGNER
RICHARD A. HARRIS .... FILM EDITOR

FLIGHT OF THE BLACK ANGEL (CTF)
LEE REDMOND .... CINEMATOGRAPHER
STUART BLATT .... PRODUCTION DESIGNER
BARRY ZETLIN .... FILM EDITOR

FLIGHT OF THE DOVES
HARRY WAXMAN .... CINEMATOGRAPHER

FLIGHT OF THE INTRUDER
FRED J. KOENEKAMP .... CINEMATOGRAPHER
JACK T. COLLIS .... PRODUCTION DESIGNER
C. TIMOTHY O'MEARS .... FILM EDITOR
PECK PRIOR .... FILM EDITOR
STEVE MIRKOVICH .... FILM EDITOR

FLIGHT OF THE NAVIGATOR
JAMES M. GLENNON .... CINEMATOGRAPHER
WILLIAM J. CREBER .... PRODUCTION DESIGNER
MICHAEL NOVOTNY .... PRODUCTION DESIGNER
MARY LOU BYRD .... COSTUME DESIGNER
JEFF S. GOURSON .... FILM EDITOR

FLIGHT OF THE PHOENIX, THE
MICHAEL LUCIANO .... FILM EDITOR

FLIGHT OF THE SPRUCE GOOSE
JERZY ZIELINSKI .... CINEMATOGRAPHER
CORKY O'HARA .... FILM EDITOR

FLIGHT TO BERLIN
PETER PRZYGODDA .... FILM EDITOR

FLIM-FLAM MAN, THE
VINCENT SAIZIS .... CINEMATOGRAPHER

FLORENCE NIGHTINGALE (TF)
JACK HILDYARD .... CINEMATOGRAPHER
MARIT ALLEN .... COSTUME DESIGNER

FLOWER DRUM SONG
IRENE SHARAFF .... COSTUME DESIGNER

FLOWERS IN THE ATTIC
FRANK BYERS .... CINEMATOGRAPHER
GIL HUBBS .... CINEMATOGRAPHER
JOHN MUTO .... PRODUCTION DESIGNER
ANN SOMERS MAJOR .... COSTUME DESIGNER
GREGORY F. PLOTTS .... FILM EDITOR

FLY, THE
MARK IRWIN .... CINEMATOGRAPHER
CAROL SPIER .... PRODUCTION DESIGNER
DENISE CRONENBERG .... COSTUME DESIGNER
RONALD SANDERS .... FILM EDITOR

FLY II, THE
ROBIN VIDGEON .... CINEMATOGRAPHER
MICHAEL S. BOLTON .... PRODUCTION DESIGNER
CHRISTOPHER RYAN .... COSTUME DESIGNER
SEAN BARTON .... FILM EDITOR

FLYING BIRD
HOWARD SMITH .... FILM EDITOR

FLYING BLIND
WILLIAM A. ELLIOT .... PRODUCTION DESIGNER

FLYING BLIND (TF)
JAMES GLENNON .... CINEMATOGRAPHER
WILLIAM A. ELLIOTT .... PRODUCTION DESIGNER
HOWARD SMITH .... FILM EDITOR

FLYING DEVILS, THE
MIKAEL SALOMON .... CINEMATOGRAPHER

FM
DAVID MYERS .... CINEMATOGRAPHER
LAWRENCE G. PAULL .... PRODUCTION DESIGNER
RICHARD SAWYER .... PRODUCTION DESIGNER
JEFF S. GOURSON .... FILM EDITOR

FOG, THE
DEAN CUNDEY .... CINEMATOGRAPHER
CRAIG STEARNS .... PRODUCTION DESIGNER
STEPHEN LOOMIS .... COSTUME DESIGNER
CHARLES BORNSTEIN .... FILM EDITOR

FOLLOW THAT BIRD
STANLEY WARNOW .... FILM EDITOR

FOLLOW THAT CAR
J. RAE FOX .... PRODUCTION DESIGNER

FOOD OF THE GODS, THE
REGINALD H. MORRIS .... CINEMATOGRAPHER

FOOL FOR LOVE
PIERRE MIGNOT .... CINEMATOGRAPHER
STEPHEN ALTMAN .... PRODUCTION DESIGNER
LUCE GRUNENWALDT .... FILM EDITOR
STEPHEN DUNN .... FILM EDITOR

FOOL KILLER, THE
ALEX PHILLIPS .... CINEMATOGRAPHER

FOOL'S PARADE
ALFRED SWEENEY .... PRODUCTION DESIGNER

FOOLIN' AROUND
PHILIP LATHROP .... CINEMATOGRAPHER
FERNANDO CARRERE .... PRODUCTION DESIGNER
JOE I. TOMPKINS .... COSTUME DESIGNER
PETER ZINNER .... FILM EDITOR

FOOLS
MICHEL HUGO .... CINEMATOGRAPHER

FOOTLOOSE
RIC WAITE .... CINEMATOGRAPHER
RON HOBBS .... PRODUCTION DESIGNER
GLORIA GRESHAM .... COSTUME DESIGNER
PAUL HIRSCH .... FILM EDITOR

FOR KEEPS
JAMES A. CRABE .... CINEMATOGRAPHER
WILLIAM J. CASSIDY .... PRODUCTION DESIGNER
COLLEEN C. ATWOOD .... COSTUME DESIGNER
JOHN G. AVILDSEN .... FILM EDITOR

FOR LOVE AND HONOR (TF)
CHARLES F. WHEELER .... CINEMATOGRAPHER

FOR PETE'S SAKE
LASZLO KOVACS .... CINEMATOGRAPHER

FOR QUEEN AND COUNTRY
RICHARD GREATREX .... CINEMATOGRAPHER
ANDREW MCALPINE .... PRODUCTION DESIGNER
CHARMIAN ADAMS .... PRODUCTION DESIGNER
STEPHEN SINGLETON .... FILM EDITOR

FOR THE LOVE OF BENJI
DON REDDY .... CINEMATOGRAPHER
LEON SEITH .... FILM EDITOR

FOR US, THE LIVING (TF)
HARRY KERAMIDAS .... FILM EDITOR

FOR YOUR EYES ONLY
ALAN HUME .... CINEMATOGRAPHER
JOHN FENNER .... PRODUCTION DESIGNER
PETER LAMONT .... PRODUCTION DESIGNER
LIZ WALLER .... COSTUME DESIGNER
JOHN GROVER .... FILM EDITOR

FORBIDDEN DANCE, THE
R. MICHAEL STRINGER .... CINEMATOGRAPHER
DON DAY .... PRODUCTION DESIGNER
SUSAN BERTRAM .... COSTUME DESIGNER
EARL WATSON .... FILM EDITOR
ROBERT EDWARDS .... FILM EDITOR

FORBIDDEN WORLD
TIM SUHRSTEDT .... CINEMATOGRAPHER
JOSEPH T. GARRITY .... PRODUCTION DESIGNER
ALLAN HOLZMAN .... FILM EDITOR

FORCE 10 FROM NAVARONE
CHRISTOPHER CHALLIS .... CINEMATOGRAPHER
HARRY WAXMAN .... CINEMATOGRAPHER
GEOFFREY DRAKE .... PRODUCTION DESIGNER
RAYMOND POULTON .... FILM EDITOR

FORCE FIVE
GIL HUBBS .... CINEMATOGRAPHER

FORCE OF ONE, A
ROGER SHEARMAN .... CINEMATOGRAPHER
JOHN BARRY† .... PRODUCTION DESIGNER
NORM BARON .... PRODUCTION DESIGNER
BERT LOVITT .... FILM EDITOR

FORCE: FIVE
RICHARD J. LAWRENCE .... PRODUCTION DESIGNER
BOB BRING .... FILM EDITOR

FORCED VENGEANCE
REXFORD METZ .... CINEMATOGRAPHER
IRVING C. ROSENBLUM .... FILM EDITOR

FORD FAIRLANE
OLIVER WOOD .... CINEMATOGRAPHER
JOHN VALLONE .... PRODUCTION DESIGNER
MARILYN VANCE-STRAKER .... COSTUME DESIGNER
MICHAEL TRONICK .... FILM EDITOR

FORD: THE MAN AND THE MACHINES (MS)
THOMAS BURSTYN .... CINEMATOGRAPHER

FOREIGN BODY
ROY STANNARD .... PRODUCTION DESIGNER
ANDREW NELSON .... FILM EDITOR

FOREIGN CORRESPONDENT
ALEXANDER GRUSZYNSKI .... CINEMATOGRAPHER

FOREIGN EXCHANGE (TF)
FRED J. KOENEKAMP .... CINEMATOGRAPHER

FOREVER YOUNG
NORMAN LANGLEY .... CINEMATOGRAPHER
JEFFREY WOODBRIDGE .... PRODUCTION DESIGNER
TUDOR GEORGE .... COSTUME DESIGNER
MAX LEMON .... FILM EDITOR

FOREVER YOUNG, FOREVER FREE
ARTHUR ORNITZ† .... CINEMATOGRAPHER
PHILIP ROSENBERG .... PRODUCTION DESIGNER

FOREVER, LULU
LISA RINZLER .... CINEMATOGRAPHER
STEVEN MCCABE .... PRODUCTION DESIGNER
CANDA CLEMENTS .... COSTUME DESIGNER
JAY FREUND .... FILM EDITOR
RALPH ROSENBLUM .... FILM EDITOR

FORGOTTEN PRISONERS: THE AMNESTY FILE (CTF)
STEVE SHAW .... CINEMATOGRAPHER
BERTALAN TIVIDAR .... PRODUCTION DESIGNER
ROBERT FLORIO .... FILM EDITOR

FORMULA, THE
JAMES A. CRABE .... CINEMATOGRAPHER
HERMAN A. BLUMENTHAL .... PRODUCTION DESIGNER
DAVID BRETHERTON .... FILM EDITOR
JOHN CARTER .... FILM EDITOR
JOHN G. AVILDSEN .... FILM EDITOR

FORT APACHE, THE BRONX
JOHN ALCOTT† .... CINEMATOGRAPHER
BEN EDWARDS .... PRODUCTION DESIGNER
CHRISTOPHER NOWAK .... PRODUCTION DESIGNER
JOHN BOXER .... COSTUME DESIGNER
RITA ROLAND .... FILM EDITOR

FORTUNE, THE
JOHN A. ALONZO .... CINEMATOGRAPHER
POLLY PLATT .... PRODUCTION DESIGNER
RICHARD SYLBERT .... PRODUCTION DESIGNER
STU LINDER .... FILM EDITOR

FORTY-DEUCE
STEVEN FIERBERG .... CINEMATOGRAPHER
KEN ELUTO .... FILM EDITOR

FOUL PLAY
DAVID M. WALSH .... CINEMATOGRAPHER
ALFRED SWEENEY .... PRODUCTION DESIGNER
PEMBROKE J. HERRING .... FILM EDITOR

FOUND MONEY (TF)
LARRY PIZER .... CINEMATOGRAPHER

FOUR ADVENTURES OF REINETTE AND MIRABELLE
MARIA-LUISA GARCIA .... FILM EDITOR

FOUR DEUCES, THE
STEPHEN M. KATZ .... CINEMATOGRAPHER
JACKSON DE GOVIA .... PRODUCTION DESIGNER

FOUR FEATHERS, THE (TF)
ERIC BOYD-PERKINS .... FILM EDITOR

FOUR FRIENDS
GHISLAIN CLOQUET† .... CINEMATOGRAPHER
DAVID CHAPMAN .... PRODUCTION DESIGNER
PATRICIA NORRIS .... COSTUME DESIGNER
BARRY MALKIN .... FILM EDITOR
MARC LAUB .... FILM EDITOR

FOUR MUSKETEERS, THE
DAVID WATKIN .... CINEMATOGRAPHER
BRIAN EATWELL .... PRODUCTION DESIGNER
RON TALSKY .... COSTUME DESIGNER
YVONNE BLAKE .... COSTUME DESIGNER
JOHN VICTOR SMITH .... FILM EDITOR

FOUR SEASONS, THE
VICTOR J. KEMPER .... CINEMATOGRAPHER
JACK T. COLLIS .... PRODUCTION DESIGNER
JANE GREENWOOD .... COSTUME DESIGNER
MICHAEL ECONOMOU .... FILM EDITOR

FOURTH MAN, THE (TF)
JAN DE BONT .... CINEMATOGRAPHER
HAL TRUSSELL .... CINEMATOGRAPHER
NATE SCHMIDT .... FILM EDITOR

FOURTH PROTOCOL, THE
PHIL MEHEUX .... CINEMATOGRAPHER
ALLAN CAMERON .... PRODUCTION DESIGNER
TIM HUTCHINSON .... PRODUCTION DESIGNER
GRAHAM WALKER .... FILM EDITOR

FOURTH STORY (CTF)
TONY IMI .... CINEMATOGRAPHER
STEVEN KARATZAS .... PRODUCTION DESIGNER
JOHN F. BURNETT .... FILM EDITOR

FOURTH WAR, THE
GERRY FISHER .... CINEMATOGRAPHER
ALAN MANZER .... PRODUCTION DESIGNER
RAY SUMMERS .... COSTUME DESIGNER
ROBERT F. SHUGRUE .... FILM EDITOR

FOURTH WISH, THE
GEOFF BURTON .... CINEMATOGRAPHER

FOX AND THE HOUND, THE (AF)
JAMES MELTON .... FILM EDITOR

FOX IN THE CHICKEN COOP, THE
DAVID GURFINKEL .... CINEMATOGRAPHER

FOXES
PAUL G. RYAN .... CINEMATOGRAPHER
MICHAEL LEVESQUE .... PRODUCTION DESIGNER
JAMES COBLENTZ .... FILM EDITOR
PETER HOLLYWOOD .... FILM EDITOR

Fo-Fo

CINEMATOGRAPHERS
PRODUCTION
DESIGNERS,
COSTUME
DESIGNERS AND
FILM EDITORS
GUIDE

I
N
D
E
X

O
F

F
I
L
M

T
I
T
L
E
S

Fo-Fr

CINEMATOGRAPHERS
PRODUCTION
DESIGNERS,
COSTUME
DESIGNERS AND
FILM EDITORS
GUIDE

I
N
D
E
X

O
F

F
I
L
M

T
I
T
L
E
S

FOXFIRE (TF)
THOMAS BURSTYN .... CINEMATOGRAPHER

FOXFIRE LIGHT
TOM ACKERMAN .... CINEMATOGRAPHER

FOXTRAP
STEVEN SHAW .... CINEMATOGRAPHER

FOXTROT
ALEX PHILLIPS .... CINEMATOGRAPHER
JOHN M. STEPHENS .... CINEMATOGRAPHER
PETER ZINNER .... FILM EDITOR

FRAGMENT OF FEAR
RAYMOND SIMM .... PRODUCTION DESIGNER
MALCOLM COOKE .... FILM EDITOR

FRANCES
LASZLO KOVACS .... CINEMATOGRAPHER
IDA RANDOM .... PRODUCTION DESIGNER
RICHARD SYLBERT .... PRODUCTION DESIGNER
PATRICIA NORRIS .... COSTUME DESIGNER
JOHN WRIGHT .... FILM EDITOR

FRANCESCO
GIUSEPPI LANCI .... CINEMATOGRAPHER
DANILO DONATI .... PRODUCTION DESIGNER
GABRIELLA CRISTIANI .... FILM EDITOR

FRANKENHOOKER
ROBERT M. BALDWIN .... CINEMATOGRAPHER
KEVIN TENT .... FILM EDITOR

FRANKENSTEIN (TF)
TREVOR WILLIAMS .... PRODUCTION DESIGNER

FRANKENSTEIN UNBOUND
ARMANDO NANNUZZI .... CINEMATOGRAPHER
MICHAEL SCOTT .... CINEMATOGRAPHER
ENRICO TOVAGLIERI .... PRODUCTION DESIGNER
FRANCA ZUCHELLI .... COSTUME DESIGNER
JAY CASSIDY .... FILM EDITOR
MARY BAUER .... FILM EDITOR

FRANTIC
WITOLD SOBOCINSKI .... CINEMATOGRAPHER
PIERRE GUFFROY .... PRODUCTION DESIGNER
ANTHONY POWELL .... COSTUME DESIGNER
SAM O'STEEN .... FILM EDITOR

FRATERNITY VACATION
PAUL G. RYAN .... CINEMATOGRAPHER
ROBERTA NEIMAN .... PRODUCTION DESIGNER
TRACY TYNAN .... COSTUME DESIGNER

FREAKY FRIDAY
CHARLES F. WHEELER .... CINEMATOGRAPHER
JACK SENTER .... PRODUCTION DESIGNER
JOHN B. MANSBRIDGE .... PRODUCTION DESIGNER

FRED ASTAIRE SHOW, THE (TV)
BOB MACKIE .... COSTUME DESIGNER

FREE RIDE
DAN WEBSTER .... PRODUCTION DESIGNER
BARBARA SCOTT .... COSTUME DESIGNER
RON HONTHANER .... FILM EDITOR

FREEBIE & THE BEAN
LASZLO KOVACS .... CINEMATOGRAPHER
FREDRIC STEINKAMP .... FILM EDITOR

FREEDOM (TF)
DONALD M. MORGAN .... CINEMATOGRAPHER
JAMES G. HULSEY .... PRODUCTION DESIGNER

FREEDOM ROAD (TF)
DANIEL LOMINO .... PRODUCTION DESIGNER
ANNE GOURSAUD .... FILM EDITOR
GEORGE FOLSEY JR.* .... FILM EDITOR

FREEWAY
FRANK BYERS .... CINEMATOGRAPHER
MIKAEL SALOMON .... CINEMATOGRAPHER

FRENCH ATLANTIC AFFAIR, THE (TF)
ALLAN JACOBS .... FILM EDITOR

FRENCH CONNECTION, THE
OWEN ROIZMAN .... CINEMATOGRAPHER
GERALD B. GREENBERG .... FILM EDITOR

FRENCH CONNECTION II
CLAUDE RENOIR .... CINEMATOGRAPHER
TOM ROLF .... FILM EDITOR

FRENCH LESSON
ANTON FURST .... PRODUCTION DESIGNER
JUDY MOORCROFT .... COSTUME DESIGNER
JIM CLARK .... FILM EDITOR

FRENCH LESSONS
CLIVE TICKNER .... CINEMATOGRAPHER

FRENCH LIEUTENANT'S WOMAN, THE
FREDDIE FRANCIS .... CINEMATOGRAPHER
ASSHETON GORTON .... PRODUCTION DESIGNER
ALLAN CAMERON .... PRODUCTION DESIGNER
NORMAN DORME .... PRODUCTION DESIGNER
TERRY PRITCHARD .... PRODUCTION DESIGNER
TOM RAND .... COSTUME DESIGNER
JOHN BLOOM .... FILM EDITOR

FRENCH POSTCARDS
BRUNO NUYTTEN .... CINEMATOGRAPHER
CATHERINE LETERRIER .... COSTUME DESIGNER
CAROL LITTLETON .... FILM EDITOR

FRENCH QUARTER
ELLEN MIROJNICK .... COSTUME DESIGNER

FRENZY
JOHN JYMPSON .... FILM EDITOR

FRESH HORSES
FRED MURPHY .... CINEMATOGRAPHER
PAUL SYLBERT .... PRODUCTION DESIGNER
COLLEEN C. ATWOOD .... COSTUME DESIGNER
DAVID ROSENBLOOM .... FILM EDITOR

FRESHMAN, THE
WILLIAM A. FRAKER .... CINEMATOGRAPHER
KEN ADAM .... PRODUCTION DESIGNER
JULIE WEISS .... COSTUME DESIGNER

FRESNO (MS)
ROBERT STEADMAN .... CINEMATOGRAPHER
BOB MACKIE .... COSTUME DESIGNER

FRIDAY THE 13TH
BARRY ABRAMS .... CINEMATOGRAPHER
VIRGINIA FIELD .... PRODUCTION DESIGNER
JOEL GOODMAN .... FILM EDITOR

FRIDAY THE 13TH, PART 2
PETER STEIN .... CINEMATOGRAPHER
VIRGINIA FIELD .... PRODUCTION DESIGNER
ELLEN LUTTER .... COSTUME DESIGNER
SUSAN E. CUNNINGHAM .... FILM EDITOR

FRIDAY THE 13TH PART 3
GERALD FEIL .... CINEMATOGRAPHER
ROBB WILSON KING .... PRODUCTION DESIGNER
GEORGE HIVELY .... FILM EDITOR

FRIDAY THE 13TH—THE FINAL CHAPTER
JOAO FERNANDES .... CINEMATOGRAPHER

FRIDAY THE 13TH PART V: A NEW BEGINNING
STEPHEN L. POSEY .... CINEMATOGRAPHER
ROBERT HOWLAND .... PRODUCTION DESIGNER

FRIDAY THE 13TH PART VI: JASON LIVES
JON KRANHOUSE .... CINEMATOGRAPHER
JOSEPH T. GARRITY .... PRODUCTION DESIGNER
PATRICK TAGLIAFERRO .... PRODUCTION DESIGNER
MARIA MANCUSO .... COSTUME DESIGNER
BRUCE GREEN .... FILM EDITOR

FRIDAY THE 13TH PART VII - THE NEW BLOOD
PAUL ELLIOTT .... CINEMATOGRAPHER
RICHARD J. LAWRENCE .... PRODUCTION DESIGNER
JACQUELINE JOHNSON .... COSTUME DESIGNER
BARRY ZETLIN .... FILM EDITOR
MARTIN JAY SADOFF .... FILM EDITOR

FRIDAY THE 13TH PART VIII: JASON TAKES MANHATTAN
BRYAN ENGLAND .... CINEMATOGRAPHER
STEVE MIRKOVICH .... FILM EDITOR

FRIDAY THE 13TH 3-D
SANDI LOVE .... COSTUME DESIGNER

FRIENDLY FIRE (TF)
KIRK AXTELL .... PRODUCTION DESIGNER
MICHAEL ECONOMOU .... FILM EDITOR

FRIENDLY PERSUASION (TF)
JAMES H. SPENCER .... PRODUCTION DESIGNER

FRIENDS
ANNE V. COATES .... FILM EDITOR

FRIENDS, LOVERS & LUNATICS
DOUGLAS KOCH .... CINEMATOGRAPHER
ALLAN FELLOWS .... PRODUCTION DESIGNER
BETH PASTERNAK .... COSTUME DESIGNER
MICHAEL MCMAHON .... FILM EDITOR

FRIENDSHIP IN VIENNA, A (CTF)
HANANIA BAER .... CINEMATOGRAPHER
BERT GLATSTEIN .... FILM EDITOR

FRIGHT NIGHT
JAN KIESSER .... CINEMATOGRAPHER
JOHN DE CUIR JR. .... PRODUCTION DESIGNER
BETTYLEE BALSAM .... COSTUME DESIGNER
ROBERT FLETCHER .... COSTUME DESIGNER
KENT BEYDA .... FILM EDITOR

FRIGHT NIGHT PART II
MARK IRWIN .... CINEMATOGRAPHER
DEAN TSCHETTER .... PRODUCTION DESIGNER
JOSEPH PORRO .... COSTUME DESIGNER
JAY CASSIDY .... FILM EDITOR

FRINGE DWELLERS, THE
DONALD MCALPINIE .... CINEMATOGRAPHER
HERBERT PINTER .... PRODUCTION DESIGNER
KERRI BARNETT .... COSTUME DESIGNER
TIM WELLBURN .... FILM EDITOR

FRISCO KID, THE
ROBERT B. HAUSER .... CINEMATOGRAPHER
JOSAN F. RUSSO .... PRODUCTION DESIGNER
TERENCE MARSH .... PRODUCTION DESIGNER
IRVING C. ROSENBLUM .... FILM EDITOR
JOHN C. HORGER .... FILM EDITOR
MAURY WINETROBE .... FILM EDITOR

FROG PRINCE, THE
MAREK DOBROWOLSKI .... PRODUCTION DESIGNER
JUDY MOORCROFT .... COSTUME DESIGNER
JIM CLARK .... FILM EDITOR

FROGS
MARIO TOSI .... CINEMATOGRAPHER

FROM BEYOND
MAC AHLBERG .... CINEMATOGRAPHER
GIOVANNI NATALUCCI .... PRODUCTION DESIGNER
LEE PERCY .... FILM EDITOR

FROM HOLLYWOOD TO DEADWOOD
PETER DEMING .... CINEMATOGRAPHER
TORI NOURAFCHAN .... PRODUCTION DESIGNER
MEG GOODWIN .... COSTUME DESIGNER
ROBERT ERICKSON .... FILM EDITOR
STEVE ADRIANSON .... FILM EDITOR

FROM NOON TIL THREE
RICHARD J. LAWRENCE .... PRODUCTION DESIGNER
MAURY WINETROBE .... FILM EDITOR

FROM RUSSIA WITH LOVE
TED MOORE .... CINEMATOGRAPHER
SYD CAIN .... PRODUCTION DESIGNER

FROM THE DEAD OF NIGHT (TF)
BERND HEINL .... CINEMATOGRAPHER
STEVE COHEN .... FILM EDITOR

FROM THE HIP
DANTE SPINOTTI .... CINEMATOGRAPHER
MICHAEL STRINGER .... PRODUCTION DESIGNER
CLIFFORD CAPONE .... COSTUME DESIGNER
STAN COLE .... FILM EDITOR

FROM THE LIFE OF THE MARIONETTES
SVEN NYKVIST .... CINEMATOGRAPHER
ROLF ZEHETBAUER .... PRODUCTION DESIGNER
PETRA VAN OELFFEN .... FILM EDITOR

FROM THE MIXED UP FILES OF MRS. BASIL E. FRANKWEILER
PHILIP ROSENBERG .... PRODUCTION DESIGNER

FRONT PAGE, THE
JORDAN CRONENWETH .... CINEMATOGRAPHER
HENRY BUMSTEAD .... PRODUCTION DESIGNER
RALPH E. WINTERS .... FILM EDITOR

FRONT, THE
MICHAEL CHAPMAN .... CINEMATOGRAPHER
CHARLES BAILEY .... PRODUCTION DESIGNER
SIDNEY LEVIN .... FILM EDITOR

FRUIT MACHINE, THE
DAVID BROCKHURST .... PRODUCTION DESIGNER
RICHARD BEDFORD .... FILM EDITOR

FUGITIVE FAMILY (TF)
ROBERT B. HAUSER .... CINEMATOGRAPHER
PETER W. WOOLEY .... PRODUCTION DESIGNER

FULFILLMENT OF MARY GRAY, THE (TF)
DAVID BRIDGES .... CINEMATOGRAPHER
JAMES G. HULSEY .... PRODUCTION DESIGNER
MILLIE MOORE .... FILM EDITOR

FULL FATHOM FIVE
PILI FLORES GUERRA .... CINEMATOGRAPHER
FERNANDO VASQUES DE VELASCO .... PRODUCTION DESIGNER
KAREN HORN .... FILM EDITOR

FULL METAL JACKET
DOUGLAS MILSOME .... CINEMATOGRAPHER
ANTON FURST .... PRODUCTION DESIGNER
KEITH PAIN .... PRODUCTION DESIGNER
LESLIE TOMKINS .... PRODUCTION DESIGNER
KEITH DENNY .... COSTUME DESIGNER
MARTIN HUNTER .... FILM EDITOR

FULL MOON HIGH
DANIEL PEARL .... CINEMATOGRAPHER

FULL MOON IN BLUE WATER
FRED MURPHY .... CINEMATOGRAPHER
NEIL SPISAK .... PRODUCTION DESIGNER
RONDI HILLSTROM DAVIS .... COSTUME DESIGNER
JILL SAVITT .... FILM EDITOR

FULL MOON IN PARIS
RENATO BERTA .... CINEMATOGRAPHER

FUN AND GAMES (TF)
DANIEL LOMINO .... PRODUCTION DESIGNER

FUN DOWN THERE
ERIC SAKS .... CINEMATOGRAPHER
PEGGY AHWESH .... CINEMATOGRAPHER
KEITH SANBORN .... FILM EDITOR
ROGER STIGLIANO .... FILM EDITOR

FUN WITH DICK AND JANE
FRED J. KOENEKAMP .... CINEMATOGRAPHER
JAMES G. HULSEY .... PRODUCTION DESIGNER
DONFELD .... COSTUME DESIGNER
DANFORD B. GREENE .... FILM EDITOR

FUNERAL HOME
MARK IRWIN .... CINEMATOGRAPHER
ROY FORGE SMITH .... PRODUCTION DESIGNER

FUNERAL IN BERLIN
KEN ADAM .... PRODUCTION DESIGNER
PETER MURTON .... PRODUCTION DESIGNER
JOHN BLOOM .... FILM EDITOR

FUNERAL, THE
AKIRO SUZUKI .... FILM EDITOR

Fr-Fu

CINEMATOGRAPHERS
PRODUCTION
DESIGNERS,
COSTUME
DESIGNERS AND
FILM EDITORS
GUIDE

I
N
D
E
X

O
F

F
I
L
M

T
I
T
L
E
S

Fu-Ga

CINEMATOGRAPHERS
PRODUCTION
DESIGNERS,
COSTUME
DESIGNERS AND
FILM EDITORS
GUIDE

**I
N
D
E
X

O
F

F
I
L
M

T
I
T
L
E
S**

346

GARDENS OF STONE
JORDAN CRONENWETH .... CINEMATOGRAPHER
ALEX TAVOULARIS .... PRODUCTION DESIGNER
DEAN TAVOULARIS .... PRODUCTION DESIGNER
JUDIANNA MAKOVSKY .... COSTUME DESIGNER
WILLA KIM .... COSTUME DESIGNER
BARRY MALKIN .... FILM EDITOR

GARDNER'S SON, THE (TF)
FRED MURPHY .... CINEMATOGRAPHER

GAS
RENE VERZIER .... CINEMATOGRAPHER
CAROL SPIER .... PRODUCTION DESIGNER
PATRICK DODD .... FILM EDITOR

GAS PUMP GIRLS
NICHOLAS VON STERNBERG .... CINEMATOGRAPHER

GATE, THE
THOMAS VAMOS .... CINEMATOGRAPHER
WILLIAM BEETON .... PRODUCTION DESIGNER
RIT WALLIS .... FILM EDITOR

GATHERING, THE (TF)
JAN SCOTT .... PRODUCTION DESIGNER

GATOR
WILLIAM A. FRAKER .... CINEMATOGRAPHER
KIRK AXTELL .... PRODUCTION DESIGNER
CARL KRESS .... FILM EDITOR
HAROLD F. KRESS .... FILM EDITOR

GAUNTLET, THE
REXFORD METZ .... CINEMATOGRAPHER
GLENN WRIGHT .... COSTUME DESIGNER
FERRIS WEBSTER .... FILM EDITOR
JOEL COX .... FILM EDITOR

GENERAL HOSPITAL (TVS)
ANN SOMERS MAJOR .... COSTUME DESIGNER

GENOCIDE (FD)
ROY WATTS .... FILM EDITOR

GENTLEMAN TRAMP, THE
NESTOR ALMENDROS .... CINEMATOGRAPHER

GENUINE RISK
DEAN LENT .... CINEMATOGRAPHER
ELISABETH A. SCOTT .... PRODUCTION DESIGNER
ANGELA BALOGH-CALIN .... COSTUME DESIGNER
CHRISTOPHER KOEFOED .... FILM EDITOR

GEORGE WASHINGTON (MS)
HARRY STRADLING, JR. .... CINEMATOGRAPHER

GEORGIA PEACHES
MICHAEL ERLERE .... PRODUCTION DESIGNER

GEORGY GIRL
JOHN BLOOM .... FILM EDITOR

GERMANY PALE MOTHER
JURGEN JURGES .... CINEMATOGRAPHER

GET CARTER
ASSHETON GORTON .... PRODUCTION DESIGNER

GET CRAZY
THOMAS DEL RUTH .... CINEMATOGRAPHER
ELAYNE CEDER .... PRODUCTION DESIGNER
KENT BEYDA .... FILM EDITOR
MICHAEL JABLOW .... FILM EDITOR

GET OUT YOUR HANDKERCHIEFS
JEAN PENZER .... CINEMATOGRAPHER

GET SMART, AGAIN! (TF)
GAYNE RESCHER .... CINEMATOGRAPHER
DONALD R. RODE .... FILM EDITOR

GET TO KNOW YOUR RABBIT
JOHN A. ALONZO .... CINEMATOGRAPHER

GETAWAY, THE
TED HAWORTH .... PRODUCTION DESIGNER
ROBERT L. WOLFE .... FILM EDITOR

GETTING EVEN
PETER LYONS COLLISTER .... CINEMATOGRAPHER
RICHARD JAMES .... PRODUCTION DESIGNER
CHARLES BORNSTEIN .... FILM EDITOR

GETTING IT RIGHT
CAROLYN AMIES .... PRODUCTION DESIGNER

GETTING IT ON!
AUSTIN MCKINNEY .... CINEMATOGRAPHER

GETTING IT RIGHT
CLIVE TICKNER .... CINEMATOGRAPHER
FRANK WALSH .... PRODUCTION DESIGNER
HAZEL PETHIG .... COSTUME DESIGNER
CHRISTOPHER KELLY .... FILM EDITOR

GETTING LUCKY
GERALD M. WILLIAMS .... CINEMATOGRAPHER
VITO ALEOTORI .... PRODUCTION DESIGNER
TONY MILLER .... FILM EDITOR

GETTING MARRIED (TF)
DANIEL LOMINO .... PRODUCTION DESIGNER

GETTING OF WISDOM, THE
DONALD MCALPINE .... CINEMATOGRAPHER
JOHN STODDART .... PRODUCTION DESIGNER
WILLIAM M. ANDERSON .... FILM EDITOR

GETTING PHYSICAL (TF)
ELAYNE CEDER .... PRODUCTION DESIGNER

GETTING STRAIGHT
LASZLO KOVACS .... CINEMATOGRAPHER
MAURY WINETROBE .... FILM EDITOR

GHOST
ADAM GREENBERG .... CINEMATOGRAPHER
JANE MUSKY .... PRODUCTION DESIGNER
RUTH MORLEY .... COSTUME DESIGNER
WALTER MURCH .... FILM EDITOR

GHOST DAD
ANDREW LASZLO .... CINEMATOGRAPHER
HENRY BUMSTEAD .... PRODUCTION DESIGNER
RICHARD CARTER .... PRODUCTION DESIGNER
WINNIE D. BROWN .... COSTUME DESIGNER
PEMBROKE J. HERRING .... FILM EDITOR

GHOST FEVER
DORA CORONA .... PRODUCTION DESIGNER
SUSAN CHEVALIER .... COSTUME DESIGNER
JAMES RUXIN .... FILM EDITOR

GHOST IN THE NOONDAY SUN
ERNEST DAY .... CINEMATOGRAPHER
RAY LOVEJOY .... FILM EDITOR

GHOST OF FLIGHT 401 , THE(TF)
DANIEL LOMINO .... PRODUCTION DESIGNER

GHOST STORY
JACK CARDIFF .... CINEMATOGRAPHER
NORMAN NEWBERRY .... PRODUCTION DESIGNER
MAY ROUTH .... COSTUME DESIGNER
TOM ROLF .... FILM EDITOR

GHOST TOWN
MAC AHLBERG .... CINEMATOGRAPHER
DON DE FINA .... PRODUCTION DESIGNER
KING WILDER .... FILM EDITOR
PETER TESCHNER .... FILM EDITOR

GHOST WARRIOR
MAC AHLBERG .... CINEMATOGRAPHER
ROBERT HOWLAND .... PRODUCTION DESIGNER
BRAD ARENSMAN .... FILM EDITOR

GHOST WRITER, THE (TF)
KENNETH MACMILLAN .... CINEMATOGRAPHER
ANGUS NEWTON .... FILM EDITOR

GHOSTBUSTERS
LASZLO KOVACS .... CINEMATOGRAPHER
JOHN DE CUIR JR. .... PRODUCTION DESIGNER
THEONI V. ALDREDGE .... COSTUME DESIGNER
DAVID BLEWITT .... FILM EDITOR
SHELDON KAHN .... FILM EDITOR

Ga-Gh

CINEMATOGRAPHERS
PRODUCTION
DESIGNERS,
COSTUME
DESIGNERS AND
FILM EDITORS
GUIDE

INDEX OF FILM TITLES

Gh-Gl

CINEMATOGRAPHERS
PRODUCTION
DESIGNERS,
COSTUME
DESIGNERS AND
FILM EDITORS
GUIDE

I
N
D
E
X

O
F

F
I
L
M

T
I
T
L
E
S

GHOSTBUSTERS II
MICHAEL CHAPMAN .... CINEMATOGRAPHER
ROBERT W. (BO) WELCH .... PRODUCTION DESIGNER
TOM DUFFIELD .... PRODUCTION DESIGNER
GLORIA GRESHAM .... COSTUME DESIGNER
DONN CAMBERN .... FILM EDITOR
SHELDON KAHN .... FILM EDITOR

GHOSTWARRIOR
PAMELA B. WARNER .... PRODUCTION DESIGNER

GHOULIES
MAC AHLBERG .... CINEMATOGRAPHER
KATHIE CLARK .... COSTUME DESIGNER

GIANT
BORIS LEVEN† .... PRODUCTION DESIGNER

GIANT SPIDER INVASION, THE
BARBARA POKRAS .... FILM EDITOR

GIDEON OLIVER (PILOT)
FRANK PRINZI .... CINEMATOGRAPHER
GARY WEIST .... PRODUCTION DESIGNER

GIFT OF LOVE, THE (TF)
CHARLES F. WHEELER .... CINEMATOGRAPHER
LARRY PIZER .... CINEMATOGRAPHER
JOHN C. HORGER .... FILM EDITOR

GIFTED ONE, THE (TF)
KEES VAN OOSTRUM .... CINEMATOGRAPHER
GIB JAFFE .... FILM EDITOR
LARRY BOCK .... FILM EDITOR

GIG, THE
JERI SOPANEN .... CINEMATOGRAPHER
LINDA BENEDICT .... COSTUME DESIGNER
RICK SHAINE .... FILM EDITOR

GILDA LIVE
ALAN METZGER .... CINEMATOGRAPHER
JAMES A. CONTNER .... CINEMATOGRAPHER
EUGENE LEE .... PRODUCTION DESIGNER
ELLEN HIVDALE .... FILM EDITOR
LYNZEE KLINGMAN .... FILM EDITOR
MUFFIE MEYER .... FILM EDITOR

GIMME AN F
TODD RAMSAY .... FILM EDITOR
TOM WALLS .... FILM EDITOR
WENDY BRICMONT .... FILM EDITOR

GINGER & FRED
ENNIO GUARNIERI .... CINEMATOGRAPHER
DANILO DONATI .... COSTUME DESIGNER
NINO BARAGLI .... FILM EDITOR
RUGGERO MASTROIANNI .... FILM EDITOR

GINGER ALE AFTERNOON
YURI NEYMAN .... CINEMATOGRAPHER
MICHAEL HELMY .... PRODUCTION DESIGNER
LORENZO DE STEFANO .... FILM EDITOR

GINGER & FRED
TONINO DELLI COLLI .... CINEMATOGRAPHER
DANTE FERRETTI .... PRODUCTION DESIGNER

GIORDANO BRUNO
ENRICO SABBATINI .... COSTUME DESIGNER

GIRL FROM LORRAINE, THE
PHILIPPE ROUSSELOT .... CINEMATOGRAPHER

GIRL HAPPY
RITA ROLAND .... FILM EDITOR

GIRL IN A SWING, THE
ROBERT GORDON .... FILM EDITOR

GIRL IN THE PICTURE, THE
DICK POPE .... CINEMATOGRAPHER
GEMMA JACKSON .... PRODUCTION DESIGNER
MARY-JANE REYNER .... COSTUME DESIGNER
BERT EELES .... FILM EDITOR

GIRL NAMED SOONER, A (TF)
JAN SCOTT .... PRODUCTION DESIGNER

GIRL OF THE LIMBERLOST, A (TF)
GORDON LONSDALE .... CINEMATOGRAPHER
TOM WELLS .... PRODUCTION DESIGNER
DAVID SAXON .... FILM EDITOR

GIRL WHO COULDN'T LOSE, THE (TF)
FRANK WATTS .... CINEMATOGRAPHER

GIRL WHO SPELLED FREEDOM, THE (TF)
MICHAEL JABLOW .... FILM EDITOR

GIRL WITH THE RED HAIR, THE
THEO VAN DE SANDE .... CINEMATOGRAPHER

GIRL, THE
TOMISLAV PINTER .... CINEMATOGRAPHER
DEREK TRIGG .... FILM EDITOR

GIRLFRIEND FROM HELL
GERRY LIVELY .... CINEMATOGRAPHER
REGINA ARGENTINE .... PRODUCTION DESIGNER
LIBBY JACOBS .... COSTUME DESIGNER
BETH CONWELL .... FILM EDITOR

GIRLFRIENDS
FRED MURPHY .... CINEMATOGRAPHER
PATRIZIA VON BRANDENSTEIN .... PRODUCTION DESIGNER
KATHERINE WENNING .... FILM EDITOR
SUZANNE PETTIT .... FILM EDITOR

GIRLS JUST WANT TO HAVE FUN
TOM ACKERMAN .... CINEMATOGRAPHER
JEFF STAGGS .... PRODUCTION DESIGNER
SARINA ROTSTEIN .... PRODUCTION DESIGNER
BETTY PECHA MADDEN .... COSTUME DESIGNER
DAVID RAWLINS .... FILM EDITOR
LORENZO DE STEFANO .... FILM EDITOR

GIRLS OF THE WHITE ORCHID (TF)
JOHN LINDLEY .... CINEMATOGRAPHER
ROBERT KINOSHITA .... PRODUCTION DESIGNER

GIVE MY REGARDS TO BROAD STREET
IAN MCMILLAN .... CINEMATOGRAPHER
ANTHONY PRATT .... PRODUCTION DESIGNER
MILENA CANONERO .... COSTUME DESIGNER
PETER BESTON .... FILM EDITOR

GLASS CELL
ROBBY MULLER .... CINEMATOGRAPHER
PETER PRZYGODDA .... FILM EDITOR

GLASS HOUSES
GEORGE FOLSEY JR.* .... FILM EDITOR

GLASS MENAGERIE, THE
BILLY WILLIAMS .... CINEMATOGRAPHER
JOHN KASARDA .... PRODUCTION DESIGNER
TONY WALTON .... PRODUCTION DESIGNER
DAVID RAY .... FILM EDITOR

GLASS MENAGERIE, THE (TF)
MICHAEL BALLHAUS .... CINEMATOGRAPHER
TERENCE MARSH .... PRODUCTION DESIGNER
TONY WALTON .... COSTUME DESIGNER
PATRICIA ZIPPRODT .... COSTUME DESIGNER
JOHN BLOOM .... FILM EDITOR

GLEAMING THE CUBE
REED SMOOT .... CINEMATOGRAPHER
DAN WEBSTER .... PRODUCTION DESIGNER
JOHN MUTO .... PRODUCTION DESIGNER
ANN SOMERS MAJOR .... COSTUME DESIGNER
JOHN WRIGHT .... FILM EDITOR

GLITCH
GEORGE ROSENBERG .... FILM EDITOR

GLITTER DOME, THE (CTF)
MICHAEL WATKINS .... CINEMATOGRAPHER
DOUGLAS HIGGINS .... PRODUCTION DESIGNER
MICHAEL S. BOLTON .... PRODUCTION DESIGNER
ALLAN JACOBS .... FILM EDITOR

GLOBAL AFFAIR, A
BUD MOLIN .... FILM EDITOR

GLORIA
FRED SCHULER .... CINEMATOGRAPHER
GEORGE C. VILLASENOR .... FILM EDITOR

GLORY
FREDDIE FRANCIS .... CINEMATOGRAPHER
DAN WEBSTER .... PRODUCTION DESIGNER
KEITH PAIN .... PRODUCTION DESIGNER
NORMAN GARWOOD .... PRODUCTION DESIGNER

GLORY DAYS
TRACY TYNAN .... COSTUME DESIGNER
EDWARD M. ABROMS .... FILM EDITOR

GLORY! GLORY! (CMS)
MIKE FASH .... CINEMATOGRAPHER
ANDRIS HAUSMANIS .... PRODUCTION DESIGNER

GLOVE, THE
GARY GRAVER .... CINEMATOGRAPHER
ROBERT FITZGERALD .... FILM EDITOR

GO TELL IT ON THE MOUNTAIN (TF)
HIRO NARITA .... CINEMATOGRAPHER
BERNARD JOHNSON .... COSTUME DESIGNER
JAY FREUND .... FILM EDITOR

GO TELL THE SPARTANS
HARRY STRADLING, JR. .... CINEMATOGRAPHER
JACK SENTER .... PRODUCTION DESIGNER
MILLIE MOORE .... FILM EDITOR

GO TOWARD THE LIGHT (TF)
ERIC VAN HAREN NOMAN .... CINEMATOGRAPHER

GO-BETWEEN, THE
GERRY FISHER .... CINEMATOGRAPHER

GOALIE'S ANXIETY AT THE PENALTY KICK, THE
ROBBY MULLER .... CINEMATOGRAPHER

GODDESS OF LOVE (TF)
GIL HUBBS .... CINEMATOGRAPHER
DOROTHY BACA .... COSTUME DESIGNER

GODFATHER, THE
GORDON WILLIS .... CINEMATOGRAPHER
DEAN TAVOULARIS .... PRODUCTION DESIGNER
ANNA HILL JOHNSTONE .... COSTUME DESIGNER
PETER ZINNER .... FILM EDITOR
WILLIAM REYNOLDS .... FILM EDITOR

GODFATHER, PART II, THE
GORDON WILLIS .... CINEMATOGRAPHER
ANGELO GRAHAM .... PRODUCTION DESIGNER
DEAN TAVOULARIS .... PRODUCTION DESIGNER
THEADORA VAN RUNKLE .... COSTUME DESIGNER
PETER ZINNER .... FILM EDITOR
RICHARD MARKS .... FILM EDITOR

GODFATHER PART III, THE
GORDON WILLIS .... CINEMATOGRAPHER
DEAN TAVOULARIS .... PRODUCTION DESIGNER
MILENA CANONERO .... COSTUME DESIGNER
BARRY MALKIN .... FILM EDITOR
LISA FRUCHTMAN .... FILM EDITOR
WALTER MURCH .... FILM EDITOR

GODS MUST BE CRAZY, THE
BUSTER REYNOLDS .... CINEMATOGRAPHER
JAMIE UYS .... FILM EDITOR

GODS MUST BE CRAZY 2, THE
BUSTER REYNOLDS .... CINEMATOGRAPHER

GODSEND, THE
NORMAN WARWICK .... CINEMATOGRAPHER
MICHAEL ELLIS .... FILM EDITOR

GODSPELL
BRIAN EATWELL .... PRODUCTION DESIGNER
ALAN HEIM .... FILM EDITOR

GOIN' COCONUTS
FRANK PHILLIPS .... CINEMATOGRAPHER
FRANK BRACHT .... FILM EDITOR

GOIN' SOUTH
NESTOR ALMENDROS .... CINEMATOGRAPHER
TOBY CARR RAFELSON .... PRODUCTION DESIGNER
WILLIAM WARE THEISS .... COSTUME DESIGNER
RICHARD CHEW .... FILM EDITOR

GOING APE!
FRANK PHILLIPS .... CINEMATOGRAPHER
ROBERT KINOSHITA .... PRODUCTION DESIGNER
ROBERT HARRIS, JR. .... COSTUME DESIGNER
JOHN W. WHEELER .... FILM EDITOR

GOING BERSERK
BOBBY BYRNE .... CINEMATOGRAPHER
JAMES SHANAHAN .... PRODUCTION DESIGNER
PETER LANDSDOWN SMITH .... PRODUCTION DESIGNER
HARRY CURTIS .... COSTUME DESIGNER
DONN CAMBERN .... FILM EDITOR

GOING HOME
PETER W. WOOLEY .... PRODUCTION DESIGNER

GOING IN STYLE
BILLY WILLIAMS .... CINEMATOGRAPHER
FRED PRICE .... PRODUCTION DESIGNER
GARY WEIST .... PRODUCTION DESIGNER
STEPHEN HENDRICKSON .... PRODUCTION DESIGNER
CARROLL TIMOTHY O'MEARA .... FILM EDITOR
ROBERT E. SWINK .... FILM EDITOR

GOING STEADY
ADAM GREENBERG .... CINEMATOGRAPHER

GOING UNDERCOVER
JOHN COQUILLON .... CINEMATOGRAPHER
JIM DULTZ .... PRODUCTION DESIGNER
ERIC BOYD-PERKINS .... FILM EDITOR

GOLD BUG, THE (TF)
DENNIS O'CONNOR .... FILM EDITOR

GOLDEN BRAID
NINO G. MARTINETTI .... CINEMATOGRAPHER
RUSSELL HURLEY .... FILM EDITOR

GOLDEN CHILD, THE
DONALD E. THORIN .... CINEMATOGRAPHER
J. MICHAEL RIVA .... PRODUCTION DESIGNER
LYNDA PARADISE .... PRODUCTION DESIGNER
WAYNE FINKELMAN .... COSTUME DESIGNER
RICHARD A. HARRIS .... FILM EDITOR

GOLDEN GIRL
STEVAN LARNER .... CINEMATOGRAPHER

GOLDEN NEEDLES
GIL HUBBS .... CINEMATOGRAPHER
MICHAEL KAHN .... FILM EDITOR

GOLDEN SEAL, THE
ERIC SAARINEN .... CINEMATOGRAPHER
DOUGLAS HIGGINS .... PRODUCTION DESIGNER
ROBERT Q. LOVETT .... FILM EDITOR

GOLDEN VOYAGE OF SINBAD, THE
JOHN STOLL .... PRODUCTION DESIGNER

GOLDENGIRL
PETER MULLINS .... PRODUCTION DESIGNER
SYDNEY Z. LITWAK .... PRODUCTION DESIGNER
GEORGE JAY NICHOLSON .... FILM EDITOR

GOLDFINGER
TED MOORE .... CINEMATOGRAPHER
KEN ADAM .... PRODUCTION DESIGNER
PETER MURTON .... PRODUCTION DESIGNER

GOLDIE AND THE BOXER (TF)
ISIDORE MANKOFSKY .... CINEMATOGRAPHER

GOLDIE HAWN SPECIAL, THE (TV)
BOB MACKIE .... COSTUME DESIGNER

GONG SHOW MOVIE, THE
RICHARD C. GLOUNER .... CINEMATOGRAPHER
ROBERT KINOSHITA .... PRODUCTION DESIGNER
JAMES MITCHELL .... FILM EDITOR

GOOD AND BAD AT GAMES
HERBERT WESTBROOK .... PRODUCTION DESIGNER
LAURENCE MÉRY CLARK .... FILM EDITOR

GOOD COPS, BAD COPS (TF)
RONALD M. LAUTORE .... CINEMATOGRAPHER
BARBARA DUNPHY .... PRODUCTION DESIGNER
CHRISTOPHER COOKE .... FILM EDITOR

GI-Go

CINEMATOGRAPHERS
PRODUCTION
DESIGNERS,
COSTUME
DESIGNERS AND
FILM EDITORS
GUIDE

INDEX OF FILM TITLES

CINEMATOGRAPHERS
PRODUCTION
DESIGNERS,
COSTUME
DESIGNERS and
FILM EDITORS
GUIDE

I
N
D
E
X

O
F

F
I
L
M

T
I
T
L
E
S

GOOD FATHER, THE
MICHAEL COULTER .... CINEMATOGRAPHER
ADRIAN SMITH .... PRODUCTION DESIGNER
PETER HOLLYWOOD .... FILM EDITOR

GOOD FELLAS
MICHAEL BALLHAUS .... CINEMATOGRAPHER
KRISTI ZEA .... PRODUCTION DESIGNER
MAHER AHMAD .... PRODUCTION DESIGNER
RICHARD BRUNO .... COSTUME DESIGNER
THELMA SCHOONMAKER .... FILM EDITOR

GOOD GUYS AND THE BAD GUYS, THE
HARRY STRADLING, JR. .... CINEMATOGRAPHER

GOOD GUYS WEAR BLACK
BEALA B. NEEL .... PRODUCTION DESIGNER
JEAN-PIERRE DORLEAC .... COSTUME DESIGNER

GOOD LUCK MISS WYCKOFF
ALEX PHILLIPS .... CINEMATOGRAPHER
JAMES D. BISSELL .... PRODUCTION DESIGNER
RITA ROLAND .... FILM EDITOR

GOOD MORNING, BABYLON
GIUSEPPI LANCI .... CINEMATOGRAPHER
GIANNI SBARRA .... PRODUCTION DESIGNER
LINA NERLI TAVIANI .... COSTUME DESIGNER
ROBERTO PERPIGNANI .... FILM EDITOR

GOOD MORNING, VIETNAM
PETER SOVA .... CINEMATOGRAPHER
ROY WALKER .... PRODUCTION DESIGNER
STEVE SPENCE .... PRODUCTION DESIGNER
KEITH DENNY .... COSTUME DESIGNER
STU LINDER .... FILM EDITOR

GOOD MOTHER, THE
DAVID WATKIN .... CINEMATOGRAPHER
HILTON ROSEMARIN .... PRODUCTION DESIGNER
RICHARD HARRISON .... PRODUCTION DESIGNER
STAN JOLLEY .... PRODUCTION DESIGNER
SUSAN BECKER .... COSTUME DESIGNER
PETER E. BERGER .... FILM EDITOR

GOOD NIGHT MY LOVE (TF)
JOSEPH R. JENNINGS .... PRODUCTION DESIGNER

GOOD NIGHT, SWEET WIFE: A MURDER IN BOSTON (TF)
JOHN TOLL .... CINEMATOGRAPHER
PETER WOOLEY .... PRODUCTION DESIGNER
ANTHONY REDMAN .... FILM EDITOR

GOOD RIDDANCE
MICHEL PROULX .... PRODUCTION DESIGNER

GOOD SOLDIER, THE (TF)
TONY PIERCE-ROBERTS .... CINEMATOGRAPHER

GOOD SPORT, A
FRED SCHULER .... CINEMATOGRAPHER

GOOD TIMES, WONDERFUL TIMES (FD)
DOV HOENIG .... FILM EDITOR

GOOD TO GO
PETER SINCLAIR .... CINEMATOGRAPHER
GIB JAFFE .... FILM EDITOR

GOOD WIFE, THE
JAMES BARTLE .... CINEMATOGRAPHER
SALLY CAMPBELL .... PRODUCTION DESIGNER
JENNIE TATE .... COSTUME DESIGNER
JOHN SCOTT .... FILM EDITOR

GOODBYE COLUMBUS
RALPH ROSENBLUM .... FILM EDITOR

GOODBYE GIRL, THE
DAVID M. WALSH .... CINEMATOGRAPHER
ALBERT BRENNER .... PRODUCTION DESIGNER
ANN ROTH .... COSTUME DESIGNER
JOHN F. BURNETT .... FILM EDITOR
MARGARET BOOTH .... FILM EDITOR

GOODBYE NEW YORK
MIKAEL SALOMON .... CINEMATOGRAPHER
VIRGINIA FIELD .... PRODUCTION DESIGNER
ALAN HEIM .... FILM EDITOR

GOODBYE PARADISE
JOHN SEALE .... CINEMATOGRAPHER
RICHARD FRANCIS-BRUCE .... FILM EDITOR

GOODBYE PEOPLE, THE
JOHN LINDLEY .... CINEMATOGRAPHER
TONY WALTON .... PRODUCTION DESIGNER
DONA GRANATA .... COSTUME DESIGNER
RICK SHAINE .... FILM EDITOR

GOODBYE PORK PIE
MICHAEL HORTON .... FILM EDITOR

GOODBYE, CHARLIE
JOHN W. HOLMES .... FILM EDITOR

GOODBYE, COLUMBUS
GERALD HIRSCHFELD .... CINEMATOGRAPHER

GOODBYE, MR. CHIPS
KEN ADAM .... PRODUCTION DESIGNER
MAURICE FOWLER .... PRODUCTION DESIGNER

GOODFELLAS
MICHAEL BALLHAUS .... CINEMATOGRAPHER
KRISTI ZEA .... PRODUCTION DESIGNER
RICHARD BRUNO .... COSTUME DESIGNER
THELMA SCHOONMAKER .... FILM EDITOR

GOONIES, THE
NICK MCLEAN .... CINEMATOGRAPHER
RICHARD CARTER .... PRODUCTION DESIGNER
J. MICHAEL RIVA .... PRODUCTION DESIGNER
RICHARD E. LA MOTTE .... COSTUME DESIGNER
MICHAEL KAHN .... FILM EDITOR

GORE VIDAL'S BILLY THE KID (TF)
DENNIS LEWISTON .... CINEMATOGRAPHER
DONALD LIGHT-HARRIS .... PRODUCTION DESIGNER

GORE VIDAL'S LINCOLN (MS)
WILLIAM WAGES .... CINEMATOGRAPHER

GORILLAS IN THE MIST
JOHN SEALE .... CINEMATOGRAPHER
JOHN GRAYSMARK .... PRODUCTION DESIGNER
KEN COURT .... PRODUCTION DESIGNER
CATHERINE LETERRIER .... COSTUME DESIGNER
STUART BAIRD .... FILM EDITOR

GORKY PARK
RALF D. BODE .... CINEMATOGRAPHER
PAUL SYLBERT .... PRODUCTION DESIGNER
RICHARD BRUNO .... COSTUME DESIGNER
DENNIS M. VIRKLER .... FILM EDITOR

GORP
MICHEL HUGO .... CINEMATOGRAPHER
WILLIAM BUTLER .... FILM EDITOR

GOSPEL (FD)
DAVID MYERS .... CINEMATOGRAPHER
GLENN FARR .... FILM EDITOR

GOSPEL ACCORDING TO VIC
MICHAEL COULTER .... CINEMATOGRAPHER
RITA MCGURN .... PRODUCTION DESIGNER
LINDY HEMMING .... COSTUME DESIGNER
JOHN GOW .... FILM EDITOR

GOTCHA!
KING BAGGOT .... CINEMATOGRAPHER
NORMAN NEWBERRY .... PRODUCTION DESIGNER
MICHAEL A. STEVENSON .... FILM EDITOR
APRIL FERRY .... COSTUME DESIGNER

GOTHAM (CTF)
MICHAEL CHAPMAN .... CINEMATOGRAPHER
CAROL SPIER .... PRODUCTION DESIGNER
LINDA MATHESON .... COSTUME DESIGNER
EVAN LOTTMAN .... FILM EDITOR

GOTHIC
MIKE SOUTHON .... CINEMATOGRAPHER
CHRISTOPHER HOBBS .... PRODUCTION DESIGNER
MICHAEL BUCHANAN .... PRODUCTION DESIGNER
VICTORIA RUSSELL .... COSTUME DESIGNER
MICHAEL BRADSELL .... FILM EDITOR

GRACE KELLY (TF)
WOODY OMENS .... CINEMATOGRAPHER
JOHN C. HORGER .... FILM EDITOR

Gr-Gr

CINEMATOGRAPHERS
PRODUCTION
DESIGNERS,
COSTUME
DESIGNERS AND
FILM EDITORS
GUIDE

I
N
D
E
X

O
F

F
I
L
M

T
I
T
L
E
S

GRACE QUIGLEY
LARRY PIZER .... CINEMATOGRAPHER
GARY WEIST .... PRODUCTION DESIGNER
RUTH MORLEY .... COSTUME DESIGNER
ROBERT REITANO .... FILM EDITOR

GRADUATE, THE
ROBERT SURTEES† .... CINEMATOGRAPHER
RICHARD SYLBERT .... PRODUCTION DESIGNER
PATRICIA ZIPPRODT .... COSTUME DESIGNER
SAM O'STEEN .... FILM EDITOR

GRADUATION DAY
DANIEL YARUSSI .... CINEMATOGRAPHER
CHRISTOPHER HENRY .... PRODUCTION DESIGNER
MARTIN JAY SADOFF .... FILM EDITOR

GRAFFITI BRIDGE
BILL BUTLER .... CINEMATOGRAPHER
VANCE LORENZINI .... PRODUCTION DESIGNER
HELEN HIATT .... COSTUME DESIGNER
REBECCA ROSS .... FILM EDITOR

GRAND PRIX
FREDRIC STEINKAMP .... FILM EDITOR

GRAND THEFT AUTO
GARY GRAVER .... CINEMATOGRAPHER

GRAND TOUR, THE (CTF)
BARBARA SCOTT .... COSTUME DESIGNER

GRANDVIEW, U.S.A.
REYNALDO VILLALOBOS .... CINEMATOGRAPHER
JAN SCOTT .... PRODUCTION DESIGNER
WAYNE FINKELMAN .... COSTUME DESIGNER
ROBERT GORDON .... FILM EDITOR

GRASS IS ALWAYS GREENER OVER THE SEPTIC TANK, THE (TF)
STEVEN B. POSTER .... CINEMATOGRAPHER

GRASSHOPPER, THE
AARON STELL .... FILM EDITOR

GRAVEYARD SHIFT
PETER STEIN .... CINEMATOGRAPHER
GARY WISSNER .... PRODUCTION DESIGNER
SARAH LEMIRE .... COSTUME DESIGNER
NORMAN SMITH .... FILM EDITOR
JIM GROSS .... FILM EDITOR
RANDY JON MORGAN .... FILM EDITOR

GRAVY TRAIN
JOHN C. HORGER .... FILM EDITOR

GRAY LADY DOWN
STEVAN LARNER .... CINEMATOGRAPHER
WILLIAM H. TUNTKE .... PRODUCTION DESIGNER
ROBERT E. SWINK .... FILM EDITOR

GREASE
BILL BUTLER .... CINEMATOGRAPHER
PHILIP JEFFRIES .... PRODUCTION DESIGNER
ALBERT WOLSKY .... COSTUME DESIGNER
JOHN F. BURNETT .... FILM EDITOR

GREASE 2
FRANK STANLEY .... CINEMATOGRAPHER
GENE CALLAHAN .... PRODUCTION DESIGNER
ROBERT DE MORA .... COSTUME DESIGNER
JOHN F. BURNETT .... FILM EDITOR

GREASED LIGHTNING
JACK SENTER .... PRODUCTION DESIGNER
CHRISTOPHER HOLMES .... FILM EDITOR
RANDY ROBERTS .... FILM EDITOR
ROBERT WYMAN .... FILM EDITOR

GREAT BALLS OF FIRE!
AFFONSO BEATO .... CINEMATOGRAPHER
DAVID NICHOLS .... PRODUCTION DESIGNER
JON SPIRSON .... PRODUCTION DESIGNER
TIM HUTCHINSON .... PRODUCTION DESIGNER
MARY KAY STOLZ .... COSTUME DESIGNER
TRACY TYNAN .... COSTUME DESIGNER
BERT LOVITT .... FILM EDITOR
LISA DAY .... FILM EDITOR
PEMBROKE J. HERRING .... FILM EDITOR

GREAT BANK HOAX, THE
WALTER LASSALLY .... CINEMATOGRAPHER
RALPH ROSENBLUM .... FILM EDITOR

GREAT BANK ROBBERY, THE
JACK POPLIN .... PRODUCTION DESIGNER

GREAT BAR 20, THE
TOM SIITER .... FILM EDITOR

GREAT BRAIN, THE
REED SMOOT .... CINEMATOGRAPHER

GREAT ESCAPE, THE
FERRIS WEBSTER .... FILM EDITOR

GREAT EXPECTATIONS (CMS)
KEITH WILSON .... PRODUCTION DESIGNER
BARRY PETERS .... FILM EDITOR

GREAT GATSBY, THE
DOUGLAS SLOCOMBE .... CINEMATOGRAPHER
GENE RUDOLF .... PRODUCTION DESIGNER
JOHN BOX .... PRODUCTION DESIGNER
ROBERT LAING .... PRODUCTION DESIGNER
THEONI V. ALDREDGE .... COSTUME DESIGNER
TOM PRIESTLEY .... FILM EDITOR

GREAT ICE RIP-OFF, THE (TF)
WILLIAM MALLEY .... PRODUCTION DESIGNER

GREAT MCCARTHY, THE
JOHN SCOTT .... FILM EDITOR

GREAT MOUSE DETECTIVE, THE (AF)
JAMES MELTON .... FILM EDITOR

GREAT MUPPET CAPER, THE
OSWALD MORRIS .... CINEMATOGRAPHER
CHARLES BISHOP .... PRODUCTION DESIGNER
HARRY LANGE .... PRODUCTION DESIGNER
TERRY ACKLAND-SNOW .... PRODUCTION DESIGNER
JULIE HARRIS .... COSTUME DESIGNER
RALPH KEMPLEN .... FILM EDITOR

GREAT OUTDOORS, THE
RIC WAITE .... CINEMATOGRAPHER
JOHN W. CORSO .... PRODUCTION DESIGNER
MARILYN VANCE-STRAKER .... COSTUME DESIGNER
SETH FLAUM .... FILM EDITOR
TOM ROLF .... FILM EDITOR
WILLIAM GORDEAN .... FILM EDITOR

GREAT RACE, THE
RALPH E. WINTERS .... FILM EDITOR

GREAT RIDE, A
DAVID WORTH .... CINEMATOGRAPHER

GREAT SANTINI, THE
RALPH WOOLSEY .... CINEMATOGRAPHER
JACK POPLIN .... PRODUCTION DESIGNER
GEORGE FOLSEY JR.* .... FILM EDITOR
HOUSELEY STEVENSON .... FILM EDITOR

GREAT SCOUT & CATHOUSE THURSDAY,THE
ALEX PHILLIPS .... CINEMATOGRAPHER
JACK MARTIN SMITH .... PRODUCTION DESIGNER
RENIE CONLEY .... COSTUME DESIGNER
SHELDON KAHN .... FILM EDITOR

GREAT SMOKEY ROADBLOCK, THE
JEAN-PIERRE DORLEAC .... COSTUME DESIGNER

GREAT TEXAS DYNAMITE CHASE, THE
MILLIE MOORE .... FILM EDITOR

GREAT TRAIN ROBBERY, THE
GEOFFREY UNSWORTH† .... CINEMATOGRAPHER
BERT DAVEY .... PRODUCTION DESIGNER
MAURICE CARTER .... PRODUCTION DESIGNER
ANTHONY MENDLESON .... COSTUME DESIGNER

GREAT WALDO PEPPER, THE
ROBERT SURTEES† .... CINEMATOGRAPHER
HENRY BUMSTEAD .... PRODUCTION DESIGNER
EDITH HEAD† .... COSTUME DESIGNER
WILLIAM REYNOLDS .... FILM EDITOR

Gr-Gu

CINEMATOGRAPHERS
PRODUCTION
DESIGNERS,
COSTUME
DESIGNERS and
FILM EDITORS
GUIDE

I
N
D
E
X

O
F

F
I
L
M

T
I
T
L
E
S

GREAT WALL, A
PETER STEIN ...... CINEMATOGRAPHER
ROBERT PRIMES ...... CINEMATOGRAPHER
GRAHAME WEINBREN ...... FILM EDITOR

GREAT WALTZ, THE
ALFRED TAYLOR ...... CINEMATOGRAPHER

GREAT WHITE HOPE, THE
JACK MARTIN SMITH ...... PRODUCTION DESIGNER
JOHN DE CUIR ...... PRODUCTION DESIGNER
WILLIAM REYNOLDS ...... FILM EDITOR

GREATEST STORY EVER TOLD, THE
WILLIAM J. CREBER ...... PRODUCTION DESIGNER
ARGYLE NELSON ...... FILM EDITOR

GREATEST, THE
HARRY STRADLING, JR. ...... CINEMATOGRAPHER
SANDRA STEWART ...... COSTUME DESIGNER
BUZZ BRANDT ...... FILM EDITOR

GREEGAGE SUMMER, THE
FREDDIE YOUNG ...... CINEMATOGRAPHER

GREEK TYCOON, THE
ANTHONY B. RICHMOND ...... CINEMATOGRAPHER
MEL BOURNE ...... PRODUCTION DESIGNER
MICHAEL STRINGER ...... PRODUCTION DESIGNER
ALAN STRACHAN ...... FILM EDITOR

GREEN CARD
GEOFFREY SIMPSON ...... CINEMATOGRAPHER
WENDY STITES ...... PRODUCTION DESIGNER
WILLIAM ANDERSON ...... FILM EDITOR

GREEN ICE
JOHN JYMPSON ...... FILM EDITOR

GREEN ROOM, THE
NESTOR ALMENDROS ...... CINEMATOGRAPHER

GREENGAGE SUMMER, THE
JOHN STOLL ...... PRODUCTION DESIGNER

GREGORY HARRISON SHOW, THE (PILOT)
ANTHONY BROCKLISS ...... PRODUCTION DESIGNER

GREGORY'S GIRL
MICHAEL COULTER ...... CINEMATOGRAPHER
ADRIENNE ATKINSON ...... PRODUCTION DESIGNER
JOHN GOW ...... FILM EDITOR

GREMLINS
JOHN HORA ...... CINEMATOGRAPHER
JAMES H. SPENCER ...... PRODUCTION DESIGNER
TINA HIRSCH ...... FILM EDITOR

GREMLINS II
JOHN HORA ...... CINEMATOGRAPHER
JAMES H. SPENCER ...... PRODUCTION DESIGNER
KENT BEYDA ...... FILM EDITOR

GREY FOX, THE
FRANK TIDY ...... CINEMATOGRAPHER
BILL BRODIE ...... PRODUCTION DESIGNER
FRANK IRVINE ...... FILM EDITOR

GREYSTOKE: THE LEGEND OF TARZAN, LORD OF THE APES
JOHN ALCOTT† ...... CINEMATOGRAPHER
SIMON HOLLAND ...... PRODUCTION DESIGNER
STUART CRAIG ...... PRODUCTION DESIGNER
NORMAN DORME ...... PRODUCTION DESIGNER
JOHN MOLLO ...... COSTUME DESIGNER
ANNE V. COATES ...... FILM EDITOR

GRIFFIN AND PHOENIX (TF)
RICHARD C. GLOUNER ...... CINEMATOGRAPHER
WILLIAM MALLEY ...... PRODUCTION DESIGNER

GRIFTERS, THE
OLIVER STAPLETON ...... CINEMATOGRAPHER
LESLIE MCDONALD ...... PRODUCTION DESIGNER
MICK AUDSLEY ...... FILM EDITOR

GRISSOM GANG, THE
FRANK J. URIOSTE ...... FILM EDITOR

GROSS ANATOMY
STEVE YACONELLI ...... CINEMATOGRAPHER
WILLIAM F. MATTHEWS ...... PRODUCTION DESIGNER
GALE PARKER SMITH ...... COSTUME DESIGNER
BUD SMITH ...... FILM EDITOR
SCOTT SMITH ...... FILM EDITOR

GROUND STAR CONSPIRACY, THE
EDWARD M. ABROMS ...... FILM EDITOR

GROUND ZERO
STEPHEN DOBSON ...... CINEMATOGRAPHER
BRIAN THOMPSON ...... PRODUCTION DESIGNER
MARGOT LINDSAY ...... COSTUME DESIGNER
DAVID PULBROCK ...... FILM EDITOR

GROUP, THE
GENE CALLAHAN ...... PRODUCTION DESIGNER
ANNA HILL JOHNSTONE ...... COSTUME DESIGNER
RALPH ROSENBLUM ...... FILM EDITOR

GROWING PAINS
JAN DE BONT ...... CINEMATOGRAPHER

GRUNT! THE WRESTLING MOVIE
EDDY VAN DER ENDEN ...... CINEMATOGRAPHER
ALLAN HOLZMAN ...... FILM EDITOR
BARRY ZETLIN ...... FILM EDITOR

GUARDIAN, THE
JOHN ALONZO ...... CINEMATOGRAPHER
GREGG FONSECA ...... PRODUCTION DESIGNER
DENISE CRONENBERG ...... COSTUME DESIGNER
SETH FLAUM ...... FILM EDITOR

GUARDIAN, THE (CTF)
TREVOR WILLIAMS ...... PRODUCTION DESIGNER

GUESS WHO'S COMING FOR CHRISTMAS (TF)
JAMES PERGOLA ...... CINEMATOGRAPHER
JOHN LEIMANIS ...... PRODUCTION DESIGNER
JANET BARTELS ...... FILM EDITOR

GUESS WHO'S COMING TO DINNER
ROBERT C. JONES ...... FILM EDITOR

GUEST, THE
LIONEL SELWYN ...... FILM EDITOR

GUIDE FOR THE MARRIEDWOMAN, A (TF)
RIC WAITE ...... CINEMATOGRAPHER

GUILTY BY SUSPICION
MICHAEL BALLHAUS ...... CINEMATOGRAPHER
LESLIE DILLEY ...... PRODUCTION DESIGNER
RICHARD BRUNO ...... COSTUME DESIGNER
PRISCILLA NEDD ...... FILM EDITOR

GUILTY CONSCIENCE
JACQUELINE SAINT ANNE ...... COSTUME DESIGNER

GUILTY OF INNOCENCE (TF)
ROBERT JESSUP ...... CINEMATOGRAPHER

GULAG (CTF)
KELVIN PIKE ...... CINEMATOGRAPHER
KEITH WILSON ...... PRODUCTION DESIGNER
JOHN JYMPSON ...... FILM EDITOR

GULLIVER'S TRAVELS
ALAN HUME ...... CINEMATOGRAPHER
MICHAEL STRINGER ...... PRODUCTION DESIGNER
ANTHONY MENDLESON ...... COSTUME DESIGNER

GUMBALL RALLY
RICHARD C. GLOUNER ...... CINEMATOGRAPHER
DODIE SHEPARD ...... COSTUME DESIGNER
STUART H. PAPPE ...... FILM EDITOR

GUMSHOE
MICHAEL SEYMOUR ...... PRODUCTION DESIGNER

GUNG HO
DONALD PETERMAN ...... CINEMATOGRAPHER
JACK G. TAYLOR ...... PRODUCTION DESIGNER
JAMES SCHOPPE ...... PRODUCTION DESIGNER
BETSY COX ...... COSTUME DESIGNER
DANIEL J. LESTER ...... COSTUME DESIGNER
DANIEL P. HANLEY ...... FILM EDITOR
MICHAEL J. HILL ...... FILM EDITOR

GUNN
PETER ZINNER .... FILM EDITOR

GUNRUNNER, THE
ALAIN DOSTIE .... CINEMATOGRAPHER
WENDELL DENNIS .... PRODUCTION DESIGNER

GUNSMOKE: THE RETURN TO DODGE (TV)
ALBERT HESCHONG .... PRODUCTION DESIGNER

GUS
FRANK PHILLIPS .... CINEMATOGRAPHER
JACK MARTIN SMITH .... PRODUCTION DESIGNER

GUYANA TRAGEDY: THE STORY OF JIM JONES (TF)
GIL HUBBS .... CINEMATOGRAPHER

GUYS AND DOLLS
IRENE SHARAFF .... COSTUME DESIGNER

GYMKATA
GODFREY A. GODAR .... CINEMATOGRAPHER
DRAGO HABAZIAN .... COSTUME DESIGNER
ROBERT A. FERRETTI .... FILM EDITOR

H

H.O.T.S.
HARVEY GENKINS .... CINEMATOGRAPHER
BARBARA POKRAS .... FILM EDITOR

H.P. LOVECRAFT'S RE-ANIMATOR
ROBERT BURNS .... PRODUCTION DESIGNER

HADLEY'S REBELLION
DAVID GOLIA .... CINEMATOGRAPHER
ERICA EDELL PHILLIPS .... COSTUME DESIGNER

HAIR
MIROSLAV ONDRICEK .... CINEMATOGRAPHER
ANN ROTH .... COSTUME DESIGNER
LYNZEE KLINGMAN .... FILM EDITOR
STANLEY WARNOW .... FILM EDITOR

HAIRSPRAY
DAVID INSLEY .... CINEMATOGRAPHER
VINCENT PERANIO .... PRODUCTION DESIGNER
VAN SMITH .... COSTUME DESIGNER
JANICE HAMPTON .... FILM EDITOR

HALF A SIXPENCE
PETER MURTON .... PRODUCTION DESIGNER
TED HAWORTH .... PRODUCTION DESIGNER

HALF MOON STREET
PETER HANNAN .... CINEMATOGRAPHER
PETER WILLIAMS .... PRODUCTION DESIGNER
ANTHONY CURTIS .... PRODUCTION DESIGNER
LOUISE FROGLEY .... COSTUME DESIGNER
RICHARD MARDEN .... FILM EDITOR

HALLOWEEN
DEAN CUNDEY .... CINEMATOGRAPHER
CRAIG STEARNS .... PRODUCTION DESIGNER
CHARLES BORNSTEIN .... FILM EDITOR

HALLOWEEN II
DEAN CUNDEY .... CINEMATOGRAPHER
J. MICHAEL RIVA .... PRODUCTION DESIGNER
MARK GOLDBLATT .... FILM EDITOR

HALLOWEEN III: SEASON OF THE WITCH
DEAN CUNDEY .... CINEMATOGRAPHER
PETER JAMISON .... PRODUCTION DESIGNER
MILLIE MOORE .... FILM EDITOR

HALLOWEEN 4: THE RETURN OF MICHAEL MYERS
PETER LYONS COLLISTER .... CINEMATOGRAPHER
CURTISS CLAYTON .... FILM EDITOR

HALLOWEEN 5
ROBERT DRAPER .... CINEMATOGRAPHER
SIMON TUKE .... COSTUME DESIGNER
JERRY BRADY .... FILM EDITOR

HALLS OF ANGER
BUD MOLIN .... FILM EDITOR

HAMBONE AND HILLIE
ROBERT KIZER .... FILM EDITOR

HAMBURGER HILL
PETER MACDONALD .... CINEMATOGRAPHER
AUSTEN SPRIGGS .... PRODUCTION DESIGNER
PETER TANNER .... PRODUCTION DESIGNER
PETER TANNER .... FILM EDITOR

HAMBURGER...THE MOTION PICTURE
KAREN GROSSMAN .... CINEMATOGRAPHER
GEORGE COSTELLO .... PRODUCTION DESIGNER
SHARI FELDMAN .... COSTUME DESIGNER
ANN E. MILLS .... FILM EDITOR
STEVEN SCHOENBERG .... FILM EDITOR

HAMLET
DAVID WATKIN .... CINEMATOGRAPHER
DANTE FERRETTI .... PRODUCTION DESIGNER
MAURIZIO MILLENOTTI .... COSTUME DESIGNER
RICHARD MARDEN .... FILM EDITOR

HAMMER
GEORGE FOLSEY JR.* .... FILM EDITOR

HAMMERSMITH IS OUT
RICHARD H. KLINE .... CINEMATOGRAPHER

HAMMETT
JOSEPH BIROC .... CINEMATOGRAPHER
PHILIP LATHROP .... CINEMATOGRAPHER
DEAN TAVOULARIS .... PRODUCTION DESIGNER
ANGELO GRAHAM .... PRODUCTION DESIGNER
LEON ERICKSON .... PRODUCTION DESIGNER
BARRY MALKIN .... FILM EDITOR
MARC LAUB .... FILM EDITOR
RANDY ROBERTS .... FILM EDITOR
ROBERT Q. LOVETT .... FILM EDITOR

HAND SIDE
MICHAEL ECONOMOU .... FILM EDITOR

HAND, THE
KING BAGGOT .... CINEMATOGRAPHER
J. MICHAEL RIVA .... PRODUCTION DESIGNER
RICHARD SAWYER .... PRODUCTION DESIGNER
VIRGINIA RANDOLPH .... PRODUCTION DESIGNER
ERNEST MISKO .... COSTUME DESIGNER
RICHARD MARKS .... FILM EDITOR

HANDFUL OF DUST, A
PETER HANNAN .... CINEMATOGRAPHER
EILEEN DISS .... PRODUCTION DESIGNER
JANE ROBINSON .... COSTUME DESIGNER
PETER COULSON .... FILM EDITOR

HANDGUN
CHARLES STEWART .... CINEMATOGRAPHER
LILLY KILVERT .... PRODUCTION DESIGNER

HANDLE WITH CARE
JORDAN CRONENWETH .... CINEMATOGRAPHER

HANDMAID'S TALE, THE
IGOR LUTHER .... CINEMATOGRAPHER
TOM WALSH .... PRODUCTION DESIGNER
COLEEN ATWOOD .... COSTUME DESIGNER
DAVID RAY .... FILM EDITOR

HANDS OF A STRANGER (TF)
LASZLO GEORGE .... CINEMATOGRAPHER

HANDS OF STEEL
GIANCARLO FERRANDO .... CINEMATOGRAPHER

HANG 'EM HIGH
RICHARD H. KLINE .... CINEMATOGRAPHER
BILL BRAME .... FILM EDITOR

HANG TOUGH
HARRY MAKIN .... CINEMATOGRAPHER
DOUGLAS HIGGINS .... PRODUCTION DESIGNER
TONY LOWER .... FILM EDITOR

HANGAR 18
PAUL HIPP .... CINEMATOGRAPHER
MICHAEL SPENCE .... FILM EDITOR

Gu-Ha

CINEMATOGRAPHERS
PRODUCTION
DESIGNERS,
COSTUME
DESIGNERS AND
FILM EDITORS
GUIDE

I
N
D
E
X

O
F

F
I
L
M

T
I
T
L
E
S

353

CINEMATOGRAPHERS
PRODUCTION
DESIGNERS,
COSTUME
DESIGNERS and
FILM EDITORS
GUIDE

I N D E X O F F I L M T I T L E S

HANGFIRE
MARK NORRIS .... CINEMATOGRAPHER
STEPHEN GREENBERG .... PRODUCTION DESIGNER
HAROLD EVANS .... COSTUME DESIGNER
PETER MARIS .... FILM EDITOR

HANGIN' WITH THE HOMEBOYS
ANGHEL DECCA .... CINEMATOGRAPHER
ISABEL BAU MADDEN .... PRODUCTION DESIGNER
MARY JANE FORT .... COSTUME DESIGNER
MICHAEL SCHWEITZER .... FILM EDITOR

HANK WILLIAMS - THE SHOW HE NEVER GAVE
BERT DUNK .... CINEMATOGRAPHER

HANKY PANKY
ARTHUR ORNITZ† .... CINEMATOGRAPHER
BEN EDWARDS .... PRODUCTION DESIGNER
CHRISTOPHER NOWAK .... PRODUCTION DESIGNER
MICHAEL BAUGH .... PRODUCTION DESIGNER
BERNARD JOHNSON .... COSTUME DESIGNER
HARRY KELLER .... FILM EDITOR

HANNA K
RICARDO ARONOVITCH .... CINEMATOGRAPHER
PIERRE GUFFROY .... PRODUCTION DESIGNER
EDITH VESPERINI .... COSTUME DESIGNER
FRANÇOISE BONNOT .... FILM EDITOR

HANNA'S WAR
ELMER RAGALYI .... CINEMATOGRAPHER
JOHN MOLLO .... COSTUME DESIGNER
ALAIN JAKUBOWICZ .... FILM EDITOR

HANNA-BARBERA HAPPYHOUR, THE (TV)
BOB MACKIE .... COSTUME DESIGNER

HANNAH AND HER SISTERS
CARLO DI PALMA .... CINEMATOGRAPHER
STUART WURTZEL .... PRODUCTION DESIGNER
JEFFREY KURLAND .... COSTUME DESIGNER
SUSAN E. MORSE .... FILM EDITOR

HANOI HILTON, THE
MARK IRWIN .... CINEMATOGRAPHER
R. CLIFFORD SEARCY .... PRODUCTION DESIGNER
RICHARD E. LA MOTTE .... COSTUME DESIGNER
PENELOPE SHAW .... FILM EDITOR

HANOVER STREET
DAVID WATKIN .... CINEMATOGRAPHER
MALCOLM MIDDLETON .... PRODUCTION DESIGNER
PHILIP HARRISON .... PRODUCTION DESIGNER
ROBERT CARTWRIGHT .... PRODUCTION DESIGNER
JOAN BRIDGE .... COSTUME DESIGNER
JAMES MITCHELL .... FILM EDITOR

HANSEL AND GRETEL
MAREK DOBROWOLSKI .... PRODUCTION DESIGNER

HANUSSEN
LAJOS KOLTAI .... CINEMATOGRAPHER

HAPPILY EVER AFTER
AFFONSO BEATO .... CINEMATOGRAPHER

HAPPY (TF)
NORM BARON .... PRODUCTION DESIGNER

HAPPY BIRTHDAY GEMINI
JAMES B. KELLEY .... CINEMATOGRAPHER
STEPHEN FANFARA .... FILM EDITOR

HAPPY BIRTHDAY TO ME
MIKLOS LENTE .... CINEMATOGRAPHER
EARL PRESTON .... PRODUCTION DESIGNER
DEBRA KAREN .... FILM EDITOR

HAPPY ENDING, THE
CONRAD HALL .... CINEMATOGRAPHER
GEORGE GRENVILLE .... FILM EDITOR

HAPPY ENDINGS (TF)
VINCENT M. CRESCIMAN .... PRODUCTION DESIGNER

HAPPY HOOKER, THE
GERALD B. GREENBERG .... FILM EDITOR

HAPPY HOOKER GOES TO HOLLYWOOD, THE
DENA ROTH .... PRODUCTION DESIGNER

HAPPY HOOKER GOES TO WASHINGTON, THE
ROBERT CARAMICO .... CINEMATOGRAPHER
BEALA B. NEEL .... PRODUCTION DESIGNER

HAPPY HOUR
JOHN DE BELLO .... FILM EDITOR

HAPPY MOTHER'S DAY - LOVE GEORGE
GEORGE GRENVILLE .... FILM EDITOR

HAPPY NEW YEAR
JAMES A. CRABE .... CINEMATOGRAPHER
WILLIAM F. MATTHEWS .... PRODUCTION DESIGNER
WILLIAM J. CASSIDY .... PRODUCTION DESIGNER
JODIE TILLEN .... COSTUME DESIGNER
MARY LOU BYRD .... COSTUME DESIGNER
JANE KURSON .... FILM EDITOR

HAPPY TOGETHER
JOE PENNELLA .... CINEMATOGRAPHER
MARCIA HINDS .... PRODUCTION DESIGNER
DONA GRANATA .... COSTUME DESIGNER
O. NICHOLAS BROWN .... FILM EDITOR

HARD CHOICES
TOM D. HURWITZ .... CINEMATOGRAPHER
DANIEL LOEWENTHAL .... FILM EDITOR

HARD CORE
PAUL SYLBERT .... PRODUCTION DESIGNER
TOM ROLF .... FILM EDITOR

HARD COUNTRY
DENNIS DALZELL .... CINEMATOGRAPHER
ED RICHARDSON .... PRODUCTION DESIGNER
JOHN A. MARTINELLI .... FILM EDITOR

HARD DAY'S NIGHT, A
GIL TAYLOR .... CINEMATOGRAPHER
RAYMOND SIMM .... PRODUCTION DESIGNER
JOHN JYMPSON .... FILM EDITOR

HARD FEELINGS
HARRY MAKIN .... CINEMATOGRAPHER
DOUGLAS HIGGINS .... PRODUCTION DESIGNER
TONY LOWER .... FILM EDITOR

HARD KNOX (TF)
RUDI FEHR .... FILM EDITOR

HARD ROCK ZOMBIES
TOM RICHMOND .... CINEMATOGRAPHER
CYNTHIA SOWDER .... PRODUCTION DESIGNER

HARD TICKET TO HAWAII
HOWARD WEXLER .... CINEMATOGRAPHER
MICHAEL HAIGHT .... FILM EDITOR

HARD TIME ON PLANET EARTH (PILOT)
FRED J. KOENEKAMP .... CINEMATOGRAPHER
JOSEPH ALTADONNA .... PRODUCTION DESIGNER
BUZZ BRANDT .... FILM EDITOR

HARD TIMES
PHILIP LATHROP .... CINEMATOGRAPHER
TREVOR WILLIAMS .... PRODUCTION DESIGNER

HARD TO HANDLE (HVD)
JOHN SCOTT .... FILM EDITOR

HARD TO HOLD
RICHARD H. KLINE .... CINEMATOGRAPHER
JOSEPH C. PACELLI .... PRODUCTION DESIGNER
PETER W. WOOLEY .... PRODUCTION DESIGNER
ROSANNA NORTON .... COSTUME DESIGNER
ROBERT WYMAN .... FILM EDITOR

HARD TO KILL
MATTHEW F. LEONETTI .... CINEMATOGRAPHER
ROBB WILSON KING .... PRODUCTION DESIGNER
JOHN F. LINK .... FILM EDITOR

HARD TRAVELING
DAVID MYERS .... CINEMATOGRAPHER
KEVIN CONSTANT .... PRODUCTION DESIGNER
KAREN MITCHELL .... COSTUME DESIGNER
SUSAN HEICK .... FILM EDITOR

HARD WAY, THE
ROBERT PRIMES ....CINEMATOGRAPHER
VICTOR J. KEMPER ....CINEMATOGRAPHER
DON MCALPINE ....CINEMATOGRAPHER
PHILIP HARRISON ....PRODUCTION DESIGNER
MARY VOGT ....COSTUME DESIGNER
FRANK MORRISS ....FILM EDITOR
TONY LOMBARDO ....FILM EDITOR

HARDBODIES
TOM RICHMOND ....CINEMATOGRAPHER
GREGG FONSECA ....PRODUCTION DESIGNER
ANDY BLUMENTHAL ....FILM EDITOR

HARDBODIES 2
TOM RICHMOND ....CINEMATOGRAPHER
ANDY BLUMENTHAL ....FILM EDITOR

HARDCORE
MICHAEL CHAPMAN ....CINEMATOGRAPHER
EDWIN O'DONOVAN ....PRODUCTION DESIGNER

HARDHAT AND LEGS (TF)
PATRIZIA VON BRANDENSTEIN ....PRODUCTION DESIGNER

HARDLY WORKING
JAMES PERGOLA ....CINEMATOGRAPHER
DON K. IVEY ....PRODUCTION DESIGNER
MICHAEL LUCIANO ....FILM EDITOR

HARDWARE
STEVE CHIVERS ....CINEMATOGRAPHER
JOSEPH BENNETT ....PRODUCTION DESIGNER
DEREK TRIGG ....FILM EDITOR

HAREM (TF)
SIMON HOLLAND ....PRODUCTION DESIGNER

HARLEM NIGHTS
WOODY OMENS ....CINEMATOGRAPHER
LAWRENCE G. PAULL ....PRODUCTION DESIGNER
JOE I. TOMPKINS ....COSTUME DESIGNER
GEORGE BOWERS ....FILM EDITOR

HARLEQUIN
BERNARD HIDES ....PRODUCTION DESIGNER
ADRIAN CARR ....FILM EDITOR

HAROLD AND MAUDE
JOHN A. ALONZO ....CINEMATOGRAPHER
MICHAEL D. HALLER ....PRODUCTION DESIGNER
WILLIAM WARE THEISS ....COSTUME DESIGNER

HARPER
CONRAD HALL ....CINEMATOGRAPHER

HARPER VALLEY P.T.A.
WILLY KURANT ....CINEMATOGRAPHER
MICHAEL ECONOMOU ....FILM EDITOR

HARRAD EXPERIMENT, THE
RICHARD H. KLINE ....CINEMATOGRAPHER
BILL BRAME ....FILM EDITOR

HARRAD SUMMER, THE
BILL BRAME ....FILM EDITOR

HARRY & SON
HENRY BUMSTEAD ....PRODUCTION DESIGNER
DEDE ALLEN ....FILM EDITOR

HARRY & WALTER GO TO NEW YORK
LASZLO KOVACS ....CINEMATOGRAPHER

HARRY AND SON
DONALD MCALPINIE ....CINEMATOGRAPHER

HARRY AND THE HENDERSONS
ALLEN DAVIAU ....CINEMATOGRAPHER
JAMES D. BISSELL ....PRODUCTION DESIGNER
DONALD B. WOODRUFF ....PRODUCTION DESIGNER
WILLIAM F. MATTHEWS ....PRODUCTION DESIGNER
MARLA DENISE SCHLOM ....COSTUME DESIGNER
PETER V. SALDUTTI ....COSTUME DESIGNER
DONN CAMBERN ....FILM EDITOR

HARRY AND TONTO
MICHAEL C. BUTLER ....CINEMATOGRAPHER
TED HAWORTH ....PRODUCTION DESIGNER
RICHARD HALSEY ....FILM EDITOR

HARRY AND WALTER GO TO NEW YORK
HARRY HORNER ....PRODUCTION DESIGNER
RICHARD BERGER ....PRODUCTION DESIGNER
DAVID BRETHERTON ....FILM EDITOR
DON GUIDICE ....FILM EDITOR
FREDRIC STEINKAMP ....FILM EDITOR

HARRY TRACY
ALLEN DAVIAU ....CINEMATOGRAPHER
KAREN BROMLEY ....PRODUCTION DESIGNER
OLGA DIMITROV ....COSTUME DESIGNER
RON WISMAN ....FILM EDITOR

HARRY'S HONG KONG (TF)
WILLIAM KENNEY ....PRODUCTION DESIGNER

HARRY'S MACHINE
RICHARD C. MEYER ....FILM EDITOR

HARRY'S WAR
REED SMOOT ....CINEMATOGRAPHER
DOUGLAS G. JOHNSON ....PRODUCTION DESIGNER
BERT LOVITT ....FILM EDITOR

HAUNTED (TF)
JACK HOFSTRA ....FILM EDITOR

HAUNTED BY HER PAST (TF)
ROY FORGE SMITH ....PRODUCTION DESIGNER

HAUNTED HONEYMOON
FRED SCHULER ....CINEMATOGRAPHER
ALAN TOMKINS ....PRODUCTION DESIGNER
TERENCE MARSH ....PRODUCTION DESIGNER
RUTH MYERS ....COSTUME DESIGNER
CHRISTOPHER GREENBURY ....FILM EDITOR

HAUNTED SUMMER
GIUSEPPE ROTUNNO ....CINEMATOGRAPHER
STEPHEN GRIMES† ....PRODUCTION DESIGNER
GABRIELLA PESCUCCI ....COSTUME DESIGNER
CESARE D'AMICO ....FILM EDITOR
RICHARD FIELDS ....FILM EDITOR

HAUNTING OF JULIA, THE
PETER HANNAN ....CINEMATOGRAPHER
BRIAN MORRIS ....PRODUCTION DESIGNER
RON WISMAN ....FILM EDITOR

HAUNTING OF M, THE
MICHAEL BOCKMAN ....FILM EDITOR

HAUNTING OF SARAH HARDY, THE (TF)
BOJAN BAZELLI ....CINEMATOGRAPHER
BERNARD GRIBBLE ....FILM EDITOR

HAVANA
OWEN ROIZMAN ....CINEMATOGRAPHER
TERENCE MARSH ....PRODUCTION DESIGNER
BERNIE POLLACK ....COSTUME DESIGNER
FREDRIC STEINKAMP ....FILM EDITOR
WILLIAM STEINKAMP ....FILM EDITOR

HAWAIIAN HEAT (TF)
CARL KRESS ....FILM EDITOR

HAWAIIANS, THE
BILL THOMAS ....COSTUME DESIGNER
RALPH E. WINTERS ....FILM EDITOR

HAWK THE SLAYER
PAUL BEESON ....CINEMATOGRAPHER
MICHAEL PICKWOAD ....PRODUCTION DESIGNER
ERIC BOYD-PERKINS ....FILM EDITOR

HAWKS
DOUGLAS MILSOME ....CINEMATOGRAPHER
PETER HOWITT ....PRODUCTION DESIGNER
CATHERINE COOKE ....COSTUME DESIGNER
MALCOLM COOKE ....FILM EDITOR

HAWMPS
DON REDDY ....CINEMATOGRAPHER
LEON SEITH ....FILM EDITOR

HAYWIRE (TF)
RENIE CONLEY ....COSTUME DESIGNER

HE KNOWS YOU'RE ALONE
GERALD FEIL ....CINEMATOGRAPHER

Ha-He

CINEMATOGRAPHERS
PRODUCTION
DESIGNERS,
COSTUME
DESIGNERS AND
FILM EDITORS
GUIDE

INDEX OF FILM TITLES

CINEMATOGRAPHERS
PRODUCTION
DESIGNERS,
COSTUME
DESIGNERS and
FILM EDITORS
GUIDE

INDEX

OF

FILM

TITLES

HE SAID, SHE SAID
STEPHEN H. BURUM .... CINEMATOGRAPHER
MICHAEL CORENBLITH .... PRODUCTION DESIGNER
DEENA APPEL .... COSTUME DESIGNER
SIDNEY LEVIN .... FILM EDITOR

HE'S FIRED, SHE'S HIRED (TF)
RICHARD LEITERMAN .... CINEMATOGRAPHER

HE'S MY GIRL
PETER LYONS COLLISTER .... CINEMATOGRAPHER
PATRICIA FIELD .... COSTUME DESIGNER
ROY WATTS .... FILM EDITOR

HE'S NOT YOUR SON (TF)
ROBERT JESSUP .... CINEMATOGRAPHER

HEAD OFFICE
GERALD HIRSCHFELD .... CINEMATOGRAPHER
ELAYNE CEDER .... PRODUCTION DESIGNER
JUDITH R. GELLMAN .... COSTUME DESIGNER
DANFORD B. GREENE .... FILM EDITOR

HEAD OVER HEELS
BOBBY BYRNE .... CINEMATOGRAPHER
PETER JAMISON .... PRODUCTION DESIGNER
ROSANNA NORTON .... COSTUME DESIGNER
CYNTHIA SCHEIDER .... FILM EDITOR

HEADIN' FOR BROADWAY
ERIC SAARINEN .... CINEMATOGRAPHER

HEALTH
EDMOND L. KOONS .... CINEMATOGRAPHER
RAJA GOSNELL .... FILM EDITOR

HEART
DARIUSZ ADAMS WOLSKI .... CINEMATOGRAPHER
JACEK LASKUS .... CINEMATOGRAPHER
VICTORIA PAUL .... PRODUCTION DESIGNER
BARBARA WEISS .... COSTUME DESIGNER
TICIA BLACKBURN .... COSTUME DESIGNER
LORENZO MARINELLI .... FILM EDITOR

HEART BEAT
LASZLO KOVACS .... CINEMATOGRAPHER
JACK FISK .... PRODUCTION DESIGNER
PATRICIA NORRIS .... COSTUME DESIGNER
ERIC JENKINS .... FILM EDITOR

HEART CONDITION
ARTHUR ALBERT .... CINEMATOGRAPHER
JOHN MUTO .... PRODUCTION DESIGNER
LOUISE FROGLEY .... COSTUME DESIGNER
DAVID FINFER .... FILM EDITOR

HEART IS A LONELY HUNTER, THE
JOHN F. BURNETT .... FILM EDITOR

HEART LIKE A WHEEL
TAK FUJIMOTO .... CINEMATOGRAPHER
JAMES WILLIAM NEWPORT .... PRODUCTION DESIGNER
WILLIAM WARE THEISS .... COSTUME DESIGNER
O. NICHOLAS BROWN .... FILM EDITOR

HEART OF DIXIE
ROBERT ELSWIT .... CINEMATOGRAPHER
GLENDA GANIS .... PRODUCTION DESIGNER
SANDRA DAVIDSON .... COSTUME DESIGNER
BONNIE KOEHLER .... FILM EDITOR

HEART OF MIDNIGHT
RAY RIVAS .... CINEMATOGRAPHER
CHRISTA MUNRO .... PRODUCTION DESIGNER
GENE RUDOLF .... PRODUCTION DESIGNER
LINDA FISHER .... COSTUME DESIGNER
PENELOPE SHAW .... FILM EDITOR

HEART OF STEEL (TF)
ROBERT W. (BO) WELCH .... PRODUCTION DESIGNER

HEART OF THE CITY (PILOT)
WOODY OMENS .... CINEMATOGRAPHER

HEART OF THE GARDEN
ARTHUR ORNITZ† .... CINEMATOGRAPHER

HEART OF THE HIGH COUNTRY (MS)
MAURICE CAIN .... PRODUCTION DESIGNER

HEART OF THE STAG
JAMES BARTLE .... CINEMATOGRAPHER
MICHAEL HORTON .... FILM EDITOR

HEARTACHES
VIC SARIN .... CINEMATOGRAPHER
GERRY HAMBLING .... FILM EDITOR
PETER BOITA .... FILM EDITOR

HEARTBEAT (HVD)
MICHAEL Z. HANAN .... PRODUCTION DESIGNER

HEARTBEEPS
CHARLES ROSHER, JR. .... CINEMATOGRAPHER
JOHN W. CORSO .... PRODUCTION DESIGNER
MADELINE ANN GRANETO .... COSTUME DESIGNER
TINA HIRSCH .... FILM EDITOR

HEARTBREAK HOTEL
STEPHEN DOBSON .... CINEMATOGRAPHER
DAN WEBSTER .... PRODUCTION DESIGNER
JOHN MUTO .... PRODUCTION DESIGNER
NORD HAGGERTY .... COSTUME DESIGNER
RAJA GOSNELL .... FILM EDITOR

HEARTBREAK KID, THE
OWEN ROIZMAN .... CINEMATOGRAPHER
RICHARD SYLBERT .... PRODUCTION DESIGNER
ANTHEA SYLBERT .... COSTUME DESIGNER

HEARTBREAK RIDGE
JACK N. GREEN .... CINEMATOGRAPHER
EDWARD C. CARFAGNO .... PRODUCTION DESIGNER
GLENN WRIGHT .... COSTUME DESIGNER
JOEL COX .... FILM EDITOR

HEARTBREAKER
MICHAEL LONZO .... CINEMATOGRAPHER
DAVID NICHOLS .... PRODUCTION DESIGNER
LARRY BOCK .... FILM EDITOR

HEARTBREAKERS
MICHAEL BALLHAUS .... CINEMATOGRAPHER
BETSY JONES .... COSTUME DESIGNER
JOHN CARNOCHEN .... FILM EDITOR

HEARTBURN
NESTOR ALMENDROS .... CINEMATOGRAPHER
JOHN KASARDA .... PRODUCTION DESIGNER
TONY WALTON .... PRODUCTION DESIGNER
ANN ROTH .... COSTUME DESIGNER
GARY JONES .... COSTUME DESIGNER
SAM O'STEEN .... FILM EDITOR

HEARTLAND
FRED MURPHY .... CINEMATOGRAPHER
PATRIZIA VON BRANDENSTEIN .... PRODUCTION DESIGNER
BILL YAHRAUS .... FILM EDITOR

HEARTS AND MINDS
LYNZEE KLINGMAN .... FILM EDITOR

HEARTS ARE TRUMP
MIKAEL SALOMON .... CINEMATOGRAPHER

HEARTS OF FIRE
ALAN HUME .... CINEMATOGRAPHER
BARBARA DUNPHY .... PRODUCTION DESIGNER
ROGER MURRAY-LEACH .... PRODUCTION DESIGNER
PIP NEWBERY .... COSTUME DESIGNER
SEAN BARTON .... FILM EDITOR

HEARTS OF THE WEST
MARIO TOSI .... CINEMATOGRAPHER
PATRICK CUMMINGS .... COSTUME DESIGNER
EDWARD A. WARSCHILKA .... FILM EDITOR

HEARTSOUNDS (TF)
RICHARD CIUPKA .... CINEMATOGRAPHER
JUDITH R. GELLMAN .... COSTUME DESIGNER
JOHN WRIGHT .... FILM EDITOR

HEAT
JAMES A. CONTNER .... CINEMATOGRAPHER
NORMAN SALLING .... COSTUME DESIGNER
JEFFREY WOLF .... FILM EDITOR

HEAT AND DUST
WALTER LASSALLY .... CINEMATOGRAPHER
MAURICE FOWLER .... PRODUCTION DESIGNER
RAM YEDEKER .... PRODUCTION DESIGNER
WILFRED SHINGLETON .... PRODUCTION DESIGNER
BARBARA LANE .... COSTUME DESIGNER
HUMPHREY DIXON .... FILM EDITOR

HEAT OF DESIRE
JOELE VAN EFFENTERRE .... FILM EDITOR

HEAT OF THE DAY, THE (TF)
CHRISTOPHER J. BRADSHAW .... PRODUCTION DESIGNER
ANDREW SUMNER .... FILM EDITOR

HEAT WAVE (CTF)
MARK IRWIN .... CINEMATOGRAPHER
RICHARD HOOVER .... PRODUCTION DESIGNER
DEBRA NEIL .... FILM EDITOR

HEAT, THE (PILOT)
MICHAEL HELMY .... PRODUCTION DESIGNER
GEOFFREY ROWLAND .... FILM EDITOR
RICHARD E. RABJOHN .... FILM EDITOR

HEATED VENGEANCE
RICHARD HALSEY .... FILM EDITOR

HEATHERS
FRANCIS KENNEY .... CINEMATOGRAPHER
JON HUTMAN .... PRODUCTION DESIGNER
RUDY DILLON .... COSTUME DESIGNER
NORMAN HOLLYN .... FILM EDITOR

HEATWAVE
VINCENT MONTON .... CINEMATOGRAPHER
ROSS MAJOR .... PRODUCTION DESIGNER
TERRY RYAN .... COSTUME DESIGNER
JOHN SCOTT .... FILM EDITOR

HEAVEN
FREDERICK ELMES .... CINEMATOGRAPHER

HEAVEN (FD)
BARBARA LING .... PRODUCTION DESIGNER
PAUL BARNES .... FILM EDITOR

HEAVEN BECOMES HELL
LARRY REVENE .... CINEMATOGRAPHER

HEAVEN CAN WAIT
WILLIAM A. FRAKER .... CINEMATOGRAPHER
EDWIN O'DONOVAN .... PRODUCTION DESIGNER
PAUL SYLBERT .... PRODUCTION DESIGNER
RICHARD BRUNO .... COSTUME DESIGNER
DON ZIMMERMAN .... FILM EDITOR
ROBERT C. JONES .... FILM EDITOR

HEAVEN HELP US
MIROSLAV ONDRICEK .... CINEMATOGRAPHER
MICHAEL MOLLY .... PRODUCTION DESIGNER
JOSEPH G. AULISI .... COSTUME DESIGNER
STEPHEN A. ROTTER .... FILM EDITOR

HEAVEN'S GATE
VILMOS ZSIGMOND .... CINEMATOGRAPHER
MAURICE FOWLER .... PRODUCTION DESIGNER
TAMBI LARSEN .... PRODUCTION DESIGNER
SPENCER DEVERILL .... PRODUCTION DESIGNER
J. ALLEN HIGHFILL† .... COSTUME DESIGNER
GERALD B. GREENBERG .... FILM EDITOR
LISA FRUCHTMAN .... FILM EDITOR
TOM ROLF .... FILM EDITOR
WILLIAM REYNOLDS .... FILM EDITOR

HEAVENLY BODIES
THOMAS BURSTYN .... CINEMATOGRAPHER
LINDSEY GODDARD .... PRODUCTION DESIGNER
SEAMUS FLANNERY .... PRODUCTION DESIGNER
JULIE GANTON .... COSTUME DESIGNER
ROBERT K. LAMBERT .... FILM EDITOR

HEAVENLY KID, THE
STEVEN B. POSTER .... CINEMATOGRAPHER
RON HOBBS .... PRODUCTION DESIGNER
MARY LOU BYRD .... COSTUME DESIGNER
CHRISTOPHER GREENBURY .... FILM EDITOR

HEDDA
DOUGLAS SLOCOMBE .... CINEMATOGRAPHER
PETER TANNER .... FILM EDITOR

HEIRESS, THE
EDITH HEAD† .... COSTUME DESIGNER

HELD HOSTAGE: THE SIS AND JERRY LEVIN STORY (TF)
DAVID GURFINKEL .... CINEMATOGRAPHER
ARIEL ROSHKO .... PRODUCTION DESIGNER
GLENDA GANIS .... PRODUCTION DESIGNER
STAN WARNOW .... FILM EDITOR

HELEN KELLER - THE MIRACLE CONTINUES (TF)
FRANK WATTS .... CINEMATOGRAPHER
ROGER HALL .... PRODUCTION DESIGNER

HELL HIGH
STEVEN FIERBERG .... CINEMATOGRAPHER
CLAIRE SIMPSON-CROZIER .... FILM EDITOR

HELL IN THE PACIFIC
CONRAD HALL .... CINEMATOGRAPHER
ANTHONY PRATT .... PRODUCTION DESIGNER

HELL NIGHT
MAC AHLBERG .... CINEMATOGRAPHER
STEVEN LEGLER .... PRODUCTION DESIGNER
TONY DI MARCO .... FILM EDITOR

HELL SQUAD
ROBERT ERNST .... FILM EDITOR

HELL'S ANGELS ON WHEELS
LASZLO KOVACS .... CINEMATOGRAPHER

HELL'S BLOODY DEVILS
ROBERT KINOSHITA .... PRODUCTION DESIGNER

HELLBOUND: HELLRAISER 2
ROBIN VIDGEON .... CINEMATOGRAPHER
MICHAEL BUCHANAN .... PRODUCTION DESIGNER

HELLFIGHTERS
VINCENT SAIZIS .... CINEMATOGRAPHER

HELLHOLE
STEPHEN L. POSEY .... CINEMATOGRAPHER

HELLO AGAIN
JAN WEINCKE .... CINEMATOGRAPHER
EDWARD PISONI .... PRODUCTION DESIGNER
WILLIAM BARCLAY .... PRODUCTION DESIGNER
RUTH MORLEY .... COSTUME DESIGNER
TRUDY SHIP .... FILM EDITOR

HELLO AGAIN
PETER C. FRANK .... FILM EDITOR

HELLO MARY LOU: PROM NIGHT II
JOHN HERZOG .... CINEMATOGRAPHER
SANDY KYBARTAS .... PRODUCTION DESIGNER
NICK ROTUNDO .... FILM EDITOR

HELLO DOLLY!
HERMAN A. BLUMENTHAL .... PRODUCTION DESIGNER
JACK MARTIN SMITH .... PRODUCTION DESIGNER
JOHN DE CUIR .... PRODUCTION DESIGNER
IRENE SHARAFF .... COSTUME DESIGNER
WILLIAM REYNOLDS .... FILM EDITOR

HELLRAISER
ROBIN VIDGEON .... CINEMATOGRAPHER
DAVID WORLEY .... CINEMATOGRAPHER
JOCELYN JAMES .... PRODUCTION DESIGNER
MICHAEL BUCHANAN .... PRODUCTION DESIGNER
JOANNA JOHNSTON .... COSTUME DESIGNER
RICHARD MARDEN .... FILM EDITOR

HELP!
DAVID WATKIN .... CINEMATOGRAPHER
RAYMOND SIMM .... PRODUCTION DESIGNER
JOHN VICTOR SMITH .... FILM EDITOR

HENNESSY
RAYMOND SIMM .... PRODUCTION DESIGNER
JOHN STOLL .... PRODUCTION DESIGNER
ERIC BOYD-PERKINS .... FILM EDITOR

CINEMATOGRAPHERS
PRODUCTION
DESIGNERS,
COSTUME
DESIGNERS AND
FILM EDITORS
GUIDE

INDEX OF FILM TITLES

He-Hi

**CINEMATOGRAPHERS
PRODUCTION
DESIGNERS,
COSTUME
DESIGNERS** and
**FILM EDITORS
GUIDE**

I
N
D
E
X

O
F

F
I
L
M

T
I
T
L
E
S

358

HIGH ROAD TO CHINA
RONNIE TAYLOR .... CINEMATOGRAPHER
GEORGE RICHARDSON .... PRODUCTION DESIGNER
ROBERT LAING .... PRODUCTION DESIGNER
BETSY HEIMANN .... COSTUME DESIGNER
JOHN JYMPSON .... FILM EDITOR

HIGH SEASON
CHRIS MENGES .... CINEMATOGRAPHER
ANDREW MCALPINE .... PRODUCTION DESIGNER
GABRIELLA CRISTIANI .... FILM EDITOR

HIGH SPIRITS
ALEX THOMSON .... CINEMATOGRAPHER
ALAN TOMKINS .... PRODUCTION DESIGNER
ANTON FURST .... PRODUCTION DESIGNER
LESLIE TOMKINS .... PRODUCTION DESIGNER
EMMA PORTEUS .... COSTUME DESIGNER
MICHAEL BRADSELL .... FILM EDITOR

HIGH TIDE
RUSSELL BOYD .... CINEMATOGRAPHER
SALLY CAMPBELL .... PRODUCTION DESIGNER
TERRY RYAN .... COSTUME DESIGNER
NICHOLAS BEAUMAN .... FILM EDITOR

HIGH-BALLIN
RENE VERZIER .... CINEMATOGRAPHER
ERIC WRATE .... FILM EDITOR

HIGHER EDUCATION
BRENTON SPENCER .... CINEMATOGRAPHER

HIGHLANDER
GERRY FISHER .... CINEMATOGRAPHER
ALLAN CAMERON .... PRODUCTION DESIGNER
TIM HUTCHINSON .... PRODUCTION DESIGNER
GILLY HEBDEN .... COSTUME DESIGNER
JAMES ACHESON .... COSTUME DESIGNER
PETER HONESS .... FILM EDITOR

HIGHPOINT
BERT DUNK .... CINEMATOGRAPHER
SEAMUS FLANNERY .... PRODUCTION DESIGNER
PATTI UNGER .... COSTUME DESIGNER
ERIC WRATE .... FILM EDITOR

HIGHWAYMAN, THE (TF)
JOHN M. STEPHENS .... CINEMATOGRAPHER

HIJACKING OF THE ACHILLE LAURO, THE (TF)
VINCENT MONTON .... CINEMATOGRAPHER
ROSS MAJOR .... PRODUCTION DESIGNER
ROBERT K. LAMBERT .... FILM EDITOR

HILLS HAVE EYES, THE
ERIC SAARINEN .... CINEMATOGRAPHER
ROBERT BURNS .... PRODUCTION DESIGNER

HILLS HAVE EYES, PART II, THE
ROBB WILSON KING .... PRODUCTION DESIGNER

HINDENBERG, THE
ROBERT SURTEES† .... CINEMATOGRAPHER
EDWARD C. CARFAGNO .... PRODUCTION DESIGNER
DONN CAMBERN .... FILM EDITOR

HIRED HAND, THE
VILMOS ZSIGMOND .... CINEMATOGRAPHER
LAWRENCE G. PAULL .... PRODUCTION DESIGNER

HIROSHIMA: OUT OF THE ASHES (TF)
NEIL ROACH .... CINEMATOGRAPHER
WILLIAM CRUISE .... PRODUCTION DESIGNER
ROBERT FLORIO .... FILM EDITOR

HIS MISTRESS (TV)
ANN LAMBERT .... COSTUME DESIGNER

HISTORY OF THE WORD, PART I
WOODY OMENS .... CINEMATOGRAPHER
HAROLD MICHELSON .... PRODUCTION DESIGNER
NORMAN NEWBERRY .... PRODUCTION DESIGNER
PATRICIA NORRIS .... COSTUME DESIGNER
JOHN C. HOWARD .... FILM EDITOR

HIT LIST
DAVID KERN .... FILM EDITOR

HIT!
ARGYLE NELSON .... FILM EDITOR

HIT, THE
JOHN A. ALONZO .... CINEMATOGRAPHER
ANDREW SANDERS .... PRODUCTION DESIGNER
MARIT ALLEN .... COSTUME DESIGNER
MICK AUDSLEY .... FILM EDITOR

HITCHER, THE
JOHN SEALE .... CINEMATOGRAPHER
DENNIS GASSNER .... PRODUCTION DESIGNER
FRANK J. URIOSTE .... FILM EDITOR

HITLER'S DAUGHTER (CTF)
FRANK TIDY .... CINEMATOGRAPHER
TONY HALL .... PRODUCTION DESIGNER
SCOTT SMITH .... FILM EDITOR

HITLER'S S.S.: PORTRAIT IN EVIL (TF)
EILEEN DISS .... PRODUCTION DESIGNER
LIZ WALLER .... COSTUME DESIGNER
JOHN SHIRLEY .... FILM EDITOR

HOG WILD
RENE VERZIER .... CINEMATOGRAPHER
CAROL SPIER .... PRODUCTION DESIGNER

HOLCROFT COVENANT, THE
GERRY FISHER .... CINEMATOGRAPHER
BRIAN ACKLAND-SNOW .... PRODUCTION DESIGNER
PETER MULLINS .... PRODUCTION DESIGNER
DEREK HYDE .... COSTUME DESIGNER
RALPH SHELDON .... FILM EDITOR

HOLLYWOOD BOULEVARD
JAMIE ANDERSON .... CINEMATOGRAPHER
AMY JONES .... FILM EDITOR

HOLLYWOOD HIGH PART II
GARY GRAVER .... CINEMATOGRAPHER
WARREN CHADWICK .... FILM EDITOR

HOLLYWOOD KNIGHTS
WILLIAM A. FRAKER .... CINEMATOGRAPHER
DAVID WORTH .... CINEMATOGRAPHER
LEE FISCHER .... PRODUCTION DESIGNER
DARRYL LEVINE .... COSTUME DESIGNER
DANFORD B. GREENE .... FILM EDITOR
SCOTT CONRAD .... FILM EDITOR
STANFORD C. ALLEN .... FILM EDITOR

HOLLYWOOD ON TRIAL (FD)
BARRY ABRAMS .... CINEMATOGRAPHER

HOLLYWOOD SHUFFLE
PETER DEMING .... CINEMATOGRAPHER
MELBA FARQUHAR .... PRODUCTION DESIGNER
ANDRE ALLEN .... COSTUME DESIGNER
W.O. GARRETT .... FILM EDITOR

HOLLYWOOD VICE SQUAD
JOHN HENDRICKS .... CINEMATOGRAPHER
MICHAEL CORENBLITH .... PRODUCTION DESIGNER
JILL OHANNESON .... COSTUME DESIGNER
JOHN BOWEY .... FILM EDITOR

HOLLYWOOD ZAP
TOM FRASER .... CINEMATOGRAPHER
JUDITH BREWER CURTIS .... COSTUME DESIGNER
RICHARD E. WESTOVER .... FILM EDITOR

HOLOCAUST (MS)
BRIAN WEST .... CINEMATOGRAPHER

HOME ALONE
JULIO MACAT .... CINEMATOGRAPHER
JOHN MUTO .... PRODUCTION DESIGNER
JAY HURLEY .... COSTUME DESIGNER
RAJA GOSNELL .... FILM EDITOR

HOME FIRES (CTF)
NICHOLAS C. SMITH .... FILM EDITOR

HOME FIRES BURNING (TF)
CHARLES BENNETT .... PRODUCTION DESIGNER
PAUL RUBELL .... FILM EDITOR

HOME FREE ALL
DANIEL LOEWENTHAL .... FILM EDITOR

Hi-Ho

CINEMATOGRAPHERS
PRODUCTION
DESIGNERS,
COSTUME
DESIGNERS AND
FILM EDITORS
GUIDE

INDEX OF FILM TITLES

359

Ho-Ho

CINEMATOGRAPHERS
PRODUCTION
DESIGNERS,
COSTUME
DESIGNERS and
FILM EDITORS
GUIDE

I
N
D
E
X

O
F

F
I
L
M

T
I
T
L
E
S

HOME IS WHERE THE HART IS
ROBERT ENNIS .... CINEMATOGRAPHER
JILL SCOTT .... PRODUCTION DESIGNER
JANE STILL .... COSTUME DESIGNER
MICHAEL TODD .... FILM EDITOR

HOME MOVIES
JAMES L. CARTER .... CINEMATOGRAPHER

HOME OF THE BRAVE
JOHN LINDLEY .... CINEMATOGRAPHER
DAVID GROPMAN .... PRODUCTION DESIGNER
SUSAN HILFERT .... COSTUME DESIGNER
LISA DAY .... FILM EDITOR

HOME REMEDY
PAMELA S. ARNOLD .... FILM EDITOR

HOME ROOM (PILOT)
RUTH E. CARTER .... COSTUME DESIGNER

HOMEBODIES
ISIDORE MANKOFSKY .... CINEMATOGRAPHER

HOMEBOY
GALE TATTERSALL .... CINEMATOGRAPHER
BRIAN MORRIS .... PRODUCTION DESIGNER
RAY LOVEJOY .... FILM EDITOR

HOMER
KAREN BROMLEY .... PRODUCTION DESIGNER

HOMER AND EDDIE
LAJOS KOLTAI .... CINEMATOGRAPHER
MICHAEL LEVESQUE .... PRODUCTION DESIGNER
HENRY RICHARDSON .... FILM EDITOR

HOMETOWN BOY MAKES GOOD (CTF)
GREGORY M. CUMMINS .... CINEMATOGRAPHER

HOMETOWN, U.S.A.
FRANK MORRISS .... FILM EDITOR

HOMEWARD BOUND (TF)
WILILAM HINEY .... PRODUCTION DESIGNER
HARRY KERAMIDAS .... FILM EDITOR

HOMEWORK
PAUL H. GOLDSMITH .... CINEMATOGRAPHER

HOMICIDE
ROGER DEAKINS .... CINEMATOGRAPHER
MICHAEL MERRITT .... PRODUCTION DESIGNER
NAN CIBULA .... COSTUME DESIGNER
BARBARA TULLIVER .... FILM EDITOR

HONEY POT, THE
JOHN DE CUIR .... PRODUCTION DESIGNER

HONEY, I SHRUNK THE KIDS
HIRO NARITA .... CINEMATOGRAPHER
GREGG FONSECA .... PRODUCTION DESIGNER
JOHN IACOVELLI .... PRODUCTION DESIGNER
CAROL BROLASKI .... COSTUME DESIGNER
MICHAEL A. STEVENSON .... FILM EDITOR

HONEYMOON ACADEMY
JOHN CABRERA .... CINEMATOGRAPHER
HUBERT C. DE LA BOUILLERIE .... FILM EDITOR

HONEYMOON KILLERS, THE
STANLEY WARNOW .... FILM EDITOR

HONEYSUCKLE ROSE
ROBBY MULLER .... CINEMATOGRAPHER
JOEL SCHILLER .... PRODUCTION DESIGNER
JO YNOCENCIO .... COSTUME DESIGNER
EVAN LOTTMAN .... FILM EDITOR
MARC LAUB .... FILM EDITOR
NORMAN GAY .... FILM EDITOR

HONKY
JIM BENSON .... FILM EDITOR

HONKY TONK FREEWAY
JOHN BAILEY .... CINEMATOGRAPHER
EDWIN O'DONOVAN .... PRODUCTION DESIGNER
FERDINANDO SCARFIOTTI .... PRODUCTION DESIGNER
ANN ROTH .... COSTUME DESIGNER
JIM CLARK .... FILM EDITOR

HONKY TONK MAN
BRUCE SURTEES .... CINEMATOGRAPHER
EDWARD C. CARFAGNO .... PRODUCTION DESIGNER
FERRIS WEBSTER .... FILM EDITOR
JOEL COX .... FILM EDITOR

HONOR BOUND
JOHN JYMPSON .... FILM EDITOR

HONORARY CONSUL, THE
PHIL MEHEUX .... CINEMATOGRAPHER
STUART BAIRD .... FILM EDITOR

HOODLUM PRIEST, THE
HASKELL WEXLER .... CINEMATOGRAPHER

HOODWINK
DEAN SEMLER .... CINEMATOGRAPHER

HOOPER
BOBBY BYRNE .... CINEMATOGRAPHER
HILYARD BROWN .... PRODUCTION DESIGNER
NORMAN SALLING .... COSTUME DESIGNER
DONN CAMBERN .... FILM EDITOR

HOORAY FOR HOLLYWOOD
BUD FRIEDGEN .... FILM EDITOR
MICHAEL J. SHERIDAN .... FILM EDITOR

HOOSIERS
FRED MURPHY .... CINEMATOGRAPHER
DAVID LUBIN .... PRODUCTION DESIGNER
DAVID NICHOLS .... PRODUCTION DESIGNER
JANE ANDERSON .... COSTUME DESIGNER
CARROLL TIMOTHY O'MEARA .... FILM EDITOR

HOPE AND GLORY
PHILIPPE ROUSSELOT .... CINEMATOGRAPHER
ANTHONY PRATT .... PRODUCTION DESIGNER
SHIRLEY RUSSELL .... COSTUME DESIGNER
IAN CRAFFORD .... FILM EDITOR

HOPSCOTCH
ARTHUR IBBETSON .... CINEMATOGRAPHER
WILLIAM J. CREBER .... PRODUCTION DESIGNER
CARL KRESS .... FILM EDITOR

HORROR PLANET
JOHN METCALFE .... CINEMATOGRAPHER
PETER BOYLE .... FILM EDITOR

HORROR SHOW, THE
MAC AHLBERG .... CINEMATOGRAPHER

HORSE'S MOUTH
ARTHUR IBBETSON .... CINEMATOGRAPHER

HORSEMAN, THE
HAROLD F. KRESS .... FILM EDITOR

HOSPITAL MASSACRE
NICHOLAS VON STERNBERG .... CINEMATOGRAPHER

HOSPITAL, THE
VICTOR J. KEMPER .... CINEMATOGRAPHER
GENE RUDOLF .... PRODUCTION DESIGNER

HOSTAGE: DALLAS
RICHARD JAMES .... PRODUCTION DESIGNER

HOT CHILD IN THE CITY
RICHARD C. GLOUNER .... CINEMATOGRAPHER

HOT DOG...THE MOVIE
PAUL G. RYAN .... CINEMATOGRAPHER
DON DE FINA .... PRODUCTION DESIGNER
STEPHEN E. RIVKIN .... FILM EDITOR
GEORGE HIVELY .... FILM EDITOR

HOT LEAD AND COLD FEET
FRANK PHILLIPS .... CINEMATOGRAPHER
JOHN B. MANSBRIDGE .... PRODUCTION DESIGNER
RON TALSKY .... COSTUME DESIGNER

HOT MOVES
GEORGE COSTELLO .... PRODUCTION DESIGNER

HOT PAINT (TF)
MADELINE ANN GRANETO .... COSTUME DESIGNER

HOT POTATO
RONALD VICTOR GARCIA .... CINEMATOGRAPHER
PETER E. BERGER .... FILM EDITOR

HOT PURSUIT
FRANK TIDY .... CINEMATOGRAPHER
WILLIAM J. CREBER .... PRODUCTION DESIGNER
TARYN DECHELLIS .... COSTUME DESIGNER
MITCHELL SINOWAY .... FILM EDITOR

HOT RESORT
FRANK FLYNN .... CINEMATOGRAPHER
BRENT SCHOENFIELD .... FILM EDITOR

HOT ROD (TF)
MICHAEL BAUGH .... PRODUCTION DESIGNER

HOT SPOT, THE
UELI STEIGER .... CINEMATOGRAPHER
CARY WHITE .... PRODUCTION DESIGNER
MARY KAY STOLZ .... COSTUME DESIGNER
WENDE PHIFER MATE .... FILM EDITOR

HOT STUFF
JAMES PERGOLA .... CINEMATOGRAPHER

HOT TARGET
ALEC MILLS .... CINEMATOGRAPHER
JOSEPHINE FORD .... PRODUCTION DESIGNER
MICHAEL HORTON .... FILM EDITOR

HOT TO TROT
VICTOR J. KEMPER .... CINEMATOGRAPHER
WILLIAM F. MATTHEWS .... PRODUCTION DESIGNER
DANIEL J. LESTER .... COSTUME DESIGNER
FRANK MORRISS .... FILM EDITOR

HOT TOMORROWS
JACQUES HAITKIN .... CINEMATOGRAPHER

HOTEL
SAM O'STEEN .... FILM EDITOR

HOTEL COLONIAL
GIUSEPPE ROTUNNO .... CINEMATOGRAPHER
NINO BARAGLI .... FILM EDITOR

HOTEL DU LAC (TF)
KENNETH MACMILLAN .... CINEMATOGRAPHER

HOTEL NEW HAMPSHIRE, THE
DAVID WATKIN .... CINEMATOGRAPHER
JOHN MEIGHEN .... PRODUCTION DESIGNER
ROBERT K. LAMBERT .... FILM EDITOR

HOTEL NEW YORK
SUZANNE FENN .... FILM EDITOR

HOTEL TERMINUS: KLAUS BARBIE, HIS LIFE AND TIMES (FD)
ALBERT JURGENSON .... FILM EDITOR
CATHERINE ZINA .... FILM EDITOR

HOUND OF THE BASKERVILLES, THE
DICK BUSH .... CINEMATOGRAPHER
ROY FORGE SMITH .... PRODUCTION DESIGNER
CHARLES KNODE .... COSTUME DESIGNER
GLENN HYDE .... FILM EDITOR
MALCOLM COOKE .... FILM EDITOR
RICHARD MARDEN .... FILM EDITOR

HOUR OF THE ASSASSIN
CUSI BARRIO .... CINEMATOGRAPHER
WILIAM FLICKER .... FILM EDITOR

HOUR OF THE STAR
CLOVIS BUENO .... PRODUCTION DESIGNER

HOUSE
MAC AHLBERG .... CINEMATOGRAPHER
GREGG FONSECA .... PRODUCTION DESIGNER
BERNADETTE O'BRIEN .... COSTUME DESIGNER
MICHAEL KNUE .... FILM EDITOR

HOUSE II: THE SECOND STORY
MAC AHLBERG .... CINEMATOGRAPHER
GREGG FONSECA .... PRODUCTION DESIGNER
MARTY NICHOLSON .... FILM EDITOR

HOUSE BY THE LAKE, THE
ROBERT SAAD .... CINEMATOGRAPHER
ROY FORGE SMITH .... PRODUCTION DESIGNER

HOUSE CALLS
DAVID M. WALSH .... CINEMATOGRAPHER
HENRY BUMSTEAD .... PRODUCTION DESIGNER
EDWARD A. WARSCHILKA .... FILM EDITOR

HOUSE OF GAMES
JUAN RUIZ-ANCHIA .... CINEMATOGRAPHER
MICHAEL MERRITT .... PRODUCTION DESIGNER
TRUDY SHIP .... FILM EDITOR

HOUSE OF GOD, THE
GERALD HIRSCHFELD .... CINEMATOGRAPHER
WILLIAM MALLEY .... PRODUCTION DESIGNER
BILLY WEBER .... FILM EDITOR
ROBERT WYMAN .... FILM EDITOR

HOUSE OF THE LONG SHADOWS
NORMAN LANGLEY .... CINEMATOGRAPHER
ROBERT DEARBERG .... FILM EDITOR

HOUSE OF THE RISING SUN
AMIR MOKRI .... CINEMATOGRAPHER

HOUSE OF USHER, THE
JOSSI WEIN .... CINEMATOGRAPHER
LEONARDO COEN CAGLI .... PRODUCTION DESIGNER
DIANNA CILLIERS .... COSTUME DESIGNER
MICHAEL J. DUTHIE .... FILM EDITOR

HOUSE ON CARROLL STREET, THE
MICHAEL BALLHAUS .... CINEMATOGRAPHER
WRAY STEVEN GRAHAM .... PRODUCTION DESIGNER
STUART WURTZEL .... PRODUCTION DESIGNER
RITA RYACK .... COSTUME DESIGNER
RAY LOVEJOY .... FILM EDITOR

HOUSE ON CHELOUCHE STREET, THE
DOV HOENIG .... FILM EDITOR

HOUSE ON SORORITY ROW, THE
TIM SUHRSTEDT .... CINEMATOGRAPHER
VINCENT PERANIO .... PRODUCTION DESIGNER

HOUSE ON TELEGRAPH HILL, THE
JOHN DE CUIR .... PRODUCTION DESIGNER

HOUSE PARTY
PETER DEMING .... CINEMATOGRAPHER
BRYAN JONES .... PRODUCTION DESIGNER
HAROLD EVANS .... COSTUME DESIGNER
EARL WATSON .... FILM EDITOR

HOUSE WHERE DEATH LIVES, THE
STEPHEN L. POSEY .... CINEMATOGRAPHER
STEVEN LEGLER .... PRODUCTION DESIGNER
ROBERT LEIGHTON .... FILM EDITOR

HOUSE WHERE EVIL DWELLS, THE
JACQUES HAITKIN .... CINEMATOGRAPHER
BARRY PETERS .... FILM EDITOR

HOUSEKEEPER, THE
DAVID HERRINGTON .... CINEMATOGRAPHER
LINDA MATHESON .... COSTUME DESIGNER
STAN COLE .... FILM EDITOR

HOUSEKEEPING
MICHAEL COULTER .... CINEMATOGRAPHER
ADRIENNE ATKINSON .... PRODUCTION DESIGNER
MARY-JANE REYNER .... COSTUME DESIGNER
MICHAEL ELLIS .... FILM EDITOR

HOUSTON KNIGHTS (PILOT)
ROY H. WAGNER .... CINEMATOGRAPHER

HOUSTON: THE LEGEND OF TEXAS (TF)
FRANK WATTS .... CINEMATOGRAPHER

HOW I GOT INTO COLLEGE
ROBERT ELWSIT .... CINEMATOGRAPHER
IDA RANDOM .... PRODUCTION DESIGNER
TARYN DECHELLIS .... COSTUME DESIGNER
KAJA FEHR .... FILM EDITOR
SONYA SONES TRAMER .... FILM EDITOR

HOW SWEET IT IS!
BUD MOLIN .... FILM EDITOR

Ho-Ho

CINEMATOGRAPHERS
PRODUCTION
DESIGNERS,
COSTUME
DESIGNERS AND
FILM EDITORS
GUIDE

Ho-Hy

CINEMATOGRAPHERS
PRODUCTION
DESIGNERS,
COSTUME
DESIGNERS and
FILM EDITORS
GUIDE

I
N
D
E
X

O
F

F
I
L
M

T
I
T
L
E
S

I

I AM THE CHEESE
DAVID QUAID .... CINEMATOGRAPHER
NICHOLAS C. SMITH .... FILM EDITOR

I COME IN PEACE
MARK IRWIN .... CINEMATOGRAPHER
NINO CANDIDO .... PRODUCTION DESIGNER
JOSEPH PORRO .... COSTUME DESIGNER
MARK HELFRICH .... FILM EDITOR

I CONFESS
TED HAWORTH .... PRODUCTION DESIGNER

I DREAM OF JEANNIE: 15 YEARS LATER (TV)
JEF BILLINGS .... COSTUME DESIGNER

I KNOW MY FIRST NAME IS STEVEN (TF)
ERIC VAN HAREN NOMAN .... CINEMATOGRAPHER
W. STEWART CAMPBELL .... PRODUCTION DESIGNER
DAVID RAMIREZ .... FILM EDITOR

I LIVE IN FEAR
SHINOBU MURAKI .... PRODUCTION DESIGNER
YOSHIRO MURAKI .... PRODUCTION DESIGNER

I LOVE YOU TO DEATH
OWEN ROIZMAN .... CINEMATOGRAPHER
LILLY KILVERT .... PRODUCTION DESIGNER
AGGIE GUERARD RODGERS .... COSTUME DESIGNER
ANNE V. COATES .... FILM EDITOR

I LOVE YOU, ALICE B. TOKLAS
PATO GUZMAN .... PRODUCTION DESIGNER
ROBERT C. JONES .... FILM EDITOR

I LOVE YOU, ROSA
DOV HOENIG .... FILM EDITOR

I MARRIED A SHADOW
BERNARD ZITZERMANN .... CINEMATOGRAPHER

I NEVER PROMISED YOU A ROSE GARDEN
BRUCE LOGAN .... CINEMATOGRAPHER
J. MICHAEL RIVA .... PRODUCTION DESIGNER
TOBY CARR RAFELSON .... PRODUCTION DESIGNER
JANE RUHM .... COSTUME DESIGNER
GARTH CRAVEN .... FILM EDITOR

I OUGHT TO BE IN PICTURES
DAVID M. WALSH .... CINEMATOGRAPHER
ALBERT BRENNER .... PRODUCTION DESIGNER
RUTH MORLEY .... COSTUME DESIGNER
SIDNEY LEVIN .... FILM EDITOR

I SAW WHAT YOU DID (TF)
WOODY OMENS .... CINEMATOGRAPHER
JAMES G. HULSEY .... PRODUCTION DESIGNER

I SENT A LETTER TO MY LOVER
FRANÇOISE BONNOT .... FILM EDITOR

I WALK THE LINE
DAVID M. WALSH .... CINEMATOGRAPHER
HAROLD F. KRESS .... FILM EDITOR

I WANNA HOLD YOUR HAND
DONALD M. MORGAN .... CINEMATOGRAPHER
PETER JAMISON .... PRODUCTION DESIGNER
ROSANNA NORTON .... COSTUME DESIGNER
FRANK MORRISS .... FILM EDITOR

I WANT TO LIVE (TF)
CHARLES F. WHEELER .... CINEMATOGRAPHER
TED HAWORTH .... PRODUCTION DESIGNER
PATRICK CUMMINGS .... COSTUME DESIGNER

I WAS A TEENAGE T.V. TERRORIST
LISA RINZLER .... CINEMATOGRAPHER

I WILL, I WILL FOR NOW
JOHN A. ALONZO .... CINEMATOGRAPHER
FERNANDO CARRERE .... PRODUCTION DESIGNER
ROBERT LAWRENCE .... FILM EDITOR

I WONDER WHO'S KILLING HER NOW?
BEALA B. NEEL .... PRODUCTION DESIGNER

I'LL BE HOME FOR CHRISTMAS (TF)
PAUL LOHMANN .... CINEMATOGRAPHER
BRAD R. LOMAN .... COSTUME DESIGNER

I'LL TAKE MANHATTAN (MS)
STEVEN B. POSTER .... CINEMATOGRAPHER

I'LL TAKE ROMANCE (TF)
PAUL MURPHY .... CINEMATOGRAPHER
CARMI GALLO .... PRODUCTION DESIGNER
PAMELA MALOUF .... FILM EDITOR

I'M DANCING AS FAST AS I CAN
JAN DE BONT .... CINEMATOGRAPHER
DAVID JENKINS .... PRODUCTION DESIGNER
JULIE WEISS .... COSTUME DESIGNER
MICHAEL BRADSELL .... FILM EDITOR

I'M DANGEROUS TONIGHT (CTF)
LEVIE ISAACS .... CINEMATOGRAPHER
LEONARD MAZZOLA .... PRODUCTION DESIGNER
CARL KRESS .... FILM EDITOR

I'M GONNA GIT YOU SUCKA
TOM RICHMOND .... CINEMATOGRAPHER
MELBA FARQUHAR .... PRODUCTION DESIGNER
CATHERINE HARDWICKE .... PRODUCTION DESIGNER
RUTH E. CARTER .... COSTUME DESIGNER
MICHAEL R. MILLER .... FILM EDITOR

I'VE HEARD THE MERMAIDS SINGING
DOUGLAS KOCH .... CINEMATOGRAPHER
VALANNE RIDGEWAY .... PRODUCTION DESIGNER
PATRICIA ROZEMA .... FILM EDITOR

I, MADMAN
BRYAN ENGLAND .... CINEMATOGRAPHER
MATTHEW JACOBS .... PRODUCTION DESIGNER
RON WILSON .... PRODUCTION DESIGNER
MARCUS MANTON .... FILM EDITOR

I, THE JURY
ANDREW LASZLO .... CINEMATOGRAPHER
ROBERT GUNDLACH .... PRODUCTION DESIGNER
CELIA BRYANT .... COSTUME DESIGNER
GARTH CRAVEN .... FILM EDITOR

ICE CASTLES
BILL BUTLER .... CINEMATOGRAPHER
JOEL SCHILLER .... PRODUCTION DESIGNER
RICHARD BRUNO .... COSTUME DESIGNER
MAURY WINETROBE .... FILM EDITOR
MELVIN SHAPIRO .... FILM EDITOR
MICHAEL KAHN .... FILM EDITOR

ICE HOUSE
BROWN COOPER .... CINEMATOGRAPHER
LYNN RUTH APPEL .... PRODUCTION DESIGNER

ICE PIRATES, THE
MATTHEW F. LEONETTI .... CINEMATOGRAPHER
DAVID M. HABER .... PRODUCTION DESIGNER
RONALD KENT FOREMAN .... PRODUCTION DESIGNER
DANIEL PAREDES .... COSTUME DESIGNER
TOM WALLS .... FILM EDITOR

ICEHOUSE
JOHN MURRAY .... FILM EDITOR

ICEMAN
IAN BAKER .... CINEMATOGRAPHER
JOSAN F. RUSSO .... PRODUCTION DESIGNER
LEON ERICKSON .... PRODUCTION DESIGNER
RONDI JOHNSON .... COSTUME DESIGNER
BILLY WEBER .... FILM EDITOR

ICEMAN COMETH, THE
RALPH WOOLSEY .... CINEMATOGRAPHER
JACK MARTIN SMITH .... PRODUCTION DESIGNER
HAROLD F. KRESS .... FILM EDITOR

IDAHO TRANSFER
BRUCE LOGAN .... CINEMATOGRAPHER

IDI AMIN DAD (FD)
NESTOR ALMENDROS .... CINEMATOGRAPHER

IDIOT, THE
SHINOBU MURAKI .... PRODUCTION DESIGNER
YOSHIRO MURAKI .... PRODUCTION DESIGNER

CINEMATOGRAPHERS
PRODUCTION
DESIGNERS,
COSTUME
DESIGNERS AND
FILM EDITORS
GUIDE

INDEX OF FILM TITLES

Id-In

CINEMATOGRAPHERS
PRODUCTION
DESIGNERS,
COSTUME
DESIGNERS AND
FILM EDITORS
GUIDE

I
N
D
E
X

O
F

F
I
L
M

T
I
T
L
E
S

IDOLMAKER, THE
ADAM HOLENDER .... CINEMATOGRAPHER
DAVID L. SNYDER .... PRODUCTION DESIGNER
RITA RIGGS .... COSTUME DESIGNER
NEIL TRAVIS .... FILM EDITOR

IF EVER I SEE YOU AGAIN
ADAM HOLENDER .... CINEMATOGRAPHER
RICK SHAINE .... FILM EDITOR

IF LOOKS COULD KILL
DOUG MILSOME .... CINEMATOGRAPHER
GUY J. COMTOIS .... PRODUCTION DESIGNER
MARY MCLEOD .... COSTUME DESIGNER
JOHN F. LINK .... FILM EDITOR

IF THINGS WERE DIFFERENT (TF)
SYDNEY Z. LITWAK .... PRODUCTION DESIGNER

IF YOU COULD SEE WHAT I HEAR
HARRY MAKIN .... CINEMATOGRAPHER

IF...
MIROSLAV ONDRICEK .... CINEMATOGRAPHER

IKE (MS)
FREDDIE YOUNG .... CINEMATOGRAPHER
PETER MURTON .... PRODUCTION DESIGNER
WARD PRESTON .... PRODUCTION DESIGNER

IKIRU
SHINOBU MURAKI .... PRODUCTION DESIGNER
YOSHIRO MURAKI .... PRODUCTION DESIGNER

IL SECRETO DEL SAHARA (MS)
DANTE FERRETTI .... PRODUCTION DESIGNER

ILL FARES THE LAND
LESLEY WALKER .... FILM EDITOR

ILLEGALLY YOURS
DANTE SPINOTTI .... CINEMATOGRAPHER
JANE MUSKY .... PRODUCTION DESIGNER
NANCY G. FOX .... COSTUME DESIGNER
RICHARD FIELDS .... FILM EDITOR
RONALD KREHEL .... FILM EDITOR

ILLUSIONIST, THE
THEO VAN DE SANDE .... CINEMATOGRAPHER

ILLUSIONS (TF)
BERT DUNK .... CINEMATOGRAPHER

ILLUSTRATED MAN, THE
JOEL SCHILLER .... PRODUCTION DESIGNER

ILLUSTRIOUS CORPSES
PASQUALINO DE SANTIS .... CINEMATOGRAPHER
RUGGERO MASTROIANNI .... FILM EDITOR

IMAGE MAKER, THE
JACQUES HAITKIN .... CINEMATOGRAPHER
EDWARD PISONI .... PRODUCTION DESIGNER

IMAGES
VILMOS ZSIGMOND .... CINEMATOGRAPHER

IMAGINE: JOHN LENNON (FD)
BERT LOVITT .... FILM EDITOR

IMMEDIATE FAMILY
JOHN W. LINDLEY .... CINEMATOGRAPHER
DAVID WILSON .... PRODUCTION DESIGNER
MARK S. FREEBORN .... PRODUCTION DESIGNER
APRIL FERRY .... COSTUME DESIGNER
JANE KURSON .... FILM EDITOR

IMMORTAL BACHELOR, THE
PASQUALINO DE SANTIS .... CINEMATOGRAPHER

IMMORTAL STORY, THE
WILLY KURANT .... CINEMATOGRAPHER

IMPOSTER, THE (TF)
MILLIE MOORE .... FILM EDITOR

IMPOSTERS
FRED MURPHY .... CINEMATOGRAPHER

IMPROMPTU
BRUNO DE KEYZER .... CINEMATOGRAPHER
GERARD DAOUDAL .... PRODUCTION DESIGNER
JENNY BEAVAN .... COSTUME DESIGNER
MICHAEL ELLIS .... FILM EDITOR

IMPROPER CHANNELS
ANTHONY B. RICHMOND .... CINEMATOGRAPHER
THOM NOBLE .... FILM EDITOR

IMPULSE
DEAN SEMLER .... CINEMATOGRAPHER
THOMAS DEL RUTH .... CINEMATOGRAPHER
JACK T. COLLIS .... PRODUCTION DESIGNER
WILLIAM A. ELLIOT .... PRODUCTION DESIGNER
DAVID HOLDEN .... FILM EDITOR

IN A SHALLOW GRAVE
JERZY ZIELINSKI .... CINEMATOGRAPHER
DAVID WASCO .... PRODUCTION DESIGNER
SHARON SEYMOUR .... PRODUCTION DESIGNER
NICHOLAS C. SMITH .... FILM EDITOR

IN BROAD DAYLIGHT (TF)
ROBERT DRAPER .... CINEMATOGRAPHER
JOHN FRICK .... PRODUCTION DESIGNER
SCOTT VICKREY .... FILM EDITOR

IN CELEBRATION
DICK BUSH .... CINEMATOGRAPHER

IN COLD BLOOD
CONRAD HALL .... CINEMATOGRAPHER
PETER ZINNER .... FILM EDITOR

IN COUNTRY
RUSSELL BOYD .... CINEMATOGRAPHER
JACKSON DE GOVIA .... PRODUCTION DESIGNER
AGGIE GUERARD RODGERS .... COSTUME DESIGNER
LOU LOMBARDO .... FILM EDITOR

IN CROWD, THE
JOSEPH T. GARRITY .... PRODUCTION DESIGNER
PETER MITCHELL .... COSTUME DESIGNER
JEFFREY WOLF .... FILM EDITOR

IN DEFENSE OF A MARRIED MAN (TF)
FRANCOIS PROTAT .... CINEMATOGRAPHER
DAVID DAVIS .... PRODUCTION DESIGNER
RALPH BRUNJES .... FILM EDITOR

IN GOD WE TRUST
CHARLES CORRELL .... CINEMATOGRAPHER
DAVID L. SNYDER .... PRODUCTION DESIGNER
LAWRENCE G. PAULL .... PRODUCTION DESIGNER
RUTH MYERS .... COSTUME DESIGNER
DAVID BLEWITT .... FILM EDITOR

IN HER OWN TIME (FD)
SUZANNE PETTIT .... FILM EDITOR

IN LIKE FLINT
VINCENT SAIZIS .... CINEMATOGRAPHER

IN LIKE FLYNN (TF)
RENE VERZIER .... CINEMATOGRAPHER

IN LOVE AND WAR (TF)
GAYNE RESCHER .... CINEMATOGRAPHER
DEBORAH LA GORGE KRAMER .... COSTUME DESIGNER

IN OUR HANDS (FD)
OLIVER WOOD .... CINEMATOGRAPHER
STANLEY WARNOW .... FILM EDITOR

IN PRAISE OF OLDER WOMEN
MIKLOS LENTE .... CINEMATOGRAPHER
WOLF KROEGER .... PRODUCTION DESIGNER
OLGA DIMITROV .... COSTUME DESIGNER

IN SEARCH OF HISTORIC JESUS
PAUL HIPP .... CINEMATOGRAPHER

IN SEARCH OF NOAH'S ARK
RICHARD SAWYER .... PRODUCTION DESIGNER

IN SELF DEFENSE (TF)
PAUL ONORATO .... CINEMATOGRAPHER

In-In

CINEMATOGRAPHERS
PRODUCTION
DESIGNERS,
COSTUME
DESIGNERS AND
FILM EDITORS
GUIDE

I
N
D
E
X

O
F

F
I
L
M

T
I
T
L
E
S

CINEMATOGRAPHERS
PRODUCTION
DESIGNERS,
COSTUME
DESIGNERS and
FILM EDITORS
GUIDE

I
N
D
E
X

O
F

F
I
L
M

T
I
T
L
E
S

INSIDERS, THE (PILOT)
ANDREW DINTENFASS .... CINEMATOGRAPHER

INSIGNIFICANCE
PETER HANNAN .... CINEMATOGRAPHER
DAVID BROCKHURST .... PRODUCTION DESIGNER
SHUNA HARWOOD .... COSTUME DESIGNER
TONY LAWSON .... FILM EDITOR

INSPECTOR CLOUSEAU
ARTHUR IBBETSON .... CINEMATOGRAPHER

INSPECTOR MORSE
LAURENCE MERY CLARK .... FILM EDITOR

INSTANT KARMA
THOMAS JEWETT .... CINEMATOGRAPHER
GEORGE EDWARDS .... PRODUCTION DESIGNER
FRANK MAZZOLA .... FILM EDITOR

INTENT TO KILL (TF)
ROBERT JESSUP .... CINEMATOGRAPHER

INTERIORS
GORDON WILLIS .... CINEMATOGRAPHER
MEL BOURNE .... PRODUCTION DESIGNER
RALPH ROSENBLUM .... FILM EDITOR

INTERNAL AFFAIRS
JOHN ALONZO .... CINEMATOGRAPHER
WALDEMAR KALINOWSKI .... PRODUCTION DESIGNER
RUDY DILLON .... COSTUME DESIGNER
ROBERT ESTRIN .... FILM EDITOR

INTERNATIONAL VELVET
TONY IMI .... CINEMATOGRAPHER
KEITH WILSON .... PRODUCTION DESIGNER
TIMOTHY GEE .... FILM EDITOR

INTERNECINE PROJECT, THE
GEOFFREY UNSWORTH† .... CINEMATOGRAPHER

INTERVIEWS WITH MY LAI VETERANS
HASKELL WEXLER .... CINEMATOGRAPHER

INTIMATE CONTACT (MS)
MAURICE CAIN .... PRODUCTION DESIGNER
LIZ WALLER .... COSTUME DESIGNER
LAURENCE MERY CLARK .... FILM EDITOR

INTO THE HOMELAND
EVE NEWMAN .... FILM EDITOR

INTO THE NIGHT
ROBERT PAYNTER .... CINEMATOGRAPHER
JOHN J. LLOYD .... PRODUCTION DESIGNER
DEBORAH NADOOLMAN .... COSTUME DESIGNER
MALCOLM CAMPBELL .... FILM EDITOR

INTO THIN AIR (TF)
ERIC SEARS .... FILM EDITOR

INTRODUCTION TO THE ENEMY
HASKELL WEXLER .... CINEMATOGRAPHER

INVADERS FROM MARS
DANIEL PEARL .... CINEMATOGRAPHER
CRAIG STEARNS .... PRODUCTION DESIGNER
LESLIE DILLEY .... PRODUCTION DESIGNER
CARIN HOOPER .... COSTUME DESIGNER
ALAIN JAKUBOWICZ .... FILM EDITOR

INVASION EARTH: THE ALIENS ARE HERE
MICHAEL NOVOTNY .... PRODUCTION DESIGNER
VICKI GRAEF .... COSTUME DESIGNER

INVASION OF THE BODY SNATCHERS
MICHAEL CHAPMAN .... CINEMATOGRAPHER
CHARLES ROSEN .... PRODUCTION DESIGNER
TED HAWORTH .... PRODUCTION DESIGNER
DOUGLAS STEWART .... FILM EDITOR

INVASION U.S.A.
JOAO FERNANDES .... CINEMATOGRAPHER
LADISLAV WILHELM .... PRODUCTION DESIGNER
FRED LONG .... COSTUME DESIGNER
DANIEL LOEWENTHAL .... FILM EDITOR
SCOTT VICKREY .... FILM EDITOR

INVISIBLE KID, THE
MICHAEL BARNARD .... CINEMATOGRAPHER
GABRIELLE GILBERT .... FILM EDITOR

INVITATION TO A GUNFIGHTER
ROBERT C. JONES .... FILM EDITOR

INVITATION TO HELL
DEAN CUNDEY .... CINEMATOGRAPHER

INVITATION TO THE WEDDING
FREDDIE YOUNG .... CINEMATOGRAPHER
ANDREW MOLLO .... PRODUCTION DESIGNER
GERRY HAMBLING .... FILM EDITOR

IPCRESS FILE, THE
KEN ADAM .... PRODUCTION DESIGNER
PETER MURTON .... PRODUCTION DESIGNER

IRISHMAN, THE
PETER JAMES .... CINEMATOGRAPHER
GRAHAM GRACE WALKER .... PRODUCTION DESIGNER
TIM WELLBURN .... FILM EDITOR

IRON EAGLE
ROBB WILSON KING .... PRODUCTION DESIGNER
GEORGE GRENVILLE .... FILM EDITOR

IRON EAGLE II
ALAIN DOSTIE .... CINEMATOGRAPHER
ROBB WILSON KING .... PRODUCTION DESIGNER
SYLVIE KRASKER .... COSTUME DESIGNER
RIT WALLIS .... FILM EDITOR

IRON MAZE
MORIO SAEGUSA .... CINEMATOGRAPHER
BONNIE KOEBLER .... FILM EDITOR

IRON TRIANGLE, THE
IRV GOODNOFF .... CINEMATOGRAPHER
ERROLL KELLY .... PRODUCTION DESIGNER
ROY WATTS .... FILM EDITOR

IRONWEED
LAURO ESCOREL .... CINEMATOGRAPHER
JENNINE CLAUDIA OPPEWALL .... PRODUCTION DESIGNER
ROBERT GUERRA .... PRODUCTION DESIGNER
JOSEPH G. AULISI .... COSTUME DESIGNER
ANNE GOURSAUD .... FILM EDITOR

IRRECONCILABLE DIFFERENCES
WILLIAM A. FRAKER .... CINEMATOGRAPHER
IDA RANDOM .... PRODUCTION DESIGNER
JOE I. TOMPKINS .... COSTUME DESIGNER
JOHN F. BURNETT .... FILM EDITOR

ISABEL'S CHOICE (TF)
FRANK BEASCOECHEA .... CINEMATOGRAPHER

ISADORA
DICK BUSH .... CINEMATOGRAPHER
LARRY PIZER .... CINEMATOGRAPHER
RUTH MYERS .... COSTUME DESIGNER

ISHI, THE LAST OF HIS TRIBE (TF)
WOODY OMENS .... CINEMATOGRAPHER

ISHTAR
BILL GROOM .... PRODUCTION DESIGNER
PAUL SYLBERT .... PRODUCTION DESIGNER
VICTORIA PAUL .... PRODUCTION DESIGNER
ANTHONY POWELL .... COSTUME DESIGNER
RICHARD P. CIRINCIONE .... FILM EDITOR
STEPHEN A. ROTTER .... FILM EDITOR
WILLIAM REYNOLDS .... FILM EDITOR

ISLAND AT THE TOP OF THE WORLD, THE
JOHN B. MANSBRIDGE .... PRODUCTION DESIGNER

ISLAND IN THE SUN
JOHN DE CUIR .... PRODUCTION DESIGNER

ISLAND OF DR. MOREAU, THE
GERRY FISHER .... CINEMATOGRAPHER
PHILIP JEFFRIES .... PRODUCTION DESIGNER
EMMA PORTEUS .... COSTUME DESIGNER
RICHARD E. LA MOTTE .... COSTUME DESIGNER
MARION ROTHMAN .... FILM EDITOR

ISLAND, THE
HENRI DECAE† .... CINEMATOGRAPHER
DALE HENNESY† .... PRODUCTION DESIGNER
ANN ROTH .... COSTUME DESIGNER
RICHARD A. HARRIS .... FILM EDITOR

ISLANDS IN THE STREAM
FRED J. KOENEKAMP .... CINEMATOGRAPHER
WILLIAM J. CREBER .... PRODUCTION DESIGNER
ROBERT E. SWINK .... FILM EDITOR

ISHTAR
VITTORIO STORARO .... CINEMATOGRAPHER

IT CAME FROM HOLLYWOOD (FD)
FRED J. KOENEKAMP .... CINEMATOGRAPHER
JANICE HAMPTON .... FILM EDITOR
BERT LOVITT .... FILM EDITOR

IT CAME UPON A MIDNIGHT CLEAR (TF)
DEAN CUNDEY .... CINEMATOGRAPHER

IT COULDN'T HAPPEN TO A NICER GUY (TF)
CHRISTOPHER HOLMES .... FILM EDITOR

IT HAD TO BE YOU
BART LAU .... CINEMATOGRAPHER
STEPHEN WOLF .... PRODUCTION DESIGNER
LESLIE HERMAN .... COSTUME DESIGNER
TOM FINAN .... FILM EDITOR

IT HAPPENED HERE
PETER SUSCHITZKY .... CINEMATOGRAPHER

IT TAKES A LOT OF LOVE
TIMOTHY GALFAS .... CINEMATOGRAPHER

IT TAKES TWO
PETER DEMING .... CINEMATOGRAPHER
RICHARD HOOVER .... PRODUCTION DESIGNER
REVE RICHARDS .... COSTUME DESIGNER
DAVID GARFIELD .... FILM EDITOR

IT WILL STAND (TF)
VICTORIA PAUL .... PRODUCTION DESIGNER

IT'S A FUNNY, FUNNY WORLD
ADAM GREENBERG .... CINEMATOGRAPHER
ALAIN JAKUBOWICZ .... FILM EDITOR

IT'S A MAD, MAD, MAD, MAD WORLD
GENE FOWLER JR. .... FILM EDITOR

IT'S ALIVE: ISLAND OF THE ALIVE
DAVID KERN .... FILM EDITOR

IT'S ALIVE III: ISLAND OF THE ALIVE
DANIEL PEARL .... CINEMATOGRAPHER

IT'S MY TURN
BILL BUTLER .... CINEMATOGRAPHER
JACKSON DE GOVIA .... PRODUCTION DESIGNER
RUTH MYERS .... COSTUME DESIGNER
BUZZ BRANDT .... FILM EDITOR
JAMES COBLENTZ .... FILM EDITOR

IT'S NEVER TOO LATE
TEO ESCAMILLA .... CINEMATOGRAPHER

IT'S NOT THE SIZE THAT COUNTS
TONY IMI .... CINEMATOGRAPHER
ROY WATTS .... FILM EDITOR

IT'S SHOWTIME
ALAN HOLZMAN .... FILM EDITOR
PETER E. BERGER .... FILM EDITOR

IZZIE & MOE (TF)
PETER STEIN .... CINEMATOGRAPHER

J

J. EDGAR HOOVER (CTF)
WARD PRESTON .... PRODUCTION DESIGNER
PATRICK KENNEDY .... FILM EDITOR

J.D.'S REVENGE
GEORGE FOLSEY JR.* .... FILM EDITOR

JABBERWOCKY
TERRY BEDFORD .... CINEMATOGRAPHER
MILLY BURNS .... PRODUCTION DESIGNER
ROY FORGE SMITH .... PRODUCTION DESIGNER
CHARLES KNODE .... COSTUME DESIGNER
MICHAEL BRADSELL .... FILM EDITOR

JACK THE RIPPER (MS)
ALAN HUME .... CINEMATOGRAPHER
ANTHONY READING .... PRODUCTION DESIGNER
JOHN BLEZARD .... PRODUCTION DESIGNER
KEITH PALMER .... FILM EDITOR

JACK'S BACK
SHELLY JOHNSON .... CINEMATOGRAPHER
PIERS PLOWDEN .... PRODUCTION DESIGNER
HARRY B. MILLER, III .... FILM EDITOR

JACKIE COLLINS' 'LUCKY CHANCES'-PARTS I-III (MS)
GAYNE RESCHER .... CINEMATOGRAPHER
JAN SCOTT .... PRODUCTION DESIGNER
JAMES GALLOWAY .... FILM EDITOR
LES GREEN .... FILM EDITOR
SUSAN HEICK .... FILM EDITOR

JACKNIFE
BRIAN WEST .... CINEMATOGRAPHER
EDWARD PISONI .... PRODUCTION DESIGNER
JOHN BLOOM .... FILM EDITOR

JACKSON COUNTY JAIL
BRUCE LOGAN .... CINEMATOGRAPHER
CAROLINE BIGGERSTAFF .... FILM EDITOR

JACOB TWO-TWO MEETS THE HOODED FANG
FRANCOIS PROTAT .... CINEMATOGRAPHER
SEAMUS FLANNERY .... PRODUCTION DESIGNER
STAN COLE .... FILM EDITOR

JACOB'S LADDER
JEFFREY L. KIMBALL .... CINEMATOGRAPHER
BRIAN MORRIS .... PRODUCTION DESIGNER
ELLEN MIROJNICK .... COSTUME DESIGNER
TOM ROLF .... FILM EDITOR

JACQUELINE BOUVIER KENNEDY (TF)
ISIDORE MANKOFSKY .... CINEMATOGRAPHER
MICHAEL BAUGH .... PRODUCTION DESIGNER
TRAVILLA .... COSTUME DESIGNER

JACQUELINE SUSANN'S ONCE IS NOT ENOUGH
JOHN DE CUIR .... PRODUCTION DESIGNER
RITA ROLAND .... FILM EDITOR

JACQUELINE SUSANN'S VALLEY OF THE DOLLS (TF)
JAN SCOTT .... PRODUCTION DESIGNER

JAGGED EDGE
MATTHEW F. LEONETTI .... CINEMATOGRAPHER
GENE CALLAHAN .... PRODUCTION DESIGNER
PETER LANDSDOWN SMITH .... PRODUCTION DESIGNER
ANN ROTH .... COSTUME DESIGNER
CONRAD BUFF IV .... FILM EDITOR
SEAN BARTON .... FILM EDITOR

JAGUAR LIVES
JOHN CABRERA .... CINEMATOGRAPHER
ANGELO ROSS .... FILM EDITOR

JAILBIRDS (TF)
BOB BRING .... FILM EDITOR

JAKE AND THE FATMAN (PILOT)
JEAN-PIERRE DORLEAC .... COSTUME DESIGNER

Is-Ja

CINEMATOGRAPHERS
PRODUCTION
DESIGNERS,
COSTUME
DESIGNERS AND
FILM EDITORS
GUIDE

INDEX OF FILM TITLES

CINEMATOGRAPHERS
PRODUCTION
DESIGNERS,
COSTUME
DESIGNERS AND
FILM EDITORS
GUIDE

Jo-Ju

CINEMATOGRAPHERS
PRODUCTION
DESIGNERS,
COSTUME
DESIGNERS AND
FILM EDITORS
GUIDE

I
N
D
E
X

O
F

F
I
L
M

T
I
T
L
E
S

CINEMATOGRAPHERS
PRODUCTION
DESIGNERS,
COSTUME
DESIGNERS AND
FILM EDITORS
GUIDE

**I
N
D
E
X

O
F

F
I
L
M

T
I
T
L
E
S**

KEY EXCHANGE
FRED MURPHY .... CINEMATOGRAPHER
DAVID GROPMAN .... PRODUCTION DESIGNER
RUTH MORLEY .... COSTUME DESIGNER
JILL SAVITT .... FILM EDITOR

KEY TO REBECCA, THE (TF)
MARIO VULPIANI .... CINEMATOGRAPHER

KGB—THE SECRET WAR
PHILIP J.C. DUFFIN .... PRODUCTION DESIGNER

KHARTOUM
HARRY WAXMAN .... CINEMATOGRAPHER
JOHN STOLL .... PRODUCTION DESIGNER

KICKBOXER
JONKRANHOUSE .... CINEMATOGRAPHER
SHAY AUSTIN .... PRODUCTION DESIGNER

KID BLUE
BILLY WILLIAMS .... CINEMATOGRAPHER
JOEL SCHILLER .... PRODUCTION DESIGNER

KID FROM NOT-SO-BIG, THE
DURINDA RICE WOOD .... COSTUME DESIGNER

KID FROM NOWHERE, THE (TF)
IDA RANDOM .... PRODUCTION DESIGNER

KID WHO LOVED CHRISTMAS, THE (TF)
HANANIA BAER .... CINEMATOGRAPHER
LINDA SUTTON .... PRODUCTION DESIGNER
BERT GLASTEIN .... FILM EDITOR

KID WITH THE 200 I.Q., THE
CHESTER KACZENSKI .... PRODUCTION DESIGNER

KIDCO
PAUL LOHMANN .... CINEMATOGRAPHER
FRED PRICE .... PRODUCTION DESIGNER
WILLIAM WARE THEISS .... COSTUME DESIGNER

KIDNAPPED
TOM DENOVE .... CINEMATOGRAPHER

KIDNAPPING OF THE PRESIDENT, THE
MIKE MOLLOY .... CINEMATOGRAPHER
DOUGLAS HIGGINS .... PRODUCTION DESIGNER

KIDS ARE ALRIGHT, THE (FD)
ANTHONY B. RICHMOND .... CINEMATOGRAPHER

KIDS AT RISK: NOBODY LISTENS! (PILOT)
KEITH L. REAMER .... FILM EDITOR

KIDS DON'T TELL (TF)
JOHN CARTWRIGHT .... PRODUCTION DESIGNER
RANDY ROBERTS .... FILM EDITOR

KILL AND KILL AGAIN
ROBERT LEIGHTON .... FILM EDITOR

KILL CRAZY
BRUCE L. FINN .... CINEMATOGRAPHER
MARK SIMON .... PRODUCTION DESIGNER
ZACK DAVIS .... FILM EDITOR

KILL ME AGAIN
JACQUES STEYN .... CINEMATOGRAPHER
MICHELLE MINCH .... PRODUCTION DESIGNER
FRANK J. JIMINEZ .... FILM EDITOR
JACQUES STEYN .... FILM EDITOR
JONATHAN SHAW .... FILM EDITOR

KILLBOTS
TOM RICHMOND .... CINEMATOGRAPHER
KATIE SPARKS .... COSTUME DESIGNER
LESLIE ROSENTHAL .... FILM EDITOR

KILLER AMONG US, A (TF)
THOMAS NEUWIRTH .... CINEMATOGRAPHER
GREG J. GRANDE .... PRODUCTION DESIGNER
RICHARD BRACKEN .... FILM EDITOR

KILLER CLOWNS
PHILIP DEAN FOREMAN .... PRODUCTION DESIGNER

KILLER ELITE, THE
PHILIP LATHROP .... CINEMATOGRAPHER
TED HAWORTH .... PRODUCTION DESIGNER
GARTH CRAVEN .... FILM EDITOR

KILLER FISH
ALBERTO SPAGNOLI .... CINEMATOGRAPHER

KILLER IN THE FAMILY, A (TF)
HANANIA BAER .... CINEMATOGRAPHER

KILLER INSIDE ME, THE
WILLIAM A. FRAKER .... CINEMATOGRAPHER
AARON STELL .... FILM EDITOR
DANFORD B. GREENE .... FILM EDITOR

KILLER PARTY
JOHN LINDLEY .... CINEMATOGRAPHER
REUBEN FREED .... PRODUCTION DESIGNER
GINA KIELLERMAN .... COSTUME DESIGNER
ERIC ALBERTSON .... FILM EDITOR

KILLER, THE
PETER PAO .... CINEMATOGRAPHER
WONG WING HANG .... CINEMATOGRAPHER
LUK MAN WAH .... PRODUCTION DESIGNER
FAN KUNG MING .... FILM EDITOR

KILLERS, THE
STUART H. PAPPE .... FILM EDITOR

KILLING AFFAIR, A
DOMINIQUE CHAPIUS .... CINEMATOGRAPHER
JOHN JAY MOORE .... PRODUCTION DESIGNER
ELIZABETH ANN SELEY .... COSTUME DESIGNER
PATRICK MCMAHON .... FILM EDITOR

KILLING DAD
GABRIEL BERISTAIN .... CINEMATOGRAPHER
EDWARD MARNIER .... FILM EDITOR

KILLING FIELDS, THE
CHRIS MENGES .... CINEMATOGRAPHER
ROGER MURRAY-LEACH .... PRODUCTION DESIGNER
ROY WALKER .... PRODUCTION DESIGNER
STEVE SPENCE .... PRODUCTION DESIGNER
JUDY MOORCROFT .... COSTUME DESIGNER
JIM CLARK .... FILM EDITOR

KILLING FLOOR, THE (TF)
JANE KURSON .... FILM EDITOR

KILLING HOUR, THE
LARRY PIZER .... CINEMATOGRAPHER

KILLING KIND
MARIO TOSI .... CINEMATOGRAPHER

KILLING OF A CHINESE BOOKIE, THE
FREDERICK ELMES .... CINEMATOGRAPHER
BRYAN RYMAN .... PRODUCTION DESIGNER

KILLING OF ANGEL STREET, THE
PETER JAMES .... CINEMATOGRAPHER
TIM WELLBURN .... FILM EDITOR

KILLING TIME, THE
PAUL H. GOLDSMITH .... CINEMATOGRAPHER
BERNT AMADEUS CAPRA .... PRODUCTION DESIGNER
JEAN-PIERRE DORLEAC .... COSTUME DESIGNER
LORENZO DE STEFANO .... FILM EDITOR

KILLJOY (TF)
ROBERT B. HAUSER .... CINEMATOGRAPHER

KIM (TF)
MICHAEL REED .... CINEMATOGRAPHER
ROGER HALL .... PRODUCTION DESIGNER
JOHN SHIRLEY .... FILM EDITOR

KIND OF LOVING, A
RAYMOND SIMM .... PRODUCTION DESIGNER

KINDERGARTEN COP
MICHAEL CHAPMAN .... CINEMATOGRAPHER
BRUNO RUBEO .... PRODUCTION DESIGNER
GLORIA GRESHAM .... COSTUME DESIGNER
SHELDON KAHN .... FILM EDITOR
WENDY BRICMONT .... FILM EDITOR

Ke-Ki

CINEMATOGRAPHERS
PRODUCTION
DESIGNERS,
COSTUME
DESIGNERS AND
FILM EDITORS
GUIDE

INDEX OF FILM TITLES

Ki-KI

CINEMATOGRAPHERS
PRODUCTION
DESIGNERS,
COSTUME
DESIGNERS AND
FILM EDITORS
GUIDE

I
N
D
E
X

O
F

F
I
L
M

T
I
T
L
E
S

Kn-La

CINEMATOGRAPHERS
PRODUCTION
DESIGNERS,
COSTUME
DESIGNERS AND
FILM EDITORS
GUIDE

I
N
D
E
X

O
F

F
I
L
M

T
I
T
L
E
S

La-La

CINEMATOGRAPHERS
PRODUCTION
DESIGNERS,
COSTUME
DESIGNERS AND
FILM EDITORS
GUIDE

I
N
D
E
X

O
F

F
I
L
M

T
I
T
L
E
S

La-Le

CINEMATOGRAPHERS
PRODUCTION
DESIGNERS,
COSTUME
DESIGNERS AND
FILM EDITORS
GUIDE

I
N
D
E
X

O
F

F
I
L
M

T
I
T
L
E
S

Le-Li

CINEMATOGRAPHERS
PRODUCTION
DESIGNERS,
COSTUME
DESIGNERS and
FILM EDITORS
GUIDE

I
N
D
E
X

O
F

F
I
L
M

T
I
T
L
E
S

Li-Li

CINEMATOGRAPHERS
PRODUCTION
DESIGNERS,
COSTUME
DESIGNERS AND
FILM EDITORS
GUIDE

I
N
D
E
X

O
F

F
I
L
M

T
I
T
L
E
S

Li-Lo

CINEMATOGRAPHERS
PRODUCTION
DESIGNERS,
COSTUME
DESIGNERS and
FILM EDITORS
GUIDE

I
N
D
E
X

O
F

F
I
L
M

T
I
T
L
E
S

380

LONGEST YARD, THE
JAMES D. VANCE .... PRODUCTION DESIGNER
ALLAN JACOBS .... FILM EDITOR
MICHAEL LUCIANO .... FILM EDITOR

LONGSHOT
ROBBY MULLER .... CINEMATOGRAPHER
JOSEPH ALTADONNA .... PRODUCTION DESIGNER
ROBB WILSON KING .... PRODUCTION DESIGNER

LONGSHOT, THE
SANDRA CULOTTA .... COSTUME DESIGNER

LOOK DOWN AND DIE
WARD PRESTON .... PRODUCTION DESIGNER

LOOK WHO'S TALKING
THOMAS DEL RUTH .... CINEMATOGRAPHER
REUBEN FREED .... PRODUCTION DESIGNER
GRAEME MURRAY .... PRODUCTION DESIGNER
MOLLY MAGINNIS .... COSTUME DESIGNER
DEBRA CHIATE .... FILM EDITOR

LOOKALIKE, THE (CTF)
NEIL ROACH .... CINEMATOGRAPHER
NORM BARON .... PRODUCTION DESIGNER
DONALD R. RODE .... FILM EDITOR

LOOKER
PAUL LOHMANN .... CINEMATOGRAPHER
DEAN E. MITZNER .... PRODUCTION DESIGNER
JACK G. TAYLOR .... PRODUCTION DESIGNER
BETSY COX .... COSTUME DESIGNER
CARL KRESS .... FILM EDITOR

LOOKIN' TO GET OUT
HASKELL WEXLER .... CINEMATOGRAPHER
JAMES SCHOPPE .... PRODUCTION DESIGNER
ROBERT F. BOYLE .... PRODUCTION DESIGNER
EVA GARDOS .... FILM EDITOR
ROBERT C. JONES .... FILM EDITOR

LOOKING FOR MR. GOODBAR
WILLIAM A. FRAKER .... CINEMATOGRAPHER
EDWARD C. CARFAGNO .... PRODUCTION DESIGNER
JODIE TILLEN .... COSTUME DESIGNER
GEORGE GRENVILLE .... FILM EDITOR

LOOKING GLASS WAR, THE
TERENCE MARSH .... PRODUCTION DESIGNER

LOOPHOLE
MICHAEL REED .... CINEMATOGRAPHER
MAURICE CAIN .... PRODUCTION DESIGNER
RALPH SHELDON .... FILM EDITOR

LOOSE CANNONS
REGINALD H. MORRIS .... CINEMATOGRAPHER
HARRY POTTLE .... PRODUCTION DESIGNER
STAN COLE .... FILM EDITOR

LOOSE SCREWS
STEPHEN FANFARA .... FILM EDITOR

LOOSE SHOES
ALAN BALSAM .... FILM EDITOR

LOOT
ANTHONY PRATT .... PRODUCTION DESIGNER

LORD JIM
FREDDIE YOUNG .... CINEMATOGRAPHER

LORD OF THE FLIES
MARTIN FUHRER .... CINEMATOGRAPHER
JAMIE LEONARD .... PRODUCTION DESIGNER
TOM PRIESTLY .... FILM EDITOR

LORD OF THE RINGS, THE (AF)
TIMOTHY GALFAS .... CINEMATOGRAPHER
DONALD W. ERNST .... FILM EDITOR

LORDS OF DISCIPLINE, THE
BRIAN TUFANO .... CINEMATOGRAPHER
JOHN GRAYSMARK .... PRODUCTION DESIGNER
ALAN CASSIE .... PRODUCTION DESIGNER
JOHN MOLLO .... COSTUME DESIGNER
MICHAEL ELLIS .... FILM EDITOR

LORDS OF FLATBUSH, THE
GLENDA GANIS .... PRODUCTION DESIGNER

LORDS OF THE DEEP
AUSTIN MCKINNEY .... CINEMATOGRAPHER

LOS ALBANILES
ALEX PHILLIPS .... CINEMATOGRAPHER

LOSIN' IT
GIL TAYLOR .... CINEMATOGRAPHER
ROBB WILSON KING .... PRODUCTION DESIGNER
RICHARD HALSEY .... FILM EDITOR

LOSS OF INNOCENCE
JOHN STOLL .... PRODUCTION DESIGNER

LOST AND FOUND
DOUGLAS SLOCOMBE .... CINEMATOGRAPHER
TREVOR WILLIAMS .... PRODUCTION DESIGNER
WILLIAM BUTLER .... FILM EDITOR

LOST ANGELS
ALEX TAVOULARIS .... PRODUCTION DESIGNER
ASSHETON GORTON .... PRODUCTION DESIGNER
JUDIANNA MAKOVSKY .... COSTUME DESIGNER
MILENA CANONERO .... COSTUME DESIGNER
DAVID GLADWELL .... FILM EDITOR

LOST BOYS, THE
MICHAEL CHAPMAN .... CINEMATOGRAPHER
ROBERT W. (BO) WELCH .... PRODUCTION DESIGNER
TOM DUFFIELD .... PRODUCTION DESIGNER
SUSAN BECKER .... COSTUME DESIGNER
ROBERT BROWN .... FILM EDITOR

LOST CAPONE, THE (CTF)
PAUL ELLIOTT .... CINEMATOGRAPHER
KAREN STERN .... FILM EDITOR

LOST EMPIRE, THE
JACQUES HAITKIN .... CINEMATOGRAPHER
WAYNE SPRINGFIELD .... PRODUCTION DESIGNER
LARRY BOCK .... FILM EDITOR

LOST HONOR OF KATHRYN BECK, THE (TF)
PETER S. LARKIN .... PRODUCTION DESIGNER

LOST HORIZON
MAURY WINETROBE .... FILM EDITOR

LOST IN AMERICA
ERIC SAARINEN .... CINEMATOGRAPHER
RICHARD SAWYER .... PRODUCTION DESIGNER
CYNTHIA BALES .... COSTUME DESIGNER
DAVID FINFER .... FILM EDITOR

LOST IN THE STARS
JACK MARTIN SMITH .... PRODUCTION DESIGNER

LOST ISLANDS, THE
DAVID GRIBBLE .... CINEMATOGRAPHER

LOST TRIBE, THE
THOMAS BURSTYN .... CINEMATOGRAPHER

LOTS OF LUCK (CTF)
REED SMOOT .... CINEMATOGRAPHER
MARK MELNICK .... FILM EDITOR

LOTTERY! (TF)
JOSEPH ALTADONNA .... PRODUCTION DESIGNER
RICHARD SAWYER .... PRODUCTION DESIGNER
STEPHEN BERGER .... PRODUCTION DESIGNER

LOUISIANA
MICHEL BRAULT .... CINEMATOGRAPHER

LOUISIANA (CTF)
IVO G. CRISTANTE .... PRODUCTION DESIGNER

LOULOU
PIERRE-WILLIAM GLENN .... CINEMATOGRAPHER

LOVE
REGINALD H. MORRIS .... CINEMATOGRAPHER
LINDA MATHESON .... COSTUME DESIGNER

CINEMATOGRAPHERS
PRODUCTION
DESIGNERS,
COSTUME
DESIGNERS and
FILM EDITORS
GUIDE

LOVE & MURDER
DAVID HERRINGTON .... CINEMATOGRAPHER
TONY HALL .... PRODUCTION DESIGNER
RON WISEMAN .... FILM EDITOR

LOVE AMONG THE RUINS (TF)
JOHN F. BURNETT .... FILM EDITOR

LOVE AND BULLETS
ANTHONY B. RICHMOND .... CINEMATOGRAPHER
FRED J. KOENEKAMP .... CINEMATOGRAPHER
JACK SENTER .... PRODUCTION DESIGNER
JOHN DE CUIR .... PRODUCTION DESIGNER
DOROTHY JEAKINS .... COSTUME DESIGNER
WILLIAM A. ANDERSON .... FILM EDITOR
MICHAEL F. ANDERSON .... FILM EDITOR

LOVE AND DEATH
GHISLAIN CLOQUET† .... CINEMATOGRAPHER
RALPH ROSENBLUM .... FILM EDITOR

LOVE AND MONEY
FRED SCHULER .... CINEMATOGRAPHER
LEE FISCHER .... PRODUCTION DESIGNER
DENNIS M. HILL .... FILM EDITOR

LOVE AND PAIN
GEOFFREY UNSWORTH† .... CINEMATOGRAPHER

LOVE AT FIRST BITE
EDWARD ROSSON .... CINEMATOGRAPHER
ALLAN JACOBS .... FILM EDITOR

LOVE AT LARGE
ELLIOT DAVIS .... CINEMATOGRAPHER
STEVEN LEGLER .... PRODUCTION DESIGNER
INGRID FERRIN .... COSTUME DESIGNER
LISA CHURGIN .... FILM EDITOR

LOVE AT STAKE
MARK IRWIN .... CINEMATOGRAPHER

LOVE BUG, THE
JOHN B. MANSBRIDGE .... PRODUCTION DESIGNER

LOVE CHILD
JAMES PERGOLA .... CINEMATOGRAPHER
DON K. IVEY .... PRODUCTION DESIGNER
ROBERT WYMAN .... FILM EDITOR

LOVE HURTS
DAVID BRIDGES .... CINEMATOGRAPHER
ADAM GREENBERG .... CINEMATOGRAPHER
ARMIN GANZ .... PRODUCTION DESIGNER
JOHN C. HORGER .... FILM EDITOR

LOVE IN A TAXI
JOSEPH MANGINE .... CINEMATOGRAPHER

LOVE IS FOREVER (TF)
DANIEL LOMINO .... PRODUCTION DESIGNER

LOVE LEADS THE WAY (TF)
DODIE SHEPARD .... COSTUME DESIGNER

LOVE LETTERS
ALEC HIRSCHFELD .... CINEMATOGRAPHER
JEANNINE CLAUDIA OPPEWALL .... PRODUCTION DESIGNER
WENDY BRICMONT .... FILM EDITOR

LOVE LINES
DUKE CALLAGHAN .... CINEMATOGRAPHER

LOVE LIVES ON (TF)
GERALD HIRSCHFELD .... CINEMATOGRAPHER
ERIC SEARS .... FILM EDITOR

LOVE ON THE GROUND
WILLIAM LUBTCHANSKY .... CINEMATOGRAPHER
NICOLE LUBTCHANSKY .... FILM EDITOR

LOVE ON THE RUN
NESTOR ALMENDROS .... CINEMATOGRAPHER

LOVE ON THE RUN (TF)
PHILIP LATHROP .... CINEMATOGRAPHER

LOVE OR MONEY
IGOR SUNARA .... CINEMATOGRAPHER
ROBERT P. KRACIK .... PRODUCTION DESIGNER
ILEANE MELTZER .... COSTUME DESIGNER
RAY HUBLEY .... FILM EDITOR

LOVE SHE SOUGHT, THE (TF)
JACK CONROY .... CINEMATOGRAPHER
JOHN LUCAS .... PRODUCTION DESIGNER
DEBRA KAREN .... FILM EDITOR

LOVE SONGS
ROBERT ALAZRAKI .... CINEMATOGRAPHER
NOELLE BOISSON .... FILM EDITOR

LOVE STORY
ROBERT C. JONES .... FILM EDITOR

LOVE STREAMS
AL RUBAN .... CINEMATOGRAPHER
PHEDON PAPAMICHAEL .... PRODUCTION DESIGNER
JENNIFER SMITH-ASHLEY .... COSTUME DESIGNER
GEORGE C. VILLASENOR .... FILM EDITOR

LOVE TAPES, THE (TF)
ELAYNE CEDER .... PRODUCTION DESIGNER

LOVE THY NEIGHBOR
ROLAND OZZIE SMITH .... CINEMATOGRAPHER

LOVE WITH A PROPER STRANGER
AARON STELL .... FILM EDITOR

LOVE, LIES AND MURDER-PARTS I & II (TF)
ISADORE MANKOFSKY .... CINEMATOGRAPHER
DONALD LIGHT-HARRIS .... PRODUCTION DESIGNER
JERRY LUDWIG .... FILM EDITOR

LOVED ONE, THE
HASKELL WEXLER .... CINEMATOGRAPHER
STUART H. PAPPE .... FILM EDITOR
ANTONY GIBBS .... FILM EDITOR

LOVELESS, THE
DOYLE SMITH .... CINEMATOGRAPHER
LILLY KILVERT .... PRODUCTION DESIGNER
NANCY KANTER .... FILM EDITOR

LOVELINES
ROBERT KINOSHITA .... PRODUCTION DESIGNER
DAVID BRETHERTON .... FILM EDITOR
FRED A. CHULACK .... FILM EDITOR

LOVELY BUT DEADLY
RICHARD S. BRUMMER .... FILM EDITOR

LOVEMAKING (TF)
JAMES G. HULSEY .... PRODUCTION DESIGNER

LOVERBOY
JOHN HORA .... CINEMATOGRAPHER
DAN LEIGH .... PRODUCTION DESIGNER
ROSANNA NORTON .... COSTUME DESIGNER
RICK SHAINE .... FILM EDITOR

LOVERS AND LIARS
TONINO DELLI COLLI .... CINEMATOGRAPHER

LOVERS AND OTHER STRANGERS
ANDREW LASZLO .... CINEMATOGRAPHER
BEN EDWARDS .... PRODUCTION DESIGNER
DAVID BRETHERTON .... FILM EDITOR

LOVESICK
GERRY FISHER .... CINEMATOGRAPHER
PHILIP ROSENBERG .... PRODUCTION DESIGNER
KRISTI ZEA .... COSTUME DESIGNER
NINA FEINBERG .... FILM EDITOR

LOVING
GORDON WILLIS .... CINEMATOGRAPHER
ROBERT LAWRENCE .... FILM EDITOR

LOVING COUPLES
PHILIP LATHROP .... CINEMATOGRAPHER
JAN SCOTT .... PRODUCTION DESIGNER
ARNOLD SCAASI .... COSTUME DESIGNER
THEONI V. ALDREDGE .... COSTUME DESIGNER
FRANK J. URIOSTE .... FILM EDITOR

Lo-Ma

CINEMATOGRAPHERS
PRODUCTION
DESIGNERS,
COSTUME
DESIGNERS AND
FILM EDITORS
GUIDE

I
N
D
E
X

O
F

F
I
L
M

T
I
T
L
E
S

Ma-Ma

CINEMATOGRAPHERS
PRODUCTION
DESIGNERS,
COSTUME
DESIGNERS AND
FILM EDITORS
GUIDE

I
N
D
E
X

O
F

F
I
L
M

T
I
T
L
E
S

MAN CALLED HAWK, A (PILOT)
JACK PRIESTLEY .... CINEMATOGRAPHER
TRACY BOUSMAN .... PRODUCTION DESIGNER

MAN CALLED HORSE, A
ROBERT B. HAUSER .... CINEMATOGRAPHER
RICHARD E. LA MOTTE .... COSTUME DESIGNER

MAN CALLED SARGE, A
DAVID GURFINKEL .... CINEMATOGRAPHER

MAN FACING SOUTHEAST
RICARDO DE ANGELIS .... CINEMATOGRAPHER
CESARE D'ANGIOLILLO .... FILM EDITOR

MAN FOR ALL SEASONS, A
TED MOORE .... CINEMATOGRAPHER
TERENCE MARSH .... PRODUCTION DESIGNER

MAN FRIDAY
ALEX PHILLIPS .... CINEMATOGRAPHER
PETER MURTON .... PRODUCTION DESIGNER
ANNE V. COATES .... FILM EDITOR

MAN FROM HONG KONG, THE
RUSSELL BOYD .... CINEMATOGRAPHER
DAVID COPPING .... PRODUCTION DESIGNER

MAN FROM SNOWY RIVER, THE
KEITH WAGSTAFF .... CINEMATOGRAPHER
LESLIE BINNS .... PRODUCTION DESIGNER
ROBIN HALL .... COSTUME DESIGNER
ADRIAN CARR .... FILM EDITOR

MAN IN LOVE, A
DEAN TAVOULARIS .... PRODUCTION DESIGNER

MAN IN LOVE, A
BERNARD ZITZERMANN .... CINEMATOGRAPHER
BRIGITTE NIERHAUS .... COSTUME DESIGNER
JOELE VAN EFFENTERRE .... FILM EDITOR

MAN IN THE BROWN SUIT, THE (TF)
BRIAN ACKLAND-SNOW .... PRODUCTION DESIGNER
JOSE MARIA TAPIADOR .... PRODUCTION DESIGNER
DONALD R. RODE .... FILM EDITOR

MAN IN THE GLASS BOOTH, THE
JOEL SCHILLER .... PRODUCTION DESIGNER
DAVID BRETHERTON .... FILM EDITOR

MAN IN THE IRON MASK, THE (TF)
FREDDIE YOUNG .... CINEMATOGRAPHER
JOHN STOLL .... PRODUCTION DESIGNER

MAN IN THE SANTA CLAUS SUIT, THE (TF)
WOODY OMENS .... CINEMATOGRAPHER

MAN IN THE SILK HAT, THE
SUZANNE BARON .... FILM EDITOR

MAN INSIDE, THE
RICARDO ARONOVITCH .... CINEMATOGRAPHER
DIDIER NAERT .... PRODUCTION DESIGNER
BRIGITTE NIERHAUS .... COSTUME DESIGNER
LUCE GRUNEWALDT .... FILM EDITOR

MAN OF FLOWERS
YURI SOKOL .... CINEMATOGRAPHER
TIM LEWIS .... FILM EDITOR

MAN OF LA MANCHA
ROBERT C. JONES .... FILM EDITOR

MAN ON A SWING
ADAM HOLENDER .... CINEMATOGRAPHER

MAN ON FIRE
GERRY FISHER .... CINEMATOGRAPHER
GIANTITO BURCHIELLARO .... PRODUCTION DESIGNER
ALBERT BARACQ .... COSTUME DESIGNER
NOELLE BOISSON .... FILM EDITOR

MAN OUTSIDE
WILLIAM WAGES .... CINEMATOGRAPHER
TONY LOMBARDO .... FILM EDITOR

MAN OUTSIDE, THE
PETER MULLINS .... PRODUCTION DESIGNER

MAN UNDER SUSPICION
JURGEN JURGES .... CINEMATOGRAPHER

MAN WHO BROKE A THOUSAND CHAINS, THE
MIKAEL SALOMON .... CINEMATOGRAPHER

MAN WHO FELL TO EARTH, THE
ANTHONY B. RICHMOND .... CINEMATOGRAPHER
MAY ROUTH .... COSTUME DESIGNER
GRAEME CLIFFORD .... FILM EDITOR

MAN WHO FELL TO EARTH, THE (TF)
JOHN B. MANSBRIDGE .... PRODUCTION DESIGNER

MAN WHO LOVED CAT DANCING, THE
ALFRED TAYLOR .... CINEMATOGRAPHER
HARRY STRADLING, JR. .... CINEMATOGRAPHER

MAN WHO LOVED WOMEN, THE
NESTOR ALMENDROS .... CINEMATOGRAPHER
JACK SENTER .... PRODUCTION DESIGNER
RODGER MAUS .... PRODUCTION DESIGNER
ANN ROTH .... COSTUME DESIGNER
RALPH E. WINTERS .... FILM EDITOR

MAN WHO LOVED WOMEN, THE (1983)
HASKELL WEXLER .... CINEMATOGRAPHER

MAN WHO SAW TOMORROW, THE
LEE COLE .... PRODUCTION DESIGNER

MAN WHO WASN'T THERE, THE
FREDERICK MOORE .... CINEMATOGRAPHER
ROBB WILSON KING .... PRODUCTION DESIGNER
SANDI LOVE .... COSTUME DESIGNER
HARRY KELLER .... FILM EDITOR

MAN WHO WOULD BE KING, THE
OSWALD MORRIS .... CINEMATOGRAPHER
ALEXANDER TRAUNER .... PRODUCTION DESIGNER
EDITH HEAD† .... COSTUME DESIGNER
RUSSELL LLOYD .... FILM EDITOR

MAN WITH BOGART'S FACE, THE
RICHARD C. GLOUNER .... CINEMATOGRAPHER
ROBERT KINOSHITA .... PRODUCTION DESIGNER
HOUSELEY STEVENSON .... FILM EDITOR

MAN WITH ONE RED SHOE, THE
RICHARD H. KLINE .... CINEMATOGRAPHER
DEAN E. MITZNER .... PRODUCTION DESIGNER
WILLIAM WARE THEISS .... COSTUME DESIGNER
BUD MOLIN .... FILM EDITOR
O. NICHOLAS BROWN .... FILM EDITOR

MAN WITH THE GOLDEN GUN, THE
OSWALD MORRIS .... CINEMATOGRAPHER
TED MOORE .... CINEMATOGRAPHER
PETER MURTON .... PRODUCTION DESIGNER

MAN WITH TWO BRAINS, THE
MICHAEL CHAPMAN .... CINEMATOGRAPHER
MARK MANSBRIDGE .... PRODUCTION DESIGNER
POLLY PLATT .... PRODUCTION DESIGNER
ELLIS COHEN .... COSTUME DESIGNER
MINA MITTELMAN .... COSTUME DESIGNER
BUD MOLIN .... FILM EDITOR

MAN WITHOUT A COUNTRY, THE (TF)
JAN SCOTT .... PRODUCTION DESIGNER

MAN, A WOMAN AND A BANK, A
JACK CARDIFF .... CINEMATOGRAPHER
ANNE PRITCHARD .... PRODUCTION DESIGNER
CARL KRESS .... FILM EDITOR

MAN, THE
JAMES G. HULSEY .... PRODUCTION DESIGNER
GEORGE JAY NICHOLSON .... FILM EDITOR

MAN, WOMAN & CHILD
RICHARD H. KLINE .... CINEMATOGRAPHER
DEAN E. MITZNER .... PRODUCTION DESIGNER
JOSEPH G. AULISI .... COSTUME DESIGNER
DAVID BRETHERTON .... FILM EDITOR

MANCHURIAN CANDIDATE, THE
RICHARD SYLBERT .... PRODUCTION DESIGNER
FERRIS WEBSTER .... FILM EDITOR

Ma-Ma

CINEMATOGRAPHERS
PRODUCTION
DESIGNERS,
COSTUME
DESIGNERS AND
FILM EDITORS
GUIDE

I
N
D
E
X

O
F

F
I
L
M

T
I
T
L
E
S

Ma-Mc

CINEMATOGRAPHERS
PRODUCTION
DESIGNERS,
COSTUME
DESIGNERS AND
FILM EDITORS
GUIDE

I N D E X O F F I L M T I T L E S

MARTIAN CHRONICLES, THE (TF)
ASSHETON GORTON .... PRODUCTION DESIGNER

MARTIANS GO HOME
PETER DEMING .... CINEMATOGRAPHER
CATHERINE HARDWICKE .... PRODUCTION DESIGNER
DON DAY .... PRODUCTION DESIGNER
ROBYN REICHEK .... COSTUME DESIGNER
M. KATHRYN CAMPBELL .... FILM EDITOR

MARTIN
MICHAEL GORNICK .... CINEMATOGRAPHER

MARTIN'S DAY
FRANK WATTS .... CINEMATOGRAPHER
TREVOR WILLIAMS .... PRODUCTION DESIGNER
LYNNE MACKAY .... COSTUME DESIGNER
DAVID DE WILDE .... FILM EDITOR

MARTY
TED HAWORTH .... PRODUCTION DESIGNER

MARVA COLLINS STORY, THE (TF)
RICHARD B. LEWIS .... PRODUCTION DESIGNER

MARVIN AND TIGE
BRIAN WEST .... CINEMATOGRAPHER
ELAYNE CEDER .... PRODUCTION DESIGNER
FABIEN TORDJMANN .... FILM EDITOR

MARY WHITE (TF)
BILL BUTLER .... CINEMATOGRAPHER
WARD PRESTON .... PRODUCTION DESIGNER

MARY, QUEEN OF SCOTS
ROBERT CARTWRIGHT .... PRODUCTION DESIGNER
TERENCE MARSH .... PRODUCTION DESIGNER

MASADA (MS)
JOHN BLOOM .... FILM EDITOR

MASCULINE FEMININE
WILLY KURANT .... CINEMATOGRAPHER

MASK
LASZLO KOVACS .... CINEMATOGRAPHER
NORMAN NEWBERRY .... PRODUCTION DESIGNER
APRIL FERRY .... COSTUME DESIGNER
MARLA DENISE SCHLOM .... COSTUME DESIGNER
TONY SCARANO .... COSTUME DESIGNER
EVA GARDOS .... FILM EDITOR

MASQUERADE
DAVID WATKIN .... CINEMATOGRAPHER
DAN DAVIS .... PRODUCTION DESIGNER
JOHN KASARDA .... PRODUCTION DESIGNER
JOHN BOXER .... COSTUME DESIGNER
SCOTT CONRAD .... FILM EDITOR

MASS APPEAL
DONALD PETERMAN .... CINEMATOGRAPHER
PHILIP JEFFRIES .... PRODUCTION DESIGNER
JOHN WRIGHT .... FILM EDITOR

MASSACRE AT CENTRAL HIGH
HARRY KERAMIDAS .... FILM EDITOR

MASSACRE IN ROME
FRANÇOISE BONNOT .... FILM EDITOR

MASSIVE RETALIATION
B.J. SEARS .... FILM EDITOR

MASTER BLASTER
FRANK FLYNN .... CINEMATOGRAPHER
ANGELO ROSS .... FILM EDITOR

MASTER GUNFIGHTER, THE
STEPHEN BERGER .... PRODUCTION DESIGNER
DANFORD B. GREENE .... FILM EDITOR
WILLIAM REYNOLDS .... FILM EDITOR

MASTER OF THE GAME (MS)
ALAN PATILLO .... FILM EDITOR

MASTERS OF MENACE
EDWARD J. PEI .... CINEMATOGRAPHER
RICHARD HUMMEL .... PRODUCTION DESIGNER
STEPHEN MYERS .... FILM EDITOR

MASTERS OF THE UNIVERSE
HANANIA BAER .... CINEMATOGRAPHER
ROBERT HOWLAND .... PRODUCTION DESIGNER
WILLIAM STOUT .... PRODUCTION DESIGNER
JULIE WEISS .... COSTUME DESIGNER
ANNE V. COATES .... FILM EDITOR

MATA HARI
DAVID GURFINKEL .... CINEMATOGRAPHER
HENRY RICHARDSON .... FILM EDITOR

MATEWAN
HASKELL WEXLER .... CINEMATOGRAPHER
DAN BISHOP .... PRODUCTION DESIGNER
NORA CHAVOOSHIAN .... PRODUCTION DESIGNER
CYNTHIA FLYNT .... COSTUME DESIGNER
SONYA POLONSKY .... FILM EDITOR

MATILDA
BORIS LEVEN† .... PRODUCTION DESIGNER
ALLAN JACOBS .... FILM EDITOR

MATING SEASON, THE (TF)
DENNIS O'CONNOR .... FILM EDITOR

MATTER OF INNOCENCE, A
PETER MULLINS .... PRODUCTION DESIGNER

MATTER OF LIFE AND DEATH, A
JACK CARDIFF .... CINEMATOGRAPHER

MATTER OF TIME, A
GEOFFREY UNSWORTH† .... CINEMATOGRAPHER

MATTERS OF THE HEART (CTF)
RON GARCIA .... CINEMATOGRAPHER
ARNOLD WHYLER .... PRODUCTION DESIGNER
EDWARD BEYER .... FILM EDITOR

MAURICE
PIERRE L'HOMME .... CINEMATOGRAPHER
BRIAN ACKLAND-SNOW .... PRODUCTION DESIGNER
JENNY BEAVEN .... COSTUME DESIGNER
JOHN BRIGHT .... COSTUME DESIGNER
KATHERINE WENNING .... FILM EDITOR

MAUSOLEUM
ROBERT BURNS .... PRODUCTION DESIGNER

MAX DUGAN RETURNS
DAVID M. WALSH .... CINEMATOGRAPHER
ALBERT BRENNER .... PRODUCTION DESIGNER
DAVID M. HABER .... PRODUCTION DESIGNER
BOB MACKIE .... COSTUME DESIGNER
RICHARD MARKS .... FILM EDITOR

MAX HAVELAAR
JAN DE BONT .... CINEMATOGRAPHER

MAXIE
FRED SCHULER .... CINEMATOGRAPHER
JOHN J. LLOYD .... PRODUCTION DESIGNER
ANN ROTH .... COSTUME DESIGNER
LYNZEE KLINGMAN .... FILM EDITOR

MAXIMUM OVERDRIVE
ARMANDO NANNUZZI .... CINEMATOGRAPHER
GIORGIO POSTIGLIONE .... PRODUCTION DESIGNER
CLIFFORD CAPONE .... COSTUME DESIGNER
EVAN LOTTMAN .... FILM EDITOR
PENELOPE SHAW .... FILM EDITOR

MAYA
OLIVER WOOD .... CINEMATOGRAPHER

MAYBE BABY (TF)
GREGORY PRANGE .... FILM EDITOR

MAYDAY AT 40,000 FEET (TF)
ROBERT KINOSHITA .... PRODUCTION DESIGNER

MAZES AND MONSTERS (TF)
LASZLO GEORGE .... CINEMATOGRAPHER

MCCABE & MRS. MILLER
VILMOS ZSIGMOND .... CINEMATOGRAPHER
LEON ERICKSON .... PRODUCTION DESIGNER
PHILIP THOMAS .... PRODUCTION DESIGNER
LOU LOMBARDO .... FILM EDITOR

CINEMATOGRAPHERS
PRODUCTION
DESIGNERS,
COSTUME
DESIGNERS AND
FILM EDITORS
GUIDE

**I
N
D
E
X**

**O
F**

**F
I
L
M**

**T
I
T
L
E
S**

MCMASTERS, THE
JOEL SCHILLER .... PRODUCTION DESIGNER

MCQ
HARRY STRADLING, JR. .... CINEMATOGRAPHER

MCVICAR
VERNON LAYTON .... CINEMATOGRAPHER
BRIAN ACKLAND-SNOW .... PRODUCTION DESIGNER
PETER BOYLE .... FILM EDITOR

ME AND HIM
HELGE WEINDLER .... CINEMATOGRAPHER
SUZANNE CAVEDON .... PRODUCTION DESIGNER
EUGENIE BAFALOUKAS .... COSTUME DESIGNER
RAIMUND BARTHELMES .... FILM EDITOR

ME AND MY KID BROTHER
MIKAEL SALOMON .... CINEMATOGRAPHER

MEADOW, THE
FRANCO DI GIACOMO .... CINEMATOGRAPHER

MEAN DOG BLUES
ROBERT B. HAUSER .... CINEMATOGRAPHER
JACK POPLIN .... PRODUCTION DESIGNER
HOUSELEY STEVENSON .... FILM EDITOR

MEAN SEASON, THE
FRANK TIDY .... CINEMATOGRAPHER
PHILIP JEFFRIES .... PRODUCTION DESIGNER
DUWAYNE DUNHAM .... FILM EDITOR

MEAN STREETS
KENT WAKEFORD .... CINEMATOGRAPHER
DAVID NICHOLS .... PRODUCTION DESIGNER
SIDNEY LEVIN .... FILM EDITOR

MEANING OF LIFE, THE
JAMES ACHESON .... COSTUME DESIGNER

MEANTIME
ROGER PRATT .... CINEMATOGRAPHER
LESLEY WALKER .... FILM EDITOR

MEATBALLS
DON WILDER .... CINEMATOGRAPHER
JUDITH R. GELLMAN .... COSTUME DESIGNER
DEBRA KAREN .... FILM EDITOR

MEATBALLS PART II
DONALD M. MORGAN .... CINEMATOGRAPHER
JAMES WILLIAM NEWPORT .... PRODUCTION DESIGNER
SANDI LOVE .... COSTUME DESIGNER
GEORGE BERNDT .... FILM EDITOR

MEATBALLS III
PETER BENISON .... CINEMATOGRAPHER
CHARLES DUNLOP .... PRODUCTION DESIGNER
MARY E. MCLEOD .... COSTUME DESIGNER
DEBRA KAREN .... FILM EDITOR

MECHANIC, THE
RICHARD H. KLINE .... CINEMATOGRAPHER

MEDEA
DANTE FERRETTI .... PRODUCTION DESIGNER

MEDIUM COOL
HASKELL WEXLER .... CINEMATOGRAPHER

MEDUSA TOUCH, THE
ARTHUR IBBETSON .... CINEMATOGRAPHER
PETER MULLINS .... PRODUCTION DESIGNER
IAN CRAFFORD .... FILM EDITOR
ANNE V. COATES .... FILM EDITOR

MEET THE APPLEGATES
MITCHELL DUBIN .... CINEMATOGRAPHER
NORMAN HOLLYN .... FILM EDITOR

MEET THE HOLLOWHEADS
CARL KRESS .... FILM EDITOR

MEETINGS WITH REMARKABLE MEN
JOHN JYMPSON .... FILM EDITOR

MEGAFORCE
MICHAEL C. BUTLER .... CINEMATOGRAPHER
JOEL SCHILLER .... PRODUCTION DESIGNER
PATRICK ROARK .... FILM EDITOR

MELANIE
RICHARD CIUPKA .... CINEMATOGRAPHER
ROY FORGE SMITH .... PRODUCTION DESIGNER

MELODY/SWALK
PETER SUSCHITZKY .... CINEMATOGRAPHER

MELVIN AND HOWARD
TAK FUJIMOTO .... CINEMATOGRAPHER
RICHARD SAWYER .... PRODUCTION DESIGNER
TOBY CARR RAFELSON .... PRODUCTION DESIGNER
CRAIG MC KAY .... FILM EDITOR

MELVIN PURVIS: G-MAN (TF)
TREVOR WILLIAMS .... PRODUCTION DESIGNER

MEMED MY HAWK
FREDDIE FRANCIS .... CINEMATOGRAPHER
PETER HONESS .... FILM EDITOR

MEMORIAL DAY (TF)
JAMES MATHERS .... CINEMATOGRAPHER
HECTOR FIGUEROA .... CINEMATOGRAPHER

MEMORIES
LARRY PIZER .... CINEMATOGRAPHER

MEMORIES NEVER DIE (TF)
RICHARD B. LEWIS .... PRODUCTION DESIGNER

MEMORIES OF ME
ANDREW DINTENFASS .... CINEMATOGRAPHER
WILLIAM J. CASSIDY .... PRODUCTION DESIGNER
ERIC H. SANDBERG .... COSTUME DESIGNER
PETER E. BERGER .... FILM EDITOR

MEMORY OF EVA RYKER, THE (TF)
PAUL ZASTUPNEVICH .... COSTUME DESIGNER

MEMPHIS BELLE
DAVID WATKIN .... CINEMATOGRAPHER
STUART DRAIG .... PRODUCTION DESIGNER
JANE ROBINSON .... COSTUME DESIGNER
JIM CLARK .... FILM EDITOR

MEN
HELGE WEINDLER .... CINEMATOGRAPHER
RAIMUND BARTHELMES .... FILM EDITOR

MEN AT WORK
TIM SUHRSTEDT .... CINEMATOGRAPHER
DINS DANIELSEN .... PRODUCTION DESIGNER
KEITH LEWIS .... COSTUME DESIGNER
CRAIG BASSETT .... FILM EDITOR

MEN DON'T LEAVE
BRUCE SURTEES .... CINEMATOGRAPHER
BARBARA LING .... PRODUCTION DESIGNER
J. ALLEN HIGHFILL† .... COSTUME DESIGNER
RICHARD CHEW .... FILM EDITOR

MEN OF RESPECT
BOBBY BUKOWSKI .... CINEMATOGRAPHER
ELIZABETH KING .... FILM EDITOR

MEN'S CLUB, THE
JOHN FLECKENSTEIN .... CINEMATOGRAPHER
KEN DAVIS .... PRODUCTION DESIGNER
LAURENCE BENNET .... PRODUCTION DESIGNER
MARIANNA ELLIOTT .... COSTUME DESIGNER
PETER MITCHELL .... COSTUME DESIGNER
WILLIAM BUTLER .... FILM EDITOR
CYNTHIA SCHEIDER .... FILM EDITOR

MENAGE
CLAUDE MERLIN .... FILM EDITOR

MEPHISTO
LAJOS KOLTAI .... CINEMATOGRAPHER

MERCENARY FIGHTERS
DANIEL SCHNEOR .... CINEMATOGRAPHER
DEAN GOODHILL .... FILM EDITOR
MICHAEL CAMPBELL .... FILM EDITOR

MERMAIDS
HOWARD ATHERTON .... CINEMATOGRAPHER
STUART WURTZEL .... PRODUCTION DESIGNER
MARIT ALLEN .... COSTUME DESIGNER
JACQUELINE CAMBAS .... FILM EDITOR

MERRY CHRISTMAS, MR. LAWRENCE
ANDREW SANDERS .... PRODUCTION DESIGNER

MES PETITES AMOREUSES
NESTOR ALMENDROS .... CINEMATOGRAPHER

MESMERIZED
PETRA VAN OELFFEN .... FILM EDITOR

MESSAGE, THE
MAURICE FOWLER .... PRODUCTION DESIGNER
JOHN BLOOM .... FILM EDITOR

MESSENGER OF DEATH
GIDEON PORATH .... CINEMATOGRAPHER
WHITNEY BROOKE WHEELER .... PRODUCTION DESIGNER
SHELLEY KOMAROV .... COSTUME DESIGNER
PETER LEE THOMPSON .... FILM EDITOR

MESSENGER, THE
CRAIG GREENE .... CINEMATOGRAPHER
GIANCARLO FERRANDO .... CINEMATOGRAPHER

MESSIAH OF EVIL
STEPHEN M. KATZ .... CINEMATOGRAPHER
SCOTT CONRAD .... FILM EDITOR

METALSTORM: THE DESTRUCTION OF JARED-SYN
MAC AHLBERG .... CINEMATOGRAPHER
PAMELA B. WARNER .... PRODUCTION DESIGNER
KATHIE CLARK .... COSTUME DESIGNER
BRAD ARENSMAN .... FILM EDITOR

METEOR
PAUL LOHMANN .... CINEMATOGRAPHER
EDWARD C. CARFAGNO .... PRODUCTION DESIGNER
CARL KRESS .... FILM EDITOR

METROPOLITAN AVENUE
STAN SALFAS .... FILM EDITOR

MIAMI BLUES
TAK FUJIMOTO .... CINEMATOGRAPHER
MAHER AHMAD .... PRODUCTION DESIGNER
EUGENIE BAFALOUKAS .... COSTUME DESIGNER
CRAIG MCKAY .... FILM EDITOR

MICHAEL KOLHAS
WILLY KURANT .... CINEMATOGRAPHER

MICKEY SPILLANE'S MIKE HAMMER: MURDER TAKES ALL (TF)
JACK DE SHIELDS .... PRODUCTION DESIGNER

MICKI & MAUDE
HARRY STRADLING, JR. .... CINEMATOGRAPHER
JACK SENTER .... PRODUCTION DESIGNER
RODGER MAUS .... PRODUCTION DESIGNER
PATRICIA NORRIS .... COSTUME DESIGNER
RALPH E. WINTERS .... FILM EDITOR

MIDAS VALLEY (MS)
RIC WAITE .... CINEMATOGRAPHER

MIDDLE AGE CRAZY
REGINALD H. MORRIS .... CINEMATOGRAPHER
KAREN BROMLEY .... PRODUCTION DESIGNER
LINDA MATHESON .... COSTUME DESIGNER
JOHN KELLY .... FILM EDITOR

MIDDLE AGE SPREAD
MICHAEL HORTON .... FILM EDITOR

MIDNIGHT
DAVID GOLIA .... CINEMATOGRAPHER

MIDNIGHT CALLER (PILOT)
JEFFREY BEECROFT .... PRODUCTION DESIGNER

MIDNIGHT COWBOY
ADAM HOLENDER .... CINEMATOGRAPHER
JOHN ROBERT LLOYD .... PRODUCTION DESIGNER
ANN ROTH .... COSTUME DESIGNER

MIDNIGHT CROSSING
HENRY VARGAS .... CINEMATOGRAPHER
ERIC WATSON .... FILM EDITOR

MIDNIGHT EXPRESS
MICHAEL SERESIN .... CINEMATOGRAPHER
EVAN HERCULES .... PRODUCTION DESIGNER
GEOFFREY KIRKLAND .... PRODUCTION DESIGNER
MILENA CANONERO .... COSTUME DESIGNER
GERRY HAMBLING .... FILM EDITOR

MIDNIGHT HOUR, THE (TF)
REXFORD METZ .... CINEMATOGRAPHER

MIDNIGHT MADNESS
FRANK PHILLIPS .... CINEMATOGRAPHER
JOHN B. MANSBRIDGE .... PRODUCTION DESIGNER
RICHARD J. LAWRENCE .... PRODUCTION DESIGNER

MIDNIGHT MAN, THE
JACK PRIESTLEY .... CINEMATOGRAPHER
JAMES D. VANCE .... PRODUCTION DESIGNER

MIDNIGHT PLEASURES
PASQUALINO DE SANTIS .... CINEMATOGRAPHER

MIDNIGHT RUN
DONALD E. THORIN .... CINEMATOGRAPHER
ANGELO GRAHAM .... PRODUCTION DESIGNER
JAMES J. MARUKAMI .... PRODUCTION DESIGNER
GLORIA GRESHAM .... COSTUME DESIGNER
BILLY WEBER .... FILM EDITOR
CHRIS LEBENZON .... FILM EDITOR
MICHAEL TRONICK .... FILM EDITOR

MIDNIGHT SPARES
GEOFF BURTON .... CINEMATOGRAPHER

MIDSUMMER NIGHT'S DREAM, A
PETER SUSCHITZKY .... CINEMATOGRAPHER

MIDSUMMER NIGHT'S SEX COMEDY, A
GORDON WILLIS .... CINEMATOGRAPHER
SPEED HOPKINS .... PRODUCTION DESIGNER
MEL BOURNE .... PRODUCTION DESIGNER
SANTO LOQUASTO .... COSTUME DESIGNER
SUSAN E. MORSE .... FILM EDITOR

MIDWAY
HARRY STRADLING, JR. .... CINEMATOGRAPHER
FRANK J. URIOSTE .... FILM EDITOR
ROBERT E. SWINK .... FILM EDITOR

MIGHTY QUINN, THE
JACQUES STEYN .... CINEMATOGRAPHER
ROGER MURRAY-LEACH .... PRODUCTION DESIGNER
DANA LYMAN .... COSTUME DESIGNER
JOHN JYMPSON .... FILM EDITOR

MIKE'S MURDER
REYNALDO VILLALOBOS .... CINEMATOGRAPHER
HUB BRADEN .... PRODUCTION DESIGNER
PETER JAMISON .... PRODUCTION DESIGNER
DEDE ALLEN .... FILM EDITOR
JEFF S. GOURSON .... FILM EDITOR

MIKEY AND NICKY
VICTOR J. KEMPER .... CINEMATOGRAPHER
PAUL SYLBERT .... PRODUCTION DESIGNER
JOHN CARTER .... FILM EDITOR
SHELDON KAHN .... FILM EDITOR

MILAGRO BEANFIELD WAR, THE
ROBBIE GREENBERG .... CINEMATOGRAPHER
JOE AUBEL .... PRODUCTION DESIGNER
BERNIE POLLACK .... COSTUME DESIGNER
DEDE ALLEN .... FILM EDITOR
JIM MILLER .... FILM EDITOR

MILES FROM HOME
ELLIOT DAVIS .... CINEMATOGRAPHER
DAVID GROPMAN .... PRODUCTION DESIGNER
NICHOLAS ROMANAC .... PRODUCTION DESIGNER
SHAY CUNLIFFE .... COSTUME DESIGNER
JANE SCHWARTZ JAFFE .... FILM EDITOR

MILK AND HONEY (TF)
GUY DUFAUX .... CINEMATOGRAPHER

MILLENNIUM
RENE OHASHI .... CINEMATOGRAPHER
CHARLES DUNLOP .... PRODUCTION DESIGNER
GENE RUDOLF .... PRODUCTION DESIGNER
OLGA DIMITROV .... COSTUME DESIGNER
RON WISMAN .... FILM EDITOR

INDEX OF FILM TITLES

CINEMATOGRAPHERS
PRODUCTION
DESIGNERS,
COSTUME
DESIGNERS AND
FILM EDITORS
GUIDE

INDEX OF FILM TITLES

MILLER'S CROSSING
BARRY SONNENFELD .... CINEMATOGRAPHER
DENNIS GASSNER .... PRODUCTION DESIGNER
RICHARD HORNUNG .... COSTUME DESIGNER
MICHAEL MILLER .... FILM EDITOR

MILLION DOLLAR MYSTERY
JACK CARDIFF .... CINEMATOGRAPHER
JACK G. TAYLOR .... PRODUCTION DESIGNER
CLIFFORD CAPONE .... COSTUME DESIGNER
JOHN W. WHEELER .... FILM EDITOR

MIND GAME
MAREK DOBROWOLSKI .... PRODUCTION DESIGNER

MIND OF MR. SOAMES, THE
BILLY WILLIAMS .... CINEMATOGRAPHER

MIND OVER MURDER (TF)
SYDNEY Z. LITWAK .... PRODUCTION DESIGNER

MINDWALK
KARL KASES .... CINEMATOGRAPHER
BAMBI BREAKSTONE .... COSTUME DESIGNER
JEAN CLAUDE PIROUE .... FILM EDITOR

MINISTRY OF VENGEANCE
TERRY DRESBACH .... COSTUME DESIGNER

MINNIE AND MOSKOWITZ
MICHAEL D. MARGULIES .... CINEMATOGRAPHER
MICHAEL ECONOMOU .... FILM EDITOR

MINSTREL MAN (TV)
SANDRA STEWART .... COSTUME DESIGNER

MIO DIO COME SONO CADUTA IN BASSO
DANTE FERRETTI .... PRODUCTION DESIGNER

MIRACLE AT BEEKMAN'S PLACE (TF)
RICHARD C. GLOUNER .... CINEMATOGRAPHER

MIRACLE MILE
THEO VAN DE SANDE .... CINEMATOGRAPHER
SHAY CUNLIFFE .... COSTUME DESIGNER
STEPHEN SEMEL .... FILM EDITOR

MIRACLE WORKER, THE (TF)
RUTH MORLEY .... COSTUME DESIGNER

MIRACLES
CYNTHIA BALES .... COSTUME DESIGNER

MIRROR CRACK'D, THE
CHRISTOPHER CHALLIS .... CINEMATOGRAPHER
MICHAEL STRINGER .... PRODUCTION DESIGNER
RICHARD MARDEN .... FILM EDITOR

MIRRORS (TF)
ROBERT L. ESTRIN .... FILM EDITOR
PAUL RUBELL .... FILM EDITOR

MISCHIEF
DONALD E. THORIN .... CINEMATOGRAPHER
PAUL PETERS .... PRODUCTION DESIGNER
MINA MITTELMAN .... COSTUME DESIGNER
O. NICHOLAS BROWN .... FILM EDITOR

MISERY
BARRY SONNENFELD .... CINEMATOGRAPHER
NORMAN GARWOOD .... PRODUCTION DESIGNER
GLORIA GRESHAM .... COSTUME DESIGNER
ROBERT LEIGHTON .... FILM EDITOR

MISFITS OF SCIENCE
ISIDORE MANKOFSKY .... CINEMATOGRAPHER

MISHIMA
JOHN BAILEY .... CINEMATOGRAPHER

MISHIMA: A LIFE IN FOUR CHAPTERS
MICHAEL CHANDLER .... FILM EDITOR

MISPLACED
IGOR SUNARA .... CINEMATOGRAPHER
MICHAEL BERENBAUM .... FILM EDITOR

MISS FIRECRACKER
ARTHUR ALBERT .... CINEMATOGRAPHER
KRISTI ZEA .... PRODUCTION DESIGNER
MAHER AHMAD .... PRODUCTION DESIGNER
MOLLY MAGINNIS .... COSTUME DESIGNER
PETER C. FRANK .... FILM EDITOR

MISS LONELY HEARTS
JUAN RUIZ-ANCHIA .... CINEMATOGRAPHER

MISS MARY
MIGUEL RODRIGUEZ .... CINEMATOGRAPHER
CESARE D'ANGIOLILLO .... FILM EDITOR

MISSING
RICARDO ARONOVITCH .... CINEMATOGRAPHER
AUGUSTIN ITUARTE .... PRODUCTION DESIGNER
PETER JAMISON .... PRODUCTION DESIGNER
JOE I. TOMPKINS .... COSTUME DESIGNER
FRANÇOISE BONNOT .... FILM EDITOR

MISSING IN ACTION
JOAO FERNANDES .... CINEMATOGRAPHER
MICHAEL BAUGH .... PRODUCTION DESIGNER
NANCY CONE .... COSTUME DESIGNER
DANIEL LOEWENTHAL .... FILM EDITOR
JOEL GOODMAN .... FILM EDITOR

MISSING IN ACTION 2—THE BEGINNING
JORGE STAHL .... CINEMATOGRAPHER
GREGG FONSECA .... PRODUCTION DESIGNER
MICHAEL BAUGH .... PRODUCTION DESIGNER
POPPY CANNON .... COSTUME DESIGNER
MARK CONTE .... FILM EDITOR
MARCUS MANTON .... FILM EDITOR

MISSION, THE
CHRIS MENGES .... CINEMATOGRAPHER
GEORGE RICHARDSON .... PRODUCTION DESIGNER
JACK STEPHENS .... PRODUCTION DESIGNER
JOHN KING .... PRODUCTION DESIGNER
STUART CRAIG .... PRODUCTION DESIGNER
ENRICO SABBATINI .... COSTUME DESIGNER
JIM CLARK .... FILM EDITOR

MISSIONARY, THE
PETER HANNAN .... CINEMATOGRAPHER
NORMAN GARWOOD .... PRODUCTION DESIGNER
SHUNA HARWOOD .... COSTUME DESIGNER
PAUL GREEN .... FILM EDITOR

MISSISISSIPPI BLUES (FD)
PIERRE-WILLIAM GLENN .... CINEMATOGRAPHER

MISSISSIPPI BURNING
PETER BIZIOU .... CINEMATOGRAPHER
GEOFFREY KIRKLAND .... PRODUCTION DESIGNER
PHILIP HARRISON .... PRODUCTION DESIGNER
AUDE BRONSON-HOWARD .... COSTUME DESIGNER
GERRY HAMBLING .... FILM EDITOR

MISSOURI BREAKS, THE
MICHAEL C. BUTLER .... CINEMATOGRAPHER
ALBERT BRENNER .... PRODUCTION DESIGNER
STEPHEN BERGER .... PRODUCTION DESIGNER
PATRICIA NORRIS .... COSTUME DESIGNER
DEDE ALLEN .... FILM EDITOR
GERALD B. GREENBERG .... FILM EDITOR
STEPHEN A. ROTTER .... FILM EDITOR

MISTRAL'S DAUGHTER (MS)
JOHN BLOOM .... FILM EDITOR

MISTRESS
NESTOR ALMENDROS .... CINEMATOGRAPHER

MISTRESS PAMEL
ARTHUR IBBETSON .... CINEMATOGRAPHER

MISUNDERSTOOD
PASQUALINO DE SANTIS .... CINEMATOGRAPHER
JOEL SCHILLER .... PRODUCTION DESIGNER
JO YNOCENCIO .... COSTUME DESIGNER
MARC LAUB .... FILM EDITOR

MITCHELL
HARRY STRADLING, JR. .... CINEMATOGRAPHER

MITZI GAYNOR SPECIALS, THE (TV)
BOB MACKIE .... COSTUME DESIGNER

MIXED BLOOD

STEFAN ZAPASNIK .... CINEMATOGRAPHER
STEVEN MCCABE .... PRODUCTION DESIGNER
SCOTT VICKREY .... FILM EDITOR

MO' BETTER BLUES

ERNEST DICKERSON .... CINEMATOGRAPHER
WYNN THOMAS .... PRODUCTION DESIGNER
RUTH E. CARTER .... COSTUME DESIGNER
SAM POLLARD .... FILM EDITOR

MOB BOSS

GARY GRAVER .... CINEMATOGRAPHER
COLIN DE ROVIN .... PRODUCTION DESIGNER
JILL CONNER .... COSTUME DESIGNER
CHRIS ROTH .... FILM EDITOR

MODERN DAY HOUDINI

STEPHEN L. POSEY .... CINEMATOGRAPHER

MODERN GIRLS

KAREN GROSSMAN .... CINEMATOGRAPHER
LAURENCE BENNET .... PRODUCTION DESIGNER
THEDA DERAMUS .... COSTUME DESIGNER
MITCHELL SINOWAY .... FILM EDITOR

MODERN PROBLEMS

EDMOND L. KOONS .... CINEMATOGRAPHER
JACK SENTER .... PRODUCTION DESIGNER
MICHAEL JABLOW .... FILM EDITOR

MODERN ROMANCE

ERIC SAARINEN .... CINEMATOGRAPHER
ED RICHARDSON .... PRODUCTION DESIGNER
DAVID FINFER .... FILM EDITOR

MODERNS, THE

TOYOMICHI KURITA .... CINEMATOGRAPHER
STEVEN LEGLER .... PRODUCTION DESIGNER
RENEE APRIL .... COSTUME DESIGNER
DEBRA T. SMITH .... FILM EDITOR
SCOTT BROCK .... FILM EDITOR

MODESTY BLAISE

RICHARD MACDONALD .... PRODUCTION DESIGNER

MOHAMMED, MESSENGER OF GOD

JACK HILDYARD .... CINEMATOGRAPHER
MAURICE FOWLER .... PRODUCTION DESIGNER

MOLIERE

BERNARD ZITZERMANN .... CINEMATOGRAPHER

MOLLY MAGUIRES, THE

TAMBI LARSEN .... PRODUCTION DESIGNER
FRANK BRACHT .... FILM EDITOR

MOM FOR CHRISTMAS, A (TF)

RON LAUTORE .... CINEMATOGRAPHER
GLENDA GANIS .... PRODUCTION DESIGNER
LES GREEN .... FILM EDITOR

MOMENT BY MOMENT

PHILIP LATHROP .... CINEMATOGRAPHER
DAVID M. HABER .... PRODUCTION DESIGNER
HARRY HORNER .... PRODUCTION DESIGNER
ALBERT WOLSKY .... COSTUME DESIGNER
JOHN F. BURNETT .... FILM EDITOR

MOMMA'S BOY

ROBBIE GREENBERG .... CINEMATOGRAPHER

MOMMIE DEAREST

PAUL LOHMANN .... CINEMATOGRAPHER
HAROLD MICHELSON .... PRODUCTION DESIGNER
WILLIAM MALLEY .... PRODUCTION DESIGNER
IRENE SHARAFF .... COSTUME DESIGNER
PETER E. BERGER .... FILM EDITOR
RICHARD A. HARRIS .... FILM EDITOR

MON ONCLE D'AMERIQUE

ALBERT JURGENSON .... FILM EDITOR

MONA LISA

ROGER PRATT .... CINEMATOGRAPHER
GEMMA JACKSON .... PRODUCTION DESIGNER
JAMIE LEONARD .... PRODUCTION DESIGNER
LOUISE FROGLEY .... COSTUME DESIGNER
LESLEY WALKER .... FILM EDITOR

MONDO NEW YORK

RICHARD FRIEDMAN .... FILM EDITOR

MONEY MOVERS

DONALD MCALPINE .... CINEMATOGRAPHER
DAVID COPPING .... PRODUCTION DESIGNER
WILLIAM M. ANDERSON .... FILM EDITOR

MONEY PIT, THE

GORDON WILLIS .... CINEMATOGRAPHER
PATRIZIA VON BRANDENSTEIN .... PRODUCTION DESIGNER
WRAY STEVEN GRAHAM .... PRODUCTION DESIGNER
RUTH MORLEY .... COSTUME DESIGNER
JACQUELINE CAMBAS .... FILM EDITOR

MONKEY GRIP

DAVID GRIBBLE .... CINEMATOGRAPHER

MONKEY HUSTLE, THE

JACK L. RICHARDS .... CINEMATOGRAPHER

MONKEY SHINES

JAMES A. CONTNER .... CINEMATOGRAPHER
CLETUS ANDERSON .... PRODUCTION DESIGNER
J. MARK HERRINGTON .... PRODUCTION DESIGNER
JIM FENG .... PRODUCTION DESIGNER
PASQUALE BUBA .... FILM EDITOR

MONSIEUR ALBERT

GHISLAIN CLOQUET† .... CINEMATOGRAPHER

MONSIGNOR

BILLY WILLIAMS .... CINEMATOGRAPHER
JOHN DE CUIR .... PRODUCTION DESIGNER
THEONI V. ALDREDGE .... COSTUME DESIGNER
PETER E. BERGER .... FILM EDITOR

MONSTER CLUB, THE

PETER TANNER .... FILM EDITOR

MONSTER IN THE CLOSET

MARK CONTE .... FILM EDITOR
RAJA GOSNELL .... FILM EDITOR

MONSTER SHARK

ANTONELLO GELENG .... PRODUCTION DESIGNER

MONSTER SQUAD

BRADFORD MAY .... CINEMATOGRAPHER
ALBERT BRENNER .... PRODUCTION DESIGNER
DAVID M. HABER .... PRODUCTION DESIGNER
MICHAEL HOFFMAN .... COSTUME DESIGNER
JAMES MITCHELL .... FILM EDITOR

MONTE WALSH

DAVID M. WALSH .... CINEMATOGRAPHER
ALBERT BRENNER .... PRODUCTION DESIGNER

MONTENEGRO

TOMISLAV PINTER .... CINEMATOGRAPHER
SYLVIA INGEMARSSON .... FILM EDITOR

MONTH IN THE COUNTRY, A

KENNETH MACMILLAN .... CINEMATOGRAPHER
LEO AUSTIN .... PRODUCTION DESIGNER

MONTY PYTHON & THE HOLY GRAIL

ROY FORGE SMITH .... PRODUCTION DESIGNER

MONTY PYTHON LIVE AT THE HOLLYWOOD BOWL (FD)

JULIAN DOYLE .... FILM EDITOR

MONTY PYTHON'S LIFE OF BRIAN

PETER BIZIOU .... CINEMATOGRAPHER
ROGER CHRISTIAN .... PRODUCTION DESIGNER
CHARLES KNODE .... COSTUME DESIGNER
HAZEL PETHIG .... COSTUME DESIGNER
JULIAN DOYLE .... FILM EDITOR

MONTY PYTHON'S THE MEANING OF LIFE

PETER HANNAN .... CINEMATOGRAPHER
HARRY LANGE .... PRODUCTION DESIGNER
RICHARD DAWKING .... PRODUCTION DESIGNER
JAMES ACHESON .... COSTUME DESIGNER
JULIAN DOYLE .... FILM EDITOR

MOON IN THE GUTTER, THE

PHILIPPE ROUSSELOT .... CINEMATOGRAPHER
HILTON MCCONNICO .... PRODUCTION DESIGNER

Mi-Mo

CINEMATOGRAPHERS
PRODUCTION
DESIGNERS,
COSTUME
DESIGNERS AND
FILM EDITORS
GUIDE

I
N
D
E
X

O
F

F
I
L
M

T
I
T
L
E
S

Mo-Mo

CINEMATOGRAPHERS
PRODUCTION
DESIGNERS,
COSTUME
DESIGNERS and
FILM EDITORS
GUIDE

I
N
D
E
X

O
F

F
I
L
M

T
I
T
L
E
S

MOON OVER PARADOR
DONALD MCALPINE .... CINEMATOGRAPHER
MARCOS FLAKSMAN .... PRODUCTION DESIGNER
PATO GUZMAN .... PRODUCTION DESIGNER
ALBERT WOLSKY .... COSTUME DESIGNER
HARRY CURTIS .... COSTUME DESIGNER
STUART H. PAPPE .... FILM EDITOR

MOON OVER THE ALLEY
PETER HANNAN .... CINEMATOGRAPHER

MOONLIGHTING
TONY PIERCE-ROBERTS .... CINEMATOGRAPHER
TONY WOLLARD .... PRODUCTION DESIGNER
BARRIE VINCE .... FILM EDITOR

MOONRAKER
JEAN TOURNIER .... CINEMATOGRAPHER
ANTON FURST .... PRODUCTION DESIGNER
CHARLES BISHOP .... PRODUCTION DESIGNER
KEN ADAM .... PRODUCTION DESIGNER
JOHN GLEN .... FILM EDITOR

MOONSHINE COUNTY EXPRESS
GARY GRAVER .... CINEMATOGRAPHER
PETER JAMISON .... PRODUCTION DESIGNER
GENE RUGGIERO .... FILM EDITOR

MOONSHINE WAR, THE
RICHARD H. KLINE .... CINEMATOGRAPHER

MOONSTRUCK
DAVID WATKIN .... CINEMATOGRAPHER
DAN DAVIS .... PRODUCTION DESIGNER
PHILIP ROSENBERG .... PRODUCTION DESIGNER
THEONI V. ALDREDGE .... COSTUME DESIGNER
LOU LOMBARDO .... FILM EDITOR

MOONWALKER
FREDERICK ELMES .... CINEMATOGRAPHER
JOHN HORA .... CINEMATOGRAPHER
BETTY PECHA MADDEN .... COSTUME DESIGNER
DAVID BLEWITT .... FILM EDITOR

MORE
RITA ROLAND .... FILM EDITOR

MORE AMERICAN GRAFFITI
CALEB DESCHANEL .... CINEMATOGRAPHER
RAYMOND G. STOREY .... PRODUCTION DESIGNER
AGGIE GUERARD RODGERS .... COSTUME DESIGNER
TINA HIRSCH .... FILM EDITOR

MORE THAN FRIENDS (TF)
SOL NEGRIN .... CINEMATOGRAPHER

MORE WILD, WILD WEST (TF)
ALBERT HESCHONG .... PRODUCTION DESIGNER

MORGAN STEWART'S COMING HOME
RICHARD E. BROOKS .... CINEMATOGRAPHER
CHARLES BENNETT .... PRODUCTION DESIGNER
MOLLY MAGINNIS .... COSTUME DESIGNER
BOB LETTERMAN .... FILM EDITOR

MORGAN!
LARRY PIZER .... CINEMATOGRAPHER

MORGAN, A SUITABLE CASE FOR TREATMENT
LARRY PIZER .... CINEMATOGRAPHER

MORNING AFTER, THE
ANDRZEJ BARTKOWIAK .... CINEMATOGRAPHER
ALBERT BRENNER .... PRODUCTION DESIGNER
KANDY STERN .... PRODUCTION DESIGNER
ANN ROTH .... COSTUME DESIGNER
JOEL GOODMAN .... FILM EDITOR

MORONS FROM OUTER SPACE
PHIL MEHEUX .... CINEMATOGRAPHER
BERT DAVEY .... PRODUCTION DESIGNER
BRIAN EATWELL .... PRODUCTION DESIGNER
MAY ROUTH .... COSTUME DESIGNER
PETER BOYLE .... FILM EDITOR

MORTAL THOUGHTS
ELLIOT DAVIS .... CINEMATOGRAPHER
HOWARD CUMMINGS .... PRODUCTION DESIGNER
HOPE HANAFIN .... COSTUME DESIGNER
TOM WALLS .... FILM EDITOR

MORTUARY
GARY GRAVER .... CINEMATOGRAPHER
RANDY SER .... PRODUCTION DESIGNER
STANFORD C. ALLEN .... FILM EDITOR

MORTUARY ACADEMY
ROY H. WAGNER .... CINEMATOGRAPHER
ELLEN KENESHA .... FILM EDITOR

MOSCOW ON THE HUDSON
DONALD MCALPINE .... CINEMATOGRAPHER
MICHAEL MOLLY .... PRODUCTION DESIGNER
PATO GUZMAN .... PRODUCTION DESIGNER
PETER ROTHE .... PRODUCTION DESIGNER
ALBERT WOLSKY .... COSTUME DESIGNER
RICHARD HALSEY .... FILM EDITOR

MOSES
ENRICO SABBATINI .... COSTUME DESIGNER
GERRY HAMBLING .... FILM EDITOR
PETER BOITA .... FILM EDITOR

MOSQUITO COAST, THE
JOHN SEALE .... CINEMATOGRAPHER
BRIAN NICKLES .... PRODUCTION DESIGNER
JOHN STODDART .... PRODUCTION DESIGNER
GARY JONES .... COSTUME DESIGNER
RICHARD FRANCIS-BRUCE .... FILM EDITOR
THOM NOBLE .... FILM EDITOR

MOST BEAUTIFUL, THE
SHINOBU MURAKI .... PRODUCTION DESIGNER
YOSHIRO MURAKI .... PRODUCTION DESIGNER

MOTEL HELL
THOMAS DEL RUTH .... CINEMATOGRAPHER
JOSEPH ALTADONNA .... PRODUCTION DESIGNER
BERNARD GRIBBLE .... FILM EDITOR

MOTHER AND DAUGHTER - THE LOVING WAR (TF)
RICHARD SAWYER .... PRODUCTION DESIGNER
MARIANNA ASTROM DEFINA .... COSTUME DESIGNER

MOTHER KUSTERS GOES TO HEAVEN
MICHAEL BALLHAUS .... CINEMATOGRAPHER

MOTHER LODE
RICHARD LEITERMAN .... CINEMATOGRAPHER
MICHAEL S. BOLTON .... PRODUCTION DESIGNER
ERIC BOYD-PERKINS .... FILM EDITOR

MOTHER LOVE-PARTS I-III (MS)
NIGEL WALTERS .... CINEMATOGRAPHER
SIMON MAGGS .... CINEMATOGRAPHER
KEN LEDSHAM .... PRODUCTION DESIGNER
LAWRENCE WILLIAMS .... PRODUCTION DESIGNER
RAY WINGROVE .... FILM EDITOR

MOTHER TERESA (FD)
EDWARD LACHMAN .... CINEMATOGRAPHER

MOTHER'S COURAGE: THE MARY THOMAS STORY, A (TF)
KING BAGGOT .... CINEMATOGRAPHER
MICHAEL MERRITT .... PRODUCTION DESIGNER
RICHARD A. HARRIS .... FILM EDITOR

MOTHER'S DAY
JOSEPH MANGINE .... CINEMATOGRAPHER

MOTHER, JUGS & SPEED
RALPH WOOLSEY .... CINEMATOGRAPHER
WALTER SCOTT HERNDON† .... PRODUCTION DESIGNER

MOTHER, MOTHER
JOAO FERNANDES .... CINEMATOGRAPHER
PENELOPE SHAW .... FILM EDITOR

MOTHERLODE
DOUGLAS HIGGINS .... PRODUCTION DESIGNER

MOTOR KINGS
BILL BUTLER .... CINEMATOGRAPHER

MOUNTAIN MEN, THE
MICHEL HUGO .... CINEMATOGRAPHER
WILLIAM KENNEY .... PRODUCTION DESIGNER
EVA RUGGIERO .... FILM EDITOR

MOUNTAINS OF THE MOON
ROGER DEAKINS .... CINEMATOGRAPHER
NORMAN REYNOLDS .... PRODUCTION DESIGNER
JENNY BEAVAN .... COSTUME DESIGNER
THOM NOBLE .... FILM EDITOR

MOVE
JACK MARTIN SMITH .... PRODUCTION DESIGNER

MOVERS & SHAKERS
ROBBIE GREENBERG .... CINEMATOGRAPHER
DONALD LIGHT-HARRIS .... PRODUCTION DESIGNER
TOM BENKO .... FILM EDITOR

MOVIE MOVIE
CHARLES ROSHER, JR. .... CINEMATOGRAPHER
BRUCE SURTEES .... CINEMATOGRAPHER
JACK FISK .... PRODUCTION DESIGNER
PATRICIA NORRIS .... COSTUME DESIGNER
GEORGE HIVELY .... FILM EDITOR

MOVING
DONALD MCALPINE .... CINEMATOGRAPHER
DAVID L. SNYDER .... PRODUCTION DESIGNER
JOE WOOD .... PRODUCTION DESIGNER
DEBORAH L. SCOTT .... COSTUME DESIGNER
ALAN BALSAM .... FILM EDITOR

MOVING OUT
VINCENT MONTON .... CINEMATOGRAPHER
ROBERT MARTIN .... FILM EDITOR

MOVING TARGET (TF)
MARK MELNICK .... FILM EDITOR

MOVING VIOLATIONS
ROBERT ELSWIT .... CINEMATOGRAPHER
CHARLES CORRELL .... CINEMATOGRAPHER
GREGORY PICKRELL .... PRODUCTION DESIGNER
RICHARD SAWYER .... PRODUCTION DESIGNER
VIRGINIA FIELD .... PRODUCTION DESIGNER
DARRYL LEVINE .... COSTUME DESIGNER
TOM WALLS .... FILM EDITOR

MOVIOLA (MS)
GAYNE RESCHER .... CINEMATOGRAPHER
MICHAEL BAUGH .... PRODUCTION DESIGNER
TRAVILLA .... COSTUME DESIGNER

MR. & MRS. BRIDGE
TONY PIERCE-ROBERTS .... CINEMATOGRAPHER
DAVID GROPMAN .... PRODUCTION DESIGNER
CAROL RAMSEY .... COSTUME DESIGNER
HUMPHREY DIXON .... FILM EDITOR

MR. BILLION
MATTHEW F. LEONETTI .... CINEMATOGRAPHER
RICHARD BERGER .... PRODUCTION DESIGNER
O. NICHOLAS BROWN .... FILM EDITOR

MR. DESTINY
ALEX THOMSON .... CINEMATOGRAPHER
MICHAEL SEYMOUR .... PRODUCTION DESIGNER
JANE GREENWOOD .... COSTUME DESIGNER
MICHAEL R. MILLER .... FILM EDITOR

MR. FROST
DOMINIQUE BRENGUIER .... CINEMATOGRAPHER
MAX BERTO .... PRODUCTION DESIGNER
JUDY SHREWSBURY .... COSTUME DESIGNER
RAY LOVEJOY .... FILM EDITOR

MR. JOHNSON
PETER JAMES .... CINEMATOGRAPHER
HERBERT PINTER .... PRODUCTION DESIGNER
ROSEMARY BURROWS .... COSTUME DESIGNER
HUMPHREY DIXON .... FILM EDITOR

MR. KLEIN
GERRY FISHER .... CINEMATOGRAPHER

MR. LOVE
ADRIENNE ATKINSON .... PRODUCTION DESIGNER
ANN HOLLYWOOD .... COSTUME DESIGNER
ALAN J. CUMNER-PRICE .... FILM EDITOR

MR. MAJESTYK
RALPH E. WINTERS .... FILM EDITOR

MR. MIKE'S MONDO VIDEO
EUGENE LEE .... PRODUCTION DESIGNER
ALAN MILLER .... FILM EDITOR
ROBERT TISCHLER .... FILM EDITOR

MR. MOM
VICTOR J. KEMPER .... CINEMATOGRAPHER
ALFRED SWEENEY .... PRODUCTION DESIGNER
NOLAN MILLER .... COSTUME DESIGNER
PATRICK KENNEDY .... FILM EDITOR

MR. NORTH
ROBIN VIDGEON .... CINEMATOGRAPHER
EUGENE LEE .... PRODUCTION DESIGNER
RITA RIGGS .... COSTUME DESIGNER
ROBERTO SILVI .... FILM EDITOR

MR. PATMAN
JOHN COQUILLON .... CINEMATOGRAPHER
TREVOR WILLIAMS .... PRODUCTION DESIGNER
WILLIAM WARE THEISS .... COSTUME DESIGNER
MAX BENEDICT .... FILM EDITOR

MR. QUILP
CHRISTOPHER CHALLIS .... CINEMATOGRAPHER
NORMAN REYNOLDS .... PRODUCTION DESIGNER
JOHN JYMPSON .... FILM EDITOR

MR. RICCO
FRANK STANLEY .... CINEMATOGRAPHER

MRS. DELAFIELD WANTS TO MARRY (TF)
DOUGLAS HIGGINS .... PRODUCTION DESIGNER

MRS. POLLIFAX - SPY
JACK POPLIN .... PRODUCTION DESIGNER

MRS. SOFFEL
RUSSELL BOYD .... CINEMATOGRAPHER
JACQUES BRADETTE .... PRODUCTION DESIGNER
LUCIANA ARRIGHI .... PRODUCTION DESIGNER
ROY FORGE SMITH .... PRODUCTION DESIGNER
SHAY CUNLIFFE .... COSTUME DESIGNER
NICHOLAS BEAUMAN .... FILM EDITOR

MS. 45
JAMES MOMEL .... CINEMATOGRAPHER

MUGGABLE MARY: STREET COP (TF)
GARY WEIST .... PRODUCTION DESIGNER

MUGSY'S GIRLS
PAUL LOHMANN .... CINEMATOGRAPHER

MUNCHIES
JONATHAN WEST .... CINEMATOGRAPHER
JOHN BALLOWE .... PRODUCTION DESIGNER
KATIE SPARKS .... COSTUME DESIGNER

MUPPET MOVIE, THE
ISIDORE MANKOFSKY .... CINEMATOGRAPHER
JOEL SCHILLER .... PRODUCTION DESIGNER
LES GOBRUEGGE .... PRODUCTION DESIGNER
GWEN CAPETANOS BOUZON .... COSTUME DESIGNER
CHRISTOPHER GREENBURY .... FILM EDITOR

MUPPETS TAKE MANHATTAN, THE
ROBERT PAYNTER .... CINEMATOGRAPHER
PAUL EADS .... PRODUCTION DESIGNER
WRAY STEVEN GRAHAM .... PRODUCTION DESIGNER
STEPHEN HENDRICKSON .... PRODUCTION DESIGNER
KAREN ROSTON .... COSTUME DESIGNER
EVAN LOTTMAN .... FILM EDITOR

MURDER AMONG FRIENDS (TF)
PAUL PETERS .... PRODUCTION DESIGNER

MURDER AT THE PTA LUNCHEON (TF)
STAN TAYLOR .... CINEMATOGRAPHER
ROY ALAN AMARAL .... PRODUCTION DESIGNER
BOB WYMAN .... FILM EDITOR

MURDER AT THE WORLD SERIES (TF)
ELAYNE CEDER .... PRODUCTION DESIGNER

MURDER BY MOONLIGHT (TF)
HAROLD MICHELSON .... PRODUCTION DESIGNER

Mo-Mu

CINEMATOGRAPHERS
PRODUCTION
DESIGNERS,
COSTUME
DESIGNERS AND
FILM EDITORS
GUIDE

INDEX OF FILM TITLES

393

Mu-Mu

CINEMATOGRAPHERS
PRODUCTION
DESIGNERS,
COSTUME
DESIGNERS AND
FILM EDITORS
GUIDE

I
N
D
E
X

O
F

F
I
L
M

T
I
T
L
E
S

394

MURDER BY DEATH
DAVID M. WALSH .... CINEMATOGRAPHER
STEPHEN GRIMES† .... PRODUCTION DESIGNER
JOHN F. BURNETT .... FILM EDITOR
MARGARET BOOTH .... FILM EDITOR

MURDER BY DECREE
REGINALD H. MORRIS .... CINEMATOGRAPHER
HARRY POTTLE .... PRODUCTION DESIGNER
KEN DAVIS .... PRODUCTION DESIGNER
JUDY MOORCROFT .... COSTUME DESIGNER
STAN COLE .... FILM EDITOR

MURDER BY MOONLIGHT (TF)
DAVID WATKIN .... CINEMATOGRAPHER
RALPH SHELDON .... FILM EDITOR
ROBERT K. LAMBERT .... FILM EDITOR

MURDER BY PHONE
REGINALD H. MORRIS .... CINEMATOGRAPHER
SEAMUS FLANNERY .... PRODUCTION DESIGNER

MURDER BY THE BOOK (TF)
JOANNE D'ANTONIO .... FILM EDITOR

MURDER C.O.D. (TF)
BERND HEINL .... CINEMATOGRAPHER
JO ANNE CHORNEY .... PRODUCTION DESIGNER
PAMELA MALOUF-CUNDY .... FILM EDITOR

MURDER IN COWETA COUNTY (TF)
LARRY PIZER .... CINEMATOGRAPHER

MURDER IN SPACE (TF)
LASZLO GEORGE .... CINEMATOGRAPHER

MURDER IN TEXAS (TF)
DONALD M. MORGAN .... CINEMATOGRAPHER
VINCENT M. CRESCIMAN .... PRODUCTION DESIGNER

MURDER LUST
T.L. LANKFORD .... PRODUCTION DESIGNER

MURDER ON LINE ONE
JOHN DE BORMAN .... CINEMATOGRAPHER
GEO CLARKE .... PRODUCTION DESIGNER
SUE WHALL .... COSTUME DESIGNER
PAVIENDA COTT .... FILM EDITOR

MURDER ON THE ORIENT EXPRESS
GEOFFREY UNSWORTH† .... CINEMATOGRAPHER
SIMON HOLLAND .... PRODUCTION DESIGNER
TONY WALTON .... PRODUCTION DESIGNER
JACK STEPHENS .... PRODUCTION DESIGNER
TONY WALTON .... COSTUME DESIGNER
ANNE V. COATES .... FILM EDITOR

MURDER ONE
LUDEK BOGNER .... CINEMATOGRAPHER
MICHAEL MCMAHON .... FILM EDITOR

MURDER STORY
MORLEY SMITH .... PRODUCTION DESIGNER
RODNEY HOLLAND .... FILM EDITOR

MURDER TIMES SEVEN (TF)
BERT DUNK .... CINEMATOGRAPHER
NORMAN GAY .... FILM EDITOR

MURDER WITH MIRRORS (TF)
BRIAN WEST .... CINEMATOGRAPHER
JANE ROBINSON .... COSTUME DESIGNER

MURDER: BY REASON OF INSANITY (TF)
SHELLEY KOMAROV .... COSTUME DESIGNER
JOHN C. HORGER .... FILM EDITOR

MURDERERS AMONG US: THE SIMON WIESENTHAL STORY (CTF)
ELMER RAGALYI .... CINEMATOGRAPHER
CHRISTOPHER WIMBLE .... FILM EDITOR
EVA GARDOS .... FILM EDITOR

MURDEROUS VISION (CTF)
ALEZ NEPOMNIASCHY .... CINEMATOGRAPHER
CHRISTOPHER HORNER .... PRODUCTION DESIGNER
ROSS ALBERT .... FILM EDITOR

MURDERS IN THE RUE MORGUE, THE (TF)
BRUNO DE KEYZER .... CINEMATOGRAPHER

MURPH THE SURF
MICHEL HUGO .... CINEMATOGRAPHER
JAMES D. VANCE .... PRODUCTION DESIGNER
HOWARD SMITH .... FILM EDITOR

MURPHY'S LAW
ALEX PHILLIPS .... CINEMATOGRAPHER
WILLIAM CRUISE .... PRODUCTION DESIGNER
SHELLEY KOMAROV .... COSTUME DESIGNER
PETER LEE THOMPSON .... FILM EDITOR

MURPHY'S LAW (PILOT)
PAUL RUBELL .... FILM EDITOR

MURPHY'S ROMANCE
WILLIAM A. FRAKER .... CINEMATOGRAPHER
JOEL SCHILLER .... PRODUCTION DESIGNER
JOE I. TOMPKINS .... COSTUME DESIGNER
SIDNEY LEVIN .... FILM EDITOR

MURPHY'S WAR
DOUGLAS SLOCOMBE .... CINEMATOGRAPHER

MUSIC BOX
PATRICK BLOSSIER .... CINEMATOGRAPHER
JEANNINE C. OPPEWALL .... PRODUCTION DESIGNER
RITA SALAZAR .... COSTUME DESIGNER
JOELE VAN EFFENTERRE .... FILM EDITOR

MUSIC LOVERS, THE
DOUGLAS SLOCOMBE .... CINEMATOGRAPHER

MUSIC MACHINE, THE
PHIL MEHEUX .... CINEMATOGRAPHER
ALAN PATILLO .... FILM EDITOR
BRIAN SMEDLEY-ASTON .... FILM EDITOR

MUSSOLINI: THE UNTOLD STORY (MS)
ROBERT STEADMAN .... CINEMATOGRAPHER

MUTANT
ALFRED TAYLOR .... CINEMATOGRAPHER

MUTINY ON THE BOUNTY
ROBERT SURTEES† .... CINEMATOGRAPHER

MY AMERICAN COUSIN
RICHARD LEITERMAN .... CINEMATOGRAPHER
HAIDA PAUL .... FILM EDITOR

MY AMERICAN UNCLE
CATHERINE LETERRIER .... COSTUME DESIGNER

MY BEAUTIFUL LAUNDRETTE
OLIVER STAPLETON .... CINEMATOGRAPHER
HUGO LUCZYC WYHOWSKI .... PRODUCTION DESIGNER
LINDY HEMMING .... COSTUME DESIGNER
MICK AUDSLEY .... FILM EDITOR

MY BEST FRIEND IS A VAMPIRE
JAMES BARTLE .... CINEMATOGRAPHER
MICHAEL MOLLY .... PRODUCTION DESIGNER
RONA LAMONT .... COSTUME DESIGNER
JANICE HAMPTON .... FILM EDITOR
GAIL YASUNAGA .... FILM EDITOR

MY BEST FRIEND'S GIRL
JEAN PENZER .... CINEMATOGRAPHER

MY BLOODY VALENTINE
RODNEY GIBBONS .... CINEMATOGRAPHER
JEAN LA FLEUR .... FILM EDITOR

MY BLUE HEAVEN
JOHN BAILEY .... CINEMATOGRAPHER
CHARLES ROSEN .... PRODUCTION DESIGNER
JOSEPH G. AULISI .... COSTUME DESIGNER
STEPHEN A. ROTTER .... FILM EDITOR

MY BODYGUARD
MICHAEL D. MARGULIES .... CINEMATOGRAPHER
JACKSON DE GOVIA .... PRODUCTION DESIGNER
STU LINDER .... FILM EDITOR

MY BOYFRIEND'S BACK
LARRY PIZER .... CINEMATOGRAPHER

MY BRILLIANT CAREER
DONALD MCALPINE .... CINEMATOGRAPHER
LUCIANA ARRIGHI .... PRODUCTION DESIGNER
ANNA SENIOR .... COSTUME DESIGNER
NICHOLAS BEAUMAN .... FILM EDITOR

My-My

CINEMATOGRAPHERS
PRODUCTION
DESIGNERS,
COSTUME
DESIGNERS AND
FILM EDITORS
GUIDE

MY CHAUFFEUR
HARRY MATHIAS .... CINEMATOGRAPHER
C.J. STRAWN .... PRODUCTION DESIGNER
CAMILE SCHROEDER .... COSTUME DESIGNER
RICHARD E. WESTOVER .... FILM EDITOR

MY COUSIN RACHEL
JOHN DE CUIR .... PRODUCTION DESIGNER

MY DARK LADY
DARREN KLOOMOK .... FILM EDITOR

MY DEMON LOVER
JACQUES HAITKIN .... CINEMATOGRAPHER
BRENTON SWIFT .... PRODUCTION DESIGNER
DOUGLAS DICK .... PRODUCTION DESIGNER
TOM MCKINLEY .... COSTUME DESIGNER
RONALD ROOSE .... FILM EDITOR

MY DINNER WITH ANDRE
JERI SOPANEN .... CINEMATOGRAPHER
DAVID MITCHELL .... PRODUCTION DESIGNER
STEVEN MCCABE .... PRODUCTION DESIGNER
JEFFREY ULLMAN .... COSTUME DESIGNER
SUZANNE BARON .... FILM EDITOR

MY FATHER'S GLORY
ROBERT ALAZRAKI .... CINEMATOGRAPHER
PIERRE GILLETTE .... FILM EDITOR

MY FATHER, MY SON (TF)
DURINDA RICE WOOD .... COSTUME DESIGNER

MY FAVORITE YEAR
GERALD HIRSCHFELD .... CINEMATOGRAPHER
CHARLES ROSEN .... PRODUCTION DESIGNER
MAY ROUTH .... COSTUME DESIGNER
RICHARD CHEW .... FILM EDITOR

MY FIRST LOVE
BERNARD ZITZERMANN .... CINEMATOGRAPHER

MY FIRST WIFE
YURI SOKOL .... CINEMATOGRAPHER
ASHER BILU .... PRODUCTION DESIGNER
TIM LEWIS .... FILM EDITOR

MY GIRL
PAUL ELLIOT .... CINEMATOGRAPHER

MY HEROES HAVE ALWAYS BEEN COWBOYS
BERND HEINL .... CINEMATOGRAPHER
RUDY DILLON .... COSTUME DESIGNER
DENNIS M. HILL .... FILM EDITOR

MY LEFT FOOT
JACK CONROY .... CINEMATOGRAPHER
AUSTEN SPRIGGS .... PRODUCTION DESIGNER
J. PATRICK DUFFNER .... FILM EDITOR

MY LIFE AS A DOG
JORGEN PERSSON .... CINEMATOGRAPHER
CHRISTER FURUBRAND .... FILM EDITOR

MY LITTLE GIRL
PIERRE L'HOMME .... CINEMATOGRAPHER
DAN LEIGH .... PRODUCTION DESIGNER
SUSAN GAMMIE .... COSTUME DESIGNER
KATHERINE WENNING .... FILM EDITOR

MY MAN ADAM
JEFF S. GOURSON .... FILM EDITOR

MY MOTHER'S SECRET LIFE (TF)
ROBBIE GREENBERG .... CINEMATOGRAPHER
ROBERT TURTURICE .... COSTUME DESIGNER

MY NAME IS BILL W. (TF)
FRED HARPMAN .... PRODUCTION DESIGNER
APRIL FERRY .... COSTUME DESIGNER
JOHN WRIGHT .... FILM EDITOR
PAUL RUBELL .... FILM EDITOR

MY NIGHT AT MAUD'S
NESTOR ALMENDROS .... CINEMATOGRAPHER

MY OLD MAN (TF)
LARRY PIZER .... CINEMATOGRAPHER
PATRIZIA VON BRANDENSTEIN .... PRODUCTION DESIGNER

MY SCIENCE PROJECT
DAVID M. WALSH .... CINEMATOGRAPHER
DAVID L. SNYDER .... PRODUCTION DESIGNER
BETSY JONES .... COSTUME DESIGNER
CARROLL TIMOTHY O'MEARA .... FILM EDITOR

MY SISTER'S CHILDREN GO TO TOWN
MIKAEL SALOMON .... CINEMATOGRAPHER

MY SISTERS CHILDREN GOES ASTRAY
MIKAEL SALOMON .... CINEMATOGRAPHER

MY STEPMOTHER IS AN ALIEN
RICHARD H. KLINE .... CINEMATOGRAPHER
CHARLES ROSEN .... PRODUCTION DESIGNER
AGGIE GUERARD RODGERS .... COSTUME DESIGNER
JACQUELINE CAMBAS .... FILM EDITOR

MY TUTOR
MAC AHLBERG .... CINEMATOGRAPHER
LINDA PEARL .... PRODUCTION DESIGNER
KRISTIN NELSON .... COSTUME DESIGNER
SIDNEY WOLINSKY .... FILM EDITOR

MY WICKED, WICKED WAYS...THE LEGEND OF ERROL FLYNN (TF)
JAMES M. GLENNON .... CINEMATOGRAPHER
ALBERT HESCHONG .... PRODUCTION DESIGNER
TRAVILLA .... COSTUME DESIGNER

MYRA BRECKINRIDGE
RICHARD MOORE .... CINEMATOGRAPHER
FRED HARPMAN .... PRODUCTION DESIGNER
JACK MARTIN SMITH .... PRODUCTION DESIGNER
DANFORD B. GREENE .... FILM EDITOR

MYSTERE
RAIMONDO CROCIANI .... FILM EDITOR

MYSTERIES
ROBBY MULLER .... CINEMATOGRAPHER

MYSTERIOUS ISLAND OF BEAUTIFUL WOMEN (TF)
KIRK AXTELL .... PRODUCTION DESIGNER

MYSTERIOUS MONSTERS, THE
DAVID MYERS .... CINEMATOGRAPHER
ROBERT K. LAMBERT .... FILM EDITOR

MYSTERIOUS TWO (TF)
ELAYNE CEDER .... PRODUCTION DESIGNER

MYSTERY OF ALEXINA, THE
BERNARD ZITZERMANN .... CINEMATOGRAPHER

MYSTERY OF FLIGHT 1501, THE (TF)
PAUL LOHMANN .... CINEMATOGRAPHER
MARCIA HINDS .... PRODUCTION DESIGNER
ED ABROMS .... FILM EDITOR

MYSTERY TRAIN
ROBBY MULLER .... CINEMATOGRAPHER
DAN BISHOP .... PRODUCTION DESIGNER
CAROL WOOD .... COSTUME DESIGNER
MELODY LONDON .... FILM EDITOR

MYSTIC PIZZA
TIM SUHRSTEDT .... CINEMATOGRAPHER
DAVID CHAPMAN .... PRODUCTION DESIGNER
MARK HAACK .... PRODUCTION DESIGNER
JENNIFER VON MAYRHAUSER .... COSTUME DESIGNER
DON BROCHU .... FILM EDITOR
MARION ROTHMAN .... FILM EDITOR

MYSTIC WARRIOR, THE (MS)
STEVAN LARNER .... CINEMATOGRAPHER
MORT RABINOWITZ .... PRODUCTION DESIGNER

MYSTIQUE
AFFONSO BEATO .... CINEMATOGRAPHER
KEN DAVIS .... PRODUCTION DESIGNER

Na-Ne

CINEMATOGRAPHERS
PRODUCTION
DESIGNERS,
COSTUME
DESIGNERS AND
FILM EDITORS
GUIDE

I
N
D
E
X

O
F

F
I
L
M

T
I
T
L
E
S

N

N A SHALLOW GRAVE
MOLLY MAGINNIS .... COSTUME DESIGNER

NADIA (TF)
FRANK BEASCOECHEA .... CINEMATOGRAPHER
DOROTHY BACA .... COSTUME DESIGNER

NADINE
NESTOR ALMENDROS .... CINEMATOGRAPHER
PAUL SYLBERT .... PRODUCTION DESIGNER
PETER LANDSDOWN SMITH .... PRODUCTION DESIGNER
ALBERT WOLSKY .... COSTUME DESIGNER
HARRY CURTIS .... COSTUME DESIGNER
SAM O'STEEN .... FILM EDITOR

NAKED APE, THE
LAWRENCE G. PAULL .... PRODUCTION DESIGNER
ROBERT L. WOLFE .... FILM EDITOR

NAKED CAGE, THE
HAL TRUSSELL .... CINEMATOGRAPHER
SHELLEY KOMAROV .... COSTUME DESIGNER

NAKED COUNTRY, THE
DAVID EGGBY .... CINEMATOGRAPHER

NAKED FACE, THE
DAVID GURFINKEL .... CINEMATOGRAPHER
WILLIAM FOSSER .... PRODUCTION DESIGNER
JAY HURLEY .... COSTUME DESIGNER
SANDRA DAVIDSON .... COSTUME DESIGNER
PHILIP SHAW .... FILM EDITOR

NAKED GUN: FROM THE FILES OF POLICE SQUAD, THE
ROBERT M. STEVENS .... CINEMATOGRAPHER
DONALD B. WOODRUFF .... PRODUCTION DESIGNER
JOHN J. LLOYD .... PRODUCTION DESIGNER
MARY E. VOGT .... COSTUME DESIGNER
MICHAEL JABLOW .... FILM EDITOR

NAKED LIE (TF)
RONALD VICTOR GARCIA .... CINEMATOGRAPHER
MATTHEW JACOBS .... PRODUCTION DESIGNER

NAKED TANGO
JUAN RUIZ-ANCHIA .... CINEMATOGRAPHER
ANTHONY PRATT .... PRODUCTION DESIGNER
PATRICIO BISSO .... COSTUME DESIGNER
DEBRA MCDERMOTT .... FILM EDITOR
LEE PERCY .... FILM EDITOR

NAME OF THE ROSE, THE
TONINO DELLI COLLI .... CINEMATOGRAPHER
DANTE FERRETTI .... PRODUCTION DESIGNER
GABRIELLA PESCUCCI .... COSTUME DESIGNER
JANE SEITZ .... FILM EDITOR

NANA
ARMANDO NANNUZZI .... CINEMATOGRAPHER

NANOU
MARTIN FUHRER .... CINEMATOGRAPHER

NARROW MARGIN
PETER HYAMS .... CINEMATOGRAPHER
JOEL SCHILLER .... PRODUCTION DESIGNER
JAMES MITCHELL .... FILM EDITOR

NASHVILLE
PAUL LOHMANN .... CINEMATOGRAPHER
DENNIS M. HILL .... FILM EDITOR
SIDNEY LEVIN .... FILM EDITOR

NASTY GIRL, THE
ALEX DE ROCHE .... CINEMATOGRAPHER
HUBERT POPP .... PRODUCTION DESIGNER
UTE TRUTHMANN .... COSTUME DESIGNER
BARBARA HENNINGS .... FILM EDITOR

NASTY HABITS
DOUGLAS SLOCOMBE .... CINEMATOGRAPHER
PETER TANNER .... FILM EDITOR

NATE AND HAYES
TONY IMI .... CINEMATOGRAPHER
JOSEPHINE FORD .... PRODUCTION DESIGNER
MAURICE CAIN .... PRODUCTION DESIGNER
NORMA MORICEAU .... COSTUME DESIGNER
JOHN SHIRLEY .... FILM EDITOR

NATIONAL LAMPOON GOES TO THE MOVIES
CHARLES CORRELL .... CINEMATOGRAPHER
TAK FUJIMOTO .... CINEMATOGRAPHER
JAMES COBLENTZ .... FILM EDITOR

NATIONAL LAMPOON'S ANIMAL HOUSE
CHARLES CORRELL .... CINEMATOGRAPHER
JOHN J. LLOYD .... PRODUCTION DESIGNER
DEBORAH NADOOLMAN .... COSTUME DESIGNER
GEORGE FOLSEY JR.* .... FILM EDITOR

NATIONAL LAMPOON'S CHRISTMAS VACATION
THOMAS ACKERMAN .... CINEMATOGRAPHER
STEPHEN MARSH .... PRODUCTION DESIGNER
MICHAEL KAPLAN .... COSTUME DESIGNER
GERALD B. GREENBERG .... FILM EDITOR

NATIONAL LAMPOON'S CLASS REUNION
PHILIP LATHROP .... CINEMATOGRAPHER
DEAN E. MITZNER .... PRODUCTION DESIGNER
JEAN-PIERRE DORLEAC .... COSTUME DESIGNER
RICHARD C. MEYER .... FILM EDITOR

NATIONAL LAMPOON'S EUROPEAN VACATION
ROBERT PAYNTER .... CINEMATOGRAPHER
ALAN TOMKINS .... PRODUCTION DESIGNER
ROBERT CARTWRIGHT .... PRODUCTION DESIGNER
GRAHAM WILLIAMS .... COSTUME DESIGNER
PEMBROKE J. HERRING .... FILM EDITOR

NATIONAL LAMPOON'S MOVIE MADNESS
CHARLES CORRELL .... CINEMATOGRAPHER
TAK FUJIMOTO .... CINEMATOGRAPHER
JAMES COBLENTZ .... FILM EDITOR

NATIONAL LAMPOON'S VACATION
VICTOR J. KEMPER .... CINEMATOGRAPHER
JACK T. COLLIS .... PRODUCTION DESIGNER
PEMBROKE J. HERRING .... FILM EDITOR

NATIVE SON
THOMAS BURSTYN .... CINEMATOGRAPHER
STEPHEN MARSH .... PRODUCTION DESIGNER
HILARY WRIGHT .... COSTUME DESIGNER
AARON STELL .... FILM EDITOR

NATURAL ENEMIES
RICHARD E. BROOKS .... CINEMATOGRAPHER

NATURAL, THE
CALEB DESCHANEL .... CINEMATOGRAPHER
ANGELO GRAHAM .... PRODUCTION DESIGNER
JAMES J. MURAKAMI .... PRODUCTION DESIGNER
MEL BOURNE .... PRODUCTION DESIGNER
SPEED HOPKINS .... PRODUCTION DESIGNER
GLORIA GRESHAM .... COSTUME DESIGNER
BERNIE POLLACK .... COSTUME DESIGNER
STU LINDER .... FILM EDITOR

NAVIGATOR, THE
GEOFFREY SIMPSON .... CINEMATOGRAPHER

NAVIGATOR: AN ODYSSEY ACROSS TIME, THE
SALLY CAMPBELL .... PRODUCTION DESIGNER
JOHN SCOTT .... FILM EDITOR

NAVY SEALS
JOHN ALONZO .... CINEMATOGRAPHER
GUY J. COMTOIS .... PRODUCTION DESIGNER
VERONICA HADFIELD .... PRODUCTION DESIGNER
BRAD LOMAN .... COSTUME DESIGNER
DON ZIMMERMAN .... FILM EDITOR

NAZI HUNTER: THE BEATE KLARSFELD STORY (TF)
DICK BUSH .... CINEMATOGRAPHER
JANE ROBINSON .... COSTUME DESIGNER

NEAR DARK
ADAM GREENBERG .... CINEMATOGRAPHER
DIAN PERRYMAN .... PRODUCTION DESIGNER
STEPHEN ALTMAN .... PRODUCTION DESIGNER
JOSEPH PORRO .... COSTUME DESIGNER
HOWARD SMITH .... FILM EDITOR

NECESSITY (TF)
REXFORD METZ .... CINEMATOGRAPHER

NECROPOLIS
ARTHUR D. MARKS .... CINEMATOGRAPHER
MARINA ZURKOW .... PRODUCTION DESIGNER
BARRY ZETLIN .... FILM EDITOR
TOM MASHELSKI .... FILM EDITOR

NEIGHBORS
GERALD HIRSCHFELD .... CINEMATOGRAPHER
PETER S. LARKIN .... PRODUCTION DESIGNER
JOHN BOXER .... COSTUME DESIGNER
JANE KURSON .... FILM EDITOR

NELSON AFFAIR, THE
JACK STEPHENS .... PRODUCTION DESIGNER
ANNE V. COATES .... FILM EDITOR

NEON MANIACS
JOSEPH MANGINE .... CINEMATOGRAPHER
OLIVER WOOD .... CINEMATOGRAPHER
KATHERINE G. VALLIN .... PRODUCTION DESIGNER
JOSEPH PORRO .... COSTUME DESIGNER

NERO WOLF (PILOT)
SOL NEGRIN .... CINEMATOGRAPHER

NEST, THE
TEO ESCAMILLA .... CINEMATOGRAPHER

NESTING, THE
JOAO FERNANDES .... CINEMATOGRAPHER

NETWORK
OWEN ROIZMAN .... CINEMATOGRAPHER
PHILIP ROSENBERG .... PRODUCTION DESIGNER
ALAN HEIM .... FILM EDITOR

NEVADA SMITH (TF)
JOHN C. HORGER .... FILM EDITOR

NEVER CRY WOLF
HIRO NARITA .... CINEMATOGRAPHER
GRAEME MURRAY .... PRODUCTION DESIGNER
MICHAEL CHANDLER .... FILM EDITOR
PETER PARASHELES .... FILM EDITOR

NEVER GIVE AN INCH
RICHARD MOORE .... CINEMATOGRAPHER

NEVER SAY NEVER AGAIN
DOUGLAS SLOCOMBE .... CINEMATOGRAPHER
LESLIE DILLEY .... PRODUCTION DESIGNER
PHILIP HARRISON .... PRODUCTION DESIGNER
STEPHEN GRIMES† .... PRODUCTION DESIGNER
CHARLES KNODE .... COSTUME DESIGNER
IAN CRAFFORD .... FILM EDITOR
ROBERT LAWRENCE .... FILM EDITOR

NEVER TOO YOUNG TO DIE
DAVID WORTH .... CINEMATOGRAPHER
DEAN TSCHETTER .... PRODUCTION DESIGNER
NED HUMPHREYS .... FILM EDITOR
PAUL SEYDOR .... FILM EDITOR
WILLIAM A. ANDERSON .... FILM EDITOR

NEVERENDING STORY, THE
JOST VACANO .... CINEMATOGRAPHER
ROLF ZEHETBAUER .... PRODUCTION DESIGNER
JANE SEITZ .... FILM EDITOR

NEVERENDING STORY II: THE NEXT CHAPTER, THE
DAVE CONNELL .... CINEMATOGRAPHER
ROBERT LAING .... PRODUCTION DESIGNER
GOETZ WEIDNER .... PRODUCTION DESIGNER
HEIDI WEBER .... COSTUME DESIGNER
CHRIS BLUNDEN .... FILM EDITOR
PETER HOLLYWOOD .... FILM EDITOR

NEW ADVENTURES OF HEIDI, THE (TF)
MICHAEL BAUGH .... PRODUCTION DESIGNER

NEW ADVENTURES OF PIPPI LONGSTOCKING, THE
ROLAND OZZIE SMITH .... CINEMATOGRAPHER
JACK SENTER .... PRODUCTION DESIGNER
STEPHEN M. BERGER .... PRODUCTION DESIGNER
JACQUELINE SAINT ANNE .... COSTUME DESIGNER
KEN ZEMKE .... FILM EDITOR

NEW CENTURIONS, THE
RALPH WOOLSEY .... CINEMATOGRAPHER
BORIS LEVEN† .... PRODUCTION DESIGNER
ROBERT C. JONES .... FILM EDITOR

NEW JACK CITY
FRANCIS KENNY .... CINEMATOGRAPHER
CHARLES C. BENNETT .... PRODUCTION DESIGNER
BERNARD JOHNSON .... COSTUME DESIGNER
STEVEN KEMPER .... FILM EDITOR

NEW KIDS, THE
STEVEN B. POSTER .... CINEMATOGRAPHER
PETER LANDSDOWN SMITH .... PRODUCTION DESIGNER
ROBB WILSON KING .... PRODUCTION DESIGNER
MOLLY MAGINNIS .... COSTUME DESIGNER
RITA ROLAND .... FILM EDITOR

NEW LEAF, A
GAYNE RESCHER .... CINEMATOGRAPHER
FREDRIC STEINKAMP .... FILM EDITOR

NEW LIFE, A
KELVIN PIKE .... CINEMATOGRAPHER
BARBARA DUNPHY .... PRODUCTION DESIGNER
LUCINDA ZAK .... PRODUCTION DESIGNER
MARY E. MCLEOD .... COSTUME DESIGNER
WILLIAM REYNOLDS .... FILM EDITOR

NEW YEAR'S EVIL
TOM ACKERMAN .... CINEMATOGRAPHER

NEW YORK STORIES
NESTOR ALMENDROS .... CINEMATOGRAPHER
SVEN NYKVIST .... CINEMATOGRAPHER
DEAN TAVOULARIS .... PRODUCTION DESIGNER
KRISTI ZEA .... PRODUCTION DESIGNER
SANTO LOQUASTO .... PRODUCTION DESIGNER
WRAY STEVEN GRAHAM .... PRODUCTION DESIGNER
JEFFREY KURLAND .... COSTUME DESIGNER
JOHN DUNN .... COSTUME DESIGNER
BARRY MALKIN .... FILM EDITOR
SUSAN E. MORSE .... FILM EDITOR
THELMA SCHOONMAKER .... FILM EDITOR

NEW YORK STORIES (LIFE WITHOUT ZOE & OEDIPUS WRECKS)
SPEED HOPKINS .... PRODUCTION DESIGNER

NEW YORK STORIES (LIFE WITHOUT ZOE)
VITTORIO STORARO .... CINEMATOGRAPHER
SOFIA COPPOLA .... COSTUME DESIGNER

NEW YORK, NEW YORK
LASZLO KOVACS .... CINEMATOGRAPHER
BORIS LEVEN† .... PRODUCTION DESIGNER
THEADORA VAN RUNKLE .... COSTUME DESIGNER
MARCIA LUCAS .... FILM EDITOR

NEWS AT ELEVEN (TF)
FRED J. KOENEKAMP .... CINEMATOGRAPHER

NEWSFRONT
VINCENT MONTON .... CINEMATOGRAPHER
JOHN SCOTT .... FILM EDITOR

NEXT MAN, THE
MICHAEL CHAPMAN .... CINEMATOGRAPHER
GENE CALLAHAN .... PRODUCTION DESIGNER
ANNA HILL JOHNSTONE .... COSTUME DESIGNER
ROBERT Q. LOVETT .... FILM EDITOR

NEXT OF KIN
STEVEN B. POSTER .... CINEMATOGRAPHER
JACK T. COLLIS .... PRODUCTION DESIGNER
DONFELD .... COSTUME DESIGNER
PETER HONESS .... FILM EDITOR

NEXT STOP, GREENWICH VILLAGE
ARTHUR ORNITZ† .... CINEMATOGRAPHER
PHILIP ROSENBERG .... PRODUCTION DESIGNER
RICHARD HALSEY .... FILM EDITOR

NEXT SUMMER
WILLIAM LUBTCHANSKY .... CINEMATOGRAPHER
MARIE-JOSEPH YOYOTTE .... FILM EDITOR

NICE GIRL LIKE ME, A
RUTH MYERS .... COSTUME DESIGNER

Ne-Ni

CINEMATOGRAPHERS
PRODUCTION
DESIGNERS,
COSTUME
DESIGNERS AND
FILM EDITORS
GUIDE

INDEX OF FILM TITLES

Ni-Ni

CINEMATOGRAPHERS
PRODUCTION
DESIGNERS,
COSTUME
DESIGNERS AND
FILM EDITORS
GUIDE

INDEX

OF

FILM

TITLES

NICE GIRLS DON'T EXPLODE
STEPHEN M. KATZ .... CINEMATOGRAPHER
SARINA ROTSTEIN .... PRODUCTION DESIGNER
BELINDA WELLS .... COSTUME DESIGNER
WENDY PHIFER MATE .... FILM EDITOR

NICHOLAS AND ALEXANDRA
FREDDIE YOUNG .... CINEMATOGRAPHER
GIL PARRONDO .... PRODUCTION DESIGNER
JOHN BOX .... PRODUCTION DESIGNER
YVONNE BLAKE .... COSTUME DESIGNER

NICK KNIGHT (PILOT)
FRANK BEASCOECHEA .... CINEMATOGRAPHER
BENJAMIN A. WEISSMAN .... FILM EDITOR

NICKEL RIDE, THE
JORDAN CRONENWETH .... CINEMATOGRAPHER
LAWRENCE G. PAULL .... PRODUCTION DESIGNER

NICKELODEON
LASZLO KOVACS .... CINEMATOGRAPHER
RICHARD BERGER .... PRODUCTION DESIGNER
NORMAN SALLING .... COSTUME DESIGNER
THEADORA VAN RUNKLE .... COSTUME DESIGNER
WILLIAM CARRUTH .... FILM EDITOR

NIGHT BEFORE,THE
RONALD VICTOR GARCIA .... CINEMATOGRAPHER

NIGHT CONFIGURATION, THE
THOMAS M. BRONSON .... COSTUME DESIGNER

NIGHT CROSSING
TONY IMI .... CINEMATOGRAPHER
ROLF ZEHETBAUER .... PRODUCTION DESIGNER
GORDON D. BRENNER .... FILM EDITOR

NIGHT EYES
RON WISMAN .... FILM EDITOR

NIGHT FRIEND
DOUGLAS KOCH .... CINEMATOGRAPHER
MICHAEL TODD .... FILM EDITOR

NIGHT GALLERY (TF)
DAVID RAWLINS .... FILM EDITOR

NIGHT GAME
FRED MURPHY .... CINEMATOGRAPHER
NEIL SPISAK .... PRODUCTION DESIGNER
ROBERT BARRERE .... FILM EDITOR

NIGHT GAMES
DENNIS LEWISTON .... CINEMATOGRAPHER
ROBERT LAING .... PRODUCTION DESIGNER

NIGHT IN HEAVEN, A
DAVID QUAID .... CINEMATOGRAPHER
WILLIAM J. CASSIDY .... PRODUCTION DESIGNER
ANNA HILL JOHNSTONE .... COSTUME DESIGNER
JOHN G. AVILDSEN .... FILM EDITOR

NIGHT IN THE LIFE OF JIMMY REARDON, A
JOHN J. CONNOR .... CINEMATOGRAPHER
JOHN R. JENSEN .... PRODUCTION DESIGNER
NORMAN NEWBERRY .... PRODUCTION DESIGNER
ROBERT DE MORA .... COSTUME DESIGNER
SUZANNE FENN .... FILM EDITOR

NIGHT, MOTHER
STEPHEN M. KATZ .... CINEMATOGRAPHER
JACKSON DE GOVIA .... PRODUCTION DESIGNER
ROBERT BLACKMAN .... COSTUME DESIGNER
SUZANNE PETTIT .... FILM EDITOR

NIGHT MOVES
BRUCE SURTEES .... CINEMATOGRAPHER
GEORGE JENKINS .... PRODUCTION DESIGNER
RITA RIGGS .... COSTUME DESIGNER
DEDE ALLEN .... FILM EDITOR
STEPHEN A. ROTTER .... FILM EDITOR

NIGHT OF COURAGE (TF)
JACK L. RICHARDS .... CINEMATOGRAPHER

NIGHT OF DARK SHADOWS
RICHARD SHORE .... CINEMATOGRAPHER
TREVOR WILLIAMS .... PRODUCTION DESIGNER

NIGHT OF THE COMET, THE
ARTHUR ALBERT .... CINEMATOGRAPHER
JOHN MUTO .... PRODUCTION DESIGNER
FRED STAFFORD .... FILM EDITOR

NIGHT OF THE CREEPS
GEORGE COSTELLO .... PRODUCTION DESIGNER
EILEEN KENNEDY .... COSTUME DESIGNER
MICHAEL KNUE .... FILM EDITOR

NIGHT OF THE FOX-PARTS I & II (MS)
JEAN-PAUL RABIE .... CINEMATOGRAPHER
CLAUDIO GUZMAN .... PRODUCTION DESIGNER
YVES CHAROY .... FILM EDITOR

NIGHT OF THE IGUANA, THE
GABRIEL FIGUEROA .... CINEMATOGRAPHER

NIGHT OF THE JUGGLER
VICTOR J. KEMPER .... CINEMATOGRAPHER
MICHAEL MOLLY .... PRODUCTION DESIGNER
STUART WURTZEL .... PRODUCTION DESIGNER
ARGYLE NELSON .... FILM EDITOR
HARVEY ROSENSTOCK .... FILM EDITOR

NIGHT OF THE LIVING DEAD
FRANK PRINZI .... CINEMATOGRAPHER
CLETUS R. ANDERSON .... PRODUCTION DESIGNER
BARBARA ANDERSON .... COSTUME DESIGNER
TOM DUBENSKY .... FILM EDITOR

NIGHT OF THE PENCILS
LEONARD SOLIS .... CINEMATOGRAPHER
MIGUEL MARIO LOPEZ .... FILM EDITOR

NIGHT OF THE SHOOTING STARS, THE
FRANCO DI GIACOMO .... CINEMATOGRAPHER
RAIMONDO CROCIANI .... FILM EDITOR

NIGHT OF THE ZOMBIES
JOHN CABRERA .... CINEMATOGRAPHER

NIGHT PARTNERS (TF)
NORM BARON .... PRODUCTION DESIGNER

NIGHT PATROL
HANANIA BAER .... CINEMATOGRAPHER
JURG WALTHERS .... CINEMATOGRAPHER
JACKIE KONG .... FILM EDITOR

NIGHT RIDER (TF)
STEVEN B. POSTER .... CINEMATOGRAPHER

NIGHT SCHOOL
MARK IRWIN .... CINEMATOGRAPHER
ROBERT REITANO .... FILM EDITOR

NIGHT SHIFT
JAMES A. CRABE .... CINEMATOGRAPHER
JACK T. COLLIS .... PRODUCTION DESIGNER
PETER LANDSDOWN SMITH .... PRODUCTION DESIGNER
DANIEL P. HANLEY .... FILM EDITOR
MICHAEL J. HILL .... FILM EDITOR

NIGHT STALKER, THE
DON BURGESS .... CINEMATOGRAPHER
STANFORD C. ALLEN .... FILM EDITOR

NIGHT STRANGLER, THE (TF)
TREVOR WILLIAMS .... PRODUCTION DESIGNER

NIGHT THE FOLLOWING DAY, THE
WILLY KURANT .... CINEMATOGRAPHER

NIGHT THE LIGHTS WENT OUT IN GEORGIA, THE
FRED BATKA .... CINEMATOGRAPHER
BILL BUTLER .... CINEMATOGRAPHER
GENE RUDOLF .... PRODUCTION DESIGNER
JOSEPH G. AULISI .... COSTUME DESIGNER
ANNE GOURSAUD .... FILM EDITOR

NIGHT THEY RAIDED MINSKY'S,THE
ANDREW LASZLO .... CINEMATOGRAPHER

NIGHT THEY SAVED CHRISTMAS, THE (TF)
DAVID WORTH .... CINEMATOGRAPHER
GEORGE COSTELLO .... PRODUCTION DESIGNER
MICHAEL Z. HANAN .... PRODUCTION DESIGNER

NIGHT VISION (TF)
PETER STEIN .... CINEMATOGRAPHER
VINCE CRESCIMAN .... PRODUCTION DESIGNER
JAMES COBLENTZ .... FILM EDITOR
MARK MELNICK .... FILM EDITOR

NIGHT WARNING
ROBBIE GREENBERG .... CINEMATOGRAPHER

NIGHT WARS
STEPHEN ASHLEY BLAKE .... CINEMATOGRAPHER

NIGHT WATCH
BILLY WILLIAMS .... CINEMATOGRAPHER
PETER MURTON .... PRODUCTION DESIGNER

NIGHT ZOO
GUY DUFAUX .... CINEMATOGRAPHER

NIGHTBREAKER (TF)
RONALD VICTOR GARCIA .... CINEMATOGRAPHER
STEPHEN E. RIVKIN .... FILM EDITOR

NIGHTBREED
ROBIN VIDGEON .... CINEMATOGRAPHER
STEVE HARDIE .... PRODUCTION DESIGNER
ANN HOLLOWOOD .... COSTUME DESIGNER
MARIE FRANCE .... COSTUME DESIGNER
MARK GOLDBLATT .... FILM EDITOR
RICHARD MARDEN .... FILM EDITOR

NIGHTFALL
DARIUSZ ADAMS WOLSKI .... CINEMATOGRAPHER

NIGHTFLOWERS
LARRY PIZER .... CINEMATOGRAPHER

NIGHTFLYERS
SHELLY JOHNSON .... CINEMATOGRAPHER
JOHN MUTO .... PRODUCTION DESIGNER
MICHAEL BINGHAM .... PRODUCTION DESIGNER
BRAD R. LOMAN .... COSTUME DESIGNER
TOM SIITER .... FILM EDITOR

NIGHTHAWKS
JAMES A. CONTNER .... CINEMATOGRAPHER
PETER S. LARKIN .... PRODUCTION DESIGNER
ROBERT DE MORA .... COSTUME DESIGNER
CHRISTOPHER HOLMES .... FILM EDITOR

NIGHTINGALES (PILOT)
FREDERICK MOORE .... CINEMATOGRAPHER

NIGHTMARE AT BITTER CREEK (TF)
JACQUES STEYN .... CINEMATOGRAPHER

NIGHTMARE AT SHADOW WOODS
RICHARD E. BROOKS .... CINEMATOGRAPHER

NIGHTMARE IN BADHAM COUNTY (TF)
JAN SCOTT .... PRODUCTION DESIGNER

NIGHTMARE ON ELM STREET, A
JACQUES HAITKIN .... CINEMATOGRAPHER
GREGG FONSECA .... PRODUCTION DESIGNER
RICK SHAINE .... FILM EDITOR

NIGHTMARE ON ELM STREET PART 2: FREDDY'S REVENGE, A
JACQUES HAITKIN .... CINEMATOGRAPHER
ARLINE GARSON .... FILM EDITOR

NIGHTMARE ON ELM STREET PART 3: DREAM WARRIORS, A
ROY H. WAGNER .... CINEMATOGRAPHER
MICK STRAWN .... PRODUCTION DESIGNER
C.J. STRAWN .... PRODUCTION DESIGNER
TERRY STOKES .... FILM EDITOR

NIGHTMARE ON ELM STREET 4: THE DREAM MASTER, A
STEVEN FIERBERG .... CINEMATOGRAPHER
C.J. STRAWN .... PRODUCTION DESIGNER
MICK STRAWN .... PRODUCTION DESIGNER
THOMAS A. O'CONNOR .... PRODUCTION DESIGNER
CHUCK WEISS .... FILM EDITOR
MICHAEL KNUE .... FILM EDITOR

NIGHTMARE ON ELM STREET 5: THE DREAM CHILD, A
PETER LEVY .... CINEMATOGRAPHER
BRENT SCHOENFIELD .... FILM EDITOR
CHUCK WEISS .... FILM EDITOR
C.J. STRAWN .... PRODUCTION DESIGNER

NIGHTMARE ON THE 13TH FLOOR (CTF)
TOM RICHMOND .... CINEMATOGRAPHER
SIDNEY KATZ .... FILM EDITOR

NIGHTMARES
GERALD PERRY FINNERMAN .... CINEMATOGRAPHER
MARIO DI LEO .... CINEMATOGRAPHER
DEAN E. MITZNER .... PRODUCTION DESIGNER
JACK G. TAYLOR .... PRODUCTION DESIGNER
MICHAEL BROWN .... FILM EDITOR

NIGHTS OF THE CITY
MARK CONTE .... FILM EDITOR

NIGHTSHADOWS
ALFRED TAYLOR .... CINEMATOGRAPHER

NIGHTSTICK
REUBEN FREED .... PRODUCTION DESIGNER

NIGHTWING
CHARLES ROSHER, JR. .... CINEMATOGRAPHER
JAMES D. VANCE .... PRODUCTION DESIGNER
JOHN C. HOWARD .... FILM EDITOR

NIGTMARE AT SHADOW WOODS
MICHAEL R. MILLER .... FILM EDITOR

NIJINSKY
DOUGLAS SLOCOMBE .... CINEMATOGRAPHER
GEORGE RICHARDSON .... PRODUCTION DESIGNER
JOHN BLEZARD .... PRODUCTION DESIGNER
PIERLUIGI BASILE .... PRODUCTION DESIGNER
ALAN BARRETT .... COSTUME DESIGNER
WILLIAM REYNOLDS .... FILM EDITOR

NIKITA
THEIRRY ARBOGAST .... CINEMATOGRAPHER
DAN WEIL .... PRODUCTION DESIGNER
OLIVIER MAUFFROY .... FILM EDITOR

NINE DEATHS OF THE NINJA
ROY H. WAGNER .... CINEMATOGRAPHER

NINE TO FIVE
REYNALDO VILLALOBOS .... CINEMATOGRAPHER
DEAN E. MITZNER .... PRODUCTION DESIGNER
JACK G. TAYLOR .... PRODUCTION DESIGNER
ANN ROTH .... COSTUME DESIGNER
PEMBROKE J. HERRING .... FILM EDITOR

NINETEEN NINETEEN
CAROLYN AMIES .... PRODUCTION DESIGNER
JANE ROBINSON .... COSTUME DESIGNER
DAVID GLADWELL .... FILM EDITOR

NINJA III - THE DOMINATION
HANANIA BAER .... CINEMATOGRAPHER
NANCY CONE .... COSTUME DESIGNER
MICHAEL J. DUTHIE .... FILM EDITOR

NINTH CONFIGURATION, THE
GERRY FISHER .... CINEMATOGRAPHER
DENNIS WASHINGTON .... PRODUCTION DESIGNER
WILLIAM MALLEY .... PRODUCTION DESIGNER
BATTLE DAVIS .... FILM EDITOR
PETER LEE THOMPSON .... FILM EDITOR

NO BLADE OF GRASS
ERIC BOYD-PERKINS .... FILM EDITOR

NO BUSINESS LIKE SHOW BUSINESS
TRAVILLA .... COSTUME DESIGNER

NO DEPOSIT, NO RETURN
FRANK PHILLIPS .... CINEMATOGRAPHER
JACK SENTER .... PRODUCTION DESIGNER
JOHN B. MANSBRIDGE .... PRODUCTION DESIGNER

NO HOLDS BARRED
FRANK BEASCOECHEA .... CINEMATOGRAPHER
JAMES SHANAHAN .... PRODUCTION DESIGNER
TOM PRYOR .... FILM EDITOR

Ni-No

CINEMATOGRAPHERS
PRODUCTION
DESIGNERS,
COSTUME
DESIGNERS AND
FILM EDITORS
GUIDE

I
N
D
E
X

O
F

F
I
L
M

T
I
T
L
E
S

399

No-No

CINEMATOGRAPHERS
PRODUCTION
DESIGNERS,
COSTUME
DESIGNERS and
FILM EDITORS
GUIDE

I
N
D
E
X

O
F

F
I
L
M

T
I
T
L
E
S

400

NOT OF THIS EARTH
HAYDEN YATES .... PRODUCTION DESIGNER
LIBBY JACOBS .... COSTUME DESIGNER
KEVIN TENT .... FILM EDITOR

NOT OF THIS WORLD (TF)
MARK IRWIN .... CINEMATOGRAPHER
PHILLIP M. LEONARD .... PRODUCTION DESIGNER
JOHN F. BURNETT .... FILM EDITOR

NOT QUITE HUMAN (TF)
ELAYNE CEDER .... PRODUCTION DESIGNER

NOT QUITE PARADISE
TONY IMI .... CINEMATOGRAPHER
JOHN STOLL .... PRODUCTION DESIGNER
CINDY PATERSON .... COSTUME DESIGNER
ALAN STRACHAN .... FILM EDITOR

NOT WITHOUT MY DAUGHTER
PETER HANNAN .... CINEMATOGRAPHER
ANTHONY PRATT .... PRODUCTION DESIGNER
NIC EDE .... COSTUME DESIGNER
TERRY RAWLING .... FILM EDITOR

NOTHING BUT THE TRUTH
MIKAEL SALOMON .... CINEMATOGRAPHER

NOTHING BUT TROUBLE
DEAN CUNDEY .... CINEMATOGRAPHER
WILLIAM SANDELL .... PRODUCTION DESIGNER
DEBORAH NADOOLMAN .... COSTUME DESIGNER
JAMES SYMONS .... FILM EDITOR
MALCOLM CAMPBELL .... FILM EDITOR

NOTHING IN COMMON
JOHN A. ALONZO .... CINEMATOGRAPHER
CHARLES ROSEN .... PRODUCTION DESIGNER
ROSANNA NORTON .... COSTUME DESIGNER
GLENN FARR .... FILM EDITOR
JANICE HAMPTON .... FILM EDITOR

NOTHING LASTS FOREVER
FRED SCHULER .... CINEMATOGRAPHER
KATHLEEN DOUGHERTY .... FILM EDITOR

NOTHING PERSONAL
ARTHUR IBBETSON .... CINEMATOGRAPHER
LASZLO GEORGE .... CINEMATOGRAPHER
GEORGE APPELBY .... FILM EDITOR

NOW AND FOREVER
DONALD MCALPINE .... CINEMATOGRAPHER

NOWHERE TO HIDE
VIC SARIN .... CINEMATOGRAPHER
RENEE APRIL .... COSTUME DESIGNER
RIT WALLIS .... FILM EDITOR

NUDE BOMB, THE
WILLIAM H. TUNTKE .... PRODUCTION DESIGNER
BURTON MILLER .... COSTUME DESIGNER
WALTER HANNEMAN .... FILM EDITOR

NUMBER ONE
MICHEL HUGO .... CINEMATOGRAPHER

NUMBER ONE WITH A BULLET
ALEX PHILLIPS .... CINEMATOGRAPHER
NORM BARON .... PRODUCTION DESIGNER
ROSALIE WALLACE .... COSTUME DESIGNER
MICHAEL J. DUTHIE .... FILM EDITOR

NUN AND THE SARGEANT, THE
ROBERT KINOSHITA .... PRODUCTION DESIGNER

NUNS ON THE RUN
MICHAEL GARFATH .... CINEMATOGRAPHER
SIMON HOLLAND .... PRODUCTION DESIGNER
SUSAN YELLAND .... COSTUME DESIGNER
DAVID MARTIN .... FILM EDITOR

NUNZIO
MEL BOURNE .... PRODUCTION DESIGNER
ANN ROTH .... COSTUME DESIGNER

NUTCRACKER
STEPHEN H. BURUM .... CINEMATOGRAPHER
MAURICE SENDAK .... PRODUCTION DESIGNER
MAURICE SENDAK .... COSTUME DESIGNER
JOHN NUTT .... FILM EDITOR
MAX BENEDICT .... FILM EDITOR

NUTCRACKER: MONEY, MADNESS AND MURDER (MS)
ISIDORE MANKOFSKY .... CINEMATOGRAPHER
JACK SENTER .... PRODUCTION DESIGNER

NUTS
ANDRZEJ BARTKOWIAK .... CINEMATOGRAPHER
ERIC W. ORBOM .... PRODUCTION DESIGNER
JOEL SCHILLER .... PRODUCTION DESIGNER
JOE I. TOMPKINS .... COSTUME DESIGNER
SIDNEY LEVIN .... FILM EDITOR

O

O LUCKY MAN
MIROSLAV ONDRICEK .... CINEMATOGRAPHER

O'HARA'S WIFE
HARRY STRADLING, JR. .... CINEMATOGRAPHER
ROBERT ZENTIS .... PRODUCTION DESIGNER
MADELINE ANN GRANETO .... COSTUME DESIGNER
GEORGE BERNDT .... FILM EDITOR

O'MALLEY (PILOT)
SOL NEGRIN .... CINEMATOGRAPHER

O.C. AND STIGGS
PIERRE MIGNOT .... CINEMATOGRAPHER
DAVID GROPMAN .... PRODUCTION DESIGNER
SCOTT BUSHNELL .... PRODUCTION DESIGNER
ELIZABETH KLING .... FILM EDITOR

OASIS, THE
ALEXANDER GRUSZYNSKI .... CINEMATOGRAPHER

OBSESSED WITH A MARRIED WOMAN (TF)
HANANIA BAER .... CINEMATOGRAPHER

OBSESSION
VILMOS ZSIGMOND .... CINEMATOGRAPHER
JACK SENTER .... PRODUCTION DESIGNER
PAUL HIRSCH .... FILM EDITOR

OBSESSION: A TASTE FOR FEAR
ROMANO ALBANI .... CINEMATOGRAPHER

OBSESSIVE LOVE (TF)
FRED J. KOENEKAMP .... CINEMATOGRAPHER
DANIEL P. HANLEY .... FILM EDITOR
MICHAEL J. HILL .... FILM EDITOR

OCTAGON, THE
MICHEL HUGO .... CINEMATOGRAPHER
JAMES SCHOPPE .... PRODUCTION DESIGNER
DANN CAHN .... FILM EDITOR

OCTOPUSSY
ALAN HUME .... CINEMATOGRAPHER
JOHN FENNER .... PRODUCTION DESIGNER
PETER LAMONT .... PRODUCTION DESIGNER
HENRY RICHARDSON .... FILM EDITOR
JOHN GROVER .... FILM EDITOR
PETER DAVIES .... FILM EDITOR

ODD AND EVEN
JUAN RUIZ-ANCHIA .... CINEMATOGRAPHER

ODD ANGRY SHOT, THE
DONALD MCALPINE .... CINEMATOGRAPHER
BERNARD HIDES .... PRODUCTION DESIGNER
BRIAN KAVANAUGH .... FILM EDITOR

ODD BALL HALL
AVRAHAM KARPICK .... CINEMATOGRAPHER

ODD COUPLE, THE
ROBERT B. HAUSER .... CINEMATOGRAPHER
FRANK BRACHT .... FILM EDITOR

ODD JOB, THE
ANTHONY CURTIS .... PRODUCTION DESIGNER
SHUNA HARWOOD .... COSTUME DESIGNER
BARRIE VINCE .... FILM EDITOR

No-Od

CINEMATOGRAPHERS
PRODUCTION
DESIGNERS,
COSTUME
DESIGNERS AND
FILM EDITORS
GUIDE

INDEX OF FILM TITLES

401

Od-On

CINEMATOGRAPHERS
PRODUCTION
DESIGNERS,
COSTUME
DESIGNERS AND
FILM EDITORS
GUIDE

I
N
D
E
X

O
F

F
I
L
M

T
I
T
L
E
S

CINEMATOGRAPHERS
PRODUCTION
DESIGNERS,
COSTUME
DESIGNERS AND
FILM EDITORS
GUIDE

ON THE EDGE
STEFAN CZAPSKY .... CINEMATOGRAPHER
DON DE FINA .... PRODUCTION DESIGNER
BERT LOVITT .... FILM EDITOR

ON THE LINE
TEO ESCAMILLA .... CINEMATOGRAPHER
PHILIP THOMAS .... PRODUCTION DESIGNER
SWANIE R. BALDRIDGE .... COSTUME DESIGNER
CURTISS CLAYTON .... FILM EDITOR

ON THE NICKEL
RIC WAITE .... CINEMATOGRAPHER
PATRICIA NORRIS .... COSTUME DESIGNER
WENDY BRICMONT .... FILM EDITOR

ON THE RIGHT TRACK
JACK L. RICHARDS .... CINEMATOGRAPHER
WILLIAM FOSSER .... PRODUCTION DESIGNER
WILLIAM BUTLER .... FILM EDITOR

ON THE YARD
LEON HARRIS .... PRODUCTION DESIGNER
EVAN LOTTMAN .... FILM EDITOR

ON THIN ICE: THE TAI BABILONIA STORY (TF)
BRIAN R.R. HEBB .... CINEMATOGRAPHER
TONY HALL .... PRODUCTION DESIGNER
SALLY PATERSON .... FILM EDITOR

ON VALENTINE'S DAY
GEORGE TIRL .... CINEMATOGRAPHER
HOWARD CUMMINGS .... PRODUCTION DESIGNER

ON WINGS OF EAGLES (MS)
ROBERT STEADMAN .... CINEMATOGRAPHER
MICHAEL BAUGH .... PRODUCTION DESIGNER

ONCE A COP...
MIKAEL SALOMON .... CINEMATOGRAPHER

ONCE AROUND
THEO VAN DE SANDE .... CINEMATOGRAPHER
DAVID GROPMAN .... PRODUCTION DESIGNER
RENEE KALFUS .... COSTUME DESIGNER
ANDREW MONDSHEIN .... FILM EDITOR

ONCE BITTEN
ADAM GREENBERG .... CINEMATOGRAPHER
GENE RUDOLF .... PRODUCTION DESIGNER
ROBERT HOWLAND .... PRODUCTION DESIGNER
JILL OHANNESON .... COSTUME DESIGNER
MARC GROSSMAN .... FILM EDITOR

ONCE IN PARIS
ROBERT Q. LOVETT .... FILM EDITOR

ONCE IS NOT ENOUGH
JOHN A. ALONZO .... CINEMATOGRAPHER
JOHN DE CUIR .... PRODUCTION DESIGNER
RITA ROLAND .... FILM EDITOR

ONCE UPON A MATRESS (TV)
BOB MACKIE .... COSTUME DESIGNER

ONCE UPON A TIME IN AMERICA
TONINO DELLI COLLI .... CINEMATOGRAPHER
CARLO SIMI .... PRODUCTION DESIGNER
JAMES SINGELIS .... PRODUCTION DESIGNER
GABRIELLA PESCUCCI .... COSTUME DESIGNER
NINO BARAGLI .... FILM EDITOR

ONCE WE WERE DREAMERS
MIKAEL SALOMON .... CINEMATOGRAPHER

ONE AND ONLY, THE
VICTOR J. KEMPER .... CINEMATOGRAPHER
EDWARD C. CARFAGNO .... PRODUCTION DESIGNER
BUD MOLIN .... FILM EDITOR

ONE COOKS, THE OTHER DOESN'T (TF)
ERICA EDELL PHILLIPS .... COSTUME DESIGNER

ONE CRAZY SUMMER
ISIDORE MANKOFSKY .... CINEMATOGRAPHER
HERMAN ZIMMERMAN .... PRODUCTION DESIGNER
BRAD R. LOMAN .... COSTUME DESIGNER
ALAN BALSAM .... FILM EDITOR

ONE CUP OF COFFEE
TOM RICHMOND .... CINEMATOGRAPHER
DAVID W. FORD .... PRODUCTION DESIGNER
KRISTINE BROWN .... COSTUME DESIGNER
MARK S. WESTMORE .... FILM EDITOR

ONE DARK NIGHT
HAL TRUSSELL .... CINEMATOGRAPHER
CRAIG STEARNS .... PRODUCTION DESIGNER
LINDA BASS .... COSTUME DESIGNER
MICHAEL SPENCE .... FILM EDITOR

ONE DEADLY SUMMER
ETTIENNE BECKER .... CINEMATOGRAPHER
JACQUES WITTA .... FILM EDITOR

ONE DOWN TWO TO GO
JAMES LEMMO .... CINEMATOGRAPHER

ONE FLEW OVER THE CUCKOO'S NEST
BILL BUTLER .... CINEMATOGRAPHER
HASKELL WEXLER .... CINEMATOGRAPHER
PAUL SYLBERT .... PRODUCTION DESIGNER
AGGIE GUERARD RODGERS .... COSTUME DESIGNER
LYNZEE KLINGMAN .... FILM EDITOR
SHELDON KAHN .... FILM EDITOR
RICHARD CHEW .... FILM EDITOR

ONE FROM THE HEART
RONALD VICTOR GARCIA .... CINEMATOGRAPHER
VITTORIO STORARO .... CINEMATOGRAPHER
ANGELO GRAHAM .... PRODUCTION DESIGNER
DEAN TAVOULARIS .... PRODUCTION DESIGNER
RUTH MORLEY .... COSTUME DESIGNER
ANNE GOURSAUD .... FILM EDITOR
RANDY ROBERTS .... FILM EDITOR
RUDI FEHR .... FILM EDITOR

ONE GOOD COP
RALF BODE .... CINEMATOGRAPHER
SANDY VENEZIANO .... PRODUCTION DESIGNER
BETSY HEIMANN .... COSTUME DESIGNER
RICHARD MARKS .... FILM EDITOR

ONE IN A MILLION: THE RON LEFLORE STORY (TF)
JORDAN CRONENWETH .... CINEMATOGRAPHER

ONE IS A LONELY NUMBER
MICHEL HUGO .... CINEMATOGRAPHER

ONE LIFE IS NOT ENOUGH (FD)
MARY HICKEY .... FILM EDITOR

ONE MAGIC CHRISTMAS
FRANK TIDY .... CINEMATOGRAPHER
BILL BRODIE .... PRODUCTION DESIGNER
OLGA DIMITROV .... COSTUME DESIGNER
SIDNEY WOLINSKY .... FILM EDITOR

ONE MORE CHANCE
JONATHAN BRAUN .... CINEMATOGRAPHER
DOV HOENIG .... FILM EDITOR

ONE MORE SATURDAY NIGHT
JAMES M. GLENNON .... CINEMATOGRAPHER
MAHER AHMAD .... PRODUCTION DESIGNER
JAY HURLEY .... COSTUME DESIGNER
GREGORY PRANGE .... FILM EDITOR

ONE MORE TIME
JACK STEPHENS .... PRODUCTION DESIGNER

ONE NIGHT STAND
JOHN SCOTT .... FILM EDITOR

ONE ON ONE
DONALD M. MORGAN .... CINEMATOGRAPHER
DONFELD .... COSTUME DESIGNER

ONE POINT OF VIEW
ALEX NEPOMNIASCHY .... CINEMATOGRAPHER

ONE POTATO, TWO POTATO
ANDREW LASZLO .... CINEMATOGRAPHER

ONE SUMMER LOVE
GERALD HIRSCHFELD .... CINEMATOGRAPHER
BARRY MALKIN .... FILM EDITOR

On-Or

CINEMATOGRAPHERS
PRODUCTION
DESIGNERS,
COSTUME
DESIGNERS and
FILM EDITORS
GUIDE

I
N
D
E
X

O
F

F
I
L
M

T
I
T
L
E
S

Ot-Ov

CINEMATOGRAPHERS
PRODUCTION
DESIGNERS,
COSTUME
DESIGNERS AND
FILM EDITORS
GUIDE

OTHER WOMAN, THE (TF)
ALBERT HESCHONG .... PRODUCTION DESIGNER

OTHER, THE
ALBERT BRENNER .... PRODUCTION DESIGNER

OUR MOTHER'S HOUSE
LARRY PIZER .... CINEMATOGRAPHER

OUR STORY
JEAN PENZER .... CINEMATOGRAPHER

OUR TIME
PETER W. WOOLEY .... PRODUCTION DESIGNER
JAMES MITCHELL .... FILM EDITOR

OUR WINNING SEASON
STEPHEN M. KATZ .... CINEMATOGRAPHER
ANGELO GRAHAM .... PRODUCTION DESIGNER
WILLIAM BUTLER .... FILM EDITOR

OUT COLD
TONY PIERCE-ROBERTS .... CINEMATOGRAPHER
LINDA PEARL .... PRODUCTION DESIGNER
LINDA BASS .... COSTUME DESIGNER
DENNIS M. HILL .... FILM EDITOR

OUT FOR JUSTICE
RIC WAITE .... CINEMATOGRAPHER
GENE RUDOLF .... PRODUCTION DESIGNER
STEPHEN M. BERGER .... PRODUCTION DESIGNER
RICHARD BRUNO .... COSTUME DESIGNER
DONALD BROCHU .... FILM EDITOR
ROBERT A. FERRETTI .... FILM EDITOR

OUT OF AFRICA
DAVID WATKIN .... CINEMATOGRAPHER
CLIFFORD ROBINSON .... PRODUCTION DESIGNER
HERBERT WESTBROOK .... PRODUCTION DESIGNER
STEPHEN GRIMES† .... PRODUCTION DESIGNER
MILENA CANONERO .... COSTUME DESIGNER
FREDRIC STEINKAMP .... FILM EDITOR
SHELDON KAHN .... FILM EDITOR
WILLIAM STEINKAMP .... FILM EDITOR
PEMBROKE J. HERRING .... FILM EDITOR

OUT OF BOUNDS
BRUCE SURTEES .... CINEMATOGRAPHER
NORMAN NEWBERRY .... PRODUCTION DESIGNER
DONNA LINSON .... COSTUME DESIGNER
KENT BEYDA .... FILM EDITOR
LARRY BOCK .... FILM EDITOR

OUT OF CONTROL
JOHN A. ALONZO .... CINEMATOGRAPHER
ALLAN HOLZMAN .... FILM EDITOR
ROBERT A. FERRETTI .... FILM EDITOR

OUT OF ORDER
JACQUES STEYN .... CINEMATOGRAPHER
NORBERT HERZNER .... FILM EDITOR

OUT OF SEASON
ARTHUR IBBETSON .... CINEMATOGRAPHER

OUT OF THE BLUE
MARC CHAMPION .... CINEMATOGRAPHER

OUT OF THE DARKNESS (TF)
BRIAN WEST .... CINEMATOGRAPHER

OUT OF TIME
FRED TAMMES .... CINEMATOGRAPHER
JOHN SHIRLEY .... FILM EDITOR

OUT OF TOWNERS, THE
ANDREW LASZLO .... CINEMATOGRAPHER

OUT ON A LIMB (MS)
BRADFORD MAY .... CINEMATOGRAPHER

OUT ON THE EDGE
WALT LLOYD .... CINEMATOGRAPHER

OUTBACK
BRIAN WEST .... CINEMATOGRAPHER

OUTFIT, THE
RALPH E. WINTERS .... FILM EDITOR

OUTING, THE
HERBERT RADITSCHING .... CINEMATOGRAPHER
ROBERT BURNS .... PRODUCTION DESIGNER
CLAUDIO CUTRY .... FILM EDITOR

OUTLAND
STEPHEN GOLDBLATT .... CINEMATOGRAPHER
MALCOLM MIDDLETON .... PRODUCTION DESIGNER
PHILIP HARRISON .... PRODUCTION DESIGNER
JOHN MOLLO .... COSTUME DESIGNER
STUART BAIRD .... FILM EDITOR

OUTLAW BLUES
JULES BRENNER .... CINEMATOGRAPHER
JACK MARTY .... PRODUCTION DESIGNER
ROSANNA NORTON .... COSTUME DESIGNER
DANFORD B. GREENE .... FILM EDITOR
SCOTT CONRAD .... FILM EDITOR

OUTLAW FORCE
JAMES MATHERS .... CINEMATOGRAPHER

OUTLAW JOSEY WALES, THE
BRUCE SURTEES .... CINEMATOGRAPHER
TAMBI LARSEN .... PRODUCTION DESIGNER
FERRIS WEBSTER .... FILM EDITOR

OUTLAWS,THE
DENNIS DALZELL .... CINEMATOGRAPHER

OUTRAGE! (TF)
PAUL ZASTUPNEVICH .... COSTUME DESIGNER

OUTRAGEOUS!
JAMES B. KELLEY .... CINEMATOGRAPHER
SANDY VENEZIANO .... PRODUCTION DESIGNER
KAREN BROMLEY .... PRODUCTION DESIGNER
GEORGE APPELBY .... FILM EDITOR

OUTRAGEOUS FORTUNE
DAVID M. WALSH .... CINEMATOGRAPHER
JAMES D. VANCE .... PRODUCTION DESIGNER
GLORIA GRESHAM .... COSTUME DESIGNER
TOM ROLF .... FILM EDITOR

OUTSIDE CHANCE (TF)
WILLY KURANT .... CINEMATOGRAPHER

OUTSIDE CHANCE OF MAXIMILIAN GLICK, THE
IAN ELKIN .... CINEMATOGRAPHER
KIM STEER .... PRODUCTION DESIGNER
RICHARD MARTIN .... FILM EDITOR

OUTSIDE WOMAN, THE (TF)
PAUL LOHMANN .... CINEMATOGRAPHER

OUTSIDER, THE
RICARDO ARONOVITCH .... CINEMATOGRAPHER
TED HAWORTH .... PRODUCTION DESIGNER
JUDY DOLAN .... COSTUME DESIGNER

OUTSIDERS, THE
STEPHEN H. BURUM .... CINEMATOGRAPHER
DEAN TAVOULARIS .... PRODUCTION DESIGNER
MARJORIE BOWERS .... COSTUME DESIGNER
ANNE GOURSAUD .... FILM EDITOR

OVER MY DEAD BODY (TF)
ERIC VAN HAREN NOMAN .... CINEMATOGRAPHER
WARD PRESTON .... PRODUCTION DESIGNER
CHRIS COOKE .... FILM EDITOR
TOM FINNEN .... FILM EDITOR

OVER THE BROOKLYN BRIDGE
ADAM GREENBERG .... CINEMATOGRAPHER
JOHN LAWLESS .... PRODUCTION DESIGNER
MARK GOLDBLATT .... FILM EDITOR

OVER THE EDGE
ANDREW DAVIS .... CINEMATOGRAPHER
JAMES WILLIAM NEWPORT .... PRODUCTION DESIGNER
ROBERT BARRERE .... FILM EDITOR

OVER THE TOP
DAVID GURFINKEL .... CINEMATOGRAPHER
JAMES SCHOPPE .... PRODUCTION DESIGNER
THOMAS M. BRONSON .... COSTUME DESIGNER
DON ZIMMERMAN .... FILM EDITOR
JAMES SYMONS .... FILM EDITOR

Ov-Pa

CINEMATOGRAPHERS
PRODUCTION
DESIGNERS,
COSTUME
DESIGNERS and
FILM EDITORS
GUIDE

INDEX OF FILM TITLES

OVERBOARD
JOHN A. ALONZO .... CINEMATOGRAPHER
JAMES SHANAHAN .... PRODUCTION DESIGNER
JIM DULTZ .... PRODUCTION DESIGNER
LAWRENCE MILLER .... PRODUCTION DESIGNER
WAYNE FINKELMAN .... COSTUME DESIGNER
SONNY BASKIN .... FILM EDITOR
DOV HOENIG .... FILM EDITOR

OWL AND THE PUSSYCAT, THE
ANDREW LASZLO .... CINEMATOGRAPHER
KEN ADAM .... PRODUCTION DESIGNER
PHILIP ROSENBERG .... PRODUCTION DESIGNER
JOHN F. BURNETT .... FILM EDITOR

OWLFARM BROTHERS, THE
MIKAEL SALOMON .... CINEMATOGRAPHER

OXFORD BLUES
JOHN STANIER .... CINEMATOGRAPHER
TERRY PRITCHARD .... PRODUCTION DESIGNER
PATRICK MOORE .... FILM EDITOR

P

P.K. AND THE KID
EDMOND L. KOONS .... CINEMATOGRAPHER
CHET ALLEN .... PRODUCTION DESIGNER
TONY LOMBARDO .... FILM EDITOR

P.O.W. THE ESCAPE
GIDEON PORATH .... CINEMATOGRAPHER
BO JOHNSON .... PRODUCTION DESIGNER
MARCIA HINDS .... PRODUCTION DESIGNER
AUDREY BANSMER .... COSTUME DESIGNER
MARCUS MANTON .... FILM EDITOR
ROY WATTS .... FILM EDITOR

PACIFIC HEIGHTS
DENNIS E. JONES .... CINEMATOGRAPHER
NEIL SPISAK .... PRODUCTION DESIGNER
ANN ROTH .... COSTUME DESIGNER
BRIDGET KELLY .... COSTUME DESIGNER
MARK WARNER .... FILM EDITOR

PACK OF LIES (TF)
KENNETH MACMILLAN .... CINEMATOGRAPHER

PACK, THE
RALPH WOOLSEY .... CINEMATOGRAPHER
WILLIAM SANDELL .... PRODUCTION DESIGNER
PETER E. BERGER .... FILM EDITOR

PACKAGE, THE
FRANK TIDY .... CINEMATOGRAPHER
MICHAEL LEVESQUE .... PRODUCTION DESIGNER
MARILYN VANCE-STRAKER .... COSTUME DESIGNER
BILLY WEBER .... FILM EDITOR
DON ZIMMERMAN .... FILM EDITOR

PADDY
CHRISTOPHER HOLMES .... FILM EDITOR

PAINT IT BLACK
LEONARD POLLACK .... COSTUME DESIGNER

PAINT YOUR WAGON
JAMES G. HULSEY .... PRODUCTION DESIGNER
ROBERT C. JONES .... FILM EDITOR

PALAIS ROYALE
SUSAN MARTIN .... FILM EDITOR

PALE RIDER
BRUCE SURTEES .... CINEMATOGRAPHER
EDWARD C. CARFAGNO .... PRODUCTION DESIGNER
GLENN WRIGHT .... COSTUME DESIGNER
JOEL COX .... FILM EDITOR

PALMERSTOWN, U.S.A. (TF)
JAMES D. BISSELL .... PRODUCTION DESIGNER

PANCHO BARNES (TF)
WILLIAM WAGES .... CINEMATOGRAPHER
MICHAEL ELIOT .... FILM EDITOR
MICHAEL F. ANDERSON .... FILM EDITOR

PANDEMONIUM
MICHEL HUGO .... CINEMATOGRAPHER
JACK DE SHIELDS .... PRODUCTION DESIGNER
ROBERTA WEINER .... COSTUME DESIGNER
ERIC JENKINS .... FILM EDITOR

PANDORA AND THE FLYING DURCHMAN
JACK CARDIFF .... CINEMATOGRAPHER

PANIC IN NEEDLE PARK
ADAM HOLENDER .... CINEMATOGRAPHER
JO YNOCENCIO .... COSTUME DESIGNER
EVAN LOTTMAN .... FILM EDITOR

PAPER CHASE, THE
GORDON WILLIS .... CINEMATOGRAPHER

PAPER DOLLS (PILOT)
JAMES A. CRABE .... CINEMATOGRAPHER

PAPER DOLLS (TF)
THOMAS DEL RUTH .... CINEMATOGRAPHER

PAPER MASK
NAT CROSBY .... CINEMATOGRAPHER
PETER COULSON .... FILM EDITOR

PAPER MOON
LASZLO KOVACS .... CINEMATOGRAPHER
POLLY PLATT .... PRODUCTION DESIGNER

PAPER TIGER
JOHN CABRERA .... CINEMATOGRAPHER

PAPERHOUSE
MIKE SOUTHON .... CINEMATOGRAPHER
FRANK WALSH .... PRODUCTION DESIGNER
GEMMA JACKSON .... PRODUCTION DESIGNER
NIC EDE .... COSTUME DESIGNER
DAN RAE .... FILM EDITOR

PAPILLON
FRED J. KOENEKAMP .... CINEMATOGRAPHER
ANTHONY MASTERS .... PRODUCTION DESIGNER
ANTHONY POWELL .... COSTUME DESIGNER
ROBERT E. SWINK .... FILM EDITOR

PARADISE
ADAM GREENBERG .... CINEMATOGRAPHER

PARADISE ALLEY
LASZLO KOVACS .... CINEMATOGRAPHER
JOHN W. CORSO .... PRODUCTION DESIGNER
EVE NEWMAN .... FILM EDITOR

PARALLAX VIEW, THE
GORDON WILLIS .... CINEMATOGRAPHER
JOHN W. WHEELER .... FILM EDITOR

PARAMEDIC
MICHAEL WATKINS .... CINEMATOGRAPHER

PARASITE
MAC AHLBERG .... CINEMATOGRAPHER
BRAD ARENSMAN .... FILM EDITOR

PARENT TRAP II (TF)
PETER STEIN .... CINEMATOGRAPHER

PARENT TRAP III (TF)
ISIDORE MANKOFSKY .... CINEMATOGRAPHER
RAYMOND G. STOREY .... PRODUCTION DESIGNER
DUANE HARTZELL .... FILM EDITOR
HOWARD KUNIN .... FILM EDITOR

PARENTHOOD
DONALD MCALPINE .... CINEMATOGRAPHER
CHRISTOPHER NOWAK .... PRODUCTION DESIGNER
TODD HALLOWELL .... PRODUCTION DESIGNER
RUTH MORLEY .... COSTUME DESIGNER
DANIEL P. HANLEY .... FILM EDITOR
MICHAEL J. HILL .... FILM EDITOR

PARENTS
ERNEST DAY .... CINEMATOGRAPHER
ROBIN VIDGEON .... CINEMATOGRAPHER
ANDRIS HAUSMANIS .... PRODUCTION DESIGNER
ARTHUR ROWSELL .... COSTUME DESIGNER
BILL PANKOW .... FILM EDITOR

PARIS BY NIGHT
ROGER PRATT .... CINEMATOGRAPHER
ANTHONY PRATT .... PRODUCTION DESIGNER
LIZ WALLER .... COSTUME DESIGNER
GEORGE AKERS .... FILM EDITOR

PARIS TROUT
ROBERT ELSWIT .... CINEMATOGRAPHER
RICHARD SHERMAN .... PRODUCTION DESIGNER
MARY ROSE .... COSTUME DESIGNER
HARVEY ROSENSTOCK .... FILM EDITOR

PARIS, TEXAS
ROBBY MULLER .... CINEMATOGRAPHER
KATE ALTMAN .... PRODUCTION DESIGNER
BIRGITTA BJERKE .... COSTUME DESIGNER
PETER PRZYGODDA .... FILM EDITOR

PARK IS MINE, THE (TF)
LASZLO GEORGE .... CINEMATOGRAPHER

PAROLE (TF)
LASZLO GEORGE .... CINEMATOGRAPHER

PART 2 SOUNDER
WALTER SCOTT HERNDON† .... PRODUCTION DESIGNER
SIDNEY LEVIN .... FILM EDITOR

PARTING GLANCES
JACEK LASKUS .... CINEMATOGRAPHER
JOHN LOGGIA .... PRODUCTION DESIGNER
SYLVIA HEISEL .... COSTUME DESIGNER
BILL SHERWOOD .... FILM EDITOR

PARTNERS
VICTOR J. KEMPER .... CINEMATOGRAPHER
GEORGE GAINES† .... PRODUCTION DESIGNER
IDA RANDOM .... PRODUCTION DESIGNER
RICHARD SYLBERT .... PRODUCTION DESIGNER
WAYNE FINKELMAN .... COSTUME DESIGNER
DANFORD B. GREENE .... FILM EDITOR
GEORGE APPELBY .... FILM EDITOR

PARTY ANIMAL, THE
BRYAN ENGLAND .... CINEMATOGRAPHER

PARTY CAMP
GARY GRAVER .... CINEMATOGRAPHER

PARTY, THE
RALPH E. WINTERS .... FILM EDITOR

PASCALI'S ISLAND
ROGER DEAKINS .... CINEMATOGRAPHER
PAM TAIT .... COSTUME DESIGNER
EDWARD MARNIER .... FILM EDITOR

PASS THE AMMO
MARK IRWIN .... CINEMATOGRAPHER
DEAN TSCHETTER .... PRODUCTION DESIGNER
REVE RICHARDS .... COSTUME DESIGNER
BILL YAHRAUS .... FILM EDITOR

PASSAGE TO INDIA, A
ERNEST DAY .... CINEMATOGRAPHER
CLIFFORD ROBINSON .... PRODUCTION DESIGNER
HERBERT WESTBROOK .... PRODUCTION DESIGNER
JOHN BOX .... PRODUCTION DESIGNER
LESLIE TOMKINS .... PRODUCTION DESIGNER
RAM YEDEKER .... PRODUCTION DESIGNER
JUDY MOORCROFT .... COSTUME DESIGNER
DAVID LEAN .... FILM EDITOR

PASSAGE, THE
PETER STEIN .... CINEMATOGRAPHER

PASSAGE, THE (1979)
MICHAEL REED .... CINEMATOGRAPHER
ALAN STRACHAN .... FILM EDITOR

PASSION
RAOUL COUTARD .... CINEMATOGRAPHER

PASSIONE D'AMORE
GABRIELLA PESCUCCI .... COSTUME DESIGNER

PASSOVER PLOT, THE
ADAM GREENBERG .... CINEMATOGRAPHER
DOV HOENIG .... FILM EDITOR

PAST CARING (TF)
KENNETH MACMILLAN .... CINEMATOGRAPHER

PAT GARRETT & BILLY THE KID
TED HAWORTH .... PRODUCTION DESIGNER
GARTH CRAVEN .... FILM EDITOR
ROBERT L. WOLFE .... FILM EDITOR

PATCH OF BLUE, A
RITA ROLAND .... FILM EDITOR

PATERNITY
BOBBY BYRNE .... CINEMATOGRAPHER
JACK T. COLLIS .... PRODUCTION DESIGNER
PETER LANDSDOWN SMITH .... PRODUCTION DESIGNER
ALBERT WOLSKY .... COSTUME DESIGNER
DONN CAMBERN .... FILM EDITOR

PATRICK
DONALD MCALPINE .... CINEMATOGRAPHER
LESLIE BINNS .... PRODUCTION DESIGNER

PATRIOT, THE
FRANK HARRIS .... CINEMATOGRAPHER
RICHARD E. WESTOVER .... FILM EDITOR

PATTI ROCKS
GREGORY CUMMINS .... CINEMATOGRAPHER

PATTON
FRED J. KOENEKAMP .... CINEMATOGRAPHER
GIL PARRONDO .... PRODUCTION DESIGNER

PATTY HEARST
BOJAN BAZELLI .... CINEMATOGRAPHER
HAROLD THRASHER .... PRODUCTION DESIGNER
JANE MUSKY .... PRODUCTION DESIGNER
RICHARD HORNUNG .... COSTUME DESIGNER
MICHAEL R. MILLER .... FILM EDITOR

PAUL'S CASE (TF)
LARRY PIZER .... CINEMATOGRAPHER

PAULINE AT THE BEACH
NESTOR ALMENDROS .... CINEMATOGRAPHER

PAWNBROKER, THE
ALBERT BRENNER .... PRODUCTION DESIGNER
RICHARD SYLBERT .... PRODUCTION DESIGNER

PEACE KILLERS, THE
STEPHEN M. KATZ .... CINEMATOGRAPHER

PEACEMAKER
THOMAS JEWELL .... CINEMATOGRAPHER
ROBERT SISSMAN .... PRODUCTION DESIGNER
DAVID DUNCAN .... FILM EDITOR

PEE-WEE HERMAN SHOW, THE (TVS)
BETSY HEIMANN .... COSTUME DESIGNER

PEE-WEE'S BIG ADVENTURE
VICTOR J. KEMPER .... CINEMATOGRAPHER
DAVID L. SNYDER .... PRODUCTION DESIGNER
MARJORIE STONE MCSHIRLEY .... PRODUCTION DESIGNER
AGGIE GUERARD RODGERS .... COSTUME DESIGNER
BILLY WEBER .... FILM EDITOR

PEEPER
JAMES MITCHELL .... FILM EDITOR

PEGGY SUE GOT MARRIED
JORDAN CRONENWETH .... CINEMATOGRAPHER
ALEX TAVOULARIS .... PRODUCTION DESIGNER
DEAN TAVOULARIS .... PRODUCTION DESIGNER
THEADORA VAN RUNKLE .... COSTUME DESIGNER
BARRY MALKIN .... FILM EDITOR

PELLE THE CONQUERER
JANUS BILLESKOV JANSEN .... FILM EDITOR

PENELOPE
RITA ROLAND .... FILM EDITOR

PENITENT, THE
ROBIN VIDGEON .... CINEMATOGRAPHER
PETER TAYLOR .... FILM EDITOR

PENITENTIARY
MARTY OLLSTEIN .... CINEMATOGRAPHER
BETSY BLANKETT .... FILM EDITOR

Pa-Pe

CINEMATOGRAPHERS
PRODUCTION
DESIGNERS,
COSTUME
DESIGNERS AND
FILM EDITORS
GUIDE

INDEX

OF

FILM

TITLES

407

CINEMATOGRAPHERS
PRODUCTION
DESIGNERS,
COSTUME
DESIGNERS AND
FILM EDITORS
GUIDE

I
N
D
E
X

O
F

F
I
L
M

T
I
T
L
E
S

PENITENTIARY II
STEPHEN L. POSEY .... CINEMATOGRAPHER
JAMES E. NOWNES .... FILM EDITOR

PENITENTIARY III
MARTY OLLSTEIN .... CINEMATOGRAPHER
MARSHALL TOOMEY .... PRODUCTION DESIGNER
JERRY N. SKEELS .... COSTUME DESIGNER
ED HARKER .... FILM EDITOR

PENN & TELLER GET KILLED
JAN WEINCKE .... CINEMATOGRAPHER
RITA RYACK .... COSTUME DESIGNER
JEFFREY WOLF .... FILM EDITOR

PENN & TELLER'S INVISIBLE THREAD (CBL)
JACEK LASKUS .... CINEMATOGRAPHER

PENNIES FROM HEAVEN
GORDON WILLIS .... CINEMATOGRAPHER
BERNIE CUTLER .... PRODUCTION DESIGNER
FRED TUCH .... PRODUCTION DESIGNER
KEN ADAM .... PRODUCTION DESIGNER
BOB MACKIE .... COSTUME DESIGNER
RICHARD MARKS .... FILM EDITOR

PENNY ANTE
JACOB ELESARI .... CINEMATOGRAPHER
ADAM WOLFE .... FILM EDITOR

PENTHOUSE, THE (TF)
RENE VERZIER .... CINEMATOGRAPHER

PEOPLE THAT TIME FORGOT, THE
ALAN HUME .... CINEMATOGRAPHER
MAURICE CARTER .... PRODUCTION DESIGNER
BARRY PETERS .... FILM EDITOR

PEOPLE, THE (TF)
JACKSON DE GOVIA .... PRODUCTION DESIGNER

PEPE
TED HAWORTH .... PRODUCTION DESIGNER

PEPPERMINT SODA
PHILIPPE ROUSSELOT .... CINEMATOGRAPHER

PERCEVAL
NESTOR ALMENDROS .... CINEMATOGRAPHER

PERFECT
GORDON WILLIS .... CINEMATOGRAPHER
MICHAEL D. HALLER .... PRODUCTION DESIGNER
MICHAEL KAPLAN .... COSTUME DESIGNER
JEFF S. GOURSON .... FILM EDITOR

PERFECT COUPLE, A
EDMOND L. KOONS .... CINEMATOGRAPHER
TONY LOMBARDO .... FILM EDITOR

PERFECT FRIDAY
TERENCE MARSH .... PRODUCTION DESIGNER

PERFECT MATCH, (TF)
RIC WAITE .... CINEMATOGRAPHER

PERFECT MURDER, THE
WALTER LASSALLY .... CINEMATOGRAPHER

PERFECT PEOPLE (TF)
CURTIS A. SCHNELL .... PRODUCTION DESIGNER
MOLLY MAGINNIS .... COSTUME DESIGNER

PERFECT STRANGERS
PAUL GLICKMAN .... CINEMATOGRAPHER
ARMAND LEBOWITZ .... FILM EDITOR

PERFECT WEAPON, THE
RUSSELL CARPENTER .... CINEMATOGRAPHER
CURTIS SCHNELL .... PRODUCTION DESIGNER
JOSEPH PORRO .... COSTUME DESIGNER
WAYNE WAHRMAN .... FILM EDITOR

PERFECT!
LYNDA PARADISE .... PRODUCTION DESIGNER

PERFORMANCE
ANTONY GIBBS .... FILM EDITOR

PERMANENT RECORD
FREDERICK ELMES .... CINEMATOGRAPHER
MICHAEL LEVESQUE .... PRODUCTION DESIGNER
STEVEN KARATZOS .... PRODUCTION DESIGNER
TRACY TYNAN .... COSTUME DESIGNER
ROBERT BROWN .... FILM EDITOR

PERMANENT VACATION
THOMAS DICILLO .... CINEMATOGRAPHER
JIM JARMUSCH .... FILM EDITOR

PERRY MASON: THE CASE OF THE DEFIANT DAUGHTER (TF)
DANIEL MCKINNY .... CINEMATOGRAPHER
PAUL STAHELI .... PRODUCTION DESIGNER
CARTER DE HAVEN IV .... FILM EDITOR

PERRY MASON: THE CASE OF THE MALIGNED MOBSTER (TF)
ROBERT SEAMAN .... CINEMATOGRAPHER
CARTER DE HAVEN IV .... FILM EDITOR

PERSONAL BEST
MICHAEL CHAPMAN .... CINEMATOGRAPHER
RICHARD CARTER .... PRODUCTION DESIGNER
RON HOBBS .... PRODUCTION DESIGNER
BUD SMITH .... FILM EDITOR

PERSONAL CHOICE
PATRICK MCMAHON .... FILM EDITOR

PERSONAL FOUL
ELIZABETH P. PALMER .... COSTUME DESIGNER

PERSONAL SERVICES
ROGER DEAKINS .... CINEMATOGRAPHER
HUGO LUCZYC WYHOWSKI .... PRODUCTION DESIGNER
SHUNA HARWOOD .... COSTUME DESIGNER
GEORGE AKERS .... FILM EDITOR

PERSONALS, THE
PETER MARKLE .... CINEMATOGRAPHER
STEPHEN E. RIVKIN .... FILM EDITOR

PET SEMATARY
PETER STEIN .... CINEMATOGRAPHER
MICHAEL Z. HANAN .... PRODUCTION DESIGNER
MARLENE STEWART .... COSTUME DESIGNER
DANIEL P. HANLEY .... FILM EDITOR
MICHAEL J. HILL .... FILM EDITOR

PETE 'N' TILLIE
JOHN A. ALONZO .... CINEMATOGRAPHER
EDITH HEAD† .... COSTUME DESIGNER
FRANK BRACHT .... FILM EDITOR

PETE'S DRAGON (AF)
FRANK PHILLIPS .... CINEMATOGRAPHER
JACK MARTIN SMITH .... PRODUCTION DESIGNER
JOHN B. MANSBRIDGE .... PRODUCTION DESIGNER
GORDON D. BRENNER .... FILM EDITOR

PETER GUNN (PILOT)
RICHARD Y. HAMAN .... PRODUCTION DESIGNER
ROBERT PERGAMENT .... FILM EDITOR

PETER THE GREAT (TV)
SHELLEY KOMAROV .... COSTUME DESIGNER

PETER VON SCHOLTEN
MIKAEL SALOMON .... CINEMATOGRAPHER

PETIT CON
GEORGES KLOTZ .... FILM EDITOR

PETRIA'S WREATH
TOMISLAV PINTER .... CINEMATOGRAPHER

PETULIA
ANTONY GIBBS .... FILM EDITOR

PEYTON PLACE: THE NEXT GENERATION (TF)
RICHARD JAMES .... PRODUCTION DESIGNER
W. STEWART CAMPBELL .... PRODUCTION DESIGNER
ERICA EDELL PHILLIPS .... COSTUME DESIGNER

PHANTASM II
DARYN OKADA .... CINEMATOGRAPHER
PHILIP J.C. DUFFIN .... PRODUCTION DESIGNER
CARLA GIBBONS .... COSTUME DESIGNER
PETER TESCHNER .... FILM EDITOR

PHANTASTS, THE
MIKAEL SALOMON .... CINEMATOGRAPHER

PHANTOM OF THE MALL
HARRY MATHIAS .... CINEMATOGRAPHER

PHANTOM OF THE MALL: ERIC'S REVENGE
HARRY MATHIAS .... CINEMATOGRAPHER
GARY T. NEW .... PRODUCTION DESIGNER
JUDY B. SWARTZ .... COSTUME DESIGNER
AMY TOMPKINS .... FILM EDITOR
GREGORY F. PLOTTS .... FILM EDITOR

PHANTOM OF THE OPERA, THE
ELEMER RAGALYI .... CINEMATOGRAPHER
TIVADA BERTALAN .... PRODUCTION DESIGNER
JOHN BLOOMFIELD .... COSTUME DESIGNER
CHARLES BORNSTEIN .... FILM EDITOR

PHANTOM OF THE PARADISE
LARRY PIZER .... CINEMATOGRAPHER
PAUL HIRSCH .... FILM EDITOR

PHAR LAP
RUSSELL BOYD .... CINEMATOGRAPHER
ANNA SENIOR .... PRODUCTION DESIGNER
LAWRENCE ESATWOOD .... PRODUCTION DESIGNER
TONY PATERSON .... FILM EDITOR

PHAROAH'S CURSE
ROBERT KINOSHITA .... PRODUCTION DESIGNER

PHASE IV
DICK BUSH .... CINEMATOGRAPHER
JOHN BARRY† .... PRODUCTION DESIGNER

PHILADELPHIA EXPERIMENT, THE
DICK BUSH .... CINEMATOGRAPHER
CHRIS CAMPBELL .... PRODUCTION DESIGNER
NEIL TRAVIS .... FILM EDITOR

PHILADELPHIA HERE I COME
MALCOLM COOKE .... FILM EDITOR

PHILIP MARLOWE - PRIVATE EYE (CMS)
JAMES SHANAHAN .... PRODUCTION DESIGNER
JANE ROBINSON .... COSTUME DESIGNER
RONALD SANDERS .... FILM EDITOR

PHOBIA
REGINALD H. MORRIS .... CINEMATOGRAPHER
BEN EDWARDS .... PRODUCTION DESIGNER
ALEIDA MAC DONALD .... COSTUME DESIGNER
STAN COLE .... FILM EDITOR

PHOTOGRAPHER, THE
KIRK AXTELL .... PRODUCTION DESIGNER

PHYNX, THE
MICHEL HUGO .... CINEMATOGRAPHER

PHYSICAL EVIDENCE
JOHN A. ALONZO .... CINEMATOGRAPHER
DAN YARHI .... PRODUCTION DESIGNER
BETSY COX .... COSTUME DESIGNER
GLENN FARR .... FILM EDITOR

PICASSO SUMMER, THE
WILLIAM DORNISCH .... FILM EDITOR

PICASSO TRIGGER
HOWARD WEXLER .... CINEMATOGRAPHER
MARK HASKINS .... PRODUCTION DESIGNER
PETER MUNNEKE .... PRODUCTION DESIGNER
MICHAEL HAIGHT .... FILM EDITOR

PICK-UP ARTIST, THE -
GORDON WILLIS .... CINEMATOGRAPHER
BILL GROOM .... PRODUCTION DESIGNER
PAUL SYLBERT .... PRODUCTION DESIGNER
COLLEEN C. ATWOOD .... COSTUME DESIGNER
ANGELO CORRAO .... FILM EDITOR
DAVID BRETHERTON .... FILM EDITOR

PICKING UP THE PIECES (TF)
PHILIP LATHROP .... CINEMATOGRAPHER
MINA MITTELMAN .... COSTUME DESIGNER

PICNIC AT HANGING ROCK
RUSSELL BOYD .... CINEMATOGRAPHER
DAVID COPPING .... PRODUCTION DESIGNER

PICTURE OF DORIAN GRAY, THE (TF)
TREVOR WILLIAMS .... PRODUCTION DESIGNER
FERRIS WEBSTER .... FILM EDITOR

PICTURE SHOW MAN, THE
GEOFF BURTON .... CINEMATOGRAPHER
DAVID COPPING .... PRODUCTION DESIGNER
NICHOLAS BEAUMAN .... FILM EDITOR

PIECE OF THE ACTION, A
DONALD M. MORGAN .... CINEMATOGRAPHER
ALFRED SWEENEY .... PRODUCTION DESIGNER
PEMBROKE J. HERRING .... FILM EDITOR

PIED PIPER, THE
PETER SUSCHITZKY .... CINEMATOGRAPHER
ASSHETON GORTON .... PRODUCTION DESIGNER

PILOT, THE
EVAN LOTTMAN .... FILM EDITOR

PIN
GUY DUFAUX .... CINEMATOGRAPHER
PATRICK DODD .... FILM EDITOR

PING PONG
NICK KNOWLAND .... CINEMATOGRAPHER
COLIN PIGOTT .... PRODUCTION DESIGNER
DAVID SPIERS .... FILM EDITOR

PINK CADILLAC
JACK N. GREEN .... CINEMATOGRAPHER
EDWARD C. CARFAGNO .... PRODUCTION DESIGNER
JOEL COX .... FILM EDITOR

PINK FLOYD - THE WALL
PETER BIZIOU .... CINEMATOGRAPHER
BRIAN MORRIS .... PRODUCTION DESIGNER
CLINTON CAVERS .... PRODUCTION DESIGNER
GERRY HAMBLING .... FILM EDITOR

PINK MOTEL
NICHOLAS VON STERNBERG .... CINEMATOGRAPHER
CHESTER KACZENSKI .... PRODUCTION DESIGNER
EARL WATSON .... FILM EDITOR

PINK PANTHER, THE
PHILIP LATHROP .... CINEMATOGRAPHER
WILLIAM WARE THEISS .... COSTUME DESIGNER
RALPH E. WINTERS .... FILM EDITOR

PINK PANTHER STRIKES AGAIN, THE
HARRY WAXMAN .... CINEMATOGRAPHER
JOHN SIDALL .... PRODUCTION DESIGNER
PETER MULLINS .... PRODUCTION DESIGNER
ALAN JONES .... FILM EDITOR

PIPE DREAMS
STEVAN LARNER .... CINEMATOGRAPHER
GLENDA GANIS .... PRODUCTION DESIGNER
ROBERT L. ESTRIN .... FILM EDITOR

PIRANHA
JAMIE ANDERSON .... CINEMATOGRAPHER
WILLIAM SANDELL .... PRODUCTION DESIGNER
MARK GOLDBLATT .... FILM EDITOR

PIRANHA II - THE SPAWNING
ROBERTO SILVI .... FILM EDITOR

PIRATE
HERVE DE LUZE .... FILM EDITOR

PIRATE MOVIE, THE
ROBIN COPPING .... CINEMATOGRAPHER
KEN ZEMKE .... FILM EDITOR

PIRATES
WITOLD SOBOCINSKI .... CINEMATOGRAPHER
PIERRE GUFFROY .... PRODUCTION DESIGNER
ANTHONY POWELL .... COSTUME DESIGNER
WILLIAM REYNOLDS .... FILM EDITOR

PIRATES OF PENZANCE, THE
DOUGLAS SLOCOMBE .... CINEMATOGRAPHER
ALAN CASSIE .... PRODUCTION DESIGNER
ELLIOT SCOTT .... PRODUCTION DESIGNER
TOM RAND .... COSTUME DESIGNER
ANNE V. COATES .... FILM EDITOR

Pi-Po

CINEMATOGRAPHERS
PRODUCTION
DESIGNERS,
COSTUME
DESIGNERS and
FILM EDITORS
GUIDE

I
N
D
E
X

O
F

F
I
L
M

T
I
T
L
E
S

410

Po-Pr

CINEMATOGRAPHERS
PRODUCTION
DESIGNERS,
COSTUME
DESIGNERS AND
FILM EDITORS
GUIDE

I N D E X   O F   F I L M   T I T L E S

411

Pr-Pr

CINEMATOGRAPHERS
PRODUCTION
DESIGNERS,
COSTUME
DESIGNERS and
FILM EDITORS
GUIDE

I
N
D
E
X

O
F

F
I
L
M

T
I
T
L
E
S

PRANKS
STEPHEN CARPENTER .... CINEMATOGRAPHER
STEPHEN CARPENTER .... FILM EDITOR

PRAY FOR DEATH
ROY H. WAGNER .... CINEMATOGRAPHER
ADRIAN H. GORTON .... PRODUCTION DESIGNER
WILLIAM BUTLER .... FILM EDITOR

PRAY FOR THE WILDCATS (TF)
WILLIAM MALLEY .... PRODUCTION DESIGNER

PRAY TV
HARRY MATHIAS .... CINEMATOGRAPHER
ERICA EDELL PHILLIPS .... COSTUME DESIGNER

PRAYER FOR THE DYING, A
MIKE GARFATH .... CINEMATOGRAPHER
EVAN HERCULES .... PRODUCTION DESIGNER
EVANGELINE HARRISON .... COSTUME DESIGNER
PETER BOYLE .... FILM EDITOR

PREDATOR
DONALD MCALPINE .... CINEMATOGRAPHER
FRANK RICHWOOD .... PRODUCTION DESIGNER
JOHN VALLONE .... PRODUCTION DESIGNER
MARILYN VANCE-STRAKER .... COSTUME DESIGNER
JOHN F. LINK .... FILM EDITOR
MARK HELFRICH .... FILM EDITOR

PREDATOR 2
PETER LEVY .... CINEMATOGRAPHER
LAWRENCE G. PAULL .... PRODUCTION DESIGNER
MARILYN VANCE-STRAKER .... COSTUME DESIGNER
MARK GOLDBLATT .... FILM EDITOR

PREPPIES
LARRY REVENE .... CINEMATOGRAPHER

PRESIDENT MUST DIE, THE
PAUL HIPP .... CINEMATOGRAPHER

PRESIDENT'S ANALYST, THE
PATO GUZMAN .... PRODUCTION DESIGNER
STUART H. PAPPE .... FILM EDITOR

PRESIDENT'S PLANE IS MISSING, THE (TF)
JAMES G. HULSEY .... PRODUCTION DESIGNER

PRESIDENT'S WOMAN
RALF D. BODE .... CINEMATOGRAPHER

PRESIDIO, THE
PETER HYAMS .... CINEMATOGRAPHER
ALBERT BRENNER .... PRODUCTION DESIGNER
KANDY STERN .... PRODUCTION DESIGNER
JAMES MITCHELL .... FILM EDITOR

PRESUMED INNOCENT
GORDON WILLIS .... CINEMATOGRAPHER
GEORGE JENKINS .... PRODUCTION DESIGNER
JOHN BOXER .... COSTUME DESIGNER
EVAN LOTTMAN .... FILM EDITOR

PRETTY BABY
SVEN NYKVIST .... CINEMATOGRAPHER
TREVOR WILLIAMS .... PRODUCTION DESIGNER
MINA MITTELMAN .... COSTUME DESIGNER
SUZANNE BARON .... FILM EDITOR
SUZANNE FENN .... FILM EDITOR

PRETTY IN PINK
TAK FUJIMOTO .... CINEMATOGRAPHER
JOHN W. CORSO .... PRODUCTION DESIGNER
MARILYN VANCE-STRAKER .... COSTUME DESIGNER
RICHARD MARKS .... FILM EDITOR

PRETTY KILL
ANDRIS HAUSMANIS .... PRODUCTION DESIGNER

PRETTY MAIDS ALL IN A ROW
CHARLES ROSHER, JR. .... CINEMATOGRAPHER
WILLIAM WARE THEISS .... COSTUME DESIGNER
BILL BRAME .... FILM EDITOR

PRETTY POISON
HAROLD MICHELSON .... PRODUCTION DESIGNER

PRETTY POLLY
ARTHUR IBBETSON .... CINEMATOGRAPHER
PETER MULLINS .... PRODUCTION DESIGNER

PRETTY SMART
BEAU PETERSON .... PRODUCTION DESIGNER
GAELLE ALLEN .... COSTUME DESIGNER
DANIEL GROSS .... FILM EDITOR

PRETTY WOMAN
CHARLES MINSKY .... CINEMATOGRAPHER
ALBERT BRENNER .... PRODUCTION DESIGNER
MARILYN VANCE-STRAKER .... COSTUME DESIGNER
PRISCILLA NEDD .... FILM EDITOR

PRETTYKILL
JOAO FERNANDES .... CINEMATOGRAPHER
TOM MERCHANT .... FILM EDITOR

PREY, THE
MICHAEL BARNARD .... FILM EDITOR

PRICELESS BEAUTY
VICTORIA PAUL .... PRODUCTION DESIGNER

PRICELESS DAY, A
LAJOS KOLTAI .... CINEMATOGRAPHER

PRICELESS GIFT, THE
NORM WALLERSTEIN .... FILM EDITOR

PRICK UP YOUR EARS
OLIVER STAPLETON .... CINEMATOGRAPHER
HUGO LUCZYC WYHOWSKI .... PRODUCTION DESIGNER
BOB RINGWOOD .... COSTUME DESIGNER
MICK AUDSLEY .... FILM EDITOR

PRIEST OF LOVE
TED MOORE .... CINEMATOGRAPHER
DAVID BROCKHURST .... PRODUCTION DESIGNER
ANTHONY POWELL .... COSTUME DESIGNER

PRIMAL SCREAM
KEITH L. REAMER .... FILM EDITOR

PRIME CUT
WILLIAM MALLEY .... PRODUCTION DESIGNER

PRIME RISK
MAC AHLBERG .... CINEMATOGRAPHER
CHRISTOPHER HENRY .... PRODUCTION DESIGNER
BERNADETTE O'BRIEN .... COSTUME DESIGNER
BRUCE GREEN .... FILM EDITOR

PRIME SUSPECT (TF)
MARIANNA ASTROM DEFINA .... COSTUME DESIGNER

PRINCE AND THE PAUPER, THE
JACK CARDIFF .... CINEMATOGRAPHER
ANTHONY PRATT .... PRODUCTION DESIGNER
MAURICE FOWLER .... PRODUCTION DESIGNER
JUDY MOORCROFT .... COSTUME DESIGNER

PRINCE JACK
HIRO NARITA .... CINEMATOGRAPHER
MICHAEL CORENBLITH .... PRODUCTION DESIGNER
BOBBIE MANNIX .... COSTUME DESIGNER
JANICE HAMPTON .... FILM EDITOR

PRINCE OF BEL AIR (TF)
HANANIA BAER .... CINEMATOGRAPHER
BRYAN RYMAN .... PRODUCTION DESIGNER

PRINCE OF DARKNESS
GARY B. KIBBE .... CINEMATOGRAPHER
DANIEL LOMINO .... PRODUCTION DESIGNER
DEANDRO SCARANO .... COSTUME DESIGNER
STEVE MIRKOVICH .... FILM EDITOR

PRINCE OF PENNSYLVANIA, THE
FRANK PRINZI .... CINEMATOGRAPHER
TOBY CORBETT .... PRODUCTION DESIGNER
CAROL WOOD .... COSTUME DESIGNER
WILLIAM SCHARF .... FILM EDITOR

PRINCE OF THE CITY
ANDRZEJ BARTKOWIAK .... CINEMATOGRAPHER
EDWARD PISONI .... PRODUCTION DESIGNER
TONY WALTON .... PRODUCTION DESIGNER
ANNA HILL JOHNSTONE .... COSTUME DESIGNER
JOHN J. FITZSTEPHENS .... FILM EDITOR

PRINCESS ACADEMY, THE
KENT WAKEFORD .... CINEMATOGRAPHER
MARTIN COHEN .... FILM EDITOR

PRINCESS AND THE CABBIE, THE (TF)
WILLIAM MC ALLISTER .... PRODUCTION DESIGNER

PRINCESS BRIDE, THE
ADRIAN BIDDLE .... CINEMATOGRAPHER
KEITH PAIN .... PRODUCTION DESIGNER
NORMAN GARWOOD .... PRODUCTION DESIGNER
PHYLLIS DALTON .... COSTUME DESIGNER
ROBERT LEIGHTON .... FILM EDITOR

PRINCESS DAISY (MS)
CHARLES ROSHER, JR. .... CINEMATOGRAPHER
ERICA EDELL PHILLIPS .... COSTUME DESIGNER
ROBERT F. SHUGRUE .... FILM EDITOR

PRINCIPAL, THE
ARTHUR ALBERT .... CINEMATOGRAPHER
BRENTON SWIFT .... PRODUCTION DESIGNER
JAMES DAVIS .... PRODUCTION DESIGNER
MARIANNA ASTROM DEFINA .... COSTUME DESIGNER
JACK HOFSTRA .... FILM EDITOR

PRINCIPLE, THE
MARK BILLERMAN .... PRODUCTION DESIGNER

PRISON
MAC AHLBERG .... CINEMATOGRAPHER
PHILIP J.C. DUFFIN .... PRODUCTION DESIGNER
STEPHEN CHUDEJ .... COSTUME DESIGNER
TED NICOLAOU .... FILM EDITOR

PRISON FOR CHILDREN (TF)
ERIC SEARS .... FILM EDITOR

PRISON SHIP: THE ADVENTURES OF TAURA, PART 1
MICHAEL NOVOTNY .... PRODUCTION DESIGNER

PRISONER OF SECOND AVENUE, THE
PHILIP LATHROP .... CINEMATOGRAPHER
ROBERT WYMAN .... FILM EDITOR

PRISONER OF ZENDA, THE
ARTHUR IBBETSON .... CINEMATOGRAPHER
JOHN J. LLOYD .... PRODUCTION DESIGNER
SUSAN YELLAND .... COSTUME DESIGNER
BUZZ BRANDT .... FILM EDITOR

PRISONERS
JAMES M. GLENNON .... CINEMATOGRAPHER
STEPHEN M. KATZ .... CINEMATOGRAPHER
JACKSON DE GOVIA .... PRODUCTION DESIGNER

PRISONERS OF INERTIA
BILL GROOM .... PRODUCTION DESIGNER
DARREN KLOOMOK .... FILM EDITOR

PRIVATE BATTLE (TF)
LARRY PIZER .... CINEMATOGRAPHER

PRIVATE BENJAMIN
DAVID M. WALSH .... CINEMATOGRAPHER
JEFFREY HOWARD .... PRODUCTION DESIGNER
ROBERT F. BOYLE .... PRODUCTION DESIGNER
BETSY COX .... COSTUME DESIGNER
SHELDON KAHN .... FILM EDITOR

PRIVATE COLLECTION
DAVID GRIBBLE .... CINEMATOGRAPHER

PRIVATE CONTENTMENT (TF)
PETER STEIN .... CINEMATOGRAPHER

PRIVATE DEBTS
FARREL LEVY .... FILM EDITOR

PRIVATE EYE (PILOT)
BRADFORD MAY .... CINEMATOGRAPHER

PRIVATE EYES, THE
JACQUES HAITKIN .... CINEMATOGRAPHER
CHRISTINE GOULDING .... COSTUME DESIGNER
VINCENT PERANIO .... PRODUCTION DESIGNER
ALAN BALSAM .... FILM EDITOR
FABIEN TORDJMANN .... FILM EDITOR
PATRICK M. CRAWFORD .... FILM EDITOR

PRIVATE FILES OF J. EDGAR HOOVER, THE
PAUL GLICKMAN .... CINEMATOGRAPHER
CHRIS LEBENZON .... FILM EDITOR

PRIVATE FUNCTION, A
TONY PIERCE-ROBERTS .... CINEMATOGRAPHER
STUART WALKER .... PRODUCTION DESIGNER
PHYLLIS DALTON .... COSTUME DESIGNER
BARRIE VINCE .... FILM EDITOR

PRIVATE HISTORY OF A CAMPAIGN THAT FAILED, THE (TF)
LINDA FISHER .... COSTUME DESIGNER

PRIVATE INVESTIGATIONS
DAVID BRIDGES .... CINEMATOGRAPHER
NICK RAFTER .... PRODUCTION DESIGNER
PIERS PLOWDEN .... PRODUCTION DESIGNER
CHARMIN ESPINOZA .... COSTUME DESIGNER
SCOTT CHESTNUT .... FILM EDITOR

PRIVATE LESSONS
JAN DE BONT .... CINEMATOGRAPHER
LINDA PEARL .... PRODUCTION DESIGNER
FRED A. CHULACK .... FILM EDITOR

PRIVATE NAVY OF SGT. O'FARRELL, THE
ROBERT KINOSHITA .... PRODUCTION DESIGNER

PRIVATE PROPERTY
BRYAN ENGLAND .... CINEMATOGRAPHER

PRIVATE RESORT
MICHAEL CORENBLITH .... PRODUCTION DESIGNER

PRIVATE SCHOOL
WALTER LASSALLY .... CINEMATOGRAPHER
IVO G. CRISTANTE .... PRODUCTION DESIGNER
FRED A. CHULACK .... FILM EDITOR

PRIVATE SESSIONS (TF)
MIKE FASH .... CINEMATOGRAPHER
CRAIG MC KAY .... FILM EDITOR

PRIVATES ON PARADE
IAN WILSON .... CINEMATOGRAPHER
LUCIANA ARRIGHI .... PRODUCTION DESIGNER
LUCIANA ARRIGHI .... COSTUME DESIGNER
JIM CLARK .... FILM EDITOR

PRIVILEGE
PETER SUSCHITZKY .... CINEMATOGRAPHER

PRIVILEGED
UELI STEIGER .... CINEMATOGRAPHER
DEREK GOLDMAN .... FILM EDITOR

PRIZE FIGHTER, THE
JACQUES HAITKIN .... CINEMATOGRAPHER
VINCENT PERANIO .... PRODUCTION DESIGNER
FABIEN TORDJMANN .... FILM EDITOR

PRIZZI'S HONOR
ANDRZEJ BARTKOWIAK .... CINEMATOGRAPHER
DENNIS WASHINGTON .... PRODUCTION DESIGNER
MICHAEL HELMY .... PRODUCTION DESIGNER
TRACY BOUSMAN .... PRODUCTION DESIGNER
DONFELD .... COSTUME DESIGNER
KAJA FEHR .... FILM EDITOR
RUDI FEHR .... FILM EDITOR

PROBLEM CHILD
PETER LYONS COLLISTER .... CINEMATOGRAPHER
GEORGE COSTELLO .... PRODUCTION DESIGNER
EILEEN KENNEDY .... COSTUME DESIGNER
DANIEL HANLEY .... FILM EDITOR
MICHAEL HILL .... FILM EDITOR

PRODIGAL, THE
FRANK STANLEY .... CINEMATOGRAPHER
WILLIAM J. CREBER .... PRODUCTION DESIGNER
BILL BRAME .... FILM EDITOR

PRODUCERS, THE
CHARLES ROSEN .... PRODUCTION DESIGNER

PROFESSIONALS, THE
CONRAD HALL .... CINEMATOGRAPHER
TED HAWORTH .... PRODUCTION DESIGNER
PETER ZINNER .... FILM EDITOR

PROGRAMMED TO KILL
VICKI GRAEF .... COSTUME DESIGNER
MICHAEL KELLY .... FILM EDITOR

Pr-Pr

CINEMATOGRAPHERS
PRODUCTION
DESIGNERS,
COSTUME
DESIGNERS AND
FILM EDITORS
GUIDE

INDEX OF FILM TITLES

Pr-Pu

CINEMATOGRAPHERS
PRODUCTION
DESIGNERS,
COSTUME
DESIGNERS AND
FILM EDITORS
GUIDE

I
N
D
E
X

O
F

F
I
L
M

T
I
T
L
E
S

PUSS IN BOOTS
AVRAHAM KARPICK .... CINEMATOGRAPHER
MAREK DOBROWOLSKI .... PRODUCTION DESIGNER

PUTNEY SWOPE
BUD SMITH .... FILM EDITOR

PUZZLE OF A DOWNFALL CHILD
ADAM HOLENDER .... CINEMATOGRAPHER
EVAN LOTTMAN .... FILM EDITOR

Q

Q
FRED MURPHY .... CINEMATOGRAPHER
ARMAND LEBOWITZ .... FILM EDITOR

Q & A
ANDRZEJ BARTKOWIAK .... CINEMATOGRAPHER
RICHARD P. CIRINCIONE .... FILM EDITOR

QUADROPHENIA
BRIAN TUFANO .... CINEMATOGRAPHER
SIMON HOLLAND .... PRODUCTION DESIGNER
MIKE TAYLOR .... FILM EDITOR

QUANTUM LEAP (PILOT)
ROY H. WAGNER .... CINEMATOGRAPHER

QUARTERBACK PRINCESS (TF)
ISIDORE MANKOFSKY .... CINEMATOGRAPHER

QUARTET
PIERRE L'HOMME .... CINEMATOGRAPHER
HUMPHREY DIXON .... FILM EDITOR

QUEEN OF HEARTS
MIKE SOUTHON .... CINEMATOGRAPHER
LINDY HEMMING .... COSTUME DESIGNER
PETER BOYLE .... FILM EDITOR

QUEENIE (MS)
ERIC SEARS .... FILM EDITOR
MICHAEL RIPPS .... FILM EDITOR

QUEENS LOGIC
AMIR MOKRI .... CINEMATOGRAPHER
EDWARD PISONI .... PRODUCTION DESIGNER
PATRICK KENNEDY .... FILM EDITOR

QUERELLE
XAVIER SCHWARZENBERGER .... CINEMATOGRAPHER
BARBARA BAUM .... COSTUME DESIGNER

QUEST FOR FIRE
CLAUDE AGOSTINI .... CINEMATOGRAPHER
BRIAN MORRIS .... PRODUCTION DESIGNER
CLINTON CAVERS .... PRODUCTION DESIGNER
GUY COMTOIS .... PRODUCTION DESIGNER
YVES LANGLOIS .... FILM EDITOR

QUEST FOR THE MIGHTY SWORD
FEDERIKO SLONISKO .... CINEMATOGRAPHER
MASSIMO LENTINI .... PRODUCTION DESIGNER
LAURA GEMSER .... COSTUME DESIGNER
KATHLEEN STRATTON .... FILM EDITOR

QUEST, THE
BRIAN KAVANAUGH .... FILM EDITOR

QUESTION OF GUILT, A (TF)
RIC WAITE .... CINEMATOGRAPHER

QUESTION OF HONOR, A (TF)
MICHAEL MOLLY .... PRODUCTION DESIGNER

QUESTION OF HONOUR, A
BRIAN WEST .... CINEMATOGRAPHER

QUICK AND THE DEAD, THE (CTF)
DICK BUSH .... CINEMATOGRAPHER
CHESTER KACZENSKI .... PRODUCTION DESIGNER
BARBARA WEISS .... COSTUME DESIGNER

QUICK CHANGE
MICHAEL CHAPMAN .... CINEMATOGRAPHER
DAVID GROPMAN .... PRODUCTION DESIGNER
JEFFREY KURLAND .... COSTUME DESIGNER

ALAN HEIM .... FILM EDITOR

QUICKER THAN THE EYE
WOLFGANG TREU .... CINEMATOGRAPHER

QUICKSILVER
THOMAS DEL RUTH .... CINEMATOGRAPHER
CHARLES ROSEN .... PRODUCTION DESIGNER
JAMES SHANAHAN .... PRODUCTION DESIGNER
BETSY COX .... COSTUME DESIGNER
KIM SECRIST .... FILM EDITOR
TOM ROLF .... FILM EDITOR

QUIET COOL
JACQUES HAITKIN .... CINEMATOGRAPHER
J. RAE FOX .... PRODUCTION DESIGNER
LYNDA BURBANK .... PRODUCTION DESIGNER
BOB BRADY .... FILM EDITOR

QUIET DUEL, THE
SHINOBU MURAKI .... PRODUCTION DESIGNER
YOSHIRO MURAKI .... PRODUCTION DESIGNER

QUIET EARTH, THE
JAMES BARTLE .... CINEMATOGRAPHER
JOSEPHINE FORD .... PRODUCTION DESIGNER
MICHAEL HORTON .... FILM EDITOR

QUIET LITTLE NEIGHBORHOOD, A PERFECT LITTLE MURDER, A (TF)
DAVID HERRINGTON .... CINEMATOGRAPHER
DONALD LIGHT-HARRIS .... PRODUCTION DESIGNER
PETER V. WHITE .... FILM EDITOR

QUIGLEY DOWN UNDER
DAVID EGGBY .... CINEMATOGRAPHER
ROSS MAJOR .... PRODUCTION DESIGNER
WAYNE FINKELMAN .... COSTUME DESIGNER
PETER BURGESS .... FILM EDITOR

QUILOMBO
LAURO ESCOREL .... CINEMATOGRAPHER

QUINTET
JEAN BOFFETY .... CINEMATOGRAPHER
LEON ERICKSON .... PRODUCTION DESIGNER
WOLF KROEGER .... PRODUCTION DESIGNER
SCOTT BUSHNELL .... COSTUME DESIGNER
DENNIS M. HILL .... FILM EDITOR

R

R.E.L.A.X. (TF)
ELAYNE CEDER .... PRODUCTION DESIGNER

R.P.M.
MICHEL HUGO .... CINEMATOGRAPHER

RABBIT TEST
ROBERT KINOSHITA .... PRODUCTION DESIGNER
STANFORD C. ALLEN .... FILM EDITOR

RABBIT, RUN
ALFRED SWEENEY .... PRODUCTION DESIGNER

RABID
RENE VERZIER .... CINEMATOGRAPHER
JEAN LA FLEUR .... FILM EDITOR

RACE FOR GLORY
JACK N. GREEN .... CINEMATOGRAPHER
CYNTHIA CHARETTE .... PRODUCTION DESIGNER
MARYANN BRANDON .... FILM EDITOR

RACE TO A YANKEE ZEPHYR
DOUGLAS MILSOME .... CINEMATOGRAPHER

RACE WITH THE DEVIL
ROBERT JESSUP .... CINEMATOGRAPHER
ALLAN JACOBS .... FILM EDITOR
JOHN F. LINK .... FILM EDITOR

RACHAEL RIVER
LINDA FISHER .... COSTUME DESIGNER

Pu-Ra

CINEMATOGRAPHERS
PRODUCTION
DESIGNERS,
COSTUME
DESIGNERS AND
FILM EDITORS
GUIDE

INDEX OF FILM TITLES

CINEMATOGRAPHERS
PRODUCTION
DESIGNERS,
COSTUME
DESIGNERS AND
FILM EDITORS
GUIDE

RAPPIN'
DAVID GURFINKEL .... CINEMATOGRAPHER
STEVE MILLER .... PRODUCTION DESIGNER
AUDE BRONSON-HOWARD .... COSTUME DESIGNER
ANDY HORVITCH .... FILM EDITOR
BERT GLATSTEIN .... FILM EDITOR
MARCUS MANTON .... FILM EDITOR

RAQUEL (TV)
BOB MACKIE .... COSTUME DESIGNER

RASCALS AND ROBBERS: THE SECRET ADVENTURES OF TOM SAWYER AND HUCKLEBERRY FINN (TF)
ALBERT HESCHONG .... PRODUCTION DESIGNER
ROSANNA NORTON .... COSTUME DESIGNER

RASHOMON
SHINOBU MURAKI .... PRODUCTION DESIGNER
YOSHIRO MURAKI .... PRODUCTION DESIGNER

RATBOY
BRUCE SURTEES .... CINEMATOGRAPHER
EDWARD C. CARFAGNO .... PRODUCTION DESIGNER
GLENN WRIGHT .... COSTUME DESIGNER
JOEL COX .... FILM EDITOR

RATINGS GAME, THE
TIM SUHRSTEDT .... CINEMATOGRAPHER

RATINGS GAME, THE (CTF)
MICHAEL CORENBLITH .... PRODUCTION DESIGNER
MARSHALL HARVEY .... FILM EDITOR

RATS, THE
RON WISMAN .... FILM EDITOR

RAVAGERS
VINCENT SAIZIS .... CINEMATOGRAPHER
RON HOBBS .... PRODUCTION DESIGNER
RON TALSKY .... COSTUME DESIGNER
MAURY WINETROBE .... FILM EDITOR

RAW DEAL
VINCENT MONTON .... CINEMATOGRAPHER
ALEX THOMSON .... CINEMATOGRAPHER
GIORGIO POSTIGLIONE .... PRODUCTION DESIGNER
JON DOWDING .... PRODUCTION DESIGNER
MAHER AHMAD .... PRODUCTION DESIGNER
CLIFFORD CAPONE .... COSTUME DESIGNER
ANNE V. COATES .... FILM EDITOR

RAWHEAD REX
JOHN METCALFE .... CINEMATOGRAPHER
LEN HUNTINGFORD .... PRODUCTION DESIGNER
ANDY HORVITCH .... FILM EDITOR

RAY MANCINI STORY, THE (TF)
JAN DE BONT .... CINEMATOGRAPHER

RAZOR'S EDGE, THE
PETER HANNAN .... CINEMATOGRAPHER
PHILIP HARRISON .... PRODUCTION DESIGNER
MALCOLM MIDDLETON .... PRODUCTION DESIGNER
SHIRLEY RUSSELL .... COSTUME DESIGNER
PETER BOYLE .... FILM EDITOR

RAZORBACK
DEAN SEMLER .... CINEMATOGRAPHER
WILLIAM M. ANDERSON .... FILM EDITOR

RE-ANIMATOR
MAC AHLBERG .... CINEMATOGRAPHER
ROBERT BURNS .... PRODUCTION DESIGNER
LEE PERCY .... FILM EDITOR

REACHING OUT
DAVID SPERLING .... CINEMATOGRAPHER

REAL GENIUS
VILMOS ZSIGMOND .... CINEMATOGRAPHER
JACK G. TAYLOR .... PRODUCTION DESIGNER
JOSAN F. RUSSO .... PRODUCTION DESIGNER
ARTHUR COBURN .... FILM EDITOR
RICHARD CHEW .... FILM EDITOR

REAL LIFE
ERIC SAARINEN .... CINEMATOGRAPHER
DAVID FINFER .... FILM EDITOR

REAL MEN
JOHN A. ALONZO .... CINEMATOGRAPHER
JAMES ALLEN .... PRODUCTION DESIGNER
WILLIAM J. CASSIDY .... PRODUCTION DESIGNER
JODIE TILLEN .... COSTUME DESIGNER
GLENN FARR .... FILM EDITOR
MALCOLM CAMPBELL .... FILM EDITOR

REAL TROUBLE
STEVEN FIERBERG .... CINEMATOGRAPHER

REARVIEW MIRROR
FRANK WATTS .... CINEMATOGRAPHER

REASON TO LIVE, A (TF)
ERIC SEARS .... FILM EDITOR

REBEL
PETER JAMES .... CINEMATOGRAPHER
BRIAN THOMPSON .... PRODUCTION DESIGNER
IGOR NAY .... PRODUCTION DESIGNER
ROGER KIRK .... COSTUME DESIGNER
MICHAEL HONEY .... FILM EDITOR

REBEL IN TOWN
ROBERT KINOSHITA .... PRODUCTION DESIGNER

REBORN
JUAN RUIZ-ANCHIA .... CINEMATOGRAPHER

RECKLESS
MICHAEL BALLHAUS .... CINEMATOGRAPHER
DAVID NICHOLS .... PRODUCTION DESIGNER
JEFFREY TOWNSEND .... PRODUCTION DESIGNER
ELLEN MIROJNICK .... COSTUME DESIGNER
ALBERT MAGNOLI .... FILM EDITOR
TONY LOMBARDO .... FILM EDITOR

RECKLESS DISREGARD (CTF)
RENE VERZIER .... CINEMATOGRAPHER
TONY LOWER .... FILM EDITOR

RECKONING, THE
RAYMOND SIMM .... PRODUCTION DESIGNER

RECOVERY
ROBERT M. STEVENS .... CINEMATOGRAPHER

RECRUITS
STEPHEN FANFARA .... FILM EDITOR

RED ALERT (TF)
RIC WAITE .... CINEMATOGRAPHER
JAMES H. SPENCER .... PRODUCTION DESIGNER

RED BADGE OF COURAGE, THE (TF)
CHARLES F. WHEELER .... CINEMATOGRAPHER
WILLIAM MALLEY .... PRODUCTION DESIGNER

RED BEARD
SHINOBU MURAK .... PRODUCTION DESIGNER
YOSHIRO MURAK .... PRODUCTION DESIGNER

RED DAWN
RIC WAITE .... CINEMATOGRAPHER
JACKSON DE GOVIA .... PRODUCTION DESIGNER
VINCENT M. CRESCIMAN .... PRODUCTION DESIGNER
THOM NOBLE .... FILM EDITOR

RED EARTH, WHITE EARTH (TF)
RENE VERZIER .... CINEMATOGRAPHER

RED HEADED STRANGER
NEIL ROACH .... CINEMATOGRAPHER
CARY WHITE .... PRODUCTION DESIGNER
LANA NELSON .... COSTUME DESIGNER
ERIC AUSTIN WILLIAMS .... FILM EDITOR

RED HEAT
MATTHEW F. LEONETTI .... CINEMATOGRAPHER
JOHN VALLONE .... PRODUCTION DESIGNER
MICHAEL CORENBLITH .... PRODUCTION DESIGNER
DAN MOORE .... COSTUME DESIGNER
CARMEL DAVIES .... FILM EDITOR
DONN ARON .... FILM EDITOR
FREEMAN DAVIES .... FILM EDITOR

RED LIGHT STING, THE (TF)
WOODY OMENS .... CINEMATOGRAPHER

Ra-Re

CINEMATOGRAPHERS
PRODUCTION
DESIGNERS,
COSTUME
DESIGNERS AND
FILM EDITORS
GUIDE

INDEX OF FILM TITLES

417

Re-Re

CINEMATOGRAPHERS
PRODUCTION
DESIGNERS,
COSTUME
DESIGNERS AND
FILM EDITORS
GUIDE

I
N
D
E
X

O
F

F
I
L
M

T
I
T
L
E
S

418

RETURN FROM WITCH MOUNTAIN
FRANK PHILLIPS .... CINEMATOGRAPHER
JACK SENTER .... PRODUCTION DESIGNER
JOHN B. MANSBRIDGE .... PRODUCTION DESIGNER
BOB BRING .... FILM EDITOR

RETURN OF A MAN CALLED HORSE, THE
RONNIE TAYLOR .... CINEMATOGRAPHER
OWEN ROIZMAN .... CINEMATOGRAPHER
W. STEWART CAMPBELL .... PRODUCTION DESIGNER
RICHARD E. LA MOTTE .... COSTUME DESIGNER
MICHAEL KAHN .... FILM EDITOR

RETURN OF BILLY JACK, THE
ROBERT SAAD .... CINEMATOGRAPHER
NICHOLAS C. SMITH .... FILM EDITOR
RAJA GOSNELL .... FILM EDITOR

RETURN OF CAPTAIN INVINCIBLE, THE
MIKE MOLLOY .... CINEMATOGRAPHER
DAVID COPPING .... PRODUCTION DESIGNER
JOHN SCOTT .... FILM EDITOR

RETURN OF FRANK CANNON (TF)
WILLIAM CRONJAGER .... CINEMATOGRAPHER

RETURN OF MARTIN GUERRE, THE
ANDRE NEAU .... CINEMATOGRAPHER
ANNE-MARIE MARCHAND .... COSTUME DESIGNER

RETURN OF MICKEY SPILLANE'S MIKE HAMMER, THE (TF)
HECTOR FIGUEROA .... CINEMATOGRAPHER

RETURN OF SUPERFLY, THE
ANGHEL DECCA .... CINEMATOGRAPHER
JEREMIE FRANK .... PRODUCTION DESIGNER
IDA GEARON .... COSTUME DESIGNER
JOHN MULLEN .... FILM EDITOR

RETURN OF SWAMP THING, THE
ROBB WILSON KING .... PRODUCTION DESIGNER
LESLIE ROSENTHAL .... FILM EDITOR

RETURN OF THE JEDI
ALAN HUME .... CINEMATOGRAPHER
FRED HOLE .... PRODUCTION DESIGNER
JAMES SCHOPPE .... PRODUCTION DESIGNER
NORMAN REYNOLDS .... PRODUCTION DESIGNER
AGGIE GUERARD RODGERS .... COSTUME DESIGNER
NILO RODIS-JAMERO .... COSTUME DESIGNER
DUWAYNE DUNHAM .... FILM EDITOR
MARCIA LUCAS .... FILM EDITOR
SEAN BARTON .... FILM EDITOR

RETURN OF THE LIVING DEAD, THE
JULES BRENNER .... CINEMATOGRAPHER
ROBERT HOWLAND .... PRODUCTION DESIGNER
WILLIAM STOUT .... PRODUCTION DESIGNER
ROBERT GORDON .... FILM EDITOR

RETURN OF THE LIVING DEAD PART II
ROBERT ELSWIT .... CINEMATOGRAPHER
CHARLES BORNSTEIN .... FILM EDITOR

RETURN OF THE MUSKETEERS, THE
BERNARD LUTIC .... CINEMATOGRAPHER
GIL PARRONDO .... PRODUCTION DESIGNER
YVONNE BLAKE .... COSTUME DESIGNER
JOHN VICTOR SMITH .... FILM EDITOR

RETURN OF THE PINK PANTHER, THE
GEOFFREY UNSWORTH† .... CINEMATOGRAPHER
TOM PRIESTLEY .... FILM EDITOR

RETURN OF THE SECAUCUS SEVEN
AUSTIN DE BESCHE .... CINEMATOGRAPHER
JOHN SAYLES .... FILM EDITOR

RETURN OF THE SOLDIER
STEPHEN GOLDBLATT .... CINEMATOGRAPHER
LUCIANA ARRIGHI .... PRODUCTION DESIGNER
SHIRLEY RUSSELL .... COSTUME DESIGNER
LAURENCE MÉRY CLARK .... FILM EDITOR

RETURN OF THE SWAMP THING
VICKI GRAEF .... COSTUME DESIGNER

RETURN TO EDEN -PARTS 1 & 2 (TF)
DEAN SEMLER .... CINEMATOGRAPHER

RETURN TO HORROR HIGH
ROY H. WAGNER .... CINEMATOGRAPHER
NANCY FORNER .... FILM EDITOR

RETURN TO MACON COUNTY
JACQUES MARQUETTE .... CINEMATOGRAPHER

RETURN TO OZ
DAVID WATKIN .... CINEMATOGRAPHER
CHARLES BISHOP .... PRODUCTION DESIGNER
NORMAN REYNOLDS .... PRODUCTION DESIGNER
RAYMOND HUGHES .... COSTUME DESIGNER
LESLIE HODGSON .... FILM EDITOR

RETURN TO PEYTON PLACE (TF)
NEIL ROACH .... CINEMATOGRAPHER

RETURN TO SNOWY RIVER
KEITH WAGSTAFF .... CINEMATOGRAPHER
LESLIE BINNS .... PRODUCTION DESIGNER
GARY WOODYARD .... FILM EDITOR

RETURN TO WATERLOO (TF)
ROGER DEAKINS .... CINEMATOGRAPHER
TERRY PRITCHARD .... PRODUCTION DESIGNER
DAVID MINGAY .... FILM EDITOR

REUBEN, REUBEN
PETER STEIN .... CINEMATOGRAPHER
PETER S. LARKIN .... PRODUCTION DESIGNER
JOHN BOXER .... COSTUME DESIGNER
SKIP LUSK .... FILM EDITOR

REUNION
BRUNO DE KEYZER .... CINEMATOGRAPHER
ALEXANDER TRAUNER .... PRODUCTION DESIGNER
MARTINE BARRAQUE .... FILM EDITOR

REVENGE
JACQUES HAITKIN .... CINEMATOGRAPHER
JEFFREY L. KIMBALL .... CINEMATOGRAPHER
MICHAEL SEYMOUR .... PRODUCTION DESIGNER
AUDE BRONSON-HOWARD .... COSTUME DESIGNER
CHRIS LEBENZON .... FILM EDITOR

REVENGE OF AL CAPONE, THE (TF)
TIM SUHRSTEDT .... CINEMATOGRAPHER
JEFF FREEMAN .... FILM EDITOR

REVENGE OF THE NERDS
KING BAGGOT .... CINEMATOGRAPHER
JAMES SCHOPPE .... PRODUCTION DESIGNER
TREVOR WILLIAMS .... PRODUCTION DESIGNER
ALAN BALSAM .... FILM EDITOR

REVENGE OF THE NERDS II: NERDS INPARADISE
CHARLES CORRELL .... CINEMATOGRAPHER
TREVOR WILLIAMS .... PRODUCTION DESIGNER
JEFFREY KURLAND .... COSTUME DESIGNER
RICHARD CHEW .... FILM EDITOR

REVENGE OF THE NINJA
DAVID GURFINKEL .... CINEMATOGRAPHER
IVO G. CRISTANTE .... PRODUCTION DESIGNER
MARK HELFRICH .... FILM EDITOR
MICHAEL J. DUTHIE .... FILM EDITOR

REVENGE OF THE PINK PANTHER
ERNEST DAY .... CINEMATOGRAPHER
JOHN SIDALL .... PRODUCTION DESIGNER
PETER MULLINS .... PRODUCTION DESIGNER
ALAN JONES .... FILM EDITOR

REVENGE OF THE STEPFORD WIVES (TF)
RIC WAITE .... CINEMATOGRAPHER

REVERSAL OF FORTUNE
LUCIANO TOVOLI .... CINEMATOGRAPHER
MEL BOURNE .... PRODUCTION DESIGNER
JUDIANNA MAKOVSKY .... COSTUME DESIGNER
LEE PERCY .... FILM EDITOR

REVOLUTION
BERNARD LUTIC .... CINEMATOGRAPHER
ASSHETON GORTON .... PRODUCTION DESIGNER
JON BUNKER .... PRODUCTION DESIGNER
JOHN MOLLO .... COSTUME DESIGNER
STUART BAIRD .... FILM EDITOR

Re-Re

CINEMATOGRAPHERS
PRODUCTION
DESIGNERS,
COSTUME
DESIGNERS and
FILM EDITORS
GUIDE

INDEX OF FILM TITLES

419

CINEMATOGRAPHERS
PRODUCTION
DESIGNERS,
COSTUME
DESIGNERS and
FILM EDITORS
GUIDE

**I
N
D
E
X

O
F

F
I
L
M

T
I
T
L
E
S**

RHINESTONE
TIMOTHY GALFAS .... CINEMATOGRAPHER
FRANK RICHWOOD .... PRODUCTION DESIGNER
ROBERT F. BOYLE .... PRODUCTION DESIGNER
THEADORA VAN RUNKLE .... COSTUME DESIGNER
THOMAS M. BRONSON .... COSTUME DESIGNER
JOHN W. WHEELER .... FILM EDITOR
STAN COLE .... FILM EDITOR

RHINOCEROS
JAMES A. CRABE† .... CINEMATOGRAPHER
JACK MARTIN SMITH .... PRODUCTION DESIGNER
BUD SMITH .... FILM EDITOR

RICH AND FAMOUS
DONALD PETERMAN .... CINEMATOGRAPHER
FRED HARPMAN .... PRODUCTION DESIGNER
JAN SCOTT .... PRODUCTION DESIGNER
THEONI V. ALDREDGE .... COSTUME DESIGNER
JOHN F. BURNETT .... FILM EDITOR

RICH BOYS
FRANK PRINZI .... CINEMATOGRAPHER

RICH GIRL
LEVIE ISAACKS .... CINEMATOGRAPHER
RICHARD MCGUIRE .... PRODUCTION DESIGNER
JANET SOBLE .... COSTUME DESIGNER
MARK HELFRICH .... FILM EDITOR
RICHARD CANDIB .... FILM EDITOR

RICH KIDS
RALF D. BODE .... CINEMATOGRAPHER
DAVID MITCHELL .... PRODUCTION DESIGNER

RICH MAN, POOR MAN (MS)
WILLIAM HINEY .... PRODUCTION DESIGNER

RICHARD PRYOR HERE AND NOW (FD)
RAYMOND BUSH .... FILM EDITOR

RICHARD PRYOR LIVE ON THE SUNSET STRIP
HASKELL WEXLER .... CINEMATOGRAPHER
MICHAEL BAUGH .... PRODUCTION DESIGNER
SHELDON KAHN .... FILM EDITOR

RICHARD'S THINGS
FREDDIE YOUNG .... CINEMATOGRAPHER
MARIT ALLEN .... COSTUME DESIGNER
LESLEY WALKER .... FILM EDITOR

RIDDANCE
LAJOS KOLTAI .... CINEMATOGRAPHER

RIDDLE OF THE SANDS, THE
CHRISTOPHER CHALLIS .... CINEMATOGRAPHER
TERRY PRITCHARD .... PRODUCTION DESIGNER
PETER HOLLYWOOD .... FILM EDITOR

RIDE A WILD PONY
JACK CARDIFF .... CINEMATOGRAPHER

RIDERS ON THE STORM
JOHN J. CONNOR .... CINEMATOGRAPHER

RIDING THE EDGE
BERNARD SALZMANN .... CINEMATOGRAPHER
JAMES SHANAHAN .... PRODUCTION DESIGNER
JAMES RUXIN .... FILM EDITOR

RIEVERS, THE
THEADORA VAN RUNKLE .... COSTUME DESIGNER

RIGHT HAND MAN, THE
PETER JAMES .... CINEMATOGRAPHER
DON SAUNDERS .... FILM EDITOR

RIGHT OF THE PEOPLE, THE (TF)
GIL HUBBS .... CINEMATOGRAPHER

RIGHT OF WAY
HOWARD SCHWARTZ .... CINEMATOGRAPHER

RIGHT STUFF, THE
CALEB DESCHANEL .... CINEMATOGRAPHER
GENE RUDOLF .... PRODUCTION DESIGNER
GEOFFREY KIRKLAND .... PRODUCTION DESIGNER
PETER ROMERO .... PRODUCTION DESIGNER
RICHARD J. LAWRENCE .... PRODUCTION DESIGNER
W. STEWART CAMPBELL .... PRODUCTION DESIGNER

RIGHT STUFF, THE   (CONTINUED)
DOUGLAS STEWART .... FILM EDITOR
GLENN FARR .... FILM EDITOR
LISA FRUCHTMAN .... FILM EDITOR
STEPHEN A. ROTTER .... FILM EDITOR
TOM ROLF .... FILM EDITOR

RIGHT TO KILL? (TF)
GAYNE RESCHER .... CINEMATOGRAPHER
JAMES G. HULSEY .... PRODUCTION DESIGNER
SCOTT CONRAD .... FILM EDITOR

RIKKY AND PETE
DAVID PARKER .... CINEMATOGRAPHER
JOSEPHONE FORD .... PRODUCTION DESIGNER
KEN SALLOWS .... FILM EDITOR

RIO CONCHOS
WILLIAM J. CREBER .... PRODUCTION DESIGNER

RIOT
PAUL SYLBERT .... PRODUCTION DESIGNER

RISING DAMP
FRANK WATTS .... CINEMATOGRAPHER
PETER WEATHERLY .... FILM EDITOR

RISING SON (CTF)
SANDI SISSEL .... CINEMATOGRAPHER
DAN LEIGH .... PRODUCTION DESIGNER
TRUDY SHIP .... FILM EDITOR

RISKY BUSINESS
BRUCE SURTEES .... CINEMATOGRAPHER
WILLIAM J. CASSIDY .... PRODUCTION DESIGNER
ROBERT DE MORA .... COSTUME DESIGNER
RICHARD CHEW .... FILM EDITOR

RITA HAYWORTH: THE LOVE GODDESS (TF)
JAN SCOTT .... PRODUCTION DESIGNER

RITA, SUE AND BOB TOO
LEN HUNTINGFORD .... PRODUCTION DESIGNER
CATHERINE COOKE .... COSTUME DESIGNER
STEPHEN SINGLETON .... FILM EDITOR

RITES OF SUMMER
JEFFREY L. GOLDSTEIN .... PRODUCTION DESIGNER

RITUALS
RENE VERZIER .... CINEMATOGRAPHER
KAREN BROMLEY .... PRODUCTION DESIGNER

RITZ, THE
JOHN BLOOM .... FILM EDITOR

RIVER NIGER, THE
MICHAEL D. MARGULIES .... CINEMATOGRAPHER

RIVER OF DEATH
AVI KARPICK .... CINEMATOGRAPHER
JOHN ROSEWARNE .... PRODUCTION DESIGNER
ROBYN SMITH .... COSTUME DESIGNER
KEN BORNSTEIN .... FILM EDITOR

RIVER OF GOLD
ALEX PHILLIPS .... CINEMATOGRAPHER

RIVER RAT, THE
JAN KIESSER .... CINEMATOGRAPHER
JOHN J. LLOYD .... PRODUCTION DESIGNER
PETER V. SALDUTTI .... COSTUME DESIGNER
DENNIS M. VIRKLER .... FILM EDITOR

RIVER'S EDGE
FREDERICK ELMES .... CINEMATOGRAPHER
JOHN MUTO .... PRODUCTION DESIGNER
CLAUDIA BROWN .... COSTUME DESIGNER
HOWARD SMITH .... FILM EDITOR
SONYA SONES TRAMER .... FILM EDITOR

RIVER, THE
VILMOS ZSIGMOND .... CINEMATOGRAPHER
CHARLES ROSEN .... PRODUCTION DESIGNER
NORMAN NEWBERRY .... PRODUCTION DESIGNER
JOE I. TOMPKINS .... COSTUME DESIGNER
SIDNEY LEVIN .... FILM EDITOR

RIVERBEND
MARCUS MANTON .... FILM EDITOR

CINEMATOGRAPHERS
PRODUCTION
DESIGNERS,
COSTUME
DESIGNERS and
FILM EDITORS
GUIDE

**I
N
D
E
X

O
F

F
I
L
M

T
I
T
L
E
S**

ROMAN SPRING OF STONE, THE
HARRY WAXMAN .... CINEMATOGRAPHER

ROMANCING THE STONE
DEAN CUNDEY .... CINEMATOGRAPHER
AUGUSTIN ITUARTE .... PRODUCTION DESIGNER
LAWRENCE G. PAULL .... PRODUCTION DESIGNER
MARILYN VANCE-STRAKER .... COSTUME DESIGNER
DONN CAMBERN .... FILM EDITOR
FRANK MORRISS .... FILM EDITOR

ROMANTIC COMEDY
DAVID M. WALSH .... CINEMATOGRAPHER
ALFRED SWEENEY .... PRODUCTION DESIGNER
JOE I. TOMPKINS .... COSTUME DESIGNER
JOHN C. HOWARD .... FILM EDITOR

ROMANTIC ENGLISHWOMAN, THE
GERRY FISHER .... CINEMATOGRAPHER
RICHARD MACDONALD .... PRODUCTION DESIGNER
RUTH MYERS .... COSTUME DESIGNER

ROMEO AND JULIET
PASQUALINO DE SANTIS .... CINEMATOGRAPHER

ROMERO
GEOFF BURTON .... CINEMATOGRAPHER

ROOFTOPS
THEO VAN DE SANDE .... CINEMATOGRAPHER
JEANNINE CLAUDIA OPPEWALL .... PRODUCTION DESIGNER
KATHLEEN DETORO .... COSTUME DESIGNER
WILLIAM REYNOLDS .... FILM EDITOR

ROOKIE, THE
JACK N. GREEN .... CINEMATOGRAPHER
JUDY CAMMER .... PRODUCTION DESIGNER
JOEL COX .... FILM EDITOR

ROOM UPSTAIRS, THE (TF)
RON HAGEN .... CINEMATOGRAPHER

ROOM WITH A VIEW, A
TONY PIERCE-ROBERTS .... CINEMATOGRAPHER
BRIAN ACKLAND-SNOW .... PRODUCTION DESIGNER
GIANNI QUARANTA .... PRODUCTION DESIGNER
JENNY BEAVEN .... COSTUME DESIGNER
JOHN BRIGHT .... COSTUME DESIGNER
HUMPHREY DIXON .... FILM EDITOR

ROOMMATE, THE
JEFF JUR .... CINEMATOGRAPHER
NICHOLAS C. SMITH .... FILM EDITOR

ROOSTER COGBURN
HARRY STRADLING, JR. .... CINEMATOGRAPHER
ROBERT E. SWINK .... FILM EDITOR

ROOTS (MS)
STEVAN LARNER .... CINEMATOGRAPHER
JAN SCOTT .... PRODUCTION DESIGNER
JOSEPH R. JENNINGS .... PRODUCTION DESIGNER
NEIL TRAVIS .... FILM EDITOR

ROOTS: THE GIFT (TF)
JOHN A. ALONZO .... CINEMATOGRAPHER
BEALA B. NEEL .... PRODUCTION DESIGNER
STANFORD C. ALLEN .... FILM EDITOR

ROSA LUXEMBURG
KAREL VACEK .... PRODUCTION DESIGNER

ROSALIE GOES SHOPPING
BERND HEINL .... CINEMATOGRAPHER

ROSARY MURDERS, THE
DAVID GOLIA .... CINEMATOGRAPHER
W. STEWART CAMPBELL .... PRODUCTION DESIGNER
JUDY DOLAN .... COSTUME DESIGNER
SAM VITALE .... FILM EDITOR

ROSE GARDEN, THE
JAN SCHLUBACH .... PRODUCTION DESIGNER
MONICA JACOBS .... COSTUME DESIGNER

ROSE KING, THE
JULIANE LORENZ .... FILM EDITOR

ROSE, THE
VILMOS ZSIGMOND .... CINEMATOGRAPHER
JAMES SCHOPPE .... PRODUCTION DESIGNER
RICHARD MACDONALD .... PRODUCTION DESIGNER
CARROLL TIMOTHY O'MEARA .... FILM EDITOR
ROBERT L. WOLFE .... FILM EDITOR

ROSEBUD
MICHAEL SEYMOUR .... PRODUCTION DESIGNER
SIMON HOLLAND .... PRODUCTION DESIGNER
THOM NOBLE .... FILM EDITOR

ROSEBUD BEACH HOTEL, THE
JOAO FERNANDES .... CINEMATOGRAPHER
DANIEL LOEWENTHAL .... FILM EDITOR

ROSELAND
ERNEST VINCZE .... CINEMATOGRAPHER
DIANE FINN CHAPMAN .... COSTUME DESIGNER
HUMPHREY DIXON .... FILM EDITOR

ROSEMARY'S BABY
WILLIAM A. FRAKER .... CINEMATOGRAPHER
RICHARD SYLBERT .... PRODUCTION DESIGNER
ANTHEA SYLBERT .... COSTUME DESIGNER
ROBERT WYMAN .... FILM EDITOR
SAM O'STEEN .... FILM EDITOR

ROSENCRANTZ AND GUILDENSTERN ARE DEAD
PETER BIZIOU .... CINEMATOGRAPHER
NICOLAS GASTER .... FILM EDITOR

ROSES ARE FOR THE RICH (TF)
SHELLEY KOMAROV .... COSTUME DESIGNER

ROSIE: THE ROSEMARY CLOONEY STORY (TF)
JEAN-PIERRE DORLEAC .... COSTUME DESIGNER

ROTTEN TO THE CORE
FREDDIE YOUNG .... CINEMATOGRAPHER

ROUGH CUT
FREDDIE YOUNG .... CINEMATOGRAPHER
TED HAWORTH .... PRODUCTION DESIGNER
TIM HUTCHINSON .... PRODUCTION DESIGNER
DOUGLAS STEWART .... FILM EDITOR

ROUGHNECKS (TF)
BEALA B. NEEL .... PRODUCTION DESIGNER

ROUND MIDNIGHT
BRUNO DE KEYZER .... CINEMATOGRAPHER
ALEXANDER TRAUNER .... PRODUCTION DESIGNER
JACQUELINE MORCEAU .... COSTUME DESIGNER
ARMAND PSENNY .... FILM EDITOR

ROXANNE
IAN BAKER .... CINEMATOGRAPHER
JACKSON DE GOVIA .... PRODUCTION DESIGNER
RICHARD BRUNO .... COSTUME DESIGNER
TISH MONAGHAN .... COSTUME DESIGNER
JOHN SCOTT .... FILM EDITOR

ROYAL FLASH
TERENCE MARSH .... PRODUCTION DESIGNER
JOHN VICTOR SMITH .... FILM EDITOR

RUBY AND OSWALD (TF)
THOMAS M. BRONSON .... COSTUME DESIGNER

RUCKUS
DON BURGESS .... CINEMATOGRAPHER

RUDE AWAKENING
TOM SIGEL .... CINEMATOGRAPHER
MEL BOURNE .... PRODUCTION DESIGNER
PEGGY FARRELL-SALTEN .... COSTUME DESIGNER
PAUL FRIED .... FILM EDITOR

RUDE BOY
JACK HAZAN .... CINEMATOGRAPHER

RULING CLASS, THE
PETER MURTON .... PRODUCTION DESIGNER
RUTH MYERS .... COSTUME DESIGNER
RAY LOVEJOY .... FILM EDITOR

RUMBLE FISH
STEPHEN H. BURUM .... CINEMATOGRAPHER
DEAN TAVOULARIS .... PRODUCTION DESIGNER
MARJORIE BOWERS .... COSTUME DESIGNER
BARRY MALKIN .... FILM EDITOR

RUMPELSTILTSKIN
DAVID GURFINKEL .... CINEMATOGRAPHER
MAREK DOBROWOLSKI .... PRODUCTION DESIGNER
TOVA NEEMAN .... FILM EDITOR

RUN
BRUCE SURTEES .... CINEMATOGRAPHER
JOHN WILLETT .... PRODUCTION DESIGNER
JACK HOFSTRA .... FILM EDITOR
STEPHEN E. RIVKIN .... FILM EDITOR

RUNAWAY
JOHN A. ALONZO .... CINEMATOGRAPHER
DOUGLAS HIGGINS .... PRODUCTION DESIGNER
BETSY COX .... COSTUME DESIGNER
GLENN FARR .... FILM EDITOR

RUNAWAY TRAIN
ALAN HUME .... CINEMATOGRAPHER
JOSEPH T. GARRITY .... PRODUCTION DESIGNER
STEPHEN MARSH .... PRODUCTION DESIGNER
KATHY DOVER .... COSTUME DESIGNER
HENRY RICHARDSON .... FILM EDITOR

RUNNER
ANTONY GIBBS .... FILM EDITOR

RUNNER STUMBLES, THE
LASZLO KOVACS .... CINEMATOGRAPHER
ALFRED SWEENEY .... PRODUCTION DESIGNER
PEMBROKE J. HERRING .... FILM EDITOR

RUNNING
LASZLO GEORGE .... CINEMATOGRAPHER
ROY FORGE SMITH .... PRODUCTION DESIGNER

RUNNING AGAINST TIME (CTF)
BRIAN HEBB .... CINEMATOGRAPHER
BARRY ROBISON .... PRODUCTION DESIGNER
HEATHER MACDOUGALL .... FILM EDITOR

RUNNING BRAVE
FRANCOIS PROTAT .... CINEMATOGRAPHER
BARBARA DUNPHY .... PRODUCTION DESIGNER
CAROL SPIER .... PRODUCTION DESIGNER
TONY LOWER .... FILM EDITOR

RUNNING HOT
TOM RICHMOND .... CINEMATOGRAPHER
ANDY BLUMENTHAL .... FILM EDITOR

RUNNING MAN, THE
THOMAS DEL RUTH .... CINEMATOGRAPHER
JACK T. COLLIS .... PRODUCTION DESIGNER
ROBERT BLACKMAN .... COSTUME DESIGNER
EDWARD A. WARSCHILKA .... FILM EDITOR
JOHN WRIGHT .... FILM EDITOR
MARK ROY WARNER .... FILM EDITOR

RUNNING MAN, THE (1963)
JOHN STOLL .... PRODUCTION DESIGNER

RUNNING ON EMPTY
GERRY FISHER .... CINEMATOGRAPHER
PHILIP ROSENBERG .... PRODUCTION DESIGNER
ROBERT GUERRA .... PRODUCTION DESIGNER
ANNA HILL JOHNSTONE .... COSTUME DESIGNER
ANDREW MONDSHEIN .... FILM EDITOR

RUNNING SCARED
PETER HYAMS .... CINEMATOGRAPHER
ALBERT BRENNER .... PRODUCTION DESIGNER
JAMES MITCHELL .... FILM EDITOR

RUNNING SCARED (1972)
ERNEST DAY .... CINEMATOGRAPHER

RUSH WEEK
JEFF MART .... CINEMATOGRAPHER
R. CLIFFORD SEARCY .... PRODUCTION DESIGNER
JEFF REINER .... FILM EDITOR

RUSSIA HOUSE, THE
IAN BAKER .... CINEMATOGRAPHER
RICHARD MACDONALD .... PRODUCTION DESIGNER
RUTH MYERS .... COSTUME DESIGNER
PETER HONESS .... FILM EDITOR

RUSSIAN ROULETTE
BRIAN WEST .... CINEMATOGRAPHER
RICHARD MARDEN .... FILM EDITOR

RUSSIAN TERMINATOR
ANTHONY NEWTON .... CINEMATOGRAPHER
ANNIKA SONEBY .... COSTUME DESIGNER

RUSSKIES
REED SMOOT .... CINEMATOGRAPHER
LINDA PEARL .... PRODUCTION DESIGNER
NANCY CONE .... COSTUME DESIGNER
ANTONY GIBBS .... FILM EDITOR

RUSTLER'S RHAPSODY
JOSE LUIS ALCAINE .... CINEMATOGRAPHER
GIL PARRONDO .... PRODUCTION DESIGNER
WAYNE FINKELMAN .... COSTUME DESIGNER
JOHN VICTOR SMITH .... FILM EDITOR

RUTHLESS PEOPLE
JAN DE BONT .... CINEMATOGRAPHER
DONALD B. WOODRUFF .... PRODUCTION DESIGNER
LILLY KILVERT .... PRODUCTION DESIGNER
ROSANNA NORTON .... COSTUME DESIGNER
ARTHUR SCHMIDT .... FILM EDITOR
GIB JAFFE .... FILM EDITOR

RYAN WHITE STORY, THE (TF)
NORM BARON .... PRODUCTION DESIGNER
ROBERT FLORIO .... FILM EDITOR

RYAN'S DAUGHTER
FREDDIE YOUNG .... CINEMATOGRAPHER

S

S.E.A.L.S.
AVRAHAM KARPICK .... CINEMATOGRAPHER

S.H.E. (TF)
MICHAEL ECONOMOU .... FILM EDITOR

S.O.B.
HARRY STRADLING, JR. .... CINEMATOGRAPHER
RODGER MAUS .... PRODUCTION DESIGNER
WILLIAM CRAIG SMITH .... PRODUCTION DESIGNER
THEADORA VAN RUNKLE .... COSTUME DESIGNER
RALPH E. WINTERS .... FILM EDITOR

S.P.Y.S.
ROBERT LAWRENCE .... FILM EDITOR

SABOTEUR: CODE NAME MORITURI
CONRAD HALL .... CINEMATOGRAPHER

SABRINA
EDITH HEAD† .... COSTUME DESIGNER

SACCO AND VANZETTI
JAN SCOTT .... PRODUCTION DESIGNER
ENRICO SABBATINI .... COSTUME DESIGNER

SACRIFICE
ANTHONY REDMAN .... FILM EDITOR

SAFARI 3000
ADAM GREENBERG .... CINEMATOGRAPHER

SAHARA
DAVID GURFINKEL .... CINEMATOGRAPHER
LUCIANO SPADONI .... PRODUCTION DESIGNER
JANE ROBINSON .... COSTUME DESIGNER

SAHARA SECRET, THE (MS)
DANTE FERRETTI .... PRODUCTION DESIGNER

SAIL AWAY (TF)
ELAYNE CEDER .... PRODUCTION DESIGNER

Ru-Sa

CINEMATOGRAPHERS
PRODUCTION
DESIGNERS,
COSTUME
DESIGNERS AND
FILM EDITORS
GUIDE

Sa-Sa

CINEMATOGRAPHERS
PRODUCTION
DESIGNERS,
COSTUME
DESIGNERS AND
FILM EDITORS
GUIDE

I
N
D
E
X

O
F

F
I
L
M

T
I
T
L
E
S

SAILOR WHO FELL FROM GRACE WITH THE SEA, THE
DOUGLAS SLOCOMBE .... CINEMATOGRAPHER
BRIAN ACKLAND-SNOW .... PRODUCTION DESIGNER
TED HAWORTH .... PRODUCTION DESIGNER
ANTONY GIBBS .... FILM EDITOR

SAILOR'S RETURN, THE
BRIAN TUFANO .... CINEMATOGRAPHER

SAINT JACK
ROBBY MULLER .... CINEMATOGRAPHER
WILLIAM CARRUTH .... FILM EDITOR

SAINT JOAN
RAYMOND SIMM .... PRODUCTION DESIGNER

SAKHAROV
HERBERT WESTBROOK .... PRODUCTION DESIGNER
KEITH PALMER .... FILM EDITOR

SALAMANDER, THE
CLAUDIO CUTRY .... FILM EDITOR

SALLY AND FREEDOM
SYLVIA INGEMARSSON .... FILM EDITOR

SALO, 120 DAYS OF SODOM
DANTE FERRETTI .... PRODUCTION DESIGNER

SALOME'S LAST DANCE
HARVEY HARRISON .... CINEMATOGRAPHER
MICHAEL BUCHANAN .... PRODUCTION DESIGNER
MICHAEL ARRALS .... COSTUME DESIGNER
TIMOTHY GEE .... FILM EDITOR

SALSA
DAVID GURFINKEL .... CINEMATOGRAPHER
MARK HASKINS .... PRODUCTION DESIGNER
CARIN HOOPER .... COSTUME DESIGNER
ALAIN JAKUBOWICZ .... FILM EDITOR

SALUTE OF THE JUGGLER, THE
DAVID EGGBY .... CINEMATOGRAPHER
RICHARD FRANCIS-BRUCE .... FILM EDITOR

SALVADOR
ROBERT RICHARDSON .... CINEMATOGRAPHER
BRUNO RUBEO .... PRODUCTION DESIGNER
KATHRYN MORRISON .... COSTUME DESIGNER
CLAIRE SIMPSON-CROZIER .... FILM EDITOR

SALVATION!
FRANCIS KENNEY .... CINEMATOGRAPHER
LESTER COHEN .... PRODUCTION DESIGNER
ELIZABETH KLING .... FILM EDITOR

SAM'S SPA
CYNTHIA FLYNT .... COSTUME DESIGNER

SAMARITAN (TF)
HANANIA BAER .... CINEMATOGRAPHER
GREGG FONSECA .... PRODUCTION DESIGNER

SAME TIME, NEXT YEAR
SHELDON KAHN .... FILM EDITOR

SAME TIME, NEXT YEAR
ROBERT SURTEES† .... CINEMATOGRAPHER
HENRY BUMSTEAD .... PRODUCTION DESIGNER
THEADORA VAN RUNKLE .... COSTUME DESIGNER

SAMMY AND ROSIE GET LAID
OLIVER STAPLETON .... CINEMATOGRAPHER
HUGO LUCZYC WYHOWSKI .... PRODUCTION DESIGNER
BARBARA KIDD .... COSTUME DESIGNER
MICK AUDSLEY .... FILM EDITOR

SAMMY STOPS THE WORLD (FD)
DAVID MYERS .... CINEMATOGRAPHER
SANTO LOQUASTO .... COSTUME DESIGNER
BILL YAHRAUS .... FILM EDITOR

SAMSON & DELILAH
GERRY FISHER .... CINEMATOGRAPHER
EDITH HEAD† .... COSTUME DESIGNER

SAMSON & DELILAH (TF)
MADELINE ANN GRANETO .... COSTUME DESIGNER

SAMURAI (TF)
PAUL PETERS .... PRODUCTION DESIGNER

SAN BERDOO (PILOT)
MICHAEL CORENBLITH .... PRODUCTION DESIGNER
TOD FEUERMAN .... FILM EDITOR

SAND PEBBLES, THE
WILLIAM REYNOLDS .... FILM EDITOR

SANDGLASS, THE
WITOLD SOBOCINSKI .... CINEMATOGRAPHER

SANDINO
HANS BURMANN .... CINEMATOGRAPHER
ENRIQUE ESTEVEZ .... PRODUCTION DESIGNER
PEDRO DEL REY .... FILM EDITOR

SANDPIPER, THE
IRENE SHARAFF .... COSTUME DESIGNER
DAVID BRETHERTON .... FILM EDITOR

SANJURO
SHINOBU MURAKI .... PRODUCTION DESIGNER
YOSHIRO MURAKI .... PRODUCTION DESIGNER

SANSHIRO SUGATA
SHINOBU MURAKI .... PRODUCTION DESIGNER
YOSHIRO MURAKI .... PRODUCTION DESIGNER

SANSHIRO SUGATA - PART TWO
SHINOBU MURAKI .... PRODUCTION DESIGNER
YOSHIRO MURAKI .... PRODUCTION DESIGNER

SANTA CLAUS: THE MOVIE
ARTHUR IBBETSON .... CINEMATOGRAPHER
MALCOLM STONE .... PRODUCTION DESIGNER
ANTHONY PRATT .... PRODUCTION DESIGNER
TIM HUTCHINSON .... PRODUCTION DESIGNER
BOB RINGWOOD .... COSTUME DESIGNER
PETER HOLLYWOOD .... FILM EDITOR

SARAH, PLAIN AND TALL (TF)
MICHAEL FASH .... CINEMATOGRAPHER
ED WITTSTEIN .... PRODUCTION DESIGNER
JOHN WRIGHT .... FILM EDITOR

SATAN'S BREW
MICHAEL BALLHAUS .... CINEMATOGRAPHER

SATAN'S PRINCESS
THOMAS F. DENOVE .... CINEMATOGRAPHER
GENEVIVE MOORE .... PRODUCTION DESIGNER
BARBARA BOGUSKI .... FILM EDITOR

SATISFACTION
THOMAS DEL RUTH .... CINEMATOGRAPHER
LYNDA PARADISE .... PRODUCTION DESIGNER
EUGENIE BAFALOUKAS .... COSTUME DESIGNER
JOEL GOODMAN .... FILM EDITOR

SATURDAY NIGHT FEVER
RALF D. BODE .... CINEMATOGRAPHER
CHARLES BAILEY .... PRODUCTION DESIGNER
PATRIZIA VON BRANDENSTEIN .... COSTUME DESIGNER
DAVID RAWLINS .... FILM EDITOR

SATURDAY THE 14TH
DANIEL LACAMBRE .... CINEMATOGRAPHER
ARLENE ALEN .... PRODUCTION DESIGNER
JOANNE D'ANTONIO .... FILM EDITOR
KENT BEYDA .... FILM EDITOR

SATURDAY THE 14TH STRIKES BACK
BERNARD F. CAPUTO .... FILM EDITOR

SATURDAY, SUNDAY, MONDAY
CARLO TAPANI .... CINEMATOGRAPHER
BENITO PERSICO .... COSTUME DESIGNER

SATURN 3
BILLY WILLIAMS .... CINEMATOGRAPHER
NORMAN DORME .... PRODUCTION DESIGNER
STUART CRAIG .... PRODUCTION DESIGNER
RICHARD MARDEN .... FILM EDITOR

SAVAGE BEACH
HOWARD WEXLER .... CINEMATOGRAPHER
JIMMY HADDER .... PRODUCTION DESIGNER
MICHAEL HAIGHT .... FILM EDITOR

SAVAGE DAWN
GERALD FEIL .... CINEMATOGRAPHER
ROBB WILSON KING .... PRODUCTION DESIGNER
GERALD B. GREENBERG .... FILM EDITOR

SAVAGE EYE, THE
HASKELL WEXLER .... CINEMATOGRAPHER

SAVAGE HARVEST
RONNIE TAYLOR .... CINEMATOGRAPHER
ALAN RODERICK-JONES .... PRODUCTION DESIGNER
BRIAN EATWELL .... PRODUCTION DESIGNER
ELLIS COHEN .... COSTUME DESIGNER
PATRICK KENNEDY .... FILM EDITOR
SCOTT WALLACE .... FILM EDITOR

SAVAGE HUNTER, A
ALEXANDER GRUSZYNSKI .... CINEMATOGRAPHER

SAVAGE IS LOOSE, THE
ALEX PHILLIPS .... CINEMATOGRAPHER
MICHAEL KAHN .... FILM EDITOR

SAVAGE ISLANDS
NORMA MORICEAU .... COSTUME DESIGNER

SAVAGE MESSIAH
DICK BUSH .... CINEMATOGRAPHER

SAVAGE SEVEN, THE
LASZLO KOVACS .... CINEMATOGRAPHER

SAVAGE STREETS
STEPHEN L. POSEY .... CINEMATOGRAPHER
BRUCE STUBBLEFIELD .... FILM EDITOR
JOHN O'CONNOR .... FILM EDITOR

SAVANNAH SMILES
STEPHEN W. GRAY .... CINEMATOGRAPHER
EVA RUGGIERO .... FILM EDITOR

SAVE THE DOG (CTF)
CHESTER KACZENSKI .... PRODUCTION DESIGNER

SAVE THE TIGER
JAMES A. CRABE† .... CINEMATOGRAPHER
JACK T. COLLIS .... PRODUCTION DESIGNER

SAVING GRACE
REYNALDO VILLALOBOS .... CINEMATOGRAPHER
GIOVANNI NATALUCCI .... PRODUCTION DESIGNER
PETER ZINNER .... FILM EDITOR

SAY AMEN, SOMEBODY
EDWARD LACHMAN .... CINEMATOGRAPHER
PAUL BARNES .... FILM EDITOR

SAY ANYTHING
LASZLO KOVACS .... CINEMATOGRAPHER
MARK MANSBRIDGE .... PRODUCTION DESIGNER
JANE RUHM .... COSTUME DESIGNER
RICHARD MARKS .... FILM EDITOR

SAY YES
ISIDORE MANKOFSKY .... CINEMATOGRAPHER
MARGARET MORRISON .... FILM EDITOR

SAYONARA
TED HAWORTH .... PRODUCTION DESIGNER

SBATTI IL MOSTRO N PRIMA PAGINA
DANTE FERETTI .... PRODUCTION DESIGNER

SCALAWAG
JOHN C. HOWARD .... FILM EDITOR

SCALPHUNTERS, THE
DUKE CALLAGHAN .... CINEMATOGRAPHER
RICHARD MOORE .... CINEMATOGRAPHER

SCANDAL
MIKE MOLLOY .... CINEMATOGRAPHER
SHINOBU MURAKI .... PRODUCTION DESIGNER
SIMON HOLLAND .... PRODUCTION DESIGNER
YOSHIRO MURAKI .... PRODUCTION DESIGNER
JANE ROBINSON .... COSTUME DESIGNER
ANGUS NEWTON .... FILM EDITOR

SCANDAL IN A SMALL TOWN (TF)
WALTER SHIPLEY .... PRODUCTION DESIGNER

SCANDALO
VITTORIO STORARO .... CINEMATOGRAPHER

SCANDALOUS
JACK CARDIFF .... CINEMATOGRAPHER
BRIAN ACKLAND-SNOW .... PRODUCTION DESIGNER
JOHN SIDALL .... PRODUCTION DESIGNER
PETER MULLINS .... PRODUCTION DESIGNER
MICHAEL BRADSELL .... FILM EDITOR

SCANNERS
MARK IRWIN .... CINEMATOGRAPHER
CAROL SPIER .... PRODUCTION DESIGNER
RONALD SANDERS .... FILM EDITOR

SCARECROW
VILMOS ZSIGMOND .... CINEMATOGRAPHER
ALBERT BRENNER .... PRODUCTION DESIGNER
JO YNOCENCIO .... COSTUME DESIGNER
CRAIG MCKAY .... FILM EDITOR
EVAN LOTTMAN .... FILM EDITOR

SCARED STRAIGHT - ANOTHER STORY (TF)
HECTOR FIGUEROA .... CINEMATOGRAPHER
HARRY KERAMIDAS .... FILM EDITOR

SCARFACE
JOHN A. ALONZO .... CINEMATOGRAPHER
ED RICHARDSON .... PRODUCTION DESIGNER
PATRICIA NORRIS .... COSTUME DESIGNER
DAVID RAY .... FILM EDITOR
GERALD B. GREENBERG .... FILM EDITOR

SCARLET LETTER, THE
ROBBY MULLER .... CINEMATOGRAPHER

SCAVENGER HUNT
RICHARD BERGER .... PRODUCTION DESIGNER
CHRISTOPHER HOLMES .... FILM EDITOR

SCENES FROM A MALL
FRED MURPHY .... CINEMATOGRAPHER
PATO GUZMAN .... PRODUCTION DESIGNER
ALBERT WOLSKY .... COSTUME DESIGNER
STUART PAPPE .... FILM EDITOR

SCENES FROM THE CLASS STRUGGLE IN BEVERLY HILLS
STEVEN FIERBERG .... CINEMATOGRAPHER
ALEX TAVOULARIS .... PRODUCTION DESIGNER
BOB KENSINGER .... PRODUCTION DESIGNER
DONA GRANATA .... COSTUME DESIGNER
ALAN TOOMAYAN .... FILM EDITOR

SCHIZOID
A. NORMAN LEIGH .... CINEMATOGRAPHER
KATHY CURTIS CAHILL .... PRODUCTION DESIGNER
ROBERT FITZGERALD .... FILM EDITOR

SCHOOL DAZE
ERNEST DICKERSON .... CINEMATOGRAPHER
WYNN P. THOMAS .... PRODUCTION DESIGNER
RUTH E. CARTER .... COSTUME DESIGNER
BARRY ALEXANDER BROWN .... FILM EDITOR

SCHOOL SPIRIT
ROBERT EBINGER .... CINEMATOGRAPHER
SONYA SONES TRAMER .... FILM EDITOR

SCOOP (TF)
ROGER PRATT .... CINEMATOGRAPHER
VIC SYMONDS .... PRODUCTION DESIGNER
DEREK BAINE .... FILM EDITOR

SCORCHERS
PETER DEMING .... CINEMATOGRAPHER

SCORCHY
MICHAEL LUCIANO .... FILM EDITOR

SCORNED AND SWINDLED (TF)
GIL HUBBS .... CINEMATOGRAPHER
PETER SMOKLER .... CINEMATOGRAPHER
BRENTON SEIFT .... PRODUCTION DESIGNER

SCOTT JOPLIN
DAVID M. WALSH .... CINEMATOGRAPHER
WILLIAM HINEY .... PRODUCTION DESIGNER
BERNARD JOHNSON .... COSTUME DESIGNER
PATRICK KENNEDY .... FILM EDITOR

Sa-Sc

CINEMATOGRAPHERS
PRODUCTION
DESIGNERS,
COSTUME
DESIGNERS AND
FILM EDITORS
GUIDE

I N D E X   O F   F I L M   T I T L E S

425

Sc-Se

CINEMATOGRAPHERS
PRODUCTION
DESIGNERS,
COSTUME
DESIGNERS AND
FILM EDITORS
GUIDE

I
N
D
E
X

O
F

F
I
L
M

T
I
T
L
E
S

SCREAM FOR HELP
ROBERT PAYNTER .... CINEMATOGRAPHER
ANTHONY READING .... PRODUCTION DESIGNER

SCREAM, PRETTY PEGGY (TF)
LEONARD J. SOUTH .... CINEMATOGRAPHER

SCREEN TEST
JEFF JUR .... CINEMATOGRAPHER
CAROL EASTMAN .... FILM EDITOR

SCREWBALLS
MIKLOS LENTE .... CINEMATOGRAPHER

SCROOGE
ROBERT CARTWRIGHT .... PRODUCTION DESIGNER
TERENCE MARSH .... PRODUCTION DESIGNER

SCROOGED
MICHAEL CHAPMAN .... CINEMATOGRAPHER
J. MICHAEL RIVA .... PRODUCTION DESIGNER
WAYNE FINKELMAN .... COSTUME DESIGNER
FREDRIC STEINKAMP .... FILM EDITOR
WILLIAM STEINKAMP .... FILM EDITOR

SCRUBBERS
ERNEST VINCZE .... CINEMATOGRAPHER
RODNEY HOLLAND .... FILM EDITOR

SCRUPLES (TF)
DANIEL PAREDES .... COSTUME DESIGNER
DONALD BROOKS .... COSTUME DESIGNER

SCUM
PHIL MEHEUX .... CINEMATOGRAPHER
MICHAEL BRADSELL .... FILM EDITOR

SEA GULL, THE
ALAN HEIM .... FILM EDITOR

SEA GYPSIES, THE
ROBERT BROWN .... FILM EDITOR

SEA OF LOVE
ADAM HOLENDER .... CINEMATOGRAPHER
JOHN JAY MOORE .... PRODUCTION DESIGNER
BETSY COX .... COSTUME DESIGNER
DAVID BLEWITT .... FILM EDITOR

SEA WOLVES, THE
TONY IMI .... CINEMATOGRAPHER
MAURICE CAIN .... PRODUCTION DESIGNER
SYD CAIN .... PRODUCTION DESIGNER
ELSA FENNELL .... COSTUME DESIGNER
JOHN GLEN .... FILM EDITOR

SEANCE ON A WET AFTERNOON
RAYMOND SIMM .... PRODUCTION DESIGNER

SEARCH AND DESTROY
RENE VERZIER .... CINEMATOGRAPHER
CAROL SPIER .... PRODUCTION DESIGNER

SECOND CHANCE
FRED J. KOENEKAMP .... CINEMATOGRAPHER

SECOND HAND HEARTS
HASKELL WEXLER .... CINEMATOGRAPHER
PETER W. WOOLEY .... PRODUCTION DESIGNER
RICHARD CARTER .... PRODUCTION DESIGNER
AMY JONES .... FILM EDITOR

SECOND SERVE (TF)
ROBBIE GREENBERG .... CINEMATOGRAPHER
JOHN C. HORGER .... FILM EDITOR

SECOND SIGHT
DANA CHRISTIAANSEN .... CINEMATOGRAPHER
DAVID M. WALSH .... CINEMATOGRAPHER
JAMES SCHOPPE .... PRODUCTION DESIGNER
CYNTHIA BALES .... COSTUME DESIGNER
DAVID RAY .... FILM EDITOR

SECOND SIGHT - A LOVE STORY (TF)
JAMES M. GLENNON .... CINEMATOGRAPHER

SECOND THOUGHTS
KING BAGGOT .... CINEMATOGRAPHER
PAUL PETERS .... PRODUCTION DESIGNER
JULIE WEISS .... COSTUME DESIGNER
NEIL TRAVIS .... FILM EDITOR

SECOND WIND
REGINALD H. MORRIS .... CINEMATOGRAPHER
KAREN BROMLEY .... PRODUCTION DESIGNER
ALEIDA MAC DONALD .... COSTUME DESIGNER

SECONDS
FERRIS WEBSTER .... FILM EDITOR

SECRET ADMIRER
VICTOR J. KEMPER .... CINEMATOGRAPHER
WILLIAM J. CASSIDY .... PRODUCTION DESIGNER
MARY E. VOGT .... COSTUME DESIGNER
DENNIS M. VIRKLER .... FILM EDITOR

SECRET CEREMONY
GERRY FISHER .... CINEMATOGRAPHER
RICHARD MACDONALD .... PRODUCTION DESIGNER

SECRET HONOR
PIERRE MIGNOT .... CINEMATOGRAPHER
JULIET WEBER .... FILM EDITOR

SECRET LIFE OF KATHY MCCORMICK (TF)
ELAYNE CEDER .... PRODUCTION DESIGNER

SECRET LIFE OF PLANTS, THE (FD)
DAVID MYERS .... CINEMATOGRAPHER
GHISLAIN CLOQUET† .... CINEMATOGRAPHER
PETER SMOKLER .... CINEMATOGRAPHER
CHRIS LEBENZON .... FILM EDITOR
ROBERT K. LAMBERT .... FILM EDITOR

SECRET OF MY SUCCESS, THE
CARLO DI PALMA .... CINEMATOGRAPHER
EDWARD PISONI .... PRODUCTION DESIGNER
PETER S. LARKIN .... PRODUCTION DESIGNER
JOSEPH G. AULISI .... COSTUME DESIGNER
PAUL HIRSCH .... FILM EDITOR

SECRET PLACES
PETER MACDONALD .... CINEMATOGRAPHER
EILEEN DISS .... PRODUCTION DESIGNER
ROBERT CARTWRIGHT .... PRODUCTION DESIGNER
JANE ROBINSON .... COSTUME DESIGNER
LAURENCE MÉRY CLARK .... FILM EDITOR

SECRET POLICEMAN'S OTHER BALL, THE (FD)
OLIVER STAPLETON .... CINEMATOGRAPHER

SECRET POLICEMAN'S THIRD BALL, THE (FD)
JOHN HACKNEY .... FILM EDITOR

SECRET WEAPONS (TF)
RICHARD CIUPKA .... CINEMATOGRAPHER

SECRETS
CHRISTOPHER CHALLIS .... CINEMATOGRAPHER
JEFFREY WOODBRIDGE .... PRODUCTION DESIGNER
ERIC BOYD-PERKINS .... FILM EDITOR

SECRETS OF A MARRIED MAN (TF)
ROBERT STEADMAN .... CINEMATOGRAPHER

SECRETS OF A MOTHER AND DAUGHTER (TF)
ELAYNE CEDER .... PRODUCTION DESIGNER

SEDUCED (TF)
TAK FUJIMOTO .... CINEMATOGRAPHER
JOEL SCHILLER .... PRODUCTION DESIGNER
ANTHONY REDMAN .... FILM EDITOR

SEDUCTION OF JOE TYNAN, THE
ADAM HOLENDER .... CINEMATOGRAPHER
DAVID CHAPMAN .... PRODUCTION DESIGNER
JO YNOCENCIO .... COSTUME DESIGNER
EVAN LOTTMAN .... FILM EDITOR

SEDUCTION, THE
TONY DI MARCO .... FILM EDITOR

SEDUCTION, THE
MAC AHLBERG .... CINEMATOGRAPHER

SEE NO EVIL, HEAR NO EVIL
VICTOR J. KEMPER .... CINEMATOGRAPHER
JAMES SINGELIS .... PRODUCTION DESIGNER
ROBERT GUNDLACH .... PRODUCTION DESIGNER
RUTH MORLEY .... COSTUME DESIGNER
ROBERT C. JONES .... FILM EDITOR

Se-Se

CINEMATOGRAPHERS
PRODUCTION
DESIGNERS,
COSTUME
DESIGNERS AND
FILM EDITORS
GUIDE

I
N
D
E
X

O
F

F
I
L
M

T
I
T
L
E
S

427

CINEMATOGRAPHERS
PRODUCTION
DESIGNERS,
COSTUME
DESIGNERS and
FILM EDITORS
GUIDE

I
N
D
E
X

O
F

F
I
L
M

T
I
T
L
E
S

SEVERED HEAD, A
RICHARD MACDONALD .... PRODUCTION DESIGNER

SEX APPEAL
LARRY REVENE .... CINEMATOGRAPHER

SEX TAPES, THE (TF)
DENNIS LEWISTON .... CINEMATOGRAPHER
DONALD LIGHT-HARRIS .... PRODUCTION DESIGNER
GREGORY PRANGE .... FILM EDITOR

sex, lies and videotape
WALT LLOYD .... CINEMATOGRAPHER
JOANNE SCHMIDT .... PRODUCTION DESIGNER

SEXTETTE
JAMES A. CRABE .... CINEMATOGRAPHER
ARGYLE NELSON .... FILM EDITOR

SGT. PEPPER'S LONELY HEARTS CLUB BAND
OWEN ROIZMAN .... CINEMATOGRAPHER
BRIAN EATWELL .... PRODUCTION DESIGNER
MAY ROUTH .... COSTUME DESIGNER
CHRISTOPHER HOLMES .... FILM EDITOR

SHADEY
NORMAN GARWOOD .... PRODUCTION DESIGNER
TUDOR GEORGE .... COSTUME DESIGNER
CHRISTOPHER KELLY .... FILM EDITOR

SHADOW BOX, THE (TF)
ADAM HOLENDER .... CINEMATOGRAPHER
ALLAN JACOBS .... FILM EDITOR

SHADOW CHASERS (TF)
JAMES ALLEN .... PRODUCTION DESIGNER

SHADOW DANCING
RENE OHASHI .... CINEMATOGRAPHER

SHADOW IN THE STREETS, A (TF)
DAVID RAWLINS .... FILM EDITOR

SHADOW OF THE HAWK
REGINALD H. MORRIS .... CINEMATOGRAPHER
O. NICHOLAS BROWN .... FILM EDITOR

SHADOW OF THE SUN - PART II (MS)
ROBERT K. LAMBERT .... FILM EDITOR
FABIEN TORDJMANN .... FILM EDITOR

SHADOW PLAY
STEVEN KARATZOS .... PRODUCTION DESIGNER

SHADOWS OF THE PEACOCK
PETER JAMES .... CINEMATOGRAPHER

SHADY
ROGER DEAKINS .... CINEMATOGRAPHER

SHAFT IN AFRICA
JOHN STOLL .... PRODUCTION DESIGNER

SHAG
BUDDY CONE .... PRODUCTION DESIGNER
MARY E. VOGT .... COSTUME DESIGNER
LAURENCE MERY CLARK .... FILM EDITOR

SHAG: THE MOVIE
PETER MACDONALD .... CINEMATOGRAPHER

SHAGGY D.A., THE
FRANK PHILLIPS .... CINEMATOGRAPHER
JOHN B. MANSBRIDGE .... PRODUCTION DESIGNER
BOB BRING .... FILM EDITOR

SHAKAZULU (MS)
ALEC MILLS .... CINEMATOGRAPHER

SHAKEDOWN
JOHN LINDLEY .... CINEMATOGRAPHER
CHARLES BENNETT .... PRODUCTION DESIGNER
PEGGY FARRELL-SALTEN .... COSTUME DESIGNER
PAUL FRIED .... FILM EDITOR

SHAMPOO
LASZLO KOVACS .... CINEMATOGRAPHER
RICHARD SYLBERT .... PRODUCTION DESIGNER
W. STEWART CAMPBELL .... PRODUCTION DESIGNER
ANTHEA SYLBERT .... COSTUME DESIGNER
ROBERT C. JONES .... FILM EDITOR

SHANGHAI SURPRISE
ERNEST VINCZE .... CINEMATOGRAPHER
DAVID MINTY .... PRODUCTION DESIGNER
JOHN SIDALL .... PRODUCTION DESIGNER
PETER MULLINS .... PRODUCTION DESIGNER
JUDY MOORCROFT .... COSTUME DESIGNER
RALPH SHELDON .... FILM EDITOR

SHANNON'S DEAL (TF)
JOHN VALLONE .... PRODUCTION DESIGNER
NEIL TRAVIS .... FILM EDITOR

SHAPE OF THINGS TO COME, THE
REGINALD H. MORRIS .... CINEMATOGRAPHER
SEAMUS FLANNERY .... PRODUCTION DESIGNER

SHARING RICHARD (TF)
STEVEN FIERBERG .... CINEMATOGRAPHER

SHARKEY'S MACHINE
WILLIAM GORDEAN .... FILM EDITOR

SHARKY'S MACHINE
WILLIAM A. FRAKER .... CINEMATOGRAPHER
WALTER SCOTT HERNDON† .... PRODUCTION DESIGNER
NORMAN SALLING .... COSTUME DESIGNER

SHARMA AND BEYOND
ERNEST VINCZE .... CINEMATOGRAPHER
MAURICE CAIN .... PRODUCTION DESIGNER
MAX LEMON .... FILM EDITOR

SHARON: PORTRAIT OF A MISTRESS (TF)
DANIEL LOMINO .... PRODUCTION DESIGNER

SHATTERED VOWS (TF)
MIKHAIL SUSLOV .... CINEMATOGRAPHER
RICHARD SAWYER .... PRODUCTION DESIGNER
TRACY TYNAN .... COSTUME DESIGNER

SHE
HARRY WAXMAN .... CINEMATOGRAPHER

SHE KNOWS TOO MUCH (TF)
TIM SUHRSTEDT .... CINEMATOGRAPHER

SHE SAID NO (TF)
KING BAGGOT .... CINEMATOGRAPHER
RON FOREMAN .... PRODUCTION DESIGNER
NICHOLAS C. SMITH .... FILM EDITOR

SHE WAS MARKED FOR MURDER (TF)
GIDEON PORATH .... CINEMATOGRAPHER

SHE'LL BE WEARING PINK PAJAMAS
CLIVE TICKNER .... CINEMATOGRAPHER

SHE'S BACK
ARTHUR D. MARKS .... CINEMATOGRAPHER
MARY HICKEY .... FILM EDITOR

SHE'S BEEN AWAY
ARDAN FISHER .... FILM EDITOR

SHE'S DRESSED TO KILL (TF)
THOMAS DEL RUTH .... CINEMATOGRAPHER
SYDNEY Z. LITWAK .... PRODUCTION DESIGNER

SHE'S GOTTA HAVE IT
ERNEST DICKERSON .... CINEMATOGRAPHER
RON PALEY .... PRODUCTION DESIGNER
WYNN P. THOMAS .... PRODUCTION DESIGNER
JOHN MICHAEL REEFER .... COSTUME DESIGNER
SPIKE LEE .... FILM EDITOR

SHE'S HAVING A BABY
DONALD PETERMAN .... CINEMATOGRAPHER
JOHN W. CORSO .... PRODUCTION DESIGNER
APRIL FERRY .... COSTUME DESIGNER
ALAN HEIM .... FILM EDITOR

SHE'S OUT OF CONTROL
DONALD PETERMAN .... CINEMATOGRAPHER
DAVID L. SNYDER .... PRODUCTION DESIGNER
JOE WOOD .... PRODUCTION DESIGNER
MARIE FRANCE .... COSTUME DESIGNER
DOV HOENIG .... FILM EDITOR

SHE-DEVIL
OLIVER STAPLETON .... CINEMATOGRAPHER
SANTO LOQUASTO .... PRODUCTION DESIGNER
ALBERT WOLSKY .... COSTUME DESIGNER
CRAIG MCKAY .... FILM EDITOR

SHEENA
PASQUALINO DE SANTIS .... CINEMATOGRAPHER
MALCOLM MIDDLETON .... PRODUCTION DESIGNER
PETER MURTON .... PRODUCTION DESIGNER
ANNALISA NASALLI-ROCCA .... COSTUME DESIGNER
RAY LOVEJOY .... FILM EDITOR

SHEER MADNESS
MICHAEL BALLHAUS .... CINEMATOGRAPHER
DAGMAR HIRTZ .... FILM EDITOR

SHEILA LEVINE IS DEAD AND LIVING IN NEW YORK
DONALD M. MORGAN .... CINEMATOGRAPHER
ARGYLE NELSON .... FILM EDITOR

SHELL GAME (TF)
GAYNE RESCHER .... CINEMATOGRAPHER
ANN LAMBERT .... COSTUME DESIGNER

SHELTERING SKY, THE
VITTORIO STORARO .... CINEMATOGRAPHER
GIANNI SILVESTRI .... PRODUCTION DESIGNER
JAMES ACHESON .... COSTUME DESIGNER
GABRIELLA CRISTIANI .... FILM EDITOR

SHENANIGANS
WALTER LASSALLY .... CINEMATOGRAPHER
RALPH ROSENBLUM .... FILM EDITOR

SHERMAN'S MARCH
ROSS MCELWEE .... FILM EDITOR

SHIELDS & YARNELL (TV)
BOB MACKIE .... COSTUME DESIGNER

SHILLINGBURY BLOWERS...THE BAND PLAYED ON, THE
FRANK WATTS .... CINEMATOGRAPHER

SHINING SEASON, A (TF)
ELAYNE CEDER .... PRODUCTION DESIGNER

SHINING STAR
ALAN METZGER .... CINEMATOGRAPHER

SHINING, THE
JOHN ALCOTT† .... CINEMATOGRAPHER
LESLIE TOMKINS .... PRODUCTION DESIGNER
ROY WALKER .... PRODUCTION DESIGNER
MILENA CANONERO .... COSTUME DESIGNER
RAY LOVEJOY .... FILM EDITOR

SHIRLEY VALENTINE
ALAN HUME .... CINEMATOGRAPHER
JOHN STOLL .... PRODUCTION DESIGNER
LESLEY WALKER .... FILM EDITOR

SHIVERS
JERZY ZIELINSKI .... CINEMATOGRAPHER
PATRICK DODD .... FILM EDITOR

SHOAH (FD)
DOMINIQUE CHAPUIS .... CINEMATOGRAPHER

SHOCK 'EM DEAD
RON CHAPMAN .... CINEMATOGRAPHER
RANDY LAPIN .... PRODUCTION DESIGNER
JACQUELINE ARONSON .... COSTUME DESIGNER
TERRY BLYTHE .... FILM EDITOR

SHOCK TREATMENT
MIKE MOLLOY .... CINEMATOGRAPHER
ANDREW SANDERS .... PRODUCTION DESIGNER
BRIAN THOMPSON .... PRODUCTION DESIGNER
SUE BLANE .... COSTUME DESIGNER
RICHARD BEDFORD .... FILM EDITOR

SHOCK WAVES
NORMAN GAY .... FILM EDITOR

SHOCKER
JACQUES HAITKIN .... CINEMATOGRAPHER
ISIS MUSSENDEN .... COSTUME DESIGNER
ANDY BLUMENTHAL .... FILM EDITOR

SHOES OF THE FISHERMAN, THE
EDWARD C. CARFAGNO .... PRODUCTION DESIGNER

SHOGUN (MS)
JOSEPH R. JENNINGS .... PRODUCTION DESIGNER

SHOOT
EARL PRESTON .... PRODUCTION DESIGNER
RON WISMAN .... FILM EDITOR

SHOOT THE MOON
MICHAEL SERESIN .... CINEMATOGRAPHER
GEOFFREY KIRKLAND .... PRODUCTION DESIGNER
W. STEWART CAMPBELL .... PRODUCTION DESIGNER
KRISTI ZEA .... COSTUME DESIGNER
GERRY HAMBLING .... FILM EDITOR

SHOOT TO KILL
MICHAEL CHAPMAN .... CINEMATOGRAPHER
RICHARD SYLBERT .... PRODUCTION DESIGNER
RICHARD BRUNO .... COSTUME DESIGNER
GARTH CRAVEN .... FILM EDITOR
GEORGE BOWERS .... FILM EDITOR

SHOOT-OUT
BERNARD JOHNSON .... COSTUME DESIGNER

SHOOTDOWN (TF)
WILLIAM WAGES .... CINEMATOGRAPHER

SHOOTER (TF)
GAYNE RESCHER .... CINEMATOGRAPHER

SHOOTING PARTY, THE
FRED TAMMES .... CINEMATOGRAPHER
MORLEY SMITH .... PRODUCTION DESIGNER
TOM RAND .... COSTUME DESIGNER
PETER DAVIES .... FILM EDITOR

SHOOTIST, THE
BRUCE SURTEES .... CINEMATOGRAPHER
ROBERT F. BOYLE .... PRODUCTION DESIGNER
DOUGLAS STEWART .... FILM EDITOR

SHORT CHANGED
RICHARD FRANCIS-BRUCE .... FILM EDITOR

SHORT CIRCUIT
NICK MCLEAN .... CINEMATOGRAPHER
DIANNE WAGER .... PRODUCTION DESIGNER
PHILIP HARRISON .... PRODUCTION DESIGNER
MARY E. VOGT .... COSTUME DESIGNER
FRANK MORRISS .... FILM EDITOR

SHORT CIRCUIT 2
JOHN MC PHERSON .... CINEMATOGRAPHER
ALICIA KEYWAN .... PRODUCTION DESIGNER
BILL BRODIE .... PRODUCTION DESIGNER
LARRY WELLS .... COSTUME DESIGNER
CONRAD BUFF IV .... FILM EDITOR

SHORT EYES
PETER SOVA .... CINEMATOGRAPHER

SHORT TIME
JOHN J. CONNOR .... CINEMATOGRAPHER
MICHAEL S. BOLTON .... PRODUCTION DESIGNER
CHRISTOPHER RYAN .... COSTUME DESIGNER
FRANK MORRISS .... FILM EDITOR

SHOUT AT THE DEVIL
MICHAEL REED .... CINEMATOGRAPHER
SYD CAIN .... PRODUCTION DESIGNER
MICHAEL J. DUTHIE .... FILM EDITOR

SHOUT, THE
MIKE MOLLOY .... CINEMATOGRAPHER
SIMON HOLLAND .... PRODUCTION DESIGNER
BARRIE VINCE .... FILM EDITOR

SHOW OF FORCE, A
JAMES GLENNON .... CINEMATOGRAPHER
SONYA POLANSKY .... PRODUCTION DESIGNER
WILLIAM J. CASSIDY .... PRODUCTION DESIGNER
KATHRYN MORRISON-PAHOA .... COSTUME DESIGNER
HENRY RICHARDSON .... FILM EDITOR

SHRIMP ON THE BARBIE, THE
FRED CHULACK .... FILM EDITOR

Sh-Sh

CINEMATOGRAPHERS
PRODUCTION
DESIGNERS,
COSTUME
DESIGNERS AND
FILM EDITORS
GUIDE

INDEX OF FILM TITLES

429

Sh-Si

CINEMATOGRAPHERS
PRODUCTION
DESIGNERS,
COSTUME
DESIGNERS AND
FILM EDITORS
GUIDE

I
N
D
E
X

O
F

F
I
L
M

T
I
T
L
E
S

SILVER CHAIR, THE (TF)
TREVOR WIMLETT .... CINEMATOGRAPHER
MALCOLM BANTHORPE .... FILM EDITOR

SILVER CITY
JOHN SEALE .... CINEMATOGRAPHER
IGOR NAY .... PRODUCTION DESIGNER
JAY HURLEY .... COSTUME DESIGNER
DON SAUNDERS .... FILM EDITOR

SILVER DREAM RACER
PAUL BEESON .... CINEMATOGRAPHER
MALCOLM MIDDLETON .... PRODUCTION DESIGNER
JUDY MOORCROFT .... COSTUME DESIGNER
PETER HOLLYWOOD .... FILM EDITOR

SILVER DREAMS
BERNARD GRIBBLE .... FILM EDITOR

SILVER STREAK
DAVID M. WALSH .... CINEMATOGRAPHER
ALFRED SWEENEY .... PRODUCTION DESIGNER
DAVID BRETHERTON .... FILM EDITOR

SILVERADO
JOHN BAILEY .... CINEMATOGRAPHER
IDA RANDOM .... PRODUCTION DESIGNER
WILLIAM A. ELLIOT .... PRODUCTION DESIGNER
KRISTI ZEA .... COSTUME DESIGNER
CAROL LITTLETON .... FILM EDITOR

SIMON
ADAM HOLENDER .... CINEMATOGRAPHER
STUART WURTZEL .... PRODUCTION DESIGNER
SANTO LOQUASTO .... COSTUME DESIGNER
NINA FEINBERG .... FILM EDITOR

SINBAD AND THE EYE OF THE TIGER
TED MOORE .... CINEMATOGRAPHER
GEOFFREY DRAKE .... PRODUCTION DESIGNER
ROY WATTS .... FILM EDITOR

SINCERELY CHARLOTTE
BRUNO DE KEYZER .... CINEMATOGRAPHER
PATRICE MERCIER .... PRODUCTION DESIGNER
ANNE BOISSEL .... FILM EDITOR

SINFUL LIFE, A
JONATHAN WEST .... CINEMATOGRAPHER
ROBERT ZENTIS .... PRODUCTION DESIGNER
SYLVIA MOSS .... COSTUME DESIGNER
JEFFREY REINER .... FILM EDITOR

SING
PETER SOVA .... CINEMATOGRAPHER
CAROL SPIER .... PRODUCTION DESIGNER
JOHN HAY .... COSTUME DESIGNER
BUD SMITH .... FILM EDITOR
JERE HUGGINS .... FILM EDITOR
SCOTT SMITH .... FILM EDITOR

SINGER AND THE DANCER, THE
RUSSELL BOYD .... CINEMATOGRAPHER
NICHOLAS BEAUMAN .... FILM EDITOR

SINGING DETECTIVE, THE (TF)
KEN WESTBURY .... CINEMATOGRAPHER

SINGING NUN, THE
RITA ROLAND .... FILM EDITOR

SINGING ON THE TREADMILL
ELMER RAGALYI .... CINEMATOGRAPHER

SINGING THE BLUES IN RED
CHRIS MENGES .... CINEMATOGRAPHER
ROBERT JOHNSON .... PRODUCTION DESIGNER
JONATHAN MORRIS .... FILM EDITOR

SINGLE BARS, SINGLE WOMEN (TF)
JUAN RUIZ-ANCHIA .... CINEMATOGRAPHER
IVO G. CRISTANTE .... PRODUCTION DESIGNER
ANN SOMERS MAJOR .... COSTUME DESIGNER

SINGLE ROOM FURNISHED
LASZLO KOVACS .... CINEMATOGRAPHER

SINS OF DORIAN GRAY, THE
LINDA MATHESON .... COSTUME DESIGNER

SINS OF INNOCENCE (TF)
ROBERT JESSUP .... CINEMATOGRAPHER
STEPHEN BERGER .... PRODUCTION DESIGNER

SINS OF THE MOTHER (TF)
JULES BRENNER .... CINEMATOGRAPHER
JOHN LEIMANIS .... PRODUCTION DESIGNER
JIM OLIVER .... FILM EDITOR

SINS OF THE PAST (TF)
DAVID L. SNYDER .... PRODUCTION DESIGNER
ANN SOMERS MAJOR .... COSTUME DESIGNER

SIROCCO BLOW, THE
JEAN-FRANÇOIS ROBIN .... CINEMATOGRAPHER

SISTER MARGARET AND THE SATURDAY NIGHT LADIES (TF)
ELAYNE CEDER .... PRODUCTION DESIGNER

SISTER, SISTER
STEPHEN M. KATZ .... CINEMATOGRAPHER
RICHARD SHERMAN .... PRODUCTION DESIGNER
BRUCE FINLAYSON .... COSTUME DESIGNER
MARION ROTHMAN .... FILM EDITOR

SIX AGAINST THE ROCK
PHILIP LATHROP .... CINEMATOGRAPHER

SIX PACK
MARIO TOSI .... CINEMATOGRAPHER
WILLIAM J. CREBER .... PRODUCTION DESIGNER
RITA ROLAND .... FILM EDITOR

SIX WEEKS
MICHAEL D. MARGULIES .... CINEMATOGRAPHER
HILYARD BROWN .... PRODUCTION DESIGNER
SANDY VENEZIANO .... PRODUCTION DESIGNER
STU LINDER .... FILM EDITOR

SIXTEEN CANDLES
BOBBY BYRNE .... CINEMATOGRAPHER
JOHN W. CORSO .... PRODUCTION DESIGNER
EDWARD A. WARSCHILKA .... FILM EDITOR

SIXTEEN DAYS OF GLORY
GIL HUBBS .... CINEMATOGRAPHER
ROBERT PRIMES .... CINEMATOGRAPHER

SIXTH AND MAIN
GWEN CAPETANOS BOUZON .... COSTUME DESIGNER
KEN JOHNSON .... FILM EDITOR

SKAG (TF)
EDMOND L. KOONS .... CINEMATOGRAPHER

SKATEBOARD, U.S.A
GENE FOWLER JR. .... FILM EDITOR

SKATETOWN, U.S.A.
DONALD M. MORGAN .... CINEMATOGRAPHER
BETSY HEIMANN .... COSTUME DESIGNER

SKETCHES
TOM WALLS .... FILM EDITOR

SKI PATROL
JOHN M. STEPHENS .... CINEMATOGRAPHER
FRED WEILER .... PRODUCTION DESIGNER
ANGEE BECKETT .... COSTUME DESIGNER
SCOTT WALLACE .... FILM EDITOR

SKIN DEEP
ISIDORE MANKOFSKY .... CINEMATOGRAPHER
RODGER MAUS .... PRODUCTION DESIGNER
NOLAN MILLER .... COSTUME DESIGNER
ROBERT PERGAMENT .... FILM EDITOR

SKIN, THE
DANTE FERRETTI .... PRODUCTION DESIGNER

SKIRMISH
PETER LYONS COLLISTER .... CINEMATOGRAPHER

SKULLDUGGERY
VINCENT SAIZIS .... CINEMATOGRAPHER

Si-Sk

CINEMATOGRAPHERS
PRODUCTION
DESIGNERS,
COSTUME
DESIGNERS AND
FILM EDITORS
GUIDE

INDEX OF FILM TITLES

CINEMATOGRAPHERS
PRODUCTION
DESIGNERS,
COSTUME
DESIGNERS AND
FILM EDITORS
GUIDE

I
N
D
E
X

O
F

F
I
L
M

T
I
T
L
E
S

SKY BANDITS
DAVID WATKIN .... CINEMATOGRAPHER
CHARLES BISHOP .... PRODUCTION DESIGNER
TONY WOLLARD .... PRODUCTION DESIGNER
BETSY HEIMANN .... COSTUME DESIGNER
PETER TANNER .... FILM EDITOR

SKY IS GREY, THE (TF)
LARRY PIZER .... CINEMATOGRAPHER

SKY RIDERS
TERRY ACKLAND-SNOW .... PRODUCTION DESIGNER

SKY'S THE LIMIT, THE (TF)
GIL HUBBS .... CINEMATOGRAPHER
ROBB WILSON KING .... PRODUCTION DESIGNER
DAVID FINFER .... FILM EDITOR

SKYJACK
VINCENT M. CRESCIMAN .... PRODUCTION DESIGNER

SKYJACKED
HARRY STRADLING, JR. .... CINEMATOGRAPHER
ROBERT E. SWINK .... FILM EDITOR

SLAM DANCE
AMIR MOKRI .... CINEMATOGRAPHER
EUGENIO ZANETTI .... PRODUCTION DESIGNER
PHILIP DEAN FOREMAN .... PRODUCTION DESIGNER
MALISSA DANIEL .... COSTUME DESIGNER
LEE PERCY .... FILM EDITOR

SLAMMER GIRLS
LARRY REVENE .... CINEMATOGRAPHER

SLAP SHOT
VICTOR J. KEMPER .... CINEMATOGRAPHER
HENRY BUMSTEAD .... PRODUCTION DESIGNER
THOMAS M. BRONSON .... COSTUME DESIGNER
DEDE ALLEN .... FILM EDITOR

SLAPSTICK OF ANOTHER KIND
ANTHONY B. RICHMOND .... CINEMATOGRAPHER
JOEL SCHILLER .... PRODUCTION DESIGNER
DOUG JACKSON .... FILM EDITOR

SLATE, WYN & ME
DAVID CONNELL .... CINEMATOGRAPHER
JEANIE CAMERON .... COSTUME DESIGNER
PETER FRIEDRICH .... FILM EDITOR

SLAUGHTER HIGH
JIM CONNOCK .... FILM EDITOR

SLAUGHTERHOUSE FIVE
MIROSLAV ONDRICEK .... CINEMATOGRAPHER
HENRY BUMSTEAD .... PRODUCTION DESIGNER

SLAUGHTERHOUSE ROCK
NICHOLAS VON STERNBERG .... CINEMATOGRAPHER

SLAVE GIRLS FROM BEYOND INFINITY
THOMAS L. CALLAWAY .... CINEMATOGRAPHER
BRUCE STUBBLEFIELD .... FILM EDITOR

SLAVES OF NEW YORK
TONY PIERCE-ROBERTS .... CINEMATOGRAPHER
DAVID GROPMAN .... PRODUCTION DESIGNER
CAROL RAMSEY .... COSTUME DESIGNER
KATHERINE WENNING .... FILM EDITOR

SLAYER, THE
EDWARD SALIER .... FILM EDITOR
ERIC BOYD-PERKINS .... FILM EDITOR

SLAYGROUND
STEPHEN SMITH .... CINEMATOGRAPHER
EDWARD PISONI .... PRODUCTION DESIGNER
NICHOLAS GASTER .... FILM EDITOR

SLEDGEHAMMER (PILOT)
TRACY TYNAN .... COSTUME DESIGNER

SLEEPAWAY CAMP
BENJAMIN DAVIS .... CINEMATOGRAPHER
SHARYN L. ROSS .... FILM EDITOR

SLEEPER
DAVID M. WALSH .... CINEMATOGRAPHER
RALPH ROSENBLUM .... FILM EDITOR

SLEEPING BEAUTY
MAREK DOBROWOLSKI .... PRODUCTION DESIGNER

SLEEPING DOGS
MICHAEL SERESIN .... CINEMATOGRAPHER

SLEEPING WITH THE ENEMY
JOHN W. LINDLEY .... CINEMATOGRAPHER
DOUG KRANER .... PRODUCTION DESIGNER
RICHARD HORNUNG .... COSTUME DESIGNER
GEORGE BOWERS .... FILM EDITOR

SLEEPWALK
FRANK PRINZI .... CINEMATOGRAPHER

SLENDER THREAD, THE
JACK POPLIN .... PRODUCTION DESIGNER

SLEUTH
KEN ADAM .... PRODUCTION DESIGNER

SLIPPER AND THE ROSE, THE
TONY IMI .... CINEMATOGRAPHER
TIMOTHY GEE .... FILM EDITOR

SLIPPER AND THE ROSE: THE STORY OF CINDERELLA, THE
RAYMOND SIMM .... PRODUCTION DESIGNER
JULIE HARRIS .... COSTUME DESIGNER

SLIPPING INTO DARKNESS
BARBARA POKRAS .... FILM EDITOR

SLIPSTREAM
FRANK TIDY .... CINEMATOGRAPHER
ANDREW MCALPINE .... PRODUCTION DESIGNER
MALCOLM STONE .... PRODUCTION DESIGNER
CATHERINE COOKE .... COSTUME DESIGNER
TERRY RAWLINGS .... FILM EDITOR

SLITHER
LASZLO KOVACS .... CINEMATOGRAPHER
ALFRED TAYLOR .... CINEMATOGRAPHER
DALE HENNESY† .... PRODUCTION DESIGNER
DAVID BRETHERTON .... FILM EDITOR

SLOW ATTACK
PETER PRZYGODDA .... FILM EDITOR

SLOW BURN (CTF)
ROBERT W. (BO) WELCH .... PRODUCTION DESIGNER
GALE PARKER-SMITH .... COSTUME DESIGNER

SLOW DANCING IN THE BIG CITY
RALF D. BODE .... CINEMATOGRAPHER
WILLIAM J. CASSIDY .... PRODUCTION DESIGNER
RUTH MORLEY .... COSTUME DESIGNER
JOHN G. AVILDSEN .... FILM EDITOR

SLUGGER'S WIFE, THE
CALEB DESCHANEL .... CINEMATOGRAPHER
J. MICHAEL RIVA .... PRODUCTION DESIGNER
RICHARD CARTER .... PRODUCTION DESIGNER
ANN ROTH .... COSTUME DESIGNER
DON BROCHU .... FILM EDITOR
GEORGE C. VILLASENOR .... FILM EDITOR

SLUGS
RICHARD E. RABJOHN .... FILM EDITOR

SLUMBER PARTY '57
ROBERT CARAMICO .... CINEMATOGRAPHER

SLUMBER PARTY MASSACRE
STEPHEN L. POSEY .... CINEMATOGRAPHER
THOMAS L. CALLAWAY .... CINEMATOGRAPHER
WENDY BRICMONT .... FILM EDITOR

SLUMBER PARTY MASSACRE II
WILLIAM FLICKER .... FILM EDITOR

SMALL CHANGE
PIERRE WILLIAM GLENN .... CINEMATOGRAPHER

SMALL CIRCLE OF FRIENDS, A
MICHAEL C. BUTLER .... CINEMATOGRAPHER
JOEL SCHILLER .... PRODUCTION DESIGNER
RANDY ROBERTS .... FILM EDITOR

SMALL KILLING, A (TF)
VINCENT M. CRESCIMAN .... PRODUCTION DESIGNER

SMALL TOWN IN TEXAS, A
ROBERT JESSUP .... CINEMATOGRAPHER
ELAYNE CEDER .... PRODUCTION DESIGNER
JOHN C. HORGER .... FILM EDITOR

SMART ALEC
JERRY N. SKEELS .... COSTUME DESIGNER

SMASH PALACE
GRAEME COWLEY .... CINEMATOGRAPHER
MICHAEL HORTON .... FILM EDITOR

SMASH, CRASH, AND BURN
CHRISTOPHER G. TUFTY .... CINEMATOGRAPHER

SMASHING TIME
RUTH MYERS .... COSTUME DESIGNER

SMILE
CONRAD HALL .... CINEMATOGRAPHER
PATRICIA NORRIS .... COSTUME DESIGNER
RICHARD A. HARRIS .... FILM EDITOR

SMILEY'S PEOPLE (MS)
KENNETH MACMILLAN .... CINEMATOGRAPHER

SMITHEREENS
CHIRINE EL KHADOM .... CINEMATOGRAPHER
FRANZ HARLAND .... PRODUCTION DESIGNER
LILLY KILVERT .... PRODUCTION DESIGNER
SUSAN SEIDELMAN .... FILM EDITOR

SMOKEY AND THE BANDIT
HENRY BUMSTEAD .... PRODUCTION DESIGNER
MARK MANSBRIDGE .... PRODUCTION DESIGNER
ANGELO ROSS .... FILM EDITOR
WALTER HANNEMAN .... FILM EDITOR
BUZZ BRANDT .... FILM EDITOR

SMOKEY AND THE BANDIT II
MICHAEL C. BUTLER .... CINEMATOGRAPHER
BERNIE CUTLER .... PRODUCTION DESIGNER
DONN CAMBERN .... FILM EDITOR
WILLIAM GORDEAN .... FILM EDITOR

SMOKEY AND THE BANDIT 3
JAMES PERGOLA .... CINEMATOGRAPHER
RON HOBBS .... PRODUCTION DESIGNER
LINDA BENEDICT .... COSTUME DESIGNER
DAVID BLEWITT .... FILM EDITOR
CHRISTOPHER GREENBURY .... FILM EDITOR

SMOKEY BITES THE DUST
GARY GRAVER .... CINEMATOGRAPHER
LARRY BOCK .... FILM EDITOR

SMOOTH TALK
JAMES M. GLENNON .... CINEMATOGRAPHER
DAVID WASCO .... PRODUCTION DESIGNER
CAROL ODITZ .... COSTUME DESIGNER
PATRICK DODD .... FILM EDITOR

SMORGASBORD
GERALD PERRY FINNERMAN .... CINEMATOGRAPHER
GENE FOWLER JR. .... FILM EDITOR

SNAP-SHOT
VINCENT MONTON .... CINEMATOGRAPHER
JON DOWDING .... PRODUCTION DESIGNER

SNO-LINE
BETH CONWELL .... FILM EDITOR

SNOW KILL (CTF)
FRANK BEASCOECHEA .... CINEMATOGRAPHER
DOUGLAS G. JOHNSON .... PRODUCTION DESIGNER
TOM PRYOR .... FILM EDITOR

SNOW WHITE
MAREK DOBROWOLSKI .... PRODUCTION DESIGNER

SNOW WHITE AND THE THREE STOOGES
JOHN W. HOLMES .... FILM EDITOR

SNOWS OF KILIMANJARO, THE
JOHN DE CUIR .... PRODUCTION DESIGNER

SO FINE
JAMES A. CONTNER .... CINEMATOGRAPHER
PAUL EADS .... PRODUCTION DESIGNER
SANTO LOQUASTO .... PRODUCTION DESIGNER
ALAN HEIM .... FILM EDITOR

SOGGY BOTTOM, U.S.A.
WARD PRESTON .... PRODUCTION DESIGNER

SOLAR CRISIS
RUSS CARPENTER .... CINEMATOGRAPHER
GEORGE JENSON .... PRODUCTION DESIGNER
ROBERT TURTURICE .... COSTUME DESIGNER

SOLARBABIES
PETER MACDONALD .... CINEMATOGRAPHER
ANTHONY PRATT .... PRODUCTION DESIGNER
JOSE MARIA ALARCON .... PRODUCTION DESIGNER
LESLIE TOMKINS .... PRODUCTION DESIGNER
BOB RINGWOOD .... COSTUME DESIGNER
CONRAD BUFF IV .... FILM EDITOR

SOLDIER OF METAL
JUAN RUIZ-ANCHIA .... CINEMATOGRAPHER

SOLDIER OF ORANGE
JOST VACANO .... CINEMATOGRAPHER

SOLDIER'S STORY, A
RUSSELL BOYD .... CINEMATOGRAPHER
WALTER SCOTT HERNDON† .... PRODUCTION DESIGNER
CAROLINE BIGGERSTAFF .... FILM EDITOR
MARK ROY WARNER .... FILM EDITOR

SOLDIER'S STORY, A (TF)
PETER SOVA .... CINEMATOGRAPHER

SOLDIER'S TALE, A
MICHAEL HORTON .... FILM EDITOR

SOLDIER, THE
ROBERT M. BALDWIN .... CINEMATOGRAPHER

SOLEMN COMMUNION
JEAN-FRANÇOIS ROBIN .... CINEMATOGRAPHER

SOLITARY MAN, THE (TF)
KIRK AXTELL .... PRODUCTION DESIGNER

SOLOMON NORTHUP'S ODYSSEY (TF)
HIRO NARITA .... CINEMATOGRAPHER

SOME CALL IT LOVING
MARIO TOSI .... CINEMATOGRAPHER

SOME GIRLS
UELI STEIGER .... CINEMATOGRAPHER
EUGENIO ZANETTI .... PRODUCTION DESIGNER
DAVID SPIERS .... FILM EDITOR

SOME KIND OF HERO
KING BAGGOT .... CINEMATOGRAPHER
JAMES SCHOPPE .... PRODUCTION DESIGNER
CHRISTOPHER GREENBURY .... FILM EDITOR

SOME KIND OF MIRACLE (TF)
JAMES H. SPENCER .... PRODUCTION DESIGNER

SOME KIND OF WONDERFUL
JAN KIESSER .... CINEMATOGRAPHER
GREGORY PICKRELL .... PRODUCTION DESIGNER
JOSAN F. RUSSO .... PRODUCTION DESIGNER
MARILYN VANCE-STRAKER .... COSTUME DESIGNER
BUD SMITH .... FILM EDITOR
SCOTT SMITH .... FILM EDITOR

SOME KINDA WOMAN
ROY H. WAGNER .... CINEMATOGRAPHER

SOME LIKE IT HOT
TED HAWORTH .... PRODUCTION DESIGNER

SOMEBODY HAS TO SHOOT THE PICTURE (CTF)
BOJAN BAZELLI .... CINEMATOGRAPHER
MICHAEL HANAN .... PRODUCTION DESIGNER
PETER ZINNER .... FILM EDITOR

Sm-So

CINEMATOGRAPHERS
PRODUCTION
DESIGNERS,
COSTUME
DESIGNERS AND
FILM EDITORS
GUIDE

I
N
D
E
X

O
F

F
I
L
M

T
I
T
L
E
S

So-So

CINEMATOGRAPHERS
PRODUCTION
DESIGNERS,
COSTUME
DESIGNERS and
FILM EDITORS
GUIDE

I
N
D
E
X

O
F

F
I
L
M

T
I
T
L
E
S

SOMEBODY KILLED HER HUSBAND
ANDREW LASZLO .... CINEMATOGRAPHER
DAVID CHAPMAN .... PRODUCTION DESIGNER
TED HAWORTH .... PRODUCTION DESIGNER
BARRY MALKIN .... FILM EDITOR

SOMEONE TO LOVE
HANANIA BAER .... CINEMATOGRAPHER

SOMEONE TO WATCH OVER ME
STEVEN B. POSTER .... CINEMATOGRAPHER
JAMES D. BISSELL .... PRODUCTION DESIGNER
JEFFREY BEECROFT .... PRODUCTION DESIGNER
JOHN JAY MOORE .... PRODUCTION DESIGNER
COLLEEN C. ATWOOD .... COSTUME DESIGNER
CLAIRE SIMPSON-CROZIER .... FILM EDITOR

SOMETHING ABOUT AMELIA (TF)
THOMAS DEL RUTH .... CINEMATOGRAPHER
WILLIAM MALLEY .... PRODUCTION DESIGNER

SOMETHING BIG
HARRY STRADLING, JR. .... CINEMATOGRAPHER
ALFRED SWEENEY .... PRODUCTION DESIGNER

SOMETHING FOR EVERYONE
RALPH ROSENBLUM .... FILM EDITOR

SOMETHING IN COMMON (TF)
BRYAN RYMAN .... PRODUCTION DESIGNER
SYDNEY Z. LITWAK .... PRODUCTION DESIGNER
PAUL RUBELL .... FILM EDITOR

SOMETHING IS WAITING
MICHELLE MINCH .... PRODUCTION DESIGNER

SOMETHING SHORT OF PARADISE
WALTER LASSALLY .... CINEMATOGRAPHER
WILLIAM F. DE SETA .... PRODUCTION DESIGNER
FRANK BRACHT .... FILM EDITOR

SOMETHING SO RIGHT (TF)
BRYAN RYMAN .... PRODUCTION DESIGNER

SOMETHING WICKED THIS WAY COMES
STEPHEN H. BURUM .... CINEMATOGRAPHER
RICHARD MACDONALD .... PRODUCTION DESIGNER
JOHN B. MANSBRIDGE .... PRODUCTION DESIGNER
RICHARD J. LAWRENCE .... PRODUCTION DESIGNER
RUTH MYERS .... COSTUME DESIGNER
ARGYLE NELSON .... FILM EDITOR

SOMETHING WILD
TAK FUJIMOTO .... CINEMATOGRAPHER
NORMA MORICEAU .... PRODUCTION DESIGNER
EUGENIE BAFALOUKAS .... COSTUME DESIGNER
CRAIG MC KAY .... FILM EDITOR

SOMETIMES A GREAT NOTION
RICHARD MOORE .... CINEMATOGRAPHER
PHILIP JEFFRIES .... PRODUCTION DESIGNER
ROBERT WYMAN .... FILM EDITOR

SOMEWHERE IN TIME
ISIDORE MANKOFSKY .... CINEMATOGRAPHER
JEAN-PIERRE DORLEAC .... COSTUME DESIGNER
JEFF S. GOURSON .... FILM EDITOR

SON OF THE MORNING STAR-PARTS I & II (MS)
KEES VAN OOSTRUM .... CINEMATOGRAPHER
CARY WHITE - 2DP
BENJAMIN A. WEISSMAN .... FILM EDITOR

SON-RISE: A MIRACLE OF LOVE (TF)
JAMES H. SPENCER .... PRODUCTION DESIGNER

SONG OF SUMMER
DICK BUSH .... CINEMATOGRAPHER

SONG REMAINS THE SAME,THE
ERNEST DAY .... CINEMATOGRAPHER

SONGWRITER
MATTHEW F. LEONETTI .... CINEMATOGRAPHER
JOEL SCHILLER .... PRODUCTION DESIGNER
STUART H. PAPPE .... FILM EDITOR
TOM WALLS .... FILM EDITOR

SONIA, 16 YEARS
MIKAEL SALOMON .... CINEMATOGRAPHER

SONNY & CHER COMEDY HOUR, THE (TVS)
BOB MACKIE .... COSTUME DESIGNER

SONNY & CHER SHOW, THE (TVS)
BOB MACKIE .... COSTUME DESIGNER

SONNY BOY
ROBERTO D'ETTORRE PIAZZOLI .... CINEMATOGRAPHER
CLAUDIO CUTRY .... FILM EDITOR

SONS
STEFAN CZAPSKY .... CINEMATOGRAPHER
JAY FREUND .... FILM EDITOR

SONS AND LOVERS
FREDDIE FRANCIS .... CINEMATOGRAPHER

SOPHIE'S CHOICE
NESTOR ALMENDROS .... CINEMATOGRAPHER
GEORGE JENKINS .... PRODUCTION DESIGNER
JOHN JAY MOORE .... PRODUCTION DESIGNER
ALBERT WOLSKY .... COSTUME DESIGNER
EVAN LOTTMAN .... FILM EDITOR

SORCERER
DICK BUSH .... CINEMATOGRAPHER
JOHN M. STEPHENS .... CINEMATOGRAPHER
JOHN BOX .... PRODUCTION DESIGNER
ROY WALKER .... PRODUCTION DESIGNER
BUD SMITH .... FILM EDITOR

SORCERESS
ALEX PHILLIPS .... CINEMATOGRAPHER
BARRY ZETLIN .... FILM EDITOR
LARRY BOCK .... FILM EDITOR

SORORITY BABES IN THE SLIMEBALL BOWL-O-RAMA
BARRY ZETLIN .... FILM EDITOR
TOM MASHELSKI .... FILM EDITOR

SOTTO, SOTTO
DANTE SPINOTTI .... CINEMATOGRAPHER
LUIGI ZITA .... FILM EDITOR

SOUL MAN
JEFF JUR .... CINEMATOGRAPHER
DON DIERS .... PRODUCTION DESIGNER
GREGG FONSECA .... PRODUCTION DESIGNER
JOHN REINHART .... PRODUCTION DESIGNER
SHARON SIMONAIRE .... COSTUME DESIGNER
DAVID FINFER .... FILM EDITOR

SOUL OF NIGGER CHARLEY, THE
GENE RUDOLF .... PRODUCTION DESIGNER

SOULTAKER
JAMES A. ROSENTHAL .... CINEMATOGRAPHER
THAD CARR .... PRODUCTION DESIGNER
JASON COLEMAN .... FILM EDITOR
MICHAEL RISSI .... FILM EDITOR

SOUND OF MUSIC, THE
BORIS LEVEN† .... PRODUCTION DESIGNER
DOROTHY JEAKINS .... COSTUME DESIGNER
WILLIAM REYNOLDS .... FILM EDITOR

SOUNDER
JOHN A. ALONZO .... CINEMATOGRAPHER
PETER W. WOOLEY .... PRODUCTION DESIGNER
SIDNEY LEVIN .... FILM EDITOR

SOUP FOR ONE
FRED SCHULER .... CINEMATOGRAPHER
PHILIP ROSENBERG .... PRODUCTION DESIGNER
DAVID RAWLINS .... FILM EDITOR

SOUP TO NUTS
LLOYD KAUFMAN .... CINEMATOGRAPHER
DANIEL LOEWENTHAL .... FILM EDITOR

SOURDOUGH
GEORGE FOLSEY JR.* .... FILM EDITOR

SOURSWEET
MIKE GARFATH .... CINEMATOGRAPHER
MICK AUDSLEY .... FILM EDITOR

SOUTH OF RENO
PHILIP J.C. DUFFIN .... PRODUCTION DESIGNER
MARC GROSSMAN .... FILM EDITOR

SOUTHERN COMFORT
ANDREW LASZLO .... CINEMATOGRAPHER
JOHN VALLONE .... PRODUCTION DESIGNER
FREEMAN DAVIES .... FILM EDITOR

SOUVENIR
FRED TAMMES .... CINEMATOGRAPHER

SOUVENIR (CTF)
BOB MORGAN .... FILM EDITOR

SOYLENT GREEN
RICHARD H. KLINE .... CINEMATOGRAPHER
EDWARD C. CARFAGNO .... PRODUCTION DESIGNER

SPACE (MS)
GAYNE RESCHER .... CINEMATOGRAPHER
JACK DE SHIELDS .... PRODUCTION DESIGNER
JOSEPH R. JENNINGS .... PRODUCTION DESIGNER
RENIE CONLEY .... COSTUME DESIGNER
ROBERT FLETCHER .... COSTUME DESIGNER
DONALD R. RODE .... FILM EDITOR
PATRICK KENNEDY .... FILM EDITOR

SPACE - PARTS 1 - 5 (MS)
HECTOR FIGUEROA .... CINEMATOGRAPHER

SPACE RAGE
TIM SUHRSTEDT .... CINEMATOGRAPHER

SPACE RAIDERS
ALEC HIRSCHFELD .... CINEMATOGRAPHER
ROBERT KIZER .... FILM EDITOR

SPACEBALLS
NICK MC LEAN .... CINEMATOGRAPHER
HAROLD MICHELSON .... PRODUCTION DESIGNER
TERENCE MARSH .... PRODUCTION DESIGNER
DONFELD .... COSTUME DESIGNER
CONRAD BUFF IV .... FILM EDITOR

SPACECAMP
LEON HARRIS .... PRODUCTION DESIGNER
RICHARD J. LAWRENCE .... PRODUCTION DESIGNER
RICHARD MACDONALD .... PRODUCTION DESIGNER
PATRICIA NORRIS .... COSTUME DESIGNER
JOHN W. WHEELER .... FILM EDITOR

SPACED INVADERS
JAMES L. CARTER .... CINEMATOGRAPHER
TONY TREMBLAY .... PRODUCTION DESIGNER
DANIEL GROSS .... FILM EDITOR
SETH GAVEN .... FILM EDITOR

SPACED OUT
JOHN METCALFE .... CINEMATOGRAPHER
PETER SINCLAIR .... CINEMATOGRAPHER

SPACEHUNTER: ADVENTURES IN THE FORBIDDEN ZONE
FRANK TIDY .... CINEMATOGRAPHER
BRENTON SWIFT .... PRODUCTION DESIGNER
JACKSON DE GOVIA .... PRODUCTION DESIGNER
JOHN R. JENSEN .... PRODUCTION DESIGNER
JULIE WEISS .... COSTUME DESIGNER
SCOTT CONRAD .... FILM EDITOR

SPARKLE
BRUCE SURTEES .... CINEMATOGRAPHER
PETER W. WOOLEY .... PRODUCTION DESIGNER
DANIEL PAREDES .... COSTUME DESIGNER

SPARTACUS
ROBERT LAWRENCE .... FILM EDITOR

SPASMS
MARK IRWIN .... CINEMATOGRAPHER

SPEAKING PARTS
PAUL SAROSSY .... CINEMATOGRAPHER
LINDA DEL ROSARIO .... PRODUCTION DESIGNER
BRUCE MCDONALD .... FILM EDITOR

SPECIAL BULLETIN (TF)
ROBB WILSON KING .... PRODUCTION DESIGNER

SPECIAL DAY, A
ENRICO SABBATINI .... COSTUME DESIGNER

SPECIAL DELIVERY
HARRY STRADLING, JR. .... CINEMATOGRAPHER
JACK POPLIN .... PRODUCTION DESIGNER
HOUSELEY STEVENSON .... FILM EDITOR

SPECIAL EFFECTS
PAUL GLICKMAN .... CINEMATOGRAPHER
ARMAND LEBOWITZ .... FILM EDITOR

SPECIAL FRIENDSHIP, A (TF)
BEN EDWARDS .... PRODUCTION DESIGNER

SPECIAL PEOPLE: BASED ON A TRUE STORY (TF)
MARK IRWIN .... CINEMATOGRAPHER
RON WISMAN .... FILM EDITOR

SPECIAL SECTION
FRANÇOISE BONNOT .... FILM EDITOR

SPECIALIST, THE
EDUARDO SERRA .... CINEMATOGRAPHER
NORM WALLERSTEIN .... FILM EDITOR

SPECTRE
ARTHUR IBBETSON .... CINEMATOGRAPHER

SPEED ZONE
FRANCOIS PROTAT .... CINEMATOGRAPHER
RICHARD HUDOLIN .... PRODUCTION DESIGNER
PAUL-ANDRE GUERIN .... COSTUME DESIGNER
MICHAEL ECONOMOU .... FILM EDITOR

SPELLBINDER
ADAM GREENBERG .... CINEMATOGRAPHER
RODGER MAUS .... PRODUCTION DESIGNER
STEVE MIRKOVICH .... FILM EDITOR

SPETTERS
JOST VACANO .... CINEMATOGRAPHER

SPHINX
ERNEST DAY .... CINEMATOGRAPHER
GIL PARRONDO .... PRODUCTION DESIGNER
TERENCE MARSH .... PRODUCTION DESIGNER
JUDY MOORCROFT .... COSTUME DESIGNER
MICHAEL F. ANDERSON .... FILM EDITOR
ROBERT E. SWINK .... FILM EDITOR

SPIDERBABY
ALFRED TAYLOR .... CINEMATOGRAPHER

SPIES (TF)
JOSEPH C. NEMEC III .... PRODUCTION DESIGNER

SPIES LIKE US
ROBERT PAYNTER .... CINEMATOGRAPHER
JOHN J. LLOYD .... PRODUCTION DESIGNER
PETER MURTON .... PRODUCTION DESIGNER
TERRY ACKLAND-SNOW .... PRODUCTION DESIGNER
DEBORAH NADOOLMAN .... COSTUME DESIGNER
MALCOLM CAMPBELL .... FILM EDITOR

SPIKE OF BENSONHURST
STEVEN FIERBERG .... CINEMATOGRAPHER
STEVEN MCCABE .... PRODUCTION DESIGNER
STAN SALFAS .... FILM EDITOR

SPIKER
RICHARD S. BRUMMER .... FILM EDITOR

SPIKES GANG, THE
BRIAN WEST .... CINEMATOGRAPHER
RALPH E. WINTERS .... FILM EDITOR

SPINOUT
RITA ROLAND .... FILM EDITOR

SPIRIT OF '76, THE
STEPHEN LIGHTHILL .... CINEMATOGRAPHER
DANIEL TALPERS .... PRODUCTION DESIGNER
SOFIA COPPOLA .... COSTUME DESIGNER
GLEN SCANTLEBURY .... FILM EDITOR

SPIRIT OF THE WIND
MARK GOLDBLATT .... FILM EDITOR

So-Sp

CINEMATOGRAPHERS
PRODUCTION
DESIGNERS,
COSTUME
DESIGNERS AND
FILM EDITORS
GUIDE

I
N
D
E
X

O
F

F
I
L
M

T
I
T
L
E
S

CINEMATOGRAPHERS
PRODUCTION
DESIGNERS,
COSTUME
DESIGNERS AND
FILM EDITORS
GUIDE

I
N
D
E
X

O
F

F
I
L
M

T
I
T
L
E
S

SPLASH
DONALD PETERMAN .... CINEMATOGRAPHER
JACK T. COLLIS .... PRODUCTION DESIGNER
JOHN B. MANSBRIDGE .... PRODUCTION DESIGNER
MAY ROUTH .... COSTUME DESIGNER
DANIEL P. HANLEY .... FILM EDITOR
MICHAEL J. HILL .... FILM EDITOR

SPLENDOR IN THE GRASS
RICHARD SYLBERT .... PRODUCTION DESIGNER

SPLIT DECISIONS
TIM SUHRSTEDT .... CINEMATOGRAPHER
MICHAEL Z. HANAN .... PRODUCTION DESIGNER
HILARY WRIGHT .... COSTUME DESIGNER
JEFF FREEMAN .... FILM EDITOR
JOHN W. WHEELER .... FILM EDITOR
THOMAS STANFORD .... FILM EDITOR

SPLIT IMAGE
ROBERT JESSUP .... CINEMATOGRAPHER
JACK MARTY .... PRODUCTION DESIGNER
WOLF KROEGER .... PRODUCTION DESIGNER
JAY KAMEN .... FILM EDITOR

SPLIT, THE
RITA ROLAND .... FILM EDITOR

SPOOK WHO SAT BY THE DOOR, THE
MICHAEL KAHN .... FILM EDITOR

SPORTING CLUB, THE
JOEL SCHILLER .... PRODUCTION DESIGNER

SPOT MARKS THE X (CTF)
MICHAEL A. STEVENSON .... FILM EDITOR

SPRAGGUE (TF)
W. STEWART CAMPBELL .... PRODUCTION DESIGNER

SPRING BREAK
STEVEN B. POSTER .... CINEMATOGRAPHER
NICHOLAS ROMANAC .... PRODUCTION DESIGNER
VIRGINIA FIELD .... PRODUCTION DESIGNER
SUSAN DENISON .... COSTUME DESIGNER
SUSAN E. CUNNINGHAM .... FILM EDITOR

SPRING FEVER
BRUNO RUBEO .... PRODUCTION DESIGNER
KIRK JONES .... FILM EDITOR
TONY LOWER .... FILM EDITOR

SPY WHO LOVED ME, THE
CLAUDE RENOIR .... CINEMATOGRAPHER
KEN ADAM .... PRODUCTION DESIGNER
PETER LAMONT .... PRODUCTION DESIGNER
JOHN GLEN .... FILM EDITOR

SPY WITH A COLD NOSE, THE
PETER MULLINS .... PRODUCTION DESIGNER

SQUAMISH FIVE, THE
RICHARD LEITERMAN .... CINEMATOGRAPHER

SQUARE DANCE
JACEK LASKUS .... CINEMATOGRAPHER
JAN SCOTT .... PRODUCTION DESIGNER
ELIZABETH MCBRIDE .... COSTUME DESIGNER
BRUCE GREEN .... FILM EDITOR

SQUEEZE, THE
ARTHUR ALBERT .... CINEMATOGRAPHER
CHRISTOPHER NOWAK .... PRODUCTION DESIGNER
SIMON WATERS .... PRODUCTION DESIGNER
JANE GREENWOOD .... COSTUME DESIGNER
HARRY KERAMIDAS .... FILM EDITOR
JOHN SHIRLEY .... FILM EDITOR

SQUEEZE, THE (1977)
DENNIS LEWISTON .... CINEMATOGRAPHER

SQUIRM
JOSEPH MANGINE .... CINEMATOGRAPHER
BRIAN SMEDLEY-ASTON .... FILM EDITOR

SQUIZZY TAYLOR
DAN BURSTALL .... CINEMATOGRAPHER

SREDNI VASHTAR (SHORT)
PETER HOLLYWOOD .... FILM EDITOR

ST. ELMO'S FIRE
STEPHEN H. BURUM .... CINEMATOGRAPHER
JAMES D. BISSELL .... PRODUCTION DESIGNER
WILLIAM SANDELL .... PRODUCTION DESIGNER
SUSAN BECKER .... COSTUME DESIGNER
RICHARD MARKS .... FILM EDITOR

ST. HELENS
JACQUES HAITKIN .... CINEMATOGRAPHER
MICHAEL ERLERE .... PRODUCTION DESIGNER
GEORGE BERNDT .... FILM EDITOR

ST. IVES
PHILIP JEFFRIES .... PRODUCTION DESIGNER
MICHAEL F. ANDERSON .... FILM EDITOR

STACKING
PAUL ELLIOTT .... CINEMATOGRAPHER
RICHARD BOWEN .... CINEMATOGRAPHER
DAVID WASCO .... PRODUCTION DESIGNER
LINDA BASS .... PRODUCTION DESIGNER
SHARON SEYMOUR .... PRODUCTION DESIGNER
PATRICK DODD .... FILM EDITOR

STACY'S KNIGHTS
RAOUL LOMAS .... CINEMATOGRAPHER
JILL OHANNESON .... COSTUME DESIGNER
BONNIE KOEHLER .... FILM EDITOR

STAINLESS STEEL AND STAR SPIES
FREDDIE YOUNG .... CINEMATOGRAPHER

STAKEOUT
JOHN SEALE .... CINEMATOGRAPHER
PHILIP HARRISON .... PRODUCTION DESIGNER
RICHARD HUDOLIN .... PRODUCTION DESIGNER
MICHAEL RIPPS .... FILM EDITOR

STAKEOUT
MARY E. VOGT .... COSTUME DESIGNER
TOM ROLF .... FILM EDITOR

STALKING MOON, THE
JACK POPLIN .... PRODUCTION DESIGNER
AARON STELL .... FILM EDITOR

STAND ALONE
TIM SUHRSTEDT .... CINEMATOGRAPHER
TOM RICHMOND .... CINEMATOGRAPHER
PAMELA B. WARNER .... PRODUCTION DESIGNER
FABIEN TORDJMANN .... FILM EDITOR

STAND AND DELIVER
TOM RICHMOND .... CINEMATOGRAPHER
MILO .... PRODUCTION DESIGNER
KATHRYN MORRISON .... COSTUME DESIGNER
NANCY RICHARDSON .... FILM EDITOR

STAND BY ME
THOMAS DEL RUTH .... CINEMATOGRAPHER
DENNIS WASHINGTON .... PRODUCTION DESIGNER
SUE MOORE .... COSTUME DESIGNER
ROBERT LEIGHTON .... FILM EDITOR

STAND UP AND BE COUNTED
HAROLD F. KRESS .... FILM EDITOR

STAND UP VIRGIN SOLDIERS
HARRY POTTLE .... PRODUCTION DESIGNER
GEOFFREY FOOT .... FILM EDITOR

STANLEY
RUSSELL BOYD .... CINEMATOGRAPHER
WILLIAM M. ANDERSON .... FILM EDITOR

STANLEY & IRIS
DONALD MCALPINE .... CINEMATOGRAPHER
JOEL SCHILLER .... PRODUCTION DESIGNER
THEONI ALDREDGE .... COSTUME DESIGNER
SIDNEY LEVIN .... FILM EDITOR

STAR 80
SVEN NYKVIST .... CINEMATOGRAPHER
JACK G. TAYLOR .... PRODUCTION DESIGNER
MICHAEL S. BOLTON .... PRODUCTION DESIGNER
ALBERT WOLSKY .... COSTUME DESIGNER
ALAN HEIM .... FILM EDITOR

STAR CHAMBER, THE
RICHARD HANNAH .... CINEMATOGRAPHER
ROBERT W. (BO) WELCH .... PRODUCTION DESIGNER
WILLIAM MALLEY .... PRODUCTION DESIGNER
PATRICIA NORRIS .... COSTUME DESIGNER
JAMES MITCHELL .... FILM EDITOR

STAR IS BORN, A
ROBERT SURTEES† .... CINEMATOGRAPHER
POLLY PLATT .... PRODUCTION DESIGNER
WILLIAM HINEY .... PRODUCTION DESIGNER
PETER ZINNER .... FILM EDITOR
SCOTT CONRAD .... FILM EDITOR

STAR IS BORN, A (1954)
IRENE SHARAFF .... COSTUME DESIGNER

STAR SEARCH (TVS)
SANDI LOVE .... COSTUME DESIGNER

STAR TRAP
WITOLD STOK .... CINEMATOGRAPHER

STAR TREK — THE MOTION PICTURE
RICHARD H. KLINE .... CINEMATOGRAPHER
HAROLD MICHELSON .... PRODUCTION DESIGNER
JOSEPH R. JENNINGS .... PRODUCTION DESIGNER
JOHN VALLONE .... PRODUCTION DESIGNER
LEON HARRIS .... PRODUCTION DESIGNER
ROBERT FLETCHER .... COSTUME DESIGNER
BILL BRAME .... FILM EDITOR
TODD RAMSAY .... FILM EDITOR

STAR TREK II: THE WRATH OF KHAN
GAYNE RESCHER .... CINEMATOGRAPHER
JOSEPH R. JENNINGS .... PRODUCTION DESIGNER
ROBERT FLETCHER .... COSTUME DESIGNER
WILLIAM DORNISCH .... FILM EDITOR

STAR TREK III: THE SEARCH FOR SPOCK
CHARLES CORRELL .... CINEMATOGRAPHER
JOHN E. CHILBERG .... PRODUCTION DESIGNER
ROBERT FLETCHER .... COSTUME DESIGNER
ROBERT F. SHUGRUE .... FILM EDITOR

STAR TREK IV: THE VOYAGE HOME
DONALD PETERMAN .... CINEMATOGRAPHER
JACK T. COLLIS .... PRODUCTION DESIGNER
JOE AUBEL .... PRODUCTION DESIGNER
PETER LANDSDOWN SMITH .... PRODUCTION DESIGNER
ROBERT FLETCHER .... COSTUME DESIGNER
PETER E. BERGER .... FILM EDITOR

STAR TREK V: THE FINAL FRONTIER
ANDREW LASZLO .... CINEMATOGRAPHER
HERMAN ZIMMERMAN .... PRODUCTION DESIGNER
NILO RODIS-JAMERO .... COSTUME DESIGNER
PETER E. BERGER .... FILM EDITOR

STAR TREK: THE NEXT GENERATION (TVS)
DURINDA RICE WOOD .... COSTUME DESIGNER

STAR WARS
GIL TAYLOR .... CINEMATOGRAPHER
JOHN BARRY† .... PRODUCTION DESIGNER
LESLIE DILLEY .... PRODUCTION DESIGNER
NORMAN REYNOLDS .... PRODUCTION DESIGNER
ROGER CHRISTIAN .... PRODUCTION DESIGNER
JOHN MOLLO .... COSTUME DESIGNER
MARCIA LUCAS .... FILM EDITOR
PAUL HIRSCH .... FILM EDITOR
RICHARD CHEW .... FILM EDITOR

STAR!
BORIS LEVEN† .... PRODUCTION DESIGNER
DONALD BROOKS .... COSTUME DESIGNER
WILLIAM REYNOLDS .... FILM EDITOR

STAR-SPANGLED GIRL
LAWRENCE G. PAULL .... PRODUCTION DESIGNER

STARCHASER: THE LEGEND OF ORION (AF)
DONALD W. ERNST .... FILM EDITOR

STARCRASH
PAUL BEESON .... CINEMATOGRAPHER
AURELIO CRUGNOLA .... PRODUCTION DESIGNER
SERGIO MONTANARI .... FILM EDITOR

STARCROSSED (TF)
GIL HUBBS .... CINEMATOGRAPHER

STARDUST
RUTH MYERS .... COSTUME DESIGNER

STARDUST MEMORIES
GORDON WILLIS .... CINEMATOGRAPHER
MEL BOURNE .... PRODUCTION DESIGNER
MICHAEL MOLLY .... PRODUCTION DESIGNER
SANTO LOQUASTO .... PRODUCTION DESIGNER
SUSAN E. MORSE .... FILM EDITOR

STARHOPS
ERIC SAARINEN .... CINEMATOGRAPHER

STARK (TF)
FRANK BEASCOECHEA .... CINEMATOGRAPHER

STARK: MIRROR IMAGE (TF)
ROBERT W. (BO) WELCH .... PRODUCTION DESIGNER

STARMAN
DONALD M. MORGAN .... CINEMATOGRAPHER
DANIEL LOMINO .... PRODUCTION DESIGNER
WILLIAM J. DURRELL, JR. .... PRODUCTION DESIGNER
MARION ROTHMAN .... FILM EDITOR

STARS AND BARS
JERZY ZIELINSKI .... CINEMATOGRAPHER
BECKY BLOCK .... PRODUCTION DESIGNER
LESLIE DILLEY .... PRODUCTION DESIGNER
STUART CRAIG .... PRODUCTION DESIGNER
ANN ROTH .... COSTUME DESIGNER
MICHAEL BRADSELL .... FILM EDITOR

STARSHIP
LEE COLE .... PRODUCTION DESIGNER

STARSHIP INVASIONS
MARK IRWIN .... CINEMATOGRAPHER
KAREN BROMLEY .... PRODUCTION DESIGNER
MILLIE MOORE .... FILM EDITOR

STARSLAMMER - PRISONSHIP
MIRIAM PREISSEL .... FILM EDITOR

STARSTRUCK
RUSSELL BOYD .... CINEMATOGRAPHER
NICHOLAS BEAUMAN .... FILM EDITOR

START THE REVOLUTION WITHOUT ME
JOHN C. HORGER .... FILM EDITOR

STARTING OVER
SVEN NYKVIST .... CINEMATOGRAPHER
GEORGE JENKINS .... PRODUCTION DESIGNER
MICHAEL MOLLY .... PRODUCTION DESIGNER
JOHN BOXER .... COSTUME DESIGNER
MARION ROTHMAN .... FILM EDITOR

STATE OF EMERGENCY, A
WILLY KURANT .... CINEMATOGRAPHER
STATE OF SEIGE
FRANCOISE BONNOT .... FILM EDITOR
STATE OF THINGS, THE
FRED MURPHY .... CINEMATOGRAPHER

STATIC
JEFF JUR .... CINEMATOGRAPHER
EMILY PAINE .... FILM EDITOR

STATIONMASTER'S WIFE
MICHAEL BALLHAUS .... CINEMATOGRAPHER

STAY HUNGRY
VICTOR J. KEMPER .... CINEMATOGRAPHER
TOBY CARR RAFELSON .... PRODUCTION DESIGNER
JOHN F. LINK .... FILM EDITOR

STAYING ALIVE
NICK MCLEAN .... CINEMATOGRAPHER
NORMAN NEWBERRY .... PRODUCTION DESIGNER
ROBERT F. BOYLE .... PRODUCTION DESIGNER
BOB MACKIE .... COSTUME DESIGNER
THOMAS M. BRONSON .... COSTUME DESIGNER
DON ZIMMERMAN .... FILM EDITOR
MARK MELNICK .... FILM EDITOR
MARK ROY WARNER .... FILM EDITOR
PETER E. BERGER .... FILM EDITOR

St-St

CINEMATOGRAPHERS
PRODUCTION
DESIGNERS,
COSTUME
DESIGNERS AND
FILM EDITORS
GUIDE

INDEX OF FILM TITLES

CINEMATOGRAPHERS
PRODUCTION
DESIGNERS,
COSTUME
DESIGNERS AND
FILM EDITORS
GUIDE

I
N
D
E
X

O
F

F
I
L
M

T
I
T
L
E
S

STITCHES
HECTOR FIGUEROA .... CINEMATOGRAPHER
RICHARD E. LA MOTTE .... COSTUME DESIGNER
JOHN DUFFY .... FILM EDITOR

STOLEN HOURS
HARRY WAXMAN .... CINEMATOGRAPHER

STOLEN: ONE HUSBAND (TF)
BOB BRING .... FILM EDITOR

STONE (TF)
LARRY PIZER.. CINEMATOGRAPHER
WOODY OMENS .... CINEMATOGRAPHER

STONE BOY, THE
JUAN RUIZ-ANCHIA .... CINEMATOGRAPHER
JOSEPH C. PACELLI .... PRODUCTION DESIGNER
GAIL VIOLA .... COSTUME DESIGNER
PAUL RUBELL .... FILM EDITOR

STONE COLD
ALEXANDER GRUSZYNSKI .... CINEMATOGRAPHER
JOHN MANSBRIDGE .... PRODUCTION DESIGNER
RICHARD JOHNSON .... PRODUCTION DESIGNER
MARK HELFRICH .... FILM EDITOR

STONE COLD DEAD
TED WATKINS .... PRODUCTION DESIGNER

STONE KILLER, THE
RICHARD MOORE .... CINEMATOGRAPHER
WARD PRESTON .... PRODUCTION DESIGNER

STONES FOR IBARRA (TF)
ROBERT BLACKMAN .... COSTUME DESIGNER

STONING IN FULLHAM COUNTY, A (TF)
LASZLO GEORGE .... CINEMATOGRAPHER
NORM BARON .... PRODUCTION DESIGNER

STONY ISLAND
TAK FUJIMOTO .... CINEMATOGRAPHER
DOV HOENIG .... FILM EDITOR

STOOGEMANIA
CHRISTOPHER G. TUFTY .... CINEMATOGRAPHER
CHARLES D. TOMLINSON .... PRODUCTION DESIGNER
JAMES RUXIN .... FILM EDITOR

STOOLIE, THE
GERALD B. GREENBERG .... FILM EDITOR

STOP MAKING SENSE
JORDAN CRONENWETH .... CINEMATOGRAPHER

STOP MAKING SENSE (FD)
JEFFREY BEECROFT .... PRODUCTION DESIGNER
LISA DAY .... FILM EDITOR

STORIE SCELLERATE
DANTE FERRETTI .... PRODUCTION DESIGNER

STORIES FROM A FLYING TRUNK
BRIAN WEST .... CINEMATOGRAPHER

STORM AND SORROW (CTF)
IVAN MARK .... CINEMATOGRAPHER
LASZLO GEORGE .... CINEMATOGRAPHER
MARIANNA MIKLOS .... FILM EDITOR
ROBERT KIMBLE .... FILM EDITOR
ZSUZSA POSAN .... FILM EDITOR

STORM BOY
GEOFF BURTON .... CINEMATOGRAPHER
DAVID COPPING .... PRODUCTION DESIGNER

STORMIN' HOME (TF)
ROBERT JESSUP .... CINEMATOGRAPHER
RICHARD JAMES .... PRODUCTION DESIGNER

STORMTROOPERS
GIUSEPPE ROTUNNO .... CINEMATOGRAPHER

STORMY MONDAY
ROGER DEAKINS .... CINEMATOGRAPHER
ANDREW MC ALPINE .... PRODUCTION DESIGNER
CHARMIAN ADAMS .... PRODUCTION DESIGNER
SANDY POWELL .... COSTUME DESIGNER
DAVID MARTIN .... FILM EDITOR

STORMY SUMMER
WILLY KURANT .... CINEMATOGRAPHER
MICHELE BOEHM .... FILM EDITOR

STORY OF A MARRIAGE (TF)
VAN BROUGHTON RAMSEY .... COSTUME DESIGNER

STORY OF ADELE H., THE
NESTOR ALMENDROS .... CINEMATOGRAPHER

STORY OF RUTH, THE
JOHN W. HOLMES .... FILM EDITOR

STORY OF WOMEN
JEAN RABIER .... CINEMATOGRAPHER
MONIQUE FARDOULIS .... FILM EDITOR

STORYTELLER , THE (PILOT)
ROGER HALL .... PRODUCTION DESIGNER

STRAIGHT OUT OF BROOKLYN
JOHN ROSNELL .... CINEMATOGRAPHER
JACK HAIGIS .... FILM EDITOR

STRAIGHT TIME
OWEN ROIZMAN .... CINEMATOGRAPHER
PAUL LOHMANN .... CINEMATOGRAPHER
RICHARD J. LAWRENCE .... PRODUCTION DESIGNER
STEPHEN GRIMES† .... PRODUCTION DESIGNER
BERNIE POLLACK .... COSTUME DESIGNER
RANDY ROBERTS .... FILM EDITOR
SAM O'STEEN .... FILM EDITOR

STRAIGHT TO HELL
TOM RICHMOND .... CINEMATOGRAPHER
ANDREW MC ALPINE .... PRODUCTION DESIGNER
PAM TAIT .... COSTUME DESIGNER
DAVID MARTIN .... FILM EDITOR

STRANDED
JEFF JUR .... CINEMATOGRAPHER
STEPHEN E. RIVKIN .... FILM EDITOR

STRANDED (TF)
PETER MOSS .... CINEMATOGRAPHER
JAMES G. HULSEY .... PRODUCTION DESIGNER
LOIS FREEMAN-FOX .... FILM EDITOR

STRANGE BEHAVIOR
LOUIS HORVATH .... CINEMATOGRAPHER
PETRA VAN OELFFEN .... FILM EDITOR

STRANGE BREW
STEVEN B. POSTER .... CINEMATOGRAPHER
DAVID L. SNYDER .... PRODUCTION DESIGNER
LARRY WELLS .... COSTUME DESIGNER
PATRICK MCMAHON .... FILM EDITOR

STRANGE COMPANIONS (TF)
DOUGLAS HIGGINS .... PRODUCTION DESIGNER

STRANGE INVADERS
LOUIS HORVATH .... CINEMATOGRAPHER
SUSANNAH MOORE .... PRODUCTION DESIGNER
LINDA MATHESON .... COSTUME DESIGNER
SUSANNA MOORE .... COSTUME DESIGNER
JOHN W. WHEELER .... FILM EDITOR

STRANGE NEW WORLD (TF)
DODIE SHEPARD .... COSTUME DESIGNER

STRANGE VOICES (TF)
HANANIA BAER .... CINEMATOGRAPHER
EMILY DRAPER .... COSTUME DESIGNER

STRANGER IN MY BED (TF)
LASZLO GEORGE .... CINEMATOGRAPHER

STRANGER IS WATCHING, A
BARRY ABRAMS .... CINEMATOGRAPHER
VIRGINIA FIELD .... PRODUCTION DESIGNER
SUSAN E. CUNNINGHAM .... FILM EDITOR

STRANGER ON MY LAND (TF)
BETSY HEIMANN .... COSTUME DESIGNER

STRANGER THAN PARADISE
TOM DICILLO .... CINEMATOGRAPHER
JIM JARMUSCH .... FILM EDITOR
MELODY LONDON .... FILM EDITOR

St-St

CINEMATOGRAPHERS
PRODUCTION
DESIGNERS,
COSTUME
DESIGNERS AND
FILM EDITORS
GUIDE

INDEX OF FILM TITLES

439

St-St

CINEMATOGRAPHERS
PRODUCTION
DESIGNERS,
COSTUME
DESIGNERS AND
FILM EDITORS
GUIDE

I
N
D
E
X

O
F

F
I
L
M

T
I
T
L
E
S

STRANGER WITHIN, THE (TF)
JIM HAYMAN .... CINEMATOGRAPHER
RAY STOREY .... PRODUCTION DESIGNER
SCOTT CONRAD .... FILM EDITOR

STRANGER'S KISS
MIKHAIL SUSLOV .... CINEMATOGRAPHER
J. MICHAEL RIVA .... PRODUCTION DESIGNER
TRACY TYNAN .... COSTUME DESIGNER

STRANGER, THE
ABEL FACELLO .... PRODUCTION DESIGNER
EDUARDO LOPEZ .... FILM EDITOR

STRANGERS KISS
WILLIAM CARRUTH .... FILM EDITOR

STRANGERS ON A TRAIN
TED HAWORTH .... PRODUCTION DESIGNER

STRAPLESS
ANDREW DUNN .... CINEMATOGRAPHER
ROGER HALL .... PRODUCTION DESIGNER
PENNY ROSE .... COSTUME DESIGNER
REBECCA HALE .... COSTUME DESIGNER
EDWARD MARNIER .... FILM EDITOR

STRAW DOGS
RAYMOND SIMM .... PRODUCTION DESIGNER
GARTH CRAVEN .... FILM EDITOR
ROBERT L. WOLFE .... FILM EDITOR

STRAWBERRY STATEMENT, THE
RALPH WOOLSEY .... CINEMATOGRAPHER

STRAY DOG
SHINOBU MURAKI .... PRODUCTION DESIGNER
YOSHIRO MURAKI .... PRODUCTION DESIGNER

STREAMERS
PIERRE MIGNOT .... CINEMATOGRAPHER
STEPHEN ALTMAN .... PRODUCTION DESIGNER
WOLF KROEGER .... PRODUCTION DESIGNER
SCOTT BUSHNELL .... COSTUME DESIGNER
NORMAN SMITH .... FILM EDITOR

STREET HAWK (TF)
JAMES ALLEN .... PRODUCTION DESIGNER

STREET HUNTER
PHIL PARMET .... CINEMATOGRAPHER
JOHN PAINO .... PRODUCTION DESIGNER
JANE TABACHNIK .... COSTUME DESIGNER
MARY HICKEY .... FILM EDITOR

STREET JUSTICE
ROLAND OZZIE SMITH .... CINEMATOGRAPHER

STREET MUSIC
RICHARD BOWEN .... CINEMATOGRAPHER
DON DE FINA .... PRODUCTION DESIGNER
MARIANNA ASTROM DEFINA .... COSTUME DESIGNER
LISA FRUCHTMAN .... FILM EDITOR

STREET SMART
ADAM HOLENDER .... CINEMATOGRAPHER
DAN LEIGH .... PRODUCTION DESIGNER
JO YNOCENCIO .... COSTUME DESIGNER
PRISCILLA ANNE NEDD .... FILM EDITOR

STREET TRASH
DAVID SPERLING .... CINEMATOGRAPHER
DENNIS WERNER .... FILM EDITOR

STREET WALKIN'
PATRICK RAND .... FILM EDITOR

STREETCAR NAMED DESIRE, A (TF)
BILL BUTLER .... CINEMATOGRAPHER
JAMES G. HULSEY .... PRODUCTION DESIGNER
TRAVILLA .... COSTUME DESIGNER

STREETS OF FIRE
ANDREW LASZLO .... CINEMATOGRAPHER
ANTHONY BROCKLISS .... PRODUCTION DESIGNER
JAMES ALLEN .... PRODUCTION DESIGNER
JOHN VALLONE .... PRODUCTION DESIGNER
DONNA LINSON .... COSTUME DESIGNER
MARILYN VANCE-STRAKER .... COSTUME DESIGNER
FREEMAN DAVIES .... FILM EDITOR
MICHAEL RIPPS .... FILM EDITOR

STREETS OF GOLD
ARTHER ALBERT .... CINEMATOGRAPHER
MARCOS FLAKSMAN .... PRODUCTION DESIGNER
JEFFREY KURLAND .... COSTUME DESIGNER
RICHARD CHEW .... FILM EDITOR

STREETS OF L.A. (TF)
ALLEN DAVIAU .... CINEMATOGRAPHER

STREETS OF MALICE (TF)
SCOTT WALLACE .... FILM EDITOR

STREETS, THE (PILOT)
FRED SCHULER .... CINEMATOGRAPHER

STREETWALKIN'
STEVEN FIERBERG .... CINEMATOGRAPHER
KAREN PERRY .... COSTUME DESIGNER

STRIKE IT RICH
ROBERT PAYNTER .... CINEMATOGRAPHER
CHRISTOPHER HOBBS .... PRODUCTION DESIGNER
TOM RAND .... COSTUME DESIGNER
THOMAS SCHWALM .... FILM EDITOR

STRIPES
BILL BUTLER .... CINEMATOGRAPHER
JAMES H. SPENCER .... PRODUCTION DESIGNER
RICHARD BRUNO .... COSTUME DESIGNER
EVA RUGGIERO .... FILM EDITOR
HARRY KELLER .... FILM EDITOR
MICHAEL LUCIANO .... FILM EDITOR

STRIPPED TO KILL
BRUCE STUBBLEFIELD .... FILM EDITOR
ZACH STAENBERG .... FILM EDITOR

STRIPPED TO KILL 2
STEPHEN MARK .... FILM EDITOR

STRIPPER
EDWARD LACHMAN .... CINEMATOGRAPHER

STRIPPER, THE
TRAVILLA .... COSTUME DESIGNER

STROKER ACE
NICK MCLEAN .... CINEMATOGRAPHER
PAUL PETERS .... PRODUCTION DESIGNER
NORMAN SALLING .... COSTUME DESIGNER
CARL KRESS .... FILM EDITOR
WILLIAM GORDEAN .... FILM EDITOR

STROSZEK
THOMAS MAUCH .... CINEMATOGRAPHER

STUCK ON YOU
LLOYD KAUFMAN .... CINEMATOGRAPHER
DARREN KLOOMOK .... FILM EDITOR
RALPH ROSENBLUM .... FILM EDITOR
RICHARD HAINES .... FILM EDITOR

STUD FARM, THE
LAJOS KOLTAI .... CINEMATOGRAPHER

STUD, THE
PETER HANNAN .... CINEMATOGRAPHER

STUDENT BODIES
ROBERT EBINGER .... CINEMATOGRAPHER
KATHRYN RUTH HOPE .... FILM EDITOR

STUDENT CONFIDENTIAL
DAVID WASCO .... PRODUCTION DESIGNER

STUDENT TEACHER, THE
STEPHEN M. KATZ .... CINEMATOGRAPHER

STUDIO 5B (PILOT)
STEVAN LARNER .... CINEMATOGRAPHER
LYNDA PARADISE .... PRODUCTION DESIGNER
HARVEY ROSENSTOCK .... FILM EDITOR

STUDS LONIGAN (MS)
JAN SCOTT .... PRODUCTION DESIGNER

STUFF, THE
PAUL GLICKMAN .... CINEMATOGRAPHER
TIM D'ARCY .... COSTUME DESIGNER
ARMAND LEBOWITZ .... FILM EDITOR

St-Su

CINEMATOGRAPHERS
PRODUCTION
DESIGNERS,
COSTUME
DESIGNERS and
FILM EDITORS
GUIDE

I
N
D
E
X

O
F

F
I
L
M

T
I
T
L
E
S

Su-Sw

CINEMATOGRAPHERS
PRODUCTION
DESIGNERS,
COSTUME
DESIGNERS and
FILM EDITORS
GUIDE

I
N
D
E
X

O
F

F
I
L
M

T
I
T
L
E
S

SUPERCARRIER (TF)
ROBERT STEADMAN .... CINEMATOGRAPHER

SUPERDAD
WILLIAM J. CREBER .... PRODUCTION DESIGNER

SUPERGIRL
ALAN HUME .... CINEMATOGRAPHER
RICHARD MACDONALD .... PRODUCTION DESIGNER
TERRY ACKLAND-SNOW .... PRODUCTION DESIGNER
MALCOLM COOKE .... FILM EDITOR

SUPERGIRL - THE MAKING OF THE MOVIE (TF)
PETER HOLLYWOOD .... FILM EDITOR

SUPERMAN
GEOFFREY UNSWORTH† .... CINEMATOGRAPHER
GENE RUDOLF .... PRODUCTION DESIGNER
JOHN BARRY† .... PRODUCTION DESIGNER
LESLIE DILLEY .... PRODUCTION DESIGNER
STUART BAIRD .... FILM EDITOR

SUPERMAN II
GEOFFREY UNSWORTH† .... CINEMATOGRAPHER
ROBERT PAYNTER .... CINEMATOGRAPHER
JOHN BARRY† .... PRODUCTION DESIGNER
MAURICE FOWLER .... PRODUCTION DESIGNER
PETER MURTON .... PRODUCTION DESIGNER
SUSAN YELLAND .... COSTUME DESIGNER
YVONNE BLAKE .... COSTUME DESIGNER
JOHN VICTOR SMITH .... FILM EDITOR
STUART BAIRD .... FILM EDITOR

SUPERMAN III
ROBERT PAYNTER .... CINEMATOGRAPHER
BERT DAVEY .... PRODUCTION DESIGNER
BRIAN ACKLAND-SNOW .... PRODUCTION DESIGNER
CHARLES BISHOP .... PRODUCTION DESIGNER
PETER MURTON .... PRODUCTION DESIGNER
TERRY ACKLAND-SNOW .... PRODUCTION DESIGNER
EVANGELINE HARRISON .... COSTUME DESIGNER
JOHN VICTOR SMITH .... FILM EDITOR
PETER HOLLYWOOD .... FILM EDITOR

SUPERMAN IV: THE QUEST FOR PEACE
ERNEST DAY .... CINEMATOGRAPHER
JOHN GRAYSMARK .... PRODUCTION DESIGNER
JOHN FENNER .... PRODUCTION DESIGNER
LESLIE TOMKINS .... PRODUCTION DESIGNER
JOHN BLOOMFIELD .... COSTUME DESIGNER
JOHN SHIRLEY .... FILM EDITOR

SUPERNATURALS, THE
PETER LYONS COLLISTER .... CINEMATOGRAPHER
GAIL VIOLA .... COSTUME DESIGNER

SUPERSTAR (FD)
BURLEIGH WARTES .... CINEMATOGRAPHER
CHUCK WORKMAN .... FILM EDITOR

SUPPORT YOUR LOCAL GUNFIGHTER
HARRY STRADLING, JR. .... CINEMATOGRAPHER

SUPPORT YOUR LOCAL SHERRIFF
HARRY STRADLING, JR. .... CINEMATOGRAPHER

SUPPOSE THEY GAVE A WAR AND NOBOBY CAME?
JACK POPLIN .... PRODUCTION DESIGNER
JOHN F. BURNETT .... FILM EDITOR

SUR
FELIX MONTI .... CINEMATOGRAPHER

SURE THING, THE
ROBERT ELSWIT .... CINEMATOGRAPHER
LILLY KILVERT .... PRODUCTION DESIGNER
DURINDA RICE WOOD .... COSTUME DESIGNER
ROBERT LEIGHTON .... FILM EDITOR

SURF II
ALEX PHILLIPS .... CINEMATOGRAPHER
JACQUELINE CAMBAS .... FILM EDITOR

SURF NAZIS MUST DIE
ROLF KESTERMANN .... CINEMATOGRAPHER

SURRENDER
JUAN RUIZ-ANCHIA .... CINEMATOGRAPHER
JON HUTMAN .... PRODUCTION DESIGNER
LILLY KILVERT .... PRODUCTION DESIGNER
BETSY HEIMANN .... COSTUME DESIGNER
WENDY BRICMONT .... FILM EDITOR

SURVIVAL GAME
AVRAHAM KARPICK .... CINEMATOGRAPHER
DIANA MORRIS .... PRODUCTION DESIGNER
CHARLES SIMMONS .... FILM EDITOR

SURVIVAL OF DANA (TF)
PETER W. WOOLEY .... PRODUCTION DESIGNER

SURVIVAL QUEST
DARYN OKADA .... CINEMATOGRAPHER
ANDREW SIEGEL .... PRODUCTION DESIGNER
CARLA GIBSON .... COSTUME DESIGNER
DON COSCARELLI .... FILM EDITOR

SURVIVAL RUN
ALEX PHILLIPS .... CINEMATOGRAPHER
CHRISTOPHER GREENBURY .... FILM EDITOR

SURVIVING (TF)
JOHN F. BURNETT .... FILM EDITOR

SURVIVOR, THE
JOHN SEALE .... CINEMATOGRAPHER

SURVIVORS, THE
BILLY WILLIAMS .... CINEMATOGRAPHER
GENE CALLAHAN .... PRODUCTION DESIGNER
JOHN JAY MOORE .... PRODUCTION DESIGNER
ANN ROTH .... COSTUME DESIGNER
RICHARD A. HARRIS .... FILM EDITOR

SUSPECT
BILLY WILLIAMS .... CINEMATOGRAPHER
STEVE SARDANIS .... PRODUCTION DESIGNER
STUART WURTZEL .... PRODUCTION DESIGNER
RITA RYACK .... COSTUME DESIGNER
RAY LOVEJOY .... FILM EDITOR

SUSPIRA
LUCIANO TOVOLI .... CINEMATOGRAPHER

SWALLOWS AND AMAZONS
SIMON HOLLAND .... PRODUCTION DESIGNER

SWAMP THING
ROBIN GOODWIN .... CINEMATOGRAPHER
DAVID NICHOLS .... PRODUCTION DESIGNER
ROBB WILSON KING .... PRODUCTION DESIGNER
RICHARD BRACKEN .... FILM EDITOR

SWAN SONG (TF)
STEPHEN BERGER .... PRODUCTION DESIGNER

SWANN IN LOVE
SVEN NYKVIST .... CINEMATOGRAPHER
FRANÇOISE BONNOT .... FILM EDITOR

SWARM, THE
FRED J. KOENEKAMP .... CINEMATOGRAPHER
STAN JOLLEY .... PRODUCTION DESIGNER
PAUL ZASTUPNEVICH .... COSTUME DESIGNER
HAROLD F. KRESS .... FILM EDITOR

SWASHBUCKLER
PHILIP LATHROP .... CINEMATOGRAPHER
JOHN ROBERT LLOYD .... PRODUCTION DESIGNER
EDWARD A. BIERY .... FILM EDITOR

SWEE' PEA
SERGIO MONTANARI .... FILM EDITOR

SWEET DREAMS
ROBBIE GREENBERG .... CINEMATOGRAPHER
ALBERT BRENNER .... PRODUCTION DESIGNER
DAVID M. HABER .... PRODUCTION DESIGNER
ANN ROTH .... COSTUME DESIGNER
MALCOLM COOKE .... FILM EDITOR

SWEET HEART'S DANCE
TAK FUJIMOTO .... CINEMATOGRAPHER
JAMES ALLEN .... PRODUCTION DESIGNER
BOBBIE READ .... COSTUME DESIGNER
ROBERT FLORIO .... FILM EDITOR

SWEET HOURS
TEO ESCAMILLA .... CINEMATOGRAPHER

SWEET LIBERTY
FRANK TIDY .... CINEMATOGRAPHER
BEN EDWARDS .... PRODUCTION DESIGNER
CHRISTOPHER NOWAK .... PRODUCTION DESIGNER
JANE GREENWOOD .... COSTUME DESIGNER
MICHAEL ECONOMOU .... FILM EDITOR

SWEET LORRAINE
RENE OHASHI .... CINEMATOGRAPHER
DAVID GROPMAN .... PRODUCTION DESIGNER
CYNTHIA FLYNT .... COSTUME DESIGNER
LAURENCE SOLOMON .... FILM EDITOR

SWEET REVENGE
VILMOS ZSIGMOND .... CINEMATOGRAPHER
WILLIAM KENNEY .... PRODUCTION DESIGNER
EVAN LOTTMAN .... FILM EDITOR
MICHAEL S. MURPHY .... FILM EDITOR
RICHARD FETTERMAN .... FILM EDITOR

SWEET RIDE, THE
JACK MARTIN SMITH .... PRODUCTION DESIGNER

SWEET WILLIAM
LES YOUNG .... CINEMATOGRAPHER
EILEEN DISS .... PRODUCTION DESIGNER
PETER COULSON .... FILM EDITOR

SWIM SUIT
LASZLO GEORGE .... CINEMATOGRAPHER

SWIMMING TO CAMBODIA
JOHN BAILEY .... CINEMATOGRAPHER
SANDY MCLEOD .... PRODUCTION DESIGNER
CAROL LITTLETON .... FILM EDITOR

SWIMSUIT (TF)
MICHAEL ERLERE .... PRODUCTION DESIGNER
DAVID ROSENBLOOM .... FILM EDITOR

SWINDLE, THE
PIERRE-WILLIAM GLENN .... CINEMATOGRAPHER

SWING SHIFT
TAK FUJIMOTO .... CINEMATOGRAPHER
PETER JAMISON .... PRODUCTION DESIGNER
ROBERT W. (BO) WELCH .... PRODUCTION DESIGNER
JOE I. TOMPKINS .... COSTUME DESIGNER
CRAIG MC KAY .... FILM EDITOR

SWINGING CHEERLEADERS, THE
ALFRED TAYLOR .... CINEMATOGRAPHER

SWISS FAMILY ROBINSON
HARRY WAXMAN .... CINEMATOGRAPHER

SWITCH
DICK BUSH .... CINEMATOGRAPHER
RODGER MAUS .... PRODUCTION DESIGNER
ELLEN MIROJNICK .... COSTUME DESIGNER
ROBERT PERGAMENT .... FILM EDITOR

SWITCHBLADE SISTERS
STEPHEN M. KATZ .... CINEMATOGRAPHER
BEALA B. NEEL .... PRODUCTION DESIGNER

SWITCHING CHANNELS
FRANÇOIS PROTAT .... CINEMATOGRAPHER
ANNE PRITCHARD .... PRODUCTION DESIGNER
CHARLES DUNLOP .... PRODUCTION DESIGNER
MARY E. MCLEOD .... COSTUME DESIGNER
THOM NOBLE .... FILM EDITOR

SWORD AND THE SORCERER, THE
JOSEPH MANGINE .... CINEMATOGRAPHER
GEORGE COSTELLO .... PRODUCTION DESIGNER
MARSHALL HARVEY .... FILM EDITOR

SWORD OF GIDEON (CTF)
CLAUDE AGOSTINI .... CINEMATOGRAPHER
TREVOR WILLIAMS .... PRODUCTION DESIGNER

SWORD OF HEAVEN
GIL HUBBS .... CINEMATOGRAPHER

SWORD OF THE BARBARIANS, THE
GIANCARLO FERRANDO .... CINEMATOGRAPHER

SWORD OF THE VALIANT
MAURICE FOWLER .... PRODUCTION DESIGNER
SHUNA HARWOOD .... COSTUME DESIGNER
BARRY PETERS .... FILM EDITOR
RICHARD MARDEN .... FILM EDITOR

SWORDKILL
MAC AHLBERG .... CINEMATOGRAPHER
PAMELA B. WARNER .... PRODUCTION DESIGNER
ROBERT HOWLAND .... PRODUCTION DESIGNER
BRAD ARENSMAN .... FILM EDITOR

SWORDS OF HEAVEN
WARREN CHADWICK .... FILM EDITOR

SYLVESTER
HIRO NARITA .... CINEMATOGRAPHER
JAMES WILLIAM NEWPORT .... PRODUCTION DESIGNER
SHARON DAY-NYE .... COSTUME DESIGNER
DAVID GARFIELD .... FILM EDITOR
HOWARD SMITH .... FILM EDITOR
SUZANNE PETTIT .... FILM EDITOR

SYLVIA
GARY HANSEN .... PRODUCTION DESIGNER
ANNE MCKAY .... COSTUME DESIGNER
MICHAEL HORTON .... FILM EDITOR

SYNGENOR
JAMES MATHERS .... CINEMATOGRAPHER
R. CLIFFORD SEARCY .... PRODUCTION DESIGNER
RHONA MEYERS .... COSTUME DESIGNER
ELLEN KENESHEA .... FILM EDITOR

T

T. R. BASKIN
GERALD HIRSCHFELD .... CINEMATOGRAPHER
ALBERT BRENNER .... PRODUCTION DESIGNER
MAURY WINETROBE .... FILM EDITOR

TABLE FOR FIVE
VILMOS ZSIGMOND .... CINEMATOGRAPHER
NORMAN NEWBERRY .... PRODUCTION DESIGNER
ROBERT F. BOYLE .... PRODUCTION DESIGNER
VICKI SANCHEZ .... COSTUME DESIGNER
BRUCE GREEN .... FILM EDITOR
MICHAEL KAHN .... FILM EDITOR

TADPOLE AND THE WHALE, THE
THOMAS BURSTYN .... CINEMATOGRAPHER
HELENE GIRARD .... FILM EDITOR

TAG
WILLY KURANT .... CINEMATOGRAPHER
TOM WALLS .... FILM EDITOR

TAGGET (CTF)
BILLY DICKSON .... CINEMATOGRAPHER
DEAN MITZNER .... PRODUCTION DESIGNER
RALPH E. WINTERS .... FILM EDITOR
ROBERT HYAMS .... FILM EDITOR

TAI-PAN
JACK CARDIFF .... CINEMATOGRAPHER
ANTHONY MASTERS .... PRODUCTION DESIGNER
BENJAMIN FERNANDEZ .... PRODUCTION DESIGNER
PIERLUIGI BASILE .... PRODUCTION DESIGNER
JOHN BLOOMFIELD .... COSTUME DESIGNER
ANTONY GIBBS .... FILM EDITOR

TAIL GUNNER JOE (TF)
RIC WAITE .... CINEMATOGRAPHER

TAKE A HARD RIDE
STANFORD C. ALLEN .... FILM EDITOR

TAKE DOWN
REED SMOOT .... CINEMATOGRAPHER
DOUGLAS G. JOHNSON .... PRODUCTION DESIGNER
RICHARD FETTERMAN .... FILM EDITOR

TAKE MY DAUGHTERS, PLEASE (TF)
SHELLEY KOMAROV .... COSTUME DESIGNER
MICHAEL S. MURPHY .... FILM EDITOR

TAKE THE MONEY AND RUN
FRED HARPMAN .... PRODUCTION DESIGNER

Sw-Ta

**CINEMATOGRAPHERS
PRODUCTION
DESIGNERS,
COSTUME
DESIGNERS** AND
**FILM EDITORS
GUIDE**

I
N
D
E
X

O
F

F
I
L
M

T
I
T
L
E
S

Ta-Ta

CINEMATOGRAPHERS
PRODUCTION
DESIGNERS,
COSTUME
DESIGNERS AND
FILM EDITORS
GUIDE

I
N
D
E
X

O
F

F
I
L
M

T
I
T
L
E
S

TEA AND THE HAREM
DOMINIQUE CHAPUIS .... CINEMATOGRAPHER

TEA IN THE HAREM
KENOUT PELTIER .... FILM EDITOR

TEACHER, THE
NORM WALLERSTEIN .... FILM EDITOR

TEACHERS
DAVID M. WALSH .... CINEMATOGRAPHER
RICHARD MACDONALD .... PRODUCTION DESIGNER
RUTH MYERS .... COSTUME DESIGNER
DON ZIMMERMAN .... FILM EDITOR

TEARAWAY
KEVIN HAYWARD .... CINEMATOGRAPHER
MICHAEL HACKING .... FILM EDITOR

TEARS IN THE RAIN (CTF)
KEN WESTBURY .... CINEMATOGRAPHER
ANN HOLLOWOOD .... COSTUME DESIGNER

TED KENNEDY, JR. STORY, THE (TF)
ALAN PATILLO .... FILM EDITOR

TEDDY BEAR HABIT, THE
BILL GROOM .... PRODUCTION DESIGNER
CYNTHIA SCHEIDER .... FILM EDITOR

TEEN WITCH
STEPHEN RICE .... PRODUCTION DESIGNER

TEEN WOLF
TIM SUHRSTEDT .... CINEMATOGRAPHER
CHESTER KACZENSKI .... PRODUCTION DESIGNER
LOIS FREEMAN-FOX .... FILM EDITOR

TEEN WOLF TOO
JULES BRENNER .... CINEMATOGRAPHER
PEG MCCLELLAN .... PRODUCTION DESIGNER
HEIDI M. KACZENSKI .... COSTUME DESIGNER
KIM SECRIST .... FILM EDITOR
HARVEY ROSENSTOCK .... FILM EDITOR
RAJA GOSNELL .... FILM EDITOR
STEVEN POLIVKA .... FILM EDITOR

TEENAGE DOLL
ROBERT KINOSHITA .... PRODUCTION DESIGNER

TEENAGE MUTANT NINJA TURTLES
JOHN FENNER .... CINEMATOGRAPHER
ROY FORGE SMITH .... PRODUCTION DESIGNER
JOHN M. HAY .... COSTUME DESIGNER
JAMES SYMONS .... FILM EDITOR
SALLY MENKE .... FILM EDITOR
WILLIAM GORDEAN .... FILM EDITOR

TELEFON
MICHAEL C. BUTLER .... CINEMATOGRAPHER
TED HAWORTH .... PRODUCTION DESIGNER
WILLIAM F. O'BRIEN .... PRODUCTION DESIGNER
JANE ROBINSON .... COSTUME DESIGNER
LUSTER BAYLESS .... COSTUME DESIGNER
DOUGLAS STEWART .... FILM EDITOR

TELEPHONE, THE
DAVID CLAESSEN .... CINEMATOGRAPHER
JIM POHL .... PRODUCTION DESIGNER
SANDRA ADAIR .... FILM EDITOR

TELL IT LIKE IT IS, BOYS
MIKAEL SALOMON .... CINEMATOGRAPHER

TELL ME A RIDDLE
FRED MURPHY .... CINEMATOGRAPHER
PATRIZIA VON BRANDENSTEIN .... PRODUCTION DESIGNER
SUZANNE PETTIT .... FILM EDITOR

TELL THEM WILLIE BOY IS HERE
CONRAD HALL .... CINEMATOGRAPHER

TEMPEST
DONALD MCALPINE .... CINEMATOGRAPHER
PATO GUZMAN .... PRODUCTION DESIGNER
PAUL EADS .... PRODUCTION DESIGNER
ALBERT WOLSKY .... COSTUME DESIGNER
DONN CAMBERN .... FILM EDITOR

TEMPEST, THE
PETER MIDDLETON .... CINEMATOGRAPHER
LESLEY WALKER .... FILM EDITOR

TENSPEED AND BROWN SHOE (TF)
STEPHEN BERGER .... PRODUCTION DESIGNER

TENANT, THE
FRANÇOISE BONNOT .... FILM EDITOR
SVEN NYKVIST .... CINEMATOGRAPHER

TENDER IS THE NIGHT (CMS)
KEN WESTBURY .... CINEMATOGRAPHER

TENDER MERCIES
RUSSELL BOYD .... CINEMATOGRAPHER
JEANNINE CLAUDIA OPPEWALL .... PRODUCTION DESIGNER
WILLIAM M. ANDERSON .... FILM EDITOR

TENDER, THE
THEO VAN DE SANDE .... CINEMATOGRAPHER
DAVID BRISBIN .... PRODUCTION DESIGNER

TENTH MAN, THE
MICHAEL STRINGER .... PRODUCTION DESIGNER

TENTH MAN, THE (TF)
ALAN HUME .... CINEMATOGRAPHER
MILLIE MOORE .... FILM EDITOR

TEQUILA SUNRISE
CONRAD HALL .... CINEMATOGRAPHER
PETER LANDSDOWN SMITH .... PRODUCTION DESIGNER
RICHARD SYLBERT .... PRODUCTION DESIGNER
JULIE WEISS .... COSTUME DESIGNER
CLAIRE SIMPSON-CROZIER .... FILM EDITOR

TERMINAL BLISS
GREGORY SMITH .... CINEMATOGRAPHER
CATHERINE TIRR .... PRODUCTION DESIGNER
BRUCE SINOFSKY .... FILM EDITOR

TERMINAL CHOICE
PATTI UNGER .... COSTUME DESIGNER

TERMINAL ENTRY
JAMES L. CARTER .... CINEMATOGRAPHER

TERMINAL FORCE
STEPHEN ASHLEY BLAKE .... CINEMATOGRAPHER
TED TUNNEY .... PRODUCTION DESIGNER
JILL CONNER .... COSTUME DESIGNER
WILLIAM SHAFFER .... FILM EDITOR

TERMINAL MAN, THE
RICHARD H. KLINE .... CINEMATOGRAPHER
FRED HARPMAN .... PRODUCTION DESIGNER
NINO NOVARESSE .... COSTUME DESIGNER
ROBERT L. WOLFE .... FILM EDITOR

TERMINATOR, THE
ADAM GREENBERG .... CINEMATOGRAPHER
GEORGE COSTELLO .... PRODUCTION DESIGNER
HILARY WRIGHT .... COSTUME DESIGNER
MARK GOLDBLATT .... FILM EDITOR

TERMS OF ENDEARMENT
ANDRZEJ BARTKOWIAK .... CINEMATOGRAPHER
HAROLD MICHELSON .... PRODUCTION DESIGNER
POLLY PLATT .... PRODUCTION DESIGNER
KRISTI ZEA .... COSTUME DESIGNER
RICHARD MARKS .... FILM EDITOR

TERROR
LES YOUNG .... CINEMATOGRAPHER

TERROR AMONG US (TF)
ROBERT B. HAUSER .... CINEMATOGRAPHER
NORM BARON .... PRODUCTION DESIGNER

TERROR AT LONDON BRIDGE (TF)
GIL HUBBS .... CINEMATOGRAPHER

TERROR IN THE AISLES (FD)
JOHN A. ALONZO .... CINEMATOGRAPHER

TERROR ON HIGHWAY 91 (TF)
BRIAN WEST .... CINEMATOGRAPHER
GREGORY BOLTON .... PRODUCTION DESIGNER

Te-Te

CINEMATOGRAPHERS
PRODUCTION
DESIGNERS,
COSTUME
DESIGNERS and
FILM EDITORS
GUIDE

I
N
D
E
X

O
F

F
I
L
M

T
I
T
L
E
S

Te-Th

CINEMATOGRAPHERS
PRODUCTION
DESIGNERS,
COSTUME
DESIGNERS AND
FILM EDITORS
GUIDE

I
N
D
E
X

O
F

F
I
L
M

T
I
T
L
E
S

Th-Th

CINEMATOGRAPHERS
PRODUCTION
DESIGNERS,
COSTUME
DESIGNERS AND
FILM EDITORS
GUIDE

I
N
D
E
X

O
F

F
I
L
M

T
I
T
L
E
S

CINEMATOGRAPHERS
PRODUCTION
DESIGNERS,
COSTUME
DESIGNERS AND
FILM EDITORS
GUIDE

INDEX

OF

FILM

TITLES

448

THRASHIN'
CHUCK COLWELL ....CINEMATOGRAPHER
CATHERINE HARDWICKE ....PRODUCTION DESIGNER
NICHOLAS C. SMITH ....FILM EDITOR

THREAT, THE
PIERRE-WILLIAM GLENN ......................................CINEMATOGRAPHER

THREE AMIGOS
RONALD W. BROWNE ....CINEMATOGRAPHER
RICHARD SAWYER ....PRODUCTION DESIGNER
DEBORAH NADOOLMAN ....COSTUME DESIGNER
MALCOLM CAMPBELL ....FILM EDITOR

THREE BAD MEN IN A HIDDEN FORTRESS
SHINOBU MURAKI ....PRODUCTION DESIGNER
YOSHIRO MURAKI ....PRODUCTION DESIGNER

THREE BROTHERS
PASQUALINO DE SANTIS ......................................CINEMATOGRAPHER
RUGGERO MASTROIANNI ....FILM EDITOR

THREE COINS IN THE FOUNTAIN
JOHN DE CUIR ....PRODUCTION DESIGNER

THREE DAYS OF THE CONDOR
OWEN ROIZMAN ....CINEMATOGRAPHER

THREE FOR THE ROAD
STEPHEN L. POSEY ....CINEMATOGRAPHER
LINDA ALLEN ....PRODUCTION DESIGNER
HILARY WRIGHT ....COSTUME DESIGNER
CHRISTOPHER GREENBURY ....FILM EDITOR

THREE FROM HAPARANDA
MIKAEL SALOMON ....CINEMATOGRAPHER

THREE FUGITIVES
HASKELL WEXLER ....CINEMATOGRAPHER
MARJORIE STONE MCSHIRLEY ....PRODUCTION DESIGNER
RICHARD CARTER ....PRODUCTION DESIGNER
APRIL FERRY ....COSTUME DESIGNER
BRUCE GREEN ....FILM EDITOR

THREE IN THE ATTIC
JACQUES MARQUETTE ....CINEMATOGRAPHER
WILLIAM J. CREBER ....PRODUCTION DESIGNER

THREE INTO TWO WON'T GO
RUTH MYERS ....COSTUME DESIGNER

THREE KINDS OF HEAT
TERRY COLE ....CINEMATOGRAPHER
ROBERT DEARBERG ....FILM EDITOR

THREE KINGS, THE (TF)
WARD PRESTON ....PRODUCTION DESIGNER
BOB BRING ....FILM EDITOR

THREE MEN AND A BABY
ADAM GREENBERG ....CINEMATOGRAPHER
DAN YARHI ....PRODUCTION DESIGNER
PETER S. LARKIN ....PRODUCTION DESIGNER
LARRY WELLS ....COSTUME DESIGNER
MICHAEL A. STEVENSON ....FILM EDITOR

THREE MEN AND A LITTLE LADY
ADAM GREENBERG ....CINEMATOGRAPHER
STUART WURTZEL ....PRODUCTION DESIGNER
LOUISE FROGLEY ....COSTUME DESIGNER
MICHAEL A. STEVENSON ....FILM EDITOR

THREE MOTHERS
GABRIELLA PESCUCCI ....COSTUME DESIGNER

THREE MUSKETEERS, THE
DAVID WATKIN ....CINEMATOGRAPHER
BRIAN EATWELL ....PRODUCTION DESIGNER

THREE O'CLOCK HIGH
BARRY SONNENFELD ....CINEMATOGRAPHER
WILLIAM F. MATTHEWS ....PRODUCTION DESIGNER
JANE RUHM ....COSTUME DESIGNER
JOE ANN FOGLE ....FILM EDITOR

THREE ON A DATE (TF)
MICHAEL BAUGH ....PRODUCTION DESIGNER

THREE SISTERS (TF)
LEONARD J. SOUTH ....CINEMATOGRAPHER

THREE SISTERS, THE
GEOFFREY UNSWORTH† ......................................CINEMATOGRAPHER

THREE SOVEREIGNS FOR SARAH (TF)
LARRY PIZER ....CINEMATOGRAPHER

THREE THE HARD WAY
ROBERT E. SWINK ....FILM EDITOR

THREE WARRIORS
BRUCE SURTEES ....CINEMATOGRAPHER
BONNIE KOEHLER ....FILM EDITOR

THREE WISHES OF BILLY GRIER, THE (TF)
FRANK STANLEY ....CINEMATOGRAPHER

THREE'S A MATCH (TF)
MICHAEL Z. HANAN ....PRODUCTION DESIGNER

THREESOME (TF)
MIKAEL SALOMON ....CINEMATOGRAPHER
ADAM HOLENDER ....CINEMATOGRAPHER

THRESHOLD
MICHEL BRAULT ....CINEMATOGRAPHER
ANNE PRITCHARD ....PRODUCTION DESIGNER
SUSAN MARTIN ....FILM EDITOR

THRILLER STORY
PIERRE-WILLIAM GLENN ......................................CINEMATOGRAPHER

THRONE OF BLOOD
SHINOBU MURAKI ....PRODUCTION DESIGNER
YOSHIRO MURAKI ....PRODUCTION DESIGNER

THROUGH NAKED EYES (TF)
JACK L. RICHARDS ....CINEMATOGRAPHER

THROW MOMMA FROM THE TRAIN
BARRY SONNENFELD ....CINEMATOGRAPHER
IDA RANDOM ....PRODUCTION DESIGNER
WILLIAM A. ELLIOT ....PRODUCTION DESIGNER
MARILYN VANCE-STRAKER ....COSTUME DESIGNER
MICHAEL JABLOW ....FILM EDITOR

THUMBTRIPPING
HARRY STRADLING, JR. ....CINEMATOGRAPHER

THUNDER ALLEY
KAREN GROSSMAN ....CINEMATOGRAPHER
JOSEPH T. GARRITY ....PRODUCTION DESIGNER
PATRICK TAGLIAFERRO ....PRODUCTION DESIGNER
DOROTHY BACA ....COSTUME DESIGNER
DAN WETHERBEE ....FILM EDITOR

THUNDER AND LIGHTNING
JAMES PERGOLA ....CINEMATOGRAPHER
ANTHONY REDMAN ....FILM EDITOR

THUNDER RUN
HARVEY GENKINS ....CINEMATOGRAPHER
BURTON LEE HARRY ....FILM EDITOR

THUNDERBALL
TED MOORE ....CINEMATOGRAPHER
KEN ADAM ....PRODUCTION DESIGNER
PETER MURTON ....PRODUCTION DESIGNER

THUNDERBOLT AND LIGHTFOOT
FERRIS WEBSTER ....FILM EDITOR

THURSDAY'S CHILD (TF)
CHARLES F. WHEELER ....CINEMATOGRAPHER

THX 1138
MICHAEL D. HALLER ....PRODUCTION DESIGNER

THY KINGDOM COME...THY WILL BE DONE (FD)
CURTIS CLARK ....CINEMATOGRAPHER
MACDONALD BROWN ....FILM EDITOR

TICKET TO HEAVEN
RICHARD LEITERMAN ....CINEMATOGRAPHER
SUSAN LONGMIRE ....PRODUCTION DESIGNER
LYNDA KEMP ....COSTUME DESIGNER
RON WISMAN ....FILM EDITOR

TIE ME UP! TIE ME DOWN!
JOSE LUIS ALCAINE ....CINEMATOGRAPHER
JOSE MARIA COSSIO ....COSTUME DESIGNER
JOSE SALCEDO ....FILM EDITOR

Ti-To

CINEMATOGRAPHERS
PRODUCTION
DESIGNERS,
COSTUME
DESIGNERS AND
FILM EDITORS
GUIDE

I
N
D
E
X

O
F

F
I
L
M

T
I
T
L
E
S

CINEMATOGRAPHERS
PRODUCTION
DESIGNERS,
COSTUME
DESIGNERS and
FILM EDITORS
GUIDE

I
N
D
E
X

O
F

F
I
L
M

T
I
T
L
E
S

Tr-Tr

CINEMATOGRAPHERS
PRODUCTION
DESIGNERS,
COSTUME
DESIGNERS AND
FILM EDITORS
GUIDE

I
N
D
E
X

O
F

F
I
L
M

T
I
T
L
E
S

TRUST
MICHAEL SPILLER .... CINEMATOGRAPHER
DANIEL OUELLETTE .... PRODUCTION DESIGNER
NICK GOMEZ .... FILM EDITOR

TRUST ME
THOMAS JEWETT .... CINEMATOGRAPHER
BARRY ZETLIN .... FILM EDITOR

TUCKER: A MAN AND HIS DREAM
VITTORIO STORARO .... CINEMATOGRAPHER
ALEX TAVOULARIS .... PRODUCTION DESIGNER
DEAN TAVOULARIS .... PRODUCTION DESIGNER
PRISCILLA ANNE NEDD .... FILM EDITOR
JUDIANNA MAKOVSKY .... COSTUME DESIGNER
MILENA CANONERO .... COSTUME DESIGNER

TUESDAY NIGHT IN MEMPHIS
ROBBY MULLER .... CINEMATOGRAPHER

TUFF TURF
WILLY KURANT .... CINEMATOGRAPHER
CRAIG STEARNS .... PRODUCTION DESIGNER
KATHIE CLARK .... COSTUME DESIGNER
MARC GROSSMAN .... FILM EDITOR

TULIPS
FRANCOIS PROTAT .... CINEMATOGRAPHER
TED WATKINS .... PRODUCTION DESIGNER
ALAN COLLINS .... FILM EDITOR
DAVID GARFIELD .... FILM EDITOR
YURI LUHOVY .... FILM EDITOR

TUMMY TROUBLE (ANIMATED SHORT)
DONALD W. ERNST .... FILM EDITOR

TUNE IN TOMORROW...
ROBERT STEVENS .... CINEMATOGRAPHER
JIM CLAY .... PRODUCTION DESIGNER
BETSY HEIMAN .... COSTUME DESIGNER
PETER BOYLE .... FILM EDITOR

TUNNEL UNDER THE WALL (CD)
STANFORD SINGER .... FILM EDITOR

TURK 182
REGINALD H. MORRIS .... CINEMATOGRAPHER
HARRY POTTLE .... PRODUCTION DESIGNER
PAUL EADS .... PRODUCTION DESIGNER
LINDA WAYNE .... COSTUME DESIGNER
STAN COLE .... FILM EDITOR

TURKISH DELIGHT
JAN DE BONT .... CINEMATOGRAPHER

TURNER & HOOCH
ADAM GREENBERG .... CINEMATOGRAPHER
JOHN DE CUIR JR. .... PRODUCTION DESIGNER
SIG TINGLOF .... PRODUCTION DESIGNER
ERIC H. SANDBERG .... COSTUME DESIGNER
GARTH CRAVEN .... FILM EDITOR

TURNING POINT, THE
ROBERT SURTEES† .... CINEMATOGRAPHER
ALBERT BRENNER .... PRODUCTION DESIGNER
ALBERT WOLSKY .... COSTUME DESIGNER
TONY FASO .... COSTUME DESIGNER
WILLIAM REYNOLDS .... FILM EDITOR

TURTLE DIARY
PETER HANNAN .... CINEMATOGRAPHER
LEO AUSTIN .... PRODUCTION DESIGNER
LIZ WALLER .... COSTUME DESIGNER
PETER TANNER .... FILM EDITOR

TWELVE CHAIRS, THE
RUTH MYERS .... COSTUME DESIGNER
ALAN HEIM .... FILM EDITOR

TWENTY-ONE
KEITH GODDARD .... CINEMATOGRAPHER
ROGER MURRAY-LEACH .... PRODUCTION DESIGNER
SUSANNAH BUXTON .... COSTUME DESIGNER
DAVID SPIERS .... FILM EDITOR

TWICE DEAD
STEPHEN RICE .... PRODUCTION DESIGNER

TWICE IN A LIFETIME
NICK MCLEAN .... CINEMATOGRAPHER
WILLIAM J. CREBER .... PRODUCTION DESIGNER
BERNIE POLLACK .... COSTUME DESIGNER
ERICA EDELL PHILLIPS .... COSTUME DESIGNER
EDWARD A. WARSCHILKA .... FILM EDITOR
ROBERT C. JONES .... FILM EDITOR

TWILIGHT TIME
TOMISLAV PINTER .... CINEMATOGRAPHER

TWILIGHT ZONE - THE MOVIE
ALLEN DAVIAU .... CINEMATOGRAPHER
JOHN HORA .... CINEMATOGRAPHER
STEVAN LARNER .... CINEMATOGRAPHER
JAMES D. BISSELL .... PRODUCTION DESIGNER
JAMES H. SPENCER .... PRODUCTION DESIGNER
RICHARD SAWYER .... PRODUCTION DESIGNER
DEBORAH NADOOLMAN .... COSTUME DESIGNER
HOWARD SMITH .... FILM EDITOR
MALCOLM CAMPBELL .... FILM EDITOR
MICHAEL KAHN .... FILM EDITOR
TINA HIRSCH .... FILM EDITOR

TWILIGHT'S LAST GLEAMING
ROBERT B. HAUSER .... CINEMATOGRAPHER
ROLF ZEHETBAUER .... PRODUCTION DESIGNER
TOM DAWSON .... COSTUME DESIGNER
IRVING C. ROSENBLUM .... FILM EDITOR
MAURY WINETROBE .... FILM EDITOR
MICHAEL LUCIANO .... FILM EDITOR

TWIN PEAKS (TF)
FRANK BYERS .... CINEMATOGRAPHER
RICHARD HOOVER .... PRODUCTION DESIGNER
SARA MARKOWITZ .... COSTUME DESIGNER
DUWAYNE DUNHAM .... FILM EDITOR

TWINS
ANDRZEJ BARTKOWIAK .... CINEMATOGRAPHER
JAMES D. BISSELL .... PRODUCTION DESIGNER
GLORIA GRESHAM .... COSTUME DESIGNER
DONN CAMBERN .... FILM EDITOR
SHELDON KAHN .... FILM EDITOR

TWINS OF EVIL
DICK BUSH .... CINEMATOGRAPHER

TWIRL (TF)
GIL HUBBS .... CINEMATOGRAPHER

TWIST AND SHOUT
JAN WEINCKE .... CINEMATOGRAPHER
JANUS BILLESKOV JANSEN .... FILM EDITOR

TWISTED JUSTICE
DAVID HUE .... CINEMATOGRAPHER
DIAN SKINNER .... PRODUCTION DESIGNER
KEVIN ACKERMAN .... COSTUME DESIGNER
GREGORY SCHORER .... FILM EDITOR

TWISTED NERVE
HARRY WAXMAN .... CINEMATOGRAPHER

TWISTED OBSESSION
JOSE LUIS ALCAINE .... CINEMATOGRAPHER
PIERRE-LOUIS THEVENET .... PRODUCTION DESIGNER
CARMEN FRIAS .... FILM EDITOR
IVETTE FRANK .... COSTUME DESIGNER

TWISTER
RENATO BERTA .... CINEMATOGRAPHER
CAROL WOOD .... COSTUME DESIGNER
ROBERTO SILVI .... FILM EDITOR

TWO ENGLISH GIRLS
NESTOR ALMENDROS .... CINEMATOGRAPHER

TWO FATHERS' JUSTICE (TF)
JOSEPH T. GARRITY .... PRODUCTION DESIGNER

TWO FOR THE MONEY
DAVID INSLEY .... CINEMATOGRAPHER
VINCENT PERANIO .... PRODUCTION DESIGNER

TWO GENTLEMEN SHARING
BILLY WILLIAMS .... CINEMATOGRAPHER

Tr-Tw

CINEMATOGRAPHERS
PRODUCTION
DESIGNERS,
COSTUME
DESIGNERS AND
FILM EDITORS
GUIDE

INDEX OF FILM TITLES

Tw-Un

CINEMATOGRAPHERS
PRODUCTION
DESIGNERS,
COSTUME
DESIGNERS AND
FILM EDITORS
GUIDE

I
N
D
E
X

O
F

F
I
L
M

T
I
T
L
E
S

454

TWO JAKES, THE
VILMOS ZSIGMOND .... CINEMATOGRAPHER
RICHARD SAWYER .... PRODUCTION DESIGNER
JEREMY RAILTON .... PRODUCTION DESIGNER
RICHARD SAWYER .... PRODUCTION DESIGNER
WAYNE A. FINKELMAN .... COSTUME DESIGNER
ANNE GOURSAUD .... FILM EDITOR

TWO JAKES, THE
VILMOS ZSIGMOND .... CINEMATOGRAPHER
WAYNE FINKELMAN .... COSTUME DESIGNER
ANNE GOURSAUD .... FILM EDITOR

TWO MOON JUNCTION
MARK PLUMMER .... CINEMATOGRAPHER
MICHELLE MINCH .... PRODUCTION DESIGNER
MARIA MANCUSO .... COSTUME DESIGNER
MARC GROSSMAN .... FILM EDITOR

TWO MRS. GRENVILLES, THE (TF)
MALCOLM MIDDLETON .... PRODUCTION DESIGNER
HERBERT WESTBROOK .... PRODUCTION DESIGNER
NOLAN MILLER .... COSTUME DESIGNER
SUSAN YELLAND .... COSTUME DESIGNER
DONALD BROOKS .... COSTUME DESIGNER

TWO MULES FOR SISTER SARA
ROBERT F. SHUGRUE .... FILM EDITOR

TWO OF A KIND
FRED J. KOENEKAMP .... CINEMATOGRAPHER
ALBERT BRENNER .... PRODUCTION DESIGNER
SPENCER DEVERILL .... PRODUCTION DESIGNER
JACK HOFSTRA .... FILM EDITOR

TWO PEOPLE
HAROLD MICHELSON .... PRODUCTION DESIGNER

TWO SOLITUDES
RENE VERZIER .... CINEMATOGRAPHER

TWO WORLDS OF ANGELITA, THE
AFFONSO BEATO .... CINEMATOGRAPHER
SUZANNE FENN .... FILM EDITOR

TWO-MINUTE WARNING
GERALD HIRSCHFELD .... CINEMATOGRAPHER
HERMAN A. BLUMENTHAL .... PRODUCTION DESIGNER
EVE NEWMAN .... FILM EDITOR
WALTER HANNEMAN .... FILM EDITOR

U

U2: RATTLE AND HUM
JORDAN CRONENWETH .... CINEMATOGRAPHER
ROBERT BRINKMANN .... CINEMATOGRAPHER
PHIL JOANOU .... FILM EDITOR

UFORIA
DAVID MYERS .... CINEMATOGRAPHER
WILLIAM MALLEY .... PRODUCTION DESIGNER
BETSY HEIMANN .... COSTUME DESIGNER
DENNIS M. HILL .... FILM EDITOR

UHF
DAVID LEWIS .... CINEMATOGRAPHER
WARD PRESTON .... PRODUCTION DESIGNER
TOM MCKINLEY .... COSTUME DESIGNER
DENNIS O'CONNOR .... FILM EDITOR

ULTIMATE THRILL, THE
ISIDORE MANKOFSKY .... CINEMATOGRAPHER

UMBRELLA WOMAN, THE
JOHN SCOTT .... FILM EDITOR

UNAPPROACHABLE, THE
JAN SCHLUBACH .... PRODUCTION DESIGNER

UNBEARABLE LIGHTNESS OF BEING, THE
SVEN NYKVIST .... CINEMATOGRAPHER
PIERRE GUFFROY .... PRODUCTION DESIGNER
ANN ROTH .... COSTUME DESIGNER
B.J. SEARS .... FILM EDITOR
STEPHEN A. ROTTER .... FILM EDITOR
VIVIEN HILLGROVE GILLIAM .... FILM EDITOR
WALTER MURCH .... FILM EDITOR

UNCLE BUCK
RALF D. BODE .... CINEMATOGRAPHER
JOHN W. CORSO .... PRODUCTION DESIGNER
MARILYN VANCE-STRAKER .... COSTUME DESIGNER
LOU LOMBARDO .... FILM EDITOR

UNCLE JOE SHANNON
BILL BUTLER .... CINEMATOGRAPHER
WILLIAM KENNEY .... PRODUCTION DESIGNER
BOBBIE MANNIX .... COSTUME DESIGNER
DON ZIMMERMAN .... FILM EDITOR

UNCLE TOM'S CABIN (CTF)
JOSEPH T. GARRITY .... PRODUCTION DESIGNER

UNCOMMON VALOR
RIC WAITE .... CINEMATOGRAPHER
STEPHEN H. BURUM .... CINEMATOGRAPHER
JACK G. TAYLOR .... PRODUCTION DESIGNER
JAMES SCHOPPE .... PRODUCTION DESIGNER
MARK MELNICK .... FILM EDITOR

UNCONQUERED (TF)
BUZZ BRANDT .... FILM EDITOR

UNDER CAPRICORN
JACK CARDIFF .... CINEMATOGRAPHER

UNDER COVER
BECKY BLOCK .... PRODUCTION DESIGNER
ERNEST MISKO .... COSTUME DESIGNER

UNDER COVER (TF)
THOMAS OLGEIRSON .... CINEMATOGRAPHER
JAMES WILLIAM NEWPORT .... PRODUCTION DESIGNER
DAVID SIMMONS .... FILM EDITOR

UNDER FIRE
JOHN ALCOTT† .... CINEMATOGRAPHER
AUGUSTIN ITUARTE .... PRODUCTION DESIGNER
TOBY CARR RAFELSON .... PRODUCTION DESIGNER
JOHN BLOOM .... FILM EDITOR
MARK CONTE .... FILM EDITOR

UNDER GROUND
HASKELL WEXLER .... CINEMATOGRAPHER

UNDER SATAN'S SON
WILLY KURANT .... CINEMATOGRAPHER

UNDER SIEGE (TF)
PETER STEIN .... CINEMATOGRAPHER
STEPHEN MARSH .... PRODUCTION DESIGNER

UNDER SUSPICION
BRUNO NUYTTEN .... CINEMATOGRAPHER
ALBERT JURGENSON .... FILM EDITOR

UNDER THE BILTMORE CLOCK
JANE MUSKY .... PRODUCTION DESIGNER

UNDER THE BOARDWALK
DON BURGESS .... CINEMATOGRAPHER
MAXINE SHEPARD .... PRODUCTION DESIGNER
DANIEL GROSS .... FILM EDITOR

UNDER THE CHERRY MOON
MICHAEL BALLHAUS .... CINEMATOGRAPHER
RICHARD SYLBERT .... PRODUCTION DESIGNER
MARIE FRANCE .... COSTUME DESIGNER
EVA GARDOS .... FILM EDITOR

UNDER THE GUN
GARY THIELTGES .... CINEMATOGRAPHER

UNDER THE INFLUENCE (TF)
ERICA EDELL PHILLIPS .... COSTUME DESIGNER

UNDER THE RAINBOW
FRANK STANLEY .... CINEMATOGRAPHER
JOEL SCHILLER .... PRODUCTION DESIGNER
PETER W. WOOLEY .... PRODUCTION DESIGNER
MIKE BUTLER .... COSTUME DESIGNER
DAVID BLEWITT .... FILM EDITOR

UNDER THE VOLCANO
GABRIEL FIGUEROA .... CINEMATOGRAPHER
JOSE RODRIGUEZ GRANADA .... PRODUCTION DESIGNER
ANGELA DODSON .... COSTUME DESIGNER
ROBERTO SILVI .... FILM EDITOR

UNDERCOVER
ALEXANDER GRUSZYNSKI .... CINEMATOGRAPHER
SHARYN L. ROSS .... FILM EDITOR

UNDERGRADS, THE (CTF)
LASZLO GEORGE .... CINEMATOGRAPHER
RON WISMAN .... FILM EDITOR

UNDERGROUND ACES
DANIEL LOMINO .... PRODUCTION DESIGNER
ARGYLE NELSON .... FILM EDITOR

UNDERGROUND TERROR
KEITH L. REAMER .... FILM EDITOR

UNE SEMAINE DE VACANCES
PIERRE-WILLIAM GLENN .... CINEMATOGRAPHER

UNFAIR EXCHANGES (TF)
ANGUS NEWTON .... FILM EDITOR

UNFAITHFULLY YOURS
DAVID M. WALSH .... CINEMATOGRAPHER
ALBERT BRENNER .... PRODUCTION DESIGNER
KRISTI ZEA .... COSTUME DESIGNER
SHELDON KAHN .... FILM EDITOR

UNFINISHED BUSINESS (TF)
GAYNE RESCHER .... CINEMATOGRAPHER

UNHEARD MUSIC, THE (FD)
CARI COUGHLIN .... FILM EDITOR
CURTISS CLAYTON .... FILM EDITOR
KENT BEYDA .... FILM EDITOR

UNHOLY ROLLERS
BARBARA POKRAS .... FILM EDITOR

UNHOLY, THE
HENRY VARGAS .... CINEMATOGRAPHER
BEVERLY SAFIER .... COSTUME DESIGNER
CHRIS CIBELLI .... FILM EDITOR
MARK MELNICK .... FILM EDITOR

UNIDENTIFIED FLYING ODDBALL, THE
PAUL BEESON .... CINEMATOGRAPHER
PETER BOITA .... FILM EDITOR

UNION CITY
EDWARD LACHMAN .... CINEMATOGRAPHER

UNKNOWN GOD, THE
TEO ESCAMILLA .... CINEMATOGRAPHER

UNMARRIED WOMAN, AN
ARTHUR ORNITZ† .... CINEMATOGRAPHER
PATO GUZMAN .... PRODUCTION DESIGNER
ALBERT WOLSKY .... COSTUME DESIGNER
STUART H. PAPPE .... FILM EDITOR

UNNAMEABLE, THE
TOM FRASER .... CINEMATOGRAPHER

UNSANE
LUCIANO TOVOLI .... CINEMATOGRAPHER
FRANCO FRATICELLI .... FILM EDITOR

UNSEEN, THE
DENA ROTH .... PRODUCTION DESIGNER
JONATHAN BRAUN .... FILM EDITOR

UNSINKABLE MOLLY BROWN, THE
FREDRIC STEINKAMP .... FILM EDITOR

UNSUB (PILOT)
FRANCIS KENNEY .... CINEMATOGRAPHER
STEPHEN GEAGHAN .... PRODUCTION DESIGNER

UNSUITABLE JOB FOR A WOMAN, AN
ANTON FURST .... PRODUCTION DESIGNER
MARIT ALLEN .... COSTUME DESIGNER

UNTIL SEPTEMBER
PHILIPPE WELT .... CINEMATOGRAPHER
HILTON MCCONNICO .... PRODUCTION DESIGNER
SEAN BARTON .... FILM EDITOR

UNTOUCHABLES, THE
STEPHEN H. BURUM .... CINEMATOGRAPHER
PATRIZIA VON BRANDENSTEIN .... PRODUCTION DESIGNER
WILLIAM A. ELLIOTT .... PRODUCTION DESIGNER
RICHARD BRUNO .... COSTUME DESIGNER
MARILYN VANCE-STRAKER .... COSTUME DESIGNER
BILL PANKOW .... FILM EDITOR
GERALD B. GREENBERG .... FILM EDITOR

UP IN SMOKE
GENE POLITO .... CINEMATOGRAPHER
LEON ERICKSON .... PRODUCTION DESIGNER
ERNEST MISKO .... COSTUME DESIGNER
DENNIS M. HILL .... FILM EDITOR
LOU LOMBARDO .... FILM EDITOR
SCOTT CONRAD .... FILM EDITOR

UP THE ACADEMY
PETER W. WOOLEY .... PRODUCTION DESIGNER
BUD MOLIN .... FILM EDITOR

UP THE CREEK
JAMES M. GLENNON .... CINEMATOGRAPHER
DANIEL MC CAULEY .... PRODUCTION DESIGNER
STEPHEN MARSH .... PRODUCTION DESIGNER
WILILAM HINEY .... PRODUCTION DESIGNER
ROBERT TURTURICE .... COSTUME DESIGNER
WILLIAM BUTLER .... FILM EDITOR

UP THE SANDBOX
GORDON WILLIS .... CINEMATOGRAPHER
HARRY HORNER .... PRODUCTION DESIGNER
ROBERT LAWRENCE .... FILM EDITOR

UP YOUR ALLEY
TOM SIITER .... FILM EDITOR

UPHILL ALL THE WAY
ROLAND OZZIE SMITH .... CINEMATOGRAPHER
CHUCK WEISS .... FILM EDITOR

UPS & DOWNS
PETER BENISON .... CINEMATOGRAPHER

UPTOWN SATURDAY NIGHT
ALFRED SWEENEY .... PRODUCTION DESIGNER

URANIUM CONSPIRACY, THE
ADAM GREENBERG .... CINEMATOGRAPHER
DOV HOENIG .... FILM EDITOR

URBAN COWBOY
REYNALDO VILLALOBOS .... CINEMATOGRAPHER
STEPHEN GRIMES† .... PRODUCTION DESIGNER
W. STEWART CAMPBELL .... PRODUCTION DESIGNER
DAVID RAWLINS .... FILM EDITOR

USED CARS
DONALD M. MORGAN .... CINEMATOGRAPHER
PETER JAMISON .... PRODUCTION DESIGNER
MICHAEL KAHN .... FILM EDITOR

UTILITIES
RICHARD LEITERMAN .... CINEMATOGRAPHER
WILLIAM BEETON .... PRODUCTION DESIGNER
JOHN KELLY .... FILM EDITOR

V

V - THE FINAL BATTLE (TF)
STEVAN LARNER .... CINEMATOGRAPHER
MORT RABINOWITZ .... PRODUCTION DESIGNER

VACATION IN HELL, A
ANN LAMBERT .... COSTUME DESIGNER

VAGABOND
PATRICK BLOSSIER .... CINEMATOGRAPHER
AGNES VARDA .... FILM EDITOR

VALDEZ IS COMING
JOEL SCHILLER .... PRODUCTION DESIGNER

VALENTINA
JUAN RUIZ-ANCHIA .... CINEMATOGRAPHER

Un-Va

CINEMATOGRAPHERS
PRODUCTION
DESIGNERS,
COSTUME
DESIGNERS AND
FILM EDITORS
GUIDE

INDEX OF FILM TITLES

Va-Vi

CINEMATOGRAPHERS
PRODUCTION
DESIGNERS,
COSTUME
DESIGNERS AND
FILM EDITORS
GUIDE

I
N
D
E
X

O
F

F
I
L
M

T
I
T
L
E
S

Vi-Wa

CINEMATOGRAPHERS
PRODUCTION
DESIGNERS,
COSTUME
DESIGNERS AND
FILM EDITORS
GUIDE

I
N
D
E
X

O
F

F
I
L
M

T
I
T
L
E
S

Wa-Wa

CINEMATOGRAPHERS
PRODUCTION
DESIGNERS,
COSTUME
DESIGNERS AND
FILM EDITORS
GUIDE

I
N
D
E
X

O
F

F
I
L
M

T
I
T
L
E
S

WALKER
DAVID BRIDGES .... CINEMATOGRAPHER
BRUNO RUBEO .... PRODUCTION DESIGNER
J. RAE FOX .... PRODUCTION DESIGNER
PAM TAIT .... COSTUME DESIGNER
THEDA DERAMUS .... COSTUME DESIGNER
ALEX COX .... FILM EDITOR
CARLOS PUENTE .... FILM EDITOR

WALKING TALL
JOSEPH ALTADONNA .... PRODUCTION DESIGNER
PHILIP JEFFRIES .... PRODUCTION DESIGNER

WALKING THE EDGE
WARREN CHADWICK .... FILM EDITOR

WALL STREET
ROBERT RICHARDSON .... CINEMATOGRAPHER
HILDA STARK .... PRODUCTION DESIGNER
JOHN JAY MOORE .... PRODUCTION DESIGNER
STEPHEN HENDRICKSON .... PRODUCTION DESIGNER
ELLEN MIROJNICK .... COSTUME DESIGNER
CLAIRE SIMPSON-CROZIER .... FILM EDITOR

WALLENBERG: A HERO'S STORY (TF)
CHARLES CORRELL .... CINEMATOGRAPHER

WALTER AND JUNE
CHRIS MENGES .... CINEMATOGRAPHER
MICK AUDSLEY .... FILM EDITOR

WALTZ ACROSS TEXAS
ROBERT ELSWIT .... CINEMATOGRAPHER
SANDRA DAVIDSON .... COSTUME DESIGNER

WANDA NEVADA
MICHAEL C. BUTLER .... CINEMATOGRAPHER
LYNDA PARADISE .... PRODUCTION DESIGNER
SCOTT CONRAD .... FILM EDITOR

WANDERERS, THE
MICHAEL CHAPMAN .... CINEMATOGRAPHER
JOHN JAY MOORE .... PRODUCTION DESIGNER
ROBERT DE MORA .... COSTUME DESIGNER
RONALD ROOSE .... FILM EDITOR
STUART H. PAPPE .... FILM EDITOR

WANTED DEAD OR ALIVE
ALEX NEPOMNIASCHY .... CINEMATOGRAPHER
PAUL EADS .... PRODUCTION DESIGNER
ROSS ALBERT .... FILM EDITOR

WAR AND LOVE
ADAM GREENBERG .... CINEMATOGRAPHER
PETER ZINNER .... FILM EDITOR

WAR AND PEACE
JACK CARDIFF .... CINEMATOGRAPHER
THOMAS MAUCH .... CINEMATOGRAPHER

WAR AND REMEMBRANCE (MS)
ALAN TOMKINS .... PRODUCTION DESIGNER
GUY COMTOIS .... PRODUCTION DESIGNER
NORM BARON .... PRODUCTION DESIGNER
WILLIAM CRUISE .... PRODUCTION DESIGNER
JOHN F. BURNETT .... FILM EDITOR
PETER ZINNER .... FILM EDITOR

WAR GAME, THE
PETER SUSCHITZKY .... CINEMATOGRAPHER

WAR GAMES
ANGELO GRAHAM .... PRODUCTION DESIGNER

WAR LORD, THE
HENRY BUMSTEAD .... PRODUCTION DESIGNER

WAR OF CHILDREN, A (TF)
SIMON HOLLAND .... PRODUCTION DESIGNER
CHRISTOPHER HOLMES .... FILM EDITOR
ERIC BOYD-PERKINS .... FILM EDITOR

WAR OF THE ROSES, THE
STEPHEN H. BURUM .... CINEMATOGRAPHER
IDA RANDOM .... PRODUCTION DESIGNER
MARK MANSBRIDGE .... PRODUCTION DESIGNER
GLORIA GRESHAM .... COSTUME DESIGNER
LYNZEE KLINGMAN .... FILM EDITOR

WAR OF THE WORLDS (PILOT)
VICKI GRAEF .... COSTUME DESIGNER

WAR PARTY
BRIAN TUFANO .... CINEMATOGRAPHER
MICHAEL BINGHAM .... PRODUCTION DESIGNER
KATHRYN MORRISON .... COSTUME DESIGNER
SEAN BARTON .... FILM EDITOR

WARGAMES
WILLIAM A. FRAKER .... CINEMATOGRAPHER
JAMES J. MURAKAMI .... PRODUCTION DESIGNER
TOM ROLF .... FILM EDITOR

WARLOCK
DAVID EGGBY .... CINEMATOGRAPHER
ROY FORGE SMITH .... PRODUCTION DESIGNER
LOUISE FROGLEY .... COSTUME DESIGNER
DAVID FINFER .... FILM EDITOR
JOHN W. HOLMES .... FILM EDITOR

WARLORDS OF ATLANTIS
ALAN HUME .... CINEMATOGRAPHER
ELLIOT SCOTT .... PRODUCTION DESIGNER
BILL BLUNDEN .... FILM EDITOR
JOHN BLOOM .... FILM EDITOR

WARLORDS OF THE 21ST CENTURY
CHRIS MENGES .... CINEMATOGRAPHER
MICHAEL HORTON .... FILM EDITOR

WARM DECEMBER, A
PEMBROKE J. HERRING .... FILM EDITOR

WARM HANDS, COLD FEET (TF)
BRYAN RYMAN .... PRODUCTION DESIGNER

WARM NIGHTS ON A SLOW MOVING TRAIN
TRACY WATT .... PRODUCTION DESIGNER

WARNING SIGN
DEAN CUNDEY .... CINEMATOGRAPHER
HENRY BUMSTEAD .... PRODUCTION DESIGNER
AGGIE GUERARD RODGERS .... COSTUME DESIGNER
ROBERT LAWRENCE .... FILM EDITOR

WARRIOR AND THE SORCERESS, THE
LEONARD SOLIS .... CINEMATOGRAPHER
MARY BERTRAM .... COSTUME DESIGNER
SILVIA RIPOLL .... FILM EDITOR

WARRIOR OF THE LOST WORLD
GIANCARLO FERRANDO .... CINEMATOGRAPHER
ANTONELLO GELENG .... PRODUCTION DESIGNER
CESARE D'AMICO .... FILM EDITOR

WARRIORS, THE
ANDREW LASZLO .... CINEMATOGRAPHER
BOBBIE MANNIX .... COSTUME DESIGNER
DAVID HOLDEN .... FILM EDITOR

WASH, THE
WALT LLOYD .... CINEMATOGRAPHER
DAVID WASCO .... PRODUCTION DESIGNER
JAY FREUND .... FILM EDITOR

WASN'T THAT A TIME!
TOM D. HURWITZ .... CINEMATOGRAPHER
PAUL BARNES .... FILM EDITOR

WATCHER IN THE WOODS, THE
ALAN HUME .... CINEMATOGRAPHER
ALAN CASSIE .... PRODUCTION DESIGNER
ELLIOT SCOTT .... PRODUCTION DESIGNER
GEOFFREY FOOT .... FILM EDITOR

WATCHERS
RICHARD LEITERMAN .... CINEMATOGRAPHER
RICHARD WILCOX .... PRODUCTION DESIGNER
MONIQUE STRANAN .... COSTUME DESIGNER
BILL FREDA .... FILM EDITOR
CAROLLE ALAIN .... FILM EDITOR

WATCHING (TF)
DEREK HYDE .... COSTUME DESIGNER

WATER
DOUGLAS SLOCOMBE .... CINEMATOGRAPHER
KEITH PAIN .... PRODUCTION DESIGNER
NORMAN GARWOOD .... PRODUCTION DESIGNER
JAMES ACHESON .... COSTUME DESIGNER
JOHN VICTOR SMITH .... FILM EDITOR

Wa-Wh

CINEMATOGRAPHERS
PRODUCTION
DESIGNERS,
COSTUME
DESIGNERS AND
FILM EDITORS
GUIDE

I
N
D
E
X

O
F

F
I
L
M

T
I
T
L
E
S

Wh-Wh

CINEMATOGRAPHERS
PRODUCTION
DESIGNERS,
COSTUME
DESIGNERS AND
FILM EDITORS
GUIDE

I
N
D
E
X

O
F

F
I
L
M

T
I
T
L
E
S

460

CINEMATOGRAPHERS
PRODUCTION
DESIGNERS,
COSTUME
DESIGNERS AND
FILM EDITORS
GUIDE

WHISPERERS, THE
RAYMOND SIMM .... PRODUCTION DESIGNER

WHISPERS
PETER BENISON .... CINEMATOGRAPHER
CHARLES DUNLOP .... PRODUCTION DESIGNER
MARY MCLEOD .... COSTUME DESIGNER
JACQUES JEAN .... FILM EDITOR

WHISTLE BLOWER, THE
FRED TAMMES .... CINEMATOGRAPHER
MORLEY SMITH .... PRODUCTION DESIGNER
RAYMOND HUGHES .... COSTUME DESIGNER
BOB MORGAN .... FILM EDITOR

WHISTLE DOWN THE WIND
RAYMOND SIMM .... PRODUCTION DESIGNER

WHITE BUFFALO, THE
PAUL LOHMANN .... CINEMATOGRAPHER
TAMBI LARSEN .... PRODUCTION DESIGNER
MICHAEL F. ANDERSON .... FILM EDITOR

WHITE DAWN, THE
MICHAEL CHAPMAN .... CINEMATOGRAPHER
DOUGLAS STEWART .... FILM EDITOR

WHITE DOG
BRUCE SURTEES .... CINEMATOGRAPHER
BRIAN EATWELL .... PRODUCTION DESIGNER

WHITE ELEPHANT
TOM D. HURWITZ .... CINEMATOGRAPHER

WHITE FANG
TONY PIERCE-ROBERTS .... CINEMATOGRAPHER
MICHAEL BOLTON .... PRODUCTION DESIGNER
LISA DAY .... FILM EDITOR

WHITE GIRL, THE
JOSEPH M. WILCOTS .... CINEMATOGRAPHER
PAUL SIMMONS .... COSTUME DESIGNER
TONY VIGNA .... FILM EDITOR

WHITE HUNTER, BLACK HEART
JACK N. GREEN .... CINEMATOGRAPHER
JOHN GRAYSMARK .... PRODUCTION DESIGNER
JOHN MOLLO .... COSTUME DESIGNER
JOEL COX .... FILM EDITOR

WHITE KNIGHTS
DAVID WATKIN .... CINEMATOGRAPHER

WHITE LIGHTNING
GEORGE JAY NICHOLSON .... FILM EDITOR

WHITE LINE FEVER
FRED J. KOENEKAMP .... CINEMATOGRAPHER
SYDNEY Z. LITWAK .... PRODUCTION DESIGNER

WHITE LIONS, THE (TF)
ROBERT JESSUP .... CINEMATOGRAPHER

WHITE MISCHIEF
ROGER DEAKINS .... CINEMATOGRAPHER
LEN HUNTINGFORD .... PRODUCTION DESIGNER
ROGER HALL .... PRODUCTION DESIGNER
MARIT ALLEN .... COSTUME DESIGNER
TOM PRIESTLEY .... FILM EDITOR

WHITE NIGHTS
AUSTEN SPRIGGS .... PRODUCTION DESIGNER
MALCOLM MIDDLETON .... PRODUCTION DESIGNER
PHILIP HARRISON .... PRODUCTION DESIGNER
RICHARD DAWKING .... PRODUCTION DESIGNER
EVANGELINE HARRISON .... COSTUME DESIGNER
FREDRIC STEINKAMP .... FILM EDITOR
WILLIAM STEINKAMP .... FILM EDITOR

WHITE OF THE EYE
LARRY MCCONKEY .... CINEMATOGRAPHER
TERRY RAWLINGS .... FILM EDITOR

WHITE PALACE
LAJOS KOLTAI .... CINEMATOGRAPHER
JEANNINE C. OPPEWALL .... PRODUCTION DESIGNER
LISA JENSEN .... COSTUME DESIGNER
CAROL LITTLETON .... FILM EDITOR

WHITE ROCK
ARTHUR WOOSTER .... CINEMATOGRAPHER

WHITE ROCK (FD)
HARVEY HARRISON .... CINEMATOGRAPHER

WHITE ROOM
PAUL SAROSSY .... CINEMATOGRAPHER
VALANNE RIDGEWAY .... PRODUCTION DESIGNER

WHITE WATER SUMMER
JEFFREY L. GOLDSTEIN .... PRODUCTION DESIGNER
DAVID RAY .... FILM EDITOR

WHO DARES WINS
SYD CAIN .... PRODUCTION DESIGNER
PETER DAVIES .... FILM EDITOR

WHO FRAMED ROGER RABBIT
DEAN CUNDEY .... CINEMATOGRAPHER
ELLIOT SCOTT .... PRODUCTION DESIGNER
ROGER CAIN .... PRODUCTION DESIGNER
WILLIAM MCALLISTER .... PRODUCTION DESIGNER
JOANNA JOHNSTON .... COSTUME DESIGNER
ARTHUR SCHMIDT .... FILM EDITOR

WHO GETS THE FRIENDS? (TF)
BRADFORD MAY .... CINEMATOGRAPHER
CYNTHIA BALES .... COSTUME DESIGNER
JOANNE D'ANTONIO .... FILM EDITOR

WHO HAS SEEN THE WIND
RICHARD LEITERMAN .... CINEMATOGRAPHER
ANNE PRITCHARD .... PRODUCTION DESIGNER

WHO IS HARRY KELLERMAN AND WHY IS HE SAYING ALL THOSE TERRIBLE THINGS ABOUT ME?
VICTOR J. KEMPER .... CINEMATOGRAPHER
HARRY HORNER .... PRODUCTION DESIGNER
BARRY MALKIN .... FILM EDITOR

WHO IS KILLING THE GREAT CHEFS OF EUROPE?
JOHN ALCOTT† .... CINEMATOGRAPHER
WERNER ACHMAN .... PRODUCTION DESIGNER
JUDY MOORCROFT .... COSTUME DESIGNER
THOM NOBLE .... FILM EDITOR

WHO IS THE BLACK DAHLIA? (TF)
JAMES G. HULSEY .... PRODUCTION DESIGNER

WHO WAS THAT LADY?
TED HAWORTH .... PRODUCTION DESIGNER

WHO WILL LOVE MY CHILDREN? (TF)
THOMAS DEL RUTH .... CINEMATOGRAPHER
JAMES G. HULSEY .... PRODUCTION DESIGNER

WHO'LL STOP THE RAIN
RICHARD H. KLINE .... CINEMATOGRAPHER
WILLIAM WARE THEISS .... COSTUME DESIGNER
JOHN BLOOM .... FILM EDITOR

WHO'S AFRAID OF VIRGINIA WOOLF?
HASKELL WEXLER .... CINEMATOGRAPHER
RICHARD SYLBERT .... PRODUCTION DESIGNER
IRENE SHARAFF .... COSTUME DESIGNER
SAM O'STEEN .... FILM EDITOR

WHO'S HARRY CRUMB?
STEPHEN M. KATZ .... CINEMATOGRAPHER
TREVOR WILLIAMS .... PRODUCTION DESIGNER
JERRY R. ALLEN .... COSTUME DESIGNER
DANFORD B. GREENE .... FILM EDITOR

WHO'S THAT GIRL?
JAN DE BONT .... CINEMATOGRAPHER
DONALD B. WOODRUFF .... PRODUCTION DESIGNER
IDA RANDOM .... PRODUCTION DESIGNER
DEBORAH L. SCOTT .... COSTUME DESIGNER
PEMBROKE J. HERRING .... FILM EDITOR

WHOLLY MOSES!
FRANK STANLEY .... CINEMATOGRAPHER
DALE HENNESY† .... PRODUCTION DESIGNER
SIDNEY LEVIN .... FILM EDITOR

WHOOPEE BOYS, THE
CHARLES ROSEN .... PRODUCTION DESIGNER
PATRICIA NORRIS .... COSTUME DESIGNER
ERIC JENKINS .... FILM EDITOR

WHORE
AMIR MOKRI .... CINEMATOGRAPHER
RICHARD LEWIS .... PRODUCTION DESIGNER
LEONARD POLLACK .... COSTUME DESIGNER

Wh-Wi

CINEMATOGRAPHERS
PRODUCTION
DESIGNERS,
COSTUME
DESIGNERS and
FILM EDITORS
GUIDE

I
N
D
E
X

O
F

F
I
L
M

T
I
T
L
E
S

WILLOW

ADRIAN BIDDLE	CINEMATOGRAPHER
ALLAN CAMERON	PRODUCTION DESIGNER
ANTHONY READING	PRODUCTION DESIGNER
MALCOLM STONE	PRODUCTION DESIGNER
TIM HUTCHINSON	PRODUCTION DESIGNER
BARBARA LANE	COSTUME DESIGNER
DANIEL P. HANLEY	FILM EDITOR
MICHAEL J. HILL	FILM EDITOR

WILLY WONKA'S CHOCOLATE FACTORY

ARTHUR IBBETSON	CINEMATOGRAPHER

WILT

NORMAN LANGLEY	CINEMATOGRAPHER
LEO AUSTIN	PRODUCTION DESIGNER
LIZ WALLER	COSTUME DESIGNER
CHRIS BLUNDEN	FILM EDITOR

WIMPS

LARRY REVENE	CINEMATOGRAPHER

WIN, PLACE OR STEAL

MARTIN BRAM	FILM EDITOR

WIND AND THE LION, THE

BILLY WILLIAMS	CINEMATOGRAPHER
RICHARD E. LA MOTTE	COSTUME DESIGNER
ROBERT L. WOLFE	FILM EDITOR

WINDOWS

GORDON WILLIS	CINEMATOGRAPHER
MEL BOURNE	PRODUCTION DESIGNER
BARRY MALKIN	FILM EDITOR

WINDRIDER

JOHN SCOTT	FILM EDITOR

WINDS OF KITTY HAWK, THE (TF)

SYDNEY Z. LITWAK	PRODUCTION DESIGNER

WINDS OF WAR, THE (MS)

STEVAN LARNER	CINEMATOGRAPHER
CHARLES CORRELL	CINEMATOGRAPHER
JACKSON DE GOVIA	PRODUCTION DESIGNER
JOHN F. BURNETT	FILM EDITOR

WINDWALKER

REED SMOOT	CINEMATOGRAPHER
JANICE HAMPTON	FILM EDITOR

WINDY CITY

REYNALDO VILLALOBOS	CINEMATOGRAPHER
WILLIAM KENNEY	PRODUCTION DESIGNER
CLIFFORD JONES	FILM EDITOR

WINNER NEVER QUITS, A (TF)

MICHAEL A. STEVENSON	FILM EDITOR

WINNIE (TF)

PAUL H. GOLDSMITH	CINEMATOGRAPHER
JOSAN F. RUSSO	PRODUCTION DESIGNER
JAMES OLIVER	FILM EDITOR

WINNING

RICHARD MOORE	CINEMATOGRAPHER

WINSTON CHURCHILL - THE WILDERNESS YEARS (MS)

LESLEY WALKER	FILM EDITOR

WINTER FLIGHT

CHRIS MENGES	CINEMATOGRAPHER
ADRIENNE ATKINSON	PRODUCTION DESIGNER
SUSAN YELLAND	COSTUME DESIGNER

WINTER KILLS

VILMOS ZSIGMOND	CINEMATOGRAPHER
NORMAN NEWBERRY	PRODUCTION DESIGNER
ROBERT F. BOYLE	PRODUCTION DESIGNER
ROBERT DE MORA	COSTUME DESIGNER
DAVID BRETHERTON	FILM EDITOR

WINTER OF OUR DISCONTENT, THE (TF)

ROBBIE GREENBERG	CINEMATOGRAPHER

WINTER OF OUR DREAMS

HENRY DANGAR	FILM EDITOR

WINTER PEOPLE

FRANÇOIS PROTAT	CINEMATOGRAPHER
CHAS. BUTCHER	PRODUCTION DESIGNER
RONALD KENT FOREMAN	PRODUCTION DESIGNER
RUTH MORLEY	COSTUME DESIGNER
THOM NOBLE	FILM EDITOR

WINTER TAN, A

JOHN WALKER	CINEMATOGRAPHER
SUSAN MARTIN	FILM EDITOR

WINTER'S FLIGHT

LESLEY WALKER	FILM EDITOR

WINTERHAWK

TOM BOUTROSS	FILM EDITOR

WIRED

TONY IMI	CINEMATOGRAPHER
BRIAN EATWELL	PRODUCTION DESIGNER
SHARI FELDMAN	COSTUME DESIGNER
ERIC SEARS	FILM EDITOR

WIRED TO KILL

TOM FRASER	CINEMATOGRAPHER

WISDOM

ADAM GREENBERG	CINEMATOGRAPHER
DENNIS GASSNER	PRODUCTION DESIGNER
MICHAEL KAHN	FILM EDITOR

WISE BLOOD

GERRY FISHER	CINEMATOGRAPHER
ROBERTO SILVI	FILM EDITOR

WISE GUYS

FRED SCHULER	CINEMATOGRAPHER
EDWARD PISONI	PRODUCTION DESIGNER
PAUL EADS	PRODUCTION DESIGNER
RICHARD BRUNO	COSTUME DESIGNER
GERALD B. GREENBERG	FILM EDITOR

WISEGUY (TF)

TOM PRIESTLY, JR.	CINEMATOGRAPHER
MARK HARRINGTON	PRODUCTION DESIGNER
GENE RANNEY	FILM EDITOR
HOWARD TERRILL	FILM EDITOR

WISH YOU WERE HERE

IAN WILSON	CINEMATOGRAPHER
CAROLYN AMIES	PRODUCTION DESIGNER
SHUNA HARWOOD	COSTUME DESIGNER
GEORGE AKERS	FILM EDITOR

WITCHBOARD

ROY H. WAGNER	CINEMATOGRAPHER
SARAH BURDICK	PRODUCTION DESIGNER
MERRILL GREENE	COSTUME DESIGNER
DANIEL DUNCAN	FILM EDITOR

WITCHERY

LORENZO BATTAGLIA	CINEMATOGRAPHER

WITCHES OF EASTWICK, THE

VILMOS ZSIGMOND	CINEMATOGRAPHER
MARK MANSBRIDGE	PRODUCTION DESIGNER
AGGIE GUERARD RODGERS	COSTUME DESIGNER
HUBERT DE LA BOULLERIE	FILM EDITOR
RICHARD FRANCIS-BRUCE	FILM EDITOR

WITCHES, THE

HARVEY HARRISON	CINEMATOGRAPHER

WITHNAIL AND I

PETER HANNAN	CINEMATOGRAPHER
MICHAEL PICKWOAD	PRODUCTION DESIGNER
ANDREA GALER	COSTUME DESIGNER
ALAN STRACHAN	FILM EDITOR

WITHOUT A CLUE

ALAN HUME	CINEMATOGRAPHER
BRIAN ACKLAND-SNOW	PRODUCTION DESIGNER
MARTYN HEBERT	PRODUCTION DESIGNER
TERRY ACKLAND-SNOW	PRODUCTION DESIGNER
JUDY MOORCROFT	COSTUME DESIGNER
PETER TANNER	FILM EDITOR

Wi-Wo

CINEMATOGRAPHERS
PRODUCTION
DESIGNERS,
COSTUME
DESIGNERS AND
FILM EDITORS
GUIDE

I
N
D
E
X

O
F

F
I
L
M

T
I
T
L
E
S

WITHOUT A TRACE
JOHN BAILEY .... CINEMATOGRAPHER
GREGORY BOLTON .... PRODUCTION DESIGNER
PAUL SYLBERT .... PRODUCTION DESIGNER
GLORIA GRESHAM .... COSTUME DESIGNER
CYNTHIA SCHEIDER .... FILM EDITOR

WITHOUT WARNING
DEAN CUNDEY .... CINEMATOGRAPHER

WITNESS
JOHN SEALE .... CINEMATOGRAPHER
STAN JOLLEY .... PRODUCTION DESIGNER
SHARI FELDMAN .... COSTUME DESIGNER
THOM NOBLE .... FILM EDITOR

WITNESS FOR THE PROSECUTION
ARTHUR IBBETSON .... CINEMATOGRAPHER

WITNESS TO A KILLING
DARYN OKADA .... CINEMATOGRAPHER

WITNESS, THE
MARIT ALLEN .... COSTUME DESIGNER

WIZ, THE
OSWALD MORRIS .... CINEMATOGRAPHER
PHILIP ROSENBERG .... PRODUCTION DESIGNER
TONY WALTON .... PRODUCTION DESIGNER
TONY WALTON .... COSTUME DESIGNER
DEDE ALLEN .... FILM EDITOR

WIZARD OF LONELINESS, THE
RICHARD BOWEN .... CINEMATOGRAPHER
JEFFREY BEECROFT .... PRODUCTION DESIGNER
STEPHANIE MASLANSKY .... COSTUME DESIGNER
LISA DAY .... FILM EDITOR

WIZARD, THE (PILOT)
JIM MILLER .... FILM EDITOR

WIZARDS (AF)
DONALD W. ERNST .... FILM EDITOR

WIZARDS OF THE LOST KINGDOM
LEONARD SOLIS .... CINEMATOGRAPHER

WOLF AT THE DOOR, THE
MIKAEL SALOMON .... CINEMATOGRAPHER
ANDRE GUERIN .... PRODUCTION DESIGNER
CHARLOTTE CLASON .... COSTUME DESIGNER
JANUS BILLESKOV JANSEN .... FILM EDITOR

WOLF LAKE
ALEX PHILLIPS .... CINEMATOGRAPHER
AUGUSTIN ITUARTE .... PRODUCTION DESIGNER

WOLFEN
GERRY FISHER .... CINEMATOGRAPHER
DAVID CHAPMAN .... PRODUCTION DESIGNER
PAUL SYLBERT .... PRODUCTION DESIGNER
JOHN BOXER .... COSTUME DESIGNER
CHRIS LEBENZON .... FILM EDITOR
DENNIS DOLAN .... FILM EDITOR
MARTIN BRAM .... FILM EDITOR

WOMAN CALLED GOLDA, A (TF)
ROBERT F. SHUGRUE .... FILM EDITOR

WOMAN IN FLAMES, A
JURGEN JURGES .... CINEMATOGRAPHER

WOMAN IN RED, THE
FRED SCHULER .... CINEMATOGRAPHER
DAVID L. SNYDER .... PRODUCTION DESIGNER
RUTH MYERS .... COSTUME DESIGNER
CHRISTOPHER GREENBURY .... FILM EDITOR

WOMAN IN THE ROOM, THE
JUAN RUIZ-ANCHIA .... CINEMATOGRAPHER

WOMAN INSIDE, THE
JOHN DUFFY .... FILM EDITOR

WOMAN NEXT DOOR, THE
MARTINE BARRAQUE .... FILM EDITOR

WOMAN OF SUBSTANCE, A (MS)
JANE ROBINSON .... COSTUME DESIGNER

WOMBLING FREE
ALAN HUME .... CINEMATOGRAPHER
PETER TANNER .... FILM EDITOR

WOMEN AT WEST POINT (TF)
SOL NEGRIN .... CINEMATOGRAPHER

WOMEN IN CAGES
BARBARA POKRAS .... FILM EDITOR

WOMEN IN LOVE
BILLY WILLIAMS .... CINEMATOGRAPHER

WOMEN OF BREWSTER PLACE, THE (TF)
ALEXANDER GRUSZYNSKI .... CINEMATOGRAPHER
SHAY AUSTIN .... PRODUCTION DESIGNER
DANIEL PAREDES .... COSTUME DESIGNER

WOMEN OF SAN QUENTIN (TF)
ROBERT STEADMAN .... CINEMATOGRAPHER

WOMEN ON THE VERGE OF A NERVOUS BREAKDOWN
JOSE LUIS ALCAINE .... CINEMATOGRAPHER
JOSE SALCEDO .... FILM EDITOR

WOMEN'S CLUB, THE
KENT WAKEFORD .... CINEMATOGRAPHER
MARTIN COHEN .... FILM EDITOR

WOMEN'S ROOM, THE (TF)
JAMES G. HULSEY .... PRODUCTION DESIGNER
RENIE CONLEY .... COSTUME DESIGNER

WON TON TON, THE DOG WHO SAVED HOLLYWOOD
RICHARD H. KLINE .... CINEMATOGRAPHER
WARD PRESTON .... PRODUCTION DESIGNER
BERNARD GRIBBLE .... FILM EDITOR

WONDERLAND
DICK POPE .... CINEMATOGRAPHER
DAVID BROCKHURST .... PRODUCTION DESIGNER
RICHARD BEDFORD .... FILM EDITOR

WOODSTOCK (FD)
STANLEY WARNOW .... FILM EDITOR
THELMA SCHOONMAKER .... FILM EDITOR

WORD, THE (MS)
MARTIN JAY SADOFF .... FILM EDITOR

WORK IS A FOUR LETTER WORD
RUTH MYERS .... COSTUME DESIGNER

WORKING BOX, THE
RAYMOND SIMM .... PRODUCTION DESIGNER

WORKING CLASS GOES TO HEAVEN, THE
DANTE FERRETTI .... PRODUCTION DESIGNER

WORKING GIRL
MICHAEL BALLHAUS .... CINEMATOGRAPHER
DOUG KRANER .... PRODUCTION DESIGNER
PATRIZIA VON BRANDENSTEIN .... PRODUCTION DESIGNER
ANN ROTH .... COSTUME DESIGNER
SAM O'STEEN .... FILM EDITOR

WORKING GIRLS
JUDY IROLA .... CINEMATOGRAPHER
KURT OSSENFORT .... PRODUCTION DESIGNER

WORKING TRASH (TF)
BRIAN CAPENER .... CINEMATOGRAPHER
SHARYN L. ROSS .... FILM EDITOR

WORLD ACCORDING TO GARP, THE
MIROSLAV ONDRICEK .... CINEMATOGRAPHER
HENRY BUMSTEAD .... PRODUCTION DESIGNER
WOODS MACINTOSH .... PRODUCTION DESIGNER
ANN ROTH .... COSTUME DESIGNER
MARY MALIN .... COSTUME DESIGNER
RONALD ROOSE .... FILM EDITOR
STEPHEN A. ROTTER .... FILM EDITOR

WORLD APART, A
PETER BIZIOU .... CINEMATOGRAPHER
BRIAN MORRIS .... PRODUCTION DESIGNER
MIKE PHILLIPS .... PRODUCTION DESIGNER
NIC EDE .... COSTUME DESIGNER
NICHOLAS GASTER .... FILM EDITOR

WORLD GONE WILD
DON BURGESS .... CINEMATOGRAPHER
DONALD LIGHT-HARRIS .... PRODUCTION DESIGNER
DONA GRANATA .... COSTUME DESIGNER
GARY A. GRIFFEN .... FILM EDITOR

WORLD IS FULL OF MARRIED MEN, THE
ANTHONY CURTIS .... PRODUCTION DESIGNER

WORLD WAR III (TF)
WILLIAM MALLEY .... PRODUCTION DESIGNER

WORLD'S GREATEST LOVER, THE
GERALD HIRSCHFELD .... CINEMATOGRAPHER
TERENCE MARSH .... PRODUCTION DESIGNER
STEVE SARDANIS .... PRODUCTION DESIGNER
RUTH MYERS .... COSTUME DESIGNER
CHRISTOPHER GREENBURY .... FILM EDITOR

WORLDS APART
AVRAHAM KARPICK .... CINEMATOGRAPHER

WORTH WINNING
ADAM GREENBERG .... CINEMATOGRAPHER
JON HUTMAN .... PRODUCTION DESIGNER
LILLY KILVERT .... PRODUCTION DESIGNER
ROBERT BLACKMAN .... COSTUME DESIGNER
SIDNEY WOLINSKI .... FILM EDITOR

WRAITH, THE
REED SMOOT .... CINEMATOGRAPHER
GARY ROCKLEN .... FILM EDITOR
SCOTT CONRAD .... FILM EDITOR

WRATH OF GOD, THE
JACK POPLIN .... PRODUCTION DESIGNER

WRECKING CREW, THE
MAURY WINETROBE .... FILM EDITOR

WRONG GUYS, THE
FRANK BYERS .... CINEMATOGRAPHER
GEORGE COSTELLO .... PRODUCTION DESIGNER
JILL OHANNESON .... COSTUME DESIGNER
FRANK J. JIMINEZ .... FILM EDITOR

WRONG IS RIGHT
FRED J. KOENEKAMP .... CINEMATOGRAPHER
EDWARD C. CARFAGNO .... PRODUCTION DESIGNER
ROY SUMMERS .... COSTUME DESIGNER
GEORGE GRENVILLE .... FILM EDITOR

WRONG SIDE OF THE ROAD
JOHN SCOTT .... FILM EDITOR

WUSA
RICHARD MOORE .... CINEMATOGRAPHER
ROBERT WYMAN .... FILM EDITOR

X

X Y & ZEE
PETER MULLINS .... PRODUCTION DESIGNER

X-RAY
NICHOLAS VON STERNBERG .... CINEMATOGRAPHER
J. RAE FOX .... PRODUCTION DESIGNER

XANADU
VICTOR J. KEMPER .... CINEMATOGRAPHER
JOHN W. CORSO .... PRODUCTION DESIGNER
BOBBIE MANNIX .... COSTUME DESIGNER
DENNIS M. VIRKLER .... FILM EDITOR

XTRO
ANDREW MOLLO .... PRODUCTION DESIGNER
NICHOLAS GASTER .... FILM EDITOR

Y

YAKUZA, THE
STEPHEN GRIMES† .... PRODUCTION DESIGNER
FREDRIC STEINKAMP .... FILM EDITOR

YAKUZA, THE
DUKE CALLAGHAN .... CINEMATOGRAPHER
DOROTHY JEAKINS .... COSTUME DESIGNER

YANKS
DICK BUSH .... CINEMATOGRAPHER
BRIAN MORRIS .... PRODUCTION DESIGNER
MILLY BURNS .... PRODUCTION DESIGNER
SHIRLEY RUSSELL .... COSTUME DESIGNER
JIM CLARK .... FILM EDITOR

YEAR MY VOICE BROKE, THE
GEOFF BURTON .... CINEMATOGRAPHER

YEAR OF LIVING DANGEROUSLY, THE
RUSSELL BOYD .... CINEMATOGRAPHER
HERBERT PINTER .... PRODUCTION DESIGNER
WENDY STITES .... PRODUCTION DESIGNER
TERRY RYAN .... COSTUME DESIGNER
WILLIAM M. ANDERSON .... FILM EDITOR

YEAR OF THE DRAGON
ALEX THOMSON .... CINEMATOGRAPHER
VICTORIA PAUL .... PRODUCTION DESIGNER
WOLF KROEGER .... PRODUCTION DESIGNER
MARIETTA CIRIELLO .... COSTUME DESIGNER
FRANÇOISE BONNOT .... FILM EDITOR

YELLOW HAIR AND THE FORTRESS OF GOLD
JOHN CABRERA .... CINEMATOGRAPHER
CLAUDIO CUTRY .... FILM EDITOR

YELLOWBEARD
GERRY FISHER .... CINEMATOGRAPHER
JOSEPH R. JENNINGS .... PRODUCTION DESIGNER
GILLY HEBDEN .... COSTUME DESIGNER
WILLIAM REYNOLDS .... FILM EDITOR

YENTL
DAVID WATKIN .... CINEMATOGRAPHER
LESLIE TOMKINS .... PRODUCTION DESIGNER
ROY WALKER .... PRODUCTION DESIGNER
JUDY MOORCROFT .... COSTUME DESIGNER
TERRY RAWLINGS .... FILM EDITOR

YES, GIORGIO
FRED J. KOENEKAMP .... CINEMATOGRAPHER
WILLIAM J. CREBER .... PRODUCTION DESIGNER
BETSY COX .... COSTUME DESIGNER
RITA RIGGS .... COSTUME DESIGNER
MICHAEL F. ANDERSON .... FILM EDITOR

YESTERDAY
RICHARD CIUPKA .... CINEMATOGRAPHER
ROY FORGE SMITH .... PRODUCTION DESIGNER
DEBRA KAREN .... FILM EDITOR

YESTERDAY'S CHILD (TF)
JOSEPH R. JENNINGS .... PRODUCTION DESIGNER

YESTERDAY'S HERO
BRIAN WEST .... CINEMATOGRAPHER
KEITH WILSON .... PRODUCTION DESIGNER
ANTONY GIBBS .... FILM EDITOR

YOJIMBO
SHINOBU MURAKI .... PRODUCTION DESIGNER
YOSHIRO MURAKI .... PRODUCTION DESIGNER

YOR, THE HUNTER FROM THE FUTURE
MARCELLO MASCIOCCHI .... CINEMATOGRAPHER
WALTER PATRICIA .... PRODUCTION DESIGNER
ENRICO LUZZI .... COSTUME DESIGNER
ALBERTO MORIANI .... FILM EDITOR

YOU BETTER WATCH OUT
RICARDO ARONOVITCH .... CINEMATOGRAPHER
CORKY O'HARA .... FILM EDITOR

YOU CAN'T GO HOME AGAIN (TF)
MARTIN BRAM .... FILM EDITOR

Wo-Yo

CINEMATOGRAPHERS
PRODUCTION
DESIGNERS,
COSTUME
DESIGNERS AND
FILM EDITORS
GUIDE

INDEX

OF

FILM

TITLES

465

CINEMATOGRAPHERS
PRODUCTION
DESIGNERS,
COSTUME
DESIGNERS AND
FILM EDITORS
GUIDE

ZELLY AND ME

MIKAEL SALOMON .... CINEMATOGRAPHER
DAVID MORONG .... PRODUCTION DESIGNER
DIANA FREAS .... PRODUCTION DESIGNER
KATHLEEN DETORO .... COSTUME DESIGNER
CINDY KAPLAN-ROONEY .... FILM EDITOR

ZERO BOYS, THE

STEVEN SHAW .... CINEMATOGRAPHER

ZINA

BRYAN LOFTUS .... CINEMATOGRAPHER
ROBERT HARGREAVES .... FILM EDITOR

ZOMBIE ISLAND MASSACRE

ROBERT M. BALDWIN .... CINEMATOGRAPHER

ZONE TROOPERS

MAC AHLBERG .... CINEMATOGRAPHER
PHILIP DEAN FOREMAN .... PRODUCTION DESIGNER
JILL OHANNESON .... COSTUME DESIGNER
TED NICOLAOU .... FILM EDITOR

ZOO GANG, THE

STEVEN LEGLER .... PRODUCTION DESIGNER
JAMES SYMONS .... FILM EDITOR

ZOO GANG, THE

ROBERT C. NEW .... CINEMATOGRAPHER

ZOOT SUIT

DAVID MYERS .... CINEMATOGRAPHER
TOM H. JOHN .... PRODUCTION DESIGNER
YVONNE WOOD .... COSTUME DESIGNER
JACQUELINE CAMBAS .... FILM EDITOR

ZORRO, THE GAY BLADE

JOHN A. ALONZO .... CINEMATOGRAPHER
ADRIAN H. GORTON .... PRODUCTION DESIGNER
HERMAN A. BLUMENTHAL .... PRODUCTION DESIGNER
GLORIA GRESHAM .... COSTUME DESIGNER
PEMBROKE J. HERRING .... FILM EDITOR
ZULUJOHN JYMPSON .... FILM EDITOR

ZULU DAWN

OUSAMA RAWI .... CINEMATOGRAPHER
PETER WILLIAMS .... PRODUCTION DESIGNER
MALCOLM COOKE .... FILM EDITOR

Ze-Zu

CINEMATOGRAPHERS
PRODUCTION
DESIGNERS,
COSTUME
DESIGNERS AND
FILM EDITORS
GUIDE

I
N
D
E
X

O
F

F
I
L
M

T
I
T
L
E
S

467

INDEX OF AGENTS & MANAGERS

CINEMATOGRAPHERS
PRODUCTION
DESIGNERS,
COSTUME
DESIGNERS AND
FILM EDITORS
GUIDE

A
G
E
N
T
S

A
N
D

M
A
N
A
G
E
R
S

A

**ADDIS-WECHSLER &
ASSOCIATES**
*(In Association with The
Robert Littman Co.)*
8444 Wilshire Blvd.
Beverly Hills, CA 90211
213/653-8867

Keith Addis
Nick Wechsler

THE AGENCY
10351 Santa Monica Blvd.
Suite 211
Los Angeles, CA 90025
213/551-3000

DOUG APATOW AGENCY
10559 Blythe Avenue
Los Angeles, CA 90064
213/202-6888

**IRVIN ARTHUR
ASSOCIATES, LTD.**
9363 Wilshire Blvd.
Suite212
Beverly Hills, CA 90210
213/278-5934

THE ARTISTS GROUP, LTD.
1930 Century Park West
Suite 403
Los Angeles, CA 90067
213/552-1100

Arnold Soloway
Hal Stalmaster

**ASSOCIATED TALENT
INTERNATIONAL**
9744 Wilshire Blvd.
Suite 360
Beverly Hills, CA 90212
213/271-4662

B

BARSKIN AGENCY
120 South Victory Blvd.
Burbank, CA 91505
818/848-5536

**BARRETT, BENSON, MCCARTT
& WESTON**
9320 Wilshire Blvd.
Suite 200
Beverly Hills, CA 90212
213/247-5500

Christopher Barrett
Jeff Benson
Bettye McCartt
Richard A. Weston

BENNETT AGENCY
150 South Barrington Avenue
Suite 1
Los Angeles, CA 90049
213/471-2251

Carole Bennett

**BRODER • KURLAND • WEBB •
UFFNER AGENCY**
8439 Sunset Blvd.
Suite 402
Los Angeles, CA 90069
213/656-9262

Bob Broder
Norman Kurland
Elliot Webb
Beth Uffner

CURTIS BROWN, LTD.
606 North Larchmont Blvd.
Suite 309
Los Angeles, CA 90004
213/461-0148

Ten Astor Place
New York, NY 10003
212/473-5400

C

CAMERA MASTERS
38C Avenue 29
Venice, CA 90291
213/306-0810
Fax: 213/822-8991

Pat Little
Carl Bressler

**CCA PERSONAL
MANAGEMENT, LTD.**
4 Court Lodge
48 Sloane Square
London SW1 W8AT England
011/44/71/730-8857

CNA & ASSOCIATES
1801 Avenue of the Stars
Suite 1250
Los Angeles, CA 90067
213/556-4343
Fax: 213/556-4633

THE COPPAGE COMPANY
11501 Chandler Blvd.
North Hollywood, CA 91601
818/980-1106

Judy Coppage

**CREATIVE ARTISTS AGENCY
(CAA)**
9830 Wilshire Blvd.
Beverly Hills, CA 90212
213/288-4545
Fax: 213/288-4800

CREATIVE TECHNIQUE
P.O. Box 311, Station F
Toronto, Ontario M4Y2L7
Canada
416/466-4173
Fax: 416/534-6243

CURTIS BROWN, LTD.
606 North Larchmont Blvd.
Suite 309
Los Angeles, CA 90004
213/461-0148

Ten Astor Place
New York, NY 10003
212/473-5400

Da-Mo

CINEMATOGRAPHERS
PRODUCTION
DESIGNERS,
COSTUME
DESIGNERS AND
FILM EDITORS
GUIDE

A
G
E
N
T
S

A
N
D

M
A
N
A
G
E
R
S

D

DATTNER & ASSOCIATES
12210 Nebraska Avenue
Suite 45
Los Angeles, CA 90025

Fay Dattner

G

PAUL GERARD TALENT AGENCY
2918 Alta Vista Drive
Newport Beach, CA 92660
714/644-7950

THE GERSH AGENCY
232 N. Cañon Drive
Beverly Hills, CA 90210
213/274-6611
Fax: 213/274-4035

Bob Gersh
Dave Gersh
Phil Gersh

THE GOLDSTEIN COMPANY
864 South Robertson Blvd.
Suite 304
Los Angeles, CA 90035
213/659-9511

Gary W. Goldstein

THE GORFAINE/SCHWARTZ AGENCY, INC.
3301 Barham Blvd.
Suite 201
Los Angeles, CA 90068
213/553-5200
Fax: 213/969-1022

Michael Gorfaine
Samuel Schwartz

THE GURIAN AGENCY
10249 Century Woods Drive
Los Angeles, CA 90067
213/550-0400

Naomi Gurian

H

HARRIS & GOLDBERG TALENT & LITERARY AGENCY, INC.
1999 Avenue of the Stars
Suite 2850
Los Angeles, CA 90067
213/553-5200
Fax: 213/557-2211

Scott Harris
Howard Goldberg

I

INTERNATIONAL CREATIVE MANAGEMENT (ICM)
8899 Beverly Blvd.
Los Angeles, CA 90048
213/550-4000

40 West 57th Street
New York, NY 10019
212/556-5600

in Italy, known as
TNA (The New Agency)
Viale Paroli, 41
Rome, Italy 00197
011/396-87.87.98

388-396 Oxford Street
London, W1 England W1N 9HE
01/629-8080

L

LAKE & DOUROUX
445 S. Beverly Drive
Suite 310
Beverly Hills, CA 90212
213/557-0700

Candace Lake
Michael Douroux

THE LANTZ OFFICE
(In Association with The Roberts Company)
888 Seventh Avenue
25th Floor
New York, NY 10106
212/586-0200

THE ROBERT LITTMAN COMPANY
(In Association with Addis-Wechsler & Associates)
409 North Camden Drive
Beverly Hills, CA 90210
213/278-1572

LONDON MANAGEMENT
235/241 Regent Street
London W1, England
011/441/493-1610

GRACE LYONS MANAGEMENT
8380 Melrose Avenue
Suite 202
Los Angeles, CA 90069
213/655-5100

M

STEPHANIE MANN AGENCY
8323 Blackburn Avenue
Suite 5
Los Angeles, CA 90048
213/653-7130

SANDRA MARSH MANAGE-MENT
14930 Ventura Blvd.
Suite 200
Sherman Oaks, CA 91403
818/905-6961

THE MILLER AGENCY
23560 Lyons Avenue
Suite 209
Santa Clarita, CA 91321
805/255-7173
Fax: 805/255-7286

Tom Miller

WILLIAM MORRIS AGENCY
151 S. El Camino Drive
Beverly Hills, CA 90212
213/274-7451

1350 Avenue of the Americas
New York, NY 10019
212/586-5100

2325 Crestmoore Road
Nashville, TN 37215
615/385-0310

31-32 Soho Square
London W12 5DG, England
01/434-2191

(continued on next page)

WILLIAM MORRIS AGENCY
(continued)

Via Giosue Carducci, 10
00187 Rome, Italy
48-6961

Lamonstrasse 9
Munich 80, West Germany
011/47/608-1234

R

**THE RICHLAND/WUNSCH/
HOHMAN AGENCY**
9220 Sunset Blvd.
Suite 311
Los Angeles, CA 90069
213/278-1955
Fax: 213/278-1156

Daniel A. Richland
Joseph Richland
Robert J. Wunsch
Robert Hohman

THE ROBERTS COMPANY
*(In Association with The
Lantz Office)*
10345 West Olympic Blvd.
Penthouse
Los Angeles, CA 90064
213/552-7800
Fax: 213/552-9324

Namcy Roberts

**ROBINSON, WEINTRAUB,
GROSS & ASSOCIATES, INC.**
*(In Association with The
Marion Rosenberg Office)*
8428 Melrose Place
Suite C
Los Angeles, CA 90069
213/653-5802
Fax: 213/653-9268

Stu Robinson
Bernie Weintraub
Ken Gross

**THE MARION ROSENBERG
OFFICE**
*(In Association with Robinson,
Weintraub, Gross & Associates)*
8428 Melrose Place
Suite C
West Hollywood, CA 90069
213/653-7383

S

**SANFORD, SKOURAS, GROSS
& ASSOCIATES**
1015 Gayley Avenue
Suite 300
Los Angeles, CA 90024
213/208-2100
Fax: 213/208-6704

Geoffrey Sanford
Spyros Skouras
Brad Gross

**THE IRV SCHECHTER
COMPANY**
9300 Wilshire Blvd., Suite 410
Beverly Hills, CA 90212
213/278-8070
Fax: 213/278-6058

Irv Schechter

**DON SCHWARTZ &
ASSOCIATES**
8749 Sunset Blvd.
Suite 200
Los Angeles, CA 90069
213/657-8910

**THE SHAPIRO/LICHTMAN
AGENCY**
8827 Beverly Blvd.
Los Angeles, CA 90048
213/859-8877
Fax: 213/859-7153

Mark Lichtman
Bob Shapiro
Martin Shapiro

**SMITH/GOSNELL/NICHOLSON
& ASSOCIATES**
P. O. Box 1166
1294 Calle de Sevilla
Pacific Palisades, CA 90272
213/459-0307
Fax: 213/4547987

Creighton Smith
Ray Gosnell
Skip Nicholson
Patty Mack

STE REPRESENTATION, LTD.
9301 Wilshire Blvd.
Suite 312
Beverly Hills, CA 90210
213/550-3982
Fax: 213/550-5991

David Eidenberg

888 Seventh Avenue
Suite 21-F
New York, NY 10106
212/246-1030
Fax: 212/246-1521

Clifford Stevens

T

TRIAD ARTISTS, INC.
10100 Santa Monica Blvd.
16th Floor
Los Angeles, CA 90067
213/556-2727
Fax: 213/551-0501

888 Seventh Avenue
Suite 1602
New York, NY 10109
212/489-8100
Fax: 212/245-2316

W

WRITERS & ARTISTS AGENCY
11726 San Vicente Blvd.
Suite 300
Los Angeles, CA 90049
213/820-2240
Fax: 213/207-3781

Joan Scott

70 West 36th Street
Suite 501
New York, NY 10018
212/947-8765

★ ★ ★ ★

Mo-Wr

CINEMATOGRAPHERS
PRODUCTION
DESIGNERS,
COSTUME
DESIGNERS AND
FILM EDITORS
GUIDE

A
G
E
N
T
S

A
N
D

M
A
N
A
G
E
R
S

CALLING ALL CREDITS!

The **Fourth Edition of CINEMATOGRAPHERS, PRODUCTION DESIGNERS, COSTUME DESIGNERS AND FILM EDITORS GUIDE** is now in preparation. It will be published in the fall of 1992. We update our records continuously. If you are a cinematographer, production designer, costume designer or film editor and you qualify to be listed (please read the Introduction for qualifications), then send us your listing information **ASAP**.

Photocopy the form on the next page.

Our editorial deadline is March 1, 1992.

(Please do not wait until then.)

Send all listing information to:

Cinematographers, Production Designers, Costume Designers and Film Editors GUIDE Fourth Edition 1837 Glendon Avenue #9 Los Angeles, CA 90025 213/471-8066 or 1/800-FILMBKS

If you are a writer *(film or television)*, a director *(film or television)*, film actor, film composer, agent, producer or studio executive, special effects or stunts coordinator and want to find out about getting listed in our other directories, call **213/471-8066** or **1/800-FILMBKS** or write to:

LONE EAGLE PUBLISHING CO.
**2337 Roscomare Road, Suite 9
Los Angeles, CA 90077
213/471-8066 • 213/471-4969 (FAX) • 1/800-FILMBKS**

★ ★ ★

The FOURTH EDITION of
CINEMATOGRAPHERS, PRODUCTION DESIGNERS, COSTUME DESIGNERS
AND FILM EDITORS GUIDE
is now in preparation.

PLEASE CHECK APPROPRIATE CATEGORY

☐ Cinematographer
☐ Production Designer
☐ Art Director
☐ Costume Designer
☐ Film Editor
☐ Other _____

DON'T BE LEFT OUT!!! Guarantee your *FREE* listing (for qualified persons)
by filling out and returning this form to us *IMMEDIATELY*.
(Photocopy as many times as necessary).

APPLICANT'S INFORMATION

Name

Company

Address

City/State/Zip

Area Code/Phone

Birth Date & Place

Home ☐   Business ☐

REPRESENTATIVE'S INFORMATION

Agent ☐   Personal Manager ☐   Attorney ☐
Business Manager ☐   Other ☐   AFM ☐

(List as many representatives as you would like. Continue listing on reverse, if necessary.)

Name

Company

Address

City/State/Zip

Area Code/Telephone

Guild/Union Affiliations

PLEASE PRINT OR TYPE

CREDITS

List your credits as follows: Please note alternate titles in parentheses. Pease note Academy and Emmy nominations/awards for your work. If you need more space, please continue on reverse side.

FEATURES: AVALON   Balitmore Pictures/Tri-Star, 1990 ★
DANCES WITH WOLVES   Orion, 1990 ★★
PRETTY WOMAN *3000*   Touchtone, 1989
TELEFEATURES: LONG ROAD HOME (TF)   Rosemont Productions, 1991

MAIL or FAX form *IMMEDIATELY* to:
**CINEMATOGRAPHERS, PRODUCTION DESIGNERS,
COSTUME DESIGNERS and FILM EDITORS GUIDE**
Fourth Edition
1837 Glendon Avenue #9
Los Angeles, CA 90025
213/471-8066 or 213/471-4969 (FAX)

Questions ???
Problems ???
Call 213/471-8066

We couldn't have said it better ourselves...

CINEMATOGRAPHERS,
PRODUCTION
DESIGNERS,
COSTUME
DESIGNERS AND
FILM EDITORS
GUIDE

NOTES

NOTES

CINEMATOGRAPHERS,
PRODUCTION
DESIGNERS,
COSTUME
DESIGNERS AND
FILM EDITORS
GUIDE

CINEMATOGRAPHERS,
PRODUCTION
DESIGNERS,
COSTUME
DESIGNERS AND
FILM EDITORS
GUIDE

INDEX OF ADVERTISERS

A special thanks to our advertisers whose support makes it possible to bring you the **CINEMATOGRAPHERS, PRODUCTION DESIGNERS, COSTUME DESIGNERS and FILM EDITORS GUIDE.**

★ ★ ★

CINEMATOGRAPHERS,
PRODUCTION
DESIGNERS,
COSTUME
DESIGNERS AND
FILM EDITORS
GUIDE

A
B
O
U
T

T
H
E

E
D
I
T
O
R

ABOUT THE EDITOR

DAVID PECCHIA, a 35 year old Los Angeles resident of ten years, is a freelance entertainment reporter best known for his annual movie roundups in the Los Angeles Times' Sunday Calendar. Movies/USA Magazine also has published a half dozen cover stories of David's and features his "Talking Pictures" movie column each and every month.